THE COMPLETE
CROSSWORD
COMPANION

THE COMPLETE
CROSSWORD
COMPANION

**The ULTIMATE PROBLEM SOLVER for
Crossword Puzzles and Word Games**

BB Bounty
Books

First published in Great Britain as two separate volumes under the titles:

Complete Crossword Reference Book
First published in 1932 by C.Arthur Pearson Limited
A revised edition published by Hamlyn under the title
The Hamlyn Crossword Dictionary
Further revised 1978
Published in 1983 by Newnes Books under the title
The Newnes Crossword Dictionary

The Pocket English Dictionary
First published 1976 by Hamlyn
Published in 1983 by Newnes Books under the title
Newnes Pocket English Dictionary
Revised and expanded 1985

This edition first published in 1998 by Chancellor Press (Bounty Books),
a division of Octopus Publishing Group Ltd
Reprinted 1990, 1991, 1992, 1998

This paperback edition published in 2007 by Bounty Books,
a division of Octopus Publishing Group Ltd
2–4 Heron Quays, London E14 4JP

An Hachette Livre UK Company

ISBN: 978-0-753716-45-8

A CIP catalogue record for this book is available from the British Library

Printed and bound in Spain

Contents

Introduction

This first section of *The Complete Crossword Companion*, the 'Crossword Reference Dictionary' is a completely revised and updated version of the work previously published by C. Arthur Pearson Ltd under the title of the *Complete Crossword Reference Book*. It is the ideal guide for the crossword enthusiast presenting in a convenient form a collection of about 130,000 carefully selected and classified words which will prove invaluable in solving and compiling crosswords.

It is really very simple to use. In crossword puzzles the number of letters in the required word is known and usually also the subject. The aim of the *Crossword Reference Dictionary* is to enable the reader to quickly find the word he wants. For this reason it has been systematically divided into a number of main subject categories, including *Armed Forces, Business, Professions and Occupations, Geography, Literature and the Arts, Natural History* and *Science and Technology*, each of which is split up into subdivisions. In these subdivisions all the relevant words will be found under the number of letters required, in lists of words of from two to fifteen (and sometimes more) letters, each list being set out in alphabetical order.

The *Crossword Reference Dictionary* not only is the indispensable companion for the crossword-puzzle fan but the encyclopedic coverage of its contents makes it a most useful general reference work in addition. Among the many valuable sections in the book are the comprehensive lists of animals, birds, fish, coins, plants, etc., and characters from mythology and literature.

ARMED FORCES
Air force ranks and appellations: British and U.S.

3 AND 4

A.C.2
A.C.1
L.A.C.
W.A.A.F.

5

major (U.S.)
pilot

6

airman
fitter
rigger

7

aviator
captain (U.S.)
colonel (U.S.)
general (U.S.)
private (U.S.)

8

armourer
corporal

mechanic
observer
sergeant

9

air gunner
bomb aimer
drum-major
navigator

10

air marshal
apprentice
balloonist
bombardier (U.S.)
nose gunner
rear gunner
tail gunner

11

aircraftman
belly gunner
second pilot

12

air commodore

group captain
major general (U.S.)
pilot officer

13

flying officer
sergeant major (U.S.)
staff sergeant (U.S.)
wing commander

14

air vice marshal
flight engineer
flight mechanic
flight sergeant
master sergeant (U.S.)
squadron leader
warrant officer

15

air chief marshal
first lieutenant (U.S.)

16

flight lieutenant
second lieutenant (U.S.)

Battles and sieges

3 AND 4

Acre
Aden
Agra
Alma (The)
Amoy
Caen
Gaza
Ivry
Jena
Kut
Laon
Loos
Lys (The)
Maas
Mons
Nile (The)
Taku
Tet
Ulm
Yser (The)
Zama

5

Aisne (The)
Alamo (The)

Arcot
Arras
Basra
Boyne (The)
Cadiz
Cairo
Crécy
Crete
Delhi
El Teb
Eylau
Genoa
Herat
Kabul
Kandy
Liège
Ligny
Maida
Malta
Marne (The)
Meuse
Miami
Narvik
Paris
Pusan
Rhine
Sedan
Selle
Somme (The)

Tagus (The)
Texel (The)
Tours
Valmy
Ypres

6

Actium
Amiens
Arbela
Argaon
Armada (The)
Arnhem
Assaye
Atbara (The)
Bagdad
Barnet
Bataan
Berlin
Burgos
Busaco
Calais
Camden
Cannae
Chusan
Coruña
Dargai

9

Delium
Dunbar
Ferrol
Guarda
Gujrat
Havana
Isonzo (The)
Jattoo
Jhansi
Lutzen
Madras
Madrid
Majuba
Malaga
Manila
Mantua
Midway
Mileto
Minden
Moscow
Nagpur
Naseby
Oporto
Orthez
Ostend
Peking
Plevna
Quebec
Rhodes
Rivoli
Rocroi
Sadowa
Saints (The)
Shiloh
Tarifa
Tobago
Tobruk
Toulon
Tudela
Tugela (The)
Ushant
Verdun
Vienna
Wagram
Warsaw

7

Aboukir
Abu Klea
Alamein
Albuera
Almansa
Almeida
Antwerp
Badajoz
Baghdad
Bapaume
Bautzen
Bousaco
Brienne
Bull Run
Cambrai
Cape Bon
Cassino
Chalons
Coimbra
Colenso
Cordova
Coronel
Corunna
Dresden
Dunkirk
Edghill
El Obeid

Falkirk
Flodden
Granada
Gwalior
Iwo Jima
Jutland
La Hogue
Leipzig
Lemberg
Lepanto
Leuthen
Lucknow
Magdala
Magenta
Marengo
Matapan
Minorca
Moselle
Moskowa (The)
Nations (The)
Newbury
Nivelle (The)
Okinawa
Orleans
Plassey
Poltava
Preston
St. Kitts
St. Lucia
Salerno
Sobraon
Solebay
Vimiera
Vitoria

8

Ardennes
Atlantic (The)
Bastille (The)
Beresina (The)
Blenheim
Bhurtpur
Borodino
Bosworth
Calcutta
Carthage
Cawnpore
Culloden
Edgehill
Flanders
Flushing
Fontenoy
Fort Erie
Hastings
Inkerman
Kandahar
Khartoum
Lake Erie
Le Cateau
Mafeking
Malakoff (The)
Marathon
Maubeuge
Medellin
Messines
Metaurus
Montreal
Navarino
Nieuport
Normandy
Omdurman
Poitiers
Potidaea
Pretoria

Przemysl
St. Mihiel
St. Pierre
Salsette
Saratoga
Spion Kop
Stirling
Suvla Bay
Syracuse
Talavera
Tiberias
Toulouse
Valencia
Waterloo
Yorktown
Zaragoza

9

Agincourt
Algeciras
Balaclava
Belle Isle
Caporetto
Chaeronea
Champagne
Charleroi
Ctesiphon
Dettingen
El Alamein
Falklands (The)
Festubert
Friedland
Gallipoli
Gaugamela
Gibraltar
Hyderabad
Kimberley
Ladysmith
Laing's Nek
Leningrad
Leyte Gulf
Louisburg
Mauritius
Melagnano
Mobile Bay
Oudenarde
Pharsalus
Port Mahon
Ramillies
Rodriguez
Saragossa
St. Quentin
St. Vincent
Salamanca
Sedgemoor
Solferino
Stormberg
Stromboli
Tarragona
Tourcoing
Trafalgar
Vicksburg
Walcheren
Worcester
Zeebrugge

10

Adrianople
Ahmednagar
Alexandria
Appomattox
Austerlitz

Brandywine
Brownstown
Bunker Hill
Camperdown
Chevy-chase
Copenhagen
Corregidor
Dogger Bank
Fort George
Gettysburg
Gravelotte
Guadeloupe
Heligoland
Imjin River
Kut-el-Amara
La Rochelle
Les Saintes
Malplaquet
Martinique
Montevideo
Montfaucon
New Orleans
Nördlingen
Paardeburg
Petersburg
Port Arthur
Porto Praya
Quatre Bras
River Plate
Sevastopol
Shrewsbury
Stalingrad
Tannenberg
Tel-el-Kebir
Tewkesbury
Tinchebray

11

Albuquerque
Bannockburn
Breitenfeld
Chattanooga
Chilianwala
Dardanelles (The)
Dien Bien Phu
Fort Niagara
Guadalcanal
Hohenlinden
Isandhlwana
Jameson Raid (The)
Marston Moor
Pearl Harbor
Philiphaugh
Philippines (The)
Pieter's Hill
Pondicherry
Prestonpans
Quiberon Bay
Rorke's Drift
Schoneveldt
Thermopylae
Ticonderoga

12 AND OVER

Antietam Creek (13)
Battle of Britain (15)
Bloemfontein (12)
Cape St. Vincent (13)
Ciudad Rodrigo (13)
Constantinople (14)

Delville Wood (12)
Falkland Islands (15)
Flodden Field (12)
Lake Champlain (13)
Little Bighorn (12)
Magersfontein (13)

Messines Ridge (13)
Neuve Chapelle (13)
Neville's Cross (13)
Passchendaele (13)
Plains of Abraham (15)
San Sebastian (12)

Seringapatam (12)
Spanish Armada (The) (13)
Stamford Bridge (14)
Trichinopoly (12)
Tsushima Strait (14)
White Mountain (13)

Military ranks and appellations

2 AND 3

A.D.C.
C.O.
C.S.M.
G.I.
N.C.O.
O.C.
R.S.M.
R.T.O.

4

goum
koul
lewa
naik
peon

5

cadet
fifer
Jäger
major
miner
piper
scout
sepoy
sowar
spahi
Tommy
Uhlan

6

batman
bomber
bowman
bugler
cornet
driver
ensign
gunner
Gurkha
hetman
hussar
lancer
marine
ranger
ranker
sapper
sutler
Zouave

7

ancient
captain

colonel
Cossack
dragoon
drummer
estafet
farrier
general
hobbler
hoplite
janizar
jemadar
lancers
marines
marshal
militia
officer
orderly
pikeman
pioneer
private
recruit
redcoat
reserve
saddler
sappers
soldier
subadar
trooper
vedette
veteran
warrior

8

adjutant
armourer
bandsman
cavalier
chasseur
commando
corporal
daffadar
decurion
deserter
doughboy
dragoons
fencible
fugelman
fusilier
havildar
infantry
janizary
Landwehr
marksman
messmate
muleteer
mutineer
partisan
rifleman
risaldar
sentinel
sergeant

spearman
turncoat
waterman

9

beefeater
berserker
brigadier
cannoneer
cannonier
centurion
combatant
commander
conductor
conscript
drum-major
estaffette
field rank
fife-major
fort-major
grenadier
guardsman
guerrilla
Home Guard
irregular
Janissary
lance-naik
man-at-arms
musketeer
paymaster
pensioner
pipe-major
signaller
subaltern
tactician
town-major
trumpeter
tradesman
vexillary
voltigeur
volunteer

10

aide-de-camp
bandmaster
bombardier
campaigner
carabineer
cavalryman
commandant
cuirassier
drummer-boy
file-leader
footguards
halberdier
instructor
Lansquenet
lieutenant
lifeguards

militiaman
other ranks
paratroops
roughrider
strategist

11

arquebusier
artillerist
auxiliaries
bashi-bazook
bersaglieri
condottiere
crack troops
crossbowman
gendarmerie
horse guards
infantryman
Landsknecht
moss-trooper
parachutist
paratrooper
rangefinder
top sergeant
Tommy Atkins

12

armour-bearer
artilleryman
brigade-major
camp-follower
ensign-bearer
field marshal
field officer
horse soldier
jemadar-major
major-general
master gunner
officer cadet
P.T. instructor
Royal Marines
Royal Signals
staff officer
storm-trooper
subadar-major
sub-conductor
territorials

13

army commander
barrack-master
brevet-colonel
bugle-corporal
color-sergeant
corporal-major
dispatch-rider
drill sergeant

first sergeant
generalissimo
lance-corporal
lance-daffadar
lance-sergeant
lifeguardsman
light infantry
machine-gunner
marine officer
mounted rifles
prisoner of war
quartermaster
risaldar major
sergeant major
staff-sergeant

14

citizen-soldier
colonel-in-chief
colour-havildar
colour-sergeant
liaison officer
master sergeant
medical officer
military police
orderly officer
provost-marshal
Royal Artillery
Royal Engineers
Royal Tank Corps
second corporal
signals officer

standard bearer
warrant officer

15

adjutant-general
corporal-of-horse
first lieutenant
gentleman-at-arms
honorary colonel
household troops
mounted infantry
orderly corporal
orderly sergeant
ordnance officer
provost sergeant

Military terms (including fortifications)

2–4

aim
ally
ammo
anfo
arm
arms
army
A.W.O.L.
band
base
bawn
belt
berm
blip
camp
defy
draw
duck
duel
dun
fife
file
fire
flag
flak
foe
foot
form
fort
foss
gas
gun
halt
host
hut
jam
jeep
kern
kit
lay
levy
line
loot
man
map
mess
mine
moat
O.C.T.U.
out

pah
park
P.I.A.T.
plan
post
P.O.W.
push
raid
ramp
rank
raze
rear
rout
ruse
sack
sap
shot
slay
slug
spot
spur
star
take
tank
tent
tilt
trap
turn
unit
van
war
ward
wing
zero

5

abort
agent
alarm
alert
annex
A.N.Z.A.C.
armed
armor
array
baton
beret
berme
beset
booty

busby
butts
cadre
cavin
cells
clean
corps
decoy
depot
depth
ditch
dogra
draft
drawn
dress
drill
enemy
enrol
equip
feint
field
fight
flank
flare
foray
fosse
fours
front
gazon
gorge
guard
guide
gurry
herse
horse
khaki
lance
lines
march
medal
mélée
mount
mufti
onset
order
party
peace
pivot
poilu
pouch
prime
radar

rally
range
ranks
redan
relay
repel
rifle
round
route
royal
sally
salvo
scale
scarp
seize
S.H.A.E.F.
shako
shell
shift
shock
shoot
siege
snipe
sonar
sonic
spoil
squad
staff
stand
storm
strap
talus
T.E.W.T.S.
track
troop
truce
unarm
vexil
wheel
wound
yield

6

abatis
ack-ack
action
affray
allies
ambush
archer

7

armour	limber	abattis	gunnery
assail	marker	advance	gun-shot
attack	merlon	aid-post	half-pay
bailey	mining	air-raid	harness
banner	mobile	airlift	holster
barbed	muster	archery	hostage
battle	mutiny	armoury	hostile
beaten	number	arsenal	hutment
billet	obsess	assault	jamming
blinds	occupy	baggage	Kremlin
blow up	oppose	barrack	landing
bonnet	orders	barrage	leaguer
bouche	orgues	basenet	liaison
brevet	outfit	bastion	looting
bunker	parade	battery	lunette
cartel	parley	battled	madrier
castle	parole	besiege	maniple
centre	patrol	bivouac	marquee
charge	pennon	bombard	martial
clayes	permit	brigade	megaton
cohort	picket	bulwark	moineau
colour	plonge	caltrop	mounted
column	pompom	canteen	neutral
combat	pompon	carbine	nuclear
convoy	primer	caserne	on guard
cordon	pursue	cavalry	outpost
corral	raider	chamade	outwing
curfew	ransom	charger	outwork
dagger	rapine	chevron	overawe
débris	rappel	citadel	overrun
decamp	ration	cold war	parados
defeat	ravage	colours	parapet
defend	rebuff	command	pennant
defier	recall	company	phalanx
defile	recoil	conquer	pillbox
deploy	reduce	counter	pitfall
desert	relais	coupure	platoon
detach	relief	crusade	plongée
detail	report	curtain	postern
disarm	resist	debouch	priming
donjon	retake	defence	protect
double	retire	defiant	provost
dugout	review	degrade	prowess
embark	riddle	destroy	pursuit
embody	rideau	détente	quarter
encamp	roster	detrain	rampart
engage	saddle	disband	rations
enlist	salute	dismiss	ravelin
enmity	sconce	dispart	redoubt
ensign	sensor	drawn up	refugee
epaule	signal	draw off	regular
escape	sketch	dungeon	remblai
escarp	sortie	echelon	remount
escort	square	ecoutes	repulse
Fabian	stores	enguard	reserve
fanion	strife	enomoty	retaken
firing	strike	entrain	retreat
fleche	stripe	envelop	reverse
foeman	stroke	environ	Riot Act
forted	subdue	epaulet	salient
fraise	submit	fallout	sand-bag
gabion	supply	fanfare	section
glacis	target	fascine	service
guards	tattoo	fatigue	sniping
guides (the)	thrust	flanker	spurred
guidon	trench	fortify	stand-by
hawhaw	trophy	fortlet	subvert
helmet	umpire	forward	support
hurter	vallum	fourgon	tactics
impact	valour	foxhole	tambour
inroad	victor	fraised	tenable
invade	volley	gallery	tilting
invest	walled	guérite	trailer
inwall	warcry	gunfire	triumph
kitbag	zareba		unarmed
legion	zigzag		uncased

13

uniform
valiant
van-foss
venture
victory
ward off
warfare
wargame
war-hoop
warlike
warpath
warsong
warworn
wheeler
windage
wounded

8

accoutre
advanced
airborne
air force
alarm gun
alliance
armament
armature
armorial
arms race
Army List
baldrick
barbette
barbican
barracks
bartizan
bawdrick
bearskin
billeted
blockade
bull's eye
camisade
camisado
campaign
casemate
casualty
chivalry
civil war
collapse
conquest
cornetcy
crusader
decimate
decisive
defended
defender
defiance
demi-lune
demolish
despatch
detonate
disarray
disenrol
dismount
dispatch
distance
division
doubling
drumhead
duelling
earth-bag
embattle
embodied
enceinte
enfilade
ensigncy

entrench
equipage
escalade
escouade
estacade
eyes left
fastness
field day
fighting
flagpost
flanking
footband
fortress
fourneau
furlough
garrison
gauntlet
gendarme
gonfalon
guerilla
half-moon
hang-fire
hedgehog
herisson
hillfort
horn-work
intrench
invasion
knapsack
last post
lay siege
lay waste
limber up
lodgment
loophole
magazine
majority
Mameluke
mantelet
marching
mark time
matériel
mess bill
militant
military
mobilize
movement
muniment
musketry
mutinous
on parade
on parole
opponent
ordnance
outflank
outguard
outlying
overcome
overkill
palisade
paradrop
passport
password
pavilion
pay corps
pipe-clay
prisoner
punitive
quarters
railhead
ramparts
rear line
rear rank
rearward
recharge
re-embark

re-embody
regiment
remounts
reprisal
resalute
retirade
retrench
reveille
ricochet
rifle-pit
roll-call
sabotage
saboteur
saluting
scout-car
security
sentry-go
services (the)
shabrack
shelling
shooting
shot-belt
siege-war
skirmish
soldiery
spotting
squadron
stampede
standard
star-fort
stockade
stoppage
storming
straddle
strategy
strength
struggle
supplies
support
surprise
surround
sword arm
tactical
tenaille
time-fuse
tortoise
training
transfer
traverse
trooping (the colour)
unallied
unbeaten
unlimber
uprising
valorous
vanguard
vanquish
vexillar
victuals
vigilant
vincible
warfarer
warhorse
warpaint
war-plume
war-whoop
watch-box
wheeling
yeomanry
zero hour

9

aggressor
alarm post

ambuscade
ambuscado
armistice
armouries
army corps
artillery
assailant
atomic war
attrition
ballistic
bandolier
banquette
barricade
barricado
battalion
batteries
battle-cry
beachhead
beleaguer
bellicose
billeting
bodyguard
bombproof
bugle call
bulldozer
cannonade
captaincy
cashiered
cavalcade
ceasefire
challenge
chevalier
colonelcy
comitadji
conqueror
covert-way
crossfire
crown-work
crow's foot
defection
defensive
defiatory
demi-gorge
desertion
devastate
discharge
disembody
disengage
dismantle
earthwork
elevation
embattled
embrasure
encompass
encounter
enfiladed
enrolment
epaulette
equipment
espionage
esplanade
eyes front
eyes right
fencibles
field rank
fire-drill
flagstaff
forage-cap
form fours
fortalice
fortifier
fortilage
fusillade
gabionade
gas attack
gladiator

14

guardroom
guerrilla
haversack
heliostat
hersillon
homograph
hostility
housewife
incursion
interdict
invalided
irregular
land force
Landsturm
legionary
lifeguard
logistics
loopholed
Luftwaffe
majorship
manoeuvre
mechanist
mercenary
militancy
musketoon
Mutiny Act
objective
offensive
officiate
onsetting
onslaught
operation
overpower
overshoot
overthrow
overwhelm
packdrill
pack train
palladium
parachute
predictor
pregnable
pressgang
projector
promotion
protector
provender
rearguard
rebellion
reconquer
red ensign
re-enforce
refortify
reinforce
rencontre
reprimand
revetment
revictual
safeguard
sally-port
scrimmage
semaphore
sentry-box
sham-fight
slaughter
slope arms
slow-march
stack arms
stand-fast
stand fire
stand-firm
stratagem
strategic
subaltern
subjugate
surrender

sword-knot
taskforce
tenaillon
terrorist
train-band
transport
treachery
tricolour
unbridged
undaunted
undrilled
unguarded
unhostile
uniformed
unopposed
unordered
unscathed
unsheathe
unstormed
unwarlike
unwounded
vigilance
war office
watchword
Wehrmacht
white flag
withstand
zigzagged

10

action left
aggressive
air-defence
ammunition
annexation
annihilate
arbalister
armipotent
attackable
battlement
blitzkrieg
blockhouse
breastwork
brevet rank
bridgehead
camel corps
camouflage
cantonment
capitulate
ceremonial
challenger
color guard
commandeer
commissary
commission
contraband
crenulated
dead ground
decampment
defendable
defensible
defilading
demobilize
demolition
deployment
desolating
desolation
despatches
detachment
detonation
direct fire
dismounted
dispatches
divisional

dragonnade
drawbridge
embodiment
encampment
enfilading
engagement
engarrison
enlistment
epaulement
epauletted
escalation
escarpment
expedition
fieldworks
flying camp
garrisoned
glasshouse
ground fire
guardhouse
hand-to-hand
heliograph
Indian file
inspection
investment
invincible
leadership
light-armed
light horse
limited war
line of fire
manoeuvres
map-reading
martial law
militarism
musketeers
muster book
muster roll
night-watch
no man's land
nuclear war
occupation
odd-numbers
operations
opposition
outgeneral
over the top
patrolling
point blank
portcullis
presidiary
prison camp
projectile
protection
provisions
quartering
quick-march
raking fire
reconquest
recruiting
re-entering
regimental
rencounter
rendezvous
reorganize
reparation
resistance
respirator
retirement
revolution
rifle range
route march
sabretache
sentry beat
sentry duty
senty post
shell-proof

siege-train
signal-fire
signalling
skirmisher
slit trench
soldiering
squad drill
state of war
sticky bomb
stronghold
subjection
subsection
submission
submissive
subversion
surrounded
sword-fight
table money
terreplein
tirailleur
trajectory
triumphant
undecisive
undefended
unequipped
unlimbered
unmolested
unsheathed
vanquisher
victorious
volunteers
vulnerable
war-council
watchtower

11

action front
action right
aides-de-camp
assaultable
barrackroom
battle-array
battledress
battlefield
battle-royal
belligerent
besiegement
bombardment
bridge-train
bulletproof
button-stick
castellated
colour party
conquerable
co-operation
countermine
defenceless
demi-bastion
devastation
disarmament
disbandment
disgarrison
double-march
drawn swords
dress parade
embarkation
emplacement
envelopment
even numbers
fatigue duty
firing party
firing squad
flag of truce
flying party

15

flying squad
foot-soldier
forced march
forlorn hope
form two deep
fortifiable
generalship
germ warfare
guerilla war
impregnable
indefensive
machicoulis
mobile force
orderly room
penetration
postern gate
present arms
protagonist
range-finder
rank-and-file
reconnoitre
recruitment
redoubtable
review order
royal salute
running-fire
safe conduct
searchlight
shock-troop
skirmishing
smokescreen
stand-to-arms
supply depot
trous-de-loup
trumpet call
unconquered
unfortified
unprotected
unsoldierly
unsupported
vincibility
war memorial

12

advanced base
advance guard
annihilation
anti-aircraft
Bailey bridge
barking-irons
battlemented
bush-fighting
capitulation
civil defence
commissariat
commissioned
conscription
counterguard
countermarch
court-martial
covering fire
demi-distance
disaffection
dropping fire
fatigue party
field colours
field-kitchen
flying column
foot-barracks
garrison town
guerrilla war
headquarters
heavy brigade
hollow square

horse-and-foot
indefensible
indirect fire
intelligence
intrenchment
invulnerable
irresistible
landing party
light brigade
light cavalry
line-of-battle
machicolated
Maltese cross
mobile column
mobilization
outmanoeuvre
platoon drill
plunging fire
protectorate
quarter-guard
remount depot
retrenchment
running fight
ruse-de-guerre
shock tactics
saluting base
shoulder-belt
shoulder-knot
siege tactics
siege warfare
staff college
surveillance
truce-breaker
ungarrisoned
unintrenched
unobstructed
unvanquished
vanquishable
white feather
working party

13

accoutrements
advanced guard
carrier pigeon
cheval-de-frise
circumvallate
co-belligerent
column-of-route
counterattack
counter-parole
counterstoke
disembodiment
encompassment
fatigue parade
field equipage
field of battle
fighting force
flying colours
fortification
guards' brigade
interior lines
invincibility
lorry workshop
machicolation
martello tower
mass formation
mounted police
mushroom cloud
order of battle
ordnance depot
pontoon-bridge
radiolocation
rallying point

re-embarkation
re-enforcement
regular troops
reinforcement
sapper officer
shoulder-strap
splinter-proof
squadron drill
storming-party
strategically
swordsmanship
trench warfare
unarmed combat
unconquerable
unsoldierlike
unsurrendered
urban guerilla
Victoria Cross
vitrified fort
war department

14

ammunition dump
auxiliary force
blockade-runner
castrametation
chevaux-de-frise
demobilization
field allowance
general reserve
mechanized army
military school
miniature-range
medical officer
musketry course
musketry school
nuclear warfare
Pyrrhic victory
reconnaissance
reinforcements
reorganization
standing orders
supreme command
trooping-season
unvanquishable
volunteer force
winter quarters

15

auxiliary forces
casualty station
circumvallation
clearing station
contravallation
counter-approach
discharge papers
dressing-station
flying artillery
guerilla warfare
intrenching tool
invulnerability
married quarters
military academy
military college
military funeral
military railway
non-commissioned
observation post
operation orders
submarine-mining
substantive rank
turning movement

Naval (British and U.S.), Fleet Air Arm, Merchant Navy (Merchant Marine) ranks and appellations

4

cook
mate
wren

5

bosun
cadet
diver
middy
pilot

6

cooper
ensign
lascar
marine
master
purser
rating
reefer
seaman
snotty
stoker
topman
writer
yeoman

7

admiral
armorer
artisan
captain
deckboy
fireman
greaser
jack-tar
look-out
messman
recruit
shipman
sideboy
skipper
steward

surgeon
trimmer
wireman

8

armourer
cabinboy
chaplain
coxswain
engineer
flag rank
gun-layer
helmsman
leadsman
messmate
motorman
ship's boy
winchman

9

air-fitter
artificer
boatswain
commander
commodore
cook's mate
donkeyman
engineman
navigator
paymaster
powder-boy
ropemaker
sailmaker
ship's cook
signalman
tugmaster

10

able seaman
apprentice
coastguard
gun captain
instructor
lieutenant
midshipman

range-taker
shipmaster
ship's baker
shipwright
torpedoman
wardmaster

11

air mechanic
branch pilot
chief stoker
electrician
extra master
flag captain
flag officer
foremastman
gunner's mate
leading wren
master's mate
mechanician
port admiral
port officer
post captain
rating pilot
rear-admiral
vice-admiral
watchkeeper

12

boy artificer
cabin steward
chief officer
chief skipper
chief steward
first officer
master-at-arms
master gunner
officers' cook
petty officer
photographer
powder monkey
P.T. instructor
schoolmaster
seaman-bugler
seaman-gunner
second master
senior purser

ship's butcher
ship's caulker
ship's surgeon
supply rating
telegraphist
third officer

13

armourer's mate
captain's clerk
chief armourer
chief engineer
fourth officer
harbourmaster
leading seaman
leading stoker
marine officer
privateersman
quartermaster
quarter rating
radio operator
sailing master
second officer
ship's corporal
signal officer
stern-sheetman
sub-lieutenant
third engineer
torpedo-gunner

14 AND 15

boarding officer
boatswain's mate
first lieutenant
flag-lieutenant
fourth engineer
half-pay officer
leading steward
lieut.-commander
officer's steward
ordinary seaman
rating observer
sailmaker's mate
second engineer
ship's carpenter
torpedo coxswain
warrant officer

Weapons and armour

3 AND 4

ABM
ammo
arm
arms
axe
ball
bill
bola
bolt
bomb
bow

butt
cane
club
colt
dag
dart
dirk
epée
flak
foil
gaff
goad
gun

helm
ICBM
jack
jet
kris
mace
mail
mine
nike
pike
ram
shot
tank

tuck
VTOL
wad
whip
Z-gun

5

A-bomb
aegis
armor
arrow

17

bilbo
birch
clean
crest
estoc
fusee
fusil
grape
H-bomb
hobit
knife
knout
lance
lasso
lathi
Maxim
poker
pouch
rifle
royal
sabre
salvo
shaft
shell
skean
skene
spear
staff
stick
sword
targe
tasse
tawse
visor
vizor

6

ack-ack
air-gun
anlace
armlet
armour
barrel
basnet
bodkin
Bofors
bonnet
buffer
bullet
cannon
carrel
casque
cudgel
cuisse
dagger
dragon
dualin
feltre
glaive
gorget
hanger
helmet
homing
jezail
lariat
lassoo
lorica
mailed
mauser
morion
mortar
musket
muzzle
napalm

petard
pistol
pom-pom
popgun
powder
primer
quarry
rapier
recoil
sallet
saturn
shield
sickle
stylet
swivel
target
tonite
tulwar
umbril
weapon
Webley
zipgun

7

anelace
armbrust
assagai
assegai
ataghan
bar-shot
baslard
bayonet
bazooka
brasset
Bren gun
buckler
carbine
calibre
cordite
couteau
cuirass
curtana
curtein
cutlass
djerrid
dualine
dudgeon
ejector
elf-bolt
espadon
firearm
fire-pot
gantlet
gasmask
greaves
grenade
gunshot
halberd
halbert
handgun
harpoon
hatchet
hauberk
holster
javelin
langrel
longbow
long tom
lyddite
machete
megaton
missile
morglay
murrion

nuclear
oil-bomb
panoply
poitrel
polaris
priming
pole-axe
poniard
quarrel
rabinet
roundel
shotgun
side-arm
sjambok
Skybolt
Sten gun
teargas
torpedo
trident
twibill
vamplet
ventail
warhead
wind-gun

8

arbalist
arquebus
attaghan
balister
ballista
bascinet
basilisk
birdbolt
blowpipe
bludgeon
brassart
broad-axe
Browning
burganet
burgonet
canister
carabine
case-shot
catapult
chamfron
charfron
chausses
claymore
corselet
crossbow
culettes
culverin
damaskin
dynamite
eel-spear
elf-arrow
falchion
falconet
field-gun
firearms
fire-ball
firelock
fireship
gadlings
gauntlet
gavelock
gunsight
half-pike
hand-pike
haquebut
howitzer
jazerant
langrage

Lewis gun
magazine
mangonel
mantelet
Maxim gun
munition
naval gun
oerlikon
ordnance
paravane
paterero
pectoral
pederero
petronel
pistolet
plastron
port-fire
pyroxyle
revolver
ricochet
ringmail
scabbard
scimitar
scorpion
shrapnel
siege-gun
spadroon
spontoon
springal
steam-gun
stiletto
stinkpot
stonebow
tomahawk
Tommy gun
umbriere
vambrace
vamplate
whin-yard
yataghan

9

angel-shot
arquebuse
arrowhead
artillery
aventaile
backpiece
ballistic
bastinado
battleaxe
Blue Water
boar-spear
Bofors gun
bomb-chest
bombshell
boomerang
Brown Bess
brownbill
carronade
cartouche
cartridge
chain-mail
chain-shot
chassepot
columbiad
defoliant
demi-lance
derringer
deterrent
detonator
espringal
face-guard
fish-spear

garde-bras
gelignite
grapeshot
guncotton
gunpowder
habergeon
half-track
hand-staff
headpiece
heavy tank
heelpiece
light tank
matchlock
Mills bomb
munitions
musketoon
needle-gun
poison gas
quaker-gun
shillalah
slow-match
slung-shot
smallarms
smallbore
spring-gun
starshell
stinkbomb
sword-cane
teeth arms
troop ship
truncheon
turret gun
ward staff
welsh-hook
xyloidine
zumbooruk

10

ammunition
arcubalist
battery gun
blind shell
Blue Streak
bowie-knife
brigandine
broadsword
burrel-shot
cannonball
cannon-shot
cataphract
coat armour
coat of mail
cross-arrow
demi-cannon
field-piece
fire-barrel
Gatling gun

grainstaff
harquebuse
knobkerrie
Lee-Enfield
machine-gun
medium tank
Minie rifle
mustard-gas
paixhan-gun
pea-shooter
powder horn
projectile
pyroxyline
recoilless
safety-fuse
six-shooter
sticky bomb
sword-stick
touchpaper

11

antitank gun
armoured car
basket sword
blunderbuss
bow and arrow
breastplate
contact-mine
cruiser tank
Dahlgren gun
depth-charge
grande-garde
gun carriage
gun-howitzer
hand-grenade
harping-iron
Jacob's-staff
Lochaber axe
morning-star
mountain-gun
powder-chest
powder flask
safety-catch
scale-armour
Snider rifle
stern-chaser
Thompson gun

12

Armstrong gun
battering ram
boarding pike
bombing plane
breech-loader
cartridge-box

conventional
cross-bar-shot
demi-culverin
double-charge
flame-thrower
fowling-piece
Lancaster gun
landing craft
Mills grenade
mitrailleuse
muzzle-loader
quarterstaff
rocket-mortar
spigot mortar
Stokes mortar
sword-bayonet
tracer bullet
trench mortar
wheel-lock dag

13

aerial torpedo
armor-piercing
ball-cartridge
cartridge-case
cat-o'-nine-tails
Damocles sword
guided missile
high-explosive
knuckleduster
life preserver
percussion cap
poisoned arrow
scalping-knife
shrapnel shell
sub-machine-gun
submarine-mine
thermonuclear
two-edged sword

14–16

anti-aircraft-gun (15)
armour-piercing (14)
ballistic missile (16)
blank cartridge (a.) (14)
Brennan torpedo (14)
flame-projector (14)
incendiary bomb (a.) (14)
lachrymatory gas (15)
miniature rifle (14)
nitroglycerine (a.) (14)
nuclear weapons (14)
powder-magazine (14)
small-bore rifle (14)

BUSINESS, PROFESSIONS AND OCCUPATIONS
Business, trade and commerce

2 AND 3

A 1
bid
B.O.T.
buy
C\A.
C.O.D.
cut

dun
E.E.C.
fee
F.O.B.
G.N.P.
H.P.
I.O.U.
job
lot

Ltd
net
owe
par
pay
r.d.
rig
S.E.T.
sum

tax
tip
V.A.T.

4

agio
back

	5	stock	hammer
bail		talon	holder
bank		taxes	honour
bear	agent	teind	import
bill	angel	tight	in cash
bond	asset	tithe	income
boom	at par	token	in debt
bull	audit	trade	indent
call	award	trend	insure
cash	batch	trust	jobber
cess	bears	usury	job lot
chip	bid up	value	labour
coin	block	wages	ledger
cost	board	worth	lender
deal	bonds	yield	liable
dear	bonus		Lloyd's
debt	brand		lock-up
deed	bribe	**6**	margin
dole	bulls		market
dues	buyer	accept	mark-up
dump	buy in	accrue	mature
duty	buy up	advice	merger
earn	by-law	agency	minute
easy	cargo	amount	nem. con.
E.F.T.A.	cheap	assets	notice
even	check	assign	octroi
fine	chips	at cost	office
firm	clear	avails	on call
fisc	clerk	bailee	oncost
free	costs	bailor	option
fund	cover	banker	one off
gain	crash	barter	outbid
G.A.T.T.	cycle	bearer	outlay
gild	debit	borrow	outlet
gilt	draft	bought	output
giro	entry	bounce	packet
glut	ex cap.	bounty	parity
gold	ex div.	bourse	pay-day
good	float	branch	paying
hire	folio	broker	pay-off
idle	funds	bubble	pay out
I.O.U.S.	gilts	budget	pledge
kite	goods	burden	plunge
lend	gross	buying	policy
levy	hedge	buy out	profit
lien	'House'	by-laws	public
loan	index	cartel	punter
long	issue	cheque	quorum
loss	labor	change	racket
mart	lease	charge	rating
mint	limit	client	realty
nett	money	corner	rebate
note	notes	coupon	recoup
owed	offer	credit	redeem
paid	order	crisis	refund
P.A.Y.E.	owing	cum. div.	remedy
poll	panic	dealer	rental
pool	paper	deal in	rentes
post	payee	debtor	report
puff	payer	defray	resale
punt	pound	demand	retail
ramp	price	dicker	return
rate	proxy	docket	salary
rent	quota	drawee	sample
ring	quote	drawer	save up
risk	rally	equity	saving
sale	rates	estate	sell in
sell	remit	excise	sell up
sink	repay	expend	set off
sold	rider	export	settle
spot	score	factor	shares
stag	scrip	figure	shorts
tare	share	fiscal	silver
term	shark	freeze	simony
turn	short	godown	specie
20 vend	sight	growth	spiral
wage	slump		

spread
staple
stocks
strike
supply
surety
surtax
syndic
tariff
taxman
teller
tender
ticket
tithes
trader
tycoon
unload
unpaid
usance
usurer
valuta
vendor
vendue
volume
wampan
wealth
wind up

7

account
actuary
advance
allonge
annuity
arrears
at sight
auction
auditor
average
backing
bad debt
balance
banking
bargain
bidding
bonanza
bullion
buy back
cambist
capital
cashier
ceiling
certify
charter
company
consols
convert
crossed
customs
cut-rate
damages
day book
dealing
declare
default
deficit
deflate
deposit
douceur
draw out
dumping
duopoly
economy
embargo

endorse
engross
entrust
ex bonus
expense
exploit
exports
factory
failure
fall due
feedback
finance
flutter
forward
freight
funding
futures
gearing
haulage
hedging
holding
imports
imprest
indorse
inflate
in funds
insured
interim
invoice
jobbers
jobbing
kaffirs
killing
lay days
leasing
lending
limited
lockout
lottery
lump sum
manager
mint par
minutes
name day
nest egg
net gain
no funds
on offer
on order
package
partner
payable
pay cash
payment
pay rise
payroll
pay slip
pension
per cent
pre-empt
premium
prepaid
pricing
product
profits
promote
pro rata
pyramid
realize
receipt
reissue
renewal
reserve
returns
revenue
rigging

royalty
salvage
selling
sell-out
service
sold out
solvent
spinoff
squeeze
stipend
storage
subsidy
surplus
swindle
takings
tax free
tonnage
trade in
trading
traffic
trustee
utility
vending
venture
war bond
war loan
warrant
way bill
wound up
write up

8

above par
acceptor
accounts
act of God
after tax
agiotage
amortize
ante-date
appraise
assignee
assigner
auditing
back bond
bailment
bank bill
bankbook
bank giro
bank loan
banknote
bank rate
bankrupt
barratry
basic pay
below par
berthage
blue chip
book debt
borrower
bottomry
business
buying in
carriage
cashbook
cash down
cash sale
clearing
commerce
consumer
contango
contract
creditor
credit to

cum bonus
currency
customer
cut-price
dealings
defrayed
delivery
director
disburse
discount
dividend
drawings
dry goods
earnings
embezzle
employee
employer
emporium
endorsee
endorser
entrepot
equities
estimate
evaluate
exchange
expenses
exporter
ex gratia
ex rights
finances
fine gold
flat rate
gold pool
goodwill
gratuity
hallmark
hammered
hard cash
hard sell
hot money
importer
in arrear
increase
indebted
industry
interest
in the red
investor
lame duck
manifest
mark down
markings
maturing
maturity
merchant
monetary
monopoly
mortgage
net price
novation
on credit
on demand
on strike
operator
ordinary
overhead
overtime
par value
passbook
pin money
poundage
price cut
price war
proceeds
producer
property

21

purchase
quit rent
rack rent
receipts
receiver
recovery
reinvest
reserves
retailer
retainer
scarcity
schedule
security
shipment
sinecure
solvency
spending
spot cash
sterling
straddle
supertax
swindler
takeover
taxation
tax dodge
taxpayer
trade gap
transfer
Treasury
turnover
undercut
unquoted
wage rate
warranty
windfall
write off

9

actuarial
ad valorem
aggregate
allotment
allowance
annuitant
ante-dated
anti-trust
appraisal
appraiser
arbitrage
arrearage
assurance
averaging
bank stock
blank bill
book value
bordereau
borrowing
brokerage
by-product
call money
call price
carry over
certified
chartered
charterer
clearance
closing bid
commodity
cost price
cum rights
death duty
debenture
debit note
deck cargo

deduction
defaulter
deflation
demurrage
depletion
depositor
directors
dishonour
easy money
easy terms
economics
economies
economize
emolument
exchequer
executive
extortion
face value
fair price
fair trade
fiat money
fiduciary
financial
financier
fine paper
firm offer
firm price
first call
first cost
flotation
franchise
free trade
fully paid
garnishee
gilt-edged
going rate
guarantee
guarantor
hard money
import tax
in arrears
incentive
income tax
indemnity
indenture
inflation
insolvent
insurance
inventory
leasehold
liability
liquidate
liquidity
list price
long-dated
mail order
marketing
middleman
mortgagee
mortgagor
near money
negotiate
net income
order book
outgoings
overdraft
overdrawn
overheads
packaging
pari passu
paymaster
pecuniary
petty cash
piecework
portfolio
preferred

price list
price ring
price rise
prime cost
principal
profiteer
promotion
purchaser
put option
quittance
quotation
ratepayer
ready cash
recession
redundant
reflation
reimburse
repayable
repayment
resources
restraint
reversion
royalties
sell short
shift work
short bill
shortfall
short time
sideline
sight bill
sold short
speculate
spot price
stamp duty
statement
stock list
stockpile
subscribe
subsidize
surcharge
syndicate
tax return
ticket day
trade fair
trademark
trade name
tradesman
traveller
treasurer
undersell
unit trust
utilities
valuation
vendition
viability
wage claim
warehouse
wealth tax
wholesale
winding up
work force
work sheet
work study
World Bank

10

acceptance
accountant
account day
accounting
accumulate
active bond
adjustment
advice note

appreciate
assessment
assignment
attachment
auctioneer
automation
average out
bank credit
bank return
bankruptcy
bear market
bearer bond
bill broker
bill of sale
block grant
bondholder
bonus issue
bonus share
bookkeeper
bucket shop
bulk buying
calculator
call option
capitalism
capitalist
capitalize
capitation
chain store
chequebook
closed shop
collateral
colporteur
commercial
commission
compensate
consortium
contraband
conversion
credit bank
credit card
credit note
credit slip
cumulative
defalcator
del credere
depreciate
depression
direct cost
dirty money
drawn bonds
elasticity
encumbered
engrossing
ergonomics
evaluation
excise duty
ex dividend
first offer
fiscal year
fixed charge
fixed costs
fixed price
fixed trust
free market
floor price
forwarding
funded debt
gross value
ground rent
growth area
honorarium
import duty
income bond
industrial
insolvency
instalment

investment
joint stock
lighterage
liquidator
living wage
long period
loss leader
management
marked down
marketable
mass market
mercantile
money order
monopolist
monopolize
moratorium
negotiable
nonpayment
no par value
note of hand
obligation
open cheque
open credit
opening bid
open market
open policy
option rate
overcharge
paper money
pawnbroker
percentage
plough back
pre-emption
preference
prepayment
price index
price level
production
profitable
profits tax
prospector
prospectus
prosperity
prosperous
provide for
purchasing
pure profit
pyramiding
quarter day
ready money
real estate
real income
recompense
redeemable
redemption
redundancy
remittance
remunerate
rock bottom
sales force
scrip issue
second-hand
securities
selling out
settlement
serial bond
share index
short bonds
short-dated
sole agency
speculator
statistics
stockpiles
stock split
subscriber
tape prices

tax evasion
ticker tape
tight money
trade cycle
trade price
trade union
ultra vires
underwrite
unemployed
upset price
wage freeze
Wall Street
wholesaler
working day
work to rule
written off

11

account book
accountancy
acquittance
advance note
advertising
arbitration
asking price
auction ring
auction sale
average bond
bank account
bank balance
bank holiday
bank of issue
bear squeeze
beneficiary
big business
bill of entry
billionaire
bimetallism
black market
blank cheque
bonded goods
bonus scheme
book-keeping
budget price
businessman
capital gain
cash account
central bank
certificate
circulation
commitments
competition
comptometer
commodities
common stock
competitive
consignment
consumption
co-operative
corporation
counterfeit
cum dividend
customs duty
days of grace
defence bond
demand curve
demand draft
deposit rate
deposit slip
devaluation
discounting
dishonoured
distributor
dividend tax

double entry
down payment
economic law
economic man
endorsement
expenditure
fixed assets
fixed charge
fixed income
fluctuation
foreclosure
free on board
freight note
Gresham's Law
gross income
high finance
hypothecate
income stock
indemnified
indirect tax
industrials
job analysis
joint return
legal tender
liquidation
loan capital
manufacture
market overt
market price
mass-produce
merchandise
middle price
millionaire
minimum wage
money-lender
negotiation
net interest
net receipts
open account
option price
outstanding
overpayment
overtrading
package deal
partnership
pay on demand
physiocrats
point of sale
postal order
poverty line
premium bond
price fixing
price freeze
property tax
purchase tax
Queer Street
raw material
realization
reinsurance
reserve bank
revaluation
rights issue
risk capital
safe deposit
sales ledger
savings bank
seigniorage
sell forward
selling day
shareholder
single entry
sinking fund
small trader
sold forward
speculation
stockbroker

stockjobber
stock market
stockpiling
stocktaking
subsistence
supermarket
syndicalism
take-home pay
takeover bid
time deposit
transaction
undercharge
undervalued
underwriter
with profits

12

above the line
account payee
ad valorem tax
amalgamation
amortization
appreciation
assembly line
balance sheet
banker's draft
banker's order
bargain price
below the line
bill of lading
board meeting
Board of Trade
bond creditor
bonded stores
bottomry bond
branch office
bridging loan
buyer's market
callable bond
capital gains
capital goods
capital stock
carrying over
carry-over day
cash and carry
caveat emptor
charter party
clearing bank
closing price
common market
compensation
consumer goods
contract note
cost of living
credit rating
current price
current ratio
customs union
Defence Bonds
denomination
depreciation
differential
direct labour
disbursement
discount rate
disinflation
distribution
Dutch auction
earned income
embezzlement
econometrics
economy drive
entrepreneur
exchange rate

23

export credit
first refusal
fiscal policy
fixed capital
floating debt
frozen assets
going concern
gold standard
hard currency
hire purchase
indirect cost
interest rate
invoice clerk
irredeemable
joint account
keep accounts
labour market
laissez-faire
life interest
liquid assets
manufacturer
marginal cost
mass-produced
maturity date
mercantilism
merchant bank
mixed economy
monetization
money changer
national bank
national debt
nearest offer
nominal price
nominal value
official list
opening price
overcapacity
pay as you earn
pay in advance
paying-in-slip
policy holder
present worth
price ceiling
price control
price current
price rigging
productivity
profiteering
profit margin
profit motive
profit taking
public sector
rate of growth
raw materials
redeployment
remuneration
remunerative
reserve price
rig the market
rising prices
running costs
sale or return
sales manager
salesmanship
severance pay
share capital
shareholding
sliding scale
social credit
soft currency
specie points
statistician
sterling area
stock in trade
stockjobbery
stockjobbing

surplus value
tax avoidance
tax collector
tax exemption
terms of trade
trade balance
trading stamp
transfer deed
treasury bill
treasury bond
treasury note
trial balance
trustee stock
underwriting
valued policy
welfare state
works council

13

acceptilation
allotment note
appropriation
articled clerk
average clause
backwardation
bank statement
blank transfer
bullion market
business cycle
clearing house
contract curve
credit account
credit control
credit squeeze
crossed cheque
current assets
discount house
dividend yield
dollar premium
Dow-Jones index
exchequer bill
free trade area
futures market
gross receipts
guarantee fund
incomes policy
interim report
issued capital
livery company
Lombard Street
long-dated bill
making-up price
non-cumulative
not negotiable
ordinary share
outside broker
overhead price
paid-up capital
par of exchange
participating
premium income
private sector
profitability
profit sharing
public company
quota sampling
rateable value
sales forecast
settlement day
share transfer
specification
Stock Exchange
switch selling
taxable income

trade discount
value added tax
vendor's shares
wasting assets
wheeler-dealer
works councils

14

account current
advance freight
apprenticeship
balance of trade
bearer security
bill of exchange
blocked account
break-even point
bureau de change
capital account
capital gearing
capitalization
consumer credit
convertibility
corporation tax
current account
current balance
debenture stock
decimalization
deferred rebate
deferred shares
deposit account
discount market
economic growth
featherbedding
fiduciary issue
finance company
floating charge
founders' shares
fringe benefits
full employment
garnishee order
general average
general manager
half-commission
holder for value
holding company
hyperinflation
infrastructure
inscribed stock
invisible trade
joint stock bank
letter of credit
limited company
liquidity ratio
Lloyd's Register
loan conversion
macro-economics
managing agents
market research
micro-economics
monthly account
mortgage broker
new issue market
nominal capital
option dealings
ordinary shares
oversubscribed
preferred stock
progress chaser
promissory note
quality control
random sampling
rate of exchange
rate of interest
receiving order

revenue account
short-term gains
social security
superannuation
surrender value
trading account
uberrimae fidei
unearned income
working capital

15

average adjuster
bonded warehouse

building society
capital employed
commission agent
consignment note
dividend warrant
exchange control
ex-gratia payment
foreign exchange
interim dividend
investment trust
labour-intensive
liquidity ratios
marine insurance
nationalization
non-contributory

political science
preference bonds
preference share
preferred shares
preference stock
public ownership
public relations
purchasing power
rationalization
redemption yield
reducing balance
secured creditor
sleeping partner
sterling balance
unissued capital

Journalism, printing and publishing

2

ad
em
en
o.p.
pi
s.c.
w.f.

3

ads
bed
box
cub
cut
die
mat
out
pie
pot
run
set
sub
web

4

back
body
bold
bulk
caps
comp
copy
cyan
dash
demy
edit
etch
face
film
flap
font
grid
lead
limp
news
open
page
pica
puff

pull
quad
ream
ruby
rule
sewn
sink
slug
stet
take
trim
type

5

beard
black
bleed
block
blurb
cameo
canon
caret
cased
chase
chill
cloth
clump
crown
daily
Didot
draft
dummy
flong
folio
forme
fount
gloss
index
leads
libel
linen
litho
metal
pearl
plate
point
print
proof
punch
quire
quote
recto

reset
roman
rough
royal
run-on
scoop
serif
sigla
solid
sorts
spine
stone
story
title
verso
xerox

6

back-up
banner
boards
ceriph
cliché
coated
cock-up
column
delete
editor
flimsy
format
galley
indent
italic
jacket
keep up
layout
leader
linage
lock up
makeup
marked
masked
matrix
minion
morgue
offset
ozalid
punch
quotes
random
review
revise

rotary
screen
serial
series
set-off
sketch
spiked
splash
weekly
weight

7

article
artwork
binding
bled off
brevier
bromide
bumping
capital
caption
cast off
clicker
diamond
display
edition
English
engrave
etching
feature
Fraktur
full out
gravure
gripper
imprint
justify
leading
literal
masking
measure
monthly
mortice
net sale
overrun
overset
preface
prelims
printer
publish
release
reprint
rewrite

sits vac
subedit
tabloid
typeset
woodcut

8

art board
ascender
bleeding
boldface
colophon
cut flush
dateline
deadline
designer
endpaper
footnote
fudge box
hairline
halftone
hardback
headband
headline
hot metal
imperial
intaglio
keyboard
linotype
monotype
obituary
paginate
photoset
print run
register
reporter
slipcase
streamer
tailband
turnover
type area
verbatim
vignette
woodpulp

9

art editor
bookplate
bourgeois
box number
brilliant
broadside
casebound
co-edition
collating
columnist
copypaper
copyright
crossword
descender
editorial
exclusive
facsimile
freelance
furniture
idiot tape
laminated
lineblock
lower case
make ready
newspaper
newsprint

nonpareil
overprint
pageproof
paperback
paragraph
photocopy
photostat
pseudonym
publisher
quarterly
sans serif
signature
small pica
stonehand
subeditor
symposium
tear sheet
the morgue
title verso
upper case
watermark
web-offset
woodblock
wrong font

10

assembling
annotation
blockmaker
body matter
broadsheet
casting box
casting-off
catch title
city editor
compositor
copyholder
copytaster
copywriter
dead matter
dirty proof
feuilleton
film critic
four colour
imposition
impression
imprimatur
interleave
journalese
journalism
journalist
lamination
leader page
lithograph
long primer
monochrome
news agency
news editor
nom-de-plume
overmatter
pagination
paraphrase
periodical
plagiarism
press agent
reverse out
separation
short story
stereotype
supplement
syndication
title verso
trade paper
typesetter

typography
vignetting
wrong fount
xerography

11

advance copy
advertising
agony column
circulation
copyfitting
crown octavo
cub reporter
display type
galley proof
great primer
half measure
letterpress
line drawing
lithography
night editor
platemaking
proofreader
running head
section-sewn
unjustified

12

block letters
book reviewer
cross heading
facing matter
feature story
illustration
keep standing
leader writer
London editor
magazine page
perfect bound
sports editor
telegraphese
works manager

13

advertisement
composing room
editor-in-chief
foreign editor
justification
literary agent
photogravure
spiral binding
stop press news
wire stitching

14–16

banner headline (14)
calendered paper (15)
colour separation (16)
dramatic critic (14)
features editor (14)
literary editor (14)
managing editor (14)
offset printing (14)
perfect binding (14)
personal column (14)
photolithography (16)
running headline (15)

Officials (including titles and religious designations)

2–4

abbé
aga
aide
amir
amma
babu
beak
beg
bey
cadi
cham
cid
curé
czar
dean
dey
doge
don
duce
duke
earl
emir
foud
graf
head
imam
inca
jam
J.P.
khan
king
lady
lama
lord
miss
M.C.
M.P.
naib
naik
page
papa
peer
pope
rank
ras
rex
shah
sir
sire
tsar
tzar
ward
whip
zaim

5

abbot
agent
ameer
baboo
baron
bedel
begum
board
boyar
canon
chief
Clare

count
dewan
divan
donna
doyen
edile
elder
emeer
envoy
ephor
friar
hakam
imaum
judge
junta
junto
jurat
kalif
laird
laity
liege
macer
mahdi
mayor
mufti
nabob
nawab
nizam
noble
pacha
pasha
padre
porte
prior
queen
rabbi
rajah
reeve
ruler
sagan
sahib
sheik
sophi
staff
state
suite
synod
thane
title
vakil
vicar
wazir

6

abbess
aedile
alcade
archon
ataman
avener
avenor
bailie
barony
bashaw
beadle
begaum
bigwig
bishop
brehon
bursar

caesar
caliph
cantor
censor
cherif
childe
consul
curate
custos
datary
deacon
deputy
despot
donzel
duenna
dynast
eparch
ephori
exarch
fecial
Führer
gauger
harman
herald
hetman
judger
kaiser
kavass
keeper
knight
legate
lictor
mikado
misses
mister
mullah
notary
nuncio
police
préfet
pretor
primus
prince
puisne
rabbin
ranger
rector
regent
sachem
satrap
sbirro
senate
sexton
sheikh
shogun
sirdar
squire
sultan
syndic
tanist
umpire
verger
vestry
vizier
warden
warder

7

alcalde
apostle

armiger
asiarch
attaché
bailiff
baronet
bellman
bencher
burgess
cacique
caloyer
cazique
commère
compère
consort
coroner
council
curator
custode
custrel
czarina
dapifer
dauphin
dogeate
donship
dowager
duchess
dukedom
duumvir
dynasty
earldom
effendi
elector
embassy
emperor
empress
enactor
eparchy
equerry
equites
esquire
estafet
exactor
fidalgo
Fuehrer
gabeler
gaekwar
Gestapo
grandee
hangman
head boy
headman
hidalgo
infanta
infante
jemadar
jerquer
justice
khalifa
khedive
kinglet
maestro
magnate
mahatma
majesty
marquis
marshal
monarch
muezzin
navarch
notable
officer
orderer

27

padisha
paladin
paritor
peerage
peeress
podesta
pontiff
praetor
prefect
prelate
premier
primacy
primate
proctor
prophet
provost
questor
referee
regency
retinue
royalty
sea-king
sea-lord
senator
senatus
shereef
sheriff
signior
skipper
speaker
steward
subadar
sub-dean
sultana
supremo
Tammany
toparch
tribune
tsarina
tzarina
vavasor
viceroy
vaivode
voivode

8

alderman
antistes
archduke
autocrat
banneret
baroness
baronial
Black Rod
blazoner
blindman
brevetcy
burgrave
canoness
cardinal
carnifex
caudillo
chafewax
chairman
chaplain
cicerone
co-bishop
cofferer
consular
co-regent
cursitor
czarevna
deaconry
deanship

deemster
delegate
diaconal
dictator
diocesan
diplomat
director
douanier
dukeling
dukeship
duumviri
emeritus
emissary
enthrone
ethnarch
genearch
guardian
head girl
headship
headsman
heptarch
hierarch
highness
hospodar
imperial
imperium
interrex
kingling
ladyship
laureate
lawgiver
lawmaker
lay elder
legation
licenser
life peer
lordling
lordship
maharaja
manciple
mandarin
margrave
marquess
marquise
martinet
mayoress
minister
ministry
monarchy
monocrat
myriarch
myrmidon
nobility
nobleman
noblesse
official
oligarch
optimacy
overlord
overseer
palatine
placeman
pontifex
princess
priorate
prioress
provisor
quaestor
recorder
regality
register
resident
sagamore
seigneur
seignior
squireen

summoner
suzerain
synarchy
talukdar
tetrarch
tipstaff
treasury
triarchy
tribunal
triumvir
tsarevna
tzarevna
verderer
viscount
wardmote
zemindar

9

ale-conner
ale-taster
archdruid
archducal
archduchy
authority
baronetcy
beglerbeg
bodyguard
bretwalda
bumbledom
burggrave
caliphate
captaincy
carmelite
cartulary
castellan
catchpole
celebrant
cellarist
centurion
chevalier
chieftain
chief whip
chiliarch
commander
commodore
constable
cordelier
court fool
cupbearer
custodian
Dalai Lama
darbyites
deaconess
decemviri
despotism
diaconate
dictatrix
dignitary
diplomate
directory
dominator
drum major
eldership
electress
envoyship
ephoralty
escheator
estafette
exarchate
exciseman
executive
exequatur
ex-officer
fort-major

goldstick
grand duke
high court
incumbent
inspector
Jack Ketch
judgeship
justiciar
knightage
landgrave
lifeguard
liveryman
lord mayor
magnifico
majarajah
majordomo
mandatary
mandatory
matriarch
mayoralty
moderator
monocracy
monsignor
oligarchy
ombudsman
Orangeman
palsgrave
patriarch
patrician
pendragon
pentarchy
policeman
polyarchy
polycracy
portfolio
portreeve
potentate
precentor
presbyter
president
pretender
princedom
principal
proconsul
registrar
reichsrat
rural dean
sacristan
secretary
seneschal
seraskier
sovereign
statesman
sub-beadle
sub-deacon
suffragan
sultaness
timocracy
town clerk
town crier
treasurer
vestryman
viscounty
vizierate
waldgrave
whipper-in
zemindari

10

agonothete
aide-de-camp
ambassador
appanagist
archbishop

archdeacon
archflamen
archimagus
archpriest
areopagite
autocrator
bergmaster
borsholder
bumbailiff
bursarship
camerlengo
carabineer
catechumen
catholicos
censorship
chancellor
chaplaincy
chartulary
chatellany
cimeliarch
cloisterer
cloistress
commandant
commissary
consulship
controller
corporator
corregidor
coryphaeus
councillor
councilman
covenanter
crown agent
czarevitch
dauphiness
deaconship
delegation
designator
dock-master
doorkeeper
enomotarch
enumerator
episcopate
excellency
fire-master
headmaster
heraldship
high master
high priest
Home Office
incumbency
inquisitor
institutor
justiciary
king-at-arms
knighthood
lay brother
legateship
legislator
lieutenant
lower house
mace-bearer
magistracy
magistrate
margravine
marquisate
mayor-elect
midshipman
ministrant
mint-master
monarchism
noblewoman
ochlocracy
officially
oligarchal
opposition

parliament
plutocracy
postmaster
prebendary
presbytery
presidency
proclaimer
procurator
prolocutor
proscriber
proveditor
pursuivant
rectorship
regentship
ringmaster
sachemship
sea captain
sextonship
shrievalty
sign manual
squirehood
squireship
statecraft
state paper
sultanship
suzerainty
tithing-man
unofficial
upper house
vice-consul
vicegerent
vice-master
vice-regent
war council
whiggarchy

11

archdapifer
archduchess
archdukedom
aristocracy
assay-master
autocratrix
burgess-ship
burgomaster
cardinalate
catercousin
chamberlain
chieftaincy
comptroller
corporation
country court
court jester
cross-bearer
crossbowman
crown lawyer
crown prince
diplomatist
directorate
directorial
earl-marshal
ecclesiarch
electorship
executioner
flag officer
functionary
good templar
grand master
grand vizier
gymnasiarch
headborough
intercessor
internuncio
justiceship

landgravine
legislatrix
legislature
lieutenancy
lord provost
marchioness
marshalship
ministerial
monarchical
monseigneur
officialdom
officiating
papal legate
papal nuncio
policewoman
pontificate
pound-keeper
praepositor
premiership
primateship
prince royal
preconsular
proctorship
protocolist
protonotary
provostship
puisne judge
queen-mother
questorship
referendary
school board
senatorship
speakership
squirearchy
stadtholder
stratocracy
subordinate
sword-bearer
tax assessor
tax gatherer
thesmothete
town council
tribuneship
triumvirate
vestry clerk
vice-regency
viceroyalty
viscountess
wreckmaster

12

agent-general
ambassadress
armour-bearer
avant-courier
bound-bailiff
carpet-knight
chairmanship
chief justice
chief of staff
churchwarden
civil servant
civil service
commendatory
commissioner
constabulary
crown-equerry
dictatorship
ecclesiastic
enfranchiser
enthronement
field officer
guardianship
headmistress

29

heir apparent
House of Lords
inspectorate
internuncius
jack-in-office
laureateship
legislatress
lord-temporal
maid of honour
mastersinger
metropolitan
muster-master
notary-public
office-bearer
parish priest
peace officer
poet laureate
prince-bishop
Privy Council
quaestorship
queen-consort
queen-dowager
queen-regnant
quindecemvir
recordership
remembrancer
sheriff-clerk
staff officer
tax collector
Trinity house
unauthorized
uncovenanted
vicar-general
viscountship
water-bailiff
witenagemote

13

administrator
archidiaconal
archimandrite

archpresbyter
archtreasurer
army commander
barrack-master
borough-master
chieftainship
chorepiscopus
color sergeant
consul-general
count palatine
county council
district judge
generalissimo
grand-seigneur
gubernatorial
high constable
inspectorship
judge-advocate
lord-spiritual
mounted police
parliamentary
prime minister
Prince of Wales
Princess Royal
public trustee
state function
states-general
statesmanship
vice-president
vigintivirate

14

archchancellor
archiepiscopal
auditor-general
chancellorship
chief constable
colour sergeant
crown solicitor
dowager-duchess
lord of the manor

gentleman-usher
high court judge
House of Commons
king's messenger
lord chancellor
lord lieutenant
lords-spiritual
medical officer
parochial board
political agent
provost-marshal
revenue officer
superintendent
town councillor
vicar-apostolic
vice-chancellor

15

advocate-general
archchamberlain
archiepiscopacy
archiepiscopate
astronomer-royal
attorney-general
cabinet minister
chamberlainship
chargé d'affaires
district officer
election auditor
governor-general
heir-presumptive
lords lieutenant
messenger-at-arms
parliamentarian
plenipotentiary
privy councillor
queen's messenger
sheriff's officer
suffragan bishop
surveyor-general
vice-chamberlain
vice-chancellors

People

2 AND 3	kid	R.S.M.	bard
	imp	she	bear
A.B.	kin	sir	beau
ace	lad	spy	bevy
ass	lob	son	bird
B.A.	M.A.	sot	blue
boy	ma	tar	boor
B.Sc.	man	us	bore
cad	me	wag	boss
cit	men	we	brat
dab	mob	wit	buck
dad	M.P.	ye	bull
D.D.	Mr.	yob	chap
deb	Mrs.	you	chum
dux	mug		clan
elf	mum		colt
fag	N.C.O.		cove
fan	nun		crew
fop	oaf	4	dame
fub	pa		dear
G.I.	pal	ally	demy
gun	pet	aunt	doer
guy	pig	babe	dull
hag	rat	baby	dolt
ham	rip	band	doxy

drip	team	droll	namer
duck	them	drone	nanny
dude	thug	dummy	Negro
dupe	tike	dunce	niece
feed	toff	duper	ninny
folk	tony	dwarf	noddy
fool	tool	eater	nomad
funk	tory	enemy	nymph
gaby	twin	exile	odist
gang	tyke	extra	ogler
gawk	tyro	fakir	owner
girl	user	felon	pacer
goer	vamp	fence	pagan
goth	waif	fiend	party
grub	ward	fifer	pater
gull	whig	filer	patsy
haji	wife	firer	payee
heel	wino	flier	payer
heir	yogi	flirt	peach
herd	zany	flock	pigmy
hero		fogey	piler
hick		fraud	pin-up
hobo	**5**	freak	piper
host		freer	porer
idol		gamin	poser
jack	adept	gaper	posse
jade	adult	gazer	proxy
jill	aider	genii	prude
jilt	airer	ghost	pryer
jury	alien	giant	puker
kith	angel	giber	punch
lass	argus	gipsy	pupil
liar	aunty	giver	puppy
loon	bairn	goose	pygmy
lout	beast	grass	quack
lush	being	groom	queen
magi	belle	guest	queer
maid	bigot	guide	racer
male	biter	hater	raker
mama	black	heavy	raver
mate	blade	hewer	rebel
mess	blood	hider	rider
mime	booby	hiker	rival
minx	bride	hodge	rogue
miss	broad	hunks	rough
mite	brute	hussy	rover
mome	bully	idiot	rower
monk	cadet	idler	sahib
muff	carle	in-law	saint
mute	cheat	issue	saver
mutt	child	jingo	scamp
nizy	choir	joker	scion
ogre	chuff	Judas	scold
papa	chump	juror	scout
peer	churl	knave	screw
peon	clare	lazar	shark
prig	clown	leper	shrew
rake	co-aid	limey	sider
roué	couch	local	silly
runt	crank	locum	siren
sage	crone	loser	sizar
salt	crony	lover	skier
sect	crook	madam	snail
seer	crowd	maker	sneak
self	cynic	mamma	sorry
sept	dandy	mater	sower
serf	darky	mimic	spark
shot	decoy	minim	sport
silk	devil	minor	squab
sire	dicer	miser	squaw
slut	diver	moron	staff
snob	do-all	mouse	stoic
soak	donce	mover	stray
star	donor	mower	sumph
swot	doter	mummy	swain
tart	dozer	muser	swell

31

taker	carver	gainer	lapper
tenor	casual	gammer	lasher
thief	chaser	gasbag	lassie
toady	client	genius	layman
tommy	clique	gentry	leader
toper	co-ally	getter	league
toyer	coaxer	geezer	leaper
tramp	codder	giglot	leaser
trier	codger	gigman	leaver
troop	co-heir	gigolo	lecher
trull	coolie	gillie	legist
trump	copier	glider	lender
twins	co-star	godson	lessee
uncle	cottar	golfer	lessor
urger	cotter	gossip	letter
vexer	cousin	granny	lifter
vixen	coward	grazer	limner
voter	craven	griper	lisper
wader	creole	grouch	lister
wench	cretin	grower	loafer
whoso	cueist	guiser	lobber
widow	damsel	guller	lodger
wight	dancer	gulper	looker
wiper	darner	gunman	loonie
witch	dauber	gunner	looter
women	debtor	gusher	lubber
wooer	defier	halter	lurker
yahoo	delver	healer	lyrist
yobbo	denier	hearer	madcap
yokel	deputy	heater	madman
youth	digger	heaver	maiden
	dipper	hector	maniac
	dodger	hedger	marine
	doodle	helper	marker
6	dotard	hermit	maroon
	double	hinter	marrer
abaser	dragon	hippie	martyr
abider	drawee	hoaxer	masher
abuser	drawer	holder	masker
admass	drazel	hooter	master
adored	driver	hopper	matron
adorer	drudge	howler	medium
agnate	dry-bob	hoyden	melter
albino	ducker	huffer	member
allies	duffer	humbug	menial
alumna	dyvour	hummer	mentor
amazon	earwig	hunter	mestee
ambler	egoist	hurler	midget
angler	elator	hussar	minion
apache	envier	hymner	misses
auntie	eraser	iceman	missis
au pair	escort	infant	missus
backer	eunuch	inmate	mister
bandit	expert	ironer	mocker
bar fly	fabler	jeerer	modist
batman	faggot	jerker	mohawk
bayard	family	jester	mohock
beater	fanner	Jesuit	moiler
beauty	father	jet set	monkey
beldam	fawner	jilter	mooter
better	feeler	jogger	moppet
bettor	fellow	jolter	mortal
bibber	female	jumper	mother
bidder	fencer	junior	mugger
bilker	Fenian	junker	mulier
blacks	fiancé	junkie	mummer
blonde	fibber	keeper	myself
bomber	filler	kicker	nagger
boozer	finder	kidder	nation
bowler	foeman	killer	native
buster	foiler	kisser	needer
cadger	forcer	knower	nephew
caller	friend	lacker	nipper
camper	gadder	lagger	nitwit
captor	gaffer	lancer	nobody
carper	gagger	lander	nodder

noodle	ringer	talker	abettor
novice	rinker	tartar	acceder
nudist	rinser	tasker	accuser
ogress	rioter	taster	adapter
old boy	ripper	tatler	admirer
old man	risker	tearer	adviser
opener	roamer	teaser	agamist
oracle	roarer	teller	aircrew
orator	rocker	tenant	also-ran
orphan	Romany	Teuton	alumnus
outlaw	rookie	theist	amateur
pandit	rotter	thrall	amorosa
panter	rouser	throng	amoroso
papist	rubber	tilter	anybody
parent	ruiner	toiler	ascetic
pariah	runner	tomboy	assizer
parter	rusher	tooter	assumer
patron	rustic	tosser	atheist
pauper	sadist	truant	athlete
pawnee	sailer	tutrix	avenger
pawner	santon	tyrant	averter
paynim	savage	umpire	babbler
pecker	savant	undoer	ballboy
pedant	scaler	uniter	bastard
peeler	scorer	urchin	batsman
peeper	scouse	vamper	beatnik
pelter	scrimp	vandal	bedmate
penman	second	vanner	bedouin
penpal	seeker	varlet	beldame
person	seizer	vendee	beloved
piecer	selves	vendor	best man
pigeon	sender	vestal	bigshot
pinner	senior	viator	blabber
placer	sentry	victim	blender
player	shadow	victor	boarder
poller	shaker	viewer	boaster
Pommie	shaman	Viking	boggler
poseur	sharer	virago	bookman
poster	shaver	virgin	bouncer
pourer	sheila	votary	bounder
pouter	shover	voyeur	breeder
prater	shower	wafter	brother
prayer	shrimp	walker	bucolic
preyer	sigher	wanton	buffoon
proser	sinner	warmer	bumpkin
prover	sipper	warner	bungler
public	sister	washer	burgher
puffer	sitter	waster	bushman
puller	skater	wearer	bustler
pumper	slayer	weeder	cackler
pundit	slicer	weeper	caitiff
punter	slider	wet-bob	captain
puppet	sloven	whiner	captive
purger	smiler	wincer	casuist
purist	smiter	winder	caveman
pusher	smoker	winker	changer
quaker	snarer	winner	chanter
quoter	sniper	wisher	Charlie
rabbit	snorer	wizard	charmer
rabble	snudge	wittol	cheater
racist	soaker	worker	checker
racker	solver	worthy	Chindit
ragtag	sparer	wretch	citizen
raider	spouse	writer	clapper
railer	squire	yapper	cleaver
rammer	square	yeoman	climber
ranter	stager	yonker	clipper
rapist	starer	zealot	clubman
rascal	stayer	zombie	cockney
rating	stoner		cognate
reader	stooge		colleen
reaper	stroke	**7**	colonel
relict	sucker		combine
relier	suitor		commons
rhymer	surety	abactor	company
rifter	tacker	abetter	compère

comrade	elegist	groupie	knoller
consort	elogist	grouser	know-all
convert	elohist	growler	laggard
convict	empiric	grown-up	landman
copycat	emptier	grubber	laugher
co-rival	enactor	grudger	leaguer
Cossack	endower	grunter	learner
coterie	endurer	guesser	legatee
counter	engager	guildry	liberal
courser	enjoyer	guzzler	limiter
courter	enticer	gymnast	loather
coxcomb	entrant	habitué	lobcock
crawler	epicure	haggler	lookout
creator	erecter	half-wit	lorette
creeper	eremite	handler	lounger
cringer	escapee	has-been	lowbrow
cripple	escaper	hatcher	lunatic
croaker	exactor	haunter	lurcher
crooner	exalter	heathen	magnate
crusher	exciter	heckler	mangler
cry baby	exposer	heiress	manikin
cuckold	failure	hell-hag	mankind
culprit	fair sex	hellier	marcher
curioso	fall-guy	heretic	marplot
cyclist	fanatic	heroine	meddler
dabbler	fancier	hipster	menacer
dabster	fantast	hoarder	mestino
dallier	fascist	hobbler	mestizo
damosel	fathead	homager	milksop
dangler	faulter	hoodlum	mingler
darling	favorer	hostage	minikin
dastard	feaster	hostess	misdoer
dawdler	feoffee	hothead	mobster
daysman	feoffor	huddler	modiste
debaser	fiancée	humbler	monitor
debater	fiddler	hurrier	moulder
defacer	fielder	husband	mounter
defamer	filcher	hustler	mourner
defiler	flapper	hymnist	mouther
defunct	flasher	imagist	mudlark
delator	fleecer	imbiber	mugwump
deluder	floater	impeder	mulatto
denizen	flouter	imposer	mumbler
derider	foister	imputer	Negress
desirer	fondler	inciter	Negrita
devisee	fopling	inducer	nettler
deviser	forager	infidel	nibbler
devisor	founder	infuser	niggard
devotee	freeman	ingrate	niggler
diarist	freezer	inhaler	nithing
dibbler	frisker	injurer	nominee
diehard	frowner	insured	oarsman
dilator	frumper	insurer	obligee
divider	fuddler	invader	obliger
diviner	fumbler	invalid	obligor
dizzard	gabbler	inviter	oddball
doubter	gallant	invoker	offerer
dowager	gambler	jackass	old fogy
dragoon	garbler	jack-tar	old girl
dreader	general	jacobin	old maid
dreamer	gentile	jangler	old salt
drifter	giggler	Jezebel	oppidan
driller	glutton	Joe Soap	opposer
drinker	gobbler	jostler	orderer
droller	goodman	juggler	outcast
drowner	gormand	jumbler	Oxonian
drubber	gossoon	juryman	paddler
dualist	gourmet	juvenal	papoose
dueller	gownman	Kantist	paragon
dullard	grandam	killjoy	partner
dweller	grandma	kindler	parvenu
edifier	grantee	kindred	patcher
egghead	granter	kingpin	patient
egotist	grantor	kinsman	patriot
ejector	grasper	kneeler	Paul Pry
elector	griffin	knocker	peasant

peruser	saluter	spurner	usurper
pervert	sandman	spurrer	utopian
piercer	saviour	stabber	utterer
pilgrim	scalder	stand-by	vacuist
pincher	scalper	stand-in	vagrant
pioneer	sceptic	starlet	vampire
plaiter	schemer	starter	vaulter
planner	scholar	stealer	vaunter
playboy	scoffer	stentor	veteran
pleadee	scolder	stepson	villain
pleader	scooper	sticker	villein
pleaser	scorner	stiller	visitor
plenist	scraper	stinger	vouchee
plodder	scraple	stinker	voucher
plotter	scrooge	stinter	voyager
plucker	scroyle	stirrer	vulture
plumper	sculler	stooper	waddler
plunger	seceder	stopper	wagerer
pounder	sectary	strayer	wakener
praiser	securer	striker	waltzer
pranker	seducer	striver	want-wit
presser	seminar	stroker	warbler
pricker	service	student	warlock
prinker	settler	studier	wastrel
private	shammer	stumper	watcher
prodigy	sharker	stylist	waterer
progeny	sharper	subduer	waverer
protégé	shedder	subject	weigher
prowler	shifter	suicide	welcher
puncher	shooter	suspect	wencher
punster	shopper	swagman	whipper
puritan	shouter	swinger	whisker
pursuer	show-off	swearer	widower
puzzler	shutter	sweater	wielder
quaffer	shyster	sweeper	windbag
queller	sibling	swiller	wise guy
querent	skimmer	swimmer	witling
querist	skipper	swinger	witness
quieter	skulker	tarrier	wolf cub
quitter	slacker	tattler	worrier
radical	slammer	taunter	wounder
rambler	slasher	templar	wrapper
ravener	sleeper	tempter	wrecker
reacher	slinger	text-man	wrester
realist	slipper	thinker	wringer
rebuker	slitter	thriver	yielder
reciter	smasher	thrower	younker
recluse	snapper	thumper	Zionist
redhead	snarler	tickler	
redskin	sniffer	tippler	
reducer	snipper	toaster	**8**
referee	snoozer	toddler	
refugee	snorter	tomfool	
refuser	snuffer	toppler	abdicant
refuter	society	tosspot	abductor
regular	soloist	tourist	absentee
relater	someone	trainee	academic
remover	soother	trainer	accepter
renewer	sophist	traitor	achiever
repiner	soprano	treader	adherent
replier	spaniel	treater	adjutant
rescuer	spanker	tricker	adulator
reserve	spanner	trifler	advocate
retaker	speaker	tripper	aesthete
retinue	speeder	trollop	agitator
reverer	speller	trooper	agnostic
reviver	spender	tropist	alarmist
rhymist	spiller	trouper	allottee
riddler	spitter	trudger	allotter
roadhog	spoiler	trustee	alter ego
royalty	sponger	truster	altruist
ruffian	sponsor	tumbler	ancestor
ruffler	sporter	twirler	ancestry
rumbler	spotter	twister	anchoret
runaway	spouter	twitter	antihero
rustler	sprayer	upstart	antipope

apostate	combiner	enjoiner	harasser
appellee	commando	enlarger	hardener
appellor	commoner	enricher	harridan
approver	commuter	enslaver	harrower
arranger	complier	ensnarer	hastener
aspirant	computer	ephesian	hazarder
assassin	consumer	erastian	hectorer
assembly	convener	eschewer	hedonist
assertor	conveyer	espouser	helpmate
assignee	coquette	esteemer	helpmeet
assignor	corporal	eulogist	highbrow
assuager	co-surety	euphuist	hijacker
attacker	cottager	Eurasian	hinderer
attestor	courtier	everyman	homicide
audience	co-worker	everyone	honourer
aularian	crackpot	evildoer	hooligan
awakener	creditor	evocator	horseman
bachelor	criminal	examinee	huckster
balancer	customer	examiner	Huguenot
bankrupt	crusader	exceeder	humanist
banterer	dalesman	exceptor	humorist
baritone	daughter	executor	humpback
barrator	deadhead	expiator	idealist
beadsman	deaf-mute	expirant	idolater
beginner	debutant	exploder	idolizer
beguiler	deceased	explorer	idyllist
believer	deceiver	exponent	imaginer
bellower	defector	extender	imbecile
benedict	defender	extoller	imitator
bestower	deferrer	fanfaron	immortal
betrayer	democrat	fatalist	impairer
bigamist	demoniac	favourer	imparter
big noise	departer	feminist	impeller
blackleg	deponent	ferreter	implorer
blazoner	depraver	figurant	impostor
blighter	depriver	finalist	improver
bluecoat	derelict	finisher	impugner
bohemian	deserter	flaunter	inceptor
bookworm	deserver	flincher	incloser
borderer	despiser	folk-hero	indictee
borrower	detainee	follower	indicter
boy scout	detainer	fomenter	indigene
braggart	detector	fondling	inductee
brethren	devourer	foregoer	inductor
brunette	diffuser	foreseer	indulger
busybody	digester	forgiver	infecter
cabalist	diner-out	fourling	inferior
caballer	dirty dog	franklin	inflamer
callgirl	disciple	freedman	informer
canaille	disponee	freshman	initiate
cannibal	disponer	fribbler	innocent
canoeist	disposer	frizzler	inquirer
carouser	disputer	front man	insister
castaway	ditheist	fugitive	insnarer
catamite	diverter	fusilier	inspirer
Catholic	divorcée	futurist	insulter
caviller	divorcer	gadabout	intended
celibate	divulger	galloper	intender
cenobite	do-gooder	gamester	intimate
champion	dogsbody	gaolbird	intruder
chaperon	drencher	garroter	investor
children	dribbler	gatherer	islander
chiliast	drunkard	genearch	jabberer
chuckler	duellist	geometer	jackaroo
cicerone	duettist	getter-on	Jacobite
cicisbeo	dullard	giantess	jailbird
civilian	effector	godchild	Jehovist
claimant	elegiast	goodwife	jingoist
clansman	elevator	gourmand	John Bull
classman	embracer	gownsman	Jonathan
clincher	emigrant	graduate	joy-rider
clodpoll	emulator	grandson	Judaizer
cognizee	enchanter	grisette	juvenile
cognizor	encloser	grumbler	kinsfolk
colonial	enforcer	habitant	lady-love
36 colonist	enhancer	hanger-on	lame duck

lamenter	numberer	quaverer	scuffler
landsman	numskull	quencher	seafarer
landsmen	nursling	quibbler	searcher
latinist	objector	quidnunc	seconder
launcher	obscurer	quietist	selector
layabout	observer	Quisling	sentinel
lay-clerk	obtainer	rakehell	sergeant
layer-out	obtruder	ransomer	shortner
laywoman	occupant	ratifier	shrieker
legalist	occupier	ravisher	shrimper
levanter	offender	reasoner	shrinker
leveller	old-timer	rebutter	shuffler
libellee	old woman	recaptor	sidekick
libeller	onlooker	receiver	sidesman
liegeman	operator	reckoner	simoniac
linesman	opificer	recliner	simperer
lingerer	opponent	recoiler	skeleton
linguist	oppugner	recorder	sketcher
listener	optimist	recreant	slattern
literate	oratress	redeemer	slugabed
literati	outliver	reformer	sluggard
litigant	outsider	refunder	slyboots
livewire	pacifier	regicide	small fry
logician	pacifist	rejecter	snatcher
loiterer	paleface	rejoicer	snuffler
looker-on	palterer	relapser	sodomite
loyalist	pamperer	relation	softener
luminary	panderer	releasee	softling
lunarian	Papalist	releaser	solecist
lutanist	paramour	reliever	solitary
luxurist	parasite	remarker	somebody
lyricist	parcener	reminder	songster
macaroni	pardoner	remitter	son-in-law
malapert	parodist	renderer	sorcerer
malaprop	partaker	renegade	spinster
maligner	partisan	repealer	spitfire
mandarin	passer-by	repeater	splitter
man-hater	patentee	repeller	spreader
mannikin	pelagian	reporter	springer
marauder	penitent	reprover	sprinter
marksman	perjurer	repulser	squaller
martinet	pesterer	reseizer	squasher
may-queen	pharisee	resenter	squatter
medalist	picaroon	reserver	squeaker
mediator	pilferer	resident	squealer
merryman	pillager	resigner	squeezer
mesmeree	plagiary	resister	squinter
messmate	playgoer	resolver	squireen
mimicker	playmate	resorter	squirter
mislayer	plebeian	restorer	stancher
mistress	poisoner	retarder	stickler
modalist	polluter	retorter	stinkard
modifier	poltroon	returner	stitcher
molester	ponderer	revealer	stowaway
monodist	popinjay	reveller	stranger
monsieur	populace	revenger	stripper
moon-calf	prattler	revolter	stroller
moonling	preparer	rewarder	strutter
moralist	presager	riffraff	stumbler
Moravian	presbyte	rifleman	suborner
motorist	presumer	rigorist	suckling
murderer	prisoner	rodomont	sufferer
murmurer	prize-man	romancer	superior
mutineer	prodigal	Romanist	superman
mutterer	producer	romantic	supposer
namesake	profaner	rotarian	surmiser
narrator	promisee	royalist	survivor
narrower	promiser	runagate	sybarite
naturist	promoter	ruralist	tacksman
neophyte	proposer	saboteur	talesman
nepotist	protégée	satanist	tartuffe
neurotic	provoker	saucebox	taxpayer
new broom	punisher	sciolist	teddy boy
newcomer	purifier	scorcher	teenager
nihilist	Puseyite	scourger	telltale
nuisance	quadroon	scrawler	tenantry

testator	aggressor	companion	driveller
theorist	alcoholic	concubine	dyspeptic
thrasher	analogist	confessor	early bird
threader	anarchist	confidant	earthling
thruster	anchoress	conformer	eccentric
thurifer	anchorite	Confucian	Edwardian
thwarter	annuitant	co-nominee	emendator
top brass	apologist	conqueror	enchanter
torturer	appellant	conscript	encomiast
townsman	applauder	consenter	energizer
traditor	applicant	consignee	energumen
traducer	appraiser	consignor	enfeebler
trampler	arch-enemy	conspirer	engrosser
trappist	assailant	constable	enlivener
trembler	associate	consulter	entangler
triplets	augmenter	contemner	entourage
truckler	authority	contender	entreater
truelove	automaton	continuer	epicurean
turncoat	bacchanal	contralto	epileptic
twaddler	backbiter	contriver	epistoler
twitcher	banqueter	converter	evacuator
two-timer	barbarian	co-patriot	everybody
underdog	bargainee	corrector	exactress
unionist	bargainer	corrupter	examinant
upholder	battleaxe	covergirl	excusator
upper ten	bedfellow	crackshot	executant
vagabond	bedlamite	creatress	executrix
vanguard	beggarman	creditrix	exhauster
vapourer	bel esprit	cricketer	exhibiter
venturer	biblicist	crookback	exhibitor
verifier	bicyclist	cut-throat	exploiter
vilifier	blockhead	daredevil	expositor
villager	bluebeard	dark horse	expounder
violator	blunderer	debauchee	exquisite
visitant	blusterer	débutante	extractor
votaress	bolsterer	declaimer	extravert
votarist	bon vivant	declarant	extrovert
wallower	bourgeois	defaulter	extremist
wanderer	boy friend	defeatist	falsifier
wayfarer	bridesman	defendant	family man
waylayer	brigadier	defrauder	favourite
waymaker	bystander	deliverer	find-fault
weakener	cabin crew	demagogue	fire-eater
weanling	Calvinist	demandant	first born
welcomer	candidate	demi-monde	flatterer
Wesleyan	canvasser	dependant	flay-flint
wheedler	careerist	depositor	fleshling
whistler	carnalist	depressor	forbidder
whitener	celebrity	depurator	forebears
whizz-kid	chain-gang	designate	foreigner
wiseacre	chantress	desperado	forfeiter
wonderer	character	despoiler	forgetter
wrangler	charlatan	destinist	formalist
wrestler	charterer	destroyer	fortifier
wriggler	chatterer	detractor	forwarder
yeomanry	chiseller	dialector	fossicker
yodeller	Christian	dialogist	foster-son
yokemate	churchman	disburser	foundling
yourself	clatterer	discerner	foundress
	clientele	discloser	fratricide
	coadjutor	disgracer	free agent
9	coalition	disguiser	freelance
	cocklaird	dispeller	free-liver
abecedary	co-heiress	disperser	freemason
aborigine	colleague	displayer	fulfiller
absconder	collegian	disprover	furtherer
abstainer	combatant	disputant	gainsayer
academist	comforter	disseizor	garnishee
accessory	commander	dissenter	garnisher
acclaimer	committee	dissident	garreteer
addressee	committer	disturber	garrotter
addresser	committor	disuniter	gathering
admiralty	commodore	divinator	gentleman
adulterer	communist	dogmatist	girl guide
adversary	community	dolly bird	Girondist
affirmant	compacter	do-nothing	go-between

godfather
godmother
Gothamite
grandpapa
grandsire
gratifier
great-aunt
greenhorn
grenadier
greybeard
groomsman
groveller
guerrilla
guest star
guineapig
half-breed
half-caste
haranguer
harbinger
harbourer
harnesser
hearkener
hell-hound
highflier
hillbilly
Hottentot
household
housewife
hunchback
hylozoist
hypocrite
ignoramus
immigrant
immolator
impeacher
impleader
inamorata
inamorato
increaser
incurable
indicator
indweller
inebriate
inflicter
informant
infractor
infringer
inhabiter
inheritor
initiator
innovator
in-patient
inscriber
insolvent
instiller
insurgent
intestate
intriguer
introvert
inveigher
inveigler
Jansenist
jay-walker
jitterbug
joculator
joint-heir
journeyer
jovialist
justifier
kidnapper
kinswoman
lackbrain
ladies' man
landowner
law-monger
lay reader

lazybones
libellant
liberator
libertine
lionheart
lip-reader
liturgist
lost sheep
loud-mouth
lowlander
magnifier
makepeace
malthorse
mammonist
mannerist
masochist
matricide
meanderer
medallist
mediatrix
messieurs
Methodist
metrician
middleman
millenary
miscreant
mitigator
moderator
modernist
modulator
monitress
moonraker
moralizer
mortgagee
mortgagor
mortifier
Mrs. Grundy
multitude
muscleman
mutilator
mythmaker
Narcissus
neglecter
neighbour
neogamist
Neptunian
next of kin
nominator
nonentity
non-smoker
nourisher
novitiate
nullifier
numerator
observant
occultist
offspring
old master
oppressor
organizer
ourselves
pacemaker
palaverer
panellist
paralytic
paranymph
parricide
part-owner
passenger
patricide
patroness
peasantry
Pecksniff
peculator
pen-friend
pen-pusher

pensioner
perceiver
perfecter
performer
permitter
personage
personnel
persuader
perturber
perverter
pessimist
pilgarlic
pinchfist
pin-up girl
plaintiff
Platonist
plunderer
plutocrat
plutonist
portioner
possessor
posterity
postponer
postulant
pot-hunter
practiser
precursor
predicant
predictor
preferrer
prelatist
presbyope
presentee
presenter
preserver
pretender
preventer
proceeder
profferer
profiteer
projector
prolonger
promissor
promulger
proselyte
prosodist
protector
protester
protruder
punctuist
purchaser
purloiner
pussyfoot
Quakeress
quickener
rabbinist
racketeer
raconteur
rainmaker
ransacker
rapturist
ratepayer
recipient
recordist
recoveree
recoverer
rectifier
redresser
reflector
refresher
regulator
rehearser
reinsurer
renouncer
renovator
represser

reprobate
requester
respecter
rhymester
ridiculer
ritualist
roisterer
Romanizer
roughneck
routinist
rubrician
ruminator
Samaritan
Sassenach
satellite
satisfier
Saturnist
saunterer
scapegoat
scarecrow
scavenger
schoolboy
scoundrel
scrambler
scratcher
scribbler
scrutator
sea-lawyer
sectarian
separator
serenader
sermonist
sexualist
shaveling
shortener
shoveller
sightseer
simpleton
skin-diver
skinflint
skylarker
slanderer
slobberer
slowcoach
slumberer
smatterer
sniveller
socialist
socialite
sojourner
solicitor
solitaire
son-of-a-gun
sophister
sophomore
spadassin
spectator
Spinozist
spiritist
spokesman
sportsman
sprinkler
sputterer
squabbler
stammerer
stargazer
star pupil
stigmatic
straggler
strangler
stretcher
stripling
strongman
struggler
stutterer
subaltern

submitter
subverter
succeeder
successor
succourer
suggester
sundowner
suppliant
supporter
surfeiter
susceptor
suspecter
suspender
sustainer
swaggerer
swallower
sweetener
sycophant
symbolist
syncopist
tactician
Talmudist
targumist
temptress
termagant
terminist
terrorist
testatrix
testifier
theorizer
thickskin
thunderer
toad-eater
tormentor
townsfolk
traitress
trapanner
traveller
traverser
trepanner
tribesman
trickster
trigamist
tritheist
truepenny
underling
unitarian
valentine
venerator
verbalist
versifier
Victorian
vigilante
visionary
volunteer
vulcanist
warmonger
wassailer
whosoever
womanizer
womankind
womenfolk
worldling
wrongdoer
xenophobe
yachtsman
young lady
youngling
youngster

10

aboriginal
aborigines
Abraham man

absolutist
accomplice
admonisher
adulterant
adulteress
adventurer
aficionado
alcoranist
allegorist
alms people
ambidexter
ambodexter
anabaptist
ancestress
anecdotist
anglophile
anglophobe
Anglo-Saxon
antagonist
antecedent
antecessor
antecursor
antichthon
antiscians
apologizer
aristocrat
assemblage
assentient
babe-in-arms
baby-sitter
bamboozler
beautifier
bed-presser
bedswerver
Belgravian
belswagger
benefactor
Benthamite
Bethlemite
better half
big brother
blackamoor
blackguard
black sheep
blasphemer
bobbysoxer
bogtrotter
bold spirit
bootlicker
borstal boy
bridegroom
bridesmaid
bureaucrat
bushranger
campaigner
capitalist
caravanner
card-player
cavalryman
centralist
changeling
chatterbox
chauvinist
cheesecake
churchgoer
Cinderella
clodhopper
cloisterer
cloistress
coadjutant
coadjutrix
cohabitant
coloratura
commonalty
competitor
complainer

confessant
confessary
confidante
considerer
contendent
contestant
controller
co-operator
coparcener
copyholder
co-relation
councillor
counsellor
countryman
crackbrain
cringeling
criticizer
crosspatch
curmudgeon
daggle-tail
daydreamer
day-tripper
declaimant
deforciant
delinquent
demoiselle
depositary
deprecator
depredator
deputation
descendant
diatribist
dilettante
diminisher
directress
discharger
discourser
discoverer
discursist
disheritor
disparager
dispraiser
dispreader
disquieter
dissembler
distracter
distruster
divineress
divisioner
dogmatizer
dominicide
dramatizer
Drawcansir
drug addict
drug pusher
dunderpate
dunderhead
Dutch uncle
dynamitard
early riser
ear-witness
elaborator
electorate
electoress
elucidator
emboldener
empiricist
empoisoner
emulatress
encourager
encroacher
engenderer
Englishman
enigmatist
enthusiast
enumerator

enunciator
epitaphist
epitomizer
equestrian
eternalist
evangelist
exhortator
expatiator
explicator
expurgator
extenuator
extirpator
eye-witness
fabricator
factionist
fagot-voter
fashionist
federalist
fire-raiser
flagellant
flourisher
fly-by-night
footballer
footlicker
forefather
foreleader
foremother
forerunner
forswearer
fosterling
foxhunter
fraternity
freeholder
free-trader
frequenter
fuddy-duddy
fund-holder
fund-raiser
Gasconader
gastronome
gentlefolk
girl friend
glacialist
goal keeper
gold-digger
goodfellow
grandchild
grand juror
grandmamma
grandniece
grand-uncle
grass widow
great-uncle
half-sister
harmonizer
hatchet man
head hunter
heliolater
heresiarch
highjacker
highlander
hitch-hiker
human being
iconoclast
identifier
ideologist
idolatress
impenitent
impoisoner
importuner
imprisoner
incendiary
individual
inhabitant
inheritrix
inquisitor

insinuator
instigator
interceder
interferer
interloper
interposer
intervener
introducer
Ishmaelite
jackadandy
jackanapes
jobbernowl
job-hunter
jolterhead
kith and kin
lady-killer
land-holder
landlubber
languisher
lawbreaker
left-winger
legitimist
liberty man
licentiate
lieutenant
literalist
loggerhead
lotus-eater
lower class
Lychnobite
machinator
magnetizer
maiden aunt
maiden lady
malefactor
malingerer
manoeuvrer
man of straw
married man
marshaller
mastermind
matchmaker
merrymaker
metaphrast
methuselah
middlebrow
militarist
mindreader
misogamist
misogynist
monarchist
moneyed man
monogamist
monologist
monomaniac
monopolist
monotheist
mountebank
mouthpiece
muddied oaf
multiplier
namby-pamby
ne'er-do-well
neutralist
nincompoop
nominalist
non-starter
notability
obstructer
occasioner
old soldier
opinionist
opium-eater
originator
orthoepist
out-patient

overrunner
overturner
painstaker
pall-bearer
panegyrist
paraphrast
past master
patronizer
peacemaker
pedestrian
Peeping Tom
pensionary
persecutor
persifleur
personator
petitioner
phenomenon
philistine
pinchpenny
plagiarist
polo player
polygamist
polyhistor
polytheist
population
positivist
pragmatist
preadamite
procreator
profligate
progenitor
prohibiter
promenader
pronouncer
propagator
prophesier
propounder
proprietor
prosecutor
Protestant
psychopath
pulverizer
pyrrhonist
quarreller
questioner
rabblement
ragamuffin
rascallion
Rechabites
recidivist
reclaimant
recognizer
recognitor
reconciler
reimburser
relinquent
rememberer
reproacher
reprobater
reproducer
republican
repudiator
restrainer
restricter
retributer
reverencer
revivalist
rhapsodist
ringleader
sacrificer
scrapegrace
Scaramouch
schematist
schismatic
scrutineer
secularist

sensualist
separatist
sermonizer
seventh son
shoplifter
shanghaier
sinecurist
slammerkin
smart aleck
snuff-taker
solemnizer
solicitant
solifidian
solitarian
son and heir
songstress
soothsayer
Sorbonnist
speculator
spoilsport
squanderer
starveling
stepfather
stepmother
stepsister
stimulator
stipulator
strategist
street arab
strokesman
subscriber
substitute
subtracter
sugar daddy
supplanter
supplicant
suppressor
surmounter
suscipient
sweetheart
sworn enemy
syllogizer
syncopater
syncretist
synonymist
tale-bearer
tale-teller
tantalizer
taskmaster
tea-drinker
televiewer
temporalty
temporizer
tenderfoot
tenderling
textualist
textuarist
themselves
thickskull
third party
threatener
timeserver
tramontane
transferee
transferer
transmuter
trespasser
troglodyte
troubadour
tub-thumper
tweedledee
tweedledum
tuft-hunter
unbeliever
undertaker
unemployed

upper class
upper crust
utopianist
vacillator
vanquished
vanquisher
Vaticanist
vegetarian
vindicator
voluptuary
wallflower
well-wisher
white friar
whomsoever
widow-maker
wine-bibber
wirepuller
withdrawer
withholder
woman-hater
worshipper
yoke-fellow
young blood
yourselves

11

abbreviator
abecedarian
academician
accompanier
accumulator
adventuress
animal lover
aristocracy
association
bandy-player
beauty queen
belligerent
beneficiary
Bible reader
bibliolater
bibliophile
bird's-nester
blackmailer
bloodsucker
blue-eyed boy
blunderhead
bourgeoisie
braggadocio
breadwinner
brotherhood
calumniator
catabaptist
cave-dweller
centenarian
chance-comer
cheer leader
cheese parer
chucklehead
clairvoyant
coalitioner
cognoscenti
co-inheritor
collitigant
commentator
complainant
condisciple
confamiliar
confiscator
conjecturer
connoisseur
conspirator
constituent
continuator

contributor
co-ordinator
deliberator
denominator
denunciator
depopulator
depreciator
detractress
devotionist
dilapidator
diluvialist
dipsomaniac
discipliner
discourager
dishonourer
dissentient
dissertator
distributor
disunionist
doctrinaire
domestician
double agent
draggle-tail
dram-drinker
drug peddler
eager beaver
electioneer
emancipator
embellisher
embroiderer
enchantress
encounterer
endeavourer
enlightener
enlisted man
enterpriser
entertainer
epigenesist
epistolizer
equilibrist
equivocator
establisher
euphemerist
exaggerator
exasperater
father-in-law
fault-finder
femme fatale
fifth column
fighting man
first cousin
flat dweller
flying squad
foot soldier
forestaller
foster-child
francophile
francophobe
freethinker
frothblower
fustilarian
galley slave
gallows bird
gatecrasher
gentlefolks
gentlewoman
ginger group
god-daughter
gormandizer
grandfather
grandmother
grandnephew
grandparent
gull-catcher
guttersnipe
half brother

hard drinker
harum-scarum
helping hand
high society
hobbledehoy
holder-forth
homo sapiens
hyperbolist
hypercritic
ideopraxist
imperialist
inaugurator
infantryman
inhabitress
inheritress
interceptor
intercessor
interrupter
interviewer
intimidater
joint-tenant
knucklehead
leaseholder
libertarian
lickspittle
lilliputian
littérateur
living image
lycanthrope
manipulator
marrying-man
masquerader
materialist
matinee idol
maxim-monger
merry Andrew
metaphorist
middle class
millenarian
millionaire
misanthrope
misbeliever
misinformer
monopolizer
moonlighter
mother-in-law
mountaineer
mouth-friend
Mrs. Malaprop
name dropper
nationalist
necessarian
neutralizer
night-walker
nondescript
non-resident
nosey-parker
opportunist
owner-driver
pacificator
panic-monger
parishioner
participant
pearly queen
pedobaptist
peripatetic
perpetrator
personality
perturbator
phenomenist
philosopher
physicalist
predecessor
prize-winner
probabilist
probationer

prodigal son
proletarian
proletariat
promulgator
propitiator
prosecutrix
protagonist
protectress
protestator
Punchinello
punctualist
purgatorian
questionist
rank and file
rapscallion
rationalist
reactionary
recommender
recompenser
religionist
replenisher
reprehender
resuscitant
reversioner
right-winger
Rosicrucian
royal family
rugby player
sabbatarian
sacrilegist
sans-culotte
scaremonger
scatterling
scoutmaster
scripturist
scrutinizer
search party
shareholder
simple Simon
singularist
sister-in-law
sleepwalker
spectatress
speculatist
speech-maker
speed-skater
spendthrift
spindlelegs
stepbrother
stockholder
stonewaller
stool pigeon
story teller
stump-orator
subordinate
suffragette
surrenderee
surrenderer
sword player
sworn friend
sympathizer
systematist
system-maker
tautologist
teetotaller
teleologist
telepathist
thanksgiver
theosophist
time-pleaser
Tommy Atkins
torch-bearer
town-dweller
traditioner
transmitter
trencherman

trend setter
undersigned
undervaluer
undesirable
Walter Mitty
war criminal
wastethrift
weathercock
wholehogger
withstander

12

abolitionist
acquaintance
advance party
antediluvian
anticourtier
appropriator
artful dodger
assassinator
awkard squad
bachelor girl
backwoodsman
barber-monger
benefactress
bible-thumper
bibliomaniac
blood brother
bluestocking
bond-creditor
bottle-friend
brother-in-law
bounty hunter
carpet-knight
chief mourner
church-member
coalitionist
collaborator
Colonel Blimp
commiserator
committeeman
communicator
competitress
complimenter
compossessor
conservative
consignatory
conquistador
contemplator
contemporary
controverter
convalescent
conventicler
conventioner
convivialist
co-respondent
corporealist
cosmopolitan
defectionist
demimondaine
demonstrator
determinator
dialectician
disciplinant
discommender
discontinuer
disenchanter
disorganizer
dispossessor
disseminator
doppelgänger
double-dealer
eavesdropper

13

educationist
elocutionist
encumbrancer
enfranchiser
equestrienne
exclusionist
excursionist
exhibitioner
experimenter
expostulator
exserviceman
extemporizer
extensionist
exterminator
extinguisher
featherbrain
filibusterer
firstnighter
foster father
foster mother
foster parent
foster sister
foundationer
gastronomist
gesticulator
globe-trotter
gospel-gossip
grey eminence
guest speaker
hair-splitter
headshrinker
heir-apparent
holidaymaker
humanitarian
impersonator
impoverisher
improvisator
inseparables
intellectual
intercipient
interlocutor
intermeddler
intermediary
interpolator
interrogator
investigator
irregularist
kleptomaniac
knight-errant
landed gentry
leading light
legacy-hunter
letter-writer
longshoreman
lounge lizard
mademoiselle
man-about-town
married woman
melancholist
mercurialist
mezzo soprano
misconstruer
misinformant
modest violet
morris dancer
natural child
near relation
neoplatonist
noctambulist
nonagenarian
obscurantist
octogenarian
old gentleman
pantophagist
participator
peace-breaker

penitentiary
perambulator
peregrinator
persona grata
philosophist
pillion-rider
poor relation
postdiluvian
postgraduate
pot-companion
precipitator
prevaricator
primogenitor
proprietress
proselytizer
public figure
quater-cousin
recriminator
redemptioner
relinquisher
remonstrator
residentiary
resolutioner
resuscitator
roller-skater
rolling stone
salvationist
scatterbrain
schoolfellow
second cousin
second fiddle
sequestrator
sexagenarian
significator
single person
sister-german
sole occupant
somnambulist
somniloquist
spiritualist
spirit-rapper
stepdaughter
stormtrooper
straightener
street-urchin
stuffed shirt
sub-committee
sublapsarian
subpurchaser
Sunday driver
swashbuckler
sworn enemies
systematizer
system-monger
tennis player
testificator
theologaster
transgressor
transmigrant
transvestite
troublemaker
truce-breaker
truncheoneer
ugly customer
ugly duckling
ultramontane
undermanager
unemployable
universalist
velocipedist
versificator
village idiot
way passenger
wicket keeper
wool gatherer
working class

adminiculator
administrator
anagrammatist
Anglo-American
Anglo-Catholic
annexationist
anthropophagi
antisocialist
apothegmatist
bibliophilist
blood relation
brother-german
bureaucratist
castle-builder
chamber-fellow
comprovincial
conceptualist
concessionist
conspiratress
conventionist
co-religionist
correspondent
daughter-in-law
deck passenger
deuterogamist
devotionalist
discriminator
distinguisher
exhibitionist
experimentist
fashion-monger
first offender
foot passenger
fortune-hunter
foster brother
fresh-air fiend
grand-daughter
hard bargainer
high churchman
hypochondriac
immaterialist
irreligionist
Job's comforter
laughing stock
life-annuitant
machiavellian
millennialist
miracle-monger
miracle-worker
misanthropist
mischief-maker
multiplicator
necessitarian
nonconformist
paterfamilias
perfectionist
philhellenist
philosophizer
predestinator
protectionist
proverbialist
reprobationer
revolutionary
sophisticator
speed merchant
spindleshanks
spiritualizer
state criminal
state prisoner
strike-breaker
tranquillizer
transmigrator
undergraduate
understrapper

14

antiaristocrat
armchair critic
billiard-player
corpuscularian
destructionist
disciplinarian
disenchantress
foster daughter
galactophagist
good-for-nothing
grammaticaster
ichthyophagist
improvisatrice
indifferentist
latitudinarian
ministerialist
misinterpreter
obstructionist
paragrammatist
philanthropist

procrastinator
prognosticator
progressionist
prohibitionist
promise-breaker
psilanthropist
quadragenarian
quodlibetarian
requisitionist
restorationist
sabbath-breaker
sacramentarian
sensationalist
sentimentalist
septuagenarian
skittles-player
squandermaniac
stamp-collector
superior person
tatterdemalion
trencher-friend
ultramontanist

undergraduette
valetudinarian
waifs-and-strays
weather prophet
whippersnapper

15

antitrinitarian
autograph hunter
circumnavigator
constitutionist
conversationist
emancipationist
experimentalist
heir-presumptive
insurrectionary
insurrectionist
intellectualist
supernaturalist
Tom, Dick, and Harry

Professions, occupations, trades, etc.

2–4

alma
ayah
babu
bard
boss
char
chef
cook
crew
diva
doc
don
dyer
gang
G.P.
gyp
hack
hand
head
herd
hind
lead
magi
maid
mate
mime
M.D.
M.O.
P.A.
page
peon
P.M.
poet
pro
P.R.O.
rep
ryot
seer
serf
spy
syce
thug
tout
vet
ward
whip

5

actor
ad-man
agent
augur
avoué
baker
bonze
boots
bosun
caddy
choir
clerk
clown
coach
comic
crier
crimp
curer
daily
egger
envoy
extra
fakir
fence
fifer
filer
finer
flier
gager
gipsy
gluer
groom
guard
guide
guild
hakim
harpy
helot
hirer
hiver
hoppo
lamia
leech
luter
mason
medic

miner
navvy
nurse
oiler
owler
pilot
piper
plyer
pupil
quack
quill
rabbi
rater
reeve
runer
scout
sewer
shoer
slave
smith
sower
staff
sweep
tamer
tawer
taxer
thief
tiler
tuner
tutor
tyler
usher
valet
viner

6

airman
archer
artist
aurist
author
bagman
bailee
bailer

bailor
balker
bandit
banker
barber
bargee
barker
barman
batman
bearer
beggar
binder
boffin
bookie
bowman
brewer
broker
bugler
burler
bursar
busker
butler
cabbie
cabman
calker
canner
carman
carter
carver
casual
censor
clergy
cleric
codist
coiner
comber
conder
con man
coolie
cooper
copper
co-star
coster
cowboy
cowman
critic
cutler
cutter

dacoit	medico	singer	actuary
dancer	mender	sircar	alewife
dealer	menial	skivvy	almoner
digger	mentor	slater	alnagar
docker	mercer	slaver	alnager
doctor	milker	slavey	analyst
dowser	miller	sleuth	ancient
draper	minter	snarer	apposer
drawer	monger	socman	Arabist
driver	morisk	sorter	arbiter
drover	mummer	souter	artisan
editor	mumper	spicer	artiste
fabler	mystic	squire	assayer
factor	nailer	stager	assizer
farmer	notary	stoker	assured
fellah	nurser	storer	assurer
feller	oboist	sutler	auditor
fictor	oilman	tabler	aviator
fisher	orator	tailor	awarder
fitter	ostler	tamper	bailiff
flayer	packer	tanner	bandman
forger	parson	tasker	barmaid
fowler	pastor	taster	bedeman
framer	patrol	teller	bellboy
fuller	pavier	termer	bellhop
gaffer	pavior	tester	birdman
ganger	pedant	tiller	blaster
gaoler	pedlar	tinker	blender
gaucho	penman	tinman	boatman
gauger	picker	tinner	bondman
gigolo	pieman	toller	bookman
gilder	pirate	touter	bottler
gillie	pitman	toyman	brigand
glazer	plater	tracer	builder
glover	player	trader	burglar
graver	porter	troupe	butcher
grocer	potboy	tubman	buttons
guider	potter	turner	callboy
guidon	priest	tycoon	cambist
gunman	pruner	typist	carrier
gunner	purser	usurer	caseman
harper	querry	vacher	cashier
hatter	rabbin	valuer	cateran
hawker	ragman	vamper	caterer
healer	ranger	vanman	caulker
heaver	ratter	vassal	cellist
hodman	reader	vender	chanter
hooper	reaper	vendor	chapman
horner	reaver	verger	chemist
hosier	rector	verser	chorist
hunter	regent	viewer	cleaner
intern	relief	waiter	clicker
issuer	renter	walker	clippie
jailer	rigger	waller	co-agent
jailor	ringer	warden	coalman
jobber	robber	warder	cobbler
jockey	roofer	warper	cockler
joiner	rooter	washer	collier
jowter	sacker	weaver	co-pilot
jurist	sailor	weeder	copyist
keeler	salter	welder	coroner
keeper	salvor	whaler	corsair
killer	sapper	worker	counsel
lackey	sartor	wright	courier
lander	sawyer	writer	cowherd
lascar	scribe		cowpoke
lawyer	sea-dog		crofter
lector	sealer		cropper
lender	-seaman	**7**	curator
loader	seiner		currier
logman	seizor	abacist	custode
lumper	seller	abigail	danseur
magian	server	acolyte	dentist
marker	setter	acolyth	dialist
master	sexton	acrobat	dietist
matron	shroff	actress	ditcher

45

dominie	marbler	spotter	boxmaker
doorman	marcher	stainer	brewster
dragman	mariner	stamper	broacher
drapier	marshal	stapler	busheler
drawboy	matador	statist	cabin boy
drayman	matelot	steerer	cellarer
dredger	mealman	steward	ceramist
dresser	meatman	surgeon	chandler
drogman	metayer	swabber	choirboy
drummer	metrist	sweeper	co-author
dustman	midwife	taborer	ciderist
famulus	milkman	tallier	claqueur
farrier	modiste	tapster	clothier
fascist	moneyer	taxi-man	coachman
faunist	monitor	teacher	codifier
fiddler	mootman	tipster	coistril
fireman	moulder	tracker	collator
fish-fag	newsboy	trainer	comedian
flesher	oculist	trapper	compiler
florist	officer	trawler	composer
flunkey	orderer	trimmer	conclave
flutist	orderly	trucker	conjurer
footboy	packman	trustee	conveyor
footman	pageboy	tumbler	coryphée
footpad	painter	turnkey	courtier
foreman	palmist	vintner	cow-leech
founder	pantler	violist	coxswain
friseur	peddler	wagoner	croupier
frogman	pianist	waister	cutpurse
fueller	picador	warrior	dairyman
furrier	planner	waterer	danseuse
gateman	planter	webster	deckhand
girdler	pleader	weigher	defender
glazier	plumber	wheeler	designer
gleaner	poacher	whetter	director
gleeman	poetess	wireman	dog-leech
glosser	postboy	woodman	domestic
graffer	postman	woolman	doughboy
grafter	presser	workman	dragoman
grainer	prestor	wrapper	druggist
granger	printer		editress
grantee	puddler		educator
grantor	rancher	**8**	embalmer
grazier	realtor		emissary
grinder	refiner	adscript	employee
gymnast	riveter	aeronaut	employer
hackler	roadman	algerine	engineer
harpist	roaster	analyser	engraver
haulier	rustler	annalist	enroller
helotry	sacrist	aphorist	epic poet
herbist	saddler	apiarist	essayist
herdman	sampler	apron-man	essoiner
heritor	samurai	arborist	exorcist
higgler	scourer	armourer	explorer
hogherd	scraper	armorist	exporter
hostler	servant	arrester	fabulist
indexer	settler	arrestor	factotum
inlayer	sharper	assessor	falconer
ironist	shearer	attorney	famulist
janitor	shipper	bagmaker	farmhand
juggler	shopboy	bagpiper	ferryman
junkman	shopman	ballader	figurant
juryman	showman	bandsman	filmstar
keelman	shunter	bargeman	finisher
knacker	silkman	bearherd	fishwife
knitter	simpler	bearward	flatfoot
laborer	skinner	bedesman	flautist
laceman	skipper	bedmaker	fletcher
linkboy	slipper	bit-maker	fodderer
linkman	smelter	bleacher	forester
lockman	snipper	boatsman	forgeman
lombard	socager	bondmaid	fugleman
mailman	soldier	bondsman	gangster
maltman	soloist	boniface	gardener
manager	spencer	botanist	gavelman
mangler	spinner	bowmaker	gendarme

glassman
goatherd
godsmith
gossiper
governor
guardian
gunsmith
hammerer
handmaid
handyman
hatmaker
haymaker
headsman
head cook
helmsman
henchman
herdsman
hired man
hireling
histrion
home help
hotelier
houseboy
huckster
huntsman
importer
improver
inkmaker
inventor
japanner
jet pilot
jeweller
jongleur
kipperer
labourer
landgirl
landlady
landlord
lapidary
larcener
larderer
leadsman
lecturer
linesman
lumberer
magician
magister
maltster
masseuse
measurer
mechanic
medalist
melodist
mercator
merchant
messager
metal-man
milkmaid
millgirl
millhand
milliner
minister
minstrel
mistress
modeller
muleteer
muralist
musician
neatherd
newshawk
novelist
onion-man
operator
optician
ordainer
ordinand

organist
outrider
overseer
pargeter
parodist
penmaker
perfumer
peterman
pewterer
picaroon
picklock
pinmaker
plagiary
plougher
polisher
portress
postiler
potmaker
preacher
prefacer
preluder
pressman
probator
procurer
promoter
prompter
prosaist
provider
psalmist
publican
pugilist
purveyor
quarrier
raftsman
ranchero
rapperee
receiver
regrater
relessee
relessor
repairer
reporter
resetter
restorer
retailer
retainer
reviewer
rewriter
rivetter
romancer
rugmaker
rumourer
salesman
satirist
sawbones
scullion
sculptor
seamster
sea-rover
seasoner
seedsman
sempster
servitor
shearman
shepherd
ship's boy
shipmate
shopgirl
showgirl
sidesman
simplist
sketcher
smuggler
soldiery
spaceman.
spearman

speedcop
spurrier
starcher
stitcher
stockman
storeman
stripper
strummer
stuntman
supplier
surveyor
swindler
tabourer
tallyman
taverner
teamster
thatcher
thespian
thresher
tin miner
tinsmith
torturer
toymaker
tripeman
truckman
turncock
turnspit
tutoress
unionist
valuator
vintager
virtuoso
vocalist
volumist
waitress
walker-on
wardress
warrener
watchman
waterman
wet nurse
whaleman
whitener
whitster
wigmaker
winnower
wool-dyer
workfolk
workhand
wrestler

9

alchemist
alluminor
anatomist
annotator
announcer
arbitress
arborator
archeress
architect
archivist
art critic
art dealer
artificer
astronaut
attendant
authoress
balladist
ballerina
bank agent
barrister
barrow boy

beefeater
beekeeper
beemaster
berserker
biologist
boanerges
boatswain
bodyguard
boilerman
bondslave
bondwoman
bookmaker
bootblack
bootmaker
buccaneer
bus driver
burnisher
cab driver
café owner
cameraman
car driver
caretaker
carpenter
casemaker
catechist
cellarman
charwoman
chauffeur
cheapjack
chorister
clarifier
clergyman
clinician
clogmaker
coalminer
coalowner
collector
columnist
colourist
comprador
concierge
conductor
conserver
cosmonaut
cost clerk
costumier
courtesan
couturier
cowfeeder
cowkeeper
cracksman
craftsman
crayonist
critickin
cymbalist
dactypist
daily help
dairymaid
decorator
decretist
desk clerk
detective
dice-maker
die-sinker
dietetist
dietitian
directrix
dispenser
dissector
distiller
doctoress
draftsman
dramatist
drawlatch
drum major
drum-maker

47

drysalter	ingrafter	pitsawyer	stableman
ecologist	innholder	planisher	stagehand
embezzler	innkeeper	plasterer	stationer
enameller	inscriber	ploughboy	stay-maker
engineman	inspector	ploughman	steersman
engrosser	intendant	pluralist	stevedore
epitomist	ironsmith	poetaster	subeditor
errand boy	itinerant	pointsman	subworker
estimator	jack-smith	policeman	succentor
examinant	job-master	pontonier	sur-master
excavator	kennel-man	pop artist	swan-upper
excerptor	lacemaker	porteress	swineherd
exchanger	lacquerer	portrayer	switchman
executive	lady's maid	portreeve	swordsman
exercitor	lampooner	postilion	syndicate
exciseman	land agent	postwoman	synoptist
exorciser	landreeve	poulterer	tablemaid
eye doctor	larcenist	practiser	tactician
fabricant	launderer	precentor	tailoress
fashioner	laundress	predicant	teataster
felt-maker	law writer	preceptor	tentmaker
figurante	legionary	prelector	test pilot
financier	librarian	priestess	therapist
film actor	linotyper	privateer	theurgist
film extra	liontamer	professor	throwster
film-maker	liveryman	profilist	timberman
fire-eater	loan agent	provedore	toolsmith
fish-curer	lockmaker	publicist	town clerk
fisherman	locksmith	publisher	towncrier
fish-woman	log-roller	pulpiteer	tire-woman
flag-maker	lumberman	puppeteer	tradesman
flax-wench	machinist	pythoness	tragedian
flyfisher	magnetist	qualifier	traveller
freelance	majordomo	quarryman	treasurer
freighter	male model	quirister	trepanner
fripperer	male nurse	racketeer	tributary
fruiterer	man-at-arms	railmaker	trumpeter
furbisher	mannequin	recruiter	tympanist
furnisher	mechanist	reformist	usherette
galvanist	medallist	rehearser	varnisher
gasfitter	memoirist	ribbonman	versifier
gazetteer	mendicant	roadmaker	vetturino
gem-cutter	mercenary	romancist	vexillary
geologist	mesmerist	ropemaker	violinist
gladiator	messenger	roundsman	volcanist
gluemaker	metallist	ruddleman	voltigeur
goldsmith	metrician	rum-runner	wadsetter
gondolier	middleman	sacristan	warrantee
gospeller	mill-owner	safemaker	warranter
governess	modelgirl	sailmaker	washerman
groundman	mortician	scarifier	waxworker
guardsman	muffin-man	scavenger	whitester
guerrilla	musketeer	scenarist	winemaker
guitarist	musketoon	scholiast	wood-reeve
gun-runner	myologist	schoolman	workwoman
harlequin	navigator	scientist	zookeeper
harmonist	negotiant	scrivener	zoologist
harpooner	neologian	scytheman	zootomist
harvester	neologist	sea-robber	
Hellenist	newsagent	secretary	
herbalist	nursemaid	ship's mate	**10**
herbarian	odd job man	shipowner	
herborist	office boy	shoeblack	able seaman
herb-woman	operative	shoemaker	accomptant
hired hand	orchestra	sightsman	accoucheur
hired help	ordinator	signalman	accountant
homeopath	osteopath	sinologue	acolothist
historian	otologist	soapmaker	advertiser
hog-ringer	outfitter	solicitor	aerologist
hop-picker	pantaloon	sonneteer	agrologist
hosteller	pasquiler	sopranist	agronomist
housemaid	paymaster	sorceress	air hostess
housewife	pedagogue	soubrette	air steward
hygienist	performer	space crew	algebraist
hypnotist	physician	spiderman	amanuensis
48 incumbent	physicist	stableboy	apothecary

apple-woman	concordist	hatcheller	pedicurist
apprentice	contractor	head porter	peltmonger
arbalister	controller	head waiter	penologist
arbitrator	copyholder	hierophant	perruquier
astrologer	copywriter	highwayman	pharmacist
astronomer	cordwainer	horn player	philologer
atmologist	cotton lord	horologist	piano tuner
auctioneer	counsellor	horsecoper	pickpocket
audit clerk	crow-keeper	horse-leech	platelayer
ballet girl	cultivator	house agent	playwright
balloonist	customs man	huckstress	politician
ballplayer	cytologist	husbandman	portionist
bandmaster	delineator	inoculator	postillion
bank robber	directress	institutor	postmaster
baseballer	disc jockey	instructor	prescriber
bassoonist	discounter	interagent	prima donna
beadswoman	discoverer	ironmonger	private eye
beautician	dishwasher	ironworker	procurator
bell-hanger	dispatcher	journalist	programmer
bell-ringer	distrainer	journeyman	pronouncer
bibliopole	distrainor	lady doctor	proprietor
bill-broker	dockmaster	land holder	prospector
billposter	dog breeder	land jobber	protractor
biochemist	dog-fancier	land waiter	proveditor
biographer	doorkeeper	land worker	puncturist
blacksmith	dramaturge	laundryman	pyrologist
bladesmith	dressmaker	law officer	quiz-master
blockmaker	drummer-boy	legislator	railwayman
bluejacket	dry cleaner	librettist	rat-catcher
bombardier	emblazoner	lighterman	recitalist
bondswoman	emboweller	lime-burner	researcher
bonesetter	enamellist	linotypist	ringmaster
bookbinder	ephemerist	liquidator	roadmender
bookholder	epitaphist	lobsterman	ropedancer
bookkeeper	epitomizer	lock-keeper	roughrider
bookseller	evangelist	lumberjack	safeblower
bootlegger	examinator	magistrate	sales force
bricklayer	explorator	management	saleswoman
brickmaker	eye-servant	manageress	schoolmarm
brushmaker	fell-monger	manicurist	scrutineer
bureaucrat	fictionist	manservant	sculptress
butterwife	file-cutter	matchmaker	sea-captain
caravaneer	filibuster	meat-hawker	seamstress
career girl	film editor	medical man	second mate
cartoonist	firemaster	militiaman	seminarist
cartwright	fire-worker	millwright	serving-man
cash-keeper	fishmonger	mineralist	sexologist
cat breeder	flight crew	ministress	ship-broker
cat burglar	flowergirl	mintmaster	ship-holder
ceramicist	fluvialist	missionary	shipmaster
chair-maker	folk-dancer	moonshiner	shipwright
chargehand	folk-singer	naturalist	shopfitter
charioteer	forecaster	nautch girl	shopkeeper
chirurgeon	frame-maker	negotiator	shopwalker
chorus girl	freebooter	news editor	signwriter
chronicler	fund raiser	newscaster	silentiary
chucker-out	fustianist	newsvendor	silk-mercer
circuiteer	gamekeeper	newswriter	silk-weaver
claim agent	game warden	night nurse	sinologist
clapper boy	geisha girl	nosologist	skirmisher
clockmaker	gear-cutter	nurseryman	slop seller
clog dancer	geneticist	obituarist	sneak thief
cloth maker	geographer	oil painter	soap-boiler
coachmaker	glee-singer	orchardist	specialist
coal-backer	glossarist	osteologer	staff nurse
coal-fitter	glue-boiler	overlooker	steersmate
coalheaver	gold-beater	panegyrist	stewardess
coal-master	gold-digger	pantrymaid	stipulator
co-assessor	gold-washer	park-keeper	stocktaker
coastguard	governante	park-ranger	stone-borer
collocutor	grammarian	pasquilant	stonemason
colloquist	gunslinger	pastry-cook	strategist
colporteur	hackney-man	pathfinder	street-ward
comedienne	hall porter	pawnbroker	supercargo
compositor	handmaiden	pearl-diver	superviser
compounder	harvestman	pediatrist	surcharger

surface-man
swan-keeper
symphonist
tally clerk
taskmaster
taxi-dancer
taxi-driver
tea-blender
tea planter
technician
technocrat
theogonist
theologian
theologist
threnodist
timekeeper
tractarian
trade union
traffic cop
trafficker
tram-driver
transactor
translator
trawlerman
treasuress
troubadour
typesetter
undertaker
veterinary
victualler
vinegrower
vivandiere
vocabulist
wage-earner
wainwright
warrioress
watchmaker
waterguard
wharfinger
wholesaler
whitesmith
winegrower
wine-waiter
wireworker
woodcarver
woodcutter
wood-monger
woodworker
wool-carder
wool-comber
wool-driver
wool-grower
wool-sorter
wool-trader
wool-winder
wool-worker
work-fellow
working man
workmaster
work people
yardmaster
zinc-worker
zoographer
zymologist

11

accompanist
accoucheuse
acoustician
adjudicator
allopathist
annunciator

antiquarian
apple-grower
arbitratrix
army officer
arquebusier
artillerist
audio typist
auscultator
bag-snatcher
ballad-maker
bank cashier
bank manager
bargemaster
basketmaker
batti-wallah
battologist
beachcomber
bell-founder
Benedictine
bill-sticker
bird-catcher
bird-fancier
bird-watcher
boatbuilder
body servant
boilermaker
boilersmith
bondservant
boot-catcher
broadcaster
bullfighter
businessman
butter-woman
candlemaker
car salesman
cattle thief
cat's-meat-man
chair-mender
chalk-cutter
chambermaid
chiffonnier
chirologist
chiromancer
chiropodist
choirmaster
chronologer
cinder-wench
cinder-woman
clock-setter
cloth-worker
coal-whipper
coffin-maker
cognoscente
collar-maker
common-crier
condisciple
condottiere
conductress
confederate
congressman
consecrator
conservator
constituent
conveyancer
coppersmith
cosmogonist
cosmologist
crane driver
crimewriter
cub reporter
cypher clerk
day-labourer
delivery man
demographer
dispensator
draughtsman

duty officer
electrician
emblematist
embroiderer
entertainer
estate agent
ethnologist
etymologist
executioner
extortioner
face-painter
factory hand
faith healer
fancy-monger
field worker
figure-maker
filing clerk
finestiller
fire brigade
fire insurer
flax-dresser
flesh-monger
fourbisseur
fringe-maker
fruit picker
funambulist
galley-slave
genealogist
ghostwriter
glass-bender
glass-blower
glass-cutter
glass-worker
grass-cutter
grave-digger
greengrocer
haberdasher
hagiologist
hairdresser
hair stylist
hardwareman
harvest lord
head foreman
head workman
hedge-priest
hedge-writer
hierologist
histologist
horse doctor
horse jockey
horse-keeper
horse trader
hospitaller
hotel-keeper
housekeeper
housemaster
housemother
hymnologist
illuminator
illusionist
illustrator
infantryman
institutist
interpreter
interviewer
iron-founder
ivory-carver
ivory-turner
ivory-worker
kennelmaid
kitchenmaid
lamplighter
land steward
laundrymaid
leading lady
ledger clerk

lifeboatman
lightkeeper
linen draper
lithologist
lithotomist
lorry driver
madrigalist
maidservant
mammalogist
master baker
mechanician
medicine man
merchantman
memorialist
metal worker
miniaturist
money-broker
money-lender
monographer
mule-spinner
music critic
music master
myographist
mysteriarch
mythologist
necrologist
necromancer
needlewoman
neurologist
neurotomist
night porter
night sister
nightworker
nomenclator
numismatist
office staff
onion-seller
opera singer
ophiologist
orientalist
orthopedist
osteologist
pamphleteer
panel-beater
pantomimist
paperhanger
parish clerk
parlourmaid
pathologist
pattenmaker
pearlfisher
penny-a-liner
petrologist
pettifogger
philatelist
philologist
piece worker
phytologist
phonologist
polyphonist
pork butcher
portraitist
preceptress
print-seller
probationer
promulgator
proofreader
property man
proprietrix
quacksalver
questionary
radiologist
rag merchant
representer
republisher
rhetorician

12

roadsweeper
safebreaker
sandwich man
Sanscritist
saxophonist
scoutmaster
scrapdealer
scrip-holder
secret agent
seditionary
servant girl
serving-maid
share-broker
sheepfarmer
shepherdess
shipbreaker
shipbuilder
ship's master
shopsteward
silk-thrower
silversmith
slaughterer
slave-driver
slave-holder
smallholder
sociologist
stage-driver
stage-player
stake-holder
steeplejack
stereotyper
stipendiary
stockbroker
stockjobber
stonecutter
storekeeper
stripteaser
sundriesman
system-maker
taxidermist
telegrapher
telephonist
ticket agent
toastmaster
tobacconist
tooth-drawer
topographer
torch-bearer
town planner
toxophilite
tragedienne
train-bearer
transcriber
transporter
travel agent
type-founder
typographer
underbearer
underletter
underwriter
upholsterer
versemonger
vine-dresser
waiting-maid
washerwoman
watchkeeper
water-doctor
water-gilder
wax-chandler
wheel-cutter
wheelwright
whitewasher
witch-doctor
wool-stapler
xylophonist
zoographist

accordionist
actor manager
ambulance man
anaesthetist
animalculist
archeologist
artilleryman
artist's model
bagpipe-maker
ballad singer
ballet dancer
ballet master
bantamweight
bellows-maker
bibliologist
bibliopegist
bibliopolist
body-snatcher
booking clerk
bus conductor
cabinet-maker
calligrapher
caricaturist
carpet-bagger
carpet-fitter
cartographer
cataclysmist
cerographist
cheesemonger
chief cashier
chimney-sweep
chiropractor
chronologist
churchwarden
circuit rider
civil servant
clarinettist
clerk of works
cloth-shearer
coach-builder
coleopterist
commissioner
conchologist
confectioner
corn chandler
cosmographer
costermonger
crafts-master
craniologist
cryptogamist
dance hostess
deep-sea diver
demonologist
demonstrator
dendrologist
dramaturgist
ecclesiastic
Egyptologist
electionist
engastrimuth
engine-driver
entomologist
entomotomist
entrepreneur
escapologist
ethnographer
experimenter
family doctor
farm labourer
film director
film producer
first officer
flying doctor
footplateman

geometrician
geriatrician
glass-grinder
glossologist
greasemonkey
guild brother
gymnosophist
gynecologist
hagiographer
haliographer
harness-maker
head gardener
headshrinker
homeopathist
horse-breaker
horse-courser
horse-knacker
hotel manager
housebreaker
housepainter
house steward
house surgeon
hydrographer
hydropathist
hypothecator
immunologist
impropriator
instructress
invoice clerk
jerry-builder
joint-trustee
jurisconsult
juvenile lead
king's counsel
knife-grinder
knife-thrower
labouring man
land surveyor
lath-splitter
leader-writer
legal adviser
lexicologist
lithographer
longshoreman
loss adjuster
lumber-dealer
maitre d'hotel
make-up artist
malacologist
man of letters
manual worker
manufacturer
mass producer
meat-salesman
mezzo soprano
metallurgist
microscopist
mineralogist
miscellanist
money-changer
monographist
morris-dancer
mosaic-artist
mosaic-worker
mythographer
newspaperman
notary public
nutritionist
obstetrician
office junior
oneirocritic
orchestrator
organ-builder
organ-grinder
orthodontist
orthographer

ovariotomist
paper-stainer
pattern-maker
pediatrician
phonographer
photographer
phrenologist
physiologist
plant manager
ploughwright
plumber's mate
plyer-for-hire
postmistress
practitioner
press officer
prestigiator
prison warder
prize-fighter
professional
propagandist
proprietress
psychiatrist
psychologist
publicity man
pupil-teacher
puppet-player
pyrotechnist
quarry master
racing driver
radiographer
receptionist
remembrancer
restaurateur
riding-master
right-hand man
rubber-grader
sales manager
scene-painter
scene-shifter
schoolmaster
screenwriter
scriptwriter
scullery-maid
seafaring man
seed-merchant
seismologist
sharecropper
sharpshooter
ship chandler
ship's husband
shoe-repairer
silver-beater
slaughterman
snake-charmer
social worker
soil mechanic
special agent
speechwriter
spice-blender
sportscaster
sportswriter
stage manager
statistician
steel erector
stenographer
stonebreaker
stonedresser
stonesquarer
street-trader
street-walker
sugar-refiner
tax-collector
technologist
telegraph boy
telegraphist
test engineer

51

therapeutist
thief-catcher
ticket-porter
timber trader
toll-gatherer
tourist agent
toxicologist
tradespeople
transplanter
trichologist
undermanager
underservant
veterinarian
waiting-woman
water diviner
warehouseman
wine merchant
wood-engraver
woollen-draper
works manager
zincographer

13

administrator
agriculturist
antique dealer
arachnologist
archaeologist
arithmetician
articled clerk
Assyriologist
barber-surgeon
bibliographer
calico-printer
campanologist
cartographist
chartographer
chicken-farmer
chirographist
choreographer
chronographer
civil engineer
clearstarcher
coffee-planter
cometographer
contrabandist
contortionist
cotton-spinner
counter-caster
counterfeiter
cranioscopist
cryptographer
dancing master
deipnosophist
dermatologist
diagnostician
diamond-cutter
draughtswoman
drawing-master
dress designer
drill sergeant
electroplater
electrotypist
emigrationist
encyclopedist
entozoologist
epigrammatist
estate manager
exhibitionist
family butcher
fencing-master
fortune-teller

freight-broker
galvanologist
game-preserver
gastriloquist
glossographer
glyphographer
ground-bailiff
gynaecologist
harbour master
hieroglyphist
horse-milliner
hospital nurse
ichthyologist
industrialist
intelligencer
joint-executor
letter-carrier
letter-founder
lexicographer
lighthouse-man
maid-of-all-work
master-builder
master mariner
mathematician
melodramatist
metaphysician
meteorologist
metoposcopist
music mistress
night-watchman
old-clothes-man
ornithologist
orthographist
park attendant
periodicalist
pharmaceutist
physiognomist
physiographer
posture-master
poultry farmer
privateersman
process-server
psalmographer
psychoanalyst
pteridologist
public speaker
queen's counsel
racing-tipster
revolutionary
revolutionist
rubber-planter
sailing master
schoolteacher
science master
shop assistant
silk-throwster
singing-master
station-master
stenographist
stereoscopist
stethoscopist
street-sweeper
sub-contractor
superintender
supernumerary
thaumaturgist
thimble-rigger
toll collector
trade unionist
tram conductor
tramcar-driver
ventriloquist
violoncellist
window-cleaner
window-dresser
writing-master

14

administratrix
anthropologist
autobiographer
bacteriologist
ballet mistress
billiard-marker
billiard-player
chamber-counsel
chimney-sweeper
citizen-soldier
classics master
colour sergeant
commissionaire
dancing partner
discount-broker
educationalist
ecclesiologist
encyclopaedist
exchange-broker
grammaticaster
handicraftsman
heresiographer
horticulturist
house decorator
house furnisher
language master
leather-dresser
manual labourer
market-gardener
medical officer
merchant-tailor
miscellanarian
money-scrivener
mother-superior
music publisher
naval pensioner
painter-stainer
pharmacologist
pneumatologist
psalmographist
reception clerk
representative
schoolmistress
ship's-carpenter
siderographist
spectacle-maker
spectroscopist
superintendent
systems analyst
tallow chandler
water-colourist
weather prophet

15

arboriculturist
assistant master
Bow Street runner
crossing-sweeper
crustaceologist
dancing mistress
diamond merchant
domestic servant
forwarding agent
gentleman-farmer
hackney coachman
heart specialist
helminthologist
hierogrammatist
historiographer
instrumentalist
insurance broker

jack-of-all-trades
musical director
numismatologist
ophthalmologist
palaeontologist
platform-speaker

portrait-painter
professional man
programme seller
provision dealer
railway engineer
resurrectionist

scripture-reader
sleeping partner
stretcher-bearer
ticket collector
tightrope walker
tonsorial artist

DOMESTIC
Clothes and materials

3

alb
bag
bib
boa
bra
cap
fez
fur
hat
hem
jam
kid
lap
mac
net
PVC
rag
rep
sox
tie
wig
zip

4

band
belt
boot
brim
cape
clog
coat
coif
cony
cope
cowl
cuff
down
drag
duck
duds
felt
frog
garb
gear
gimp
gown
gros
haik
hide
hood
hose
jute
képi
kilt
lace
lamé
lawn

leno
maud
maxi
mesh
mini
mink
mitt
moff
muff
mule
mull
pelt
poke
repp
robe
ruff
sack
sari
sash
shag
shoe
silk
slip
sock
spur
stud
suit
tapa
toga
togs
tutu
vamp
veil
vest
wool
wrap

5

abaya
amice
amict
apron
baize
batik
beige
benjy
beret
bezan
boots
braid
budge
busby
capoc
caxon
chaps
cloak
clogs
cloth

clout
crape
crash
crêpe
denim
dhoti
dicky
dress
drill
ephod
ermin
fanon
fichu
finos
floss
frill
frock
gauze
get-up
glove
gunny
habit
haick
heels
inkle
jabot
jasey
jeans
jippo
jupon
jussi
khaki
lacet
lapel
Levis
linen
lisle
middy
mitre
mitts
moiré
mufti
nylon
orlon
orris
pants
parka
plaid
pleat
plume
plush
pumps
quoif
rayon
romal
ruche
sable
sabot
sagum
satin
scarf

serge
shako
shawl
shift
shirt
skirt
slops
smock
snood
spats
stays
stock
stola
stole
stuff
suede
surah
tabby
tails
tammy
toile
topee
toque
train
trews
tulle
tunic
tweed
twill
vamps
V-neck
voile
weeds

6

alpaca
angola
angora
anorak
aridas
baftas
banian
barret
basque
beaver
bengal
berlin
bikini
biggin
blazer
blouse
boater
bob-wig
bodice
bolero
bonnet
bonten
bootee

bouclé
bowler
bow tie
braces
briefs
brogan
brogue
buckle
burlap
buskin
bustle
button
byssus
cabeca
caftan
calash
calico
camlet
canvas
capoch
capote
chintz
cloche
coatee
collar
collet
corset
cossas
cotton
cravat
crepon
cyprus
dacron
damask
diadem
diaper
dickey
dimity
dirndl
dolman
domino
dornic
dorsel
dowlas
duffel
ear-cap
edging
ermine
fabric
fag-end
faille
fedora
ferret
fibule
flares
fleece
foxfur
frieze
fringe
gaiter
garter
girdle
guimpe
gurrah
gusset
hankie
helmet
humbum
insole
jacket
jerkin
jersey
joseph
jumper
juppon
kaftan

kersey
kimono
kirtle
lappet
lining
linsey
livery
madras
mantle
mantua
marmot
merino
mitten
mobcap
mohair
moreen
mundil
muslin
nutria
nylons
panama
patten
peltry
peplum
peruke
pleats
pompon
poncho
pongee
poplin
puttee
PVC mac
raglan
ratine
reefer
riband
ribbon
rigout
rochet
ruffle
russet
samite
sandal
sarong
sateen
sendal
sequin
serape
sheath
shoddy
shorts
slacks
sleeve
smalls
soneri
stamin
sunhat
tabard
taminy
tartan
ticken
tights
tippet
tissue
tobine
toison
top-hat
toquet
torque
toupee
toupet
tricot
trilby
trunks
T-shirt
tucker

turban
tussah
tuxedo
tweeds
ulster
velure
velvet
visite
waders
wampum
weeper
whites
wimple
wincey
woolly
zonnar

7

abb wool
acrilan
anarak
anorak
apparel
art-silk
bandana
bandeau
batiste
bay-yarn
beveren
biretta
blanket
blucher
bocking
bottine
brocade
brogans
buckram
burnous
bycoket
byssine
calotte
camblet
cambric
capuche
cantoon
cassock
casuals
challis
chamois
chapeau
chemise
chenille
chimere
chlamys
chopine
chrisom
civvies
clobber
clothes
coating
cockade
coronet
corsage
costume
cow-hide
crochet
crounet
cut-away
delaine
doeskin
dogskin
dollman
dornock
doublet

drabbet
drawers
drip-dry
egrette
epaulet
ermelin
fallals
falsies
felt hat
felting
filibeg
flannel
flat hat
floroon
flounce
foulard
frislet
frounce
fur coat
fustian
gaiters
galloon
gantlet
garment
gaskins
genappe
gingham
grogram
grogan
guipure
G-string
gymslip
handbag
hat-band
hessian
hoggers
hogskin
holland
homburg
hosiery
jaconet
lasting
latchet
layette
leather
legging
leghorn
leotard
loafers
lockram
Mae West
malines
maniple
mantlet
matting
mechlin
minever
miniver
montero
morocco
muffler
nacarat
nankeen
necktie
nightie
oilskin
organza
orleans
orphrey
overall
paisley
paletot
pallium
panties
parasol
partlet

pattens
pelisse
periwig
petasus
pigskin
pugaree
purflew
puttees
pyjamas
raiment
rompers
rosette
sacking
sarsnet
satinet
scarlet
singlet
slip-ons
slipper
spencer
sporran
stammel
stetson
suiting
sunsuit
surcoat
surtout
sweater
tabaret
tabinet
taffeta
taffety
tatting
ticking
tiffany
top coat
top-knot
tricorn
tunicle
turn-ups
tussore
twinset
uniform
vandyke
velours
vesting
vesture
webbing
wellies
wetsuit
whittle
wiggery
woollen
worsted
yashmak

8

aigrette
appliqué
babouche
baffetas
baldrick
barathea
barracan
bathrobe
baudekin
bearskin
bed linen
bedsocks
biggonet
blancard
bloomers
bluchers

boat-neck
body-belt
bombasin
bonelace
bootikin
bottines
breeches
brocatel
brodekin
buckskin
Burberry
burnoose
bycocket
camisole
cardigan
carlisle
cashmere
Celanese
chagreen
chaperon
chasuble
chausses
chaussure
chenille
chesible
cloaking
cloth cap
clothing
coiffure
collaret
corduroy
cordwain
corporal
corselet
cracowes
cretonne
culottes
dagswain
deerskin
diamanté
dress tie
drilling
dungaree
earmuffs
ensemble
Fair Isle
fatigues
fillibeg
fingroms
flannels
florence
fontange
footwear
frilling
frippery
frontlet
froufrou
furbelow
gabarage
galoshes
gambeson
gambroon
gauntlet
glad rags
gold lamé
gossamer
gumboots
gymshoes
half-hose
headband
hipsters
homespun
jackboot
Jacquard
jodhpurs
jump suit

kerchief
knickers
knitwear
lambskin
leggings
lingerie
mantelet
mantilla
material
moccasin
moleskin
moquette
muffetee
muslinet
musquash
nainsook
neckband
négligée
nightcap
oilcloth
opera hat
organdie
osnaburg
overalls
overcoat
overshoe
paduasoy
pelerine
piccadil
pinafore
playsuit
plumelet
polo-neck
ponyskin
prunella
prunello
pullover
raincoat
rose-knot
sandshoe
sarcanet
sealskin
scapular
shagreen
shalloon
Shantung
sheeting
shirring
shirting
shoelace
shot silk
skiboots
skipants
skullcap
slippers
smocking
sneakers
snoeshoe
sombrero
stitchel
stocking
straw hat
sundress
sunshade
surplice
swanskin
swimsuit
tabbinet
taglioni
tailcoat
tapestry
tarboosh
tarlatan
terai-hat
Terylene
Thai silk

trimming
trousers
two-piece
umbrella
valentia
vallancy
vestment
wardrobe
woollens
wristlet

9

alice band
astrakhan
baby linen
balaclava
bandolier
beachwear
bedjacket
billycock
blond lace
blue jeans
bombazine
bowler hat
brassiere
broadbrim
bushshirt
calamanco
camelhair
caparison
cassimere
cerecloth
chantilly
clump boot
cocked hat
comforter
Courtelle
crinoline
Cuban heel
dalmatica
décolleté
dog collar
dress coat
dress suit
duffle bag
dungarees
epaulette
fermillet
fingering
fleshings
flipflops
floss silk
forage cap
frockcoat
full dress
full skirt
fur collar
gaberdine
galoshes
gambadoes
garibaldi
gauntlets
georgette
Glengarry
greatcoat
grosgrain
haircloth
hairshift
hairpiece
headdress
headscarf
high heels
hoop skirt
horsehair

housecoat
huckaback
Inverness
jack boots
jockey cap
justi-coat
kid gloves
knee socks
lambswool
levantine
linen mesh
loincloth
longcloth
long dress
long skirt
long socks
millinery
miniskirt
moiré silk
nightgown
nightwear
neckcloth
organzine
overdress
overshoes
panama hat
pantalets
pantaloon
paramatta
patchwork
pea jacket
peaked cap
percaline
petticoat
pina cloth
pixie hood
plimsolls
plus-fours
point lace
polonaise
pourpoint
polyester
press stud
quoiffure
redingote
round-neck
sackcloth
sack dress
safety pin
sailcloth
sailor cap
sailor hat
sanbenito
satinette
scapulary
school cap
scoop-neck
separates
sharkskin
sheepskin
shovel hat
shower cap
silk serge
sloppy joe
slouch hat
snowshoes
sou'wester
spun rayon
stockings
stomacher
strapless
strouding
suede coat
sunbonnet
swansdown
sweatband

sword belt
tarpaulin
towelling
track suit
trilby hat
trousseau
underwear
velveteen
vestments
waistband
waistcoat
wedge heel
wide-awake
wristband
zucchetto

10

angora wool
ankle socks·
balbriggan
ballet shoe
bathing cap
beaverteen
Berlin wool
bishop's-cap
blanketing
bobbin lace
bobbysocks
boiler suit
bombazette
broadcloth
brocatello
bushjacket
buttonhole
canonicals
cassinette
chatelaine
chemisette
chinchilla
court dress
court shoes
coverchief
crepe soles
cricket cap
cummerbund
diving suit
drainpipes
dress shoes
embroidery
epauletted
Eton collar
Eton jacket
fancy dress
fearnought
feather boa
florentine
foot mantle
foresleeve
fustanella
gold thread
grass cloth
grass skirt
habiliment
halterneck
Havana pelt
hodden-gray
hodden-grey
horsecloth
Irish linen
jersey silk
jersey wool
kerseymere
khaki drill
lounge suit

mackintosh
mess jacket
middy skirt
mock velvet
mousseline
needlecord
new clothes
nightdress
nightshirt
old clothes
opera cloak
overblouse
Oxford bags
pantaloons
party dress
persiennes
piccadilly
pillow lace
pilot-cloth
pith helmet
plastic mac
print dress
rabbitskin
riding-hood
roquelaure
sailorsuit
scratch wig
seersucker
shoebuckle
shoe string
slingbacks
sportscoat
suspenders
tablecloth
table linen
thrown silk
trench coat
trousering
turtle-neck
tussah silk
underpants
waterproof
windjammer
wing collar
wraparound

11

Aran sweater
battledress
bellbottoms
best clothes
black patent
candystripe
canvas shoes
cap and bells
cheesecloth
clodhoppers
cloth-of-gold
crash-helmet
deerstalker
diving dress
Dolly Varden
dreadnought
farthingale
flannelette
flared skirt
football cap
hammer cloth
hand-me-downs
Harris tweed
herringbone
Honiton lace
Kendal green
leather coat

leatherette
leopardskin
mechlin lace
morning coat
mortarboard
neckerchief
nettlecloth
Norfolk suit
panty girdle
Phrygian cap
pilot jacket
pinstripes
ready-to-wear
regimentals
riding habit
shoe leather
shoulder bag
slumberwear
stiff collar
stockinette
suede jacket
tam-o'-shanter
tennis dress
tennis skirt
torchon lace
trencher cap
trouser suit
tussore silk
watered silk
wellingtons
widow's weeds
windcheater
yachting cap

12

antigropelos
asbestos suit
bathing dress
billycock hat
body stocking
bolting cloth
business suit
cardinal's hat
cavalry twill
chastity belt
collar and tie
college scarf
crêpe-de-chine
dinner jacket
divided skirt
donkey jacket
dress clothes
dressing gown
Easter bonnet
evening dress
football boots
galligaskins
handkerchief
Indian cotton
knee breeches
leather skirt
lumber jacket
moiré antique
monkey jacket
morning dress
plain clothes
pleated skirt
service dress
shirtwaister
sleeping suit
sportsjacket
underclothes
wedding dress
Welsh flannel

13

Anthony Eden
Bermuda shorts
cashmere shawl
chinchilla fur
football scarf
leather jacket
Norfolk jacket
patent leather
pinafore dress
platform soles
Russia leather

spatterdashes
swaddling band
underclothing

14

artificial silk
bathing costume
chamois leather
Fair Isle jumper
knickerbockers
Morocco leather

riding breeches
Shetland jumper
shoulder strap
swaddling cloth
undress uniform

15

maribou feathers
mourning clothes
ostrich feathers
tarpaulin jacket

Dances

3

bop
hop
jig

4

ball
jive
jota
juba
kolo
reel

5

bebop
caper
fling
mambo
polka
rondo
rumba
samba
tango
twist
valse
waltz

6

bolero
boston
bourée

cancan
cha-cha
chassé
corant
colipee
gallop
minuet
morisk
morris
pavane
redowa
shimmy
valeta

7

beguine
coranto
fox-trot
gavotte
lancers
la volta
madison
mazurka
morisco
one-step
rondeau
two-step

8

bunny-hug
cake-walk
capriole
chaconne
cotillon

courante
danseuse
fandango
galliard
habanera
hornpipe
hulahula
huy-de-guy
rigadoon
saraband
tap-dance

9

arabesque
barndance
bossa nova
cha-cha-cha
clog dance
écossaise
farandole
folkdance
gallopade
jitterbug
paso doble
Paul Jones
pirouette
polonaise
poussette
quadrille
rock 'n' roll

10

boston reel
charleston

hey-de-guize
pooka-pooka
saltarello
strathspey
sword-dance
tambourine
tarantella
torch dance
turkey-trot
tripudiary

11

contra-dance
jolly miller
morris dance
rock and roll
square-dance
varsovienne

12

country dance
maypole dance
palais-glide
state-lancers
tripudiation

13

eightsome reel
Helston flurry
Highland fling

Drinks (wines, spirits, non-alcoholic beverages, etc.)

3

ale
bub
cha
fix
gin
kir
nog
rum
rye

tea

4

arak
asti
bass
beer
bock
bols

cola
fizz
flip
grog
hock
kava
marc
mead
mild
milk
moët

mumm
ouzo
port
raki
reid
rosé
sack
sake
saki
stum
tent

wine
wort

5

arack
ayala
bohea
broth
bumbo
byrrh
capri
chica
cider
cocoa
congo
cream
daisy
hooch
hyson
Irish
irroy
julep
kvass
lager
Maçon
Médoc
mobby
morat
negus
noyau
padra
pekoe
perry
plonk
punch
purre
quass
shrub
sirop
smash
stout
tafia
toddy
Tokay
tonic
vichy
winox

6

alegar
arrack
Barsac
Beaune
bitter
Bovril
brandy
bubbly
canary
cassis
caudle
claret
coffee
Cognac
Cooper
egg-nog
elixir
geneva
Gibson
gimlet
grappa
Graves
junora

kirsch
kummel
liquor
Lisbon
Malaga
masdeu
mastic
muscat
oolong
perkin
Pernod
pimint
pontac
porter
posset
poteen
ptisan
pulque
rickey
Saumur
Scotch
shandy
sherry
spirit
squash
stingo
Strega
swipes
volnay
wherry
whisky

7

alcohol
ale-gill
alicant
aquavit
bitters
bourbon
Campari
catawba
Chablis
Chandon
Chianti
cobbler
cordial
curaçao
egg-flip
Falerno
gin fizz
gin sour
hock-clip
koumiss
liqueur
low-wine
mace ale
Madeira
Malmsey
Marsala
martini
Moselle
Orvieto
pale ale
perrier
pink gin
Pomerol
Pommard
Pommery
Pouilly
pulchra
ratafia
red wine
retsina
samshoo

sherbet
sloe-gin
spirits
stinger
tequila
tintara
twankay
vibrona
vouvray
whiskey

8

absinthe
Advocaat
alkermes
anisette
aperitif
Assam tea
bees'-wing
beverage
block tea
bock-beer
Bordeaux
brick tea
Burgundy
charneco
China tea
cider cup
ciderkin
Clicquot
coca-cola
cocktail
Drambuie
dry wines
Dubonnet
eau-de-vie
espresso
florence
gin-sling
green tea
Guinness
highball
Hollands
Horlick's
hydromel
lemonade
montilla
muscadel
muscatel
nightcap
oopak tea
padra tea
pekoe tea
pilsener
Pol Roger
pouchong
prasites
punt y mes
ramboose
red biddy
red wines
roederer
ruby port
rum-punch
rum-shrub
St. Julien
sangaree
Sauterne
schnapps
sillabub
skim-milk
souchong
sour milk
syllabub

tia maria
verjuice
vermouth
vin blanc
wish-wash

9

altar wine
angostura
Anjou wine
applejack
aqua vitae
barley-pop
birch wine
bitter ale
black beer
Bollinger
brut wines
Ceylon tea
champagne
chocolate
claret cup
Cointreau
copa de oro
cuba libre
elder wine
Falernian
ginger-ale
ginger-pop
grenadine
gunpowder
Hall's wine
hermitage
Heidsieck
hippocras
iced water
Indian tea
lager beer
limejuice
Manhattan
metheglin
milk-punch
mint julep
mulled ale
muscadine
oolong-tea
orangeade
orange-gin
St. Emilion
St. Raphael
salutaris
Scotch ale
slivovitz
small-beer
soda water
soft drink
still-hock
sundowner
tarragona
tawny port
white lady
white port
white wine
Wincarnis

10

Beaujolais
bitter beer
black-strap
bloody mary
café-au-lait
calcavella

cappuccino
chartreuse
clary-water
constantia
dry martini
frontiniac
genevrette
ginger beer
ginger wine
goldwasser
horse's neck
iced drinks
Jamaica rum
lime-squash
malt liquor
malted milk
malt whisky
maraschino
Mateus Rosé
mickey finn
Moselle cup
mulled wine
Munich beer
pale sherry
raisin wine
Rhine wines
Rhône wines
rye whiskey
sack posset
shandygaff
soft drinks
spruce beer
still wines
sweet wines
tanglefoot
tonic water
usquebaugh
twankay tea
vichy water
white capri
white wines

11

aguardiente
amontillado
apollinaris
apple brandy
barley broth
barleywater
benedictine
black velvet
Bristol milk
cider-brandy
citron water

Courvoisier
cowslip wine
dry monopole
Irish coffee
Irish whisky
John Collins
lemon squash
montefiasco
mountain-dew
Niersteiner
orange-pekoe
peach brandy
Plymouth gin
potash water
pouchong tea
Saint Julien
scuppernong
soda and milk
southong tea
spring water
tomato juice
vin de Graves
vintage wine

12

champagne cup
cherry brandy
crème de cacao
crème-de-menthe
Cyprus sherry
Fernet-Branca
ginger brandy
Grand Marnier
ice-cream soda
India pale ale
Irish whiskey
kirschwasser
Malvern water
mulled claret
old fashioned
orange brandy
orange squash
peach bitters
Perrier-Jouet
red wine punch
Rhenish wines
Saint Emilion
Saint Raphael
sarsaparilla
Scotch whisky
seltzer water
still Moselle
treacle water
vin ordinaire

13

aërated waters
aperitif wines
apricot brandy
bijou cocktail
bronx cocktail
Château-Lafite
Contrexéville
dandelion wine
Darjeeling tea
Falernian wine
ginger cordial
Liebfraumilch
liqueur brandy
liqueur whisky
mineral waters
orange bitters
pink champagne
planters' punch
prairie oyster
seidlitz water
sherry cobbler
sparkling hock
sparkling wine
Touraine wines
Veuve Clicquot

14

bamboo-cocktail
blended whiskey
champagne cider
champagne punch
Château-Margaux
French vermouth
Johannisberger
Moët and Chandon
Piper-Heidsieck
Rob Roy cocktail
sparkling-wines
vermouth cassis
white wine punch

15

cascade-cocktail
champagne-cognac
duchess-cocktail
green chartreuse
Italian vermouth
martini-cocktail
sacramental wine
sparkling waters
tintara burgundy

Food

3 AND **4**	fare	ice	mint
	fat	jam	mush
bap	fish	jowl	oxo
bean	flan	junk	pâté
beef	fool	kale	pie
bran	fowl	lamb	pork
bun	game	lard	puff
cake	ghee	lean	rice
cate	grub	loaf	rob
chop	ham	loin	roe
curd	hare	lung	roll
Edam	hash	meat	roux
egg	herb	milk	rusk

sago	steak	oxtail	giblets
snow	stock	paella	glucose
soup	sugar	panada	goulash
soy	sweet	pastry	gristle
stew	syrup	pepper	gruyère
suet	taffy	pickle	haricot
tart	tansy	pilaff	houmous
veal	toast	pillau	jam roll
whey	tripe	polony	jam tart
yolk	viand	posset	ketchup
	wafer	potage	lasagne
	yeast	potato	Marmite
5		quiche	meat pie
		rabbit	mustard
aioli	**6**	ragout	oatcake
aspic		raisin	oatmeal
bacon	almond	rasher	pancake
blood	batter	relish	paprika
bombe	biffin	salami	pickles
brawn	blintz	sea-pie	plum jam
bread	bonbon	simnel	plum pie
brose	Bovril	sorbet	popcorn
broth	brains	sowens	potargo
candy	brunch	sponge	pottage
chili	burger	sundae	poultry
clove	butter	supper	praline
cream	canapé	sweets	pretzel
crêpe	casein	tiffin	pudding
crust	caviar	tit-bit	ramekin
curds	cheese	toffee	rarebit
curry	collop	tongue	ravioli
dough	comfit	trifle	rhubarb
dulse	congee	viands	rice bun
filet	cookie	waffle	risotto
flour	crowdy	walnut	rissole
fruit	crumbs	yogurt	sapsago
fudge	cutlet		sausage
gigot	dainty		saveloy
glaze	dinner	**7**	savoury
Gouda	éclair		seafood
gravy	eggnog	bannock	sherbet
gruel	entrée	banquet	sirloin
gumbo	faggot	bath bun	soufflé
heart	fillet	beef tea	Stilton
honey	flitch	biltong	strudel
icing	fodder	biscuit	succado
jelly	fondue	blossom	sucrose
joint	fumado	borscht	tapioca
juice	gammon	bouilli	tartlet
kebab	garlic	brisket	teacake
liver	gâteau	broiler	treacle
lunch	ginger	brownie	truffle
manna	grease	calipee	venison
melba	greens	caramel	vinegar
melts	grouse	catchup	
mince	haggis	caviare	
mocha	hot dog	cheddar	**8**
pasta	hot-pot	chicken	
pasty	humbug	chicory	allspice
patty	hummus	chowder	aperitif
pilaf	jujube	chutney	apple jam
pilau	jumble	cobloaf	apple pie
pilaw	junket	compote	bath chap
pilta	kelkel	confect	béchamel
pizza	kidney	corn cob	biscotin
prune	leaven	cracker	bouillon
pulse	lights	crumpet	chestnut
roast	mousse	currant	chop suey
salad	muffin	custard	chow mien
salmi	mutton	dariole	coleslaw
sauce	noodle	dessert	confetti
scone	nougat	fig cake	conserve
skirt	noyeau	fritter	consommé
snack	nut oil	galette	couscous
syrup	oliver	game pie	cracknel
spice	omelet	gelatin	cream bun

cross bun
dainties
date roll
déjeuner
delicacy
dog's-meat
doughnut
dripping
dumpling
fishmeal
flapjack
flummery
frumenty
frosting
fruit pie
hardbake
hazelnut
hotchpot
hung beef
ice cream
iced cake
Julienne
kedgeree
lamb chop
loblolly
lollipop
luncheon
macaroni
macaroon
marzipan
meatball
meringue
mince pie
mishmash
molasses
mushroom
olive oil
omelette
parmesan
pemmican
porridge
preserve
racahout
raisinée
rice cake
rollmops
roly poly
ryebread
salad oil
salpicon
salt fish
salt junk
salt pork
sandwich
seedcake
skim milk
slapjack
soda cake
sparerib
squab pie
steak pie
stuffing
turnover
undercut
victuals
whitepot

9

antipasti
appetizer
arrowroot
beefsteak
breakfast
bridecake

bubblegum
cassareep
casserole
cassonade
chipolata
chocolate
chump-chop
comfiture
condiment
confiture
corn bread
corn salad
crackling
cream cake
croquette
Easter egg
entremets
forcemeat
fricassee
fried eggs
fried fish
fruit cake
fruit tart
galantine
Genoa cake
giblet pie
gravy soup
hamburger
hard sauce
honeycomb
Irish stew
lemon curd
loafsugar
lobscouse
lump sugar
macedoine
margarine
marmalade
mincemeat
mint sauce
mutton ham
mutton pie
nutriment
pigeon pie
potato pie
potpourri
pound cake
puff paste
raised pie
schnitzel
scotch egg
seasoning
shellfish
shortcake
sour cream
sourdough
spaghetti
stirabout
succotash
sugarloaf
sugar-plum
sweetmeat
swiss roll
tipsy cake
vegetable
white meat
whole meal
wild honey

10

apple sauce
apricot jam
bath oliver

beefburger
bêche-de-mer
blancmange
blanquette
Bombay duck
bosh butter
breadstuff
bridescake
brown bread
buttermilk
cannelloni
capillaire
cheesecake
chelsea bun
comestible
confection
corned beef
cornflakes
cottage pie
currant bun
delicacies
dog biscuit
estouffade
fig pudding
flesh broth
frangipane
French loaf
fricandeau
fruit salad
giblet soup
ginger cake
girdle cake
gloucester
gorgonzola
grape sugar
ground rice
guava jelly
ham and eggs
hodge-podge
hotch-potch
ice pudding
indian corn
jugged hare
lamb cutlet
maple sugar
marrow bone
mayonnaise
minced meat
mock turtle
mutton chop
pepper cake
peppermint
poached egg
potted fish
potted meat
pudding pie
puff pastry
raisin loaf
rhubarb pie
rolled oats
saccharine
salmagundi
salt butter
sauerkraut
shortbread
shortcrust
simnel cake
sponge cake
stale bread
stewed meat
sugar candy
sustenance
sweetbread
tea biscuit
temse bread
tenderloin

tinned food
turtle soup
vermicelli
water gruel
white bread
white sauce

11

baked Alaska
Banbury cake
barley sugar
bonne bouche
cassava cake
chiffon cake
cream cheese
curry powder
frankfurter
French bread
gingerbread
golden syrup
green turtle
griddle cake
ham sandwich
hors d'oeuvre
hot cross bun
iron rations
jam sandwich
meat biscuit
meat pudding
medlar jelly
milk pudding
olla podrida
oyster patty
peppermints
plum pudding
raisin bread
refreshment
rice biscuit
rice pudding
sago pudding
sausage roll
short pastry
stewed fruit
suet pudding
tagliatelle
wedding cake
Welsh mutton
Welsh rabbit
wheaten loaf
wine biscuit

12

apple fritter
birthday cake
burnt almonds
butterscotch
chip potatoes
clotted cream
Cornish pasty
corn-on-the-cob
curds and whey
Danish pastry
dunmow flitch
eggs and bacon
finnan haddie
guarana-bread
hasty pudding
Julienne soup
liver sausage
lobster patty
maid of honour
marshmallow

61

merry thought
mullagatawny
mulligatawny
nutmeg butter
peanut butter
pease pudding
plum porridge
pumpernickel
quartern loaf
refreshments
shepherd's pie
ship's biscuit
steak pudding
sweet and sour
tripe de roche
Welsh rarebit

13

apple dumpling
béchamel sauce
bouillabaisse
cheddar cheese

chili con carne
Christmas cake
confectionery
cottage cheese
custard-coffin
flitch of bacon
German sausage
gigot de mouton
ginger pudding
gruyère cheese
Oxford sausage
roll and butter
salad dressing
scotch collops
sirloin of beef
sponge pudding
Stilton cheese
veal-and-ham pie

14

almond hardbake
apple charlotte

bologna sausage
bread and butter
bread and cheese
caramel custard
charlotte russe
haunch of mutton
household bread
mashed potatoes
mock-turtle soup
parmesan cheese
saddle of mutton
toasted teacake
turkish delight
wholemeal bread

15

bakewell pudding
black-cap pudding
bubble and squeak
chocolate éclair
Devonshire cream
haunch of venison

Furniture, fittings, and personal effects
See also **Kitchen utensils and requisites.**

3

bag
bar
bed
bin
can
cot
fan
hod
ink
mat
nib
nog
pad
ped
pen
pew
pin
rug
urn
vat

4

ambo
bath
bowl
bunk
butt
case
cask
cist
comb
cott
crib
desk
door
etui
form
gong
hi-fi
lamp

mull
oven
poke
rack
sack
safe
seal
seat
sofa
tank
tape
till
trap
tray
trug
vase
wick

5

apron
arras
basin
bench
besom
bidet
blind
board
broom
chair
chest
china
cigar
clock
cloth
coign
couch
cover
crate
creel
crock
cruet
cruse

diota
divan
doily
dosel
doser
duvet
flask
flisk
glass
globe
grill
guard
jesse
joram
jorum
label
laver
leash
light
linen
mural
paper
paten
patin
piano
pouch
purse
quill
quilt
radio
razor
scrip
shade
shelf
skeel
slate
spill
stand
stool
stoup
strop
suite
swing
table

tache
tapis
tongs
tools
torch
towel
traps
trunk
twine
vesta
watch

6

air-bed
ash-bin
ash-can
awning
basket
beaker
bicker
bucket
bunker
bureau
camera
carafe
carboy
carpet
carver
casket
castor
cheval
chowry
coffer
consol
cooker
cradle
day-bed
dishes
dosser
drapet
drawer
duster

fender
fly-net
forfex
fridge
geyser
goblet
goglet
hamper
hat-box
hearth
heater
hookah
hoppet
hussif
ink-pot
ice-box
ladder
keeler
kit-bag
kurkee
locker
log bin
loofah
mangle
mirror
mobile
napery
napkin
needle
noggin
oilcan
pallet
patera
patine
pelmet
pencil
piggin
pillow
plaque
pomade
posnet
pottle
pouffe
punkah
punnet
red ink
rocker
saddle
salver
scales
sconce
scovel
screen
settee
settle
shovel
shower
siphon
sponge
starch
string
syphon
tablet
teapot
tea set
tea urn
thread
throne
tiller
tin box
tinder
toy box
trevet
tripod
trivet
trophy

tureen
valise
wallet
window
wisket
zip-bag

7

adaptor
aerator
amphora
andiron
armoire
ash-tray
baggage
bath mat
bathtub
bedding
beeswax
bellows
blanket
blotter
bolster
brasier
brazier
broiler
bunk bed
cabinet
camp bed
canteen
chalice
chamois
chopper
cistern
cobiron
coir-mat
commode
compact
costrel
counter
cue-rack
cutlery
curtain
cushion
door-mat
down-bed
drapery
dresser
drugget
dustbin
dust-pan
epergne
flacket
flasket
fly-rail
fuse-box
gas-fire
gas ring
goggles
griddle
hair-oil
hammock
hassock
hip bath
holdall
horn-cup
ink-horn
knocker
lagging
lantern
lectern
lighter
matches
matting

monocle
netsuke
oil-lamp
ottoman
padlock
pannier
percher
pianino
pianola
picture
pillion
pin-case
playpen
pomatum
pottager
pot-hook
roaster
rundlet
rush-mat
saccule
sadiron
samovar
sampler
sand-box
satchel
scraper
shelves
shoebox
show-box
skimmer
soap-box
sofa-bed
steamer
stopper
stopple
syringe
tallboy
tambour
tankard
tea-cosy
tea-tray
tent-bed
thermos
thimble
tin-case
toaster
tobacco
tool kit
trammel
trolley
truckle
tumbler
tun-dish
valance
wardian
wash-tub
what-not
whisket
wine-bag
woodcut
work-bag
workbox
wringer
yule-log

8

ale bench
angel bed
armchair
banister
barbecue
bassinet
bed cover
bed linen

bed quilt
bedstaff
bedstead
bed-straw
bird-bath
bird-cage
bookcase
bookends
borachio
camp-bath
card-case
cashbook
cathedra
causeuse
cellaret
chair-bed
chattels
clay pipe
coat-hook
colander
coverlet
crockery
cupboard
curtains
cuspidor
decanter
demi-john
ditty-box
dog-chain
doorbell
doorknob
door-step
egg-timer
endirons
eyeglass
fauteuil
field-bed
firewood
flock-bed
fly paper
foot-bath
fuse wire
gallipot
gasalier
handbell
hangings
hat-brush
hatstand
heirloom
hip flask
holdfast
inkstand
jalousie
knapsack
lamp-wick
lanthorn
latchkey
linoleum
lipstick
loo table
love seat
matchbox
mattress
nail-file
note-book
oak chest
oilcloth
ornament
penknife
pianette
pipe-rack
postcard
press-bed
quill-pen
radiator
reticule

63

road-book
saddlery
scissors
sea chest
shoehorn
shoelace
show-case
sink unit
sitz-bath
slop bowl
slop pail
snuffbox
snuffers
soap dish
speculum
spittoon
stair-rod
standish
steel pen
suitcase
sun-blind
table-mat
tabouret
tantalus
tape-line
tapestry
tea-board
tea-caddy
tea-chest
tea-cloth
tea-table
trencher
tridarne
triptych
tweezers
umbrella
vestiary
vestuary
wall-safe
wardrobe
watch-key
water-can
water-pot
water tap
wax cloth
wax light
wineskin
wireless

9

barometer
bathtowel
bedspread
black-jack
bookshelf
book-stand
boot-brush
bric-à-brac
cakestand
camp-chair
camp-stool
cane-chair
cantharus
card-table
carpet-bag
carpeting
case-knife
casserole
china bowl
chinaware
cigarette
clack-dish
clasplock
club chair

coffee-cup
coffee-pot
comb-brush
container
corkscrew
crumb-tray
cullender
cushionet
davenport
deck chair
devonport
directory
dishcloth
dish-clout
dish-cover
dog-basket
dog-collar
dog-kennel
dust-brush
dust-sheet
Dutch oven
easy chair
egg boiler
eiderdown
equipment
face towel
faldstool
fire-board
fire-brush
fire-grate
fire-guard
fire-irons
fireplace
fish-knife
fish-plate
flower-pot
food-mixer
foot-board
footstool
frying-pan
gas-burner
gas-cooker
gas-geyser
girandole
gold-plate
gout-stool
hairbrush
hair tonic
hall table
hand-towel
haversack
high chair
horsewhip
housewife
ink-bottle
ink-holder
inventory
jack-towel
jewel case
kitchener
lamp-shade
lampstand
letter-box
light bulb
loving-cup
marquetry
master-key
mouse-trap
muffineer
music book
nail brush
newspaper
nick-nacks
nipperkin
notepaper
ornaments

paillasse
palliasse
paper clip
paper-rack
parchment
pepper-pot
perdonium
pewter pot
pier-glass
pier-table
piggy-bank
plate-rack
porringer
portfolio
port glass
pot-hanger
pot-pourri
pounce-box
powder-box
punchbowl
punkah-fan
quail-pipe
radiogram
rush-light
safety-pin
scrutoire
secretary
serviette
shakedown
shoe-brush
shower-cap
sideboard
side-light
side-table
slop-basin
spin-drier
sponge-bag
sprinkler
stair rods
stamp-case
steel wool
stopwatch
string-box
sword-cane
table bell
table hook
table lamp
tableware
tea-kettle
telephone
timepiece
timetable
tinder-box
tin-opener
toothpick
underfelt
vanity-box
wall-clock
wallpaper
wall-light
wash-basin
wash-board
wash-stand
water-butt
water-tank
wax candle
wax polish
window-box
wine glass
work table

10

air-cushion
alarm clock

alarm watch
bedclothes
biscuit-box
boot polish
broomstick
brown paper
buck-basket
cabbage net
calefactor
candelabra
canterbury
ceiling fan
chandelier
chessboard
chiffonier
chopsticks
clamp-irons
clothes peg
clothes pin
coal bucket
coal bunker
coat hanger
crumb-brush
crumb cloth
curtain rod
dandy-brush
deep-freeze
disfurnish
dishwasher
down pillow
dumb-waiter
elbow-chair
escritoire
featherbed
finger-bowl
fire-basket
fire-bucket
fire-escape
firescreen
fire-shovel
fish-basket
fish-carver
fish-kettle
fish-trowel
flesh-brush
floor-cloth
flower-bowl
fly-catcher
fly-swotter
foot-warmer
fourposter
garbage-can
gas-bracket
gas-lighter
gramophone
grand piano
hair lotion
hair pomade
jardinière
knife-board
langsettle
lead pencil
letter-rack
loose cover
marking ink
musical box
music-stand
music-stool
napkin ring
needle-book
needle-case
needlework
night-light
nutcracker
opera glass
overmantel

pack-saddle
pack-thread
paper-knife
paper-stand
pencil-case
peppermill
persian mat
persian rug
pewter dish
photograph
pianoforte
piano stool
pile carpet
pillowcase
pillowslip
pincushion
plate-glass
pocket-book
prayer-book
rattan-cane
razor-strop
riding-whip
rolling-pin
saddle-bags
salt-cellar
scatter rug
sealing-wax
secretaire
shower-bath
soda syphon
spectacles
spirit lamp
stamp-album
stationery
step-ladder
strip light
tablecloth
table linen
tablespoon
television
time-keeper
time-switch
tobacco-jar
toilet roll
toothbrush
toothpaste
truckle-bed
trug-basket
trundlebed
typewriter
upholstery
vapour-bath
warming-pan
wash basket
wassail-cup
watch-chain
watch-glass
watch-guard
watch-light
watch-stand
window-seat
wine-bottle
wine-cooler
work basket
wrist-watch

11

account book
address book
airing horse
alarum clock
alarum watch
attaché case
basket chair

bed-hangings
billiard-cue
bolster-case
book matches
boot-scraper
braising-pan
butter-print
butter-stamp
button-stick
candelabrum
candlestick
centrepiece
chafing-dish
cheese board
cheval-glass
chiffonnier
clothes-hook
clothes-line
coal-scuttle
coffee table
coir-matting
counterpane
curtain hook
curtain rail
curtain ring
despatch-box
dining-table
dinner-table
dispatch-box
dredging-box
dripping-pan
Dutch carpet
finger-glass
fire-lighter
first-aid box
floor polish
flour-dredge
footcushion
foot-scraper
fountain-pen
gaming-table
garden chair
hearth brush
knick-knacks
lamp-chimney
leather case
linen basket
minute glass
minute watch
mosquito-net
nut-crackers
ormolu clock
paper-basket
paperweight
picture-rail
pipe-lighter
pocket flask
pocket-glass
pocket-knife
porridge-pot
portmanteau
primus stove
pumice-stone
reading lamp
roll-top desk
saddle-cloth
safety-razor
scuttle-cask
shopping bag
siphon-stand
slate-pencil
stair-carpet
straw pillow
syphon-stand
table napkin
table-runner

tape-measure
tea-canister
thermometer
tin-lined box
tissue paper
tobacco pipe
toilet-cover
toilet-table
tooth-powder
vacuum flask
vinaigrette
waffle-irons
washing line
wash-leather
wassail-bowl
waste-basket
water heater
watering-can
watering-pot
window blind
writing-desk

12

adhesive tape
antimacassar
bedside light
bedside table
blotting book
bottle-opener
bucking stool
camp-bedstead
candleholder
candle-sconce
carpet beater
chaise longue
chesterfield
churchwarden
clothes-brush
clothes drier
clothes-horse
console table
cottage piano
cup and saucer
despatch-case
dessert-spoon
dispatch-case
dressing-case
drinking-horn
Dutch dresser
electric bulb
electric fire
electric iron
electric lamp
fan regulator
field-glasses
fish-strainer
flour-dredger
flower-basket
folding stool
gate-leg table
gladstone bag
hot-water tank
hubble-bubble
ironing board
ironing table
judgment-seat
kitchen table
kneehole desk
knife-cleaner
looking-glass
lucifer match
nail-scissors
nutmeg-grater
opera-glasses

packing cloth
packing paper
packing sheet
paraffin lamp
picnic basket
picnic hamper
playing cards
porridge-bowl
postage stamp
reading glass
record-player
refrigerator
roasting-jack
rocking chair
rocking horse
standard lamp
straw bolster
sweating-bath
table lighter
table service
tallow-candle
tape recorder
thermos flask
tin-lined case
toasting fork
tobacco pouch
toilette case
trestle table
turkey carpet
visitors' book
upright piano
walking-staff
walking stick
washing board
water pitcher
Welsh dresser
wicker basket
Windsor chair
wine decanter
writing table
writing paper

13

billiard balls
billiard table
blotting paper
carpet sweeper
chopping block
chopping knife
cribbage board
dressing-table
electric clock
electric stove
feather pillow
feeding bottle
filing cabinet
florence flask
folding screen
medicine glass
netting needle
newspaper rack
packing needle
persian blinds
persian carpet
petrol-lighter
ping-pong table
quizzing-glass
razor-stropper
roulette table
sewing-machine
smoothing-iron
sounding-board
straw mattress
styptic pencil

65

turnover table
umbrella stand
vacuum cleaner
visiting-cards
washhand-stand
window curtain
witney blanket

14

anglepoise lamp
billiard marker
chamber-hanging

chest-of-drawers
cocktail-shaker
eiderdown quilt
electric cooker
electric geyser
electric kettle
feather bolster
glove-stretcher
hot water bottle
kitchen dresser
meerschaum pipe
tobacco stopper
Venetian blinds
washing machine

15

electric blanket
feather mattress
garden furniture
gate-legged table
Japanese lantern
knitting needles
mosquito curtain
pestle and mortar
photograph album
photograph frame
pneumatic pillow

Games, sports and pastimes

3

ace
art
bat
bet
bob
bow
box
bye
cue
cup
die
fun
gym
hux
lap
l.b.w.
lie
lob
lov
nap
oar
out
pam
peg
put
rod
set
ski
sod
tag
taw
tig
tir
top
toy
win
won

4

arts
bait
ball
bias
bite
boat
brag
club
crib
dice
dive
draw

epée
faro
foil
fore
foul
gala
game
goal
golf
grab
hunt
jack
jazz
judo
king
knar
knur
love
ludo
luge
main
mate
meet
mime
miss
mora
Oaks
odds
pace
pawn
play
polo
pool
punt
quiz
race
ride
ring
rink
ruff
shot
sice
side
skip
slam
slip
snap
solo
spar
suit
swim
team
toss
tote
trap

trey
trip
trot
turf
vole
volt
walk
whip
wide
xyst
yoga
yo-yo

5

amuse
arena
baign
bails
bandy
basto
batik
bingo
bogey
boule
bowls
boxer
caddy
capot
cards
chase
cheat
chess
clubs
dance
darts
Derby
deuce
dicer
diver
dormy
drama
drawn
drive
dummy
extra
field
fives
fluke
glaze
hobby
joker
joust
kayle

kendo
knave
lasso
links
lists
loser
lotto
lucky
match
mount
music
ombre
opera
paced
pacer
party
pitch
point
poker
prize
queen
quits
racer
rafia
reins
relay
revel
rider
rifle
rodeo
rugby
rummy
samba
score
skate
skier
slice
slide
slosh
spade
spoon
sport
spurt
stalk
start
stump
stunt
swing
throw
touch
track
train
trial
trump
vault

veney
wager
whist
yacht

6

aikido
archer
ballet
banker
basset
battue
bewits
bowler
bowman
boxing
bridge
casino
cinque
cobnut
cockal
course
crafts
crambo
crease
crochet
cup tie
dealer
defeat
discus
diving
domino
driver
dyeing
ecarté
euchre
falcon
finish
fluker
flying
gambit
gamble
gammon
gillie
gobang
go-kart
googly
gully
gymnic
hazard
header
hiking
hockey
hunter
hurdle
huxing
jetton
jigger
jockey
karate
kicker
knight
kung-fu
lariat
leg-bye
loader
lobber
manege
marker
mashie
masque
maying
no-ball
not-out

outing
outrun
pacing
paddle
peg-top
pelota
piquet
pistol
player
poetry
punter
putter
puzzle
quoits
rabbit
racing
racket
raffle
rattle
recite
record
revoke
riddle
riding
rowing
rubber
rugger
runner
scorer
second
see-saw
shinny
shinty
single
skater
skiing
slalom
slider
soccer
soirée
squash
stroke
stumps
T'ai chi
tarocs
tenace
tennis
tierce
tip-cat
toss-up
travel
trophy
umpire
unfair
venery
victor
vigaro
wicket
winner
xystos
yorker

7

agonism
agonist
allonge
amateur
ambs-ace
ames-ace
angling
archery
athlete
auction
average

bathing
batsman
batting
beagles
benefit
bezique
bicycle
boating
bone ace
bowling
bran-pie
bruiser
canasta
carving
cassino
century
charade
checker
chicane
codille
collage
concert
contest
cookery
cooking
cooncan
cricket
croquet
curling
cycling
cyclist
dancing
diabolo
dice-box
discard
doddart
doubles
drawing
dribble
driving
etching
fencing
fielder
fishery
fishing
fluking
forward
fowling
fox hunt
gambler
glasses
glazing
gliding
golf bag
gunning
gymnast
hunting
hurling
innings
joy-ride
ju-jitsu
jumping
keep fit
last lap
leaping
loggats
lottery
love all
love set
low bell
macramé
mahjong
marbles
may-pole
misdeal
montant

mosaics
netball
oarsman
oarsmen
off-side
old-maid
outdoor
outride
pageant
pallone
pastime
pat ball
picquet
pitcher
play day
playing
pontoon
pottery
potting
primero
pushpin
putting
rackets
reading
referee
regatta
reversi
rinking
roadhog
running
sailing
saltant
scooter
scoring
scratch
sculler
sea trip
shuffle
singing
singles
skating
ski jump
sliding
snooker
St. Leger
stadium
starter
sub-aqua
surfing
tilting
tinchel
tombola
top spin
tourney
trained
trainer
trapeze
'vantage
vaulter
wagerer
walking
wargame
weaving
weights
whip top
winning
wrestle
writing

8

all-fours
antiques
appliqué
aquatics

67

baccarat
baseball
boat race
boundary
canoeing
carnival
carolina
catapult
ceramics
champion
charades
cheating
chessmen
climbing
commerce
contract
counters
coursing
cribbage
cup final
dead heat
deck golf
dominoes
doublets
drag-hunt
draughts
duelling
eurythme
eventing
exercise
face card
fair play
falconry
fielding
flat race
football
foot race
forfeits
fox chase
full back
game laws
gin rummy
goal line
golf ball
golf club
gymkhana
handball
handicap
harriers
high jump
hurdling
jiu-jitsu
jousting
juggling
knitting
korfball
lacrosse
leapfrog
long jump
long stop
love game
lucky-dip
marathon
may games
motoring
movement
natation
ninepins
olympiad
olympics
out-field
outsider
painting
palestra
pall-mall
patience

ping-pong
pole jump
pony race
pope Joan
printing
proverbs
pugilism
pugilist
pyramids
quatorze
racquets
rambling
roulette
rounders
sack race
sculling
sculpture
shooting
sing-song
skipping
skittles
sledding
softball
somerset
spadille
sparring
sporting
stalking
stumping
swimming
teamwork
teetotum
third-man
tiny golf
toboggan
training
tray-trip
trial run
tricycle
trotting
tumbling
turf club
umpiring
vaulting
vauntlay
walkover
wall-game
woodwork
yachting

9

advantage
adventure
agonistes
agonistic
amusement
archeress
athletics
aunt-sally
babyhouse
badminton
bagatelle
ball games
bandalore
bicycling
bilboquet
billiards
bob cherry
breakdown
broad jump
bull board
bull feast
bullfight
camelling

challenge
checkmate
cherry pit
chicanery
clock golf
close time
cockfight
cockmatch
conqueror
court-card
cricketer
cup winner
deck games
decoy duck
dirt track
dog racing
drawn game
dumbbells
embrocado
engraving
entertain
equitancy
fairy tale
fancy ball
fish spear
frivolity
gardening
gate money
goal posts
golf clubs
grand slam
gymnasium
gymnastic
hatha yoga
hopscotch
horseplay
horserace
ice hockey
joy riding
lampadist
lob bowler
make merry
marooning
marquetry
megaphone
merrimake
merriment
merriness
motorboat
newmarket
night club
nine holes
novelette
overmatch
pacemaker
pageantry
palestric
palmistry
pedalling
philately
plaything
pole vault
prize-ring
programme
promenade
racehorse
racestand
reception
relay race
repasture
revelment
revel rout
river trip
rolly poly
scorching
scorecard

scrapbook
showplace
shrimping
ski runner
skylarker
sleighing
smock race
solitaire
spectacle
sportsman
springing
square-leg
stalemate
stool ball
stopwatch
storybook
stroke oar
summerset
symposiac
symposium
tablegame
tabletalk
test match
tie dyeing
tip and run
torch race
touch line
trap stick
trial game
trial race
trump card
untrained
victoress
vingt-et-un
wandering
water jump
water polo
whipper-in
whirligig
whistling
woodcraft
wrestling
yacht-race
yachtsman

10

acrobatics
agonistics
agonothete
backgammon
ballooning
basket-ball
bat-fowling
battledoor
battledore
bear garden
blind harry
challenger
chessboard
collecting
competitor
conundrums
cover-point
cricket-bat
cup-and-ball
deck quoits
deck tennis
derby sweep
doll's house
dumb crambo
eel fishing
embroidery
enamelling
equitation

fancy dress
fast bowler
feathering
feuilleton
field games
fishing net
fishing rod
fisticuffs
fives court
flat racing
flop-dragon
fly-fishing
fox-hunting
goalkeeper
goalkicker
grandstand
greasy pole
groundbait
gymnastics
handspring
handy-dandy
hippodrome
hobby horse
hockey ball
hockey club
hotcockles
hucklebone
humming-top
hunting box
hurdle race
ice dancing
ice sailing
ice skating
kettle pins
lace making
lampadrome
landing net
lansquenet
lawn tennis
ledger line
lob bowling
masquerade
midget golf
Monte Carlo
needlework
opposition
palestrian
pancratist
pancratium
paper chase
pony racing
pot hunting
prison base
prize fight
racecourse
raceground
recreation
relaxation
riding pony
riding whip
rollicking
rotary club
roundabout
rowing club
saturnalia
scoreboard
scratch man
sea bathing
shovepenny
shuffle cap
silk screen
ski running
skylarking
slow bowler
snapdragon
somersault

stirrup cup
strokesman
surf riding
sweepstake
switchback
table bowls
tap dancing
tarantella
tauromachy
team spirit
tennis ball
thimblerig
tomfoolery
tournament
travelling
trial match
trick track
tricycling
victorious
volley ball
weighing-in
whirlabout
word making

11

agonistical
athleticism
barley-brake
bear baiting
bull baiting
bumblepuppy
calligraphy
chariot race
chess player
competition
competitive
county match
cricket ball
croquet ball
deck cricket
Derby winner
dicing house
disportment
diving board
fast bowling
field sports
fishing line
five hundred
flaconnade
fleet-footed
fluking-iron
folk dancers
free fishery
garden party
general post
grand circle
grass skiing
gymnasiarch
hang gliding
happy family
heavyweight
hide-and-seek
high jumping
high pitched
hockey stick
horse racing
horse riding
hunt counter
hunting horn
ice yachting
indian clubs
inter-county
lawn bowling
lightweight

lithography
long jumping
magic square
make-believe
masquerader
merrymaking
minute watch
oarsmanship
open-air life
picnic party
pillow fight
pole jumping
prawning net
prize giving
prizewinner
promenading
protagonist
public stand
regatta card
riding horse
river sports
rouge-et-noir
rough riding
sand sailing
schottische
shovel board
show jumping
shuttlecock
sightseeing
single stick
skateboard
skating club
skating rink
skittle pool
slot machine
slow bowling
snowballing
soap bubbles
span-counter
spelling bee
springboard
stirrup lamp
stonewaller
summersault
sweepstakes
sword player
table tennis
tale telling
tennis court
tent pegging
theatre-goer
tobogganing
top-spinning
totalisator
toxophilite
trap-and-ball
trick riding
trolmydames
trout-stream
uncontested
unexercised
water skiing
whipping-top
wild fowling
winning crew
winning side
winning team
wood cutting
world record
yacht racing

12

bantamweight
billiard ball

bird's nesting
bobsleighing
bowling alley
brass rubbing
bullfighting
butterfly net
calisthenics
championship
club swinging
cockfighting
competitress
consequences
cricket match
curling stone
deer stalking
draughtboard
drinking bout
field glasses
figure skater
first-nighter
flower making
glass blowing
googly bowler
hoodman-blind
horsemanship
housewarming
hunting-horse
huntsmanship
jigsaw puzzle
losing hazard
magic lantern
marathon race
marking board
medicine ball
merry-go-round
miss milligan
mixed bathing
mixed doubles
nimble footed
novel reading
obstacle race
Olympic games
opera glasses
parallel bars
parlour games
pitch-and-toss
pleasure trip
point-to-point
pole vaulting
professional
prize fighter
prize winning
pyrotechnics
Pythian games
racing stable
rock climbing
roller skater
rope climbing
rope spinning
rope throwing
sand yachting
scotch-hopper
shrimping net
skipping rope
skittle alley
speed skating
starting post
state lottery
steeplechase
stilt walking
stirrup strap
storytelling
swimming gala
table croquet
table turning
tennis player

69

tennis racket
theatre-going
thoroughbred
tiddley-winks
tittle-tattle
wicket keeper
winning horse
winter sports

13

alectoromachy
alectryomachy
aquatic sports
auction bridge
ballad singing
blindman's buff
bubble blowing
camera obscura
Christmas tree
chuck farthing
cribbage board
cricket ground
cricket stumps
croquet mallet
deck billiards
divertisement
double or quits
entertainment
featherweight
figure skating
fishing tackle
googly-bowling
ground-angling
hare-and-hounds
horizontal bar
international
Isthmian games

jigsaw puzzles
jollification
machine junket
model yachting
motor cruising
musical chairs
Olympian games
parlour tricks
pillion riding
prisoner's base
prize fighting
record breaker
roller skating
roulette table
speed merchant
spirit rapping
sportsmanship
squash rackets
stalking horse
starting point
steeplechaser
sword fighting
ten-pin bowling
track and field
vantage ground
vaulting horse
victor ludorum
weight lifting
wicket keeping
winning hazard

14

all-in wrestling
billiard marker
billiard player
bladder angling

children's party
coin collecting
contract bridge
discus-throwing
divertissement
double patience
downhill skiing
driving licence
ducks-and-drakes
hunt-the-slipper
hunt-the-thimble
long-arm balance
mountaineering
record breaking
rubicon bezique
shove-halfpenny
steeplechasing
thimblerigging
weight training

15

ballroom dancing
cinderella dance
consolation race
crossword puzzle
Derby sweepstake
dirt track racing
greyhound racing
javelin throwing
king-of-the-castle
Old English bowls
public enclosure
short-arm balance
stamp collecting
talking pictures
three-legged race
unsportsmanlike
youth hostelling

Jewellery, gems, etc.

3 AND 4

bead
clip
gaud
gem
jade
jet
onyx
opal
ring
ruby
sard
stud
torc

carat
clasp
coral
crown
ivory
jewel
lapis
links
nacre
paste
pearl
tiara
topaz
watch

5

agate
aglet
amber
badge
beads
beryl
bezel
bijou
brait
bugle
cameo

6

albert
amulet
anklet
armlet
augite
bangle
bauble
brooch
diadem
enamel
fibula
garnet

gewgaw
iolite
ligure
locket
olivet
pearls
pyrope
quartz
signet
sphere
spinel
telesm
tiepin
torque
turkis
wampum
zircon

7

abraxas
adamant
annulet
armilla
asteria
axinite
cat's eye
chaplet
coronet

crystal
diamond
eardrop
earring
emerald
espinel
euclase
faceted
filigree
jacinth
jewelry
olivine
pendant
peridot
regalia
ringlet
rubicel
sardine
sardius
sceptre
smaragd
spangle
telesia
trinket

8

adularia
aigrette

amethyst
armillet
carcanet
cardiace
corundum
diopside
hallmark
hyacinth
intaglio
liginite
necklace
pectoral
rock ruby
sapphire
sardonyx
scarf-pin
shirt-pin
sunstone

9

balas ruby
black onyx
black opal
breast-pin
brilliant
carbuncle
carnelian
cornelian
cufflinks
foil-stone
gold watch
jadestone
jewellery

marcasite
medallion
moonstone
morganite
moss-agate
paillette
phenacite
press stud
pyreneite
seed pearl
starstone
thumbring
trinketry
turquoise

10

adderstone
amber beads
andalusite
aquamarine
black pearl
bloodstone
chalcedony
chrysolite
coral beads
glass beads
madrepearl
Mocha stone
rhinestone
signet ring
topazolite
tourmaline
watch-chain

watchstrap
water opal
wristwatch

11

aiguillette
alexandrite
bostrychite
cameo brooch
chalcedonyx
chrysoberyl
chrysophrase
colophonite
crocidolite
lapis lazuli
slave bangle
wedding-ring

12 AND OVER

bead necklace (12)
chain bracelet (13)
coral necklace (13)
crystal necklace (15)
engagement ring (14)
eternity ring (12)
link bracelet (12)
mother-of-pearl (13)
mourning brooch (14)
mourning ring (13)
pearl necklace (13)
precious stone (13)

Kitchen utensils and requisites

3

bin
can
cup
hob
jar
jug
lid
mop
mug
pan
pot
tap
tin
tub
urn

4

bowl
coal
cosy
dish
ewer
fork
grid
hook
iron
lard
oven
pail
peel

rack
salt
sink
soap
soda
spit
suet
trap
tray

5

airer
basin
besom
broom
broth
brush
caddy
china
cover
crock
cruet
doily
dough
drier
flour
glass
grate
grill
gruel
hatch
herbs

jelly
joint
knife
ladle
match
mixer
mould
paste
plate
poker
range
sauce
scoop
shelf
sieve
spice
spoon
steel
stock
stove
sugar
table
timer
tongs
towel
whisk
wiper
yeast

6

ash-pan
beaker

beater
boiler
bottle
bucket
burner
butter
candle
carver
caster
cooker
cupful
drawer
duster
eggbox
eggcup
fender
filter
flagon
funnel
gas-jet
geyser
grater
grease
haybox
heater
ice-box
jugful
juicer
kettle
larder
mangle
mincer
pantry
pastry

pepper
pickle
polish
pot-lid
recipe
salver
saucer
scales
shovel
sifter
skewer
slicer
starch
tea-cup
tea-pot
tea-urn
trivet
tureen
vessel

7

basting
blender
bluebag
broiler
butlery
cake-tin
cambrel
canteen
chopper
coal-bin
coal-box
cuisine
cutlery
dishmat
dishmop
drainer
dresser
dust-bin
dust-pan
freezer
griller
grinder
infuser
kneader
kneeler
milk-jug
panikin
pie-dish
pitcher
platter
potager
sapples
saltbox
scuttle
seether
skillet
spatula
steamer
stew-pan

tea-cosy
tea-tray
terrine
toaster
tumbler
vinegar
wash-tub

8

bread bin
canister
cauldron
clapdish
colander
covercle
cream-jug
crockery
cupboard
dish rack
egg-slice
eggspoon
eggwhisk
fish fork
flan ring
flat-iron
gas stove
gridiron
hotplate
matchbox
meatsafe
oilcloth
oilstove
patty pan
saucepan
scissors
shoe box
slop bowl
stockpot
strainer
tea caddy
teacloth
teaplate
teaspoon
water jug

9

can opener
casserole
chinaware
coffee-cup
coffee pot
corkscrew
crumb tray
dishcloth
dish cover
egg beater
egg boiler
firegrate

fire-irons
fireplace
fish-knife
fish-plate
fish-slice
flue brush
frying-pan
gas burner
gas cooker
gas geyser
gravy boat
muffineer
pepper-box
pepper-pot
plate-rack
porringer
slop basin
soupspoon
sugar bowl
tea kettle
tin opener
wineglass

10

apple corer
biscuit box
bread board
bread knife
broomstick
butter dish
coffee mill
cook's knife
dishwasher
egg poacher
fish carver
fish kettle
floor cloth
flour crock
gas lighter
ice freezer
jelly mould
knife board
liquidizer
milk boiler
pan scourer
pepper mill
percolator
rolling pin
rotisserie
salamander
salt cellar
tablecloth
tablespoon
waffle iron

11

baking sheet
bread grater

butter knife
coalscuttle
dinner plate
dripping pan
flour dredge
meat chopper
paring knife
porridge pot
pudding bowl
sugar dredge
tea canister
water filter

12

breakfast-cup
carving knife
dessertspoon
double boiler
fishstrainer
flour dredger
hot cupboard
ironing board
kitchen range
knife cleaner
knife machine
measuring cup
nutmeg grater
porridge bowl
potato masher
potato peeler
pudding basin
pudding cloth
refrigerator
thermos flask
toasting fork

13

chopping board
coffee grinder
lemon squeezer
saucepan brush
water softener

14

crockery washer
fuelless cooker
galvanized pail
knife sharpener
mincing machine
pressure cooker
scrubbing brush

15

vegetable cutter

EDUCATION
Educational terms

3

cap
C.S.E.
D.E.S.

don
fag
G.C.E.
gyp
Pop

4

bump
crib
dean

demy
digs
exam
form
gate

gown
hall
head
hood
I.L.E.A.
poly
swot
term
test

5

backs
bedel
class
coach
gaudy
grant
house
lines
pupil
scout
sizar
study
tawse
tutor

6

A-level
beadle
bodley
bursar
course
day boy
degree
eights
fellow
Hilary
incept
locals
locker
master
matron
O-level
optime
reader
rector
school
sconce
senate
tripos
warden

7

academy
battels
Bodley's
bull-dog

burgess
bursary
captain
college
crammer
diploma
dominie
faculty
gestalt
head boy
honours
lecture
monitor
nursery
prefect
proctor
project
provost
reading
scholar
seminar
smalls
student
teacher
teach-in
the high
torpids
tuition

8

academic
ad eundem
backward
emeritus
encaenia
examinee
famulist
graduate
guidance
head girl
homework
learning
lecturer
little-go
manciple
May races
mistress
red-brick
research
roll-call
semester
seminary
send down
statutes
textbook
tuck-shop
tutorial
vacation
viva voce
wrangler

9

art master
art school
bilateral
classroom
collegian
day school
dormitory
great hall
pedagogue
playgroup
preceptor
prelector
president
principal
professor
refectory
registrar
scale post
scholarly
schoolboy
selection
speech day
streaming
sub-rector
trimester

10

blackboard
chancellor
collegiate
commonroom
day release
dining-hall
eleven-plus
exhibition
extra-mural
fellowship
fives court
form-master
illiteracy
imposition
instructor
laboratory
sabbatical
schooldays
schoolgirl
schoolmarm
schoolmate
schoolroom
school year
Sheldonian
university

11

convocation
examination

games master
head teacher
holiday task
housemaster
matriculate
mortarboard
music master
polytechnic
responsions
scholarship
school hours

12

aptitude test
exhibitioner
headmistress
kindergarten
master of arts
night-classes
public orator
pupil-teacher
schoolfellow
schoolmaster
Sunday school

13

adult learning
co-educational
comprehension
comprehensive
doctor of music
grammar school
matriculation
mature student
schoolteacher
science master
supply teacher
undergraduate
vice-principal

14

bachelor of arts
common entrance
junior wrangler
language master
Open University
schoolmistress
senior wrangler
vice-chancellor

15

doctor of science
master of science
school inspector
secondary modern

Oxford and Cambridge colleges

(C.) = Cambridge; (m.) = mixed;
(O.) = Oxford; (p.p.h.) = permanent private hall; (w.) = women.

3 – 5

B.N.C. (O.) (Brasenose)
Caius (C.) (Gonville and)

Clare (C.) (m)
Hall (C.) (Trinity Hall)
House (O.) (Christ Church)
Jesus (C. and O.)

Keble (O.)
King's (C.) (m)
New (O.)
Oriel (O.)

6

Darwin (C.) (m)
Exeter (O.)
Girton (C.) (w)
Merton (O.)
New Hall (C.) (w.)
Queens' (C. and O.)
Selwyn (C.) (m)
Wadham (O.)

7

Balliol (O.)
Christ's (C.)
Downing (C.)
Linacre (O.)
Lincoln (O.)
New Hall (C.) (w)
Newnham (C.) (w)
St. Anne's (O.)
St. Cross (O.)
St. Hugh's (O.) (w)
St. John's (C. and O.)
Trinity (C. and O.)
Wolfson (C. and O.)

8

All Souls (O.)
Emmanuel (C.)
Hertford (O.)
Magdalen (O.)
Nuffield (O.)
Pembroke (C. and O.)
St. Hilda's (O.) (w)
St. Peter's (O.)

9 AND 10

Brasenose (O.) (9)
Churchill (C.) (m) (9)
Clare Hall (C.) (m) (9)
Greyfriars (O.) (p.p.h.) (10)
Hughes Hall (C.) (w) (10)
Magdalene (C.) (9)
Mansfield (O.) (p.p.h.) (9)
Peterhouse (C.) (10)
St. Antony's (O.) (9)
Saint Hugh's (O.) (w) (10)
Saint John's (C. and O.) (10)
Somerville (O.) (w) (10)
University (O.) (10)
Worcester (O.) (9)

11 AND 12

Campion Hall (O.) (p.p.h.) (11)
Christ Church (O.) (12)
Fitzwilliam (C.) (11)
Regent's Park (O.) (p.p.h.) (11)
St. Benet's Hall (O.) (p.p.h.) (12)
St. Catharine's (C.) (12)
St. Catherine's (O.) (12)
St. Edmund Hall (O.) (12)
Saint Hilda's (O.) (w) (11)
Saint Peter's (O.) (11)
Sidney Sussex (C.) (m) (12)
Trinity Hall (C.) (11)

13 AND OVER

Corpus Christi (C. and O.) (13)
Gonville and Caius (C.) (16)
Lady Margaret Hall (O.) (w) (1
Lucy Cavendish (C.) (w) (13)
Saint Benet's Hall (O.)
(p.p.h.) (15)
Saint Catharine's (C.) (15)
Saint Catherine's (O.) (15)
Saint Edmund Hall (O.) (15)
St. Edmund's House (C.) (14)

Some boys' schools

(c.) = "College", as distinct from "School," in title.

4 – 6

Dover (c.) (5)
Durham (6)
Eltham (c.) (6)
Epsom (c.) (5)
Eton (c.) (4)
Exeter (6)
Fettes (c.) (6)
Harrow (6)
Leys (The) (4)
Oakham (6)
Oundle (6)
Radley (c.) (6)
Repton (6)
Rugby (5)
St. Bees (6)
Stowe (5)
Trent (c.) (5)

7

Bedales
Bedford
Bloxham
Clifton (c.)
Dulwich (c.)
Felsted
Lancing (c.)
Loretto
Malvern (c.)
Mercers'
Oratory

Rossall
St. Paul's
Taunton
The Leys
Warwick

8

Abingdon
Ardingly (c.)
Beaumont (c.)
Blue Coat
Brighton (c.)
Denstone (c.)
Downside
Highgate
Mill Hill
St. Albans
St. Olave's
Sedbergh
Whitgift

9

Blundell's
Bradfield (c.)
Bryanston
Cranbrook
Cranleigh
Dean Close
Liverpool (c.)
Sherborne

Tonbridge
Uppingham
Wakefield

10

Ampleforth (c.)
Birkenhead
Bromsgrove
Cheltenham (c.)
Eastbourne (c.)
Haileybury (c.)
Royal Naval (c.)
Shrewsbury
Stoneyhurst (c.)
Summerhill
Wellington (c.)
Winchester (c.)

11

Berkhamsted
Eton College
Framlingham (c.)
Giggleswick
Gordonstoun
Leatherhead
(St. John's)
Marlborough (c.)
Westminster

12

Charterhouse
City of London
King's College (Schoo
Monkton Combe

13

Bedford Modern
Bedford School
Wolverhampton

14

Blue Coat School
Hurstpierpoint (c.)
Wellingborough

15

Christ's Hospital
Imperial Service (c.)
King's, Canterbury
Magdalen College
(School)
Merchant Taylors'

FAMOUS PEOPLE
Admirals

3 – 5

Anson (Lord)
Bacon
Blake
Boyle
Brand
Brock
Broke
Byng
Cowan
Dewar
Dewey
Drake
Field
Hawke
Hood (Lord)
Hope
Howes (Lord)
James
Jones
Keith
Kerr
Keyes (Lord)
Mahan
May
Milne
Moore
Noble
Rooke
Scott
Sims
Stark
Togo
Tovey
Tromp
Tryon

6

Beatty (Lord)
Bridge
Brueys
Calder
Colomb
Darlan
Duncan
Fisher (Lord)
Fraser
Horton
Howard (Lord)
Jerram

Jervis
Keppel
Madden
Nelson (Lord)
Nimitz
Oliver
Parker
Popham
Porter
Ramsay
Rawson
Rodney (Lord)
Rupert (Prince)
Ruyter
Scheel
Scheer
Shovel

7

Burnaby
Burnett
Dampier
de Chair
Doenitz
Exmouth (Lord)
Hopkins
Jackson
Markham
Rainier
Raleigh
Ronarch
Seymour
Sturdee
von Spee
Watkins

8

Berkeley
Boscawen
Caldwell
Cochrane (Lord)
Cockburn
Colville
Craddock
Custance
de Robeck
de Ruyter
Fanshawe
Farragut

Jellicoe (Lord)
Mark Kerr
Muselier
Richmond
Saunders
Saumarez
Tyrwhitt
Villaret
van Tromp
Yamamoto

9

Albemarle
Arbuthnot
Beresford (Lord)
Callaghan
Chatfield (Lord)
Duckworth
Effingham
Fremantle
St. Vincent (Lord)
von Hipper
Warrender

10

Codrington
Cunningham
Evan-Thomas
Kempenfelt
Mountevans (Lord)
Somerville
Troubridge
Villeneuve
von Tirpitz

11 AND 12

Collingwood (11)
Culme-Seymour (12)
Elphinstone (11)
Mountbatten (Lord) (11)
Wester-Wemyss (Lord) (12)

13 AND OVER

Cork and Orrery (Lord) (13)
Rozhdestvensky (14)

Celebrities
1. The World of Entertainment: theatre, opera, ballet, films, the circus, television, radio, music (classical, jazz, folk, pop, etc.).

3 AND 4

Baez, Joan
Bass, Alfie
Bilk, Acker
Bron, Eleanor
Cash, Johnny
Coco (the clown)
Cole, George

Cole, Nat King
Cook, Peter
Day, Doris
Day, Robin
Dean, James
Dors, Diana
Ford, John
Fury, Billy
Getz, Stan

Gish, Lillian
Hall, Henry
Hall, Sir Peter
Hess, Dame Myra
Hope, Bob
Joad, Prof. Cyril
John, Elton
Kean, Edmund
Kerr, Deborah

Lean, David
Lee, Christopher
Lee, Peggy
Lunt, Alfred
Lynn, Vera
Marx brothers
Monk, Thelonious
More, Kenneth
Muir, Frank

75

Nunn, Trevor
Peck, Gregory
Piaf, Edith
Ray, Satyajit
Reed, Carol
Reid, Beryl
Rix, Brian
Ross, Annie
Sim, Alistair
Swan, Donald
Tati, Jacques
Took, Barrie
Tree, Sir Herbert
Wise, Ernie
Wise, Robert
Wood, Sir Henry
York, Michael
York, Susannah

5

Adler, Larry
Allen, Chesney
Allen, Dave
Arden, John
Askey, Arthur
Baker, Dame Janet
Baker, Richard
Baker, Sir Stanley
Basie, Count
Bates, Alan
Benny, Jack
Black, Cilla
Blair, David
Boult, Sir Adrian
Bowie, David
Brain, Dennis
Bream, Julian
Brice, Fanny
Brook, Peter
Bryan, Dora
Clark, Lord
Clark, Petula
Cooke, Alistair
Costa, Sam
Cukor, George
Davis, Bette
Davis, Colin
Davis, Miles
Davis, Sammy
Dench, Judi
Dolan, Anton
Dyall, Valentine
Dylan, Bob
Evans, Dame Edith
Faith, Adam
Felix, Julie
Finch, Peter
Flynn, Errol
Fonda, Henry
Fonda, Jane
Frost, David
Gable, Clark
Gabor, Zsa Zsa
Garbo, Greta
Gigli, Beniamino
Gobbi, Tito
Gould, Elliot
Grade, Lord
Grant, Cary
Greco, Juliette
Green, Hughie
Haley, Bill
Handl, Irene
Hines, Earl

Holly, Buddy
Horne, Kenneth
Horne, Lena
James, Sid
Jones, Tom
Kazan, Elia
Kelly, Barbara
Kelly, Grace
Kempe, Rudolf
Korda, Alexander
La Rue, Danny
Leigh, Vivien
Lloyd, Harold
Losey, Joseph
Magee, Patrick
Marks, Alfred
Mason, James
Melba, Dame Nellie
Melly, George
Miles, Sir Bernard
Mills, Bertram
Mills, Mrs.
Moore, Dudley
Moore, Gerald
Mount, Peggy
Negus, Arthur
Niven, David
Ogdon, John
Pears, Peter
Quinn, Anthony
Reith, Lord
Scott, Terry
Smith, Bessie
Smith, Maggie
Somes, Michael
Sousa, John
Starr, Ringo
Stern, Isaac
Swann, Sir Michael
Sykes, Eric
Tatum, Art
Teyte, Dame Maggie
Terry, Ellen
Tynan, Kenneth
Wayne, John
Welch, Raquel
Welsh, Alex
Worth, Irene

6

Adrian, Max
Ashton, Sir Frederick
Bacall, Lauren
Barber, Chris
Bardot, Brigitte
Barnet, Lady (Isobel)
Barnum, P. T.
Bassey, Shirley
Baylis, Lilian
Bechet, Sidney
Bogart, Humphrey
Boulez, Pierre
Braden, Bernard
Brando, Marlon
Burney, Fanny
Burton, Richard
Callas, Maria
Caruso, Enrico
Casals, Pablo
Cleese, John
Colyer, Ken
Cooper, Gary
Curran, Sir Charles
Curzon, Clifford

Cusack, Cyril
Cushing, Peter
de Sica, Vittorio
Disney, Walt
Dowell, Anthony
Duncan, Isadora
Fields, Gracie
Fields, W. C.
Finney, Albert
Greene, Sir Hugh
Garson, Greer
Godard, Jean-Luc
Goring, Marius
Groves, Sir Charles
Harlow, Jean
Heston, Charlton
Hiller, Dame Wendy
Hobson, Harold
Howard, Frankie
Irving, Sir Henry
Jacobs, David
Jagger, Mick
Joplin, Scott
Keaton, Buster
Kemble, Fanny
Kramer, Stanley
Lennon, John
Lidell, Alvar
Lillie, Beatrice
Miller, Glenn
Miller, Jonathan
Mingus, Charlie
Monroe, Marilyn
Moreau, Jeanne
Morley, Robert
Morton, Jelly Roll
Mostel, Zero
Nerina, Nadia
Newman, Nanette
Newman, Paul
Norden, Dennis
Oliver, King
O'Toole, Peter
Parker, Charlie
Parker, Dorothy
Powell, Dilys
Previn, André
Quayle, Anthony
Renoir, Jean
Robson, Dame Flora
Rogers, Ginger
Rooney, Mickey
Savile, Jimmy
Seegar, Peggy
Seegar, Pete
Sibley, Antoinette
Sinden, Donald
Snagge, John
Talbot, Godfrey
Tauber, Richard
Taylor, Elizabeth
Temple, Shirley
Waller, Fats
Waring, Eddie
Warner brothers
Warner, David
Welles, Orson
Wilder, Billy
Wilder, Gene
Wolfit, Sir Donald

7

Andrews, Eamonn
Andrews, Julie

76

Astaire, Fred
Baillie, Isobel
Beecham, Sir Thomas
Bennett, Alan
Bennett, Jill
Bentine, Michael
Bentley, Dick
Bergman, Ingmar
Bergman, Ingrid
Blondin, Charles
Bogarde, Dirk
Brubeck, Dave
Chaplin, Sir Charles
Chester, Charlie
Cocteau, Jean
Collins, Judy
Connery, Sean
Corbett, Harry
Donegan, Lonnie
Donovan
Dougall, Robert
Douglas, Kirk
Edwards, Jimmy
Feldman, Marty
Fellini, Federico
Ferrier, Kathleen
Fonteyn, Dame Margot
Freeman, John
Garland, Judy
Garnett, Alf
Garrick, David
Gielgud, Sir John
Goldwyn, Sam
Goosens, Léon
Goodman, Benny
Guiffre, Jimmy
Guthrie, Sir Tyrone
Guthrie, Woody
Hammond, Joan
Hancock, Sheila
Hancock, Tony
Handley, Tommy
Harding, Gilbert
Hawkins, Jack
Hendrix, Jimi
Hepburn, Audrey
Hepburn, Katherine
Hoffman, Dustin
Holiday, Billie
Hopkins, Antony
Houdini, Harry
Jackson, Glenda
Jackson, Mahalia
Jacques, Hattie
Karloff, Boris
Kendall, Kenneth
Kennedy, Ludovic
Kubrick, Stanley
Lympany, Moira
MacColl, Ewan
Markova, Alicia
Menunin, Yehudi
Montand, Yves
Monteux, Pierre
Murdoch, Richard
Novello, Ivor
Nureyev, Rudolph
Olivier, Lord
Pavlova, Anna
Pickles, Wilfred
Rambert, Dame Marie
Rantzen, Esther
Redford, Robert
Richard, Cliff
Roberts, Rachel
Rodgers, Richard

Rushton, William
Russell, Jane
Russell, Ken
Sargent, Sir Malcolm
Secombe, Harry
Sellers, Peter
Seymour, Lynn
Shankar, Ravi
Shearer, Moira
Sherrin, Ned
Siddons, Mrs Sarah
Simmons, Jean
Sinatra, Frank
Stevans, Cat
Stewart, James
Swanson, Gloria
Ulanova, Galina
Ustinov, Peter
Vaughan, Frankie
Vaughan, Sarah
Whicker, Alan
Wheldon, Huw
Withers, Googie

8

Anderson, Lindsay
Anderson, Marian
Ashcroft, Dame Peggy
Beerbohm, Sir Max
Brambell, Wilfred
Bygraves, Max
Campbell, Mrs Pat
Chisholm, George
Christie, Julie
Clements, Sir John
Coltrane, John
de Valois, Dame Ninette
Dietrich, Marlene
Dimbleby, Richard
Eastwood, Clint
Flanagan, Bud
Flanders, Michael
Fletcher, Cyril
Grenfell, Joyce
Guinness, Sir Alec
Harrison, George
Harrison, Rex
Helpmann, Sir Robert
Hoffnung, Gerard
Holloway, Stanley
Horowitz, Vladimir
Laughton, Charles
Lawrence, Gertrude
Liberace
Matthews, Jessie
Milligan, Spike
Mitchell, Joni
Mulligan, Gerry
Nijinski, Vaslav
Oistrakh, David
Oistrakh, Igor
Paganini, Niccolò
Pickford, Mary
Polanski, Roman
Redgrave, Sir Michael
Redgrave, Vanessa
Robinson, Edward G.
Robinson, Eric
Robinson, Robert
Scofield, Paul
Stephens, Robert
Streeter, Fred
Truffaut, François
Visconti, Luchino

Williams, Andy
Williams, John
Williams, Kenneth
Zeppelin, Led

9

Antonioni, Michelangelo
Armstrong, Louis
Ashkenazy, Vladimir
Barenboim, Daniel
Barrymore, John
Belafonte, Harry
Bernhardt, Sarah
Brannigan, Owen
Cardinale, Claudia
Chevalier, Maurice
Christoff, Boris
Courtenay, Tom
Dankworth, John
Davenport, Bob
Diaghilev, Serge
Ellington, Duke
Gillespie, Dizzy
Grisewood, Freddy
Engelmann, Franklin
Fairbanks, Douglas
Hampshire, Susan
Hitchcock, Alfred
Humphries, Barry
Klemperer, Otto
Leadbelly
Lyttelton, Humphrey
McCartney, Paul
Monkhouse, Bob
Morecombe, Eric
Pleasance, Donald
Plowright, Joan
Preminger, Otto
Reinhardt, Django
Reinhardt, Max
Sternberg, Joseph von
Streisand, Barbra
Thorndike, Dame Sybil

10

Barbirolli, Sir John
Eisenstein, Sergei
Fitzgerald, Ella
Littlewood, Joan
Michelmore, Cliff
Muggeridge, Malcolm
Richardson, Sir Ralph
Rubinstein, Artur
Rutherford, Dame Margaret
Sutherland, Joan

11 AND OVER

Attenborough, David (12)
Attenborough, Sir Richard (12)
Beiderbecke, Bix (11)
Chipperfield, Mary (12)
Fischer-Dieskau, Dietrich (14)
Granville-Barker, Harley (15)
Hammerstein, Oscar (11)
Springfield, Dusty (11)
Stradivarius, Antonio (12)
Terry-Thomas (11)

77

2. Sports and Games

ath. = athletics; *box.* = boxing; *crc.* = cricket; *fb.* = football; *gf* = golf;
gym. = gymnastics; *hr.* = horseracing; *mr.* = motor-racing;
mt. = mountaineering; *sj.* = showjumping; *sw.* = swimming; *ten.* = tennis;
yt. = yachting

3 AND 4

Ali, Muhammed *box.*
Amis, Dennis, *crc.*
Ashe, Arthur *ten.*
Best, George *fb.*
Borg, Bjorn *ten.*
Clay, Cassius *box.*
Cobb, Ty *baseball*
Endo, Yukio *gym.*
Fox, Uffa *yt.*
Hill, Graham *mr.*
Hoad, Lew *ten.*
Hunt, James *mr.*
Hunt, Sir John *mt.*
John, Barry *rugby*
Kim, Nellie *gym.*
King, Billie Jean *ten.*
Law, Denis *fb.*
Lock, Tony *crc.*
May, Peter *crc.*
Moss, Stirling *mr.*
Read, Phil *motor-cycling*
Ruth, 'Babe' *baseball*
Snow, John *crc.*
Wade, Virginia *ten.*
Webb, Capt. M. *sw.*

5

Banks, Gordon *fb.*
Brown, Joe *mt.*
Bueno, Maria *ten.*
Busby, Sir Matthew *fb.*
Clark, Jim *mr.*
Close, Brian *crc.*
Court, Margaret *ten.*
Curry, John *skating*
Davis, Joe, *billiards*
Evans, Godfrey *crc.*
Evert, Chris *ten.*
Grace, Dr W. G. *crc.*
Greig, Tony *crc.*
Hobbs, Sir John *crc.*
Hogan, Ben *gf*
Irwin, Hale *gf*
Jones, Ann *ten.*
Keino, Kip *ath.*
Knott, Alan *crc.*
Kodes, J. *ten.*
Laker, Jim *crc.*
Lauda, Niki *mr.*
Laver, Rod *ten.*
Lloyd, Clive *crc.*
Louis, Joe *box.*
Moore, Ann *sj.*
Moore, Bobby *fb.*
Perry, Fred, *ten.*
Pirie, Gordon *ath.*
Revie, Don *fb.*
Roche, Tony *ten.*
Scott, Sheila *aviation*
Sloan, James *hr.*
Smith, Harvey *sj.*
Smith, Stan *ten.*
Spitz, Mark *sw.*
Wills, Helen *ten.*

6

Barker, Sue *ten.*
Bedser, Alec *crc.*
Benaud, Richard *crc.*
Broome, David *sj.*
Bugner, Joe *box.*
Casals, Rosemary *ten.*
Cooper, Henry *box.*
Dexter, Ted *crc.*
Drobny, Jaroslav *ten.*
Edrich, John *crc.*
Fangio, Juan *mr.*
Foster, Brendan *ath.*
Fraser, Dawn *sw.*
Gibson, Althea *ten.*
Hutton, Sir Len *crc.*
Kanhai, Rohan *crc.*
Keegan, Kevin *fb.*
Korbut, Olga *gym.*
Lillee, Dennis *crc.*
Liston, Sonny *box.*
Merckx, Eddy *cycling*
Palmer, Arnold *gf*
Peters, Mary *ath.*
Player, Gary *gf*
Ramsey, Sir Alf *fb.*
Sobers, Sir Gary *crc.*
Smythe, Pat *sj.*
Stolle, Fred *ten.*
Taylor, Roger *ten.*
Thoeni, G. *skiing*
Titmus, Fred *crc.*
Turpin, Randolph *box.*
Wilkie, David *sw.*

7

Boycott, Geoffrey *crc.*
Brabham, Jack *mr.*
Bradman, Sir Don *crc.*
Compton, Dennis *crc.*
Connors, Jimmy *ten.*
Cowdrey, Colin *crc.*
Dempsey, Jack *box.*
Elliott, Herb *ath.*
Emerson, Roy *ten.*
Ferrari, Enzio *mr.*
Fischer, Bobby *chess*
Foreman, George *box.*
Frazier, Joe *box.*
Greaves, Jimmy *fb.*
Hillary, Sir Edmund *mt.*
Hopkins, Thelma *ath,
hockey*
Jacklin, Tony *gf*
Johnson, Amy *aviation*
Mottram, Buster *ten.*
Nastase, Ilie *ten.*
Piggott, Lester *hr.*
Spassky, Boris *chess*
Stewart, Jackie *mr.*
Surtees, John *mr.*
Tabarly, Eric *yt.*
Tensing, Sherpa *mt.*
Thomson, Jeff *crc.*
Trevino, Lee *gf*

Trueman, Freddie *crc.*
Worrell, Sir Frank *crc.*

8

Brinkley, Brian *sw.*
Chappell, Greg *crc.*
Chappell, Ian *crc.*
Charlton, Bobby *fb.*
Charlton, Jack *fb.*
Comaneci, Nadia *gym.*
Connolly, Maureen *ten.*
Cordobés, El *bullfighting*
Cousteau, Jacques-Yves
diving
Docherty, Tommy *fb.*
Elvstrom, Paul *yt.*
Gligorić, Svetozar *chess*
Graveney, Tom *crc.*
Latynina, Larissa *gym.*
Marciano, Rocky *box.*
Matthews, Sir Stanley *fb.*
McClaren, Bruce *mr.*
Mortimer, Angela *ten.*
Newcombe, John *ten.*
Nicklaus, Jack *gf*
Phillips, Capt. Mark *sj.*
Richards, Sir Gordon *hr.*
Rosewall, Ken *ten.*
Weiskopf, Tom *gf*

9

Bannister, Dr Roger *ath.*
Bonington, Chris *mt.*
D'Oliveira, Basil *crc.*
Goolagong, Evonne *ten.*
Johansson, Ingomar *box.*
Lindbergh, Charles *aviation*
Patterson, Floyd *box.*
Pattisson, Rodney *yt.*
Underwood, Derek *crc.*

10 AND OVER

Barrington, Jonah *squash*
(10)
Blanchflower, Danny *fb.*
(12)
Capablanca, José *chess* (10)
Chichester, Sir Francis *yt.*
(10)
Constantine, Sir Leary *crc.*
(11)
Fittipaldi, Emerson *mr.* (10)
Fredericks, Roy *crc.* (10)
Illingworth, Ray *crc.* (11)
Lonsbrough, Anita *sw.* (10)
Oosterhuis, Peter *gf* (10)
Schockemohle, Alwin *sj.*
(12)
Turischeva, Ludmila *gym.*
(10)
Weissmuller, Johnny *sw.* (11)

3. Other prominent people

3 AND 4

Beit, Alfred (S. African financier)
Cid, The (Spanish hero)
Eddy, Mrs Mary Baker (U.S. founder of Christian Science)
Fox, George (Eng. preacher)
Fry, Elizabeth (Eng. social reformer)
Hus, Jan (Bohemian religious reformer)
Hall, Marshall (Eng. physiologist)
Hill, Octavia (Eng. social reformer)
Hill, Sir Rowland (Eng. pioneer in postal services)
Jung, Carl Gustav (Swiss psychoanalyst)
Kant, Immanuel (Ger. philosopher)
Kidd, Capt. William (Sc. pirate)
Knox, John (Sc. religious reformer)
Kun, Bela (Communist leader in Hungary)
Lee, Ann (Eng. founder of Society of Shakers)
Low, David (N.Z.-born cartoonist)
Luce, Henry Robinson (U.S. publisher)
Marx, Karl (Ger. Socialist)
Mond, Ludwig (Ger.-born chemist)
Penn, William (Eng. Quaker, founder of Pennsylvania)
Polo, Marco (It. explorer)
Salk, Jonas Edward (U.S. scientist)

5

Acton, John Dalberg, Lord (Eng. historian)
Adams, Henry (U.S. historian)
Adler, Alfred (Austrian psychologist)
Amati, Nicolò (Italian violin-maker)
Astor, John Jacob (U.S. millionaire)
Astor, Nancy, Viscountess (first woman in Br. House of Commons)
Bacon, Roger (philosopher)
Baird, John Logie (Sc. pioneer in TV)
Banks, Sir Joseph (Eng. naturalist)
Barth, Karl (Swiss theologian)
Booth, William (founder of the Salvation Army)
Botha, General Louis (Boer leader)

Clive, Robert (Indian Empire pioneer)
Freud, Sigmund (Austrian pioneer psychoanalyst)
'Grock' (Adrien Wettach) (Swiss clown)
Hegel, Georg Wilhelm Friedrich (Ger. philosopher)
Herzl, Theodor (Hung.-born founder of Zionism)
Karsh, Yousuf (Armenian-born photographer)
Keble, John (Eng. divine)
Zeiss, Carl (Ger. optical instrument maker)

6

Alcock, Sir John William (pioneer aviator)
Attila (King of the Huns)
Barker, Sir Herbert Atkinson (Eng. specialist in manipulative surgery)
Baruch, Bernard Mannes (U.S. financier)
Besant, Mrs Anne (Eng. theosophist)
Boehme, Jakob (Ger. theosophist)
Butler, Mrs Josephine (Eng. social reformer)
Calvin, John (Fr. theologian)
Capone, Al (U.S. gangster)
Caslon, William (Eng. typefounder)
Cavell, Nurse Edith (Eng. patriot)
Caxton, William (first Eng. printer)
Cicero, Marcus Tullius (Roman statesman and writer)
Diesel, Rudolf (Ger. engineer)
Dunant, Henri (Swiss founder of International Red Cross)
Euclid (Greek mathematician)
Fokker, Anton (Dutch aviation pioneer)
Graham, Billy (U.S. evangelist)
Halley, Edmond (Eng. astronomer)
Hearst, William Randolph (U.S. newspaper publisher)
Keynes, John Maynard (Eng. economist)
Luther, Martin (Ger. church reformer)
Mellon, Andrew William (U.S. financier)
Mesmer, Friedrich Franz (Ger. hypnotist)

Morgan, John Pierpont (U.S. financier)
Petrie, William Flinders (Eng. archaeologist)
Planck, Max (Ger. physicist – formulated quantum theory)
Stopes, Dr Marie (Eng. pioneer in family planning)
Tagore, Rabindrath (Indian poet and philosopher)
Turpin, Dick (Eng. highwayman)
Wesley, John (founder of Methodism)
Wright, Orville (U.S. pioneer aviator)
Wright, Wilbur (U.S. pioneer aviator)
Wyclif, John (Eng. religious reformer)

7

Abelard, Peter (Fr. philosopher)
Aga Khan (Ismaili leader)
Atatürk, Kemal (Turkish soldier and statesmen)
Bleriot, Louis (Fr. aviator)
Blondin, Charles (Fr. acrobat)
Boyd-Orr, John, Baron (Sc. nutritionist)
Buchman, Frank (U.S. founder of Moral Rearmament)
Cassini, Giovanni Domenico (It. astronomer)
Celsius, Anders (Sw. inventor of Centigrade thermomenter)
Ehrlich, Paul (Ger. bacteriologist)
Erasmus, Desiderius (Dutch religious reformer and theologian)
Haeckel, Ernest Heinrich (Ger. naturalist)
Houdini, Harry (Erich Weiss) (Hung.-born magician and conjurer)
Leblanc, Nicolas (Fr. chemist)
Linacre, Thomas (Eng. founder of Royal College of Physicians)
Lumière, August and Louis (Fr. pioneers of cinematography)
MacEwen, Sir William (Sc. surgeon)
Scribner, Charles (U.S. publisher)
Spinoza, Benedict (Dutch philosopher)
Steiner, Rudolf (Hung.-born philosopher and educationalist)

Tussaud, Mme Marie
(Swiss-born modeller in
wax)

8

Avicenna (Arab
philosopher)
Bancroft, George (U.S.
historian)
Berkeley, George (Irish
philosopher)
Carnegie, Andrew (Sc.-born
philanthropist)
Earheart, Amelia (U.S.
aviator)
Grimaldi, Joseph (Eng.
clown)
Larousse, Pierre Athanase
(Fr. encyclopaedist)
Mercator, Geradus (Flemish
geographer)
Negretti, Enrico (It.-born
instrument-maker)
Nuffield, William Richard
Morris, Viscount (motor
manufacturer and
philanthropist)
Sheraton, Thomas (Eng.
cabinet-maker)
Wedgwood, Josiah (Eng.
potter)

9

Arbuthnot, Alexander
(printer of first bible,
1579, in Scotland)
Aristotle (Greek
philosopher)
Arkwright, Sir Richard
(inventor)
Blackwell, Dr. Elisabeth
(first Eng. registered
woman doctor)

Blavatsky, Madame Helena
(Russian-born
theosophist)
Courtauld, Samuel (Eng.
silk manufacturer)
Descartes, René (Fr.
philospher)
Gutenberg, Johannes (Ger.
founder of western
printing)
Heidegger, Martin (Ger.
philosopher)
Macgregor, Rober ('Rob
Roy') (Sc. rebel)
Nietzsche, Friedrich (Ger.
philosopher)
Pankhurst, Mrs. Emmeline
(Eng. suffragette leader)

10

Bernadotte, Jean Baptiste
(Fr. general and king of
Sweden)
Cagliostro, Alessandro
(Guiseppe Balsamo) (It.
alchemist)
Flammarion, Camille (Fr.
astronomer)
Guggenhiem, Meyer (U.S.
financier)
Macpherson, Aimée Semple
(U.S. evangelist)
Max-Müller, Friedrich
(Ger.-born philologist and
orientalist)
Montessori, Maria (It.
founder of Montessori
educational method)
Rothermere, Harold Sidney
Harmsworth, Viscount
(Eng. newspaper
publisher)
Rothschild, Meyer Amshel
(Ger. financier)
Rutherford, Daniel (Sc.
discoverer of nitrogen)

Schweitzer, Dr. Albert
(Alsatian musician and
medical missionary)
Stradivari, Antonio (It.
violin-maker)
Swedenborg, Emanuel (Sw.
theologian)
Vanderbilt, Cornelius (U.S.
financier)

11

Beaverbrook, William
Maxwell Aitken, 1st
Baron (Canadian-born
newspaper publisher)
Chippendale, Thomas (Eng.
furniture designer)
Hippocrates (Greek
physician)
Machiavelli (It. political
reformer)
Nightingale, Florence (Eng.
pioneer in training
nurses)
Northcliffe, Alfred
Harmsworth, Viscount
(Irish-born newspaper
owner)
Shaftesbury, Anthony
Ashley Cooper, 7th Earl
(Eng. philanthropist)
Wilberforce, Samuel (Eng.
divine)
Wilberforce, William (Eng.
abolitionist)

12

Krishnamurti, Jiddu
(Indian mystic)
Schopenhauer, Arthur (Ger.
philosopher)
Wittgenstein, Ludwig
(Austrian-born
philosopher)

Explorers

3 AND 4

Back
Beke
Bird
Byrd
Cam
Cook
Diaz
Gama
Gann
Hore
Leif
Park
Polo
Rae
Ross (Sir John)
Rut

5

Anson (Lord George)
Baker

Brown (Lady)
Bruce (General)
Burke
Cabot
Clark
Davis
Drake (Sir Francis)
Dyatt
Dyott (Commander)
Evans (Capt.)
Fuchs
Gomez
Hanno
Hedin
Lewis
Mosto
Nares (Sir George)
Necho
Nuyts
Oates (Capt.)
Ojeda
Parry (Admiral)
Peary (Admiral)

Penny (Capt.)
Prado
Scott (Capt.)
Smith (Capt.)
Speke (Capt.)
Terry
Welzl
Wills

6

Andrée
Austin (Capt.)
Baffin
Balboa
Barnes
Barrow (Sir John)
Bellot
Bering
Burton (Sir Richard)
Cabral
Conway (Sir Martin)

Generals, field marshals, air marshals, etc.

3 – 5

Adam
Baird
Blood
Bols
Botha
Bruce
Byng
Clark
Clive
Condé
Craig
Dawes
Dayan
de Wet
Duff
Dyer
Foch
Giap
Gort
Gough
Grant
Haig
Hart
Horne
Ismay
Jacob
Jodl
Junot
Lee
Leese
Maude
Milne
Model
Monro
Moore
Munro
Murat
Neill
Ney
Nye
Paget
Parma
Patch
Peck
Pile
Raban
Robb
Saxe
Shea
Slim
Smuts
Soult
Sulla
Tojo
Tully
Weeks
White
Wolfe
Wood

6

Barrow
Buller
Butler
Caesar
Capper
Creagh
Crerar
Cronje
Daxout
Douglas
Dundas
Eugene
French
Giraud
Gordon
Göring
Graham
Harris
Hunter
Joffre
Keitel
Koniev
Mangin
Marius
Moltke
Murray
Napier
Newall
Outram
Patton
Pétain
Plumer
Pompey
Portal
Raglan
Rommel
Rundle
Rupert (Prince)
Scipio
Spaatz
Tedder
Trajan
Wilson
Zhukov

7

Allenby
Blücher
Bradley
Cadorna
Capello
Dempsey
Fairfax
Gamelin
Gaselee
Gatacre
Gonzalo

Gourand
Haldane
Joubert
Leclerc
Lyautey
McMahon
MacMunn
Masséna
Maurice
Maxwell
Methuen
Mortier
Nivelle
O'Connor
Roberts
Salmond
Sherman
Simpson
Stewart
Turenne
Weygand
Wingate

8

Birdwood
Brancker
Browning
Campbell
Chetwode
Cromwell
De Gaulle
Freyberg
Galliéni
Gleichen
Hamilton
Hannibal
Havelock
Ironside
Lockhart
Napoleon
Pershing
Radetsky
Saunders
Skobelev
Townsend
Urquhart
von Bülow
von Kluck
Wolseley

9

Alexander
Berthelot
Boulanger
Cambridge
Chermside
Connaught

Dundonald
Garibaldi
Harington
Higginson
Kitchener
Lyttelton
Ludendorf
Macdonald
Miltiades
Nicholson
Rawlinson
Robertson
Trenchard
Wellesley
Willcocks

10

Alanbrooke
Auchinleck
Bernadotte
Chelmsford
Cornwallis
Eisenhower
Falkenhayn
Hindenburg
Kesselring
Kuropatkin
Montgomery
Voroshilov
Wellington

11

Abercrombie
Baden-Powell
Brackenbury
de Castelnau
Marlborough
Ochterlonie
Strathnairn
Wallenstein

12 AND 13

Hunter-Weston (12)
Smith-Dorrien (12)
von Mackensen (12)
von Rundstedt (12)
Younghusband (12)

14 AND 15

Forestier-Walker (15)
Garnet-Wolseley (14)
Napier of Magdala (15)

Politicians and statesmen:
a selection

3 AND 4

Amin
Blum

Burr
Cato
Chou

Clay
Foot
Fox

Grey
Hess
Hull

Meir
Pitt
Pym
Rhee
Root
Rusk
Tito

5

Banda
Benés
Bevan
Bevin
Burke
Ciano
Cleon
Desai
Hiero
Hoare
Hoxha
Husak
Jagan
Kadar
Laval
Lenin
Marat
Nehru
Perón
Sadat
Simon
Smith
Smuts
Solon

6

Bhutto
Borgia
Brandt
Caesar
Castro
Cavour
Chiang
Cobden
Cripps

Cromer
Curzon
Danton
Dubcek
Dulles
Franco
Gadafy
Gandhi
Hitler
Horthy
Kaunda
Mobutu
Mosley
Nasser
Pétain
Powell
Rhodes
Samuel
Stalin

7

Acheson
Allende
Batista
Bolivar
Bormann
Giscard
Gomulka
Halifax
Hampden
Himmler
Kennedy
Kosygin
Kreisky
Lumumba
Masaryk
Menzies
Mintoff
Molotov
Nkrumah
Nyerere
Parnell
Pearson
Ptolemy
Redmond
Reynaud

Salazar
Sukarno
Trotsky
Trudeau
Vorster
Webster

8

Adenauer
Augustus
Ayub Khan
Bismarck
Brezhnev
Bulganin
Cromwell
Daladier
De Gaulle
De Valera
Dollfuss
Duvalier
Goebbels
Hamilton
Kenyatta
Lycurgus
Makarios
Montfort
Morrison
Napoleon
O'Higgins
Pericles
Pinochet
Podgorny
Pompidou
Ulbricht
Verwoerd
Welensky

9

Alexander
Ben Gurion
Bonaparte
Bourguiba
Chou En-Lai
Churchill

Clarendon
Dionysius
Garibaldi
Ho Chi Minh
Mussolini
Richelieu
Salisbury
Strafford

10

Buonaparte
Clemenceau
Hindenburg
Khrushchev
Lee Kuan-Yew
Mao Tse-Tung
Metternich
Ribbentrop
Sekou Touré
Talleyrand

11

Boumédienne
Castlereagh
Chamberlain
Cleisthenes
Robespierre
Shaftesbury

12

Bandaranaike
Hammarskjöld
Kemal Atatürk
Mendès-France
Themistocles

13 AND OVER

Chiang Kai-Shek (13)
Giscard d'Estaing (15)
Hailé Selassié (13)

Presidents of the United States

4 AND 5

Adams, John
Adams, John Quincy
Ford, Gerald
Grant, Ulysses S.
Hayes, Rutherford B.
Nixon, Richard M.
Polk, James K.
Taft, William
Tyler, John

6

Arthur, Chester A.
Carter, Jimmy
Hoover, Herbert
Munroe, James
Pierce, Franklin
Taylor, Zachary

Truman, Harry
Wilson, Woodrow

7

Harding, Warren G.
Jackson, Andrew
Johnson, Andrew
Johnson, Lyndon B.
Kennedy, John F.
Lincoln, Abraham
Madison, James

8

Buchanan, James
Coolidge, Calvin

Fillmore, Millard
Garfield, James A.
Harrison, Benjamin
Harrison, William
McKinley, William
Van Buren, Martin

9

Cleveland, Grover
Jefferson, Thomas
Roosevelt, Franklin D.
Roosevelt, Theodore

10

Eisenhower, Dwight
Washington, George

Prime ministers of Great Britain

4 AND 5

Bute, Lord
Derby, Lord
Eden, Sir Anthony
Grey, Lord
Heath, Edward
North, Lord
Peel, Sir Robert
Pitt, William (the Younger)

6

Attlee, Clement
Pelham, Henry
Wilson, Sir Harold

7

Asquith, Herbert
Baldwin, Stanley
Balfour, Arthur
Canning, George
Chatham, Lord (Wm Pitt
    the Elder)

Grafton, Duke of
Russell, Lord John
Walpole, Sir Robert

8

Aberdeen, Lord
Bonar Law, Andrew
Disraeli, Benjamin
Goderich, Lord
Perceval, Spencer
Portland, Duke of
Rosebery, Lord

9

Addington, Henry
Callaghan, James
Churchill, Sir Winston
Gladstone, William
Grenville, George
Grenville, Lord
Liverpool, Lord
MacDonald, Ramsay

Macmillan, Harold
Melbourne, Lord
Newcastle, Duke of
Salisbury, Marquis of
Shelburne, Lord

10

Devonshire, Duke of
Palmerston, Lord
Rockingham, Marquis of
Wellington, Duke of
Wilmington, Lord

11 AND OVER

Beaconsfield, Lord (12)
Campbell-Bannerman, Sir
    Henry (17)
Chamberlain, Neville (11)
Douglas-Home, Sir Alec (11)
Lloyd George, David (11)

Scientists and engineers

3 AND 4

Aird
Ball
Bell
Bohr
Bose
Coué
Davy
Ford
Gall
Gibb
Gold
Hahn
Hale
Hero
Hess
Howe
Koch
Low
Ohm
Paré
Ray
Reed
Swan
Watt
Wren

5

Bacon
Banks
Barry
Boole
Boyle
Bragg
Brahe
Crick

Curie
Debye
Ewing
Fermi
Galen
Gamow
Gauss
Haber
Henri
Hertz
Hooke
Jacob
Jeans
Joule
Klein
Krebs
Lodge
Maxim
Monod
Morse
Pauli
Pliny
Segrè
Smith
Volta
White

6

Ampère
Brunel
Bunsen
Calvin
Cardew
Dalton
Darwin
Dawson
Edison

Euclid
Froude
Fulton
Halley
Harvey
Hubble
Hughes
Hutton
Huxley
Jenner
Kekulé
Kelvin
Kepler
Kuiper
Liebig
Lister
Mendel
Morgan
Napier
Nernst
Newton
Pascal
Pavlov
Planck
Ramsay
Rennie
Roscoe
Stokes
Thales
Watson

7

Andrews
Banting
Charles
Compton
Coulomb

Coulson
Crookes
Daimler
Da Vinci
Doppler
Faraday
Fleming
Galileo
Galvani
Huggins
Huygins
Kendrew
Lamarck
Lockyer
Lorentz
Marconi
Maxwell
Medawar
Moseley
Newmann
Pasteur
Pauling
Piccard
Ptolemy
Röntgen
Rumford
Seaborg
Siemens
Thomson
Tyndall
Virchow
Wallace
Whitney

8

Agricola
Bessemer

Blackett
Chadwick
Crompton
De Forest
Einstein
Foucault
Franklin
Goodyear
Harrison
Herschel
Humboldt
Lawrence
Linnaeus
Malpighi
Mercator
Millikan
Rayleigh

Roentgen
Thompson
Van Allen
Van't Hoff
Zeppelin

9

Aristotle
Armstrong
Arrhenius
Becquerel
Bernoulli
Cavendish
De Broglie
Descartes

Eddington
Fibonnaci
Gay-Lussac
Heaviside
Kirchhoff
Lankester
Mendeleev
Michelson
Priestley

10

Archimedes
Cannizzaro
Copernicus
Fahrenheit

Heisenberg
Hipparchus
Paracelsus
Rutherford
Stephenson
Torricelli

11 AND OVER

Grosseteste (11)
Le Chatelier (11)
Leeuwenhoek (11)
Oppenheimer (11)
Schrödinger (11)
Szent-Györgyi (12)
Van der Waals (11)

GEOGRAPHY
References for geographical lists

Adr. Adriatic Sea
Aeg. Aegean Sea
Af. Africa
Afghan. Afghanistan
Alg. Algeria
Am. America
Antarc. Antarctic (Ocean)
Arab. Arabia
   Arabian Sea
Arc. Arctic (Ocean)
Arg. Argentina
Asia M. Asia Minor
Atl. Atlantic Ocean
Aust. Austria
Austral. Australia
Balt. Baltic (Sea)
Bangla. Bangladesh
Belg. Belgium
Boliv. Bolivia
Braz. Brazil
Bulg. Bulgaria
C.Am. Central America
Can. Canada
Cen. Af. Rep. Central
   African
   Republic
Ch. Is. Channel Islands
Cors. Corsica
Cze. Czechoslovakia
Den. Denmark
E. Af. East Africa
E. Ger. East Germany
E.I. (East Indies
Eng. England

Eth. Ethiopia
Eur. Europe
Fin. Finland
Fr. France
Ger. Germany
Gr. Greece
Him. Himalayas
Hung. Hungary
Ind. India
   Indian Ocean
Indo. Indonesia
Ire. Ireland
   Republic of
   Ireland
Isr. Israel
It. Italy
Jap. Japan
Jord. Jordan
Malag. Rep. Malagasy
   Republic
Malay. Malaysia
Med. Mediterranean (Sea)
Mex. Mexico
Mon. Mongolia
Moroc. Morocco
Moz. Mozambique
N.Af North Africa
N.Am. North America
Nep. Nepal
N. Guin. New Guinea
Neth. Netherlands
N.I. Northern Ireland
Nig. Nigeria
Nor. Norway

N.Z. New Zealand
Pac. Pacific Ocean
Pak. Pakistan
Papua Papua New Guinea
P.D.R. Yemen People's
   Democratic Republic of
   Yemen
Philip. Philippines
Pol. Poland
Port. Portugal
Pyr. Pyrenees
Rom. Romania
S.A. South Africa
S.Am. South America
Sard. Sardinia
Saudi Saudi Arabia
Scot. Scotland
Sib. Siberia
Sic. Sicily
Sp. Spain
Sri Sri Lanka
Swed. Sweden
Swit. Switzerland
Thai. Thailand
Tanz. Tanzania
Tas. Tasmania
Turk. Turkey
Venez. Venezuela
Viet. Vietnam
W.Af. West Africa
W.Ger. West Germany
W.I. West Indies
Yug. Yugoslavia

Bays, bights, firths, gulfs, sea lochs, loughs, and harbours
B. = Bay. Bi. = Bight. F. = Firth. Fi. = Fiord. G. = Gulf.
Har. = Harbour. L. = Loch (Scottish). Lou = Lough (Irish.) S. = Sea.

2 – 4

Acre, B. of (Isr.)
Aden, G. of (Arab.)
Awe, L. (Scot.)
Clew, B. (Ire.)
Ewe, L. (Scot.)
Fyne, L. (Scot.)

Gilp, L. (Scot.)
Goil, L. (Scot.)
Kiel, B. (Ger.)
Long, L. (Scot.)
Luce, B. (Scot.)
Lyme B. (Eng.)
Ob, G. of (U.S.S.R.)

Riga, G. of (U.S.S.R.)
Siam, G. of (Asia)
Suez, G. of (Red S.)
Tay, F. of (Scot.)
Tees, B. (Eng.)
Tor B. (Eng.)
Wash, The (Eng.)

5

Aqaba, G. of (Arab.)
Algoa B. (S.A.)
Benin, Bi. of (W.Af.)
Blind B. (N.Z.)
Broom, L. (Scot.)

Chi-Li, G. of (China)
Clyde, F. of (Scot.)
Cutch, G. of (Ind.)
Enard B. (Scot.)
Evans B. (N.Z.)
False B. (S.A.)
Forth, F. of (Scot.)
Foyle, Lou. (Ire.)
Fundy, B. of (Can.)
Genoa, G. of (It.)
Hawke B. (N.Z.)
Izmir, G. of (Turk.)
James B. (Can.)
Leven, L. (Scot.)
Lions, G. of (Med.)
Lorne, F. of (Scot.)
Moray F. (Scot.)
Otago Har. (N.Z.)
Papua, G. of (N. Guin.)
Paria, G. of (S. Am.)
Table B. (S.A.)
Tunis, G. of (N.Af.)

6

Aegina, G. of (Gr.)
Aylort, L. (Scot.)
Baffin B. (Can.)
Bantry B. (Ire.)
Bengal, B. of (Ind.)
Biafra, Bi. of (W. Af.)
Biscay, B. of (Fr.)
Botany B. (Austral.)
Broken B. (Austral.)
Cambay, G. of (Ind.)
Cloudy B. (N.Z.)
Colwyn B. (Wales)
Danzig, G. of (Pol.)
Darien, G. of (S. Am.)
Denial B. (Austral.)
Dingle B. (Ire.)
Drake's B. (U.S.A.)
Dublin B. (Ire.)
Galway B. (Ire.)
Guinea, G. of (W.Af.)
Hervey B. (Austral.)
Hudson B. (Can.)
Ijssel S. (Neth.)
Linnhe, L. (Scot.)
Lübeck B. (Ger.)
Manaar, G. of (Ind.)
Mexico, G. of (Mex.)
Mounts B. (Eng.)
Naples, B. of (It.)
Panama, G. of (C. Am.)
Plenty, B. of (N.Z.)
St. Malo, G. of (Fr.)
Sharks B. (Austral.)
Smyrna, G. of (Turk.)
Solway F. (Scot.)
Sunart, L. (Scot.)
Swilly, Lou. (Ire.)
Sydney Har. (Austral.)
Tasman B. (N.Z.)

Tonkin, G. of (S. China S.)
Venice, G. of (It.)
Walvis B. (S.A.)
Zuider S. (Neth.)

7

Aboukir B. (Med.)
Argolis, G. of (Gr.)
Baffin's B. (Can.)
Belfast Lou. (N.I.)
Boothia, G. of (Can.)
Bothnia, G. of (Swed.)
Bustard B. (Austral.)
Chaleur B. (Can.)
Delagoa B. (S.A.)
Donegal B. (Ire.)
Dornoch F. (Scot.)
Dundalk B. (Scot.)
Finland, G. of (U.S.S.R.)
Fortune B. (Can.)
Halifax B. (Austral.)
Hudson's B. (Can.)
Kaipara Har. (N.Z.)
Lepanto, G. of (Gr.)
Moreton B. (Austral.)
Pe-Chi-Li, G. of (China)
Pegasus B. (N.Z.)
Persian G. (Asia)
Salerno, G. of (It.)
Snizort, L. (Scot.)
Taranto, G. of (It.)
Tarbert, L. (Scot.)
Trieste, G. of (Adr.)
Trinity B. (Can.)
Volcano B. (Jap.)

8

Cagliari, G. of (It.)
Campeche, B. of (Mex.)
Cardigan B. (Wales)
Cromarty F. (Scot.)
Delaware B. (U.S.A.)
Georgian B. (Can.)
Hammamet, G. of (N. Af.)
Hang-Chow B. (China)
Honduras, G. of (C. Am.)
Liau-Tung, G. of (China)
Martaban, G. of (Burma)
Pentland F. (Scot.)
Plymouth Har. (Eng.)
Portland B. (Austral.)
Portland Har. (Eng.)
Quiberon B. (Fr.)
Salonika, G. of (Gr.)
San Jorge, G. of (S. Am.)
San Pablo B. (U.S.A.)
Spencer's G. (Austral.)
Thailand, G. of (Asia)
Tongking, G. of (S. China S.)
Tremadoc B. (Wales)
Weymouth Bay (Eng.)

9

Admiralty B. (N.Z.)
Broughton B. (Austral.)
Buzzard's B. (U.S.A.)
Cambridge G. (Austral.)
Discovery B. (Austral.)
Encounter B. (Austral.)
Frobisher B. (Can.)
Galveston B. (U.S.A.)
Geographe B. (Austral.)
Hermitage B. (Can.)
Inverness F. (Scot.)
Mackenzie B. (Can.)
Morecambe B. (Eng.)
Notre Dame B. (Can.)
Placentia B. (Can.)
St. Bride's B. (Wales)
St. George's B. (Can.)
St. George's B. (S. Am.)
Saint Malo, G. of (Fr.)
San Matias, G. of (S. Am.)
St. Vincent G. (Austral.)
Van Diemen G. (Austral.)
Venezuela, G. of (S. Am.)

10 AND OVER

Barnstaple B. (Eng.) (10)
Bridgewater B. (Eng.) (11)
California, G. of (Mex.) (10)
Canterbury Bi. (N.Z.) (10)
Carmarthen B. (Wales) (10)
Carpentaria, G. of (Austral.) (11)
Chesapeake B. (U.S.A.) (10)
Christiania Fi. (Nor.) (11)
Conception B. (Can.) (10)
Great Australian Bi. (Austral.) (15)
Heligoland B. (Ger.) (10)
Pomeranian B. (Baltic S.) (10)
Port Jackson B. (Austral.) (11)
Port Philip B. (Austral.) (10)
Portsmouth Har. (Eng.) (10)
Princess Charlotte B. (Austral.) (17)
Ringkøbing Fi. (Den.) (1)
Robin Hood's B. (Eng.) (10)
Saint Bride's B. (Wales) (11)
St. Lawrence, G. of (Can.) (10)
Saint Lawrence, G. of (Can.) (13)
Saint Vincent, G. of (Austral.) (12)
San Francisco B. (U.S.A.) (12)
Southampton Water (Eng.) (16)
Tehuantepec, G. of (Mex.) (12)

Capes, headlands, points, etc.

C. = Cape.   Hd. = Head, or Headland.   N. = Ness.   Pt. = Point.

3 AND 4

Aird Pt. (Scot.)
Ann, C. (U.S.A.)

Ayre Pt. (Eng.)
Baba, C. (Turk.)
Bon, C. (N. Af.)
Busa, C. (Crete)

Cod, C. (U.S.A.)
Cruz, C. (S. Am.)
East C. (N.Z.)
East Pt. (Can.)

Farr Pt. (Scot.)
Fear, C. (U.S.A.)
Fife N. (Scot.)
Fogo, C. (Can.)

Frio, C. (Braz.)
Frio, C. (W. Af.)
Hoe Pt. (Scot.)
Horn, C. (S. Am.)
Howe, C. (Austral.)
Icy C. (Can.)
King, C. (Jap.)
Krio, C. (Crete)
Loop Hd. (Ire.)
May, C. (U.S.A.)
Nao, C. (It.)
Naze (The) (Eng.)
Naze (The) (Nor.)
Nord, C. (Nor.)
Noss Hd. (Scot.)
Nun, C. (W. Af.)
Race, C. (Can.)
Roxo, C. (Can.)
Sima, C. (Jap.)
Slea Hd. (Ire.)
Soya, C. (Jap.)
Sur Pt. (S. Am.)
Toe Hd. (Scot.)
Turn N. (Scot.)
York, C. (Austral.)

5

Adieu, C. (Austral.)
Amber, C. (E. Af.)
Aniva, C. (U.S.S.R.)
Bauer, C. (Austral.)
Brims N. (Scot.)
Byron, C. (Austral.)
Clark Pt. (Can.)
Clare, C. (Ire.)
Corso, C. (Cors.)
Creus, C. (Sp.)
Dunge N. (Eng.)
Gallo, C. (Gr.)
Gaspé, C. (Can.)
Lopez, C. (W. Af.)
Malia, C. (Gr.)
Mirik, C. (W. Af.)
Negro, C. (W. Af.)
North C. (N.Z.)
North C. (Nor.)
Orme's Hd. (Wales)
Otway, C. (Austral.)
Quoin Pt. (S.A.)
Roray Hd. (Scot.)
Sable, C. (Can.)
Sable, C. (U.S.A.)
Sandy C. (Austral.)
San Ho, C. (Viet.)
Sheep Hd. (Ire.)
Slade Pt. (Austral.)
Sleat Pt. (Scot.)
Slyne Hd. (Ire.)
South C. (China)
Spurn Hd. (Eng.)
Start Pt. (Eng.)
Tavoy Pt. (Burma)
Troup Hd. (Scot.)
Verde, C. (W. Af.)
Wiles, C. (Austral.)
Worms Hd. (Wales)
Wrath, C. (Scot.)
Yakan, C. (Sib.)

6

Andres Pt. (S. Am.)
Bantam, C. (Indo.)

Barren, C. (Austral.)
Beachy Hd. (Eng.)
Blanco, C. (N. Af.)
Blanco, C. (S. Am.)
Branco, C. (S. Am.)
Breton, C. (Can.)
Buddon N. (Scot.)
Burrow Hd. (Scot.)
Burrow Pt. (Scot.)
Carmel, C. (Isr.)
Castle Pt. (N.Z.)
Comino, C. (Sard.)
Cuvier, C. (Austral.)
De Gata, C. (Spain)
De Roca, C. (Port)
Dodman Pt. (Eng.)
Dunnet Hd. (Scot.)
Egmont, C. (N.Z.)
Formby Hd. (Eng.)
Friars Pt. (U.S.A.)
Galley Hd. (Ire.)
Gallon Hd. (Scot.)
Glossa, C. (Turk.)
Lizard (The) (Eng.)
Orford N. (Eng.)
Palmas, C. (W. Af.)
Prawle Pt. (Eng.)
Recife, C. (S.A.)
Rhynns Pt. (Scot.)
St. Abb's Hd. (Scot.)
St. Bees Hd. (Eng.)
St. Mary, C. (Can.)
St. Paul, C. (W. Af.)
Sambro, C. (Can.)
Sanaig Pt. (Scot.)
Sidero, C. (Crete)
Sorell, C. (Austral.)
Tarbat, N. (Scot.)
Tarifa, C. (Sp.)
Tolsta Hd. (Scot.)
Wad Nun, C. (N. Af.)
Whiten Hd. (Scot.)
Yerimo, C. (Jap.)

7

Agulhas, C. (S.A.)
Arisaig Pt. (Scot.)
Bengore Hd. (N.I.)
Bismark, C. (Green.)
Bizzuto, C. (It.)
Blanche, C. (Austral.)
Charles, C. (U.S.A.)
Clogher Hd. (Ire.)
Colonna, C. (Gr.)
Comorin, C. (Ind.)
De Palos, C. (Sp.)
De Penas, C. (Sp.)
De Sines, C. (Port.)
Formosa, C. (W. Af.)
Gregory, C. (Can.)
Gris-Nez, C. (Fr.)
Haytian, C. (W.I.)
Icy Cape (Can.)
Kataska, C. (Jap.)
Kennedy, C. (U.S.A.)
La Hague, C. (Fr.)
Leeuwin, C. (Austral.)
Matapan, C. (Gr.)
Milazzo, C. (Sic.)
Mondego, C. (Port)
Mumbles Hd. (Wales)
Needles, The (Eng.)
Negrais, C. (Burma)
Orlando, C. (Sic.)

Ortegal, C. (Sp.)
Rattray Hd. (Scot.)
Romania, C. (Malay.)
Runaway, C. (N.Z.)
St. Lucia, C. (S.A.)
San Blas, C. (U.S.A.)
São Tomé, C. (Braz.)
Spartel, C. (N. Af.)
Strathy Pt. (Scot.)
Tegupan Pt. (Mex.)
Teulada, C. (Sard.)
The Horn (S. Am.)
The Naze (Eng.)
The Naze (Nor.)
Toe Head (Scot.)
Upstart, C. (Austral.)
Vincent, C. (U.S.A.)
Yang-tsi, C. (China)

8

Bathurst, C. (Can.)
Cambodia Pt. (Thai.)
East Cape (N.Z.)
Espichel, C. (Port.)
Fairhead, C. (N.I.)
Farewell, C. (Green.)
Farewell, C. (N.Z.)
Fife Ness (Scot.)
Flattery, C. (U.S.A.)
Foreland (The) (Eng.)
Gallinas Pt. (S. Am.)
Good Hope, C. of (S.A.)
Greenore Pt. (Ire.)
Hangklip, C. (S.A.)
Hartland Pt. (Eng.)
Hatteras, C. (U.S.A.)
Kaliakra, C. (Bulg.)
Kinnaird Hd. (Scot.)
Land's End (Eng.)
Loop Head (Ire.)
Maranhao, C. (Braz.)
Melville, C. (Austral.)
Palliser, C. (N.Z.)
Palmyras Pt. (Ind.)
Patience, C. (Jap.)
St. Albans Hd. (Eng.)
St. David's Hd. (Wales)
St George, C. (Can.)
St. Gowan's Hd. (Wales)
San Diego, C. (S. Am.)
San Lucas, C. (Mex.)
São Roque, C. (Braz.)
Sidmouth, C. (Austral.)
Slea Head (Ire.)
Sordwana Pt. (S.A.)
Strumble Hd. (Wales)
Sumburgh Hd. (Scot.)
Sur Point (U.S.A.)
Thorsden, C. (Arc.)
Turn Ness (Scot.)
Vaticano, C. (It.)

9

Bonavista, C. (Can.)
Brims Ness (Scot.)
Canaveral, C. (U.S.A.)
Carvoeira, C. (Port.)
Claremont Pt. (Austral.)
De Talbert Pt. (Fr.)
Dungeness (Eng.)
East Point (Can.)
Esquimaux, C. (Can.)

87

Farr Point (Scot.)
Girardeau, C. (U.S.A.)
Granitola, C. (Sic.)
Guardafin, C. (E. Af.)
Inishowen Hd. (Ire.)
Mendocino, C. (U.S.A.)
Murchison, C. (Can.)
Nash Point (Wales)
North Cape (N.Z.)
North Cape (Nor.)
Ormes Head (Wales)
Roray Head (Scot.)
Saint Abbs Hd. (Scot.)
Saint Bees Hd. (Eng.)
St. Francis, C. (Can.)
Saint Mary, C. (Can.)
Saint Paul, C. (W. Af.)
St. Vincent, C. (Port.)
Sand Patch Pt. (Austral.)
Sandy Cape (Austral.)
Sandy Cape (Tas.)
Santo Vito, C. (Sic.)
Sheep Head (Ire.)
Slyne Head (Ire.)
South Cape (China)
Spurn Head (Eng.)
Streedagh Pt. (Ire.)
The Lizard (Eng.)
Trafalgar, C. (Sp.)
Troup Head (Scot.)
Vaternish Pt. (Scot.)
Worms Head (Wales)

10

Beachy Head (Eng.)
Breakheart Pt. (Can.)
Buddon Ness (Scot.)
Burrow Head (Scot.)
Clark Point (Can.)
Conception Pt. (U.S.A.)
Duncansbay Hd. (Scot.)
Dunnet Head (Scot.)
Finisterre, C. (Sp.)
Galley Head (Ire.)
Gallon Head (Scot.)

Great Ormes Hd. (Wales)
Greenstone Pt. (Scot.)
Orford Ness (Eng.)
Palmerston, C. (Austral.)
Quoin Point (S.A.)
Rayes Point (S. Am.)
Saint Lucia, C. (S.A.)
St. Margaret Pt. (Can.)
St. Matthieu Pt. (Fr.)
San Antonio Pt. (Mex.)
San Lorenzo, C. (S. Am.)
Santa Maria, C. (Port.)
Selsey Bill (Eng.)
Slade Point (Austral.)
Sleat Point (Scot.)
Snettisham Pt. (Can.)
Start Point (Eng.)
Tarbat Ness (Scot.)
Tavoy Point (Burma)
The Needles (Eng.)
Tolsta Head (Scot.)
Walsingham, C. (Can.)
Washington, C. (Arc.)
Whiten Head (Scot.)

11

Andres Point (S. Am.)
Bengore Head (N.I.)
Bridgewater, C. (Austral.)
Castle Point (N.Z.)
Catastrophe, C. (Austral.)
Clogher Head (Ire.)
De San Adrian, C. (Sp.)
Dodman Point (Eng.)
Downpatrick Hd. (N.I.)
Flamborough Hd. (Eng.)
Friars Point (U.S.A.)
Little Ormes Hd. (Wales)
Lizard Point (Eng.)
Mumbles Head (Wales)
Murraysburg, C. (S.A.)
Prawle Point (Eng.)
Rattray Head (Scot.)
Rhynns Point (Scot.)
Saint Albans Hd. (Eng.)

Saint David's Hd. (Wales)
Saint Gilda's Pt. (Fr.)
Saint Gowan's Hd. (Wales)
Sanaig Point (Scot.)
The Foreland (Eng.)
Three Points, C. (W. Af.)
Tribulation, C. (Austral.)

12 AND OVER

Ardnamurchan Pt. (Scot.)
(12)
Arisaig Point (Scot.) (12)
Breakheart Point (Can.)
(15)
Cape of Good Hope (S.A.)
(14)
Cayenne Point (E. Af.) (12)
Claremont Point (Austral.)
(14)
Conception Point (U.S.A.)
(15)
Downpatrick Head (N.I.)
(15)
Duncansbay Head (Scot.)
(14)
Flamborough Head (Eng.)
(15)
Gracias a Dios, C. (C. Am.)
(12)
Inishowen Head (Ire.) (13)
North Foreland (Eng.) (13)
Northumberland, C.
(Austral.) (14)
Palmuras Point (Ind.) (13)
Portland Bill (Eng.) (12)
Saint Margaret Pt. (Can.)
(13)
Sand Patch Point (Austral.)
(14)
San Francisco, C. (S. Am.)
(12)
Strumble Head (Wales) (12)
Sumburgh Head (Scot.) (12)
Tegupan Point (Mex.) (12)
Vaternish Point (Scot.) (14)

Capital cities of the world

3 AND 4

Aden (P.D.R. Yemen)
Apia (W. Samoa)
Bern (Swit.)
Bonn (W. Ger.)
Doha (Qatar)
Lima (Peru)
Lomé (Togo)
Male (Maldives)
Oslo (Nor.)
Rome (It.)
San'a (Yemen)
Suva (Fiji)

5

Accra (Ghana)
Agana (Guam)
Ajman (Ajman)
Amman (Jordan)

Berne (Swit.)
Cairo (Egypt)
Dacca (Bangla.)
Dakar (Senegal)
Dubai (Dubai)
Hanoi (N. Viet.)
Kabul (Afghan.)
Lagos (Nig.)
La Paz (Boliv.)
Macao (Macao)
Paris (Fr.)
Praia (Cape Verde Is.)
Quito (Ecuador)
Rabat (Moroc.)
Sanaa (Yemen)
Seoul (S. Korea)
Sofia (Bulg.)
Sucre (Boliv.)
Tokyo (Jap.)
Tunis (Tunisia)
Vaduz (Liechtenstein)
Zomba (Malawi)

6

Ankara (Turk.)
Athens (Gr.)
Bagdad (Iraq)
Bamako (Mali)
Bangui (Cen. Af. Rep.)
Banjul (Gambia)
Beirut (Lebanon)
Belice } (Belice)
Belize }
Bissau (Guinea - Bissau)
Bogotá (Colombia)
Brunei (Brunei)
Dublin (Ire.)
Habana } (Cuba)
Havana }
Kigali (Rwanda)
Kuwait (Kuwait)
Lisbon (Port.)
London (U.K.)
Luanda (Angola)

Lusaka (Zambia)
Madrid (Sp.)
Malabo (Equatorial Guinea)
Manama (Bahrain)
Maputo (Mozambique)
Maseru (Lesotho)
Masqat (Oman)
Mexico (Mexico)
Monaco (Monaco)
Moroni (Comoro Is.)
Moscow (U.S.S.R.)
Muscat (Oman)
Nassau (Bahamas)
Niamey (Niger)
Ottawa (Can.)
Panama (Panama)
Peking (China)
Prague (Cze.)
Riyadh (Saudi)
Roseau (Dominica)
Saigon (S. Viet.)
Taipei (Taiwan)
Tehran (Iran)
Thimbu } (Bhutan)
Thimpu ∫
Tirana (Albania)
Vienna (Aust.)
Warsaw (Pol.)

7

Abidjan (Ivory Coast)
Algiers (Alg.)
Andorra (Andorra)
Baghdad (Iraq)
Bangkok (Thai.)
Caracas (Venez.)
Colombo (Sri)
Conakry (Guinea)
Cotonou (Benin)
Douglas (Isle of Man)
El Aaiun (W. Sahara)
Gangtok (Sikkim)
Jakarta (Indo.)
Kampala (Uganda)
Managua (Nicaragua)
Mbabane (Swaziland)
Nairobi (Kenya)
Nicosia (Cyprus)
Rangoon (Burma)
St. John's (Antigua)
San José (Costa Rica)
São Tomé (São Tomé and
   Principé)
Sharjah (Sharjah)
Stanley (Falkland Is.)
Tripoli (Libya)
Valetta (Malta)
Vatican (Vatican)
Yaoundé (Cameroun)

8

Abu Dhabi (Abu Dhabi)
Asunción (Paraguay)
Belgrade (Yug.)
Brasilia (Braz.)
Brussels (Belg.)
Budapest (Hung.)
Canberra (Austral.)
Cape Town (S.A.)
Castries (St. Lucia)
Damascus (Syria)
Djibouti (Djibouti)
Freetown (Sierra Leone)
Fujairah (Fujairah)
Gaborone (Botswana)
Hamilton (Bermuda)
Helsinki (Fin.)
Katmandu (Nep.)
Khartoum (Sudan)
Kingston (Jamaica)
Kinshasa (Zaïre)
Lilongwe (Malawi)
Monrovia (Liberia)
N'Djamena (Chad)
New Delhi (Ind.)
Plymouth (Montserrat)
Pretoria (S.A.)
St. Helier (Jersey)
The Hague (Neth.)
Santiago (Chile)
Valletta (Malta)
Victoria (Hong Kong)
Victoria (Seychelles)
Windhoek (Namibia)

9

Amsterdam (Neth.)
Bucharest (Rom.)
Bujumbura (Burundi)
Edinburgh (Scot.)
Gaberones (Botswana)
Grand Turk (Turks and
   Caicos Is.)
Guatemala (Guatemala)
Islamabad (Pak.)
Jamestown (St. Helena)
Jerusalem (Isr.)
Kingstown (St. Vincent)
Mogadishu (Somalia)
Nukualofa (Tonga)
Phnom Penh (Cambodia)
Port Louis (Mauritius)
Porto Novo (Benin)
Pyongyang (N. Korea)
Reykjavik (Iceland)
St. George's (Grenada)
Salisbury (Rhodesia)

San Marino (San Marino)
Singapore (Singapore)
Stockholm (Swed.)
Ulan Bator (Mon.)
Vientiane (Laos)

10

Addis Ababa (Eth.)
Basseterre (St. Christopher-
   Nevis-Anguilla)
Bridgetown (Barbados)
Copenhagen (Den.)
East Berlin (E. Ger.)
Georgetown (Cayman Is.)
Georgetown (Guyana)
Kuwait City (Kuwait)
Libreville (Gabon)
Luxembourg (Luxembourg)
Mexico City (Mexico)
Montevideo (Uruguay)
Nouakchott (Mauritania)
Ougadougou (Upper Volta)
Paramaribo (Surinam)
Quezon City (Philip.)
Tananarive (Malag. Rep.)
Washington (U.S.A.)
Wellington (N.Z.)

11 AND OVER

Brazzaville (Congo) (11)
Buenos Aires (Arg.) (11)
Dar es Salaam (Tanz.) (11)
Guatemala City
   (Guatemala) (13)
Kuala Lumpur (Malay.) (11)
Luang Prabang (Laos) (12)
Medina as-Shaab (P.D.R.
   Yemen) (13)
Port-au-Prince (Haiti) (12)
Port Moresby (Papua) (11)
Port of Spain (Trinidad and
   Tobago) (11)
Ras al-Khaimah (Ras
   al-Khaimah) (12)
St. Peter Port (Guernsey)
   (11)
San Salvador (El Salvador)
   (11)
Santa Isabel (Equatorial
   Guinea) (11)
Santo Domingo (Dominican
   Rep.) (12)
Tegucigalpa (Honduras)
   (11)
Uaboe District (Nauru) (13)
Umm al-Qaiwain (Umm
   al-Qaiwain) (12)
Vatican City (Vatican) (11)

Channels, passages, sounds, and straits

Ch. = Channel. P. = Passage. Sd. = Sound. St(s). = Strait(s).

Note.—The land references are to give a general idea as to location.

3 AND 4

Bass St. (Austral.)
Coll, P. of (Scot.)
Cook St. (N.Z.)

Fox Ch. (Can.)
Jura Sd. (Scot.)
Mona P. (W.I.)
Nore (The) (Eng.)
Palk St. (Ind.)

5

Cabot St. (Can.)
Davis St. (Can.)
Dover, Sts. of (Eng.)

89

Downs (The) (Eng.)
Korea St. (Jap.)
Menai Sts. (Wales)
Minch (The) (Scot.)
North Ch. (Scot.)
Ormuz, St. of (Iran)
Puget Sd. (U.S.A.)
Sleat, Sd. of (Scot.)
Smith Sd. (Can.)
Sound (The) (Swed.)
Sunda, St. of (E.I.)

Formosa St. (China)
Foveaux St. (N.Z.)
Georgia, St. of (Can.)
Le Maire St. (S. Am.)
Malacca St. (Malaya)
Messina, St. of (It.)
Molucca P. (E.I.)
Otranto, St. of (It.)
Pamlico Sd. (U.S.A.)
The Nore (Eng.)
Yucatan Ch. (Mex.)

The Solent (Eng.)
Van Diemen St. (Jap.)

10

Dogger Bank (N. Sea)
Golden Gate (U.S.A.)
Golden Horn (Turk.)
Kilbrennan Sd. (Scot.)
King George Sd. (Austral.)
Little Belt (The) (Den.)
Mozambique Ch. (E. Af.)

6

Achill Sd. (Ire.)
Barrow St. (Can.)
Bering St. (Pac.)
Denmark St. (Green.)
Harris, St. of (Scot.)
Hecate St. (Can.)
Hudson St. (Can.)
Nootka Sd. (Can.)
Panama Canal (C. Am.)
Queen's Ch. (Austral.)
Solent (The) (Eng.)
Torres St. (Austral.)
Tromsø Sd. (Nor.)

8

Cattegat (The) (Den.)
Colonsay, P. of (Scot.)
Kattegat (The) (Den.)
Magellan St. (S. Am.)
Plymouth Sd. (Eng.)
Spithead (Eng.)
The Downs (Eng.)
The Minch (Scot.)
The Sound (Swed.)
Windward P. (W.I.)

9

Bonifacio, St. of (Med.)
Bosphorus (The) (Turk.)
Gibraltar, Sts. of (Spain)
Great Belt (The) (Den.)
Lancaster Sd. (Can.)
St. George's Ch. (Eng.)
Scapa Flow (Scot.)
Skagerrak (Nor. and Den.)
Suez Canal (Af.)

11 AND OVER

Bab-el-Mandeb St. (Red S.)
  (11)
Caledonian Canal (Scot.)
  (15)
Dardanelles (The) (Turk.)
  (11)
Goodwin Sands (Eng.) (12)
Hampton Roads (U.S.A.)
  (12)
Northumberland St. (Can.)
  (14)
Pas de Calais (Fr.) (11)
Queen Charlotte Sd. (Can.)
  (14)
Saint George's Ch. (Eng.)
  (12)
The Bosphorus (Turk.) (12)
The Dardanelles (Turk.)
  (14)
The Great Belt (Den.) (12)
The Little Belt (Den.) (13)

7

Behring St. (Sib.)
Bristol Ch. (Eng.)
Cuillin Sd. (Scot.)
Dolphin St. (Can.)
English Ch. (Eng.)
Florida St. (U.S.A.)

Counties: United Kingdom and Republic of Ireland

(E.) = England.   (Ire.) = Republic of Ireland.   (N.I.) = Northern Ireland.   (S.) =
Scotland.   (W.) = Wales.

Note.—As the names of some counties are commonly used in shortened form, both
full and shortened names are given in this list. It also includes county names no
longer officially in use.

3 AND 4

Avon (E.)
Ayr (S.)
Beds (E.)
Bute (S.)
Cork (Ire.)
Down (N.I.)
Fife (S.)
Kent (E.)
Leix (Ire.)
Mayo (Ire.)
Oxon (E.)
Ross (S.)
York (E.)

5

Angus (S.)
Banff (S.)
Berks (E.)

Bucks (E.)
Cavan (Ire.)
Clare (Ire.)
Clwyd (W.)
Derby (E.)
Devon (E.)
Dyfed (W.)
Elgin (S.)
Essex (E.)
Flint (W.)
Gwent (W.)
Hants (E.)
Herts (E.)
Hunts (E.)
Kerry (Ire.)
Lancs (E.)
Meath (Ire.)
Moray (S.)
Nairn (S.)
Notts (E.)
Perth (S.)
Powys (W.)
Salop (E.)

Sligo (Ire.)
Wilts (E.)

6

Antrim (N.I.)
Argyll (S.)
Armagh (N.I.)
Brecon (W.)
Carlow (Ire.)
Dorset (E.)
Dublin (Ire.)
Durham (E.)
Forfar (S.)
Galway (Ire.)
Lanark (S.)
London (E.)
Offaly (Ire.)
Orkney (S.)
Oxford (E.)
Radnor (W.)
Staffs (E.)

Surrey (E.)
Sussex (E.)
Tyrone (N.I.)

7

Bedford (E.)
Borders (S.)
Central (S.)
Cumbria (E.)
Denbigh (W.)
Donegal (Ire.)
Dundalk (Ire.)
Gwynedd (W.)
Kildare (Ire.)
Leitrim (Ire.)
Lincoln (E.)
Lothian (S.)
Norfolk (E.)
Renfrew (S.)
Rutland (E.)
Selkirk (S.)

Suffolk (E.)
Tayside (S.)
Warwick (E.)
Wexford (Ire.)
Wicklow (Ire.)

8

Aberdeen (S.)
Anglesey (W.)
Ayrshire (S.)
Cardigan (W.)
Cheshire (E.)
Cornwall (E.)
Grampian (S.)
Hereford (E.)
Hertford (E.)
Highland (S.)
Kilkenny (Ire.)
Limerick (Ire.)
Longford (Ire.)
Monaghan (Ire.)
Monmouth (E.)
Pembroke (W.)
Roxburgh (S.)
Somerset (E.)
Stafford (E.)
Stirling (S.)

9

Berkshire (E.)
Caithness (S.)
Cambridge (E.)
Cleveland (E.)
Dunbarton (S.)
Edinburgh (S.)
Fermanagh (N.I.)
Glamorgan (W.)
Hampshire (E.)
Inverness (S.)
Leicester (E.)
Merioneth (W.)
Middlesex (E.)
Northants (E.)
Roscommon (Ire.)
Tipperary (Ire.)
Waterford (Ire.)
Westmeath (Ire.)

Wiltshire (E.)
Worcester (E.)
Yorkshire (E.)

10

Banffshire (S.)
Buckingham (E.)
Caernarvon (W.)
Carmarthen (W.)
Cumberland (E.)
Derbyshire (E.)
Devonshire (E.)
East Sussex (E.)
Flintshire (W.)
Gloucester (E.)
Haddington (S.)
Humberside (E.)
Huntingdon (E.)
Kincardine (S.)
Lancashire (E.)
Linlithgow (S.)
Merseyside (E.)
Midlothian (S.)
Montgomery (W.)
Nottingham (E.)
Perthshire (S.)
Shropshire (E.)
Sutherland (S.)
West Sussex (E.)

11 & 12

Argyllshire (S.) (11)
Bedfordshire (E.) (12)
Berwickshire (S.) (12)
Clackmannan (S.) (11)
Denbighshire (W.) (12)
Dorsetshire (E.) (11)
East Lothian (S.) (11)
Forfarshire (S.) (11)
Isle of Wight (E.) (11)
King's County (Ire.) (11)
Lanarkshire (S.) (11)
Lincolnshire (E.) (12)
Londonderry (N.I.) (11)
Mid Glamorgan (W.) (12)
Northampton (E.) (11)
Oxfordshire (E.) (11)

Queen's County (Ire.) (12)
Radnorshire (W.) (11)
Renfrewshire (S.) (12)
Rutlandshire (E.) (12)
Strathclyde (S.) (11)
Tyne & Wear (E.) (11)
Warwickshire (E.) (12)
West Lothian (S.) (11)
West Midlands (E.) (12)
Westmorland (E.) (11)

13 & 14

Aberdeenshire (S.) (13)
Brecknockshire (W.) (14)
Cambridgeshire (E.) (14)
Cardiganshire (W.) (13)
Dunbartonshire (S.) (14)
Dumfriesshire (S.) (13)
Glamorganshire (W.) (14)
Herefordshire (E.) (13)
Hertfordshire (E.) (13)
Inverness-shire (S.) (14)
Kircudbright (S.) (13)
Leicestershire (E.) (14)
Merionethshire (W.) (14)
Monmouthshire (E.) (13)
Northumberland (E.) (14)
North Yorkshire (E.) (14)
Pembrokeshire (W.) (13)
Somersetshire (E.) (13)
South Glamorgan (W.) (14)
South Yorkshire (E.) (14)
Staffordshire (E.) (13)
West Glamorgan (W.) (13)
West Yorkshire (E.) (13)
Worcestershire (E.) (14)

15 & 16

Buckinghamshire (E.) (15)
Caenarvonshire (W.) (15)
Carmarthenshire (W.) (15)
Gloucestershire (E.) (15)
Huntingdonshire (E.) (15)
Montgomeryshire (W.) (15)
Northamptonshire (E.) (16)
Nottinghamshire (E.) (15)
Ross and Cromarty (S.) (15)

Countries and continents
Note.—This list includes names of former countries.

3 AND 4

Anam (Asia)
Asia
Bali (Asia)
Chad (Af.)
Cuba (W.I.)
D.D.R. (E. Ger.)
Eire (Eur.)
Fiji (S. Pac.)
G.D.R. (E. Ger.)
Guam (Pac.)
Iran (Asia)
Iraq (Asia)
Java (Asia)
Laos (Asia)
Mali (Af.)

Nejd (Asia)
Oman (Asia)
Peru (S. Am.)
Siam (Asia)
Togo (Af.)
U.A.R. (Af.)
U.S.A. (N. Am.)
U.S.S.R. (Asia, Eur.)

5

Annam (Asia)
Benin (Af.)
Burma (Asia)
Chile (S. Am.)
China (Asia)

Congo (Af.)
Corea (Asia)
Egypt (Af.)
Fiume (Eur.)
Gando (Af.)
Ghana (Af.)
Haiti (W.I.)
India (Asia)
Italy (Eur.)
Japan (Asia)
Kandy (Asia)
Kenya (Af.)
Khmer (Asia)
Korea (Asia)
Libya (Af.)
Lydia (Asia)
Malta (Med.)

Natal (Af.)
Nauru (Pac.)
Nepal (Asia)
Niger (Af.)
Papua (E.I.)
Qatar (Asia)
Spain (Eur.)
Sudan (Af.)
Syria (Asia)
Tchad (Af.)
Texas (N. Am.)
Tibet (Asia)
Timor (E.I.)
Tonga (Pac.)
Tunis (Af.)
Wales (Eur.)
Yemen (Asia)
Zaïre (Af.)

6

Africa
Angola (Af.)
Arabia (Asia)
Azores (Atl.)
Belice⎫
Belize⎰(C. Am.)
Bhutan (Asia)
Brazil (S. Am.)
Brunei (E.I.)
Canada (N. Am.)
Ceylon (Asia)
Cyprus (Med.)
Epirus (Eur.)
Europe
France (Eur.)
Gambia (Af.)
Greece (Eur.)
Guinea (Af.)
Guyana (S. Am.)
Hawaii (Pac.)
Israel (Asia)
Johore (Asia)
Jordan (Asia)
Kuwait (Asia)
Latvia (Eur.)
Malawi (Af.)
Malaya (Asia)
Mexico (N. Am.)
Monaco (Eur.)
Muscat (Asia)
Norway (Eur.)
Panama (S. Am.)
Persia (Asia)
Poland (Eur.)
Ruanda (Af.)
Russia (Eur., Asia)
Rwanda (Af.)
Serbia ⎫
Servia ⎰(Eur.)
Sicily (Eur.)
Sikkim (Asia)
Soudan (Af.)
Sweden (Eur.)
Taiwan (Asia)
Tobago (W.I.)
Turkey (Eur., Asia)
Ulster (Eur.)
Uganda (Af.)
Urundi (Af.)
92 Zambia (Af.)

7

Albania (Eur.)
Algeria (Af.)
Andorra (Eur.)
Antigua (W.I.)
America
Armenia (Asia)
Ashanti (Af.)
Assyria (Asia)
Austria (Eur.)
Bahamas (W.I.)
Bahrain (Arab.)
Bavaria (Eur.)
Belgium (Eur.)
Bermuda (Atl.)
Bohemia (Eur.)
Bolivia (S. Am.)
Britain (Eur.)
Burundi (Af.)
Croatia (Eur.)
Dahomey (Af.)
Denmark (Eur.)
Ecuador (S. Am.)
England (Eur.)
Eritrea (Af.)
Estonia (Eur.)
Faeroes (Atl.)
Finland (Eur.)
Formosa (Asia)
Germany (Eur.)
Grenada (W.I.)
Holland (Eur.)
Hungary (Eur.)
Iceland (Eur.)
Ireland (Eur.)
Jamaica (W.I.)
Lebanon (Asia)
Lesotho (Af.)
Liberia (Af.)
Livonia (Eur.)
Macedon (Eur.)
Morocco (Af.)
Namibia (Af.)
Nigeria (Af.)
Prussia (Eur.)
Romania ⎫
Rumania ⎰(Eur.)
St. Kitts (W.I.)
São Tomé (Atl.)
Sarawak (Asia)
Senegal (Af.)
Somalia (Af.)
Sumatra (E.I.)
Sumeria (Asia)
Surinam (S. Am.)
Tangier (Af.)
Tartary (Asia)
Tripoli (Af.)
Tunisia (Af.)
Ukraine (Eur.)
Uruguay (S. Am.)
Vatican (Eur.)
Vietnam (Asia)

8

Barbados (W.I.)
Botswana (Af.)
Bulgaria (Eur.)
Burgundy (Eur.)
Cambodia (Asia)
Cameroun (Af.)
Colombia (S. Am.)
Djibouti (Af.)

Dominica (W.I.)
Ethiopia (Af.)
Honduras (S. Am.)
Hong Kong (Asia)
Malagasy (Af.)
Malaysia (Asia)
Maldives (Ind.)
Mongolia (Asia)
Pakistan (Asia)
Paraguay (S. Am.)
Portugal (Eur.)
Rhodesia (Af.)
Roumania (Eur.)
St. Helena (Atl.)
Salvador (C. Am.)
Sardinia (Med.)
Scotland (Eur.)
Sri Lanka (Asia)
Tanzania (Af.)
Tasmania (Austral.)
Thailand (Asia)
Togoland (Af.)
Trinidad (W.I.)
Zanzibar (Af.)
Zimbabwe (Af.)
Zululand (Af.)

9

Abyssinia (Af.)
Argentina (S. Am.)
Argentine, The (S. Am.)
Australia
Babylonia (Asia)
Caledonia (Eur.)
Cameroons (Af.)
Costa Rica (C. Am.)
Gibraltar (Eur.)
Greenland (Arc.)
Guatemala (C. Am.)
Hindustan (Asia)
Indochina (Asia)
Indonesia (E.I.)
Lithuania (Eur.)
Luxemburg (Eur.)
Macedonia (Eur.)
Manchuria (Asia)
Mauritius (Ind.)
New Guinea (E.I.)
Nicaragua (C. Am.)
Nyasaland (Af.)
Palestine (Asia)
Pondoland (Af.)
San Marino (Eur.)
Singapore (Asia)
Swaziland (Af.)
The Gambia (Af.)
Transvaal (Af.)
Venezuela (S. Am.)

10

Antarctica
Bangladesh (Asia)
Basutoland (Af.)
California (N. Am.)
Cape Colony (Af.)
Damaraland (Af.)
El Salvador (C. Am.)
Ivory Coast (Af.)
Luxembourg (Eur.)
Madagascar (Af.)

Mauretania } (Af.)
Mauritania }
Montenegro (Eur.)
Montserrat (W.I.)
Mozambique (Af.)
New Zealand (Pac.)
North Korea (Asia)
Seychelles (Ind.)
Shan States (Asia)
Somaliland (Af.)
South Korea (Asia)
South Yemen (Asia)
Tanganyika (Af.)
Upper Volta (Af.)
Yugoslavia (Eur.)

11

Afghanistan (Asia)
Australasia
Baluchistan (Asia)
Cochin China (Asia)
Cook Islands (Pac.)
Dutch Guiana (S. Am.)
East Germany (Eur.)
French Congo (Af.)
Malay States (Asia)
Mashonaland (Af.)
Mesopotamia (Asia)
Namaqualand (Af.)
Netherlands (Eur.)
New Hebrides (Pac.)
Philippines (Asia)
Saudi Arabia (Asia)
Sierra Leone (Af.)
South Africa
Soviet Union (Asia, Eur.)
Switzerland (Eur.)
Transjordan (Asia)
Vatican City (Eur.)
West Germany (Eur.)

12

Bechuanaland (Af.)
Belgian Congo (Af.)
Cocos Islands (Ind.)
Faroe Islands (Atl.)
French Guiana (S. Am.)
Great Britain (Eur.)
Guinea-Bissau (Af.)
Indian Empire (Asia)
Matabeleland (Af.)
Newfoundland (N. Am.)
North America
North Vietnam (Asia)
Ruanda-Urundi (Af.)
South America
South Vietnam (Asia)
The Argentine (S. Am.)
United States (N. Am.)

13

Afars and Issas (Af.)
Barbary States (Af.)
Cayman Islands (W.I.)
Comoro Islands (Af.)
Khmer Republic (Asia)
Liechtenstein (Eur.)
Norfolk Island (Pac.)
Trucial States (Asia)
United Kingdom (Eur.)

14

Cape of Good Hope (Af.)
Congo Free State (Af.)
Czechoslovakia (Eur.)
Gilbert Islands (Pac.)
Irish Free State (Eur.)

Maldive Islands (Ind.)
Mariana Islands (Pac.)
Papua-New Guinea (E.I.)
Pitcairn Island (Pac.)
Society Islands (Pac.)
Solomon Islands (Pac.)

15

British Honduras (C. Am.)
Caroline Islands (Pac.)
Christmas Island (Pac.)
Falkland Islands (Atl.)
Holy Roman Empire (Eur.)
Northern Nigeria (Af.)
Northern Ireland (Eur.)
Orange Free State (Af.)
Southern Nigeria (Af.)
South-West Africa (Af.)

16 AND OVER

Cape Verde Islands (Af.)
(16)
Congolese Republic (Af.)
(17)
Dominican Republic (W.I.)
(17)
Equatorial Guinea (Af.) (16)
Malagasy Republic (Af.)
(16)
São Tomé and Principé (Af.)
(18)
United Arab Emirates
(Asia) (18)
United Arab Republic (Af.,
Asia) (18)
Vatican City State (Eur.)
(16)

Geographical terms

3

ait
alp
bay
ben
bog
cay
col
cwm
dam
fen
lea
map
sea
tor
voe

4

aber
bank
beck
berg
bill
burn

cape
city
comb
cove
crag
croy
dale
dell
dene
dike
doab
dune
east
eyot
ford
glen
gulf
hill
holm
holt
inch
isle
lake
land
lane
loam
loch

lock
marl
mead
mere
mesa
moor
mull
naze
ness
pass
peak
pole
pond
port
race
reef
rill
road
rock
sike
spit
sudd
syke
tarn
town
tump
vale

wadi
weir
west
wind
wold
wood
wynd
zone

5

abyss
alley
atlas
atoll
bayou
bight
brook
canal
chart
chasm
chine
cliff
clime
coast
combe

93

creek
crest
croft
delta
donga
downs
drift
duchy
fault
field
fiord
fjord
firth
fleet
ghaut
glade
globe
gorge
grove
haven
heath
hithe
hurst
hythe
inlet
islet
karoo
kloof
kopje
knoll
lande
llano
loess
lough
marsh
mound
mount
mouth
north
oasis
ocean
plain
point
polar
poles
reach
ridge
river
sands
scarp
shelf
shire
shoal
shore
slade
sound
south
state
swale
swamp
swang
sward
weald

6

alpine
arctic
boreal
canton
canyon
circar
clough
colony
colure

common
county
cranny
crater
defile
desert
dingle
divide
domain
empery
empire
eyalet
forest
geyser
glacis
hamlet
harbor
inland
inning
island
isobar
jungle
lagoon
maidan
meadow
morass
nullah
orient
pampas
parish
polder
rapids
ravine
region
riding
rillet
runlet
runnel
seaway
sierra
skerry
spinny
steppe
strait
strath
stream
street
suburb
summit
talook
tropic
tundra
upland
valley
warren

7

airport
austral
bogland
channel
clachan
commune
compass
contour
country
cutting
deltaic
drought
eastern
enclave
eparchy
equator
estuary

euripus
exclave
georama
glacier
habitat
harbour
highway
hillock
hilltop
hommock
hornito
hummock
hundred
iceberg
ice-floe
insular
isthmus
kingdom
lakelet
lowland
midland
new town
oceanic
plateau
polders
prairie
rivulet
rosland
satrapy
savanna
seaport
seaside
spurway
straits
thicket
torrent
tropics
village
volcano
western

8

affluent
alluvial
alluvium
altitude
brooklet
cantonal
cataract
crevasse
currents
district
dominion
downland
easterly
eastward
eminence
eminency
environs
foreland
frontier
headland
highland
high road
hillside
home-park
interior
isthmian
landmark
latitude
littoral
lowlands
mainland
midlands

moorland
mountain
neap-tide
northern
occident
oriental
post-town
province
quagmire
republic
salt lake
seaboard
seacoast
seashore
sheading
snow-line
southern
sub-polar
toparchy
township
tropical
volcanic
westerly
westward
wild land
woodland

9

antarctic
antipodal
antipodes
backwater
backwoods
cadastral
capricorn
catchment
cisalpine
coastline
continent
coral reef
fleet-dike
foothills
heathland
highlands
landslide
longitude
marshland
monticule
north-east
northerly
northward
north-west
peninsula
precipice
rockbound
salt-marsh
sandbanks
shore-line
south-east
southerly
southmost
southward
south-west
stewartry
streamlet
sub-alpine
tableland
territory
tetrarchy
trade wind
tributary
wapentake
waterfall
watershed

waterside
westwards

10

co-latitude
county town
equatorial
escarpment
fluviatile
frigid zone
garden city
geographer
Gulf Stream
hemisphere
interfluve
land-locked
margravate
market town
meridional
metropolis
mountainet
no-man's-land
occidental
palatinate
peninsular
plantation
polar-angle
population
presidency

projection
promontory
quicksands
sandy beach
south downs
spring tide
table-shore
tidal creek
torrid zone
water table
wilderness

11

archipelago
bergschrund
circumpolar
cisatlantic
continental
conurbation
coral island
countryside
equinoctial
morningland
mountainous
northwardly
polar circle
polar region
river course
septentrion
subtropical

territorial
tetrarchate
tidal waters
transalpine
transmarine
trout stream
ultramarine
watercourse

12

equatorially
landgraviate
magnetic pole
northeastern
northwestern
principality
protectorate
southeastern
southernmost
southwestern
stratosphere
ultramontane
virgin forest

13

deltafication
extratropical
intertropical

magnetic north
Mediterranean
mother country
neighbourhood
northeasterly
northeastward
northwesterly
northwestward
polar distance
septentrional
southeasterly
southeastward
southwesterly
southwestward
temperate zone
transatlantic
virgin country
watering place

14 AND 15

acclimatization (15)
circummeridian (14)
circumnavigate (14)
irrigation canal (15)
magnetic equator (15)
Mercator's chart (14)
north frigid zone (15)
south frigid zone (15)
tropic of cancer (14)

Islands

Arch. = Archipelago   I. = Island.   Is. = Islands.   (v.) = volcanic.

2 – 4

Adi (Pac.)
Amoy (China)
Aran (Ire.)
Arru Is. (Indo.)
Bali (Indo.)
Bay Is. (C. Am.)
Bere (Ire.)
Bua (Adr.)
Buru (Indo.)
Bute (Scot.)
Ceos (Gr.)
Coll (Scot.)
Cook Is. (Pac.)
Cuba (W.I.)
Dago (Fin.)
Dogs, I. of (Eng.)
Eigg (Scot.)
Elba (Med.)
Ewe (Scot.)
Farn Is. (Eng.)
Faro (Balt.)
Fiji Is. (Pac.)
Fohr (Ger.)
Gozo (Med.)
Guam (Pac.)
Hall Is. (Pac.)
Herm (Ch. Is.)
High I. (Ire.)
Holy I. (Scot.)
Hoy (Scot.)
Idra (Gr.)
Iona (Scot.)
Java (Indo.)
Jura (Scot.)

Kei Is. (Indo.)
Long I. (U.S.A.)
Low Arch. (Pac.)
Man, I. of (Eng.)
May, I. of (Scot.)
Milo (Gr.)
Moen (Den.)
Muck (Scot.)
Mull, I. of (Scot.)
Oahu (Pac.)
Paxo (Gr.)
Rat Is. (Pac.)
Ré (Fr.)
Rum (Scot.)
Saba (W.I.)
Sark (Ch. Is.)
Scio (Gr.)
Skye (Scot.)
Sulu Is. (Indo.)
Sylt (Ger.)
Syra (Gr.)
Tory (Ire.)
Ulva (Scot.)
Unst (Scot.)
Uist (Scot.)
Yap (Pac.)
Yell (Scot.)
Yezo (Jap.)
Zea (Gr.)
Zebu (Indo.)

5

Abaco (W.I.)
Aland Is. (Balt.)

Albay (Indo.)
Arran (Scot.)
Banca (Malay)
Banda (Indo.)
Banks (S. Pac.)
Barra (Heb.)
Bonin Is. (Pac.)
Caldy (Wales)
Canna (Scot.)
Capri (It.)
Ceram (Indo.)
Cheja (Korea)
Chios (Gr.)
Clare (Ire.)
Clear (Ire.)
Cocos Is. (Ind.)
Corfu (Gr.)
Corvo (Atl.)
Crete (Med.)
Dabaz (Scot.)
Delos (Gr.)
Disco (Arc.)
Disko (Arc.)
Eagle I. (Ire.)
Ellis (U.S.A.)
Farne Is. (Eng.)
Fayal (Atl.)
Ferro (Atl.)
Foula (Scot.)
Funen (Den.)
Goree (Atl.)
Gozzo (Med.)
Haiti (W.I.)
Hart's I. (U.S.A.)
Hatia (Ind.)
Hondo (Jap.)

Hydra (Gr.)
Ibiza (Med.)
Inyak (S.A.)
Islay (Scot.)
Ivica (Med.)
Lewis (Scot.)
Leyte (Philip.)
Lissa (Adr.)
Lobos Is. (S. Am.)
Lundy I. (Eng.)
Luzon (Philip.)
Malta (Med.)
Matsu (China)
Melos (Gr.)
Milos (Gr.)
Nauru (Pac.)
Naxos (Gr.)
Nevis (W.I.)
Oesel (Balt.)
Ormuz (Iran)
Papua (E.I.)
Paros (Gr.)
Parry Is. (Arc.)
Pearl Is. (Pac.)
Pelew Is. (E.I.)
Pelew Is. (Pac.)
Pemba (Af.)
Perim (Af.)
Pines, I. of (Pac. and W.I.)
Pinos (S. Am.)
Rhode I. (U.S.A.)
Rugen (Ger.)
Sable I. (Can.)
Samoa (Pac.)
Samos (Gr.)
Skyro (Gr.)

Spice Is. (Indo.)
Sunda Is. (Indo.)
Texel (Neth.)
Timor (Malay)
Tiree (Scot.)
Tonga (Pac.)
Turk's I. (W.I.)
Voorn (Neth.)
Wight, I. of (Eng.)
Zante (Gr.)

6

Achill (Ire.)
Aegina (Gr.)
Albany (Austral.)
Anamba Is. (Indo.)
Andros (Gr.)
Azores (Atl.)
Baffin (Can.)
Bahama Is. (W.I.)
Banana Is. (Atl.)
Bissao (Atl.)
Borkum (Ger.)
Borneo (Indo.)
Bounty Is. (N.Z.)
Brazza (Adr.)
Burray (Scot.)
Caicos Is. (W.I.)
Calamo (Gr.)
Candia (Med.)
Canary Is. (Atl.)
Cayman Is. (W.I.)
Cerigo (Med.)
Cherso (It.)
Chiloe (S. Am.)
Chusan (China)
Comoro Is. (Af.)
Crozet Is. (Ind.)
Cyprus (Med.)
Dursey (Ire.)
Easter I. (Pac.)
Ellice Is. (Pac.)
Euboea (Aeg.)
Faeroes (Atl.)
Flores (Atl.)
Flores (Indo.)
Gilolo (Indo.)
Gomera (Can.)
Hainan (China)
Harris (Scot.)
Hawaii (Pac.)
Honshu (Jap.)
Imbros (Aeg.)
Inagua (W.I.)
Ionian Is. (Med.)
Ischia (It.)
Ithaca (Med.)
Iturup (Jap.)
Jaluit (Pac.)
Jersey (Ch. Is.)
Jethou (Ch. Is.)
Kishni (Iran)
Kodiak (Pac.)
Kurile Is. (Pac.)
Kyushu (Jap.)
Labuan (Malay.)
Lambay (Ire.)
Lemnos (Aeg.)
Lerins Is. (Fr.)
Lesbos (Aeg.)
Lesina (Adr.)
Limmos (Aeg.)
Lipari Is. (Med.)
Lombok (Malay)

Marajo (S. Am.)
Marken (Neth.)
Negros (Indo.)
Oleron (Fr.)
Orkney Is. (Scot.)
Patmos (Med.)
Penang (Malay)
Philae (Nile)
Pomona (Scot.)
Puffin I. (Wales)
Quemoy (China)
Rhodes (Med.)
Robben (S. A.)
Rottum (Neth.)
St. John (W.I.)
St. Paul (Ind.)
Samsoe (Den.)
Sangir Is. (Indo.)
Savage I. (Pac.)
Scarba (Scot.)
Scilly Is. (Eng.)
Sicily (Med.)
Staffa (Scot.)
Staten I. (U.S.A.)
Stroma (Scot.)
Tahiti (Pac.)
Taiwan (China)
Thanet, I. of (Eng.)
Tholen (Neth.)
Tobago (W.I.)
Trömso (Nor.)
Tubugi Is. (Pac.)
Usedom (Ger.)
Ushant (Fr.)
Vaigen (Indo.)
Virgin Is. (W.I.)

7

Aegades Is. (Med.)
Aeolian Is. (v.) (Med.)
Amboina (Indo.)
Ameland (Neth.)
Andaman Is. (Ind.)
Antigua (W.I.)
Bahamas (W.I.)
Bahrain Is. (Arab.)
Balleny Is. (Antarc.)
Behring Is. (Pac.)
Bermuda (Atl.)
Bernera (Scot.)
Bourbon (Ind.)
Cabrera (Med.)
Capraja (Med.)
Caprera (Med.)
Celebes (Indo.)
Channel Is. (Eng.)
Chatham Is. (Pac.)
Chincha Is. (S. Am.)
Corisco (Af.)
Corsica (Med.)
Cumbrae (Scot.)
Curaçao (W.I.)
Curzola (Adr.)
Dampier Is. (Austral.)
Dinding Is. (Malay.)
Diomede Is. (Arc.)
Domingo (W.I.)
Falster (Balt.)
Fanning (Pac.)
Fehmeru (Balt.)
Flannan Is. (Scot.)
Formosa (China)
Frisian Is. (Neth.)
Gambier Is. (Pac.)

Gilbert Is. (Pac.)
Gotland (Balt.)
Grenada (W.I.)
Hayling I. (Eng.)
Iceland (v.) (Atl.)
Ichaboe (Af.)
Ireland
Jamaica (W.I.)
Johanna (Af.)
Kamaran (Red S.)
Kandava (Pac.)
Keeling Is. (Ind.)
Kolonev (Rus.)
Laaland (Den.)
Leeward Is. (W.I.)
Liakhov Is. (Arc.)
Lofoten Is. (Nor.)
Loo Choo Is. (China)
Loyalty Is. (Pac.)
Madeira (Atl.)
Mageroe (Arc.)
Majorca (Med.)
Maldive Is. (Ind.)
Massowa (Red S.)
Mayotte (Af.)
Minicoy (Ind.)
Minorca (Sp.)
Molokai (Pac.)
Molucca Is. (Indo.)
Mombasa (Af.)
Mykonos (Gr.)
Nicobar Is. (Ind.)
Norfolk I. (Austral.)
Nossi Be (v.) (Af.)
Oceania (Pac.)
Orkneys (Scot.)
Phoenix Is. (Pac.)
Portsea I. (Eng.)
Princes Is. (Turk.)
Purbeck, I. of (Eng.)
Rathlin (N.I.)
Reunion (Ind.)
Roanoke (U.S.A.)
Rockall (Atl.)
Rotumah (Pac.)
St. Agnes (Eng.)
St. Kilda (Scot.)
St. Kitts (Pac.)
St. Lucia (W.I.)
St. Marie (Af.)
Salamis (Gr.)
São Tomé (Af.)
Sheppey, I. of (Eng.)
Sherbro (Af.)
Shikoka (Jap.)
Society Is. (Pac.)
Socotra (Ind.)
Solomon Is. (Pac.)
Stewart I. (N.Z.)
Sumatra (Indo.)
Sumbawa (Indo.)
Tenedos (Med.)
Ternate (Indo.)
Tortola (W.I.)
Tortuga (W.I.)
Tuamotu (Pac.)
Watling I. (W.I.)
Whalsay (Scot.)

8

Alderney (Ch. Is.)
Aleutian Is. (Pac.)
Amirante Is. (Ind.)
Andamans (Ind.)

Anglesey (Wales)
Antilles Is. (W.I.)
Aucklands Is. (N.Z.)
Balearic Is. (Med.)
Barbados (Is.) (W.I.)
Bermudas (Is.) (Atl.)
Berneray (Scot.)
Billiton (Indo.)
Bismark Arch. (Pac.)
Bissagos Is. (Af.)
Bornholm (Balt.)
Campbell (N.Z.)
Canaries (Atl.)
Caribbee Is. (W.I.)
Caroline Is. (Pac.)
Colonsay (Scot.)
Copeland Is. (Ire.)
Cyclades Is. (Gr.)
Desertas (Atl.)
Desirade (W.I.)
Dominica (W.I.)
Fair Isle (Scot.)
Falkland Is. (Atl.)
Flinders (Austral.)
Friendly Is. (Pac.)
Furneaux Is. (Austral.)
Guernsey (Ch. Is.)
Hebrides (Scot.)
Hokkaido (Jap.)
Hong Kong (China)
Inchcolm (Scot.)
Jan Mayen (Arc.)
Kangaroo Is. (Austral.)
Kermadec Is. (Pac.)
Krakatoa (v.) (Indo.)
Ladrones (Pac.)
Leucadia (Med.)
Lord Howe Is. (Austral.)
Magdalen Is. (Can.)
Malicolo (Pac.)
Mallorca (Med.)
Manihiki Is. (Pac.)
Marianne Is. (Pac.)
Marshall Is. (Pac.)
Melville (Am. and Austral.)
Mindanao (Philip.)
Miquelon (Can.)
Mitylene (Gr.)
Moluccas (Indo.)
Otaheite (Pac.)
Pitcairn Is. (Pac.)
Portland, I. of (Eng.)
Pribilof Is. (Pac.)
Pribylov Is. (Pac.)
Quelpart (Korea)
Rothesay (Scot.)
St. Helena (Atl.)
St. Martin (W.I.)
St. Thomas (Af. and W.I.)
Sakhalin (U.S.S.R.)
Salsette (Ind.)
Sandwich Is. (Pac.)
Scillies (Eng.)
Sri Lanka (Asia)
Shetland Is. (Scot.)
Starbuck (Pac.)
Tasmania (Austral.)
Thousand Is. (N. Am.)
Thursday I. (Austral.)
Tortugas Is. (U.S.A.)
Trinidad (W.I.)
Unalaska (U.S.A.)
Valentia (Ire.)
Victoria (Can.)
Viti-Levu (Fiji)
Vlieland (Neth.)

Windward Is. (W.I.)
Zanzibar (Af.)

9

Admiralty Is. (Pac.)
Anticosti (Can.)
Arranmore (Ire.)
Ascension (Atl.)
Belle Isle (Fr.)
Beverland (Neth.)
Buccaneer Arch. (Ind.)
Cape Verde Is. (Atl.)
Cerigotto (Med.)
Christmas I. (Pac. and Ind.)
Dordrecht (Neth.)
Elephanta (Ind.)
Eleuthera (W.I.)
Ellesmere (N. Am.)
Erromanga (Scot.)
Falklands (Atl.)
Galapagos Is. (v.) (Pac.)
Greenland (Arc.)
Halmahera (Indo.)
Inchkeith (Scot.)
Inishturk (Ire.)
Isle of Man (Eng.)
Isle of May (Scot.)
Lampedusa (Med.)
Langeland (Den.)
Louisiade Arch (E.I.)
Manhattan (U.S.A.)
Margarita (W.I.)
Marquesas Is. (Pac.)
Mauritius (Ind.)
Melanesia (Pac.)
Nantucket (U.S.A.)
Negropont (Gr.)
New Guinea (E.I.)
Norderney (Ger.)
Polynesia (Pac.)
Porto Rico (W.I.)
Raratonga (Pac.)
Rodrigues (Ind.)
Saghalien (U.S.S.R.)
Saint John (W.I.)
St. Michael (Atl.)
St. Nicolas (Atl.)
Saint Paul (Ind.)
St. Vincent (W.I.)
Santa Cruz (W.I.)
Santorini (v) (Gr.)
Sardinia (Med.)
Scarpanto (Med.)
Shetlands (Scot.)
Singapore (Asia)
Stromboli (v.) (Med.)
Teneriffe (Atl.)
Timor Laut Is. (Pac.)
Vancouver (Can.)
Vanua Levu (Fiji)
Walcheren (Neth.)
Wellesley Is. (Austral.)

10

Ailsa Craig (Scot.)
Bay Islands (C. Am.)
Calamianes (Indo.)
Cape Barren I. (Austral.)
Cape Breton I. (Can.)
Cephalonia (Gr.)
Dirk Hartog (Austral.)
Dodecanese (Med.)

Fernando Po (Af.)
Formentera (Med.)
Fortune Bay I. (Can.)
Friendlies (Pac.)
Grenadines (W.I.)
Guadeloupe (W.I.)
Heligoland (N. Sea)
Holy Island (Scot.)
Inchgarvie (Scot.)
Inishshark (Ire.)
Isle of Dogs (Eng.)
Isle of Skye (Scot.)
Isle of Mull (Scot.)
Kuria Muria Is. (Arab.)
Laccadives (Arab.)
Long Island (U.S.A.)
Madagascar (Af.)
Manitoulin Is. (Pac.)
Martinique (W.I.)
Micronesia (Pac.)
Montserrat (W.I.)
Navigators' I. (Pac.)
New Britain (Pac.)
New Siberia (Arc.)
New Zealand (Pac.)
North Devon (Arc.)
Nova Zembla (Arc.)
Philippine Is. (Asia)
Puerto Rico (W.I.)
Rat Islands (Pac.)
Ronaldshay (Scot.)
Saint Agnes (Eng.)
Saint Kilda (Scot.)
Saint Kitts (W.I.)
Saint Lucia (W.I.)
Saint Marie (Af.)
Sandlewood I. (Malay.)
Seychelles (Ind.)
Skerryvore (Scot.)
West Indies (Atl.)

11

Cook Islands (Pac.)
Eagle Island (Ire.)
Grand Canary (Atl.)
Guadalcanal (Pac.)
Hall Islands (Pac.)
Hart's Island (U.S.A.)
Isle of Pines (Pac. and W.I.)
Isle of Wight (Eng.)
Isola Grossa (Adr.)
Lindisfarne (Scot.)
Lundy Island (Eng.)
Mascarenene Is. (Ind.)
Monte Cristo (It.)
New Hebrides (Pac.)
North Island (N.Z.)
Pantellaria (Med.)
Philippines (Asia)
Rhode Island (U.S.A.)
Sable Island (Can.)
Saint Helena (Atl.)
Saint Martin (W.I.)
Saint Thomas (W.I.)
Scilly Isles (Eng.)
Southampton (Can.)
South Island (N.Z.)
Spitsbergen (Arc.)

12

Baffin Island (N. Am.)
Bougainville (Pac.)

97

British Isles
Easter Island (Pac.)
Great Britain (U.K.)
Great Cumbrae (Scot.)
Inaccessible I. (Atl.)
Isle of Thanet (Eng.)
Mariagalante (W.I.)
Melville Land (Arc.)
New Caledonia (Pac.)
Newfoundland (Can.)
Novaya Zemlya (Arc.)
Prince Albert (Can.)
Prince Edward I. (Can.)
Puffin Island (Wales)
Saint Michael (Atl.)
Saint Nicolas (Atl.)
Saint Vincent (W.I.)
Savage Island (Pac.)

South Georgia (Atl.)
Staten Island (U.S.A.)
Turks' Islands (W.I.)

13 AND OVER

D'Entrecastreaux Is.
  (Austral.) (15)
Isle of Portland (Eng.) (14)
Isle of Purbeck (Eng.) (13)
Isle of Sheppey (Eng.) (13)
Juan Fernandez (Pac.) (13)
Kerguelen Land (Pac.) (13)
Little Cumbrae (Scot.) (13)
Martha's Vineyard (U.S.A.)
  (15)

Norfolk Island (Pac.) (13)
North Somerset (Arc.) (14)
Prince of Wales I. (Malay.)
  (13)
Queen Charlotte Is. (Can.)
  (14)
St. Bartholomew (W.I.) (13)
St. Christopher (W.I.) (13)
South Shetlands (Atl.) (14)
Stewart Island (N.Z.) (13)
Thursday Island (Austral.)
  (14)
Tierra del Fuego (Chile) (14)
Tristan da Cunha (Atl.) (14)
Watling Island (Atl.) (13)
West Spitsbergen (Arc.) (15)

Lakes, inland lochs, etc.

3 AND 4

Aral (U.S.S.R.)
Ard (Scot.)
Awe (Scot.)
Bala (Wales)
Bay (Phil.)
Bear (U.S.A.)
Biwa (Jap.)
Chad (Af.)
Como (It.)
Derg (Ire.)
Dore (Can.)
Earn (Scot.)
Eil (Scot.)
Erie (Can and U.S.A.)
Erne (N.I.)
Ewe (Scot.)
Eyre (Austral.)
Ha Ha (Can.)
Iseo (It.)
Key (Ire.)
Kivu (Af.)
Mead (U.S.A.)
Ness (Scot.)
Oahu (N.Z.)
Ree (Ire.)
Ryan (Scot.)
Sego (U.S.S.R.)
Shin (Scot.)
Tana (Eth.)
Tay (Scot.)
Thun (Swit.)
Utah (U.S.A.)
Van (Turk.)
Voil (Scot.)
Zug (Swit.)

5

Abaya (Eth.)
Allen (Ire.)
Baker (Can.)
Camm (Can.)
Elton (U.S.S.R.)
Enara (Fin.)
Etive (Scot.)
Frome (Austral.)
Garda (It.)
Garry (Can.)
Ghana (Can.)

Hamun (Afghan.)
Honey (U.S.A.)
Huron (Can. and U.S.A.)
Ilmen (U.S.S.R.)
Kossu (Af.)
Leven (Scot.)
Lochy (Scot.)
Loyal (Scot.)
Malar (Swed.)
Maree (Scot.)
Minto (Can.)
Mjøsa (Nor.)
Moero (Af.)
Morar (Scot.)
Mweru (Af.)
Neagh (N.I.)
Moore (Austral.)
Nevis (Scot.)
Nyasa (Af.)
Onega (U.S.S.R.)
Payne (Can.)
Rainy (Can.)
Shiel (Scot.)
Talka (Can.)
Taupo (N.Z.)
Tsano (Eth.)
Tumba (Af.)
Urmia (Iran)
Volta (Ghana)
Wener (Swed.)
Yssel (Neth.)

6

Albert (Af.)
Arkaig (Scot.)
Assynt (Scot.)
Austin (Austral.)
Baikal (Sib.)
Buloke (Austral.)
Chilka (Ind.)
Edward (Af.)
Ennell (Ire.)
Geneva (Swit.)
George (Af. and Austral.)
Indian (U.S.A.)
Itasca (U.S.A.)
Kariba (Af.)
Khanka (Asia)
Ladoga (U.S.S.R.)

Lomond (Scot.)
Lugano (Swit.)
Mahood (Can.)
Malawi (Af.)
Nasser (Egypt)
Oneida (U.S.A.)
Peipus (U.S.S.R.)
Placid (U.S.A.)
Quoich (Scot.)
Rideau (Can.)
Rudolf (Af.)
St. John (Can.)
Shasta (U.S.A.)
Shirwa (Af.)
Simcoe (Can.)
Stuart (Can.)
Te Anau (N.Z.)
Tuz Gol (Turk.)
Vanern (Swed.)
Viedma (S. Am.)
Vyrnwy (Wales)
Wanaka (N.Z.)
Wenham (U.S.A.)
Wetter (Swed.)
Zürich (Swit.)

7

Abitibi (Can.)
Balaton (Hung.)
Balkash (Asia)
Benmore (N.Z.)
Blanche (Austral.)
Caillou (U.S.A.)
Caspian (Asia)
Chapala (Mex.)
Dead Sea (Asia)
Etawney (Can.)
Fannich (Scot.)
Galilee (Asia)
Hirakud (Ind.)
Hjelmar (Swed.)
Idi Amin (Af.)
Katrine (Scot.)
Koko Nor (China)
Lachine (Can.)
Leopold (Af.)
Loch Eil (Scot.)
Loch Tay (Scot.)
Lucerne (Swit.)

Muskoka (Can.)
Nipigon (Can.)
Okhrida (Turk.)
Ontario (Can. and U.S.A.)
Perugia (It.)
Quesnal (Can.)
Rannoch (Scot.)
Rosseau (Can.)
Rybinsk (U.S.S.R.)
Seistan (Afghan.)
Sempach (Swit.)
Sheelin (Ire.)
Tarbert (Scot.)
Texcoco (Mex.)
Tezcuco (Mex.)
Torrens (Austral.)
Tyrrell (Austral.)

8

Akamyara (Af.)
Balkhash (Asia)
Bear Lake (U.S.A.)
Chowilla (Austral.)
Cooroong (Austral.)
Drummond (U.S.A.)
Gairdner (Austral.)
Grasmere (Eng.)
Hirfanli (Turk.)
Humboldt (Austral.)
Issyk-Kul (Asia)
Kakhovka (U.S.S.R.)
Kawarthi (Can.)
Kootenay (Can.)
La Crosse (U.S.A.)
Loch Ness (Scot.)
Loch Ryan (Scot.)
Luichart (Scot.)
Maggiore (It.)
Manipuri (N.Z.)
Manitoba (Can.)
Mareotis (Egypt)
Menteith (Scot.)
Menzaleh (Egypt)
Michigan (U.S.A.)

Reindeer (Can.)
Seaforth (Scot.)
Sese Soko (Af.)
Stefanie (Af.)
Superior (U.S.A.)
Tarawera (N.Z.)
Titicaca (Peru)
Tungting (China)
Victoria (Af.)
Wakatipu (N.Z.)
Winnipeg (Can.)
Xaltocan (Mex.)

9

Argentino (S. Am.)
Athabaska (Can.)
Bangweolo (Af.)
Champlain (N. Am.)
Constance (Swit.)
Ennerdale (Eng.)
Eucumbene (Austral.)
Great Bear (Can.)
Great Salt (U.S.A.)
Hindmarsh (Austral.)
Honey Lake (U.S.A.)
Killarney (Ire.)
Kuibyshev (U.S.S.R.)
Lochinvar (Scot.)
Loch Leven (Scot.)
Loch Maree (Scot.)
Loch Nevis (Scot.)
Maracaibo (Venez.)
Maravilla (S. Am.)
Neuchâtel (Swit.)
Nicaragua (Am.)
Nipissing (Can.)
Playgreen (Can.)
Tengri-Nor (Tibet)
Thirlmere (Eng.)
Trasimeno (It.)
Ullswater (Eng.)
Wastwater (Eng.)
Wollaston (Can.)
Yssel Lake (Neth.)

10

Brokopondo (S. Am.)
Great Slave (Can.)
Hawes Water (Eng.)
Ijsselmeer (Neth.)
Indian Lake (U.S.A.)
Lackawanna (U.S.A.)
Loch Lomond (Scot.)
Lough Neagh (N.I.)
Michikamau (Can.)
Mistassini (Can.)
Roguaguado (Boliv.)
Rotomahana (N.Z.)
Rydal Water (Eng.)
Serpentine (Eng.)
Tanganyika (Af.)
Windermere (Eng.)
Xochimilco (Mex.)

11 AND OVER

Albert Edward Nyanza (Af.) (18)
Albert Nyanza (Af.) (12)
Bitter Lakes (Egypt) (11)
Cabora Bassa (Af.) (11)
Coniston Water (Eng.) (13)
Derwentwater (Eng.) (12)
Diefenbaker (Can.) (11)
Grand Coulee (U.S.A.) (11)
Great Salt Lake (U.S.A.) (13)
Great Slave Lake (Can.) (14)
Lake of the Woods (Can. and U.S.A.) (14)
Lesser Slave Lake (Can.) (15)
Loch Katrine (Scot.) (11)
Loch Tarbert (Scot.) (11)
Pontchatrain (U.S.A.) (12)
The Cooroong (Austral.) (11)
Timiskaming (Can.) (11)
Victoria Nyanza (Af.) (14)
Virginia Water (Eng.) (13)
Winnipegosis (Can.) (12)
Yellowstone (U.S.A.) (11)

Mountains

H. = Hill. Hs. = Hills. M. = "Mountain," commonly used *after* name. Ms. = Mountains. Mt = "Mount," "Monte," or "Mont," commonly used *before* name. (v.) = volcanic.

2–4

Abu, Mt. (Ind.)
Aboo, Mt. (Ind.)
Alps Ms. (Eur.)
Blue Ms. (Austral. and U.S.A.)
Caha Ms. (Ire.)
Cook M. (N.Z.)
Ebal, Mt. (Jord.)
Elk Ms. (U.S.A.)
Etna, Mt. (v.) (Sic.)
Fuji, Mt. (v.) (Jap.)
Harz Ms. (Ger.)
Ida, Mt. (Crete)
Iron M. (U.S.A.)
Jura Ms. (Eur.)
K2 (Him.)
Kea (v.) (Hawaii)
Kibo, Mt. (Tanz.)
Kong Ms. (Af.)

Naga Hs. (Ind.)
Qara Ms. (Arab.)
Rigi, Mt. (Swit.)
Rosa, Mt. (Alps.)
Ural Ms. (U.S.S.R.)
Zug M. (Ger.)

5

Adams M. (U.S.A.)
Altai Ms. (Him.)
Andes Ms. (S. Am.)
Athos, Mt. (Gr.)
Atlas Ms. (Af.)
Baker (v.) (U.S.A.)
Barry Ms. (Austral.)
Black Ms. (U.S.A. and Wales)
Blanc, Mt. (Alps)
Brown M. (N. Am.)

Cenis, Mt. (Alps)
Eiger (Swit.)
Djaja, Mt. (Indo.)
Downs, The (Hs.) (Eng.)
Ghats, The (Ms.) (Ind.)
Green Ms. (U.S.A.)
Hecla (v.) (Iceland)
Kamet, Mt. (Him.)
Kenia, Mt. (E. Af.)
Kenya, Mt. (E. Af.)
Logan, Mt. (Yukon)
Maipu (v.) (Arg.)
Mönch (Swit.)
Ochil Hs. (Scot.)
Ophir, M. (Malay.)
Overo (v.) (S. Am.)
Pelée (v.) (W.I.)
Rocky Ms. (N. Am.)
Sinai, Mt. (Arab.)
Table M. (S.A.)
Tabor, Mt. (Isr.)

99

Vinta, Mt. (U.S.A.)
White, Ms. (U.S.A.)
Wolds, The (Hs.) (Eng.)

6

Ararat, Mt. (Turk.)
Averno, Mt. (v.) (It.)
Balkan Ms. (Eur.)
Beluha (Him.)
Bogong, Mt. (Austral.)
Carmel, Mt. (Isr.)
Darwin, Mt. (S. Am.)
Elbruz (U.S.S.R.)
Erebus (v.) (Antarc.)
Galtee Ms. (Ire.)
Hayden, Mt. (U.S.A.)
Hermon, Mt. (Asia)
Hooker, M. (Can.)
Hoosac Ms. (U.S.A.)
Juncal (v.) (S. Am.)
Kazbek, Mt. (U.S.S.R.)
Lennox Hs. (Scot.)
Lhotse, Mt. (Him.)
Makalu, Mt. (Him.)
Masaya (v.) (C. Am.)
Mendip Hs. (Eng.)
Mourne Ms. (Ire.)
Nelson, Mt. (Tas.)
Nuptse, Mt. (Him.)
Olives, Mt. of (Isr.)
Pamirs (Asia)
Pindus Ms. (Gr.)
Robson (Can.)
Sahama (v.) (S. Am.)
Sangay (v.) (S. Am.)
Scafel, Mt. (Eng.)
Sidlaw Hs. (Scot.)
Sorata (2 Ms.) (S. Am.)
Taunus Ms. (Ger.)
Terror (v.) (Antarc.)
Tolima (v.) (S. Am.)
Vosges Ms. (Fr.)

7

Balkans Ms. (Eur.)
Ben More (Scot.)
Bernima, Mt. (Alps)
Big Horn Ms. (U.S.A.)
Bow Fell Mt. (Eng.)
Brocken, Mt. (Ger.)
Cascade Ms. (N. Am.)
Cazambe, Mt. (S. Am.)
Cheviot Hs. (Eng.)
Dapsang, Mt. (Him.)
Darling, Mt. (Austral.)
El Potra, Mt. (S. Am.)
Everest, Mt. (Him.)
Hoffman, Mt. (U.S.A.)
Illampa, Mt. (Boliv.)
Jaintia Ms. (Assam)
Jonsong, Mt. (Him.)
Jorullo (v.) (Mex.)
Kilauea (v.) (Pac.)
La Pelée (v.) (W.I.)
Lebanon, Mt. (Leb.)
Lookout M. (U.S.A.)
Malvern Hs. (Eng.)
Mamturk Ms. (Ire.)
Mendips Hs. (Eng.)
Milanji, Mt. (Af.)
Miltsin, Mt. (Af.)
M'Kinley (Alaska)

Nilgiri Hs. (Ind.)
Pennine Ms. (Eng.)
Peteroa (v.) (S. Am.)
Pilatus, Mt. (Swit.)
Orizaba (Mex.)
Quizapu (v.) (S. Am.)
Rainier, Mt. (U.S.A.)
Rhodope, Mt. (Turk.)
Rockies Ms. (N. Am.)
Roraima, Mt. (S. Am.)
Ruahine, Mt. (N.Z.)
San José (v.) (S. Am.)
San Juan Ms. (U.S.A.)
Simplon, Mt. (Swit.)
Siwalik Hs. (Ind.)
Skiddaw, Mt. (Eng.)
Snowdon, Mt. (Wales)
St. Elias, Mt. (Can. and Gr.)
Sudetes Ms. (Eur.)
Tomboro (v.) (Jap.)
Vindhya Ms. (Ind.)
Vulcano (v.) (It.)
Wenchow, Mt. (China)
Whitney, Mt. (U.S.A.)

8

Anapurna (Him.)
Aravalli Ms. (Ind.)
Auvergne Ms. (Fr.)
Ben Nevis (Scot.)
Ben Venue (Scot.)
Ben Wyvis (Scot.)
Ben-y-Gloe (Scot.)
Catskill Ms. (U.S.A.)
Caucasus Ms. (Eur.)
Cheviots (Hs.) (Eng.)
Chiltern Hs. (Eng.)
Cotopaxi (v.) (Ecuad.)
Cotswold Hs. (Eng.)
Demavend, Mt. (Iran)
Edgehill (H.) (Eng.)
Estrelle, Mt. (Port.)
Flinders Ms. (Austral.)
Fujiyama (v.) (Jap.)
Goatfell, Mt. (Scot.)
Haramokh, Mt. (Him.)
Hualalai (v.) (Pac.)
Illimani, Mt. (Bol.)
Jungfrau, Mt. (Swit.)
Katahdin, Mt. (U.S.A.)
Kinabalu (v.) (Born.)
Koh-i-Baba (Afghan.)
Krakatoa (v.) (Indo.)
Kuenluiv Ms. (Asia)
McKinley, Mt. (Alaska)
Moorfoot Hs. (Scot.)
Mulhacén, Mt. (Sp.)
Nilgiris Hs. (Ind.)
Pennines (Hs.) (Eng.)
Pentland Hs. (Scot.)
Preseley Ms. (Wales)
Pyrenees Ms. (Eur.)
Quantock Hs. (Eng.)
Rajmahal Hs. (Ind.)
Rushmore, Mt. (U.S.A.)
Scawfell, Mt. (Eng.)
Snaefell, Mt. (I. of Man)
Sulaiman, Ms. (Ind.)
Tarawera, Mt. (N.Z.)
The Downs (Hs.) (Eng.)
The Ghats (Ms.) (Ind.)
The Wolds (Hs.) (Eng.)
Tien Shan Ms. (Asia)
Townsend, Mt. (Austral.)

Vesuvius (v.) (It.)
Wrangell, Mt. (Can.)
Yablonoi Ms. (Asia)

9

Aconcagua (v.) (Arg.)
Adam's Peak (Sri)
Allegheny Ms. (U.S.A.)
Annapurna (Him.)
Apennines (It.)
Ben Lawers (Scot.)
Ben Lomond (Scot.)
Black Dome Mt. (U.S.A.)
Blue Ridge Ms. (U.S.A.)
Breithorn (Alps)
Cairntoul (Scot.)
Carstensz (Indo.)
Chilterns (Hs.) (Eng.)
Chumalari, Mt. (Him.)
Communism (U.S.S.R.)
Cotswolds (Hs.) (Eng.)
Cuchullin Hs. (Skye)
Dardistan, Mt. (Ind.)
Faucilles Ms. (Fr.)
Grampians (Ms.) (Scot.)
Helvellyn, Mt. (Eng.)
Himalayas (Ms.) (Asia)
Hindu-Kush Ms. (Asia)
Itaculomi, Mt. (S. Am.)
Karakoram, Mt. (Asia)
Koseiusko, Mt. (Austral.)
Lafayette, Mt. (U.S.A.)
Las Yeguas (v.) (Chile)
Lenin Peak (U.S.S.R.)
Licancaur, Mt. (Chile)
Liverpool (Austral.)
Maladetta, Mt. (Pyr.)
Mont Blanc (Alps)
Mont Cenis (Alps)
Mont Perdu (Pyr.)
Monte Rosa (Alps)
Naga Hills (Ind.)
Parnassus, Mt. (Gr.)
Pic du Midi (Pyr.)
Pike's Peak (U.S.A.)
Rakaposhi (Him.)
Ruwenzori Ms. (Uganda and Zaïre)
Solfatara (v.) (It.)
St. Bernard (Pass) (Swit.)
St. Gothard, Mt. (Swit.)
Stromboli (v.) (Med.)
Thian-Shan Ms. (Asia)
Tongariro (v.) (N.Z.)
Tupungato (v.) (S. Am.)
Wind River Ms. (U.S.A.)

10

Adirondack Ms (U.S.A.)
Ben Macdhui (Scot.)
Cairngorms (Scot.)
Cantabrian Ms. (Sp.)
Carpathian Ms. (Eur.)
Cedar Berge, Mt. (S.A.)
Chimborazo (v.) (Ecuad.)
Chumallari, Mt. (Him.)
Dent du Midi (Swit.)
Dhaulagiri, Mt. (Him.)
Diablerets, Mt. (Swit.)
Erzgebirge (Ger.)
Graian Alps (Eur.)
Khyber Pass (Afghan., Pak.)

Koshtan Tau (U.S.S.R.)
Kuh-i-Taftan (v.) (Iran)
Kwathlamba, Mt. (S.A.)
Lammermuir Hs. (Scot.)
Laurentian Ms. (Can.)
Matterhorn, The (Alps)
Moel Fammau, Mt. (Wales)
Monte Corno (It.)
Nanga-Devi (Him.)
Ochil Hills (Scot.)
Pinlimmon, Mt. (Wales)
Saint Elias (Can. and Gr.)
Wellington, Mt. (Tas.)
Wetterhorn, The (Swit.)

11

Appalachian Ms. (U.S.A.)
Bernese Alps (Swit.)
Carpathians (Ms.) (Eur.)
Citlaltepec, Mt. (Mex.)
Descapezado (v.) (Chile)
Dinaric Alps (Eur.)
Drachenfels, Mt. (Ger.)
Drakensberg Ms. (S.A.)
Drakenstein, Mt. (S.A.)
Hochstetter, Mt. (N.Z.)
Kilimanjaro, Mt. (Tanz.)
La Sonfrière (v.) (W.I.)
Lennox Hills (Scot.)
Livingstone Ms. (Af.)

Mendip Hills (Eng.)
Nanga Parbat (Him.)
Ortler Spitz (Aust.)
Owen Stanley Ms. (Papua)
Pennine Alps (Eur.)
Schreckhorn (Swit.)
Sidlow Hills (Scot.)
Sierra Madre Ms. (Mex.)
Splugen Pass (Swit.)
Stelvio Pass (It.)
Swabian Alps (Ger.)
Vatnajökull (Iceland)

12

Bougainville, Mt. (Papua)
Cheviot Hills (Eng.)
Godwin Austen, Mt. (Him.)
Ingleborough, Mt. (Eng.)
Jaintia Hills (Ind.)
Kanchenjunga, Mt. (Him.)
Kinchinjunga, Mt. (Him.)
Llullaillaco (v.) Chile
Malvern Hills (Eng.)
Maritime Alps (Fr., It.)
Nilgiri Hills (Ind.)
Peak District (Eng.)
Popocatepetl (v.) (Mex.)
Roncesvalles (v.) (Pyr.)
Saint Gothard, Mt. (Swit.)
Schiehallion, Mt. (Scot.)

Sierra Morena, Mt. (Sp.)
Sierra Nevada Ms. (Sp.)
Siwalik Hills (Ind.)
Tinguiririca (v.) (Chile)
Zoutpansberg, Mt. (S.A.)

13 AND OVER

Black Dome Peak (U.S.A.
  (13)
Carrantuohill, Mt. (Ire.)
  (13)
Chiltern Hills (Eng.) (13)
Cotswold Hills (Eng.) (13)
Fichtelgebirge (Ger.) (14)
Finsteraahorn, Mt. (Swit.)
  (13)
Grossglockner, Mt. (Alps)
  (13)
Knockmealdown, Mt. (Ire.)
  (13)
Mont Aux Sources (Lesotho)
  (14)
Mount of Olives (Isr.) (13)
Pentland Hills (Scot.) (13)
Pidurutalagala (Sri) (14)
Riesengebirge Ms. (Eur.)
  (13)
Skaptarjökull (v.) Iceland (13)
Table Mountain (S.A.) (13)
Tabor Mountain (Isr.) (13)

Oceans and seas

3 AND 4

Aral S. (U.S.S.R.)
Azov, S. of (U.S.S.R.)
Dead S. (Jord., Isr.)
Java S. (Indo.)
Kara S. (U.S.S.R.)
Red S. (Egypt, Arab.)
Ross S. (Antarc.)
Sava S. (Indo.)
Sulu S. (Philip.)

5

Banda S. (Indo.)
Black S. (Eur., Turk.)
Ceram S. (Indo.)
China S. (China)
Coral S. (Indo.)
Irish S. (Brit. Isles)
Japan, S. of (Jap.)
Malay S. (Malay.)
North S. (Eur.)
Timor S. (Indo.)
White S. (U.S.S.R.)

6

Aegean S. (Gr., Turk.)
Arctic O.

Baltic S. (N. Eur.)
Bering S. (Pac.)
Flores S. (Indo.)
Gaelic S. (Brit. Isles)
Indian O.
Ionian S. (Gr.)
Laptev S. (U.S.S.R.)
Scotia S. (Antarc.)
Tasman S. (Austral.)
Yellow S. (China)

7

Andaman S. (Indo.)
Arabian S. (Ind.)
Arafura S. (Austral.)
Barents S. (U.S.S.R.)
Behring S. (Pac.)
Caspian S. (U.S.S.R., Iran)
Celebes S. (Indo.)
Marmora, S. of (Turk.)
Molucca S. (Indo.)
Okhotsk, S. of (U.S.S.R.)
Pacific O.
Weddell S. (Antarc.)

8

Adriatic S. (Med.)
Amundsen S. (Antarc.)

Atlantic O.
Beaufort S. (Can.)
Ligurian S. (It.)
Macassar S. (Indo.)
McKinley S. (Green.)
Sargasso S. (Atl.)

9

Antarctic O.
Caribbean S. (Am.)
East China S. (China)
Greenland S. (Green.)
Norwegian S. (Nor.)
Zuider Zee }
Zuyder Zee } (Neth.)

10 AND OVER

Bellingshausen S. (Antarc.)
  (13)
East Siberian S. (U.S.S.R.)
  (12)
King Haakon VIII S.
  (Antarc.) (14)
Mediterranean S. (Eur., Af.)
  (13)
South China S. (China) (10)
Tyrrhenian S. (W. Med. (10)

Ports

3 AND 4

Acre (Isr.)
Aden (P.D.R. Yemen)
Akko (Isr.)
Amoy (China)
Baku (U.S.S.R.)
Bar (Yug.)
Bari (It.)
Cebu (Philip.)
Cobh (Ire.)
Cork (Ire.)
Elat (Isr.)
Erie (U.S.A.)
Hull (Eng.)
Ilo (Peru)
Kiel (W. Ger.)
Kobe (Jap.)
Okha (U.S.S.R.)
Oran (Alg.)
Oslo (Nor.)
Para (Braz.)
Pula (Yug.)
Riga (U.S.S.R.)
Safi (Moroc.)
Suez (Egypt)
Tain (Scot.)
Tema (Ghana)
Wick (Scot.)

5

Akyab (Burma)
Arica (Chile)
Basra (Iraq)
Beira (Moz.)
Belem (Braz.)
Brest (Fr.)
Cadiz (Fr.)
Canea (Gr.)
Ceuta (Moroc.)
Colon (Panama)
Corfu (Gr.)
Dakar (Senegal)
Delft (Neth.)
Dover (Eng.)
Eilat (Isr.)
Emden (W. Ger.)
Gaeta (It.)
Galle (Sri.)
Genoa (It.)
Haifa (Isr.)
Havre (Le) (Fr.)
Izmir (Turk.)
Kerch (U.S.S.R.)
Kochi (Jap.)
Kotor (Yug.)
Lagos (Nig.)
Leith (Scot.)
Lulea (Swed.)
Malmö (Swed.)
Mocha (Yemen)
Osaka (Jap.)
Ostia (It.)
Palma (Sp.)
Palos (Sp.)
Pusan (S. Korea)
Rabat (Moroc.)
Reval (U.S.S.R.)
Scapa (Scot.)
Trani (It.)

Varna (Bulg.)
Wisby (Swed.)
Yalta (U.S.S.R.)
Ystad (Swed.)

6

Agadir (Moroc.)
Ahmedi (Yemen)
Ancona (It.)
Ashdod (Isr.)
Balboa (Panama)
Bastia (Cors.)
Beirut (Lebanon)
Bergen (Nor.)
Bilbao (Sp.)
Bombay (Ind.)
Bremen (W. Ger.)
Calais (Fr.)
Callao (Peru)
Cannes (Fr.)
Chalna (Pak.)
Chefoo (China)
Cochin (Ind.)
Danzig (Pol.)
Dieppe (Fr.)
Douala (Cameroun)
Dunbar (Scot.)
Dundee (Scot.)
Durban (S.A.)
F'derik (Mauritania)
Ferrol (Sp.)
Gdansk (Pol.)
Gdynia (Pol.)
Haldia (Ind.)
Hankow (China)
Hobart (Tas.)
Izmail (U.S.S.R.)
Jeddah (Saudi)
Kalmar (Swed.)
Kandla (Ind.)
Kuwait (Kuwait)
Larvik (Nor.)
Lisbon (Port.)
Lobito (Angola)
London (Eng.)
Madras (Ind.)
Malaga (Sp.)
Manila (Philip.)
Matadi (Zaire)
Mtwara (Tanz.)
Naples (It.)
Narvik (Nor.)
Nelson (N.Z.)
Odense (Den.)
Odessa (U.S.S.R.)
Oporto (Port.)
Ostend (Belg.)
Padang (Indo.)
Patras (Gr.)
Penang (Malay.)
Ramsey (I. of Man)
Recife (Braz.)
Rhodes (Gr.)
Rijeka (Yug.)
Santos (Braz.)
Sittwe (Burma)
Skikda (Alg.)
Smyrna (Turk.)
Suakin (Sudan)
Swatow (China)

Sydney (Austral.)
Tainan (Taiwan)
Tetuán (Moroc.)
Toulon (Fr.)
Tromsö (Nor.)
Venice (It.)
Weihai (China)
Wismar (E. Ger.)

7

Aalborg (Den.)
Abidjan (Ivory Coast)
Ajaccio (Cors.)
Algiers (Alg.)
Antwerp (Belg.)
Bangkok (Thai.)
Belfast (N.I.)
Bushire (Iran)
Cardiff (Wales)
Cattaro (Yug.)
Cayenne (Fr. Guiana)
Chatham (Eng.)
Colombo (Sri)
Corunna (Sp.)
Cotonou (Benin)
Dampier (Austral.)
Detroit (U.S.A.)
Donegal (Ire.)
Dundalk (Ire.)
Dunkirk (Fr.)
Foochow (China)
Funchal (Sp.)
Geelong (Austral.)
Grimsby (Eng.)
Guaymas (Mex.)
Halifax (Can.)
Hamburg (W. Ger.)
Harwich (Eng.)
Hodeida (Yemen)
Horsens (Den.)
Houston (U.S.A.)
Jakarta (Indo.)
Karachi (Pak.)
Keelung (Taiwan)
Kitimat (Can.)
La Plata (Arg.)
Larnaca (Cyprus)
Leghorn (It.)
Le Havre (Fr.)
Marsala (It.)
Melilla (Moroc.)
Messina (It.)
Mogador (Moroc.)
Mombasa (Kenya)
New York (U.S.A.)
Norfolk (U.S.A.)
Okhotsk (U.S.S.R.)
Palermo (It.)
Piraeus (Gr.)
Rangoon (Burma)
Rostock (E. Ger.)
Salerno (It.)
San Juan (Puerto Rico)
Seattle (U.S.A.)
Stettin (Pol.)
Swansea (Wales)
Tallinn (U.S.S.R.)
Tangier (Moroc.)
Tilbury (Eng.)
Tobarao (Braz.)

Trapani (It.)
Trieste (It.)
Tripoli (Libya)
Yingkow (China)
Youghal (Ire.)

8

Abù Dhabi
Adelaide (Austral.)
Alicante (Sp.)
Arrecife (Sp.)
Auckland (N.Z.)
Benghazi (Libya)
Bordeaux (Fr.)
Boulogne (Fr.)
Brindisi (It.)
Brisbane (Austral.)
Budapest (Hung.)
Calcutta (Ind.)
Cape Town (S.A.)
Cocanada (Ind.)
Coquimbo (Chile)
Cuxhaven (W. Ger.)
Damietta (Egypt)
Djibouti (Djibouti)
Dunleary (Ire.)
Elsinore (Den.)
Europort (Neth.)
Falmouth (Eng.)
Flushing (Neth.)
Freetown (Sierra Leone
Gisborne (N.Z.)
Göteborg (Swed.)
Greenock (Scot.)
Hakodate (Jap.)
Halmstad (Swed.)
Helsinki (Fin.)
Holyhead (Wales)
Honfleur (Fr.)
Hong Kong
Honolulu (Hawaii)
Istanbul (Turk.)
Kakinada (Ind.)
Kingston (Jam.)
La Guiara (Venez.)
La Coruña (Sp.)
Llanelli (Wales)
Macassar (Indo.)
Makassar (Indo.)
Matarini (Peru)
Montreal (Can.)
Moulmein (Burma)
Nagasaki (Jap.)
Nakhodka (U.S.S.R.)
Navarino (Gr.)
Newhaven (Eng.)
New Haven (U.S.A.)
Nyköping (Swed.)
Paradeep (Indo.)
Pechenga (U.S.S.R.)
Pembroke (Wales)
Penzance (Eng.)
Plymouth (Eng.)
Portland (Eng.)
Port Said (Egypt)
St. Helier (Ch. Is.)
Sandwich (Eng.)
Szczecin (Pol.)
Shanghai (China)
Taganrog (U.S.S.R.)

Takoradi (Ghana)
Tamatave (Malag. Rep.)
Tientsin (China)
Tiksi Bay (U.S.S.R.)
Vera Cruz (Mex.)
Weymouth (Eng.)
Yokohama (Jap.)

9

Algeciras (Sp.)
Amsterdam (Neth.)
Archangel (U.S.S.R.)
Ardrossan (Scot.)
Avonmouth (Eng.)
Baltimore (U.S.A.)
Barcelona (Sp.)
Cartagena (Sp. and
  Colombia)
Cherbourg (Fr.)
Churchill (Can.)
Cristobal (Panama)
Devonport (Eng.)
Dubrovnik (Yug.)
Esquimalt (Can.)
Essaouira (Moroc.)
Flensburg (W. Ger.)
Fos-sur-Mer (Fr.)
Freemantle (Austral.)
Galveston (U.S.A.)
Gibraltar (Med.)
Gravesend (Eng.)
Guayaquil (Equador)
Helsingör (Den.)
Hiroshima (Jap.)
Kagoshima (Jap.)
Kaohsiung (Taiwan)
King's Lynn (Eng.)
Kolobrzeg (Pol.)
Las Palmas (Sp.)
Leningrad (U.S.S.R.)
Liverpool (Eng.)
Lyttelton (N.Z.)
Mbuji-Mayi (Zaïre)
Melbourne (Austral.)
Mossel Bay (S.A.)
Nantucket (U.S.A.
Newcastle (Eng. and
  Austral.)
Owen Sound (Can.)
Port Arzew (Alg.)
Pensacola (U.S.A.)
Port Klang (Malay.)
Port Louis (Mauritius)
Portmadoc (Wales)
Port Mahon (Sp.)

Port Natal (S.A.)
Porto Novo (Benin)
Port Royal (Jam.)
Port Sudan (Sudan)
Rotterdam (Neth.)
Scapa Flow (Scot.)
Sheerness (Eng.)
Singapore
Stavangar (Nor.)
Stockholm (Swed.)
Stornaway (Scot.)
Trondheim (Nor.)
Vancouver (Can.)
Zeebrugge (Belg.)

10

Alexandria (Egypt)
Barnstaple (Eng.)
Bridgeport (U.S.A.)
Casablanca (Moroc.)
Charleston (U.S.A.)
Chittagong (Ind.)
Colchester (Eng.)
Constantsa (Rom.)
Copenhagen (Den.)
East London (S.A.)
Felixstowe (Eng.)
Folkestone (Eng.)
George Town (Malay.)
Gothenburg (Swed.)
Hammerfest (Nor.)
Hartlepool (Eng.)
Hermopolis (Gr.)
Jersey City (U.S.A.)
La Rochelle (Fr.)
Los Angeles (U.S.A.)
Marseilles (Fr.)
Montego Bay (Jam.)
Montevideo (Uruguay)
New Bedford (U.S.A.)
New Orleans (U.S.A.)
Nouadhibou (Mauretania)
Pernambuco (Braz.)
Perth Amboy (U.S.A.)
Port Arthur (China)
Portsmouth (Eng. and
  U.S.A.)
Rock Harbour (U.S.A.)
San Juan Bay (Peru)
Simonstown (S.A.)
Sunderland (Eng.)
Teignmouth (Eng.)
Travemünde (W. Ger.)
Vlissingen (Neth.)
Whitstable (Eng.)

11

Bremerhaven (W. Ger.)
Buenos Aires (Arg.)
Christiana (Nor.)
Cinque Ports (Eng.)
Dar es Salaam (Tanz.)
Dun Laoghaire (Ire.)
Grangemouth (Scot.)
Helsingborg (Swed.)
Hermoupolis (Gr.)
Masulipatam (Ind.)
Pearl Harbor (Hawaii)
Pondicherry (Ind.)
Port Glasgow (Scot.)
Port Jackson (Austral.)
Port Moresby (Papua)
Port of Spain (Trinidad)
Richard's Bay (S.A.)
Saint Helier (Ch. Is.)
St. Peter Port (Ch. Is.)
Shimonoseki (Jap.)
Southampton (Eng.)
Three Rivers (Can.)
Trincomalee (Ind.)
Vladivostok (U.S.S.R.)

12

Barranquilla (Colombia)
Buenaventura (Colombia)
Kotakinabalu (Malay.)
Masulipatnam (Ind.)
Mina al-Ahmadi (Kuwait)
Milford Haven (Wales)
North Shields (Eng.)
Port Adelaide (Austral.)
Port Harcourt (Nig.)
Port Sunlight (Eng.)
Puerto Hierro (Venez.)
Rio de Janeiro (Braz.)
San Francisco (U.S.A.)

13 AND 14

Christiansund (Nor.) (13)
Constantinople (Turk.) (14)
Frederikshavn (Den.) (13)
Middlesbrough (Eng.) (13)
Mina Hassan Tani (Moroc.) (14)
Petropavlovsk (U.S.S.R.) (13)
Port Elizabeth (S.A.) (13)
Puerto Cabello (Venez.) (13)
Santiago de Cuba (Cuba) (14)
Wilhelmshaven (W. Ger.) (13)

Provinces, cantons, districts, regions, dependent states, etc.

3 AND 4

Ain (Fr.)
Aube (Fr.)
Aude (Fr.)
Bari (It.)
Bern (Swit.)
Cher (Fr.)
Diu (Ind.)
Eure (Fr.)
Fars (Iran)

Gard (Fr.)
Gaza (Isr.)
Gers (Fr.)
Goa (Ind.)
Ica (Peru)
Iowa (U.S.A.)
Jaen (Sp.)
Jura (Fr.)
Kano (Nig.)
Kum (Iran)
Leon (Sp.)

Lima (Peru)
Lot (Fr.)
Lugo (Sp.)
Nord (Fr.)
Ohio (U.S.A.)
Oise (Fr.)
Orne (Fr.)
Oudh (Ind.)
Pale (The) (Ire.)
Para (Braz.)
Pegu (Burma)

Pisa (It.)
Rome (It.)
Saar (Ger.)
Sind (Pak.)
Sus (Moroc.)
Tarn (Fr.)
Uri (Swit.)
Utah (U.S.A.)
Var (Fr.)
Vaud (Swit.)
Zug (Swit.)

5

Achin (Indo.)
Adana (Turk.)
Aisne (Fr.)
Anjou (Fr.)
Assam (Ind.)
Baden (Ger.)
Bahia (Braz.)
Banat (Eur.)
Basel (Swit.)
Béarn (Fr.)
Beira (Port.)
Berne (Swit.)
Berry (Fr.)
Bihar (Ind.)
Cadiz (Sp.)
Ceara (Braz.)
Doubs (Fr.)
Drome (Fr.)
Eifel (Ger.)
Eupen (Belg.)
Fayum (Egypt)
Genoa (It.)
Goiás (Braz.)
Hamar (Nor.)
Hejaz (Saudi)
Herat (Afghan.)
Hesse (Ger.)
Honan (China)
Hopeh (China)
Hunan (China)
Hupeh (China)
Idaho (U.S.A.)
Indre (Fr.)
Isère (Fr.)
Judea (Asia)
Jujuy (Arg.)
Kansu (China)
Khiva (Asia)
Kirin (China)
Kwara (Nig.)
Lagos (Nig.)
La Paz (Boliv.)
Lecce (It.)
Liège (Belg.)
Loire (Fr.)
Lucca (It.)
Maine (U.S.A. and Fr.)
Marne (Fr.)
Meuse (Fr.)
Milan (It.)
Morea (Gr.)
Namur (Belg.)
Nubia (Sudan)
Ojaca (Mex.)
Oruro (Boliv.)
Otago (N.Z.)
Padua (It.)
Parma (It.)
Pavia (It.)
Perak (Malay.)
Posen (Pol.)
Rhône (Fr.)
R.S.F.S.R. (U.S.S.R.)
Sabah (Malay.)
Sahel (Af.)
Salta (Arg.)
Savoy (It.)
Seine (Fr.)
Simla (Ind.)
Sivas (Turk.)
Somme (Fr.)
Surat (Ind.)
Tacna (Chile)
Tavoy (Burma)

Tepic (Mex.)
Terai (Ind.)
Texas (U.S.A.)
Tibet (China)
Tigre (Eth.)
Tokay (Hung.)
Tomsk (U.S.S.R.)
Tyrol (Aust.)
Vizeu (Port.)
Weald (The) (Eng.)
Yonne (Fr.)
Yukon (Can.)

6

Aargau (Swit.)
Alaska (U.S.A.)
Alisco (Mex.)
Allier (Fr.)
Alsace (Fr.)
Anhwei (China)
Apulia (It.)
Aragon (Sp.)
Ariège (Fr.)
Artois (Fr.)
Bashan (Asia)
Basque Prov.
Bengal (Ind.)
Bergen (Nor.)
Biscay (Sp.)
Bombay (Ind.)
Bosnia (Yug.)
Cachar (Ind.)
Creuse (Fr.)
Crimea (U.S.S.R.)
Dakota (U.S.A.)
Darfur (Sudan)
Emilia (It.)
Epirus (Gr.)
Faenza (It.)
Fukien (China)
Geneva (Swit.)
Gerona (Sp.)
Ghilan (Iran)
Glarus (Swit.)
Guiana (S. Am.)
Hawaii (U.S.A.)
Hedjaz (Saudi)
Huelva (Sp.)
Huesca (Sp.)
Iloilo (Philip.)
Johore (Ind.)
Judaea (Asia)
Kansas (U.S.A.)
Karroo (S.A.)
Kaspan (Iran)
Kerala (Ind.)
Kerman (Iran)
Kielce (Pol.)
Ladakh (Ind.)
Landes (Fr.)
Latium (It.)
Latvia (U.S.S.R.)
Lerida (Sp.)
Levant (Asia)
Loiret (Fr.)
Loreto (Port.)
Lozère (Fr.)
Lublin (Pol.)
Madras (Ind.)
Málaga (Sp.)
Manche (Fr.)
Mantua (It.)
Marico (S.A.)
Mercia (Eng.)

Mergui (Burma)
Modena (It.)
Molise (It.)
Murcia (Sp.)
Mysore (Ind.)
Nelson (N.Z.)
Nevada (U.S.A.)
Nièvre (Fr.)
Novara (It.)
Oaxaca (Mex.)
Oregon (U.S.A.)
Orense (Sp.)
Orissa (Ind.)
Oviedo (Sp.)
Pahang (Malay.)
Pampas (S. Am.)
Paraná (Braz.)
Poitou (Fr.)
Potosi (Boliv.)
Punjab (Ind. and Pak.)
Quebec (Can.)
Rivers (Nig.)
Sahara (Af.)
St. Gall (Swit.)
Sarthe (Fr.)
Saxony (Ger.)
Scania (Swed.)
Schwyz (Swit.)
Scinde (Ind.)
Serbia (Yug.)
Shansi (China)
Shensi (China)
Sicily (It.)
Sokoto (Nig.)
Sonora (Mex.)
Soudan (Af.)
Styria (Aust.)
Swabia (Ger.)
Sylhet (Ind.)
Thrace (Gr.)
Ticino (Swit.)
Toledo (Sp.)
Tromsø (Nor.)
Ulster (N.I.)
Umbria (It.)
Upsala (Swed.)
Valais (Swit.)
Vendée (Fr.)
Veneto (It.)
Viborg (Den.)
Vienne (Fr.)
Vosges (Fr.)
Wessex (Eng.)
Yunnan (China)
Zamora (Sp.)
Zurich (Swit.)

7

Abruzzi (It.)
Alabama (U.S.A.)
Alagoas (Braz.)
Alberta (Can.)
Algarve (Port.)
Almeria (Sp.)
Antwerp (Belg.)
Arizona (U.S.A.)
Armenia (U.S.S.R.)
Aveyron (Fr.)
Bavaria (Ger.)
Bohemia (Cze.)
Bokhara (Asia)
Brabant (Belg.)
Caceres (Sp.)
Castile (Sp.)

Chiapas (Mex.)
Corrèze (Fr.)
Côte-d'Or (Fr.)
Croatia (Yug.)
Drenthe (Neth.)
Durango (Mex.)
Eritrea (Eth.)
Estonia (U.S.S.R.)
Ferrara (It.)
Finmark (Nor.)
Florida (U.S.A.)
Galicia (Pol. and Sp.)
Galilee (Isr.)
Gascony (Fr.)
Georgia (U.S.S.R. and
　U.S.A.)
Granada (Sp.)
Grisons (Swit.)
Guienne (Fr.)
Gujarat (Ind.)
Hanover (Ger.)
Haryana (Ind.)
Hérault (Fr.)
Hidalgo (Mex.)
Holland (Neth.)
Huanuco (Peru)
Indiana (U.S.A.)
Iquique (Chile)
Jalisco (Mex.)
Jutland (Den.)
Karelia (U.S.S.R.)
Kashmir (Ind. and Pak.)
Kiangsi (China)
Lapland (Eur.)
Leghorn (It.)
Liguria (It.)
Limburg (Neth.)
Linares (Chile)
Logroño (Sp.)
Lucerne (Swit.)
Malacca (Malay.)
Manipur (Ind.)
Marches (It.)
Mayenne (Fr.)
Mendoza (Arg.)
Montana (U.S.A.)
Moravia (Cze.)
Munster (Ire.)
Navarre (Sp.)
New York (U.S.A.)
Ontario (Can.)
Orléans (Fr.)
Paraíba (Braz.)
Perugia (It.)
Picardy (Fr.)
Potenza (It.)
Prussia (Ger.)
Ravenna (It.)
Riviera (The) (Fr., It.)
Samaria (Asia)
Santa Fé (Arg.)
Sarawak (Malay.)
Segovia (Sp.)
Sennaar (Sudan)
Sergipe (Braz.)
Seville (Sp.)
Siberia (U.S.S.R.)
Silesia (Pol.)
Simaloa (Mex.)
Sondrio (It.)
Tabasco (Mex.)
Tafilet (Moroc.)
Tanjore (Ind.)
Teheran (Iran)
Thurgau (Swit.)
Tripura (Ind.)

Tucuman (Arg.)
Tuscany (It.)
Ukraine (U.S.S.R.)
Utrecht (Neth.)
Venetia (It.)
Vermont (U.S.A.)
Waldeck (Ger.)
Western (Nig.)
Wyoming (U.S.A.)
Yucatan (Mex.)
Zealand ⎱
Zeeland ⎰ (Neth.)

8

Alentejo (Port.)
Alicante (Sp.)
Amazonas (Braz.)
Anatolia (Turk.)
Ardennes (Fr.)
Arkansas (U.S.A.)
Asturias (Sp.)
Auckland (N.Z.)
Brittany (Fr.)
Bukovina (Eur.)
Burgundy (Fr.)
Calabria (It.)
Calvados (Fr.)
Campania (It.)
Campeche (Mex.)
Carniola (Aust.)
Carolina (U.S.A.)
Caucasia (U.S.S.R.)
Charente (Fr.)
Chekiang (China)
Coahuila (Mex.)
Colorado (U.S.A.)
Columbia (U.S.A.)
Dalmatia (Yug.)
Dauphiné (Fr.)
Delaware (U.S.A.)
Dordogne (Fr.)
Ferghana (Turk.)
Flanders (Belg.)
Florence (It.)
Fribourg (Swit.)
Girgenti (It.)
Gothland (Swed.)
Guerrero (Mex.)
Hainault (Belg.)
Hannover (Ger.)
Haut Rhin (Fr.)
Hawke Bay (N.Z.)
Holstein (Ger.)
Illinois (U.S.A.)
Kandahar (Afghan.)
Kentucky (U.S.A.)
Kirgizia (U.S.S.R.)
Korassan (Iran)
Kordofan (Sudan)
Kweichow (China)
Labrador (Can.)
Leinster (Ire.)
Liaoning (China)
Limousin (Fr.)
Lombardy (It.)
Lorraine (Fr.)
Lothians (The) (Scot.)
Lowlands (Scot.)
Luristan (Iran)
Lyonnais (Fr.)
Macerata (It.)
Manitoba (Can.)
Maranhao (Braz.)
Maryland (U.S.A.)

Michigan (U.S.A.)
Missouri (U.S.A.)
Moldavia (Rom. and
　U.S.S.R.)
Mongolia (China and
　U.S.S.R.)
Morbihan (Fr.)
Nagaland (Ind.)
Nebraska (U.S.A.)
Normandy (Fr.)
Norrland (Swed.)
Oberland (Swit.)
Oklahoma (U.S.A.)
Palencia (Sp.)
Parahiba (Braz.)
Peshawar (Ind.)
Piacenza (It.)
Piedmont (It.)
Provence (Fr.)
Roumelia (Turk.)
Ruthenia (Eur.)
Saarland (Ger.)
Salonika (Gr.)
Salzburg (Aust.)
Sardinia (It.)
Shantung (China)
Sinkiang (China)
Slavonia (Eur.)
Slovakia (Cze.)
Slovenia (Yug.)
Syracuse (It.)
Szechwan (China)
Taranaki (N.Z.)
Tarapaca (Chile)
Thessaly (Gr.)
Tiaxcala (Mex.)
Tongking (Asia)
Trentino (It.)
Tsinghai (China)
Valdivia (Chile)
Valencia (Sp.)
Vaucluse (Fr.)
Vera Cruz (Mex.)
Victoria (Austral.)
Virginia (U.S.A.)
Wallonia (Belg.)
Westland (N.Z.)
Wimmeria (Austral.)

9

Alto Adige (It.)
Andalusia (Sp.)
Appenzell (Swit.)
Aquitaine (Fr.)
Asia Minor (Asia)
Astrakhan (U.S.S.R.)
Carinthia (Aust.)
Catalonia (Sp.)
Champagne (Fr.)
Chihuahua (Mex.)
Connaught (Ire.)
Dakahlieh (Egypt)
Entre Rios (Arg.)
Franconia (Ger.)
Friesland (Neth.)
Groningen (Neth.)
Guipuzcoa (Sp.)
Hadramaut (Arab.)
Highlands (Scot.)
Kamchatka (U.S.S.R.)
Karnataka (Ind.)
Khuzestan (Iran)
Kwangtung (China)
Languedoc (Fr.)

105

Linköping (Swed.)
Lithuania (U.S.S.R.)
Louisiana (U.S.A.)
Macedonia (Gr.)
Meghalaya (Ind.)
Melanesia (Pac.)
Michoacan (Mex.)
Minnesota (U.S.A.)
Neuchâtel (Swit.)
New Forest (Eng.)
New Jersey (U.S.A.)
New Mexico (U.S.A.)
Nivernais (Fr.)
Nuevo Leon (Mex.)
Oedenburg (Hung.)
Oldenburg (Ger.)
Overyssel (Neth.)
Palestine (Asia)
Patagonia (S. Am.)
Polynesia (Pac.)
Pomerania (Ger. and Pol.)
Potteries (The) (Eng.)
Queretaro (Mex.)
Rajasthan (Ind.)
Rajputana (Ind.)
Rhineland (Ger.)
Saint Gall (Swit.)
Salamanca (Sp.)
Samarkand (Asia)
Saragossa (Sp.)
Schleswig (Ger.)
Southland (N.Z.)
Tamil Nadu (Ind.)
Tarragona (Sp.)
Tennessee (U.S.A.)
Thayetmyo (Burma)
Thuringia (Ger.)
Transvaal (S.A.)
Trebizond (Turk.)
Trondheim (Nor.)
Turkestan (Asia)
Turkistan (Asia)
Turkmenia (Asia)
Villareal (Port.)
Wallachia (Rom.)
Wisconsin (U.S.A.)
Zacatecas (Mex.)

10

Adrianople (Turk.)
Azerbaijan (U.S.S.R.)
Baffinland (Can.)
Basilicata (It.)
Belorussia (U.S.S.R.)
Bessarabia (U.S.S.R.)
Burgenland (Aust.)
California (U.S.A.)
Canterbury (N.Z.)
East Africa
East Anglia (Eng.)
Eure-et-Loir (Fr.)
Gelderland (Neth.)
Griqualand (S.A.)
Guanajuato (Mex.)
Haute-Loire (Fr.)
Haute-Marne (Fr.)
Haute-Saône (Fr.)
Kazakhstan (U.S.S.R.)
Kermanshah (Iran)
Lambayeque (Peru)
Loir-et-Cher (Fr.)
Mazandaran (Iran)
Micronesia (Pac.)
Mid-Western (Nig.)

Montenegro (Yug.)
New Castile (Sp.)
Nova Scotia (Can.)
Old Castile (Sp.)
Overijssel (Neth.)
Palatinate (Ger.)
Pernambuco (Braz.)
Pontevedra (Sp.)
Queensland (Austral.)
Rawalpindi (Pak.)
Rohilkhand (Ind.)
Roussillon (Fr.)
Senegambia (Af.)
Slave Coast (Af.)
Tamaulipas (Mex.)
Tavastehus (Fin.)
Tenasserim (Burma)
Valladolid (Sp.)
Valparaiso (Chile)
Vorarlberg (Aust.)
Washington (U.S.A.)
Waziristan (Pak.)
West Africa
West Bengal (Ind.)
West Indies (Carib.)
Westphalia (Ger.)

11

Baluchistan (Pak.)
Bourbonnais (Fr.)
Brandenburg (Ger.)
Byelorussia (U.S.S.R.)
Connecticut (U.S.A.)
Côtes-du-Nord (Fr.)
East-Central (Nig.)
Estremadura (Port. and Sp.)
Great Karroo (S.A.)
Guadalajara (Sp.)
Guelderland (Neth.)
Hautes-Alpes (Fr.)
Haute-Savoie (Fr.)
Haute-Vienne (Fr.)
Herzegovina (Yug.)
Hesse-Nassau (Ger.)
Ile-de-France (Fr.)
Lower Saxony (Ger.)
Maharashtra (Ind.)
Matto Grosso (Braz.)
Mecklenburg (Ger.)
Minas Gerais (Braz.)
Mississippi (U.S.A.)
North Africa
North Dakota (U.S.A.)
Northumbria (Eng.)
Pas de Calais (Fr.)
Peloponnese (Gr.)
Quintana Roo (Mex.)
Rhode Island (U.S.A.)
Schwarzwald (Ger.)
South Dakota (U.S.A.)
Sudetenland (Ger.)
The Lothians (Scot.)
Unterwalden (Swit.)
Uzbekhistan (U.S.S.R.)
Valle d'Aosta (It.)
West Prussia (Pol.)
White Russia (U.S.S.R.)
Württemberg (Ger.)

12

Benue-Plateau (Nig.)
British Isles (Eur.)

Franche-Comté (Fr.)
Haute-Garonne (Fr.)
Heilungkiang (China)
Hohenzollern (Ger.)
Huancavelica (Peru)
Indre-et-Loire (Fr.)
Latin America
Little Russia (U.S.S.R.)
Lot-et-Garonne (Fr.)
Lower Austria (Aust.)
New Brunswick (Can.)
Newfoundland (Can.)
New Hampshire (U.S.A.)
North Brabant (Neth.)
North-Central (Nig.)
North-Eastern (Nig.)
North Holland (Neth.)
North-Western (Nig.)
Pennsylvania (U.S.A.)
Rio de Janeiro (Braz.)
Saskatchewan (Can.)
Schaffhausen (Swit.)
Schleswig-Holstein (Ger.)
Seine-et-Marne (Fr.)
South-Eastern (Nig.)
South Holland (Neth.)
Tadzhikistan (U.S.S.R.)
The Potteries (Eng.)
Transylvania (Rom.)
Turkmenistan (U.S.S.R.)
Upper Austria (Aust.)
Uttar Pradesh (Ind.)
West Virginia (U.S.A.)

13

Andhra Pradesh (Ind.)
Canary Islands (Sp.)
Christiansand (Nor.)
Emilia-Romagna (It.)
Espirito Santo (Braz.)
Ille-et-Vilaine (Fr.)
Inner Mongolia (China)
Madhya Pradesh (Ind.)
Massachusetts (U.S.A.)
New South Wales (Austral.)
North Carolina (U.S.A.)
Outer Mongolia (U.S.S.R.)
Rhondda Valley (Wales)
Romney Marshes (Eng.)
San Luis Potosi (Mex.)
Santa Catarina (Braz.)
Saxe-Altenberg (Ger.)
Saxe-Meiningen (Ger.)
South Carolina (U.S.A.)
Tarn-et-Garonne (Fr.)
Transbaikalia (U.S.S.R.)
Witwatersrand (S.A.)

14 AND OVER

Alpes-Maritimes (Fr.) (14)
Alsace-Lorraine (Fr.) (14)
Baden-Württemberg (Ger.) (16)
Baltic Provinces (U.S.S.R.) (15)
Basque Provinces (Sp.) (14)
Bihar and Orissa (Ind.) (14)
British Columbia (Can.) (15)
Central America (14)
Channel Islands (U.K.) (14)
District of Columbia (U.S.A.) (18)

Entre-Douro-e-Minho (Port.) (16)
Griqualand West (S.A.) (14)
Hautes-Pyrénées (Fr.) (14)
Himachal Pradesh (Ind.) (15)
Loire-Atlantique (Fr.) (15)
Lower California (Mex.) (15)
Northern Ireland (U.K.) (15)

North Rhine-Westphalia (Ger.) (20)
North-West Frontier (Pak.) (17)
Orange Free State (S.A.) (15)
Rhenish Prussia (Ger.) (14)
Rio Grande do Sul (Braz.) (14)
Santa Catharina (Braz.) (14)

Saxe-Coburg-Gotha (Ger.) (15)
Schaumburg-Lippe (Ger.) (15)
South Australia (Austral.) (14)
Southern Africa (14)
United Provinces (Ind.) (15)
Western Australia (Austral.) (16)

Rivers

R. = River, and is inserted where "River" commonly follows the name.

1–3

Aar (Swit.)
Ain (Fr.)
Aln (Eng.)
Axe (Eng.)
Bug (Pol., U.S.S.R.)
Cam (Eng.)
Dee (Eng.)
Don (Scot.)
Ems (Ger.)
Esk (Scot.)
Exe (Eng.)
Fal (Eng.)
Fly (Papua)
Hex R. (S.A.)
Hsi (China)
Hue (Asia)
Ili (Asia)
Ill (Fr.)
Inn (Aust.)
Ket (Sib.)
Kur (U.S.S.R.)
Kwa (Af.)
Lea (Eng.)
Lee (Ire.)
Lek (Neth.)
Lot (Fr.)
Lys (Fr. and Belg.)
Nen (Eng.)
Ob (Sib.)
Oka (U.S.S.R.)
Po (It.)
Red R. (U.S.A.)
Rur (Eur.)
Rye (Eng.)
Sid (Eng.)
Sow (Eng.)
Syr (U.S.S.R.)
Taw (Eng.)
Tay (Scot.)
Tom (Sib.)
Ure (Eng.)
Usa (U.S.S.R.)
Usk (Wales)
Var (Fr.)
Wey (Eng.)
Wye (Eng.)
Wye (Wales)
Y (Neth.)
Yeo (Eng.)
Zab (Turk.)

4

Adda (It.)
Adur (Eng.)
Aire (Eng.)

Aire (Scot.)
Alma (U.S.S.R.)
Amur (Asia)
Anio (It.)
Arno (It.)
Arun (Eng.)
Avon (Eng.)
Bann (N.I.)
Beas (Ind.)
Bure (Eng.)
Cart (Scot.)
Cher (Fr.)
Cole (Eng.)
Coln (Eng.)
Dart (Eng.)
Doon (Scot.)
Dora (It.)
Dove (Eng.)
Duna (U.S.S.R.)
Earn (Scot.)
Ebro (Sp.)
Eden (Eng.)
Eden (Scot.)
Elbe (Ger.)
Enns (Aust.)
Erne (Ire.)
Fall (U.S.A.)
Geba (W. Af.)
Gila (U.S.A.)
Gota (Swed.)
Ha Ha (Can.)
Isar (Ger.)
Isis (Eng.)
Juba (E. Af.)
Kama (U.S.S.R.)
Kusi (Ind.)
Lahn (Ger.)
Lech (Ger.)
Lena (Sib.)
Loir (Fr.)
Lune (Eng.)
Lynd (Austral.)
Maas (Neth.)
Main (Ger.)
Main (Ire.)
Mole (Eng.)
Mooi (S. A.)
Naze (Eng.)
Neva (U.S.S.R.)
Nida (U.S.S.R.)
Nile (Af.)
Nith (Scot.)
Oder (Cze, E. Ger., Pol.)
Ohio (U.S.A.)
Oise (Fr.)
Ouse (Eng.)
Oxus (Asia)
Peel (Austral.)

Peel (Can.)
Pina (U.S.S.R.)
Prah (Af.)
Ravi (Ind.)
Rede (Eng.)
Roer (Eur.)
Ruhr (Ger.)
Saar (Fr., Ger.)
Salt R. (U.S.A.)
Save (Fr.)
Spey (Scot.)
Styr (Spain)
Suck (Ire.)
Suir (Ire.)
Swan (Austral.)
Taff (Wales)
Tana (E. Af.)
Tara (Sib.)
Tarn (Fr.)
Tawe (Wales)
Tees (Eng.)
Test (Eng.)
Thur (Swit.)
Tons (Ind.)
Towy (Wales)
Tyne (Eng.)
Umea (Swed.)
Ural (U.S.S.R.)
Vaal (S. Af.)
Vire (Fr.)
Waag (Hung.)
Waal (Neth.)
Wash (Eng.)
Wear (Eng.)
Yana (Sib.)
Yare (Eng.)

5

Abana (Syr.)
Adige (It.)
Adour (Fr.)
Agout (Fr.)
Aisne (Fr.)
Alice (Austral.)
Allan (Scot.)
Allen (Scot.)
Aller (Ger.)
Annan (Scot.)
Avoca (Austral.)
Benue (W. Af.)
Black R. (U.S.A.)
Blood R. (S. A.)
Bober (Ger.)
Bogie (Scot.)
Boyne (Ire.)
Brent (Eng.)
Bride (Ire.)

Camel (Eng.)
Clyde (Scot.)
Colne (Eng.)
Congo (Af.)
Desna (U.S.S.R.)
Devon (Scot.)
Douro (Port., Sp.)
Dovey (Wales)
Drave (Hung.)
Drina (Yug.)
Eider (Ger.)
Etive (Scot.)
Feale (Ire.)
Forth (Scot.)
Foyle (Ire.)
Frome (Eng.)
Gogra (Ind.)
Green R. (U.S.A.)
Gumti (Ind.)
Habra (N. Af.)
Havel (Ger.)
Huang (China)
Hugli (Ind.)
Hunza (Ind.)
Ikopa (E. Af.)
Indus (Ind.)
Isère (Fr.)
Ishim (U.S.S.R.)
James R. (U.S.A.)
Jelum (Ind.)
Jumna (Ind.)
Kabul R. (Afghan.)
Kafue (Af.)
Karun (Iran.)
Katun (Sib.)
Koros (Hung.)
Kowie (S.A.)
Kuram (Afghan.)
Lagan (N. Ire.)
Lenea (U.S.S.R.)
Leven (Scot.)
Liard (Can.)
Loire (Fr.)
Marne (Fr.)
Maroo (Rom.)
Memel (Ger.)
Menam (China)
Meuse (Belg.)
Miami (U.S.A.)
Minho (Port. and Sp.)
Moose (Can.)
Neath (Wales)
Neuse (U.S.A.)
Niger (Af.)
Oglio (It.)
Onega (U.S.S.R.)
Otter (Eng.)
Peace R. (Can.)
Pecos (U.S.A.)

Pei Ho (China)
Perak (Malay.)
Plate (S. Am.)
Pruth (Rom.)
Purus (S. Am.)
Rance (Fr.)
Reuss (Swit.)
Rhine
(Ger., Neth., Swit.)
Rhone (Fr., Swit.)
Saale (Ger.)
Saone (Fr.)
Seine (Fr.)
Shari (E. Af.)
Sheaf (Eng.)
Shiel (Scot.)
Shire (Af.)
Snake R. (U.S.A.)
Somme (Fr.)
Spree (Ger.)
Stolp (U.S.S.R.)
Stour (Eng.)
Sugar (U.S.A.)
Sulir (Swit.)
Swale (Eng.)
Tagus (Port.)
Tamar (Eng.)
Tapti (Ind.)
Tarim (China)
Teffe (S. Am.)
Teifi (Wales)
Teign (Eng.)
Teith (Scot.)
Temes (Hung.)
Tiber (It.)
Tisza (Hung.)
Traun (Aust.)
Trent (Can.)
Trent (Eng.)
Tweed (Scot.)
Usuri (Asia)
Volga (U.S.S.R.)
Volta (W. Af.)
Warta (Pol.)
Welle (Af.)
Werra (Ger.)
Weser (Ger.)
Xiugo (S. Am.)
Yonne (Fr.)
Yssel (Neth.)
Yukon (Can.)
Zaïre (Af.)
Zenta (Hung.)

6

Agogno (It.)
Aguada (Sp.)
Alagon (Sp.)
Albany (Can.)
Albert (Austral.)
Allier (Fr.)
Amazon (S. Am.)
Angara (U.S.S.R.)
Arinos (S. Am.)
Atbara (Af.)
Barrow (Ire.)
Barwon (Austral.)
Beauly (Scot.)
Bolsas (Mex.)
Brazos (U.S.A.)
Buller (N.Z.)
Calder (Eng.)

Canton R. (China)
Caroni (S. Am.)
Carron (Scot.)
Chenab (Ind.)
Coquet (Eng.)
Crouch (Eng.)
Danube (Eur.)
Dihong (Ind.)
Draava (Hung.)
Elster (Ger.)
Foyers (Scot.)
Fraser (Can.)
French (Can.)
Gambia (Af.)
Gandak (Ind.)
Ganges (Ind.)
Grande (S. Am.)
Grande (U.S.A., Mex.)
Grande (W. Af.)
Hamble (Eng.)
Hawash (E. Af.)
Hudson (U.S.A.)
Humber (Eng.)
Irtish (U.S.S.R.)
Irwell (Eng.)
Itchen (Eng.)
Japura (Braz.)
Jhelum (Ind.)
Jordan
(Isr., Jord., Syria)
Kagera (Af.)
Kaveri (Ind.)
Kennet (Eng.)
Komati (E. Af.)
Kwanza (W. Af.)
Lehigh (U.S.A.)
Leitha (Hung.)
Liffey (Ire.)
Loddon (Eng.)
Loddon (Austral.)
Lomami (Af.)
Medina (Eng.)
Medway (Eng.)
Mekong (Asia)
Mersey (Eng.)
Mincio (It.)
Mobile (U.S.A.)
Modder R. (S.A.)
Mohawk (U.S.A.)
Moldau (Cze.)
Monnow (Eng.)
Morava (Cze.)
Moskva (U.S.S.R.)
Murray R. (Austral.)
Neckar (Ger.)
Neisse (Ger.)
Nelson (Can.)
Neutra (Hung.)
Niemen (U.S.S.R.)
Ogowai (Af.)
Oneida (U.S.A.)
Orange (S.A.)
Orwell (Eng.)
Ottawa (Can.)
Paraná (S. Am.)
Parima (Braz.)
Parret (Eng.)
Platte (U.S.A.)
Porali (Ind.)
Pungwe (E. Af.)
Pungwe (S.A.)
Racket (U.S.A.)
Ribble (Eng.)
Roding (Eng.)
Rother (Eng.)
Rovuma (E. Af.)

Rufiji (E. Af.)
Sabine (U.S.A.)
Sarthe (Fr.)
St. Paul (W. Af.)
Salwin (Burma)
Sambre (Belg., Fr.)
Santee (U.S.A.)
Scioto (U.S.A.)
Seneca (U.S.A.)
Sereth (Rom.)
Severn (Can.)
Severn (Eng., Wales)
Slaney (Ire.)
Stroma (Balkans)
Sunday (S.A.)
Sutlej (Ind.)
Sutluj (Ind.)
Swilly (Ire.)
Tamega (Port.)
Tanaro (It.)
Teviot (Scot.)
Thames (Can.)
Thames (Eng.)
Thames (N.Z.)
Theiss (Hung.)
Ticino (Swit.)
Tigris (Iraq., Turk.)
Tormes (Sp.)
Tornio (Fin.)
Tugela (S.A.)
Tummel (Scot.)
Ubangi (Af.)
Viatka (U.S.S.R.)
Vienne (Fr.)
Vltava (Cze.)
Wabash (U.S.A.)
Waihou (N.Z.)
Wandle (Eng.)
Warthe (Pol.)
Weaver (Eng.)
Wensum (Eng.)
Wharfe (Eng.)
Wipper (Ger.)
Witham (Eng.)
Yarrow (Scot.)
Yavari (S. Am.)
Yellow R. (China)
Zarang (Iran)
Zontag (S.A.)

7

Abitibi (Can.)
Alabama (U.S.A.)
Big Blue R. (U.S.A.)
Buffalo (S.A.)
Calabar (Af.)
Catawba (U.S.A.)
Cauvery (Ind.)
Chambal (Ind.)
Chelmer (Eng.)
Chumbal (Ind.)
Darling (Austral.)
Derwent (Eng.)
Deveron (Scot.)
Dnieper (U.S.S.R.)
Dunajec (Pol.)
Durance (Fr.)
Ettrick (Scot.)
Feather (U.S.A.)
Fitzroy (Austral.)
Gamtoos (S.A.)
Garonne (Fr.)

Gauritz (S.A.)
Genesee (U.S.A.)
Gilbert (Austral.)
Glenelg (Austral.)
Glommen (Nor.)
Guapore (S. Am.)
Heri Rud (Afghan.)
Hoang Ho (China)
Hooghli (Ind.)
Hwangho (China)
Juniata (U.S.A.)
Kanawha (Ind.)
Kubango (Af.)
Lachlan (Austral.)
La Plata (S. Am.)
Limpopo (S.A.)
Lualaba (Af.)
Luangwa (Af.)
Lugendi (Af.)
Madeira (S. Am.)
Marañón (S. Am.)
Maritza (Gr.)
Mattawa (Can.)
Mayenne (Fr.)
Meklong (Thail.)
Moselle (Eur.)
Muluyar (N. Af.)
Murghab (Afghan.)
Narbuda (Ind.)
Niagara (N. Am.)
Niagara (U.S.A.)
Olifant (S.A.)
Orinoco (S. Am.)
Orontes (Syria)
Paraıba (S. Am.)
Paraná (Braz.)
Parsnip (Can.)
Passaic (U.S.A.)
Pechora (U.S.S.R)
Potomac (U.S.A.)
Rubicon (It.)
San Juan (S. Am.)
Sankuru (Af.)
St. Johns (U.S.A.)
Salween (Burma)
Schelde (Belg., Neth.)
Scheldt (Belg., Neth.)
Selenga (Asia)
Semliki (Af.)
Senegal (Af.)
Shannon (Ire.)
Spokane (U.S.A.)
Sungari (Asia)
Surinam (S. Am.)
Suwanee (U.S.A.)
Tampico (Mex.)
Tapajos (S. Am.)
Thomson (Austral.)
Tobique (Can.)
Torridge (Eng.)
Trinity (U.S.A.)
Ucayali (S. Am.)
Uruguay (S. Am.)
Vistula (Pol.)
Walkato (N.Z.)
Warrego (Austral.)
Washita (U.S.A.)
Waveney (Eng.)
Welland (Eng.)
Wichita (U.S.A.)
Yangtse (China)
Yarkand (Asia)
Yenesei (Sib.)
Ystwith (Wales)
Yuruari (S. Am.)
Zambezi (Af.)

8

Amu Darya (Asia)
Arkansas (U.S.A.)
Beaulieu (Eng.)
Beresina (U.S.S.R.)
Big Black R. (U.S.A.)
Blue Nile (Af.)
Brisbane R. (Austral.)
Campaspe (Austral.)
Cape Fear R. (U.S.A.)
Chambezi (Af.)
Cherwell (Eng.)
Chindwin (Burma)
Clarence (Austral.)
Colorado R. (U.S.A.)
Columbia (N. Am.)
Delaware (U.S.A.)
Demerara (S. Am.)
Dniester (U.S.S.R.)
Evenlode (Eng.)
Gallinas (W. Af.)
Gatineau (Can.)
Georgina (Austral.)
Godavari (Ind.)
Goulburn (Austral.)
Great Kei (S.A.)
Guadiana (Spain)
Hankiang (China)
Huallaga (S. Am.)
Humboldt (U.S.A.)
Itimbiri (Af.)
Kankakee (U.S.A.)
Kelantan (Malay.)
Kennebec (U.S.A.)
Klondyke R. (Can.)
Kootenay (N. Am.)
Mahanadi (Ind.)
Mazaruni (S. Am.)
Merrimac (U.S.A.)
Missouri (U.S.A.)
Mitchell (Austral.)
Nebraska (U.S.A.)
Ob Irtish (U.S.S.R.)
Paraguay (S. Am.)
Parahiba (S. Am.)
Putumayo (S. Am.)
Red River (U.S.A.)
Richmond (Austral.)
Rimouski (Can.)
Rio Negro (S. Am.)
Rio Tinto (Sp.)
Saguenay (Can.)
St. Claire (Can.)
Santiago (S. Am.)
Savannah (U.S.A.)
Syr Daria (U.S.S.R.)
Tunguska (Sib.)

Umvolosi (S.A.)
Wanganui (N.Z.)
Wansbeck (Eng.)
Windrush (Eng.)
Winnipeg (Can.)

9

Abbitibee (Can.)
Churchill (Can.)
Crocodile R. (S.A.)
East River (U.S.A.)
Esmeralda (S. Am.)
Essequibo (S. Am.)
Euphrates (Iraq., Turk.,
　Syria)
Gala Water (Scot.)
Great Fish R. (S.A.)
Great Ouse (Eng.)
Guadalete (Spain)
Indigirka (U.S.S.R.)
Irrawaddy (Burma)
Kalamazoo (U.S.A.)
Kizil Uzen (Iran)
Mackenzie (Can.)
Mallagami (Can.)
Miramichi (Can.)
Mirimichi (Can.)
Missimabi (Can.)
Nipisquit (Can.)
Paranaíba (S. Am.)
Penobscot (U.S.A.)
Pilcomayo (S. Am.)
Rede River (Eng.)
Rio Branco (S. Am.)
Rio Grande (Braz.)
Rio Grande (U.S.A., Mex.)
Rio Grande (W. Af.)
Saint John (Can.)
Saint Paul (W. Af.)
Salt River (U.S.A.)
Tennessee (U.S.A.)
Tocantins (S. Am.)
Toombudra (Ind.)
Umsimvubu (S.A.)
Umsimkulu (S.A.)
White Nile (Af.)
Wisconsin (U.S.A.)
Zarafshan (Asia)

10

Allenwater (Scot.)
Black River (U.S.A.)
Blackwater (Eng.)

Blackwater (Ire.)
Blood River (S.A.)
Great Slave R. (Can.)
Green River (U.S.A.)
Hawkesbury (Austral.)
Kizil Irmak (Turk.)
Lackawanna (U.S.A.)
Macquarrie (Austral.)
Manzanares (Sp.)
Monagahela (U.S.A.)
Paranahiba (S. Am.)
Parramatta (Austral.)
Sacramento (U.S.A.)
San Joaquin (U.S.A.)
Saint John's (U.S.A.)
St. Lawrence (Can.)
Shat-el-Arab (Asia)
Shenandoah (U.S.A.)
Snake River (U.S.A.)
White River (U.S.A.)
Yarra Yarra (Austral.)

11 AND OVER

Big Black River (U.S.A.)
　(13)
Big Blue River (U.S.A.) (12)
Big Horn River (U.S.A.) (12)
Big Sandy River (U.S.A.)
　(13)
Big Sioux River (U.S.A.)
　(13)
Bonaventure (Can.) (11)
Brahmaputra (Ind.) (11)
Desaguadero (S. Am.) (11)
Ettrickwater (Scot.) (12)
Great Kanawka (U.S.A.)
　(12)
Guadalquivir (Sp.) (12)
Mississippi (U.S.A.) (11)
Modder River (S.A.) (11)
Murray-Darling (Austral.)
　(13)
Rappahannock (U.S.A.) (12)
Restigouche (Can.) (11)
Rio del Norte (Mex.) (11)
Saint Claire (Can.) (11)
Saint Lawrence (Can.) (13)
São Francisco (Braz.) (12)
Saskatchewan (Can.) (12)
Shubenacadia (Can.) (12)
Susquehanna (U.S.A.) (11)
Upper Paraná (S. Am.) (11)
Yangtse Kiang (China) (12)
Yarrowwater (Scot.) (11)
Yellow River (China) (11)

Towns and cities: United Kingdom

(E.) = England.　(N.I.) = Northern Ireland.　(S.) = Scotland.　(W.) = Wales

3 AND 4

Alva (S.)
Ayr (S.)
Bala (W.)
Barr (S.)
Bath (E.)
Bray (E.)
Bude (E.)
Bury (E.)
Clun (E.)
Deal (E.)

Diss (E.)
Duns (S.)
Elie (S.)
Ely (E.)
Eton (E.)
Eye (E.)
Holt (E.)
Holt (W.)
Hove (E.)
Hull (E.)
Hyde (E.)
Ince (E.)

Kirn (S.)
Leek (E.)
Looe (E.)
Luss (S.)
Lydd (E.)
Mold (W.)
Muff (N.I.)
Nigg (S.)
Oban (S.)
Pyle (W.)
Reay (S.)
Rhyl (W.)

Rona (S.)
Ross (E.)
Ryde (E.)
Rye (E.)
Shap (E.)
Stow (S.)
Uig (S.)
Usk (E.)
Ware (E.)
Wark (E.)
Wem (E.)
Wick (S.)

Yarm (E.)
York (E.)

5

Acton (E.)
Alloa (S.)
Alton (E.)
Annan (S.)
Appin (S.)
Avoch (S.)
Ayton (S.)
Bacup (E.)
Banff (S.)
Beith (S.)
Blyth (E.)
Bourn (E.)
Brora (S.)
Bunaw (S.)
Busby (S.)
Calne (E.)
Ceres (S.)
Chard (E.)
Cheam (E.)
Chirk (W.)
Clova (S.)
Clune (S.)
Colne (E.)
Cowes (E.)
Crail (S.)
Crewe (E.)
Cupar (S.)
Denny (S.)
Derby (E.)
Doagh (N.I.)
Downe (S.)
Dover (E.)
Egham (E.)
Elgin (S.)
Ellon (S.)
Epsom (E.)
Errol (S.)
Filey (E.)
Flint (W.)
Fowey (E.)
Frome (E.)
Fyvie (S.)
Glynn (N.I.)
Goole (E.)
Govan (S.)
Hawes (E.)
Hedon (E.)
Hurst (E.)
Hythe (E.)
Insch (S.)
Islay (S.)
Keady (N.I.)
Keiss (S.)
Keith (S.)
Kelso (S.)
Lairg (S.)
Largo (S.)
Larne (N.I.)
Leeds (E.)
Leigh (E.)
Leith (S.)
Lewes (E.)
Louth (E.)
Louth (N.I.)
Luton (E.)
March (E.)
Nairn (S.)
Neath (W.)
Nevin (W.)
Newry (N.I.)

Olney (E.)
Omagh (N.I.)
Otley (E.)
Perth (S.)
Poole (E.)
Reeth (E.)
Ripon (E.)
Risca (E.)
Rugby (E.)
Salen (S.)
Sarum (E.)
Selby (E.)
Stoke (E.)
Stone (E.)
Tebay (E.)
Tenby (W.)
Thame (E.)
Toome (N.I.)
Towyn (W.)
Tring (E.)
Troon (S.)
Truro (E.)
Wells (E.)
Wigan (E.)

6

Aboyne (S.)
Alford (E.)
Alford (S.)
Alston (E.)
Amlwch (W.)
Antrim (N.I.)
Ashton (E.)
Augher (N.I.)
Bangor (W.)
Barnet (E.)
Barrow (E.)
Barton (E.)
Barvas (S.)
Batley (E.)
Battle (E.)
Bawtry (E.)
Beauly (S.)
Bedale (E.)
Belcoo (N.I.)
Belper (E.)
Beragh (N.I.)
Bervie (S.)
Biggar (S.)
Bodmin (E.)
Bognor (E.)
Bolton (E.)
Bo'ness (S.)
Bootle (E.)
Boston (E.)
Brecon (W.)
Bruton (E.)
Buckie (S.)
Builth (W.)
Bungay (E.)
Burton (E.)
Buxton (E.)
Callan (N.I.)
Carney (N.I.)
Carron (S.)
Castor (E.)
Cawdor (S.)
Cobham (E.)
Comber (N.I.)
Comrie (S.)
Conway (W.)
Crieff (S.)
Cromer (E.)
Cullen (S.)

Culter (S.)
Darwen (E.)
Dollar (S.)
Drymen (S.)
Dudley (E.)
Dunbar (S.)
Dundee (S.)
Dunlop (S.)
Dunnet (S.)
Dunoon (S.)
Durham (E.)
Dysart (S.)
Ealing (E.)
Eccles (E.)
Edzell (S.)
Epping (E.)
Exeter (E.)
Findon (S.)
Forfar (S.)
Forres (S.)
Girvan (S.)
Glamis (S.)
Goring (E.)
Hanley (E.)
Harlow (E.)
Harrow (E.)
Havant (E.)
Hawick (S.)
Henley (E.)
Hexham (E.)
Howden (E.)
Huntly (S.)
Ilford (E.)
Ilkley (E.)
Ilsley (E.)
Irvine (S.)
Jarrow (E.)
Kendal (E.)
Killin (S.)
Kilmun (S.)
Lanark (S.)
Lauder (S.)
Leslie (S.)
Leyton (E.)
Linton (S.)
Lochee (S.)
London (E.)
Ludlow (E.)
Lurgan (N.I.)
Lynton (E.)
Lytham (E.)
Maldon (E.)
Malton (E.)
Marlow (E.)
Masham (E.)
Meigle (S.)
Moffat (S.)
Morley (E.)
Naseby (E.)
Nelson (E.)
Neston (E.)
Newark (E.)
Newent (E.)
Newlyn (E.)
Newton (E.)
Norham (E.)
Oakham (E.)
Oldham (E.)
Ormsby (E.)
Ossett (E.)
Oundle (E.)
Oxford (E.)
Penryn (E.)
Pewsey (E.)
Pinner (E.)
Pladda (S.)

Pudsey (E.)
Putney (E.)
Ramsey (E.)
Raphoe (N.I.)
Redcar (E.)
Reston (S.)
Rhynie (S.)
Ripley (E.)
Romney (E.)
Romsey (E.)
Rosyth (S.)
Rothes (S.)
Ruabon (W.)
Rugely (E.)
Ruthin (W.)
St. Ives (E.)
Seaham (E.)
Seaton (E.)
Selsey (E.)
Settle (E.)
Shotts (S.)
Shrule (N.I.)
Snaith (E.)
Strood (E.)
Stroud (E.)
Sutton (E.)
Thirsk (E.)
Thorne (E.)
Thurso (S.)
Tongue (S.)
Totnes (E.)
Walton (E.)
Watton (E.)
Weston (E.)
Whitby (E.)
Widnes (E.)
Wigton (E.)
Wilton (E.)
Wishaw (S.)
Witham (E.)
Witney (E.)
Wooler (E.)
Yarrow (S.)
Yeovil (E.)

7

Airdrie (S.)
Alnwick (E.)
Andover (E.)
Appleby (E.)
Arundel (E.)
Ashford (E.)
Aylsham (E.)
Balfron (S.)
Balloch (S.)
Bampton (E.)
Banavie (S.)
Banbury (E.)
Barking (E.)
Beccles (E.)
Bedford (E.)
Belfast (N.I.)
Belford (E.)
Belleek (N.I.)
Berwick (E.)
Bewdley (E.)
Bexhill (E.)
Bickley (E.)
Bilston (E.)
Bourton (E.)
Bowfell (E.)
Bowmore (S.)
Braemar (S.)
Brandon (E.)

Brechin (S.)
Bristol (E.)
Brixham (E.)
Brodick (S.)
Bromley (E.)
Burnham (E.)
Burnley (E.)
Burslem (E.)
Caistor (E.)
Caledon (N.I.)
Canobie (S.)
Cantyre (S.)
Carbost (S.)
Carbury (W.)
Cardiff (W.)
Cargill (S.)
Carluke (S.)
Carrick (N.I.)
Catford (E.)
Cawston (E.)
Charing (E.)
Chatham (E.)
Cheadle (E.)
Cheddar (E.)
Chesham (E.)
Chester (E.)
Chorley (E.)
Clacton (E.)
Clifton (E.)
Clogher (N.I.)
Crathie (S.)
Crawley (E.)
Croydon (E.)
Culross (S.)
Cumnock (S.)
Cwmbran (W.)
Darsley (E.)
Datchet (E.)
Dawlish (E.)
Denbigh (W.)
Denholm (S.)
Dervock (N.I.)
Devizes (E.)
Dorking (E.)
Douglas (E.)
Douglas (S.)
Dundrum (N.I.)
Dunkeld (S.)
Dunmore (N.I.)
Dunning (S.)
Dunster (E.)
Elstree (E.)
Enfield (E.)
Evanton (S.)
Everton (E.)
Evesham (E.)
Exmouth (E.)
Fairlie (S.)
Falkirk (S.)
Fareham (E.)
Farnham (E.)
Feltham (E.)
Fintona (N.I.)
Galston (S.)
Gifford (S.)
Gilford (N.I.)
Glasgow (S.)
Glenarm (N.I.)
Glencoe (S.)
Glossop (E.)
Golspie (S.)
Gosport (E.)
Gourock (S.)
Granton (S.)
Grimsby (E.)
Guthrie (S.)

Halifax (E.)
Halkirk (S.)
Hampton (E.)
Harwich (E.)
Haworth (E.)
Helston (E.)
Heywood (E.)
Hitchin (E.)
Honiton (E.)
Hornsea (E.)
Hornsey (E.)
Horsham (E.)
Ipswich (E.)
Ixworth (E.)
Kenmore (S.)
Kessock (S.)
Keswick (E.)
Kilmory (S.)
Kilmuir (S.)
Kilsyth (S.)
Kinross (S.)
Kington (E.)
Kintore (S.)
Lamlash (S.)
Lancing (E.)
Langton (E.)
Larbert (S.)
Ledbury (E.)
Leyburn (E.)
Lifford (N.I.)
Lincoln (E.)
Lisburn (N.I.)
Lybster (S.)
Macduff (S.)
Maesteg (W.)
Malvern (E.)
Margate (E.)
Matlock (E.)
Maybole (S.)
Meldrum (S.)
Melrose (S.)
Melvich (S.)
Methven (S.)
Molesey (E.)
Monikie (S.)
Moreton (E.)
Morpeth (E.)
Mossley (E.)
Muthill (S.)
Newbury (E.)
Newport (E.)
Newport (W.)
Newport (E.)
Newtown (W.)
Norwich (E.)
Oldbury (E.)
Overton (E.)
Padstow (E.)
Paisley (S.)
Peebles (S.)
Penrith (E.)
Polmont (S.)
Poolewe (S.)
Portree (S.)
Portsoy (S.)
Poulton (E.)
Prescot (E.)
Preston (E.)
Rainham (E.)
Reading (E.)
Redhill (E.)
Redruth (E.)
Reigate (E.)
Renfrew (S.)
Retford (E.)
Romford (E.)

Rossall (E.)
Royston (E.)
Runcorn (E.)
Saddell (S.)
St. Asaph (W.)
St. Neots (E.)
Salford (E.)
Saltash (E.)
Sandown (E.)
Sarclet (S.)
Saxelby (E.)
Scourie (S.)
Seaford (E.)
Selkirk (S.)
Shifnal (E.)
Shipley (E.)
Shipton (E.)
Silloth (E.)
Skipton (E.)
Spilsby (E.)
Staines (E.)
Stanley (S.)
Stilton (E.)
Strathy (S.)
Sudbury (E.)
Sunbury (E.)
Swanage (E.)
Swansea (W.)
Swindon (E.)
Swinton (E.)
Tarbert (S.)
Tarland (S.)
Taunton (E.)
Tayport (S.)
Telford (E.)
Tenbury (E.)
Tetbury (E.)
Thaxted (E.)
Tilbury (E.)
Torquay (E.)
Tranent (S.)
Turriff (S.)
Tundrum (S.)
Twyford (E.)
Ullster (S.)
Ventnor (E.)
Walsall (E.)
Waltham (E.)
Wantage (E.)
Wareham (E.)
Warwick (E.)
Watchet (E.)
Watford (E.)
Weobley (E.)
Wickwar (E.)
Windsor (E.)
Winslow (E.)
Winster (E.)
Wisbeck (E.)
Worksop (E.)
Wrexham (W.)
Yetholm (S.)

8

Aberavon (W.)
Aberdare (W.)
Aberdeen (S.)
Abergele (W.)
Aberlady (S.)
Abingdon (E.)
Abington (S.)
Ahoghill (N.I.)
Alfreton (E.)
Alnmouth (E.)

Amesbury (E.)
Ampthill (E.)
Arbroath (S.)
Armadale (S.)
Arrochar (S.)
Auldearn (S.)
Axbridge (E.)
Aycliffe (E.)
Bakewell (E.)
Ballater (S.)
Ballybay (N.I.)
Banchory (S.)
Barmouth (W.)
Barnsley (E.)
Barrhill (S.)
Beattock (S.)
Berkeley (E.)
Beverley (E.)
Bicester (E.)
Bideford (E.)
Blantyre (S.)
Bolsover (E.)
Brackley (E.)
Bradford (E.)
Brampton (E.)
Bridgend (W.)
Bridport (E.)
Brighton (E.)
Bromyard (E.)
Broseley (E.)
Burghead (S.)
Caerleon (E.)
Camborne (E.)
Canisbay (S.)
Cardigan (W.)
Carlisle (E.)
Carnwath (S.)
Caterham (E.)
Chepstow (E.)
Chertsey (E.)
Clevedon (E.)
Clovelly (E.)
Coventry (E.)
Crediton (E.)
Creetown (S.)
Cromarty (S.)
Dalkeith (S.)
Dalmally (S.)
Daventry (E.)
Debenham (E.)
Dedworth (E.)
Deptford (E.)
Dewsbury (E.)
Dingwall (S.)
Dirleton (S.)
Dolgelly (W.)
Dufftown (S.)
Dumfries (S.)
Dunbeath (S.)
Dunblane (S.)
Dungiven (N.I.)
Dunscore (S.)
Earlston (S.)
Egremont (E.)
Eversley (E.)
Eyemouth (S.)
Fakenham (E.)
Falmouth (E.)
Findhorn (S.)
Fortrose (S.)
Foulness (E.)
Glenluce (S.)
Grantham (E.)
Grantown (E.)
Greenlaw (S.)
Greenock (S.)

111

Hadleigh (E.)
Hailsham (E.)
Halstead (E.)
Hamilton (S.)
Hastings (E.)
Hatfield (E.)
Hawarden (W.)
Helmsley (E.)
Hereford (E.)
Herne Bay (E.)
Hertford (E.)
Hilltown (N.I.)
Hinckley (E.)
Holbeach (E.)
Holyhead (W.)
Holywell (W.)
Hunmanby (E.)
Ilkeston (E.)
Inverary (S.)
Inverury (S.)
Jeantown (S.)
Jedburgh (S)
Keighley (E.)
Kidwelly (W.)
Kilbride (S.)
Kilniver S.)
Kilrenny (S.)
Kinghorn (S.)
Kingston (E.)
Kirkwall (S.)
Knighton (E.)
Lampeter (W.)
Langholm (S.)
Latheron (S.)
Lavenham (E.)
Lechlade (E.)
Leuchars (S.)
Liskeard (E.)
Llanelly (W.)
Llanrwst (W.)
Loanhead (S.)
Longtown (E.)
Lynmouth (E.)
Markinch (S.)
Marykirk (S.)
Maryport (E.)
Midhurst (E.)
Minehead (E.)
Moniaive (S.)
Monmouth (E.)
Montrose (S.)
Monymusk (S.)
Muirkirk (S.)
Nantwich (E.)
Neilston (S.)
Newburgh (S.)
Newhaven (E.)
Newmilns (E.)
Nuneaton (E.)
Ormskirk (E.)
Oswestry (E.)
Pembroke (W.)
Penicuik (S.)
Penzance (E.)
Pershore (E.)
Peterlee (E.)
Petworth (E.)
Pevensey (E.)
Pitsligo (S.)
Plaistow (E.)
Plymouth (E.)
Pooltiel (S.)
Portrush (N.I.)
Pwllheli (W.)
Quiraing (S.)
Ramsgate (E.)

Redditch (E.)
Rhayader (W.)
Richmond (E.)
Ringwood (E.)
Rochdale (E.)
Rothbury (E.)
Rothesay (S.)
St. Albans (E.)
St. Fergus (S.)
St. Helens (E.)
Saltburn (E.)
Sandgate (E.)
Sandwich (E.)
Sedbergh (E.)
Shanklin (E.)
Shelford (E.)
Shipston (E.)
Sidmouth (E.)
Skegness (E.)
Skerries (W.)
Skifness (W.)
Sleaford (E.)
Southend (E.)
Spalding (E.)
Stafford (E.)
Stamford (E.)
Stanhope (E.)
Stanwell (E.)
Stirling (S.)
Stockton (E.)
Strabane (N.I.)
Stratton (E.)
Strichen (S.)
Surbiton (E.)
Swaffham (E.)
Talgarth (W.)
Talisker (S.)
Tamworth (E.)
Taransay (S.)
Thetford (E.)
Thornaby (E.)
Tiverton (E.)
Traquair (S.)
Tredegar (W.)
Tregaron (W.)
Trillick (N.I.)
Tunstall (E.)
Uckfield (E.)
Ullapool (S.)
Uxbridge (E.)
Wallasey (E.)
Wallsend (E.)
Wanstead (E.)
Westbury (E.)
Wetheral (E.)
Wetherby (E.)
Weymouth (E.)
Whithorn (S.)
Woodford (E.)
Woodside (S.)
Woolwich (E.)
Worthing (E.)
Yarmouth (E.)

9

Aberaeron (W.)
Aberdovey (W.)
Aberfeldy (S.)
Aberffraw (W.)
Aberfoyle (S.)
Aldeburgh (E.)
Aldershot (E.)

Allendale (E.)
Alresford (E.)
Ambleside (E.)
Ardrossan (S.)
Ashbourne (E.)
Ashburton (E.)
Avonmouth (E.)
Aylesbury (E.)
Ballintra (N.I.)
Ballymena (N.I.)
Ballymore (N.I.)
Banbridge (N.I.)
Beaumaris (W.)
Belturbet (N.I.)
Berridale (S.)
Bettyhill (S.)
Blackburn (E.)
Blacklarg (S.)
Blackpool (E.)
Blandford (E.)
Blisworth (E.)
Bracadale (S.)
Bracknell (E.)
Braeriach (S.)
Braintree (E.)
Brentford (E.)
Brentwood (E.)
Brighouse (E.)
Broadford (S.)
Broughton (E.)
Broughton (S.)
Buckhaven (S.)
Bushmills (N.I.)
Cairntoul (S.)
Callander (S.)
Cambridge (E.)
Carstairs (S.)
Carnarvon (W.)
Carnforth (E.)
Castleton (E.)
Chesilton (E.)
Chingford (E.)
Clitheroe (E.)
Coleraine (N.I.)
Congleton (E.)
Cookstown (N.I.)
Cranborne (E.)
Cranbrook (E.)
Crewkerne (E.)
Criccieth (W.)
Cricklade (E.)
Cuckfield (E.)
Dartmouth (E.)
Devonport (E.)
Doncaster (E.)
Donington (E.)
Droitwich (E.)
Dronfield (E.)
Dumbarton (S.)
Dungannon (N.I.)
Dungeness (E.)
Dunstable (E.)
Edinburgh (S.)
Ellesmere (E.)
Faversham (E.)
Ferintosh (S.)
Festiniog (W.)
Fishguard (W.)
Fleetwood (E.)
Fochabers (S.)
Gateshead (E.)
Glaslough (N.I.)
Godalming (E.)
Gravesend (E.)
Greenwich (E.)
Grinstead (E.)

Guildford (E.)
Harrogate (E.)
Haslemere (E.)
Haverhill (E.)
Hawkhurst (E.)
Holmfirth (E.)
Ilchester (E.)
Immingham (E.)
Inchkeith (S.)
Inveraray (S.)
Inverness (S.)
Johnstone (S.)
Kettering (E.)
Kildrummy (S.)
Killybegs (N.I.)
King's Lynn (E.)
Kingswear (E.)
Kingussie (S.)
Kircubbin (N.I.)
Kirkcaldy (S.)
Lambourne (E.)
Lancaster (E.)
Leadhills (S.)
Leicester (E.)
Lichfield (E.)
Liverpool (E.)
Llanberis (W.)
Llandudno (W.)
Lochgelly (S.)
Lochinvar (S.)
Lochnagar (S.)
Lockerbie (S.)
Logierait (S.)
Longridge (E.)
Lowestoft (E.)
Lyme Regis (E.)
Lymington (E.)
Maidstone (E.)
Mansfield (E.)
Mauchline (S.)
Middleton (E.)
Milngavie (S.)
Moneymore (N.I.)
Newcastle (E.)
Newcastle (N.I.)
Newmarket (E.)
New Radnor (W.)
New Romney (E.)
Northwich (E.)
Otterburn (E.)
Pembridge (E.)
Penistone (E.)
Penkridge (E.)
Penyghent (E.)
Peterhead (S.)
Pickering (E.)
Pitlochry (S.)
Pontypool (E.)
Portadown (N.I.)
Port Ellen (S.)
Portcawl (W.)
Portmadoc (W.)
Prestwick (S.)
Rasharkin (N.I.)
Riccarton (S.)
Rochester (E.)
Rostrevor (N.I.)
Rotherham (E.)
Rothiemay (S.)
St. Andrews (S.)
St. Austell (E.)
St. Fillans (S.)
Salisbury (E.)
Saltcoats (S.)
Saltfleet (E.)
Sevenoaks (E.)

Sheerness (E.)
Sheffield (E.)
Sherborne (E.)
Shieldaig (S.)
Slamannan (S.)
Smethwick (E.)
Southgate (E.)
Southport (E.)
Southwell (E.)
Southwold (E.)
Starcross (E.)
Stevenage (E.)
Stewarton (S.)
Stockport (E.)
Stokesley (E.)
Stourport (E.)
Stranraer (S.)
Stratford (E.)
Strathdon (S.)
Strontian (S.)
Tarporley (E.)
Tavistock (E.)
Tenterden (E.)
Thornhill (S.)
Tobermory (S.)
Todmorden (E.)
Tomintoul (S.)
Tonbridge (E.)
Tovermore (N.I.)
Towcester (E.)
Tynemouth (E.)
Ulverston (E.)
Upminster (E.)
Uppingham (E.)
Uttoxeter (E.)
Wainfleet (E.)
Wakefield (E.)
Warkworth (E.)
Welshpool (W.)
Weybridge (E.)
Whernside (E.)
Wimbledon (E.)
Wincanton (E.)
Wokingham (E.)
Woodstock (E.)
Worcester (E.)
Wymondham (E.)

10

Abbotsford (S.)
Accrington (E.)
Achnasheen (S.)
Aldborough (E.)
Altrincham (E.)
Anstruther (S.)
Applecross (S.)
Ardrishaig (S.)
Auchinleck (S.)
Ballantrae (S.)
Ballybofir (N.I.)
Ballyclare (N.I.)
Ballyhaise (N.I.)
Ballymoney (N.I.)
Ballyroney (N.I.)
Barnstaple (E.)
Beaminster (E.)
Bedlington (E.)
Bellingham (E.)
Billericay (E.)
Birkenhead (E.)
Birmingham (E.)
Blackadder (S.)

Bridgnorth (E.)
Bridgwater (E.)
Bromsgrove (E.)
Broxbourne (E.)
Buckingham (E.)
Cader Idris (W.)
Caernarvon (W.)
Canterbury (E.)
Carmarthen (W.)
Carnoustie (S.)
Carshalton (E.)
Carsphairn (S.)
Castlederg (N.I.)
Castlefinn (N.I.)
Castletown (S.)
Chelmsford (E.)
Cheltenham (E.)
Chichester (E.)
Chippenham (E.)
Chulmleigh (E.)
Coatbridge (S.)
Coggeshall (E.)
Colchester (E.)
Coldingham (S.)
Coldstream (S.)
Crickhowel (W.)
Cullompton (E.)
Cushenhall (N.I.)
Dalbeattie (S.)
Darlington (E.)
Donaghadel (N.I.)
Dorchester (E.)
Drumlithie (S.)
Dukinfield (E.)
Eastbourne (E.)
East Linton (S.)
Eccleshall (E.)
Farningham (E.)
Ffestiniog (W.)
Folkestone (E.)
Freshwater (E.)
Galashiels (S.)
Gillingham (E.)
Glengariff (N.I.)
Glenrothes (S.)
Gloucester (E.)
Halesworth (E.)
Hartlepool (E.)
Haslingdon (E.)
Heathfield (E.)
Horncastle (E.)
Hornchurch (E.)
Hungerford (E.)
Hunstanton (E.)
Huntingdon (E.)
Ilfracombe (E.)
Johnshaven (S.)
Kenilworth (E.)
Kilconnell (N.I.)
Kilcreggan (S.)
Killenaule (S.)
Kilmainham (S.)
Kilmalcolm (S.)
Kilmarnock (S.)
Kilwinning (S.)
Kincardine (S.)
Kingsbarns (S.)
Kingsclere (E.)
Kirkmaiden (S.)
Kirkoswald (E.)
Kirkoswald (S.)
Kirriemuir (S.)
Launceston (E.)
Leamington (E.)
Lennoxtown (S.)
Leominster (E.)

Lesmahagow (S.)
Linlithgow (S.)
Littleport (F.)
Livingston (S.)
Llandovery (W.)
Llanfyllin (W.)
Llangadock (W.)
Llangollen (W.)
Llanidloes (W.)
Maidenhead (E.)
Malmesbury (E.)
Manchester (E.)
Markethill (N.I.)
Mexborough (E.)
Micheldean (E.)
Middlewich (E.)
Mildenhall (E.)
Milnathort (S.)
Montgomery (W.)
Motherwell (S.)
Nailsworth (E.)
Nottingham (E.)
Okehampton (E.)
Orfordness (E.)
Pangbourne (E.)
Patrington (E.)
Peacehaven (E.)
Pittenweem (S.)
Plinlimmon (W.)
Pontefract (E.)
Portaferry (N.I.)
Porth Nigel (W.)
Portishead (E.)
Portobello (S.)
Portsmouth (E.)
Potter's Bar (E.)
Presteigne (W.)
Ravenglass (E.)
Rockingham (E.)
Ronaldsay (S.)
Rutherglen (S.)
Saintfield (N.I.)
St. Leonards (E.)
Saxmundham (E.)
Shepperton (E.)
Sheringham (E.)
Shrewsbury (E.)
Stalbridge (E.)
Stonehaven (S.)
Stonehouse (S.)
Stoneykirk (S.)
Stowmarket (E.)
Strangford (N.I.)
Stranorlar (N.I.)
Strathaven (S.)
Strathearn (S.)
Strathmore (S.)
Sunderland (E.)
Tanderagee (N.I.)
Teddington (E.)
Teignmouth (E.)
Tewkesbury (E.)
Thamesmead (E.)
Torrington (E.)
Trowbridge (E.)
Tweedmouth (S.)
Twickenham (E.)
Warminster (E.)
Warrington (E.)
Washington (E.)
Wednesbury (E.)
Wellington (E.)
West Calder (S.)
Westward Ho (E.)
Whitchurch (E.)
Whithaven (E.)

Whitstable (E.)
Whittlesey (E.)
Willenhall (E.)
Wilsontown (S.)
Winchelsea (E.)
Winchester (E.)
Windermere (E.)
Windlesham (E.)
Wirksworth (E.)
Withernsea (E.)
Wolsingham (E.)
Woodbridge (E.)
Workington (E.)

11

Aberchirder (S.)
Abergavenny (E.)
Aberystwyth (W.)
Ballycastle (N.I.)
Ballygawley (N.I.)
Balquhidder (S.)
Bannockburn (S.)
Basingstoke (E.)
Blairgowrie (S.)
Bognor Regis (E.)
Bournemouth (E.)
Braich-y-Pwll (W.)
Bridlington (E.)
Buntingford (E.)
Campbeltown (S.)
Carrickmore (N.I.)
Charlestown (S.)
Cleethorpes (E.)
Cockermouth (E.)
Crossmaglen (N.I.)
Cumbernauld (S.)
Downpatrick (N.I.)
Draperstown (N.I.)
Drummelzier (S.)
Dunfermline (S.)
East Retford (E.)
Ecclefechan (S.)
Enniskillen (N.I.)
Fettercairn (S.)
Fort William (S.)
Fraserburgh (S.)
Glastonbury (E.)
Great Marlow (E.)
Guisborough (E.)
Haltwhistle (E.)
Hampton Wick (E.)
Hatherleigh (E.)
Helensburgh (S.)
High Wycombe (E.)
Ingatestone (E.)
Invergordon (S.)
Kirkmichael (S.)
Letterkenny (N.I.)
Leytonstone (E.)
Littlestone (E.)
Londonderry (N.I.)
Lossiemouth (S.)
Lostwithiel (E.)
Ludgershall (E.)
Lutterworth (E.)
Mablethorpe (E.)
Machynlleth (W.)
Magherafelt (N.I.)
Manningtree (E.)
Market Rasen (E.)
Marlborough (E.)
Maxwelltown (S.)
Much Wenlock (E.)

Musselburgh (S.)
New Brighton (E.)
Newton Abbot (E.)
Northampton (E.)
Oystermouth (W.)
Petersfield (E.)
Pocklington (E.)
Port Glasgow (S.)
Portglenone (N.I.)
Port Patrick (S.)
Prestonpans (S.)
Pultneytown (S.)
Randalstown (N.I.)
Rathfryland (N.I.)
Rawtenstall (E.)
St. Margaret's (E.)
Scarborough (E.)
Shaftesbury (E.)
Southampton (E.)
South Molton (E.)
Stalybridge (E.)
Stourbridge (E.)
Strathblane (S.)
Tattershall (E.)
Wallingford (E.)
Walthamstow (E.)
Westminster (E.)
Whitechurch (E.)
Woodhall Spa (E.)

12

Attleborough (E.)
Auchterarder (S.)
Ballachulish (S.)
Bexhill-on-Sea (E.)
Castleblaney (N.I.)
Castle Dawson (N.I.)
Castle Rising (E.)
Castlewellan (N.I.)
Chesterfield (E.)
Christchurch (E.)
East Kilbride (S.)
Five Mile Town (N.I.)
Fort Augustus (S.)
Gainsborough (E.)
Garelochhead (S.)
Great Grimsby (E.)
Great Malvern (E.)
Hillsborough (N.I.)
Huddersfield (E.)
Ingleborough (E.)
Inishtrahull (N.I.)

Innerleithen (S.)
Lawrencekirk (S.)
Llandilofawr (W.)
Llantrissant (W.)
Long Stratton (E.)
Loughborough (E.)
Macclesfield (E.)
Milton Keynes (E.)
Morecambe Bay (E.)
North Berwick (E.)
North Shields (E.)
North Walsham (E.)
Peterborough (E.)
Portmahomack (S.)
Shoeburyness (E.)
Shottesbrook (E.)
Slieve Donard (N.I.)
South Shields (E.)
Stewartstown (N.I.)
Stoke-on-Trent (E.)
Strathpeffer (S.)
Tillicoultry (S.)

13

Auchtermuchty (S.)
Barnard Castle (E.)
Berkhampstead (E.)
Bishop's Castle (E.)
Boroughbridge (E.)
Brightlingsea (E.)
Brookeborough (N.I.)
Burton-on-Trent (E.)
Bury St. Edmunds (E.)
Carrickfergus (N.I.)
Castle Douglas (S.)
Chipping Ongar (E.)
Cockburnspath (S.)
Dalmellington (S.)
Derrygonnelly (N.I.)
Finchampstead (E.)
Godmanchester (E.)
Great Yarmouth (E.)
Haverfordwest (W.)
Higham Ferrers (E.)
Inverkeithing (S.)
Inverkeithnie (S.)
Kidderminster (E.)
Kirkby Stephen (E.)
Kirkcudbright (S.)
Kirkintilloch (S.)
Knaresborough (E.)
Littlehampton (E.)

Lytham St. Annes (E.)
Market Deeping (E.)
Market Drayton (E.)
Melcombe Regis (E.)
Melton Mowbray (E.)
Merthyr Tydfil (W.)
Middlesbrough (E.)
Newton Stewart (S.)
Northallerton (E.)
Rothiemurchus (S.)
Saffron Walden (E.)
Shepton Mallet (E.)
Wolverhampton (E.)

14

Berwick-on-Tweed (E.)
Bishop Auckland (E.)
Bishops Waltham (E.)
Chipping Barnet (E.)
Chipping Norton (E.)
Hemel Hempstead (E.)
Kirkby Lonsdale (E.)
Market Bosworth (E.)
Mortimer's Cross (E.)
Newtown Stewart (N.I.)
Stockton-on-Tees (E.)
Stony Stratford (E.)
Sutton Courtney (E.)
Tunbridge Wells (E.)
Wellingborough (E.)
West Hartlepool (E.)
Wootton Basset (E.)

15

Ashton-under-Lyne (E.)
Barrow-in-Furness (E.)
Burnham-on-Crouch (E.)
Castle Donington (E.)
Leighton Buzzard (E.)
Newcastle-on-Tyne (E.)
St. Leonards-on-Sea (E.)
Stratford-on-Avon (E.)
Sutton Coldfield (E.)
Weston-super-Mare (E.)

16

Bishop's Stortford (E.)
Welwyn Garden City (E.)

Towns and cities: United States

4

Gary
Lima
Reno
Troy
York
Waco

5

Akron
Boise
Bronx

Butte
Flint
Miami
Omaha
Ozark
Salem
Selma
Tulsa
Utica

6

Albany
Austin

Bangor
Biloxi
Boston
Camden
Canton
Dallas
Dayton
Denver
Duluth
El Paso
Eugene
Fresno
Lowell
Mobile
Nassau

Newark
Oxnard
Peoria
St. Paul
Tacoma
Toledo
Topeka
Tucson
Urbana

7

Abilene
Anaheim

Atlanta
Boulder
Brooklyn
Buffalo
Chicago
Columbus
Concord
Detroit
Hampton
Hoboken
Houston
Jackson
Lincoln
Madison
Memphis
Modesto
New York
Norfolk
Oakland
Orlando
Phoenix
Raleigh
Reading
Roanoke
St. Louis
Saginaw
San Jose
Seattle
Spokane
Wichita
Yonkers

8

Berkeley
Dearborn
Green Bay
Hannibal

Hartford
Honolulu
Lakeland
Las Vegas
New Haven
Oak Ridge
Palo Alto
Pasadena
Portland
Richmond
San Diego
Santa Ana
Savannah
Stamford
Stockton
Syracuse
Wheeling

9

Anchorage
Annapolis
Arlington
Baltimore
Bethlehem
Cambridge
Champaign
Charlotte
Cleveland
Des Moines
Fairbanks
Fort Wayne
Fort Worth
Galveston
Hollywood
Johnstown
Kalamazoo
Lancaster

Lexington
Long Beach
Manhattan
Milwaukee
Nashville
New London
Northeast
Princeton
Riverside
Rochester
Waterbury
Worcester
Ypsilanti

10

Atomic City
Baton Rouge
Birmingham
Charleston
Cincinnati
Evansville
Greensboro
Greenville
Harrisburg
Huntsville
Jersey City
Kansas City
Little Rock
Long Branch
Los Angeles
Louisville
Miami Beach
Montgomery
New Bedford
New Orleans
Pittsburgh
Providence

Sacramento
Saint Louis
San Antonio
Washington
Youngstown

11

Albuquerque
Cedar Rapids
Chattanooga
Grand Rapids
Minneapolis
Newport News
Palm Springs
Schenectady
Springfield

12 AND OVER

Atlantic City (12)
Beverly Hills (12)
Colorado Springs (15)
Corpus Christi (13)
Fayetteville (12)
Fort Lauderdale (14)
Independence (12)
Indianapolis (12)
Jacksonville (12)
New Brunswick (12)
Niagara Falls (12)
Oklahoma City (12)
Philadelphia (12)
Poughkeepsie (12)
St. Petersburg (12)
Salt Lake City (12)
San Francisco (12)
Santa Barbara (12)

Towns and cities: rest of the world

3 AND 4

Agra (Ind.)
Aix (Fr.)
Ava (Burma)
Baku (U.S.S.R.)
Bâle (Swit.)
Bari (It.)
Bray (Ire.)
Brno (Cze.)
Cali (Colombia)
Cobh (Ire.)
Cork (Ire.)
Fez (Moroc.)
Gaza (Isr.)
Gera (E. Ger.)
Giza (Egypt)
Homs (Syria and Libya)
Hue (Viet.)
Kano (Nig.)
Kiel (W. Ger.)
Kiev (U.S.S.R.)
Kobe (Jap.)
Köln (W. Ger.)
Lamu (Kenya)
Laon (Fr.)
Lodz (Pol.)
Luta (China)
Lvov (U.S.S.R.)
Lyon (Fr.)

Metz (Fr.)
Nice (Fr.)
Omsk (U.S.S.R.)
Oran (Alg.)
Pécs (Hung.)
Pisa (It.)
Riga (U.S.S.R.)
Sian (China)
Suez (Egypt)
Suhl (E. Ger.)
Tour (Fr.)
Troy (Asia M.)
Tyre (Lebanon)
Ufa (U.S.S.R.)
Vigo (Sp.)

5

Ajmer (Ind.)
Alwar (Ind.)
Arras (Fr.)
Aswan (Egypt)
Balla (Ire.)
Basel } (Swit.)
Basle }
Basra (Iraq)
Boyle (Ire.)
Beira (Moz.)
Brest (Fr. and U.S.S.R.)

Cadiz (Sp.)
Clare (Ire.)
Cuzco (Peru)
Delhi (Ind.)
Dijon (Fr.)
Essen (W. Ger.)
Galle (Sri)
Genoa (It.)
Ghent (Belg.)
Gorky (U.S.S.R.)
Hague (Neth.)
Haifa (Isr.)
Halle (E. Ger.)
Herat (Afghan.)
Izmir (Turk.)
Jaffa (Isr.)
Jidda (Saudi)
Kandy (Sri)
Kazan (U.S.S.R.)
Kells (Ire.)
Kotah (Ind.)
Kyoto (Jap.)
Liege (Belg.)
Lille (Fr.)
Lyons (Fr.)
Mainz (W. Ger.)
Malmö (Swed.)
Mecca (Saudi)
Memel (U.S.S.R.)
Milan (It.)

115

Minsk (U.S.S.R.)
Mosul (Iraq)
Namur (Belg.)
Nancy (Fr.)
Osaka (Jap.)
Ostia (It.)
Padua (It.)
Parma (It.)
Patna (Ind.)
Perth (Austral.)
Pinsk (U.S.S.R.)
Poona (Ind.)
Posen (Pol.)
Pskov (U.S.S.R.)
Pusan (S. Korea)
Rabat (Moroc.)
Reims (Fr.)
Rouen (Fr.)
Sidon (Lebanon)
Siena (It.)
Simla (Ind.)
Sligo (Ire.)
Trent (It.)
Trier (W. Ger.)
Turin (It.)
Varna (Bulg.)
Vilna (U.S.S.R.)
Wuhan (China)
Yalta (U.S.S.R.)
Ypres (Belg.)

6

Aachen (W. Ger.)
Abadan (Iran)
Aleppo (Syria)
Amiens (Fr.)
Anshan (China)
Arklow (Ire.)
Arnhem (Neth.)
Bantry (Ire.)
Baroda (Ind.)
Berber (Sudan)
Bergen (Nor.)
Bhopal (Ind.)
Bilbao (Sp.)
Bombay (Ind.)
Bochum (W. Ger.)
Bremen (W. Ger.)
Bruges (Belg.)
Calais (Fr.)
Canton (China)
Carlow (Ire.)
Cashel (Ire.)
Cassel (W. Ger.)
Dairen (China)
Danang (Viet.)
Danzig (Pol.)
Darwin (Austral.)
Dieppe (Fr.)
Dinant (Belg.)
Durban (S.A.)
Erfurt (E. Ger.)
Fushun (China)
Galway (Ire.)
Gdansk (Pol.)
Geneva (Swit.)
Harbin (China)
Hobart (Austral.)
Howrah (Ind.)
Ibadan (Nig.)
Imphal (Ind.)
Indore (Ind.)

Jaipur (Ind.)
Jhansi (Ind.)
Juarez (Mex.)
Kanpur (Ind.)
Kassel (W. Ger.)
Kaunas (U.S.S.R.)
Kohima (Ind.)
Krakow (Pol.)
Lahore (Pak.)
Leiden (Neth.)
Le Mans (Fr.)
Leyden (Neth.)
Lobito (Angola)
Lübeck (W. Ger.)
Lublin (Pol.)
Madras (Ind.)
Manila (Philip.)
Medina (Saudi)
Meerut (Ind.)
Mukden (China)
Munich (W. Ger.)
Mysore (Ind.)
Nagoya (Jap.)
Nagpur (Ind.)
Nantes (Fr.)
Napier (N.Z.)
Naples (It.)
Nelson (N.Z.)
Odessa (U.S.S.R.)
Oporto (Port.)
Ostend (Belg.)
Puebla (Mex.)
Quebec (Can.)
Quetta (Pak.)
Rampur (Ind.)
Recife (Braz.)
Reggio (It.)
Regina (Can.)
Rheims (Fr.)
Seville (Sp.)
Shiraz (Iran)
Smyrna (Turk.)
Soweto (S.A.)
Sparta (Gr.)
St. Malo (Fr.)
Sydney (Austral.)
Tabriz (Iran)
Thebes
  (Gr. and Egypt)
Tiflis (U.S.S.R.)
Tobruk (Libya)
Toulon (Fr.)
Trèves (W. Ger.)
Tsinan (China)
Venice (It.)
Verdun (Fr.)
Verona (It.)
Zagreb (Yug.)
Zurich (Swit.)

7

Ajaccio (Fr.)
Alençon (Fr.)
Alma-Ata (U.S.S.R.)
Antwerp (Belg.)
Athlone (Ire.)
Avignon (Fr.)
Babylon (Asia)
Badajoz (Sp.)
Bandung (Indo.)
Bayonne (Fr.)
Benares (Ind.)
Blarney (Ire.)
Bologna (It.)

Breslau (Pol.)
Calgary (Can.)
Clonmel (Ire.)
Coblenz (W. Ger.)
Cologne (W. Ger.)
Cordoba (Sp. and Arg.)
Corinth (Gr.)
Cottbus (E. Ger.)
Donetsk (U.S.S.R.)
Dongola (Sudan)
Dresden (E. Ger.)
Dundalk (Ire.)
Dunedin (N.Z.)
Dunkirk (Fr.)
Erzerum (Turk.)
Granada (Sp.)
Gwalior (Ind.)
Halifax (Can.)
Hamburg (W. Ger.)
Hanover (W. Ger.)
Homburg (W. Ger.)
Irkutsk (U.S.S.R.)
Isfahan (U.S.S.R.)
Jericho (Asia)
Jodhpur (Ind.)
Kalinin (U.S.S.R.)
Karachi (Pak.)
Kharkov (U.S.S.R.)
Kildare (Ire.)
Koblenz (W. Ger.)
Kunming (China)
Lanchow (China)
La Plata (Arg.)
Le Havre (Fr.)
Leipzig (E. Ger.)
Lemberg (U.S.S.R.)
Lourdes (Fr.)
Lucerne (Swit.)
Lucknow (Ind.)
Malines (Belg.)
Mansura (Egypt)
Mashhad (Iran)
Memphis (Egypt)
Messina (It.)
Mombasa (Kenya)
München (W. Ger.)
Mycenae (Gr.)
Nanking (China)
Orléans (Fr.)
Palermo (It.)
Palmyra (Syria)
Piraeus (Gr.)
Pompeii (It.)
Potsdam (E. Ger.)
Ravenna (It.)
Rostock (E. Ger.)
St. John's (Can.)
Salerno (It.)
San Remo (It.)
Sapporo (Jap.)
Tallinn (U.S.S.R.)
Tangier (Moroc.)
Tbilisi (U.S.S.R.)
Taiyuan (China)
Tel Aviv (Isr.)
Toronto (Can.)
Trieste (It.)
Uppsala (Swed.)
Utrecht (Neth.)
Vatican (It.)
Vilnius (U.S.S.R.)
Wexford (Ire.)
Wicklow (Ire.)
Yakutsk (U.S.S.R.)
Yerevan (U.S.S.R.)
Youghal (Ire.)

8

Acapulco (Mex.)
Adelaide (Austral.)
Agartala (Ind.)
Alicante (Sp.)
Amritsar (Ind.)
Auckland (N.Z.)
Augsburg (W. Ger.)
Besançon (Fr.)
Bordeaux (Fr.)
Boulogne (Fr.)
Brisbane (Austral.)
Bulawayo (Rhodesia)
Calcutta (Ind.)
Carthage (N. Af.)
Cawnpore (Ind.)
Clontarf (Ire.)
Dortmund (W. Ger.)
Drogheda (Ire.)
Edmonton (Can.)
Florence (It.)
Grenoble (Fr.)
Göteborg (Swed.)
Haiphong (Viet.)
Hamilton (Can.)
Hannover (W. Ger.)
Ismailia (Egypt)
Istanbul (Turk.)
Jamalpur (Ind.)
Kandahar (Afghan.)
Kilkenny (Ire.)
Kingston (Can.)
Lausanne (Swit.)
Limerick (Ire.)
Listowel (Ire.)
Mafeking (S.A.)
Mandalay (Burma)
Mannheim (W. Ger.)
Maynouth (Ire.)
Montreal (Can.)
Nagasaki (Jap.)
Novgorod (U.S.S.R.)
Nürnberg (W. Ger.)
Omdurman (Sudan)
Pamplona (Sp.)
Peshawar (Pak.)
Port Said (Egypt)
Przemysl (Pol.)
Rathdrum (Ire.)
Salonika (Gr.)
Salzburg (Aust.)
Sao Paulo (Braz.)
Sarajevo (Yug.)
Schwerin (E. Ger.)
Shanghai (China)
Shenyang (China)
Shillong (Ind.)
Soissons (Fr.)
Smolensk (U.S.S.R.)
Srinagar (Ind.)
Surabaja (Indo.)
Syracuse (It.)
Tangiers (Moroc.)
Tashkent (U.S.S.R.)
The Hague (Neth.)
Tientsin (China)
Timbuktu (Mali)
Toulouse (Fr.)
Valencia (Sp.)
Varanasi (Ind.)
Victoria (Can.)
Winnipeg (Can.)
Yokohama (Jap.)
Zanzibar (Tanz.)
Zaragoza (Sp.)

9

Abbeville (Fr.)
Agrigento (It.)
Ahmedabad (Ind.)
Allahabad (Ind.)
Astrakhan (U.S.S.R.)
Bangalore (Ind.)
Barcelona (Sp.)
Beersheba (Isr.)
Brunswick (W. Ger.)
Byzantium (Turk.)
Cartagena (Sp. and
  Colombia)
Changchun (China)
Cherbourg (Fr.)
Cherkessk (U.S.S.R.)
Chungking (China)
Connemara (Ire.)
Darmstadt (W. Ger.)
Dordrecht (Neth.)
Eindhoven (Neth.)
Frankfurt (E. Ger.)
Frankfurt (W. Ger.)
Gibraltar (Eur.)
Hiroshima (Jap.)
Hyderabad (Ind. and Pak.)
Innsbruck (Aust.)
Karaganda (U.S.S.R.)
Killarney (Ire.)
Kimberley (S.A.)
Krivoi Rog (U.S.S.R.)
Kuibyshev (U.S.S.R.)
Ladysmith (S.A.)
Las Palmas (Sp.)
Leningrad (U.S.S.R.)
Ljubljana (Yug.)
Magdeburg (E. Ger.)
Maracaibo (Venez.)
Marrakech ⎫
Marrakesh ⎬ (Moroc.)
Marseille (Fr.)
Melbourne (Austral.)
Monterrey (Mex.)

Newcastle (Austral.)
Nuremberg (W. Ger.)
Panmunjon (Korea)
Roscommon (Ire.)
Rotterdam (Neth.)
Samarkand (U.S.S.R.)
Santander (Sp.)
Saragossa (Sp.)
Stuttgart (W. Ger.)
Tipperary (Ire.)
Trondheim (Nor.)
Vancouver (Can.)
Volgograd (U.S.S.R.)
Waterford (Ire.)
Wiesbaden (W. Ger.)
Wuppertal (W. Ger.)

10

Alexandria (Egypt)
Baden Baden (W. Ger.)
Bad Homburg (W. Ger.)
Bratislava (Cze.)
Casablanca (Moroc.)
Chandigarh (Ind.)
Chittagong (Bangla.)
Darjeeling (Ind.)
Düsseldorf (W. Ger.)
Gothenburg (Swed.)
Heidelberg (W. Ger.)
Jamshedpur (Ind.)
Königsberg (U.S.S.R.)
Lubumbashi (Zaïre)
Marseilles (Fr.)
Port Arthur (China)
Sevastopol (U.S.S.R.)
Shillelagh (Ire.)
Simonstown (S.A.)
Stalingrad (U.S.S.R.)
Strasbourg (Fr.)
Sverdlovsk (U.S.S.R.)
Trivandrum (Ind.)

Valparaiso (Chile)
Versailles (Fr.)

11

Armentières (Fr.)
Bahia Blanca (Arg.)
Ballymurphy (Ire.)
Bhubaneswar (Ind.)
Fredericton (Can.)
Grahamstown (S.A.)
Guadalajara (Mex.)
Helsingborg (Swed.)
Kaliningrad (U.S.S.R.)
Novosibirsk (U.S.S.R.)
Saarbrücken (W. Ger.)
Sharpeville (S.A.)
Vladivostok (U.S.S.R.)

12

Bloemfontein (S.A.)
Christchurch (N.Z.)
Johannesburg (S.A.)
Niagara Falls (Can.)
Rio de Janeiro (Braz.)
San Sebastian (Sp.)

13 AND OVER

Aix-la-Chapelle (W. Ger.)
  (13)
Belo Horizonte (Braz.) (13)
Charlottetown (Can.) (13)
Clermont-Ferrand (Fr.) (15)
Constantinople (Turk.) (14)
Dnepropetrovsk (U.S.S.R.)
  (14)
Karl-Marx-Stadt (E. Ger.) (13)
Pietermaritzburg (S.A.) (16)
Port Elizabeth (S.A.) (13)

Waterfalls, the largest

Churchill (9) *Can.*
Gavarnie (8) *Fr.*
Giessbach (9) *Swit.*
Guaira (6) *Braz.*
Hamilton (8) *Can.*
Krimmler (8) *Aust.*

Multnomah (9) *U.S.A.*
Niagara (7) *Can.-U.S.A.*
Ribbon (6) *U.S.A.*
Roraima (7) *Guyana*
Salto Angel (10) *Venez.*
Sete Quedas (10) *Braz.*

Stanley (7) *Zaire*
Sutherland (10) *N.Z.*
Trümmelbach (11) *Swit.*
Vettisfos (9) *Nor.*
Victoria (8) *Zambia*
Yosemite, Upper (13) *U.S.A.*

Weather

3 AND 4

bise
calm
cold
cool
damp
dark
dry
dull
east
fog
föhn
gale

gust
hail
haze
hazy
heat
hot
icy
mild
mist
rain
smog
snow
tide
veer

warm
west
wet
wind

5

cirri
cloud
dusty
eurus
flood
foehn

foggy
frost
gusty
light
misty
muggy
north
rainy
sleet
snowy
south
storm
sunny
windy

117

6

arctic
auster
bright
chilly
cirrus
clouds
cloudy
colder
deluge
floods
freeze
frosty
hot day
lowery
meteor
mizzle
mizzly
nimbus
normal
samiel
shower
simoom
simoon
solano
squall
starry
stormy
sultry
torrid
trades
vortex
warmer
wet day
winter
wintry
zephyr

7

backing
blowing
climate
clouded
cold day
coldish
cumulus
cyclone
drizzle
drought
dry-bulb
fogbank
freshen
fresher
freshet
hailing
hottish
icy-cold
mistral
monsoon
muggish
pampero
rainbow

raining
set fair
showery
sirocco
snowing
squally
stratus
summery
sunspot
tempest
thunder
tornado
typhoon
veering
warm day
warmish
wintery

8

autumnal
blizzard
cold snap
cyclonic
dead-calm
doldrums
downpour
easterly
east wind
eddy wind
fireball
freezing
heatwave
hot night
hurlwind
landwind
levanter
lowering
meteoric
nubilous
overcast
rainfall
rainless
snowfall
sunlight
thundery
tropical
westerly
west wind
wet night
windless

9

cold night
drift wind
drizzling
dry season
hailstorm
hard frost
harmattan
hoarfrost
hurricane

lightning
moonlight
northeast
northerly
northwest
north wind
nor'-wester
raincloud
sea breeze
snow-storm
southeast
southerly
southwest
south wind
sou'-wester
starlight
tidal wave
trade wind
unclouded
unsettled
warm night
whirlwind
zephyrous

10

arctic cold
black frost
changeable
depression
euroclydon
freshening
frostbound
hot climate
hot weather
land breeze
March winds
monsoonish
pouring-wet
Scotch mist
storm-cloud
waterspout
wet weather
white frost

11

anticyclone
cats and dogs
cold climate
cold weather
dull weather
etesian wind
foul weather
hard weather
lowering sky
mackerel sky
meteorology
mild weather
rain or shine
rainy season
stiff breeze
storm signal

summer cloud
temperature
tempestuous
thunderbolt
thunderclap
warm weather
wind backing
wind veering

12

anticyclonic
April showers
atmospherics
cirrocumulus
cirrostratus
currocumulus
currostratus
easterly wind
equinoctials
freezing rain
mackerel gale
shooting star
storm brewing
thundercloud
thunderstorm
tropical heat
tropical rain
weather glass
westerly wind
windy weather

13 AND 14

aurora borealis (14)
autumn weather (13)
cumulostratus (13)
frosty weather (13)
meteorological (14)
moonlight night (14)
northeast wind (13)
northerly wind (13)
northwest wind (13)
sheet lightning (14)
southeast wind (13)
southerly wind (13)
southwest wind (13)
starlight night (14)
summer weather (13)
thunder-shower (13)
torrential rain (14)
weather report (13)
weather prophet (14)
wintry weather (13)

15

forked lightning
meteoric showers
prevailing winds
summer lightning
tropical climate

LAW AND GOVERNMENT
Legal terms

2

J.P.
K.C.
Q.C.

3 AND 4

abet
act
bail
bar
bars
case
dock
D.P.P.
fair
fee
fine
gaol
I.O.U.
jury
law
lien
m'lud
oath
plea
quit
rape
rent
riot
rob
seal
stay
sue
suit
tort
use
will
writ

5

alien
arson
award
bench
cause
clerk
costs
court
crime
false
forge
fraud
guilt
in rem
judge
juror
legal
libel
mulct
order
penal
plead
poach
police
prize
proof

quash
right
rules
steal
trial
trust
usher
usury
valid

6

access
action
affirm
appeal
arrest
attorn
bailee
bigamy
breach
charge
commit
deceit
de jure
disbar
duress
elegit
equity
escrow
estate
felony
fiscal
forger
guilty
Hilary
incest
injury
insult
junior
legacy
malice
master
motion
murder
pardon
parole
piracy
police
prison
puisne
remand
repeal
set-off
surety
surtax

7

accused
alimony
assault
assizes
bailiff
battery
bequest
borstal
bribery
capital

case law
caution
circuit
codicil
consent
control
convict
coroner
counsel
cruelty
custody
damages
de facto
defence
divorce
ex parte
faculty
forgery
garnish
hanging
harming
hearsay
illegal
impeach
inquest
justice
land tax
larceny
lawless
lawsuit
licence
neglect
non suit
offence
penalty
perjury
precept
probate
proving
querent
release
reserve
Riot Act
robbery
servant
service
sheriff
slander
statute
summary
summons
suspect
tel-quel
treason
trustee
verdict
warrant
witness

8

absolute
abstract
act of god
act of law
advocate
advowson
attorney
barratry
birching

bottomry
brawling
burglary
camera
canon law
chancery
civil law
coercion
contract
covenant
criminal
deed poll
disorder
distress
drafting
entailed
estoppel
eviction
evidence
executor
felo de se
fidelity
forensic
guardian
homicide
in camera
indecent
judgment
judicial
law agent
law lords
legal aid
licensee
litigant
majority
murderer
novation
nuisance
perjuror
petition
pleading
preamble
prisoner
receiver
recorder
reprieve
Salic law
sedition
sentence
Shops Act
stealing
subpoena
sui juris
testator
trespass
tribunal
Truck Act
true bill
unlawful
validity

9

abduction
accessory
acquittal
ademption
agreement
allotment
annulment

attainder
barrister
blackmail
bona fides
cestui que
champerty
code of law
collusion
common law
copyright
defendant
de son tort
deviation
discharge
dismissal
distraint
embracery
endowment
equitable
execution
executory
extortion
fee simple
feoffment
Gaming Act
good faith
grand jury
guarantee
guarantor
high court
income tax
indemnity
innocence
intestacy
intestate
judiciary
land court
licensing
endowment
litigious
loitering
mala fides
mandatory
murderous
not guilty
not proven
Old Bailey
plaintiff
precatory
precedent
privilege
probation
procedure
refresher
registrar
remission
restraint
servitude
solicitor
statutory
summing-up
surrender
testament
testimony

10

alienation
appearance
assessment
assignment
attachment
attornment
bankruptcy
common pleas

common riot
confession
connivance
conspiracy
corruption
decree nisi
deed of gift
defamation
disclaimer
enticement
estate duty
executrix
eye witness
finance act
forfeiture
fraudulent
gaming acts
government
gun licence
hard labour
high treason
illegality
impediment
in chambers
indictment
injunction
inter vivos
judicature
King's Bench
land tenure
law sitting
Law Society
legitimacy
limitation
liquor laws
litigation
magistrate
misconduct
misprision
negligence
next friend
parliament
Poor Law Act
post mortem
prize court
procurator
prosecutor
respondent
revocation
separation
settlement
trespasser
ultra vires

11

advancement
affiliation
appointment
arbitration
arrangement
assize court
association
attestation
civil wrongs
composition
concealment
condonation
congé d'élire
county court
criminal law
death duties
debtors' acts
deportation
dissolution

disturbance
enabling act
enforcement
engrossment
examination
extenuating
extradition
fair comment
fieri facias
foreclosure
impeachment
infanticide
issue of writ
king's pardon
maintenance
market overt
mayor's court
obstruction
prerogative
prosecution
Queen's Bench
regulations
requisition
restitution
root of title
royal assent
sheriff's act
stamp duties
stipendiary
subornation
suicide pact
third degree
trespassing
Vagrancy Act
vesting deed

12

adjudication
bona vacantia
case of thorns
causa proxima
caution money
caveat emptor
charter party
Companies Act
compensation
constabulary
conveyancing
co-respondent
crime and tort
cross-examine
crown witness
death penalty
disaffection
embezzlement
encroachment
express trust
ferae naturae
grand assizes
guardianship
Habeas Corpus
imprisonment
infringement
inherent vice
interpleader
intimidation
joint tenancy
king's proctor
land transfer
Lord Advocate
lord of appeal
manslaughter
mensa et thoro
misbehaviour

misdemeanour
misdirection
oral evidence
pendente lite
prescription
privy council
prostitution
Queen's Pardon
ratification
royal charter
royal warrant
sheriff clerk
supreme court
taxing master
testamentary

13

administrator
age of marriage
ancient lights
apportionment
appropriation
burden of proof
charging order
common assault
consideration
court of appeal
Court of Arches
criminal libel
damage feasant
ejection order
ejusdem generis
Ground Game Act
hereditaments
housebreaking
illegal action
interlocutory
judge advocate
justification
law of property
letters patent
lord president
parliamentary
petty sessions
public trustee
quantum meruit
recognisances
right of appeal
search warrant
simple larceny
statute barred
treasure trove
trial by combat
trial by ordeal
Witchcraft Act

14

act of indemnity
administration
Admiralty Court
choses in action
common nuisance
common sergeant
companies court
concealed fraud
conjugal rights
county judgment
court of justice
criminal appeal
default summons
false pretences
identification

identity parade	special licence	attorney-general	contempt of court
local authority	wrongful arrest	autrefois acquit	emergency powers
lord chancellor		benefit of clergy	latent ambiguity
naturalization		charitable trust	local government
oyer and terminer	**15**	commercial court	marital coercion
penal servitude		commissary court	marriage licence
Queen's evidence	act of bankruptcy	compound a felony	official secrets
Queen's pleasure	act of parliament	compound larceny	power of attorney
second division	Act of Settlement	consistory court	quarter sessions

Parliamentary and political

2

M.P.
P.M.
U.N.

3

act
bar
C.B.I.
C.I.A.
E.E.C.
gag
I.R.A.
K.G.B.
law
opt
P.L.O.
red
sit
tax
T.U.C.

4

ayes
bill
coup
Dail
D.O.R.A.
Duma
gain
left
lord
mace
N.A.T.O.
noes
oath
pact
pass
peer
poll
rump
seat
Tory
veto
'vide
vote
vuli
Whig
whip
writ

5

agent
amend

bylaw
chair
clerk
count
draft
edict
elect
enact
house
junta
legal
lobby
Nazis
order
paper
party
Provo
purge
rally
right
S.E.A.T.O.
sit-in
valid
voter

6

assent
backer
ballot
budget
caucus
clause
colony
commie
Cortes
decree
divide
enosis
Fabian
Führer
govern
heckle
Labour
leader
Maoism
member
motion
nation
picket
policy
putsch
quorum
recess
record
reform
report
ruling
secede
senate

sirkar
speech
strike
summon
swaraj
tariff
teller
tyrant

7

adjourn
Al Fatah
anarchy
barrack
borough
boycott
cabinet
canvass
censure
chamber
closure
cold war
Comecon
Commons
commune
council
deficit
détente
dissent
elector
embargo
fascism
fascist
federal
finance
gallery
Hansard
heckler
hot line
Knesset
lock out
liberal
mandate
Marxism
neutral
new left
opening
outvote
pairing
passage
politic
poor law
premier
primary
prolong
radical
reading
recount
re-elect

re-enact
Riksdag
senator
session
speaker
statute
toryism
tribune
tyranny
vacancy
Zionism
Zionist

8

apartheid
assembly
Black rod
blockade
caudillo
chairman
Chiltern (Hundreds)
commissar
commoner
Congress
democrat
dictator
dissolve
division
dominion
election
elective
feminism
free vote
Gerousia
home rule
hustings
left-wing
majority
minister
ministry
minority
national
official
politics
prorogue
republic
rollback
schedule
Sobranye
Storting
suffrage
Tanaiste
Treasury
triumvir
unionism
unionist
whiggery
woolsack

121

9

amendment
anarchism
ballot-box
Barebone's
bicameral
Bundestag
coalition
Cominform
Comintern
committee
communism
communist
democracy
deterrent
Eduskunta
exchequer
first lord
legislate
ombudsman
politburo
poujadist
president
red guards
Reichstag
right-wing
sanctions
secretary
shire-moot
show trial
socialism
socialist
Stalinism
Taoiseach
terrorism

10

block grant
by-election
capitalism
chancellor
collective

conference
devolution
government
guillotine
invalidate
monarchism
Monday Club
opposition
parliament
Plaid Cymru
plebiscite
psephology
radicalism
referendum
republican
resolution
revolution
scrutineer
sitting-day
Third Reich
Third World
trade union
Trotskyism
unicameral
Warsaw Pact
White House
white paper

11

adjournment
back-bencher
ballot-paper
bye-election
casting vote
coexistence
congressman
constituent
containment
co-operative
demarcation
dissolution
divine right
enfranchise

finance bill
imperialist
independent
legislation
legislative
legislature
McCarthyism
nationalist
package deal
party leader
prerogative
private bill
reactionary
revisionism
statute book
suffragette
syndicalism
syndicalist
Tammany Hall
Witenagemot
yeoman-usher

12

commissioner
Common Market
Commonwealth
conservatism
Conservative
constituency
constitution
dictatorship
division lobby
domino theory
federal union
House of Lords
house of peers
invalidation
lord advocate
lord chairman
privy council
reading clerk
snap division
ways and means
welfare state

13

demonstration
deputy-speaker
disengagement
free trade area
home secretary
international
lord president
lord privy seal
prime minister
shadow cabinet
single chamber
trade unionist
United Nations
vote of censure

14

constitutional
deputy chairman
deputy premier
deputy sergeant
gerrymandering
lord chancellor
representative
sergeant-at-arms
social democrat

15

attorney-general
cabinet minister
clerk of the house
general election
Marxist-Leninist
minister of state
people's republic
personality cult
totalitarianism

LITERATURE AND THE ARTS
Art

2 AND 3

air
art
bur
del.
exc.
fec.
hue
inc.
inv.
key
mat
oil
op
pop
sit

4

airy
arts

base
body
burr
bust
chic
dada
daub
draw
etch
flat
form
gild
halo
icon
ikon
limn
line
lipo
mass
nude
pinx.
pose
size

tone
wash

5

akkhr
batik
bloom
blush
board
brush
burin
cameo
chalk
couch
delin.
draft
easel
ember
Fauve
fecit
frame

genre
gesso
glaze
glory
gloss
grave
hatch
inert
japan
lay-in
lumia
magot
model
mount
mural
nabis
paint
pietà
prime
print
putto
rebus
salon

scene
sculp
secco
shade
Stijl
study
stump
tondo
torso
trace
vertu
virtu

6

action
artist
ashcan
cachet
canvas
colour
crayon
cubism
depict
design
doctor
ectype
emblem
emboss
enamel
engild
flambé
fresco
fylfot
gothic
ground
kitcat
kit-kat
limner
mastic
medium
mobile
mosaic
niello
nimbus
object
ormolu
ox-gall
pastel
patina
pencil
pinxit
plaque
plaster
purism
reflex
relief
rhythm
rococo
school
sculpt.
shadow
sitter
sketch
statue
studio
uncial

7

abbozzo
academy
acrylic
atelier

amorino
archaic
aureole
baroque
Bauhaus
bottega
bachiru
biscuit
camaieu
cartoon
carving
cissing
classic
collage
contour
Dadaism
daubing
De Stijl
diagram
diptych
draught
drawing
etching
excudit
faience
Fauvism
felt tip
gilding
glazing
gouache
graphic
hot tone
impaint
impasto
lacquer
lino-cut
lunette
montage
mordant
orphism
outline
painter
palette
picture
pigment
plastic
profile
realism
remodel
replica
reredos
rococco
scumble
shading
sketchy
stabile
stencil
stipple
support
surface
tableau
tempera
texture
tracery
T-square
varnish
vehicle
woodcut

8

abstract
academic
acid bath
acrolith

anaglyph
aquatint
armature
arriccio
artistic
blue four
charcoal
concours
cool tone
diaglyph
drypoint
engraver
figurine
fixative
freehand
frottage
Futurism
gargoyle
graffiti
grouping
hatching
half-tone
handling
idealism
intaglio
intonaco
luminist
majolica
makimono
monotype
mounting
negative
oil paint
ornament
painting
panorama
pastiche
penumbra
plein air
portrait
repoussé
romantic
seascape
seicento
statuary
symmetry
tachisme
tapestry
tectonic
tesserae
throwing
trecento
triglyph
triptych
vignette
warm tone

9

aggregate
alla prima
anti-cerne
appliqué
aquarelle
aquatinta
arabesque
asymmetry
ball-point
bas-relief
blockbook
bric-à-brac
cartridge
cartouche
cloisonné
colourist

crow quill
damascene
damaskeen
dichroism
distemper
emblemata
embossing
encaustic
engraving
facsimile
geometric
gradation
grisaille
grotesque
highlight
hot colour
indelible
indian ink
intimiste
japanning
landscape
lay figure
lithotint
mahlstick
mannerism
marquetry
maulstick
mezzotint
miniature
modelling
neo-gothic
oil colour
oleograph
painterly
phototype
polyptych
primitive
ready made
recession
sculpture
scumbling
serigraph
statuette
still-life
stippling
strapwork
stretcher
Symbolist
tailpiece
tattooing
tenebrism
Totentanz
Vorticism
woodblock
xylograph

10

accidental
achromatic
altogether
anaglyphic
anaglyptic
Art Nouveau
atmosphere
automatism
avant-garde
background
biomorphic
body colour
caricature
cartellino
cerography
classicism
cool colour

cornucopia
dead colour
embossment
embroidery
fitch brush
flat colour
foreground
full length
hair pencil
half-length
India paper
Jugendstil
kinetic art
lithograph
mezzotinto
monochrome
naturalism
night piece
organic art
paint brush
pen and wash
pencilling
photograph
pietra dura
plasticity
portcrayon
Raphaelism
Raphaelite
Romanesque
serigraphy
silhouette
silk screen
Surrealism
synthesism
terracotta

turpentine
warm colour
xylography

11

academician
alto-relievo
aquatinting
battle piece
calligraphy
chiaroscuro
chinoiserie
chromograph
cinquecento
colour print
composition
concrete art
connoisseur
draughtsman
eclecticism
electrotype
engravement
foreshorten
found object
french chalk
ground plane
heliochrome
heliochromy
iconography
illusionism
imprimatura
life drawing

lithography
masterpiece
neo-romantic
oil painting
pavement art
perspective
photography
pointillism
portraiture
poster paint
primitivism
renaissance
restoration
scenography
stained glass
stereochromy
tessellation
tracing linen
tracing paper
watercolour

12

alkyd colours
bird's eye view
illustration
palette knife
scraper board

13

black and white
complementary

daguerreotype
decorative art
etching needle
expressionism
glass painting
Impressionism
Neo-Classicism
neoplasticism
Pre-Raphaelite
primary colour
social realism
tactile values
underpainting

14 AND OVER

action painting (14)
cabinet picture (14)
chromatography (14)
constructivism (14)
conversation piece (17)
draughtsmanship (15)
foreshortening (14)
Neo-Impressionism (16)
Neo-Romanticism (14)
pavement artist (14)
picture gallery (14)
plaster of paris (14)
portrait painter (15)
Post-Impressionism (17)
representational (16)
socialist realism (16)
steel engraving (14)
vanishing point (14)

Artists, architects, sculptors, cartoonists, etc.

3 AND 4

Adam
Arp
Bell
Bird
Bone
Both
Burn
Caro
Cima
Cole
Cox
Cuyp
Dadd
Dali
Dick
Dine
Dix
Dodd
Doré
Dou
Dufy
Dyce
Dyck
Egg
Etty
Eves
Eyck
Faed
Fehr
Ford
Gabo
Gere

Gill
Gogh
Good
Gore
Gow
Goya
Gris
Gros
Guys
Hals
Hand
Hart
Hemy
Herp
Holl
Home
Hone
Hook
Hunt
Jack
John
Kane
Kerr
King
Klee
Lam
Lamb
Lane
Lear
Lee
Lely
Lion
Low
Maes

Marc
May
Miró
Mola
Nash
Neer
Opie
Owen
Poy
Puy
Pyne
Reid
Reni
Rich
Rohe
Ross
Ryn
Sant
Shaw
Sime
Sims
Spee
Swan
Todd
Toft
Tuke
Wade
Wain
Ward
Watt
Webb
West
Wood
Wren

5

Aalto
Abbey
Adams
Allan
Allen
Amiet
Appel
Bacon
Baily
Balla
Banks
Barry
Barye
Bates
Beale
Bezzi
Blake
Boehm
Bosch
Bough
Brett
Brock
Brown
Bundy
Burra
Carra
Clark
Clint
Cohen
Cooke
Corot

Cross	Poole	Clouet	Mesdac
Cossa	Prout	Colton	Millet
Costa	Pugin	Conder	Monaco
Cotes	Redon	Cooper	Morley
Craig	Rodin	Copley	Morone
Crane	Rooke	Corbet	Morris
Credi	Rossi	Cotman	Müller
Crome	Sands	Cowper	Murray
Danby	Scott	Cozens	Newton
David	Segna	Currie	Nisbet
Davie	Short	Dahmen	Noland
Davis	Sleap	Dawson	Oliver
Degas	Small	Derain	Olsson
Devis	Smith	De Wint	O'Neill
Dixon	Soane	Dobson	Palmer
Drury	Soest	Draper	Panini
Durer	Speed	Duccio	Parker
Ensor	Staël	Dunbar	Parton
Ernst	Stark	Elwell	Paxton
Foley	Steen	Erlach	Pegram
Frink	Steer	Ferber	Penley
Frith	Stone	Fildes	Perret
Furse	Stott	Fisher	Pettie
Gaddi	Studd	Forbes	Piombo
Gaudi	Tobey	Foster	Pisano
Gaunt	Tonks	Fraser	Potter
Gibbs	Unwin	Fuller	Ramsay
Giles	Uwins	Fuseli	Renoir
Gotch	Velde	Geddes	Ribera
Goyen	Vonet	Gellée	Ridley
Grant	Watts	Gérard	Rivera
Grosz	Wells	Gibson	Rivers
Haden	White	Gilman	Robbia
Haghe	Wiens	Ginner	Robert
Hayes	Woods	Giotto	Romano
Innes	Wyatt	Girtin	Romney
Johns	Wyeth	Glover	Rothko
Jones	Wylie	Gordon	Rubens
Keene	Yeats	Graham	Ruskin
Kelly	Zoppo	Greuze	Sadler
Klein		Guardi	Sandby
Klimt		Gulich	Sandys
Lance	**6**	Hacker	Seddon
Leech		Harral	Serres
Leger	Abbott	Haydon	Seurat
Lemon	Albers	Heckel	Sisley
Le Vau	Allori	Hilton	Smirke
Lewis	Archer	Holmes	Smythe
Lippi	Arnold	Howard	Spence
Lotto	Ashton	Hudson	Stokes
Lowry	Barker	Hughes	Storck
Lucas	Barton	Hunter	Storey
Manet	Baskin	Ingres	Strang
Maris	Behnes	Jagger	Strube
Mason	Benson	Joseph	Stuart
Mauve	Benton	Kaprow	Stubbs
Moira	Berman	Kettle	Tadema
Monet	Bettes	Keyser	Tanguy
Moore	Bewick	Knight	Tayler
Munch	Birley	Laroon	Taylor
Nebot	Bodley	Laszlo	Thomas
Nervi	Boxall	Lavery	Titian
Nicol	Braque	Lawson	Turner
Noble	Briggs	Leader	Vacher
Nolde	Brough	Lebrun	Van Ryn
North	Brunel	Ledoux	Varley
Orpen	Buchel	Legros	Vernet
Palma	Burnet	Le Nain	Walker
Pater	Burton	Leslie	Waller
Payne	Butler	Linton	Wallis
Penny	Calder	Mabuse	Walton
Piper	Callow	McEvoy	Wardle
Plaas	Campin	Manson	Warhol
Platt	Carter	Marini	Watson
Ponte	Casson	Martin	Weekes
Ponti	Claude	Massys	Weenix

125

Weyden
Wilkie
Wilson
Windus
Wright
Wyllie
Yeames

7

Alberti
Aretino
Baldung
Barlach
Bassano
Bateman
Beechey
Belcher
Bellini
Bennett
Berchem
Bernini
Bomberg
Bonnard
Boucher
Bramley
Bridell
Brouwer
Calvert
Cameron
Campion
Cellini
Cézanne
Chagall
Chardin
Charles
Cheston
Chirico
Christo
Cimabue
Clausen
Cockram
Collier
Collins
Connard
Corinth
Cortona
Courbet
Cranach
Cundell
Dalziel
Daniell
Daumier
Da Vinci
De Hooch
De Lazlo
Dicksee
Dighton
Douglas
Downman
Duchamp
Edridge
Edwards
El Greco
Emanuel
Epstein
Flaxman
Fouquet
Fox-Pitt
Francia
Gabriel
Garstin
Gauguin
Gertlin
Gibbons

Gilbert
Gillray
Goodall
Goodwin
Greaves
Gregory
Gropius
Guarini
Guevara
Guthrie
Harding
Hartung
Hayward
Herbert
Herring
Hobbema
Hockney
Hofland
Hogarth
Hokusai
Holbein
Holland
Holroyd
Hoppner
Hopwood
Horsley
Housman
Indiana
Israels
Jackson
Jaggers
Johnson
Kneller
Knights
Kooning
Lambert
Lancret
Lanteri
Lessore
Linnell
Llander
Lucidel
Macbeth
Maccoll
Maclise
Maillol
Mansart
Maratti
Martini
Matisse
Memlinc
Merritt
Meunier
Michaux
Millais
Morandi
Morisot
Morland
Morrice
Murillo
Nasmith
Nattier
Neumann
Orcagna
Orchard
Osborne
Pacchia
Parrish
Parsons
Pasmore
Peacock
Peruzzi
Phidias
Philips
Phillip
Phil May

Philpot
Picabia
Picasso
Pickard
Pinwell
Pomeroy
Poussin
Poynter
Prinsep
Rackham
Raeburn
Raphael
Riviere
Roberts
Rouault
Roussel
Russell
Sargent
Schetky
Schiele
Shannon
Sickert
Siddall
Simpson
Smetham
Solomon
Spencer
Stanley
Stevens
Teniers
Tenniel
Thirtle
Thomson
Tiepolo
Uccello
Ugolino
Utrillo
Van Dyck
Van Eyck
Van Gogh
Vermeer
Watteau
Webster
Westall
Whiting
Woolner
Wynants
Zoffany

8

Allinson
Angelico
Armitage
Armstead
Aumonier
Beaumont
Beckmann
Beerbohm
Boccioni
Boffrand
Boughton
Brabazon
Bramante
Brancusi
Brangwyn
Brearley
Brooking
Brueghel
Calderon
Callcott
Calthorp
Carracci

Chambers
Chantrey
Crawhall
Creswick
Daubigny
De Keyser
De Laszlo
Delaunay
Del Prete
Deverell
Dietrich
Dressler
Dubuffet
Eastlake
Fielding
Fontaine
Frampton
Garofalo
Ghiberti
Giovanni
Gottlieb
Hartwell
Hepworth
Herkomer
Highmore
Hilliard
Hodgkins
Holloway
Houghton
Ibbetson
Inchbold
Jacobsen
Jan Steen
John Opie
Johnston
Jordaens
Kaufmann
Kirchner
Kokoshka
Kollwitz
Lambardo
Landseer
Lawrence
Leighton
Leonardo
Logsdail
Macallum
Macquoid
Magritte
Maitland
Mantegna
Marshall
Masaccio
Melville
Mondrian
Montalba
Montegna
Muirhead
Mulready
Munnings
Naviasky
Nevinson
Niemeyer
Palladio
Paolozzi
Paul Nash
Perugino
Phillips
Pissarro
Pontormo
Redgrave
Reynolds
Richmond
Ricketts
Robinson
Rossetti

Rousseau
Rugendas
Rushbury
Saarinen
Sassetta
Scamozzi
Schinkel
Segonzac
Severini
Simmonds
Solimena
Stanhope
Stothard
Stringer
Sullivan
Terbosch
Tinguely
Topolski
Vanbrugh
Van Goyen
Van Steen
Vasarely
Verbeeck
Veronese
Vlaminck
Waterlow
Wheatley
Whistler
Willcock
Williams
Woodward
Zakharov
Zurbarán

Donatello
Farington
Feininger
Fragonard
Franz Hals
Friedrich
Gastineau
Géricault
Giorgione
Griffiths
Grünewald
Guido Reni
Halswelle
Hatherell
Hawksmoor
Henderson
Honthorst
Hurlstone
Jawlensky
Kandinsky
Kemp-Welch
Kokoschka
Lancaster
Lanfranco
La Thangue
Lee-Hankey
Lightfoot
Llewellyn
Louis Wain
MacGregor
MacKennal
McLachlan
McWhirter
Martineau
Maundrell
Mazzolino
Mestrovic
Mondriaan
Nicholson
Northcote
Pisanello
Rembrandt
Salisbury
Sansovino
Schalcken
Singleton
Stanfield
Steenwyck
Stevenson
Strudwick
Thornhill
Velasquez
Verrochio
Waterford
Whitcombe

10

Alma-Tadema
Archipenko
Botticelli
Breenbergh
Brockhurst
Burne-Jones
Caravaggio
Cattermole
Cruikshank
Del Pacchia
di Giovanni
Fiddes-Watt
Friedenson
Fulleylove
Giacometti
Glendening
Holman-Hunt
Jan van Eyck
Kennington
La Fresnaye
Lethbridge
Liebermann
Lorenzetti
Mackintosh
Meissonier
Michelozzo
Modigliani
Onslow Ford
Orchardson
Peppercorn
Pollaiuolo
Praxiteles
Richardson
Rowlandson
Saint-Aubin
Sanmicheli
Shackleton
Simon Vonet
Somerville
Sutherland
Swynnerton
Tintoretto
Van der Goes
Van der Meer
Van de Velde
Waterhouse
Winstanley

11

Apollodorus
Copley Heath

Della Robbia
Farquharson
Fra Angelico
Ghirlandaio
Hondecoeter
Le Corbusier
Lloyd Wright
Margaritone
Pickersgill
Poelenburgh
Polycleitus
Polykleitos
Rippingille
San Severino
Somerscales
Thornycroft
Van der Plaas
Van Ruisdael

12 AND OVER

Brunelleschi (12)
de Hondecoeter (13)
Della Francesca (14)
de Loutherbourg (14)
Fantin-Latour (12)
Ford Madox Brown (14)
Gainsborough (12)
Gaudier-Brzeska (14)
Grandma Moses (12)
Haynes-Williams (14)
Heath Robinson (13)
Huchtenburgh (12)
Hughes-Stanton (13)
Lawes Witteronge (15)
Leonardo da Vinci (15)
Lichtenstein (12)
Loutherbourg (12)
Michelangelo (12)
Middleton-Todd (13)
Muirhead-Bone (12)
Puvis de Chavannes (16)
Rauschenberg (12)
Rembrandt van Ryn (15)
Sassoferrato (12)
Sidney Cooper (12)
Spencer Pryse (12)
Toulouse-Lautrec (15)
Van der Weyden (12)
Van Huchtenburgh (15)
Van Ochtervelt (13)
Winterhalter (12)
Witherington (12)

9

Ackermann
Alexander
Appleyard
Aston Webb
Bakhinzen
Beardsley
Biederman
Bonington
Botticini
Branwhite
Caldecot
Canaletto
Collinson
Constable
Correggio
Delacroix
d'Erlanger
Donaldson

Authors, poets, dramatists, etc.

3 AND 4

Amis
Ayer
Ball
Baum
Bede
Bell
Benn
Bolt
Buck
Cary
Coke
Cole

Dane
Day
Dell
Duse
Eden
Eyre
Ford
Fox
Fry
Fyfe
Gay
Gide
Glyn
Gray

Grey
Hall
Hart
Hay
Hine
Home
Hood
Hook
Hope
Hugo
Hume
Hunt
Hyne
Inge

Joad
Kant
King
Knox
Kyd
Lamb
Lang
Lear
Lee
Livy
Loos
Loti
Lyly
Lynd

Mais
Mann
Marx
Mill
More
Muir
Nash
Ovid
Owen
Poe
Pope
Pugh
Read
Reid
Rowe
Ruck
Sade
Sala
Shaw
Sims
Snow
Tate
Vane
Vega
Ward
West
Wood
Wren
Zola

5

Acton
Adams
Aesop
Agate
Aiken
Albee
Arden
Arlen
Auden
Ayres
Bacon
Barry
Barth
Bates
Behan
Betti
Beyle
Blake
Bloom
Blunt
Bowen
Bruce
Bunin
Burke
Burns
Byron
Cable
Caine
Camus
Capek
Clare
Colum
Couch
Croce
Dante
Dario
Defoe
Diver
Donne
Doyle
Dumas
Eliot
Ellis

Evans
Field
Freud
Frost
Gibbs
Gogol
Gorki
Gosse
Gower
Grimm
Hardy
Harte
Hegel
Heine
Henry
Henty
Homer
Hulme
Ibsen
Innes
Irwin
James
Jeans
Jones
Joyce
Kafka
Keats
Keith
Keyte
Lever
Lewis
Locke
Lodge
Logue
Lorca
Lucan
Lucas
Mason
Milne
Moore
Murry
Noyes
Ngugi
Odets
O'Dowd
Ogden
O'Hara
Orczy
Orton
Otway
Ouida
Paine
Pater
Peake
Peele
Pepys
Plato
Pliny
Pound
Praed
Prior
Raine
Reade
Ridge
Rilke
Rolle
Sagan
Scott
Shute
Smart
Smith
Spark
Stark
Staël
Stein
Stern

Stowe
Swift
Synge
Taine
Tasso
Twain
Tynan
Udall
Varro
Verne
Walsh
Waugh
Wells
Wilde
Woolf
Wyatt
Yeats
Yonge
Young
Zweig

6

Adcock
Aldiss
Anstey
Aragon
Archer
Arnold
Asimov
Austen
Bailey
Balzac
Barham
Barrie
Begbie
Belloc
Bellow
Benson
Besant
Besier
Binyon
Borrow
Brecht
Bridie
Brieux
Briggs
Brontë
Brooke
Brophy
Browne
Bryant
Buchan
Bunyan
Burgin
Burney
Butler
Caesar
Chekov
Church
Cicero
Clarke
Clough
Conrad
Cooper
Coward
Cowley
Cowper
Crabbe
Cronin
Curzon
Darwin
Daudet
Davies
Dekker

Dennis
Dobson
Dryden
Dunbar
Duncan
Empson
Ervine
Euclid
Ennius
Evelyn
Farnol
Fichte
Fonson
France
Frazer
Freund
Froude
Ganpat
George
Gibbon
Godwin
Goethe
Gordon
Graeme
Graham
Graves
Greene
Hallam
Hamsun
Harris
Hawkes
Haynes
Hemans
Henley
Hesiod
Hobbes
Holmes
Holtby
Horace
Howard
Howitt
Hughes
Huxley
Ian Hay
Ibañez
Irving
Jacobs
Jepson
Jerome
Jonson
Jowett
Junius
Keller
Kuprin
Landor
Lao-Tse
Larkin
Lawson
Le Sage
London
Lowell
Ludwig
Lytton
Mailer
Malory
Mannin
Marcel
Martyn
Miller
Milton
Morgan
Mörike
Morris
Munthe
Murray
Musset

Necker
Nerval
Newman
O'Brien
O'Casey
Ogilvy
O. Henry
O'Neill
Onions
Orwell
Parker
Pascal
Pellew
Pepler
Petőfi
Pindar
Pinter
Pinero
Proust
Racine
Raynal
Rhodes
Riding
Rohmer
Rowley
Ruskin
Sandys
Sapper
Sappho
Sardou
Sartre
Savage
Sayers
Scribe
Sedley
Seneca
Sidney
Sladen
Snaith
Soutar
Squire
Steele
Sterne
Tagore
Taylor
Temple
Thomas
Thorne
Thrale
Undset
Valery
Villon
Virgil
Waller
Walton
Watson
Wesker
Weyman
Wilson
Wotton
Wilcox

7

Abelard
Addison
Alfieri
Anouilh
Aquinas
Ariosto
Baldwin
Beddoes
Beeding
Belasco
Bennett

Bentham
Bentley
Berchet
Bergson
Bernard
Birrell
Blunden
Boswell
Brandes
Bridges
Bullett
Burgess
Caedmon
Camoens
Campion
Carlyle
Carroll
Chapman
Chaucer
Chekhov
Cheyney
Claudel
Clayton
Clemens
Cobbett
Colette
Collier
Collins
Corelli
Craigie
Crashaw
Deeping
Delaney
Dickens
Diderot
Dodgson
Doughty
Douglas
Drayton
Dreiser
Dunsany
Durrell
Emerson
Erasmus
Erskine
Flecker
Forster
Foscolo
Frankau
Freeman
Galileo
Gallico
Garnett
Gaskell
Gautier
Gilbert
Gissing
Glossop
Golding
Gregory
Haeckel
Haggard
Hakluyt
Hartley
Hassall
Hazlitt
Herbert
Herrick
Hewlett
Heywood
Hichens
Hocking
Hopkins
Housman
Howells
Hueffer

Ionesco
Jimenez
Johnson
Juvenal
Kinross
Kipling
Leacock
Leblanc
Lehmann
Le Queux
Lessing
Lindsay
Macleod
McKenna
Malraux
Manzoni
Marryat
Marlowe
Marston
Martial
Marvell
Maugham
Mauriac
Maurois
Maurras
Mazzini
Mencken
Mérimée
Meynell
Moffatt
Molière
Montagu
Murdoch
Nabokov
Newbolt
Nichols
Ogilvie
Osborne
Oxenham
Patmore
Peacock
Plummer
Pushkin
Rastell
Richter
Rimbaud
Rolland
Romains
Ronsard
Rostand
Rushkin
Russell
Sadleir
Sarasin
Saroyan
Sassoon
Service
Shelley
Simenon
Simonov
Sitwell
Skelton
Solinus
Southey
Spencer
Spender
Spenser
Spinoza
Stevens
Strauss
Surtees
Tacitus
Terence
Thomson
Thoreau
Tolkien

Tolstoy
Ustinov
Vachell
Vaughan
Walkley
Wallace
Walpole
Webster
Whitman
Wickham
Withers
Zetland

8

Albanesi
Alington
Andersen
Anderson
Andreyev
Apuleius
Atherton
Aumonier
Barbusse
Beaumont
Beerbohm
Bensusan
Berkeley
Berryman
Betjeman
Bindloss
Bjornson
Bradbury
Browning
Bushnell
Calthrop
Campbell
Catullus
Cervantes
Chambers
Christie
Clouston
Congreve
Conquest
Cornford
Crichton
Crockett
Crompton
Cummings
Davidson
Day Lewis
De la Mare
De Musset
Disraeli
Donleavy
Drummond
Du Bellay
Faulkner
Fielding
Flaubert
Fletcher
Fontaine
Forester
Goncourt
Goodyear
Grierson
Grimshaw
Guedalla
Hamilton
Heinlein
Hoffmann
Ibbetson
Ingemann
Johnston
Kavanagh

129

Kingsley
Kingston
Knoblock
Koestler
Laforgue
Lagerlöf
Langland
Lawrence
Leibnitz
Leishman
Lonsdale
Leopardi
Lovelace
Ludovici
Macaulay
MacNeice
Mallarmé
Melville
Meredith
Merriman
Michelet
Mirabeau
Mitchell
Mortimer
Palgrave
Pattison
Perrault
Petrarch
Plutarch
Ponsonby
Quennell
Rabelais
Rattigan
Reynolds
Rossetti
Rousseau
Sabatini
Salinger
Sandburg
Schiller
Shadwell
Sheridan
Sidgwick
Sillitoe
Sinclair
Smollett
Stendhal
Stephens
Strachey
Sturgess
Suckling
Taffrail
Tennyson
Thompson
Thurston
Tibullus
Tourneur
Traherne
Trollope
Turgenev
Vanbrugh
Verlaine
Voltaire
Vonnegut
Walbrook
Wheatley
Whittier
Williams
Zane Grey
Zangwill

9

Adam Smith
Addinsell

Aeschylus
Ainsworth
Aldington
Alec Waugh
Anita Loos
Antoninus
Aristotle
Bartimeus
Ben Jonson
Berta Ruck
Blackmore
Blackwood
Boccaccio
Bottomley
Boyd Cable
Bret Harte
Burroughs
Cervantes
Corneille
Churchill
Coleridge
D'Annunzio
David Hume
Delafield
De la Roche
De Quincey
Descartes
Dickenson
Dos Passos
Dudintsev
Du Maurier
Eddington
Edgeworth
Etheridge
Ehrenburg
Euripides
Froissart
Giraudoux
Goldsmith
Goncharov
Gutenberg
Guy Thorne
Hall Caine
Hauptmann
Hawthorne
Heidegger
Hemingway
Herodotus
Heyerdahl
Hölderlin
Isherwood
Kaye-Smith
La Bruyère
La Fontaine
Lamartine
Leigh Hunt
Lermontov
Linklater
Lomonosov
Lord Byron
Lucretius
MacCarthy
Mackenzie
Macrobius
Madariaga
Mansfield
Mark Twain
Masefield
Massinger
Maud Diver
Middleton
Mitchison
Montaigne
Nietzsche
Oppenheim
Pasternak

Pemberton
Pett Ridge
Priestley
Radcliffe
Robertson
Rochester
Ruby Ayres
Sackville
Sax Rohmer
Schreiner
Shenstone
Sholokhov
Sophocles
Spielmann
Stacpoole
Steinbeck
Stevenson
Suetonius
Swinburne
Thackeray
Tomlinson
Trevelyan
Turgeniev
Van Druton
Wodehouse
Wycherley
Zuckmayer

10

Ballantyne
Barrington
Baudelaire
Birmingham
Boldrewood
Brett Young
Chatterton
Chesterton
Conan Doyle
don Marquis
Dostoevsky
Drinkwater
Dürrenmatt
Elinor Glyn
Emil Ludwig
Fitzgerald
Galsworthy
Hungerford
Hutchinson
Jack London
Jane Austen
John Buchan
Jules Verne
Longfellow
Lope de Vega
Lord Lytton
Maupassant
Mayakovsky
Mcgonagall
Mickiewicz
Mrs. Gaskell
Muriel Hine
Noel Coward
Oscar Wilde
Phillpotts
Pierre Loti
Pirandello
Propertius
Pryce-Jones
Quintilian
Richardson
Ronaldshay
Saintsbury
Saint-Simon
Sean O'Casey

Strindberg
Sutton Vane
Tarkington
Thucydides
Victor Hugo
Williamson
Wordsworth

11

Abercrombie
Apollinaire
Dostoievski
Garcia Lorca
Grillparzer
Kierkegaard
Maeterlinck
Montesquieu
Montherlant
Omar Khayyam
Ravenscroft
Sainte-Beuve
Shakespeare
Tocqueville
Watts-Dunton
Yevtushenko

12

Aristophanes
Beaumarchais
Bulwer Lytton
Chesterfield
De Selincourt
Fiona Macleod
Hans Andersen
Hergesheimer
Macchiavelli
Quiller-Couch
Rider Haggard
Robbe-Grillet
Rose Macaulay
Solzhensitsyn
Storm Jameson
Wittgenstein
Wyndham Lewis

13

Andrew Marvell
Arnold Bennett
Baroness Orczy
Cecil Day Lewis
Cosmo Hamilton
Edgar Allan Poe
Ford Madox Ford
Hilaire Belloc
Jeffrey Farnol
Jerome K. Jerome
Ohlenschlager
Rouget de Lisle
Sackville-West
Sinclair Lewis
Stacy Aumonier
Upton Sinclair
Wilkie Collins

14

Agatha Christie
Compton-Burnett
Eden Philpotts

Lecomte de Lisle
Marcus Aurelius
Middleton Murry
Rafael Sabatini
Rudyard Kipling
Storer Clouston
Temple Thurston

Warwick Deeping

15

Beverley Nichols
Booth Tarkington

Granville Barker
La Rochefoucauld
Millington Synge
Pierre de Ronsard
Somerset Maugham
Valerius Flaccus
Washington Irving (16)

Building and architecture

3

bar
bay
hip
hut
inn
mew
pub
spa
sty
won

4

apse
arch
area
bank
barn
bema
byre
café
cage
cell
cyma
club
cowl
crib
dado
dais
dike
dome
door
exit
fane
flag
flat
flue
gaol
gate
grot
hall
jail
jamb
keep
khan
kiln
kirk
lath
lift
lock
loft
mart
maze
mews
mill
mint
moat
mole
nave

nook
oast
ogee
oven
pale
pane
pave
pier
pile
plan
post
quay
rail
ramp
rink
roof
room
ruin
sash
seat
shed
shop
sill
sink
site
slat
stay
step
stud
tile
tomb
town
trap
vane
vill
vyse
wair
wall
wing
wood
xyst
yard
yate

5

abbey
abode
aisle
alley
ambry
annex
attic
bayed
block
booth
bower
brace
brest
brick
build

built
cabin
choir
coign
compo
court
crypt
dairy
depot
domed
Doric
drain
eaves
entry
erect
fence
flats
floor
forum
gable
glass
glaze
grate
grout
gully
harem
hotel
house
hovel
hydro
igloo
ionic
jetty
joint
joist
jutty
kiosk
kraal
latch
ledge
lobby
lodge
manse
mitre
newel
niche
order
oriel
paned
panel
patio
plank
pound
putty
quoin
rails
ranch
range
scape
serai
sewer
shaft

shelf
shell
slate
slatt
socle
solar
spire
stack
stage
stair
stake
stall
stand
steps
stile
stone
store
stove
strut
study
suite
tabby
thorp
tiled
tourn
tower
trone
truss
Tudor
vault
villa
wharf
works

6

access
adytum
alcove
alette
annexe
arbour
arcade
ashlar
ashler
asylum
atrium
aviary
bakery
batten
belfry
bourse
bricks
canopy
casino
castle
cellar
cement
châlet
chapel
chevet

chunam
church
cilery
cimbia
cinema
cintre
circus
closet
coffer
coigne
column
coping
corbel
corona
coving
crèche
cupola
dagoba
débris
design
dogana
donjon
drains
dug-out
ecurie
estate
exedra
façade
fascia
fillet
finial
fresco
friary
fylfot
gablet
garage
garret
girder
glazed
godown
Gothic
grange
grille
grotto
gutter
hangar
hearth
hog-pen
hog-sty
hostel
impost
inwall
Ionian
kennel
ladder
lanary
larder
lean-to
linhay
lintel
locker
lock-up
loggia
log-hut
louver
louvre
lyceum
mantel
market
mihrab
mitred
morgue
mortar
mosaic
mosque
mud hut

museum
mutule
niched
Norman
office
outlet
pagoda
palace
paling
pantry
parget
paving
perron
pharos
piazza
pigsty
pillar
pinery
plinth
poling
portal
priory
prison
purlin
putlog
quarry
rabbet
rafter
rancho
recess
refuge
rococo
ropery
rosery
rubble
rustic
saloon
saw-pit
school
scroll
shanty
smiddy
smithy
soffit
spence
square
stable
stairs
staith
stores
stucco
studio
subway
tarsia
tavern
temple
tender
thatch
thorpe
tilery
tiling
timber
tolsey
trench
trough
turret
unroof
untile
veneer
vestry
vihara
vinery
vintry
vivary
volute
wattle

wicket
wigwam
window
xystos
zaccho
zareba
zenana

7

academy
acroter
air duct
air flue
alcazar
almonry
ambitus
ancones
annulet
anticum
arcaded
archway
armoury
atelier
balcony
ballium
baroque
bastion
bedroom
bossage
boudoir
brewery
builder
butlery
butment
buttery
cabinet
cafenet
canteen
capitol
cassino
castlet
ceiling
chamber
chancel
chantry
château
chevron
chimney
choltry
cistern
cob-wall
college
compost
conduit
convent
cornice
cortile
cottage
crocket
cubicle
culvert
curtain
deanery
demesne
domical
dooring
doorway
doucine
dovecot
dungeon
edifice
embassy
entasis
eustyle

factory
farmery
fernery
fixture
fluting
foundry
fullery
gallery
gateway
granary
grapery
grating
groined
grounds
hay loft
herbary
hip roof
hogcote
hospice
hot-wall
hydrant
impasto
jib door
joinery
juffers
kennels
keyhole
kitchen
knocker
kremlin
landing
lantern
lattice
laundry
lazaret
library
lunette
mansard
mansion
masonry
megaron
mill dam
minaret
minster
moellon
mud wall
mullion
munnion
nailery
narthex
nogging
nunnery
nursery
obelisk
oratory
ossuary
out-gate
paddock
pantile
parapet
parlour
passage
pension
pentice
pentile
piggery
pillbox
plaster
portico
postern
pugging
pug mill
pyramid
quarrel
railing
rebuild

rectory
re-edify
reeding
rejoint
repairs
reredos
rockery
roofing
rostrum
rotunda
sanctum
sawmill
seabank
seawall
section
shebeen
shelves
shelter
shingle
shutter
slating
spicery
stadium
staging
station
steeple
storied
surgery
systyle
tambour
tannery
taproom
tegular
terrace
theatre
tie-beam
tracery
tracing
transom
trellis
turncap
unbuilt
unpaved
untiled
vachery
varnish
vaulted
veranda
viaduct
village
voluted

8

abat-jour
abattoir
abat-voix
abutment
air-drain
airtight
anteroom
apophyge
approach
aquarium
arboured
atheneum
backdoor
backroom
ballroom
baluster
banister
basement
basilica
bathroom
building

bungalow
buttress
caliduct
caryatid
casement
causeway
cavation
cenotaph
cesspool
chaptrel
chatelet
cincture
cloister
clubroom
cockloft
coliseum
comptoir
concrete
contract
corn loft
corridor
cow house
cradling
crescent
cromlech
cross-tie
cupboard
curb roof
cutchery
darkroom
dead wall
decorate
detached
doghouse
domicile
door case
door nail
doorpost
doorsill
doorstep
dovecote
dovetail
dowel pin
drainage
draughty
dry store
dry stove
dust stove
dust hole
dwelling
elevator
emporium
entrance
entresol
epistyle
erection
espalier
estimate
excavate
fanlight
fireclay
fish weir
flagging
flashing
flatting
flooring
freehold
fretwork
frontage
fusarole
gargoyle
geodesic
grillage
grouting
handrail
hen house

hoarding
hoistway
home farm
hospital
hostelry
hothouse
ice house
intrados
jalousie
keystone
kingpost
kingwood
lathwork
lavatory
legation
lichgate
lift well
log cabin
loghouse
lychgate
madhouse
magazine
memorial
mill pond
monolith
monument
mortuary
moulding
newsroom
openwork
orangery
outhouse
overhang
palisade
panelled
pantheon
pavement
pavilion
pedestal
pediment
pentroof
pilaster
pinnacle
plashing
platform
plumbing
pointing
pothouse
propylon
refinery
registry
rockwork
rood loft
roof tree
ropewalk
sacristy
sail-loft
sale room
scaffold
seminary
seraglio
showroom
skirting
skylight
slop-shop
smeltery
snuggery
soil pipe
solarium
spanroof
stabling
stuccoed
sudatory
sun-proof
taphouse
tectonic

tenement
terminus
toll-gate
townhall
transept
trapdoor
triglyph
tympanum
underpin
upstairs
vicarage
wainscot
wardroom
waxworks
well hole
well room
windmill
windowed
woodwork
workroom
workshop
ziggurat

9

acropolis
acroteria
aerodrome
alarm bell
alignment
almshouse
apartment
arabesque
arch-brick
architect
archivolt
archstone
aerostyle
art school
ashlaring
athenaeum
bakehouse
bay window
bede house
bell gable
bell tower
belvedere
bivaulted
boathouse
bow window
brick clay
brick kiln
brick dust
campanile
cartouche
cathedral
ceilinged
cellarage
centering
chop house
claustral
clay slate
clay stone
cloakroom
clubhouse
coalhouse
cocoonery
coffer dam
colonnade
colosseum
construct
consulate
cooperage
copestone
courtyard

133

10

cross-beam
crown-post
day school
decastyle
distemper
doorplate
doorstead
doorstone
dormitory
dowelling
drain trap
dripstone
earthbank
elevation
embrasure
episenium
eremitage
escalator
esplanade
estaminet
excavator
farmhouse
ferestral
firebrick
fireplace
fir-framed
fishgarth
flagstone
flashings
floriated
framework
frontdoor
frontroom
gallery
garreting
gatehouse
gravel pit
grotesque
guardroom
guestroom
guildhall
gullyhole
gymnasium
headstone
hermitage
hexastyle
homestall
homestead
hypocaust
hypostyle
infirmary
interaxal
interaxis
ironworks
jettyhead
jut-window
kalsomine
kerbstone
Kitchener
labyrinth
lazaretto
leasehold
letterbox
lift-shaft
linenfold
Lob's pound
mausoleum
metalling
mezzanine
modillion
monastery
music hall
music room
octastyle
octostyle
orphanage

oubliette
outer door
outer gate
palladian
pargeting
parquetry
parsonage
parthenon
partition
party-wall
pay office
penthouse
peristyle
pillarbox
playhouse
pleasance
pontifice
poorhouse
pressroom
prize ring
promenade
quicklime
race-stand
rail-fence
rainproof
raintight
refectory
rendering
reservoir
residence
residency
rest-house
ring-fence
sallyport
scagliola
scantling
sectional
spareroom
staircase
stillroom
stinktrap
stockroom
stonewall
stonework
storeroom
stretcher
structure
swinecote
synagogue
tablature
tenements
threshold
tile-drain
tollbooth
tollhouse
tower-room
townhouse
treillage
triforium
turf-house
turnstile
undermine
underprop
undrained
vestibule
wallpaper
wall-plate
warehouse
wastepipe
watertank
whitewash
windproof
windtight
winevault
wiregauze
workhouse

à la grecque
antechapel
antetemple
araeostyle
arc-boutant
architrave
archivault
backstairs
ball-flower
balustered
balustrade
bargeboard
bedchamber
bell-turret
brick-built
brick earth
cantilever
catafalque
chapellany
chimney cap
chimney pot
clerestory
clock tower
coachhouse
coalcellar
common room
conversion
Corinthian
court house
covered way
crenulated
cripplings
cross-aisle
crown glass
culver-tail
damp-course
decoration
decorative
depository
dining hall
dining room
dispensary
distillery
ditriglyph
dome-shaped
doorhandle
doricorder
double-hung
double lock
dowel joint
drawbridge
dryingroom
Dutch tiles
earth house
embankment
enrockment
engine-room
excavation
facia panel
fir-wrought
first floor
fives court
flint glass
flock paper
forcing-pit
foundation
garden city
glass-house
grandstand
Greek cross
greenhouse
grotto-work
ground-plan
ground-sill

guardhouse
habitation
hipped roof
hippodrome
hunting box
hypaethral
intramural
Ionic order
Ionic style
jerry-built
laboratory
lady chapel
lancet arch
Latin cross
lazar-house
lighthouse
lumber-room
maisonette
manor house
market town
monopteros
necropolis
Norman arch
overmantel
panopticon
persiennes
plastering
plate glass
portcullis
post office
powder-house
propylaeum
proscenium
pycnostyle
quadrangle
repointing
repository
robing-room
rock-temple
Romanesque
roof garden
rose garden
rose window
roundhouse
roundtower
rubblework
sanatorium
sanitarium
settlement
skew bridge
skyscraper
slaked lime
smokestack
space frame
state house
stillatory
storehouse
streetdoor
structural
tetrastyle
tiring-room
Tudor style
undercroft
university
unoccupied
untenanted
varnishing
ventilator
vestry room
watch-house
watch-tower
water-tower
way-station
white-limed
wicket gate
window sash

windscreen
wine-cellar

11

antechamber
barge-course
caravansary
castellated
cementation
cementatory
chain-bridge
columbarium
compartment
concert hall
contabulate
coping stone
corbel steps
cornerstone
counterfort
curtail step
distempered
door knocker
dovetailing
drawing room
dress circle
entablature
entablement
finger plate
florid style
foundations
frieze-panel
glass-mosaic
ground-floor
hearthstone
lattice work
load-bearing
louvre-board
luffer board
machicoulis
mantelpiece
manufactory
market-cross
morning room
observatory
oeil-de-boeuf
office block
oriel window
out-building
picture rail
plasterwork
postern gate
postscenium
public house
purpose-built
reading room
reconstruct
renaissance
reservatory
residential
Roman cement

rustication
sarcophagus
scaffolding
shooting box
staddle roof
stringboard
sub-contract
summer house
superstruct
tessellated
tiled hearth
trelliswork
Turkish bath
Tuscan order
undercoated
unfurnished
uninhabited
ventilation
wainscoting
war memorial
water supply
weathercock
whitewashed
window frame
window glass
window ledge
wire grating
wooden house
wrought iron

12

amphitheatre
araeosystyle
archbuttress
architecture
assembly room
auction rooms
building site
caravanserai
chapel of ease
chimneypiece
chimneyshaft
cockle stairs
conservatory
construction
constructure
country house
covered court
culver-tailed
dormer window
draught-proof
dressing-room
entrance hall
floor timbers
folding doors
garden suburb
geodesic dome
guest chamber
half-timbered
Ionian column

kitchen range
labour-saving
lake dwelling
lightning-rod
lock-up garage
louvre window
machicolated
mansion house
meeting house
mission house
outer gateway
pantechnicon
parquet floor
penitentiary
power station
purbeck stone
retiring-room
spiral stairs
sub-struction
sub-structure
subterranean
sweating room
three-ply wood
tower bastion
town planning
tracing cloth
tracing linen
tracing paper
unmodernized
unornamental
unornamented
untenantable
unventilated
urban renewal
valance board
venetian door
wainscotting
weatherproof
winter garden

13

amphiprostyle
ancient lights
architectonic
architectural
assembly rooms
back staircase
breakfast room
butler's pantry
chimney corner
compass window
contabulation
coursing joint
Dutch clinkers
dwelling house
dwelling place
encaustic tile
entrance lobby
establishment

ferro-concrete
Grecian temple
lattice window
machicolation
martello tower
master builder
Norman doorway
portland stone
satellite town
skirting board
specification
sub-contractor
sweating house
transom window
triumphal arch
uninhabitable
vaulting shaft
venetian blind
vinyl emulsion
wattle and daub

14

architectonics
catherine wheel
central heating
drying cupboard
filling station
flying buttress
lath and plaster
mezzanine floor
office building
picture gallery
portland cement
powder magazine
reconstruction
superstructure
threshing floor
venetian window
wayside station
whispering dome

15

air conditioning
dampproof course
discharging arch
electric heating
feather boarding
foundation stone
hydraulic cement
pleasure gardens
pleasure grounds
refreshment room
spiral staircase
vitruvian scroll
weather boarding
withdrawing room

Characters in literature

Some characters from **Ben Jonson, Charlotte Brontë, Lord Byron, Chaucer,** and **Congreve**

List of works from which the following characters are taken, with reference numbers.

Ben Jonson

Ref. No.	Title	
1.	Alchemist, The	(12 letters)
2.	Bartholomew Fayre	(16 ,,)
3.	Cynthia's Revels	(14 ,,)
4.	Devil is an Ass, The	(15 ,,)
5.	Epicoene	(8 ,,)
6.	Every Man in his Humour	(19 ,,)
7.	Every Man out of his Humour	(22 ,,)
8.	Magnetick Lady, The	(16 ,,)
9.	New Inn, The	(9 ,,)
10.	Poetaster, The	(12 ,,)
11.	Sad Shepherd, The	(14 ,,)
12.	Sejanus	(7 ,,)
13.	Volpone	(7 ,,)
14.	(Various)	

Lord Byron

Ref. No.	Title	
15.	Don Juan	(7 letters)
16.	(Various)	

Charlotte Brontë

17.	Jane Eyre	(8 letters)
18.	Professor, The	(12 ,,)
19.	Shirley	(7 ,,)
20.	Villette	(8 ,,)

Chaucer (Geoffrey)

21.	Canterbury Tales	(15 letters)

Congreve (William)

22.	Double Dealer, The	(15 letters)
23.	Love for Love	(11 ,,)
24.	Mourning Bride, The	(16 ,,)
25.	Old Bachelor, The	(14 ,,)
26.	Way of the World, The	(16 ,,)

Note: The numbers in brackets indicate *the works* in which the characters appear.

3 AND 4

Alp (16)
Anah (16)
Azo (16)
Baba (15)
Beck (20)
Busy (2)
Cash (6)
Cave (19)
Cob (6)
Cos (3)
Daw (5)
Dent (17)
Dudu (15)
Echo (3)
Ella (21)
Eyre (17)
Face (1)
Fly (9)
Gale (19)
Hall (19)
Hogg (19)
Home (20)
Hugo (16)
Inez (15)
Lara (16)
Lucy (25)
May (21)
Nero (12)
Otho (16)
Paul (18, 20)
Prue (23)
Pug (4)
Raby (15)
Rud (17)
Seyd (16)
Wasp (1)
Whit (2)
Zara (24)

Arete (3)
Asper (7)
Beppo (16)
Betty (25)
Brisk (7, 22)
Burns (17)
Celia (13)
Chloe (10)
Cotta (12)
Cupid (3)
Donne (19)
Frail (23)
Froth (22)
Gabor (16)
Hedon (3)
Jenny (23)
Julia (10)
Kaled (16)
Laura (16)
Leila (15, 16)
Lloyd (17)
Lolah (15)
Lorel (11)
Lovel (9)
Lupus (10)
Manly (4)
Mason (17)
Minos (10)
Mitis (7)
Moore (19)
Moria (3)
Morus (3)
Mosca (13)
Neuha (16)
Osman (24)
Poole (17)
Pryor (19)
Roger (21)
Rufus (12)
Scott (19)
Selim (16)
Shift (7)
Snowe (20)
Steno (16)
Surly (1)
Tipto (9)
Topas (21)

Varro (12)
Ulric (16)
Waspe (2)
Whipp (19)
Yorke (19)

6

Albius (10)
Alison (21)
Arcite (21)
Arnold (16)
Asotus (3)
Bessie (17)
Caesar (10)
Canace (21)
Common (1)
Conrad (16)
Crites (3)
Damian (21)
Dapper (1)
Deliro (7)
Drusus (12)
Earine (11)
Emilia (21)
Ferret (9)
Foible (9)
Formal (6)
Gallus (10)
Giaour (The) (16)
Gelaia (3)
Graham (20)
Haidee (15)
Harold (16)
Hassan (16)
Horace (10)
Jaques (14)
Jeremy (23)
Kitely (6)
Lambro (15)
Legend (23)
Luscus (10)
Malone (19)
Mammon (1)
Marina (16)
Marino (16)

Maxime (21)
Medora (16)
Morose (5)
Myrrha (16)
Opsius (12)
Overdo (2)
Pliant (1)
Plyant (22)
Polish (8)
Reuter (18)
Setter (25)
Silvia (25)
Simkin (21)
St. John (Mr.) (17)
Subtle (1)
Symkin (21)
Tartar (dog) (19)
Tattle (23)
Temple (17)
Thopas (21)
Virgil (10)
Walter (21)
Werner (16)
Wittol (16)

7

Abolson (21)
Almeria (24)
Anaides (3)
Apicata (12)
Arbaces (16)
Astarte (16)
Azaziel (16)
Baillie (21)
Beleses (16)
Belinda (25)
Belmour (25)
Bertram (16)
Bobadil (6)
Boultby (19)
Bretton (20)
Buckram (23)
Buffone (7)
Clement (6)
Corvino (13)

5

Abbot (17)
Aesop (10)
Alken (11)

9

10

8

11

Ned Careless (22)
Nightingale (2)
Paulina Home (20)
Robert Moore (19)
Roger Formal (6)
Simon Simkin (21)
Stralenheim (16)
Tom Quarlous (2)
Tribulation (1)

12

Asinius Lupus (10)
Brocklehurst (17)
Captain Bluff (25)
Carlo Buffone (7)
Harold Childe (16)
Harry Baillie (21)
John Seacombe (18)
Joseph Wittol (25)
Lady Wishfort (26)
Lord Tynedale (18)
Margaret Hall (19)
Matthew Yorke (19)
Monsieur Paul (18, 20)
Poore Persoun (The) (21)
Rev. Cyril Hall (19)

Richard Mason (17)
Sardanapalus (16)
St. John Rivers (17)
Symond Symkyn (21)

13

Dr. John Bretton (20)
Edward Belmour (25)
Edward Kno'well (6)
Epicure Mammon (1)
Georgiana Reed (17)
Hortense Moore (19)
Hugh of Lincoln (21)
Humphrey Waspe (2)
James Helstone (19)
James Loredano (16)
John Littlewit (2)
Lady Loadstone (8)
Lady Pinchbeck (15)
Lady Touchwood (22)
Lord Touchwood (22)
Magnetick Lady (The) (8)
Marino Faliero (16)
Master Stephen (6)
Miss Marchmont (20)
Miss Scatcherd (17)
Mrs. Crimsworth (18)

Philip Nunnely (19)
Rev. Mr. Sweeting (19)
Sir Paul Plyant (22)

14

Augustus Caesar (10)
Augustus Malone (19)
Captain Bobadil (6)
Captain Keeldar (19)
Edward Mirabell (22)
Francis Foscari (16)
Justice Clement (6)
Rev. Peter Malone (19)
Shirley Keeldar (19)
Wilful Witwould (26)

15

Anthony Witwould (26)
Clerk of Oxenford (21)
Ezekiel Edgworth (2)
Fastidious Brisk (7)
George Downright (6)
Hon. John Seacombe (18)
Madame Eglantine (21)
Sir Joseph Wittol (25)

Some characters from **Charles Dickens**
List of works from which the following characters are taken, with reference numbers.

Ref. No.	Title			Ref. No.	Title		
1.	Barnaby Rudge	(12 letters)		14.	Martin Chuzzlewit	(16 letters)	
2.	Battle of Life, The	(15	")	15.	Master Humphrey's Clock	(20	")
3.	Bleak House	(10	")	16.	Mudfog Papers, The	(15	")
4.	Chimes, The	(9	")	17.	Nicholas Nickleby	(16	")
5.	Christmas Carol, A	(15	")	18.	Old Curiosity Shop, The	(19	")
6.	Cricket on the Hearth, The	(21	")	19.	Oliver Twist	(11	")
7.	David Copperfield	(16	")	20.	Our Mutual Friend	(15	")
8.	Dombey and Son	(12	")	21.	Pickwick, or The Pickwick Papers	(8 or 17 ")	
9.	Edwin Drood	(10	")	22.	Sketches by Boz	(13	")
10.	Great Expectations	(17	")	23.	Tale of Two Cities, A	(16	")
11.	Hard Times	(9	")				
12.	Haunted Man, The	(13	")				
13.	Little Dorrit	(12	")				

Note: The numbers in brackets indicate *the works* in which the characters appear.

2 – 4

Aged (The) (10)
Bell (16)
Bet (19)
Bray (17)
Bung (22)
Cobb (1)
Cute (4)
Dick (19)
Fang (19)
Fern (4)
Fips (14)
Fogg (21)
Gamp (14)
Gay (8)
Grip (bird) (1)
Grub (21)
Hawk (17)
Heep (7)

Hugh (1)
Jane (22)
Jip (dog) (7)
Jo (3)
Joe (21)
Jupe (11)
Kit (18)
Knag (14)
Mary (21)
Meg (4)
Mell (7)
Muff (16)
'Nemo' (3)
Peel (21)
Pell (21)
Peps (8)
'Pip' (10)
Pott (21)
Prig (14)
Pyke (17)

Riah (20)
Rosa (3)
Rugg (13)
Slug (16)
Slum (18)
Tigg (14)
Tim (5)
Tox (8)
Veck (4)
Wade (13)
Wegg (20)

5

Agnes (7)
Alice (15)
Bates (19)
Betsy (19)
Bevan (14)

Biddy (10)
Bloss (22)
Boxer (6)
Brass (18)
Brick (14)
Brown (8, 22)
'Caddy' (3)
Casby (13)
Chick (8)
Choke (14)
Clare (3)
Crupp (7)
Daisy (1)
Diver (14)
Drood (9)
Dumps (22)
Emily (7)
Evans (22)
Fagin (19)
Filer (4)

7

6

Fleming (19)
Gargery (10)
Garland (18)
Gazingi (17)
General (13)
Granger (8)
Gridley (3)
Grimwig (19)
Grinder (18)
Groffin (21)
Heyling (21)
Hopkins (21)
Jackman (24)
Jackson (21)
Jaggers (10)
Jeddler (2)
Jellyby (3)
Jiniwin (18)
Jinkins (21)
Jobling (3, 14)
Jorkins (7)
Kenwigs (17)
Larkins (7, 22)
Lewsome (14)
Loggins (22)
Macklin (22)
Manette (23)
Manners (22)
Meagles (13)
Mowcher (7)
Mrs. Heep (7)
Mrs. Pott (21)
Nadgeth (14)
Neckett (3)
Newcome (2)
Nubbles (18)
Nupkins (21)
O'Bleary (22)
Overton (22)
Pawkins (14)
Peecher (20)
Pipchin (8)
Plummer (6)
Podsnap (20)
Redburn (15)
Richard (4)
Sampson (20)
Scadder (14)
Scrooge (5)
Simpson (22)
Skewton (8)
Slammer (21)
Slowboy (6)
Slunkey (21)
Smangle (21)
Smauker (21)
Snagsby (3)
Snawley (17)
Snubbin (21)
Snuffin (17)
Sparsit (11)
Spenlow (7)
Squeers (17)
Stryver (23)
Swidger (12)
Taunton (22)
'The Aged' (10)
'Tiny Tim' (5)
Tippins (20)
Todgers (14)
Tom Cobb (1)
Tomkins (22)
Trotter (21)
Trundle (21)
Wackles (18)
Wemmuck (10)

Whimple (10)
Whisker (pony) (18)
Wickham (8)
Wilkins (22)
Wobbler (13)

8

Ada Clare (3)
Alphonse (17)
Aunt Jane (22)
Bachelor (The) (18)
Bagstock (7)
Barnacle (13)
Beckwith (12)
Beverley (22)
Blathers (19)
Brandley (10)
Bravassa (17)
Brittles (19)
Brownlow (19)
Bull's Eye (dog) (19)
Carstone (3)
Chadband (3)
Chitling (19)
Claypole (19)
Cleriker (10)
Cluppins (21)
Cratchit (5)
Crummles (17)
Crumpton (22)
Cruncher (23)
Crushton (21)
Dingwall (22)
Diogenes (dog) (8)
Dr. Lumbey (17)
Dr. Strong (7)
Fielding (6)
Finching (13)
Fladdock (14)
Flammell (22)
Fledgeby (20)
Gashford (1)
Haredale (1)
Harleigh (22)
Havisham (10)
Hortense (3)
Humphrey (15)
Jarndyce (3)
Jem Grove (18)
Jennings (22)
La Creevy (17)
Langford (12)
Ledbrain (16)
Ledbrook (17)
Lenville (17)
Littimer (7)
Lobskini (22)
Losberne (19)
Magwitch (10)
Micawber (7)
Miss Knag (17)
Miss Wade (13)
Mrs. Bloss (22)
Mrs. Crupp (7)
Mrs. Gowan (13)
Mrs. Lupin (14)
Mrs. Perch (8)
Mrs. Rudge (1)
Mrs. Tibbs (22)
Nicholas (22)
Nickleby (17)
Old Lobbs (21)
Peggotty (7)
Petowker (17)

Pickwick (21)
Plornish (13)
Robinson (22)
Skettles (8)
Skiffins (10)
Skimpole (3)
Slinkton (10)
Smithers (22)
Snitchey (2)
Sparkins (22)
Sparkler (13)
Stiggins (21)
Tetterby (12)
Toby Veck (4)
Tom Pinch (14)
Tom Scott (18)
Tom Smart (21)
Traddles (7)
Trotwood (7)
Uncle Tom (22)
Westlock (14)
Whiffers (21)
Will Fern (4)
Woolford (22)

9

Amy Dorrit (13)
Belvawney (17)
Betsy Prig (14)
Bill Sikes (19)
Blackpool (11)
Bob Sawyer (21)
Bounderby (11)
Boythorne (3)
Charlotte (19)
Cherryble (17)
Chickweed (19)
'Cleopatra' (8)
Compeyson (10)
Dr. Blimber (8)
Dr. Jeddler (2)
Dr. Jobling (14)
Dr. Slammer (21)
Evrémond (23)
Fleetwood (22)
Gattleton (22)
Gradgrind (11)
Gregsbury (17)
Grewgious (9)
Harthouse (11)
Headstone (20)
Jem Hutley (21)
Joe Willet (1)
Leo Hunter (21)
Lightwood (20)
Lillyvick (17)
'Lord Peter' (22)
Malderton (22)
Mantalini (17)
Maplesone (22)
Markleham (7)
Miss Flite (3)
Miss Gwynn (21)
Miss Miggs (1)
Miss Mills (7)
Miss Pross (23)
Mrs. Bedwin (19)
Mrs. Briggs (22)
Mrs. Budger (21)
Mrs. Corney (19)
Mrs. Craggs (2)
Mrs. Dadson (22)

Mrs. Dowler (21)
Mrs. Harris (14)
Mrs. Hubble (10)
Mrs. Hunter (21)
Mrs. Jarley (18)
Mrs. Lammle (20)
Mrs. Maylie (19)
Mrs. Merdle (13)
Mrs. Milvey (20)
Mrs. Parker (22)
Mrs. Pegler (11)
Mrs. Peploe (22)
Mrs. Raddle (21)
Mrs. Stubbs (22)
Mrs. Varden (1)
Mrs. Wilfer (20)
Murdstone (7)
Ned Dennis (1)
Nell Trent (18)
Old Orlick (10)
Pardiggle (3)
Pecksniff (14)
Phil Squod (3)
Potterson (20)
Riderhood (20)
Ruth Pinch (14)
Sam Weller (21)
Sarah Gamp (14)
Silas Wegg (20)
Sludberry (22)
Smallweed (3)
Snodgrass (21)
Spruggins (22)
Swiveller (18)
Tackleton (6)
Tappertit (1)
'The Bagman' (21)
'The Cherub' (20)
'The Fat Boy' (21)
Tom Codlin (18)
Towlinson (8)
Uncle Bill (22)
Uriah Heep (7)
Veneering (20)
Verisopht (17)
Walter Gay (8)
Wickfield (7)
Will Marks (15)
Wisbottle (22)
Witherden (18)
Woodcourt (3)
Wrayburne (20)

10

Alice Brown (8)
Aunt Martha (2)
Ayresleigh (21)
Betsy Clark (22)
Bill Barker (22)
Bill Barley (10)
Billsmethi (22)
Bitherston (8)
Chevy Slyme (14)
Chuzzlewit (14)
'Cymon' Tuggs (22)
Dame Durden (3)
Doctor Peps (8)
Edwin Drood (9)
Emma Porter (22)
Flintwinch (13)
Heathfield (13)
Henry Gowan (13)
'Honest John' (22)

Jack Bamber (21)
Jack Bunsby (8)
Jem Larkins (22)
Job Trotter (21)
Joe Gargery (10)
John Carker (8)
John Dounce (22)
John Grueby (8)
John Harman (20)
John Willet (1)
'Kit' Nubbles (18)
Kittlebell (22)
Knight Bell (16)
Little Dick (19)
Little Paul (8)
MacStinger (8)
Mark Tapley (14)
Mary Graham (14)
Miss Benton (15)
Mrs. Bardell (21)
Mrs. Clenham (13)
Mrs. Crewler (7)
Mrs. Gargery (10)
Mrs Garland (18)
Mrs. General (13)
Mrs. Grudden (17)
Mrs. Jellyby (3)
Mrs. Jiniwin (18)
Mrs. Kenwigs (17)
Mrs. Macklin (22)
Mrs. Meagles (13)
Mrs. Nubbles (18)
Mrs. Parsons (22)
Mrs. Pipchin (8)
Mrs. Skewton (8)
Mrs. Sparsit (11)
Mrs. Squeers (17)
Mrs. Swidger (12)
Mrs. Taunton (22)
Mrs. Todgers (14)
Mrs. Wackles (18)
Mrs. Whimple (10)
Mrs. Wickham (8)
Paul Dombey (8)
Rosa Dartle (7)
Rose Maylie (19)
Rouncewell (3)
Sally Brass (18)
Sempronius (22)
Signor Jupe (11)
Simon Tuggs (22)
Sliderskew (17)
Smallweed (3)
Sowerberry (19)
Stareleigh (21)
Steerforth (7)
Tony Weller (21)
Turveydrop (3)
Williamson (22)
Wititterly (17)

11

Abel Garland (18)
Arthur Gride (17)
Balderstone (22)
Bella Wilfer (20)
Betsey Quilp (18)
Betty Higden (20)
Bob Cratchit (5)
Cecilia Jupe (11)
Copperfield (7)
Daniel Quilp (18)
Doctor Wosky (22)

Dolge Orlick (10)
Dora Spenlow (7)
Edith Dombey (8)
Emily Wardle (21)
Emma Peecher (20)
Fanny Dombey (8)
Fanny Dorrit (13)
Frank Milvie (20)
Gabriel Grub (21)
'Game Chicken' (The) (8)
Ham Peggotty (7)
Harry Maylie (19)
Jack Hopkins (21)
Jack Redburn (15)
Jacob Barton (22)
James Carker (8)
Jarvis Lorry (23)
Jemima Evans (22)
Jesse Hexham (20)
John Browdie (17)
John Chivery (7)
John Dawkins (19)
John Edmunds (21)
John Evenson (22)
John Jobling (14)
John Podsnap (20)
John Smauker (21)
John Wemmock (10)
Joseph Tuggs (22)
Lady Dedlock (3)
Lady Tippins (20)
Linkinwater (17)
Little Emily (7)
Louisa Chick (8)
Lucretia Tox (8)
Misses Brown (22)
Miss Gazingi (17)
Miss Larkins (7)
Miss Mowcher (7)
Monflathers (18)
Mrs. Brandley (10)
Mrs. Clupping (21)
Mrs. Crummles (17)
Mrs. Dingwall (22)
Mrs. Fielding (6)
Mrs. Finching (13)
Mrs. Gummidge (7)
Mrs. Micawber (7)
Mrs. Nickleby (17)
Mrs. Plornish (13)
Mrs. Sparkler (13)
Mrs. Tetterby (12)
Newman Noggs (17)
Oliver Twist (19)
Perrybingle (6)
Percy Noakes (22)
Peter Magnus (21)
Polly Toodle (8)
Pumblechook (10)
Robin Toodle (8)
Slackbridge (11)
Snevellicci (17)
Solomon Peel (21)
Solomon Pell (21)
Susan Nipper (8)
Susan Weller (21)
Sweedlepipe (14)
'The Bachelor' (18)
Tim Cratchit (5)
Toby Crackit (19)
Tom Chitling (19)
Tony Jobling (3)
Tracy Tupman (21)
Tulkinghorn (3)
Uncle George (22)
Uncle Robert (22)

141

12

Abel Magwitch (10)
Agnes Fleming (19)
Alderman Cute (4)
Alfred Jingle (21)
Alfred Lammle (20)
Amelia Martin (22)
'Artful Dodger' (The) (19)
Aunt Margaret (22)
Barnaby Rudge (1)
Bayham Badger (3)
Bully Stryver (23)
Charley Bates (19)
Colonel Diver (14)
Doctor Lumbey (17)
Doctor Strong (7)
Dr. Parker Peps (8)
Edith Granger (8)
Edward Cuttle (8)
Edward Dorrit (13)
Elijah Pogram (14)
Emily Taunton (22)
Emma Haredale (1)
Emma Micawber (7)
Esther Hawdon (3)
Fanny Cleaver (20)
Fanny Squeers (17)
Feenix Cousin (8)
George Gordon (1)
Grace Jeddler (2)
Honeythunder (9)
Horace Hunter (22)
Joe, the 'Fat Boy' (21)
John Jarndyce (3)
John Westlock (14)
Julia Manners (22)
Kate Nickleby (17)
Koeldwethout (17)
Little Dorrit (13)
Lizzie Hexham (20)
Lord Barnacle (13)
Lucie Manette (23)
Madeline Bray (17)
Major Pawkins (14)
Martha Endell (7)
Mary Fielding (6)
Matilda Price (17)
Milly Swidger (12)
Miss Bravassa (17)
Miss Havisham (10)
Miss La Creevy (17)
Miss Ledbrook (17)
Miss Skiffins (10)
Miss Willises (22)
Miss Woolford (22)
Montague Tigg (14)
Mrs. Gradgrind (11)
Mrs. Maplesone (22)
Mrs. Markleham (7)
Mrs. Pardiggle (3)
Mrs. Veneering (20)
Mulberry Hawk (17)
Noah Claypole (19)
'Peepy' Jellyby (3)
Philip Pirrip (10)
Philip Redlaw (12)
Sampson Brass (18)
Samuel Briggs (22)
Samuel Weller (21)
Solomon Daisy (1)
Solomon Gills (8)
Sophy Crewler (7)
Stoney Briggs (8)
Sydney Carton (23)
Thomas Sapsea (9)

Tilly Slowboy (6)
Tite Barnacle (13)
Tom Gradgrind (11)
Tom Malderton (22)
William Guppy (3)
William Sikes (19)

13

Alfred Tomkins (22)
Anabella Allen (21)
Arthur Clenham (13)
Augustus Minns (22)
Belinda Pocket (10)
Belinda Waters (22)
Benjamin Stagg (1)
Bertha Plummer (6)
'Bob the Grinder' (8)
Brook-Dingwall (22)
Captain Bunsby (8)
Captain Cuttle (8)
Captain Dowler (21)
Captain George (3)
Captain Hawdon (3)
Captain Purday (22)
Captain Waters (22)
Charles Darnay (23)
Charles Timson (22)
Charley Hexham (23)
Clara Peggotty (7)
Dick Swiveller (18)
Doctor Blimber (8)
Doctor Jeddler (2)
Doctor Jobling (14)
Doctor Manette (23)
Dodson and Fogg (21)
Dr. John Jobling (14)
Edward Chester (1)
Edward Sparkler (13)
Emily Peggotty (7)
Emily Smithers (22)
Ernest Defarge (23)
Flora Finching (13)
Gabriel Varden (1)
George Heyling (21)
George Nupkins (21)
George Sampson (20)
George Swidger (12)
Harriet Beadle (13)
Harriet Carker (8)
Herbert Pocket (10)
Jane Murdstone (7)
Jerry Cruncher (23)
Joseph Overton (22)
Lavinia Wilfer (20)
Lord Verisopht (17)
Madame Defarge (23)
Maria Crumpton (22)
Marion Jeddler (2)
Mary Ann Raddle (21)
Matthew Pocket (10)
Michael Bumple (22)
Michael Warden (2)
Minnie Meagles (13)
Miss Belvawney (17)
Misses Ken'wigs (The) (17)
Misses Wackles (The) (18)
Miss Lillerton (22)
Miss Potterson (20)
Mistress Alice (15)
Mrs. Macstinger (8)
Mrs. Rouncewell (3)
Mrs. Sowerberry (19)
Mrs. Williamson (22)
Peg Sliderskew (17)

Philip Swidger (12)
Professor Muff (16)
Rachael Wardle (21)
Ralph Nickleby (17)
Richard Babley (7)
Sally Tetterby (12)
Samuel Slumkey (21)
Samuel Wilkins (22)
Septimus Hicks (22)
Seth Pecksniff (14)
Thomas Groffin (21)
Tumley Snuffim (17)
Watkins Tottle (22)
William Barker (22)
William Dorrit (13)

14

Abbey Potterson (20)
Agnes Wickfield (7)
Alexander Trott (22)
Allen Woodcourt (3)
Amelia Crumpton (22)
Anthony Jeddler (2)
Augustus Cooper (22)
Augustus Moddle (14)
Barnet Skettles (8)
Bentley Drummle (10)
Betsey Cluppins (21)
Betsey Trotwood (7)
Captain Boldwig (21)
Caroline Wilson (22)
Cecilia Bobster (17)
'Charlotta' Tuggs (22)
Charles Tuggs (22)
Chickenstalker (4)
Daniel Peggotty (7)
'Dot' Peerybingle (6)
Edward Plummer (6)
Edwin Cherryble (17)
Florence Dombey (8)
Francis Spenlow (7)
Frank Cheeryble (17)
Frederick Trent (18)
General Scadder (14)
Harold Skimpole (3)
Hiram Grewgious (9)
Honoria Dedlock (3)
Isabella Wardle (21)
Jefferson Brick (14)
Johnny Tetterby (12)
Lavinia Spenlow (7)
Master Humphrey (15)
Mercy Pecksniff (14)
'Merry' Pecksniff (14)
Monsieur Rigaud (13)
Mrs. Betty Higden (20)
Mrs. Copperfield (7)
Mrs. Peerybingle (6)
Mrs. Polly Toodle (8)
Mrs. Snevellicci (17)
Nicodemus Dumps (22)
Octavius Budden (22)
Reginald Wilfer (20)
Reuben Haredale (1)
Rev. Frank Milvey (20)
Roger Riderhood (20)
Samuel Pickwick (21)
Serjeant Buzfuz (21)
Signor Lobskini (22)
Simon Tappertit (1)
Sir John Chester (1)
Sophia Tetterby (12)
'The Game Chicken' (8)
Therese Defarge (23)

Thomas Traddles (7)
Tim Linkinwater (17)
William Swidger (12)

15

Alexander Briggs (22)
Alexander Budden (22)
Alfred Mantalini (17)
Benjamin Britain (2)
Caroline Jellyby (3)
'Cherry' Pecksniff (14)
Clarissa Spenlow (7)
Clemency Newcome (2)
Conkey Chickweed (19)
Cornelia Blimber (8)
'Dolphus Tetterby (12)
Dora Copperfield (7)
Ebenezer Scrooge (5)

Edward Murdstone (7)
Estella Havisham (10)
Eugene Wrayburne (20)
Ferdinand Barnacle (13)
Frederick Dorrit (13)
General Fladdock (14)
Georgina Podsnap (20)
Godfrey Nickleby (17)
Henrietta Boffin (20)
Henry Wititterly (17)
Hon. Elijah Pogram (14)
Horatio Sparkins (22)
'Horatio St. Julien' (22)
James Steerforth (7)
John Peerybingle (6)
Jonas Chuzzlewit (14)
Josephine Sleary (11)
Josiah Rounderby (11)
Julia Wititterly (17)
Lavinia Dingwall (22)

Louisa Gradgrind (11)
MacChoakumchild (11)
Madame Mantalini (17)
Mary Peerybingle (6)
Miss Snevellicci (17)
Monsieur Defarge (23)
Mrs. Joseph Porter (22)
Nathaniel Pipkin (21)
Nathaniel Winkle (21)
Nicodemus Boffin (20)
Ninetta Crummles (17)
Paul Sweedlepipe (14)
Professor Mullet (14)
Richard Carstone (3)
Serjeant Snubbin (21)
Sir Joseph Bowley (4)
Sir Mulberry Hawk (17)
Smallweed Family (3)
Teresa Malderton (22)
'The Artful Dodger' (17)

Some characters from **Dryden, George Eliot, Fielding,** and **Goldsmith**.
List of works from which the following characters are taken, with reference numbers.

Dryden

Ref. No.   Title
1. Absalom and Achitophel
                              (20 letters)
2. (Various)

George Eliot·
11. Adam Bede   (8 letters)
12. Clerical Life, Scenes
    from   (12 or 22 „)
13. Daniel Deronda   (13   „   )
14. Felix Holt   (9   „   )
15. Middlemarch   (11   „   )
16. Mill on the Floss, The   (17   „   )
17. Romola   (6   „   )
18. Silas Marner   (11   „   )
19. Spanish Gipsy, The   (15   „   )

Fielding (Henry)

Ref. No.   Title
3. Amelia   (6 letters)
4. Jonathan Wild   (12   „   )
5. Joseph Andrews   (13   „   ).
6. Mock Doctor, The   (13   „   )
7. Pasquin   (7   „   )
8. Tom Jones   (8   „   )
9. Tom Thumb   (8   „   )
10. (Various)

Goldsmith (Oliver)
20. Citizen of the World, The (20 letters)
21. Good-Natured Man, The   (17   „   )
22. She Stoops to Conquer   (18   „   )
23. Vicar of Wakefield, The   (19   „   )
24. (Various)

Note: The numbers in brackets indicate *the works* in which the characters appear.

2 – 4

Agag (1)
Amri (1)
Arod (1)
Bath (3)
Bede (11)
Cass (18)
Cei (17)
Cora (1)
Dane (18)
Doeg (1)
Holt (14)
Iras (2)
Juan (19)
Juno (dog) (11)
Lisa (17)
Lyon (14)
Maso (11)
Moss (16)
Og (1)
Omri (1)
Rann (11)
Rock (20)
Saul (1)
Snap (4)
Tibs (20)

Wild (4)
Wyld (4)

5

Adams (5)
Amiel (1)
Balak (1)
Bardo (17)
Booby (5)
Booth (3)
Burge (11)
Caleb (1)
Calvo (17)
David (1)
Deane (16)
Dorax (2)
Edwin (24)
Eppic (18)
Fanny (5)
Garth (15)
Glegg (16)
Gomaz (2)
Guest (16)
Jakin (16)
Jonas (1)

Jones (8)
Kezia (16)
Lofty (21)
Macey (18)
Moody (2)
Nadab (1)
Nello (17)
Place (7)
Sagan (1)
Sheva (1)
Tessa (17)
Tibbs (20)
Vincy (15)
Wakem (16)
Whang (20)
Zadoc (1)
Zarca (19)
Zelis (20)
Zimri (1)

6

Abdael (1)
Adriel (1)
Alexas (2)
Amelia (3)

Antony (2)
Arnold (23)
Badger (10)
Barton (12)
Bennet (3)
Blaize (24)
Blifil (8)
Brooke (15)
Casson (11)
Crispe (23)
Dobson (16)
Dr. Rock (20)
Elvira (2)
Emilia (2)
Garnet (21)
Gilfil (12)
Hingpo (20)
Honour (8)
Irwine (11)
Jarvis (21)
Jasper (6)
Jerwyn (14)
La Ruse (4)
Marlow (22)
Marner (11)
Massey (11)
Melema (17)

143

Michal (1)
Morris (11)
Olivia (21)
Phaleg (1)
Pounce (5)
Poyser (11)
Pullet (16)
Quaver (10)
Romola (17)
Shimel (1)
Skeggo (23)
Sorrel (11)
Square (8)
Squint (20)
Supple (8)
Waters (8)
Wilmot (23)

7

Absalom (1)
Andrews (5)
Annabel (1)
Artemis (2)
Aurelia (2)
Bagshot (4)
Beatrix (2)
Bellamy (2)
Benaiah (1)
Blister (10)
Bridget (8)
Brigida (17)
Buzzard (3)
Camillo (2)
Chettam (15)
Celadin (2)
Cennini (17)
Croaker (21)
Davilow (13)
Debarry (14)
Deronda (13)
Diggory (22)
Dominic (2)
Fedalma (19)
Glasher (13)
Gregory (6)
Grizzle (9)
Honoria (2)
Jim Salt (11)
Leonora (2)
Lumpkin (22)
Lydgate (15)
Mariana (10)
Maximin (2)
Meyrick (13)
Mrs. Bede (11)
Neville (22)
Phaedra (2)
Spanker (23)
Spindle (24)
Squeeze (20)
Tancred (2)
Tankard (7)
Tempest (20)
Thimble (4)
Western (8)
Wilkins (8)

8

Adam Bede (11)
Almanzar (2)
Angelina (2, 24)
Atkinson (3)

Aunt Moss (16)
Blueskin (4)
Bob Jakin (16)
Burchell (23)
Casaubon (15)
Chererel (5)
Dempster (12)
Didapper (5)
Don Silva (19)
Dr. Blifil (8)
Foxchase (7)
Goodwill (10)
Harrison (3)
Hastings (22)
Ladislaw (15)
Leonidas (2)
Leontine (21)
Lovegold (10)
Melantha (2)
Mordecai (13)
Mrs. Glegg (16)
Mrs. Tabbs (20)
Primrose (23)
Rabsheka (1)
Richland (21)
'Sandy Jim' (11)
Ser Cioni (17)
Seth Bede (11)
Slipslop (5)
Soderini (17)
Straddle (4)
Syllabub (20)
Theodore (2)
Thwackum (8)
Tom Jones (8)
Transome (14)
Tulliver (16)
Violante (2)
Williams (23)
Winthrop (18)

9

Allworthy (8)
Aunt Glegg (16)
Beau Tibbs (20)
Bellaston (8)
Boabdelin (2)
Charlotte (6)
Cleanthes (2)
Constance (2)
Dolabella (2)
Dubardieu (21)
Felix Holt (14)
Glumdalca (9)
Guiscardo (2)
Heartfree (4)
Honeywood (21)
Jenkinson (23)
Lady Booby (5)
Limberham (2)
Lord Place (7)
Lucy Deane (16)
Major Bath (3)
Mary Garth (15)
Monna Lisa (17)
Mrs. Bennet (3)
Mrs. Blaize (24)
Mrs. Blifil (8)
Mrs. Honour (8)
Mrs. Irvine (11)
Mrs. Poyser (11)
Mrs. Pullet (16)
Mrs. Waters (8)
Nonentity (20)

Partridge (8)
Rufus Lyon (14)
Sir Jasper (6)
Thornhill (23)
Tinderbox (20)
Trulliber (5)
Ventidius (2)
Will Booth (3)
Woodville (21)

10

Achitophel (1)
Amos Barton (12)
Aunt Pullet (16)
Bellarmine (5)
Caleb Garth (15)
Dr. Harrison (3)
Dr. Primrose (23)
Esther Lyon (14)
Goody Brown (8)
Grandcourt (13)
Hardcastle (22)
Huncamunca (9)
Ishbosheth (1)
Jenny Jones (8)
Joshua Rann (11)
Mark Antony (2)
Mrs. Croaker (21)
Mrs. Davilow (13)
Mrs. Glasher (13)
Mrs. Symonds (22)
Mrs. Western (8)
Mrs. Wilkins (8)
Northerton (8)
Sigismunda (2)
Tito Melema (17)
Torrismond (2)
Whitefield (8)

11

Ben Jochanan (1)
Black George (8)
Cadwallader (15)
Celia Brooke (15)
Count La Ruse (4)
Dinah Morris (11)
Dollallolla (9)
Donnithorne (11)
Dr. Nonentity (20)
Farebrother (15)
Ferravecchi (17)
Fitzpatrick (8)
Flamborough (23)
Godfrey Cass (18)
Hetty Sorrel (11)
Jack Spindle (24)
King Tancred (2)
Lachtia Snap (4)
Lady Tempest (20)
Lord Grizzle (9)
MacFlecknoe (2)
Miss Bridget (8)
Miss Neville (21)
Mrs. Primrose (23)
Mrs. Slipslop (5)
Mrs. Transome (14)
Mrs. Tulliver (16)
Parson Adams (5)
Peter Pounce (5)
Philip Wakem (16)
Silas Marner (18)
Tim Syllabub (20)

Tom Tulliver (16)
Tony Lumpkin (22)
Totty Poyser (11)
William Dane (18)
Young Marlow (22)

Squire Badger (10)
Stephen Guest (16)
Will Ladislaw (15)

13

Daniel Deronda (13)
Dolly Winthrop (18)
Harry Foxchase (7)
Janet Dempster (12)
Jonathan Burge (11)
Joseph Andrews (5)
Lady Bellaston (8)
Lady Thornhill (23)
Maynard Gilfil (12)
Matthew Jermyn (14)
Molly Straddle (4)
Moses Primrose (23)
Mrs. Hardcastle (22)
Mrs. Whitefield (8)
Nancy Lammeter (18)
Philip Debarry (14)
Pietro Cennini (17)
Romola di' Bardi (17)
Rosamond Vincy (15)
Sophia Western (8)
Squire Tankard (7)
Squire Western (8)
Theodosia Snap (4)
Thomas Thimble (4)

14

Adolphus Irwine (11)
Arabella Wilmot (23)
Carolina Skeggs (23)
Deborah Wilkins (8)
Dorothea Brooke (15)
Edward Casaubon (15)
Frederick Vincy (15)
George Primrose (23)
Harold Transome (14)
Jenny Tinderbox (20)
Kate Hardcastle (22)
Maggie Tulliver (16)
Maximus Debarry (14)
Miss Hardcastle (22)
Mrs. Cadwallader (15)
Mrs. Fitzpatrick (8)
Olivia Primrose (23)
Sophia Primrose (23)

15

Augustus Debarry (14)
Leontine Croaker (21)
Mrs. Lydia Glasher (13)
Olivia Woodville (21)
Parson Trulliber (5)
Sir James Chettam (15)
Squire Thornhill (23)
Thomas Heartfree (4)

12

Bardo di 'Bardi (17)
Bartle Massey (11)
Captain Booth (8)
Don Sebastian (2)
Featherstone (15)
Francesco Cei (17)
Friar Dominic (2)
Geoffrey Snap (4)
Hester Sorrel (11)
Jonathan Wild (4)
Jonathan Wyld (4)
Lady Chererel (12)
Lawyer Squint (20)
Lucy Goodwill (10)
Lydia Glasher (13)
Martin Poyser (11)
Miss Richland (21)
Monna Brigida (17)
Mrs. Allworthy (8)
Mrs. Heatfree (4)
Mrs. Partridge (8)

Some characters from **Jane Austen, Charles Kingsley, Kipling,** and **Longfellow**
List of works from which the following characters are taken, with reference numbers.

Jane Austen

Ref. No.	Title	
1.	Emma	(4 letters)
2.	Lady Susan	(9 „)
3.	Mansfield Park	(13 „)
4.	Northanger Abbey	(15 „)
5.	Persuasion	(10 „)
6.	Pride and Prejudice	(17 „)
7.	Sense and Sensibility	(19 „)
8.	Watsons, The	(10 „)

Charles Kingsley

16.	Alton Locke	(10 letters)
17.	Hereward the Wake	(15 „)
18.	Two Years Ago	(11 „)
19.	Westward Ho!	(10 „)
20.	Yeast	(5 „)
21.	(Various)	

Rudyard Kipling

Ref. No.	Title	
9.	Captains Courageous	(18 letters)
10.	Day's Work, The	(11 „)
11.	Life's Handicap	(13 „)
12.	Naulahka, The	(11 „)
13.	Soldiers Three	(13 „)
14.	Stalky and Co	(11 „)
15.	(Various)	

Longfellow

22.	Evangeline	(10 letters)
23.	Golden Legend, The	(15 „)
24.	Hiawatha	(8 „)
25.	Hyperion	(8 „)
26.	Kavanagh	(8 „)
27.	Miles Standish	(13 „)
28.	(Various)	

Note: The numbers in brackets indicate *the works* in which the characters appear.

3 – 5

Alden (27)
Algar (17)
Allen (4)
Basil (22)
Bates (1)
Brady (9)
Bukta (10)
Cary (19)
Chinn (10)
Croft (5)
Darcy (6)
Doone (13)
Drake (19)
Elsie (23)

Elton (1)
Emma (1)
Estes (12)
Fawne (10)
Felix (23)
Four (14)
'Foxy' (14)
Grant (3)
Hogan (13, 14)
Hurst (6)
Kamal (15)
Kim (15)
King (14)
Leigh (19)
Lewis (12, 21)
Locke (16)

Mason (14)
Maxim (12)
Mowis (22)
M'Turk (14)
Nixon (14)
Nolan (12)
O'Hara (13)
Osseo (24)
Penn (9)
Platt (9)
Price (3)
Prout (14)
Scott (10)
Shadd (13)
Slane (13)
Smith (4, 20)

Sneyd (3)
Titus (23)
Troop (9)
Tulke (14)
Uriel (23)
Ward (3)
White (14)
Yates (3)
Yeo (19)
Zouch (19)

6

Alfgar (17)
Ansell (14)

145

Arnoul (17)
Beetle (14)
Bennet (6)
Blayne (13)
Blazes (13)
Briggs (18)
Burton (21)
Carson (14)
Cheyne (9)
Clewer (14)
Conrad (21)
Coulan (13)
Dabney (14)
Elliot (5)
Elsley (18)
Folsom (10)
Gadsby (13, 15)
Gallio (13)
Godiva (17)
Godwin (17)
Harper (10)
Harvey (18)
Howard (8)
Hunter (8)
Jasoda (13)
Kinzey (9)
Lilian (16)
Maffin (13)
Mahbub (15)
Mannel (9)
Martin (1, 2, 9, 14)
Martyn (10)
McPhee (10)
Mellot (18)
Morton (7)
Mutrie (12)
Norris (3)
O'Brien (8)
Palmer (7)
Raynes (14)
Sefton (14)
Stalky (14)
Steele (7)
Swayne (14)
Tarvin (12)
Thorpe (4)
Tilney (4)
Verney (17)
Vernon (2)
Watson (8)
Weston (1)
Willis (18)
Wilton (10)
Winter (19)

7

Baldwin (17)
Berkley (25)
Bertram (3)
Bingley (6)
Brandon (7)
Campian (19)
Collins (6)
Corkran (14)
Curtiss (13)
De Sussa (13)
Dr. Grant (3)
Edwards (8)
Fairfax (1)
Ferrars (7)
Fleming (25)
Gilbert (28)
Gillett (14)
Hartopp (14)

Headley (18)
Heckler (12)
Holdock (10)
Hypatia (21)
Johnson (2)
Learoyd (11, 13)
Leblanc (22)
Leofric (17)
Lilinau (22)
Lucifer (23)
Mackage (21)
Mackesy (13)
Manders (14)
Mildred (15)
Morland (4)
Mullins (13)
Nokomis (24)
Osborne (8)
Oxenham (19)
Oweenee (24)
Parsons (19)
Pelagia (21)
Perowne (14)
Pycroft (15)
Raleigh (19)
Rattray (14)
Salters (9)
Sheriff (12)
Simmons (13)
Vaughan (26)
Vaurien (20)
Wardrop (10)
Wenonah (24)

8

Aben-Ezra (21)
Basselin (28)
Bingleys (The) (6)
Campbell (14, 18)
Crawford (3)
Dan Troop (9)
Dashwood (7)
De Bourgh (6)
De Courcy (2)
Dick Four (14)
Dumachus (23)
Fastrada (23)
Felician (22)
Filomena (28)
Gardiner (6)
Gottlieb (23)
Grenvile (19)
Harrison (14)
Hereward (17)
Hiawatha (24)
Hyperion (25)
Jan Chinn (10)
Jennings (7)
Jervoise (13)
Kavanagh (26)
Lady Bath (19)
Limmason (11)
Long Jack (9)
Lynedale (16)
M'Cartney (10)
McRimmon (10)
Miss Carr (8)
Mrs. Allen (4)
Mrs. Blake (8)
Mrs. Estes (12)
Mrs. Hurst (6)
Mrs. Leigh (19)
Mrs. Price (3)
Mrs. Sneyd (3)

Mulvaney (13)
Musgrave (8)
Newbroom (20)
Ortheris (13)
Passmore (19)
Preciosa (28)
Salterne (19)
Schaefer (9)
Standish (27)
Stettson (14)
Threegan (13)
Thurnall (18)
Tom Platt (9)
Torfrida (17)
Treboaze (18)
Tregarva (20)
Vavasour (18)
Waltheof (1)
Will Cary (19)

9

Andromeda (21)
Armsworth (18)
Ashburton (25)
Azacanora (19)
Carmathan (12)
Churchill (1, 26)
Collinson (14)
Dave Lewis (12)
Deercourt (13)
Elizabeth (21)
Finlayson (15)
Hitchcock (10)
John Alden (27)
John Chinn (10, 15)
Knightley (1)
Lavington (20)
Lightfoot (17)
MacDonald (9)
Maria Ward (3)
McAndrews (15)
Middleton (7)
Minnehaha (24)
Miss Bates (1)
Miss Sneyd (3)
Mrs. Cheyne (9)
Mrs. Harvey (18)
Mrs. McPhee (10)
Mrs. Mutrie (12)
Mrs. Norris (3)
Mrs. Palmer (7)
Mrs. Purvis (8)
Mrs. Vernon (2)
Mrs. Watson (8)
Mrs. Weston (1)
Nick Bady (9)
Priscilla (27)
Rushworth (3)
Sam Watson (8)
Stangrave (18)
Tim Coulan (13)
Victorian (28)
Vieuxbois (20)
Wentworth (5)
Woodhouse (1)

10

Alton Locke (16)
Amyas Leigh (19)
Anne Elliot (5)
Dinah Shadd (13)
Dirkovitch (11)

Disko Troop (9)
Dr. Thurnall (18)
Earl Godwin (17)
Emma Watson (8)
Evangeline (22)
Fanny Price (3)
Findlayson (10)
Godwinsson (17)
Jane Bennet (6)
John Briggs (18)
John Thorpe (4)
King Ranald (17)
Lady Godiva (17)
Lady Vernon (2)
Lajeunesse (22)
Lucy Steele (7)
Mainwaring (2)
Miss Kinzey (9)
Miss Martin (10)
Miss M'Kenna (13)
Miss Morton (7)
Mrs. De Sussa (13)
Mrs. Edwards (8)
Mrs. Holdock (10)
Mrs. Johnson (2)
Mrs. Mullins (13)
Prometheus (28)
Strickland (11)
Tom Bertram (3)
Willoughby (7)

11

Alfred Chinn (10)
Barraclough (11)
Bracebridge (2)
Count of Lara (28)
Count Robert (17)
Dundas Fawne (10)
Earl Leofric (17)
Fanny Norris (3)
Frances Ward (3)
Harry Verney (20)
Henry Tilney (4)
Hinchcliffe (15)
James Burton (21)
Jane Fairfax (1)
Jerry Blazes (13)
John Gillett (14)
John Learoyd (11)
John Oxenham (19)
Kate Sheriff (12)
Lady Bertram (3)
Lady Osborne (8)
Lionel Chinn (10)
Lord Osborne (8)
Lucy Ferrars (7)
Lydia Bennet (6)
Mary Edwards (8)
Megissogwon (24)
Mudjekeewis (24)
Mrs. Dashwood (7)
Mrs. Gardiner (6)
Mrs. Jennings (7)
Paul Fleming (25)
René Leblanc (22)

Rev. Mr. Howard (8)
Rev. Mr. Norris (3)
Shawondasee (24)
Susan Vernon (2)
Thomas Leigh (19)
Tom Musgrave (8)
Tom Thurnall (18)

12

Abbot Leofric (17)
Admiral Croft (5)
Brimblecombe (19)
Brugglesmith (10)
Captain Leigh (19)
Colonel Nolan (12)
Dick Grenvile (19)
Earl of Mercia (17)
Earl of Wessex (17)
Eustace Leigh (19)
Frank Headley (18)
Harriet Smith (4)
Harvey Cheyne (9)
Jack Thurnall (18)
Jasper Purvis (8)
John Dashwood (7)
Julia Bertram (3)
Lady de Bourgh (6)
Lady de Courcy (2)
Lady Grenville (19)
Lord Lynedale (16)
Lucy Passmore (19)
Maria Bertram (3)
Mary Crawford (3)
Miss Bingleys (The) (6)
Miss Newbroom (20)
Miss Standish (27)
Mrs. Rushworth (3)
Paul Tregarva (19)
Pau-Puk-Keewis (24)
Robert Martin (1)
Robert Watson (8)
Rose Salterne (19)
Salvation Yeo (19)
Samuel Burton (21)
Sandy Mackage (16)
Uncle Salters (9)
William Price (3)

13

Admiral Winter (19)
Ali Baba Mahbub (15)
Alicia Johnson (2)
Bellefontaine (22)
Captain Gadsby (13, 15)
Captain Hunter (8)
Captain Maffin (13)
Captain 'O'Brien (13)
Captain Willis (18)
Colonel Dabney (14)
Corporal Slane (13)
Edmund Bertram (3)
Edward Ferrars (7)
Eleanor Tilney (4)

Emma Deercourt (13)
Emma Woodhouse (1)
Fanny Dashwood (7)
Father Campian (19)
Father Parsons (19)
Henry Crawford (3)
Henry Dashwood (7)
Humphrey Chinn (10)
John Middleton (7)
Julia Crawford (3)
Lady Middleton (7)
Lancelot Smith (20)
Little Mildred (15)
Lord Vieuxbois (20)
Major Campbell (18)
Mark Armsworth (18)
Mary Armsworth (18)
Mary Ashburton (25)
Miles Standish (27)
Raymond Martin (14)
Robert Ferrars (7)
Simon Salterne (19)
Thomas Bertram (3)
William Martin (10)

14

Captain Raleigh (19)
Cecilia Vaughan (26)
Colonel Brandon (7)
Earl Godwinsson (17)
Edward Thurnall (18)
Elinor Dashwood (7)
Emanuel Pycroft (15)
Father Felicien (22)
Frank Churchill (1)
Isabella Thorpe (4)
Miss Mainwaring (2)
Nicholas Tarvin (12)
Oliver Basselin (28)
Penelope Watson (8)
Rev. John Gillett (14)
Robert of Sicily (28)
Sir James Martin (2)
Thomas Thurnall (18)
Walter of Varila (21)

15

Amos Barraclough (11)
Catherine Vernon (2)
Elizabeth Bennet (6)
Elizabeth Watson (8)
Hereward the Wake (17)
Humphrey Gilbert (28)
Lady Susan Vernon (2)
Martin Lightfoot (17)
Private Mulvaney (13)
Private Ortheris (13)
Raphael Aben-Ezra (21)
Richard Grenvile (19)
Sergeant Mullins (13)
Sir Francis Drake (19)
Squire Lavington (20)
Valentia Headley (18)

Some characters from **Lord Lytton**
List of works from which the following characters are taken, with reference numbers.

Ref. No.	Title		Ref. No.	Title	
1.	Alice	(5 letters)	11.	Money	(5 letters)
2.	Caxtons, The	(10 „)	12.	My Novel	(7 „)
3.	Devereux	(8 „)	13.	Night and Morning	(15 „)
4.	Ernest Maltravers	(16 „)	14.	Parisians, The	(12 „)
5.	Eugene Aram	(10 „)	15.	Pelham	(6 „)
6.	Godolphin	(9 „)	16.	Richelieu	(9 „)
7.	Harold	(6 „)	17.	Rienzi	(6 „)
8.	Kenelm Chillingly	(16 „)	18.	Sea Captain, The	(13 „)
9.	Last Days of Pompeii, The	(20 „)	19.	Strange Story, A	(13 „)
10.	Last of the Barons, The	(18 „)	20.	What will he do with it?	(18 „)
			21	Zanoni	(6 „)

Note: The numbers in brackets indicate *the works* in which the character appear.

3 AND 4

Aram (5)
Bolt (2)
Butt (8)
Dale (12)
Haco (7)
Ione (9)
King (14)
Lee (10)
Love (13)
Moor (5)
Odo (7)
Pike (2)
Rolf (7)
Vane (14)
Wood (5)

5

Algar (7)
Alice (1)
Alred (7)
Alton (14)
Alwyn (10)
Babel (15)
Bedos (15)
Bevil (14)
Boxer (13)
Bruce (12)
Bruse (7)
Burbo (9)
Clare (6)
Clump (13)
Crane (20)
Cutts (20)
Digby (8, 12)
Donce (1)
Dumas (21)
Duval (14)
Edith (7)
Emlyn (8)
Faber (19)
Frost (20)
Gates (10)
Githa (7)
Gower (2)
Grant (15)
Graul (10)
Green (13, 15)
Grimm (14)
Gurth (7)
Hales (5)
Hobbs (4)
Hodge (4)
Jones (4, 13, 19)

Julia (9)
Lloyd (19)
Lucia (17)
Luigi (17)
Lydon (9)
Madge (10)
Medon (9)
Merle (20)
Mills (20)
Nicot (21)
Niger (9)
Nixon (5)
Nydia (9)
Olave (7)
Pansa (9)
Paolo (21)
Payan (21)
Poole (20)
Price (13)
Rugge (20)
Rymer (3)
Sharp (13)
Smith (13, 15)
Sosia (9)
Speck (2)
Steen (8)
Stirn (12)
Tiddy (1, 4)
Thyra (7)
Vance (20)
Vebba (7)
Vesey (11)
Waife (20)
Willy (20)

6

Aubrey (1)
Avenel (12)
Ayesha (19)
Barlow (13)
Beavor (13)
Beevor (18)
Belton (15)
Benson (6)
Benzoni (3)
Birnie (13)
Blount (11)
Bovill (8)
Bowles (8)
Briggs (15)
Bungey (10)
Burley (12)
Burton (20)
Butler (1, 4)
Calton (15)

Caxton (2, 12)
Cetoxa (21)
Cibber (3)
Clarke (5)
Conway (15)
Crampe (20)
Currie (12)
Darvil (1, 4)
Dawson (15)
Dawton (15)
Derval (19)
Diomed (9)
Dubois (3)
Dysart (5)
Elmore (5)
Evelyn (11)
Favant (13)
Fleuri (3)
Forman (19)
Fulvia (9)
Godwin (7)
Gordon (8, 15)
Grayle (19)
Greggs (20)
Harold (7)
Haroun (19)
Hébert (14)
Herman (2)
Howard (1)
Jarvis (12)
Jeeves (19)
Jonson (15)
Justis (1)
Lebeau (14)
Legard (1)
Leslie (Mr.) (1, 12)
Lester (5)
Locket (8)
Losely (20)
Lovell (10)
Lufton (15)
Lumley (1)
Malden (6)
Mallet (7)
Margot (15)
Merton (1)
Mivers (8)
Morcar (7)
Morgan (12)
Morley (14, 20)
Morton (13)
Nevile (10)
Newman (1)
Norman (18)
Onslow (1)
Orsini (17)
Oswald (3)

Pelham (15)
Pietro (19)
Pisani (21)
Poyntz (19)
Rameau (14)
Renard (14)
Rienzi (17)
Ritson (15)
Rivers (10)
Rodolf (17)
Scales (10)
Simcox (4)
Siward (7)
Sloman (19)
Smythe (19)
Somers (8, 10)
Sporus (9)
Sprott (12)
Spruce (20)
Square (2)
Steele (3)
St. John (3)
St. Just (21)
Sultan (dog) (1)
Sweyne (7)
Tibson (5)
Tostig (7)
Trevor (6)
Uberto (19)
Vernon (6)
Vertot (14)
Vigors (19)
Violet (18)
Vivian (2)
Vyvyan (20)
Warner (10)
Watson (13)
Welles (10)
Zanoni (21)

7

Aberton (15)
Addison (3)
Adeline (17)
Alljack (12)
Arbaces (9)
Arundel (18)
Bacourt (14)
Baldwin (7)
Baradas (16)
Barnard (3)
Bawtrey (8)
Belvoir (6, 8)
Bolding (2)
Bullion (2)

Earl Agar (7)
Erpingham (6)
Fairfield (12)
Fairthorn (20)
Fillgrave (5)
Giraumont (13)
Glanville (15)
Godolphin (6)
Guloseton (15)
Hasselton (3)
Hazeldean (12)
Hennequin (14)
Job Jonson (15)
Jockleton (3)
Joe Spruce (20)
John Clump (13)
John Green (13)
Johnstone (6)
John Vesey (11)
King Louis (XIV) (3)
Lady Frost (20)
Lady Janet (14)
Lascelles (4)
Lemercier (14)
L'Estrange (12)
Liancourt (13)
Loubinsky (14)
Macgregor (3)
Marmaduke (10)
M'Catchley (12)
Millinger (6)
Montreuil (3)
Mrs. Avenel (12)
Mrs. Bowles (8)
Mrs. Butler (1)
Mrs. Caxton (2, 12)
Mrs. Elmore (5)
Mrs. Leslie (1, 12)
Mrs. Merton (1)
Mrs. Morley (14)
Mrs. Morton (13)
Mrs. Poyntz (19)
Mrs. Somers (8)
Mrs. Trevor (6)
Nelthorpe (15)
Nick Alwyn (10)
Paul Grimm (14)
Plaskwith (13)
Radclyffe (6)
Réné Dumas (21)
Richelieu (16)
Roseville (15)
Russelton (15)
Saxingham (1, 4)
Stalworth (3)
Stollhead (20)
St. Quintin (15)
Taillefer (7)
Templeton (1, 4)
Tetraides (9)
Thornhill (12)
Tom Bowles (8)
Townshend (15)
Trevanion (6)
Uncle Jack (2)
Vaudemont (13)
Warburton (15)
Westbrook (1)
Woodstock (15)
Woodville (10)

10

Adam Warner (10)
Beaudesert (2)

Bennington (15)
Brotherton (8)
Caleb Price (13)
Castruccio (4)
Chillingly (8)
Dame Newman (1)
Dame Ursula (17)
Dartington (6)
de Vandemar (14)
Dick Avenel (12)
Dolly Poole (20)
Doningdale (4)
Don Saltero (3)
Dr. Dosewell (12)
Earl Godwin (7)
Eugene Aram (5)
Fra Moreale (17)
Frank Vance (20)
Glenmorris (15)
Graham Vane (14)
Guy Bolding (2)
Guy Darrell (20)
Hal Peacock (2)
Helen Digby (12)
Hildebrand (7)
Jane Poyntz (19)
John Avenel (12)
John Bovill (8)
John Burley (12)
John Vernon (6)
Kate Morton (13)
King Edward (IV) (10)
King Harold (7)
Lady Dawton (15)
Lady Pelham (15)
Lethbridge (8)
Lord Belton (15)
Lord Calton (15)
Lord Dorset (10)
Lord Rivers (10)
Lord Scales (10)
MacBlarney (2)
Maltravers (1, 4)
Mandeville (6)
Marc le Roux (14)
Midgecombe (6)
Millington (15)
Miss Lockit (8)
Miss Starke (12)
Mrs. Bawtrey (8)
Mrs. Bertram (12)
Mrs. Cameron (8)
Mrs. Campion (8)
Mrs. Compton (8)
Mrs. Darrell (20)
Mrs. Dealtry (5)
Mrs. Egerton (12)
Mrs. Holwell (5)
Mrs. Lyndsay (20)
Mrs. Mervale (21)
Mrs. Pompley (12)
Nora Avenel (12)
Peter Hales (5)
Porpustone (10)
Rainsforth (2)
Riccabocca (12)
Richard Lee (10)
Robert Butt (8)
Saunderson (8)
Shallowell (6)
Snivelship (3)
Sophy Waife (20)
Stefanello (17)
Stratonice (9)
Tom Stowell (12)
Toolington (15)

Ulverstone (2)
Will Somers (10)

11

Abbé Vertpré (14)
Alban Morley (20)
Alice Darval (1, 4)
Bolingbroke (3)
Carrucarius (9)
Clutterbuck (15)
Count Cetoxa (21)
Dame Dealtry (5)
de Maintenon (3)
de Malvoisin (10)
de Montaigne (1, 4)
de Ventadown (1, 4)
Duke of Alton (14)
Farmer Bruce (12)
Fitzosborne (7)
Flora Vyvyan (20)
Friar Bungey (10)
Henry Nevile (10)
Henry Pelham (15)
Henry St. John (3)
Hugh Withers (10)
Jessie Wiles (8)
John Stokton (10)
John Tibbets (2)
John Walters (4)
Jonas Elmore (5)
Julia Elmore (5)
Julius Faber (19)
Kenelm Digby (8)
Kitty Caxton (2)
Lady Arundel (18)
Lady Delmour (6)
Lady Oldtown (15)
Longueville (10)
Lord Belvoir (6)
Lord Chester (15)
Lord Clinton (15)
Lord Montagu (10)
Lord Taunton (4)
Lord Vincent (15)
Lord Warwick (10)
Louise Duval (14)
Louis Grayle (19)
Malesherbes (21)
Marie Oswald (3)
Meeing Willy (20)
Miles Square (2)
Miss Chapman (20)
Mrs. Ashleigh (19)
Mrs. Beaufort (13)
Mrs. Haughton (20)
Mrs. Plimmins (13)
Mrs. Primmins (2)
Mrs. Saunders (20)
Paul Louvier (14)
Percy Norman (18)
Printer Pike (2)
Proteus Bolt (2)
Rev. Mr. Aubrey (1)
Rev. Mr. Merton (1)
Richard King (14)
Robespierre (21)
Roger Morton (13)
'Sisty' Caxton (2)
Squire Nixon (5)
Uncle Roland (2, 12)
Viola Pisoli (21)

12

Alfred Evelyn (11)
Allen Fenwick (19)
Arthur Morton (13)
Austin Caxton (2)
Baron di Porto (17)
Beau Fielding (3)
Captain Smith (13)
Clara Douglas (11)
Cola di Rienzi (17)
Count Baldwin (7)
Count de Passy (14)
Count William (7)
Dame Darkmans (5)
Daniel Clarke (5)
De Finisterre (14)
Dr. Riccabocca (12)
Dr. Shallowell (6)
Duc de St. Simon (3)
Earl of Mercia (7)
Edgar Ferrier (14)
Father Uberto (17)
Francis Vance (20)
General Grant (15)
George Howard (1)
George Legard (1)
George Morley (20)
Giles Tibbets (2)
Jacob Bunting (5)
James Holwell (5)
Jane Houseman (5)
Jasper Losely (20)
Lady Bonville (10)
Lady Delville (6)
Lady Franklin (11)
Lady Haughton (19)
Lady Montfort (20)
Lady Vargrave (1, 4)
Lily Mordaunt (8)
Lord Bonville (10)
Lord Dartmore (15)
Lord Falconer (6)
Lord Fitzhugh (10)
Lord Hastings (10)
Lord Lilburne (13)
Lord Luscombe (15)
Lord Montfort (20)
Lord Plympton (6)
Lord Thetford (8)
Lord Vargrave (1, 4)
Madame Beavor (13)
Madame Vertot (14)
Maéstro Páolo (21)
Miss Asterisk (14)
Miss Brabazon (19)
Misses Burton (20)
Miss Paulding (15)
Miss Trafford (15)
Mrs. Braefield (8)
Mrs. Brimstone (15)
Mrs. Dollimore (15)
Mrs. Fairfield (12)
Mrs. Hazeldean (12)
Mrs. M'Catchley (12)
Mrs. Plaskwith (13)
Mrs. Shinfield (4)
Mrs. St. Quintin (15)
Mrs. Templeton (4)
Parson Quinny (15)
Peter Dealtry (5)
Philip Morton (13)
Ralph Rumford (15)
Randal Leslie (12)
Raoul De Fulke (10)
Rev. Mr. Dumdrum (12)

Rev. Mr. Summers (5)
Robin Hilyard (10)
Sharpe Currie (12)
Sibyll Warner (10)
Simon Gawtrey (13)
Sir Guy Nevile (10)
Sir John Comers (10)
Sir John Vesey (11)
Squire Lester (5)
Squire Tibson (5)
Tirabaloschi (4)
Vipont Morley (20)
Von Schomberg (4)
Walter Lester (5)
William Waife (20)
Will Peterson (2)

13

Abbé Montreuil (3)
Adolphus Poole (20)
Adrian Colonna (17)
Angelo Villani (17)
Arabella Crane (20)
Armand Monnier (14)
Audley Egerton (12)
Blanche Caxton (2, 12)
Bob Saunderson (8)
Bridget Greggs (20)
Captain Norman (18)
Charles Merton (1)
Colonel Dysart (5)
Colonel Elmore (5)
Colonel Legard (1)
Colonel Morley (14, 20)
Colonel Poyntz (19)
Count Devereux (3)
Count Hamilton (3)
de Grantmesnil (14)
de Rochebriant (14)
Duke of Orleans (16)
Earl of Warwick (10)
Ellinor Lester (5)
Evelyn Cameron (1)
Francis Vivian (2)
Gaetano Pisani (21)
George Belvoir (8)
George Clinton (15)
Georgina Vesey (11)
Gerald Danvers (8)
Gianni Colonna (17)
Goody Darkmans (5)
Gustave Rameau (14)
Gustavus Donce (1)
Hugues Maigrot (7)
Isaura Cicogna (14)
Isora D'Alvarez (3)
Jeremiah Smith (13)
John Courtland (5)
John Russelton (15)
John Stalworth (8)
Joseph Hartopp (20)
Lady Babbleton (15)
Lady Delafield (19)
Lady Doltimore (1)
Lady Erpingham (6)
Lady Glenalvon (8)
Lady Hasselton (3)
Lady Jane Babel (15)
Lady Lascelles (4)
Lady Mary Babel (15)
Lady Nelthorpe (15)
Lady Roseville (15)
Lady Trevanion (2)
Leopold Lufton (15)

Leopold Smythe (19)
Lord Castleton (2)
Lord Doltimore (1)
Lord Erpingham (6)
Lord Guloseton (15)
Lord L'Estrange (12)
Lord Saxingham (1, 4)
Louise Corinne (14)
Lumley Ferrers (4)
Madame de Maury (14)
Madame Laurent (15)
Madame Liehbur (6)
Madge Darkmans (5)
Marion de Lorme (16)
Mark Fairfield (12)
Martino Orsini (17)
Mary Westbrook (1)
Mike Callaghan (20)
Ned Porpustone (10)
Nicholas Alwyn (10)
Nina di Raselli (17)
Prince Richard (10)
Rev. Caleb Price (13)
Richard Avenel (12)
Richard Nevile (10)
Rinaldo Orsini (17)
Robert Hilyard (10)
Rowland Lester (5)
Seymour Conway (15)
Sir John Merton (1)
Sir Peter Hales (5)
Squire Rollick (2)
Thomas Mervale (21)
William Losely (20)
William Mallet (7)

14

Aubrey Devereux (3)
Augustus Lufton (15)
Benjamin Lufton (15)
Bishop of Bayeux (7)
Caroline Merton (1)
Cecilia Travers (8)
Colonel Cleland (3)
Colonel Danvers (4)
Colonel Egerton (12)
Colonel Pompley (12)
Count de la Roche (10)
Dorothy Dealtry (5)
Duke of Clarence (10)
Earl of Hereford (7)
Fanny Millinger (6)
Fanny Trevanion (2)
Farmer Sinclair (15)
Frank Hazeldean (12)
Gaffer Solomons (12)
'Gentleman Waife' (20)
Geoffrey Lester (5)
Gerald Devereux (3)
Giovanni Orsini (17)
Giulio Franzini (12)
Henry Johnstone (6)
Howard de Howard (15)
Humfrey Heyford (10)
Irene di Gabrini (17)
John Chillingly (8)
Lady Bennington (15)
Leopold Travers (8)
Lilian Ashleigh (19)
Lionel Haughton (20)
Lord Bennington (15)
Lord Dartington (6)
Lord Doningdale (4)
Lord Glenmorris (15)

151

Lord Rainsforth (2)
Lord Ulverstone (2)
Madeline Lester (5)
Margaret Poyntz (19)
Martino di Porto (17)
Matilda Darrell (20)
Morton Devereux (3)
Mrs. Bracegirdle (3)
Percy Godolphin (6)
Queen Elizabeth (10)
Richard Strahan (19)
Robert Beaufort (13)
Rodolf of Saxony (17)
Roland de Caxton (2)
Rolf of Hereford (7)
Sidney Beaufort (13)
Sir Henry Nevile (10)
Sir Kenelm Digby (8)
Stephen Colonna (17)
Teresa Cesarini (4)
Timothy Alljack (12)
Walter Melville (8)

15

Adrien de Mauprat (16)
Albert Trevanion (2)

Anthony Hamilton (3)
Arabella Fossett (20)
Armand Richelieu (16)
Arthur Godolphin (6)
Augustine Caxton (2)
Augustus Saville (6)
Beatrice di Negra (12)
Boulainvilliers (3)
Captain Barnabas (12)
Captain Dashmore (12)
Captain de Caxton (2)
Captain Haughton (20)
Catherine Morton (13)
Cecco del Vecchio (17)
Charles Haughton (20)
Clarence Glyndon (21)
Constance Vernon (6)
Corporal Bunting (5)
David Mandeville (6)
Duke of Aspindale (6)
Earl of Erpingham (6)
Earl of Worcester (10)
Evelyn Templeton (1)
Francisco Pietro (17)
Frederick Blount (11)
George Blackwell (13)
Gertrude Douglas (15)
Gilbert Ashleigh (19)

Harley L'Estrange (12)
Haughton Darrell (20)
Jemima Hazeldean (12)
Jessica Haughton (20)
Julian Montreuil (3)
Julie de Mortemar (16)
Katherine Nevile (10)
Lady Longueville (10)
Lanfranc of Pavia (7)
Leonardo Raselli (14)
Lord Bolingbroke (3)
Lucien Duplessis (14)
Major MacBlarney (2)
Margaret of Anjou (10)
Marmaduke Nevile (10)
Pandulfo di Guido (17)
Peter Chillingly (8)
Raoul de Vandemar (14)
Rev. Mr. Lethbridge (8)
Richard Cromwell (3)
Richard Houseman (5)
Sally Chillingly (8)
Sarah Chillingly (8)
Sibyl Chillingly (8)
Sir Philip Derval (19)
Sir Ralph Rumford (15)
Sir Robert Welles (10)
Squire Hazeldean (12)

Some characters from **Meredith**, **Milton** and **Thomas Moore**
List of works from which the following characters are taken, with reference numbers.

George Meredith

Ref. No.	Title		
1.	Beauchamp's Career	(16 letters)	
2.	Egoist, The	(9	„)
3.	Evan Harrington	(14	„)
4.	Harry Richmond	(13	„)
5.	Rhoda Fleming	(12	„)
6.	Richard Feverel	(14	„)
7.	One of our Conquerors	(18	„)
8.	Sandra Belloni	(13	„)
9.	Vittoria	(8	„)
10.	(Various)		

John Milton

Ref. No.	Title		
11.	Comus	(5 letters)	
12.	Paradise Lost	(12	„)
13.	Paradise Regained	(16	„)
14.	(Various)		

Thomas Moore

15.	Fudge Family in Paris, The	(21 letters)	
16.	Irish Melodies	(13	„)
17.	Lalla Rookh	(10	„)
18.	(Various)		

Note: The numbers in brackets indicate *the works* in which the characters appear.

3 – 5

Alvan (10)
Azim (17)
Beppo (9)
Berry (6)
Camph (10)
Chloe (10)
Chump (8)
Comus (11)
Corte (9)
Dagon (12)
Dale (2)
Diana (10)
Drew (1)
Ellen (16)
Forey (6)
Forth (3)
Fudge (15)
Goren (3)
Hafed (17)
Hinda (17)
Julia (18)
Kilne (3)
Kirby (10)
Lea (18)

Moody (5)
Mount (6)
Nama (18)
Ople (10)
Pole (6)
Powys (9)
Puff (18)
Rizzo (9)
Rosa (18)
Selim (17)
Uriel (12)

6

Abdiel (12)
Aliris (17)
Arioch (12)
Austin (1)
Azazel (12)
Azazil (12)
Barmby (7)
Barnes (3)
Belial (12)

Benson (6)
Blaize (6)
Boulby (5)
Burman (7)
Busshe (2)
Callet (7)
Connor (15)
Corney (2)
Dacier (10)
Dalila (14)
Daphne (13)
Denham (1)
Durham (2)
Eccles (5)
Eglett (10)
Farina (10)
Gammon (5)
Graves (7)
Harley (6)
Kionis (4)
Laxley (3)
Lespel (1)
Lovell (5)
Lowton (3)

Manoah (14)
Nereus (11)
Noorka (10)
Oggler (1)
O'Ruark (16)
Oxford (2)
Pompey (13)
Radnor (7)
Raikes (3)
Romara (9)
Samfit (5)
Scipio (13)
Sedley (9)
Semele (13)
Strike (3)
Summer (8)
Syrinx (13)
Tethys (11)
Tinman (10)
Turbot (1)
Uploft (3)
Waring (5)
Zaraph (18)
Zelica (17)

7

Ammiani (9)
Amymone (13)
Antiopa (13)
Asmadai (12)
Bagarag (10)
Barrett (8)
Beamish (10)
Belloni (8)
Beltham (4)
Billing (5)
Calisto (13)
Clymene (13)
Cougham (1)
Culling (1)
De Craye (2)
Durance (7)
Eveleen (16)
Farrell (10)
Feverel (6)
Fleming (5)
Gambier (8, 9)
Gosstre (8)
Grossby (3)
Hackbut (5)
Halkett (1)
Harapha (14)
Jocelyn (3)
Killick (1)
Latters (5)
Lycidas (14)
Lydiard (1)
Mohanna (17)
Namouna (17)
Ottilia (4)
Parsley (3)
Pelleas (13)
Pempton (7)
Peridon (7)
Perkins (3)
Phillis (18)
Piavens (9)
Pierson (9)
Raphael (12)
Romfrey (1)
Sabrina (11)
Saracco (9)
Sedgett (5)
Shagpat (10)
Skepsey (7)
Sowerby (7)
St. Kevin (16)
Thyrsis (14)
Tuckham (1)
Warwick (10)
Weyburn (10)
Wicklow (5)
Zophiel (12)

8

Al Hassan (17)
Bakewell (6)
Blancove (5)
Blandish (6)
Bob Fudge (15)
Braintop (8)
Crossjay (2)
De Saldar (3)
Dr. Corney (2)
Dunstane (10)
Fenellan (7)
Feramorz (17)
Ithuriel (12)

Lancelot (13)
Miss Dale (2)
Mortimer (6)
Mrs. Berry (6)
Mrs. Chump (8)
Mrs. Forey (6)
Mrs. Mount (6)
Patterne (2)
Pericles (8, 10)
Redworth (10)
Richmond (4)
Shrapnel (1)
Thompson (6)
Tim Fudge (15)
Ugo Corte (9)
Vittoria (9)
Whitford (2)
Woodseer (10)

9

Adela Pole (8)
Alciphron (18)
Anemolius (18)
Armstrong (5)
Balderini (9)
Baskelett (1)
Beauchamp (1)
Beelzebub (12)
Blathenoy (7)
Cogglesby (3)
de Pyrmont (9)
Fadladeen (17)
Fionnuala (15)
Fleetwood (10)
Ilchester (4)
Jenkinson (2)
Lady Camph (10)
Maccabeus (13)
Middleton (2)
Mrs. Boulby (5)
Mrs. Burman (7)
Mrs. Harley (6)
Mrs. Lovell (5)
Mrs. Samfit (5)
Mrs. Sedley (9)
Nourmahal (17)
O'Donoghue (16)
Pellemore (13)
Phil Fudge (15)
St. Senanus (18)
Todhunter (6)
Tom Blaize (6)
Wentworth (6)

10

Adramelech (12)
Barrington (3)
Barto Rizzo (9)
Biddy Fudge (15)
Danisburgh (10)
de Croisnel (1)
Desborough (6)
Dr. Shrapnel (1)
Harrington (3)
Lady Busshe (2)
Lady Eglett (10)
Lalla Rookh (17)
Lord Laxley (3)
Lord Ormont (10)
Mark Tinman (10)
Miss Denham (1)
Mrs. Culling (1)

Mrs. Fleming (5)
Mrs. Lydiard (1)
Mrs. Wicklow (5)
Orator Puff (18)
Von Rüdiger (10)

11

Beau Beamish (10)
Blackington (7)
Dr. Middleton (2)
General Ople (10)
Jenny Denham (1)
Lady Feverel (6)
Lady Gosstre (8)
Lady Jocelyn (3)
Lady Romfrey (1)
Lenkenstein (9)
Lord of Rosna (16)
Lord Romfrey (1)
Major Waring (5)
Mountfalcon (6)
Mountstuart (2)
Mrs. Mortimer (6)
Percy Dacier (10)
Percy Waring (5)
Quidascarpi (9)
Ralph Morton (6)
Rose Jocelyn (3)
Roy Richmond (4)
Tom Bakewell (6)
Tripehallow (1)
Weisspriess (9)
Wilfrid Pole (8)

12

Adrian Harley (6)
Arabella Pole (8)
Carlo Ammiani (9)
Colonel Corte (9)
Cornelia Pole (8)
Count Ammiani (9)
Countess Lena (9)
Diana Warwick (10)
Duchess Susan (10)
Emma Dunstane (10)
Farmer Blaize (6)
George Lowton (3)
George Uploft (3)
Harry Jocelyn (3)
Harry Latters (5)
Lady Blandish (6)
Lady Patterne (2)
Laetitia Dale (2)
Laura Piavens (9)
Luigi Saracco (9)
Madame Callet (7)
Master Gammon (5)
Merthyr Powys (9)
Mrs. Beauchamp (1)
Mrs. Blathenoy (7)
Mrs. Cogglesby (3)
Mrs. Jenkinson (2)
Mrs. Wentworth (6)
Nataly Radnor (7)
Phelim Connor (15)
Robert Eccles (5)
Runningbrook (8)
Saint Senanus (18)
Squire Uploft (3)
Tom Cogglesby (3)
Victor Radnor (7)
William Moody (5)

153

13

Aminta Farrell (10)
Austin Feverel (6)
Captain Oxford (2)
Colney Durance (7)
Dahlia Fleming (5)
Daniel Skepsey (7)
Drummond Forth (3)
Dudley Sowerby (7)
Emilia Belloni (8)
Farmer Fleming (5)
Gower Woodseer (10)
Grancey Lespel (1)
Harapha of Gath (14)
Harry Richmond (4)
Horace De Craye (2)
John Todhunter (6)
Justice Harley (6)
Lawyer Perkins (3)
Luciano Romara (9)
'Mel' Harrington (3)
Mrs. Doria Forey (6)
Mrs. Harrington (3)
Sandra Belloni (8)
Shibli Bagarag (10)
Squire Beltham (4)
Timothy Turbot (1)

14

Anthony Hackbut (5)
Butcher Billing (5)
Captain Gambier (8, 9)
Caroline Strike (3)
Cecilia Halkett (1)
Clara Middleton (2)
Colonel De Craye (2)
Colonel Halkett (1)
Doctor Shrapnel (1)
Edward Blancove (5)
Evan Harrington (3)
Everard Romfrey (1)
Hippias Feverel (6)
Janet Ilchester (4)
Jonathan Eccles (5)
Lord Danisburgh (10)
Lucy Desborough (6)
Major de Pyrmont (9)
Margaret Lovell (5)
Matthew Weyburn (10)
Mrs. Mountstuart (2)
Nevil Beauchamp (1)
Richard Feverel (6)
Ripton Thompson (6)
Septimus Barmby (7)
Simeon Fenellan (7)

Thomas Redworth (10)
Vernon Whitford (2)
William Fleming (5)

15

Algernon Feverel (6)
Anna Lenkenstein (9)
Antonio Pericles (10)
Austin Wentworth (6)
Captain Fenellan (7)
Charlotte Eglett (10)
Countess Ammiani (9)
Dartrey Fenellan (7)
Earl of Fleetwood (10)
Lady Blackington (7)
Lena Lenkenstein (9)
Lord Mountfalcon (6)
Noorna fin Noorka (10)
Princess Ottilia (4)
Priscilla Graves (7)
Renée de Croisnel (1)
Robert Armstrong (5)
Rosamund Culling (1)
Samson Agonistes (14)
Sir George Lowton (3)

Some characters from **Sir Walter Scott**
List of works from which the following characters are taken, with reference numbers.

Ref. No.	Title			Ref. No.	Title		
1.	Abbot, The	(8 letters)		21.	Legend of Montrose, The	(19 ,,)	
2.	Anne of Geierstein	(16 ,,)		22.	Marmion	(7 ,,)	
3.	Antiquary, The	(12 ,,)		23.	Monastery, The	(12 ,,)	
4.	Aunt Margaret's Mirror	(19 ,,)		24.	Old Mortality	(12 ,,)	
5.	Betrothed, The	(12 ,,)		25.	Peveril of the Peak	(16 ,,)	
6.	Black Dwarf, The	(13 ,,)		26.	Pirate, The	(9 ,,)	
7.	Bridal of Triermain, The	(20 ,,)		27.	Quentin Durward	(14 ,,)	
8.	Bride of Lammermoor, The	(20 ,,)		28.	Redgauntlet	(11 ,,)	
9.	Castle Dangerous	(15 ,,)		29.	Rob Roy	(6 letters)	
10.	Count Robert of Paris	(18 ,,)		30.	Rokeby	(6 ,,)	
11.	Fair Maid Of Perth, The	(18 letters)		31.	St. Ronan's Well	(12 ,,)	
12.	Fortunes of Nigel, The	(18 ,,)		32.	Surgeon's Daughter, The	(19 ,,)	
13.	Guy Mannering	(12 ,,)		33.	Talisman, The	(11 ,,)	
14.	Heart of Midlothian, The	(20 ,,)		34.	Tapestried Chamber, The	(20 ,,)	
15.	Highland Widow, The	(16 ,,)		35.	Two Drovers, The	(13 ,,)	
16.	Ivanhoe	(7 ,,)		36.	Waverley	(8 ,,)	
17.	Kenilworth	(10 ,,)		37.	Woodstock	(9 ,,)	
18.	Lady of the Lake, The	(16 ,,)					
19.	Laird's Jock, The	(13 letters)					
20.	Lay of the Last Minstrel, The	(23 ,,)					

Note: The numbers in brackets indicate *the works* in which the characters appear.

3 AND 4

Adie (23)
Anna (Princess) (10)
Anne (Princess) (27)
Bean (36)
Beg (11)
Dods (31)
Eva (11)
Faa (13)
Gow (11)
Gray (8, 32)
Lee (37)
Lyle (21)

René (King) (2)
Tuck (16)
Weir (28)

5

Abney (37)
Allan (13)
Allen (24)
André (27)
Aston (37)
Aymer (16)
Bevis (horse) (22)

Binks (31)
Blair (11)
Block (2)
Blood (25)
Boeuf (16)
Brand (18)
Brown (29)
Caxon (3)
Clegg (25)
Croye (Countess) (27)
Deans (14)
Edgar (t)
Edith (Lady) (16)
Eppie (31)

Evans (25)
Ewart (28)
Glass (14)
Hadgi (33)
Hakim (33)
Hamet (16)
Harry (11)
Howie (36)
Irene (33)
Isaac (16)
Jabos (13)
Luira (dog) (18)
Mengs (2)
Nixon (28)
Norna (26)
North (Lord) (25)
Olave (26)
Penny (13)
Ralph (25)
Smith (17)
Timms (35)
Tinto (8, 31)
Troil (26)
Urgan (18)
Vanda (5)
Wamba (16)
Wilsa (12)

6

Airlie (Earl of) (21)
Alasco (17)
Alison (17)
Amelot (5)
Amoury (33)
Andrew (13)
Anselm (11)
Arnold (16)
Ashton (8)
Avenel (Lady of) (23)
Aylmer (37)
Badger (17)
Bailie (13)
Baliol (15)
Bayard (horse) (18)
Benjie (28)
Bennet (23)
Bertha (10)
Bibbet (37)
Blount (17)
Blower (31)
Bowyer (17)
Brakel (25)
Browne (34)
Bulmer (31)
Butler (14)
Caspar (2)
Cedric (16)
Copley (17)
Damien (16)
de Lacy (5)
de Vaux (7)
Elliot (6)
Empson (25)
Faggot (28)
Foster (17)
Foxley (28)
Geddes (28)
Glover (11)
Graeme (1)
Gyneth (7)
Halcro (26)
Hamako (33)
Happer (23)
Hastie (28)

Hector (21)
Hudson (25)
Inglis (24)
Jarvie (29)
Jin Vin (12)
Jobson (29)
Judith (12)
Lesley (27)
Louise (11)
Lumley (24)
Maclan (11)
Martha (10)
Martin (28)
Mattie (29)
Mervyn (13)
Mornay (27)
Morris (29)
Morton (Earl of) (1, 23, 24)
Norman (8)
Quitam (29)
Ramsay (12)
Red-Cap (12)
Robert (Count) (10)
Rob Roy (29)
Rowena (16)
Seyton (1)
Sharpe (24)
Stubbs (14)
Tacket (23)
Talbot (36)
Tormot (11)
Tyrrel (31)
Ulrica (10, 16)
Ursula (9)
Varney (17)
Vernon (29)
Vipont (16)
Warden (23)
Watley (25)
Wilson (14)
Winnie (8)

7

Abdalla (16)
Ackland (37)
Aikwood (3)
Aldrick (25)
Ambrose (1, 16, 28)
Anthony (9, 31)
Arnheim (2)
Baldwin (Count) (10, 16)
Balfour (24)
Barston (25)
Beaujeu (12, 36)
Berkely (Lady) (9)
Bertram (13)
Berwine (5)
Bidmore (Lord) (31)
Bletson (37)
Bridget (1)
Brydone (23)
Calista (33)
Cargill (31)
Corsand (13)
Crosbie (28)
de Boeuf (16)
de Bracy (16)
Dinmont (13)
Dorothy (11)
Douglas (18)
Dubourg (29)
Durward (27)
El Hadgi (33)
El Hakim (33)

Elspeth (3, 13)
Eustace (16, 23)
Feltham (12)
Fenella (25)
Fleming (1, 9, 14)
Francis (11, 27)
Glossin (13)
Godfrey (23)
Gosling (17)
Gourlay (8)
Grahame (24)
Guthrie (27)
Hartley (32)
Hayston (8)
Herries (Lord) (1)
Hesketh (35)
Hillary (32)
Hinchup (14)
Ivanhoe (16)
Joliffe (37)
Kennedy (13)
Kenneth (Sir) (33)
Langley (6)
Latimer (28)
Leopold (33)
MacEagh (21)
MacIvor (36)
MacTurk (31)
Malachi (28)
Margery (5)
Marmion (22)
Matilda (30)
Maxwell (12, 24, 28)
Meg Dods (31)
Mertoun (26)
Mowbray (31)
Neville (3)
Nosebag (36)
Oldbuck (3)
Pacolet (26)
Peebles (28)
Peveril (25)
Ramorny (11)
Rattray (12)
Rebecca (16)
Redmond (30)
Robsart (17)
Ruthven (Lord) (1)
Saladin (33)
Sampson (13)
Scholey (26)
Sellock (25)
Shafton (23, 29)
Staples (17)
Stephen (16)
Taffril (3)
Tancred (10)
Tomkins (37)
Torquil (11)
Tresham (29)
Trotter (31)
Vanwelt (5)
Vincent (12)
Wakeman (25)
Waldeck (3)
Wayland (17)
Wenlock (5)
Wilfrid (29)

8

Alberick (5, 33)
Alice Lee (37)
Anderson (31)
Argentin (2)

Baldrick (5)
Berenger (5)
Bohemond (Prince) (10)
Boniface (1, 23)
Bullsegg (36)
Burleigh (Lord) (21)
Campbell (14, 15, 21, 28)
Cantrips (28)
Carleton (25)
Christie (12, 23)
Clifford (33, 37)
Colkitto (21)
Conachar (11)
Dalgarno (Lord) (12)
Dalgetty (21)
Damiotti (4)
Debbitch (25)
de Multon (33)
Dennison (24)
de Wilton (22)
Engelred (16)
Evandale (Lord) (24)
Fairford (28)
Falconer (4, 36)
Fitzurse (Lord) (16)
Flammock (5)
Forester (4)
Geraldin (Lord) (3)
Guenevra (33)
Headrigg (24)
Henry Gow (11)
Henry Lee (37)
Hereward (10)
Hermione (12)
Ingelram (23)
Jamieson (32)
Jellicot (37)
King René (2)
Lapraick (28)
l'Hermite (2, 27)
Locksley (16)
Macaulay (21)
Macready (29)
Margaret (Ladye) (20)
Melville (1)
Menteith (Earl of) (21)
Meredith (28)
Misbegot (3)
Mrs. Allan (13)
Mrs. Glass (14)
Musgrave (20)
Nicholas (23)
Olifaunt (12)
O'Todshaw (13)
Pauletti (Lady) (12)
Pleydell (13)
Porteous (14)
Protocol (13)
Quodling (25)
Rentowel (36)
Ringwood (12)
Scriever (36)
Spitfire (37)
Staunton (14)
Steenson (28)
Swanston (28)
Texartis (10)
Trapbois (12)
Turnbull (28)
Waltheof (11)
Waverley (36)
Wetheral (16)
Wildfire (11)
Wildrake (37)
Woodcock (1)
156 Wycliffe (30)

9

Agelastes (10)
Albert Lee (37)
Aldovrand (5)
Alice Bean (36)
Alice Gray (8)
Annot Lyle (21)
Armstrong (6, 12, 19)
Bellenden (24)
Bickerton (14)
Biederman (2)
Bimbister (26)
Bindloose (31)
Blackless (33)
Brengwain (5)
Cadwallon (5)
Chiffinch (25)
Christian (25)
Cleveland (Duchess of)
(25, 26)
Clippurse (36)
Constance (22)
Cranstoun (20)
Cresswell (25)
de la Marck (27)
de Moncada (32)
de Valence (9)
Dick Tinto (8, 31)
Elshender (6)
Friar Tuck (16)
Galbraith (29)
Gellatley (36)
Guendolen (7)
Howleglas (1)
Inglewood (29)
Jack Jabos (13)
Jock Penny (13)
John Mengs (2)
Johnstone (13)
Josceline (33)
Lady Binks (31)
Lady Edith (16)
Lochinvar (22)
Lord North (25)
MacAlpine (29)
MacGregor (29)
MacIntyre (14)
MacTavish (15)
Major Weir (28)
Malvoisin (16)
Mannering (13)
Maugrabin (27)
Mayflower (37)
Merrilies (13)
Middlemas (32)
Mortcloke (13)
Mrs. Aylmer (37)
Mrs. Baliol (15)
Mrs. Blower (31)
Mumblazen (17)
Ochiltree (3)
Poundtext (24)
Ratcliffe (6)
Rewcastle (6)
Risingham (30)
Sturmthal (2)
Thoulouse (10)
Touchwood (31)
Turnpenny (28)
Twigtythe (36)
Wackbairn (14)
Wakefield (35)
Woodville (34)
Yellowley (26)
Zimmerman (2)

10

Alice Brand (18)
Amy Robsart (16)
Anne Bulmer (23)
Athelstane (16)
Aunt Judith (12)
Beaumanoir (16)
Bingo Binks (Sir) (31)
Blind Harry (11)
Blinkinsop (28)
Bridgeward (1, 23)
Colonel Lee (37)
Cranbourne (25)
Croftangry (11)
Dame Martin (28)
Davie Deans (14)
Desborough (37)
Donald Bean (36)
Dr. Damiotti (4)
Dryfesdale (1)
Earnscliff (6)
Effie Deans (14)
Enguerraud (33)
Flockheart (36)
Gabriel Faa (13)
Geierstein (2)
Gideon Gray (32)
Glee-Maiden (The) (11)
Grinderson (3)
Hammerlein (27)
Hatteraick (13)
Holdenough (37)
Howlaglass (13)
Hugo de Lacy (5)
Humgudgeon (37)
Huntingdon (Earl of) (33)
Ian Vanwelt (5)
Jacob Aston (37)
Jacob Caxon (3)
Jamie Howie (36)
Jenny Caxon (3)
Jerningham (25)
Lucy Ashton (8)
Meiklewham (31)
Mrs. Crosbie (28)
Mrs. Nosebag (36)
Murdochson (14)
Nanty Ewart (28)
Ned Shafton (29)
Old Dorothy (11)
Old Elspeth (3)
Penfeather (31)
Phillipson (2)
Quackleben (31)
Ravenswood (8)
Rough Ralph (25)
Saddletree (14)
Scambister (26)
Sir Kenneth (33)
Stanchells (29)
Sweepclean (3)
Theodorick (33)
Tibb Tacket (23)
Tom Hillary (32)
Toschach Beg (11)
Tressilian (17)
Whitecraft (25)
Will Badger (17)

11

Abel Sampson (13)
Adam Hartley (32)
Annie Winnie (8)

Auld Elspeth (13)
Balderstone (8)
Bet Jamieson (32)
Blandeville (36)
Bradwardine (36)
Brenda Troil (26)
Bridgenorth (25)
Chamberlain (25)
Claud Halcro (26)
Claverhouse (8)
Count Robert (10)
Craigdallie (11)
Craigengelt (8)
Dame Hinchup (14)
Dame Margery (5)
David Ramsay (12)
de Crevecour (27)
Diana Vernon (29)
Donnerhugel (2)
Dumbiedikes (14)
Fairbrother (14)
Fairservice (29)
Father Blair (11)
Frank Tyrrel (31)
Giles Bailie (13)
Glendinning (1)
Goldiebirds (3)
Graneagowl (21)
Henry Morton (24)
Henry Warden (23)
Isaac of York (16)
James Sharp (13)
Jeanie Deans (14)
John Balfour (24)
John Grahame (24)
John Guthrie (27)
John Mowbray (31)
John Ramorny (11)
Lady Berkely (9)
Lady Fleming (1)
Lord Bidmore (31)
Lord Herries (1)
Lord Ruthven (1)
Lucy Bertram (13)
MacMurrough (36)
Magnus Troil (26)
Martin Block (2)
Mary Fleming (1)
Montreville (32)
Mrs. Cantrips (28)
Mucklewrath (24)
Mysie Happer (23)
Nicol Jarvie (29)
Pate Maxwell (28)
Plantagenet (33)
Princess Ann (27)
Ralph Morton (24)
Redgauntlet (28)
Robin Hastie (28)
Roderick Dhu (18)
Rougedragon (28)
Silas Morton (24)
Simon Glover (11)
Sir Henry Lee (37)
Smotherwell (11)
Tam O'Todshaw (13)
Thomas Blood (25)
Tomahourich (35)
Walkingshaw (28)
Wild Wenlock (5)

12

Adam Woodcock (1)
Adrian Brakel (25)

Ailie Dinmont (13)
Andrew Wilson (14)
Arthur Mervyn (13)
Balmawhapple (36)
Baron Arnheim (2)
Basil Mertoun (26)
Bittlebrains (Lord) (8)
Black Feltham (12)
Blattergrowl (3)
Buonaventura (28)
Captain Brown (13)
Cholmondeley (25)
Cisly Sellock (25)
Clara Mowbray (31)
Clement Blair (11)
Colonel Blood (25)
Count Baldwin (10)
Damian de Lacy (5)
Dougal Cratur (The) (29)
Dr. Gideon Gray (32)
Dr. Quackleben (31)
Eachin MacIan (11)
Earl of Airlie (21)
Earl of Morton (23)
Earl of Oxford (2)
Ellen Douglas (18)
Flora MacIvor (36)
Frank Hayston (8)
Frank Kennedy (13)
Giles Gosling (17)
Glendinnings (The) (23)
Gowkthrapple (36)
Guy Mannering (13)
Hector Maclan (11)
Henry Bertram (13)
Hobbie Elliot (6)
Jock Scriever (36)
John Christie (12)
John Porteous (14)
Joseph Jobson (29)
Joshua Geddes (28)
Knockwinnock (3)
Lady Forester (39)
Lady Pauletti (12)
Lady of Avenel (23)
Little Benjie (28)
Lord Burleigh (21)
Lord Dalgarno (12)
Lord Evandale (24)
Lord Fitzurse (16)
Lord Geraldin (3)
Major Neville (3)
Malagrowther (12)
Martin Tacket (23)
Mary Campbell (14)
Master Bibbet (37)
Master Bowyer (17)
Meg Merrilies (13)
Mother Red-Cap (12)
Mrs. Bickerton (14)
Mucklebackit (3)
Nelly Trotter (31)
Old Alice Gray (8)
Old Mortality (24)
Osbaldistone (29)
Pate Macready (29)
Peter Peebles (28)
Princess Anna (10)
Ralph Hesketh (35)
Ralph Latimer (28)
Randal de Lacy (5)
Reuben Butler (14)
Roland de Vaux (7)
Roland Graeme (1)
Rose Flammock (5)
Sir Josceline (33)

Sister Ursula (9)
Squire Foxley (28)
Thomas Copley (17)
Tom Turnpenny (28)
Vanbust Brown (13)
Wayland Smith (17)
Wild Spitfire (37)
William Evans (25)
Witherington (32)

13

Abbot Boniface (23)
Abbot Ingleram (23)
Adam Zimmerman (2)
Ailsie Gourlay (8)
Allan Fairford (28)
Allan Macaulay (21)
Angus Macaulay (21)
Anthony Foster (17)
Baillie Jarvie (29)
Brother Bennet (23)
Caltain Lumley (24)
Christal Nixon (28)
Colonel Ashton (8)
Colonel Morton (24)
Colonel Talbot (36)
Cornet Grahame (24)
Corporal Timms (36)
Dandie Dinmont (13)
Darsie Latimer (28)
de Grantmesnil (16)
Dousterswivel (3)
Edie Ochiltree (3)
Eppie Anderson (31)
Father Ambrose (1)
Father Eustace (23)
Fergus MacIvor (36)
Fleecebumpkin (35)
General Browne (34)
George Wakeman (25)
Goody Jellicot (37)
Hector MacTurk (31)
Holdfast Clegg (25)
Jenkin Vincent (12)
Jenny Dennison (24)
John Armstrong (19)
John Bindloose (31)
John of Moidart (21)
John Rewcastle (6)
Jonathan Brown (29)
Joseph Tomkins (37)
Joshua Bletson (37)
Josiah Cargill (31)
Julian Peveril (25)
Kate Chiffinch (25)
Kettledrummle (24)
Lady Bellenden (24)
Ladye Margaret (20)
Lord Woodville (34)
MacAnaleister (29)
Madge Wildfire (14)
Major Falconer (4)
Martin Waldeck (3)
Matthew Foxley (28)
Meg Murdochson (14)
Mother Bridget (1)
Nelly Christie (12)
Nigel Olifaunt (12)
O'Neale Redmond (30)
Peter Protocol (13)
Ralph de Wilton (22)
Ranald MacEagh (21)
Richard Walley (25)

Ringan Aikwood (3)
Robert of Paris (Count) (10)
Roger Wildrake (37)
Sir Bingo Binks (31)
Sir Hugo de Lacy (5)
Sir Jacob Aston (37)
Stephen Butler (14)
Thomas Ackland (36)
William Ashton (8)

14

Adonbec el Hakim (33)
Augusta Bidmore (31)
Baldwin de Oyley (16)
Blondel de Nesle (33)
Brother Ambrose (16)
Captain Hillary (32)
Captain MacTurk (31)
Clement Dubourg (29)
Colonel Grahame (24)
Corporal Inglis (24)
Cuddie Headrigg (24)
Dame Whitecraft (25)
Davie Gellatley (36)
de Bois Guilbert (16)
Dirk Hatteraick (13)
Dominie Sampson (13)
Duncan Campbell (21)
Earl of Menteith (21)
Earl of Seaforth (21)
Edith Bellenden (24)
Edward Waverley (36)
Elspeth Brydone (23)
Eric Scambister (26)
Father Boniface (1)
Father Waltheof (11)
Geoffrey Hudson (25)
George Staunton (14)
Gilbert Glossin (13)
Grace Armstrong (6)
Harry Wakefield (35)
Heatherblutter (36)
Helen MacGregor (29)
Henry Cranstoun (20)
Jabesh Rentowel (36)
Jemima Forester (4)
Jessie Cantrips (28)
John Phillipson (2)
John Whitecraft (25)
Julia Mannering (13)
Lady Penfeather (31)
Maggie Steenson (28)

Major Bellenden (24)
Major Galbraith (29)
Malcolm Fleming (9)
Margaret Blower (12)
Margaret Ramsay (12)
Maria MacIntyre (3)
Martha Trapbois (12)
Nicholas Blount (17)
Nicholas Faggot (28)
Paulus Pleydell (13)
Peter Proudtext (24)
Philip Forester (4)
Piercie Shafton (23)
Prince Bohemond (10)
Quentin Durward (27)
Richard Grahame (24)
Robert Melville (1)
Runnion Rattray (12)
Sir Gibbs Amoury (33)
Sir John Ramorny (11)
Thomas de Multon (33)
Thomas Turnbull (28)
Wilkin Flammack (5)
William Crosbie (28)
William Maxwell (24)
Willie Steenson (28)
Zamet Maugrabin (27)
Zarah Christian (25)
Zilia de Moncada (32)

15

Abdallah el Hadgi (33)
Adam Craigdallie (11)
Adie of Aikenshaw (23)
Albert Malvoisin (16)
Archie Armstrong (12)
Arnold Biederman (2)
Augustus Bidmore (31)
Balfour of Burley (24)
Brother Nicholas (23)
Captain Campbell (15)
Captain Carleton (9)
Captain Porteous (14)
Captain Waverley (36)
Catherine Glover (11)
Catherine Seyton (1)
Claus Hammerlein (27)
Countess of Croye (27)
Count Geierstein (2)
Deborah Debbitch (25)
Duncan Galbraith (29)
Edgar Ravenswood (8)

Edward Christian (25)
Ephraim Macbriar (24)
Erminia Pauletti (12)
Eveline Berenger (5)
Father Howleglas (1)
Flibbertigibbet (17)
General Campbell (28)
Geraldin Neville (3)
Hamish MacGregor (29)
Hamish MacTavish (15)
Hector MacIntyre (3)
Hector of the Mist (21)
Hubert Ratcliffe (6)
Jeanie MacAlpine (29)
Joceline Joliffe (37)
Jonathan Oldbuck (3)
Lady Mary Fleming (1)
Lady Plantagenet (14)
Lady Rougedragon (28)
Lawrence Scholey (26)
Lawrence Staples (17)
Lawyer Clippurse (36)
Madame Cresswell (25)
Madge Murdochson (14)
Magdalene Graeme (1)
Malcolm Misbegot (3)
Miss Walkingshaw (28)
Monsieur Dubourg (29)
Mordaunt Mertoun (26)
Murdoch Campbell (21)
Peter Bridgeward (1, 23)
Philip Malvoisin (16)
Phoebe Mayflower (37)
Raymond Berenger (5)
Richard Musgrave (20)
Richard Waverley (36)
Robert MacGregor (29)
Rob-Roy MacGregor (29)
Rose Bradwardine (36)
Simon of Hackburn (6)
Sir Damian de Lacy (5)
Sir Randal de Lacy (5)
Sir Thomas Copley (17)
Squire Inglewood (29)
Stephen Wetheral (16)
The Dougal Cratur (29)
Thomas Chiffinch (25)
Torquil of the Oak (11)
Tristan l'Hermite (2, 27)
Valentine Bulmer (31)
Wandering Willie (28)
Widow Flockheart (36)
Wilfrid Wycliffe (30)
Willie Johnson (13)

Characters from **Shakespeare**
List of plays from which the following characters are taken, with reference numbers.

Ref. No.	Title			Ref. No.	Title		
1.	All's Well that Ends Well	(20 letters)		12.	King Henry VI, Part 1	(7 or 11	)
2.	Antony and Cleopatra	(18	)	13.	King Henry VI, Part 2	(7 or 11	)
3.	As You Like It	(11	)	14.	King Henry VI, Part 3	(7 or 11	)
4.	Comedy of Errors, A	(15	)	15.	King Henry VIII	(9 or 13	)
5.	Coriolanus	(10	)	16.	King John	(8	)
6.	Cymbeline	(9	)	17.	King Lear	(8	)
7.	Hamlet (Prince of Denmark)	(6	)	18.	King Richard II	(9 or 13	)
8.	Julius Caesar	(12	)	19.	King Richard III	(10 or 14	)
9.	King Henry IV, Part 1	(7 or 11	)	20.	Love's Labour's Lost	(16 letters)	
10.	King Henry IV, Part 2	(7 or 11	)	21.	Macbeth	(7	)
11.	King Henry V	(6 or 10	)	22.	Measure for Measure	(17	)
				23.	Merchant of Venice, The	(19	)

Ref. No.	Title				Ref. No.	Title			
24.	Merry Wives of Windsor	(19	„	)	31.	Tempest, The	(10	„	)
25.	Midsummer Night's				32.	Timon of Athens	(13	„	)
	Dream, A	(21	„	)	33.	Titus Andronicus	(15	„	)
26.	Much Ado About				34.	Troilus and Cressida	(18	„	)
	Nothing	(19	„	)	35.	Twelfth Night; or,			
27.	Othello, The Moor of					What You Will	(12	„	)
	Venice	(7	„	)	36.	Two Gentlemen of			
28.	Pericles, Prince of Tyre	(8	„	)		Verona	(20	„	)
29.	Romeo and Juliet	(14	„	)	37.	Winter's Tale, The	(14	„	)
30.	Taming of the Shrew, The	(19	„	)					

Note: The numbers in brackets indicate *the plays* in which the characters appear.

(A.-B. of) = Archbishop of.   (B. of) = Bishop of.   (Card.) = Cardinal.   (C. of) = Count of.
(C'ess of) = Countess of.   (D. of) = Duke of.   (D'ess of) = Duchess of.   (E. of) = Earl of.
(K. of) = King of.   (M. of) = Marquis of.   (P. of) = Prince of.   (P'ess of) = Princess of.   (Q. of) = Queen of.

3 AND 4

Adam (3)
Ajax (34)
Anne (Lady) (19)
Bona (14)
Cade (13)
Cato (8)
Davy (10)
Dick (13)
Dion (37)
Dull (20)
Eros (2)
Fang (10)
Ford (24)
Ford (Mrs.) (24)
Grey (11)
Grey (Lady) (14)
Grey (Lord) (19)
Hero (26)
Hume (13)
Iago (27)
Iden (13)
Iris (31)
Jamy (11)
John (10)
John (Don) (26)
John (K.) (16)
Juno (31)
Kent (E. of) (17)
Lear (K.) (17)
Lion (25)
Luce (4)
Lucy (12)
Moth (20, 25)
Nym (11, 24)
Page (24)
Page (Mrs.) (24)
Peto (9, 10)
Puck (25)
Ross (Lord) (18)
Ross (21)
Say (Lord) (13)
Snug (25)
Time (37)
Vaux (13, 15)
Wart (10)
York (A.-B. of) (9, 10, 19)
York (D'ess of) (18, 19)
York (D. of) (11, 18, 19)

5

Aaron (33)
Abram (29)

Alice (11)
Angus (21)
Ariel (31)
Bagot (18)
Bates (11)
Belch (35)
Bigot (16)
Biron (20)
Blunt (9, 10)
Boult (28)
Boyet (20)
Bushy (18)
Butts (15)
Caius (6, 24)
Casca (8)
Celia (3)
Ceres (31)
Cinna (8)
Cleon (28)
Clown (22, 35)
Corin (3)
Court (11)
Curan (17)
Curio (35)
Denny (15)
Diana (1, 28)
Edgar (17)
Egeus (25)
Elbow (22)
Essex (E. of) (16)
Evans (24)
Flute (25)
Froth (22)
Ghost (7)
Gobbo (23)
Gower (10, 11, 28)
Green (18)
Helen (6, 34)
Henry (19)
Henry (K.) (9, 10, 11, 12, 13, 15)
Henry (P.) (16)
Julia (36)
Lafeu (1)
Louis (Dauphin) (11, 16)
Louis (K.) (14)
Louis (Lord) (19)
Lucio (22)
March (E. of) (9)
Maria (20)
Melun (16)
Menas (2)
Milan (D. of) (36)
Mopsa (37)
Osric (7)
Paris (29, 34)

Pedro (Don) (26)
Percy (9, 10, 18)
Percy (Lady) (9)
Peter (13, 22)
Phebe (3)
Philo (2)
Pinch (4)
Poins (9, 10)
Priam (34)
Queen (6)
Regan (17)
Robin (24)
Romeo (29)
Rugby (24)
Sands (Lord) (15)
Snare (10)
Snout (25)
Speed (36)
Timon (32)
Tubal (23)
Varro (8)
Viola (35)
Wales (P. of) (9, 10, 19)

6

Adrian (31)
Aegeon (4)
Aeneas (34)
Albany (D. of) (17)
Alexas (2)
Alonso (31)
Amiens (3)
Angelo (4, 22)
Antony (2)
Armado (20)
Arthur (16)
Audrey (3)
Banquo (21)
Basset (12)
Bianca (27, 30)
Blanch (16)
Blount (19)
Bottom (25)
Brutus (5, 8)
Bullen (15)
Cadwal (6)
Caesar (2)
Caphis (32)
Cassio (27)
Chiron (33)
Cicero (8)
Clitus (8)
Clotten (22)
Cobweb (25)

159

Curtis (30)
Dehnis (3)
Dorcas (37)
Dorset (M. of) (19)
Dromio (4)
Dumain (20)
Duncan (K.) (21)
Edmund (14, 17)
Edward (13)
Edward (K.) (19)
Edward (P. of Wales) (14, 19)
Elinor (16)
Emilia (27, 37)
Exeter (D. of) (11, 14)
Fabian (35)
Feeble (10)
Fenton (24)
France (K. of) (1, 17)
France (P'ess of) (20)
Gallus (2)
George (13, 14, 19)
Grumio (30)
Gurney (16)
Hamlet (7)
Hecate (21)
Hector (34)
Helena (1, 25)
Henry V (K.) (11)
Hermia (25)
Horner (13)
Imogen (6)
Isabel (11)
Jaques (3)
Juliet (22, 29)
Launce (36)
Le Beau (3)
Lennox (21)
Lovell (15)
Lucius (8, 32, 33)
Marina (28)
Morgan (6)
Morton (10, 19)
Mouldy (10)
Mr. Ford (24)
Mr. Page (24)
Mutius (33)
Nestor (34)
Oberon (25)
Oliver (3)
Olivia (35)
Orsino (35)
Oswald (17)
Oxford (D. of) (14)
Oxford (E. of) (19)
Pedant (30)
Philip (K.) (16)
Pierce (18)
Pistol (10, 11, 24)
Portia (8, 23)
Quince (25)
Rivers (Earl) (19)
Rivers (Lord) (14)
Rogero (37)
Rumour (10)
Scales (Lord) (13)
Scarus (2)
Scroop (9, 10, 18)
Scroop (Lord) (11)
Seyton (21)
Shadow (10)
Silius (2)
Silvia (36)
Simple (24)
Siward (21)
160 Strato (8)

Surrey (D. of) (18)
Surrey (E. of) (15, 19)
Talbot (12)
Talbot (Lord) (12)
Tamora (33)
Taurus (2)
Thaisa (28)
Thisbe (25)
Thomas (22)
Thurio (36)
Tranio (30)
Tybalt (29)
Tyrrel (19)
Ursula (26)
Venice (D. of) (23, 27)
Verges (26)
Vernon (9, 12)
Wolsey (Lord) (15)

7

Adriana (4)
Aemilia (4)
Agrippa (2)
Alarbus (33)
Alencon (D. of) (12)
Antenor (34)
Antonio (23, 26, 31, 35, 36)
Arragon (P. of) (23)
Aumerle (D. of) (18)
Bedford (D. of) (11, 12)
Berkley (Earl) (18)
Bertram (1)
Bourbon (D. of) (11)
Brandon (15)
Calchas (34)
Caliban (31)
Camillo (37)
Capulet (29)
Capulet (Lady) (29)
Cassius (8)
Catesby (19)
Cerimon (28)
Charles (3)
Charles (Dauphin) (11)
Charles (K.) (11)
Claudio (22, 26)
Conrade (26)
Costard (20)
Cranmer (A.-B.) (15)
Dauphin, The (12, 16)
Dionyza (28)
Don John (26)
Douglas (E. of) (9)
Eleanor (13)
Escalus (22, 29)
Escanes (28)
Flavius (8, 32)
Fleance (21)
Gloster (D'ess of) (18)
Gloster (D. of) (11, 14, 19)
Gloster (E. of) (12)
Gloster (P. of) (10)
Goneril (17)
Gonzalo (31)
Gregory (29)
Helenus (34)
Henry IV (K.) (9, 10)
Henry VI (K.) (12, 13, 14)
Herbert (19)
Horatio (7)
Hostess (30)
Hotspur (9, 10)
Iachimo (6)
Jessica (23)

Laertes (7)
Lavinia (33)
Leonato (26)
Leonine (28)
Leontes (37)
Lepidus (2)
Lincoln (B. of) (15)
Lord Say (13)
Lorenzo (23)
Lucetta (36)
Luciana (4)
Macbeth (21)
Macbeth (Lady) (21)
Macduff (21)
Macduff (Lady) (21)
Malcolm (21)
Marcius (5)
Mardian (2)
Mariana (1, 22)
Martext (3)
Martius (33)
Mercade (20)
Messala (8)
Michael (13)
Michael (Sir) (9, 10)
Miranda (31)
Montano (27)
Morocco (P. of) (23)
Mowbray (18)
Mowbray (Lord) (10)
Mrs. Ford (24)
Mrs. Page (24)
Nerissa (23)
Norfolk (D. of) (14, 15, 18, 19)
Octavia (2)
Ophelia (7)
Orlando (3)
Orleans (D. of) (11)
Othello (27)
Paulina (37)
Perdita (37)
Phrynia (32)
Pisanio (6)
Proteus (36)
Publius (8, 33)
Pucelle (12)
Pyramus (25)
Quickly (Mrs.) (9, 10, 11, 24)
Quintus (33)
Richard (13, 14, 19)
Richard (K.) (18, 19)
Salanio (23)
Salerio (23)
Sampson (29)
Setebos (31)
Shallow (10, 24)
Shylock (23)
Silence (10)
Silvius (3)
Simpcox (13)
Slender (24)
Solinus (4)
Stanley (13, 14)
Stanley (Lord) (19)
Suffolk (D. of) (13, 15)
Suffolk (E. of) (12)
Theseus (25)
Thryeus (2)
Titania (25)
Travers (10)
Troilus (34)
Ulysses (34)
Urswick (19)
Valeria (5)
Varrius (2, 22)

Vaughan (19)
Velutus (5)
Warwick (E. of) (10, 11, 12, 13, 14)
William (3)

8

Abhorson (22)
Achilles (34)
Aemilius (33)
Aufidius (5)
Baptista (30)
Bardolph (9, 10, 11, 24)
Bardolph (Lord) (10)
Bassanio (23)
Beatrice (26)
Beaufort (12)
Beaufort (Card.) (13)
Belarius (6)
Benedick (26)
Benvolio (29)
Bernardo (7)
Borachio (26)
Bouchier (Card.) (19)
Bullcalf (10)
Burgundy (D. of) (11, 12, 17)
Campeius (Card.) (15)
Canidius (2)
Capucius (15)
Charmian (2)
Clarence (D. of) (10, 19)
Claudius (8)
Claudius (K.) (7)
Clifford (13)
Clifford (Lord) (13, 14)
Colville (5)
Cominius (5)
Cordelia (17)
Cornwall (D. of) (17)
Cressida (34)
Cromwell (15)
Dercetas (2)
Diomedes (2, 34)
Dogberry (26)
Don Pedro (26)
Edward VI (K.) (19)
Eglamour (36)
Falstaff (9, 10, 24)
Fastolfe (12)
Florence (D. of) (1)
Florizel (37)
Fluellen (11)
Gadshill (9)
Gardiner (15)
Gargrave (13)
Gertrude (Q.) (7)
Gratiano (23, 27)
Griffith (15)
Harcourt (10)
Hastings (Lord) (10, 14, 19)
Hermione (37)
Humphrey (10, 13)
Isabella (22)
Jack Cade (13)
Jourdain (13)
King John (16)
King Lear (17)
Lady Anne (19)
Lady Grey (14)
Lawrence (29)
Leonardo (23)
Leonatus (6)
Ligarius (8)

Lodovico (27)
Lord Grey (19)
Lord Ross (18)
Lucentio (30)
Lucilius (8, 32)
Lucullus (32)
Lysander (25)
Malvolio (35)
Margaret (12, 13, 19, 26)
Margaret (Q.) (14)
Marullus (8)
Mecaenas (2)
Menelaus (34)
Menteith (21)
Mercutio (29)
Montague (29)
Montague (Lady) (29)
Montague (M. of) (14)
Mortimer (9, 12, 14)
Mortimer (Lady) (9)
Mountjoy (11)
Old Gobbo (23)
Overdone (Mrs.) (22)
Pandarus (34)
Pandulph (Card.) (16)
Panthino (36)
Parolles (1)
Patience (15)
Pembroke (E. of) (14, 16)
Pericles (28)
Philario (6)
Philemon (28)
Philotus (32)
Pindarus (8)
Polonius (7)
Polydore (6)
Prospero (31)
Rambures (11)
Ratcliff (19)
Reignier (12)
Reynaldo (7)
Richmond (E. of) (19)
Roderigo (27)
Rosalind (3)
Rosaline (20)
Rotheram (19)
Salarino (23)
Seleucus (2)
Somerset (D. of) (13, 14)
Stafford (13)
Stafford (Lord) (14)
Stephano (23, 31)
Thaliard (28)
Timandra (32)
Titinius (8)
Trinculo (31)
Vicentio (22)
Violenta (1)
Virgilia (5)
Volumnia (5)
Whitmore (13)
Williams (11)

9

Agamemnon (34)
Aguecheek (35)
Alexander (34)
Antigonus (37)
Antiochus (28)
Apemantus (32)
Archibald (9, 10)
Arviragus (6)
Autolycus (37)
Balthazar (4, 23, 26, 29)

Bassianus (33)
Biondello (30)
Brabantio (27)
Caithness (21)
Cambridge (E. of) (11)
Cassandra (34)
Chatillon (16)
Cleomenes (37)
Cleopatra (2)
Constance (16)
Cornelius (6, 7)
Cymbeline (6)
Dardanius (8)
Deiphobus (34)
Demetrius (2, 25, 33)
Desdemona (27)
Dolabella (2)
Donalbain (21)
Elizabeth (19)
Enobarbus (2)
Erpingham (11)
Ferdinand (31)
Ferdinand (K.) (20)
Fitz-Peter (16)
Fitzwater (Lord) (18)
Flaminius (32)
Francisca (22)
Francisco (7, 31)
Frederick (3)
Friar John (29)
Glansdale (12)
Glendower (9)
Grandpree (11)
Guiderius (6)
Guildford (15)
Helicanus (28)
Henry VIII (K.) (15)
Hippolyta (25)
Hortensio (30)
Katharina (30)
Katharine (15, 20)
Katharine (P'ess) (11)
Lady Percy (9)
Lancaster (D. of) (18)
Lancaster (P. of) (9, 10)
Longsword (16)
Lord Lovel (19)
Lord Sands (15)
Lychorida (28)
Macmorris (11)
Mamillius (37)
Marcellus (7)
Mareshall (16)
Moonshine (25)
Nathaniel (20)
Patroclus (34)
Petruchio (30)
Polixenes (37)
Richard II (K.) (18)
Rousillon (C. of) (1)
Rousillon (C'ess of) (1)
Salisbury (E. of) (11, 12, 13, 16, 18)
Sebastian (31, 35)
Servilius (32)
Simonides (28)
Southwell (13)
Tearsheet (10)
Thersites (34)
Trebonius (8)
Valentine (35, 36)
Ventidius (2, 32)
Vincentio (30)
Voltimand (7)
Volumnius (8)
Woodville (12)

161

Worcester (E. of) (9, 10)
Young Cato (8)

10

Alcibiades (32)
Andromache (34)
Andronicus (33)
Anne Bullen (15)
Antipholus (4)
Archidamus (37)
Barnardine (22)
Brakenbury (19)
Buckingham (D. of) (13, 15, 19)
Calphurnia (8)
Canterbury (A.-B. of) (11, 15, 19)
Coriolanus (5)
Duke of York (11, 18, 19)
Earl of Kent (17)
Earl Rivers (19)
Euphronius (2)
Fortinbras (7)
Henry Percy (9, 10, 18)
Holofernes (20)
Hortensius (32)
Jaquenetta (20)
John Talbot (12)
King Henry V (10)
Longaville (20)
Lord Rivers (14)
Lord Scales (13)
Lord Scroop (11)
Lord Talbot (12)
Lysimachus (28)
Marc Antony (2)
Margarelon (34)
Menecrates (2)
Montgomery (14)
Mrs. Quickly (9, 10, 11, 24)
Prince John (10)
Proculeius (2)
Richard III (K.) (19)
Saturninus (33)
Sempronius (32)
Sir Michael (9, 10)
Somerville (14)
Starveling (25)
Touchstone (3)
Willoughby (Lord) (18)
Winchester (B. of) (15)

11

Abergavenny (Lord) (15)
Artimidorus (8)
Bishop of Ely (11, 19)
Bolingbroke (13, 18)
Dame Quickly (9, 10)
Doctor Butts (15)
Doctor Caius (24)
Duke of Milan (36)
Earl Berkley (18)
Earl of Essex (16)
Earl of March (9, 14)
James Gurney (16)
John of Gaunt (18)
King Henry IV (9, 10)
King Henry VI (12, 13, 14)
Lady Capulet (29)
Lady Macbeth (21)
Lady Macduff (21)
Lord Mowbray (10)

Lord Stanley (19)
Mrs. Anne Page (24)
Mrs. Overdone (22)
Mustardseed (25)
Peasblossom (25)
Philostrate (25)
Plantagenet (12, 13, 14)
Prince Henry (16)
Robert Bigot (16)
Rosencrantz (7)
Westminster (A.-B. of) (18)
William Page (24)
Young Siward (21)

12

Decius Brutus (8)
Duke of Albany (17)
Duke of Exeter (11, 14)
Duke of Oxford (14)
Duke of Surrey (18)
Duke of Venice (23, 27)
Earl of Oxford (19)
Earl of Surrey (15, 19)
Falconbridge (16)
Falconbridge (Lady) (16)
Guildenstern (7)
Julius Caesar (8)
Junius Brutus (5)
King of France (1, 17)
Lady Montague (29)
Lady Mortimer (9)
Lord Bardolph (10)
Lord Clifford (13, 14)
Lord Hastings (10, 14, 19)
Lord Stafford (14)
Marcus Brutus (8)
Popilius Lena (8)
Sir Hugh Evans (24)
Sir Nathaniel (20)
Sir Toby Belch (35)
Thomas Horner (13)
Three Witches (21)
Titus Lartius (5)
Westmoreland (E. of) (9, 10, 11, 14)
Young Marcius (5)

13

Alexander Iden (13)
Doll Tearsheet (10)
Duchess of York (18, 19)
Duke of Alencon (12)
Duke of Aumerle (18)
Duke of Bedford (11, 12)
Duke of Bourbon (11)
Duke of Gloster (11, 14, 19)
Duke of Norfolk (14, 15, 18, 19)
Duke of Orleans (11)
Duke of Suffolk (13, 15)
Earl of Douglas (9)
Earl of Gloster (17)
Earl of Suffolk (12)
Earl of Warwick (10, 11, 12, 13, 14)
Friar Lawrence (29)
Hubert de Burgh (16)
Joan la Pucelle (12)
King Henry VIII (15)
King Richard II (18)
Lord Fitzwater (18)
Owen Glendower (9)

Prince of Wales (10, 19)
Queen Margaret (14)
Sir Thomas Grey (11)
Young Clifford (13)

14

Cardinal Wolsey (15)
Christopher Sly (30)
Duke of Burgundy (11, 12, 17)
Duke of Clarence (10, 19)
Duke of Cornwall (17)
Duke of Florence (1)
Duke of Somerset (13, 14)
Earl of Pembroke (14, 16)
Earl of Richmond (19)
Edmund Mortimer (9, 12)
Hostess Quickly (9, 10)
Justice Shallow (10)
King Richard III (19)
Launcelot Gobbo (23)
Lord Willoughby (18)
Marcus Antonius (8)
Metellus Cimber (8)
Northumberland (E. of) (9, 10, 14, 18)
Northumberland (Lady) (10)
Octavius Caesar (2, 8)
Peter of Pomfret (16)
Pompeius Sextus (2)
Prince Humphrey (10)
Queen Elizabeth (19)
Queen Katharine (15)
Sextus Pompeius (2)
Sir James Blount (19)
Sir James Tyrrel (19)
Sir John Stanley (13)
Sir Walter Blunt (9, 10)
Sir William Lucy (12)
Smith the Weaver (13)
Tullus Aufidius (5)
Walter Whilmore (13)

15

Aemilius Lepidus (8)
Bishop of Lincoln (15)
Dromio of Ephesus (4)
Duke of Lancaster (18)
Earl of Cambridge (11)
Earl of Salisbury (11, 12, 13, 16, 18)
Earl of Worcester (9, 10)
Edmund of Langley (18)
Lord Abergavenny (15)
Margery Jourdain (13)
Marquis of Dorset (19)
Menenius Agrippa (5)
Prince of Arragon (23)
Prince of Morocco (23)
Robin Goodfellow (25)
Sicinius Volutus (5)
Sir Anthony Denny (15)
Sir Hugh Mortimer (14)
Sir John Falstaff (9, 10, 24)
Sir John Fastolfe (12)
Sir John Mortimer (14)
Sir Nicholas Vaux (15)
Sir Thomas Lovell (15)
Titus Andronicus (33)

Some characters from **Shelley, Sheridan** and **Smollett**
List of works from which the following characters are taken, with reference numbers.

Percy Bysshe Shelley

Ref. No.	Title	
1.	Cenci, The	(8 letters)
2.	Prometheus Unbound	(17 ,,)
3.	Swellfoot the Tyrant	(18 ,,)
4.	(Various)	

Ref. No.	Title	
9.	School for Scandal, The	(19 letters)
10.	St. Patrick's Day	(13 ,,)
11.	Trip to Scarborough, A	(18 ,,)

Richard Brinsley Sheridan

Ref. No.	Title	
5.	Critic, The	(9 letters)
6.	Duenna, The	(9 ,,)
7.	Pizarro	(7 ,,)
8.	Rivals, The	(9 ,,)

Tobias Smollett

Ref. No.	Title	
12.	Count Fathom	(11 letters)
13.	Humphry Clinker	(14 ,,)
14.	Peregrine Pickle	(15 ,,)
15.	Roderick Random	(14 ,,)
16.	Sir Launcelot Greaves	(19 ,,)

Note: The numbers in brackets indicate *the works* in which the characters appear.

3 AND 4

Asia (2)
Cora (7)
Crab (15)
Fag (8)
Ione (2)
Ivy (13)
Joey (15)
Lory (11)
Loyd (13)
Lucy (8)
Mab (4)
Puff (5)
Quin (13)
Rosy (10)
Trip (9)

5

Acres (8)
Cenci (1)
Clara (6)
Crowe (16)
Dakry (3)
Daood (4)
David (8)
Flint (10)
Frail (14)
Gawky (15)
Gomez (7)
Gwynn (13)
Jones (13)
Julia (8)
Lewis (13)
Lopez (6)
Maria (9)
Moses (3, 9)
Oakum (15)
Ocean (2)
Orano (7)
Pipes (14)
Probe (11)
Rifle (15)
Rolla (7)
Scrag (14)
Snake (9)
Sneer (5)
Strap (15)

6

Alonzo (7)
Amanda (11)
Andrea (1)

Apollo (2)
Banter (15)
Barton (13)
Bumper (9)
Clumsy (11)
Cythna (4)
Dangle (5)
Darnel (16)
Dr. Rosy (10)
Duenna (The) (6)
Elvira (7)
Emilia (14)
Fathom (12)
Ferret (16)
Gobble (16)
Hassan (4)
Hatton (5)
Hoyden (11)
Ianthe (4)
Jermyn (13)
Julian (4)
Louisa (6)
Mahmud (4)
Mammon (3)
Martin (13)
Marzio (1)
Morgan (15)
Murphy (13)
Norton (13)
Oregan (13)
Orsino (1)
Pallet (14)
Pickle (14)
Random (15)
Rattle (15)
Rowley (9)
Simper (15)
Teazle (9)
Thomas (8)
Townly (11)
Vandal (15)
Weazel (15)
Willis (13)
Zuluga (7)

7

Adonais (4)
Alastor (4)
Almagro (7)
Ataliba (7)
Baynard (13)
Bowling (15)
Bramble (13)
Bulford (13)
Buzzard (13)

Camillo (1)
Candour (9)
Celinda (12)
Clinker (13)
Coupler (11)
Cringer (15)
Davilla (7)
Dick Ivy (13)
Dr. Lewis (13)
Fashion (11)
Freeman (15)
Giacomo (1)
Gonzalo (7)
Greaves (16)
Griskin (13)
Gwyllim (13)
Hopkins (5)
Jackson (15)
Jenkins (13)
Macully (13)
Maddalo (4)
Melford (13)
Mendoza (6)
Mercury (2)
Milfart (13)
Mrs. Loyd (13)
O'Connor (10)
Olimpio (1)
Panthea (2)
Pizarro (7)
Raleigh (5)
Rattlin (15)
Savella (1)
Silenus (4)
Snapper (15)
Solomon (3)
Sparkle (15)
Surface (9)
Taurina (3)
Thicket (15)
Trounce (10)
Ulysses (4)
Wagtail (15)
Whiffle (15)

8

Absolute (8)
Backbite (9)
Bernardo (1)
Besselia (16)
Bob Acres (8)
Burleigh (5)
Campbell (13)
Careless (9)
Crabshaw (16)

163

Crabtree (9, 14)
Crampley (15)
Cropdale (13)
Dallison (13)
Dennison (13)
Hatchway (14)
Hercules (2)
Languish (8)
Las Casas (7)
Lauretta (10)
La Varole (11)
Lavement (15)
Loveless (11)
Malaprop (8)
Marmozet (15)
Melville (8)
Mendlegs (11)
Molopoyn (15)
Mrs. Gawky (15)
Mrs. Gwynn (13)
Mrs. Jones (13)
Narcissa (15)
O'Donnell (15)
Orozembo (7)
O'Trigger (8)
Phillips (13)
Plagiary (5)
Purganax (3)
Queen Mab (4)
Rosalind (4)
Staytape (15)
St. Irvyne (4)
Straddle (15)
Swillpot (15)
Thompson (15)
Tom Pipes (14)
Trunnion (14)
Valverde (7)
Williams (15)

9

Ahasuerus (4)
Berinthia (11)
Credulous (10)
Don Carlos (6)
Don Jerome (6)
Dr. Wagtail (15)
Faulkland (8)
Ferdinand (6)
Gauntlett (14)
Hugh Strap (15)
Lady Frail (14)
Lismahago (13)
Mackshane (15)
Mary Jones (13)
Mrs. Dangle (5)
Mrs. Jermyn (13)
Mrs. Norton (13)
Mrs. Weazel (15)
Mrs. Willis (13)
Quiverwit (15)
Sneerwell (9)
Strutwell (15)
Swellfoot (3)
The Duenna (6)
Tilburing (5)
Zephaniah (3)

10

Constancia (4)
Count Cenci (1)
Demogorgon (2)
Doctor Rosy (10)
Don Antonio (6)
Donna Clara (6)
Father Paul (6)
Foppington (11)
Helen Gwynn (13)
John Thomas (13)
Lady Teazle (9)
Lord Rattle (15)
Miss Hoyden (11)
Mitchelson (13)
Mrs. Bramble (13)
Mrs. Candour (9)
Mrs. Gwyllim (13)
Mrs. Jenkins (13)
Mrs. Snapper (15)
Prometheus (2)
Ritornello (5)
Rory Random (15)
Tom Bowling (15)
Tom Fashion (11)

11

Cadwallader (14)
Count Fathom (12)
Donna Louisa (6)
Dr. Mackshane (15)
Harry Bumper (9)
Iona Taurina (3)
Jack Rattlin (15)
Lady Bulford (13)
Lady Griskin (13)
Letty Willis (13)
Miss Snapper (15)
Miss Sparkle (15)
Miss Withers (15)
Mrs. Lavement (15)
Mrs. Malaprop (8)
Peter Teazle (9)
Saint Ervyne (4)
Squire Gawky (15)
Tim Cropdale (13)

12

Captain Crowe (16)
Captain Oakum (15)
Count Maddalo (4)
Don Ferdinand (6)
Ensign Murphy (13)
Gosling Scrag (14)
Isaac Mendoza (6)
Lord Burleigh (5)
Lord Straddle (15)
Lord Swillpot (15)
Lydia Melford (13)
Master Rowley (9)
Miss Williams (15)
Mrs. Credulous (10)
Mrs. Mary Jones (13)

Whiskerandos (5)
Witch of Atlas (4)

13

Aurelia Darnel (16)
Captain Oregan (15)
Captain Weazel (15)
Colonel Townly (11)
Corporal Flint (10)
Earl Strutwell (15)
Father Francis (6)
Joseph Surface (9)
Julia Melville (8)
Justice Gobble (16)
Lady Sneerwell (9)
Launcelot Crab (15)
Lord Quiverwit (15)
Lydia Languish (8)
Mrs. Helen Gwynn (13)
Oliver Surface (9)

14

Captain Whiffle (15)
Charles Surface (9)
Clumsy Tunbelly (11)
Dougal Campbell (13)
Francesco Cenci (1)
Hawser Trunnion (14)
Humphry Clinker (13)
Justice Buzzard (13)
Laetitia Willis (13)
Lord Foppington (11)
Lucius O'Trigger (8)
Matthew Bramble (13)
Roderick Random (15)
Sir Harry Bumper (9)
Sir John Sparkle (15)
Sir Peter Teazle (9)
Squire Dallison (13)
Sunders Macully (13)
Tabitha Bramble (13)
Watkin Phillips (13)

15

Anthony Absolute (8)
Captain Absolute (8)
Cardinal Camillo (1)
Charles Dennison (13)
Earl of Leicester (5)
Emilia Gauntlett (14)
Father Augustine (6)
Ferdinand Fathom (12)
Peregrine Pickle (14)
Serjeant Trounce (10)
Timothy Crabshaw (16)
Tyrant Swellfoot (3)
Winifred Jenkins (13)

Some characters from **Southey, Spenser** and **Tennyson**
List of works from which the following characters are taken, with reference numbers.

Robert Southey
Ref.
No.   Title
1. Curse of Kehama, The   (16 letters)
2. Madoc   (5 „)
3. Roderick, the Last of
   the Goths   (8 „)
4. Thalaba the Destroyer   (19 „)
5. (Various)

Edmund Spenser
Ref.
No.   Title
6. Colin Clout's Come
   Home Again   (24 letters)
7. Faerie Queene, The   (15 „)
8. Shephearde's Calender,
   The   (22 „)
9. (Various)

Lord Tennyson
10. Enoch Arden   (10 letters)
11. Idylls of the King   (15 „)

12. (Various)

Note: The numbers in brackets indicate *the works* in which the characters appear.

3 AND 4

Alma (7)
Ate (7)
Atin (7)
Azla (1)
Azub (3)
Baly (1)
Cid (The) (5)
Dony (7)
Dora (12)
Dove (5)
Ebba (3)
Enid (11)
Flur (11)
Hoel (2)
Ida (12)
Lee (10)
Lot (11)
Lucy (7)
Mary (5)
Maud (12)
Ray (10)
Rose (12)
Una (7)

5

Alice (12)
Amias (7)
Anton (11)
Arden (10)
Aswad (4)
Balan (11)
Balin (11)
Belge (7)
Bleys (11)
Brute (7)
Celia (7)
Clare (12)
Cleon (7)
Clout (6)
Cuddy (8)
David (King) (2)
Dolon (7)
Doorm (11)
Edyrn (11)
Error (7)
Eudon (3)
Furor (7)
Guyon (7)
Indra (1)
Isolt (11)
Isond (11)

Laila (4)
Madoc (2)
Moath (4)
Odoar (3)
Orpas (3)
Pedro (3)
Phaon (7)
Talus (7)
Torre (11)
Tyler (5)
Urban (3)
Urien (2)
Willy (8)
Yamen (1)
Yniol (11)
Ysolt (11)

6

Abessa (7)
Action (6)
Adicia (7)
Alcyon (9)
Amavia (7)
Amidas (7)
Amoret (7)
Astery (9)
Aullay (1)
Aylmer (12)
Briana (7)
Burbon (7)
Cavall (dog) (11)
Coatel (2)
Diggon (8)
Donica (5)
Dubrie (11)
Duessa (7)
Elaine (11)
Elissa (7)
Favila (3)
Gareth (11)
Gawain (11)
Glauce (7)
Godiva (12)
Godmer (7)
Guisla (3)
Guizor (7)
Harold (12)
Igerna (11)
Ignaro (7)
Iseult (11)
Isolde (11)
Jasper (5)
Julian (3)

Kehama (1)
Khawla (4)
Lilian (12)
Llaian (2)
Magued (3)
Mammon (7)
Medina (7)
Merlin (11)
Modred (11)
Moorna (5)
Munera (7)
Newman (5)
Oenone (12)
Oneiza (4)
Orelio (horse) (3)
Oriana (12)
Orraca (Queen) (5)
Paeana (7)
Pelago (3)
Quiara (5)
Romano (3)
Ronald (12)
Senena (2)
Serena (7)
Sergis (7)
Shedad (4)
Terpin (7)
The Cid (5)
Thenot (8)
Theron (dog) (3)
Timias (7)
Turpin (7)
Vivian (12)
Vivien (11)
Witiza (3)
Yeruti (5)
Ygerne (11)
Yseult (11)
Zeinab (4)

7

Acrasia (7)
Adeline (12)
Aemelia (7)
Aladine (7)
Aloadin (4)
Amphion (12)
Aragnol (9)
Argante (7)
Artegal (7)
Arvalan (1)
Aveugle (7)
Cambina (7)

Casyapa (1)
Corydon (7)
Cynetha (2)
Dagonet (11)
Diamond (7)
Egilona (3)
Ereenia (1)
Ettarre (11)
Everard (12)
Favinia (3)
Fidessa (7)
Galahad (11)
Geraint (11)
Gorlois (11)
Ibrahim (3)
Igrayne (11)
Lavaine (11)
Lincoya (2)
Lynette (11)
Lyonors (11)
Maimuna (4)
Maleger (7)
Malinal (2)
Mariana (12)
Marinel (7)
Melibee (7)
Mohareb (4)
Monnema (5)
Mordure (7)
Morrell (8)
Padalon (1)
Penlake (5)
Perissa (7)
Philtra (5)
Pollear (1)
Rudiger (5)
Rusilla (3)
Samient (7)
Sansfoy (7)
Sansjoy (7)
Sansloy (7)
Sir Owen (5)
Thalaba (4)
Ulysses (12)

8

Abdaldar (4)
Adosinda (3)
Alcahman (3)
Alphonso (3)
Amalahta (2)
Annie Lee (10)
Arthegal (7)
Bevidere (11)
Blandina (7)
Bracidas (7)
Busirane (7)
Calepine (7)
Calidore (7)
Claribel (7–12)
Clarinda (7)
Erillyab (2)
Eurytion (7)
Ferraugh (7)
Florimel (7)
Florinda (3)
Fradubio (7)
Gaudiosa (3)
Gauvaine (11)
Geryoneo (7)
Gloriana (7)
Harpalus (6)
Helinore (7)
Hobbinol (8)

Hodeirak (4)
Hudibras (7)
Jane Grey (12)
Ladurlad (1)
Lancelot (11)
Lucifera (7)
Maccabee (3)
Madeline (12)
Malbecco (7)
Margaret (12)
Mercilla (7)
Meridies (11)
Muscarol (9)
Nealling (1)
Numacian (3)
Occasion (7)
Oliphant (7)
Orgoglio (7)
Palinode (8)
Phaedria (7)
Placidas (7)
Pollente (7)
Pyrocles (7)
Radigond (7)
Roderick (King) (3)
Rosalind (8)
Sanglier (7)
Satyrane (7)
Sir Anton (11)
Sir Guyon (7)
Sir Torre (11)
Sisibert (3)
Siverian (3)
Spumador (7)
St. Dubrie (11)
Thomalin (8)
Triamond (7)
Trompart (7)
Wat Tyler (5)

9

Abdalazis (3)
Abulcacem (3)
Amaryllis (6)
Anguisant (11)
Archimage (7)
Archimago (7)
Astrophel (8)
Belphoebe (7)
Bladamour (7)
Brigadore (7)
Britomart (7)
Cadwallon (2)
Charyllis (6)
Corfiambo (7)
Cymochles (7)
Dame Celia (7)
Espriella (5)
Eumnestes (7)
Fourdelis (7)
Grantorto (7)
Grenville (12)
Guinevere (11)
Gwenhidwy (11)
Hermesind (3)
King David (2)
Lady Clare (12)
Llewellyn (2)
Lorrimite (1)
Malecasta (7)
Malengrin (7)
Mirabella (7)
Philip Ray (10)

Philotine (7)
Pithyrian (5)
Portamour (7)
Priscilla (7)
Rosalinda (9)
Ruddymane (7)
Scudamore (7)
Sir Sergis (7)
Sir Terpin (7)
Tezozomoe (2)
The Soldan (7)

10

Blandamour (7)
Bruncheval (7)
Colin Clout (6)
Count Eudon (3)
Count Pedro (3)
Cradlemont (11)
Doctor Dove (5)
Enoch Arden (10)
Kirkrapine (7)
Lady Godiva (12)
Lord Ronald (12)
Marriataby (1)
Pastorella (7)
Sanglamore (7)
Sir Dagonet (11)
Sir Galahad (11)
Sir Geraint (11)
Sir Lavaine (11)
Sir Paridel (7)
Sir Pelleas (11)
Theodofred (3)
Vere de Vere (12)
Waterproof (12)

11

Britomaris (7)
Count Julian (3)
Davie Diggon (8)
Lady Lyonors (11)
Queen Orraca (5)
Saint Dubrie (11)
Sir Bedivere (11)
Sir Calepine (7)
Sir Calidore (7)
Sir Claribel (7)
Sir Ferraugh (7)
Sir Hudibras (7)
Sir Lancelot (11)
Sir Persaunt (11)
Sir Satyrane (7)
Sir Trevisan (7)
Sir Tristram (11)
Yuhidthiton (2)

12

Blatant Beast (The) (7)
Braggadochio (7)
Dame Helinore (7)
King Roderick (3)
Lady Gaudiosa (3)
Lady Jane Grey (12)
Oliver Newman (5)
Prince Pelayo (3)
Sir Percivale (11)
Sir Perimones (11)
Sir Pertolope (11)
Sir Scudamore (7)

13 AND OVER

Chindasuintho (3)
Emma Plantagenet (2)
Father Maccabee (3)
Lady of Shalott (12)
Marian Margaret (6)
Red-Cross Knight (7)
Richard Penlake (5)
Saint Gualberto (5)
Sir Aylmer Aylmer (12)
Sir Richard Grenville (12)
Sir Shan Sanglier (7)
Sir Walter Vivian (12)
Squire of Dames, The (7)
Will Waterproof (12)

Some characters from **Thackeray**
List of works from which the following characters are taken, with reference numbers.

Ref. No.	Title		Ref. No.	Title	
1.	Adventures of Philip, The	(21 letters)	10.	Major Gahagan, The Adventures of	(27 letters)
2.	Barry Lyndon	(11 ,,)	11.	Newcomes, The	(11 ,,)
3.	Book of Snobs, The	(14 ,,)	12.	Pendennis	(9 ,,)
4.	Catherine	(9 ,,)	13.	Rebecca and Rowena	(16 ,,)
5.	Denis Duval	(10 ,,)	14.	Shabby Genteel Story, A	(19 ,,)
6.	Fatal Boots, The	(13 ,,)	15.	Vanity Fair	(10 ,,)
7.	Great Hoggarty Diamond, The	(23 ,,)	16.	Virginians, The	(13 ,,)
8.	Henry Esmond	(11 ,,)	17.	Wolves and the Lamb, The	(19 ,,)
9.	Lovel the Widower	(15 ,,)			

Note: The numbers in brackets indicate *the works* in which the characters appear.

3 AND 4

Bell (12)
Bond (1)
Bows (12)
Bull (3)
'Cat' (4)
Craw (6)
Cuff (15)
Drum (7)
Gann (14)
Gray (3)
Grig (3)
Hall (4)
Holt (8)
Huff (2)
Hunt (1)
Kew (11)
Laws (16)
Legg (3)
Levy (5)
Maw (3)
Moss (15)
Nabb (6)
Page (5, 17)
Pash (7)
Pump (3)
Quin (2)
Ruck (7)
Runt (1, 2)
Sago (3)
Tagg (3)
Tidd (7)
Veal (15)
Ward (16)
Wing (5)
Wirt (3)
Wood (4)

5

Amory (12)
Arbin (5)

Baker (9)
Barry (2)
Bates (6)
Becky (14, 15)
Bevil (5)
Biggs (10)
Bluck (15)
Boots (9)
Bowls (15)
Brady (2)
Brock (4)
Bulbo (15)
'Carry' (14)
Chuff (3)
Clap (15)
Clink (15)
Clump (15)
Crabb (14)
Crump (3)
Daisy (mare) (2)
Denis (5)
Dobbs (4)
Dr. Maw (3)
Duffy (19)
Dumps (3)
Duval (5)
Fagan (2)
Fitch (14)
Flint (5)
Foker (12, 16)
Freny (2)
Gates (7)
Gorer (dog) (15)
Gumbo (16)
Hagan (16)
Hayes (4)
Hicks (3)
Higgs (15)
Hobbs (3)
Hugby (3)
Jowls (2)
Ketch (4)
Kicks (6)
Lovel (9)
Macan (10)

Macer (3)
March (Lord) (16)
Mohun (8)
O'Dowd (3, 15)
Piper (9)
Pippi (2)
Ponto (3)
Prior (9, 17)
Query (7)
Rudge (5)
Sambo (15)
Score (4)
Screw (2)
Sharp (15)
Smith (7)
Straw (7)
Tiggs (3)
Tizzy (3)
Toole (2)
Trial (1, 16)
Tufto (3)
Walls (1)
Wamba (13)
Wolfe (16)

6

Bagwig (Lord) (2, 3)
Barker (5)
Barlow (17)
Bayham (12)
Baynes (1)
Beales (5)
Bidois (5)
Billee (12)
Binnie (11)
Blades (3)
Briggs (15)
Brough (7)
Bungay (12)
Caffin (5)
Cedric (13)
Corbet (8)

9

Altamount (12)
Augustine (14)
Batchelor (9)
Bell Brady (2)
Bellenden (9)
Bernstein (16)
Bloundell (12)
Bob Stokes (7)
Bob Stubbs (6)
Broadbent (16)
Catherine (4)
Charlotte (1)
Clavering (12)
de la Motte (5)
de Saverne (5)
Dinwiddie (16)
Doctor Maw (3)
Dr. Barnard (5)
Dr. Johnson (2, 16)
Dr. Portman (12)
Dr. Snorter (6)
Dr. Squills (15)
Farintosh (11)
Firebrace (16)
Flowerdew (15)
Geoghegan (16)
Goldsmith (2)
Jack Ketch (4)
James Gann (14)
Joe Swigby (14)
John Hayes (4)
'Jos' Sedley (15)
Lady Barker (9)
Lady Fanny (16)
Lady Maria (16)
Laura Bell (12)
Lightfoot (12)
Lilywhite (10)
Lord Mohun (8)
Macdragon (3)
Mackenzie (11)
Marrowfat (3)
Mary Smith (7)
Miss Brett (12)
Miss Prior (17)
Miss Pybus (12)
Miss Rudge (5)
Montholen (10)
Mrs. Barker (5)
Mrs. Baynes (1)
Mrs. Bonner (12)
Mrs. Brough (7)
Mrs. Fermin (1)
Mrs. Firkin (15)
Mrs. Glowry (15)
Mrs. Gretel (4)
Mrs. Haller (12)
Mrs. Jowler (10)
Mrs. Rummer (12)
Mrs. Scales (5)
Mrs. Sedley (15)
Mrs. Stokes (7)
Mrs. Tinker (15)
Mrs. Tusher (8)
Mrs. Weston (5)
Nora Brady (2)
Pendennis (1, 12)
Pinkerton (15)
Pontypool (12)
Rev. Mr. Holt (8)
Rev. Mr. Runt (2)
Rev. Mr. Veal (15)
Robin Hood (13)
Rory Barry (2)

Roundhand (7)
Sheepskin (8)
Swishtail (6, 15)
Tom Caffin (5)
Tom Esmond (8)
Tom Measom (5)
Tom Parrot (5)
Whitfield (16)

10

Agnes Duval (5)
Athelstane (13)
Becky Sharp (15)
Biddy Brady (2)
Bonnington (9, 17)
Bullingdon (2)
Castlewood (8, 16)
Cissy Lovel (9)
Coplestone (8)
Denis Duval (5)
Dick Steel (8)
Doctor Wing (5)
Eliza Kicks (6)
Fitzboodle (9)
Fred Bayham (12)
Goodenough (1)
Gus Hoskins (7)
Harry Barry (2)
Harry Foker (12)
Henry Foker (12)
Jack Morris (16)
James Wolfe (16)
John Brough (7)
John Howell (17)
Kicklebury (17)
Killblazes (7)
King George (16)
Lady Lyndon (2)
Lady Rowena (13)
Lord Bagwig (2)
Lord Steyne (15)
Mackanulty (10)
Maid Marian (13)
Major Macan (10)
Major Macer (3)
Major O'Dowd (15)
Major Ponto (3)
Mary Barlow (17)
Mary Waters (6)
Miss Clancy (2)
Miss Hunkle (12)
Miss Kiljoy (2)
Miss Pierce (12)
Miss Snobky (2)
Miss Swarby (15)
Mrs. Barnard (5)
Mrs. Brandon (1)
Mrs. Bulcher (10)
Mrs. Lambert (16)
Mrs. Macarty (14)
Mrs. Mugford (1)
Mrs. Penfold (1)
Mrs. Twysden (1)
Mrs. Wapshot (12)
Mrs. Woolsey (1)
Mrs. Worksop (8)
Mysie Brady (2)
Nan Fantail (4)
Peter Brock (4)
Peter Denis (5)
Peter Hobbs (4)
Phil Murphy (2)
Pocahontas (16)
Poly Anthus (3)

Pump Temple (3)
Rev. Mr. Crisp (15)
Rev. Mr. Jowls (2)
Sextonbury (3)
Silverkoop (4)
Solomonson (6)
Sukey Rudge (5)
'The Captain' (1)
Tom Hookham (5)
Tom Humbold (16)
Tom Sniffle (3)
Tom Wheeler (7)
Tufton Hunt (1)
Ulick Brady (2)
Warrington (12, 16)
Washington (16)
Will Esmond (16)

11

'Andrea' Fitch (14)
Andrew Fitch (14)
Baron de Barr (5)
Barry Lyndon (2)
Biddlecombe (9)
Black George (horse) (2)
Bryan Lyndon (2)
Bute Crawley (15)
Captain Bull (3)
Captain Craw (6)
Captain Grig (3)
Captain Legg (3)
Captain Page (17)
Captain Quin (2)
Captain Wood (4)
Chowder Loll (10)
Claude Duval (5)
Collingwood (15)
Countess Ida (2)
Dick Bedford (9)
Dick Bunting (6)
Doctor Dobbs (4)
Doctor Piper (9)
Dr. Swishtail (6, 15)
Earl of March (16)
Edward Bevil (5)
Eliza Stubbs (6)
Emily Blades (3)
Ensign Hicks (10)
Essex Temple (3)
Fotheringay (12)
General Lake (10)
General Sago (3)
Harry Esmond (8)
Henry Esmond (8)
Jack Spiggot (3)
James Binnie (11)
Julia Jowler (10)
Juliana Gann (14)
King Richard (13)
Lady Crawley (15)
Lady Hawbuck (3)
Lady Scraper (3)
Lady Tiptoff (7)
Lord Buckram (3)
Lucy Hawbuck (3)
Major Thrupp (10)
Mary Pinhorn (9)
Miss Clopper (6)
Miss Crawley (15)
Miss Saltire (15)
Miss Sowerby (1)
Miss Swindle (15)
Montanville (9)
Montfitchet (1)

Mrs. Hoggarty (7)
Mrs. Hollyock (15)
Mrs. Jellicoe (5)
Mrs. Manasseh (6)
Mrs. Mountain (16)
Mrs. Titmarsh (7)
Peggy O'Dwyer (2)
Pitt Crawley (15)
Pompey Hicks (3)
Popham Lovel (9)
Prince Bulbo (15)
Raymond Gray (3)
Robert Gates (7)
Roger Hooker (5)
Roger Lyndon (2)
Samuel Arbin (5)
Simon de Bary (2)
Stiffelkind (6)
Susan Stubbs (6)
Theo Lambert (16)
Thistlewood (12)
Thomas Flint (5)
Tom Tufthunt (14)
Van Den Bosch (16)

12

Agnes Twysden (1)
Alderman Pash (7)
Amelia Sedley (15)
Bella Macarty (14)
Betsy Brisket (6)
Blanche Amory (12)
Captain Baker (9)
Captain Biggs (10)
Captain Denis (5)
Captain Duffy (10)
Captain Fagan (2)
Captain Freny (2)
Captain Prior (9)
Caroline Gann (14)
Cecilia Lovel (9)
Chesterfield (16)
Clive Newcome (11)
Colonel Wolfe (16)
Count Gahagan (10)
Donnerwetter (14)
Dr. Goodenough (1)
Dr. von Glauber (15)
Emily Scraper (3)
Ensign Dobble (6)
Ensign Famish (3)
Ethel Newcome (11)
General Tufto (3)
General Wolfe (16)
George Fermin (1)
George Weston (5)
Helena Flower (2)
Hetty Lambert (16)
Honoria Brady (2)
Jack Costigan (12)
Jack Lockwood (8)
John Jorrocks (15)
Joseph la Rose (4)
Joseph Sedley (15)
Joseph Weston (5)
Lady de Mogyns (3)
Lady Golloper (3)
Lady Ribstone (12)
Linda Macarty (14)
Little Billee (12)
Little Sister (The) (1)
Lord Cinqbars (14)
Lord Ringwood (1)
Major Danvers (16)

Major Gahagan (10)
Mary Malowney (6)
Michael Brady (2)
Mick Hoggarty (7)
Miss Delamere (9)
Miss Tingwood (1)
Morgan Doolan (12)
Mrs. Lightfoot (12)
Mrs. Newbright (15)
Mrs. Pendennis (12)
Philip Fermin (1)
Prince Arthur (13)
Prince Victor (2)
Rachel Esmond (16)
Rebecca Sharp (15)
Redmond Barry (2)
Reginald Cuff (15)
Selina Stokes (7)
Thomas Stubbs (6)
Ulysses Brady (2)

13

Barnes Newcome (11)
Beatrix Esmond (8)
Belinda Brough (7)
Bryan Hawkshaw (8)
Captain Dobble (6)
Captain Fizgig (7)
Captain Franks (16)
Captain Punter (2)
Captain Steele (5)
Captain Strong (12)
Captain Waters (6)
Carrickfergus (14)
Catherine Hall (4)
Charles Lyndon (2)
Clarence Baker (9)
Colonel Dobbin (15)
Colonel Esmond (8)
Colonel Jowler (10)
Comte de Florac (11)
Cornet Gahagan (10)
Corporal Brock (4)
Corporal Clink (15)
Countess of Kew (11)
Count of Chalus (13)
Doctor Barnard (5)
Doctor Johnson (16)
Earl of Tiptoff (7)
Emily Costigan (12)
Ensign Macarty (14)
Fanny Mountain (16)
Francis Esmond (8)
General Baynes (1)
George Osborne (15)
Goody Billings (4)
Hester Lambert (16)
Hon. Poly Anthus (3)
Jack Firebrace (16)
Joseph Addison (8)
Kitty Lorrimer (3)
Lady Clavering (12)
Lady Pontypool (12)
Letty Lovelace (3)
Lord Firebrace (8)
Lydia den Bosch (16)
Martha Crawley (15)
Martin Lambert (16)
Matilda Briggs (15)
Miss Bellenden (9)
Miss Bonnyface (2)
Miss Pinkerton (15)
Mrs. Blenkinsop (15)
Mrs. Bonnington (9, 17)

Mrs. Goodenough (1)
Mrs. Silverkoop (4)
Parson Sampson (8, 16)
Philip Purcell (2)
Rawdon Crawley (15)
Robert Swinney (7)
Rosa Mackenzie (11)
Sir Peter Denis (5)
Snobley Snobky (3)
Talbot Twysden (1)
Thomas Bullock (4)
Thomas Gregson (5)
Thomas Trippet (4)
Tobias Tickler (2)
Violet Crawley (15)
William Dobbin (15)

14

Agnes de Saverne (5)
Arabella Briggs (15)
Belinda Bulcher (10)
Betty Flannigan (15)
Blanche Twysden (1)
Captain Clopper (6)
Captain Osborne (15)
Captain Pearson (5)
Captain Shandon (12)
Captain Thunder (2)
Captain Touchit (17)
Catherine Hayes (4)
Colonel Cramley (3)
Colonel Lambert (16)
Colonel Newcome (11)
Colonel Snobley (3)
Cornelius Barry (2)
Corporal Steele (8)
Count de Saverne (5)
Dora Warrington (16)
Earl of Ringwood (1)
Elizabeth Prior (9)
Ensign Macshame (4)
Frederick Lovel (9)
General Bulcher (10)
General Tinkler (10)
George Milliken (17)
Godfrey Gahagan (10)
Gregory Gahagan (10)
Helen Pendennis (12)
Horace Milliken (17)
Lady Castlewood (8, 16)
Lady Fanny Rakes (7)
Lady Huntingdon (13)
Lady Kicklebury (17)
Lady Warrington (16)
Laura Pendennis (12)
Lord Bullingdon (2)
Lord Castlewood (8, 16)
Lord Sextonbury (3)
Magdalen Crutty (6)
Major Pendennis (12)
Mdlle Augustine (14)
Michael Cassidy (1)
Mrs. Biddlecombe (9)
Mrs. Blackbrooks (15)
Mrs. Juliana Gann (14)
Mrs. Montfitchet (1)
Princess Olivia (2)
Rev. Bute Crawley (15)
Rev. Mr. Flowerdew (15)
Richard Bedford (9)
Samuel Titmarsh (7)
Sir Pitt Crawley (15)
Sir Popham Baker (9)
Thomas Billings (4)

Thomas Clodpole (4)
von Galgenstein (4)
Wilfred Ivanhoe (13)

15

Arthur Pendennis (1, 12)
Captain Costigan (12)
Captain Macheath (5)
Captain Macmurdo (15)
Captain Westbury (8)

Captain Woolcomb (1)
Charles Honeyman (11)
Charlotte Baynes (1)
Dr. Tobias Tickler (2)
Flora Warrington (16)
General Braddock (16)
George Marrowfat (3)
Harry Warrington (16)
Henry Warrington (16)
Isabella Macarty (14)
Jemima Pinkerton (15)
Lady Jane Crawley (15)

Lady Jane Preston (7)
Marquis of Bagwig (3)
Marquis of Steyne (15)
Misses Pinkerton (The) (15)
Miss Fotheringay (12)
Miss Montanville (9)
Mrs. Cecilia Lovel (9)
Queen Berengaria (13)
Ringwood Twysden (1)
Rosalind Macarty (14)
Sir George Esmond (8)
Sir John Hawkshaw (8)

Some characters from **Anthony Trollope**
List of works from which the following characters are taken, with reference numbers.

Ref. No.	Title		
1.	Alice Dugdale	(12 letters)	
2.	American Senator, The	(18 „)	
3.	Barchester Towers	(16 „)	
4.	Dr. Thorne	(8 „)	
5.	Editor's Tales, An	(14 „)	
6.	Eustace Diamonds, The	(18 „)	
7.	Framley Parsonage	(16 „)	
8.	Frau Frohmann	(12 „)	
9.	Is He Popenjoy?	(12 „)	
10.	Lady of Launay, The	(15 letters)	

Ref. No.	Title		
11.	Last Chronicle of Barset, The	(24 „)	
12.	La Vendée	(8 „)	
13.	Ralph the Heir	(12 „)	
14.	Small House at Allington, The	(24 „)	
15.	Tales of all Countries	(19 „)	
16.	Telegraph Girl, The	(16 „)	
17.	Three Clerks, The	(14 „)	
18.	Warden, The	(9 „)	

Note: The numbers in brackets indicate *the works* in which the characters appear.

3 AND 4

Bean (2)
Bell (18)
Bold (3, 7, 18)
Bolt (9)
Boom (17)
Bull (8)
Cann (6)
Cox (13)
Dale (11, 14)
Dove (6)
Dunn (11)
Erle (6)
Fawn (6)
Gazy (18)
Grey (6)
Hall (16)
Hoff (8)
Jack (horse) (2)
Knox (9)
Love (14)
Lund (15)
Nogo (17)
Pie (3, 4)
Pile (13)
Pole (7)
Ring (15)
Toff (9)
Trow (15)
Watt (5)

5

Anton (8)
Baker (4)
Boyce (11; 14)
Brown (5, 15, 16, 17)
Brush (17)
Bunce (18)
Carey (13)
Crump (11, 14)
Dandy (horse) (6, 7)

Davis (17)
Denot (12)
Dobbs (14)
Donne (5)
Eames (11, 14)
Fooks (13)
Foret (12)
Fritz (15)
Gager (6)
Glump (13)
Green (2, 4, 9, 11, 16)
Grice (2)
Handy (18)
Hearn (14)
Heine (15)
Hiram (18)
Janet (4)
Jones (7, 9, 15, 17)
Joram (13)
Knowl (10)
Krapp (8)
Lebas (12)
Lupex (14)
Mason (11)
Miles (10)
Moggs (13)
Moody (18)
M'Ruen (17)
Muntz (8)
Nobbs (2)
Oriel (4, 11)
Penge (2)
Plume (12)
Pratt (11, 14)
Price (9)
Pryor (10)
Regan (5)
Ribbs (2)
Robin (7)
Romer (4)
Runce (2)
Sally (16)
Scott (17)
Sharp (5)

Slope (3)
Smith (5, 9, 15)
Snape (9, 17)
Stein (12)
Stemm (13)
Tozer (7, 11)
Tudor (17)
Tweed (1)
Upton (15)
Vigil (17)
Wheal (17)

6

Apjohn (4)
Arabin (3, 7, 9, 14)
Athill (4)
Aunt Ju (9)
Austen (7)
Battle (9)
Bawwah (13)
Baxter (11)
Bergen (15)
Bonner (13)
Boodle (6)
Botsey (2)
Brumby (5)
Buffle (11, 14)
Bunfit (6)
'Caudle' (14)
Clarke (4)
Cobard (8)
Cobble (1)
Conner (14)
Cooper (2)
Croft (11, 14)
Currie (2)
D'Elbée (12)
Draper (11)
Dr. Bold (18)
Duplay (12)
Fiasco (14)
Finney (18)

Apollo Crosbie (14)
Babette Seppel (8)
Bishop Grantly (3, 18)
Bishop Proudie (4, 7, 11)
Blanch Robarts (7)
Captain Boodle (6)
Captain Glomax (2)
Charles O'Brien (15)
Charles Puffle (5)
Clara Hittaway (6)
Dean Greystock (6)
de Montmorenci (5)
Eleanor Duplay (12)
Farmer Cloysey (15)
Father Conolin (8)
General Bonner (13)
Georgiana Fawn (6)
Gerald Robarts (7)
Godfrey Holmes (15)
Gregory Newton (13)
Griffenbottom (13)
Helena Gresham (4)
Henry Lovelace (9)
Herbert Onslow (15)
Herr Schlessen (8)
Hetta Houghton (9)
Janet Rossiter (1)
John Broughton (15)
Jonathan Brown (5)
Joseph Cradell (14)
Josephine Bull (8)
Josiah Crawley (11)
Kate Coverdale (15)
Katie Woodward (17)
Lady Demalines (11)
Lady Fanny Dale (14)
Lady Hartletop (7, 11, 14)
Lady Penwether (2)
Lady Scatcherd (4)
Lady Underwood (13)
Linda Woodward (17)
Lord Boanerges (7)
Lord Hartletop (11)
Lord Mistletoe (2)
Lord Polperrow (13)
Macasser Jones (17)
Madame Goesler (6)
Major Caneback (2)
Major Rossiter (1)
Mary Jane Wheal (17)
Mathew Spriggs (18)
Michael Molloy (5)
Miss Dunstable (4, 7)
Miss Godolphin (2)
Miss Le Smyrger (15)
Miss Partridge (11)
Mrs. Clantanham (3)
Mrs. Goodenough (18)
Mrs. Mainwaring (2)
Norah Geraghty (17)
Olivia Proudie (3)
Patience Oriel (4)
Peter Frohmann (8)
Rev. Caleb Oriel (4)
Samuel Grantly (18)
Sarah Thompson (7)
Selina Gresham (4)
Signora Neroni (3)
Sir Omicron Pie (3, 4)
Sophia Wanless (1)
Vesey Stanhope (18)
Wilfred Thorne (3)

14

Alphabet Precis (17)
Amalia Frohmann (8)
Augusta Protest (3)
Bertie Stanhope (3)
Captain De Baron (9)
Churchill Smith (5)
Clara Van Siever (11)
Clary Underwood (17)
Countess of Care (9)
Dick Scatterall (17)
Eleanor Harding (18)
Emily Dunstable (5)
Erle Barrington (6)
Fanny Arkwright (15)
Fidus Neverbend (17)
Francis Gresham (4)
Frank Greystock (6)
Fraulein Tendel (8)
Fritz Schlessen (8)
General Talboys (15)
Gilbert de Salop (17)
Gregory Masters (2)
Grizzel Grantly (18)
Harry Arkwright (15)
Harry Stubbings (2)
Henry Arkwright (15)
Isabella Holmes (15)
Jacques Chapeau (12)
Lady Brotherton (9)
Lady Linlithgow (6)
Lady Margaretta (14)
Larry Twentyman (2)
Lord Brotherton (9)
Lord Carruthers (6)
Lucinda Roanoke (16)
Lydia St. Quinten (5)
Mary Anne Neefit (13)
Maryanne Ruffle (5)
Matilda Johnson (18)
Mrs. Harold Smith (7)
Parson Rossiter (1)
Parry Coverdale (15)
Parry Underwood (13)
Reginald Morton (2)
Rev. Arthur Donne (5)
Rev. Mark Robarts (7)
Senator Gotobed (2)
Sir John Purefoy (2)
Sir Lamda Mewmew (3)
Valentine Scott (17)
Verax Corkscrew (17)

15

Adelaide De Baron (9)
Adolphus Crosbie (11, 14)
Anastasia Bergen (15)
Arabella Trefoil (2)
Archibald Currie (2)
Augusta De Courcy (4)
Baroness Baumann (9)
Beatrice Gresham (4)
Canon Holdenough (9)
Christopher Dale (14)
Conrad Mackinnon (15)
Conway Dalrymple (11)
Dr. Vesey Stanhope (3, 18)
Elizabeth Garrow (15)
Farmer Greenacre (3)

Florinda Grantly (18)
Griselda Grantly (7, 11)
Hon. John De Courcy (4, 14)
Jacintha Pigtail (17)
Jonathan Crumple (18)
Jonathan Oldbuck (15)
Julius Mackenzie (5)
Lady Mountfencer (9)
Lieutenant Smith (9)
Lizzie Greystock (6)
Lord Mountfencer (9)
Madame de Lescure (12)
Major Mackintosh (6)
Malchen Frohmann (8)
Martha Dunstable (7)
Mortimer Gazebee (11, 14)
Mrs. Patmore Green (9)
Oliva Q. Fleabody (9)
Onesiphorus Dunn (11)
Orlando Hittaway (6)
Rev. Caleb Thumble (11)
Rev. Mr. Mainwaring (2)
Septimus Harding (11, 18)
Serjeant Burnaby (13)
Sir George Walker (15)
Sir Raffle Buffle (11)
Violet Effingham (6)

Composers

3 – 5

Arne
Bach
Balfe
Bart
Bax
Berg
Berio
Bizet
Bliss
Bloch
Brian
Bruch
Byrd
Cage
Carse
Cowen
Cui
Dufay
Dukas
Elgar
Falla
Fauré
Finck
Friml
Gatty
Gaul
Gluck
Grieg
Haydn
Henze
Holst
Ibert
Ives
Jones
Kern
Lehar
Liszt
Lully
Marks
Nono
Orff
Parry
Ravel
Rosse
Satie
Shaw
Smyth
Sousa
Spohr
Suppé
Tosti
Verdi
Weber
Weill
Wolf
Ysaye

6

Ansell
Arnold
Barber
Bartok
Berlin
Bishop
Boulez
Brahms
Bridge
Busoni

Chopin
Clarke
Coates
Coward
Czerny
Delius
Demuth
Duparc
Dvořák
Enesco
Foster
Foulds
Franck
German
Gillet
Glinka
Gounod
Handel
Isolde
Kodaly
Liadov
Mahler
Morley
Mozart
Norton
Parker
Philip
Piston
Pleyel
Quantz
Rameau
Ronald
Schütz
Searle
Seiber
Stuart
Tallis
Taylor
Viotti
Wagner
Waller
Walton
Webern
Wesley

7

Albeniz
Bantock
Bazzini
Bellini
Bennett
Berlioz
Blacher
Borodin
Britten
Cleaver
Copland
Corelli
Debussy
Delibes
Dowland
Dunhill
Frankel
Fricker
Galuppi
Gibbons
Godfrey
Hermann
Ireland
Janáček

Joachim
Ketelby
Lambert
Lutyens
Martinů
Menotti
Milhaud
Nicolai
Nielsen
Novello
Poulenc
Puccini
Purcell
Quilter
Rodgers
Rossini
Roussel
Smetana
Stainer
Strauss
Tartini
Tippett
Torelli
Vivaldi
Weelkes

8

Albinoni
Ancliffe
Boughton
Brockman
Bruckner
Chabrier
Cimarosa
Couperin
Dohnanyi
Fletcher
Gabrieli
Gershwin
Glazunov
Grainger
Granados
Holbrook
Honegger
Kreisler
Mascagni
Massenet
Messager
Messiaen
Monckton
Paganini
Palmgren
Panufnik
Petrassi
Pizzetti
Raybould
Respighi
Schnabel
Schubert
Schumann
Scriabin
Sibelius
Stanford
Sullivan
Svendsen
Telemann
Tosselli
Victoria
Vittoria
Wagenaar

9 AND 10

Addinsell (9)
Balakirev (9)
Beethoven (9)
Bernstein (9)
Boccherini (10)
Buxtehade (9)
Cherubini (9)
Cole Porter (10)
Donizetti (9)
Hindemith (9)
Kabalevsky (10)
Locatelli (9)
Macdowell (9)
Meyerbeer (9)
Miaskovsky (10)
Monteverdi (10)
Mussorgsky (10)
Offenbach (9)
Pachelbel (9)
Paisiello (9)
Palestrina (10)
Pergolesi (9)
Ponchielli (10)
Prokofiev (9)
Rawsthorne (10)
Rodriguez (9)
Rubinstein (10)
Saint Saëns (10)
Scarlatti (9)
Schoenberg (10)
Schönberg (9)
Skalkottas (10)
Stravinsky (10)
Vieuxtemps (10)
Villa-Lobos (10)
Waldteufel (10)

11

Dimitriesen
Dittersdorf
Humperdinck
Leoncavallo
Mendelssohn
Moussorgsky
Rachmaninov
Stockhausen
Tchaikovsky
Wolf-Ferrari

12 AND OVER

Coleridge Taylor (15)
Dallapiccola (12)
Josquin des Pres (14)
Khachaturian (12)
Maxwell Davies (13)
Lennox-Berkeley (14)
Rachmaninoff (12)
Racine Fricker (13)
Rimsky Korsakov (14)
Richard Strauss (14)
Shostakovich (12)
Sterndale Bennett (16)
Tschaikovsky (12)
Vaughan Williams (15)

Music, musical instruments and terms

1–3

air
alt
bar
bis
bow
cue
do
doh
duo
fa
fah
gue
hum
jig
key
kit
la
lah
lay
mi
P.
Piu
pop
Pp.
rag
ray
re
run
sax
si
soh
sol
tie
ut
va
vox
zel

4

alla
alto
arco
aria
ayre
band
bard
base
bass
beat
bell
brio
clef
coda
drum
duet
echo
fife
fine
flat
fret
glee
gong
harp
high
hold
horn
hymn
jazz

kent
koto
lead
Lied
lilt
lute
lyre
mass
mode
mood
mort
mute
neum
node
note
oboe
opus
part
peal
pean
pipe
poco
port
reed
reel
rest
root
sign
sing
slur
solo
song
stop
tace
time
toll
tone
trio
tuba
tune
turr
vamp
vina
viol
vivo
voce
vola
wind
wood

5

acuta
adapt
album
arsis
assai
atone
banjo
basso
basta
baton
bebop
bells
blare
blues
bones
brass
breve
bugle

canon
canto
carol
cello
cento
chant
cheng
chime
choir
chord
clang
clank
corno
croma
crook
croon
crwth
dance
dirge
ditty
dolce
drone
duple
etude
elegy
étude
flute
forte
fugal
fugue
galop
gamba
gamut
gigue
grace
grave
knell
kyrie
largo
lento
lyric
major
march
metre
mezzo
minim
minor
molto
motet
motif
naker
nebel
neume
nodal
nonet
notes
octet
opera
organ
paean
pause
pavan
pedal
piano
pieno
piper
pitch
polka
primo
quill
rebec
reeds

regal
resin
rondo
round
sansa
scale
scena
score
segno
segue
senza
shake
shalm
sharp
shawn
sitar
sixth
slide
snare
soave
sol-fa
sound
stave
strad
strum
suite
swell
swing
tabor
tacet
tardo
tempo
tenor
theme
third
thrum
tonic
triad
trill
trite
trope
tuner
tutti
twang
valse
vibes
viola
vocal
voice
volee
volta
volti
waits
waltz
wrest
yodel
zinke

6

accent
adagio
anthem
arioso
atabal
atonal
attune
aubade
ballad
ballet
beemol

bolero	scales	cadence	natural
bridge	sennet	cadency	ocarina
bugler	septet	cadenza	octette
cadent	serial	calando	offbeat
cantor	sestet	calypso	organum
catgut	sextet	cantata	pandora
chaunt	shanty	canzona	pan-pipe
chimes	shofar	canzone	phonica
choral	singer	caprice	pianino
choric	sonata	celesta	pianist
chorus	spinet	'cellist	pianola
citole	stanza	cembalo	pibroch
contra	string	chamade	piccolo
corona	subito	chanson	piffero
cornet	tabour	chanter	pomposo
crooks	tabret	chikara	posaune
cymbal	tam-tam	chorale	prelude
da capo	tenuto	cithara	ragtime
damper	tercet	cithern	quartet
design	tierce	clapper	quintet
diesis	timbal	clarion	recital
ditone	timbre	clavier	refrain
divoto	tirade	con brio	reprise
drones	tom-tom	concert	requiem
duetto	treble	conduct	rescore
dulcet	trigon	cornett	ripieno
eighth	tucket	counter	romance
encore	tune up	cremona	rondeau
euphon	tuning	crooner	rondino
fading	tymbal	crotalo	rosalia
fiddle	tzetze	cymbals	roulade
figure	unison	czardas	sackbut
finale	up-beat	descant	sambuca
follia	vamper	descend	sambuke
fugato	veloce	descent	saxhorn
gallop	ventil	diagram	scherzo
giusto	vielle	dichord	schisma
graces	violin	discord	sciolto
ground	vivace	distune	scoring
guitar	volata	dittied	secondo
hammer	volume	drummer	septole
intone	warble	epicede	serpent
Ionian	zambra	euphony	settina
jingle	zincke	eutonia	settino
kettle	zither	fagotto	seventh
legato		fanfare	singing
Lieder		fermata	sistrum
litany	**7**	fiddler	sithara
lutist		fistula	skiffle
lydian	aeolian	flatten	slurred
lyrist	aeolist	flutina	soloist
manual	agitato	flutist	soprano
medley	allegro	fuguist	sordine
melody	alt-horn	furioso	sordono
minuet	amoroso	gavotte	sospiro
monody	andante	gittern	spinnet
motive	angelot	gravita	stopped
nobile	animato	gravity	stretto
oboist	apotome	G-string	strophe
octave	apotomy	harmony	sub-bass
off-key	arghool	harpist	subject
pavane	arietta	hautboy	syncope
phrase	ariette	juke-box	taborer
plagal	ars nova	keynote	taboret
player	attuned	locrian	tambour
presto	bagpipe	lullaby	tambura
quaver	ballade	maestro	theorbo
rattle	bandore	marimba	tibicen
rebeck	baryton	mazurka	timbrel
record	bassist	measure	timpani
revert	bassoon	mediant	timpano
rhythm	bazooka	melisma	tipping
rounds	bellows	melodic	toccata
rubato	bitonal	mistune	tone-row
sacbut	bravura	musette	tremolo
178 sancho		musical	triplet

trumpet
tubicen
tuneful
ukelele
upright
vespers
vibrato
vihuela
violist
violone
warbler
whistle
zithern
zufflolo

8

absonant
absonous
addition
alto-clef
antiphon
arch-lute
arpeggio
autoharp
bagpipes
baritone
barytone
bassetto
bass-drum
bass-horn
bass note
bass oboe
bass-viol
beat-time
bell harp
berceuse
canticle
canzonet
carillon
castanet
castrato
cavatina
chaconne
cheville
clappers
clarinet
clavecin
claviary
composer
composto
con amore
con anima
concerto
confusco
conjusto
continuo
couranto
cromorna
crotchet
deep-tone
demi-tone
diapason
diatonic
diminish
ding-dong
distance
doloroso
dominant
down beat
drumbeat
drum-head
duettist
dulcimer
eleventh

energico
ensemble
entr'acte
euphonic
euphonon
exercise
falsetto
fandango
fantasia
fantasie
flautist
folk-song
forzando
galement
galliard
gemshorn
grazioso
half-note
harmonic
harp lute
hawk-bell
high note
hornpipe
infinito
interval
intonate
isotonic
Jew's-harp
jongleur
keyboard
key-bugle
knackers
lentando
libretto
ligature
lutanist
lutenist
madrigal
maestoso
major key
melodeon
melodics
melodist
melodize
minor key
minstrel
mirliton
miserere
moderato
modulate
monotone
monotony
movement
musicale
musician
nocturne
notation
notturno
obligato
operatic
operetta
oratorio
organist
ostinato
overture
pan-pipes
part-song
pastoral
phantasy
phrasing
Phrygian
pianette
plectrum
post horn
psaltery
quantity

recorder
reed pipe
register
resonant
response
rhapsody
rigadoon
saraband
semitone
septette
sequence
serenade
serenata
sestetto
sextette
sforzato
side drum
smorzato
sonatina
songster
spiccato
spinette
staccato
sticcado
subtonic
symmetry
symphony
syntonic
tabourer
tabouret
tamboura
tell-tale
terzetto
threnody
timoroso
tonalist
tonality
tone down
tone poem
trap-drum
tremando
triangle
trichord
trombone
tympanon
tympanum
vigoroso
virginal
virtuosi
virtuoso
vocalist
voce colo
warbling
wood-wind
zambomba

9

accordion
acoustics
all-breve
allemande
alto-viola
andamento
andantino
antiphony
arabesque
archilute
atonality
bagatelle
balalaika
banjoline
barcarole
bass-flute
bird-organ

bombardon
bow-string
brass-band
brillante
bugle-horn
cacophony
cantabile
capriccio
castanets
celestina
charivari
chromatic
clarionet
claviharp
coach-horn
conductor
consonate
contralto
cornopean
crescendo
dead-march
death-bell
decachord
deep-toned
dissonant
dithyramb
drone-pipe
drumstick
dulcitone
elbow-pipe
elevation
euphonism
euphonium
euphonize
extempore
fiddle-bow
flageolet
flute-stop
folk-music
furibondo
gallopade
generator
glissando
grace-note
gradation
grandioso
Gregorian
guitarist
half-shift
hand organ
harmonica
harmonics
harmonium
harmonize
hexachord
high-pitch
high-toned
homophony
imbroglio
immusical
impromptu
improvise
in harmony
interlude
intonation
inversion
irregular
jazz music
lagrimoso
languente
larghetto
leger-line
leitmotif
mandoline
mandolute
melodious

metronome
mezzo-voce
modulator
monochord
monophony
monotonic
mouth harp
music-book
obbligato
octachord
orchestra
part music
pastorale
phonetics
pianolist
pitch-pipe
pizzicato
plainsong
polonaise
polychord
polyphony
polytonal
pricksong
quadrille
quartette
quintette
recording
reed organ
rehearsal
resonance
rhythmics
ricercare
roundelay
saxophone
semibreve
semitonic
septimole
seraphine
sforzando
siciliana
siciliano
signature
slow march
soft pedal
solfeggio
sollecito
sopranist
sostenuto
sotto-voce
sound-post
spiritosa
spiritual
strascino
succentor
symphonic
syncopate
tablature
tabourine
tail-piece
tambourin
tenor bass
tenor clef
tenor horn
tenor tuba
tenor viol
tessitura
theorbist
time-table
timpanist
trillando
trumpeter
tubophone
tympanist
union-pipe
unmusical
untunable

variation
viola alto
violinist
voluntary
vox humana
whistling
xylophone

10

accidental
adaptation
affettuoso
allegretto
appoggiato
attunement
background
bandmaster
barcarolle
base-spring
basset-horn
bassoonist
binotonous
bull fiddle
cantillate
canzonetta
chiroplast
chitlarone
chorus girl
clarichord
clavichord
colorature
concertina
con-spirito
continuato
contrabass
cor anglais
cornettist
dance-music
demiditone
diastaltic
diminuendo
discordant
disharmony
dissonance
dissonancy
dolcemente
double bass
double time
dulcet-tone
embouchure
enharmonic
Eolian harp
Eolian lyre
euphonicon
euphonious
extraneous
flügelhorn
folk-singer
fortissimo
French harp
French horn
gramophone
grand piano
grand opera
ground bass
harmonicon
harp-string
homophonic
hurdy-gurdy
incidental
instrument
intermezzo
intonation
kettle-drum

lentamente
light opera
major chord
major scale
minor chord
minor scale
minstrelsy
mixolydian
modulation
monotonous
mouth-organ
mouth-piece
musica viva
musicology
opera buffa
opera music
ophicleide
orchestral
pentachord
percussion
pianissimo
pianoforte
polyphonic
prima donna
recitative
recitativo
ritardando
ritornello
semiquaver
sourdeline
sousaphone
staphyline
Stradivari
Strathspey
strepitoso
string-band
stringendo
submediant
supertonic
suspension
symphonion
symphonist
syncopated
syncopator
tamboureen
tambourine
tarantella
tetrachord
tin whistle
tonic chord
tonic major
tonic minor
tonic-sol-fa
triple-time
trombonist
troubador
tuning fork
twelve-tone
undulation
variamento
vibraphone
vistomente
vocal music
zumpé piano

11

accelerando
Aeolian harp
Aeolian lyre
alla capella
alto-ripieno
arrangement
ballad opera
barrel-organ

bene-placito
broken chord
canned music
capriccioso
church music
clairschach
clarion note
composition
concertante
contra-basso
contrapunto
contra-tenor
counterpart
decrescendo
demi-cadence
diatessaron
discordance
discordancy
equisonance
extemporize
fiddlestick
figured-bass
finger-board
first violin
graphophone
Guido's scale
harmoniphon
harmonizing
harpsichord
high-pitched
hunting-horn
hydraulicon
incantation
madrigalist
mandolinist
minnesinger
music-master
natural note
nickelodeon
opera bouffe
orchestrate
passing-bell
passing-note
piano-violin
polyphonism
prestissimo
progression
quarter note
quarter-tone
rallentando
rock and roll
sacred music
saxophonist
senza rigore
solmization
string music
subsemitone
symphonious
syncopation
transposing
tridiapason
unaccordant
viola d'amore
viol da gamba
violoncello
vivacissimo
voce-di-petto
voce-di-testa
volti-subito

12

accordionist
acoustic bass
allegrissimo

appassionata
appoggiatura
assai-allegro
augmentation
bass baritone
boogie-woogie
cembal d'ambre
chamber music
chromaticism
clarinettist
comedy ballet
concert grand
concert-pitch
contrapuntal
cottage piano
counterpoint
counter-tenor
divertimento
double-octave
extravaganza
false cadence
fiddle-string
funeral march
glockenspiel
inharmonious
instrumental
mezzo-relievo
mezzo-soprano
military band
musicologist
opéra comique
orchestrator
organ-grinder
organ recital
pandean-pipes
passion music

penny whistle
philharmonic
philomusical
polytonality
repercussion
sesquialtera
sounding-post
spheremelody
Stradivarius
thorough-bass
tuning-hammer
ukulele-banjo
viola da gamba
vocalization

13

accompaniment
bagpipe player
choral singing
conservatoire
cornet-à-piston
disharmonious
harmonic chord
musical comedy
music festival
operatic music
orchestration
ranz-des-vaches
sacred concert
sol-fa notation
staff notation
string octette
string quartet
superdominant

swanee whistle
terpsichorean
tetradiapason
transposition
violoncellist

14 AND OVER

Ambrosian chant (14)
banjo-mandoline (14)
brass instrument(s) (15, 16)
chromatic scale (14)
demisemiquaver (14)
direct interval (14)
double-tongueing (15)
electronic music (15)
fife-and-drum band (15)
flute-flageolet (14)
Gregorian chant (14)
Highland bagpipe (15)
instrumentalist (15)
instrumentation (15)
Lowland bagpipe (14)
mandoline player (15)
musical director (15)
musical festival (15)
musique concrète (15)
regimental band (14)
string quartette (15)
symphony concert (15)
tintinnabulary (14)
tintinnabulate (14)
tintinnabulation (16)
triple-tongueing (15)
wind instrument(s) (14, 15)

Poetry, prose, and grammar

2 AND 3

do
ego
lay
ms
nō
nôh
ode
pun
tag
wit

4

agon
bard
case
coda
copy
dual
duan
Edda
epic
epos
foot
form
gest
glee
hymn
lamb
idyl

mime
mood
myth
noun
past
pean
play
plot
poem
poet
quip
rime
root
rule
rune
saga
scan
song
tone
verb
weak
word

5

affix
blurb
canto
caret
carol
casal
codex

colon
comma
dirge
ditty
drama
elegy
elide
epode
essay
fable
farce
folio
geste
gloss
haiku
humor
ictus
idiom
idyll
Iliad
image
index
infix
irony
lyric
maxim
metre
motif
novel
paean
poesy
prose
psalm

quote
rhyme
rondo
runic
scald
scene
shift
slang
stich
style
sylva
tense
theme
tilde
triad
Vedas
verse
vowel

6

accent
active
adonic
adverb
Aeneid
alcaic
annals
anthem
aorist
aptote
ballad

181

bathos	**7**	Sapphic	language
chanty		sarcasm	laureate
chorus	adjunct	scaldic	libretto
clause	anagram	semiped	limerick
cliché	analogy	servile	logogram
climax	analyse	setting	lyricism
comedy	anapest	sextain	madrigal
crisis	antonym	spondee	metaphor
critic	apocope	stichic	metrical
dactyl	apology	strophe	mispoint
dative	article	subject	mock epic
define	ballade	syncope	morpheme
derive	berhyme	synonym	negative
digram	bucolic	systole	nonsense
dipody	cadence	tiercet	Ossianic
ending	caesura	tragedy	oxymoron
epodic	cantata	trilogy	paradigm
epopee	cedilla	triolet	particle
finite	chanson	triplet	partsong
future	choreus	trochee	pastoral
gender	collate	villain	personal
genius	content	virelay	phonetic
gerund	context	Vulgate	Pindaric
gnomic	couplet	war song	poetical
govern	decline	western	positive
heroic	descant		prologue
hiatus	diction		quantity
homily	digraph	**8**	quatrain
hubris	distich		relative
humour	eclogue	ablative	rhapsody
hybris	edition	absolute	rhetoric
hymnal	elegiac	acrostic	romantic
hyphen	elision	allusion	scanning
iambic	epicene	alphabet	scansion
iambus	epigram	amoebean	scenario
jargon	epistle	analysis	sentence
kabuki	epitaph	anapaest	singular
lacuna	fantasy	anaphora	solecism
legend	fiction	anti-hero	stanzaic
lyrist	Georgic	antiphon	suspense
macron	harmony	apodosis	swan song
mantra	Homeric	archaism	syntaxis
memoir	homonym	assonant	systolic
monody	idyllic	asterisk	temporal
neuter	imagery	balladry	threnody
number	inflect	caesural	thriller
object	introit	canticle	tribrach
parody	journal	chiasmus	trimeter
pathos	lampoon	choliamb	triptote
period	leonine	choriamb	unpoetic
person	lexicon	clerihew	versicle
phrase	litotes	contrast	vignette
pidgin	lyrical	critique	vocative
plural	meiosis	dactylic	whodunit
poetic	mimesis	definite	word play
poetry	nemesis	dieresis	
prefix	novella	dialogue	
review	Odyssey	discrete	**9**
rhythm	paradox	doggerel	
riddle	parsing	dramatic	accidence
rondle	passive	ellipsis	adjective
satire	peanism	enclitic	ampersand
simile	perfect	epic poem	anapestic
sketch	persona	epigraph	Anglicism
slogan	phoneme	epilogue	anonymous
sonnet	poetics	epitrite	anthology
stanza	polemic	euphuism	apocopate
stress	present	feminine	archetype
strong	pronoun	folktale	Asclepiad
suffix	prosaic	footnote	assonance
symbol	prosody	full-stop	biography
syntax	proverb	generate	birthsong
thesis	psalter	genitive	broadside
umlaut	refrain	glossary	burlesque
verbal	regular	guttural	cacophony
zeugma	requiem	horation	catharsis

classical
conjugate
consonant
criticism
decastich
diaeresis
dipthong
dithyramb
ditrochee
elegiacal
enclitics
etymology
euphemism
facsimile
flashback
formative
free verse
Gallicism
gerundive
grammatic
hemistich
hendiadys
hexameter
hexastich
hypallage
hyperbole
idiomatic
imperfect
inflexion
inversion
irregular
leitmotiv
lyric poem
masculine
metaplasm
minor poet
monometer
monorhyme
nonostich
neologism
objective
parataxis
partitive
past tense
phillipic
philology
Pindarism
platitude
poetaster
pot boiler
potential
preterite
pricksong
principal
privative
prose poem
prosodian
prosodist
quartette
quotation
recension
reddition
reflexive
roundelay
sea chanty
semantics
semicolon
semivowel
soliloquy
syllepsis
symbolism
symposium
symptosis
synalepha
syntactic
telestich

terza rima
trisagion
Virgilian

10

accusative
amphibrach
amphimacer
anapaestic
anarthrous
anastrophe
anastrophy
antagonist
antepenult
anticlimax
antiphonal
antiphonic
apostrophe
apposition
atmosphere
avant-garde
bestseller
blank verse
bowdlerize
caricature
choliambic
choriambic
choriambus
circumflex
colloquial
comparison
declension
definition
definitive
derivation
derivative
dissonance
dolichorus
epenthesis
epenthetic
generative
government
grammarian
hexametric
hyperbaton
hyphenated
imperative
impersonal
indefinite
infinitive
inflection
intonation
involution
linguistic
manuscript
metathesis
mock heroic
morphology
neuter verb
nom de plume
nominative
ottava rima
palindrome
paraphrase
participle
passion play
pentameter
Petrarchan
picaresque
plagiarism
pluperfect
pronominal
provection
reciprocal

short story
similitude
spoonerism
subjective
synaeresis
tetracolon
tetrameter
tetrastich
transitive
unpoetical
vernacular

11

alexandrine
amphibology
anacoluthon
antiphrasis
antistrophe
aposiopesis
association
ballad style
bibliomancy
catastrophe
chansonette
comic relief
comparative
concordance
conjunction
conjunctive
constituent
declination
descriptive
disjunctive
dissyllabic
dissyllable
dithyrambic
dithyrambus
future tense
ghost writer
grammatical
hemistichal
heteroclite
hudibrastic
linguistics
lyric poetry
miracle play
oblique case
parenthesis
portmanteau
preposition
proposition
punctuation
regular verb
reiterative
subjunctive
subordinate
substantive
superlative
suppression
syntactical
tragicomedy
trimetrical

12

alliteration
alliterative
alphabetical
anteposition
antibacchius
antimetrical
antiphonical
antiphrastic

antistrophic
archilochian
bibliography
deponent verb
dissyllabify
distributive
epigrammatic
episodically
epithalamium
etymological
grammaticism
grammaticize
heteroclitic
hexametrical
indeclinable
intransitive
metaphorical
minnesingers
nursery rhyme
onomatopoeia
perfect tense
poet laureate
postposition
prescriptive
present tense
prothalamium

13 AND OVER

antepenultimate (15)
definite article (15)
epigrammatical (14)
frequentative (13)
future perfect (13)
historic present (15)
hysteron proteron (16)
indicative mood (14)
interrogative (13)
inverted commas (14)
irregular verb (13)
lyrical poetry (13)
objective case (13)
personification (15)
poetic licence (13)
positive degree (14)
possessive case (14)
science fiction (14)
split infinitive (15)
transformation (14)
ungrammatical (13)

Theatre, opera, ballet, cinema, television and radio

2 AND 3

act
arc
bit
bow
box
cue
dub
fan
gag
ham
hit
mug
nō
pan
pit
rag
rep
run
set
tag
TV
wig

4

bill
book
boom
busk
cast
clap
clip
crew
dais
diva
duet
Emmy
epic
exit
film
flop
foil
gala
gods
grid
hero
idol
joke
lead
line
live
mask
mike
mime
mute
part
play
prop
role
rush
shot
show
skit
solo
spot
star
take
team
turn
wing

5

actor
ad lib
agent
angel
apron
aside
baton
break
clown
comic
debut
decor
drama
dry up
enact
exode
extra
farce
flies
focus
foyer
heavy
hokum
house
lines
mimer
mimic
movie
on cue
opera
Oscar
piece
props
radio
revue
scene
stage
stall
stunt
telly
usher
wings

6

acting
action
appear
backer
ballet
barker
big top
boards
buskin
camera
chorus
cinema
circle
circus
claque
comedy
critic
dancer
direct
dubbed
effect
encore
finale
flyman
kabuki

lights
make-up
masque
method
motley
movies
mummer
nautch
number
on tour
one act
parody
patron
patter
player
podium
prompt
puppet
recite
repeat
ring up
rushes
satire
screen
script
season
serial
series
singer
sitcom
sketch
speech
stalls
stooge
studio
talent
talkie
ticket
tights
timing
tinsel
troupe
TV show
viewer
walk-on
warm-up
writer

7

acrobat
actress
all-star
amateur
balcony
benefit
bit part
booking
buffoon
cabaret
callboy
cartoon
casting
catcall
catwalk
channel
charade
chorine
circuit
clapper
close-up
commère

company
compère
concert
console
costume
curtain
dancing
danseur
deadpan
dress up
drive in
dubbing
fan club
farceur
fantasy
feature
film set
gallery
heroine
ingenue
juggler
leg show
leotard
long run
matinée
mimicry
mummery
musical
mystery
new wave
on stage
overact
pageant
perform
phone-in
Pierrot
players
playing
playlet
pop star
portray
prelude
present
preview
produce
program
recital
reciter
re-enact
resting
revival
rostrum
scenery
show biz
showman
sponsor
stadium
stagery
staging
stand-in
stardom
starlet
support
tableau
talkies
theatre
the gods
tragedy
trailer
trilogy
trouper
tumbler
upstage

variety
vehicle
viewing
western

8

applause
artistry
audience
audition
backdrop
bioscope
burletta
carnival
chat show
Cinerama
clapping
clowning
coliseum
comedian
conjurer
coryphée
costumer
coulisse
danseuse
dialogue
director
disguise
dramatic
dumb show
duologue
entr'acte
entrance
epilogue
exit line
farceuse
fauteuil
festival
figurant
film crew
film star
film unit
filmgoer
first act
funny man
ham actor
interval
juggling
libretto
live show
location
magician
male lead
morality
newsreel
offstage
operatic
operetta
overture
parterre
pastoral
peep show
pictures
pit stall
platform
playbill
playgoer
première
producer
prologue
prompter
protasis
quiz show
rehearse

ring down
scenario
set piece
showbill
side show
smash hit
stagebox
star turn
straight
stripper
subtitle
telecast
Thespian
third act
tragical
travesty
typecast
wardrobe
wigmaker

9

animation
announcer
arabesque
backcloth
backstage
ballerina
bandstand
barnstorm
bit player
box office
broadcast
burlesque
cameraman
character
chorus boy
cinematic
clip joint
cloakroom
Columbine
conjuring
costumier
coulisses
criticism
cyclorama
discovery
double act
down stage
dramatics
dramatist
dramatize
drop scene
entertain
entrechat
exhibiter
figurante
film actor
film extra
fimstrip
first lead
flashback
floorshow
folkdance
full house
gala night
guest star
Harlequin
impromptu
interlude
limelight
love scene
low comedy
major role
melodrama

minor role
monodrama
monologue
movie star
movie-goer
music hall
night club
orchestra
panel game
pantaloon
pantomime
pas de deux
performer
photoplay
Pierrette
pirouette
pit-stalls
play-actor
playhouse
portrayal
programme
prompt-box
publicity
punch-line
quartette
rehearsal
repertory
represent
second act
slapstick
soap opera
soliloquy
soubrette
spectacle
spectator
spotlight
stage door
stagehand
stage left
stage-name
stage play
take a part
tap dancer
the boards
title role
tragedian
usherette
wisecrack

10

afterpiece
appearance
auditorium
chorus girl
clapper-boy
comedienne
comedietta
comic opera
commercial
continuity
coryphaeus
crowd scene
denouement
disc jockey
drama group
dramaturge
dramaturgy
fantoccini
filmscript
film house
first night
footlights
get the bird
high comedy

hippodrome
histrionic
horse opera
horror film
impresario
in the round
in the wings
junior lead
intermezzo
leading man
legitimate
librettist
marionette
masquerade
microphone
movie actor
music drama
newscaster
on location
opera buffa
opera house
performing
play-acting
playwright
prima donna
production
prompt-book
properties
proscenium
Pulcinella
puppet-show
rave notice
rave review
recitation
repertoire
repetiteur
ringmaster
screenplay
silent film
sound track
stagecraft
stage fever
stage right
star player
striptease
substitute
sword-dance
tap dancing
tear-jerker
television
theatre box
theatrical
torchdance
travelogue
understudy
variety act
vaudeville
walk-on part
wide screen

11

accompanist
all-star cast
art director
balletomane
barnstormer
black comedy
broadcaster
cap and bells
Cinemascope
circus-rider
cliff-hanger
comedy drama
comic relief

185

commentator
concert hall
credit title
cutting room
dance troupe
documentary
drama critic
drama school
dramatic art
dress circle
electrician
entertainer
equilibrist
exeunt omnes
feature film
film theatre
fire curtain
folkdancing
funambulist
greasepaint
Greek chorus
histrionics
illusionist
impersonate
kitchen-sink
leading lady
legerdemain
light comedy
matinée idol
method actor
miracle play
opera bouffe
opera singer
pantomimist
Passion play
performance
picture show
problem play
protagonist
psychodrama
Punchinello
scene change
set designer
set the scene
showmanship
show-stopper
sound effect
spectacular
stage design
stage effect
stage fright
stage player
stage school
stage-struck
star billing
star quality
star-studded
talent scout
technicolor
terpsichore

thaumaturgy
theatregoer
theatreland
theatricals
Thespian art
tragedienne
tragicomedy
trick-riding
unrehearsed
upper circle
variety show
ventriloquy
word-perfect

12

academy award
actor-manager
amphitheatre
ballet-dancer
balletomania
choreography
cinema studio
clapperboard
concert party
credit titles
dramaturgist
dressing-room
exotic dancer
extravaganza
film director
film festival
film producer
first-nighter
Grand Guignol
harlequinade
impersonator
introduction
juvenile lead
make-up artist
melodramatic
method acting
minstrel show
modern ballet
morality play
name in lights
natural break
opera glasses
orchestra pit
principal boy
Punch and Judy
puppet-player
scene-painter
scene-shifter
scene-stealer
screenwriter
scriptwriter
show business
silver screen

song and dance
sound effects
stage manager
stage whisper
starring role
steal the show
stock company
straight part
top of the bill

13

ballet dancing
burlesque show
cinematograph
contortionist
curtain-raiser
dance festival
emergency exit
entertainment
musical comedy
projectionist
Russian ballet
safety curtain
sleight-of-hand
sound engineer
studio manager
thaumaturgics
theatre school
ventriloquist

14 AND 15

acrobatic troupe (15)
ballet-mistress (14)
classical ballet (15)
continuity girl (14)
dancing academy (14)
domestic comedy (14)
dramatic critic (14)
dramatic society (15)
prima ballerina (14)
property master (14)
school of acting (14)
school of dancing (15)
shooting script (14)
situation comedy (15)
slide projector (14)
smoking concert (14)
sound-projector (14)
stage carpenter (14)
stage properties (15)
strolling player (15)
tableaux-vivants (15)
talking pictures (15)
tightrope-walker (15)
touring company (14)
variety theatre (14)

MEASUREMENT
Coins and currency

2 AND 3

as
cob
dam
ecu
far

lat
leu
lev
mil
mna
pie
ree

rei
sen
sho
sol
sou
won
yen

4

anna
baht
beka
biga
buck

cash
cent
daum
dime
doit
joey
}
kran
lira
mail
mark
merk
mite
obol
para
peag
peso
pice
rand
real
rial
ryal
tael
unik
yuan

5

angel
asper
belga
betso
broad
colon
conto
copec
crown
daric
dinar
ducat
eagle
franc
groat
krona
krone
liard
libra
litas
livre
locho
louis
medio
mohar
mohur
noble
obang
paolo
pence
pengo
penny
plack
pound
rupee
sceat
scudi
scudo
semis
soldo
stica
styca
sucre
sycee
tical
toman
uncia
unite
zloty

6

amania
balboa
baubee
bawbee
bezart
condor
copang
copeck
décime
doblon
dollar
escudo
florin
forint
fuorte
gourde
guinea
gulden
heller
kopeck
lepton
markka
nickel
pagode
peseta
rouble
sceatt
sequin
shekel
stater
stiver
talari
talent
tanner
tester
teston
thaler
tomaun
zechin

7

angelot
bolivar
carolus
centava
centavo
centime
cordoba
crusado
denarii
drachma
guilder
jacobus
lempira
milreis
moidore
ngusang
piastre
pistole
quarter
sextans
stooter
testoon
unicorn

8

ambrosin
denarius
didrachm
doubloon

ducatoon
farthing
florence
groschen
half anna
half mark
johannes
kreutzer
louis d'or
maravedi
napoleon
new pence
new penny
picayune
quetzale
sesterce
shilling
sixpence
stotinka

9

boliviano
cuartillo
didrachma
dupondius
gold broad
gold noble
gold penny
half ackey
half angel
half broad
half crown
half groat
halfpenny
pistareen
rixdollar
rose-noble
schilling
sestertii
sovereign
spur royal
two mohars
two mohurs
yellow boy

10

broad piece
crown piece
double pice
easterling
first brass
gold stater
half florin
half guinea
half laurel
quadrussis
sestertium
silverling
stour-royal
threepence
threepenny
tripondius
venezolano

11

Briton crown
double crown
double eagle
george noble
guinea piece

half guilder
half thistle
silver penny
spade guinea
tetradrachm
twelvepenny
two guilders

12 AND 13

double sequin (12)
half farthing (12)
half rose-noble (13)
half sovereign (13)
mill sixpence (12)
quarter angel (12)
quarter dollar (13)
quarter florin (13)
quarter laurel (13)
quarter noble (12)
silver-stater (12)
sixpenny piece (13)
tribute penny (12)
twenty dollars (13)
twopenny piece (13)
two-pound piece (13)

14 AND OVER

barbadoes penny (14)
five-guinea piece (15)
five-pound piece (14)
Hong Kong dollar (14)
quarter guilder (14)
three farthings (14)
threepenny piece (15)
twenty shillings (15)
two-guilder piece (15)
two-guinea piece (14)

Time (including specific dates, periods, seasons, annual festivals, etc.)

(H.) = Hindu. (I) = Islam. (J.) = Jewish months (variously spelt). (R.) = Roman.

2 – 4

Ab (J.)
Abib (J.)
A.D.
Adar (j.)
aeon
age
ages
ago
A.M.
B.C.
B.S.T.
date
dawn
day
Elul (J.)
eon
era
ever
fast
G.M.T.
Holi (H.)
hour
Ides (R.)
Iyar (J.)
July
June
last
late
Lent
May
morn
noon
now
N.S.
oft
once
O.S.
P.M.
slow
soon
span
term
then
tick
time
week
when
Xmas
year
yore
Yuga (H.)
Yule

5

adays
after
again
alway
April
bells
clock
cycle
daily
dated
early

epact
epoch
Fasti (R.)
feast
first
flash
horal
jiffy
Kalpa (H.)
later
March
month
never
night
Nisan (J.)
nones
of old
often
quick
reign
Sivan (J.)
spell
Tebet (J.)
teens
times
Tisri (J.)
to-day
trice
until
watch
while

6

always
annual
August
autumn
before
betime
brumal
Cisleu
curfew
decade
Diwali (H.)
Easter
faster
feriae
ferial
Friday
future
heyday
hourly
hiemal
Julian
Kislev (J.)
Lammas
lately
latest
May day
memory
mensal
midday
minute
modern
moment
Monday
morrow

o'clock
off-day
pay-day
period
record
rhythm
season
second
seldom
Shebat (J.)
slower
slowly
spring
summer
Sunday
sunset
Tammuz (J.)
Tebeth (J.)
termly
timely
timous
Tishri (J.)
ultimo
Veadar (J.)
Veader (J.)
vernal
vesper
weekly
whilom
whilst
winter
yearly

7

almanac
already
ancient
anights
antique
bedtime
betimes
by and by
Calends (R.)
century
chiliad
Chisleu (J.)
dawning
daytime
diurnal
dog days
earlier
epochal
equinox
estival
eternal
etesian
evening
fast day
fête day
half-day
harvest
Heshvan (J.)
high day
hock-day
holiday
holy day
instant

interim
January
jubilee
lady day
lay-days
lustrum
mail day
mid-Lent
midweek
monthly
morning
new moon
nightly
noonday
October
post-day
proximo
quartan
quarter
quicker
quickly
quintan
Ramadan (I.)
regency
rent day
sabbath
slowest
sundial
sundown
sunrise
tea time
tertian
Thammuz (J.)
timeful
time gun
timeous
tonight
triduan
Tuesday
undated
wartime
weekday
weekend
whilere
workday
Xmas day
yestern

8

aestival
annually
antecede
antedate
anterior
biennial
bimensal
birthday
biweekly
calendar
carnival
chiliasm
chiliast
day by day
daybreak
dead-slow
December
domesday

doomsday
duration
earliest
eggtimer
estivate
eternity
eventide
every day
February
festival
forenoon
formerly
futurist
futurity
gangweek
Georgian
gloaming
half-past
half-term
half-time
half-year
hibernal
high noon
Hock-tide
Hogmanay
holidays
holy week
interval
kalendar
latterly
leap year
Lord's day
mealtime
menology
midnight
minutely
natal day
new style
noontide
noon-time
November
nowadays
nundinal
oft-times
old style
overtime
past time
periodic
postpone
punctual
quickest
Ramadhan (I.)
right now
Saturday
seasonal
seed time
semester
se'nnight
sidereal
slow time
sometime
speedily
Stone Age
Thursday
time ball
time bill
timeless
tomorrow
twilight
untimely
up to date
vacation
whenever
Yuletide
zero hour

9

Adar Shani (J.)
aforetime
after ages
afternoon
afterward
All Hallow
anciently
antedated
antelucan
antiquity
bimonthly
Boxing Day
Candlemas
centenary
Christmas
civil year
close time
continual
decennary
decennial
diurnally
diuturnal
Easter Day
Edwardian
Ember days
Ember fast
Ember tide
Ember week
eternally
feast days
fortnight
fruit time
Gregorian
Halloween
hard times
hereafter
hodiernal
honeymoon
hourglass
immediate
indiction
instantly
lean years
Low Sunday
lunar year
lunch time
market day
Martinmas
matutinal
menstrual
midsummer
midwinter
nightfall
night-time
nightward
novitiate
octennial
overnight
past times
peace time
postponed
premature
presently
quarterly
quick time
quotidian
recurrent
return day
right away
September
sexennial
sometimes
speech day
sunrising

Thermidor
ticket.day
timepiece
timetable
triennial
trimester
Victorian
Wednesday
whole time
yesterday
yestereve

10

aftertimes
afterwards
All Hallows
antecedent
antemosaic
anteriorly
anticipate
beforehand
before time
behind time
biennially
bimestrial
centennial
chiliastic
chronogram
continuous
days of yore
dinner time
diuturnity
Easter term
Ember weeks
estivation
Father Time
fence month
Good Friday
half-yearly
hebdomadal
Hilary term
isochronal
lunar cycle
lunar month
Michaelmas
Middle Ages
millennium
natalitial
occasional
oftentimes
olden times
Palm Sunday
quarter day
record time
seasonable
septennial
sexagesima
Shrovetide
solar month
sowing-time
spring time
summer term
summertime
sunsetting
synchronal
Theban year
thereafter
tiffin time
time enough
timekeeper
time server
time signal
triverbial
twelfth day

unpunctual
vespertine
watch night
wedding day
Whit Sunday
winter time
working day

11

All Fools' Day
All Souls' Day
anniversary
antecedence
antemundane
antenuptial
antepaschal
anteriority
Bank Holiday
behindtimes
bicentenary
Black Monday
Chalk Sunday
chronograph
chronometer
closing time
continually
cosmic clock
discount day
Elizabethan
everlasting
fashionable
fortnightly
half holiday
harvest home
harvest time
hebdomadary
holiday time
immediately
interregnum
isochronism
isochronous
jubilee year
Judgment Day
leisure time
millenarian
New Year's Day
New Year's Eve
Passion Week
prehistoric
prematurely
present time
pudding time
punctuality
quadrennial
quartz clock
Rosh Hashonah (J.)
seeding time
settling day
synchronism
synchronize
synchronous
thenceforth
time bargain
Tudor period
twelvemonth
ultramodern
Whitsuntide
yesternight

12

afterthought
All Saints' Day   189

antediluvial
antediluvian
antemeridian
anticipation
Ash Wednesday
betrothal day
bicentennial
carbon dating
Christmas Day
Christmas Eve
continuously
duodecennial
early closing
Easter Sunday
Embering days
emergent year
hebdomatical
luncheon time
Midsummer Day
Midsummer Eve
occasionally
old-fashioned
platonic year
Plough Monday
post-diluvial
post-diluvian
post-meridian
postponement

postprandial
quadragesima
quinquennial
red-letter day
Rogation days
Rogation week
sidereal year
standard time
synchronized
tercentenary
time contract
tricentenary
tropical year
twelfth night

13

All Hallowmass
All Hallowtide
April Fools' Day
breakfast time
calendar month
Childermas day
Christmastide
Christmastime
Edwardian days
everlastingly

golden jubilee
golden wedding
Gregorian year
holiday season
lunisolar year
Michaelmas Day
once upon a time
Shrove Tuesday
silver wedding
thenceforward
Trinity Sunday
Valentine's Day

14 AND 15

behind the times (14)
biological clock (15)
day in and day out (14)
early closing day (15)
early Victorian (14)
Maundy Thursday (14)
Michaelmas term (14)
prehistoric age(s) (14–15)
sabbatical year (14)
synchronization (15)
synodical month (14)
Walpurgis night (14)

Weights and measures

(A.) = Argentina	(I.) = India	(print.) = printing
(B.) = Brazil	(Ice.) = Iceland	(R.) = Russia
(b.) = bread	(Indo.) = Indonesia	(Rom.) = Roman
(C.) = Canada	(Ire.) = Ireland	(S.) = Spain
(c.) = coal	(It.) = Italy	(s.) = silk or cotton
(Ch.) = China	(J.) = Japan	(S.A.) = South Africa
(E.) = Egypt	(liq.) = liquids	(SI) = Système International:
(elec.) = electricity	(M.) = Malta	metric system
(Eth.) = Ethiopia	(Malay.) = Malaysia	(T.) = Turkey
(F.) = France	(min.) = mining	(Thai.) = Thailand
(f.) = fish	(Mor.) = Morocco	(U.S.) = United States
(G.) = Greece	(N.) = Norway	(v.) = various commodities
(H.) = Hebrew	(O.) = Oriental	(w.) = wool
(Hon.) = Honduras	(pap.) = paper	(w.y.) = worsted yarn

Note: Words with no references against them are British weights or measures not necessarily confined to particular commodities. Many of the units listed are no longer in use.

1 – 3

A4 (pap.)
amp (elec.)
are (SI)
as (Rom.)
A.S.A.
aum (S.A.)
B.S.I.
B.T.U.
cab (H.)
cho (J.)
cor (H.)
cm. (SI)
cwt.
day
D.I.N.
dwt.
el
em (print.)

en (print.)
erg
fen (Ch.)
g. (SI)
hin (H.)
kat (E.)
keg
ken (J.)
kg.
kin (J. and Ch.)
km.
kor (H.)
lac (I.)
lb.
lea (s.)
li (Ch.)
log (H.)
m.
mho (elec.)
mil

mow (Ch.)
mu
niu (Thai.)
ohm (elec.)
oka (E.)
oke (T.)
pic (E.)
piu (It.)
rai (Thai.)
ri (J.)
rod
sen (Thai.)
sho (J.)
SI
sun (J.)
tan (Ch.)
to (J.)
tod (w.)
ton
tot

tun (liq.)
vat (liq.)
wah (Thai.)
wey (w.)

4

acre.
area
bale (v.)
bath (H.)
bind (f.)
boll
butt (liq.)
cade (f.)
case (v.)
cask (liq.)
ch'ih (Ch.)
chop (Ch.)

comb
curd
coss (I.)
cran (f.)
darg
demy (pap.)
drah (Mor.)
dram
drop
drum (v.)
dyne
epha (H.)
feet
foot
funt (R.)
gill
gram (SI)
half
hand (horses)
hank (w.y.)
hath (I.)
heml (E.)
hide
hour
inch
keel (c.)
kela (E.)
kilo (SI)
knot
koku (J.)
koss (I.)
kwan (J.)
lakh (I.)
last (f., w.)
link
load (min.)
maze (f.)
mile
mina (H.)
muid (S.A.)
nail
natr (Eth.)
oket (Eth.)
omer (H.)
onza (A.)
pace
pail (lard)
pair
palm
peck
pike (G.)
pint
pipe (liq.)
pole
pood (R.)
post (pap.)
pund (N.)
raik (I.)
ream (pap.)
reed (H.)
reel (s.)
rood
rope
rotl (E.)
sack (c. w.)
seam
seer (I.)
span
step
tael (Ch.)
tare
tola (I.)
tret
troy
ts'un (Ch.)
unit

vara (Hon.)
volt (elec.)
warp (f.)
watt (elec.)
week
wrap (w.y.)
yard
year

5

almud (T.)
anker (S.A.)
ardeb (E.)
bahar (I.)
barge (c.)
baril (G.)
barre (I.)
bekah (H.)
bidon (liq.)
bigha (I.)
brace
cable
candy (I.)
carat
catty (Ch.)
cawny (I.)
chain
cloff
clove
coomb
count (w.y.)
crore (I.)
crown (pap.)
cubic
cubit
cycle
danda (I.)
ephah (H.)
galon (A.)
gauge
gerah (H.)
grain
gross
hertz (elect.)
homer (H.)
kileh (T.)
leash
legua (A.)
liang (Ch.)
libra (B.)
litre (SI)
livre (F. and G.)
masha (I.)
maund (I.)
mease
meter   (SI)
metre
minim (liq.)
month
obole
ocque (G.)
okieh (E.)
ounce
pally (I.)
pearl
perch
picul (Ch.)
piede (M.)
plumb
point (print.)
pound
proof
pugil
purse (T.)

qirat (E.)
quart
quire (pap.)
quota
royal (pap.)
sajen (R.)
shaku (J.)
sheet (pap.)
shock (U.S.)
sicca (I.)
skein (s.)
stere (SI)
stone
stoup (liq.)
terce (liq.)
therm
tithe
toise (F.)
token (pap.)
tonne
trone
truss
tsubo (J.)
ungul (I.)
vedro (R.)
verst (R.)
yojan (I.)

6

ampère (elec.)
aroura (E. and G.)
arroba (A. and B.)
arshin (T.)
assize
bandle (Ire.)
barrel (v.)
batman (T.)
bundle (v.)
bushel
cantar (E. and T.)
casing (pap.)
cental (C. and U.S.)
cental (B. and G.)
chatak (I.)
chopin (liq.)
cottah (I.)
cuarta (A.)
djerib (T.)
double
drachm
endaze (T.)
fanega (S.)
fathom
feddan (E.)
firkin
firlot
fother
gallon (liq.)
gramme (SI)
kantar (Eth.)
kentle
league
libbra (M.)
megohm (elec.)
metric
micron (SI)
minute
modius
moiety
morgen (S.A.)
noggin
obolus (G.)
octant
octave

octavo
oxgang
parsec
pocket (hops)
pottle (liq.)
quarto (pap.)
rotolo (M.)
sajene (R.)
schene (E.)
second
shekel (H.)
shtoff (R.)
staten (G.)
suttle
talent (G.)
thrave (Ice.)
thread (s.)
tierce (liq.)
visham (I.)
weight

7

acreage
boiling
caldron (c.)
Celsius
centner
century
chalder
chittak (I.)
coulomb (elec.)
dangali (I.)
drachma (G.)
ellwand
furlong
half-aum (S.A.)
half-ton
hectare (SI)
koonkee (I.)
leaguer (S.A.)
maximum
measure
megaton
mileage
minimum
minimus
modicum
outsize
pailful
per cent.
quantar (E.)
quartan
quantum
quarter
quinary
quintal
röntgen
sarplar (w.)
scruple
seamile
spindle (s.)
stadium (G.)
stature
stremma (G.)
ternary
ternion
tonnage

8

alqueire (B.)
angstrom
caroteel (O.)

191

chaldron (c.)
chaudron (c.)
chetvert (R.)
cubic ton
distance
division
elephant (pap.)
foolscap (pap.)
freezing
half hour
half inch
half mile
hogshead (liq.)
imperial (pap.)
infinity
kassabah (E.)
kilogram
kilowatt (elec.)
kincatty (Ch.)
metrical
mutchkin (liq.)
parasang (Iran)
plateful
puncheon (liq.)
roentgen
quantity
quartern (b.)
ship-load (c.)
short ton (C. and U.S.)
spoonful
toll dish
tonelada (A.)
yardwand
zolotnik (R.)

9

altimetry
amplitude
areometry
bisegment
cubic foot
cubic inch
cubic yard
cuartilla (A.)
decalitre (SI)
decametre (SI)
decilitre (SI)
decimetre (SI)
decistere (F.)

dekalitre (SI)
dekametre (SI)
dimension
foot-pound
half ounce
half pound
hectogram (SI)
isometric
kilocycle
kilohertz (elec.)
kilolitre (SI)
kilometre (SI)
large sack (c.)
light year
long dozen
megacycle
megahertz (elec.)
metric ton
milestone
milligram (SI)
nanometre (SI)
net weight
quadruple
quarterly
quintuple
sea league
three-fold
yardstick

10

barleycorn
barrel-bulk
centesimal
centigrade
centilitre (SI)
centimetre (SI)
centistere (F.)
cubic metre (SI)
dead-weight
decagramme (SI)
decigramme (SI)
dessiatine (R.)
dessyatine (R.)
double-demy (pap.)
double-post (pap.)
dry measure
eighth-part
Fahrenheit
fifty-fifty

fluid ounce
hectolitre (SI)
hectometre (SI)
kilogramme (SI)
lunar month
microfarad (elec.)
millesimal
millilitre (SI)
millimetre (SI)
millionary
quadrantal (Rom.)
square foot
square inch
square mile
square yard
super-royal (pap.)
tripartite
tron weight
troy weight

11

avoirdupois
baker's dozen
centigramme (SI)
day's journey
double-crown (pap.)
double-royal (pap.)
equibalance
equidistant
fluid drachm
half and half
hand-breadth
heavyweight
hectogramme (SI)
imperial-cap (pap.)
long hundred
  (eggs and f.)
long measure
milligramme (SI)
pennyweight
shipping ton
short weight
square metre (SI)
tape-measure
thermal unit
thermometer
trone weight
two-foot rule
wine measure
yard measure

12

angström unit
areometrical
auncel weight
bantam-weight
boiling point
cable's length
cubic measure
eleventh part
equidistance
great hundred
hair's breadth
half-quartern
measured mile
metric system
printer's ream (pap.)
quantitative
quartern loaf (b.)
Réaumur scale
water measure

13

calendar month
decimal system
feather-weight
freezing point
hundredweight
hypermetrical
inside measure
linear measure
medicine glass
square measure
three-foot rule

14

cubic decimetre (SI)
double-foolscap (pap.)
double-imperial (pap.)
outside measure
zenith distance

15

centigrade scale
cubic centimetre (SI)
square decimetre (SI)

NATURAL HISTORY   (1) LIVING CREATURES
Animals

2 AND 3

ai
ape
ass
bat
bok
cat
cob
cow
cub
cur
dam
doe
dog
dso

dzo
elk
ewe
fox
gib
gnu
goa
hog
kid
kob
ky
man
nag
ox
pad
pig

ram
rat
roe
sai
seg
sow
tat
teg
tit
tod
tup
ure
wat
yak
zho
zo

4

alce
anoa
atoc
atok
barb
bear
boar
buck
bull
cain
calf
cavy
colt
cony

			6
coon	vari	loris	agouti
dauw	vole	magot	aliped
deer	wolf	major	alpaca
dieb	zebu	manis	angola
dood	zobo	manul	angora
douc	zuna	maral	argali
eyra		meles	aye-aye
fawn		moose	baboon
foal	**5**	morse	badger
gaur		mouse	bandar
girl		nandu	barrow
goat	addax	nyala	bawsin
gyal	aguti	okapi	bawson
hack	alces	oribi	bayard
hare	ammon	otary	beaver
hart	ariel	otter	beeves
hind	arnee	ounce	bovine
ibex	beast	panda	bronco
jade	bhyle	pekan	brumby
joey	bidet	phoca	burhel
jomo	biped	pongo	cabiai
kine	bison	potto	castor
koba	bitch	poyou	cattle
kudu	bongo	punch	cayman
lamb	brach	puppy	cayuse
lion	brock	ranny	cervus
lynx	bruin	rasse	chacma
maki	burro	ratel	chetah
mare	camel	royal	coaiti
mice	caple	sable	cosset
mico	capra	saiga	cougar
mink	capul	sajou	coyote
moco	chiru	sasin	craber
mohr	civet	screw	dassie
moke	coati	serow	desman
mole	coney	sheep	dickey
mule	coypu	shoat	dik-dik
mona	crone	shrew	dobbin
musk	cuddy	simia	dog fox
napu	daman	skunk	donkey
neat	dhole	sloth	dragon
nout	dingo	sorel	dzeren
nowt	dipus	sorex	dzeron
oryx	drill	spade	ermine
oxen	dsomo	spado	farrow
paca	eland	spitz	fennec
paco	equus	staig	ferret
pala	fauna	steed	fisher
pard	felis	steer	fox bat
peba	filly	stirk	galago
pika	fitch	stoat	garran
poka	gayal	swine	garron
pony	genet	tabby	gavial
pudu	goral	talpa	gerbil
puma	grice	tapir	gibbon
quey	grise	tatou	ginnet
rane	gyall	taxel	gopher
reem	harpy	tayra	grison
roan	hinny	tiger	grivet
runt	horse	tucan	guemal
rusa	hound	urial	guenon
saki	hutia	urson	hacker
seal	hyena	ursus	halfer
seeg	hyrax	vison	hangul
shou	indri	vixen	heifer
skug	inuus	waler	hircus
sore	izard	whale	hogget
stag	jocko	whelp	howler
stot	jumbo	yapok	hybrid
suni	kaama	zebra	impala
tahr	kalan	zerda	jackal
tegg	kevel	zibet	jaguar
topi	koala	zizel	jennet
unau	kyloe	zoril	jerboa
urus	lemur	zorra	
urva	llama	zorro	

193

jument
kalong
kelpie
keltie
kitten
koodoo
kyloes
langur
lechwe
lionel
malkin
mammal
margay
marmot
marten
mawkin
merino
messin
monkey
morkin
musk ox
musmon
mustac
nahoor
nilgai
ocelet
onager
oorial
ovibos
pallah
panter
porker
possum
pygarg
python
quagga
quokka
rabbit
racoon
red fox
reebok
renard
rhebok
rhesus
roarer
rodent
ronion
sajoin
sambar
sambur
sarlac
sarlyk
sea-ape
sea cow
serval
shammy
shelty
sorrel
sponge
suslik
taguan
tajacu
talbot
taurec
tapeti
tarpan
teledu
tenrec
thamin
theave
tomeat
tupala
vermin
vervet
vicuna
walrus

wapiti
warine
weasel
weeper
wether
wivern
wombat
wow-wow
wyvern
yapock

7

acouchy
ant-bear
assapan
aurochs
banting
bettong
bighorn
blesbok
blue cat
bonasus
boshbop
Bovidae
brawner
brocket
broncho
bubalis
buffalo
bulchin
bullock
bushcat
bush pig
caracal
caribou
cervine
cetacea
chamois
cheetah
cheslip
cheviot
chikari
chimera
chincha
clumber
colobus
courser
dasypus
dasyure
dolphin
draft-ox
eanling
Echidna
echimyd
epizoan
epizoon
ermelin
fatling
finback
fitchet
fitchew
foumart
fur seal
galla ox
gazelle
gelding
gemsbok
genette
giraffe
glutton
gorilla
grampus
griffin
griffon

grizzly
guanaco
hackney
hamster
huanaco
hystrix
jacchus
jackass
jumbuck
karagan
keitloa
kidling
klipdas
lagomys
lambkin
lemming
leopard
leveret
libbard
linsang
lioness
macacus
macaque
madoqua
mammoth
manatee
mangaby
Manx cat
maracan
marikin
mariput
markhor
marmose
megamys
meerkat
minever
miniver
mole-rat
mongrel
monture
morling
mormops
moschus
mouflon
muntjak
musiman
musk rat
mustang
mustela
mycetes
mycetis
mylodon
narwhal
nasalis
noctule
nylghau
opossum
palfrey
panther
pardale
peccary
polecat
potoroo
pricket
primate
procyon
pterope
raccoon
red deer
reed rat
rietbok
rock doe
roe deer
rorqual
sagouin
saimiri

sambhur
sapajou
sapling
sassaby
sciurus
scorpio
sea-bear
sea-lion
serpent
sheltie
siamang
soliped
sondeli
sounder
souslik
spitter
sumpter
tadpole
tamanoa
tamarin
tarsier
tatouay
thiller
tigress
toxodon
twinter
unicorn
urocyon
vampire
vansire
vicuana
viverra
wallaby
wart-hog
wheeler
wild cat
wild dog
wistiti
zamouse
zorille

8

aardvark
aardwolf
anteater
antelope
babirusa
bathorse
behemoth
black fox
black rat
bontebok
brant fox
brown rat
bull-calf
bushbaby
bushbuck
cachalot
cacholot
capuchin
capucine
capybara
cavicorn
chimaera
chipmuck
chipmunk
civet-cat
colocola
cotswold
cricetus
demi-wolf
dinosaur
dormouse
duckbill

elephant
entellus
filander
galloway
gin-horse
grysbock
hedgehog
hedgepig
hoggerel
hog steer
hylobate
indigene
kangaroo
kinkajou
kolinsky
lamantin
lamentin
macropus
mammalia
mandrill
mangabey
mantiger
marmoset
mastodon
meriones
milch-cow
mongoose
moufflon
musk deer
musquash
packmule
pangolin
physeter
platypus
polliwig
pollywog
polo pony
porkling
porpoise
red panda
reedbuck
reindeer
Rodentia
ruminant
sea-otter
serotine
sewer-rat
shorling
sika deer
sirenian
springer
squirrel
staggard
stallion
stinkard
suilline
suricate
surmulot
tabby-cat
talapoin
tiger cat
tortoise
twinling
ungulata
viscacha
wallaroo
wanderoo
war-horse
warrigal
water-hog
water-rat
weanling
wild boar
wild goat
yeanling
yearling

9

adelopode
alligator
amphioxus
amphipoda
Angola cat
annellata
anthobian
arctic fox
armadillo
bandicoot
barbastel
batrachia
bay-duiker
bezantler
black bear
black buck
blue whale
brood-mare
brown bear
carnivore
carpincho
cart-horse
catamount
chameleon
chickadee
chickaree
coalmouse
colemouse
commensal
deermouse
delundung
dicotyles
didelphys
dinoceras
draught-ox
dray-horse
dromedary
dziggetai
eared seal
flying fox
glyptodon
grimalkin
ground-hog
gruntling
guineapig
honey-bear
ichneumon
lagomorph
leviathan
malt-horse
marsupial
megalonyx
monoceros
monotreme
mousedeer
orang-utan
pachyderm
pack-horse
pademelon
padymelon
percheron
petaurist
phalanger
pipistrel
polar bear
porcupine
post-horse
predacean
prong-buck
prong-horn
quadruman
quadruped
racehorse
rearmouse

reermouse
reremouse
rosmarine
shearling
shoreling
shrew-mole
silver fox
sitatunga
southdown
spatangus
springbok
steerling
stonebuck
stud-horse
tchneuman
thylacine
todlowrie
tree hyrax
tree shrew
trematode
trematoid
waterbuck
watervole
white bear
wild horse
wolverene
wolverine
woodchuck
woodshock
youngling
zoophagon

10

amorphozoa
amphibials
angora goat
angwantibo
animalcule
anthropoid
articulata
babiroussa
barasingha
Barbary ape
birch mouse
buckjumper
camelopard
cardophagi
catarrhine
chevrotain
chimpanzee
chinchilla
chiroptera
chousingha
coach-horse
cockatrice
cottontail
Diphyodont
dolichotis
draft-horse
fallow deer
fieldmouse
fistulidae
giant panda
halmaturus
hartebeest
hippogriff
hippogryff
housemouse
human-being
Kodiak bear
Malay tapir
marsupials
monotremes
muscardine

musk beaver
natterjack
paddymelon
Persian cat
pichiciago
pilot whale
pine marten
prairie dog
pygmy shrew
quadricorn
quadrumana
raccoon dog
rhinoceros
right whale
river horse
rock badger
rock rabbit
ruminantia
saki monkey
scavernick
shrew-mouse
starveling
Thecodonts
vampire bat
vespertilio
wildebeest
wishtonwish
woolly lemur

11

American elk
anoplothere
barbastelle
black cattle
blood-sucker
branchireme
brown hyena
chlamyphore
digitigrade
douroucouli
entomophaga
fistulidans
flying lemur
flying mouse
fox squirrel
Grevy's zebra
grizzly-bear
horned-horse
insectivora
jumping deer
kangaroo rat
killer whale
Megatherium
mountain cat
orang-outang
pipistrelle
prairie wolf
Pterodactyl
red kangaroo
red squirrel
rock wallaby
sea elephant
snow leopard

12

anthropoglot
Barbary sheep
Bengal monkey
catamountain
chlamyphorus
chrysochlore
draught-horse

elephant seal
ferae-naturae
flittermouse
grey squirrel
harvest mouse
hippopotamus
horseshoe bat
klipspringer
Megalosaurus
mountain hare
mountain lion
pachydermata
Paleotherium
pouched mouse
rhesus monkey
rock squirrel
scheltopusik
Shetland pony
spider monkey
spotted hyena
striped hyena

tree kangaroo
water opossum
woolly monkey

13

Abyssinian cat
Anoplotherium
Australian cat
Bactrian camel
bearded lizard
carriage horse
Chapman's zebra
Cheirotherium
chinchilla cat
European bison
galeopithecus
golden hamster
hermaphrodite
Indian buffalo

laughing hyena
mountain zebra
Parry's wallaby
polyprotodont
ring-tail coati
sable antelope
semnopithecus
shorthorn bull
solidungulate
spiny anteater
Tasmanian wolf
tree porcupine

14

Australian bear
bridled wallaby
Burchell's zebra
crab-eating seal
dormouse-possum

flying squirrel
Indian elephant
Indian pangolin
Isabelline bear
laughing hyaena
marmoset monkey
Patagonian cavy
snoeshoe rabbit
Tasmanian devil

15

African elephant
American buffalo
Bennett's wallaby
flying phalanger
rabbit bandicoot
sabretooth tiger
Tasmanian possum
Thomson's gazelle

Birds

2 AND 3

auk
cob
daw
emu
fum
hen
jay
ka
kae
kea
kia
mew
moa
owl
pen
pie
poe
roc
ruc
tit
tui

4

alca
anas
arco
aves
barb
baya
bird
bubo
chat
cock
coot
crax
crow
dodo
dove
duck
erne
eyas
fowl
gawk
gier

guan
gull
hawk
hern
huia
ibis
kaka
kite
kiwi
knot
koel
lark
loom
loon
lory
mina
myna
naff
nias
nyas
pauw
pavo
pern
pica
piet
pope
pout
rail
rhea
rixy
rock
rook
ruff
rukh
runt
rype
shag
skua
smee
smew
sora
sore
swan
taha
teal
tern
tody
wavy

wren
xema
yaup
yunx
zati

5

agami
ajuru
amsel
amzel
ardea
biddy
bongo
booby
bowet
brant
bucco
capon
chick
claik
colin
crake
crane
creak
daker
didus
diver
drake
dunny
eagle
egret
eider
finch
galah
ganza
glede
goose
grebe
harpy
heron
hobby
jager
junco
larus
lowan

lyrie
macaw
madge
mavis
merle
minah
miner
monal
murre
mynah
nandu
noddy
ornis
ortyx
ousel
ouzel
owlet
pewet
pewit
picus
pipit
pitta
poult
purre
quail
radge
raven
reeve
robin
rodge
sacre
saker
sally
sasia
saury
scape
scarf
scaup
scray
senex
serin
shama
sitta
skite
snipe
solan
soree
spink

stare
stilt
stint
stork
strix
swift
tarin
terek
topau
topet
twite
umbre
urubu
veery
virgo
wader
wagel
whaup
wonga

6

aiglet
aigret
alcedo
alcyon
avocet
avoset
babbler
bantam
barbet
bonxie
bowess
brolga
buffel
bulbul
cagmag
canary
chough
chukar
citril
condor
corbie
corvus
coucal
cuckoo
culver
curlew
cushat
cygnet
cygnus
darter
dipper
drongo
ducker
dunlin
eaglet
einack
elanet
falcon
fulmar
galeen
gambet
gander
gannet
garrot
gentoo
godurt
godwit
gorhen
grakle
grouse
hacket
hagden
hareld

hoazin
hoopoe
hoopoo
jabiru
jacana
jaeger
jerkin
kakapo
kiddow
lanner
leipoa
linnet
loriot
magpie
marrot
martin
menura
merlin
merops
merula
missel
monaul
mopoke
mot-mot
musket
nandow
nestor
oriole
osprey
oxbird
parrot
paster
pavone
peahen
pecker
peewit
pernis
pigeon
plover
poulet
pouter
powter
puffin
pullet
pygarg
queest
quelea
redcap
reeler
roberd
roller
rotche
ruddoc
scobby
scoter
sea-bar
sea-cob
sea-mew
sea-pie
shrike
shrite
sicsac
siskin
smeath
strich
strick
sultan
tarsel
tercel
thrush
tirwit
tomtit
toucan
towhee
tringa

turbit
Turdus
turkey
turner
turtle
waggel
weaver
wigeon
willet
witwal
yaffle
ynambu
zivola
zoozoo

7

apteryx
attagas
attagen
awl-bird
babbler
barn owl
bee-bird
bittern
blue-cap
bluetit
buceros
bull-bat
bummalo
bunting
buphaga
bustard
buzzard
cackler
caponet
cariama
carvist
cat-bird
cheeper
chewink
chicken
ciconia
coaltit
coarser
cobswan
colibri
columba
corella
cotinga
courlan
cow-bird
creeper
cropper
Cuculus
dorhawk
dorking
dottrel
doucher
dovekie
dovelet
dum-bird
dunnock
egg-bird
emu-wren
fantail
fen duck
fern owl
fig-bird
fin-foot
flusher
gadwell
gavilan
gobbler
gorcock

gorcrow
goshawk
gosling
grackle
grallae
greylag
hacket
halcyon
harfang
harrier
hawk owl
hen-harm
hickway
hoatzin
horn owl
ice-bird
impeyan
jacamar
jackass
jackdaw
jacksaw
jacobin
jashawk
jedcock
kamichi
kestrel
killdee
kinglet
lagopus
lapwing
lavrock
Leghorn
lentner
lich-owl
lorilet
mallard
manakin
manikin
marabou
maracan
martlet
megamys
migrant
modwall
moorhen
motacil
moth-owl
mudlark
muggent
ortolan
oscines
ostrich
oven-tit
pandion
partlet
peacock
peafowl
pelican
penguin
percher
peterel
phaeton
phoenix
pinnock
pintado
pintail
pochard
poe-bird
poultry
puttock
quabird
quetzel
raddock
rantock
redhead
redpoll

197

redwing
robinet
rooster
rosella
rotchie
ruddock
sakenet
sawbill
scammel
scooper
sea-crow
sea-fowl
seagull
sea-hawk
senegal
seriema
serinus
shirley
simargh
sirgang
skimmer
skylark
snow-owl
sparrow
squacco
staniel
stannel
stanyel
stumpie
sturnus
sunbird
swallow
swimmer
tadorna
tanager
tarrock
tiercel
tinamou
tinamus
titlark
titling
touraco
tree tit
trochil
tumbler
turakoo
vulture
vulturn
wagtail
wapacut
warbler
waxbill
waxwing
weebill
whooper
widgeon
wimbrel
witlock
witwall
wood owl
wrybill
wryneck
yeldrin

8

accentor
aigrette
alcatras
amadavat
arapunga
avadavit
beam-bird
becafico
bee-eater

bell-bird
blackcap
bluebird
blue-wren
boat-bill
boat-tail
bobolink
bob-white
bockelet
bockeret
brancher
brevipen
bush chat
bush lark
calandra
calangay
caneroma
caracara
cargoose
clot-bird
cockatoo
cockerel
coquimbo
corn bird
curassow
cursores
cutwater
dabchick
daker-hen
dandy-hen
didapper
dinornis
dipchick
dorr-hawk
dotterel
duck-hawk
duckling
dun-diver
eagle-owl
estridge
fauvette
fig-eater
finnikin
firetail
fish-hawk
flamingo
flycatcher
gairfowl
gamecock
gang-gang
garefowl
garganey
great tit
grey teal
grosbeak
guachero
hawfinch
hazel-hen
hemipode
hernshaw
hickwall
hornbill
hula-bird
keskidee
killdeer
kingbird
landrail
langshan
lanneret
laverock
lorikeet
love-bird
lyrebird
marabout
marsh tit
megapode

mina bird
mire crow
moorcock
moorfowl
moorgame
morillon
musk duck
mute swan
mynabird
nestling
nightjar
notornis
nuthatch
paitrick
parakeet
paroquet
peachick
petchary
pheasant
plungeon
popinjay
puff-bird
redshank
redstart
ring dove
ring-tail
rock dove
screamer
scrub-tit
sea-eagle
shelduck
shoebill
shoveler
sittella
snowy owl
songbird
songlark
songster
starling
struthio
swamphen
tanagers
tantalus
tawny owl
thrasher
thresher
throstle
titmouse
tomnoddy
tragopan
tuke-nose
umbrette
waterhen
wheatear
whimbrel
whinchat
whip-bird
whistler
white-ear
white-eye
wildfowl
woodchat
woodcock
wood duck
woodlark
xanthura
yeldring
yeldrock
yoldring
zopilote

9

accipiter
albatross

andorinha
ant-thrush
autophagi
bean goose
beccafico
bell-minah
bergander
birgander
blackbird
black cock
black duck
black swan
blacktail
black tern
blue crane
bower-bird
brambling
broadbill
brown hawk
bullfinch
buzzardet
campanero
cassowary
cereopsis
chaffinch
chatterer
chevalier
chickling
church owl
cockatiel
columbine
cormorant
corncrake
crossbill
dandy-cock
deinornis
dowitcher
eagle-hawk
eider duck
field-duck
fieldfare
field wren
fig parrot
figpecker
firecrest
francolin
French pie
friar-bird
fringilla
frogmouth
gallinule
gerfalcon
gier-eagle
glaucopis
goldcrest
golden-eye
goldfinch
goldspink
goosander
grassbird
grass wren
great skua
grey heron
grossbeak
guillemot
guinea-hen
gyrfalcon
heathbird
heathcock
heronshaw
horned owl
Jenny-wren
jerfalcon
kittiwake
lint-white
log-runner

lorrikeet
macartney
mallemuck
mango bird
marshbird
merganser
merulidan
mouse-hawk
mud-sucker
muscicapa
natatores
night hawk
ossifrage
paradisea
paraquito
pardalote
parrakeet
parroquet
partridge
peregrine
phalarope
pied-goose
ptarmigan
quachilto
razorbill
redbreast
red grouse
rhynchops
rifle-bird
ring-ousel
rosefinch
rossignol
sandpiper
scratcher
scrub-bird
scrub-fowl
scrub-wren
shearbill
sheldrake
shitepoke
shoveller
shrike-tit
silver-eye
skunk-bird
snake-bird
snow goose
sooty tern
spinebill
spoonbill
stick-bird
stilt-bird
stock-dove
stonechat
stone-hawk
storm-bird
strigidae
swamp-hawk
swine-pipe
talegalla
tetraonid
thickhead
thornbill
tiercelet
trochilus
trumpeter
turnstone
waterbird
waterfowl
water-rail
wedgebill
wheat-bird
whiteface
whitetail
widow-bird
wild goose
willow tit

windhover
woodspite
wyandotte

10

aberdevine
ant-catcher
Arctic skua
Arctic tern
bell-magpie
bird of prey
blight-bird
blue-bonnet
blue-breast
blue-throat
boobook owl
brent goose
budgerigar
budgerygah
burrow-duck
butter-bird
butterbump
canary bird
canvas-back
chiffchaff
coddy-moddy
cow-bunting
crested tit
crow-shrike
demoiselle
didunculus
dishwasher
dollar bird
dusky minah
dusky robin
ember goose
eurylaimus
eyas-musket
fledgeling
flycatcher
fratercula
goatmilker
goatsucker
goldhammer
grassfinch
greenfinch
greenshank
grey falcon
grey parrot
grey plover
ground dove
ground lark
ground robin
guinea-fowl
gymnocitta
hen-harrier
honeyeater
honey-guide
hooded crow
jungle-fowl
kingfisher
king parrot
kookaburra
love-parrot
magpie-lark
mallee-fowl
maned-goose
meadow-lark
mutton-bird
night heron
night raven
noisy-minah
nutcracker
parson-bird

peewee-lark
petty-chaps
pratincole
ramphastos
regent-bird
rock parrot
rock pigeon
salpinctes
sanderling
sandgrouse
sandmartin
sassorolla
screech-owl
sea-swallow
shearwater
silver-gull
solan goose
song shrike
song thrush
summer-duck
tailor-bird
talegallus
tit-warbler
tree-runner
tropic-bird
turkey-cock
turtle dove
water-ousel
wattle-bird
weasel-coat
whidah-bird
white brant
white egret
white stork
whydah-bird
willow wren
wonga-wonga
woodgrouse
woodpecker
wood-pigeon
wood-shrike
yaffingale
yellow-bird
yellowlegs
zebra finch

11

apostle-bird
banded stilt
black falcon
black martin
bonebreaker
bristle-bird
brush-turkey
bush-creeper
butcher-bird
Canada goose
carrion crow
cattle egret
chanticleer
cock-sparrow
conirostres
corn bunting
Dorking fowl
dragoon-bird
fairy martin
fallow finch
flock pigeon
frigate-bird
fruit-pigeon
gallows-bird
gnat-snapper
golden eagle
grallatores

grey wagtail
harrier-hawk
herring gull
hooded robin
house martin
humming-bird
insectivora
kestrel-hawk
king penguin
lammergeier
leatherhead
leptodactyl
lily-trotter
magpie-goose
meadow-pipit
mocking-bird
mulga parrot
Muscovy duck
nightingale
Pacific gull
plain-turkey
powerful-fowl
procellaria
pterodactyl
punchinello
quail-thrush
querguedule
rainbow-bird
reed bunting
reed warbler
rock warbler
scarlet ibis
scissor-bill
sea-pheasant
shell-parrot
shrike-robin
singing-bird
snow-bunting
soldier-bird
sparrowhawk
stone curlew
stone plover
storm petrel
tree-creeper
tree sparrow
tree swallow
wall-creeper
whitethroat
whooper swan
wood-swallow
yellow robin

12

Adele penguin
adjutant bird
burrowing-owl
capercaillie
cardinal-bird
crested grebe
cuckoo-shrike
curvirostral
dentirostres
falcon-gentle
fairy penguin
fissirostres
golden oriole
golden plover
grass warbler
ground thrush
hedge sparrow
honey-buzzard
house sparrow
marsh harrier
marsh warbler

199

missel-thrush
mistel-thrush
mourning-dove
musophagidae
nutmeg-pigeon
painted quail
pallid-cuckoo
peaceful dove
pink cockatoo
razor-grinder
red-head finch
sage-thrasher
sedge warbler
shrike-thrush
stone-chatter
stone's-mickle
stormy petrel
stubble-goose
stubble-quail
swamp-harrier

tachydromian
tenuirosters
tiger-bittern
turbit-pigeon
turner-pigeon
water-wagtail
white goshawk
yellowhammer

13

Baltimore bird
barnacle goose
black cockatoo
carrier pigeon
coachwhip-bird
crested pigeon
fantail pigeon

long-tailed tit
mistletoe-bird
musk parrakeet
owlet-nightjar
oystercatcher
plain-wanderer
recurviroster
red-wattle bird
rosella parrot
secretary bird
shining parrot
spider-catcher
stink-pheasant
swallow-shrike
tumbler-pigeon
turkey-buzzard
white cockatoo
willow warbler
yellow bunting
yellow wagtail

14

babbling thrush
bird of paradise
canvas-back duck
diamond sparrow
double-bar finch
golden pheasant
horned screamer
king-lory parrot
Manx shearwater
mountain thrush
nankeen kestrel
rhinoceros-bird
robin-redbreast
silver pheasant
spotted harrier
tawny frogmouth
welcome swallow
whistling eagle

Dogs

3 AND 4

chow
cur
lym
minx
peke
pom
pug
pup
rach
rug
tike
tyke

5

bitch
boxer
brach
cairn
corgi
dhole
dingo
hound
husky
laika
pi-dog
pooch
puppy
spitz
whelp

6

bandog
barbet
basset
beagle
borzoi
canine
cocker
collie
Eskimo
gun-dog
jowler
lap-dog
limmer

pariah
poodle
pug-dog
pye-dog
pyrame
ranger
ratter
saluki
setter
shough
talbot
toy dog

7

beardie
bird-dog
bulldog
clumber
deer-dog
dry-foot
griffon
harrier
lion-dog
lurcher
mastiff
mongrel
pointer
samoyed
spaniel
starter
tarrier
terrier
tumbler
whippet
wolf-dog

8

Airedale
Alsatian
Blenheim
chow-chow
coach-dog
demi-wolf
Derby dog
Doberman
elkhound

field-dog
foxhound
hound-dog
house dog
keeshond
Labrador
papillon
Pekinese
St. Hubert
sealyham
sheepdog
spitz dog
springer
turnspit
watchdog
water-dog

9

badger dog
boarhound
buckhound
chihuahua
dachshund
Dalmatian
deerhound
Eskimo dog
Great Dane
greyhound
harehound
Kerry blue
limehound
Llewellyn
Molossian
Pekingese
police dog
red setter
retriever
St. Bernard
Schnauzer
staghound
wolfhound
yellow dog

10

Bedlington
bloodhound

Clydesdale
dachshund
elterwater
fox terrier
Iceland dog
Maltese dog
otter hound
Pomeranian
prairie dog
schipperke
Welsh corgi
Welsh hound

11

Afghan hound
basset hound
Bruxelloise
bull mastiff
bull terrier
carriage dog
Irish setter
Kerry beagle
King Charles
Skye terrier

12

Belvoir hound
Cairn terrier
Dandy Dinmont
gazelle hound
German collie
Gordon setter
Irish spaniel
Irish terrier
Newfoundland
Saint Bernard
Saintongeois
shepherd's dog
water spaniel
Welsh terrier

13

Alpine spaniel
border terrier

Boston terrier	
cocker spaniel	**14** AND **15**
Dandie Dinmont	Aberdeen terrier (15)
English setter	Airedale terrier (15)
French bulldog	blue Gascon hound (15)
Scotch terrier	Brussels griffon (15)
southern hound	clumber spaniel (14)
Sussex spaniel	Cuban bloodhound (15)

Egyptian bassett (15)	Norfolk springer (15)
English springer (15)	porcelaine hound (15)
golden retriever (15)	Pyrenean mastiff (15)
Highland terrier (15)	Scottish terrier (15)
Irish wolfhound (14)	Siberian wolf-dog (15)
Japanese spaniel (15)	springer spaniel (15)
Lakeland terrier (15)	Thibetan mastiff (15)
Norfolk spaniel (14)	Tibetan mastiff (14)

Fish, etc.

2–4

amia
bass
bib
blay
bley
bret
brit
burt
cale
carp
chad
char
chub
clam
cod
coho
crab
cusk
dab
dace
dar
dare
dart
dorn
dory
eel
eft
elva
esox
fash
file
fin
gar
ged
goby
grig
hake
huck
huso
id
ide
jack
kelt
keta
ling
lipp
lomp
luce
mago
mort
newt
opah
orc
orca
orfe
parr
peal
pike
pope
pout

quab
ray
roe
rudd
ruff
sapo
scad
scar
scup
shad
snig
sole
tai
tau
tope
tuna
tusk
zant

5

ablen
ablet
allis
angel
apode
banny
beroe
binny
bleak
bleck
bogue
boops
bream
brill
charr
cisco
cobia
cuddy
cudle
doree
dorse
elops
fleck
fusus
gadus
gibel
gummy
guppy
julis
loach
loche
maray
minim
moray
morse
mugil
muray
murry
mysis
myxon

nurse
perch
phoca
piper
pogge
porgy
poulp
powan
prawn
reeve
roach
roker
ruffe
saith
salmo
saury
scrod
scurf
sepia
sewin
shark
skate
smelt
smolt
smout
smowt
snook
solen
sprag
sprat
sprod
squid
sudak
sweep
tench
toado
togue
torsk
troll
trout
tunny
twait
whale
whelk
whiff
witch

6

alburn
alevin
allice
anabas
barbel
beakie
belone
beluga
blenny
blower
bonito
bounce

bowfin
braise
buckie
burbot
caplin
caranx
cepola
cheven
chevin
clupea
cockle
comber
conger
cultch
cuttle
dagoba
dentex
diodon
doctor
dugong
dun-cow
ellops
finnan
gadoid
ganoid
gardon
ginkin
goramy
grilse
groper
gunnel
gurnet
hilsah
hussar
isopod
jerkin
kipper
launce
loligo
margot
meagre
medusa
megrim
milter
minnow
morgay
mud-eel
mullet
mussel
narwal
otaria
oyster
partan
plaice
pollan
porgie
poulpe
puffer
puller
quahog
redcap
red-cod

201

red-eye
remora
robalo
rochet
romero
roughy
ruffin
runner
sabalo
sadina
saithe
salmon
samlet
sander
sardel
sauger
saurel
saynay
scarus
scurff
sea-ape
sea-bat
sea-cow
sea-dog
sea-egg
sea-fox
sea-hog
sea-owl
sea-pad
sea-pig
sephen
shanny
shiner
shrimp
snacol
soosoo
sucker
tailor
tarpon
tarpum
tautog
tawtog
tiburo
tomcord
trygon
turbit
turbot
twaite
ulican
urchin
vendis
wapper
weever
whaler
winkle
wirrah
wrasse
zander
zeidae
zingel

7

abalone
acaleph
actinia
ale-wife
anchovy
asterid
batfish
bergylt
bloater
blue-cap
blue-eye
bocking

bonetta
box-fish
brassie
bubbler
bummalo
calamar
capelin
cat-fish
catodon
cetacea
cichlid
cidaris
cod-fish
codling
cow-fish
crabite
croaker
crucian
crusien
cyprine
dog-fish
dolphin
drummer
dun-fish
echinus
eel-fare
eel-pout
escolar
fiddler
fin-back
fin-fish
garfish
garpike
garvock
girrock
gladius
goldney
gourami
gournet
grampus
grouper
grundel
grunter
gudgeon
gunard
gwiniad
gwyniad
haddock
halibut
herling
herring
homelyn
houting
jewfish
keeling
lampern
lamprey
latchet
lobster
long-tom
mahseer
manatee
manchet
merling
monodon
moon-egg
morwong
mud-fish
muraena
murexes
murices
narwhal
nautili
oar-fish
octopus
old-wife

pandore
pegasus
pen-fish
pig-fish
pointer
pollack
pollard
pollock
polypus
pomfret
quinnet
rat-tail
red-fish
reef-eel
ripsack
rock-cod
ronchil
ronquil
rorqual
sand-eel
sardine
sawfish
schelly
scomber
sea-bear
sea-calf
sea-fish
sea-lion
sea-pike
sea-wolf
shadine
silurus
skegger
smerlin
snapper
sock-eye
spawner
sphyrna
squalus
sterlet
stripey
sun-fish
thwaite
tiddler
top-knot
torgoch
torpedo
tub-fish
ulichon
umbrine
vendace
whiting
worm-eel
xippias

8

acalepha
albacore
albicore
ammodyte
anableps
anguilla
asterias
band-fish
barnacle
bill fish
blue fish
boarfish
bullhead
cachalot
cackerel
calamory
cetacean
coalfish

corystes
crawfish
crayfish
dapedium
dapedius
dragonet
drum-fish
eagle-ray
errantes
eulachon
exocetus
file-fish
fin-scale
fire-fish
flagtail
flatfish
flathead
flounder
forktail
fox-shark
frog-fish
gillaroo
gilt-head
glass-eel
goatfish
goldfish
graining
grayling
green eel
grub-fish
gymnotus
hair-tail
halicore
hand-fish
horn-beak
horn-fish
jentling
John Dory
jugulars
kelp-fish
king crab
king-fish
lady-fish
lancelet
land crab
lump-fish
lung-fish
mackerel
melanure
menhaden
moon-fish
moray eel
mormyrus
nannygai
numbfish
ophidion
pickerel
pigmy-eel
pilchard
pipe-fish
polyneme
Poor John
porpoise
raft-fish
red perch
rock-cale
rock-fish
rockling
sail-fish
salt-fish
sand-fish
sardelle
saw-shark
sea-devil
sea-horse
sea-perch

sea robin
shore-eel
siskiwit
snake-eel
sparling
spelding
speldrin
speldron
spirling
springer
spurling
starfish
sting-ray
sturgeon
sun-bream
surf-fish
tarwhine
teraglin
testacea
thornbut
thrasher
thresher
toad-fish
trevalla
troutlet
tusk-fish
water-fox
weed-fish
wolf-fish

9

acalephae
acipenser
angel-fish
Argentine
ascidians
asteroida
barracuda
blackfish
black sole
blue nurse
blue shark
blue sprat
bony bream
bulltrout
bummaloti
calamarys
chaetodon
cling-fish
cole-perch
conger eel
coral fish
coryphene
cover-clip
crampfish
crustacea
devil fish
dolphinet
echinidan
engraulis
finny-scad
fire-flair
fish-royal
fortesque
frost-fish
globe-fish
golomynka
grey nurse
hard-belly
hardyhead
hippodame
houndfish
hybodonts
jaculator

jellyfish
John Dorée
jollytail
kingstone
mango fish
menominee
murray cod
pilot fish
porbeagle
pyllopodo
razor fish
red mullet
river crab
roundhead
sand-lance
saury-pike
schnapper
sea-mullet
sea-needle
sea-nettle
sea-urchin
sheat-fish
silver-eel
spear-fish
stargazer
stingaree
sting-fish
stink-fish
stockfish
stomapoda
suctorian
surmullet
sweetlips
swordfish
thorn-back
threadfin
tittlebat
troutling
trumpeter
tunny fish
whitebait
whitefish
wobbegong

10

amblyopsis
amphytrite
angel-shark
angler fish
banstickle
barracoota
barracouta
basket fish
black bream
black whale
blind shark
blue groper
blue puller
bottle-nose
brown trout
butterfish
cestracion
clouded eel
clypeaster
cock-paddle
coelacanth
cowanyoung
ctenoidans
cuttlefish
demoiselle
dragon-fish
echinoderm
fiddle-fish
fingerling

fistularia
flute-mouth
flying fish
ganoidians
garter fish
ghost-shark
giant toado
goblin-fish
great skate
grey mullet
groundling
hammerhead
hermit crab
holothuria
knight-fish
loggerhead
lumpsucker
mirror dory
morris pike
Moses perch
parrot-fish
pearl perch
periwinkle
pigmy perch
pycnodonts
rapier fish
red gurnard
red morwong
red rockcod
ribbon-fish
rudder-fish
Samsonfish
sand-hopper
sand-mullet
sandy sprat
sea-garfish
sea-leopard
sea poacher
sea-unicorn
silver dory
silverfish
silverside
sperm whale
square-tail
sturionian
sucker-fish
tailor-fish
tassel-fish
tiger shark
tongue-sole
triple-tail
turret-fish
velvet-fish
weaver-fish
whale-shark
white shark
yellow-tail
zebra shark

11

balance-fish
banded toado
bellows-fish
black-angler
blue-pointer
bridled goby
brown-groper
brown-puller
carpet-shark
carp-gudgeon
chanda perch
common skate
common toado
crested goby

cycloidians
electric eel
electric ray
finner-whale
five-fingers
golden perch
green turtle
gurnet perch
herring-cale
hippocampus
jackass-fish
javelin-fish
Jumping-Joey
kingsnapper
leatherskin
leopard-fish
lepidosiren
little tunny
man-o'-war fish
Moorish idol
orange perch
peacock-fish
peacock-sole
pennant-fish
prickleback
pterichthys
rainbow-fish
red bullseye
red fire-fish
rock-whiting
salmon-trout
sand-whiting
school-shark
scleroderms
sea-elephant
sea-scorpion
silver-belly
silver perch
silver toado
smooth toado
soldier-crab
soldier-fish
starry toado
stickleback
stonelifter
surgeon-fish
swallow-fish
tallegalane
trumpet-fish
whistle-fish
wolf-herring

12

basking shark
black drummer
black rock-cod
blue trevally
coachwhip ray
cucumber-fish
dipterygians
dusky morwong
fan-tailed ray
fatherlasher
fighting-fish
forehead-fish
gargoyle-fish
giant herring
gray tusk-fish
oyster-blenny
painted saury
piked dog-fish
plectognathi
Plesiosaurus
rainbow-trout

rat-tailed ray
river garfish
rock flathead
scarlet bream
sentinel crab
silver mullet
smooth angler
Stout Long-Tom

13

allports perch
banded-pigfish
barred-garfish
Barred Long-Tom
black king-fish
black-trevally
branchiostoma
climbing perch
dactylopterus
dusky flathead
entomostracan
findon-haddock
finnan-haddock
flying gurnard
giant boar-fish
horse-mackerel

leafy seahorse
leatherjacket
long-finned eel
magpie-morwong
marbled angler
mountain-trout
ox-eyed herring
porcupine-fish
Red-Indian fish
salmon catfish
salt-water fish
sandpaper-fish
scarlet angler
Sergeant Baker
silver batfish
silver drummer
snub-nosed dart
southern tunny
spiny flathead
spiny seahorse
striped angler
thresher-shark
tiger-flathead

14

banded sea-perch

black stingaree
branchiostegan
brown-sweetlips
butterfly-bream
enaliosaurians
estuary cat-fish
Greenland-shark
Greenland-whale
king barracouta
king parrot-fish
little numbfish
Macquarie perch
many-banded sole
marine annelida
one-finned shark
painted gurnard
purple sea-perch
red gurnet-perch
river blackfish
short-finned eel
shovel-nosed ray
Slender Long-Tom
smooth flathead
spotted whiting
striped catfish
striped gudgeon
striped sea-pike
white horse-fish

15

acanthopterygii
Australian perch
Australian smelt
beaked coral-fish
bottle-nose shark
common stingaree
crusted flounder
crusted weed-fish
edriophthalmata
frigate mackerel
hairback herring
little cling-fish
little conger eel
long-finned perch
marbled flathead
painted dragonet
short sucker-fish
small-headed sole
smooth stingaree
spangled grunter
Spanish mackerel
spermaceti whale
spotted cat-shark
spotted eagle-ray
spotted pipe-fish
white-spotted ray

Fossils, shells, etc.

(f.s.) = fossil shell (s.) = shell

---

4 AND 5

amber
auger
baler
chama (s.)
chank (s.)
conch (s.)
cone (s.)
donax (s.)
drill (s.)
galea
gaper (s.)
murex (s.)
peuce
razor (s.)
snail (s.)
tooth (s.)
tulip (s.)
Venus (s.)
whelk (s.)

6

bonnet (s.)
buckie (s.)
chiton (s.)
cockle (s.)
cowrie
crinoid
fornix (s.)
helmet (s.)
jingle (s.)
limpet (s.)
macoma (s.)
matrix
mussel (s.)
natica (s.)
nerite (s.)

Ogygia
oyster (s.)
quahog (s.)
tellin (s.)
triton (s.)
trivea (s.)
turban (s.)
volute (s.)
winkle (s.)

7

abalone (s.)
artemis (s.)
astarte (s.)
Babylon
crabite
crinoid
discoid (s.)
fungite
muscite
neptune (s.)
ovulite
piddock (s.)
scallop (s.)
zoolite

8

ammonite (f.s.)
argonaut (s.)
ark shell (s.)
balanite
buccinum (s.)
capstone
ceratite
choanite
cololite

conchite (f.s.)
dendrite
dog whelk (s.)
ear shell (s.)
echinite
epiornis
escallop (s.)
favosite
fig shell (s.)
galerite
janthina (s.)
mangelia (s.)
muricite
mytilite
nautilus (s.)
penshell (s.)
phyllite
ram's horn (f.s.)
retinite
scaphite (f.s.)
sea snail
solenite (f.s.)
strombus (s.)
testacel (s.)
topshell (s.)
trochite
tunshell (s.)
volulite (f.s.)
volutite (f.s.)

9

aepiornis
alasmodon (s.)
alcyonite
belemnite
buccinite (f.s.)
cancerite
carpolite

clam shell (s.)
comb shell (s.)
cone shell (s.)
Conularia
copralite
corallite
crow stone
dicynodon
encrinite
fan mussel (s.)
file shell (s.)
foot shell (s.)
frog shell (s.)
giant clam (s.)
harp shell (s.)
hippurite
horn shell (s.)
lima shell (s.)
lithocarp
lithophyl
marsupite
miliolite (f.s.)
moon shell } (s.)
moon snail }
muscalite (f.s.)
nautilite
nummulite
ostracite (f.s.)
palmacite
patellite (f.s.)
polymorphe (s.)
reliquiae
rock-borer (s.)
serpulite (f.s.)
slip shell (s.)
star shell (s.)
stone lily
strombite (f.s.)
tellinite (f.s.)
trilobite

turbinite (f.s.)
turrilite (f.s.)
tusk shell (s.)

10

agate shell
batrachite
canoe shell (s.)
confervite
dendrolite
entomolite
entrochite
euomphalus (f.s.)
gyrogonite
odontolite
palmacites
periwinkle (s.)
razor shell (s.)
screw shell (s.)
snake stone (f.s.)
tiger shell (s.)
tubiporite
ulodendron
wentletrap (s.)
wing oyster (s.)
xanthidium

11

asterialite
asterolepis

basket shell (s.)
carpet shell (s.)
cetotolites
cheirolepis
dinotherium
fairy stones
finger shell (s.)
finger stone
furrowshell (s.)
gongiatites (f.s.)
helmet shell (s.)
ichthyolite
madreporite
margin shell
milleporite
mohair shell (s.)
needle shell }
needle whelk } (s.)
ornitholite
oyster drill (s.)
rhyncholite
sting winkle (s.)
strobolites
sunset shell (s.)
tiger cowrie (s.)
trough shell (s.)
turtle shell (s.)

12

amphibiolite
brocade shell (s.)
Chinaman's hat (s.)

cornu-ammonis (f.s.)
deinotherium
figured stone
holoptychis
Hungarian cap (s.)
lantern shell (s.)
macrotherium
megalichthys
pandora shell (s.)
pelican's foot (s.)
pentacrinite
saddle oyster (s.)
slipper shell (s.)
spindle shell (s.)
sundial shell (s.)
trumpet shell (s.)
zamiostrobus

13 AND 14

bothrodendron (13)
carboniferous (13)
conchyliaceous (f.s.) (14)
dolichosaurus (13)
lepidodendron (13)
lithoglyphite (13)
nacreous shells (s.) (14)
necklace shell (s.) (13)
palaeontology (13)
porphyry shell (s.) (13)
staircase shell (s.) (14)
syringodendron (14)
woodcock shell (s.) (13)

Insects, etc.

3 AND 4

ant
bee
bot
boud
bug
cleg
cob
dart
dor
flea
fly
frit
gnat
goat
grig
grub
lema
lice
mida
mite
moth
nit
pug
pupa
puss
puxi
sow
tant
tau
tick
wasp
zimb

5

acera
aphid
aphis
atlas
borer
brize
cimex
comma
culex
drake
drone
egger
emmet
eruca
hawk
imago
julus
larva
louse
midge
musca
ox-fly
pulex
splex
tinea
vespa

6

acarus
ant cow

aphids
aptera
ash-fly
bedbug
bee fly
beetle
blatta
botfly
breese
breeze
burnet
buzzer
caddis
chafer
chegre
chigoe
chigre
chinch
cicada
cicala
cimbex
cimiss
coccus
cocoon
crabro
dayfly
diurna
dog-bee
dog-fly
dorfly
earwig
elater
epeira
eupoda

evania
gadfly
hop-fly
hopper
hornet
jigger
lappet
larvae
locust
maggot
mantis
maybug
may-fly
midget
mygale
saw-fly
scarab
sow-bug
sphinx
spider
squill
termes
Thecla
Thrips
tipula
tsetse
veneer
weevil

7

acerans
agrilus

205

antenna
ant-hill
ant-lion
aphides
athalia
bean fly
beehive
bee moth
blowfly
boat fly
bruchus
bull-bee
bull fly
cheslip
coronet
crambus
cricket
culicid
cyclica
daphnia
deer-fly
diopsis
diptera
duck-ant
epeirid
epizoon
fig gnat
firefly
fish fly
fulgora
gallfly
globard
grayfly
gum moth
hexapod
hine-bee
horn-bug
hornfly
June bug
katydid
lady-cow
lampfly
microbe
papilio
path fly
pismire
puceron
pug moth
rose-bug
rotifer
salamis
sand fly
sawback
shad fly
skipper
stylops
termite
tin-worm
tortrix
wasp-fly
wax-moth
wood-ant

8

acaridan
adder-fly
antennae
arachnid
black ant
black-fly
braconid
bullhead
calandra

calandre
calomela
case-moth
cerambyx
chelifer
cocktail
Colorado
corn-moth
crane-fly
dog-louse
drake-fly
drone-bee
drone-fly
dybiscus
ephemera
erotylus
erycinia
flesh-fly
fossores
fruit-fly
gall-gnat
gall-wasp
gammarus
glow worm
goat-moth
green-fly
hawk-moth
honey-bee
horse-fly
house-fly
Isoptera
lace-lerp
ladybird
leaf-moth
lecanium
longhorn
mealy-bug
milleped
mosquito
mucivora
multiped
myriapod
natantes
night-fly
nocturna
parasite
paropsis
pedipalp
phyllium
pupipara
puss moth
queen ant
queen-bee
rotifera
sand-flea
sand-wasp
scolytus
sparkler
stone-fly
tenebrio
tetrapod
tung-tung
water-bug
water-fly
wheat-fly
white ant
white fly
woodlice
wood-mite
wood-moth

9

Amazon act
anopheles

aphid pest
arachnida
brimstone
bumble-bee
burrel-fly
butterfly
buzzardet
caddis fly
canker-fly
cedar-moth
centipede
chrysalis
churrworm
cicindela
clavicorn
cochineal
cockroach
corn-aphis
corn borer
crab-louse
cynipides
dermestes
dipterans
dorbeetle
dragon-fly
driver-ant
dumbledor
eggar-moth
egger-moth
eumenidae
fig-psylla
flying-ant
forest-fly
forficula
gall-midge
ghost-moth
grain-moth
hemiptera
hornet fly
humble-bee
ichneumon
lac-insect
leaf-louse
longicorn
membracid
millepede
orange-bug
orange-tip
pine-aphis
plant-lice
rug-weevil
sheep-lice
sheep-tick
spider-fly
squash-bug
sugar-mite
tanystoma
tarantula
tarentula
thysamura
tiger moth
tree-louse
tsetse-fly
tumblebug
turnip-fly
warble-fly
water-flea
wax-insect
wax-worker
wheat-moth
whirlygig
wood-borer
wood-louse
worker ant
worker bee
xylophaga

10

acacia-moth
bark-weevil
bird-spider
blister-fly
bluebottle
boll-weevil
bombardier
burnet moth
cabbage-fly
carpet moth
cheese-mite
chrysomela
coccinella
cockchafer
coleoptera
corn-weevil
death-watch
digger wasp
dolphin-fly
dorr-beetle
dung beetle
dynastidan
entomolite
ephemerans
fan-cricket
fen-cricket
flea-beetle
fritillary
frog-hopper
goat-chafer
hairstreak
hessian-fly
horse-emmet
jigger flea
lantern-fly
lappet moth
leaf-insect
leaf-roller
looper-moth
musk beetle
neuroptera
orthoptera
phylloxera
pine-weevil
plant-louse
red admiral
rice-weevil
ring-barker
rosechafer
saltigrade
sand-hopper
scarabeus
seed-weevil
sheep-louse
silver-fish
soldier ant
Spanish fly
stag beetle
star-psylla
stone-flies
timber-moth
twig-psylla
veneer moth
vorticella
willow-moth
winter-moth
wolf-spider
xylophagan

11

ametabolian
apple-sucker

arachnidans
auger beetle
balm-cricket
beehawk moth
black beetle
cabbage moth
cantharides
capharis bug
caterpillar
chalcia wasp
clothes moth
codling moth
coprophagan
cryptophago
drinker moth
Emperor moth
entomophaga
Ephemeridae
flour weevil
gallinipper
grain beetle
grasshopper
green-bottle
horse-marten
Hymenoptera
leaf-bag moth
Lepidoptera
mole-cricket
painted lady
pine-girdler
scorpion-fly

snout-beetle
sponge-flies
stick-insect
subulicorns
swallow-tail
terebrantia
tetrapteran
thysanurans
tiger-beetle
timber-borer
Trichoptera
tussock-moth
vine-fretter
water beetle
water-skater
wattle moths
wheel-animal
wood-fretter

12

bent-wing moth
buzzard-clock
cabbage white
carpenter ant
carpenter bee
cecropia moth
cinnabar moth
clerid-beetle
diadem spider

dimerosomata
flower-beetle
ground beetle
horned-clerid
horse-stinger
milk-white ant
money-spinner
pinhole-borer
red-cedar moth
Rhynchophera
saprophagans
scarab beetle
spruce sawfly
sycamore-moth
walking-stick
water-boatman
wattle-psylla
white admiral

13

black-lecanium
daddy-long-legs
diamond beetle
fig-leaf beetle
giant wood-moth
goliath-beetle
green wood-moth
ichneumon-wasp
jumping-spider

leather-jacket
lime-tree borer
mangold beetle
purple emperor
shot-hole borer
slender-weevil
tailed-emperor

14

bag-shelter moth
bimia-longicorn
cabbage-root fly
Colorado beetle
death's-head moth
elephant-beetle
fig-branch borer
Hercules beetle
ichneumon flies
ironbark saw-fly

15

furniture beetle
seedling-gum-moth
striped hawk-moth
thickset-chalcid
wheel-animalcule
yellow-longicorn

Marine growths, etc.

4 – 6

algae (5)
astrea (6)
coral (5)
dulse (5)
fungia (6)
kelp (4)
laver (5)
limpet (6)
mussel (6)
naiads (6)
polyp (5)
sponge (6)
tang (4)
tangle (6)
varec (5)
ware (4)
wrack (5)

7 AND 8

actinia (7)
agar agar (8)
alcyonic (8)
astraea (7)
badioga (7)
barnacle (8)
blubber (7)
calycle (7)
eschara (7)
fungite (7)
gulf weed (8)
polypary (8)
polypus (7)
porifera (8)
red algae (8)
red coral (8)
sea moss (7)

seaweed (7)
seawrack (8)
tubipore (8)
zoophyte (8)

9

alcyoneae
alcyonite
bathybius
blue algae
Irish moss
madrepore
millepore
nullipore
pink coral
sea nettle
zoophytes

10 AND OVER

abrotanoid (10)
acorn barnacle (13)
alva marina (10)
animal flower (12)
bladder kelp (11)
bladderwrack (12)
brown algae (10)
coral zoophytes (14)
goose barnacle (13)
lithodendron (12)
lithogenous (11)
lithophyte (12)
marine plants (12)
milliporite (11)
sea anemone (10)
tubiporite (10)

Molluscs

3 – 5

bulla
chank
clam
clio
ensis
gaper
helix
murex
mya
sepia
slug

snail
solen
spat
squid
unio
venus
whelk

6

buckie
chiton

cockle
cuttle
dodman
dolium
isopod
limpet
loligo
mantle
mussel
naiads
nerite
ostrea
oyster

pecten
quahog
sea ear
teredo
triton
voluta
winkle

7

acerans
actaeon

aplysia
ascidia
balanus
bivalve
diceras
eschera
etheria
glaucus
isopod
mollusc
mytilus
nauplii
octopod
octopus
patella
piddock
polyzoa
purpura
quahaug
scallop
scollop
sea hare
spirula
taccata
tellina

8

anodonta
argonaut
blue-nose
buccinum
decapoda
mollusca
nautilus
ostracea
pagurian
pedireme
sea lemon
spirifer
strombus
teredine
tridacna
tunicary

9

acephalan
clausilia
dentalium

dolabella
gastropod
giant clam
hodmandod
lithodome
ostracian
pteropods
scaphopod
shellfish

10

amphineura
amphitrite
brachiopod
cephalopod
conchifera
cuttlefish
date-mussel
haliotidae
heteropoda
periwinkle
razorshell

stone borer
stone eater

11

dragon shell
fasciolaria
gasteropoda
pearl oyster
river oyster
siphonifers
terebratula
trachelipod

12 AND OVER

boring mussel (12)
cyclobranchiata (15)
entomostomata (13)
lamellibranch (13)
tectibranchiata (15)

Reptiles and amphibians

3 – 5

aboma
adder
agama
anole
anura
asp
aspic
boa
bom
cobra
draco
eft
elaps
emys
frog
gecko
guana
hydra
jiboa
kaa
krait
kufi
mamba
newt
olm
pama
rana
skink
snake
toad
viper
waral
worm

6

anolis
caiman
cayman
daboia
dipsas
dragon

gavial
hydrus
iguana
karait
lizard
moloch
mugger
python
Sauria
taipan
triton
turtle
worrel

7

axolotl
chelone
coluber
gharial
ghavial
hicatee
labarri
lacerta
langaha
monitor
ophidia
paddock
rattler
saurian
scincus
serpent
snapper
tadpole
testudo
tuatara
urodela
varanus
zonurus

8

acontias
amphibia

anaconda
asp viper
basilisk
bull frog
cat snake
cerastes
chelonia
Congo eel
dinosaur
dragonet
fox snake
hiccatee
horn toad
jararaca
keelback
lachesis
matamata
moccasin
pit viper
rat snake
red snake
ringhals
sand fish
sand toad
sea snake
slow-worm
terrapin
tortoise
tree frog
typhlops

9

alligator
batrachia
blind-worm
blue krait
boomslang
chameleon
corn snake
crocodile
dart snake
eyed skink
galliwasp

giant frog
giant toad
green toad
hamadryad
horned asp
king cobra
king snake
marsh frog
Ophidians
pine snake
Pterosaur
puff adder
ring snake
terrapeen
tree snake
water newt
whip snake
wolf snake

10

amphibians
black mamba
black snake
bushmaster
clawed frog
cockatrice
copperhead
coral snake
Cotylosaur
dabb lizard
death adder
Diplodocus
edible frog
eyed lizard
false viper
fer-de-lance
glass snake
grass snake
green mamba
green racer
green snake
hellbender
horned frog

Mosasaurus
natterjack
night adder
Plesiosaur
river snake
rock python
salamander
sand lizard
sea serpent
smooth newt
tic polonga
tiger snake
wall lizard
water pilot
water snake

11

banded krait
black cayman
carpet viper
cottonmouth
crested newt

flying snake
Gaboon viper
gartersnake
gila monster
green lizard
green turtle
horned viper
Ichthyosaur
Indian cobra
lace monitor
leopard frog
midwife toad
Ophiosaurus
Pterodactyl
rattlesnake
royal python
smooth snake
Stegosaurus
Surinam toad
thorn lizard
thorny devil
Triceratops
water lizard
water python

12

Brontosaurus
chained snake
chicken snake
flying lizard
green tree boa
horned iguana
horned lizard
Hylaesaurus
Komodo dragon
leopard snake
pond tortoise

13 AND OVER

aquatic lizard (13)
boa constrictor (14)
brown tree snake (14)
coach-whip snake (14)
cobra de capello (14)
Dolichosaurus (13)
egg-eating snakes (15)

fire salamander (14)
four-lined snake (14)
frilled lizard (13)
giant tortoise (13)
golden tree frog (14)
golden tree snake (15)
green pit viper (13)
green tree frog (13)
Himalayan viper (14)
horn-nosed viper (14)
Ichthyosaurus (13)
long-nosed viper (14)
Nile crocodile (13)
painted terrapin (15)
rat-tailed snake (14)
Russell's viper (13)
saw-scaled viper (14)
schaapsticker (13)
snake-eyed skink (14)
snapping turtle (14)
spade-foot toad (13)
spotted lizard (13)
Tyrannosaurus (13)
water moccasin (13)

NATURAL HISTORY   (2) PLANTS
Cereals, etc.

3 AND 4

bere
bigg
bran
corn
dari
dohl
dura
far
gram
malt
meal
oats
poar
rice
rye
sago
zea

5

brank
durra

emmer
ervum
fundi
grama
grist
grout
maize
mummy
paddy
panic
pulse
spelt
straw
typha
wheat

6 AND 7

barley (6)
casava (6)
corncob (7)
darnel (6)
dhurra (6)

farina (6)
groats (6)
hominy (6)
mealie (6)
meslin (6)
millet (6)
nocake (6)
raggee (6)
rokeage (7)
shorts (6)
sorghum (7)
tapioca (7)
zea mays (7)

8 AND 9

arrowroot (9)
buckwheat (9)
espiotte (8)
garavance (9)
mangcorn (8)
middlings (9)
pearl rice (9)

pot barley (9)
seed corn (8)
seed grain (9)
semolina (8)
sweet corn (9)

10 AND OVER

barleycorn (10)
barleymeal (10)
German millet (12)
Guinea corn (10)
Indian corn (10)
Indian millet (12)
mountain rice (12)
pearl barley (11)
pearl millet (11)
Scotch barley (12)
spring wheat (11)
summer wheat (11)
turkey wheat (11)
winter barley (11)
winter wheat (11)

Flowers

3 AND 4

aloe
arum
balm
flag
geum
iris
ixia
lily
lote
may

musk
pink
rose
weld
whin
wold

5

agave
aspic

aster
avens
blite
briar
broom
canna
daisy
erica
faham
flora
gilia
gorse

henna
lilac
linum
lotus
lupin
orris
ox-eye
oxlip
padma
pagle
pansy
peony

petal
phlox
poker
poppy
sepal
stock
tansy
thyme
tulip
viola
yucca
yulan

6

acacia
acaena
alpine
arnica
azalea
balsam
bellis
bennet
borage
cactus
cistus
clover
coleus
cosmea
cosmos
crocus
dahlia
datura
fennel
iberis
kochia
lupine
madder
mallow
malope
mimosa
myrtle
nerine
nuphar
orchid
orchis
paigle
reseda
rocket
rosula
salvia
scilla
sesame
silene
sundew
thrift
violet
wattle
zinnia

7

aconite
alonsoa
aloysia
alyssum
anchusa
anemone
begonia
blawort
blewert
blossom
bouquet
bugloss

campion
candock
catmint
chaplet
chelone
chicory
clarkia
cowslip
cup rose
cytisus
day lily
deutzia
dittany
dog rose
festoon
freesia
fuchsia
gazania
genista
gentian
gerbera
godetia
heather
hyacine
jacinth
jasmine
jessamy
jonquil
kingcup
lantana
linaria
lobelia
lupinus
marybud
may-lily
melissa
milfoil
mimulus
nelumbo
nemesia
nigella
nosegay
opuntia
papaver
petunia
picotee
primula
rambler
sea-pink
seringa
spiraea
statice
succory
syringa
tagetes
tea rose
thistle
ursinia
verbena
vervain
witloof

8

abutilon
acanthus
achillia
ageratum
amaranth
angelica
arum lily
asphodel
aubretia
auricula
bartonia

bedstraw
bignonia
bluebell
buddleia
calamint
camellia
capsicum
catchfly
clematis
cockspur
cyclamen
daffodil
dianthus
dicentra
dropwort
erigeron
foxglove
gardenia
geranium
girasole
gladiola
gladiole
glaucium
gloriosa
gloxinia
harebell
helenium
hepatica
hibiscus
hottonia
hyacinth
japonica
laburnum
larkspur
lavatera
lavender
magnolia
marigold
martagon
moss rose
musk rose
myosotis
nenuphat
nymphaea
oleander
phacetia
phormium
plumbago
pond lily
primrose
rock-rose
scabious
skull-cap
snowdrop
stapelia
starwort
sweetpea
tigridia
toad-flax
tuberose
valerian
veronica
viscaria
wild rose
wisteria
woodbind
woodbine
xanthium

9

Aaron's-rod
achimines
amaryllis

anagallis
aquilegia
buttercup
calendula
campanula
candytuft
carnation
carthamus
celandine
cherry pie
China rose
cineraria
clove pink
cockscomb
colt's foot
columbine
coreopsis
corn-poppy
dandelion
digitalis
dog violet
dove's foot
edelweiss
eglantine
forsythia
gladiolus
golden rod
hollyhock
hydrangea
jessamine
kniphofia
lotus lily
mayflower
moon daisy
narcissus
nemophila
pimpernel
polygonum
pyrethrum
saxifrage
speedwell
spikenard
sunflower
tiger lily
twayblade
verbascum
water flag
waterlily
wolf's-bane

10

agapanthus
amaranthus
bell flower
caffre lilly
calliopsis
China aster
chionodoxa
cinquefoil
coquelicot
cornflower
corn violet
crane's-bill
crow flower
damask rose
delphinium
Easter lily
fritillary
gaillardia
gelder rose
golden drop
gypsophila
heart's-ease
helianthus

heliophila
heliotrope
immortelle
lady's-smock
limnanthes
marguerite
mignonette
nasturtium
nightshade
orange lily
ox-eye-daisy
penny-royal
pentstemon
periwinkle
poinsettia
polianthus
potentilla
ranunculus
snapdragon
sweet briar
wallflower
white poppy
wind flower

11

antirrhinum
blood flower
cabbage rose
calandrinia

calceolaria
cheiranthus
convallaria
convolvulus
cotoneaster
everlasting
fig marigold
forget-me-not
gillyflower
globeflower
guelder rose
helichrysum
honey-flower
honeysuckle
kidney-vetch
London pride
loosestrife
love-in-a-mist
meadowsweet
pelargonium
pepper elder
poppy mallow
ragged robin
rambler rose
red-hot poker
schizanthus
sea lavender
spear flower
sweet rocket
sweet sultan
tiger flower

wild flowers
wood anemone
xeranthemum

12

apple blossom
autumn crocus
cuckoo-flower
heather bells
horn-of-plenty
Iceland poppy
Jacob's ladder
lady's slipper
old man's-beard
pasque flower
rhododendron
salpiglossis
shirley poppy
Solomon's seal
sweet william
virgin's bower

13

alpine flowers
blanket flower

bleeding heart
bougainvillea
Bristol flower
cherry blossom
Christmas rose
chrysanthemum
creeping jenny
eschscholtzia
grape-hyacinth
huntsman's horn
marsh marigold
orange blossom
passion flower
sweet calabash
traveller's joy
trumpet flower
water hyacinth

14 AND 15

Canterbury bell (14)
cardinal flower (14)
Christmas flower (15)
lily of the valley (15)
lords and ladies (14)
love-in-idleness (14)
Michaelmas daisy (15)
shepherd's purse (14)
star of Bethlehem (15)

Fruit

3 AND 4

akee
Cox
crab
date
fig
gage
gean
haw
hep
hip
kaki
lime
mast
nut
ogen
pear
pepo
plum
pome
rasp
skeg
sloe
ugli
uva

5

abhal
agava
agave
apple
arnot
betel
cubeb
drupe
eleot
grape

grout
guava
lemon
lichi
mango
melon
merry
morel
morus
olive
papaw
peach
pecan
prune
whort
whurt

6

almond
ananas
banana
biffin
cedrat
cherry
citron
citrus
cobnut
colmar
damson
drupel
durian
egriot
elk nut
groser
lichee
longan
loquat

lychee
mammee
medlar
muscat
nutmeg
orange
papaya
pawpaw
peanut
pignut
pippin
pomelo
quince
raisin
rennet
russet
samara
walnut
zapote

7

apricot
avocado
buckeye
bullace
capulin
catawba
cedrate
cheston
coconut
corinth
costard
currant
deal-nut
dessert
dog-wood
filbert
genipap

golding
hog-plum
karatas
kumquat
litchee
mahaleb
malmsey
mayduke
morello
naartje
pompion
pumpkin
quashey
rhubarb
satsuma
tangelo
wilding

8

allspice
bayberry
beechnut
bergamot
betelnut
bilberry
buckmast
burgamot
calabash
cat's-head
chestnut
coquilla
cream-nut
date-plum
dogberry
earthnut
fenberry
fig-apple
fox grape

211

hastings
hazelnut
honeydew
ivory nut
japonica
jonathan
mandarin
may apple
mulberry
muscadel
muscatel
musk pear
oleaster
pearmain
plantain
prunello
quandong
queening
rambutan
spondias
sweeting
tamarind
Valencia
whitsour

9

alkekengi
apple-john
aubergine
beechmast
blueberry
brazilnut
buck's horn
butternut
canteloup
carmelite
cherimoya
chokepear
corozo nut
crab-apple

cranberry
damascene
drupaceae
elvas plum
greengage
groundnut
hindberry
king apple
love apple
melocoton
mirabelle
monkey pot
muscadine
musk-apple
musk-melon
nectarine
ortanique
oxycoccus
persimmon
pineapple
pistachio
rambootan
rambostan
raspberry
star apple
tamarinds
tangerine
victorine
Worcester

10

adam's apple
bird cherry
blackberry
blackheart
breadfruit
cantaloupe
charentais
clementine
clingstone
corozo nuts

cream-fruit
damask plum
dried fruit
elderberry
gooseberry
granadilla
grapefruit
Indian date
loganberry
Madeira nut
mangosteen
marking nut
melocotoon
orange musk
pome-citron
pompelmous
queen apple
redcurrant
stone fruit
strawberry
watermelon
wild cherry
winter pear

11

anchovy pear
bitter apple
blood orange
candleberry
China orange
chokecherry
coquilla nut
French berry
granny smith
huckleberry
hurtleberry
Jaffa orange
leathercoat
monkey bread
myrtle berry

navel orange
pomegranate
pompelmoose
russet apple
scuppernong
winter apple

12

bitter almond
blackcurrant
chaumontelle
Chester grape
chocolate nut
cochineal fig
cooking apple
custard apple
passionfruit
pistachio nut
Victoria plum
white currant
whortleberry
winter cherry
winter citron

13 AND OVER

alligator pear (13)
Barbados cherry (14)
Blenheim orange (14)
Cape gooseberry (14)
Catherine pear (13)
conference pear (14)
cornelian cherry (15)
golden delicious (15)
mandarin orange (14)
morello cherry (13)
preserved fruit (14)
Seville orange (13)

Herbs and spices

3 – 5

anise
balm
basil
bay
chive
clary
cress
cumin
dill
grass
mace
mint
myrrh
rape
rue
sage
senna
tansy
thyme
woad

6

bennet
betony

borage
capers
chilli
chives
cloves
endive
fennel
galega
garlic
ginger
hyssop
isatis
lovage
lunary
nutmeg
orpine
savory
sesame
simple
sorrel

7

aconite
burdock
caraway
catmint

cayenne
chervil
chicory
comfrey
dittany
frasera
gentian
henbane
juniper
lettuce
milfoil
mustard
oregano
panicum
paprika
parsley
pot herb
rampion
saffron
succory
vanilla

8

agrimony
angelica
camomile

cinnamon
hog's-bean
lavender
lungwort
marigold
marjoram
mouse ear
plantain
purslane
rosemary
samphire
spicknel
tarragon
turmeric
waybread
wormwood

9

baneberry
bear's foot
chickweed
coriander
coronopus
eyebright
fenugreek
finocchio

goose foot
groundsel
hellebore
horehound
liquorice
sea fennel
sweet herb
tormentil

10
hyoscyamus
lemon thyme
motherwort
penny royal

peppermint
watercress
willow herb

11
dog's cabbage
dragon's head
hedge hyssop
horseradish
pot marigold
pot marjoram
sweet rocket
swine's cress
winter green

12 AND OVER
adder's tongue (12)
Florence fennel (14)
medicinal herbs (14)
mournful widow (13)
mustard and cress (15)
southernwood (12)
summer savory (12)
sweet marjoram (13)
thoroughwort (12)
winter savory (12)

Plants

3
box
cos
ers
hop
ivy
nep
oat
pea
pia
poa
rue
rye
seg
tod
yam
zea

4
aira
akee
alfa
aloe
anil
arum
bean
beet
bent
bigg
bulb
cane
coca
coco
coix
cole
corn
crab
dill
diss
dock
doob
dorn
fern
flag
flax
gale
geum
goss
hemp
herb
holm
ilex

iris
jute
kail
kale
kali
kans
leek
ling
mint
moss
musa
nard
peat
pipi
race
rape
reed
rice
root
rush
ruta
sage
sago
sida
sium
sloe
sola
spud
tare
taro
thea
tree
tutu
ulex
vine
wald
weed
weld
whin
woad
wold
wort

5
agave
ajuga
algae
alpia
anise
apium
aster
brake
brank

briar
broom
bugle
cacao
canna
cicer
clary
clove
cress
cumin
daisy
dicot
dryas
dwale
erica
eruca
ficus
fitch
fungi
furze
glaux
goman
gorse
gourd
grass
grias
henna
holly
liana
liane
lotus
loufa
madia
maize
medic
morel
moril
mucor
mudar
musci
napal
olive
orach
orris
oryza
oshac
osier
oxlip
paddy
palas
panic
poker
radix
rheum
rubia

rubus
runch
savin
savoy
scrog
sedge
shrub
sison
solah
stole
sumac
swede
tacca
tamus
tansy
thorn
thyme
trapa
tucum
vetch
vicia
vinca
viola
vitis
wahoo
wapon
wheat
whort
withy
wrack
yucca
yupon
zamia

6
acorus
alisma
amomum
aninga
arbute
bamboo
barley
batata
bejuco
betony
biblus
borage
bryony
burnet
cactal
cactus
caltha
cassia

213

catnip
cicely
cicuta
cissus
cistus
clover
cockle
conium
conyza
croton
cynara
daphne
darnel
dodder
eddoes
elaeis
endive
eringo
eryngo
exogen
fennel
ferula
fescue
filago
fimble
fiorin
frutex
fungus
funkia
fustet
galium
garlic
garrya
gervan
gnetum
gromil
guills
henbit
hervea
hyssop
iberis
indigo
jujube
juncus
kalmia
kiekie
kousso
lichen
locust
loofah
lupine
madder
maguey
mallow
manioc
marram
matico
milium
millet
mimosa
myrica
myrtle
nardoo
nerium
nettle
nubbin
oilnut
orache
orchid
orchis
origan
osmund
oxalis
paigle
pampas
peanut

peplis
pepper
potato
privet
protea
quinoa
quitch
raggee
rattan
reseda
ruscus
sabine
savine
savory
scilla
secale
sesame
sesban
seseli
smilax
sorrel
spurge
squash
squill
stolon
styrax
sumach
sundew
teasel
teazel
tutsan
urtica
viscum
wicker
yamboo
yarrow

7

absinth
aconite
alcanna
alhenna
all-good
all-heal
althaea
aquatic
arabine
arbutus
awlwort
azarole
barilla
bartram
begonia
bistort
bogbean
bracken
bramble
bugwort
bulbule
bulrush
burdock
bur-reed
calamus
calypso
campion
caraway
carduus
cassada
cassado
cassava
catmint
chicory
clivers
clot-bur

columba
comfrey
cowbane
cowhage
cow-itch
cow-weed
creeper
cudbear
cudweed
cup moss
cytisus
dionaea
dittany
dogbane
dog's rue
ear-wort
ehretia
elatine
esparto
eugenia
euryale
euterpe
felwort
festuca
ficaria
figwort
fitweed
foggage
foxtail
frogbit
fumaria
funaria
genista
gentian
ginseng
gladwyn
gutwort
hardock
heather
hemlock
herbage
honesty
hop-bind
hop-bine
hop-vine
humulus
ipomaea
jasmine
Jew's ear
juniper
karatas
kedlack
lucerne
lychnis
madwort
melilot
monocot
munjeet
mustard
opuntia
panicum
papyrus
pareira
parella
parelle
primula
pumpion
pumpkin
quamash
quassia
ragwort
rambler
rampion
rhatany
rhubarb
robinia

saffron
saligot
salsify
sanicle
sarcina
saw-wort
sencion
senecio
seringa
solanum
sonchus
spiraea
statice
syringa
talipot
taliput
tannier
thistle
tobacco
trefoil
truffle
turpeth
uncaria
vanilla
verbena
vervain
waratah
zalacca
zanonia
zedoary
zizania

8

acanthus
agrimony
air plant
amphigen
anthemis
asphodel
banewort
barberry
barometz
bearbind
bear's ear
bellwort
berberis
berberry
bilberry
bindweed
bogberry
bogwhort
boxthorn
brassica
bullweed
bullwort
calamint
camomile
cannabis
capsicum
carraway
cassweed
catchfly
cat's tail
centaury
cerealia
cetraria
charlock
chayroot
choyroot
cinchona
cinnamon
cleavers
clematis
clubmoss

clubrush
cocculus
cockspur
cockweed
coleseed
cornflag
cornrose
costmary
cowberry
cowgrass
cow-wheat
crithmum
crow silk
damewort
danewort
dewberry
diandria
dog briar
dog grass
dog's bane
dolichos
downweed
dropwort
duckmeat
duckweed
dumb-cane
earth nut
earth-pea
echinops
eggplant
eglatere
eleusine
epiphyte
erigeron
erisimum
euonymus
feverfew
finochio
fireweed
flaxweed
fleabane
fleawort
flixweed
foxglove
fragaria
fumitory
galangal
garcinia
gillenia
girasole
gloxinia
glumales
glyceria
gratiola
gromwell
hare's ear
hartwort
hawkweed
hawthorn
hibiscus
hockherb
ice plant
isnardia
knapweed
lacebark
larkspur
lavender
lungwort
lustwort
male fern
mandrake
mangrove
marjoram
mat grass
may bloom
mezereon

milkweed
monocarp
moonseed
moonwort
mulewort
mushroom
myosotis
nut grass
oenanthe
oleander
oleaster
orchanet
peat moss
phormium
pilewort
pink root
plantlet
plantule
pond weed
prunella
puffball
purslane
putchock
red algae
rib grass
roccella
rock-rose
rosebush
rosemary
rye grass
sainfoin
saltwort
scammony
seedling
sengreen
septfoil
shamrock
simaruba
skull-cap
smallage
soapwort
sourdock
sow bread
starwort
strobile
sun-plant
sweetsop
tamarack
tamarisk
tara fern
tarragon
tea plant
tentwort
tickweed
toad-flax
tree-fern
tremella
triticum
tuberose
turk's cap
turmeric
turnsole
valerian
veratrum
veronica
viburnum
victoria
wall-moss
wall-wort
wartwort
water-poa
wild oats
wild rose
wind seed
with-wine
woodbine

woodroof
woodruff
woodsage
woodwart
wormwood
wrightia
xanthium
zingiber

9

abrotanum
aerophyte
amaryllis
ampelosis
arbor-vine
arsesmart
artemisia
artichoke
asclepias
balsamine
basil weed
bean caper
bearberry
bent grass
bird's foot
bloodroot
bloodwort
blue algae
briar-root
brooklime
brookmint
brookweed
broomcorn
broomrape
burstwort
candytuft
canebrake
caprifole
cardamine
cariopsis
carrageen
caryopsis
celandine
cetrarine
chamomile
chaparral
chaya root
cherry-bay
chickweed
china root
choke-weed
cineraria
club-grass
coal plant
cockscomb
cock's head
colchicum
colocynth
colt's foot
columbine
commensal
coniferae
coral wort
coriander
corn poppy
corn salad
cotyledon
cramp-bark
crataegus
crowberry
cuckoo bud
culver key
cyclamine
decagynia

decandria
desert rod
didynamia
digitalis
digitaria
dittander
dockcress
doob grass
duck's foot
duck's meat
dulcamara
dyer's weed
eglantine
elaeagnus
equisetum
euphorbia
euphrasia
evergreen
evolvulus
eyebright
fenugreek
fever root
feverwort
gamagrass
gelanthus
germander
glasswort
golden cup
golden rod
goose corn
grapewort
grasspoly
ground ivy
groundnut
groundsel
hair grass
hoarhound
honeywort
horehound
horsefoot
horsetail
hypericum
Indian fig
jessamine
Job's tears
kite's foot
knee holly
knot grass
lark's heel
laserwort
liquorice
liverwort
milk vetch
mistletoe
monk's hood
moschatel
mousetail
nepenthes
nicotiana
patchouli
pellitory
pilularia
pimpernel
planticle
poison ivy
poison oak
pyracanth
rafflesia
rocambole
rosmarine
safflower
saintfoin
saxifrage
smartweed
snakeroot
snakeweed

215

snowberry
soap plant
socotrine
spearmint
spearwort
speedwell
spikenard
spirogyra
spoonwort
stellaria
stonecrop
sugarbeet
sugar cane
sun spurge
sweet flag
sweet john
sweet root
sweet rush
sweet wood
sweet wort
taraxacum
thallogen
theobroma
thorn-bush
toadstool
tonka bean
toothwort
tormentil
trifolium
twayblade
umbilicus
villarsia
wakerobin
wall cress
waterlath
waterwort
wax myrtle
whitecrop
widow wail
wincopipe
wolf's bane
wolf's claw
wormgrass
woundwort
xanthosia

10

adam's apple
adder grass
agrostemma
alabastrus
amaranthus
angiosperm
arbor vitae
asarabacca
beccabunga
bitterwort
brome grass
brown algae
butterbush
butterweed
butterwood
butterwort
cascarilla
cassumunar
cellulares
cinquefoil
cloudberry
corn cockle
corn rocket
cotton rose
cottonweed
couch grass
cow parsley

crake berry
crotalaria
devil's club
diadelphia
dog's fennel
dog's poison
dog's tongue
dracontium
elacampane
elaeococca
entophytes
eriocaulon
eriophoron
escallonia
eupatorium
fimble-hemp
friar's cowl
fritillary
furrow weed
gaultheria
globe daisy
globularia
goldenhair
goldy locks
goose grass
grass-wrack
gymnosperm
helianthus
hemp nettle
herds grass
honey stalk
Indian corn
Indian reed
Indian shot
Jew's mallow
kidney-wort
king's spear
knapbottle
lycopodium
maidenhair
manila hemp
mock orange
mock privet
muscardine
nasturtium
nightshade
nipplewort
panic grass
passiflora
pennyroyal
peppermint
pepperwort
periwinkle
poker plant
potentilla
race ginger
ranunculus
rest harrow
rhein berry
rhinanthus
rose acacia
rose mallow
saprophyte
sarracenia
setterwort
shave grass
silver weed
sneezewort
sow thistle
Spanish nut
speargrass
spleenwort
stavesacre
stitchwort
stonebreak
stork's bill

sweet briar
sweet brier
swine bread
swinegrass
swordgrass
throatwort
tiger's foot
touch-me-not
tragacanth
tropaeolum
Venus's comb
wall pepper
water plant
way thistle
whitethorn
wild indigo
willow herb
willow weed
witch hazel
wolf's peach
wood sorrel
yellow-root
yellow-wort

11

bear's breech
bishop's weed
blackbonnet
bottle gourd
brank ursine
calceolaria
calcyanthus
canary grass
chanterelle
coffee plant
contrayerva
convolvulus
corn parsley
cotton grass
cotton plant
crest marine
cuckoo's meat
dame's violet
dog's cabbage
dog's mercury
dracunculus
dragon's head
Dragon's wort
Dutch clover
erythronium
everlasting
fescue grass
fig marigold
finger grass
fuller's weed
giant cactus
giant fennel
guelder rose
hart's tongue
holy thistle
honeysuckle
humble plant
Iceland moss
Indian berry
Indian cress
indigo plant
ipecacuanha
kidney vetch
laurustinus
London pride
marram grass
marsh mallow
meadow-sweet
milk thistle

millet grass
moon trefoil
moving plant
myoporaceae
oyster plant
pedicedaris
pelargonium
pepper grass
poison sumac
prickly pear
red-hot poker
ribbon grass
ripple grass
scurvy grass
sempervivum
serpentaria
snail clover
snail flower
sparrow wort
stagger bush
star thistle
sulphur-wort
swallow-wort
sweet cicely
sweet cistus
sweet potato
swine's cress
thorough wax
tinkar's root
tonquin bean
tussac grass
twitch grass
viper's grass
water radish
water violet
white clover
white darnel
winter berry
winter bloom
winter cress
wintergreen
wood anemone
xanthoxylum
zygophyllum

12

adderstoupie
aerial plants
bladderwrack
buffalo grass
Christ's thorn
coloquintida
compass plant
corn marigold
cow's lungwort
custard apple
deadly carrot
dragon's blood
echinocactus
erythroxylon
feather grass
fennel flower
fool's parsley
German millet
globe thistle
hound's tongue
Indian millet
Indian turnip
mangel wurzel
melon thistle
palma christi
pickerel weed
pitcher plant
quaking grass

reindeer moss
rhododendron
sarsaparilla
snail trefoil
Solomon's seal
southern wood
Spanish broom
Spanish grass
spear thistle
swine thistle
timothy grass
tobacco plant
torch thistle
Venus flytrap
Venus's sumack
vinegar plant
virgin's bower
water parsnip
water pitcher
water soldier
white campion
whitlow grass
whortleberry

winter cherry
xanthorrhiza
yellow rattle

13

chrysanthemum
crown imperial
dog's-tail grass
elephant grass
elephant's foot
eschscholtzia
flowering fern
flowering rush
globe amaranth
golden thistle
Indian tobacco
meadow saffron
raspberry bush
Scotch thistle
spike lavender
summer cypress

sweet marjoram
traveller's joy
Venus's fly trap
vervain mallow
viper's bugloss
wall pennywort
water calamint
water crowfoot
water hyacinth
wayfaring tree

14

blackberry bush
blue couch grass
carline thistle
distaff thistle
fuller's thistle
giant groundsel
golden lungwort
golden mouse-ear

gooseberry bush
mountain sorrel
prince's feather
sensitive plant
shepherd's pouch
shepherd's purse
shepherd's staff
snake's-head iris
Spanish bayonet
starch hyacinth
treacle mustard
wood nightshade

15

golden saxifrage
Italian rye grass
shepherd's needle
Venus's navelwort
virginia creeper
woody nightshade

Trees, shrubs, etc.

2 AND 3

asa
ash
bay
bo
box
elm
fig
fir
gum
haw
hip
hop
ivy
may
nut
oak
sap
tea
tod
yew

4

acer
akee
aloe
arum
atap
balm
bark
bass
bead
beam
bole
cork
dali
dari
date
deal
holm
huon
hura
ilex
jaca

lana
leaf
lime
lote
milk
mowa
palm
pear
pine
pipe
plum
roan
root
rose
shea
sloe
sorb
teak
teil
twig
upas
vine

5

abele
Abies
acorn
agave
alder
almug
amber
anise
anona
apple
arbor
areca
Argan
aspen
balsa
Banga
beech
birch
cacao
carob
cedar

clove
copse
coral
durio
dwarf
ebony
elder
fagus
fruit
glade
glory
grass
grove
guava
hazel
holly
judas
karri
kauri
larch
lemon
lilac
macaw
mahwa
mango
maple
mulga
myall
nyssa
oaken
olive
osier
palay
papaw
peach
pecan
pipal
plane
plank
quina
roots
rowan
salix
sapan
smoke
sumac
taxus

thorn
tilia
tingi
trunk
tsuga
tuart
tulip
ulmus
walan
yulan
xamia

6

abroma
acacia
almond
aralia
arbute
balsam
bamboo
banana
banyan
baobab
bog-oak
bombax
bo-tree
bottle
branch
brazil
butter
button
carica
cashew
catkin
caudex
cedrat
cerris
cerrus
cherry
citron
coffee
cornel
daphne
deodar
fustic

217

gatten
ginkgo
illipe
jarrah
kittul
kumbuk
laurel
lignum
linden
locust
mallee
manuka
mastic
medlar
mimosa
nargil
nettle
orange
pawpaw
pepper
pinery
poplar
privet
quince
redbud
red fir
red gum
rubber
sallow
sappan
she-oak
sissoo
sorrel
souari
spruce
sumach
sylvan
tallow
timber
titoki
tupelo
veneer
vinery
walnut
wampee
wattle
wicken
willow

7

ailanto
amboyna
aniseed
Arbutus
ash tree
avocado
banksia
bay tree
blossom
blue gum
boxwood
buckeye
cabbage
camphor
cam-wood
canella
catalpa
champac
coconut
conifer
coquito
corylus
cowtree
cypress

daddock
dammara
determa
dogwood
dottard
duramen
elk-wood
elm tree
emblica
fan palm
fig tree
fir cone
fir tree
foliage
genipap
gum tree
hemlock
hickory
hog palm
holm oak
jasmine
jugians
juniper
king gum
kumquat
lentisk
logwood
margosa
mastich
moringa
nut pine
oakling
oak tree
oil palm
orchard
platane
pollard
quercus
red pine
redwood
sandbox
sanders
sapling
sapwood
Sequoia
service
shittah
shittim
silk oak
snow-gum
sour-sop
spindle
tanghin
varnish
wallaba
wax palm
wax tree
wych-elm

8

agalloch
agalwood
alburnum
allspice
arbuscle
ash grove
bass wood
beam tree
beachnut
benjamin
black gum
box elder
calabash
castanea

chestnut
cinchona
coco-palm
coco-tree
cork tree
crab-tree
date palm
date plum
doom-palm
eucalypt
fraxinus
gardenia
giant gum
guaiacum
hardbeam
hawthorn
holly-oak
hornbeam
ironbark
ironwood
jack tree
jack wood
kingwood
laburnum
lima wood
long jack
magnolia
mahogany
mangrove
manna-ash
milk tree
mulberry
musk wood
mustaiba
palmetto
palm tree
pandanus
pear tree
pinaster
pine cone
pine tree
pistacia
pockwood
raintree
red cedar
red maple
rosewood
royal oak
sago palm
sapindus
scrub-oak
searwood
seedling
silky oak
sugar gum
swamp oak
sweet-bay
sweet gum
sycamore
tamarind
tamarisk
taxodium
toon-wood
white ash
white fir
white gum
white oak
wistaria
witch-elm

9

adansonia
ailanthus
aloes wood

alpine fir
angophora
araucaria
balsam fir
blackwood
brown pine
buckthorn
bud-scale
butternut
calambour
china tree
chincapin
crab apple
Cupressus
deciduous
erythrine
evergreen
forest oak
fruit tree
grapevine
greenwood
ground ash
ground oak
hackberry
ivory palm
jacaranda
Judas tree
kokrawood
lance wood
lentiscus
maracauba
mustahiba
paper bark
plane tree
quickbeam
rowan tree
sandarach
sapan wood
sapodilla
saskatoon
sassafras
satinwood
Scotch elm
Scotch fir
Scotch pine
screw-pine
shade tree
shell-bark
silver fir
sloethorn
snake-wood
sour-gourd
spicewood
stone pine
suradanni
terebinth
thorn tree
tigerwood
toothache
touch-wood
tulip tree
whitebeam
white pine
whitewood
woodlayer
yacca wood
zebra wood

10

agallochum
almond tree
artocarpus
balaustine
blackthorn

blue spruce
brazilwood
breadfruit
bunji-bunji
bunya-bunya
burra-murra
butter tree
coastal-tea
coccomilia
coniferous
cotton tree
cottonwood
Douglas fir
eucalyptus
fiddle wood
flindersia
flooded gum
garlic-pear
green-heart
hackmatack
holly berry
Indian date
japati palm
letter wood
lilly-pilly
manchineel
mangosteen
orange-ball
orange wood
palisander
paper birch
pine needle
prickly ash
quercitron

sandalwood
sand-cherry
sand-myrtle
silk-cotton
silver-bell
sneeze-wood
Spanish fir
strawberry
sugar-maple
swamp maple
tall wattle
thyine wood
weeping ash
white cedar
white thorn
wild cherry
witch hazel
woolly butt
yellow-wood

11

Algerian fir
bean trefoil
black walnut
black wattle
black willow
bottle-brush
cedar wattle
chrysobalan
coconut palm
cootamundra

copper beech
cypress pine
elaeocarpus
eriodendron
golden chain
golden mohur
hoary poplar
honey locust
Japan laurel
leper-wattle
lignum vitae
mountain ash
phoenix-palm
pomegranate
quicken tree
red-iron bark
red mahogany
sideroxylon
silver birch
stringybark
white poplar
white spruce
white willow

12

almond willow
betel-nut palm
caryophyllus
crow's-foot elm
cucumber tree
custard apple

flowering ash
golden wattle
horse-chestnut
monkey-puzzle
Norway spruce
silver-wattle
Spanish cedar
tree of heaven
umbrella palm
virgin's-bower
weeping birch
wellingtonia
white cypress
winter cherry
xylobalsamum

13 AND OVER

bird's-eye maple (13)
campeachy wood (13)
Cedar of Lebanon (14)
Christmas tree (13)
cornus florida (13)
dog-wood wattle (13)
galactodendron (14)
horse-chestnut (13)
Japanese cedar (13)
partridge wood (13)
sunshine wattle (14)
toxicodendron (13)
trembling poplar (15)
weeping willow (13)

Vegetables

3 AND 4

bean
beet
cole
corn
faba
kale
leek
neep
okra
pea(s)
sage
soy(a)
yam

5

caper
chard
chick
chili
chive
cibol
colza
cress
fitch
gourd
maize
onion
orach
pease
pulse
savoy
swede

6

carrot
celery
daucus
endive
fennel
garlic
girkin
greens
lentil
marrow
nettle
orache
porret
potato
radish
sprout
tomato
turnip

7

batatas
cabbage
cardoon
chicory
gherkin
haricot
hotspur
lactuca
lettuce
mustard
parsley
parsnip

pea bean
peppers
pimento
pompion
pumpkin
salsify
seakale
shallot
skirret
spinach
sprouts
zanonia

8

beetrave
beetroot
borecole
broccoli
capsicum
celeriac
chickpea
colewort
cucumber
eggplant
eschalot
hastings
kohlrabi
lima bean
mushroom
plantain
scallion
soyabean
tickbean
zucchini

9

artichoke
asparagus
aubergine
broad bean
calabrese
courgette
curly kale
dandelion
green peas
horsebean
mangetout
marrowfat
red pepper
split peas
sweetcorn
turban-top
turnip top

10

adzuki bean
beet radish
cos lettuce
cow parsnip
French bean
kidney bean
King Edward
red cabbage
runner bean
scorzonera
turnip tops
watercress
Welsh onion

11

cauliflower
French beans
green pepper
haricot bean
horseradish
scarlet bean
spinach beet
sweet potato

water radish
water rocket

12

bamboo shoots
chat potatoes
corn on the cob
giant shallot

savoy cabbage
Spanish onion
spring onions
spring greens
white cabbage

13 AND OVER

broccoli sprouts (15)

Brussels sprouts (15)
globe artichoke (14)
horse cucumber (13)
ladies' fingers (13)
marrowfat peas (13)
purple broccoli (14)
scarlet runners (14)
spring cabbage (13)
tankard turnip (13)
vegetable marrow (15)

PEOPLES AND LANGUAGES
African tribes

3

Ewe
Fon
Ibo
Ijo
Iru
Suk
Tiv
Vai
Yao

4

Agni
Baga
Bena
Bete
Bini
Bisa
Bubi
Fang
Fula
Guro
Haya
Hehe
Hima
Hutu
Lala
Lozi
Mali
Meru
Nama
Nupe
Nyao
Teso
Yako
Zulu

5

Afars
Anuak
Bamum
Bantu
Bassa
Baule
Bemba
Chewa
Chopi
Dinka
Dogon
Galla
Ganda
Gissi
Grebo
Hausa
Iraqu
Kamba
Lulua
Lunda
Masai
Mende
Mossi
Nandi
Ngoni
Nguni
Nguru
Pygmy
Riffs
Rundi
Shona
Sotho
Swazi
Tonga
Tussi
Tutsi
Venda
Xhosa

6

Angoni
Bakota
Balega
Basuto
Bateke
Bayaka
Chagga
Fulani
Herero
Ibibio
Kikuyu
Kpwesi
Lumbwa
Luvale
Murozi
Ngwato
Rolong
Sambaa
Senufo
Somali
Sukuma
Thonga
Tlokwa
Tsonga
Tswana
Tuareg
Veddah
Warega
Yoruba

7

Ashanti
Baganda
Bakweii
Bambara
Bangala

Bapende
Barotse
Barundi
Basonge
Batonka
Batutsi
Berbers
Bunduka
Bushmen
Dagomba
Griquas
Mashona
Namaqua
Nilotes
Samburu
Shillak
Songhai
Turkana
Watutsi

8

Bergdama
Bushongo
Kipsigis
Mamprusi
Mandingo
Matabele
Tallensi

9 AND OVER

Bangarwanda (11)
Bathlaping (10)
Hottentots (10)
Karamojong (10)
Kgalagedi (9)
Lunda-Bajokwe (12)

American Indian peoples

3 AND 4

Cree
Crow
Fox
Hopi
Hupa
Iowa
Maya
Moki
Pima
Sauk

Ute
Yuma
Zuni

5

Blood
Caddo
Campa
Creek

Haida
Huron
Incas
Kansa
Kiowa
Lipan
Miami
Moqui
Nahua
Omaha
Osage
Sioux

Teton
Wappo
Yaqui
Yuchi
Yunca

6

Abnaki
Apache

Aymara
Aztecs
Biloxi
Caribs
Cayuga
Cocopa
Dakota
Dogrib
Kichai
Mandan
Micmac
Mixtec
Mohave
Mohawk
Navaho
Nootka
Ojibwa
Oneida
Ostiak
Ottawa
Paiute
Pawnee
Pequot
Pericu
Piegan
Pueblo
Quakaw
Salish
Santee
Sarcee

Seneca
Toltec
Warrau

7

Abenaki
Arapaho
Araucan
Arikara
Catawba
Chilcal
Chinook
Choctaw
Hidatsa
Mapuche
Mohegan
Mohican
Natchez
Ojibway
Orejone
Quechua
Shawnee
Stonies
Tlingit
Tonkawa
Wichita
Wyandot

8

Aguaruna
Cherokee
Cheyenne
Comanche
Delaware
Illinois
Iroquois
Kickapoo
Kootenay
Kwakiutl
Menomini
Muskogee
Nez Percé
Onondaga
Powhatan
Quichuan
Seminole
Shoshoni
Shushwap

9

Algonkian
Algonquin
Apalachee
Ashochimi
Blackfeet

Chickasaw
Chipewyan
Chippeway
Flatheads
Karankawa
Menominee
Penobscot
Tuscarora
Winnebago

10

Araucanian
Assiniboin
Athabascan
Bella Coola
Leni-Lenapé
Minnetaree
Montagnais
Shoshonean

11 AND 12

Narraganset (11)
Pasamaquoddy (12)
Root-diggers (11)
Susquehanna (11)

Languages, nationalities, and races

2 AND 3

Edo
Ewe
Fon
Fur
Ga
Gur
Hun
Ibo
Ido
Ila
Jew
Kru
Kui
Kwa
Lao
Luo
Mon
Shi
Tiv
Twi
Vai
Wa
Wu
Yao

4

Akan
Ambo
Arab
Avar
Bali
Beja
Bini
Bodo
Boer

Celt
Chad
Copt
Dane
Efik
Erse
Fang
Finn
Garo
Gaul
Ge'ez
Gogo
Gond
Grig
Igbo
Kelt
Kurd
Lala
Lapp
Lari
Lett
Loma
Lozi
Luba
Mano
Manx
Moor
Moxu
Naga
Nuba
Nuer
Nupe
Pali
Pedi
Pict
Pole
Russ
Scot
Sena

Serb
Shan
Sikh
Slav
Sobo
Susu
Teso
Thai
Tswa
Turk
Urdu
Wend
Zend
Zulu

5

Acoli
Aleut
Aryan
Asian
Attic
Bantu
Bassa
Batak
Bemba
Benga
Berta
Bhili
Bulom
Bussi
Carib
Chaga
Chopi
Croat
Cuban
Cymry
Czech

Dayak
Dinka
Doric
Dutch
Dyold
Dyula
Fante
Frank
Galla
Ganda
Gbari
Gipsy
Gondi
Greek
Gypsy
Hadza
Hausa
Hindi
Idoma
Indic
Ionic
Iraqi
Irish
Kadai
Kafir
Kamla
Karen
Kazak
Khasi
Khmer
Kissi
Kongo
Lambi
Lango
Latin
Lenge
Lomwe
Malay
Mande

221

Maori
Masai
Mossi
Munda
Nandi
Naron
Negro
Ngala
Nguni
Nkore
Norse
Nyong
Nyoro
Oriya
Oscan
Punic
Roman
Ronga
Rundi
Sango
Saudi
Saxon
Scots
Shilh
Shona
Sinic
Sotho
Swazi
Swede
Swiss
Tamil
Temne
Tigré
Tonga
Uzbeg
Venda
Welsh
Wolof
Xhosa
Yupik
Zande

6

Acholi
Aeolic
Afghan
Altaic
Arabic
Arawak
Argive
Aymara
Baltic
Baoule
Basque
Berber
Bokmal
Brahui
Breton
Briton
Bulgar
Celtic
Chokwe
Coptic
Creole
Cymric
Danish
Dorian
Eskimo
Fijian
French
Fulani
Gaelic
Gallic
Gascon

German
Gothic
Hebrew
Herero
Ibibio
Indian
Inupik
Ionian
Italic
Jewess
Jewish
Judaic
Kabyle
Kaffir
Kanuri
Kikuyu
Korean
Kpelle
Kpessi
Kurukh
Libyan
Luvale
Manchu
Mongol
Navaho
Ndonga
Nepali
Ngbaka
Ngombe
Norman
Nsenga
Nubian
Nyanja
Ostman
Papuan
Parian
Parsee
Patois
Polish
Pushto
Pushtu
Rajput
Romaic
Romany
Rwanda
Ryukyu
Sabine
Samoan
Sérère
Sindhi
Slavic
Slovak
Somali
Soviet
Sukuma
Syriac
Syrian
Telegu
Teuton
Theban
Thonga
Tongan
Trojan
Tsonga
Tswana
Tuareg
Tungus
Turkic
Tuscan
Viking
Votyak
Yankee
Yemeni
Yoruba
Zenaga

7

Acadian
African
Amharic
Angolan
Arabian
Aramaic
Aramean
Armoric
Asiatic
Avestan
Bagirmi
Balanta
Balochi
Bambara
Bedouin
Belgian
Bengali
Bisayan
British
Burmese
Bushmen
Catalan
Chechen
Chilean
Chinese
Cornish
Cypriot
Dagomba
Dalicad
Dialect
English
Finnish
Fleming
Flemish
Frisian
Gambian
Gaulish
Guarani
Haitian
Hamitic
Hebraic
Hessian
Hittite
Iberian
Ilocano
Iranian
Israeli
Italian
Karanga
Khoisan
Kirghiz
Kurdish
Kuwaiti
Laotian
Laotien
Lappish
Latvian
Lingala
Lombard
Lugbara
Maduran
Malinke
Maltese
Mandyak
Manxman
Marathi
Mexican
Moorish
Mordvin
Morisco
Mozareb
Mulatto
Nahuatl
Nauruan

Ndebele
Negress
Ngbandi
Nilotic
Nynorsk
Ottoman
Pahlavi
Palaung
Persian
Prakrit
Punjabi
Quechua
Romance
Romansh
Russian
Rwandan
Samiote
Samoyed
Sandawe
Santali
Semitic
Serbian
Shilluk
Siamese
Slovene
Songhai
Spanish
Spartan
Swahili
Swedish
Tagalog
Tibetan
Tigrina
Turkish
Ugandan
Umbrian
Umbundu
Venetic
Walloon
Yiddish
Zairese
Zambian

8

Abderite
Akkadian
Albanian
Algerian
American
Andorran
Antiguan
Armenian
Assamese
Assyrian
Austrian
Balinese
Bavarian
Bermudan
Bohemian
Bolivian
Cambrian
Canadian
Chaldaic
Chaldean
Chamorro
Cherokee
Corsican
Cushitic
Cyrenaic
Delphian
Dutchman
Egyptian
Estonian
Ethiopic

Etruscan	Sicilian	Mauritian	Paraguayan
Eurasian	Slavonic	Mongolian	Patagonian
Frankish	Spaniard	Negrillos	Philippine
Gallican	Sudanese	Nepaulese	Philistine
Georgian	Sumerian	Norwegian	Phoenician
Germanic	Teutonic	Ostrogoth	Polynesian
Ghanaian	Tunisian	Pakistani	Pomeranian
Gujarati	Turanian	Provencal	Portuguese
Gujariti	Turkomen	Red Indian	Rajasthani
Guyanese	Vandalic	Rhodesian	Senegalese
Hawaiian	Visigoth	Roumanian	Serbo-Croat
Hellenic	Welshman	Samaritan	Singhalese
Helvetic		Sardinian	Venezuelan
Honduran		Sere Mundu	Vernacular
Illyrian	**9**	Sinhalese	Vietnamese
Irishman		Sri Lankan	
Japanese	Abkhasian	Sundanese	
Javanese	Afrikaans	Taiwanese	**11**
Kashmiri	Afrikaner	Tanzanian	
Kimbundu	Anatolian	Tocharian	Afro-Asiatic
Kingwana	Armorican	Ukrainian	Argentinian
Kuki-Chin	Barbadian	Ulotrichi	Azerbaijani
Kukuruku	Bengalese	Uruguayan	Bangladeshi
Kwanyama	Brazilian		Greenlander
Lebanese	Bulgarian		Indo-Hittite
Liberian	Byzantian	**10**	Indo-Iranian
Makassar	Byzantine		Mauretanian
Malagasy	Cambodian	Abyssinian	Palestinian
Malawian	Cantonese	Afrikander	Scots Gaelic
Mandarin	Caucasian	Algonquian	Sino-Tibetan
Mandingo	Ceylonese	Anglo-Saxon	Trinidadian
Mandinka	Chari-Nile	Australian	
Memphian	Cheremiss	Autochthon	
Moroccan	Cimmerian	Babylonian	**12**
Moru-Madi	Colombian	Circassian	
Negritos	Congolese	Costa Rican	Basic English
Nepalese	Dravidian	Ecuadorian	Byelorussian
Nigerian	Esperanto	Englishman	Indo-European
Nuba-Fula	Esquimaux	Finno-Ugric	King's English
Nyamwesi	Ethiopian	Florentine	Moru-Mangbetu
Octoroon	Frenchman	Guatemalan	mother tongue
Old Norse	Hanseatic	High German	New Zealander
Old Saxon	Hibernian	Hindustani	Plattdeutsch
Parthian	Hottentot	Indonesian	Scandinavian
Pelasgic	Hungarian	Israelitic	Tibeto-Burman
Peruvian	Icelander	Lithuanian	
Phrygian	Icelandic	Melanesian	
Prussian	Israelite	Mingrelian	**13**
Romanian	Jordanian	Monegasque	
Romansch	Kabardian	Neapolitan	Pidgin English
Rumanian	Kannarese	Nicaraguan	Queen's English
Sanskrit	Low German	Nicobarese	Rhaeto-Romanic
Scotsman	Malayalam	Niger-Congo	Serbo-Croatian
Scottish	Malaysian	Panamanian	

RELIGION AND MYTHOLOGY
Biblical characters

3	Ahab	Mark	Caleb
	Amos	Mary	David
Asa	Baal	Moab	Demas
Eve	Boaz	Noah	Devil (The)
God	Cain	Paul	Elihu
Ham	Esau	Ruth	Enoch
Job	Jael	Saul	Herod
Lot	Joab	Shem	Hiram
	John		Hosea
	Jude		Isaac
4	Leah	**5**	Jacob
	Levi		James
Abel	Luke	Aaron	Jesse
Adam	Magi (The)	Annas	Jesus

Joash
Jonah
Judas
Laban
Linus
Lydia
Micah
Moses
Nahum
Naomi
Peter
Satan
Sihon
Silas
Simon
Titus
Uriah
Uriel
Zadok

6

Abijah
Andrew
Balaam
Christ
Daniel
Darius
Dorcas
Elijah
Elisha
Esther
Festus
Gehazi
Gideon
Haggai
Isaiah

Jairus
Joseph
Joshua
Judith
Kohath
Miriam
Naaman
Naboth
Nathan
Philip
Pilate
Rachel
Reuben
Samson
Samuel
Simeon
Sisera
Thomas
Uzziah
Yahweh

7

Abraham
Absalom
Ananias
Azariah
Clement
Delilah
Eleazar
Ephraim
Ezekiel
Gabriel
Japheth
Jehovah
Jezebel
Joiakim

Lazarus
Lucifer
Malachi
Matthew
Meshach
Michael
Obadiah
Pharaoh
Raphael
Shallum
Solomon
Stephen
Timothy
Zebulon

8

Abednego
Barnabas
Benjamin
Caiaphas
Gamaliel
Habakkuk
Hezekiah
Issachar
Jeremiah
Jeroboam
Jonathan
Maccabee
Matthias
Mordecai
Nehemiah
Philemon
Rehoboam
Sapphira
Shadrach
Zedekiah

9

Abimelech
Bathsheba
Jehoiakim
Nathanael
Nicodemus
Thaddaeus
Zacchaeus
Zachariah
Zacharias
Zechariah
Zephaniah

10

Bartimaeus
Belshazzar
Holofernes
Methuselah
Theophilus

11

Bartholomew
Jehoshaphat
Melchizedek
Sennacherib

13 AND 14

Mary Magdalene (13)
John the Baptist (14)
Nebuchadnezzar (14)
Pontius Pilate (13)

Mythology

2 AND 3

Aah
Aea
Ahi
Ali
Amt
Ana
Anu
Aon
Ate
Bel
Bes
Con
Cos
Dis
Ea
elf
Eos
Eru
fay
Fum
Ge
Gog
Heh
Hel
Ida
Ino
Io
Ira
Lar

Ler
Lif
Mab
Min
Neo
Nix
Nox
Nut
On
Ops
Pan
Pax
Ra
Ran
Roe
Set
Shu
Sol
Sua
Tiw
Tyr
Ule
Uma
Ve

4

Abae
Abas
Abia

Abii
Acis
Agni
Ajax
Amam
Amen
Amor
Amsi
Amsu
Anit
Ankh
Annu
Anpu
Apia
Apis
Area
Ares
Argo
Asia
Askr
Aten
Atys
Auge
Baal
Bakh
Bast
Beda
Beli
Bias
Bilé
Bran

Buto
Ceyx
Chac
Chin
Clio
Core
Danu
Deva
Dice
Dido
Dino
Donu
Duse
Dwyn
Echo
Eden
Elli
Enna
Enyo
Eris
Eros
Esus
Fama
Faun
Frig
Fury
Gaea
gods
gram
Gwyn
Gyes

Hapi
Hebe
Heno
Hera
hero
Hest
Idas
Ikto
Ilia
Ilus
Iole
Iris
Irus
Isis
Issa
Itys
Iynx
jinn
Jove
Juno
Kali
kama
Lear
Leda
Leto
Llyr
Lofn
Loki
Maia
Mara
Mark
Mars
Math
Moly
Mors
muse
Myth
Nabu
Naga
Nebu
Nick
Nike
Nila
Nubu
Nudd
Odin
ogre
Pasi
Peri
Pero
pixy
Ptah
Puck
Rahu
Raji
Rama
Rhea
Roma
saga
Selk
Shai
Sita
Siva
Soma
Styx
Susa
tabu
Tadg
Thia
Thor
Troe
Troy
Tupa
Tyro
Upis
Vata

Vayu
Wasi
Xulu
Yama
Yggr
Ymir
Yoga
Yuga
yule
Zeus
Zume

5

Abila
Acron
Actor
Aedon
Aegir
Aegis
Aegle
Aello
Aenea
Aesir
Aeson
Aesop
Aetna
Agave
Ahura
Alope
Amata
Ammon
Amset
Anava
angel
Anher
Anhur
Anius
Antea
Anxor
Anxur
Apepi
Arawn
Arete
Argos
Argus
Ariel
Arimi
Arion
Armes
Artio
Asius
Atlas
Attis
Aulis
Bacis
Barce
Belus
Bennu
Beroe
Bitol
Biton
Bogie
Borvo
Bragi
Butis
Byrsa
Cacus
Cales
Canis
Capra
Capys
Carna
Ceres
Chaos

Cilix
Circe
Coeus
Creon
Crete
Cupid
Cyane
Dagda
Dagon
Damon
Danaê
Dares
Delos
demon
Deuce
Deuse
devas
Diana
Dione
Dirce
djinn
Dolon
Donar
Doris
Dryad
Durga
dwarf
Dyaus
Dylan
Edoni
Egypt
elfin
elves
embla
Enlil
Epeus
Epona
Erato
Estas
Evius
faery
fairy
Fates
Fauna
Fides
Flora
Freya
Freyr
Fulla
Gades
Galar
Galli
Garme
genii
Getae
ghoul
giant
Gihil
gnome
Gorge
Grail
Gwyar
Gyges
Gymir
Hades
Harpy
Helen
Helle
Herse
Homer
Honor
Horae
Horta
Horus
houri
Hydra

Hylas
Hymen
Hymir
Iamus
Iapyx
Iason
Ichor
Idmon
Idyia
Ilama
Ilium
Indra
Ionia
Iphis
Irene
Istar
Iulus
Ixion
Janus
Jason
Jorth
Kaboi
Kabul
Ladon
Laius
Lamia
Lamus
lares
Lethe
Liber
Linus
Lludd
Lotis
Lugus
Lycus
Macar
Macha
Maera
Magog
Manes
Maron
Mazda
Medea
Medon
Melia
Metis
Midas
Mimas
Mimir
Minos
Mitra
Moira
Molus
Momus
Monan
Mothi
Mullo
Muses
naiad
Nanda
Nandi
Nemon
Niobe
Nisus
Nixie
Norna
norns
Nymph
Orcus
Oread
Orion
Paean
Pales
Panes
Paris
Pavan

Perse	Aegypt	Cratos	Hermes
Phaon	Aeneas	Creios	Hesiod
Phyto	Aeneid	Creusa	Hestia
Picus	Aeolus	Crissa	Heyoka
pigmy	Aerope	Crocus	Hroptr
pisky	Aethra	Cronus	Huginn
pixie	Africa	Cybele	Hyades
Pluto	Agenor	Cycnus	Hygeia
Poeas	Aglaia	Cyrene	Hyllus
Priam	Agrius	Damona	Ianthe
Pwyll	Alecto	Danaus	Iarbas
Remus	Aletes	Daphne	Iasion
Rimac	Aleuas	Daulis	Iasius
Rudra	Aloeus	Daunus	Icarus
Sakra	Althea	Delius	Ilaira
Salus	Amazon	Delphi	Iliona
santa	Amen-Ra	Dictys	Inferi
satyr	Ampyse	Dipsas	Iolaus
Sesha	Amycus	Dirona	Iphias
Sibyl	Amydon	Dodona	Ishtar
Sinis	Anapus	Dragon	Iseult
Sinon	Andros	Dryads	Isolde
Siren	Angont	Dryope	Ismene
Skuld	Antium	Dumuzi	Italus
Sulis	Anubis	Durinn	Ithaca
Supay	Anukit	Echion	Ithunn
sylph	Aphaca	Egeria	Itonia
Syren	Apollo	Egesta	Kobold
taboo	Aquilo	Elatus	Kraken
Tages	Araxes	Elymus	Kvasia
Talos	Arctos	Empusa	Latona
Tanen	Arthur	Eostre	Lilith
tarot	Asgard	Eponae	Lucina
Ta-urt	Asopus	Erebus	Lycaon
Theia	Athena	Euneus	Lyceus
Thoas	Athene	Europa	Maenad
Thoth	Athens	Evadne	Mamers
Thule	Atreus	Evenus	Mammon
Thyia	Augeas	Faerie	Marica
Titan	Aurora	Faunus	Medusa
Tohil	Avatar	Febris	Megara
Tonan	Avalon	Fenrir	Memnon
Troll	Bacabs	Fenris	Mentor
Uazit	Baldur	fetish	Merlin
Uller	Balius	Fidius	Merman
Urien	Battus	Fimila	Merops
Urthr	Baucis	Fjalar	Mestra
Ushas	Befana	Foliot	Mictla
Vanir	Bendis	Fornax	Miming
Venti	Benshi	Frigga	Mintha
Venus	Bestla	Furies	Minyas
Vesta	Bitias	Furnia	Mithra
Woden	Boreas	Galeus	Moccos
Wotan	Brahma	Ganesh	Moirae
Xquiq	Byblis	Gemini	Moloch
Zamna	Byblus	Genius	Mopsus
Zelia	Cabiri	Geryon	Munnin
Zetes	Cadmus	Ghanna	Mygdon
	Calais	Glance	Mythic
6	Canens	Goblin	naiads
	Cardea	Gorgon	Narada
	Caryae	Graces	Natose
Abaris	Castor	Graeae	Nectar
Abdera	Caurus	Haemon	Neleus
Abeona	Celeus	Haemus	Nereid
Abydos	Charis	Hafgan	Nereus
Acamus	Charon	Hamhit	Nergal
Achaei	cherub	Haokah	Nessus
Achaia	Chione	Hather	Nestor
Actaea	Chiron	Hecale	Ninlil
Admeta	Chryse	Hecate	Nireus
Adonis	Clotho	Hector	Niskai
Aeacus	Clytie	Hecuba	Nomius
Aeetes	Codrus	Helice	Nornas
Aegeus	Comana	Helios	nymphs
Aegina	Consus	Hellen	Oberon

226

Oeneus	sprite	Ampelus	Cinyras
Oenone	Sthanu	Amphion	Cleobis
Oeonus	Syrinx	Ampycus	Clymene
Ogmios	Talaus	Amymone	Cocytus
ogress	Tammuz	Amyntor	Copreus
Ogyges	Tarvos	Anaburn	Coronis
Ogygia	Tereus	Anagnia	Creteus
Oileus	Tethys	Anaphae	Curetes
Olenus	Teucer	Anaurus	Cyaneae
Ophion	Thalia	Ancaeus	Cyclops
oracle	Theano	Angitia	Cythera
Ormuzd	Themis	Anigrus	Dactyls
orphic	Thetis	Antaeus	Daphnis
Orthia	Thisbe	Antenor	Delphus
Orthus	Thunor	Anteros	Demeter
Osiris	Thyone	Anthene	demi-god
Palici	Tiamat	Antiope	Diomede
Pallas	Titans	Antissa	Dwynwen
Pallos	Tityus	Aphetae	Echemus
Panope	Tlaloc	Aphytos	Echidna
Paphus	Tmolus	Arachne	Ehecatl
Parcae	Triton	Arcadia	Electra
Peleus	Typhon	Arestor	Elicius
Pelias	Ulixes	Ariadne	Elpenor
Pelion	Umbria	Arsinoë	Elysian
Pelops	Undine	Artemis	Elysium
Peneus	Urania	Asathor	Epaphus
Perdix	Uranus	Astarte	Epigoni
Peryda	Utgard	Asteria	Erigone
Phenix	Utopia	Astraea	Erinyes
Pheres	Vacuna	Ataguju	erl-king
Phoebe	Valkyr	Athamas	Eumaeus
Pholus	Varuna	Atropos	Eumelus
Phylas	Vishnu	Autonoë	Eunomia
Pirene	Vulcan	Auxesia	Euryale
Pistor	Xangti	Avatars	Eurybia
Plutus	Xelhua	Avernus	Euterpe
Polias	Xolotl	Bacchae	Evander
Pollux	Xuthus	Bacchus	evil eye
Pomona	Yaksha	banshee	Exadius
Prithi	Zancle	banshie	Februus
Prithu	Zethus	Belenos	Feronia
Pronax	zombie	Bellona	Formiae
Psyche		Beltane	Fortuna
Pulaha		Bifrost	Fylgjur
Pushan	**7**	bogyman	Galatea
Pyrrha		Bochica	Galleus
Python	Abderus	Bona Dea	Gargara
Rhenea	Acarnam	Brahman	Gelanor
Rhesus	Acastus	Branwen	Glaucus
Rhodes	Acerbas	Brauron	Gnossos
Rhodos	Acestes	Briseis	Goibniu
Rumina	Achaeus	Bromius	Gordius
Safekh	Achates	Brontes	Gorgons
Samana	Acheron	brownie	Grannus
Sancus	Acoetes	Busiris	Gremlin
Sappho	Actaeon	Caeneus	griffin
Saturn	Achtaeus	Calchas	Grimnir
Satyrs	Admetus	Calypso	Gryphon
Scylla	Aegaeon	Camelot	Gungnir
Scyros	Aegiale	Camenae	Halesus
sea-god	Aenaria	Camilla	Hamoneu
Selene	Aepytus	Canopus	hanuman
Semele	Aesacus	Capella	Harpies
Semnai	Aetolus	Caranus	Helenus
Sestus	Agamede	Carneus	Helicone
Sethon	Agyieus	Cecrops	Hesione
Sibyls	Ahriman	Celaeno	Hilaira
Sigeum	Alastor	centaur	Hor-Amen
Simois	Alcides	Cepheus	Hun-Ahpu
Sirens	Alcmene	Cercyon	Hunbatz
Sirona	Alcyone	Cessair	Hurakan
Somnus	Alpheus	Chelone	Hydriad
Sothis	Aluberi	Chimera	Hygeian
Sphinx	Amathus	Chloris	Hylaeus
spirit	Amazons	Chryses	Iacchus

Ialemus
Iapetus
Icarius
Idalium
Idothea
Iguvium
Inarime
incubus
Inferno
Iobates
Ioskeha
Ismenos
Itzamna
Iztal Ix
Iztat Ix
Jocasta
Jupiter
Juturna
Krishna
Laeradh
Laertes
Laocoon
Laodice
Larunda
Latinus
Lavinia
Leander
Lemures
Lorelei
Lothurr
Lynceus
Macaria
Machaon
Maenads
Maponos
Megaera
Menippe
Mercury
mermaid
Metylto
Michabo
Midgard
Minerva
Mithras
Mordred
Morrigu
Musaeus
Mvrddin
Nemesis
Nephele
Neptune
Nereids
Nokomis
Nycteus
Nysaeus
Oceanus
Ocyrhoe
Oeagrus
Oedipus
Ogygian
Old Nick
Olympia
Olympus
Omphale
Onniont
oracles
Orestes
Ormenus
Orphean
Orpheus
Ortygia
Pandion
Pandora
Parvati
Pegasus
Penates

Perseis
Perseus
Petasus
Phegeus
Phemius
Phineus
Phoebus
Phoenix
Phorcus
Phrixus
Phyllis
Pierian
Pleiads
Pleione
Plouton
Pluvius
Polites
Priapus
Procles
Procris
Proetus
Proteus
Pryderi
Purusha
Pylades
Pyramus
Pyrrhus
Pythias
Qabanil
Racumon
Renenet
Rhamnus
Rhoecus
Rhoetus
Rig-Veda
Robigus
Romulus
Rubicon
Rukmini
Samblin
Scandea
Scaptia
Scheria
Scythia
Segesta
Selleis
Serapis
Setebos
Sicinus
Silenus
Skirnir
Soranus
Spright
sprites
Stentor
Stimula
sylphid
Talarea
Telamon
Telemus
Temenus
Thaumas
Theonoe
Theseus
Thialfi
Titania
Triopas
Tristan
Troilus
Ulysses
unicorn
Unktahe
vampire
Veionis
Venilia
vestals

Vintios
Virbius
Vitharr
Walkyrs
Wayland
Wieland
wood god
Xanthus
Xibalba
Xmucane
Yakshas
Yolcuat
Zagreus
Zipacna

8

Abantias
Absyrtus
Academus
Achelons
Achilles
Acidalia
Aconteus
Acontius
Acrisius
Adrastia
Adrastus
Aeacides
Aegimius
Aegyptus
Aeneades
Agamedes
Aganippe
Aglauros
Akha-Kanet
Alberich
Albiorix
Alcathoe
Alcestis
Alcimede
Alcinous
Alcmaeon
Amaethon
Amalthea
Ambrosia
Anacreon
Anatarho
Anchiale
Anchises
Anemotis
Angharad
Antemnae
Anthedon
Anthemus
Anthylla
Anticlea
Antigone
Antiphus
Apaturia
Apidonus
Apollyon
Appareus
Arcesius
Arethusa
Argonaut
Arianrod
Ascanius
Asterion
Astraeus
Astyanax
Ataensic
Atalanta
Atlantis
Avernian

basilisk
Bebryces
Bedivere
Belisama
bogeyman
Bolthorn
Branchus
Bubastis
Bylazora
Caduceus
Caeculus
Calliope
Callisto
Camaxtli
Camazotz
Capaneus
Carmenta
Castalia
Celaenae
centaurs
Centeotl
Cephalus
Cerberus
Cercopes
Chalybes
Chantico
Charites
Chimaera
Chryseis
Cimmerii
Cipactli
Cocidius
Coroebus
Cretheus
Crommyon
Cyclades
Cylopes
Cyllarus
Cynosura
Cytherea
Daedalus
Damascus
Damastes
Damocles
Dardanus
Deianira
Dervones
Dionysos
Dionysus
Dioscuri
Dodonian
Doybayba
Draupnir
El Dorado
Elivager
Endymion
Enigorio
Entellus
Enyalius
Epicaste
Epidanus
Eriphyle
Eteocles
Eteoclus
Eumolpus
Euphemus
Euryabus
Euryclea
Eurydice
Eurynome
Faesulae
Farbauti
Favonius
folklore
Fornjotr
Ganymede

Gigantes
Gilgames
good folk
Govannon
Gucumatz
Halcyone
Harmonia
Haroeris
Heliadae
Heracles
Hercules
Hermione
Hersilia
Hesperus
Hyperion
Iardanes
Ilithyia
Illatici
Iphicles
Jarnsaxa
Jurupari
Keridwen
Kukulcan
Labdacus
Lachesis
Lampetie
Lancelot
Laodamas
Laodamia
Laomedon
Lapithae
Libertas
Libitina
Lupercus
Maeander
Mama Nono
Marpessa
Megareus
Melampus
Meleager
Menelaus
Merodach
Minotaur
Morpheus
Mulciber
Myrtilus
Narayana
Nausicaa
Niflheim
Nin-Lilla
Oceanids
Odysseus
Oenomaus
Olympian
Orithyia
Othrerir
Pacarina
Palaemon
Pandarus
Panopeus
Panthous
paradise
Parjanya
Pasiphaë
Pasithea
Pelasgus
Penelope
Pentheus
Pephredo
Percival
Periphas
Pessinus
Phaethon
Philemon
Phintias
Phlegyas

Phoronis
Picumnus
Pierides
Pilumnus
Pisander
Pittheus
Pleiades
Podarces
Polyxena
Porthaon
Poseidon
Prithivi
Proximae
Psamathe
Pulastya
Quiateot
Quirinal
Quirinus
Ragnarok
Rakshasa
Rhodopis
Rosmerta
Rubezahl
Sahadeva
Sarawati
Sarpedon
Schedius
Sciathus
Seriphos
Silvanus
Sipontum
Sisyphus
Sparsana
Srikanta
succubus
Summanus
Talassio
talisman
Tantalus
Tartarus
Tecmessa
Telephus
Terminus
Thamyri
Thanatos
Theogony
Thyestes
Tiresias
Tithonus
Tonatiuh
Tristram
Ucalegon
Valhalla
Valkyrie
Vasudeva
Vesuvius
Victoria
Virginia
Visvampa
Wakinyan
water god
Waukkeon
werewolf
Xpiyacoc
Yadapati
Zalmoxis
Zephyrus

9

Acherusia
Achilleum
Acmonides
Adsullata
Aegialeus

Aegisthus
Aethiopia
Agamemnon
Agathyrsi
Alcathous
Alcyoneus
Amalivaca
Ambrosial
Amphrysus
Anaxarete
Andraemon
Androclus
Androgeus
Andromeda
Antandrus
Antevorta
Aphrodite
Areithous
Areopagus
Argonauts
Aristaeus
Ascalabus
Asclepius
Ashtoreth
Assoracus
Autolycus
Automeden
Aventinus
Bacchante
Bosphorus
Brunhilde
Bucentaur
Bzyantium
Cassandra
Cerberean
Chalcodon
Charybdis
Chthonius
Clitumnus
Coatlicue
Cockaigne
Concordia
Cytherean
Davy Jones
Deiphobus
Demophoon
Dervonnae
Deucalion
Diancecht
Diespiter
Dionysius
Domdaniel
Enceladus
Epidaurus
Eumenides
Euphorbus
Eurybates
Eurypylus
Eurysaces
Excalibur
Fabia Gens
Fairyland
fairy tale
Faustulus
Ferentina
Feretrius
Fjawrgynn
Friar Tuck
Gagurathe
Gargaphin
Ghisdubar
Guinivere
Hamadryad
Harmakhis
Heimdallr
Hippolyte

hobgoblin
Holy Grail
Hypsipyle
Idacanzas
Idomeneus
Indigetes
Iphigenia
Iphimedia
Ixiomides
Jotunheim
Lyonesse
Melanthus
Melisande
Melpomene
Menoeceus
Menoetius
Metaneira
Missibizi
Mnemosyne
Mnestheus
Nanahuatl
Narcissus
Noncomala
Nyctimene
Oceanides
Orgiastic
Palamedes
Pandareos
Pandrosos
Parnassus
Patroclus
Pelopidae
Periander
Philammon
Philomela
Phoroneus
Pirithous
Polydamas
Polydorus
Polynices
Polyphron
Portumnus
Postvorta
Pudicitia
Pygmalion
Quahootze
Rakshasas
Rediculus
Rigasamos
Robin Hood
Sagittary
Salmoneus
Samavurti
Saturnius
Scamander
Scyllaeum
Sibylline
Siegfried
Sthenelus
Strophius
Taranucus
Tawiscara
Telchines
Telegonus
Thersites
Thymoetes
Tisamenus
Tisiphone
Toutiorix
Uxellimus
Valkyrean
Valkyries
Vasishtha
Vertumnus
Walpurgis
white lady

229

wood nymph
Xbakiyalo
Xbalanque
Yggdrasil
Zacynthus
Zerynthus

10

Abantiades
Achillides
Aetholides
Ahsonnutli
Ahura Mazda
Ambisagrus
Amisodarus
Amnisiades
Amphiaraus
Amphictyon
Amphitrite
Amphitryon
Andromache
Antilochus
Antitaurus
Arcesilaus
Archemoros
Berecyntia
Bussumarus
Callirrhoe
Cassiopeia
changeling
Cihuacoatl
cockatrice
compitalia
cornucopia
Corybantes
Cyparissus
Delphinium
Eileithyia
Eldhrimnir
Emathiades
Epimenides
Epimetheus
Erechtheum
Erechtheus
Erymanthus
Euphrosyne
fisher king
Galinthias
Gwenhwyvar
Hamadryads
Heliopolis
Hephaestus
Hesperides
Hippocrene
Hippodamia
Hippogriff

Hippolytus
Hippomedon
Hippothous
Horbehutet
Juggernaut
Kaneakeluh
King Arthur
leprechaun
Lifthrasir
little folk
Maid Marian
Mama Quilla
Melanippus
Melanthius
Menestheus
mundane egg
Nausithous
Necessitas
Nilmadhava
Onocentaur
Pachacamac
Palladinus
Pallantias
Parnassian
Persephone
Phlegethon
Phosphorus
Pigwidgeon
Plisthenes
Polydectes
Polydeuces
Polyhymnia
Polymestor
Polyphemus
Porphyrion
Prajapatis
Procrustes
Prometheus
Proserpina
Qebhsennuf
Rhea Silvia
Round Table
Sakambhari
Samothrace
Santa Claus
Saptajihiva
sea serpent
Strophades
Talthybius
Telemachus
Tlepolemus
Trophonius
Utgardloki
Visvakarma
Visvamitra
Vrihaspati
Vukub-Cakix
Wonderland
Yajneswara

Yoganindra

11

Aesculapius
Alaghom Naom
Alalcomenae
Amphilochus
Anna Perenna
Antaeopolis
Anthesteria
Aphrodisias
Apocatequil
Arimaspians
Atius Tirawa
Awonawilona
Bellerophon
Britomartis
Canopic jars
Cuervaperi
Dam Gal Nunna
Eileithyias
Enigohatgea
Erysichton
Eurysthenes
Ginnungagap
Gladsheimir
Harpocrates
Heracleidae
mythologist
mythologize
Nantosvelta
Neoptolemus
Pandora's box
Penthesilea
Philoctetes
Polyphontes
Protesilaus
Savitripati
Scamandrius
Sraddhadeva
Symplegades
Terpsichore
Thrasymedes
Triptolemus
troglodytes
Ultima Thule
Vishnamvara

12

Acca Larentia
Achaemenides
Acroceraunia
Agathodaemon
Aius Locutius

Ancus Martius
Belatucadrus
Chrysothemis
Clytemnestra
Erichthonius
Gigantomachy
Golden Fleece
Hippocentaur
Hyperboreans
Hypermnestra
Jormundgandr
Kittanitowit
Mount Olympus
mythographer
mythological
Pallas Athene
Purushattama
Quetzalcoatl
Rhadamanthus
Tezcatlipoca
Theoclymenus
Trismegistus
Wandering Jew
white goddess
Xochiquetzal
Yohualticitl
Yudhishthira

13 AND OVER

Achilleus Dromos (15)
Apochquiahuayan (15)
Apple of Discord (14)
Augean stables (13)
Calydonian Hunt (14)
Colonus Hippius (14)
Damocles' sword (13)
Elysian Fields (13)
Father Christmas (15)
Halirrhathius (13)
Hermaphroditus (14)
Huitzilopochtli (15)
Itsikamahidis (13)
Jupiter Elicius (14)
Jupiter Pluvius (14)
Laestrygonians (14)
Llew Llaw Gyffes (14)
Mayan Mythology (14)
Never Never Land (14)
Oonawieh Unggi (13)
Phoebus Apollo (13)
Quetzalcohuatl (14)
Tloque Nahuaque (14)
Tonacatecutli (13)
Tuatha de Danann (14)
Walpurgis night (14)
Yoalli Ehecatl (13)

Religion, ecclesiastical terms, etc.

2-4

abbé
alb
alms
amen
apse
ark
ave
Baal

bier
bon
chan
cope
cowl
curé
dana
dean
Ebor
Eden

Eve
evil
ewer
fane
fast
font
God
guni
hadj
hajj

hell
holy
host
hymn
icon
idol
I.H.S.
Imam
I.N.R.I.
jah

Jain
Jew
joss
ka'ba
lama
lay
Lent
mass
monk
nave
N. or M.
nun
obit
pall
pew
pica
pie
pome
pope
pray
pyx
R.I.P.
rite
rood
rupa
sect
see
sext
sin
Siva
soul
Sufi
text
Toc H
Veda
veil
vow
Xmas
yang
yin
yoga
Zen
Zion

5

abbey
abbot
abdal
agape
aisle
Allah
altar
amice
angel
Arian
banns
beads
Bible
bigot
bless
bodhi
burse
canon
carol
chant
chela
choir
credo
creed
cross
curia
Dagon
deify
deism

deist
deity
demon
devil
dirge
dogma
double
druid
elder
ephod
exeat
faith
fakir
friar
glory
godly
grace
Grail
guild
hades
hafiz
Hindu
image
imaum
Islam
Kaaba
karma
Koran
laity
lauds
logos
manse
matin
mitre
morse
myrrh
pagan
papal
pasch
paten
piety
pious
prior
psalm
purim
rabbi
relic
saint
Sarum
Satan
selah
stole
Sudra
Sunna
sutra
synod
taboo
terce
Torah
tract
vedic
vicar
vigil
zazen

6

abbacy
abbess
adamic
Advent
adytum
anoint
anthem
ashram

aumbry
banner
beadle
Belial
bikkhu
bikshu
bishop
Brahma
Buddha
burial
cantor
censer
chapel
cherub
chrism
Christ
church
cierge
clergy
cleric
corban
culdee
cruets
curacy
curate
deacon
decani
dervis
devout
dharma
divine
donary
dossal
dunker
Easter
Elohim
Exodus
ferial
flamen
friary
gloria
Gospel
hallow
heaven
Hebrew
Hegira
heresy
hermit
homily
housel
hymnal
I-ching
intone
Jesuit
Jewess
Jewish
Judaic
keblah
latria
lavabo
lector
legate
Levite
litany
living
mantra
martyr
matins
missal
Mormon
mosaic
Moslem
mosque
mullah
Muslim
mystic

novice
nuncio
oblate
octave
ordain
orders
orison
pagoda
painim
palmer
papacy
papism
papist
parish
Parsee
parson
pastor
popery
prayer
preach
priest
primus
proper
psalms
pulpit
purana
Quaker
rector
repent
ritual
rochet
rosary
rubric
sacred
Saddhu
sangha
santon
schism
scribe
seraph
sermon
server
Shaker
shaman
Shiite
Shinto
shrine
shrive
sinful
sinner
solemn
Sofism
spirit
Sunday
suttee
Talmud
tantra
te deum
temple
theism
trance
triune
tunker
verger
vestry
virgin
Vishnu
votive
Wahabi

7

Aaronic
Abaddon
abelian

231

acolyte
acolyth
Adamite
advowee
Alcoran
Alkoran
alms-bag
ampulla
angelic
angelus
animism
apostle
Arahant
atheism
atheist
baptism
baptist
baptize
beatify
Beghard
Beguard
Beguine
bigotry
biretta
Brahman
Brahmin
calvary
cassock
chalice
chancel
chaplet
chapter
charity
chrisom
Cluniac
collect
confirm
convent
convert
croslet
crozier
crusade
dataria
deanery
decanal
deified
dervise
dervish
devilet
diocese
diptych
diviner
docetae
Elohist
epistle
Essenes
eternal
evangel
exegete
faculty
fasting
frontal
Galilee
gaudete
Gehenna
Genesis
gentile
glorify
gnostic
goddess
godhead
godhood
godless
godlike
godling
godship

gradine
gradual
gremial
hassock
heathen
heretic
hexapla
holy day
hosanna
impiety
incense
infidel
introit
Jainism
Jehovah
Judaism
Judaize
Lady Day
lamaism
Lateran
lectern
lection
liturgy
Lollard
low mass
madonna
maniple
mattins
messiah
mid-Lent
minaret
minster
miracle
mission
muezzin
mystics
narthex
nirvana
nocturn
numbers
nunnery
oratory
ordinal
orphrey
Our Lady
penance
peshito
pietist
pilgrim
piscina
pontiff
popedom
prayers
prebend
prelate
prester
primacy
primate
profane
prophet
psalter
puritan
Quakery
Ramadan
rebirth
rectory
requiem
reredos
retable
retreat
Sabbath
sacring
sainted
saintly
sanctum
Saracen

satanic
saviour
sedilia
service
Shaster
Shastra
Sivaite
sontane
steeple
stipend
sub-dean
Sunnite
synodal
tantric
tempter
tonsure
trinity
tunicle
unblest
unction
unfrock
Vatican
Vedanta
vespers
Vulgate
worship
Xmas day

8

ablution
aceldama
acephali
advowson
agnostic
agnus dei
alleluia
almighty
altarage
anathema
anchoret
Anglican
anointed
antiphon
antipope
antistes
apostasy
apostate
apparels
Arianism
Arminian
atheneum
ave maria
beatific
benifice
bénitier
biblical
brethren
breviary
Buddhism
Buddhist
cantoris
capuchin
cardinal
carmelin
catacomb
canonize
cathedral
Catholic
cemetery
cenobite
cenotaph
chasuble
cherubim
chimere

chrismal
christen
ciborium
cincture
clerical
compline
conclave
confalon
corporal
covenant
creation
credence
crucifer
crucifix
dalmatic
deaconry
deifical
demoness
devilish
devilkin
devotion
diaconal
dies irae
diocesan
disciple
ditheism
ditheist
divinity
divinize
doctrine
Donatism
donatist
doxology
druidess
druidism
ebionite
elements
Ember Day
enthrone
epiphany
episcopy
epistler
Erastian
Essenism
Eternity
ethereal
Eusebian
evensong
evermore
evildoer
exegesis
exegetic
exorcist
faithful
feretory
foot-pace
frontlet
futurist
God's acre
Hail Mary
heavenly
hell fire
hierarch
high mass
hinayana
holy name
homilies
holy rood
Holy Week
Huguenot
hymn book
idolater
idolatry
immortal
indevout
infernal

Jesuitic
Jesuitry
Judaizer
lay-clerk
libation
literate
lord's day
Lutheran
lych-gate
mass-book
mahayana
minister
ministry
minorite
miserere
modalist
Mohammed
monachal
monastic
moravian
nativity
navicula
Nazarene
nethinim
novatian
obituary
oblation
offering
ordinary
orthodox
paganism
pantheon
papistry
pardoner
Passover
pharisee
pontifex
preacher
predella
priestly
prioress
prophecy
prophesy
Proverbs
psalmist
Puseyism
Puseyite
quietism
quietist
Ramadhan
recollet
redeemer
religion
response
reverend
reverent
rogation
Romanism
Romanist
Romanize
sacristy
Sadducee
sanctify
sanctity
satanism
sequence
seraphim
sidesman
skullcap
Sunnites
superior
surplice
swastika
tenebrae
thurible
thurifer

transept
trimurti
triptych
unbelief
unbishop
unchurch
venerate
versicle
vestment
viaticum
vicarage
zoolatry

9

ablutions
alleluiah
allelujah
All Hallow
All Saints
alms bason
altar tomb
anchorite
anointing
antipapal
apocrypha
apostolic
archangel
archfiend
archiarcy
Ascension
athenaeum
atonement
baptismal
beatitude
Beelzebub
beneficed
bishopric
bismillah
black mass
blasphemy
Calvinism
Candlemas
Carmelite
catechism
cathedral
celestial
cere-cloth
Christian
Christmas
churching
clergyman
co-eternal
communion
confessor
Cordelier
cremation
Dalai Lama
dalmatica
damnation
deaconess
dedicated
desecrate
diaconate
dissenter
dissident
dominical
eagle-wood
Easter day
Easter eve
Ember Days
Ember Fast
Ember Tide
episcopal
epistoler

eucharist
eutychian
evangelic
gospeller
Gregorian
Halloween
hierarchy
hierogram
hierology
high mass
holy ghost
holy water
incumbent
induction
interment
interdict
Islamitic
Jansenism
Jansenist
Jesuitism
joss-stick
Lammas Day
lay reader
Lazarists
Lazarites
Levitical
Leviticus
Low Church
Low Sunday
Mahomedan
Maronites
martyrdom
Methodism
Methodist
moderator
monachism
monastery
Mormonism
mundatory
Mussulman
Nestorian
obeisance
offertory
orthodoxy
ostensory
pantheism
pantheist
paraclete
Parseeism
patriarch
Pentecost
pharisaic
plainsong
prayer mat
prayer rug
preaching
precentor
presbyter
priestess
proselyte
prothesis
purgatory
pyrolatry
Quakerism
quasimodo
quicunque
reading-in
reconvert
red rubric
reliquary
religieux
religious
repentant
responses
reverence
ritualism

ritualist
rural dean
sabbatism
sabianism
sacrament
sacrifice
sacrilege
sacristan
salvation
sanctuary
Scripture
semi-Arian
sepulchre
shamanism
solemnity
solemnize
spiritual
sub-beadle
subdeacon
subrector
succentor
suffragan
suffrages
sutteeism
synagogue
synergism
synodical
teleology
Testament
theatines
theocracy
theomachy
theomancy
theopathy
theophany
theosophy
Theravada
tritheism
Vaishnava
Vajrayana
venerable
vestments
Waldenses

10

Abelonians
absolution
abstinence
aladinists
Albigenses
alkoranist
All Hallows
altar bread
altar cloth
altar cross
altar light
altar piece
altar steps
altar table
Anabaptism
Anabaptist
anointment
antichrist
apocalypse
apostolate
apotheosis
archbishop
archdeacon
archflamen
archimagus
archpriest
armageddon
assumption
Athanasian

233

baptistery
benedicite
Bernardine
Bethlemite
bible class
biblically
black friar
Brahminism
Buddhistic
Carthusian
catechumen
Celestines
ceremonial
cherubical
chronicles
church army
churchgoer
church work
churchyard
Cistercian
confessant
confession
conformist
consecrate
consistory
cosmolatry
devotional
ditheistic
divination
Dominicans
doxologize
dragonnade
Eastertide
ecumenical
Ember Weeks
episcopacy
episcopate
epistolary
evangelism
evangelist
evangelize
free chapel
Free Church
Genevanism
gnosticism
Good Friday
gospel side
gymnosophy
halleluiah
hallelujah
hallowmass
heathenism
heaven-born
heliolater
heliolatry
heptateuch
hierocracy
High Church
high priest
holy orders
holy spirit
hylotheism
hyperdulia
iconoclasm
iconoclast
iconolater
iconolatry
idolatress
impanation
indulgence
infallible
invocation
irreligion
irreverent
juggernaut
lady chapel

lay brother
lectionary
magnificat
mariolatry
meditation
ministrant
missionary
Mohammedan
monotheism
monotheist
monstrance
omnipotent
ophiolatry
ordination
Palm Sunday
Pentateuch
pentecost
pharisaism
pilgrimage
prayer book
prayer flag
prebendary
presbytery
priesthood
prophetess
Protestant
puritanism
rectorship
redemption
repentance
reproaches
revelation
rock temple
rood screen
sacerdotal
sacrosanct
sanctified
sanctifier
schismatic
scriptural
septuagint
sepulchral
Sexagesima
Shrovetide
subdeanery
syncretism
tabernacle
temptation
39 articles
Tridentine
unanointed
unbaptized
unbeliever
uncanonize
unclerical
unorthodox
veneration
white friar
Whit Sunday
worshipper
Zend-Avesta

11

acephalites
agnosticism
All Souls' Day
altar screen
antepaschal
antependium
antiphonary
apotheosize
archdiocese
arches court
Arminianism

aspersorium
baldeochino
Benedictine
benediction
benedictory
bibliolatry
bibliomancy
black rubric
blasphemous
Bodhisattva
Catabaptist
Catholicism
chalice veil
celebration
chrismation
chrismatory
Christendom
christening
church house
commination
communicant
consecrator
convocation
crematorium
crucifixion
deification
desecration
devotionist
divine light
doxological
ecclesiarch
episcopalia
epistle-side
Erastianism
eschatology
eternal life
evangelical
evening hymn
everlasting
exhortation
fire-worship
freethinker
Geneva Bible
genuflection
hagiography
Hare Krishna
hierarchism
hierography
humeral veil
immortality
incarnation
inquisition
intercessor
irreligious
irreverence
Karmathians
Latin Church
Lord's supper
Lutheranism
miracle play
mission room
Mohammedism
Nicene Creed
parishioner
œcumenical
passing bell
passionists
passion play
Passion Week
paternoster
patron saint
Pedobaptism
pharisaical
Plymouthism
pontificate
pontifician

prayer wheel
priestcraft
procession
proselytism
proselytize
protomartyr
purificator
Reformation
religionary
religionism
religionist
religiosity
reservation
ritualistic
Roman Church
sacramental
sacring-bell
Sadduceeism
sarcophagus
scientology
Socinianism
theosophist
trinitarian
unbeneficed
uncanonical
undedicated
unorthodoxy
unrighteous
Wesleyanism
Whitsuntide
Zoroastrian

12

All Saints' Day
annunciation
altar frontal
archdeaconry
Ascension Day
Ash Wednesday
Augustinians
Bible Society
chapel of ease
choir service
Christianity
Christmas Day
Christmas Eve
church living
church parade
churchwarden
confessional
confirmation
Confucianism
congregation
consecration
consistorial
devil worship
discipleship
disciplinant
disestablish
dispensation
ditheistical
Easter Sunday
Ecclesiastes
ecclesiastic
ecclesiology
enthronement
episcopalian
evangelicism
exomologesis
frankincense
hot gospeller
image worship
intercession
interdiction

Low Churchman	Anglican music	prayer-meeting	high priesthood
metropolitan	Anglo-Catholic	Protestantism	Maundy Thursday
mission house	antichristian	Quinquagesima	Orthodox Church
New Testament	antiepiscopal	Roman Catholic	Oxford Movement
nunc dimittis	Apostles' Creed	reincarnation	psilanthropism
Old Testament	archarchitect	Sacerdotalism	psilanthropist
omnipresent	archbishopric	Salvation Army	reconsecration
postillation	archdeaconate	sanctuary-lamp	redemptionists
Presbyterian	baptismal shell	scripturalist	Reformed Church
purification	beatification	Shrove Tuesday	Rogation Sunday
Quadragesima	bidding prayer	Swedenborgian	sacramentarian
reconsecrate	burial service	Tractarianism	sanctification
reconversion	burnt offering	Trinity Sunday	sign of the cross
red letter day	canonical hour	unconsecrated	transmigration
religionless	ceremoniarius	unevangelical	trine immersion
residentiary	Christianlike	way of the cross	Trinitarianism
Resurrection	church service		vicar apostolic
Rogation Days	confessionary		
Rogation Week	convocational	**14**	**15**
Salvationist	Corpus Christi		
sanctus bell	credence table	antiscriptural	antievangelical
spiritualism	devotionalist	black letter day	antiministerial
Sunday school	Eastern Church	burnt sacrifice	antitrinitarian
superfrontal	excommunicate	church assembly	Athanasian Creed
thanksgiving	glorification	communion table	cardinal virtues
Unitarianism	High Churchman	crutched friars	Episcopalianism
universalism	holy innocents	Easter offering	excommunication
unscriptural	incense burner	ecclesiastical	harvest festival
vicar general	lord spiritual	Ecclesiasticus	infernal regions
	miracle worker	ecclesiologist	Jehovah's Witness
13	mission church	evangelicalism	metropolitanate
	Mohammedanism	evangelization	Mothering Sunday
All Hallowmass	Nonconformist	extreme unction	Presbyterianism
All Hallows Eve	paschal candle	fire-worshipper	suffragan bishop
All Hallowtide	pastoral staff	fundamentalism	transfiguration
	pectoral cross	Gregorian chant	

Saints

Note.—The numbers of letters mentioned do not include "St" or "Saint," for which allowances should be made when necessary.

3 AND **4**	Alban	Andrew	**7**
	Amand	Anselm	
Abb	André	Ansgar	Ambrose
Ann	Asaph	Bertin	Anschar
Anne	Barbe	Brieuc	Anthony
Bee	Basil	Claire	Austell
Bede	Bavon	Cosmas	Barbara
Bega	Bride	Fabian	Bernard
Cyr	Bruno	Fergus	Bridget
Ebba	Clair	Gallus	Cecilia
Gall	Clara	George	Charles
Jean	David	Helena	Clement
Joan	Denis	Heiler	Crispin
John	Elias	Hilary	Damascus
Jude	Genny	Hubert	Dominic
Just	Giles	Jerome	Dorothy
Loe	Hilda	Joseph	Dunstan
Luce	James	Ludger	Elsinus
Lucy	Kilda	Magnus	Emidius
Luke	Louis	Martha	Etienne
Mark	Lucia	Martin	Eustace
Mary	Marie	Maurus	Francis
Paul	Olave	Michel	Germain
Roch	Paola	Monica	Gregory
Zeno	Peter	Philip	Isodore
		Pierre	Joachim
		Thomas	Leonard
5	**6**	Ursane	Matthew
		Ursula	Maurice
Agnes	Albert	Valery	Michael
Aidan	Andrea	Xavier	Nazaire

Nicolas
Pancras
Patrick
Raphael
Raymond
Romuald
Saviour
Stephen
Swithin
Swithun
Vincent
William

Eusebius
Ignatius
Lawrence
Longinus
Margaret
Nicholas
Placidus
Vericona
Walpurga
Waltheof
Winifred
Zenobius

Fredewith
Hyacinthe
Joan of Arc
Mamertius
Sebastian
Servatius
Sylvester
Valentine
Walpurgis

Hippolytus (10)
Jeanne d'Arc (10)
Mercuriale (10)
Peter Martyr (11)
Philip Neri (10)
Scholastica (11)
Symphorien (10)
Zaccharias (10)

8

Aloysius
Augustus
Barnabas
Benedict
Bernhard
Damianus
Denevick
Donatian

9

Apollonia
Augustine
Catherine
Christina
Demetrius
Eanswythe
Elizabeth
Exuperius

10 AND 11

Apollinaris (11)
Athanasius (10)
Bartholomew (11)
Bernardino (10)
Benhardino (11)
Bonaventura (11)
Christopher (11)
Ethelburga (10)
Eustochium (10)
Gallo Abbato (11)
Gaudentius (10)

12 AND OVER

Anthony of Padua (14
Bridget of Sweden (1£
James the Great (13)
James the Less (12)
John the Baptist (14)
Louis of Toulouse (15
Mary Magdalene (13)
Nicholas of Bari (14)
Nicholas of Myra (14)
Simon Stylites (13)
Thomas Aquinas (13)
Vincent Ferrer (13)

SCIENCE AND TECHNOLOGY
Agriculture

3

awn
bin
cob
cod
cow
cub
dig
ear
erf
ewe
far
feu
gid
hay
hep
hip
hoe
hog
ket
kex
kid
kip
lea
moo
mow
pig
pip
ram
ret
rye
sow
ted
teg
tup
vag
vat
zea

4

akee
aril

avel
bale
barn
bawn
beam
beef
bent
bere
bigg
boon
bran
bull
byre
calf
cart
clay
corn
cote
crop
culm
curb
drey
dung
farm
foal
gait
galt
gape
harl
haum
herd
hind
hink
holt
hops
hull
husk
kine
lamb
lime
loam
lyme
malm
mare
marl

meal
milk
neat
neep
nide
nout
nowt
oast
oats
odal
paco
peat
pest
pone
quey
rabi
rake
rape
resp
rime
root
roup
runn
rust
ryot
sand
scab
seed
sere
shaw
silo
skep
skug
slob
sock
soil
soya
span
stot
teff
toft
tope
tore
udal
vale

vega
weed
wold
yean
zebu

5

ammon
aphid
araba
baler
beans
bhyle
biddy
borax
bosky
bothy
braxy
briza
calve
carse
cavie
chaff
churn
clevy
closh
couch
croft
crone
crops
dairy
ditch
drill
drove
durra
ergot
ervum
farcy
fruit
fungi
gavel
gebur

glume
grain
grass
graze
guano
halfa
hards
haugh
haulm
hedge
hilum
hoove
horse
humus
kulak
lande
llano
lobby
maize
mower
mummy
ovine
plant
ranch
rumen
sewel
sheep
sheth
shoat
shuck
spelt
spuds
staig
stall
stich
stipa
stock
straw
swill
tilth
tiver
tuber
veldt
vimen
vives
vomer
wagon
wheat
withe
withy
worms
yield

6

angora
animal
arable
arista
barley
basset
beeves
binder
bosket
bottle
butter
carney
cattle
cereal
clover
colter
corral
cowman
cratch
cutter

digger
disbud
dobbin
drover
earing
eatage
écurie
enspan
fallow
farina
farmer
fodder
forage
furrow
gargol
garran
gaucho
gimmer
gluten
grains
grange
harrow
heifer
hogget
hogsty
hopper
huller
incult
inning
inspan
intine
jument
linhay
llanos
malkin
manger
manure
mealie
merino
milium
millet
milsey
mowing
nubbin
padnag
pampas
piglet
pigsty
plough
podzol
polder
porker
potato
punner
raggee
rancho
realty
reaper
roller
runrig
sheave
silage
socage
sowans
sowing
stable
steppe
stover
tanist
tomand
travis
trough
turnip
turves
warble
weevil

7

acidity
aerator
alfalfa
amidine
anthrax
avenage
binding
boscage
budding
bulchin
bullock
buttery
cabbage
calving
combine
compost
copland
cornage
coulter
cowherd
cowshed
demesne
digging
dipping
docking
drought
droving
eanling
erosion
farming
fee-tail
foaling
foldage
foot rot
forcing
fox trap
gadsman
granger
grazing
hallier
harvest
hay cart
hay rick
hedging
herding
hogcote
hop pole
hunkers
implant
infield
innings
kidling
lamb-ale
lambing
laniary
layland
leasowe
lucerne
maizena
marlite
milk can
milking
misyoke
morling
multure
murrain
novalia
nursery
pabular
paddock
panicum
pannage
pasture
peonage

piggery
pinetum
pinfold
polders
popcorn
poultry
prairie
praties
predial
provine
pruning
pulping
pummace
radicel
raking
rancher
reaping
rearing
retting
rhizome
rokeage
rundale
rustler
ryotwar
sickled
slanket
spancel
stacker
station
stooker
stubble
stuckle
subsoil
swinery
tantony
tascall
tax cart
threave
thwaite
tillage
tilling
tractor
trammel
trekker
trotter
udaller
vaquero
vitular
wagoner
windrow
yardman

8

agronomy
branding
breeding
clipping
cropping
ditching
drainage
elevator
ensilage
farmyard
forestry
gleaning
grafting
hayfield
haymaker
haystack
haywagon
hopfield
kohlrabi
landgirl
loosebox

milkcart
pedigree
pig-swill
plougher
rootcrop
rotation
shearing
sheep-dip
vineyard
watering
wireworm

9

agrimotor
agroville
allotment
cornfield
dairy-farm
dairymaid
disc drill
fertility
fungicide
gathering

grassland
harrowing
harvester
haymaking
hop-picker
horserake
husbandry
implement
incubator
livestock
pasturage
penthouse
phosphate
pig trough
ploughing
rice field
screening
separator
shorthorn
sugar beet
sugar cane
swineherd
thrashing
threshing
trenching
winnowing

10

agronomist
battery hen
cattle cake
cultivator
fertilizer
harvesting
husbandman
irrigation
mould-board
plantation
rounding-up
self-binder
transplant
weed killer
wheatfield

11

agriculture
cake crusher
chaff cutter
chicken farm
crude plough

cultivation
fertilizing
germination
insecticide
motor plough
pastureland
poultry farm
reclamation
stock-taking
water-trough
weed control

12

agricultural
feeding-stock
fermentation
horticulture
insemination
market garden
smallholding
swathe turner
turnip cutter

Astronomy

(a.) = asteroid.   (c.) = constellation.   (c.p.) = constellation (popular name).
(g.) = group of stars.   (p.) = planet.   (s.) = noted star.   (sa.) = large satellite.

2 – 4

Apus (c.)
Ara (c.)
Argo (c.)
belt
Bull (c.p.)
coma
Crab (c.p.)
Crow (c.p.)
Crux (c.)
Cup (c.p.)
Eros
Grus (c.)
halo
Hare (c.p.)
Hebe
Io
Juno
Leo (c.)
limb
Lion (c.p.)
Lynx (c.) (c.p.)
Lyra (c.)
Lyre (c.p.)
Mars (p.)
Mira (s.)
Moon
Net (c.p.)
Node
nova
orb
Pavo (c.)
pole
Ram (c.p.)
Rhea (sa.)
Star
Sun
Swan (c.p.)
Vega (s.)
Wolf (c.p.)

5

Algol (s.)
Altar (c.p.)
Apollo
Ariel (sa.)
Aries (c.)
Arrow (c.p.)
Ceres
Cetus (c.)
Clock (c.p.)
comet
Crane (c.p.)
Deneb (s.)
Digit
Dione (sa.)
Draco (c.)
Eagle (c.p.)
Earth (p.)
epact
epoch
error
flare
giant
Hamal (s.)
Hyads (g.)
Hydra (c.)
Indus (c.)
label
Lepus (c.)
Libra (c.)
lunar
Lupus (c.)
Mensa (c.)
Musca (c.)
nadir
Norma (c.)
orbit
Orion (c.)
phase
Pluto (p.)

Regel (s.)
Rigel (s.)
solar
space
Spica (s.)
stars
Titan (sa.)
Tucan (c.p.)
Twins (c.p.)
umbra
Venus (p.)
Vesta (a.)
Vrigo (c.)

6

albedo
Altair (s.)
Antlia (c.)
apogee
Aquila (c.)
Archer (c.p.)
astral
Auriga (c.)
aurora
binary
Boötes (c.)
Bolide
Caelum (c.)
Cancer (c.)
Castor (s.)
colure
Corona
corvus (c.)
crater
Crater (c.)
Cygnus (c.)
Dipper
domify
Dorado (c.)

Dragon (c.p.)
Europa (sa.)
Fishes (c.p.)
Fornax (c.)
galaxy
Gemini (c.)
gnomon
Hyades (g.)
Hydrus (c.)
Icarus (a.)
Indian (c.p.)
Lizard (c.p.)
lunary
meteor
moonet
nebula
Oberon (sa.)
Octans (c.)
Octant (c.p.)
octile
Pallas (a.)
parsec
Pictor (c.)
Pisces (c.)
planet
Plough (g.)
Pollux (s.)
pulsar
quasar
Radius
Saturn (p.)
Scales (c.p.)
Sirius (s.)
sphere
Square (c.p.)
sun-dog
syzygy
Taurus (c.)
Tethys (sa.)
triton (sa.)
Tucana (c.)

Uranus (p.)
vector
vertex
Viking
Virgin (c.p.)
Volans (c.)
zenith
zodiac

7

Airpump (c.p.)
Alphard (s.)
Antares (s.)
apogean
auroral
azimuth
big-bang
Canopus (s.)
Capella (s.)
Centaur (c.p.)
Cepheid
Cepheus (c.) (c.p.)
cluster
Columba (c.)
cometic
Dog Star (s.)
Dolphin (c.p.)
eclipse
equator
equinox
Furnace (c.p.)
gibbous
Giraffe (c.p.)
Jupiter (p.)
Lacerta (c.)
Mariner
Mercury (p.)
metonic
mock sun
nebulae
nebular
Neptune (p.)
new moon
Peacock (c.p.)
Pegasus (c.)
perigee
Perseus (c.)
Phoenix (c.) (c.p.)
Polaris (s.)
Procyon (s.)
Proxima (s.)
radiant
Regulus (s.)
Sagitta (c.)
Scorpio (c.)
Sea goat (c.p.)
Serpens (c.)
Serpent (c.p.)
Sextans (c.)
Sextant (c.p.)
sextile
spectra
sputnik
stellar
sunspot
Titania (sa.)
transit
Unicorn (c.p.)

8

Achernar (s.)
aerolite

aerolith
almagest
Alpherat (s.)
altitude
aphelion
Aquarius (c.)
Arcturus (s.)
asterism
asteroid
Callisto (sa.)
canicula
Circinus (c.)
cometary
Denebola (s.)
draconic
ecliptic
epicycle
Equuleus (c.)
Eridanus (c.)
evection
Explorer
fireball
free fall
full moon
Ganymede (sa.)
Great Dog (c.p.)
Hercules (c.) (c.p.)
latitude
Leo Minor (c.)
Loadstar (s.)
Lodestar (s.)
meridian
meteoric
Milky Way
nutation
occulted
parallax
parhelia
penumbra
perigean
Pleiades (g.)
Pole Star (s.)
quadrant
quadrate
quartile
quintile
red giant
red shift
Scorpion (c.p.)
Sculptor (c.)
Ship Argo (c.p.)
sidereal
solstice
spectrum
spheroid
starless
stellary
sublunar
systemic
tetragon
Triangle (c.p.)
universe
Van Allen
Vanguard
variable
zodiacal

9

aerolitic
Aldebaran (s.)
Andromeda (c.) (c.p.)
ascendant
ascension
astrology

astronomy
azimuthal
black hole
canicular
celestial
Centaurus (c.)
Chamaelon (c.)
Chameleon (c.p.)
Compasses (c.p.)
cosmogeny
cosmology
Curtation
Delphinus (c.)
draconian
elevation
ephemeris
epicyclic
firmament
Fomalhaut (s.)
Great Bear (c.p.)
hour angle
light-year
Little Dog (c.p.)
longitude
lunisolar
magnitude
meteorite
meteoroid
meteorous
Minuteman
Monoceros (c.)
Nubeculae
Noah's Dove (c.p.)
novilunar
Ophiuchus (c.)
parhelian
planetary
planetoid
planetule
Ploughman (c.p.)
Ptolemaic
reflector
refractor
Reticulum (c.)
satellite
solar wind
star-gazer
starlight
sublunary
supernova
Sword-fish (c.p.)
synodical
telescope
Telescope (c.p.)
trioctile
uranology
Ursa Major (c.)
Ursa Minor (c.)
Via Lactea
Vulpecula (c.)

10

aberration
altazimuth
apparition
asteroidal
astrologer
astrometer
astonomer
astronomic
Atlantides (g.)
atmosphere
Betelgeuse (s.)
brightness

Canis Major (c.)
Canis Minor (c.)
Cassiopeia (c.) (c.p.)
Charioteer (c.p.)
cometarium
Copernican
cosmic rays
Crab nebula
depression
discoverer
dispositor
double star
earthshine
elongation
exaltation
extra-solar
Flying Fish (c.p.)
Greyhounds (c.p.)
hour circle
Little Bear (c.p)
Little Lion (c.p.)
lunar cycle
lunar month
lunar probe
Microscope (c.p.)
North Star
opposition
outer space
perihelion
Piscis Aust. (c.)
precession
prominence
quadrature
refraction
retrograde
rudolphine
Sea Monster (c.p.)
siderolite
star-gazing
supergiant
terminator
trajectory
Triangulum (c.)
uranoscopy
Watersnake (c.p.)
white dwarf

11

astrography
astronomize
blazing star
Capricornus (c.)
conjunction
declination
Evening Star (p.)
falling star
giant planet
Hunter Orion (c.p.)
last quarter
Little Horse (c.p.)
metemptosis
meteorolite
minor planet
Morning Star (p.)
neutron star
occultation
photosphere
observatory
planetarium
Sagittarius (c.)
solar system
Southern Fly (c.p.)
spectrology
Telescopium (c.)   239

terrestrial
uranography
Water-bearer (c.p.)
Winged Horse (c.p.)

spectroscope
spiral galaxy
uranographic
Van Allen Belt
variable star

Bird of Paradise (c.p.)
Camelopardalis (c.)
Corona Borealis (c.)
interplanetary
Musca Australis (c.)
radio astronomy
radio telescope
right ascension
Sculptor's Tools (c.p.)
summer solstice
transit of Venus
vertical circle
winter solstice
Wolf-Rayet star
zenith distance

12

astronautics
astronomical
astrophysics
Charles's Wain (g.)
chromosphere
doppler shift
eccentricity
first quarter
Flying-dragon (c.p.)
Halley's comet
Horologium (c.)
intermundane
interstellar
lunar eclipse
lunar rainbow
Microscopium (c.)
Saturn's rings
shooting star
sidereal time
solar eclipse
Southern Fish (c.p.)

13

Alpha Centauri (s.)
Berenice's Hair (c.p.)
Canes Venatici (c.)
Coma Berenices (c.)
constellation
Crux Australis (c.)
meteorography
Northern Crown (c.p.)
Painter's Easel (c.p.)
River Eridanus (c.p.)
Serpent-bearer (c.p.)
sidereal clock
Southern Cross (c.p.)
Southern Crown (c.p.)
zodiacal light

14

annular eclipse
Aurora Borealis

15 AND 16

Alphonsine tables (16)
armillary sphere (15)
astronomical unit (16)
Aurora Australis (15)
celestial sphere (15)
Corona Australis (c.) (15)
Fraunhofer lines (15)
Magellanic Clouds (16)
meteoric showers (15)
Piscis Australis (c.) (15)
Sculptor's Chisel (c.) (15)

Biology, botany, and zoology

2 AND 3

ADH
ADP
ATP
bud
CNS
cud
DNA
ear
egg
ER
eye
FAD
fin
gel
gum
gut
IAA
jaw
lip
NAD
ova
pod
rib
RNA
rod
sap
sex

4

anal
anus
apex
axon
bark
bile
bird
body

bone
bulb
burr
cell
claw
cone
cork
corm
cyst
food
foot
gall
gene
germ
gill
haem
hair
hand
head
hoof
host
iris
leaf
lens
life
limb
lung
milk
NADH
NADP
neck
node
ovum
palp
pith
pome
pore
root
salt
seed
skin

stem
tail
urea
vein
wilt
wing
wood
yolk

5

actin
aorta
aster
auxin
berry
birth
blood
bract
brain
calyx
chyle
chyme
cilia
class
cline
clone
codon
colon
cutin
cycad
cycle
death
digit
drupe
druse
fauna
femur
fibre
flora

fruit
genus
gland
gonad
graft
heart
hilum
humus
hymen
ileum
imago
larva
latex
liver
lymph
molar
mouth
mucus
NADPH
nasal
nasty
nerve
order
organ
ovara
ovary
ovule
penis
petal
phage
plant
pubic
pubis
pupil
ramus
resin
scale
semen
sense
sepal
shell

shoot
sinus
skull
smell
sperm
spine
spore
stoma
style
sweat
taste
testa
thigh
tibia
touch
trunk
tuber
urine
vagus
villi
virus
whorl
wrist
xylem

6

achene
aerobe
albino
allele
amnion
animal
annual
anther
artery
atrium
biceps
biotic
botany
branch
bulbil
caecum
canine
carpal
carpel
caudal
chitin
climax
cloaca
coccyx
cocoon
coelum
cornea
cortex
dermis
dormin
embryo
enamel
energy
enzyme
facial
faeces
family
fibril
fibrin
fibula
floral
flower
foetus
forest
floral
fusion
gamete
gemmae

genome
girdle
growth
gullet
hybrid
hyphae
joints
labial
labium
labrum
lamina
larynx
leaves
lignin
mammal
mantle
marrow
mucous
muscle
mutant
nastic
nectar
neural
neuron
oocyte
oogamy
palate
pappus
pectin
pelvic
pelvis
phloem
phylum
pistil
plasma
pollen
purine
radius
rectum
retina
runner
sacrum
sexual
spinal
spleen
stamen
stigma
stolon
sucker
tactic
tannin
telome
tendon
tenson
testis
thorax
tissue
tongue
turgor
ureter
uterus
vagina
vessel
vision
zygote

7

abdomen
adenine
adipore
adrenal
aerobic
albumen
anatomy

annulus
antenna
antigen
asexual
atavism
auricle
biology
biotope
bipolar
bladder
bronchi
cambium
capsule
cardiac
carotid
cell sap
chaetae
chalaza
chiasma
chorion
cochlea
conifer
corolla
cranial
cranium
creeper
cristae
culture
cuticle
cutting
diploid
dormant
ecdysis
ecology
elastin
enteron
epiboly
epigeal
gastric
genital
gizzard
glottis
habitat
haploid
hearing
hepatic
histone
hormone
humerus
incisor
insulin
isogamy
jejunum
keratin
lacteal
linkage
mammary
medulla
meiosis
mitosis
myotome
nectary
nostril
nucleus
oogonia
organic
osmosis
oviduct
petiole
pharynx
pigment
pinnate
plastid
plumule
protein
pyloric

radicle
rhachis
rhizoid
rhizome
root cap
species
spindle
sternum
stomach
stomata
suberin
synapse
syngamy
systole
tapetum
tap root
teleost
tetanus
thallus
thyroid
trachea
triceps
trophic
tropism
urethra
vacuole
viscera
vitamin
zoology

8

abductor
abscisin
acoelous
acrosome
adductor
aeration
alkaloid
allogamy
alveolus
amoeboid
anaerobe
antibody
apospory
appendix
auditory
autogamy
bacteria
biennial
bile duct
bisexual
blastula
brachial
carapace
carotene
cellular
cell wall
cerebral
cerebrum
chordate
clavicle
cleavage
clitoris
coenzyme
collagen
cytology
dendrite
duodenum
ectoderm
efferent
egestion
endoderm
feedback
flagella

flatworm
follicle
ganglion
genetics
genitals
genotype
germ cell
holdfast
holozoic
homodont
hypogeal
inner ear
lamellae
lenticel
life span
ligament
mast cell
maxillae
membrane
meristem
mesoderm
midbrain
moulting
movement
muscular
mutation
mycelium
nerve net
nucellus
ontogeny
pancreas
papillae
parasite
pectoral
perianth
pericarp
perineum
placenta
plankton
polarity
polysome
pregnant
prop root
protozoa
receptor
ribosome
root hair
ruminant
sclereid
seedling
skeleton
spiracle
symbiont
syncarpy
taxonomy
tegument
tentacle
thalamus
tracheid
tympanum
vascular
vertebra
virology
zoospore

9

adrenalin
allantois
amino acid
anabolism
anaerobic
anisogamy
antennule

appendage
arteriole
autonomic
basal body
branchial
branching
capillary
carnivore
cartilage
cellulase
cellulose
centriole
chiasmata
chromatid
chromatin
chrysalis
commensal
community
corpuscle
cotyledon
cytoplasm
Darwinism
diaphragm
digestion
dominance
dura mater
dysploidy
ecosystem
ectoplasm
endocrine
endoplasm
endostyle
epidermis
eukaryote
evolution
excretion
excretory
exodermis
fertilize
forebrain
germinate
gestation
guttation
gynaecium
haemocoel
halophyte
herbivore
hindbrain
histology
homospory
hypocotyl
ingestion
inhibitor
internode
intestine
life cycle
life forms
megaspore
micropyle
middle ear
migration
mutagenic
nephridia
nerve cell
notochord
nucleolus
olfactory
oogenesis
operculum
optic lobe
organelle
organogeny
oxidation
pacemaker
perennial
pericycle

phagocyte
phellogen
phenotype
phylogeny
pituitary
proboscis
pulmonary
recessive
reflex arc
reticulum
retractor
sclerotic
sebaceous
secretion
secretory
selection
sieve cell
sieve tube
sporangia
Sporogony
sterility
stone cell
substrate
succulent
symbiosis
tricuspid
umbilical
unisexual
ventricle
xerophyte

10

acoelomate
actomyosin
alimentary
androecium
antheridia
anticlinal
aortic arch
apical cell
archegonia
autecology
biological
blastocoel
blastocyst
blastoderm
blastomere
blastopore
bronchiole
catabolism
centromere
centrosome
cerebellum
chemotaxis
chromomere
chromosome
coleoptile
copulation
dehiscence
dermatogen
entemology
epididymis
epiglottis
epithelium
fibrinogen
generation
geotropism
glomerulus
grey matter
guard cells
hemocyanin
hemoglobin
herbaceous
hereditary

heterodont
homocercal
homozygous
hygrophyte
hypophysis
incubation
inhibition
integument
interferon
Krebs cycle
Lamarckism
leaf sheath
leucoplast
locomotion
lymphocyte
mesenteron
metabolism
monoecious
morphology
mother cell
mycorrhiza
negentropy
nerve fibre
neural tube
nitrifying
nucleotide
oesophagus
omnivorous
osteoblast
osteoclast
parasitism
parenchyma
pathogenic
periosteum
phelloderm
photonasty
phototaxis
physiology
pineal body
polyploidy
population
prokaryote
prothallus
protoplasm
pyramidine
saprophyte
sarcolemma
schizogony
sieve plate
splanchnic
sporophyte
subspecies
succession
synecology
vegetation
vegetative
vertebrate
viviparity

11

aestivation
allelomorph
antibiotics
archenteron
autotrophic
autotropism
carbon cycle
carboxylase
carnivorous
chlorophyll
chloroplast
collenchyma
competition
conjugation

deamination
dessication
endothelium
environment
erythrocyte
exoskeleton
facultative
gall bladder
gametophyte
genetic code
germination
Golgi bodies
haemocyanin
haemoglobin
heterospory
hibernation
homeostatic
homeostatis
infundibulum
inheritance
loop of Henle
monoculture
muscle fibre
nematoblast
nucleic acid
orientation
parturition
pericardium
pinocytosis
plasmolysis
polar bodies
pollination
polypeptide
pseudopodia
respiration

somatic cell
spermatozoa
sub-cellular
tapetal cell
thermotaxis
triploblast
white matter
zooplankton

12

all-or-nothing
archesporium
back-crossing
bacteriology
biochemistry
buccal cavity
central canal
chondroblast
denitrifying
diploblastic
distribution
ectoparasite
endoparasite
endoskeleton
fermentation
flexor muscle
gastrulation
heliotropism
heterocercal
heterogamete
heterozygous
hypothalamus
invagination

invertebrate
mammary gland
medullary ray
microbiology
mitochondria
myelin sheath
nerve impulse
palaeobotany
phospholipid
phototropism
red blood cell
reductionism
reproduction
sclerenchyma
smooth muscle
spermatozoid
telolecithal

13

accommodation
bacteriophage
bicuspid valve
binary fission
cephalization
chemoreceptor
decomposition
dental formula
erector muscle
extracellular
Fallopian tube
fertilization
hermaphrodite
homoiothermic

insectivorous
intracellular
marine biology
mitochondrion
morphogenesis
multinucleate
ovoviviparity
palisade cells
parthenocarpy
photoreceptor
phytoplankton
plasmodesmata
proprioceptor
striped muscle
thermotropism
thigmotropism
translocation
transpiration

14 AND 15

Brunner's glands (14)
chemosynthesis (14)
extensor muscle (14)
Haversian canal (14)
multiple fission (15)
osmoregulation (14)
oxyhaemoglobin (14)
parthenogenesis (15)
photoperiodism (14)
photosynthesis (14)
poikilothermic (14)
polysaccharide (14)
vascular bundle (14)

Chemistry and metallurgy

2 AND 3

azo
DDT
DNA
E.M.F.
fat
gas
ion
oil
ore
pH
pKa
PVC
RNA
sol
TCP
tin
TNT

4

acid
acyl
alum
aryl
atom
base
bond
cell
clay
coal
coke
enol

gold
iron
keto
lead
lime
meta
mica
mole
neon
rust
salt
slag
soda
spin
zinc

5

aldol
alkyl
alloy
amide
amine
amino
anion
anode
arene
argon
basic
beryl
borax
boron
brass
chalk

ester
ether
ethyl
freon
glass
group
imine
invar
ionic
lipid
metal
model
molal
molar
monad
nylon
oxide
ozone
phase
radon
redox
resin
roast
smelt
solid
steel
sugar
vinyl
xenon

6

acetal
acetic

acetyl
acidic
adduct
aerate
alkali
alkane
alkene
alkyne
ammine
atomic
aufbau
barium
biuret
bleach
borane
borate
bronze
buffer
butane
carbon
cation
cerium
chrome
cobalt
copper
curium
dipole
dry ice
energy
enzyme
erbium
ethane
ferric
galena

243

gangue
gypsum
halide
helium
indium
iodate
iodide
iodine
iodite
iodize
isomer
ketone
ligand
liquid
litmus
methyl
nickel
octane
olefin
osmium
oxygen
period
phenol
phenyl
potash
proton
quartz
raceme
radium
reduce
refine
retort
ribose
rutile
silica
silver
sinter
sodium
solute
starch
sterol
sulfur
teepol
teflon
thymol

7

acetate
acetone
acidity
aerosol
alchemy
alcohol
alumina
amalgam
ammonia
analyse
aniline
anodize
antacid
arsenic
bauxite
benzene
bismuth
bonding
bromate
bromide
bromine
cadmium
caesium
calcium
carbide
cathode
chemist

chloric
cyanate
cyanide
diamond
dioxide
element
entropy
ferment
fermium
ferrate
ferrous
formate
gallium
gelatin
glucose
hafnium
halogen
holmium
hydrate
hydride
iridium
isotope
krypton
lithium
mercury
methane
mineral
monomer
naptha
neutral
neutron
niobium
nitrate
nitride
nitrite
nucleon
orbital
organic
osmosis
osmotic
oxidant
oxidize
oxyacid
pentane
peptide
pig iron
plastic
polymer
propane
protein
pyrites
quantum
quinine
reagent
rhenium
rhodium
silicon
soluble
solvent
spectra
spelter
sucrose
sulfate
sulfide
sulfite
sulphur
terbium
terpene
thorium
thulium
titrate
toluene
tritium
uranium
valence
valency

vitamin
vitriol
wolfram
yttrium

8

actinide
actinium
aldehyde
alkaline
aluminum
ammonium
analysis
antimony
aromatic
asbestos
astatine
Bakelite
Bessemer
caffeine
carbolic
carbonic
carbonyl
cast iron
catalyst
charcoal
chemical
chlorate
chloride
chlorine
chromate
chromite
chromium
cinnabar
corundum
covalent
cryolite
cyanogen
diatomic
diborane
didymium
disilane
dissolve
electron
europium
emission
enthalpy
ethylene
firedamp
fluoride
fluorine
francium
fructose
glycerol
graphite
gunmetal
half-life
haloform
hematite
hydrated
hydrogen
hydroxyl
ideal gas
inert gas
iodoform
kerosene
kinetics
litharge
lone pair
lutetium
magnesia
marsh gas
masurium
methanol

molecule
nichrome
nicotine
nitrogen
nobelium
noble gas
non-metal
oxyanion
paraffin
particle
peroxide
phosgene
platinum
polonium
pot metal
reactant
reaction
refining
rock salt
rubidium
samarium
saturate
scandium
selenium
silicate
solution
spectrum
suboxide
sulphate
sulphide
sulphite
tantalum
test tube
thallium
titanium
tungsten
unit cell
unstable
vanadium
water gas

9

acetylene
acylation
alchemist
alcoholic
aliphatic
allotropy
aluminate
aluminium
americium
amino acid
anhydrous
anti-knock
apparatus
aqua regia
bell metal
berkelium
beryllium
brimstone
carbonate
carbonium
catalysis
cellolose
chemistry
chokedamp
colombium
corrosion
deuterium
diazonium
duralumin
galvanize
germanium
haematite

histamine
homolysis
hydration
hydroxide
indicator
inorganic
insoluble
isomerism
lanthanum
limestone
limewater
magnesium
magnetite
manganese
metalloid
millerite
molecular
monatomic
neodymium
neptunium
nitration
nitronium
oxidation
palladium
periodic
permalloy
petroleum
phosphate
phosphide
plutonium
polar bond
polyester
polythene
polyvinyl
potassium
quicklime
rare gases
reductant
reduction
ruthenium
resonance
saltpetre
semi-metal
solvation
stability
strontium
sulphuric
synthesis
synthetic
tellurium
titration
vulcanite
ytterbium
zirconium

10

acetic acid
alkalinity

allotropes
amphoteric
analytical
bimetallic
bond energy
bond length
carnallite
catenation
chalybeate
chemically
chloroform
dative bond
double bond
dysprosium
electronic
enantiomer
exothermic
flotation
formic acid
free energy
gadolinium
heavy water
hydrolysis
isocyanide
laboratory
lactic acid
lanthanide
latent heat
lawrencium
mass number
metallurgy
mischmetal
molybdenum
Muntz metal
natural gas
neutralize
nitric acid
nucleotide
oxalic acid
phosphorus
polyatomic
polymerize
promethium
rare earths
saccharide
solubility
technetium
transition
whitemetal
zinc blende
zwitterion

11

acetylation
benzoic acid
bicarbonate
californium
cassiterite

cholesterol
crystallize
cyclohexane
dehydration
einsteinium
electrolyte
elimination
endothermic
equilibrium
free radical
German steel
ground state
hydrocarbon
hydrocyanic
hydroxonium
laughing gas
litmus paper
mendelevium
Muntz's metal
naphthalene
non-metallic
nucleophile
phosphorous
pitchblende
polystyrene
precipitate
prussic acid
quicksilver
radioactive
ribonucleic
sal ammoniac
Schiff's base
sublimation
substituent
tautomerism
transuranic
wrought iron

12

acetaldeyde
alkali metals
alkyl halides
atomic number
atomic weight
benzaldehyde
blast furnace
carbohydrate
carbonic acid
chlorination
condensation
covalent bond
deliquescent
diamagnetism
disaccharide
displacement
dissociation
distillation
electrolysis

electrophile
fermentation
formaldehyde
German silver
Haber process
halogenation
hydrochloric
hydrogen bond
permanganate
praseodymium
Prince's metal
protactinium
rate constant
sulphonamide
tartaric acid
zone refining

13

Bessemer steel
carbon dioxide
chain reaction
chromium steel
giant molecule
lattice energy
molecular mass
paramagnetism
periodic table
petrochemical
precipitation
radioactivity
reaction order
recrystallize
semiconductor
sulphuric acid
trisaccharide

14 AND OVER

Born-Haber cycle (14)
Britannia metal (14)
carbon monoxide (14)
carboxylic acid (14)
Chile saltpetre (14)
decarbonization (15)
deoxyribonucleic (16)
electrochemical (15)
esterification (14)
Grignard reagent (15)
monosaccharide (14)
organo-metallic (14)
oxidizing agent (14)
phosphor bronze (14)
photosynthesis (14)
polysaccharide (14)
reaction profile (15)
saponification (14)
trinitrotoluene (15)

Dyes, paints and colours

3

bay
dun
hue
jet
lac
red
tan
vat

4

acid
anil
ashy
bice
bise
blue
buff
cyan

dark
deep
drab
ebon
ecru
fast
fawn
food
gilt
gold

gray
grey
hoar
jade
kohl
lake
navy
pale
pink
puce

roan
room
rose
ruby
rust
sage
weld
woad
wold

5

amber
argal
argol
ashen
azoic
azure
basic
beige
black
brown
camel
chica
coral
cream
diazo
ebony
flame
grain
green
gules
hazel
henna
hoary
ivory
khaki
lemon
light
lilac
livid
mauve
murex
ocher
ochre
ochry
olive
orpin
paint
roset
rouge
ruddy
sable
sandy
sepia
snowy
sooty
stain
swart
tawny
ulmin
umber
white

6

anotta
anotto
archil
auburn
aureat
azured
bablah
bistre

bluish
cerise
cherry
chrome
claret
cobalt
copper
damask
direct
enamel
fallow
flaxen
fulvid
fustic
ginger
golden
greeny
indigo
isabel
kermes
lac dye
litmus
madder
marone
maroon
minium
modena
morone
murrey
orange
pastel
purple
reseda
roucou
rubian
rubied
rubric
rufous
russet
sallow
sanded
sienna
silver
sorrel
spotty
Tyrian
umbery
vermil
violet
virent
yellow

7

alkanet
almagra
annotta
annotto
apricot
arnotto
aureate
barwood
bezetta
camboge
camwood
carmine
carroty
cassius
catechu
cerulin
cesious
chermes
citrine
coupler
crimson

cudbear
cyanine
darkish
dracina
dracine
emerald
filemot
flavine
fulvous
fuscous
gamboge
grayish
greyish
grizzle
grizzly
hazelfy
ingrain
logwood
magenta
mahaleb
minious
mordant
mottled
munjeet
nacarat
nankeen
natural
neutral
old gold
piebald
pigment
pinkish
plunket
reddish
red lead
rubican
ruby red
russety
saffron
scarlet
silvern
silvery
sinopia
sinopis
sky blue
solvent
spotted
stammel
streaky
striped
sulphur
swarthy
verdant
vermiel
watchet
whiting
whitish
xanthic
zaphara

8

alizarin
amaranth
amethyst
ashy pale
blood red
brownish
caesious
cardinal
carotene
cerulean
chay-root
chestnut
chromule

cinnabar
croceous
disperse
glaucous
greenish
gridelin
grizzled
iron grey
jet black
lavender
litharge
luteolin
mazarine
navy blue
nut brown
oak stain
ochreous
off-white
pea green
purplish
rose hued
rubrical
saffrony
sanguine
sap green
sapphire
saxe blue
sea green
speckled
streaked
titanium
verditer
viridian
xanthine
xanthium

9

alizarine
argentine
aubergine
azure tint
bone black
brilliant
carnation
chaya root
chocolate
coal black
cochineal
colour box
columbine
coralline
curcumine
developer
double dye
draconine
duck green
dun colour
Dutch pink
dyer's weed
dye stuffs
encrimson
envermeil
erythrean
ertythrine
euchloric
foliomort
Indian red
jade green
kalsomine
lampblack
leaf-green
lily white
lime green
myrobalan

oil colour
oxidation
pigmental
prasinous
puniceous
purpureal
purpurine
quercetin
royal blue
rufescent
safflower
sallowish
santaline
sapan wood
sap colour
sarcoline
Saxon blue
sky colour
silver grey
snow white
steel blue
turkey red
turquoise
verdigris
verditure
vermilion
vinaceous
virescent
white-lead
willowish
yellowish
zinc-white

10

alutaceous
apple green
aquamarine
atramental
aurigerous
Berlin blue
body colour
Brazil wood
Braziletto
burnt umber
carthamine
cobalt-blue

coquelicot
double-dyed
endochrome
erubescent
flavescent
florentine
French navy
giallolina
grass green
heliotrope
indigo blue
indigotine
ivory white
morbidezza
mosaic gold
ochraceous
olivaceous
olive green
powder blue
puce colour
quercitrin
roan colour
rose colour
ruby colour
salmon pink
smaragdine
snowy white
spadiceous
Spanish red
stone ochre
strawberry
swartiness
terra-cotta
terre verte
violaceous
whity-brown

11

aerial tints
anthocyanin
ash-coloured
atramentous
bombycinous
bottle green
burnt orange
burnt sienna

chlorophyll
chrome green
cineritious
cinnamon red
crimson lake
dun-coloured
ferruginous
feuillemort
fiesta pink
flame colour
flesh colour
fluorescent
incarnadine
king's yellow
lateritious
lemon yellow
liver colour
mandarining
neutral tint
orange tawny
peach colour
peacock blue
stone colour
straw colour
terra sienna
ultramarine
Venetian red
viridescent
water colour
yellow ochre

12

airforce blue
Avignon berry
cherry colour
chrome colour
claret colour
chrome yellow
copper colour
dragon's blood
Egyptian blue
electric blue
emerald green
ferruginated
feuillemorte
golden yellow

grain colours
Indian madder
Indian yellow
Lincoln green
midnight blue
Naples yellow
Persian berry
pillar-box red
Prussian blue
rose-coloured
sapphire blue
Spanish black
Spanish brown
Spanish white
thenard's blue
Tyrian purple

13

Adrianople red
auripigmentum
cadmium yellow
chestnut brown
couleur de rose
cream-coloured
fibre-reactive
flame-coloured
flesh-coloured
peach-coloured
rainbow-tinted
Scheele's green
straw-coloured
trout-coloured
versicoloured
yellow colours

14 – 15

atramentaceous (14)
Brunswick black (14)
Brunswick green (14)
chocolate colour (15)
copper-coloured (14)
divers-coloured (14)
Frankfort black (14)
highly coloured (14)
quercitron bark (14)

Engineering
See also **Instruments** and **Tools and simple machines**

2 AND 3

ace
amp
B.H.P.
cam
cog
dam
E.M.F.
erg
fan
fit
gab
hob
H.P.
hub
I H.P.
ion
key

lag
nut
ohm
oil
ram
rig
R.P.M.
sag
tap
tew
tie
U.H.F.
V.H.F.

4

arch
axle

beam
belt
bolt
burr
cast
coak
cone
cowl
flaw
flux
fuel
fuse
gear
gibs
glue
hasp
hook
hose
jack

kiln
lens
lift
link
lock
loom
main
mill
mine
nail
nave
oily
pawl
pile
pipe
plan
plug
pump
rack

rail
reel
road
rope
rung
rust
shop
skid
slag
slue
stay
stop
stud
suck
sump
tamp
tank
test
tire
tool
tram
tube
turn
tyre
unit
vane
vent
void
volt
weir
weld
wire
work
worm

5

alloy
anode
binac
blast
braze
cable
chair
chase
civil
clamp
cleat
compo
crane
crank
crate
deuce
dowel
drill
drive
elbow
emery
felly
flawy
flows
flume
flush
force
gauge
girder
grace
H-beam
helix
hinge
hoist
ingot
input
jantu
jenny

jewel
joint
joist
keyed
laser
level
lever
lewis
maser
miner
model
motor
mould
oakum
oiler
pedal
pivot
plant
power
press
pylon
quern
radar
radio
ratch
relay
resin
rigid
rivet
rough
rusty
screw
shaft
short
shunt
slack
slide
sling
smelt
spoke
spool
spout
stamp
steam
still
strap
strut
stulm
swage
swape
taper
tewel
tommy
tools
tooth
T-rail
train
valve
video
waste
wedge
wharf
wheel
willy
wiper
works
X-rays

6

analog
aerial
anneal
axunge
barrel

bit-end
blower
bobbin
boiler
bridge
buffer
burner
camber
clutch
coppin
cotter
couple
cradle
cut-out
damper
derail
duplex
dynamo
energy
engine
fitter
flange
flashe
funnel
geyser
gutter
hinged
hooter
ingate
intake
jigger
kibble
lacing
ladder
lamina
latten
magnet
milled
mining
moment
monkey
nipple
nozzle
oil can
oil gas
output
petrol
pinion
piston
pulley
punkah
rarefy
repair
retard
rigger
rocket
roller
rotary
rundle
sagger
saw pit
sheave
siding
sleeve
sluice
smiddy
smithy
socket
solder
spigot
static
stoker
strain
stress
strike
sucker

switch
swivel
system
tackle
taglia
tappet
temper
tender
thrust
tie-bar
tie-rod
tinned
toggle
torque
tripod
trolly
tubing
tunnel
tuyere
uncoil
vacuum
washer
welded
welder
windle

7

adapter
air duct
airfoil
air pipe
air pump
air tube
air trap
artisan
autocar
autovac
battery
bearing
belting
booster
bracket
cab tyre
caisson
casting
cathode
chafery
chamfer
chimney
cistern
clacker
column
conduit
cutting
derrick
digital
drawbar
drawing
dry dock
dry pile
dynamic
exciter
exhaust
eyebolt
factory
ferrule
firebox
fitting
forging
founder
foundry
fulcrum
furnace
fuse box

gas trap
gearing
gimbals
gudgeon
hydrant
inertia
jointer
journal
lagging
lockage
lock-nut
machine
magneto
manhole
mill cog
mill dam
milling
monitor
moulded
moulder
mud hole
mud sill
nuclear
Ohm's law
oil fuel
oil lamp
oil pump
pattern
pig iron
pinhole
pontoon
program
pug mill
rag bolt
railway
ratchet
reactor
refract
rejoint
riveter
road bed
roadway
sawmill
scissel
seabank
seawall
shackle
shuttle
sleeper
smelter
soup pan
spindle
stamper
stand-by
statics
stopper
succula
suction
sump-pit
support
syringe
tamping
telefer
templet
tension
test bay
testing
thimble
tie-beam
tilting
tinfoil
tin mine
tinning
torsion
tracing
tramcar

tramway
treadle
trendle
trolley
turbine
turning
unrivet
unscrew
ventage
viaduct
voltage
voltaic
welding
wet dock
wringer
wrought

8

acentric
air brake
air valve
annealed
aqueduct
axletree
balancer
ball cock
bevelled
bridging
caliduct
camshaft
cam wheel
cassette
castings
cast iron
catenary
chainlet
chauffer
cog wheel
compound
computer
concrete
corn mill
coupling
cradling
cryotron
cylinder
Davy lamp
dead lift
declutch
draw gear
draw link
edge rail
electric
elevator
engineer
enginery
eolipile
fan blast
feed pipe
feed pump
fireclay
fireplug
flywheel
fracture
friction
fuse clip
galvanic
gas gauge
gas mains
gas works
gland nut
governor
gradient
hardware

hot blast
hot press
ignition
injecter
injector
ink stone
insulate
ironwork
irrigate
Jacquard
joint box
junk ring
klystron
laminate
land roll
leverage
limekiln
linch pin
linotype
lock gate
lock sill
lock weir
loop line
machinal
magnetic
main line
mechanic
mill pond
mill race
momentum
monorail
monotype
moulding
movement
mud valve
oilstone
oil store
oil stove
operator
ozonizer
pendulum
penstock
pile shoe
platform
polarity
pressure
puddling
pump gear
pump hood
purchase
radiator
rag wheel
railroad
recharge
refinery
register
repairer
repolish
rheostat
rigidity
ring bolt
rotatory
shearing
silk mill
skew arch
smeltery
smelting
soft iron
software
spinnery
split pin
stamping
standard
starling
stone pit
stopcock

strength
stuffing
tail race
tapering
telotype
tempered
template
terminal
textbook
throttle
tidegate
tide mill
tile kiln
time ball
tinplate
tractile
traction
tractive
train oil
tram rail
tramroad
turbojet
turnpike
tympanum
unclutch
uncoiled
unsolder
velocity
water gas
windmill
wind pump
wire-draw
wireless
wood mill
workable
workshop
wormgear

9

acoustics
air engine
air filter
air vessel
amplifier
artificer
bevel gear
brakedrum
brakepipe
brick kiln
blue light
blueprint
cast steel
chain belt
chain pump
clockwork
condenser
conductor
cotter pin
craftsman
crosshead
cyclotron
datum-line
dead level
diaphragm
disc brake
disk brake
dynamical
earthwork
eccentric
electrify
electrize
electrode
equirotal
escalator

female die
fire brick
fish joint
fishplate
floodgate
fog signal
foot valve
force pump
framework
funicular
galvanism
galvanist
galvanize
gas engine
gas fitter
gas geyser
gas holder
gasometer
gas retort
gearwheel
horse mill
hydraulic
hydrostat
idle wheel
induction
inductive
inertness
injection
insertion
insulated
insulator
ironsmith
ironworks
jet engine
knife edge
laminated
lewis bolt
Leyden jar
limelight
lubricant
lubricate
machinery
machinist
magnetist
magnetize
male screw
man engine
master key
mechanics
mechanism
mechanist
mechanize
mild steel
millstone
mine shaft
mud sluice
nodal line
nose piece
off-spring
oil engine
oil geyser
perforate
petrol can
piston rod
pneumatic
polarizer
porous pot
power loom
programme
propeller
prototype
pump break
pump spear
pump stock
radiation
rectifier

reflector
regulator
repairing
reparable
reservoir
resultant
rheomotor
rheophore
road metal
roughcast
sandpaper
scapement
shop board
shunt coil
sliderule
smack mill
soapworks
soldering
spring box
spur wheel
stanchion
steam pipe
stiffener
stock lock
stoke hole
structure
superheat
telephone
tempering
tin lining
tin mining
train road
transform
trunk line
tunnel pit
turntable
twin cable
unscrewed
vibration
voltatype
vulcanite
vulcanize
waste weir
watermark
water tank
well drain
wheelrace
whip graft
white heat
winepress
wire gauze
wire wheel
worm wheel
X-ray plant

10

accelerate
air machine
alarm gauge
alternator
anelectric
automation
automobile
bevel wheel
broad gauge
cantilever
caseharden
centigrade
clack valve
coach screw
combustion
crankshaft
crown wheel

dead weight
derailment
dielectric
discharger
disc wheels
dish wheels
diving bell
donkey pump
drawbridge
earth plate
economizer
efficiency
electrical
electronic
embankment
emery cloth
emery paper
emery wheel
engine room
escapement
fire escape
flange rail
fluid drive
footbridge
fuse holder
galvanized
gas turbine
glass paper
goods train
goods truck
grid system
gudgeon pin
guillotine
hair spring
heart wheel
hogger pump
horsepower
hydrophore
Indian fire
inertitude
inflexible
instrument
insulating
insulation
iron heater
irrigation
isodynamic
laboratory
lamination
leaf bridge
lewis joint
lock paddle
locomotive
lubricator
macadamize
magnetizer
male thread
mechanical
nodal point
paper cable
pentaspast
percolator
petrol tank
piledriver
pneumatics
powder mill
powerhouse
power-plant
programmer
pulverizer
pump-handle
recondense
refraction
rejointing
resistance
revolution

rubber-wire
safety-lamp
scoop-wheel
self-acting
skew bridge
smokestack
soap boiler
socket pipe
socket pole
solid state
spokeshave
stationary
steam gauge
stiffening
streamline
structural
swing wheel
swivel hook
telegraphy
telescopic
television
telpherage
temper heat
thermopile
thermostat
toll bridge
torque tube
transients
transistor
tunnelling
unclutched
unpatented
unsoldered
voltaic arc
voltaplast
water crane
water power
watertight
water tower
waterwheel
waterwings
waterworks
wave motion
well-boring
windtunnel
wiped joint

11

accelerator
accumulator
aerodynamics
air fountain
anelectrode
atomic clock
bell founder
bell foundry
block system
Bramah press
brush wheels
cable laying
candlepower
carburetter
carburettor
compression
computation
contrivance
coupling box
coupling pin
damask steel
diamagnetic
driving band
driving belt
dynamometer
edge railway

electrician
electricity
electric jar
electrolyze
electrolyte
electronics
endless belt
engineering
exhaust pipe
female screw
frame bridge
gas governor
graving dock
gutta percha
helical gear
incinerator
inking table
iron filings
iron founder
iron foundry
laminations
latten-brass
lock chamber
low pressure
lubrication
machine-tool
maintenance
manilla rope
manufactory
mechanician
mini-computer
mono-railway
narrow gauge
oil purifier
oil strainer
perforation
piledriving
pilot engine
power factor
rack-railway
rarefaction
reconstruct
retardation
revolutions
rolling mill
rubber cable
safety valve
searchlight
service pipe
skeleton key
socket joint
steam boiler
steam engine
steam hammer
stuffing box
suction pipe
suction pump
summit level
superheater
swing bridge
switchboard
synchronism
synchronize
synchrotron
tappet valve
toggle joint
transformer
transmitter
trundle head
tube railway
underground
uninsulated
voltaic pile
vulcanizing
warping bank
water cement

water engine
water furrow
water hammer
water supply
welding heat
wind furnace
wire drawing
wire grading
workmanship
wrought iron

12

acceleration
anti-friction
arterial road
artesian well
assembly line
balance wheel
belt fastener
blast furnace
block machine
block signals
canalization
chain reactor
coaxial cable
counterpoise
danger signal
diamagnetism
diesel engine
differential
disc coupling
disintegrate
donkey engine
double acting
driving shaft
driving wheel
dry-core cable
eccentric rod
eduction pipe
electric bulb
electric fire
electric fuse
electric iron
electric wire
electrolysis
electromotor
endless screw
engine driver
exhaust valve
female thread
flexible wire
floating dock
flying bridge
flying pinion
founder's dust
founder's sand
gas condenser
gas container
gas regulator
hanging valve
high pressure
hydraulic ram
hydrodynamic
inking roller
installation
jewel bearing
lubrification
machine tools
magnetomotor
make-and-break
manilla paper
marine boiler
marine engine
master spring

negative pole
non-conductor
nuclear power
oxy-acetylene
palification
paratonnerre
pattern maker
petrol engine
petrol filter
plummer block
polarization
pressure pump
pyro-electric
radiator muff
ratchet wheel
Réaumur scale
rolling press
rolling stock
service cable
short circuit
shunt winding
single acting
sleeve button
slitting mill
solar battery
specific heat
spinning mill
stamping mill
steam heating
steam turbine
steam whistle
suction valve
synchronized
terminal post
thermocouple
toothed wheel
transmission
unmechanical
unmechanized
vibratiuncle
water battery
water turbine
wheel-and-axle
wheel cutting
working model

13

buffing spring
civil engineer
compound-wound
contrate wheel
control theory
Cornish boiler
Cornish engine
counterweight
direct current
draught engine
drummond light
eccentric gear
electric cable
electric clock
electric fluid
electric light
electric motor
electric stove
electrifiable
electrization
electromagnet
engine-turning
expansion gear
ferrumination
flexible cable
floodlighting
fluid flywheel

friction balls
friction cones
inflexibility
injection cock
insulated wire
kinetic energy
lifting bridge
liquid starter
lubrification
magnetic fluid
magnetization
movement maker
non-conducting
overshot wheel
pneumatic tyre
pontoon bridge
pressure gauge
printing press
rack-and-pinion
roller bearing
series winding
shock absorber
snifting valve
standard gauge
telegraph line
telegraph pole
telegraph wire
telephone line
telephone wire
thermo-current
throttle valve
thrust bearing
water drainage
wave mechanics
whirling table
X-ray apparatus

14

analog computer
blowing machine
contra rotation
diesel-electric
discharge valve
discharging rod
disintegration
eccentric strap
eccentric wheel
electric cooker
electric cut-out
electric kettle
electrodynamic
electrostatics
electrothermic
explosive rivet
floating bridge
friction clutch
friction wheels
galvanized iron
hydraulic-press
insulated cable
lubricating oil
magnetic needle
multi-core cable
nuclear reactor
petrol strainer
plaster of paris
pneumatic drill
portable engine
reconstruction
resino-electric
resultant force
shellac-varnish
shunt regulator
thermo-electric

251

three-core cable
traction engine
universal joint
vitreo electric
voltaic battery
washing machine
wave telegraphy

15 AND 16

brake horsepower

block signalling
Centigrade scale
concentric cable
digital computer
electric battery
electric circuit
electric current
electric machine
electrification
electrochemical
electrodynamics
electrokinetics
electromagnetic

electronegative
electronic brain
electropositive
expansion engine
Fahrenheit scale
friction rollers
galvanic battery
hydraulic cement
insulating paper
irrigation canal
linotype machine
machine language
magnetic battery

magneto-electric
ohmic resistance
perpetual motion
pressure machine
railway engineer
smelting furnace
specific gravity
spigot-and-socket
synchrocyclotron (16)
tensile strength
water-tube boiler

Instruments
See also **Engineering** and **Tools and simple machines**

4 – 6

abacus
agate
camera
clock
dial
dynamo
filter
flange
fleam
flume
funnel
gauge
gasket
grid
gauge
lancet
laser
lens
lever
maser
megger
meter
nozzle
octant
octile
orrery
pole
probe
relay
rule
ruler
scale
square
style
tester
tool
trocar
toner
tube
U-tube
valve

7

aerator
ammeter
aneroid
balance
bearing
bellows
binocle
caltrop
compass

counter
divider
doubler
pH meter
quadrat
scriber
sextant
snubber
sundial
T-square
turbine
vernier
wet-bulb

8

analyser
biograph
bioscope
boot-jack
boot-last
boot-tree
calipers
computer
detector
diagraph
gasmeter
horologe
iriscope
manostat
odometer
ohm-meter
otoscope
quadrant
receiver
recorder
rheostat
solenoid
spy glass
udometer
waywiser
wireless
zootrope

9

acoumeter
aeolipile
aerometer
altimeter
altometer
ambulator
antimeter
apparatus

arcograph
areometer
astrolabe
atmometer
auriscalp
auxometer
backstaff
barograph
barometer
baroscope
clepsydra
compasses
condenser
cornmeter
cosmolabe
dynameter
dynometer
eidograph
engiscope
eriometer
excitator
flow meter
gasometer
garoscope
generator
graduator
gyroscope
heliostat
hodometer
holometer
hour glass
litholabe
lithotome
logometer
lucimeter
magnifier
manometer
marigraph
megaphone
megascope
metronome
microtome
microtron
nilometer
oleometer
optigraph
optometer
pedometer
periscope
polygraph
polyscope
pyrometer
pyroscope
rain gauge
rectifier
retractor

rheometer
rheoscope
rheotrope
rotameter
saccarium
scarifier
set-square
shot gauge
slide rule
sonometer
steelyard
tasimeter
taximeter
telegraph
telephone
telescope
televisor
tellurion
tide gauge
trebuchet
voltmeter
wattmeter
wind gauge
zoeotrope

10

acetimeter
acidimeter
altazimuth
anemograph
anemometer
anemoscope
angioscope
anglemeter
astrometer
astroscope
audiometer
audiophone
balling-gun
binoculars
calculator
calorifier
chiroplast
clinometer
collimator
cometarium
cross-staff
cryophorus
cyanometer
cyclograph
declinator
drosometer
duplicator
ear-trumpet

elaeometer
elaiometer
endiometer
field glass
goniometer
gravimeter
heliograph
heliometer
helioscope
heliotrope
hydrometer
hydrophore
hydroscope
hyetograph
hyetometer
hygrometer
hygroscope
lactometer
lactoscope
litrameter
macrometer
metrograph
micrometer
microphone
microscope
multimeter
multiplier
night glass
nitrometer
noctograph
ombrometer
operameter
ozonometer
pantagraph
pantograph
pantometer
pelvimeter
pentagraph
phonograph
phonoscope
photometer
photophone
piezometer
plane-table
planimeter
pleximeter
pole-finder
protractor
pulsimeter
radiometer
respirator
spirometer
steam-gauge
tachometer
teinoscope
theodolite
thermostat
transistor
tribometer
tuning-fork
typewriter

viscometer
voltameter
water-clock
water-gauge
water-meter
water-poise

11

actinograph
actinometer
aleurometer
alkalimeter
atmidometer
beam compass
calorimotor
cardiograph
chlorometer
chronograph
chronometer
chronoscope
clog almanac
comptometer
conchometer
cosmosphere
craniometer
dendrometer
depth-finder
diagnometer
dynamometer
eccaleobion
eclipsareon
elatrometer
graphometer
indigometer
locatograph
magnetophon
odontograph
optical lens
plantascope
pluviameter
pluviometer
poking stick
polarimeter
polariscope
polemoscope
pseudoscope
range-finder
salinometer
seismograph
seismometer
seismoscope
sideroscope
sliding-rule
spherograph
spherometer
stereometer
stereoscope
stethometer
stethoscope

teleprinter
thaumatrope
thermometer
thermoscope
torsiograph
transformer
transmitter
zymosimeter

12

aethrioscope
alcoholmeter
arithmometer
assay balance
averruncator
blanchimeter
bow compasses
burning glass
camera lucida
centrolinead
chondrometer
control valve
declinometer
ductilimeter
electrepeter
electrometer
electrophone
electroscope
ellipsograph
elliptograph
endosmometer
enorthotrope
evaporometer
field glasses
galactometer
galvanometer
galvanoscope
harmonometer
inclinometer
kaleidoscope
laryngoscope
machine ruler
magnetograph
magnetometer
measuregraph
microcoustic
night glasses
opera glasses
oscillograph
otacousticon
perambulator
psychrometer
reading glass
scarificator
sliding scale
spectrometer
spectroscope
speed-counter
sphygmometer

thermocouple
tuning hammer
weather glass
zenith sector

13

alcoholimeter
alcoholometer
bubble chamber
burning mirrow
camera obscura
chromatometer
diaphanometer
dipleidoscope
dipping needle
electric meter
electrophorus
esthesiometer
Geiger counter
parallel ruler
pneumatometer
potentiometer
pressure gauge
probe scissors
pyrheliometer
reflectometer
refractometer
saccharometer
sidereal clock
spring balance
sympiesometer
watt-hour meter

14

aesthesiometer
air thermometer
circumferentor
desk calculator
diffractometer
dinactinometer
geothermometer
hydrobarometer
interferometer
manifold writer
ophthalmoscope
radio telescope
sonic altimeter
wire micrometer

15

chemical balance
digital computer
magnifying glass
mariner's compass
solar microscope

Mathematics

2 AND 3

add
arc
cos
csc
Ln
log

p.c.
set
tan

4

area

axes
axis
base
cone
cube
edge
face
line

loci
math
mean
plus
ring
root
sine
term

unit
zero

5

acute
angle
chord
conic
cosec
cotan
cubic
curve
equal
focal
focus
force
graph
group
index
lemma
limit
locus
maths
minus
plane
point
power
probe
proof
radii
range
ratio
slope
solid

6

centre
choice
circle
conics
conoid
convex
cosine
cuboid
degree
divide
domain
equals
factor
height
matrix
maxima
median
minima
minute
modulo
moment
motion
normal
number
oblate
oblong
obtuse
period
radial
radian
radius
random
scalar
secant
sector
series

sphere
square
subset
vector
vertex
volume

7

algebra
average
cissoid
complex
concave
conical
cycloid
decagon
divisor
ellipse
evolute
hexagon
indices
inverse
mapping
maximum
minimum
modulus
nonzero
numeral
oblique
octagon
percent
polygon
produce
prolate
problem
pyramid
rhombic
rhombus
scalene
section
segment
subtend
surface
tangent
theorem
trapeze
unitary

8

abscissa
addition
analysis
binomial
bisector
calculus
centroid
circular
codomain
constant
converse
cosecant
cube root
cuboidal
cylinder
diagonal
diameter
dihedral
distance
division
elliptic
equation
friction

frustrum
function
geometer
geometry
gradient
helicoid
heptagon
identity
infinity
integers
integral
involute
matrices
meridian
momentum
multiply
negative
new maths
operator
ordinate
osculate
parabola
parallel
pentagon
positive
quadrant
quartile
quotient
rational
rhomboid
rotation
sequence
spheroid
subtract
symmetry
triangle
trigonal
variable
velocity

9

amplitude
asymptote
Cartesian
chi-square
corollary
cotangent
directrix
dodecagon
ellipsoid
expansion
factorize
frequency
geometric
half-angle
hexagonal
hyperbola
identical
imaginary
increment
induction
inflexion
intersect
isosceles
logarithm
Napierian
numerator
numerical
octagonal
parabolic
parameter
perimeter
polygonal
polyhedra

primitive
quadratic
rectangle
remainder
resultant
spherical
trapezium
trapezoid

10

arithmetic
concentric
continuity
decahedron
derivative
dimensions
eigenvalue
epicycloid
equivalent
expression
hyperbolic
hypotenuse
hypothesis
irrational
kinematics
multiplier
octahedron
orthogonal
osculation
paraboloid
percentage
polyhedral
polyhedron
polynomial
proportion
regression
right angle
semi-circle
square root
statistics
stochastic
tangential
unit vector

11

approximate
associative
coefficient
combination
commutative
coordinates
denominator
determinant
eigenvector
equiangular
equilateral
equilibrium
exponential
geometrical
hyperboloid
icosahedron
integration
isomorphism
orthocentre
permutation
probability
progression
real numbers
rectangular
rectilinear
right-angled
subtraction

symmetrical
tetrahedron
translation

semicircular
straight line
substitution
trigonometry

quadrilateral
right bisector
solid geometry

12

acceleration
conic section
differential
dodecahedron
eccentricity
harmonic mean
intersection
least squares
number theory

13

approximation
circumference
geometric mean
linear algebra
parallelogram
perpendicular
plane geometry
power function

14 AND 15

arithmetic mean (14)
binomial theorem (15)
complex numbers (14)
convexo-concave (14)
differentiation (15)
multiplication (14)
natural numbers (14)
rational numbers (15)
transformation (14)

Medicine

2 AND 3

ana
arm
ear
ECT
ENT
eye
fit
flu
hip
ill
jaw
leg
lip
LSD
pox
pus
rib
tic
toe
VD
wen

4

ache
acne
ACTH
ague
back
bile
bleb
boil
bone
burn
chin
clap
clot
cold
corn
cure
cyst
damp
derm
diet
disk
dope
dose
drug
face
falx
foot

gena
germ
gore
gout
hand
head
heal
heel
iris
knee
lame
limb
lint
lobe
lung
mole
nail
neck
nose
otic
ovum
pain
pang
pill
rale
rash
rete
scab
scar
shin
sick
skin
sore
stye
swab
tolu
ulna
vein
ward
wart
weal
womb
X-ray
yaws

5

achor
acute
agony
algid
algor
aloes

ancon
angst
aorta
ataxy
aural
belly
blend
blood
botch
bowel
brain
cheek
chest
chill
chyle
cilia
colio
colon
copos
cough
cramp
croup
dress
drops
elbow
ether
faint
femur
fever
gland
heart
joint
lance
leech
liver
lymph
M and B
mania
mouth
mucus
mumps
myopy
navel
nerve
nurse
opium
ovary
ozena
palsy
penis
phial
plica
polio
probe

pulse
reins
rheum
rigor
salts
salve
scald
scalp
scurf
semen
senna
serum
sinus
skull
sleep
sling
spasm
sperm
spine
sprue
stoma
stone
stool
stupe
swoon
tabes
teeth
thigh
thumb
tibia
tonic
torso
toxin
truss
ulcer
unfit
urine
uvula
virus
wound
wrist
X-rays

6

ailing
angina
anemia
antrum
apepsy
armpit
artery
asthma

ataxia
aurist
axilla
bellon
biceps
bruise
bulimy
bunion
cancer
canker
caries
clinic
cornea
coryza
deflux
dengue
doctor
dorsal
dosage
dropsy
earlap
eczema
elixir
emetic
fester
fibula
finger
flexor
foment
gargle
gather
goitre
gravel
gripes
grippe
growth
gullet
healer
health
heroin
herpes
idiocy
infect
infirm
insane
iodine
iritis
kidney
larynx
lesion
lotion
lunacy
maimed
malady
maniac
matron
matter
megrim
muscle
myopia
opiate
oxygen
pelvis
pepsin
phenol
phenyl
physic
pimple
plague
pleura
poison
potion
powder
quinsy
radium
ranula

remedy
renule
retina
saliva
scurvy
sepsis
spleen
splint
sprain
stitch
stupor
tablet
tannin
tartar
temple
tendon
tetany
thorax
throat
thrush
thymol
tissue
tongue
tonsil
torpor
trance
tremor
trepan
troche
tumour
typhus
unwell
uterus
vagina
vomica

7

abdomen
abscess
acidity
aconite
adenoid
adipose
ailment
albumen
aliment
allergy
alopecy
amnesia
anaemia
anatomy
anconal
anodyne
antacid
anthrax
antigen
apepsia
aphasia
arsenic
aseptic
aspirin
atrophy
autopsy
bandage
bilious
blister
boracic
bromide
bubonic
calomel
cardiac
cascara
catarrh
caustic

cautery
chafing
chloral
choking
cholera
chronic
cocaine
cranium
cupping
curable
culture
cuticle
deltoid
dentist
dietary
dieting
disease
dissect
draught
dresser
dysopsy
earache
eardrum
empyema
endemic
enteric
erosion
eupepsy
fasting
femoral
fistula
forceps
forearm
formula
gastric
glottis
gumboil
harelip
healing
healthy
hormone
humerus
hygiene
illness
insulin
invalid
knuckle
leprosy
leprous
linctus
lockjaw
lozenge
lumbago
luminal
lunatic
malaria
massage
measles
medical
menthol
microbe
mixture
morphia
myalgia
nervous
nostrum
occiput
oculist
operate
organic
otalgia
palsied
panacea
patella
patient
pharynx

pillbox
pink-eye
plaster
polypus
pustule
pyretic
quinine
recover
rickets
roseola
scabies
scalpel
seasick
sick-bay
stamina
starved
sterile
sternum
stertor
stomach
stunned
styptic
sunburn
surgeon
surgery
symptom
syncope
syringe
tetanus
therapy
thyroid
toxemia
trachea
triceps
tympana
typhoid
vaccine
veronal
vertigo
vitamin
wet-pack
whitlow
wry-neck

8

abortion
abrasion
acidity
acidosis
adenoids
adhesion
albumina
amputate
aneurysm
antibody
antidote
apoplexy
appendix
Asian flu
asphyxia
atropine
backache
bacteria
baldness
beri beri
blue pill
botulism
caffeine
cataract
club foot
collapse
compress
creosote
cystitis

dandruff
deafness
debility
deceased
deformed
delirious
delirium
delivery
demented
dementia
diabetes
diagnose
diseased
dressing
drop-foot
dropsied
dyslexia
emulsion
epidemic
epilepsy
excision
eyedrops
fainting
feverish
first aid
flat feet
forehead
formalin
fracture
freckles
fumigate
ganglion
gangrene
glaucoma
hay fever
headache
heat spot
hiccough
hip joint
hospital
hygienic
hypnotic
hysteria
impetigo
incision
infected
inflamed
insanity
iodoform
irritant
jaundice
lameness
laudanum
laxative
lethargy
ligament
ligature
liniment
magnesia
malarial
mal-de-mer
medicine
membrane
mescalin
migraine
morphine
narcosis
narcotic
neuritis
neurotic
ointment
otoscope
overdose
paranoia
paranoic
paranoid

paroxysm
pastille
phthisis
pleurisy
poisoned
poultice
ptomaine
pulmonic
recovery
Red Cross
remedial
rest cure
revivify
ringworm
sanitary
schizoid
sciatica
sedative
shingles
shoulder
sickness
sickroom
smallpox
sneezing
specific
surgical
swelling
syphilis
tapeworm
terminal
tincture
underfed
uric acid
varicose
vertebra
vomiting
wheezing
windpipe

9

adrenalin
alleviate
allopathy
ambulance
analgesic
antalkali
antitoxin
arthritis
asthmatic
bedridden
blindness
Caesarean
carbuncle
cartilage
castor oil
catalepsy
cauterize
chilblain
cirrhosis
cold cream
contagion
contusion
cortisone
curvature
deformity
delirious
dentistry
deodorant
diagnosis
diaphragm
diathermy
dietetics
dietetist
dietician

digestion
digestive
disinfect
dislocate
dissector
doctoring
dropsical
dysentery
dyspepsia
emaciated
emollient
epileptic
eye lotion
eyestrain
faintness
frost-bite
gastritis
gathering
germicide
giddiness
glycerine
hartshorn
healthful
heartburn
hepatitis
hunchback
hygienist
hypnotism
hypnotist
hysterics
impactation
infirmary
influenza
inoculate
invalided
isolation
isoniazid
leucaemia
leukaemia
liquorice
listerine
liver spot
long-sight
medicated
medicinal
menopause
monomania
nephritis
neuralgia
nightmare
nostalgia
novocaine
nux vomica
open-heart
operation
osteopath
paralysis
paralytic
phlebitis
physician
pneumonia
poisoning
poisonous
pregnancy
psychosis
psychotic
pulmonary
pulsation
pyorrhoea
radionics
rheumatic
rock-fever
sclerosis
silicosis
sinusitis
soporific

squinting
sterilize
stiff neck
stiffness
stimulant
stone dead
stone deaf
stretcher
sunstroke
toothache
treatment
umbilicus
underdose
unhealthy
vaccinate
vasectomy
water cure

10

albuminous
amputation
antibiotic
anti-poison
antiseptic
apoplectic
apothecary
aureomycin
blood count
brain fever
breastbone
bronchitis
chicken pox
chloroform
collar bone
concussion
congestion
contortion
convalesce
convulsion
cotton wool
depression
diphtheria
dipsomania
disability
dispensary
dispensing
dissecting
dissection
double bind
emaciation
enervation
epidemical
epiglottis
Epsom salts
erysipelas
eucalyptus
euthanasia
fibrositis
flatulence
fumigation
gingivitis
gonorrhoea
healthless
heat stroke
hemorrhage
homoeopath
hydropathy
hypodermic
incubation
indisposed
infectious
inhalation
insanitary

257

interferon
ionization
knock-kneed
laryngitis
lung cancer
medicament
meningitis
metabolism
nettle rash
ophthalmia
orthocaine
osteopathy
out-patient
oxygen tent
palliative
penicillin
pestilence
post mortem
psychiatry
quarantine
recuperate
relaxation
rheumatism
sanatorium
sanitarium
scarlatina
shell-shock
short sight
sickle-cell
specialist
spinal cord
stammering
starvation
stone blind
strengthen
strychnine
stuttering
tourniquet
tracheitis
transplant
unremedied
urethritis

11

acupuncture
albuminuria
aminobutene
anaesthetic
anti-pyretic
asthmatical
astigmatism
bandy-legged
barbiturate
biliousness
calabar bean
circulation
cod-liver oil
colour-blind
consumption
consumptive
corn plaster

dengue fever
disablement
dislocation
embrocation
epileptical
face-lifting
finger stall
fomentation
frostbitten
haemophilia
haemorrhage
homoeopathy
hydrophobia
hypothermia
inoculation
intercostal
intravenous
jungle fever
mustard bath
nursing home
palpitation
peritonitis
perspiration
prickly heat
psittacosis
radiography
restorative
sal volatile
seasickness
spina bifida
stethoscope
stomach-pump
suppuration
temperature
thalidomide
therapeutic
tonsillitis
tracheotomy
transfusion
trench fever
typhus fever
unconscious
vaccination
vivisection
yellow fever

12

appendicitis
carbolic acid
chemotherapy
convalescent
cough lozenge
cough mixture
court plaster
day blindness
degeneration
disinfectant
disinfection
Dover's powder
enteric fever
friar's balsam

gastric fever
group therapy
growing pains
heart disease
hospital case
homoeopathic
hysterectomy
immunization
inflammation
menstruation
neurasthenia
Politzer's bag
prescription
prophylactic
psychiatrist
radiotherapy
recuperation
recuperative
sarsaparilla
scarlet fever
skin-grafting
spinal column
streptococci
streptomycin
subcutaneous
taka diastase
talcum powder
tartar emetic
tertian fever
thyroid gland
tuberculosis
typhoid fever
unremediable
zinc ointment

13

adipose tissue
anti-spasmodic
bubonic plague
contraception
convalescence
duodenal ulcer
dusting powder
elephantiasis
eucalyptus oil
fever hospital
gamma globulin
German measles
hydrocephalus
indisposition
ipecacuanha
lead poisoning
malarial fever
materia medica
medical school
medicine glass
mononucleosis
mortification
non-contagious
osteomyelitis
pharmacopoeia

poliomyelitis
pyretic saline
radioactivity
St Vitus's-dance
schizophrenia
shooting pains
shoulder blade
smelling salts
social disease
sterilization
stretcher case
tranquillizer
varicose veins
whooping cough

14

Achilles tendon
angina pectoris
blood poisoning
Bright's disease
cascara segrada
conjunctivitis
corticosteroid
corticotrophin
floating kidney
Gregory's powder
hallucinations
hallucinogenic
housemaid's-knee
medical student
medicine bottle
mucous membrane
mustard plaster
night blindness
organic disease
pasteurization
patent medicine
plastic surgery
psychoanalysis
Seidlitz powder
smelling bottle

15

Addison's disease
adhesive plaster
alimentary canal
blackwater fever
counter-irritant
delirium tremens
endocrine glands
Eustachian tubes
linseed poultice
locomotor ataxia
manic depression
medicine dropper
radiation hazard
radium treatment
unconsciousness
water on the brain

Minerals (including metals, ores, precious stones, rocks, etc.)

3 AND 4

bort
clay
coal

gold
iron
jade
jet
lead

mica
onyx
opal
rock
ruby

sard
spar
talc
tin
tufa

wad
wadd
zinc

5

agate
albin
argil
baria
beryl
chert
emery
flint
fluor
magma
ochre
prase
shale
slate
spalt
steel
topaz

6

albite
aplome
augite
basalt
blende
cobalt
copper
davina
dipyre
doggar
egeran
gabbro
galena
garnet
gneiss
gypsum
humite
indium
iolite
jargon
jasper
kaolin
kunkur
marble
mesole
mundic
nappal
nickel
ophite
ormolu
pewter
pinite
plasma
pumice
pyrope
quartz
radium
rutile
schorl
silica
silver
sinter
sodium
sphene
tombac
xylite
yenite
zircon

7

adamant
alumina
alunite
amianth
anatase
aphrite
arsenic
asphalt
axilite
azurite
barytes
bauxite
biotime
bismuth
bitumen
barnite
breccia
cadmium
calcite
calcium
calomel
cat's-eye
cuprite
cyprine
desmine
diamond
diorite
edelite
emerald
epidote
epigene
erinite
euclase
fahlerz
fahlore
felsite
felspar
fuscite
gassoul
glucina
granite
greisen
helvine
hessite
hyalite
ice spar
iridium
jargoon
kyanite
lignite
lithium
mengite
mercury
nacrite
olivine
peridot
petzite
pycnite
pyrites
realgar
romeine
sahlite
sinoper
sinople
syenite
talcite
thorite
thorium
thulite
tripoli
uranium
wolfram
yttrium
zeolite

zeuxite
zincite
zoisite
zurlite

8

achirite
adularia
amethyst
andesite
antimony
aphanite
asbestos
blue John
austerite
bronzite
calamine
calc-spar
cast iron
chabasie
chlorite
chromite
chromium
cinnabar
corundum
cryolite
dendrite
diallage
diopside
dioptase
dolerite
dolomite
embolite
epsomite
essonite
feldspar
felstone
fireclay
fluorite
graphite
hematite
hyacinth
idocrase
ilmenite
jasponyx
konilite
laterite
lazulite
ligurite
limonite
lirocone
lomonite
meionite
melanite
mesolite
mesotype
micanite
mimetene
monazite
napolite
nemalite
nephrite
obsidian
orpiment
pagodite
pea stone
petalite
platinum
plumbago
porphyry
prehnite
psammite
pyroxene
ragstone

reussite
rhyolite
rock cork
rock salt
rock soap
rock wood
sapphire
sardonyx
selenite
siberite
siderite
smaltine
sodalite
spinelle
stellite
stibnite
stilbite
thallium
tin stone
titanium
trachyte
trap-rock
triphane
tungsten
turmalin
vesuvian
voltzite
weissite
wood opal
wood rock
worthite
xanthite
xylonite
yanolite

9

alabaster
allophane
almandine
aluminium
alum shale
alum slate
amianthus
amphibole
anamesite
anglesite
anomalite
anorthite
aphrisite
argentite
argillite
aromatite
arquifoux
asphaltum
baikalite
basaltine
boltonite
brick-clay
brown-coal
brown-spur
byssolite
carbonado
carbuncle
carnelian
carnalite
cat-silver
cerussite
ceylanite
chabasite
chabazite
chalybite
cobaltine
cornelian
corn stone

earth flax
elaeolite
elaterite
erythrine
erythrite
eudyalite
eukairite
firestone
fluorspar
galactite
gmelinite
granilite
granulite
graystone
graywacke
grenatite
greystone
greywacke
haematite
heavy spar
horn slate
hornstone
indianite
ittnerite
johannite
killinite
latrobite
laumonite
lenzinite
limbilite
limestone
lodestone
magnesite
magnesium
magnetite
malachite
manganese
marcasite
margarite
marmatite
melaphyre
mellitite
meteorite
mica slate
mispickel
moonstone
moorstone
muscovite
nagyagite
natrolite
necrolite
necronite
nepheline
niccolite
noumeaite
omphacite
ozokerite
pargasite
pearl spar
pectolite
pegmatite
periclase
phenacite
phonolite
physalite
pleonaste
plinthite
potassium
proustite
pyrophane
quartzite
raphilite
rhodonite
rhombspar
rubellite
sandstone

satin spar
scapolite
scheelite
scolecite
soapstone
spinthere
spodumene
strontium
sylvanite
tantalite
tautalite
tellurium
torbanite
torrelite
tremolite
turnerite
turquoise
veinstone
vulcanite
wavellite
wernerite
willemite
withamite
witherite
woodstone
xanthocon
zinc bloom
zirconite

10

actinolite
amianthoid
amygdaloid
anthracite
aquamarine
aventurine
azure stone
batrachite
bergmanite
beudantite
bismuthite
bloodstone
calaverite
cannel coal
cervantite
chalcedony
chonikrite
chrysolite
clinkstone
cross-stone
diallogite
dyscrasite
eagle stone
false topaz
floatstone
gabbronite
glauberite
glaucolite
glottalite
greenstone
heterosite
heulandite
hornblende
hornsilver
hydrophane
hyperstene
indicolite
iridosmine
iron glance
karpholite
Kentish rag
koupholite
lead glance
lepidolite

malacolite
meerschaum
melaconite
mica schist
mocho stone
molybdenum
nussierite
nuttallite
orthoclase
osmiridium
paranthine
phosphorus
picrosmine
polyhalite
pyrochlore
pyrolusite
rathoffite
redruthite
retinalite
rock butter
rose quartz
sapphirine
sardachate
saussurite
serpentine
sismondine
smaragdite
sparry iron
sphalerite
stalactite
stalagmite
staurolite
stephanite
talc schist
thomsonite
topazolite
tourmaline
vanadinite
villarsite
websterite
zinc blende

11

alexandrite
amblygonite
amphibolite
amphiboloid
Babbit metal
black silver
brewsterite
cassiterite
chlorophane
chondrodite
chromic iron
chrysoberyl
cobalt bloom
crichtonite
crocidolite
dendrachate
diving stone
epistilbite
ferrachrome
figure stone
franklinite
hypersthene
Iceland spar
iron pyrites
lapis lazuli
libethenite
milky quartz
molybdenite
Muller glass
muschel kalk
napoleonite

needlestone
octahedrite
phillipsite
pitchblende
polymignite
psilomelane
pyrallolite
pyrargyrite
pyrosmalite
rock crystal
sillimanite
smithsonite
smoky quartz
sordavalite
sphaerulite
tetradymite
thumerstone
titanic iron
yttrocerite

12

cobalt glance
copper glance
forest marble
greyweathers
jeffersonite
kupfernickel
mineral black
mineral green
mineral resin
montmartrite
mountain cork
mountain milk
mountain soap
murchisonite
oriental ruby
puddingstone
pyrargillite
pyromorphite
quartz schist
somervillite
Spanish chalk
specular iron
sprig crystal
tetrahedrite
woolastonite

13

agaric mineral
anthophyllite
chlorophaeite
cinnamon stone
cleavelandite
copper pyrites
emerald copper
kerosene shale
needle zeolite

14 AND 15

antimony glance
arkose sandstone
bituminous coal
brown haematite
Cairngorm stone
chlorite schist
elastic bitumen
graphic granite
hydromica schist
mountain leather
quartz porphyry

Physics

2 AND 3

a.c.
bar
bel
e.m.f.
erg
gas
lux
mev
ohm
rpm
UHF
VHF

4

atom
cell
dyne
flux
foci
halo
heat
kaon
lens
mach
mass
muon
node
pile
pion
pole
rays
spin
tube
volt
watt
wave
work
X-ray

5

anode
curie
cycle
diode
earth
farad
field
fluid
focus
force
image
joule
laser
lever
light
lumen
maser
meson
motor
phase
pitch
power
prism
radar
radio
shell

solid
sonic
sound
speed
valve
weber

6

ampere
atomic
baryon
camera
charge
corona
dipole
energy
fusion
impact
isobar
kelvin
lepton
liquid
magnet
moment
motion
newton
optics
period
photon
plasma
proton
quanta
torque
triode
vacuum
vector
weight

7

ammeter
aneroid
battery
beta ray
calorie
candela
cathode
Celsius
circuit
coulomb
crystal
current
damping
decibel
density
dry cell
elastic
element
entropy
fission
gaseous
gravity
hyperon
impulse
inertia
machine
maxwell
neutron
nuclear

nucleon
nucleus
nuclide
optical
orbital
pi-meson
quantum
reactor
röntgen
spectra
statics
thermal
torsion
voltage
voltaic

8

adhesion
aerofoil
antinode
beat note
betatron
brownian
cohesion
duo-diode
dynamics
electric
electron
emission
free fall
friction
graviton
half-life
infra-red
isogonic
kilowatt
kinetics
klystron
magnetic
magneton
molecule
momentum
negative
negatron
neutrino
overtone
particle
pendulum
polaroid
positive
positron
pressure
rest mass
roentgen
solenoid
spectrum
subshell
velocity

9

acoustics
adiabatic
amplifier
amplitude
antimeson
barometer
black body
bolometer

capacitor
coherence
condenser
conductor
cyclotron
electrode
frequency
gamma rays
generator
gyroscope
harmonics
impedance
induction
insulator
isoclinic
Leyden jar
magnetism
magnetron
manometer
mechanics
plutonium
potential
radiation
radio wave
real image
rectifier
resonance
spark coil
vibration
viscosity
voltmeter

10

aberration
absorption
achromatic
antilepton
antimatter
antiproton
atomic bomb
atomic mass
ballistics
binoculars
cathode ray
Centigrade
conduction
convection
cosmic rays
dielectric
dispersion
electrical
Fahrenheit
heavy water
horsepower
inductance
ionization
kinematics
latent heat
microscope
omega meson
oscillator

precession
reflection
refraction
relativity
resistance
ripple tank
scattering
shunt-wound
supersonic
thermionic
thermopile
transistor
vacuum tube
wavelength

11

accelerator
band spectra
capacitance
capillarity
centrifugal
centripetal
compression
conductance
declination
diffraction
electricity
falling body
focal length
gravitation
hypercharge
newton-metre
oscillation
positronium
radioactive
resistivity
restitution
series-wound
solar energy
spectrogram
statcoulomb
synchrotron
temperature
transformer
transuranic

12

acceleration
angstrom unit
antiparticle
atomic number
atomic weight
beta particle
centre of mass
cloud chamber
conductivity
critical mass
diamagnetism
eccentricity

electrolysis
electroscope
interference
kilowatt-hour
oscilloscope
permittivity
polarization
specific heat
spectrograph
wave equation

13

alpha particle
bubble chamber
chain reaction
critical angle
discharge tube
elastic impact
electric field
electric motor
electric power
electromagnet
electromotive
electron shell
electrostatic
geiger counter
gravitational
induction coil
kinetic energy
magnetic field
magnetic poles
paramagnetism
photoelectric
quantum number
quantum theory
radioactivity
rectification
scintillation
semiconductor
standing waves
thermal capacity
transmutation

14 AND OVER

centre of gravity (15)
electric current (15)
electric energy (14)
electrification (15)
electromagnetic (15)
electrostatics (14)
ferromagnetism (14)
nuclear reactor (14)
Planck's constant (15)
potential energy (15)
specific gravity (15)
terminal velocity (16)
thermodynamics (14)
thermoelectric (14)
Wheatstone bridge (16)

Poisons

4 AND 5

acids
agene
bane
coca
drug

dwale
ergot
fungi
lysol
nitre
opium
toxin

upas
venom

6

alkali

brucia
cicuta
curare
heroin
iodine
ourali
phenol

7

aconite
alcohol
ammonia
aniline
arsenic
atropia
atropin
bromine
brucina
brucine
cadmium
calomel
caustic
chloral
coal gas
cocaine
gamboge
henbane
hyoscin
hypoxia
markuri
veronal
violine
vitriol
woorali
woorara
woralli
wourali

8

antidote
antimony
atropina
atropine
botulism
chlorine
chromium
ergotine
morphine
nicotine
oenanthe
paraquat
pearl ash
phosgene

ptomaine
ratsbane
selenium
soap lees
sulfonal
veratrum

9

amanitine
antiarine
baneberry
beryllium
chromates
colchicum
colocynth
croton oil
echidnine
grapewort
hellebore
herbicide
lead ethyl
mercurial
monkshood
nux vomica
potassium
rat poison
spit venom
strychnia
toadstool
white lead
wolf's bane
zinc ethyl

10

antiseptic
aqua fortis
belladonna
chloroform
cyanic acid
mustard gas
nightshade
nitric acid
oxalic acid
phosphorus

picric acid
salmonella
snake venom
strychnine
thorn apple
weed-killer

11

olue vitriol
boracic acid
caustic soda
dog's mercury
insecticide
lead acetate
luna caustic
prussic acid
snake poison
sugar of lead

12

barbiturates
bitter almond
carbonic acid
fool's parsley
pharmacolite
water hemlock
white arsenic

13 AND OVER

allantotoxicum (14)
carbonate of lead (15)
carbonic oxide (13)
carbon monoxide (14)
caustic alkali (13)
caustic potash (13)
deadly nightshade (16)
hydrocyanic acid (15)
irritant poisons (15)
meadow saffron (13)
narcotic poisons (15)
sulphuric acid (13)
yellow arsenic (13)

Sciences

5 AND 6

augury (6)
botany (6)
conics (6)
logic (5)
optics (6)

7

algebra
anatomy
biology
cookery
ecology
farming
finance
geodesy
geogony
geology
gunnery

history
hygiene
myology
orology
otology
pandect
phonics
physics
poetics
science
statics
surgery
tanning
trivium
weaving
zoology
zootomy

8

aerology

agronomy
analysis
atmology
barology
bio-assay
biometry
breeding
bryology
calculus
commerce
cytology
dairying
dosology
dynamics
ethology
etiology
eugenics
forestry
genetics
geometry
glyptics
horology

kinetics
medicine
mycology
nosology
ontology
penology
pharmacy
politics
pomology
posology
rheology
rhetoric
sinology
sitology
spherics
taxonomy
tidology
tocology
topology
typology
virology
zymology

263

9

acoustics
aerometry
aetiology
agriology
aitology
allopathy
altimetry
anemology
annealing
areometry
astronomy
barometry
biometrics
bleaching
cartology
chemistry
chiropody
chorology
cosmology
dentistry
dietetics
diplomacy
economics
embalming
emetology
engraving
ethnology
gardening
geography
gnomonics
harmonics
histology
horometry
husbandry
hydrology
hygrology
hymnology
ichnology
lithology
mammalogy
mechanics
micrology
neurology
ophiology
orography
osteology
otography
pathology
petrology
philology
phonetics
phonology
phytogeny
phytology
phytotomy
radiology
sitiology
sociology
surveying
taxidermy
telephony
uranology
zoography

10

actinology
aerography
aesthetics
apiculture
archaeology
arithmetic
ballistics

bathymetry
biophysics
cardiology
catoptrics
cell biology
chromatics
clinometry
conchology
craniology
demography
dendrology
docimology
Egyptology
embryology
energetics
entomology
entomotomy
enzymology
eudiometry
game theory
gastrology
geophysics
homeopathy
hydraulics
hydrometry
hydropathy
hygrometry
hypsometry
immunology
kinematics
lexicology
metallurgy
microscopy
morphology
nematology
nephrology
nosography
obstetrics
odontology
oneirology
organology
osteopathy
pedagogics
pediatrics
phlebology
photometry
phrenology
physiology
planimetry
pneumatics
potamology
psychiatry
psychology
relativity
seismology
selenology
semeiology
somatology
spasmology
spermology
splenology
splenotomy
statistics
technology
telegraphy
teratology
topography
toxicology
trepanning
typography

11

aeronautics
aerostatics

agriculture
anemography
arachnology
archaeology
arteriology
arteriotomy
campanology
carcinology
cartography
chondrology
chronometry
climatology
cosmography
craniometry
criminology
cupellation
cybernetics
dermatology
dermography
desmography
diacoustics
electricity
electronics
engineering
entozoology
ethnography
foundations
games theory
geomedicine
gynaecology
haematology
heliography
homoeopathy
hydrography
hyetography
ichthyology
ichthyotomy
lichenology
linguistics
mathematics
methodology
micrography
myodynamics
neurography
ornithology
osteography
paleography
petrography
photography
phytography
probability
prophylaxis
pteridology
radiography
sericulture
skeletology
spectrology
stereometry
stereoscopy
stethoscopy
stratigraphy
thanatology
uranography
ventilation
watch-making

12

aerodynamics
amphibiology
anthropology
architecture
astrophysics
atomic theory
auscultation

biochemistry
biogeography
brachygraphy
chronography
cometography
cytogenetics
econometrics
electropathy
epidemiology
epirrheology
floriculture
geochemistry
horticulture
hydrostatics
lexicography
lymphography
microbiology
nephrography
neuroanatomy
neurobiology
number theory
oceanography
opthalmology
organography
ornithoscopy
palaeography
pharmacology
physiography
pisciculture
pneumatology
protozoology
real analysis
seismography
silviculture
spectroscopy
spermatology
stratigraphy
sylviculture
syndesmology
synosteology
trigonometry
zoophytology

13

anthropometry
arboriculture
arteriography
bioenergetics
cephalography
chondrography
chrematistics
climatography
combinatorics
crustaceology
endocrinology
geochronology
geomorphology
helminthology
hydrodynamics
hydrokinetics
ichthyography
land measuring
land surveying
lichenography
linear algebra
marine biology
matrix algebra
meteorography
palaeontology
pharmaceutics
psychophysics
psychotherapy
quantum theory
saccharometry

sedimentology
splanchnology
stoichiometry
wave mechanics
zoophysiology

14

architectonics
bioclimatology
chromatography
cinematography
electrobiology

electrostatics
fluid mechanics
hippopathology
hydrophytology
macroeconomics
microeconomics
natural history
natural science
parapsychology
photogrammetry
phytopathology
psychonosology
radiochemistry
symptomatology

syndesmography
thermodynamics

15

computer science
crystallography
electrodynamics
electrokinetics
material science
neurophysiology
psychopathology
thermochemistry

Tools and simple machines
See also **Engineering** and **Instruments**.

3

adz
awl
axe
bit
die
dog
fan
gad
gin
hod
hoe
jig
loy
saw
zax

4

adze
bill
bore
brog
burr
cart
celt
crab
file
fork
frow
gage
hink
hook
jack
last
loom
mall
maul
mule
nail
pick
pike
plow
rake
rasp
rule
sock
spud
tool
trug
vice
whim

5

anvil
auger
basil
beele
bench
besom
betty
bevel
blade
borer
brace
burin
chuck
churn
clamp
clams
clasp
cleat
cramp
crane
croom
croze
cupel
dolly
drill
flail
flang
forge
gauge
gavel
gouge
hoist
incus
jacks
jemmy
jimmy
knife
lathe
level
lever
mower
parer
plane
plumb
preen
prise
prong
punch
quern
quoin
ratch
razor

sarse
screw
sieve
spade
spike
spile
spill
swage
temse
tommy
tongs
tromp
trone
wedge
winch

6

barrow
beetle
bender
blower
bodkin
borcer
bow-saw
brayer
broach
burton
chaser
chisel
colter
crevet
cruset
dibber
dibble
doffer
dredge
driver
fanner
faucet
ferret
folder
gimlet
graver
hackle
hammer
harrow
jagger
jigger
jig saw
ladder
mallet
mortar

muller
oliver
pallet
pencil
pestle
pitsaw
planer
pliers
plough
pontee
pooler
rammer
rasper
reaper
riddle
ripsaw
rubber
sander
saw-set
screen
scythe
segger
shears
shovel
sickle
sifter
skewer
sledge
slicer
square
stiddy
stithy
strike
tackle
tenter
trepan
trowel
tubber
turrel
wimble
wrench

7

boaster
bradawl
capstan
catling
cautery
chamfer
chip-axe
chopper
cleaver

265

couloir
coulter
crampon
crisper
crowbar
cuvette
derrick
diamond
dog-belt
drudger
fistuca
forceps
fretsaw
fruggin
gradine
grainer
grapnel
grub axe
hacksaw
handsaw
hatchel
hatchet
hay fork
jointer
mandrel
mattock
nippers
nut hook
pickaxe
piercer
pincers
plummet
pole axe
pounder
pricker
salt-pan
scalpel
scauper
scraper
screwer
scriber
seed lop
spaddle
spanner
spittle
sprayer
strocal
tenoner
thimble
trestle
triblet
T-square
twibill
twister
whip-saw
whittle
woolder

8

bark mill
bar shear
beakiron
bench peg
bill hook
bistoury
bloomary
blowlamp
blowpipe
boathook
bowdrill
bull nose
butteris
calender
calipers

canthook
centre bit
chopness
crow mill
crucible
die stock
dowel bit
drill bow
edge tool
filatory
fire kiln
flame gun
flax comb
gavelock
gee cramp
glass pot
handloom
handmill
hand vice
hay knife
horse hoe
lapstone
lead mill
mitre box
molegrip
muck rake
nut screw
oilstone
paint pad
panel saw
picklock
pinchers
plumb bob
polisher
power saw
prong-hoe
puncheon
reap hook
saw wrest
scissors
scuffler
shoehorn
slate axe
stiletto
strickle
tenon saw
throstle
tooth key
tweezers
twist bit
watercan
water ram
weed hook
windlass
windmill

9

belt punch
bench hook
bolt auger
boot crimp
canker bit
cannipers
can opener
centrebit
compasses
corkscrew
cotton gin
cramp iron
curry comb
cutter bar
dog clutch
draw knife

draw-plate
excavator
eyeleteer
fillister
fining pot
fork chuck
gas pliers
hammer axe
handbrace
handscrew
handspike
holing axe
hummeller
implement
jackknife
jackplane
jackscrew
lace frame
lawnmower
nail punch
nut wrench
pitch fork
plane iron
planisher
plumbline
plumbrule
screwjack
scribe awl
shearlegs
sheep hook
steelyard
sugar mill
tin opener
try square
turf spade
turn bench
turnscrew
watermill

10

bush harrow
churn staff
claspknife
clawhammer
cold chisel
crane's bill
cultivator
dray plough
drift bolts
drillpress
drillstock
emery wheel
fire engine
fire escape
firing iron
grindstone
instrument
masonry bit
masticator
mitre block
motor mower
mould board
nail drawer
paintbrush
perforator
pipe wrench
safety lamp
screw press
sleek stone
snowplough
spokeshave
steam press
stepladder
tenterhook

thumbscrew
thumbstall
tilt hammer
trip hammer
turf cutter
turnbuckle
watercrane
watergauge
waterlevel
wheel brace

11

breast drill
chaff cutter
chain blocks
chain wrench
cheese press
cigar cutter
countersink
crazing mill
crisping pin
crosscut saw
drill barrow
drill harrow
drill plough
fanning mill
grubbing hoe
helvehammer
jagging iron
machine tool
monkey block
paint roller
ploughshare
pointed awl
pruning hook
rabbet plane
reaping-hook
sawing stool
screwdriver
single-edged
skim coulter
snatch block
spirit level
squaring rod
steam hammer
stone hammer
straw cutter
strike block
stubble rake
sward cutter
swingplough
tapemeasure
turfing iron
two-foot rule
warping hook
warping post
weeding fork
weeding hook
weeding rhim
wheelbarrow

12

barking irons
belt adjuster
brace-and-bits
branding iron
breastplough
caulking tool
counter gauge
cradle scythe
cramping iron
crimping iron

crisping iron
curling tongs
drill grubber
driving shaft
driving wheel
emery grinder
flour dresser
glass furnace
hat stretcher
hydraulic ram
mandrel lathe
marline spike
monkey wrench
pruning knife
pulley blocks
running block
scribing iron
sledge hammer
sliding bevel
socket chisel
stone breaker
straightedge
straightener
swingle knife
touch needles
trench plough
turfing spade
turning lathe

water bellows
weeding tongs

13

butcher's broom
chopping block
chopping knife
cylinder press
electric drill
grappling-iron
hydraulic jack
mowing machine
packing needle
scribing block
sewing machine
soldering bolt
soldering iron
sowing machine
spinning jenny
spinning wheel
stocking frame
subsoil plough
three-foot rule
two-hole pliers
weeding chisel

14

blowing machine
carding machine
draining engine
draining plough
pneumatic drill
reaping machine
shepherd's crook
smoothing plane
swingling knife
three-metre rule
thrusting screw
weeding forceps

15

carpenter's bench
crimping machine
dredging machine
drilling machine
envelope machine
entrenching tool
pestle and mortar
pump screwdriver
weighing machine
whitworth thread

TRANSPORT
Aviation and space travel

3 AND 4

ace
air
bank
bay
bump
buzz
car
crew
dive
dope
drag
fin
flap
fly
fuel
gap
gas
hull
jet
kite
knot
land
lane
leg
lift
loop
mach
nose
prop
rev
rib
roll
slip
span
spar
spin
tail
taxi

trim
UFO
veer
wash
wind
wing
yaw
york
zoom

5

aloft
apron
bends
cabin
cargo
chock
chord
cleat
climb
craft
crash
crate
ditch
drift
flaps
flier
float
glide
pitch
plane
prang
pylon
radar
range
rev up
rigid
slots

stall
strut
stunt
valve

6

aerial
airbus
airman
airway
basket
beacon
bomber
camber
canard
cruise
cut out
drogue
fabric
flight
floats
flying
gas-bag
glider
hangar
intake
launch
module
nose-up
octane
piston
ram jet
refuel
rocket
rudder
runway
wash-in
yawing

7

aileron
air base
aircrew
airdrop
air flow
air foil
air lane
airlift
airline
airport
air-raid
airship
aviator
ballast
balloon
banking
biplane
birdman
bale out
bomb bay
capsule
ceiling
cellule
charter
chassis
chopper
clipper
cockpit
compass
contact
co-pilot
cowling
descent
ejector
fairing
fighter
flyover
flypast

gliding
gondola
helibus
inflate
landing
lift-off
Mae West
nacelle
nose-cap
on board
pancake
payload
re-entry
ripcord
rolling
sponson
sputnik
tail fin
take-off
taxiing
twin-jet
wingtip

8

aerodyne
aerofoil
aeronaut
aerostat
air brake
airborne
aircraft
airfield
air force
airframe
airliner
air route
air scoop
airscrew
airspace
airspeed
airstrip
airwoman
altitude
approach
anhedral
autogiro
aviation
aviatrix
ballonet
bomb-rack
buoyancy
corridor
cruising
decalage
dihedral
drip-flap
elevator
envelope
flat spin
fuel pipe
fuselage
grounded
gyrostat
heliport
in flight
intercom
jet pilot
jet plane
joystick
moonshot
non-rigid
nose-cone
nosedive
nose down

pitching
pulse-jet
radiator
seaplane
sideslip
spaceman
squadron
stopover
streamer
subsonic
tail-boom
tail-skid
tail unit
terminal
throttle
triplane
turbojet
twin-tail
volplane
warplane
wind cone
windsock
wing-flap
Zeppelin

9

aerodrome
aeroplane
air intake
air pocket
airworthy
altimeter
amphibian
astrodome
astronaut
autopilot
backplate
cabin crew
carlingue
cosmonaut
countdown
crash-land
crow's-foot
delta-wing
dirigible
empennage
fuel gauge
fuel intake
gyroplane
jet bomber
launch pad
launching
lift-wires
longerons
low-flying
monocoque
monoplane
navigator
overshoot
parachute
power dive
propeller
rudder bar
sailplane
satellite
semi-rigid
spacecrew
spaceship
spacesuit
spacewalk
stability
stratojet
sweepback
tailplane

test pilot
touch down
turboprop
twin-screw
wind gauge

10

aerobatics
aero-engine
aeronautic
aerostatic
air balloon
air control
air defence
air hostess
air service
air steward
air support
air traffic
anemometer
ballooning
balloonist
cantilever
cargo plane
dive bomber
flight deck
flight path
flight plan
flying boat
ground crew
helicopter
hydroplane
jet fighter
landing run
mach number
outer space
oxygen mask
pilot plane
robot plane
rudder-post
slipstream
solo flight
spacecraft
space probe
splashdown
stabilizer
stewardess
supersonic
test flight
V-formation

11

aeronautics
aerostatics
afterburner
air terminal
air umbrella
blind flying
combat plane
ejector-seat
flying speed
free balloon
ground speed
heat barrier
heavy bomber
kite-balloon
laminar flow
landing deck
landing gear
leading-edge
loop the loop
moon landing

mooring-mast
ornithopter
parachutist
retro-rocket
retractable
sesquiplane
slotted wing
soft landing
space centre
space flight
space rocket
space travel
stabilizers
stunt flying
vapour trail
weather-vane

12

aerodynamics
airfreighter
air-sea rescue
arrester gear
beacon lights
belly landing
control tower
crash landing
ejection seat
fighter pilot
flying circus
flying saucer
gliding-angle
jet-propelled
landing light
landing speed
landing wires
launching pad
maiden flight
manned rocket
night fighter
pilot balloon
pressure suit
pursuit plane
radar scanner
radial-engine
sound barrier
space capsule
space station
space vehicle
trailing-edge

13 AND OVER

aircraft-carrier (15)
airworthiness (13)
control-column (13)
cruising speed (13)
decompression (15)
engine-mounting (14)
escape-velocity (14)
forced landing (13)
ground control (13)
heavier-than-air (14)
in-line-engines (13)
lighter-than-air (14)
looping the loop (14)
radio-location (13)
semi-retractable (15)
shock-absorber (13)
space traveller (14)
stalling-speed (13
troop-transport (14)
undercarriage (13)
weightlessness (14)

Boats and ships
See also **Nautical terms**

3 AND 4

ark
bac
bark
boat
brig
buss
caic
cog
cot
dhow
dory
four
gig
grab
hoy
hulk
junk
koff
pair
pram
proa
punt
raft
saic
scow
ship
snow
sub
T.B.D.
tub
tug
yawl

5

balsa
barge
batel
boyer
canoe
caper
casco
coble
craft
E-boat
eight
ferry
fifie
float
funny
hopper
kayak
ketch
kobil
liner
P-boat
praam
Q-ship
razee
R-boat
scull
shell
skiff
sloop
smack
tramp
U-boat
umiak

whiff
xebec
yacht

6

argosy
banker
barque
bateau
bawley
bireme
bug-eye
caique
carvel
coggle
cooper
cutter
decker
dinghy
dogger
droger
dugout
galeas
galiot
galley
hopper
hooker
launch
lorcha
lugger
packet
pirate
puffer
pulwar
puteli
PT boat
randan
sampan
sealer
settee
slaver
tanker
tartan
tender
tosher
trader
trough
vessel
wafter
whaler
wherry

7

airboat
almadie
budgero
bumboat
caravel
carrack
carrier
clinker
clipper
coaster
cockler
collier
coracle
corsair

cruiser
currach
dredger
drifter
drogher
dromond
eel punt
felucca
flyboat
four-oar
frigate
galleon
galliot
gondola
gunboat
hog-boat
ice-boat
lighter
man-o'-war
minisub
monitor
muletta
pair-oar
permagy
pinnace
piragua
pirogue
polacca
pontoon
rowboat
sea-sled
shallop
shoaler
spy boat
steamer
tonkong
tow boat
trawler
trireme
tugboat
warship

8

baghalak
bilander
car ferry
coalship
cockboat
corocole
corvette
dahabeah
dahabiya
derelict
eight-oar
fireboat
fireship
flagship
galleass
galliass
gallivat
hoogarts
hoveller
ice yacht
Indiaman
ironclad
keelboat
lifeboat
longboat
mailboat

man-of-war
netlayer
sailboat
schooner
showboat
smuggler
steam-tug
tilt-boat
trimaran
waterbus
well-boat
woodskin

9

bomb-ketch
bucentaur
cable ship
canal boat
cargo boat
catamaran
crocodile
depot ship
destroyer
ferryboat
fire-float
freighter
frigatoon
funny-boat
guard boat
guard ship
horse-boat
houseboat
hydrofoil
jollyboat
lightship
minelayer
motorboat
oil tanker
outrigger
peter-boat
pilot boat
pilot ship
powerboat
privateer
prize ship
river boat
rotor ship
sand yacht
sheer-hulk
slave dhow
speedboat
steamboat
steamship
storeship
submarine
swampboat
transport
troopship
tunny-boat
two-decker
whaleboat
wheelboat

10

advice boat
barge-yacht
barkentine

battleship
bomb vessel
brigantine
cattleboat
chain-ferry
cockleboat
Deal lugger
flying boat
four-master
hovercraft
hydroplane
icebreaker
monkey-boat
motor yacht
narrowboat
nuclear sub
ocean liner
ore-carrier
packet-boat
paddleboat
patrol boat
picket boat
pirate-ship
quadrireme
repair-ship
rescue boat
rivercraft
rowing boat
royal barge
sloop-of-war
small craft
submarine
supply ship
survey ship
target ship
tea-clipper
turret ship
victualler
Viking ship
windjammer
watercraft

11

barquentine
capital ship

chasse-marée
cockleshell
dreadnought
fishing boat
galley foist
hydroglider
merchantman
minesweeper
motor launch
motor vessel
mystery ship
naval vessel
pilot cutter
prize vessel
quinquereme
racing shell
Rob-Roy canoe
sailing boat
sailing ship
sardine boat
slavetrader
steam launch
steam vessel
submersible
three-decker
three-master
torpedo boat
victual ship

12

cabin cruiser
coasting boat
coasting ship
despatch boat
East Indiaman
ferry steamer
fishing smack
heavy cruiser
landing barge
landing craft
light cruiser
merchant ship
motor drifter
motor trawler
pirate cutter

pleasure boat
police launch
pontoon crane
river gunboat
sailing barge
sailing craft
sculling boat
square-rigger
steam gondola
survey vessel
Thames bawley
training ship

13

battlecruiser
Bermuda cutter
Canadian canoe
container ship
double-sculler
four-oared boat
hovelling-boat
motor lifeboat
paddle-steamer
passenger-boat
passenger-ship
sailing vessel
ship-of-the-line
trading vessel

14 AND **15**

aircraft-carrier (15
cable-laying ship (15)
cable-repair ship (15)
coasting vessel (14)
despatch cutter (14)
eight-oared boat (14)
electric launch (14)
flotilla leader (14)
seaplane tender (14)
submarine chaser (15)
topsail schooner (15)
torpedo-gunboat (14)
Yorkshire coble (14)

Motoring

2 AND **3**

A.A.
c.c.
air
cam
can
cap
car
cog
fan
fit
gas
G.T.
hub
h.p.
jam
jet
key
lap
lug
map

M.O.T.
nut
oil
pin
pit
R.A.C.
rev
rim
rod
run
ton
top

4

axle
belt
body
bolt
boot
boss

bulb
bush
clip
coil
dash
disc
door
drum
flat
fuse
gear
hood
hoot
horn
idle
jack
lane
lock
nail
park
pink
plug

pump
road
roll
rope
seat
skid
sump
tail
tank
test
tire
tour
tube
tyre
veer
wing

5

apron
brake

cable
chain
chart
choke
clamp
coupé
cover
crank
cut in
drive
float
frame
gauge
joint
knock
lay-by
level
lever
model
motor
on tow
pedal
rally
rev up
rivet
rotor
route
scale
screw
sedan
shaft
shift
spark
speed
spoke
squab
stall
start
ton up
tools
tread
U-turn
valve
wheel
wiper
works

6

adjust
big end
bonnet
bumper
bypass
camber
car tax
charge
clutch
cut out
dazzle
de-icer
de luxe
detour
dickey
divert
driver
dynamo
engine
fitter
flange
funnel
garage
gasket
grease
handle

hooter
hot rod
hubcap
idling
klaxon
lock-up
louvre
mascot
milage
mirror
octane
oilcan
one-way
petrol
pile up
pinion
piston
saloon
signal
spokes
spring
swerve
switch
tappet
timing
torque

7

air hose
airlock
axle-box
battery
bearing
blowout
bollard
build-up
bus lane
bus stop
carpark
carport
cat's eye
chassis
contact
control
cooling
dipping
drive-in
driving
exhaust
fanbelt
flyover
gearbox
give way
goggles
gudgeon
hardtop
highway
joyride
L driver
L plates
licence
linkage
locknut
log book
luggage
magneto
map-case
mileage
misfire
missing
mixture

muffler
no entry
non-skid

offside
oil-feed
parking
pillion
pinking
pull out
reverse
roadhog
roadmap
roadtax
rolling
run into
seizing
service
skidpan
spindle
springs
starter
test run
toolkit
top gear
touring
towrope
traffic
trailer
viaduct
warning
wingnut

8

air brake
air inlet
airtight
armature
arterial
Autobahn
backfire
back seat
bodywork
brakerod
camshaft
cat's eyes
clearway
coasting
converge
coupling
crankpin
cruising
cul-de-sac
cylinder
declutch
delivery
dipstick
driveway
fastback
fast lane
feed pipe
feed pump
flat tyre
flywheel
foglight
footpump
freezing
friction
fuelpipe
fuel tank
garaging
gasoline
gradient
guide-rod
handpump
ignition
inlet cam
knocking

manifold
missfire
motoring
motorist
motorway
mudguard
nearside
oil gauge
oncoming
open road
overhaul
overpass
overtake
overturn
pavement
prowl car
puncture
radiator
rattling
rear axle
rear lamp
ring road
roadside
road sign
road test
roofrack
rush hour
side road
sideslip
silencer
skidding
skid mark
slip road
slow down
slow lane
speeding
squad car
stock car
tail skid
tail gate
taxi rank
throttle
tire pump
two-speed
tyre pump

9

air filter
alignment
anti-glare
autoroute
back wheel
ball-valve
batteries
brakedrum
brakeshoe
breakdown
bus driver
cab driver
car driver
car polish
chain-link
chauffeur
clearance
coachwork
concourse
condenser
cotter pin
crank axle
crankcase
crossroad
cutting in
dashboard
dashlight

271

defroster
dipswitch
direction
dirt track
diversion
estate car
filler cap
footbrake
framework
free-wheel
front axle
front seat
fuel gauge
gear lever
generator
Grand Prix
grease-box
grease-gun
guarantee
handbrake
headlight
hit-and-run
inner tube
insurance
limousine
lubricate
motorbike
motorcade
motor show
nipple key
oil filter
overdrive
passenger
patrol car
petrol can
piston rod
point duty
police car
racing car
rear light
reflector
revving up
road sense
road works
saloon car
spare tire
spare tyre
sports car
spotlight
switch off
taximeter
third gear
tire lever
T-junction
tramlines
trunk road
two-seater
tyre lever
underpass
underseal
wheel base
wheel spin
white line

10

access road
adjustment
amber light
anti-dazzle
antifreeze
bevelwheel
bottom gear
box-spanner
brakeblock

brake pedal
broken down
car licence
coachbuilt
combustion
commutator
crankshaft
crossroads
dickey seat
dry battery
four-seater
front wheel
gear casing
gear change
green light
gudgeon pin
headlights
horsepower
inlet valve
insulation
lighting up
low-tension
lubricator
motorcycle
overtaking
petrol pump
petrol tank
piston ring
private car
radial tire
radial tyre
rear mirror
rev counter
right of way
roadworthy
roundabout
safety belt
signalling
spare wheel
speed limit
streamline
suspension
tachometer
thermometer
third-party
three-speed
toll bridge
touring car
traffic cop
traffic jam
two-wheeler
upholstery
ventilator
wheelbrace
windscreen
wing mirror

11

accelerator
accessories
accumulator
blind corner
brake-lining
built-up area
carburetter
carburettor
carriageway
clutch pedal
compression
convertible
crash helmet
decarbonize
de-luxe model
distributor

driving test
exhaust pipe
exhaust port
feeler-gauge
front lights
highway code
ignition key
interrupter
lorry driver
lubrication
luggage rack
motor spirit
needle-valve
number plate
oil pressure
overhauling
overheating
over-revving
owner-driver
petrol gauge
pre-ignition
racing model
radiator cap
request stop
reverse gear
reverse turn
rotary valve
screen-wiper
self-starter
sliding roof
speedometer
sports model
streamlined
sunshine roof
synchromesh
tappet valve
through road
ticking over
trafficator
vacuum brake
valve-timing
wheel wobble

12

acceleration
approach road
arterial road
ball-bearings
breakdown van
clutch-spring
coachbuilder
contact-screw
countershaft
cylinder head
diesel engine
differential
double-decker
driving-chain
driving-shaft
exhaust valve
float-chamber
freewheeling
fuel injection
gear changing
lock-up garage
miles per hour
motor scooter
motor vehicle
motorcyclist
parking light
parking meter
parking place
petrol filter

pillion rider
racing driver
ratchet-wheel
registration
repair outfit
road junction
running-board
single-decker
sparking plug
steering gear
transmission
two-speed gear
warning light

13

admission-pipe
breakdown gang
chain-adjuster
connecting rod
cooling system
driving mirror
fluid flywheel
hydraulic jack
induction pipe
inspection pit
licence-holder
pillion-riding
pressure-gauge
rack-and-pinion
roller-bearing
servo-assisted
shock absorber
shooting brake
speed merchant
starting motor
steering wheel
traffic signal

14

adjusting-screw
circuit-breaker
compression tap
contact-breaker
double-declutch
driving licence
exhaust-cam axle
filling station
friction-clutch
grease-injector
lighting-up time
lubricating oil
luggage-carrier
miles per gallon
propeller shaft
reclining seats
reversing lights
service station
starting handle
steering column
third-party risk
three-speed gear
universal joint

15

carriage-builder
dual carriageway
instrument panel
insurance policy
seating capacity
windscreen wiper

Nautical terms

See also **Boats and ships**

2 AND 3

A.B.
aft
A1
bay
bow
box
cat
cay
C.I.F.
con
cox
ebb
fay
fid
F.O.B.
fog
guy
H.M.S.
hog
jaw
jib
lee
log
man
nut
oar
ply
ram
rig
R.M.
R.N.
rum
run
sag
sea
set
SOS
tar
top
tow
way
yaw

4

ahoy
alee
back
bale
beam
beat
bend
bitt
boom
bows
brig
bunk
bunt
buoy
calk
calm
coak
comb
cott
crew
deck
dive
dock

down
dune
east
eddy
fake
fend
flag
floe
flow
foam
fore
foul
frap
furl
gaff
gale
gang
gear
girt
grog
hank
hard
haul
haze
hazy
head
helm
hold
hove
hulk
hull
jack
junk
keel
knot
land
last
lead
leak
line
list
load
loof
luff
lute
mast
mess
mine
mist
mole
moor
navy
neap
oars
peak
pier
poop
port
prow
punt
quay
raft
rail
rake
rank
rate
rear
reef
ride
roll
rope

rove
rung
sail
scud
seam
ship
sink
skid
slip
slue
spar
stay
stem
step
surf
swab
swig
tack
taut
tend
tide
tilt
toss
trim
trip
vang
veer
voya
waft
wake
wapp
warp
wave
wear
west
whip
wind
wing
yard
yarn

5

aback
abaft
abeam
afore
afoul
after
ahead
ahull
aloft
apeak
aport
atrip
avast
awash
beach
belay
belee
below
berth
bibbs
bight
bilge
bilts
bitts
blirt
block
board

bosun
bower
bowse
brace
brail
bream
briny
cabin
cable
cadet
canal
cargo
caulk
chain
chart
check
chock
clamp
cleat
craft
crank
cuddy
davit
depth
diver
douse
downs
dowse
draft
drift
embay
entry
fanal
flake
fleet
float
fluke
foggy
gauge
grave
gusty
hands
hatch
haven
hawse
hitch
hoist
horse
jetty
jutty
kedge
kevel
lay-to
lay up
leach
leaky
leech
ligan
liner
lobby
lurch
metal
misty
naval
north
oakum
ocean
order
orlop
panch
pitch

273

prick	carina	reefed	capsize
prize	comber	reefer	capstan
prore	convoy	rigged	captain
radar	course	rigger	cast off
radio	crotch	rocket	catfall
range	cruise	rudder	cathead
refit	debark	sailor	cat's-paw
rhumb	diving	saloon	channel
right	double	salute	charter
roads	driver	salvor	claw off
ropes	earing	sculls	coaling
route	embark	sealer	coaming
rower	engine	seaman	cockpit
royal	ensign	seaway	compass
sally	escort	sheets	conning
salve	fathom	shroud	cordage
salvo	fender	signal	corsair
sands	fo'c'sle	sinker	counter
screw	for'ard	sinnet	cresset
sheer	fother	splice	cringle
sheet	funnel	squall	cyclone
shelf	furled	square	deadeye
shoal	galley	stocks	deep-sea
shore	gasket	stormy	degauss
siren	gromet	strake	dismast
skeet	gunnel	strand	dockage
sling	halser	stream	dog-vane
sound	hawser	tackle	dolphin
spars	hounds	tender	drabler
spoom	hove-to	thwart	draught
sprit	inship	tiller	dry-dock
steer	jetsam	timber	dunnage
stern	jetson	toggle	ease off
storm	jigger	towage	ebb-tide
surge	kedger	unbend	embargo
swell	lading	unbitt	eye-bolt
swing	lateen	uncoil	fairway
thole	launch	undock	fishery
tidal	lay-off	unfurl	flotsam
trice	leeway	unlade	flotson
truck	Lloyd's	unload	fogbank
truss	locker	unmoor	foghorn
waist	manned	unship	foretop
watch	marina	vessel	forward
weigh	marine	voyage	founder
wharf	marker		freight
wheel	maroon		freshen
windy	marque	**7**	freshet
woold	masted		futtock
wreck	mayday	aground	gangway
	mid-sea	athwart	gimbals
6	mizzen	backing	go about
	moored	bale out	go below
aboard	mutiny	ballast	grapnel
adrift	nautic	beached	grating
afloat	neaped	bearing	graving
anchor	needle	beating	grommet
armada	offing	bilboes	gudgeon
ashore	on deck	blister	gun-deck
astern	outfit	boarder	gunnage
aweigh	paddle	bobstay	gun-port
awning	patrol	bollard	gun-room
balker	pay off	boomkin	gunwale
batten	pay out	bowline	guy-rope
beacon	pennon	bow wave	half pay
becket	Pharos	boxhaul	halyard
billow	pillow	bracing	harbour
bonnet	pintle	breaker	harpoon
bridge	piracy	bulwark	haul off
bumkin	pirate	bunkage	head off
bunker	piston	buntine	head sea
burton	pooped	bunting	headway
cablet	poppet	buoyage	heave to
canvas	raider	caboose	horizon
career	rating	calking	iceberg
	ratlin	can-buoy	icefloe

inboard
inshore
Jack Tar
jib boom
jibstay
keelage
keelson
landing
laniard
lanyard
lashing
lastage
latches
leaking
lee-gage
lee side
lee tide
leeward
listing
loading
logbook
logline
logreel
lookout
luffing
lugsail
maintop
mariner
marines
marline
marling
matelot
mistral
monsoon
moorage
mooring
mudhook
oarsman
oceanic
offward
old salt
on board
outport
oversea
painter
pennant
pooping
port-bar
quayage
rafting
rations
ratline
reefing
reeming
ride out
rigging
rollers
rolling
rope-end
rostrum
rowlock
rundown
sailing
salvage
scupper
scuttle
seacard
seafolk
sea-lane
sea-legs
seamark
sea-ooze
sea-room
seasick
seaward
set sail

sextant
shallow
shelves
shipper
shipway
shrouds
sick-bay
sinking
skipper
skysail
slipway
spanker
spencer
squally
stand-by
steward
stopper
stowage
tacking
tackled
tackler
tactics
tempest
thimble
tonnage
top deck
top mast
topping
topsail
topside
tornado
torpedo
towline
towpath
towrope
transom
trysail
typhoon
unladen
unsling
unslung
veering
waftage
ward off
warping
wavelet
waveson
wet dock
whistle
wrecked
wrecker
yardarm

8

anchored
anteport
aplustre
approach
armament
at anchor
aweather
backstay
backwash
barbette
bargeman
barnacle
beam-ends
bearings
becalmed
berthage
berthing
binnacle
boat-deck
boathook

bolt-rope
bowsprit
broach to
bulkhead
bulwarks
buntline
castaway
caulking
claw away
club-haul
coasting
crossing
cruising
cutwater
dead slow
deadwood
deckhand
derelict
disembay
ditty-bag
ditty-box
dockyard
dogwatch
doldrums
doubling
downhaul
drifting
driftway
easterly
eastward
even keel
fife-rail
flag-rank
floating
flotilla
fogbound
foot-rope
forefoot
foremast
forepeak
foresail
foreship
forestay
forewind
free-port
gaffsail
go aboard
go ashore
halliard
hard-alee
hatchway
headfast
head into
headwind
helmless
helmsman
high seas
high tide
hornpipe
hull-down
icebound
icefield
iron-sick
jackstay
jettison
jury mast
keelhaul
keel over
land ahoy!
landfall
landmark
landsman
landward
land wind
larboard
lead-line

leeboard
lee shore
lifebelt
lifebuoy
lifeline
load-line
loblolly
logboard
long haul
low water
magazine
mainboom
main deck
mainmast
mainsail
mainstay
mainyard
make sail
maritime
martinet
masthead
mastless
messmate
midships
moorings
moulinet
mutineer
mutinous
nauscopy
nautical
navigate
neap tide
ordnance
outboard
overrake
overseas
paravane
periplus
picaroon
pierhead
pilotage
plimsoll
poop deck
porthole
portoise
portside
pratique
pumproom
put about
put to sea
quarters
reef-knot
re-embark
ride easy
ride hard
roadster
sail-loft
sail-room
sail-yard
salvable
salvager
sandbank
scudding
seaborne
sea-chest
seafarer
seagoing
sea-rover
shallows
shark-net
sheer off
ship ahoy
shipmate
shipment
ship oars
shipping

275

sounding
spy-glass
squadron
standard
stand off
staysail
steerage
sternage
sternway
stowaway
stranded
streamer
submerge
tackling
tafferel
taffrail
thole-pin
timoneer
tranship
traverse
unbuoyed
uncoiled
underset
under way
unfurled
vanguard
wall-knot
wardroom
waterman
water-rot
waterway
waveworm
westerly
westward
west wind
windlass
wind-rode
wind-sail
windward
woolding
wreckage
yachting

9

about-ship
admiralty
affreight
afterdeck
air-funnel
all aboard
alongside
amidships
anchorage
anchoring
back-stays
bargepole
barnacles
beaconage
below deck
bilge-keel
bilge-pump
blue peter
boardable
boat drill
broadside
bunkering
captaincy
careenage
chartered
chartroom
close haul
coastwise
companion
corposant

crossjack
crosstree
crosswind
crow's nest
Davy Jones
dead-water
deck cargo
demurrage
departure
disanchor
discharge
disembark
doggerman
dogshores
dress ship
drift-sail
driftwood
Elmo's-fire
false keel
firedrill
floodmark
flood-tide
flying jib
foreshore
foundered
gangboard
gangplank
gather way
groundage
half-hitch
hard aport
high water
hoist sail
holystone
house-flag
houseline
hurricane
jack-block
jack-staff
jack-stays
kentledge
land ahead
lobscouse
lower deck
maelstrom
mainbrace
mainsheet
manoeuvre
midstream
minefield
minute-gun
mizzentop
naumachia
navicular
navigable
navigator
neptunian
northerly
northward
north wind
ocean lane
orlop deck
outrigger
overboard
parbuckle
periscope
press-gang
privateer
prize-crew
promenade
quicksand
recharter
reckoning
red ensign
reef-point
refitment

revictual
rhumb-line
roadstead
rockbound
royal mast
Royal Navy
rum-runner
sailcloth
seafaring
sea-letter
sea-robber
seaworthy
semaphore
sheething
shipboard
shipowner
ship's crew
shipshape
shipwreck
shoreward
sick-berth
sidelight
sight land
southerly
southward
south wind
sou'wester
spindrift
spinnaker
spritsail
stanchion
starboard
stateroom
steersman
sternfast
sternmost
sternpost
stokehold
storm-beat
stormsail
stormstay
stretcher
tarpaulin
telescope
tide-table
tophamper
trade wind
twin-screw
two-decker
unballast
uncharted
unharbour
unlighted
unsounded
upper deck
water-line
water-sail
whirlwind
wind-bound
wring-bolt
yachtsman

10

A1 at Lloyd's
aboard ship
after-guard
after-hatch
after-sails
alongshore
anchorable
anchor buoy
anchor hold
astarboard
ballasting

batten down
Bermuda rig
bilgewater
blue ensign
bluejacket
breakwater
bootlegger
breastfast
bridge deck
cargo space
cast anchor
casting-net
catch a crab
chain-cable
chain-plate
charthouse
coal-bunker
cork-jacket
cross-piece
crosstrees
deadlights
degaussing
diving-bell
dockmaster
downstream
drop anchor
drop astern
embarkment
engine room
escutcheon
fathomless
fiddlehead
figurehead
fore-and-aft
forecastle
forge ahead
freightage
freshwater
frostbound
full-rigged
gaff rigged
harbourage
heavy-laden
high-and-dry
hollow-mast
jigger-mast
Jolly Roger
jury-rigged
jury rudder
landlocked
landlubber
lateen sail
lateen yard
lay a course
liberty-man
life-jacket
lighterage
lighthouse
lookout-man
loxodromic
manoeuvres
marine soap
marker buoy
martingale
middle deck
midshipman
mizzenmast
mizzensail
mizzenstay
navigating
navigation
night-watch
ocean-going
orthodromy
parcelling
pilothouse

pipe aboard
port of call
powder-room
prize-court
prize-money
quarantine
raking fire
reduce sail
rendezvous
reshipment
rope-ladder
round-house
rudderless
rudder post
Samson post
seamanlike
seamanship
ship-broker
shipmaster
shipwright
signalling
skyscraper
slack-water
spring-tide
square-sail
stanchions
stay-tackle
stern-board
stern-frame
sternsheet
submariner
supercargo
take in sail
tally-clerk
tidal basin
tidal river
tiller-rope
topgallant
unfathomed
unfordable
upperworks
water-borne
waterspout
watertight
wheel-house
wring-staff

11

abandon ship
beachcomber
belaying pin
captainship
centreboard
chafing-gear
close-hauled
compass card
compass rose
contact mine
debarkation
depth-charge
dismastment
diving bell
diving suit
dock charges
echo-sounder
embarcation
embarkation
escape hatch
foam-crested
fore-topmast
foul weather
gallows-tops
get under way
go alongside

graving-dock
ground-swell
harbour dues
harness-cask
hug the shore
innavigable
keelhauling
landing deck
lifeboatman
loblolly-boy
loxodromics
maintopmast
maintopsail
make headway
marine store
mess steward
middle watch
mizzen course
monkey-block
naval rating
orthodromic
overfreight
paddle wheel
port charges
port of entry
press-of-sail
quarterdeck
range-finder
reconnoitre
riding-light
sailing date
Samson's-post
searchlight
seasickness
sheet anchor
shipbreaker
ship's doctor
ship's papers
sliding-keel
snatch-block
sounding-rod
south-wester
spanking boom
spring a leak
standing off
station-bill
steerage-way
stern-chaser
sternsheets
storm signal
three-masted
thwartships
tidal waters
torpedo tube
unballasted
unchartered
under canvas
under-masted
unnavigable
unnavigated
unsheltered
unsoundable
waistcloths
waterlogged
weather-gage
weathermost
weather-roll
weather side
weigh anchor
white ensign

12

air-sea rescue
between-decks

bill of lading
breeches-buoy
cable's-length
canvas length
caulking iron
change course
collision-mat
companionway
conning tower
counter-brace
displacement
double-banked
double-braced
double-manned
equinoctials
fishing fleet
floating dock
futtock-plate
ground-tackle
hard-aweather
jack-o'-lantern
jacob's ladder
lateen-rigged
line of battle
longshoreman
magnetic mine
maiden voyage
man overboard
marine boiler
marine engine
marline-spike
measured mile
minesweeping
naval command
navigability
orthodromics
outmanoeuvre
outward-bound
Plimsoll line
Plimsoll mark
privateering
recommission
ride at anchor
ship-chandler
shipping line
ship's husband
slack in stays
square-rigged
starboard bow
stream anchor
studding sail
tourist class
training ship
transhipment
Trinity House
undercurrent
unfathomable
war-insurance
weatherboard
weatherbound
weather cloth
weatherglass
weatherproof
westerly wind
will-o'-the-wisp

13

affreightment
cat-o'-nine-tails
close quarters
compass signal
dead reckoning
deck passenger
fishing-tackle

floating light
grappling-iron
high-water mark
hurricane deck
life-preserver
mizzen rigging
naval dockyard
naval ordnance
navigableness
north-east wind
northerly wind
north-west wind
order-of-battle
re-embarkation
royal dockyard
ship-of-the-line
south-east wind
southerly wind
south-west wind

spilling-lines
starboard beam
starboard side
steering-wheel
weather report

14

circumnavigate
compass-bearing
disembarkation
futtock shrouds
hard-astarboard
letter-of-marque
Lloyd's Register
mushroom-anchor
naval architect
powder magazine

prevailing wind
running-rigging
schooner-rigged
screw-propeller
ship's-carpenter
swivel-rowlocks
topgallant mast

15

Admiralty Office
circumnavigable
command of the sea
companion ladder
marine insurance
mariner's compass
operation orders
victualling yard

Vehicles

3 AND 4

auto
bier
biga
bike
bus
cab
car
cart
dan
drag
dray
duck
fly
gig
jeep
loco
mini
pram
skis
sled
tank
taxi
tram
trap
tube
van
wain

5

bogey
bogie
brake
brett
buggy
chair
coach
coupé
cycle
dilly
float
lorry
moped
motor
pulka
sedan
sulky

tonga
train
truck
wagon

6

banger
barrow
Berlin
calash
chaise
dodgem
dennet
doolie
drosky
engine
fiacre
gingle
go-cart
hansom
hearse
jalopy
landau
limber
litter
oxcart
pulkha
saloon
sledge
sleigh
surrey
tandem
tender
tonga
tri-car
troika
waggon
whisky

7

amtrack
autobus
autocar
bicycle
britzka
caboose
cacolet

caravan
cariole
chariot
dogcart
droshky
flivver
fourgon
growler
gyrocar
hackery
hackney
haywain
helibus
kibitka
mail car
mail-van
minibus
minicab
minicar
omnibus
phaeton
pullman
railcar
railbus
scooter
sidecar
taxicab
tilbury
tonneau
tractor
trailer
tramcar
trolley
trundle
tumbrel
tumbril
turnout
vis-á-vis
voiture

8

barouche
brakevan
britzska
brougham
cablecar
carriage

clarence
curricle
cycle-car
dustcart
equipage
goods van
handcart
ice-yacht
jump-seat
mail-cart
milk-cart
motorbus
motorcar
old crock
pushcart
quadriga
rickshaw
roadster
rockaway
runabout
sociable
stanhope
steam-car
toboggan
tricycle
victoria

9

ambulance
amphibian
applecart
bandwagon
bath-chair
boat-train
bob-sleigh
box-wagon
bubblecar
bulldozer
cabriolet
charabanc
diligence
dining car
dodgem car
dormobile
guard's van
hansom cab
ice skates
landaulet

land rover
limousine
mail-coach
mail-train
milkfloat
motorbike
motorcade
muletrain
palanquin
prison van
saloon car
sand yacht
sportscar
streetcar
stretcher
wagonette
water-cart

post-chaise
pullman car
sedan chair
smoking car
snowplough
spring-cart
stagecoach
state coach
tip-up lorry
touring car
tramway-car
trolley-bus
trolley-car
velocipede
waggonette
war chariot
wheelchair

12

baby carriage
coach-and-four
coach-and-pair
furniture-van
hackney-coach
invalid chair
luggage train
magic carpet
motor scooter
pantechnicon
perambulator
railway train
three-wheeler
watering-cart

10

automobile
Black Maria
boneshaker
chapel cart
conveyance
donkey-cart
fire-engine
four-in-hand
glass coach
goods train
goods truck
hackney cab
invalid cab
hand-barrow
jinricksha
locomotive
motorcoach
motorcycle
motor lorry

11

armoured car
brewer's dray
bullock cart
caterpillar
delivery van
four-wheeler
goods waggon
gun-carriage
horse-litter
jaunting-car
landaulette
mail phaeton
sleeping car
state landau
steam engine
steamroller
three-in-hand
waggon train
wheelbarrow

13

ambulance cart
electric truck
governess cart
mourning-coach
penny-farthing
state carriage
steam-carriage
wheel-carriage

14 AND 15

ambulance wagon (14)
bathing-machine (14)
hackney carriage (15)
invalid carriage (15)
luggage trailer (14)
railway carriage (15)
traction-engine (14)

MISCELLANEOUS
Abbreviations

1 AND 2

A	ampere
A.A.	Automobile Association, Anti-aircraft, Alcoholics Anonymous
A.B.	ablebodied seaman
A.C.	alternating current
a/c	account
A.D.	Anno Domini (In the year of our Lord)
A.F.	Admiral of the Fleet
A.G.	Adjutant-General
a.m.	ante meridiem (before noon)
A1	First-class in Lloyd's Register
AS	Anglo-Saxon
A.V.	Authorised Version
Av.	avenue, average
b.	born, bowled
B.A.	Bachelor of Arts
B.C.	Before Christ, British Columbia
B.D.	Bachelor of Divinity
b.l.	bill of lading
B.M.	British Museum
B.P.	British Pharmacopœia
b.p.	boiling point
Bp.	Bishop

B.S.	Bachelor of Surgery, Bachelor of Science
Bt.	Baronet
C.	centigrade, Conservative
c.	caught, chapter, cents, circa
ca.	circa (around, about)
C.A.	chartered accountant
C.B.	Companion of the Bath, confined to barracks
C.C.	cricket club, county council
C.E.	Church of England, civil engineer
C.F.	Chaplain to the Forces
ch.	chapter
C.I.	Channel Islands
C.J.	Chief Justice
cl.	class, clause
cm.	centimetre
C.O.	commanding officer, Colonial Office
Co.	company, county
c/o	care of
Cr.	creditor
C.U.	Cambridge University
d.	daughter, old penny, old pence, died
D.C.	direct current, District of Columbia (U.S.)
D.D.	Doctor of Divinity
DM	Deutschemark

do.	ditto	lb.	libra (pound)
D.P.	displaced person	L.C.	Lord Chanceller
D.R.	District Railway	l.c.	lower case (printing)
Dr.	drachm, drachma, doctor, debtor	Ld.	limited, lord
D.V.	deo volente (God willing)	L.F.	low frequency
E.	east	L.P.	low pressure
ea.	each	L.T.	low tension
E.C.	east-central	Lt.	Lieutenant, light
Ed.	editor	M.	monsieur, member, thousand
E.E.	electrical engineer, errors excepted		(mille)
e.g.	exempli gratia (for example)	m.	metre(s), mile(s), masculine,
E.I.	East Indies		married
eq.	equal	M.A.	Master of Arts
E.R.	Elizabeth Regina (Queen), East	M.B.	Bachelor of Medicine
	Riding (Yorkshire)	M.C.	Master of Ceremonies, Military
ex.	example, without, from		Cross
F.	Fahrenheit	M.D.	Doctor of Medicine
f.	feminine, francs, forte	ME	Middle English
F.A.	Football Association	mf.	Mezzoforte
F.C.	football club	mg.	milligram
ff.	fortissimo	M.I.	mounted infantry
F.M.	field-marshal, frequency	M.M.	Military Medal
	modulation	MM.	Messieurs (Fr.)
F.O.	Foreign Office	mm.	millimetre(s)
fo.	folio	M.O.	medical officer
Fr.	French, Friday	Mo.	Missouri, month
ft.	foot, feet	M.P.	Member of Parliament
G.B.	Great Britain	M.R.	Master of the Rolls
G.C.	George Cross	Mr.	mister
G.I.	general issue (U.S.A.)	MS.	manuscript
Gk.	Greek	Mt.	mount
gm.	gram(s)	M.T.	mechanical transport
G.M.	George Medal, Grand Master	N.	newton, north, nitrogen
G.P.	General Practitioner	n.	neuter, noun
G.R.	Georgius Rex (King George)	N.B.	North Britain, nota bene (note well)
Gr.	Greek	N.E.	north-east
gr.	grain(s), grammar, gross	N.F.	National Front
gs.	guineas	No.	number (numero)
Gt.	great	N.P.	new paragraph
h.	hour(s)	n.p.	new pence
H.C.	House of Commons	nr.	near
H.E.	high explosive, His (Her)	N.S.	New style, Nova Scotia
	Excellency	N.T.	New Testament
H.F.	high frequency	N.W.	north-west
hf.	half	N.Y.	New York
H.H.	His (Her) Highness	N.Z.	New Zealand
H.M.	His (Her) Majesty	O.	Ohio, oxygen
H.O.	Home Office	ob.	obiit (died)
h.p.	high pressure, horsepower	O.C.	Officer Commanding
H.Q.	headquarters	O.E.	Old English , Old Etonian(s)
hr.	hour	O.M.	Order of Merit
H.T.	high tension	Op.	opus (work)
HZ	Hertz	o.p.	out of print
Ia.	Iowa	Or.	Oregon
id.	idem (the same)	O.S.	old style
i.e.	id est (that is)	O.T.	Old Testament
in.	inch(es)	O.U.	Oxford University
Is.	island	oz.	ounce(s)
I.W.	Isle of Wight	P.	Prince, President
J.	Joule, judge	p.	page, penny, pence, piano
Jn.	junction	P.C.	Police Constable, Privy Councillor
J.P.	Justice of the Peace	p.c.	per cent., post card
Jr.	junior	p.d.	per diem, potential difference
K	kelvin	pd.	paid
K.C.	King's Counsel, Knight	pf.	pianoforte
	Commander	pl.	plural, place
kc	kilocycle	P.M.	Prime Minister, Provost Marshal,
K.G.	Knight of the Garter		Past Master, Postmaster
kg.	kilogram(s)	p.m.	post meridiem, post mortem
km.	kilometre(s)	P.O.	post office, postal order
K.P.	Knight of St. Patrick	pp.	pages, pianissimo
Ks.	Kansas	p.p.	Per procuration (by proxy)
K.T.	Knight of the Thistle	P.S.	postscript
Kt.	knight	Pt.	part, port
L.	Latin, Liberal	pt.	pint, point
l	litre	q.	query, question

Q.C.	Queen's Counsel	A.P.M.	Assistant Provost Marshal
Q.M.	Quartermaster	Apr.	April
qr.	quarter	A.R.A.	Associate of the Royal Academy
qt.	quart	Ark.	Arkansas
q.v.	quod vide (which see)	A.R.P.	Air Raid Precautions
R.	Réaumur, Royal, Rex (King),	arr.	arrive(s, ed)
	Regina (Queen), right, rupee	A.T.C.	Air Training Corps
R.A.	Royal Academician, Royal Artillery	A.T.S.	Auxiliary Territorial Service
R.C.	Roman Catholic	Aug.	August
Rd.	road	aux.	auxiliary
R.E.	Royal Engineers	ave.	avenue
R.M.	Royal Mail, Royal Marines	B.B.C.	British Broadcasting Corporation
R.N.	Royal Navy	B.C.L.	Bachelor of Civil Law
Rs.	Rupees	bde.	brigade
R.U.	Rugby Union	B.E.F.	British Expeditionary Force
ry.	railway	b.h.p.	Brake horsepower
S.	Saint, second, singular, shilling,	B.M.A	British Medical Association
	son, south	B.M.J	British Medical Journal
S.A.	South Africa	B.O.T.	Board of Trade
s.c.	small capitals (printing)	Bro.	brother
S.E.	south-east	B.Sc.	Bachelor of Science
s.g.	specific gravity	B.T.U.	British Thermal Unit(s)
S.J.	Society of Jesus	B.V.M.	Blessed Virgin Mary
S.M.	Sergeant-Major	B.W.G.	Birmingham Wire Gauge
sq.	square	cap.	capital
sr.	senior	C.B.E.	Commander of the British Empire
s.s.	same size, steamship		(Order)
St.	Saint, street, stone (wt.), stumped	C.B.I.	Confederation of British Industry
S.W.	south-west	C.I.A.	Central Intelligence Agency
T.B.	torpedo-boat, tuberculosis	C.I.D.	Criminal Investigation
T.D.	Territorial Decoration		Department
TV	television	C.I.E.	Companion of the Indian Empire
u.c.	upper case (printing)		(Order)
U.K.	United Kingdom	c.i.f.	cost, insurance, freight
U.N.	United Nations	C.I.O.	Congress of Industrial
U.S.	United States		Organizations (U.S.)
V	volt	C.M.G.	Companion of St. Michael and St.
v.	verb, versus (against)		George (Order)
Va.	Virginia	co.	company
V.C.	Victoria Cross	c.o.d.	cash on delivery
V.D.	Volunteer Decoration, Venereal	col.	Colonel, column
	Disease(s)	C.P.R.	Canadian Pacific Railway
v.g.	very good	C.S.M.	Company Sergeant-Major
V.O.	Victorian Order	C.V.O.	Commander of the Victorian
V.R.	Victoria Regina (Queen)		Order
W.	watt, west	cwt.	hundredweight
W.C.	water closet, West Central	D.A.G.	Deputy Adjutant-General
W.D.	War Department	D.B.E.	Dame Commander of the British
w.f.	wrong fount (printing)		Empire (Order)
W.O.	War Office, Warrant Officer	D.C.L.	Doctor of Civil Law
wt.	weight	D.C.M.	Distinguished Conduct Medal
yd.	yard	DDT	dichlorodiphenyl
yr.	your		trichlorocethane
		Dec.	December
		deg.	degree(s)

3

		D.E.S.	Department of Education and
			Science
A.A.A.	Amateur Athletic Association,	D.F.C.	Distinguished Flying Cross
	American Automobile	D.F.M.	Distinguished Flying Medal
	Association	div.	Dividend
A.A.G.	Assistant Adjutant-General	D.L.O	Dead Letter Office
ABC	alphabet	D.N.A.	deoxyribonucleic acid
Abp.	archbishop	D.O.E.	Department of the Environment
A.C.A.	Associate of the Institute of	doz.	dozen
	Chartered Accountants	D.S.C.	Distinguished Service Cross
A.C.F.	Army Cadet Force	D.Sc.	Doctor of Science
A.C.W.	Aircraftwoman	D.S.M.	Distinguished Service Medal
A.D.C.	aide-de-camp, amateur dramatic	D.S.O.	Distinguished Service Order
	club	dwt.	pennyweight
adj.	adjective	E.E.C.	European Economic Community
Adm.	Admiral	e.m.e.	electro-motive force
adv.	adverb	E.N.E.	east-north-east
A.E.U.	Amalgamated Engineering Union	E.S.E.	east-south-east
A.O.C.	Army Ordnance Corps	Esq.	Esquire
A.O.D.	Army Ordnance Dept.	Etc.	etcetera
A.O.F.	Ancient Order of Foresters	f.a.s.	free alongside ship

F.A.A.	Fleet Air Arm	K.L.I.	King's Light Infantry
F.B.A.	Fellow of the British Academy	Knt.	knight
F.B.I.	Federal Bureau of Investigation	Lab.	Labour
F.C.A.	Fellow of the Institute of Chartered Accountants	l.b.w.	leg before wicket
		L.C.C.	London County Council
F.C.S.	Fellow of the Chemical Society	L.C.J.	Lord Chief Justice
Feb.	February	l.c.m.	lowest common multiple
fem.	feminine	L.D.S.	Licentiate in Dental Surgery
F.G.S.	Fellow of the Geological Society	LL.B.	Bachelor of Laws
F.I.A.	Fellow of the Institute of Actuaries	LL.D.	Doctor of Laws
		loq.	loquitur (speaks)
Fig.	figure	L.S.D.	lysergic acid diethylamide
F.L.A.	Fellow of the Library Association	L.s.d.	Libræ (pounds); solidi (shillings); denarii (pence)
f.o.b.	free on board		
F.R.S.	Fellow of the Royal Society	L.S.E.	London School of Economics
fur.	furlong	Ltd.	Limited
F.Z.S.	Fellow of the Zoological Society	Maj.	Major
gal.	gallon(s)	Mar.	March
G.B.E.	Knight Grand Cross of the British Empire	M.B.E.	Member of the British Empire (Order)
G.C.A.	Ground Control Approach (Aviation)	M.C.C.	Marylebone Cricket Club
		M.F.B.	Metropolitan Fire Brigade
G.C.B.	Knight Grand Cross of the Bath	M.F.H.	Master of Foxhounds
G.C.F.	greatest common factor	mil.	military
G.C.M.	greatest common measure	min.	mineralogy
Gen.	General	Mme.	Madame
G.H.Q.	General Headquarters	M.O.D.	Ministry of Defence
Gib.	Gibraltar	M.O.T.	Ministry of Transport
G.L.C.	Greater London Council	m.p.h.	miles per hour
G.M.T.	Greenwich mean time	M.Sc.	Master of Science
G.O.C.	General Officer Commanding	MSS.	Manuscripts
G.O.M.	grand old man	M.T.B.	motor torpedo boat
G.P.O.	General Post Office	M.V.O.	Member of the Royal Victorian Order
G.T.C.	Girl's Training Corps		
gym.	gymnasium	N.C.O.	non-commissioned officer
H.A.C.	Hon. Artillery Company	neg.	negative
H.B.M.	His (Her) Britannic Majesty	N.F.S.	National Fire Service
h.c.f.	highest common factor	n.h.p.	nominal horsepower
Heb.	Hebrew(s)	N.N.E.	north-north-east
H.I.H.	His (Her) Imperial Highness	N.N.W.	north-north-west
H.I.M.	His (Her) Imperial Majesty	Nos.	numbers
H.L.I.	Highland Light Infantry	N.P.G.	National Portrait Gallery
H.M.S.	His (Her) Majesty's ship or Service	N.R.A.	National Rifle Association
		N.S.W.	New South Wales
Hon.	honorary, Honourable	N.U.J.	National Union of Journalists
H.R.H.	His (Her) Royal Highness	N.U.M.	National Union of Mineworkers
hrs.	hours	N.U.R.	National Union of Railwaymen
I.B.A.	Independent Broadcasting Authority	N.U.S.	National Union of Seamen, National Union of Students
I.C.S	Indian Civil Service	N.U.T.	National Union of Teachers
i.h.p.	indicated horsepower	O.B.E.	Officer of the British Empire (Order)
I.H.S.	Jesus, Saviour of men (Iesus Hominum Salvator)		
		Obs.	obsolete
I.L.O	International Labour Organization	Oct.	October
		Ont.	Ontario
I.L.P.	Independent Labour Party	Ord.	order, ordinary, ordnance, ordained
Inc.	incorporated		
I.O.F.	Independent Order of Foresters	O.T.C.	Officers' Training Corps
I.O.U.	(acknowledgment of debt)	Pan.	Panama
I.O.W.	Isle of Wight	par.	paragraph, parish, parallel
I.R.A.	Irish Republican Army	P.G.M.	Past Grand Master
I.S.O	Imperial Service Order	Ph. D.	Doctor of Philosophy
I.T.V.	Independent Television	P.L.O.	Palestine Liberation Organization
I.U.D.	intra-uterine device		
Jan.	January	P.M.G.	Postmaster-General
Jas.	James	pop.	population
Jos.	Joseph	P.P.C.	Pour prendre congé (to take leave)
jun.	junior	P.R.A.	President of the Royal Academy
Kan.	Kansas	P.R.O.	Public Relations Officer
K.B.E.	Knight Commander of the British Empire (Order)	pro.	professional
		P.T.O.	please turn over
K.C.B.	Knight Commander of the Bath	P.V.C.	polyvinyl chloride
K.G.B.	Komitet Gosudarstvennoi Bezopasnosti (Committee of State Security)	P.W.D.	Public Works Department
		q.e.d.	quod erat demonstrandum (which was to be demonstrated)
K K K.	Ku-Klux-Klan		

q.e.f.	quod erat faciendum (which was to be done)
Q.M.G.	Quartermaster-General
Q.M.S.	Quartermaster-Sergeant
Que.	Quebec
R.A.C.	Royal Armoured Corps, Royal Automobile Club
R.A.F.	Royal Air Force
R.A.M.	Royal Academy of Music
R.B.A.	Royal Society of British Artists
R.C.M.	Royal College of Music
R.C.P.	Royal College of Physicians
R.C.S.	Royal College of Surgeons
ref.	reference
Rev.	Reverend
R.F.A.	Royal Field Artillery
R.G.A.	Royal Garrison Artillery
R.H.A.	Royal Horse Artillery
R.I.P.	requiescat in pace (may he (or she) rest in peace)
R.M.A.	Royal Military Academy
R.M.C.	Royal Military College
R.M.S.	Royal Mail steamer
R.N.R.	Royal Naval Reserve
R.S.M.	Regimental Sergeant-Major
R.S.O.	Railway Sorting Office
R.T.C.	Royal Tank Corps
R.T.O.	Railway Transport Officer
R.U.C.	Royal Ulster Constabulary
R.Y.S.	Royal Yacht Squadron
S.C.C.	Sea Cadet Corps
Sec.	secretary
sen.	senior
seq.	sequens (the following)
Soc.	society
S.P.G.	Society for the Propagation of the Gospel
S.S.E.	south-south-east
S.S.W.	south-south-west
Stg.	sterling
str.	stroke (rowing)
S.W.G.	standard wire gauge
T.B.D.	torpedo-boat destroyer
T.N.T.	trinitrotoluene (explosive)
T.U.C.	Trades Union Congress
typ.	typography
U.D.A.	Ulster Defence Association
U.D.I.	unilateral declaration of independence
uhf	ultra-high frequency
ult.	ultimo (last month)
U.N.O.	United Nations Organisation
U.S.A.	United States of America
V.A.D.	Voluntary Aid Detachment
Ven.	The Venerable
vhf	very high frequency
Vet.	veterinary surgeon
V.I.P.	very important person
viz.	videlicet (namely)
Vol.	volunteer
vol.	volume
W.M.S.	Wesleyan Missionary Society
W.N.W.	west-north-west
W.P.C.	Woman Police Constable
W.S.W.	west-south-west

4

ACTH	adrenocorticotrophin
actg.	acting
Adjt.	adjutant
advt.	advertisement
anon.	anonymous
A.Q.M.G	Assistant Quartermaster-General
A.R.A.M.	Associate of the Royal Academy of Music
A.R.C.M.	Associate of the Royal College of Music
asst.	assistant
B.A.O.R.	British Army of the Rhine
Bart.	baronet
Beds.	Bedfordshire
Brit.	British
Bros.	brothers
B.Th.U.	British Thermal Unit
Capt.	Captain
Cent.	centigrade
C.E.R.N.	Conseil Européen pour la Recherche Nucléaire
C.E.T.S.	Church of England Temperance Society
C. of E.	Church of England
Coll.	college
Corp.	Corporal, corporation
C.U.A.C.	Cambridge University Athletic Club
C.U.B.C.	Cambridge University Boat Club
C.U.C.C.	Cambridge University Cricket Club
D.A.A.G.	Deputy Assistant Adjutant General
Dept.	department
D.H.S.S.	Department of Health and Social Security
D.Lit.	Doctor of Literature
D.O.R.A.	Defence of the Realm Act
E. & O.E.	errors and omissions excepted
Ebor.	Eboracum (York)
E.C.S.C.	European Coal and Steel Community
E.F.T.A.	European Free Trade Association
elec.	electrical, electricity
E.N.S.A.	Entertainments National Service Association
Epis.	Episcopal
exam.	examination
F.I.D.O.	Fog Investigation Dispersal Operation
F.R.A.M.	Fellow of the Royal Academy of Music
F.R.A.S.	Fellow of the Royal Astronomical Society
F.R.C.P.	Fellow of the Royal College of Physicians
F.R.C.S.	Fellow of the Royal College of Surgeons
F.R.G.S.	Fellow of the Royal Geographical Society
F.R.S.L.	Fellow of the Royal Society of Literature
G.A.T.T.	General Agreement on Tariffs and Trade
G.C.I.E.	Knight Grand Commander of the Indian Empire (Order)
G.C.M.G.	Knight Grand Cross of St. Michael and St. George (Order)
G.C.S.I.	Knight Grand Commander of the Star of India (Order)
G.V.C.O.	Knight Grand Cross of the Victorian Order
geog.	geography
geom.	geometry
gram.	grammar
inst.	instant (in the present month), institution, Institute
I. of W.	Isle of Wight

K.C.I.E. Knight Commander of the Indian Empire (Order)
K.C.M.G. Knight Commander (of the Order of) St. Michael and St. George
K.C.V.O. Knight Commander of the Royal Victorian Order
L.R.A.M. Licentiate of the Royal Academy of Music
L.R.C.M. Licentiate of the Royal College of Music
L.R.C.P. Licentiate of the Royal College of Physicians
masc. masculine
math. mathematics
mech. mechanics
memo. memorandum
M.I.E.E. Member of the Institution of Electrical Engineers
M.I.M.E. Member of the Institution of Mechanical Engineers
Mlle. Mademoiselle
M.R.C.P. Member of the Royal College of Physicians
M.R.C.S. Member of the Royal College of Surgeons
Mus.B. Bachelor of Music
Mus.D. Doctor of Music
Myth. mythology
N.A.T.O. North Atlantic Treaty Organization
N.E.D.C. National Economic Development Commission
O.E.C.D. Organization for Economic Co-operation and Development
O.E.E.C. Organization for European Economic Co-operation
O.H.M.S. On His (Her) Majesty's Service
O.U.A.C. Oxford University Athletic Club
O.U.B.C. Oxford University Boat Club
O.U.C.C. Oxford University Cricket Club
O.U.D.S. Oxford University Dramatic Society
P.A.Y.E. pay as you earn
pref. preference
pres. present
Prof. professor
prox. proximo (next month)
R.A.M.C. Royal Army Medical Corps
R.A.O.B. Royal Antediluvian Order of Buffaloes
R.A.O.C. Royal Army Ordnance Corps
R.A.S.C. Royal Army Service Corps
R.A.V.C. Royal Army Veterinary Corps
R.C.M.P. Royal Canadian Mounted Police
recd. received
Regt. regiment
R.E.M.E. Royal Electrical and Mechanical Engineers
R.I.B.A. Royal Institute of British Architects
R.N.V.R. Royal Naval Volunteer Reserve
R.S.V.P. Répondez s'il vous plaît (please reply)
R.W.G.M. Right Worshipful Grand Master
Sept. September
S.P.C.K. Society for Promoting Christian Knowledge
sp. gr. specific gravity

Supt. superintendent
Surg. surgeon
T.H.W.M. Trinity High-water Mark
Toc H Talbot House
T.G.W.U. Transport and General Workers' Union
W.A.A.F. Women's Auxiliary Air Force
W.Cdr. Wing Commander
W.J.A.C. Women's Junior Air Corps
W.R.N.S. Women's Royal Naval Service
Xmas. Christmas
Y.M.C.A. Young Men's Christian Association
Y.W.C.A. Young Women's Christian Association
zool. zoology

5

A.A.Q.M.G. Acting Assistant Quartermaster-General
ad lib. ad libitum (as much as desired)
Anzac. Australian and New Zealand Army Corps
A.R.I.B.A. Associate of the Royal Institute of British Architects
Assoc. associate, association
A.S.T.M.S. Association of Scientific Technical and Managerial Staffs
Bart's. St. Bartholomew's Hospital
Corpn. corporation
D.A.D.O.S. Deputy Assistant Director of Ordnance Services
D.A.Q.M.G. Deputy Assistant Quartermaster-General
D. Litt. Doctor of Letters
Elect. electrical, electricity
et seq. et sequens (and what follows)
ex div. without dividend
F.R.I.B.A. Fellow of the Royal Institute of British Architects
Hants. Hampshire
ht. wkt. hit wicket
incog. incognito
Lieut. Lieutenant
Litt.D. Doctor of Letters
L.R.C.V.S. Licentiate of the Royal College of Veterinary Surgeons
Lt.-Col. Lieutenant-Colonel
Lt.-Com. Lieutenant-Commander
Lt.-Gen. Lieutenant-General
Lt.-Gov. Lieutenant-Governor
Mlles. Mesdemoiselles
M.R.C.V.S. Member of the Royal College of Veterinary Surgeons
N.A.A.F.I. Navy, Army and Air Force Institutes
N.S.P.C.C. National Society for the Prevention of Cruelty to Children
P. and O. Peninsular and Oriental
photo. photograph
R.A.F.V.R. Royal Air Force Volunteer Reserve
Recce. reconnaissance
R.S.P.C.A. Royal Society for the Prevention of Cruelty to Animals
Rt. Hon. Right Honourable

Rt. Rev.	Right Reverend
Salop.	Shropshire
S.E.A.T.O.	South-east Asia Treaty Organization
Sergt.	Sergeant
Suppl.	supplement(al, ary)
Treas.	treasurer
U.N.R.R.A.	United Nations Relief and Rehabilitation Administration
Xtian	Christian

6 AND OVER

Cantab. (6)	of Cambridge
Cantuar. (7)	of Canterbury
Col.-Sergt. (8)	Colour-Sergeant
Dunelm. (6)	of Durham
E. and O.E. (6)	Errors and omissions excepted
Lieut.-Col. (8)	Lieutenant-Colonel
Lieut.-Gen. (8)	Lieutenant-General
Lieut.-Gov. (8)	Lieutenant-Governor

Lit. Hum. (6)	Literæ Humaniores (classics)
Maj.-Gen. (6)	Major General
Matric. (6)	matriculation
Messrs. (6)	Messieurs
M. Inst. C.E. (7)	Member of the Institution of Civil Engineers
nem. con. (6)	nemine contradicente (none objecting)
Non-com. (6)	non-commissioned officer
per pro. (6)	per procurationem (by proxy)
prelim. (6)	preliminary
pro tem. (6)	pro tempore (for the time being)
prox. acc. (7)	proxime accessit (a close second)
U.N.E.S.C.O. (6)	United Nations Educational Scientific and Cultural Organization
verb. sap. (7)	verbum sapienti (a word to the wise)

French Revolutionary Calendar

Nivôse (6) *snow, Dec.*
Floréal (7) *blossom, April*
Ventôse (7) *wind, Feb.*
Brumaire (8) *fog, Oct.*
Fervidor (8) *heat, July*
Frimaire (8) *sleet, Nov.*
Germinal (8) *seed, March*

Messidor (8) *harvest, June*
Pluviôse (8) *rain, Jan.*
Prairial (8) *pasture, May*
Fructidor (9) *fruit, Aug.*
Thermidor (9) *heat, July*
Vendémiaire (11) *vintage, Sept.*

Group terms

3 AND 4

band (of musicians)
bevy (of larks, quails, roes, or women)
box (of cigars)
brew (of beer)
case (of whisky or wine)
cast (of hawks)
cete (of badgers)
clan (people)
club (people)
crew (oarsmen or sailors)
crop (of farm produce)
down (of hares)
dule (of doves)
fall (of woodcock)
form (at schools)
four (card-players, oarsmen, or polo team)
gang (of elk, hooligans, labourers, slaves, or thieves)
hand (at cards)
herd (of asses, buffalo, cattle, cranes, deer, giraffes, goats, or oxen)
host (of angels)
hunt (hounds and hunters)
husk (of hares)
knob (of pochards, teal, toads, or widgeon)
leap (of leopards)
lepe (of leopards)
lot (in auctioneering)
meet (of hounds and hunters)
mess (military and naval)

mute (of hounds)
nest (of machine-guns, mice, rabbits, or wasps)
nide (of pheasants)
nine (baseball team)
pace (of asses)
pack (of grouse, hounds, wolves, or cards)
pair (of oarsmen and various)
park (of guns or cars)
peal (of bells)
pile (of arms)
pod (of whiting or peas)
pony (betting; £25)
pool (various)
posy (of flowers)
rag (of colts)
rope (of onions or pearls)
rout (of wolves)
run (of poultry)
rush (of pochards)
sect (of religious people)
set (of various articles)
show (of agricultural products, dogs, horses, etc.)
side (of players)
six (of cub scouts, sportsmen)
sord (of mallards or wild-fowl)
stud (of horses and mares)
sute (of mallards or wild-fowl)
trio (of musicans)
team (of ducks, horses, oxen, or players)
tuft (of grass)

285

walk (of snipe)
wing (of plovers)
wisp (of snipe)
wood (trees)
yoke (of oxen)

5

batch (of bread and various)
bench (of bishops or magistrates)
blast (of hunters)
blush (of boys)
board (of directors)
brace (of bucks, partridges, etc.)
brood (of hens)
bunch (of flowers, grapes, teal, or widgeon)
caste (of bread)
charm (of goldfinches)
class (of children at schools)
clump (of trees)
copse (trees)
covey (of grouse, partridges, or other birds)
crowd (of people)
doylt (of tame swine)
draft (of police or soldiers)
drove (of cattle or kine)
eight (oarsmen)
field (hunters, race-horses, or runners)
fiver (money; £5)
fleet (of motor-cars or ships)
flock (of birds, pigeons, or sheep)
flush (at cards)
genus (of animals or plants)
grand (money; £1000 or $1000)
group (photographic and various)
guard (soldiers)
hoard (of gold, etc.)
horde (of savages)
leash (of bucks or hounds)
party (of people)
plump (of wildfowl)
posse (of police)
pride (of lions)
scrum (at rugby football)
sedge (of bitterns or herons)
sheaf (of corn)
shoal (of fish)
siege (of herons)
skein (of geese, silk, or wool)
skulk (of foxes)
sloth (of bears)
squad (of beaters or soldiers)
staff (of officials or servants)
stalk (of foresters)
stand (of arms)
state (of princes)
swarm (of bees and other insects)
table (of bridge or whist players)
tribe (of goats or people)
trick (at cards)
troop (of boy-scouts, brownies, cavalry, kangaroos, lions, or monkeys)
truss (of hay)
twins (people)
watch (of nightingales or sailors)

6

barren (of mules)
basket (of strawberries)
budget (of papers)
bundle (of asparagus, firewood, and various)
caucus (of politicians)

cellar (of wine)
clique (of people)
clutch (of eggs)
colony (of gulls or people)
covert (of coots)
desert (of lapwings)
double (in betting)
eleven (cricket and other teams)
faggot (of sticks)
family (of people or sardines)
flight (of aeroplanes, doves, dunlins, or pigeons)
gaggle (of geese)
galaxy (of beauties)
harras (of horses)
kennel (of dogs)
kindle (of kittens)
labour (of moles)
litter (of cubs, pigs, pups, or whelps)
melody (of harpers)
monkey (in betting; £500)
museum (of antiques, works of art, etc.)
muster (of peacocks or soldiers)
nation (of people)
outfit (of clothes or sails)
packet (of cigarettes)
parade (of soldiers)
punnet (of strawberries)
quorum (minimum number of people)
rayful (of knaves)
rubber (at cards)
school (of porpoises or whales)
sextet (of musicians)
sleuth (of bears)
spring (of teal)
stable (of horses)
string (of pearls or racehorses)
tenner (money; £10)
throng (of people)
trophy (of arms, etc.)
troupe (of actors, dancers, or minstrels)
twelve (lacrosse team)
vestry (parochial assembly)

7

battery (of guns)
bouquet (of flowers)
brigade (of troops)
clamour (of rooks)
clouder (of cats)
cluster (of grapes or stars)
company (of actors, capitalists, or widgeon)
council (advisers or local authorities)
dopping (of sheldrakes)
draught (of butlers)
fifteen (rugby football team)
gallery (of pictures)
library (of books or music)
nosegay (of flowers)
orchard (of fruit trees)
quartet (of musicians)
service (of china or crockery)
sounder (of boars or swine)
spinney (of trees)
thicket (of trees)
vintage (of wine)

8

assembly (of people)
audience (of people)
building (of rooks)
division (of troops)

flotilla (of boats)
jamboree (of boy-scouts)
paddling (of ducks)
partners (in business or games)
regiment (of soldiers)
richesse (of martens)
sequence (at cards)
squadron (of cavalry or ships)
triplets (people)

9

army corps (of troops)
badelynge (of ducks)
committee (people)
community (of people or saints)
cowardice (of curs)
gathering (of people and the clans)
morbidity (of majors)
orchestra (of musicians)
shrubbery (of shrubs)
subtiltie (of sergeants)
syndicate (of capitalists)

10

assemblage (of clergy and various)
buttonhole (of flowers)
chattering (of choughs)
collection (of stamps, works of art, etc.)
commission (committee of enquiry)
detachment (of police or soldiers)
exaltation (of larks)
exhibition (of commercial products,
     pictures, works of art, etc.)
observance (of hermits)
shrewdness (of apes)
simplicity (of subalterns)

11 AND OVER

confraternity (brotherhood, usually
     religious) (13)
congregation (of birds or worshippers) (12)
constellation (of stars) (13)
convocation (of clergy or university
     authorities) (11)
murmuration (of starlings) (11)

Heraldry

2 – 4

arms
band
bar
bend
boar
dawl
delf
enty
erne
fess
fret
garb
gore
gray
kite
lion
or
orle
pale
pall
paly
pean
pile
posé
rose
semé
vair
vert

5

alant
animé
armed
azure
badge
barry
baton
bendy
bouche
bowed

breys
cable
chief
crest
cross
eagle
erect
ermin
fesse
field
fusil
garbe
gorge
gules
gurge
gyron
label
motto
pheon
rebus
rompu
sable
scarp
torse
waved

6

aiglet
apaumy
argent
armory
at gaze
attire
baston
bazant
bendil
bevile
bezant
billet
blazon
border
buckle

canton
charge
checky
chequy
cleché
cotise
couché
coward
dexter
dragon
ermine
escrol
etoile
falcon
fillet
flanch
fleury
florid
fretty
fylfot
garter
ground
guttée
heater
herald
jessed
knight
manche
mascle
maunch
mullet
naiant
Norroy
pallet
rebate
rustre
sejant
shield
square
timbre
vairée
vested
voided
voider

volant
vorant
wivern
wyvern

7

adorsed
adossed
alberia
annulet
arrière
arrondi
attired
barruly
bearing
bendlet
bevilly
bordure
bottony
brisure
cadency
chapter
chevron
clarion
courant
croslet
dolphin
dormant
emblaze
embowed
embrued
enarmed
endorse
engoulé
engrail
ermelin
estoile
fretted
fructed
gardant
griffin
Ich Dien

leopard
lioncel
lozenge
lozengy
martlet
miniver
nombril
passant
potence
purpure
quarter
raguled
rampant
roundel
salient
saltire
sea-lion
sexfoil
shafted
sinople
statant
swallow
torqued
torteau
trefoil
unicorn

heraldic
insignia
Lyon King
mantling
naissant
opinicus
ordinary
renverse
roundlet
sea-horse
sinister
standard
tincture
tressure

Clarenceux
coat-of-arms
cross-patée
difference
emblazoner
empalement
escalloped
escutcheon
fesse-point
fleur-de-lis
fleur-de-lys
king-at-arms
knighthood
pursuivant
quartering
quatrefoil
quintefoil
rebatement
surmounted

9

aquilated
arraswise
banderole
blazoning
carbuncle
cartouche
chevronel
combatant
diapering
displayed
embattled
enveloped
environed
erminites
estoillee
florettée
hatchment
lionceaux
lioncelle
Lyon-Court
regardant
scutcheon
spur-rowel
supporter

11 AND OVER

bend-sinister (12)
bendy-sinister (13)
bicapitated (11)
College of Arms (13)
counter-paled (12)
counter-passant (14)
countervair (11)
cross-crosslet (13)
cross-fleury (11)
cross-patencée (13)
Earl Marshal (11)
emblazonment (12)
engrailment (11)
escarbuncle (11)
escutcheoned (12)
garde-visure (11)
Garter King of Arms (16)
grant of arms (11)
heraldic emblem (14)
honour point (11)
inescutcheon (12)
Lyon King at Arms (14)
marshalling (11)
quarter arms (11)
Somerset herald (14)
transfluent (11)
unscutcheoned (13)

8

affronté
allerion
armorist
aversant
barrulet
bevilled
blazonry
caboched
caboshed
chaperon
couchant
crescent
dancetty
emblazon
englante
enmanché
erminois
escallop
gonfalon
haurient

10

barrybendi
barry-bendy
bicorporal
cinquefoil

Law sittings

Hilary (6)   Easter (6)   Trinity (7)   Michaelmas (10)

Names: boys
Including abbreviations, nicknames, and some common foreign names.

3

	Dan	Ian	Ken
	Dec	Ira	Kid
Abe	Don	Ivo	Len
Alf	Eli	Jay	Leo
Ali	Ely	Jem	Mac
Ben	Gus	Jim	Mat
Bob	Guy	Job	Max
Boy	Hal	Joe	Mee
Col	Hay	Jon	Ned
Dai	Hew	Jos	Nye

Pan	Goth	Toby	Dadoo
Pat	Gwyn	Tony	Damon
Pip	Hans	Vane	Darch
Ray	Hope	Vere	Darcy
Rea	Hugh	Walt	D'arcy
Reg	Hugo	Will	David
Rex	Hume	Wing	Davie
Rod	Hyam	Winn	Denis
Roy	Iain	Wray	Denny
Sam	Ifor	Wynn	Denys
Sid	Ikey	Yule	Derby
Tam	Ioan		Derek
Ted	Iohn		Dicky
Tim	Ivan	**5**	Drake
Tom	Ivor		Drogo
Vic	Jack	Aaron	Earle
	Jake	Abdul	Eddie
4	Jean	Abner	Edgar
	Jess	Abram	Edwin
Abel	Jock	Airay	Edwyn
Adam	Joel	Alban	Eille
Agar	Joey	Albat	Eldon
Alan	John	Algie	Eliab
Alec	Josh	Allan	Ellis
Algy	Juan	Alred	Eliot
Ally	Jude	Alroy	Elaye
Alma	Karl	Alves	Emery
Alva	Kaye	Alwin	Emile
Amos	Keir	Alwyn	Enoch
Andy	Kemp	Amand	Ernie
Axel	Kent	André	Ernst
Bald	King	Angus	Evans
Bart	Lacy	Anson	Ewart
Beau	Leon	Anton	Eyles
Bede	Leri	Archy	Felix
Bell	Lexy	Ariel	Franc
Bert	Loel	Askew	Frank
Bill	Luke	Athol	Franz
Boyd	Lyle	Aubyn	Frith
Buck	Lynd	Aurel	Fritz
Bury	Lyon	Aymar	Garth
Cain	Marc	Baden	Gavin
Carl	Mark	Barry	Geoff
Cary	Matt	Barty	Glyde
Cass	Mick	Basil	Glynn
Ciro	Mike	Beaty	Govan
Dahl	Muir	Bermy	Grant
Deri	Neil	Berty	Guido
Dick	Nero	Bevis	Harry
Dirk	Nick	Billy	Haydn
Dion	Noah	Bobby	Hebel
Duff	Noel	Booth	Henri
Duke	Ogle	Boris	Henry
Earl	Olaf	Brian	Herne
Eddy	Orme	Bruce	Heron
Eden	Otho	Bryan	Hiram
Edye	Otis	Bunny	Hyman
Elon	Otto	Cairn	Hymie
Emil	Owen	Caius	Iltyd
Eric	Page	Candy	Inigo
Eros	Paul	Carew	Innes
Esau	Penn	Carne	Isaac
Esra	Pery	Carol	Jabez
Euan	Pete	Cecil	Jacky
Evan	Phil	Clare	Jacob
Ewen	Pung	Claud	Jaime
Eyre	René	Clive	James
Ezra	Rhys	Clyde	Jamie
Fitz	Riou	Colet	Jason
Flem	Rory	Colin	Jemmy
Fred	Ross	Conan	Jerry
Fulk	Saul	Cosmo	Jesse
Gary	Sean	Cyril	Jevan
Glen	Seth	Cyrus	Jewel
Glyn	Stan	Dacre	Jimmy
	Theo	Daddy	Johan

Jonah	Speke	Crease	Hector
Jonas	Starr	Crusoe	Hedley
Jules	Steve	Curran	Henryk
Keith	Storm	Dallas	Henzel
Kenny	Tabor	Damian	Herman
Kevin	Taffy	Daniel	Hervey
Larry	Teddy	Dansil	Hilary
Leigh	Titus	Delves	Hilton
Lewin	Tommy	Declan	Hinton
Lewis	Trant	Demian	Hobart
Lexie	Tubby	Dennis	Holman
Lisle	Tudor	Dermot	Horace
Lloyd	Ulick	Derric	Howard
Louis	Usher	Dickie	Howell
Luigi	Wahab	Donald	Hubert
Lyall	Wally	Dougal	Hylton
Lynch	Willy	Dryden	Ignace
Major	Wolfe	Dudley	Inglis
Manly	Wyatt	Dugald	Irvine
Massy	Wylie	Duggie	Israel
Mavor	Wynne	Duncan	Jackey
Mayor	Wyvil	Dundas	Jackie
Meyer	Yorke	Dunlop	Jacomb
Micky		Earley	Jairus
Miles		Edmond	Janion
Monty	**6**	Edmund	Japhet
Moses		Eduard	Jasper
Moule	Adolph	Edward	Jerome
Myles	Adrian	Egbert	Jervis
Myrie	Aeneas	Eggert	Jeston
Neill	Albert	Eldred	Johann
Nigel	Albion	Elliot	Johnny
Odden	Alexis	Ernest	Joseph
Oprin	Alfred	Erroll	Joshua
Oriel	Alston	Ervine	Josiah
Orpen	Amilek	Esmond	Julian
Oscar	Andrew	Eugene	Julien
Osman	Angelo	Evelyn	Julius
Oswyn	Anselm	Fabian	Justin
Paddy	Anthon	Felton	Kersey
Paget	Antony	Fergus	Kirwan
Paton	Archer	Forbes	Laddie
Pedro	Archie	Franck	Lamley
Pelan	Armand	Freddy	Lawley
Percy	Arnold	Garnet	Leslie
Perry	Arthur	Gasper	Lionel
Peter	Aubrey	Gaston	Loftus
Phené	August	George	Lucien
Piers	Austin	Gerald	Ludwig
Power	Averil	Gerard	Lupton
Punch	Aylmer	Gideon	Luther
Ralph	Alywin	Gilbee	Magnus
Ramon	Balbus	Giulio	Mansel
Raoul	Baliol	Godwin	Marcel
Remus	Barney	Gonvil	Marcus
Renée	Baston	Gordon	Marten
Rider	Bedwyr	Graeme	Martin
Robin	Bennie	Graham	Mattos
Roden	Berend	Gregan	Mauris
Roger	Bertie	Gregor	Melvin
Rolfe	Blosse	Grizel	Merlin
Rollo	Braham	Grogan	Merrik
Romeo	Briton	Gunner	Mervyn
Romer	Brodie	Gunter	Mickie
Rowan	Brutus	Gustof	Millis
Royce	Bryden	Gwilym	Milton
Rufus	Bulwer	Hallam	Minden
Ryder	Caesar	Hamish	Montie
Sandy	Calvin	Hamlet	Moritz
Saxon	Carlos	Hamlyn	Morris
Scott	Caspar	Harold	Morvyn
Serge	Cedric	Harrel	Mostyn
Shane	Cicero	Harris	Murphy
Silas	Claude	Harrow	Murray
Simon	Conrad	Hayden	Nainby
290 Speed	Conway	Haydon	Nairne

Napier
Nathan
Nelson
Nevile
Nevill
Nickel
Nicols
Ninian
Norman
Norris
Norton
Nowell
Oliver
Onslow
Osbert
Osmond
Oswald
Pascoe
Pelham
Philip
Pierre
Powell
Prince
Rafael
Ramage
Ramsay
Randle
Ranson
Raphel
Ratsey
Rawden
Rayner
Reggie
Rendle
Reuben
Rhodes
Rippin
Robbie
Robert
Roddie
Rodger
Roland
Ronald
Rowley
Rowlie
Royden
Rudolf
Rupert
Samson
Samuel
Sander
Saurin
Sefton
Selwyn
Seumas
Shafto
Sidney
Simeon
Simons
Sinbad
Square
Squire
Steven
Stiven
St. John
Stuart
Sydney
Thomas
Tizard
Tobias
Trefor
Trevor
Vashon
Verney
Vernon
Vicary

Victor
Vivian
Vyvyan
Wallis
Walter
Warren
Watkin
Wesley
Willem
Willie
Wolsey
Yehudi
Xavier

7

Abraham
Ackroyd
Ainslie
Aladdin
Alfonso
Alister
Almeric
Alsager
Amadeus
Ambrose
Anatole
Andries
Aneurin
Anthony
Antoine
Antonio
Artemas
Artemus
Auguste
Baldwin
Balfour
Barclay
Barnaby
Barnard
Beaufoi
Bernard
Bertram
Berwald
Buckler
Burnard
Calvert
Cameron
Carlyon
Catesby
Charles
Charley
Chawner
Chester
Chewton
Clayton
Clement
Clinton
Compton
Connell
Crispin
Cyprian
Dalison
Dalziel
Dandini
Delancy
Denison
Derrick
Desmond
Dillwyn
Dominic
Donovan
Douglas
Downing
Duerdin

Eardley
Edouard
Emanuel
Emilius
Ephraim
Etienne
Eustace
Everard
Faraday
Faulder
Fielder
FitzRoy
Francis
Frankie
Freddie
Gabriel
Gaspard
Geoffry
Geraint
Gervais
Gervase
Gilbert
Gilmour
Gladwyn
Gloster
Godfrey
Goronwy
Grahame
Gregory
Gunther
Gustave
Hadrian
Herbert
Hermann
Hewlett
Hilaire
Hildred
Horatio
Humbert
Humphry
Ibrahim
Ingleby
Isidore
Jackson
Jacques
Jaffray
Jalland
Jeffrey
Jocelyn
Justice
Kenneth
Knyvett
Lachlan
Lambart
Lambert
Lennard
Leonard
Leopold
Lindsay
Lindsey
Lorimer
Lucifer
Ludovic
Madison
Malcolm
Matthew
Maurice
Maxwell
Maynard
Merrick
Michael
Montagu
Neville
Nicolas
Orlando
Orpheus

Orville
Osborne
Paladin
Patrick
Perseus
Pheroze
Phineas
Pierrot
Quentin
Quintin
Randall
Ranulph
Raphael
Raymond
Raymund
Redvers
Reynard
Richard
Roderic
Rodolph
Romulus
Ronayne
Rowland
Rudolph
Rudyard
Russell
Rutland
Sergius
Seymour
Shachel
Sheldon
Sigmund
Solomon
Spencer
Spenser
Stanley
St. Aubyn
St. Clair
Stenson
Stephen
Steuart
Stewart
St. Leger
Terence
Tertius
Timothy
Trenham
Ughtred
Ulysses
Umberto
Vaughan
Vauncey
Vincent
Wallace
Warwick
Westley
Wilfred
Wilfrid
Wilhelm
William
Winston
Wyndham
Ximenes
Zachary
Zebedee

8

Achilles
Adolphus
Alasdair
Alastair
Algernon
Alisdair
Alistair

291

Aloysius
Alphonse
Alphonso
Annesley
Antonius
Aristide
Augustus
Aurelius
Balliser
Bancroft
Banister
Barnabas
Bartlemy
Beaumont
Bedivere
Belgrave
Benjamin
Bernardi
Bertrand
Campbell
Carleton
Champion
Charnock
Clarence
Clementi
Clements
Clifford
Crauford
Crawford
Cuthbert
Diarmaid
Dominick
Ebenezer
Emmanuel
Ethelred
Faithful
FitzHugh
Florizel
François
Franklin
Frederic
Geoffrey
Geoffroy
Giovanni
Guiseppe
Greville
Gustavus
Hamilton
Harcourt
Harrison
Havelock
Herbrand

Hereward
Hezekiah
Horatius
Humphrey
Ignatius
Immanuel
Ironside
Jeremiah
Jonathan
Joscelyn
Josephus
Kingsley
Lancelot
Laurence
Lavallin
Lawrance
Lawrence
Leonhard
Leonidas
Llewelyn
Llywelyn
Lutwyche
Maddison
Maitland
Marshall
Martival
Meredith
Montague
Mortimer
Nicholas
Octavius
Oliphant
Ormiston
Oughtred
Paulinus
Perceval
Percival
Peregrin
Peterkin
Philemon
Randolph
Randulph
Reginald
Robinson
Roderick
Ruaraidh
Sandford
Scoltock
Secundus
Septimus
Sherlock
Siegmund

Sinclair
Spensley
Stafford
St. George
Sylvanus
Thaddeus
Theobald
Theodore
Trelawny
Valdimar
Vladimir
Wolseley

9

Abernethy
Abimeleck
Alaistair
Alexander
Allardyce
Almosnino
Alphonsus
Arbuthnot
Archibald
Aristotle
Armstrong
Athelstan
Augustine
Bartimeus
Beauchamp
Christian
Constable
Cornelius
Courtenay
Courteney
Creighton
Demetrius
Dionysius
Ethelbert
Ferdinand
Fortescue
Francisco
Frederick
Gascoigne
Glanville
Granville
Hazledine
Honoratus
Josceline
Llewellyn

Mackenzie
Marmaduke
Martineau
Nathaniel
Outhwaite
Peregrine
Rodriguez
Rupprecht
Sackville
Salvatore
Sebastian
Siegfried
Sigismund
Stanislas
Sylvester
Thaddaeus
Theodoric
Valentine
Valentino
Wilbraham
Zachariah
Zechariah

10 AND OVER

Athanasius (10)
Athelstane (10)
Barrington (10)
Bartholomew (11)
Carmichael (10)
Chesterfield (12)
Christopher (11)
Constantine (11)
Cruickshank (11)
Fitzherbert (11)
Fitzpatrick (11)
Haliburton (10)
Hildebrand (10)
Llewhellin (10)
Maximilian (10)
Pierrepont (10)
Ravenscroft (11)
Sacheverel (10)
Skeffington (11)
Somerville (10)
Stanislaus (10)
Theodosius (10)
Theophilus (10)
Tyrrhenian (10)
Washington (10)
Willoughby (10)

Names: girls
Including abbreviations, nicknames, and some common foreign names.

3

Ada
Ame
Amy
Ann
Ave
Bee
Dot
Eda
Ena
Eva
Eve
Fay
Flo
Gay
Heë

Ida
Ina
Isa
Ivy
Iza
Jen
Joy
Kay
Kit
Liz
Lot
Mai
May
Meg
Nan
Pam
Pat

Peg
Pen
Ray
Rio
Sue
Una
Val
Viv
Yda
Zia
Zoë

4

Aase
Aimé

Alba
Alma
Alys
Anna
Anne
Anny
Avis
Baba
Babs
Bebe
Bess
Beth
Caré
Cely
Clea
Cleo
Cora

Dawn	Niki	Cissy	Karin
Dido	Nina	Clair	Katey
Dodo	Nino	Clara	Katie
Dora	Nita	Clare	Kitty
Edie	Nora	Coral	Laila
Edna	Olga	Daisy	Laura
Edye	Oona	Delia	Lelia
Ella	Pola	Della	Letty
Elma	Puss	Denes	Lilia
Elsa	Rena	Diana	Lilly
Else	Rita	Diane	Lizzy
Emma	Rosa	Dilys	Lorna
Emmy	Rose	Dinah	Lotta
Enid	Rosy	Dodie	Lotty
Erna	Ruby	Dolly	Lucia
Esme	Ruth	Donie	Lucie
Etta	Sara	Donna	Lydia
Etty	Sita	Dorah	Lynne
Evie	Spry	Doris	Mabel
Fifi	Suky	Dreda	Madge
Gaby	Susy	Dulce	Maeve
Gage	Syme	Edith	Magda
Gail	Tess	Effie	Maggy
Gene	Tina	Eilsa	Mamie
Gola	Vera	Elena	Manie
Gwen	Vida	Elfie	Manon
Gwyn	Viki	Elise	Maria
Hebe	Vita	Eliza	Marie
Hope	Viva	Ellen	Matty
Ilse	Zena	Ellie	Maude
Inez	Zita	Elsie	Mavis
Ione	Zooe	Emily	Meave
Iris		Emmie	Megan
Irma		Erica	Mercy
Isla	**5**	Essie	Merry
Isma		Ethel	Milly
Ivey	Abbie	Ettie	Minna
Jane	Adela	Faith	Mitzi
Jean	Adele	Fanny	Moira
Jess	Aggie	Feona	Molly
Jill	Agnes	Filia	Morag
Joan	Ailsa	Fiona	Moyra
Judy	Aimee	Fleur	Myrle
June	Alice	Flora	Nancy
Kate	Aline	Freda	Nanny
Katy	Altha	Gabie	Naomi
Kaye	Angel	Gemma	Nelly
Lala	Anita	Gerty	Nessa
Leah	Annie	Gipsy	Nesta
Lena	April	Grace	Netta
Lila	Arbel	Greer	Ninie
Lily	Arden	Greta	Ninny
Lina	Avice	Gussy	Niobe
Lisa	Avril	Hazel	Norah
Lita	Barbi	Helen	Norma
Liza	Becky	Henny	Olive
Lois	Bella	Hetty	Pansy
Lola	Belle	Hilda	Patsy
Lucy	Berta	Honor	Patty
Lulu	Beryl	Hulda	Paula
Lynn	Bessy	Hylda	Pearl
Maie	Betty	Idina	Peggy
Mana	Biddy	Innes	Penny
Mary	Bobby	Irene	Phebe
Maud	Budie	Isold	Pippa
Meta	Buena	Janet	Pixie
Mimi	Bunty	Janey	Polly
Mina	Carol	Janie	Poppy
Moll	Carré	Janny	Queen
Mona	Caryl	Jenny	Renée
Muff	Cathy	Jessy	Rhoda
Muir	Cecil	Joann	Rhona
Myra	Celia	Joyce	Robin
Nell	Chloe	Julia	Rosie
Nena	Chune	Julie	Sadie
Neva	Circe	Karen	Sally

293

Sarah
Sasie
Sonia
Susan
Susie
Sybil
Tania
Tanya
Tanis
Teify
Terka
Thora
Trudy
Urith
Venis
Venus
Vesta
Vicki
Viola
Vivie
Wanda
Wendy
Zeeta
Zelia

6

Agatha
Aileen
Airlie
Alicia
Alison
Almond
Althea
Amanda
Amelia
Amelie
Anabel
Angela
Anthea
Armyne
Astrid
Audrey
Aurora
Awdrey
Azelle
Babbie
Beatie
Benita
Bertha
Bessie
Bettie
Bibbie
Biddie
Billie
Binnie
Birdie
Blanch
Blonde
Bobbie
Brenda
Brigid
Carmen
Carrie
Cecile
Cecily
Celina
Cherry
Cicely
Cissie
Claire
Connie
Daphne
Davina
Debbie

Denise
Doreen
Dorice
Dulcie
Editha
Edwina
Edythe
Eileen
Elaine
Elinor
Emilie
Esther
Eunice
Evelyn
Eyleen
Fannie
Fatima
Felice
Galena
Gerrie
Gertie
Gleana
Gladys
Gloria
Godiva
Gracie
Greeba
Gretel
Gussie
Gwenda
Gwynne
Hattie
Hannah
Helena
Hester
Hilary
Honora
Honour
Ileana
Imelda
Imogen
Ingrid
Ioanna
Isabel
Ishbel
Isobel
Isolde
Jackie
Janice
Jeanie
Jeanne
Jemima
Jennie
Jessie
Joanne
Joanna
Judith
Juliet
Kirsty
Lalage
Lallie
Lassie
Leonie
Lesley
Leslie
Lettie
Levina
Lilian
Lilias
Lillah
Lillie
Lizzie
Lorina
Lottie
Louisa
Louise

Lucilla
Lucile
Maggie
Maidie
Maimie
Maisie
Marcia
Margot
Marian
Marion
Marnie
Martha
Marthe
Mattie
Maxine
Melita
Mercia
Meriel
Mignon
Millie
Mimosa
Minnie
Miriam
Mollie
Monica
Moulie
Muriel
Murtle
Myrtle
Nadine
Nancie
Nancye
Nellie
Nelsie
Nessie
Nettie
Nicole
Noreen
Odette
Olivia
Paddie
Pamela
Parnel
Pattie
Pegeen
Peggie
Pernel
Persis
Petula
Phoebe
Pinkie
Poppet
Poppie
Popsie
Portia
Psyche
Rachel
Ramona
Regina
Renira
Richie
Robina
Rosina
Rowena
Roxana
Sabina
Sabine
Salome
Sandra
Sappho
Seabel
Selina
Seonad
Sharon
Sheena
Sheila

Sicele
Simone
Sophia
Sophie
Stella
Sybell
Sylvia
Tamsin
Teresa
Tertia
Tessie
Thalia
Thecla
Thelma
Tootie
Trixie
Ulrica
Ursula
Verity
Verona
Violet
Vivian
Vivien
Vyvyen
Willow
Winnie
Yvette
Yvonne

7

Abigail
Adeline
Alberta
Alethea
Alfrida
Ameline
Ankaret
Annabel
Annette
Anstice
Antonia
Antonie
Ariadne
Asenath
Athenia
Augusta
Aurelia
Babette
Barbara
Barbary
Beatrix
Belinda
Bettina
Billy Jo
Blanche
Blodwen
Blossom
Bridget
Camilla
Cecilia
Cherrie
Clarice
Claudia
Colette
Colleen
Coralie
Cynthia
Damozel
Darling
Deborah
Deirdre
Delysia
Diamond
Dolores

Dorinda
Dorothe
Dorothy
Dorrice
Dulcima
Eleanor
Elfreda
Elfrida
Ellenor
Ellinor
Elspeth
Emerald
Emiline
Estelle
Etienne
Eudoxia
Eugenia
Eugenie
Evaline
Eveline
Fayette
Felicia
Fenella
Feodora
Florrie
Flossie
Frances
Georgia
Gertrud
Gillian
Gladden
Gwennie
Gwenyth
Gwladys
Gwyneth
Gwynnie
Harriet
Heather
Hellena
Horatia
Hypatia
Janette
Janitha
Jessica
Jocelyn
Johanna
Juliana
Lavinia
Leoline
Leonora
Letitia
Lettice
Lettuce
Lillian
Lillias
Lisbeth
Lucille
Mabelle
Mafalda
Margery
Marjery
Marjory
Matilda
Maureen
Melanie
Michèle
Mildred
Minerva
Miralda
Miranda
Myfanwy
Nanuoya
Natalie
Natasha
Nigella
Ninette

Octavia
Ophelia
Ottilie
Palmyra
Pandora
Paulina
Pauline
Perdita
Phillis
Phyllis
Queenie
Rebecca
Rhodena
Ricarda
Roberta
Rosalie
Rosella
Rosetta
Rosette
Shambra
Sidonia
Susanna
Susanne
Suzanne
Sybilla
Tabitha
Tatiana
Theresa
Therese
Titania
Tootles
Valerie
Valetta
Vanessa
Venetia
Winsome
Yolande
Zirphie

8

Adelaide
Adrienne
Albertha
Amabelle
Angelica
Angelina
Angeline
Angharad
Arabella
Araminta
Atalanta
Beatrice
Berenice
Cammilla
Carlotta
Carolina
Caroline
Cathleen
Catriona
Christie
Chrystal
Clemency
Clotilde
Consuelo
Cordelia
Cornelia
Dorothea
Dorothie
Drusilla
Dulcinia
Eleanora
Eleanore
Elfriede
Ellaline

Emmeline
Euphemia
Evelinda
Everalda
Felicity
Filomena
Florence
Francine
Georgina
Germaine
Gertrude
Gretchen
Grizelda
Grizelle
Harriett
Hermione
Hortense
Isabella
Jeanette
Jennifer
Jeromina
Julianna
Julietta
Juliette
Katharin
Kathleen
Laburnum
Laetitia
Lavender
Lorraine
Lucretia
Madeline
Magdalen
Marcella
Marcelle
Margaret
Marianne
Mariette
Marigold
Marjorie
Marvella
Michelle
Mireille
Morwenna
Murielle
Nathalie
Nathanie
Patience
Patricia
Penelope
Petronel
Philippa
Primrose
Prudence
Prunella
Raymonde
Rebeccah
Reinagle
Reinelde
Rosalind
Rosamond
Rosamund
Rosemary
Samantha
Sapphire
Seabelle
Sheelagh
Susannah
Tallulah
Theodora
Veronica
Victoria
Violetta
Virginia
Vivienne
Vourneen

Winifred

9

Albertine
Alexandra
Ambrosine
Anastasia
Annabelle
Britannia
Cassandra
Catherine
Celestine
Charlotte
Christian
Christina
Christine
Clarenore
Cleopatra
Clothilde
Columbine
Constance
Corisande
Desdemona
Eglantine
Elisabeth
Elizabeth
Ermengard
Ernestine
Esmeralda
Esperance
Francisca
Frederica
Gabrielle
Georgiana
Geraldine
Guglielma
Guinivere
Gwendolen
Gwenllian
Harriette
Henrietta
Henriette
Hortensia
Hyacinthe
Iphigenia
Josephine
Kathailin
Katharine
Katherine
Madeleine
Magdalena
Magdalene
Maraquita
Margarita
Melisande
Millicent
Pepronill
Pierrette
Priscilla
Rosabelle
Rosaritta
Stephanie
Theodosia
Thomasina
Valentine
Winefride

10 AND 11

Alexandrina (11)
Antoinette (10)
Bernadette (10)

295

Christabel (10)
Christiana (10)
Christobel (10)
Cinderella (10)
Clementina (10)
Clementine (10)
Constantia (10)
Desiderata (10)

Ermentrude (10)
Ethelwynne (10)
Evangelina (10)
Evangeline (10)
Fredericka (10)
Gwendolene (10)
Gwendoline (10)
Hildegarde (10)

Irmentrude (10)
Jacqueline (10)
Margaretta (10)
Margherita (10)
Marguerite (10)
Petronella (10)
Philippina (10)
Wilhelmina (10)

Nine Muses

Calliope (8) *epic*
Clio (4) *history*
Erato (5) *love songs*
Euterpe (7) *lyric poetry*
Melpomene (9) *tragedy*

Polyhymnia (10) *sacred poetry*
Terpsichore (11) *choral song and dance*
Thalia (6) *comedy and idyllic poetry*
Urania (6) *astronomy*

Palindromes

3

aba
aga
aha!
ala
ama
ana
asa
ava
bab
bib
bob
bub
dad
did
dod
dud
eke
ere
eve
ewe
eye
gag
gig

gog
hah!
huh!
mam
mim
mum
nan
non
nun
oho!
oxo
pap
pep
pip
pop
pup
s.o.s.
tat
tit
tot
tut!
wow
zuz

4

abba
anna
boob
deed
dood
ecce
keek
ma'am
noon
otto
peep
poop
sees
toot

5

alula
anana
civic
kayak
level

madam
minim
put-up
radar
refer
rotor
sagas
sexes
shahs
sohos
solos
tenet

6 AND OVER

Able was I ere I saw l (19)
marram (6)
pull-up (6)
redder (6)
repaper (7)
reviver (7)
rotator (7)
terret (6)

Seven Deadly Sins

accidie (7)
acedia (6) } *sloth*
anger (5)
covetousness (12)
envy (4)
gluttony (8)
lust (4)
pride (5)
sloth (5)
vainglory (9) *pride*

Seven Virtues

charity (7)
faith (5)
fortitude (9)
hope (4)
justice (7)
love (4) *charity*
prudence (8)
temperance (10)

Seven Wonders of the World

The Pyramids of Egypt
The Hanging Gardens of Babylon
The Tomb of Mausolus
The Temple of Diana at Ephesus
The Colossus of Rhodes
The Statue of Zeus by Phidias
The Pharos of Alexandria
            or
The Palace of Cyrus (cemented with gold)

Signs of the Zodiac

Aquarius (8), *Water-bearer*
Aries (5) *Ram*
Cancer (6) *Crab*
Capricorn (9), *Goat*
Capricornus (11), *Goat*
Gemini (6), *Twins*
Leo (3), *Lion*
Libra (5), *Balance*
Pisces (6), *Fishes*
Sagittarius (11), *Archer*
Scorpio (7), *Scorpion*
Taurus (6), *Bull*
Virgo (5), *Virgin*

THE ESSENTIAL ENGLISH DICTIONARY

'The Essential English Dictionary' gives concise and accurate definitions of about 12 000 of the most important words in current use in English. Special attention has been taken to cover modern, technical, and informal meanings. An additional feature is the inclusion of over 2000 idioms and idiomatic phrasal verbs (such as *take off*). Distinct senses of words are numbered separately, with the most common or important meaning placed first. Easy-to-read pronunciations based on the International Phonetic Alphabet have been given only for words that might cause some difficulty (see *Key to symbols used in pronunciation* below).

The wide coverage of this dictionary with its emphasis on modernity, together with its compact size and clear typeface, will make it an invaluable aid at school, at the office and in the home.

Abbreviations used in the Dictionary

adj	adjective	*infin*	infinitive	*pt*	past tense
adv	adverb	*interj*	interjection	*r*	reflexive
aux	auxiliary	*n*	noun	*s*	singular
cap	capital	*neg*	negative	*sl*	slang
conj	conjunction	*pl*	plural	*tab*	taboo
def art	definite article	*poss*	possessive	*Tdmk*	trademark
esp	especially	*pp*	past participle	*US*	United States
f	feminine	*prep*	preposition	*v*	verb
indef art	indefinite article	*pres*	present tense	*vi*	verb intransitive
inf	informal	*pron*	pronoun	*vt*	verb transitive

Key to symbols used in pronunciation

Vowels

i:	*meet*	u	p*u*t	ai	*fly*
i	b*i*t	u:	sh*oo*t	au	h*ow*
e	g*e*t	ʌ	c*u*t	ɔi	b*oy*
æ	h*a*t	ə	*ago*	iə	h*ere*
ɑ:	h*ear*t	ə:	s*ir*	ɛə	*air*
ɔ	h*o*t	ei	l*a*te	uə	p*oor*
ɔ:	*ough*t	ou	g*o*		

Consonants

θ	*th*in	ʃ	*sh*ip
ð	*th*en	3	mea*s*ure
ŋ	si*ng*	tʃ	*ch*in
j	*y*es	dʒ	*g*in

[1] indicates that the following syllable is stressed as in ago (əˈgou).

ı placed under an *n* or *l* indicates that the *n* or *l* is pronounced as a syllable as in *button* (ˈbʌtn̩) and *flannel* (ˈflænl̩).

Irregular verbs

Infinitive	Past Tense	Past Participle	Infinitive	Past Tense	Past Participle
abide	abode or abided	abode *or* abided	beware[2]		
			bid	bid	bidden *or* bid
arise	arose	arisen	bind	bound	bound
awake	awoke *or* awaked	awoke *or* awaked	bite	bit	bitten *or* bit
			bleed	bled	bled
be	was	been	blow	blew	blown
bear[1]	bore	borne *or* born	break	broke	broken
beat	beat	beaten	breed	bred	bred
become	became	become	bring	brought	brought
begin	began	begun	build	built	built
bend	bent	bent	burn	burnt *or* burned	burnt *or* burned
bet	bet	bet			

302

Infinitive	Past Tense	Past Participle	Infinitive	Past Tense	Past Participle
burst	burst	burst	hurt	hurt	hurt
buy	bought	bought	keep	kept	kept
can	could		kneel	knelt	knelt
cast	cast	cast	knit	knitted or knit	knitted or knit
catch	caught	caught	know	knew	known
choose	chose	chosen	lay	laid	laid
cling	clung	clung	lead	led	led
come	came	come	lean	leant or leaned	leant or leaned
cost	cost	cost	leap	leapt or leaped	leapt or leaped
creep	crept	crept	learn	learnt or	learnt or
crow	crowed or crew	crowed		learned	learned
cut	cut	cut	leave	left	left
deal	dealt	dealt	lend	lent	lent
dig	dug or digged	dug or digged	let	let	let
do	did	done	lie	lay	lain
			light	lit or lighted	lit or lighted
draw	drew	drawn	lose	lost	lost
dream	dreamed or	dreamed or	make	made	made
	dreamt	dreamt	may	might	
drink	drank	drunk	mean	meant	meant
drive	drove	driven	meet	met	met
dwell	dwelt	dwelt	mow	mowed	mown
eat	ate	eaten	must		
fall	fell	fallen	ought		
feed	fed	fed	panic	panicked	panicked
feel	felt	felt	pay	paid	paid
fight	fought	fought	picnic	picnicked	picnicked
find	found	found	put	put	put
flee	fled	fled	quit	quitted or quit	quitted or quit
fling	flung	flung	read	read	read
fly	flew	flown	rid	rid or ridded	rid or ridded
forbid	forbade or	forbidden or	ride	rode	ridden
	forbad	forbid	ring	rang	rung
forget	forgot	forgotten or	rise	rose	risen
		forgot	run	ran	run
forgive	forgave	forgiven	saw	sawed	sawn or sawed
forsake	forsook	forsaken	say	said	said
freeze	froze	frozen	see	saw	seen
get	got	got	seek	sought	sought
give	gave	given	sell	sold	sold
go	went	gone	send	sent	sent
grind	ground	ground	set	set	set
grow	grew	grown	sew	sewed	sewn or sewed
hang[3]	hung or	hung or	shake	shook	shaken
	hanged	hanged	shall	should	
have	had	had	shear	sheared	sheared or
hear	heard	heard			shorn
hide	hid	hidden or hid	shed	shed	shed
hit	hit	hit	shine	shone	shone
hold	held	held	shoe	shod	shod

Irregular verbs

Infinitive	Past Tense	Past Participle	Infinitive	Past Tense	Past Participle
shoot	shot	shot	stink	stank or stunk	stunk
show	showed	shown	stride	strode	stridden
shrink	shrank or shrunk	shrunk or shrunken	strike	struck	struck
			string	strung	strung
shut	shut	shut	strive	strove	striven
sing	sang	sung	swear	swore	sworn
sink	sank	sunk	sweep	swept	swept
sit	sat	sat	swell	swelled	swollen or swelled
sleep	slept	slept			
slide	slid	slid	swim	swam	swum
sling	slung	slung	swing	swung	swung
slink	slunk	slunk	take	took	taken
slit	slit	slit	teach	taught	taught
smell	smelt or smelled	smelt or smelled	tear	tore	torn
			tell	told	told
sow	sowed	sown or sowed	think	thought	thought
speak	spoke	spoken	throw	threw	thrown
speed	sped or speeded	sped or speeded	thrust	thrust	thrust
			traffic	trafficked	trafficked
spell	spelt or spelled	spelt or spelled	tread	trod	trodden or trod
spend	spent	spent			
spill	spilt or spilled	spilt or spilled	wake	woke	woken
spin	spun	spun	wear	wore	worn
spit	spat or spit	spat or spit	weave	wove	woven or wove
split	split	split	weep	wept	wept
spread	spread	spread	will	would	
spring	sprang	sprung	win	won	won
stand	stood	stood	wind	wound	wound
steal	stole	stolen	wring	wrung	wrung
stick	stuck	stuck	write	wrote	written
sting	stung	stung			

[1] when *bear* means *give birth to* the past participle is always *born*.

[2] used only in the infinitive or as an imperative.

[3] the preferred form of the past tense and past participle when referring to death by hanging is *hanged*.

A

a, an *indef art* one; each; every; any; some.

aback *adv* **taken aback** taken by surprise; disconcerted; flabbergasted.

abandon *vt* **1** leave behind with no intention of returning; desert; forsake. **2** give up; fail to complete. **abandon oneself (to)** yield, submit, or give in (to).

abashed *adj* ashamed; embarrassed.

abate *vi* lessen; die down. *vt* reduce; subdue; suppress. **abatement** *n.*

abattoir ('æbɒtwɑ:) *n* slaughterhouse.

abbess *n* female head of nuns in an abbey or nunnery.

abbey *n* **1** community of monks or nuns. **2** buildings occupied by such a community. **3** church attached to such a community.

abbot *n* male head of monks in an abbey or monastery.

abbreviate *vt* shorten (a word or phrase). **abbreviation** *n.*

abdicate *vi,vt* renounce or relinquish (the throne, one's powers, etc.). **abdication** *n.*

abdomen *n* lower part of the body between the diaphragm and pelvis; belly. **abdominal** *adj.*

abduct *vt* take (a person) away unlawfully; kidnap. **abduction** *n.* **abductor** *n.*

aberration *n* deviation from the usual, right, or natural course, condition, etc. **aberrant** *adj.*

abet *vt* (-tt-) assist or encourage in crime or wrongdoing.

abeyance *n* **in abeyance** in a state of inactivity; suspended.

abhor *vt* (-rr-) have an intense horror of; loathe; detest. **abhorrence** *n.* **abhorrent** *adj.*

abide *vt* (abode *or* abided) tolerate; bear. *vi* **1** stay; remain. **2** reside; dwell. **abide by** keep to; remain close or faithful to.

ability *n* **1** power; capacity; means. **2** competence; skill.

abject *adj* **1** downcast; humiliated. **2** despicable; shocking. **3** humble. **abjectly** *adv.*

ablaze *adj* **1** on fire; in flames; burning fiercely. **2** displaying strong passion or ardour.

able *adj* **1** having the power, capacity, opportunity, or means (to). **2** competent; skilled. **ably** *adv.* **able-bodied** *adj* physically fit; strong.

abnormal *adj* irregular; unnatural; deviant. **abnormality** *n.* **abnormally** *adv.*

aboard *adv,prep* on or in(to) a ship, aircraft, etc.

abode[1] *n* place of residence; dwelling; home.

abode[2] *v* a *pt* and *pp* of **abide.**

abolish *vt* do away with; put an end to; ban. **abolition** *n.*

abominable *adj* loathsome; detestable; dreadful. **abominably** *adv.*

Aborigine (æbə'ridʒini) *n also* **Aboriginal** person belonging to a race of original native inhabitants, esp. of Australia. **Aboriginal** *adj.*

abort *vt* **1** terminate (a pregnancy); perform an abortion on. **2** cancel or destroy (a project, mission, etc.) before completion. *vi* **1** miscarry. **2** fail to function successfully; terminate before completion. **abortive** *adj.* **abortion** *n* **1** operation carried out to remove a foetus from the womb. **2** miscarriage. **3** disastrous failure.

abound *vi* exist or have in great quantity; be plentiful.

about *prep* **1** of; concerning; relating to; connected with. **2** near or close to; around. **about to** ready or preparing to; on the point of. ~*adv* **1** approximately. **2** nearby; close at hand. **3** around; here and there; to and fro.

above *adv* higher up; overhead. *prep* **1** over; higher than. **2** more or greater than. **3** in authority over; superior to. **4** beyond (suspicion, reproach, etc.). *adj also* **above-mentioned** mentioned or written above or before. **above all** more than anything. **aboveboard** *adv* openly; without deception. *adj* open; straightforward; honest; legal.

abrasion *n* **1** wearing down by rubbing. **2** graze on the skin. **abrasive** *adj* **1** producing abrasion. **2** harsh; grating. *n* something used for wearing down or smoothing a surface.

abreast *adv* side by side; level with. **keep abreast of** keep up or up-to-date with.

abridge *vt* cut (a novel, play, etc.); condense. **abridgement** *n.*

abroad *adv* **1** in or to a foreign country. **2** in circulation; at large.

abrupt *adj* 1 unexpected and sudden. 2 curt; short; brusque. **abruptly** *adv*. **abruptness** *n*.

abscess *n* pus-filled sore.

abscond *vi* leave without permission; run away, esp. after committing a crime. **absconder** *n*.

absent *adj* ('æbsənt) 1 away; not in attendance. 2 lacking; missing; not present. *v* **absent oneself** (əb'sent) stay away. **absence** *n*. **absentee** *n* person, such as an employee or landlord, who is absent. **absenteeism** *n*. **absent-minded** *adj* forgetful or vague, esp. when preoccupied. **absent-mindedly** *adv*. **absent-mindedness** *n*.

absolute *adj* total; utter; complete. **absolutely** *adv*.

absolve *vt* release from blame, sin, obligation, etc.; pardon; exonerate. **absolution** *n*.

absorb *vt* 1 take in or soak up. 2 assimilate. 3 engross; engage fully. **absorbent** *adj*. **absorbing** *adj*. **absorption** *n*.

abstain *vi* 1 refrain from registering one's vote. 2 refrain from indulging in certain pleasures, such as drinking alcohol. **abstention** *n* withholding of one's vote. **abstinence** *n* state or period of self-denial.

abstract *adj* ('æbstrækt) having no material existence; not concrete; conceptual. *n* ('æbstrækt) brief account; summary; résumé. *vt* (əb'strækt) take away; remove. **abstraction** *n*. **abstract art** *n* art depicting ideas or objects through form, colour, and line rather than natural or actual representation.

absurd *adj* ridiculous; silly; ludicrous. **absurdity** *n*. **absurdly** *adv*.

abundant *adj* plentiful. **abundance** *n*. **abundantly** *adv*.

abuse *vt* (ə'bju:z) 1 use or treat badly or unfairly; misuse. 2 insult; be rude to. *n* (ə'bju:s) 1 ill-treatment; misuse; violation. 2 insulting behaviour or language. **abusive** *adj*.

abyss (ə'bis) *n* deep bottomless pit or gulf. **abysmal** (ə'bizməl) *adj* 1 bottomless; deep. 2 dreadful; shocking. **abysmally** *adv*.

academy *n* 1 school or college offering specialized training. 2 association of distinguished scholars. **academic** *adj* 1 relating to a university, college, etc. 2 theoretical or intellectual rather than practical or technical. *n* university teacher or researcher. **academically** *adv*.

accelerate *vt,vi* make or become faster; speed up. **acceleration** *n*. **accelerator** *n* control pedal in a motor vehicle that is used for regulating speed; throttle.

accent *n* ('æksent) 1 type of pronunciation associated with a particular region, social class, etc. 2 stress placed on a syllable or word. 3 written or printed symbol occurring in some languages to indicate stress, vowel quality, etc. 4 emphasis. *vt* (æk'sent) stress; mark with an accent. **accentuate** *vt* emphasize; draw attention to. **accentuation** *n*.

accept *vt* 1 take something that is offered; receive. 2 agree (to); admit. 3 tolerate; put up with. **acceptable** *adj*. **acceptance** *n*.

access *n* 1 way in or to; approach. 2 opportunity, means, or permission to enter, reach, use, etc. **accessible** *adj* reachable; approachable.

accessory *n* 1 one of an additional set of items. 2 person who assists in or conceals knowledge of a crime.

accident *n* unforeseen event or occurrence, often having unpleasant consequences. **by accident** by chance; unexpectedly. **accidental** *adj*. **accidentally** *adv*.

acclaim *vt* show approval by cheering; applaud; hail; praise. *n also* **acclamation** enthusiastic approval; applause; praise.

acclimatize *vt,vi* make or become conditioned or used (to). **acclimatization** *n*.

accommodate *vt* 1 provide room or space for; house; shelter. 2 adjust (to); reconcile. **accommodation** *n*.

accompany *vt* go with; escort; join in or take part in with. **accompaniment** *n* 1 something that belongs or occurs with something else. 2 music that is played to support a solo performance.

accomplice *n* partner in crime or wrongdoing.

accomplish *vt* achieve; attain; complete successfully. **accomplished** *adj* talented; skilful; proficient, esp. in social graces; refined. **accomplishment** *n* 1 successful completion; achievement. 2 skill; refinement; proficiency.

accord *vt,vi* agree; correspond; match up (to). *n* harmony; agreement. **of one's own accord** on one's own initiative; voluntarily. **accordance** *n.* **in accordance with** in agreement with; conforming to. **according** *adv* **according to 1** as laid down or stipulated by. **2** as stated or shown by; on the evidence of. **3** in relation to; dependent on. **accordingly** *adv* **1** therefore; so. **2** as the situation demands.

accordion *n* portable box-shaped musical instrument with bellows and keys.

accost *vt* **1** approach (someone) in order to converse, question, etc. **2** solicit.

account *n* **1** report of an event, etc. **2** explanation. **3** banking service or a credit service at a store, etc. **4** sum of money deposited at a bank. **5** statement of money transactions. **6** importance; esteem. **on account** on credit. **on account of** because of. **on any/no account** for no reason whatever. **take into account** *or* **take account of** allow for. *vi* **account for 1** give reasons for; explain. **2** make a reckoning of; count. **3** capture; kill. **accountable** *adj* responsible (for). **accountant** *n* professional person who investigates the business and financial transactions of an individual or organization. **accountancy** *n.*

accumulate *vt,vi* amass or collect over a period. **accumulation** *n.* **accumulative** *adj.*

accurate *adj* precise; correct; exactly right. **accuracy** *n.* **accurately** *adv.*

accuse *vt* charge (a person) with a crime, mistake, fault, etc.; blame. **accusation** *n.*

accustom *vt* familiarize; acquaint; acclimatize.

ace *n* **1** playing card having a single pip. **2** pilot who has destroyed a large number of enemy aircraft. **3** champion. *adj sl* first-rate; excellent.

ache *vi* **1** feel a steady dull pain. **2** yearn; long (for). *n* steady dull pain.

achieve *vt* attain; gain. **achievement** *n.*

acid *n* sour-tasting chemical compound that turns litmus red and dissolves in water to produce hydrogen ions. *adj* **1** sharp; sourtasting. **2** sarcastic; caustic. **acidic** *adj.* **acidity** *n.* **acid rain** *n* rain containing pollutants produced by industrial processes, harmful to crops, etc.

acknowledge *vt* **1** recognize that something is true or right; admit. **2** respond to. **acknowledgment** *or* **acknowledgement** *n.*

acne ('ækni) *n* skin disorder affecting mainly the face and upper part of the body, which become covered with pimples and blackheads.

acorn *n* nut that is the fruit of the oak.

acoustic *adj* relating to sound or the sense of hearing. **acoustics** *n* **1** *s* branch of physics concerned with the study of soundwaves. **2** *pl* properties of a concert hall, room, etc., that affect the way sounds are heard.

acquaint *vt* inform; familiarize; introduce. **acquaintance** *n* **1** someone one knows, but not as a close or intimate friend. **2** personal knowledge. **acquaintanceship** *n.*

acquiesce *vi* agree tacitly; assent; comply. **acquiescence** *n.* **acquiescent** *adj.*

acquire *vt* obtain, esp. gradually or with some effort; take possession of; get. **acquisition** *n.* **acquisitive** *adj* eager to possess.

acquit *vt* (-tt-) pronounce not guilty; discharge. **acquit oneself** perform; behave; conduct oneself.

acre *n* unit of land area equal to approx. 4000 sq m (4840 sq yds). **acreage** *n* total number of acres in any given area.

acrobat *n* performer on a trapeze, tightrope, etc.; gymnast. **acrobatic** *adj.* **acrobatics** *n s or pl* gymnastic feats or exercises.

across *prep,adv* **1** from one side to another. **2** over on the other side (of). **come across** meet or discover unexpectedly.

acrylic *adj* relating to a type of synthetic fibre.

act *vi* **1** operate; function; behave; perform; do (something). **2** perform in a play. **3** pretend; feign. *vt* take the role of; play. *n* **1** single deed; action. **2** law passed by Parliament. **3** major division of a play, opera, etc., consisting of a number of scenes. **4** performer(s) in a show, circus, etc., or the performance itself.

action *n* **1** process of doing something; act; deed. **2** gesture; movement. **3** mechanism; movement of mechanical parts. **4** lawsuit.

activate *vt* make active; stir; agitate; cause to react.

active *adj* **1** in operation; functioning. **2** taking a positive part. **3** lively; busy. **actively** *adv*. **activist** *n* person working for a particular political cause.

activity *n* **1** movement; motion. **2** something that keeps one occupied or busy.

actor *n* performer in the theatre, on television, or in films. **actress** *f n*.

actual *adj* having real existence; not imaginary. **actually** *adv* really; as a matter of fact; in fact.

actuary *n* expert adviser on insurance, pensions, etc. **actuarial** *adj*.

acupuncture *n* Eastern method of medical treatment using sharp needles to puncture certain areas of the skin.

acute *adj* **1** having a keen sense of hearing, smell, etc. **2** perceptive; quick-witted; shrewd. **3** severe; critical. **4** *med* reaching crisis point; not chronic. **acute accent** *n* symbol placed over certain vowels in some languages, as in *café*. **acute angle** *n* angle of less than 90°. **acutely** *adv*. **acuteness** *n*.

adamant *adj* insistent; firm. **adamantly** *adv*.

Adam's apple *n* popular name for the thyroid cartilage of the larynx.

adapt *vt* modify to suit a different purpose or situation. *vi* adjust to a new environment or set of conditions. **adaptable** *adj*. **adaptation** *n*. **adaptor** *n*.

add *vt,vi* **1** put together; join; give as something extra. **2** calculate the sum (of); total. **3** state further; go on to say. **add to** supplement; increase. **addition** *n*. **additional** *adj* extra. **additive** *adj,n*.

adder *n* viper.

addict *n* ('ædikt) **1** person who has become physically dependent on something, esp. a drug. **2** enthusiast; fanatic. **be(come) addicted to** (ə'diktid) be(come) totally dependent on. **addiction** *n*. **addictive** *adj*.

address *n* **1** postal location of a house, office, etc. **2** speech given before an audience. *vt* **1** write the address on. **2** speak directly to. **addressee** *n*.

adenoids *pl n* mass of enlarged tissue in the pharynx.

adept *adj* skilful; adroit; deft. **adeptly** *adv*. **adeptness** *n*.

adequate *adj* **1** sufficient; just enough; acceptable; satisfactory. **2** able to cope; capable. **adequacy** *n*. **adequately** *adv*.

adhere *vi* stick; hold. *vt* stick; glue; gum. **adhere to** keep to; uphold; observe strictly; abide by. **adherent** *adj*. **adhesion** *n*. **adhesive** *n* substance such as glue, gum, or paste, used for sticking things together. *adj* relating to such a substance.

ad hoc *adj* used for a specified purpose.

adjacent *adj* adjoining; situated beside; next to.

adjective *n* part of speech qualifying a noun. **adjectival** *adj*.

adjoin *vt* be situated next to; border on. **adjoining** *adj*.

adjourn *vt,vi* discontinue or suspend (a meeting, court session, etc.) with the intention of resuming at a later time. **adjournment** *n*.

adjudicate *vi,vt* judge; settle; select (a winner). **adjudication** *n*. **adjudicator** *n*.

adjust *vt* make a minor alteration to; modify; change. *vi* change to fit in with new requirements; adapt. **adjustable** *adj*. **adjustment** *n*.

ad-lib *vi* (-bb-) compose (a speech, lines in a play, etc.) without previous preparation; improvise.

administer *vt* **1** *also* **administrate** govern; control as an official. **2** dispense; hand out; issue. **administrative** *adj*. **administrator** *n*. **administration** *n* **1** management; control; process of governing. **2** body of managers, governors, etc.

admiral *n* highest ranking naval officer. **admiralty** *n* state department responsible for naval affairs.

admire *vt* have a high regard for; respect; look up to; approve of. **admirable** *adj*. **admiration** *n*. **admirer** *n*.

admit *vt* (-tt-) **1** grant entry to. **2** confess; accept blame for. **3** accept as true; agree to. **admissible** *adj* acceptable; allowable. **admission** *n* **1** permission or opportunity to enter. **2** fee charged for entrance. **3** confession. **4** acknowledgment; acceptance. **admittance** *n* right of entry; access.

ado *n* fuss; confused excitement; commotion.

adolescence *n* period between puberty and adulthood. **adolescent** *n,adj*.

adopt *vt* **1** take (another person's child) into one's own family as a legal guardian. **2** take up (someone else's suggestion, plan, etc.). **3** give formal approval to; choose. **adoption** *n.*

adore *vt* love ardently; worship; have great affection for. **adorable** *adj.* **adoration** *n.*

adorn *vt* decorate; embellish; enhance. **adornment** *n.*

adrenaline *n* hormone secreted in the body or produced synthetically that is used to accelerate heart action, raise blood sugar levels, etc.

adrift *adj* **1** cut loose from a mooring; unattached; drifting. **2** off the point; not concise.

adroit *adj* skilfully quick; resourceful; adept. **adroitly** *adv.* **adroitness** *n.*

adulation *n* **1** unqualified or uncritical praise. **2** flattery. **3** unquestioning devotion.

adult *n* **1** person who is grown up or mature. **2** fully grown animal or plant. *adj* **1** mature; of age; fully grown. **2** intended for adults. **adulthood** *n.*

adultery *n* extra-marital sexual intercourse.

advance *vi* **1** move forwards or upwards; proceed. **2** show improvement; progress. *vt* **1** take further; move ahead. **2** pay out (money) before it is due. *n* **1** movement forwards. **2** progress. **3** amount paid before payment is due. *adj* issued in advance. **advancement** *n.* **in advance** beforehand; ahead.

advantage *n* favourable position, circumstances, etc.; privilege; benefit. **advantageous** *adj.*

adventure *n* exciting journey or experience, usually involving risks or hazards. **adventurous** *adj* daring; bold; willing to take risks.

adverb *n* part of speech qualifying a verb. **adverbial** *adj.*

adverse *adj* hostile; in opposition; antagonistic. **adversity** *n* distressing circumstances; misfortune.

advertise *vt,vi* give public information (of goods for sale, vacancies, etc.); announce. **advertiser** *n.* **advertisement** *n* public announcement in the press, on televison, etc.; note of goods for sale, etc.

advice *n* opinion or recommendation given in order to help someone make a decision.

advise *vt,vi* give advice (to); recommend. **adviser** *n.* **advisable** *adj* wise; worth recommending.

advocate *vt* ('ædvəkeit) recommend; urge. *n* ('ædvəkət) **1** supporter; believer. **2** (in Scotland) barrister.

aerial *n* system of conducting rods for receiving or transmitting radio or television signals; antenna. *adj* of, in, or from the air.

aerobics *n* system of rhythmical physical exercises to improve body fitness through increased oxygen consumption.

aerodynamics *n* study of the behaviour of aircraft, missiles, etc., in relation to airflow. **aerodynamic** *adj.* **aerodynamically** *adv.*

aeronautics *n* study of flight. **aeronautic** *or* **aeronautical** *adj.*

aeroplane *n* aircraft propelled by jet engines or propellers and kept aloft by aerodynamic forces.

aerosol *n* container dispensing a fine spray of pressurized liquid, gas, etc.

aesthetic (i:s'θetik) *adj* **1** pleasing to one's sense of beauty. **2** relating to aesthetics. **aesthetics** *n* branch of philosophy concerned with the concept and study of beauty in art.

afar *adv* far away; from or at a distance.

affair *n* **1** matter; concern; business. **2** sexual relationship, esp. an extra-marital one; liaison. *pl n* personal, business, or political matters.

affect[1] *vt* **1** influence; alter; cause to change. **2** move; arouse emotionally.

affect[2] *vt* feign; simulate; pretend. **affectation** *n* falseness of manner or style; insincerity.

affection *n* fondness; love; strong liking. **affectionate** *adj.* **affectionately** *adv.*

affiliate *vt,vi* join or unite (with) as a member; associate. **affiliation** *n.*

affinity *n* **1** relationship, esp. by marriage. **2** close connection; resemblance. **3** empathetic attraction; strong liking.

affirm *vt,vi* testify as to truth or validity; substantiate; assent. **affirmation** *n.* **affirmative** *adj* positive; assertive. *n* the answer 'yes'.

affix *vt* (ə'fiks) fasten; attach. *n* ('æfiks) prefix or suffix.

afflict *vt* cause distress, pain, or suffering; torment. **affliction** *n* 1 torment; grief. 2 disease; sickness; disability.

affluent *adj* wealthy; prosperous; rich. **affluence** *n*.

afford *vt* 1 have money, time, etc., to spare (for). 2 be able to risk. 3 offer; provide; allow.

affront *vt* insult or offend, esp. publicly. *n* public insult; display of disrespect.

afield *adv* far away; a long way off.

afloat *adj,adv* 1 floating. 2 solvent.

afoot *adj,adv* under way; in the offing.

aforesaid *adj* *also* **aforementioned** previously referred to.

afraid *adj* 1 frightened; apprehensive; fearful. 2 sorry; regretful.

afresh *adv* from the beginning; again; anew.

aft *adv* towards or at the stern.

after *prep* 1 following; later than. 2 in pursuit of. 3 in spite of; in view of. 4 concerning. 5 in imitation of. **after all** when everything is considered. *~adv* 1 behind. 2 subsequently. **take after** resemble. *~conj* subsequent to the time that. **after-care** *n* help, treatment, supervision, etc., given to a person discharged from hospital or prison. **after-effect** *n* delayed effect, esp. of a drug. **afterlife** *n* life after death. **aftermath** *n* 1 period of devastation following a war, disaster, etc. 2 disastrous consequence. **afternoon** *n* period between midday and evening. **afterthought** *n* thought or idea that occurs later or incidentally. **afterwards** *adv* at a later time; subsequently.

again *adv* 1 once more; any more. 2 additionally; further; besides. **again and again** repeatedly; many times.

against *prep* 1 in contact with; next to; close to; up as far as. 2 in opposition to; competing with. 3 not in favour of. 4 contrasting with. 5 in order to prevent.

age *n* 1 period of time during which a person or thing has existed. 2 era; epoch; period. 3 *also pl inf* a long time. *vi,vt* grow or cause to grow or look old(er). **aged** *adj* 1 ('eidʒid) very old. 2 (eidʒd) of the age of.

agenda *n* list of items to be discussed or dealt with; programme.

agent *n* 1 person representing or working on behalf of a client. 2 something that produces a change or effect. **agency** *n* 1 company providing services or goods and operating on behalf of a client. 2 influence; mediating power.

aggravate *vt* 1 make worse; exacerbate. 2 irritate; annoy. **aggravation** *n*.

aggression *n* feeling or display of hostility, anger, etc. **aggressive** *adj*. **aggressively** *adv*. **aggressor** *n*.

aggrieved *adj* suffering from injustice; feeling unfairly treated.

aghast *adj* horrified; dumbfounded; shocked.

agile *adj* quick; alert; nimble. **agility** *n*.

agitate *vt* 1 shake or stir violently. 2 worry; make anxious; trouble. *vi also* **agitate** for publicly campaign and fight for. **agitator** *n*.

aglow *adj* glowing; shining; alight.

agnostic *n* person who believes that an immaterial being such as God cannot be the subject of real knowledge. **agnosticism** *n*.

ago *adv* in the past.

agog *adj* eager and excited.

agony *n* intense and prolonged pain or suffering; torment; anguish. **agonize** *vi,vt* suffer or cause agony or extreme distress.

agrarian *adj* relating to agricultural land or landed property.

agree *vi* 1 consent. 2 correspond; match; tally. 3 think or feel the same (as). 4 make a joint decision. 5 suit; go well with. *vt* 1 settle; arrange terms of. 2 acknowledge; concede; consent to. **agreeable** *adj* 1 willing to consent. 2 pleasant. **agreement** *n* 1 consent; permission. 2 deal or contract between parties. 3 accordance; harmony.

agriculture *n* practice or study of farming. **agricultural** *adj*. **agriculturalist** *n*.

ahead *adv* further on; in front; in advance. **go ahead** continue; proceed; advance.

aid *vt,vi* help; assist; facilitate. *n* help; assistance; support. **in aid of** for; in order to help.

ailment *n* particular illness or disease.

aim *vt,vi* 1 point or direct (a gun, etc.) towards a target. 2 direct (one's efforts, remarks, etc.) towards a particular object. **aim at** *or* **for** 1 try to achieve; strive for. 2 mean or intend for. *~n* 1 act of aiming. 2 goal; target; purpose. **aimless** *adj*

having no particular goal or purpose. **aimlessly** *adv.* **aimlessness** *n.*

air *n* **1** mixture of gases, consisting chiefly
of nitrogen (78 per cent) and oxygen (21 per
cent), that is essential for respiration. **2** layer
of air surrounding the earth; atmosphere. **3**
light breeze. **4** impression or aura. **5** bearing; manner. **6** tune; melody. **by air** transported by aircraft. **clear the air** remove
tension or discord. **in the air** not yet settled.
into thin air without a trace; completely.
on/off the air being/not being broad-
cast. **walk** *or* **tread on air** feel elated. **airs**
pl n affectations. ∼*vt* **1** expose to fresh air;
ventilate. **2** declare openly; make public.
vt,vi dry in warm air. **airborne** *adj* in or
supported or carried by air. **airtight** *adj*
preventing the passage of air into or out of;
impermeable. **airy** *adj* **1** open to the fresh
air; well ventilated. **2** carefree; unconcerned.
3 light as air; graceful. **4** insubstantial;
speculative. **airily** *adv.* **airiness** *n.*

air-conditioning *n* system for controlling
flow and humidity of air within a building.

aircraft *n* machine, such as an aeroplane,
helicopter, or glider, that is capable of flight
through the air.

aircraft carrier *n* warship with special
decks for operational aircraft.

airfield *n* extensive level area for take-off
and landing of aircraft.

airforce *n* branch of a nation's armed services concerned with military aircraft.

airgun *n* gun discharged by compressed
air.

air hostess *n* stewardess on an aircraft.

airlift *n* transportation by air of people,
food, etc., esp. in an emergency when surface routes are cut. *vt* transport using an airlift.

airline *n* organization offering transportation by scheduled flights for people and
cargo. **airliner** *n.*

airmail *n* **1** letters and parcels conveyed by
aircraft. **2** system for sending such mail. *vt*
send (mail) by air.

airport *n* system of buildings, runways,
hangars, etc., providing facilities for aircraft, passengers, and cargo.

air-raid *n* military attack by enemy aircraft.

airship *n* self-propelled aircraft kept aloft
by buoyancy.

aisle *n* **1** gangway or open passageway separating blocks of seats in a theatre, church,
etc. **2** area on either side of a church, usually
separated from the nave by a series of pillars
and arches.

ajar *adj,adv* partially open.

alabaster *n* form of gypsum that is white
and opaque or translucent, used for statues,
ornaments, etc.

alarm *n* **1** warning signal, such as a bell or
shout. **2** sudden fear or anxiety; panic;
fright. *vt* **1** frighten; shock; horrify. **2** alert
to possible danger.

alas *interj* expression of regret, sadness,
etc.

albatross *n* large sea-bird with webbed
feet.

albeit *conj* even though; although.

albino *n* person or animal with unnatural
colouring in skin and eyes.

album *n* **1** book used for the display of
photographs, stamps, etc. **2** long-playing
record.

alcohol *n* **1** intoxicating substance produced by fermenting sugar in a liquid. **2** any
drink containing such a substance. **alcoholic** *adj* containing alcohol. *n* person
addicted to alcohol. **alcoholism** *n* addiction to alcohol.

alcove *n* recess or niche.

alderman *n* senior councillor of a city or
borough.

ale *n* type of light-coloured beer.

alert *adj* watchful; quick to respond. **alertness** *n.*

algebra *n* branch of mathematics in which
numbers, quantities, and variables are represented by symbols whose manipulation is
governed by generalized rules and relationships. **algebraic** *adj.*

alias *adv* also known as. *n* assumed name;
pseudonym.

alibi *n* claim that someone accused of a
crime was elsewhere at the time that it was
committed.

alien *adj* **1** foreign; strange. **2** not part of;
contrary. *n* foreigner. **alienate** *vt* estrange;
cast out; cause to become indifferent or
detached, esp. from society. **alienation** *n.*

alight[1] *adj* **1** on fire; lit up. **2** bright; shining.

alight² *vi* (alighted *or* alit) **1** dismount; get down (from). **2** settle or perch (on). **alight on** find unexpectedly; seize; light on.

align *vt,vi* **1** bring into line (with); line up; straighten. **2** form an alliance (with); cooperate. **alignment** *n.*

alike *adj* similar; appearing the same; resembling. *adv* similarly; in the same way.

alimentary canal (æli'mentəri) *n* system of organs in the body, including the stomach and intestines, through which food passes.

alimony *n* allowance paid to one marriage partner by the other following a legal separation.

alive *adj* **1** living; existing. **2** active; vigorous.

alkali ('ælkəlai) *n* chemical base that is soluble in water. **alkaline** *adj.*

all *adj* **1** every one of; the whole of. **2** complete; total. *adv* entirely; completely; totally. **all but** very nearly; almost. **all in all** taking everything into consideration. **in all** altogether; in total.

allay *vt* alleviate; assuage; appease; relieve.

allege (ə'ledʒ) *vt* claim as true; assert; avow. **allegation** (æli'geiʃən) *n.*

allegiance (ə'li:dʒəns) *n* loyalty, esp. to a sovereign; fidelity.

allegory ('æligəri) *n* story, painting, etc. in which moral values and other qualities are personified. **allegorical** (æli'gɔrik) *adj.*

allelula *interj,n* hallelujah.

allergy ('ælədʒi) *n* physical reaction of the body caused by extreme sensitivity to certain substances. **allergic** (ə'lə:dʒik) *adj.*

alleviate *vt* relieve (pain or suffering); allay. **alleviation** *n.*

alley *n* **1** *also* **alleyway** narrow passageway or street. **2** lane used in skittles, ten-pin bowling, etc.

alliance *n* **1** treaty of mutual friendship and help between nations. **2** relationship so formed. **3** nations so involved. **4** close relationship; union. **allied** *adj* **1** joined by alliance; united. **2** related; connected.

alligator *n* large reptile, chiefly of the southern US, related to the crocodile but having a shorter broader snout.

alliteration *n* repetition of the initial sound, usually a consonant, in a group of words.

allocate *vt* assign; distribute; share out. **allocation** *n.*

allot *vt* (-tt-) allocate. **allotment** *n* **1** plot of rented land for cultivation. **2** assignment.

allow *vt* **1** permit; let. **2** set aside. **3** grant; permit to have; concede. **allow for** make provision for. **allowable** *adj* permissible. **allowance** *n* **1** regular amount of money paid to a dependant. **2** sum of money allocated for certain tasks, responsibilities, etc. **3** concession; toleration. **make allowances for 1** excuse. **2** take into account.

alloy *n* metallic material consisting of a mixture of metals, as in bronze and brass, or of metals and nonmetals, as in steel.

allude *v* **allude to** refer indirectly to.

allure *vt* entice; attract; fascinate. *n* attraction; fascination. **allurement** *n.*

ally *n* ('ælai) **1** member of an alliance. **2** sympathetic person; supporter. *vt,vi* (ə'lai) unite; join (with).

almanac ('ɔ:lmənæk) *n* book containing a calendar, with astronomical and astrological information, etc., for the year.

almighty *adj* **1** omnipotent; supremely or divinely powerful. **2** *sl* tremendous; great. **the Almighty** *n* God.

almond *n* **1** tree related to the plum and peach. **2** smooth oval nut in a hard shell produced by this tree. *adj* of an oval shape like an almond.

almost *adv* nearly; close to; not quite.

alms (ɑ:mz) *pl n* money or gifts donated as charity to the poor. **almshouse** *n* building founded to provide accommodation and food for the poor and aged.

aloft *adj,adv* high up; overhead.

alone *adj,adv* by oneself; by itself; apart; isolated; separate; unaccompanied.

along *prep* **1** from one end to the other. **2** on any part of the length of. *adv* **1** onwards; forwards. **2** together (with); accompanying. **all along** all the time. **alongside** *adv,prep* along the side of; beside; parallel to.

aloof *adj* distant; haughty or reserved; uninvolved. *adv* at a distance; with reserve.

aloud *adv* using a normal speaking voice; not silently; out loud.

alphabet *n* system of letters or other symbols used for writing in a particular language. **alphabetical** *adj* following the order of the letters of the alphabet. **alphabetically** *adv.*

alpine *adj* relating to mountains or a mountainous region.

already *adv* by now, by then; previously.

Alsatian *n* breed of dog resembling a wolf in appearance and often used by the police or as a guard dog.

also *adv* in addition; as well; too; besides.

altar *n* **1** table in a Christian church at which the Eucharist is celebrated. **2** table or platform used for offerings or sacrifices to a deity.

alter *vt,vi* change; give or take on a new form or appearance; modify. **alteration** *n.*

alternate *adj* (ɔl'tɜːnət) every other or second one; first one then the other. *vi,vt* ('ɔltəneit) switch repeatedly from one to the other; take or arrange in turn. **alternately** *adv.* **alternation** *n.* **alternative** *n* the second of two possibilities or choices. *adj* offering a choice between two things.

although *conj* though; even though; in spite of the fact that.

altitude *n* height of an aircraft, mountain, etc., esp. that above sea level.

alto *n* **1** male singing voice or musical instrument with a range between tenor and treble. **2** contralto.

altogether *adv* **1** completely; totally; absolutely; all; utterly; entirely. **2** on the whole. **3** added together; in total.

aluminium *n* silvery metallic element extracted mainly from bauxite and widely used in lightweight alloys.

always *adv* all the time; without exception; regularly.

am *v* 1st person singular form of **be** in the present tense.

amalgamate *vi,vt* join together; merge; unite; combine. **amalgamation** *n.*

amass *vt,vi* bring or come together; accumulate; collect.

amateur *n* person who is an unpaid participator in an activity such as sport or the arts. *adj* **1** not professional. **2** *also* **amateurish** lacking in skill or polish; of a rather low standard.

amaze *vt* fill with surprise or wonder; astonish; astound. **amazement** *n.* **amazingly** *adv.*

ambassador *n* minister or diplomat sent abroad by the Government as an official representative.

amber *n* yellowish-brown fossil resin often used for jewellery. *adj* **1** of a yellowish-brown or dull orange colour. **2** made of amber.

ambidextrous *adj* able to use either hand with equal skill. **ambidexterity** *n.*

ambiguous *adj* having more than one possible meaning; open to interpretation. **ambiguity** *n.* **ambiguously** *adv.*

ambition *n* **1** desire or will to achieve fame, power, position, etc. **2** desired object or goal; aim. **ambitious** *adj.* **ambitiously** *adv.*

ambivalent (æm'bivələnt) *adj* having conflicting or uncertain feelings; undecided. **ambivalence** *n.* **ambivalently** *adv.*

amble *vi* **1** walk at an easy and leisurely pace; stroll; saunter. **2** (of a horse) move slowly lifting both legs on the same side of the body together. *n* leisurely pace.

ambulance *n* vehicle designed and equipped to convey sick or injured people to hospital.

ambush *n* **1** act of lying in wait in order to make a surprise attack. **2** such an attack, the concealed place from which such an attack is launched, or the attackers themselves. *vt* attack (an enemy) by ambush.

amen *interj* word meaning 'so be it' spoken or sung at the end of a prayer, hymn, etc.

amenable *adj* **1** willing; agreeable; responsive. **2** legally responsible; answerable. **3** capable of being tested or judged.

amend *vt* rectify; correct; modify. **make amends** make up (for); compensate. **amendment** *n.*

amenity *n* often *pl.* useful service or facility intended to make life easier or more comfortable.

amethyst *n* precious stone of crystallized quartz that is usually purple or mauve.

amiable *adj* pleasant; likeable; friendly. **amiability** *n.* **amiably** *adv.*

amicable *adj* friendly; not hostile. **amicably** *adv.*

amid *or* **amidst** *prep* among or amongst; in the midst of.

amiss *adj* faulty; defective; wrong. *adv* wrongly; incorrectly. **take amiss** feel wronged or hurt (by), often unjustifiably.

ammonia *n* colourless pungent gas, containing nitrogen and hydrogen, used in the manufacture of fertilizers and of other chemicals.

ammunition *n* 1 bullets, missiles, etc., that can be fired from a gun or other offensive weapon. 2 information or points of argument used against someone in debate, criticism, etc.

amnesty *n* general pardon given esp. to political prisoners.

amoeba *n* microscopic single-celled animal having a constantly changing shape.

among *or* **amongst** *prep* 1 in the middle of; surrounded by; in company with; together with. 2 between; shared by.

amoral (ei'mɔrəl) *adj* outside the sphere of morality. **amorality** *n.*

amorous *adj* concerned with or displaying love; affectionate. **amorously** *adv.* **amorousness** *n.*

amorphous *adj* having no distinct form, shape, or structure.

amount *n* 1 quantity; extent; whole. 2 sum; total. *v* **amount to 1** add up to; come to. 2 be equal or equivalent to; have the same function as.

ampere *n* unit used to measure electric current.

amphetamine *n* drug that stimulates the central nervous system, used for the relief of nasal congestion, hay fever, etc.

amphibian *n* 1 cold-blooded animal, such as the frog or newt, that usually lives on land as an adult but breeds in water. 2 vehicle able to function both on land and water. **amphibious** *adj.*

amphitheatre *n* large arena enclosed by rising tiers of seats.

ample *adj* 1 plenty; more than enough; sufficient. 2 of generous proportions; large. **amply** *adv.*

amplify *vt* increase the intensity of (an electrical signal). *vt, vi* explain in greater detail; expand (on). **amplification** *n.* **amplifier** *n* electrical device, used in radios, televisions, etc., for reproducing a signal at increased intensity.

amputate *vt, vi* sever (a limb or part of a limb) usually by surgery. **amputation** *n.*

amuse *vt* 1 entertain, esp. by speaking or acting in a humorous way. 2 keep pleasantly busy or occupied. **amusement** *n.*

an *indef art* used before an initial vowel sound and sometimes *h*. See **a.**

anachronism *n* 1 representation of an object, event, etc., in too early a historical period; chronological error. 2 something no longer useful or suitable in the present age. **anachronistic** *adj.*

anaemia *n* deficiency of red blood cells causing pale appearance of the skin, fatigue, etc. **anaemic** *adj.*

anaesthetic (ænis'θetik) *n* substance administered before an operation to produce loss of sensation or unconsciousness. **anaesthetist** *n* (ə'ni:sθətist) person trained to administer anaesthetics. **anaesthetize** *vt* (ə'ni:sθətaiz) administer anaesthetics to.

anagram *n* word or phrase whose letters can be transposed to form a new word or phrase.

anal ('einəl) *adj* relating to the anus.

analogy (ə'nælədʒi) *n* comparison that serves to draw attention to a similarity between things. **analogous** (ə'næləgəs) *adj.*

analyse ('ænəlaiz) *vt* break down (a substance, situation, etc.) into constituent parts or stages for examination. **analysis** *n, pl* **analyses** (ə'nælisi:z). **analytic** (ænə'litik) *or* **analytical** *adj.* **analyst** ('ænəlist) *n* 1 person who analyses. 2 psychoanalyst.

anarchy ('ænəki) *n* 1 form of society in which established forms of government and law are not recognized. 2 disorder; lawlessness. **anarchist** *n* supporter of anarchy.

anatomy (ə'nætəmi) *n* study or science of the physical structure of animals and plants. **anatomical** (ænə'tɔmikəl) *adj.* **anatomist** (ə'nætəmist) *n.*

ancestor ('ænsestə) *n* person from whom one is descended; forefather. **ancestral** (æn'sestrəl) *adj.* **ancestry** ('ænsəstri) *n.*

anchor *n* 1 heavy steel or iron object used for holding fast a vessel in the water. 2 something that offers security and stability. *vt, vi* hold fast with the anchor. **anchorage** *n* 1 place where a vessel may be anchored or the fee charged. **2** stability; firm or sound basis.

anchovy ('æntʃəvi) *n* small fish of the herring family with a strong salty flavour.

ancient *adj* **1** relating to a very early or remote historical period. **2** very old.

ancillary *adj* auxiliary; secondary; subsidiary.

and *conj* **1** as well as; in addition to. **2** then; after. **3** also; too.

anecdote ('ænikdout) *n* short witty account or story.

anemone (ə'nemɔni) *n* **1** woodland plant producing white, red, or deep blue flowers. **2** sea anemone.

anew *adv* afresh; again.

angel *n* **1** spiritual being in the Christian religion who is one of God's attendants and messengers, usually depicted as having human form with wings. **2** sweet kindhearted person. **angelic** (æn'dʒelik) *adj*.

anger *n* feeling of intense annoyance or irritation; rage. *vt* make angry; enrage; infuriate.

angle¹ *n* **1** difference in direction between two intersecting lines or planes, measured in degrees. **2** shape formed by such lines or planes. **3** projecting corner. **4** point of view; aspect. *vt* **1** move or place at an angle; bend into an angle. **2** direct at a particular audience; bias.

angle² *vi* **1** fish with a rod, line, and bait. **2** *also* **angle for** seek (compliments, favours, etc.), esp. by devious means. **angler** *n*.

Anglican *adj* relating to the Church of England. *n* member of the Church of England. **Anglicanism** *n*.

angry *adj* **1** extremely cross or annoyed; enraged. **2** sore and inflamed. **angrily** *adv*.

anguish *n* intense anxiety and distress; agony; torment.

angular *adj* **1** having sharp corners or many angles. **2** bony; gaunt.

animal *n* living organism capable of spontaneous movement; creature. *adj* **1** relating to an animal or animals. **2** physical as opposed to spiritual; carnal.

animate *adj* ('ænimɔt) living; capable of spontaneous movement. *vt* ('ænimeit) give life or movement to; make active. **animation** *n*.

aniseed *n* seed yielding an aromatic oil with a strong liquorice flavour, used in medicines, drinks, etc.

ankle *n* joint that connects the foot and the leg.

annex *vt* (ə'neks) **1** take possession of by conquest. **2** join; attach; incorporate. *n* ('æneks) *also* **annexe** additional building usually set apart from the main block of a hotel, hospital, etc.

annihilate *vt* wipe out completely; destroy; obliterate. **annihilation** *n*.

anniversary *n* **1** date of a significant event which occurred in some previous year. **2** celebration of this.

announce *vt* declare; proclaim; make known. **announcement** *n*. **announcer** *n* person who introduces programmes, reads news bulletins, etc., on radio or television.

annoy *vt,vi* irritate; bother; vex. **annoyance** *n*.

annual *adj* **1** occurring once a year. **2** valid for one year. **3** lasting for one growing season. *n* **1** plant that lasts for one growing season only. **2** book or periodical published in a new edition each year. **annually** *adv*.

annuity (ə'nju:iti) *n* sum of money paid out in instalments at regular intervals.

annul (ə'nʌl) *vt* (-ll-) declare (a law, marriage contract, etc.) invalid or no longer binding.

anoint *vt* rub or smear with oil, esp. ritually as an act of consecration. **anointment** *n*.

anomaly (ə'nɔmɔli) *n* something that is out of place or deviates from the common rule. **anomalous** *adj*.

anonymous (ə'nɔnimɔs) *adj* **1** *sometimes shortened to* **anon** having no acknowledged author. **2** unknown. **anonymity** (ænɔ'nimiti) *n*.

anorak *n* waterproof jacket with a hood.

anorexia (nervosa) *n* medical condition characterized by loss of appetite and distaste for food caused by obsession with need for weight loss.

another *adj* **1** additional; further. **2** different; separate. *pron* **1** one more. **2** a different or new one. **3** a comparable or similar one.

answer *n* **1** reply or response (to a question). **2** solution (to a problem). *vt,vi* reply or respond (to); acknowledge. *vt* solve.

answer for accept responsibility or blame for. **answer to** match or correspond to (a description). **answerable** *adj* responsible; liable; accountable.

ant *n* small insect that typically lives in a complex highly organized colony.

antagonize *vt* provoke; incite; arouse hostility by attacking. **antagonism** *n*. **antagonist** *n*. **antagonistic** *adj*.

antelope *n* deer-like animal with hollow horns such as the gazelle or springbok.

antenatal *adj* relating to the period of pregnancy; before birth.

antenna (æn'tenə) **1** *pl* **antennae** (æn'teni:) one of a pair of sensitive organs on the head of an insect, crustacean, etc.; feeler. **2** *pl* **antennas** radio aerial.

anthem *n* patriotic song; hymn of praise.

anthology *n* collection of poems, stories, etc.

anthropology *n* study of mankind and man's social and cultural relationships. **anthropological** *adj*. **anthropologist** *n*.

anti-aircraft *adj* designed for defence against enemy aircraft.

antibiotic (æntibai'ɔtik) *n* chemical substance, such as penicillin, used to destroy certain bacteria. *adj* relating to an antibiotic.

antibody *n* protein in the blood that counteracts harmful bacteria.

anticipate *vt* **1** realize or recognize beforehand; predict; foresee. **2** expect; look forward to; await. **anticipation** *n*.

anticlimax *n* drop in mood from excitement to flatness, seriousness to absurdity, etc.

anticlockwise *adj,adv* moving in a direction opposite to that followed by the hands of a clock.

antics *pl n* playful jokes, tricks, or gestures.

anticyclone *n* area of high atmospheric pressure producing calm settled weather.

antidote ('æntidout) *n* substance or agent used to counteract harmful effects; remedy.

antifreeze *n* substance that lowers the freezing point of a liquid, used esp. in car radiators.

antique *n* valuable piece of furniture, work of art, etc., belonging to an earlier period. *adj* **1** old and valuable. **2** antiquated. **antiquated** *adj* obsolete; out-of-date; old-fashioned. **antiquity** (æn'tikwiti) *n* **1** quality of being very old. **2** period before the Middle Ages; distant past.

anti-Semitic (æntisə'mitik) *adj* discriminating against Jews. **anti-Semite** (ænti'semait) *n*. **anti-Semitism** (ænti'semitizəm) *n*.

antiseptic *adj* relating to the destruction of undesirable microorganisms; preventing decay. *n* an antiseptic substance.

antisocial *adj* **1** contrary to the norms of society. **2** unsociable; shunning the company of others.

antithesis (æn'tiθisis) *n, pl* **antitheses** (æn'tiθisi:z) direct contrast; opposite. **antithetical** (ænti'θetikəl) *adj*.

antler *n* branched bony outgrowth on the head of a male deer or similar animal.

anus *n* opening at the lower end of the rectum.

anvil *n* iron or steel block on which metal is hammered and shaped.

anxious *adj* **1** nervous; worried; uneasy; apprehensive; tense. **2** keen; eager. **anxiety** *n*. **anxiously** *adv*.

any *adj* **1** some; several. **2** whichever; no matter which. **3** one of many; every. **at any rate/in any case** anyway; moreover; besides; anyhow; however. ~*pron* **1** anybody; anything. **2** some. *adv* at all; to an extent. **anybody** *pron, n* a person; no matter who; anyone. **anyhow** *adv* **1** besides; anyway. **2** haphazardly; with no particular care or organization; not systematically. **anyone** *pron,n* anybody. **anything** *pron,n* a thing; no matter what or which; something. ~*adv* at all; remotely. **anyway** *adv* **1** in any case; well; besides; anyhow; after all. **2** carelessly; anyhow. **anywhere** *adv* **1** to or at any place. **2** at all; anything.

apart *adv* **1** separately; independently. **2** into parts or pieces. **3** at a distance; away. **apart from** after considering; aside from; other than.

apartheid (ə'pɑːtaid) *n* system of racial segregation, esp. in South Africa.

apartment *n* **1** *chiefly US* flat, usually in a block. **2** suite of rooms.

apathy *n* lack of sympathy, feeling, interest, etc.; listlessness; complete indifference. **apathetic** *adj*.

ape *n* short-tailed or tailless primate, such as the chimpanzee or gorilla.

aperture *n* **1** opening or slit. **2** diaphragm in a lens system that limits the diameter of a light beam entering a camera, etc. **3** diameter of such a diaphragm.

apex ('eipeks) *n, pl* **apexes** *or* **apices** ('æpisi:z) highest point; vertex; tip; pinnacle.

aphid ('eifid) *n* small insect that feeds on plant juices.

apiece *adv* each; for each one.

apology *n* **1** statement expressing regret for an offence, error, failure, etc. **2** poor substitute. **apologetic** *adj* sorry; making an apology. **apologetically** *adv.* **apologize** *vi* make an apology or excuse.

apostle (ə'posəl) *n* one of Christ's twelve disciples.

apostrophe (ə'postrəfi) *n* written or printed symbol (') used to show omission of a letter or letters, or to denote the possessive case.

appal *vt* (-ll-) fill with abhorrence; shock; horrify; disgust.

apparatus *n* equipment, machinery, tools, etc., required for a particular purpose.

apparent *adj* **1** seeming; ostensible. **2** evident; clear; obvious. **apparently** *adv.*

appeal *vi* **1** apply to a higher authority for the reversal of a decision. **2** plead; beseech; call (for). **3** appear attractive (to); please. *n* **1** application to a higher authority. **2** plea; request; entreaty. **3** attractiveness; ability to arouse interest. **appealing** *adj* attractive; arousing interest, sympathy, pity, etc.

appear *vi* **1** come into view; become visible. **2** arrive. **3** seem; give the impression (of). **4** become clear or obvious; emerge. **5** give a public performance. **6** become available. **7** present oneself in court, before a tribunal, etc. **appearance** *n* **1** coming into view. **2** arrival. **3** outward manifestation; impression; aspect; look. **4** public performance. **5** attendance in court. **keep up appearances** maintain an outward show of respectability, affluence, etc.

appease *vt* **1** pacify; soothe. **2** assuage; ease; allay; relieve. **appeasement** *n.*

appendix *n, pl* **appendixes** *or* **appendices** (ə'pendisi:z) **1** small blind functionless tube attached to the lower abdomen. **2** section containing supplementary information at the end of a book. **appendicitis** *n* inflammation of the appendix.

appetite *n* **1** desire to satisfy bodily needs, esp. for food. **2** craving; capacity. **appetizing** *adj* able to stimulate the appetite; tasty.

applaud *vi,vt* **1** show appreciation (of) by clapping. **2** commend; praise. **applause** *n.*

apple *n* edible round fruit with a red, green, or yellow skin.

apply *vt* **1** use in a practical or appropriate way; employ; put into practice. **2** cover with; put on. **3** concentrate; give attention to. *vi* **1** make a formal request (for a job, money, etc.). **2** be appropriate; have a bearing (on). **appliance** *n* piece of equipment; tool; machine; instrument. **applicable** *adj* relevant; appropriate; able to be applied. **applicant** *n* person applying for a job, place, etc.; candidate. **application** *n* **1** formal request; claim. **2** putting into practice (of relevant knowledge, skills, etc.). **3** act of applying (paint, ointment, etc.). **4** close attention; concentration.

appoint *vt* **1** select for a job, position, etc. **2** assign; allocate. **3** arrange for a particular time; fix. **appointment** *n* **1** fixed meeting; engagement. **2** selection or nomination for a job, position, etc. **3** job or position for which a person is selected.

apportion *vt* share out; allot; distribute. **apportionment** *n.*

appraise *vt* estimate the quality or value of; assess. **appraisal** *n.*

appreciate *vt* **1** be grateful for; recognize the worth of. **2** realize; understand; be aware of. *vi* increase in value. **appreciation** *n.* **appreciable** *adj* considerable; large enough to be assessed.

apprehend *vt* **1** arrest and take into custody. **2** be anxious about; fear; dread. *vt,vi* comprehend; grasp. **apprehension** *n* **1** anxiety; fear; caution; dread. **2** understanding; conception. **3** arrest. **apprehensive** *adj* worried; anxious; cautious; uneasy; doubtful.

apprentice *n* person under contract to an employer whilst learning a trade. *vt* engage or place as an apprentice.

approach *vt,vi* draw close or closer (to); near; advance. *vt* **1** make contact with in order to obtain advice, a favour, etc. **2** begin to tackle; start working on; deal with. **3** approximate; come close to being. *n* **1** act of drawing near; advance. **2** initial contact; overture. **3** method of working, acting, thinking, etc. **4** approximation. **5** way in or to; access. **approachable** *adj* **1** accessible; able to be contacted. **2** friendly; easy to get on with.

appropriate *adj* (ə'proupriət) suitable for a particular purpose or set of circumstances; relevant; apt. *vt* (ə'prouprieit) **1** take possession of; take for one's own use. **2** set aside; allocate. **appropriately** *adv.* **appropriation** *n.*

approve *vt* give consent for; sanction. **approve of** have a favourable opinion of; believe to be good or right. **approval** *n* **1** consent; permission. **2** favourable opinion. **on approval** on free trial before deciding whether or not to buy.

approximate *adj* (ə'prɔksimət) roughly calculated; estimated; about right. *vt,vi* (ə'prɔksimeit) come close to what is required or expected; be roughly right. **approximately** *adv.*

apricot *n* small fleshy fruit that is similar to the peach, with a soft reddish-orange skin.

April *n* fourth month of the year.

apron *n* **1** loose covering worn over the front of the body to protect one's clothes and tied round the waist. **2** part of a stage that projects in front of the curtain.

apse *n* semicircular domed recess situated at the east end of a church.

apt *adj* **1** fitting; appropriate; to the point. **2** likely; inclined; liable. **3** quick to learn; clever. **aptly** *adv.* **aptitude** *n* talent, skill, or ability; flair.

aquarium *n, pl* **aquariums** *or* **aquaria** (ə'kwɛəriə) tank or pool for fish and aquatic plants.

Aquarius (ə'kwɛəriəs) *n* eleventh sign of the zodiac represented by the water carrier.

aquatic *adj* relating to or living in water.

aqueduct *n* channel constructed to direct a flow of water, esp. one built as a bridge.

arable *adj* (of land) able to be ploughed in order to produce crops.

arbitrary *adj* **1** not fixed by law; discretionary. **2** impulsive; capricious. **arbitrarily** *adv.*

arbitrate *vt,vi* settle (a dispute); mediate (between). **arbiter** *or* **arbitrator** *n.* **arbitration** *n.*

arc *n* **1** curved segment of a circle. **2** something shaped like an arc, such as a rainbow. **3** luminous electrical discharge between two electrodes. *vi* form an arc.

arcade *n* **1** series of arches and columns. **2** covered passageway or gallery, esp. one lined with shops.

arch[1] *n* **1** curved structure built to bear a load over an opening. **2** *also* **archway** opening, passageway, gateway, etc., with an arch. **3** curve; bow. **4** part of the sole of the foot between the ball and heel. *vt,vi* **1** span with an arch; curve over. **2** produce or form into a curve or bow.

arch[2] *adj* **1** chief; principal. **2** mischievous; cunning.

archaeology (ɑːki'ɔlədʒi) *n* scientific study of ancient remains and artefacts. **archaeological** (ɑːkiə'lɔdʒikəl) *adj.* **archaeologist** (ɑːki'ɔlədʒist) *n.*

archaic (ɑː'keiik) *adj* no longer in current use; out-of-date; old; belonging to the past.

archbishop *n* bishop having jurisdiction over an ecclesiastical province.

archduke *n* prince of the imperial dynasty of Austria. **archduchess** *n* **1** wife or widow of an archduke. **2** princess of the imperial dynasty of Austria. **archduchy** (ɑːtʃ'dʌtʃi) *n* territory ruled by an archduke or archduchess.

archery *n* art of shooting with a bow and arrows. **archer** *n.*

archetype ('ɑːkitaip) *n* **1** prototype. **2** ideal or completely typical example or model; standard type. **archetypal** *or* **archetypical** (ɑːki'tipikəl) *adj.*

archipelago (ɑːki'peləgou) *n* chain or scattered group of islands.

architecture *n* **1** art of designing buildings and other constructions. **2** style of building or design. **3** buildings taken collectively. **architect** *n* **1** person trained in architecture. **2** planner; organizer; mastermind.

archives ('ɑːkaivz) *pl n* **1** collection of historical records and documents. **2** place where such a collection is kept. **archivist** ('ɑːkivist) *n* person in charge of archives.

arctic *adj* **1** relating to regions surrounding the earth's North Pole. **2** extremely cold.

ardent *adj* fervent; zealous; vigorously enthusiastic; earnest; passionate. **ardently** *adv.* **ardour** *n.*

arduous *adj* hard and laborious; extremely difficult; exhausting; requiring great effort. **arduously** *adv.*

are *v* plural form of **be** in the present tense.

area *n* 1 extent of a specific surface, piece of ground, geometric figure, etc. 2 open space; region; locality. 3 section or part. 4 range or scope of something.

arena *n* 1 central area for performers in an amphitheatre, stadium, etc. 2 scene of activity.

argue *vi* quarrel; attack verbally. *vi,vt* debate; have a heated discussion (about); present (a case) for or against; reason. **argument** *n.* **argumentative** *adj* quarrelsome; inclined to argue.

arid *adj* 1 extremely dry and infertile; parched. 2 dull; not stimulating. **aridity** *n.*

Aries ('eəri:z) *n* first sign of the zodiac represented by the ram.

arise *vi* (arose; arisen) 1 rise; get up; stand up. 2 come about; occur; happen; start.

aristocracy *n* 1 class of privileged people of the highest rank; nobility. 2 government by such a class. **aristocrat** *n.* **aristocratic** *adj.*

arithmetic *n* (ə'riθmətik) 1 manipulation of numbers by addition, subtraction, multiplication, and division. 2 mathematical calculations. *adj* (æriθ'metik) *also* **arithmetical** relating to arithmetic.

arm[1] *n* 1 upper limb extending from the shoulder to the wrist. 2 sleeve. 3 support for the arm on a chair or seat. 4 anything resembling an arm in appearance or function. **armchair** *n* easy chair with supports for the arms. **armhole** *n* opening in a garment for the arm to pass through. **armpit** *n* hollow under the arm where it joins the shoulder.

arm[2] *vt,vi* 1 equip (with weapons and ammunition). 2 prepare (for a confrontation, discussion, etc.). **arms** *pl n* weapons; firearms. **armament** *n* 1 equipment for fighting; weaponry. 2 armed force. 3 preparation for a war or battle.

armour *n* 1 protective covering of metal formerly worn in battle. 2 hard protective shell or covering of certain animals. **-armour-plated** *adj* *also* **armoured** fitted with a protective covering of steel against bullets, shells, torpedoes, etc.

army *n* 1 organized military force. 2 horde; large organized group.

aroma *n* distinctive smell given off by food, wine, perfume, etc. **aromatic** *adj.*

arose *v* *pt* of **arise.**

around *prep* 1 round the outside of; surrounding; enclosing. 2 from place to place within; about; at various points on. 3 round rather than straight across. 4 at approximately; about. *adv* 1 on all sides; in a circle. 2 somewhere near; in the vicinity; about. 3 round; with a circular movement. **get around** travel widely; circulate.

arouse *vt* stimulate; provoke interest, anger, etc., in; awake. *vt,vi* rouse; wake. **arousal** *n.*

arrange *vt* 1 put into some kind of order or pattern; form. 2 fix; make plans for. 3 come to agreement about; settle on. 4 adapt (music) for a different instrument. **arrangement** *n.* **arranger** *n.*

array *n* 1 arranged selection or display; assortment. 2 dress; clothing. *vt* 1 dress lavishly; adorn. 2 arrange in order; set out.

arrears *pl n* outstanding payments; accumulated debts. **In arrears** behind in one's payments.

arrest *vt* 1 seize and detain by lawful authority; apprehend. 2 hinder; check; stop. *n* 1 act of arresting or state of being arrested. 2 hindrance; check; stoppage. **under arrest** held in detention. **arresting** *adj* attracting attention.

arrive *vi* 1 reach a destination. 2 happen; occur. 3 *inf* achieve success. **arrive at** reach. **arrival** *n.*

arrogant *adj* proud; haughty; conceited. **arrogance** *n.* **arrogantly** *adv.*

arrow *n* 1 slender pointed missile shot from a bow. 2 symbol used to indicate direction, etc.

arsenic *n* poisonous brittle grey metallic element.

arson *n* crime of maliciously setting fire to property.

art *n* 1 process of creative activity, esp. painting and drawing. 2 works resulting from such a process. 3 creative or practical skill. **arts** *n pl or s* university course(s) such as modern languages, literature, history, and philosophy.

artefact *n also* **artifact** man-made object.

artery *n* **1** thick-walled tubular vessel that conveys oxygenated blood from the heart. **2** major road, railway, or other channel of communication. **arterial** *adj*.

artful *adj* cunning; crafty; ingenious. **artfully** *adv*.

arthritis *n* painful inflammation of a joint or joints. **arthritic** *adj*.

artichoke *n* **1** *also* **globe artichoke** thistle-like plant with large edible fleshy flower heads. **2** *also* **Jerusalem artichoke** sunflower with an edible tuber.

article *n* **1** small object; item. **2** newspaper or magazine report. **3** clause or section in a document. **4** the words *a* or *an (indefinite articles)* or *the (definite article)* preceding a noun or noun phrase. **articled** *adj* bound by written contract; apprenticed.

articulate *v* (ɑːˈtikjuleit) *vt,vi* speak clearly. *vt* express precisely or coherently. *adj* (ɑːˈtikjulit) **1** fluent; coherent. **2** able to speak. **articulated** *adj* having two or more jointed or pivoted sections. **articulation** *n*.

artifact *n* artefact.

artificial *adj* **1** man-made; synthetic. **2** feigned; not spontaneous. **artificial respiration** *n* method for restoring natural breathing. **artificially** *adv*.

artillery *n* **1** large-calibre guns; cannon. **2** troops or military units trained in their use.

artist *n* **1** creative person, esp. a painter or sculptor. **2** skilful practitioner of a craft, etc. **3** professional performer. **artistic** *adj* **1** creative; skilled. **2** beautiful; aesthetically pleasing. **3** relating to art. **artistically** *adv*.

as *conj* **1** when; just at the time that. **2** in the manner that; like. **3** that which; what; whatever. **4** because; since. *prep,conj* to the extent (that); of the same amount (that). *prep* in the role or capacity of.

asbestos *n* any of several incombustible fibrous minerals used for thermal insulation and in flameproof and building materials.

ascend *vt,vi* climb; mount; rise. **ascent** *or* **ascension** *n*. **the Ascension** ascent of Christ into heaven.

ascertain *vt* determine by inquiry; discover; find out.

ascribe *vt* attribute (a work of art, blame, etc.); assign.

ash[1] *n* widespread deciduous tree with compound leaves, winged seeds, and a durable wood used as timber.

ash[2] *n* **1** grey powdery residue of something that has been burnt. **2** fine material thrown from an erupting volcano. **ashes 1** human remains after cremation. **2** ruins. **ashen** *adj* pallid. **ashtray** *n* receptacle for cigarette ends, ash, etc.

ashamed *adj* **1** full of shame (for); remorseful. **2** reluctant or refusing (to).

ashore *adv,adj* towards or on land.

aside *adv* **1** on or to one side. **2** into a secluded place. **3** out of one's thoughts, consideration, etc. **4** in reserve. **aside from** apart from. ~*n* confidential or seemingly confidential statement.

ask *vt,vi* **1** put a question to (concerning). **2** make a request for. *vt* **1** enquire about. **2** invite. **ask after** request news of. **ask for trouble/it** behave provocatively.

askew *adv* at an angle; awry. *adj* crooked.

asleep *adj* sleeping. **fall asleep** pass into a state of sleep.

asparagus *n* young edible shoots of a plant of the lily family.

aspect *n* **1** direction towards which something faces; outlook. **2** appearance. **3** point of view; angle.

asphalt *n* dark naturally occurring material used in road surfacing and roofing materials. *vt* cover with asphalt.

aspire *vi* have ambitious plans, desires, etc.; yearn for. **aspiration** *n*.

aspirin *n* mild pain-relieving drug, usually taken in tablet form.

ass *n* **1** donkey. **2** fool; stupid person.

assail *vt* attack; assault. **assailant** *n,adj*.

assassinate *vt* murder (a public figure), esp. for political reasons. **assassin** *n* murderer; hired killer. **assassination** *n*.

assault *n* **1** violent or sudden attack. **2** *law* threat of attack. *vt* **1** make an assault on. **2** rape.

assemble *vt,vi* **1** come or bring together; collect. **2** fit together; construct. **assembly** *n*.

assent *n* **1** agreement; acceptance. **2** consent. *vi* agree to; accept.

assert *vt* **1** declare as true. **2** insist upon; maintain. **assert oneself** act authoritatively or boldly. **assertion** *n*. **assertive** *adj*.

assess *vt* **1** determine the value or amount of; evaluate. **2** judge the worth or importance of. **assessment** *n*.

asset *n* possession, quality, etc., that is useful or of value. **assets** *pl n* capital; property.

assign *vt* **1** allot; give to; set apart for; fix. **2** nominate; select for; appoint to. **assignation** *n* arrangement to meet secretly or illicitly; tryst. **assignment** *n*.

assimilate *vt,vi* **1** absorb or become absorbed; incorporate. **2** adjust or become adjusted. *vt* digest (food). **assimilation** *n*.

assist *vt,vi* help; give support (to); work in a subordinate capacity (for). **assistance** *n*. **assistant** *n*.

associate *v* (ə'sousieit) **associate with** *vt* link or connect (with). *vi* keep company (with). *n* (ə'sousiit, -eit) **1** partner; colleague. **2** acquaintance; companion. *adj* (ə'sousiit) **1** having equal or nearly equal status with others. **2** having only partial rights. **association** *n* **1** connection. **2** organized group; society.

assorted *adj* **1** of various kinds; miscellaneous. **2** classified; sorted. **ill-assorted** badly matched. **assortment** *n*.

assuage *vt* make less severe; ease; lessen.

assume *vt* **1** take for granted; accept; suppose. **2** undertake; take on. **3** adopt; feign; affect. **assumed** *adj* **1** false; fictitious. **2** taken for granted. **assumption** *n*.

assure *vt* **1** make certain; ensure. **2** inform confidently; promise; guarantee. **assurance** *n* **1** promise; guarantee. **2** certainty. **3** self-confidence. **4** life or endowment insurance. **assuredly** *adv* definitely.

asterisk *n* symbol (*) used in print to indicate an omission, cross reference, etc. *vt* mark with an asterisk.

asthma ('æsmə) *n* disorder, often allergic, causing difficulty in breathing, wheezing, etc. **asthmatic** *adj,n*.

astonish *vt* fill with surprise or wonder; amaze; astound. **astonishment** *n*.

astound *vt* surprise greatly; astonish.

astray *adv,adj* away from what is right or expected.

astride *adv,adj,prep* with a leg on each side (of).

astrology *n* prediction of human characteristics, activities, etc., based on the motion and relative positions of celestial bodies. **astrological** *adj*. **astrologer** *n*.

astronaut *n* person trained and adapted to space travel. **astronautical** *adj*. **astronautics** *n*.

astronomy *n* study of the universe and the celestial bodies contained in it. **astronomer** *n*. **astronomical** *or* **astronomic** *adj* **1** relating to astronomy or the celestial bodies. **2** huge; immense.

astute *adj* cunning; sly; clever; perceptive; quick. **astutely** *adv*. **astuteness** *n*.

asunder *adv,adj* apart; in(to) pieces.

asylum *n* **1** temporary refuge; place of shelter; sanctuary. **2** mental hospital.

at *prep* **1** in; close to; next to. **2** towards; in the direction of. **3** towards or around a specified time. **4** in a state of; engaged in. **5** during. **6** in exchange for; for the price of. **7** about; concerning.

ate *v* *pt* of **eat**.

atheism *n* disbelief in the existence of God. **atheist** *n*.

athlete *n* person skilled in running, hurdling, shot putting, or other track and field sports. **athletics** *n* track and field sports. **athletic** *adj*.

atlas *n* book containing maps.

atmosphere *n* **1** gaseous layer surrounding the earth or other celestial body. **2** air in an enclosed space. **3** gaseous medium. **4** prevailing mood; feeling. **5** unit of pressure. **atmospheric** *adj*.

atom *n* **1** minute entity of which chemical elements are composed, consisting of a central nucleus around which electrons orbit. **2** very small amount. **atom bomb** *n* also **atomic bomb** bomb in which energy is derived from nuclear fission. **atomic** *adj*. **atomic energy** *n* energy derived from nuclear fission or fusion. **atomize** *vt* reduce (a liquid, such as perfume) to a fine spray by forcing it through a nozzle. **atomizer** *n*.

atone *vi* make amends (for a sin, error, etc.); expiate. **atonement** *n*.

atrocious *adj* **1** extremely cruel; wicked; appalling; horrifying. **2** *inf* of very poor quality. **atrociously** *adv.* **atrocity** *n* cruel and appalling act or behaviour.

attach *vt,vi* join; connect; fasten. *vi* 1 attribute; ascribe. 2 adhere; be inherent in. **attached to** 1 fond of; devoted to. 2 assigned or brought in as a specialist. **attachment** *n.*

attaché *n* member of staff of an embassy or legation. **attaché case** *n* small rectangular case for carrying documents, etc.

attack *vt* 1 make a physical or verbal assault on; assail; set upon. 2 seize upon; take up with vigour. 3 act or play offensively. 4 affect adversely. *n* 1 physical or verbal assault. 2 offensive action. 3 bout of illness.

attain *vt,vi* succeed in reaching; achieve; obtain; get. **attainable** *adj.* **attainment** *n.*

attempt *vt* try (to do or accomplish something); endeavour. *n* 1 effort, often unsuccessful. 2 attack.

attend *vt,vi* be present (at); go regularly (to). *vi* pay attention (to); listen (to). **attend to** 1 deal with; handle; manage. 2 look after; tend; minister. **attendance** *n* 1 act of attending; presence. 2 number of persons present. **attendant** *n* person employed to assist, guide, look after, etc. *adj* associated or accompanying. **attention** *n* 1 concentrated thought. 2 observation; notice. **call** *or* **bring attention to** point out. **pay attention to** 1 take notice of; attend. 2 take care of. **stand to attention**. adopt a formal alert stance, esp. on military occasions. **attentive** *adj* 1 listening carefully; observant. 2 thoughtful; polite.

attic *n* room just below the roof; garret.

attitude *n* 1 opinion; judgement; policy; disposition. 2 position of the body; pose. **strike an attitude** assume a theatrical pose.

attorney *n* 1 person with legal authority to act for another. 2 *US* lawyer.

attract *vt* 1 excite pleasure, anticipation, etc., in; fascinate. 2 cause to approach; draw towards. **attraction** *n.* **attractive** *adj* 1 pleasing to look at; alluring; appealing. 2 interesting; pleasing.

attribute *vt* (ə'tribjuːt) **attribute to** consider as produced by, resulting from, or belonging to; ascribe to. *n* ('ætribjuːt) property; quality; feature. **attribution** *n.*

atypical (ei'tipikəl) *adj* not typical; unrepresentative.

aubergine *n* tropical plant with a deep purple egg-shaped fruit, eaten as a vegetable.

auburn *n,adj* reddish-brown.

auction *n* public sale in which items are sold to the highest bidder. *vt* sell by auction. **auctioneer** *n* person conducting an auction.

audacious *adj* 1 fearlessly bold. 2 impudent; forward.

audible *adj* able to be heard. **audibly** *adv.*

audience 1 group of spectators, listeners, etc. 2 formal hearing or interview granted by someone in authority.

audiovisual *adj* involving both hearing and sight.

audit *n* professional examination of business accounts. *vt,vi* examine by or perform audit(s). **auditor** *n.*

audition *n* trial in which an actor, singer, musician, etc., demonstrates his ability or his aptitude for a role. *vt,vi* give a trial hearing (to).

auditorium *n, pl* **auditoriums** *or* **auditoria** part of a theatre, hall, etc., where the audience is seated.

augment *vt,vi* increase; enlarge; extend. **augmentation** *n.*

August *n* eighth month of the year.

aunt *n* 1 sister of one's mother or father. 2 wife of one's uncle.

au pair *n* foreign girl who undertakes housework, etc., in return for board and lodging. *adv* as an au pair.

aura *n* 1 distinctive air or quality of a person or thing; charisma. 2 apparent emanation surrounding an object, etc.

aural *adj* relating to hearing.

austere *adj* severe; strict; harsh; not luxurious. **austerely** *adv.* **austerity** *n.*

authentic *adj* genuine; real; not faked; from a reliable source. **authentically** *adv.* **authenticity** *n.*

author *n* 1 writer of a book, script, article, etc. 2 originator; creator. **authorship** *n.*

authoritative *adj* possessing, exercising, or claiming authority. **authoritatively** *adv.* **authorize** *vt* empower; sanction; give permission for. **authorization** *n.*

authority n **1** power or right to command and enforce obedience. **2** official body or group having such power. **3** position commanding such power. **4** delegated power. **5** acknowledged expert or trustworthy written work. **6** power or influence. **authoritarian** adj favouring the enforcement of obedience; opposed to individual freedom; nondemocratic. n an authoritarian person.

autistic adj living in a fantasy world; abnormally introspective. **autism** n.

autobiography n person's biography written by that person; personal biography. **autobiographical** adj.

autograph n handwritten signature. vt write an autograph in; sign.

automatic adj **1** operated or regulated by mechanical means; self-acting. **2** performed or produced without conscious thought or effort. **3** inevitable. n self-loading weapon firing continuously on depression of the trigger. **automatically** adv. **automation** n automatic operation of industrial processes or equipment.

autonomous adj self-governing; self-sufficient; independent. **autonomously** adv. **autonomy** n.

autumn n season between summer and winter.

auxiliary adj additional; supporting; extra; ancillary. n helper; assistant. **auxiliary verb** verb used to express tense, mood, etc., of another verb.

avail n **to** or **with no avail** in vain; without success. v **avail oneself of** make use of; help oneself to.

available adj obtainable; ready for use; accessible. **availability** n.

avalanche n **1** heavy fall of snow and ice down a mountainside. **2** large pile or heap that has accumulated suddenly and rapidly.

avenge vt,vi seek vengeance (for); punish in retaliation.

avenue n **1** wide road or drive, esp. one lined with trees. **2** means of achieving; way; opening.

average n **1** sum of a set of numbers or quantities divided by their total number; mean value. **2** representative or typical amount, value, etc. **on average** typically; usually. ~adj **1** typical; representative; usual. **2** constituting or worked out as an average. vt **1** perform or receive an amount calculated as an average. **2** calculate an average. vi amount to an average.

averse adj disinclined; unwilling; against. **aversion** n strong dislike; repulsion.

aviary n enclosure or large cage for birds.

aviation n art or science of flying aircraft. **aviator** n airman; pilot.

avid adj eager; enthusiastically dedicated or keen. **avidity** n. **avidly** adv.

avocado (ævɔ'kɑːdou) n also **avocado pear** fleshy pear-shaped tropical fruit with a dark green or purple skin.

avoid vt keep away from or out of; evade; refrain from. **avoidable** adj. **avoidance** n.

avow vt declare; claim; admit openly. **avowal** n.

await vt **1** wait for; expect. **2** be ready or in store for.

awake v (awoke or awaked; awaked) vt,vi wake; wake up; rouse. vt arouse; stir; stimulate.

awaken vt,vi awake.

award vt give as a prize; grant. n prize; grant.

aware adj conscious (of); having knowledge; well-informed. **awareness** n.

away adv **1** to or at a place further off. **2** apart; at a distance; separately. **3** out of one's possession. **4** without hesitation; immediately. **5** until there is nothing left. **do away with 1** abolish; get rid of. **2** murder; kill. **get away with** do without being noticed or caught. ~adj absent; not at home.

awe n feeling of absolute wonder, fear, reverence, etc. vt fill with awe; dumbfound. **awe-inspiring** adj overwhelming; magnificent; tremendous. **awesome** adj capable of producing awe. **awe-struck** adj also **awe-stricken** filled with awe.

awful adj terrible; dreadful; very bad. **awfully** adv inf very; extremely.

awhile adv briefly; for a while.

awkward adj **1** clumsy, ungainly. **2** difficult to deal with; tricky; inconvenient. **awkwardly** adv. **awkwardness** n.

awl n small tool used for boring holes in leather, wood, etc.

awning n sheet of canvas attached to a frame to provide cover and protection from the weather.

awoke *v pt* of **awake.**

awry (ə'rai) *adj* **1** crooked; askew. **2** wrong; amiss.

axe *n* chopping tool with a long handle and a broad blade. **have an axe to grind** act from selfish motives or a vested interest. ~*vt* **1** chop or fell with an axe. **2** cut back or reduce drastically.

axis *n, pl* **axes** ('æksiːz) **1** line about which something rotates or is symmetrical. **2** reference line on a graph by which a point is located. **3** main central stem of a plant.

axle *n* rod or shaft that allows an attached wheel to revolve.

azalea *n* flowering shrub related to the rhododendron.

B

babble *vi,vt* **1** speak incoherently and continuously: chatter. **2** burble; murmur. *n* **1** fast incoherent speech. **2** burbling sound; murmur.

babe *n* baby.

baboon *n* large monkey.

baby *n* **1** newborn child; infant. **2** newborn animal. *vt* treat as a baby; lavish care on. **babyish** *adj.* **baby-sit** *vi* (-tt-) look after a baby for a short time while the parents are out. **baby-sitter** *n.*

bachelor *n* **1** unmarried man. **2** person who holds a first degree from a university or college.

bacillus *n* any of various rod-shaped bacteria.

back *n* **1** that part of the body extending from the base of the neck to the buttocks. **2** corresponding part of an animal. **3** spine; backbone. **4** side or part that is opposite the front; reverse. **5** place furthest away from the front; rear. **6** part of a garment that covers the back. **7** defence player in football, hockey, etc. **behind one's back** without one's knowledge; deceitfully. **get/put one's back up** antagonize; provoke; anger. ~*vt* **1** bet on to win. **2** support; sponsor. **3** provide a musical accompaniment for. *vt,vi* move backwards; reverse. **back down** withdraw a claim, challenge, etc.; admit fault. **back onto** have the back or rear bordering on. **back out** withdraw one's support. **back up** support; encourage; confirm.

~*adv* **1** backwards; towards the rear. **2** in or into the past. **3** to a previous or earlier place, state, condition, owner, etc. **4** in reply; in return. **back to front** with the back and front reversed. **go back on** break (a promise). **take back** revoke; cancel. ~*adj* **1** situated behind. **2** from the past; overdue; not current.

backbencher *n* British member of Parliament without a ministerial position.

backbone *n* **1** spine. **2** stamina; courage; spirit.

backdate *vt* make effective from an earlier date.

backfire *vi* **1** produce an explosion of fuel mixture in an internal-combustion engine. **2** have unintended and unfortunate consequences.

backgammon *n* board game for two players, each using fifteen pieces, which are moved according to the throws of two dice.

background *n* **1** place, setting, scene etc., at the back or in the distance. **2** person's class, education, experience, etc. **3** context through which historical, political, or social events may be understood.

backhand *n* stroke in tennis made with the back of the hand facing the direction of the shot. **backhanded** *adj* **1** relating to a backhand. **2** with underlying sarcasm.

backing *n* **1** sponsorship; support. **2** musical accompaniment.

backlash *n* **1** recoil occurring when machinery parts are badly worn or faulty. **2** hostile reaction; repercussions.

backlog *n* accumulated work, arrears, etc., requiring attention.

backside *n inf* buttocks; bottom.

backstage *adv* **1** behind the stage, esp. in the wings, dressing-rooms, etc. **2** at the back of the stage. *adj* taking place behind or at the back of the stage.

backstroke *n* type of stroke made when swimming on one's back.

backward *adj* **1** slow to learn or progress; underdeveloped. **2** directed towards the back or rear. **3** towards or fixed in the past. **4** bashful; shy. *adv* backwards. **backwardness** *n.*

backwards *adv* **1** towards the back or rear. **2** in reverse. **3** into the past. **4** back to a poorer state or condition. **know backwards** know thoroughly.

backwater *n* **1** stretch of water cut off from the main stream. **2** isolated place unaffected by changes occurring elsewhere.

bacon *n* cured meat from the back or sides of a pig.

bacteria *pl n* group of microscopic vegetable organisms causing putrefaction, fermentation, disease, etc. **bacterial** *adj.*

bad[1] *adj* **1** not good; below standard; poorer than average. **2** disobedient; naughty. **3** harmful; injurious. **4** sinful; wicked. **5** sick; unwell. **6** not fresh; rotten. **7** distressing; upsetting. **8** unpleasant; distasteful. **badly** *adv* **1** unsatisfactorily; poorly. **2** very much; urgently; seriously. **bad-tempered** *adj* cross; irritable.

bad[2] *v* a *pt* of **bid**.

bade (beid, bæd) *v* a *pt* of **bid**.

badge *n* **1** emblem worn or displayed to indicate rank, membership, etc. **2** distinguishing mark or characteristic.

badger *n* nocturnal burrowing animal with a black and white striped head. *vt* pester.

badminton *n* game similar to tennis played with lightweight rackets and a shuttlecock.

baffle *vt* perplex; bewilder; stump; mystify.

bag *n* **1** container of leather, paper, etc., used for carrying things in. **2** loose or sagging fold of skin. *v* (-gg-) *vt* **1** put into a bag. **2** *inf* claim; seize first. *vi* hang loosely; sag; bulge. **baggage** *n* luggage. **baggy** *adj* hanging loosely; not tight. **bagginess** *n.*

bagpipes *pl n* musical instrument consisting of a set of reed pipes and a wind-bag. **bagpiper** *n.*

bail[1] *n* **1** sum of money that is pledged to secure the release of a person from custody on condition that he appears in court on a specified date. **2** procedure allowing such a sum of money to be pledged. *vt* **bail out** rescue (a person, company, etc.) esp. by giving financial assistance.

bail[2] *n* small wooden bar placed across the stumps of a wicket.

bail[3] *vt,vi* *also* **bail out** remove (water) from the bottom of a boat with a bucket or can.

bailiff *n* **1** official employed by a sheriff to serve writs, collect fines, summon juries, etc. **2** landowner's agent.

bait *n* **1** things such as worms, maggots, etc., used by an angler to lure and catch fish. **2** food or other enticement used to lure animals into a trap. **3** enticement; temptation. *vt* **1** prepare (a line or trap) with bait. **2** lure; entice. **3** taunt; persecute.

bake *vi,vt* cook (bread, cakes, etc.) in an oven. **baker** *n* person who bakes or sells bread, cakes, etc. **bakery** *n* **1** room where bread, cakes, etc., are baked. **2** baker's shop.

balance *n* **1** apparatus for weighing consisting of two pans suspended from either end of a horizontal bar, which has a central pivot. **2** equilibrium. **3** emotional or mental stability; rationality. **4** compatibility; equality of distribution; harmony. **5** equality between credit and debit totals. **6** remainder; amount left over. **in the balance** not yet decided. ~*vt* **1** weigh on a balance. **2** keep or put in a state of balance. **3** calculate the totals of. *vi* have equal totals. *vt,vi* place in or achieve equilibrium. **balance sheet** *n* statement of accounts showing a company's financial position for a given period.

balcony *n* **1** enclosed platform built on to the outside of a wall of a building usually with access from within. **2** gallery of seats above the circle in a theatre.

bald *adj* **1** having no hair, esp. on the head. **2** threadbare; badly worn. **3** bare; having no vegetation. **4** plainly expressed; blunt. **baldly** *adv.* **baldness** *n.*

bale[1] *n* large bundle or package. *vt* pack into a bale.

bale[2] *vi* **bale out** make an emergency parachute jump.

ball[1] *n* **1** spherical object used in games such as football, golf, or tennis. **2** any spherical object. **3** rounded fleshy part of the thumb, sole of the foot, etc. **balls** *pl n* *sl* testicles. **on the ball** aware; quick to react.

ball[2] *n* grand social event with music and dancing, refreshments, etc. **have a ball** enjoy oneself enormously. **ballroom** *n* hall or large room used for dancing.

ballad *n* narrative poem that is usually set to music.

ballast *n* **1** any heavy material used to stabilize a ship, balloon, etc. **2** mixture of gravel and sand used in building.

ballerina *n* female ballet dancer.

ballet *n* **1** theatrical dance form requiring a conventional and highly developed technique. **2** performance in which a story is told through dance and mime. **3** music written for such a performance. **4** company of dancers.

ballistics *n* study of the motion of projectiles. **ballistic** *adj* relating to projectiles or ballistics.

balloon *n* **1** inflatable coloured rubber bag used as a toy or for decoration. **2** large impermeable bag filled with gas lighter than air that enables it to rise in the air, often having a basket for passengers, scientific instruments, etc. *vi* fly in a balloon. *vt, vi* inflate or swell.

ballot *n* **1** system of voting using tickets, cards, slips, etc. **2** tickets or cards used in voting. **3** number of votes cast. *vt, vi* vote or put to the vote by ballot.

bamboo *n* tropical treelike grass with hard hollow stems, which are often used for making furniture.

ban *vt* (-nn-) prohibit; declare to be illegal; forbid. *n* order or rule prohibiting certain goods, behaviour, etc.

banal (bə'nɑːl) *adj* commonplace; trite; mundane.

banana *n* tropical fruit that is long or crescent shaped with a thick yellow skin.

band[1] *n* **1** small group of people. **2** group of musicians, esp. one playing woodwind, brass, and percussion instruments for dancing or marching. *v* **band together** form into a united group.

band[2] *n* **1** flat strip of cloth, rubber, metal, etc., used as a fastening or for decoration. **2** coloured stripe. **3** waveband.

bandage *n* strip of cloth used to keep a dressing in place over a wound, support a sprain, etc. *vt* cover with a bandage.

bandit *n* outlawed robber.

bandy *adj* bow-legged. *vt* **1** exchange (words, blows, etc.). **2** throw or pass to and fro.

bang *n* **1** loud noise as of an explosion; report. **2** knocking noise. **3** slam. **4** sharp hit or blow. *vt, vi* **1** make a loud explosive sound. **2** knock loudly; rap. **3** slam. **4** hit; strike. **banger** *sl* **1** sausage. **2** old car. **3** firework that explodes with a bang.

bangle *n* ornamental band worn as a bracelet.

banish *vt* **1** exile; expel. **2** dispel. **banishment** *n.*

banister *n* support rail on a staircase.

banjo *n* long-necked instrument of the guitar family with a circular body.

bank[1] *n* **1** slope; embankment. **2** large mound or pile. *vt also* **bank up** form into a mound; heap up.

bank[2] *n* **1** institution dealing in deposits and withdrawals of money, loans, exchange of currencies, etc. **2** building occupied by such an institution. **3** place reserved for the safekeeping of some valuable commodity. *vt* deposit in a bank. *vi* have an account with a bank. **bank on** rely on. **bankbook** *n* book containing a record of a person's financial transactions with a bank. **banker** *n* professional expert in banking; financier. **banking** *n* business of running a bank or similar institution. **bank holiday** *n* public holiday on which banks are traditionally closed. **banknote** *n* paper note issued by a bank as money. **Bank Rate** *n* rate of interest charged by the Bank of England to the banking system. **bankrupt** *adj* insolvent. *n* person who is declared bankrupt by a court. **bankruptcy** *n.*

banner *n* **1** flag or ensign, esp. one carried in a procession. **2** something that represents a principle, particular cause, etc.

banquet *n* lavish entertainment and feast given for a large number of guests.

baptize *vt, vi* initiate into the Christian faith with the rite of immersing in or sprinkling with water. **baptism** *n.* **Baptist** *n* member of a Christian denomination believing in baptism as an expression of personal faith. *adj* relating to such a denomination.

bar *n* **1** straight piece of wood, metal, etc., used as part of an enclosure, lever, etc. **2** stripe; band. **3** slab of chocolate, soap, etc. **4** barrier; obstruction. **5** counter from which drinks or refreshments are served. **6** room in a hotel or public house where alcoholic drinks are served. **7** *also* **barline** vertical stroke on a stave in a musical score. **8** notes or music occurring between such strokes. **the Bar** professional body of barristers. **barmaid** *n* woman employed to serve drinks in a hotel or public house. **barman** *n.*

barbarian *n* savage or uncivilized person. *adj* uncivilized; not cultured. **barbaric** *adj also* **barbarous** cruel; savage; brutal; inhuman. **barbarism** *n also* **barbarity** cruelty; brutality; uncivilized behaviour.

barbecue ('bɑ:bikju:) *n* 1 grid or grill used on an open fire for cooking meat, vegetables, etc. 2 party held in the open air at which barbecued food is served. *vt* cook on a barbecue.

barber *n* person who cuts men's hair, trims beards, etc.

barbiturate *n* drug used as a sedative.

bare *adj* 1 unclothed; naked. 2 uncovered; unadorned. 3 plain; undecorated. 4 having no vegetation. 5 mere; hardly sufficient. *vt* uncover; make bare. **bareness** *n.* **barefoot** *adj,adv* having no covering on the foot. **barely** *adv* 1 hardly; only just; scarcely. 2 austerely; not elaborately.

bargain *n* 1 agreement between parties; deal. 2 something bought cheaply; good buy. **Into the bargain** moreover; besides. ~*vi* barter; haggle; make a deal. **bargain for** be prepared for; expect.

barge *n* large flat-bottomed boat used esp. for carrying cargo on canals. *vi* 1 bump (into); collide; push rudely. 2 interrupt; enter noisily.

baritone *n* male singing voice or musical instrument with a range between bass and tenor.

bark[1] *n* 1 loud cry of a dog or wolf. 2 gruff angry voice. *vi,vt* 1 (of a dog or wolf) utter a loud harsh cry. 2 speak in a gruff voice.

bark[2] *n* outer covering of the trunk and branches of a tree. *vt* scrape the skin or outer layer of.

barley *n* cereal plant with spiked ears used for food and to make malt for brewing and distilling. **barley-sugar** *n* boiled sweet made from sugar.

barn *n* farm building used for storing hay, housing livestock, etc.

barnacle *n* crustacean that attaches itself to rocks, the timber of boats, etc.

barometer *n* 1 instrument for measuring atmospheric pressure. 2 anything that indicates or warns of change.

baron *n* 1 nobleman of the lowest rank. 2 *inf* magnate. **baronial** *adj.* **baroness** *n* 1 wife or widow of a baron. 2 woman of a rank that is equivalent to that of a baron. **baronet** *n* man of a rank between that of a baron and a knight. **baronetcy** *n.*

barracks *n pl or s* building used for the accommodation of soldiers.

barrel *n* 1 cylindrical wooden or metal container. 2 tube of a gun through which the bullet or shell is discharged. *vt* put into a barrel.

barren *adj* 1 infertile; sterile. 2 unproductive; bare. 3 dull; uninteresting. **barrenness** *n.*

barricade *n* obstruction hastily set up as a barrier against an advancing enemy. *vt* block with a barricade.

barrier *n* 1 gate, fence, etc., intended to prevent access. 2 something that screens or protects. 3 hindrance; impediment.

barrister *n* lawyer having the right to practise in a court of law.

barrow[1] *n* cart pushed by hand; wheelbarrow.

barrow[2] *n* burial mound.

barter *vi,vt* trade by exchanging goods or commodities. *vi* haggle. *n* exchange of goods by bartering.

base[1] *n* 1 bottom; support on which something is constructed or rests. 2 foundation; basis. 3 main ingredient or element. 4 starting point. 5 headquarters. 6 establishment set up by the armed forces. 7 marked position on a baseball pitch. 8 sour-tasting chemical substance that turns litmus blue. *vt* 1 take as a foundation or starting point. 2 locate; situate. **baseball** *n* game for two sides of nine players each, on a diamond-shaped pitch using a hard ball and wooden bat. **basement** *n* room or set of rooms built below ground level.

base[2] *adj* 1 mean; despicable. 2 inferior; worthless. **baseness** *n.*

bash *inf vt* hit hard; slog. *n* rough blow. **have a bash** try; attempt.

bashful *adj* shy; embarrassed. **bashfully** *adv.* **bashfulness** *n.*

basic *adj* 1 fundamental; main. 2 elementary; primary. 3 relating to a chemical base. **basics** *pl n* fundamental or underlying principles. **basically** *adv.*

basin *n* **1** bowl used for mixing foods, holding liquids, etc. **2** sink; washbasin. **3** area of land drained by a river.

basis *n, pl* **bases** ('beisi:z) **1** underlying principle; foundation. **2** main part.

bask *vi* **1** expose oneself to the warmth of the sun, a fire, etc. **2** display enjoyment of publicity, glory, etc.

basket *n* **1** receptacle made of cane, straw, etc. **2** metal hoop with a net attached used as the goal in basketball. **basketball** *n* game for two sides of five or six players each, using a large ball which must be shot through a metal hoop fixed to a board in order to score. **basketry** *n* art of making baskets.

bass[1] (beis) *n* **1** lowest range of male singing voice. **2** musical instrument having the lowest range of its type. **3** double bass.

bass[2] (bæs) *n, pl* **bass** sea fish with a spiny dorsal fin; perch.

bassoon *n* woodwind instrument that is lower in tone than an oboe and having a mouthpiece fitted with a double reed. **bassoonist** *n.*

bastard *n* **1** illegitimate child. **2** *inf* unpleasant or cruel person.

bat[1] *n* wooden implement used for hitting a ball in various games. **off one's own bat** unassisted and on one's own initiative. ~*vi,vt* (-tt-) strike or play with a bat. **batsman** *n, pl* **-men** person who bats in cricket.

bat[2] *n* small nocturnal mammal that is able to fly.

batch *n* **1** quantity of loaves, cakes, etc., baked at the same time. **2** set; group.

bath *n* **1** large tub that is filled with water and used for washing the whole body. **2** act of sitting or lying in a bath in order to wash oneself. **3** water in a bath. **baths** *pl n* building housing public baths, swimming pool, etc. ~*vi,vt* wash in a bath. **bathroom** *n* room containing a bath and often a toilet and washbasin.

bathe *vi* **1** swim. **2** have a bath. *vt* **1** wash in order to cleanse or soothe. **2** cover with light, colour, etc. **bathing costume** *n* garment worn when bathing, swimming, etc.

baton *n* **1** small stick used to conduct an orchestra. **2** stick carried by the runner in a relay race. **3** staff of office.

battalion *n* military unit of three or four companies.

batter[1] *vt,vi* beat severely and repeatedly; pound.

batter[2] *n* mixture of flour, eggs, and milk used in cooking.

battery *n* **1** electrical device used as the source of current in radios, torches, vehicles, etc. **2** collection of cages for intensive rearing of chickens, turkeys, etc. **3** unlawful attack on a person. **4** prepared position for artillery, the artillery itself, or a military unit operating in it. **5** array; number.

battle *n* **1** fighting between organized forces or armies. **2** hard struggle; fight. *vi* **1** fight in a battle. **2** struggle; strive. **battlefield** *n* site of a battle. **battleship** *n* large armoured warship.

battlement *n* parapet with indentations, used for defence.

bauxite *n* claylike substance that is the chief ore of aluminium.

bawl *vt,vi* shout or cry loudly; howl; bellow. *n* howl.

bay[1] *n* coastal inlet.

bay[2] *n* **1** window area projecting beyond the face of a building. **2** recess; alcove. **3** area set aside for parking or loading and unloading a vehicle. **4** storage area in an aircraft.

bay[3] *n* type of laurel tree whose aromatic leaves are used as a seasoning.

bay[4] *n* bark or deep cry of a hound. **at bay 1** facing and warding off a pursuer. **2** in check; at a distance. ~*vt,vi* bark; howl.

bay[5] *n* horse with a reddish-brown body and black mane and tail. *adj,n* reddish-brown.

bayonet *n* short blade attached to the muzzle of a rifle. *vt* stab with a bayonet.

be *vi* (*pres t s* am, are, is; *pl* are. *pt s* was, were, was; *pl* were. *pp* been) **1** exist. **2** occur; take place. **3** equal; have the character of. **4** remain; stay. **5** continue to do or act. *v aux* (used to form the passive).

beach *n* expanse of sand, pebbles, etc., on the seashore. **beachcomber** *n* person who makes a living by collecting things washed ashore by the sea.

bead n 1 small ball strung together with others to make a necklace, rosary, etc. 2 small drop; globule. vt decorate with beads.

beak n horny jaw of a bird; bill.

beaker n 1 glass for drinking from; tumbler. 2 small glass cylinder used in chemical experiments.

beam n 1 thick piece of timber or steel used to support a floor or roof; joist; girder. 2 shaft of light; ray. 3 radio or radar signal. 4 radiant smile. vt,vi 1 send out (a ray of light, radio signal, etc.). 2 smile radiantly.

bean n 1 type of plant producing pods containing seeds. 2 pod or seeds of such a plant often eaten as a vegetable. **full of beans** cheerful and energetic; ebullient.

bear[1] v (bore; borne) vt 1 take the weight of; support. 2 hold; carry. 3 accept responsibility for. 4 pp **born** give birth to. 5 yield (fruit); produce. 6 tolerate; endure. 7 display; wear. 8 possess; have. 9 conduct (oneself). vi follow or move in the direction of. **bring to bear** exert influence; effect. **bear on** 1 push or press against. 2 be relevant to; relate to. **bear out** confirm; furnish proof of. **bear up** cope cheerfully; manage. **bearer** n.

bear[2] n 1 large carnivorous mammal with black, brown, or white shaggy fur. 2 person who sells stocks and buys them back after the price has dropped.

beard n 1 hair growth on the chin and sides of the face. 2 tuft or growth resembling a beard.

bearing n 1 person's carriage, posture, deportment, etc. 2 relevance; significance. 3 angle measured from north or some other fixed direction. 4 machine part that supports or guides another moving part. **bearings** pl n 1 position or direction determined by reference to fixed points. 2 awareness of one's situation; orientation.

beast n 1 animal, esp. when distinguished from man. 2 brutal person. **beastly** inf adj disgusting, nasty. **beastliness** n.

beat v (beat; beaten) vt 1 strike hard; hit. 2 thrash; flog. 3 hammer; bang. 4 whisk; stir vigorously. 5 flap; move up and down. 6 defeat in a contest. 7 do better than; surpass. 8 overcome. vi 1 throb; pulsate. 2 pound; bang. 3 produce a rhythmical sound. 4 move up and down. **beat up** assault and injure severely. ~n 1 throb; pulsation. 2 blow; bang; stroke. 3 rhythmical sound. 4 basic unit by which the duration of musical notes is measured. 5 stressed syllable or note in poetry or music. 6 type of popular music with a strongly marked rhythm and beat.

beauty n 1 quality or qualities appealing to the senses or intellect and conforming to a certain standard of excellence, attractiveness, etc. 2 exceptionally lovely woman. 3 exceptionally good example of something. **beautiful** adj. **beautifully** adv.

beaver n 1 aquatic rodent with webbed feet and a strong broad tail. 2 fur of the beaver. vi work hard and enthusiastically.

because conj for the reason that; since. **because of** on account of; due to.

beckon vi,vt summon with a gesture of the hand or head. n summoning gesture.

become v (became; become) vi 1 grow, change, or develop into; start to be. 2 happen (to); befall. vt suit; make attractive. **becoming** fetching; attractive.

bed n 1 piece of furniture designed for sleeping on. 2 small plot of ground for growing flowers or vegetables. 3 bottom of the sea, a river, etc. 4 layer of rock. vt (-dd-) 1 plant in a bed. 2 sl have sexual intercourse with. **bed down** find a place to sleep. **bedclothes** pl n covers used on a bed. **bedding** n mattress, covers, pillows, etc., used on a bed. **bedridden** adj confined to bed, esp. through illness. **bedroom** n room used for sleeping in. **bed-sitter** n also **bed-sit** one-roomed accommodation, usually with cooking and washing facilities. **bedspread** n top cover for a bed.

bedraggled adj spattered with mud or dirt.

bee n insect that produces wax and converts nectar into honey. **have a bee in one's bonnet** be obsessed or fanatical. **beehive** n box-like or domed construction for keeping bees in.

beech n deciduous tree with a smooth bark and shiny oval leaves.

beef n 1 meat from a cow, bull, etc. 2 cow, bull, etc., used for its meat. **beefy** adj 1 containing or having the flavour of beef. 2 muscular and strong.

been *v pp* of **be.**

beer *n* alcoholic drink made from malt and flavoured with hops.

beet *n* **1** *also* **beetroot** plant with a round red root, which is eaten as a vegetable. **2** *also* **sugar beet** plant with a whitish root, which is used as a source of sugar.

beetle *n* insect with wings, which are modified to form a hard protective shell.

befall *vi,vt* (befell; befallen) happen (to); occur, esp. by chance.

befit *vt,vi* (-tt-) be right or suitable (for).

before *adv* on a previous occasion; earlier. *prep* **1** previous to. **2** in front of. **3** in the presence of. *conj* **1** until or up to the time that. **2** rather than; sooner than. **beforehand** *adj,adv* early; in advance.

befriend *vt* take care of as a friend.

beg *vt,vi* (-gg-) **1** ask for (money, food, etc.). **2** beseech; implore; plead (with). **beggar** *n.*

begin *vt,vi* (-nn-) (began; begun) start; commence; bring into being. **beginner** *n* person at an early stage of learning; novice. **beginning** *n* start; starting place; early stage; outset. **beginnings** *pl n* **1** origin; early background. **2** early indication of potential or development.

begonia *n* plant with showy red, green, or greyish leaves and red, yellow, or white flowers.

begrudge *vt* resent; wish to deny; grudge.

beguile *vt,vi* charm; bewitch; hoodwink.

behalf *n* **on behalf of** in the name of; representing.

behave *vi* **1** act; react; function. **2** conduct (oneself). **behaviour** *n.*

behead *vt* execute by severing the head; decapitate.

behind *adv,adj* **1** following; after. **2** in a place that is further back. **3** behindhand. *prep* **1** at the back of; beyond. **2** not so advanced as. **3** remaining; left over. *n inf* buttocks. **behindhand** *adj,adv* in arrears; late.

behold *vt,vi* (beheld) see; look (at). *interj* look!

beige *adj,n* light greyish-brown; fawn.

being *n* **1** living creature. **2** existence; living state.

belated *adj* arriving or happening too late. **belatedly** *adv.*

belch *vi,vt* **1** expel wind noisily from the stomach through the mouth. **2** send out in large quantities; gush. *n* **1** act of belching. **2** blast; burst.

belfry *n* tower in which bells are hung.

belie *vt* **1** give the wrong impression of. **2** show to be false.

believe *vt,vi* **1** consider to be true or right; accept. **2** think; assume. *vi* subscribe to a particular faith. **believe in** have faith in; trust; be convinced of the existence of. **believable** *adj.* **believer** *n.* **belief** *n* **1** something believed; opinion. **2** creed; faith. **3** trust; acceptance.

belittle *vt* undervalue; disparage.

bell *n* **1** hollow metal instrument that produces a ringing sound when struck. **2** electrical device that produces a ringing or buzzing sound. **ring a bell** seem vaguely familiar.

belligerent *adj* warlike; aggressive. **belligerence** *n.* **belligerently** *adv.*

bellow *vi,vt* roar loudly; bawl. *n* deep-throated roar or shout.

bellows *n pl or s* device that expands and contracts to produce a strong draught of air.

belly *n* **1** abdomen. **2** stomach. **3** part of something that bulges.

belong *v* **belong to 1** be owned by. **2** be a member of. **3** be part of a set with; go with; fit. *vi* have an allotted place. **belongings** *pl n* personal possessions.

below *adv* at a place lower down; underneath. *prep* lower or further down than; under.

belt *n* **1** strip of leather, cloth, etc., worn round the waist. **2** band; strip. **3** region or zone with specific characteristics. **4** slap; blow; sharp hit. **below the belt** unfairly; against the rules. ~*vt* **1** fasten with a belt. **2** *sl* strike; beat. **3** *also* **belt out** sing, play, or shout loudly. *vi* race; travel fast. **belt up** *sl* stop talking.

bemoan *vt,vi* moan (about); lament; deplore.

bemused *adj* **1** lost in thought. **2** dazed; confused.

bench *n* **1** long wooden or stone seat. **2** work table; counter. **3** seat occupied by a judge or magistrate.

bend *v* (bent) *vt* **1** make into a bow or curved shape. **2** turn or curve in a particular direction. **3** subdue; coerce. *vi* **1** curve. **2** stoop; bow. *n* curve. **round the bend** mad; crazy.

beneath *adv* underneath; below. *prep* **1** concealed under; lower than. **2** in an inferior or subordinate position than. **3** unacceptable to.

benefactor *n* person who donates a large sum of money; patron. **beneficial** *adj* advantageous; helpful. **beneficiary** *n* recipient of a legacy, annuity, etc.

benefit *n* **1** advantage; privilege; good. **2** welfare or insurance payment. *vt,vi* do good to or be good for.

benevolent *adj* **1** kindly; good-natured. **2** charitable; generous. **benevolence** *n.* **benevolently** *adv.*

benign (bi'nain) *adj* **1** gentle; friendly. **2** not malignant.

bent *v pt* and *pp* of **bend.** *adj* **1** crooked; curved. **2** *sl* dishonest, corrupt. **bent on** determined to. ∼*n* inclination; penchant.

benzene *n* colourless sweet-smelling liquid containing carbon and hydrogen and used as a solvent.

bequeath *vt* leave (money, property, etc.) esp. by will. **bequest** *n* something bequeathed.

bereaved *adj* deprived (of) by death. **bereavement** *n.*

bereft *adj* deprived; completely lacking (in).

beret ('berei) *n* flat circular cap of wool, felt, etc.

berry *n* soft stoneless fruit of various trees or bushes.

berserk (bə'zə:k) *adj* in a frenzy; wild and violent.

berth *n* **1** sleeping place in a ship, train, caravan, etc. **2** mooring place. *vi,vt* moor; dock.

beseech *vt* implore; entreat.

beset *vt* (besetting; beset) **1** trouble; plague. **2** attack; assail.

beside *prep* at the side of; adjacent to; by. **beside oneself** overcome; out of control. **besides** *adv* **1** moreover; furthermore; anyway. **2** additionally; as well. *prep* in addition to; apart from.

besiege *vt* **1** surround and attack (a city, fortress, etc.). **2** assail with demands, requests, etc.

best *adj* **1** of the highest quality. **2** most suitable or desirable. *adv* in the best way. *n* the highest possible standard; utmost. **best man** *n* man who looks after a bridegroom. **best-seller** *n* book or other product that sells exceptionally well.

bestial *adj* **1** brutal; coarse and savage; carnal. **2** relating to a beast.

bestow *vt* give; confer; endow. **bestowal** *n.*

bet *n* **1** pledge between parties to pay a sum of money to the one who successfully predicts the outcome of a future event. **2** sum of money pledged. **3** predicted outcome. **4** course of action. *vt,vi* (-tt-; bet) **1** place a bet (on); gamble. **2** *inf* predict. **betting shop** *n* premises of a bookmaker.

betray *vt* **1** disclose information about or expose to an enemy. **2** be unfaithful or disloyal to. **3** show signs of; reveal inadvertently. **betrayal** *n.*

better *adj* **1** of a higher quality; superior. **2** more suitable or desirable. **3** no longer sick; recovering. **better off** richer; having a greater advantage. *adv* more; to a greater extent. **had better** ought to; should. ∼*n* **1** the more excellent or desirable. **2** superior; person of higher worth. **get the better of** outwit; defeat. ∼*vt* improve upon. **betterment** *n* improvement.

between *prep* **1** in a space or interval separating two places, moments in time, etc. **2** shared by. **3** through joint effort or contribution. *adv* in or towards the middle.

beverage *n* any drink except water.

beware *vt,vi* be wary (of); take heed (of).

bewilder *vt* puzzle; confuse; perplex. **bewilderment** *n.*

bewitch *vt* charm as if by a spell; enchant.

beyond *prep* **1** farther away than; on the far side of. **2** outside the control or limits of. *adv* farther away.

biannual *adj* occurring twice a year. **biannually** *adv.*

bias *n* **1** prejudice; distorted outlook. **2** tendency; inclination. **3** diagonal line or cut. **biased** *adj* partial; prejudiced.

bib *n* **1** piece of cloth worn under the chin by a baby whilst eating. **2** part of an apron, pinafore, etc., that covers the front of the body above the waist.

Bible *n* collection of sacred writings of the Christian Church. **biblical** *adj*.

bibliography *n* list of works relating to a particular subject, author, etc. **bibliographical** *adj*. **bibliographer** *n*.

biceps *pl n* muscles of the upper arm.

bicker *vi* squabble; quarrel, esp. over trivial matters.

bicycle *also* **cycle** *or* **bike** *n* vehicle with two wheels propelled by pedalling. *vi* ride a bicycle.

bid *v* (-dd-; bad, bade, *or* bid; bidden *or* bid) *vt,vi* **1** offer to buy for a certain sum, esp. at an auction. **2** ask; command. *vt* express in greeting. **bidder** *n*.

bidet ('bi:dei) *n* small bath used for washing the genital area.

biennial *adj* occurring once every two years or lasting for two years. *n* plant with a two-year life cycle. **biennially** *adv*.

big *adj* **1** large; great; not small. **2** important; substantial. **3** generous. *adv* with authority; in a big way.

bigamy *n* crime of marrying another partner when a former marriage is still valid. **bigamist** *n*. **bigamous** *adj*.

bigot *n* offensively intolerant or prejudiced person. **bigoted** *adj*. **bigotry** *n*.

bike *n,vi* short for **bicycle**.

bikini *n* woman's two-piece bathing costume.

bile *n* fluid secreted by the liver. **bilious** *adj* suffering from excessive secretion of bile in the liver.

bilingual *adj* able to speak two languages.

bill¹ *n* **1** statement of money owed; invoice. **2** law or act of Parliament in draft form. **3** poster or notice. **4** programme of events. **5** *US* banknote. *vt* **1** present an account to; invoice. **2** put on a programme; schedule.

bill² *n* bird's beak.

billiards *n* game played with a long cue and a number of balls on a table usually fitted with pockets.

billion *n* **1** (in Britain) one million million. **2** (esp. in the US) one thousand million.

billow *n* **1** large sea-wave. **2** surging mass. *vi, vt* swell up; surge.

bin *n* storage container.

binary *adj* **1** composed of two parts. **2** relating to the number two.

bind *v* (bound) *vt,vi* **1** tie or entwine; wrap round tightly. **2** cohere; stick. *vt* **1** restrict; place under an obligation or contract. **2** confine; trap; constrain. **3** fasten together (pages) inside a cover. **4** sew the edge of to prevent fraying, for decoration, etc. *n inf* restricting circumstance; constraint. **binder** *n* folder with clasps for holding together loose sheets of paper. **binding** *n* **1** cover of a book. **2** edging material or tape. *adj* restricting; obligatory. **bindweed** *n* plant that twines round a support or the stems of other plants.

bingo *n* gambling game in which players match up numbers on a chart with those picked out at random.

binoculars *pl n* optical instrument consisting of a pair of small telescopes joined together.

biochemistry *n* study of the chemical compounds occurring in plants and animals. **biochemical** *adj*. **biochemist** *n*.

biography *n* account of a person's life written by someone else. **biographical** *adj*. **biographer** *n*.

biology *n* study of living organisms. **biological** *adj*. **biologically** *adv*. **biologist** *n*.

birch *n* **1** tree with a slender grey or white trunk. **2** bundle of birch twigs used as a whip. *vt* flog; thrash.

bird *n* warm-blooded feathered egg-laying vertebrate with forelimbs modified as wings.

birth *n* **1** act of being born or producing offspring. **2** origin; beginning. **3** descent; lineage. **birth certificate** *n* official document issued when a child's birth is registered. **birth control** *n* method or practice of contraception. **birthday** *n* anniversary of a person's birth. **birthmark** *n* blemish on the skin formed before birth. **birth rate** *n* ratio of live births in relation to a given population.

biscuit *n* crisp flat cake made from baked dough.

bisect *vt* **1** divide into two equal parts. **2** split; cut across. **bisection** *n*.

bisexual *adj* able to respond sexually to a person of either sex. *n* person who is bisexual.

bishop *n* 1 high-ranking clergyman with authority over a diocese. 2 chess piece able to move diagonally across squares of the same colour.

bison *n* N American animal of the ox family with a shaggy coat and humped back; buffalo.

bistro ('bi:strou) *n* small restaurant or bar.

bit[1] *n* 1 small piece or amount. 2 short while. **a bit** a little; somewhat; rather. **bit by bit** gradually. **do one's bit** do one's duty; contribute. **every bit as** equally as. **not a bit** not at all.

bit[2] *n* 1 mouthpiece attached to a bridle for controlling a horse. 2 metal drill used with a brace.

bitch *n* 1 female dog. 2 *sl* malicious woman. *vi* speak maliciously; grumble. **bitchy** *adj*.

bite *vt,vi* (bit; bitten) 1 press, cut, or sink into with the teeth. 2 have a tendency to attack with the teeth, fangs, etc. 3 sting; smart. 4 corrode; eat into. 5 take bait. 6 grip; hold fast. *n* 1 act of biting. 2 piece bitten off; morsel. 3 mark or swelling caused by biting. 4 something to eat; snack. 5 strong grip. **biting** *adj* 1 harsh; keen. 2 sarcastic; hurtful.

bitter *adj* 1 having a harsh taste. 2 resentful; rancorous; deeply hostile. 3 distressing; hard to bear. 4 extremely cold; icy. *n* type of beer with a strong flavour of hops. **bitterly** *adv*. **bitterness** *n*.

bivalve *n* mollusc having two hinged shells.

bizarre *adj* weird; odd; strange.

black *adj* 1 of the colour of coal, jet, etc. 2 extremely dark; unlit. 3 extremely dirty. 4 grim; bleak. 5 enraged; angry. 6 dark-skinned. **black economy** *n* unofficial economic activity involving income not reported for tax purposes. **black market** *n* system of illicit trading. **black pudding** sausage made from pork fat and blood. ~*n* 1 dark colour having no hue. 2 darkness. 3 *cap* Negro; dark-skinned person. **black and blue** heavily bruised. ~*vt* 1 blacken. 2 *inf* boycott; ban. **black out** 1 obliterate. 2 extinguish; plunge into darkness. 3 pass out; lose consciousness. **blackout** *n* 1 power failure. 2 extinguishing of lights in cities, etc., in order to prevent iden-

tification by enemy aircraft. 3 temporary loss of consciousness or memory. **blackness** *n*. **blacken** *vt,vi* make or become black; darken. *vt* defame.

blackberry *n* edible purplish-black fruit.

blackbird *n* songbird in which the male has black plumage with a yellow beak and the female is brown.

blackboard *n* large board that can be written on with chalk.

blackcurrant *n* small round edible black berry that grows on a cultivated bush.

blackguard ('blæga:d) *n* scoundrel; rogue.

blackhead *n* spot with a black surface that clogs a pore on the skin.

blackleg *n* person who acts against the interests of a trade union, esp. by refusing to strike. *vi* (-gg-) act as a blackleg.

blackmail *n* crime of demanding payment in exchange for not disclosing discreditable information. *vt* threaten by means of blackmail. **blackmailer** *n*.

blacksmith *n* craftsman who works with iron.

bladder *n* sac in the body that functions as a receptacle for urine.

blade *n* 1 sharp-edged or cutting part of a knife, sword, etc. 2 long flat leaf of grass. 3 shoulder blade. 4 flat broad end of a propeller, oar, etc.

blame *n* responsibility for a crime, error, fault, etc. *vt,vi* attribute blame (to); find fault (with). **blameless** *adj* innocent; faultless.

blanch *vt* 1 make lighter in colour; bleach. 2 plunge (vegetables, meat, etc.) into boiling water. *vi* become pale with fear, nausea, etc.

blancmange (bla'mɔndʒ) *n* dessert made from milk, cornflour, and flavouring.

bland *adj* 1 not highly flavoured or seasoned. 2 mild; temperate. 3 unemotional; without passion. **blandly** *adv*. **blandness** *n*.

blank *adj* 1 not written on or filled in. 2 bare; undecorated. 3 uncomprehending; expressionless. 4 uninspired. **blank verse** unrhymed verse. ~*n* 1 empty space. 2 mental confusion. 3 written or printed dash. 4 gun cartridge having powder but no bullet. **draw a blank** fail to obtain the required information during an investigation. *v* **blank out** blot out; obliterate.

blanket *n* **1** woollen bed cover. **2** thick layer; cover. *vt* cover up.

blare *vt,vi* **1** shout or sound loudly; proclaim. **2** shine harshly. *n* **1** loud noise; blast. **2** blinding light; glare; blaze.

blasé ('blɑːzei) *adj* no longer capable of being shocked, excited, etc.; cool and sophisticated.

blaspheme *vi* curse; swear; utter profanities. *vt* act irreverently towards. **blasphemous** *adj*. **blasphemy** *n*.

blast *n* **1** explosion. **2** loud explosive noise; blare. **3** strong sudden rush of air, flames, water, etc. *interj sl* exclamation of anger, frustration, etc. *vt,vi* **1** blow up; destroy by explosion. **2** produce a sudden loud noise. **3** force an opening (in); breach. **blastoff** *n* launching of a rocket.

blatant *adj* flagrant; conspicuous; undisguised. **blatancy** *n*. **blatantly** *adv*.

blaze *n* **1** roaring fire; bright flame. **2** bright light; glare. **3** passionate display; outburst. *vi* **1** burn vigorously; flare. **2** glare; shine harshly.

blazer *n* jacket, esp. one worn as part of a school or club uniform.

bleach *vt,vi* whiten through heat or the action of chemicals. *n* substance used for bleaching clothes, the hair, etc.

bleak *adj* **1** desolate and exposed. **2** grim; dismal; unfavourable. **bleakly** *adv*. **bleakness** *n*.

bleat *vt,vi* **1** (of a sheep or goat) utter a high-pitched cry. **2** moan plaintively; whine; complain. *n* cry of a sheep or goat.

bleed *v* (bled) *vi* **1** lose blood. **2** suffer extreme anguish. *vt* **1** drain blood from. **2** draw off (liquid, gas, etc.). **bleeding** *adj* utter. *adv sl* extremely; very.

bleep *n* noise produced by an electronic device. *vi* make a short high-pitched sound.

blemish *n* **1** discoloured mark on the skin. **2** stain or flaw. *vt* spoil; mar; tarnish.

blend *vt,vi* **1** mix (different varieties of tea, tobacco, etc.). **2** combine (colours). **3** merge; form a mixture. *vi* harmonize; mix well. *n* blended mixture. **blender** *n* machine for blending vegetables, liquids, etc.

bless *vt* **1** make holy; consecrate. **2** call for God's aid or protection for. **blessed**

with (blest) endowed or favoured with; granted. **blessed** ('blesid) *adj* holy; sacred.

blessing *n* **1** statement or ceremony invoking God's aid or protection. **2** divine gift; sanction. **3** good fortune.

blew *v pt* of **blow**[1].

blight *n* **1** plant disease caused by fungi, insects, etc. **2** something that mars or impedes growth. *vt* **1** cause blight in. **2** spoil; destroy.

blind *adj* **1** deprived of the power of sight. **2** unable or unwilling to understand or tolerate. **3** made reckless by passion. **4** concealed; unseen. **5** closed at one end. *adv also* **blindly 1** without being able to see. **2** without proper information or preparation. *vt* **1** make blind. **2** dazzle. **3** deprive of reason or judgment. *n* length of material on a roller used as a shade for a window. **blindness** *n*. **blindfold** *n* strip of cloth placed over the eyes and tied at the back of the head. *vt* place a blindfold over (the eyes).

blink *vt,vi* **1** rapidly open and shut (the eyes). **2** flash on and off. *n* **1** rapid opening and shutting of the eyes. **2** flash; twinkle. **blinkers** *pl n* **1** direction indicators on a motor vehicle. **2** part of a horse's bridle that prevents sideways vision.

bliss *n* state of ecstatic happiness. **blissful** *adj*. **blissfully** *adv*.

blister *n* **1** small swelling or bubble on the skin produced by friction, burning, etc. **2** bubble of paint. *vt,vi* produce blisters.

blithe *adj* **1** carefree; light-hearted. **2** thoughtless; casual. **blithely** *adv*. **blitheness** *n*.

blitz *n* heavy attack, such as an air-raid. *vt* make an intensive attack on.

blizzard *n* violent snowstorm.

bloat *vt,vi* swell; inflate.

blob *n* **1** drop of liquid, dirt, etc. **2** blurred shape or form. *vt* (-bb-) splash or mark with blobs.

bloc *n* united group of countries, political parties, etc.

block *n* **1** solid piece of stone, wood, etc.; slab; brick; chunk. **2** building comprising a number of offices, flats, etc. **3** group of things fastened together or arranged in rows. **4** obstruction; obstacle; blockage. **5** psychological or mental barrier. *vt also* **block up 1** obstruct; cause a blockage in; stop up. **2** veto; impede; prevent. **blockade** *n* obstruction, esp. of a port or harbour by military forces. *vt* obstruct with a blockade. **blockage** *n* something that blocks, obstructs, or impedes.

bloke *n inf* man.

blond *adj* fair-haired. *n* man with fair hair. **blonde** *f n.* **blondness** *n.*

blood *n* **1** red fluid circulating through the veins and arteries of the body. **2** lineage; descent. **in cold blood** ruthlessly; in a calculated way. **bloodcurdling** *adj* terrifying; ghastly. **blood pressure** *n* pressure of the blood against the inner walls of the arteries. **bloodshed** *n* violent killing; slaughter. **bloodstream** *n* flow of blood through the body. **bloodthirsty** *adj* sadistic; delighting in violence. **bloodthirstiness** *n.* **bloody** *adj* covered or stained with blood; gory. *adj,adv sl* damned; extremely. *vt* stain with blood. **bloodiness** *n.* **bloody-minded** *adj* obstinate; pigheaded; perverse. **bloody-mindedness** *n.*

bloom *n* **1** flower(s); blossom. **2** healthy glow. **3** shiny surface of various fruits. *vi* **1** flower; blossom. **2** flourish; develop vigorously.

blossom *n* flower(s), esp. of a fruit tree. *vi* **1** flower; produce blossom. **2** begin to grow or develop.

blot *n* **1** ink stain. **2** eyesore. **3** damage to one's character or reputation. *vt* (-tt-) **1** stain; mark. **2** use an absorbent material to soak up. **blot out** obscure completely; obliterate. **blot one's copybook** spoil one's reputation or record; blunder. **blotting paper** *n* absorbent paper used esp. to soak up excess ink.

blotch *n* stain; discolouration; patch. *vt,vi* produce stains or patches. **blotchy** *adj.*

blouse *n* woman's garment that is similar to a shirt.

blow[1] *v* (blew; blown) *vt,vi* **1** send out (air) through the mouth or nose; exhale. **2** move through or by air or wind. **3** produce the sound of a whistle, trumpet, the wind, etc. **4** fuse; burn out. **blow out** extinguish or be extinguished. **blow over** subside; pass. **blow up 1** explode or cause an explosion. **2** lose one's temper. **3** inflate. **4** enlarge (a photograph). ~*n* **1** expulsion of air; puff. **2** act of blowing or sound produced by a

whistle, trumpet, etc. **blowy** *adj* windy; blustery.

blow[2] *n* **1** heavy stroke or hit with the hand or a weapon. **2** sudden shock or disappointment; setback. **come to blows** start to fight.

blubber *n* thick layer of subcutaneous fat of a whale, seal, etc. *vt,vi* sob; cry noisily.

blue *n* colour in the spectrum that is the colour of a clear sky. **out of the blue** suddenly; without warning; from nowhere. **the blues 1** state of depression; dejectedness. **2** type of music created by Black Americans. ~*adj* **1** of the colour blue. **2** depressed; unhappy. **3** *inf* obscene. **bluebell** *n* woodland plant with blue bell-shaped flowers. **blue-blooded** *adj* of royal or aristocratic descent. **blueprint** *n* **1** photocopy of plans or drawings. **2** original model; prototype.

bluff *vt,vi* feign confidence in order to deceive about one's true motives, resources, etc. *n* act of deception. **call someone's bluff** act in a way that forces someone to reveal his true motives, resources, etc.; challenge.

blunder *n* stupid, tactless, or clumsy mistake. *vi* **1** make a stupid or tactless mistake. **2** move clumsily; stumble.

blunt *adj* **1** not sharp; unable to cut well. **2** outspoken; forthright; direct. *vt,vi* make or become blunt(er). *vt* make less sensitive; dull. **bluntly** *adv.* **bluntness** *n.*

blur *vt,vi* (-rr-) **1** make or become hazy, indistinct, or vague. **2** smear; smudge. *n* **1** something that is indistinct in outline or vague. **2** smudge.

blurt *vt,vi* *also* **blurt out** reveal (a secret), esp. when confused or under pressure.

blush *vi* become red in the face with embarrassment, shame, etc.; flush. *n* **1** reddening of the cheeks. **2** hint of redness on a flower, fruit, etc.

bluster *vt,vi* speak or act in a forceful and often boastful manner; swagger. *vi* blow strongly; be windy. **blustery** *adj.*

boar *n* **1** wild pig. **2** uncastrated male domestic pig.

board *n* **1** plank of wood. **2** shaped piece of wood or other material designed for a specific purpose, such as an ironing board or chess board. **3** cardboard. **4** notice board or blackboard. **5** body of directors, governors, or other officials; committee. **6** meals provided for residents in a hotel, hostel, etc. **go by the board** be ignored or rejected. **on board** on a ship, aircraft, etc.; aboard. ~*vt,vi* go on to a ship, aircraft, etc.; embark. *vt also* **board up** enclose or cover with boards of wood. *vt* provide lodgings for. *vi* live in lodgings. **boarder** *n* **1** child at boarding school. **2** lodger. **boarding house** *n* small private establishment offering cheap accommodation. **boarding school** *n* school with living accommodation for pupils. **board room** *n* committee room where a board meets.

boast *vi* exaggerate or speak proudly of one's own achievements or qualities; brag. *vt* be the proud possessor of. *n* exaggerated or proud statement. **boastful** *adj.* **boastfully** *adv.* **boastfulness** *n.*

boat *n* small vessel for travelling on water. **in the same boat** in the same situation or predicament. **miss the boat** miss an opportunity. ~*vi* travel in a boat, esp. for pleasure.

bob *vt,vi* (-bb-) **1** move up and down esp. in a liquid. **2** nod or jerk (the head). **3** bow or curtsy. *n* **1** jerky movement. **2** bow or curtsy.

bodice *n* top part of a woman's dress.

body *n* **1** the whole physical structure of a human being or other vertebrate. **2** torso; trunk. **3** corpse. **4** main or central part. **5** mass; expanse. **6** corporate group of people. **7** object or solid. **8** consistency or fullness, esp. of wine. **bodily** *adj* physical; corporeal. *adv* by lifting or using the body. **bodyguard** *n* person giving physical protection to another. **bodywork** *n* covering for the shell or framework of a vehicle.

bog *n* **1** area of waterlogged land, usually of peat. **2** *sl* lavatory. **bogged down** unable to make progress; hindered. **boggy** *adj.*

bogus *adj* fake; sham.

boil[1] *vt,vi* **1** produce gas or vapour from a liquid by the action of heat. **2** cook by heating in liquid. *vi* seethe; become agitated. **boil down** reduce in quantity by boiling. **boil down to** amount to; result in. **boil over** overflow or spill whilst boiling. *n* **on the boil 1** approaching boiling point. **2** in operation; functioning well. **boiler** *n*

vessel producing steam to drive an engine. **boiling point** *n* **1** temperature at which a liquid boils. **2** moment at which one loses one's temper or a situation becomes explosive.

boil[2] *n* inflamed pus-filled sore on the skin.

boisterous *adj* unruly; noisy and unrestrained. **boisterously** *adv.* **boisterousness** *n.*

bold *adj* **1** courageous; unafraid; daring. **2** clear; distinct. **boldly** *adv.* **boldness** *n.*

bolster *n* long pillow or cushion. *vt also* **bolster up** reinforce; encourage; boost.

bolt *n* **1** metal bar used to fasten a door, window, etc. **2** screw or pin used with a nut. **3** clap of thunder or flash of lightning. **make a bolt for it** run away quickly. ~*vt* **1** secure or fasten with a bolt. **2** eat hurriedly; gulp down. *vi* **1** jump up suddenly. **2** run off unexpectedly. *adv* **bolt upright** with one's back straight and rigid.

bomb *n* explosive device. **go like a bomb 1** travel at high speed. **2** be highly successful. ~*vt,vi* attack with bombs. **bombard** *vt* **1** attack repeatedly with bombs, missiles, etc. **2** direct series of questions, complaints, etc., at. **bombardment** *n.* **bombardier** (bombə'diə) *n* noncommissioned officer below a sergeant in the Royal Artillery. **bomber** *n* **1** aircraft designed to carry bombs. **2** person who attacks with bombs. **bombshell** *n* unexpected event causing great shock or distress.

bond *n* **1** something that binds, such as a rope or chain. **2** close intimate relationship; tie. **3** obligation; duty. **4** company or government certificate issued as a guarantee of repayment of money lent. **bonded warehouse** warehouse storing imported goods until duty is paid. **bondage** *n* slavery.

bone *n* hard tissue that makes up the skeleton of the body. **have a bone to pick** have something to criticize or quarrel about. **make no bones about** have no hesitation or doubt about. ~*vt* remove the bones from (meat). **bonemeal** *n* animal food or fertilizer made from crushed bones. **bony** *adj* **1** having many bones. **2** having prominent bones. **3** resembling a bone.

bonfire *n* fire lit out of doors.

bonnet *n* **1** hat kept in place with ribbons tied under the chin. **2** hinged section at the front of a vehicle that covers the engine or luggage compartment.

bonus *n* additional payment, dividend, etc.

booby trap *n* **1** concealed or disguised explosive device intended to blow up when touched. **2** object or trap used by a practical joker to surprise or scare an unsuspecting victim. **booby-trap** *vt* (-pp-) set up a booby trap in or for.

book *n* **1** set of printed pages bound together; volume. **2** written work, such as a novel or textbook. **3** pack of stamps, tickets, etc. **by the book** strictly according to the rules. ~*vt,vi* reserve (a seat, ticket, etc.) in advance. *vt* record (a person's name) prior to prosecution on a minor charge. **book-keeping** *n* accounting system or practice of keeping records of business transactions. **bookkeeper** *n.* **booklet** *n* small book; brochure. **bookmaker** *n* person running a business to accept bets, esp. in horseracing.

boom *vi* **1** produce a deep resonant sound. **2** thrive; prosper. *n* **1** deep resonant sound. **2** period or state of prosperity.

boomerang *n* curved piece of wood used as a missile and designed to follow a course back to the user when thrown.

boor *n* uncouth coarse person. **boorish** *adj.*

boost *n* **1** push or shove upwards. **2** increase; rise. **3** encouragement; help. *vt* **1** lift up with a push. **2** increase; expand. **3** improve; promote. **booster** *n.*

boot *n* **1** type of footwear usually covering the leg up to the knee. **2** stout shoe worn for walking, climbing, playing football, etc. **3** luggage compartment in a vehicle, usually situated at the rear. **4** *inf* kick. **the boot** *sl* dismissal; sack. ~*vt* **1** kick. **2** *also* **boot out** expel or dismiss unceremoniously.

booth *n* **1** enclosed cubicle. **2** covered stall at a market or fair.

booze *inf n* alcoholic drink. *vi* drink heavily.

border *n* **1** stretch of land constituting a frontier or boundary. **2** edge; margin. **3** flower bed along the edge of a lawn, path, etc. *vt,vi* function as a border or boundary (to). **border on** lie adjacent to. **2** verge on; come close to. **borderline** *n* **1** boundary line. **2** intermediate area or category. *adj* marginal; in between.

bore[1] *vt,vi* **1** drill (a hole) in. **2** dig or make (a tunnel, shaft, etc.), esp. in order to extract oil, minerals, etc. *n* **1** tunnel or shaft. **2** hollow part of a gun barrel. **3** calibre of a gun.

bore[2] *vt* exhaust or frustrate by being dull, repetitious, etc. *n* tedious or dreary person, task, etc. **boredom** *n.*

bore[3] *v pt* of **bear**[1].

born *v pt* of **bear**[1] (def 4) when used in the passive. *adj* possessing a specified innate quality.

borne *v pp* of **bear**[1].

borough *n* **1** town or district represented in Parliament. **2** area having own local council.

borrow *vt,vi* **1** take or accept on loan. **2** incorporate into one's own language; adopt. **borrower** *n.*

borstal *n* establishment for young offenders.

bosom *n* **1** breast or chest, esp. of a woman; bust. **2** centre of love or comfort.

boss *inf n* employer, manager, or foreman. *vt,vi* control or manage, esp. domineeringly. **bossy** *adj* overbearing; inclined to dominate. **bossiness** *n.*

botany *n* science or study of plants. **botanical** *adj.* **botanist** *n.*

botch *vt,vi* bungle; make a bad job of. *n* mess; clumsy repair.

both *pron,adj* each of two taken together. *conj* **both...and...** firstly...and secondly...

bother *vt* disturb; worry; annoy; trouble. *vi* concern oneself; take trouble or care. *n* **1** fuss; commotion. **2** trouble; anxiety. *interj* exclamation of mild impatience or annoyance.

bottle *n* long glass or plastic vessel with a narrow neck, for holding liquids. *vt,vi* pour into a bottle. **bottle up** repress or hide (emotions). **bottle bank** *n* large container in public area where glass bottles, etc., are deposited for recycling. **bottleneck** *n* something that restricts the flow of traffic, goods on a production line, etc.

bottom *n* **1** lowest part; base; foot. **2** seabed, riverbed, etc. **3** worst or most inferior position. **4** *inf* buttocks. **at bottom** fundamentally; basically. **get to the bottom of** investigate the truth or cause of. ~*adj* lowest. **bottomless** *adj* **1** extremely deep. **2**

seemingly endless or inexhaustible. **bottommost** *adj* **1** very lowest. **2** most basic.

bough *n* branch of a tree.

bought *v pt* and *pp* of **buy**.

boulder *n* large stone or rock.

bounce *vi,vt* **1** rebound or cause to spring back after striking or being thrown. **2** jump or throw up and down; jerk. *vi* (of a cheque) be returned by a bank as unacceptable. *n* **1** rebound; springing back. **2** jump; jerk. **3** exuberance; ebullience. **bouncing** *adj* very healthy or robust. **bouncy** *adj* exuberant; high-spirited. **bounciness** *n.*

bound¹ *v pt* and *pp* of **bind**. *adj* **bound to** certain to; sure to. **bound up with** *or* **in** closely involved with.

bound² *vi* leap; spring. *n* jump; bounce; leap.

bound³ *vt* restrict; limit. *n* boundary; limit. **boundless** *adj* inexhaustible; limitless.

bound⁴ *adj* heading towards; destined for.

boundary *n* something that marks the edge or limit of an area of land.

bouquet *n* **1** (bou'kei, bu:-) bunch of flowers, esp. one elaborately arranged or displayed. **2** (bu:'kei) aroma of a wine.

bourgeois ('buəʒwɑ:) *adj* of the middle class, esp. when regarded as conservative and materialistic. *n* member of the middle class. **bourgeoisie** (buəʒwa:'zi:) *n* middle class.

bout *n* **1** boxing contest; fight. **2** short period; spell.

boutique *n* small shop, esp. one selling clothes.

bow¹ (bau) *vt,vi* bend (the body or head) forwards as an act of respect, submission, etc. *vi* yield; submit; comply. **bow down 1** yield. **2** submit. ~*n* bending of the body or lowering of the head.

bow² (bou) *n* **1** weapon from which arrows are shot, consisting of a supple piece of wood pulled into a curved shape by a taut string. **2** rod strung with horsehair used for playing a violin, cello, etc. **3** decorative knot having two loops and two loose ends. **4** curve; arc. *vi,vt* **1** draw a bow across (a violin, cello, etc.). **2** curve; bend. **bow-legged** (bou'legid, -'legd) *adj* having the legs curving outwards; bandy.

bow³ (bau) *n* front or forward end of a ship or boat.

bowels *pl n* **1** intestines. **2** deepest or innermost part.

bowl¹ *n* shallow basin or dish. **bowler** *n* also **bowler hat** hat with a hard rounded crown and narrow brim.

bowl² *n* heavy ball used in bowls, tenpin bowling, etc. *vt,vi* **1** roll (a ball) or travel smoothly along the ground. **2** deliver (a ball) to the batsman in cricket. **bowl along** travel fast and comfortably. **bowl over 1** knock to the ground. **2** overwhelm; astound. **bowler** *n* person who bowls in cricket. **bowling** *n* tenpin bowling or skittles. **bowls** *n* game played with weighted balls on a level grass pitch.

box¹ *n* **1** flat-bottomed container sometimes with a lid. **2** compartment for a small number of spectators, situated at the side of an auditorium. **3** cubicle; booth. **4** horsebox. **5** witness box. **6** section of printed matter enclosed within a border. **the box** *sl* television. ~*vt* pack into a box. **box in 1** enclose; board up. **2** corner or jam so as to prevent movement. **Boxing day** *n* first weekday after Christmas day. **box office** *n* booking office in a theatre, cinema, etc.

box² *vi,vt* **1** fight in a boxing match (against). **2** punch; hit with the fist. *n* blow of the fist; punch; cuff. **boxer** *n* **1** person who fights in a boxing match. **2** breed of smooth-haired dog, similar to a bulldog. **boxing** *n* sport in which two opponents fight with the fists using padded gloves.

boy *n* male child. **boyhood** *n.* **boyish** *adj.* **boyfriend** *n* male friend, esp. one with whom one has a romantic relationship.

boycott *vt* refuse to deal with (another nation, group, etc.) or buy (goods). *n* practice or instance of boycotting.

bra *n* also **brassiere** woman's undergarment worn to support the bosom.

brace *n* **1** tool into which a drill or bit is fitted for boring holes. **2** beam or girder used for strengthening or supporting a wall. **3** metal band fixed to the teeth to correct their alignment. **4** pair, esp. of game birds. **braces** *pl n* pair of straps worn over the shoulders and fastened to the waistband of a pair of trousers. ~*vt* strengthen or support with a brace. *vt,vi* invigorate; freshen.

brace oneself prepare oneself for impending pain, shock, etc.

bracelet *n* ornamental chain or band worn round the wrist.

bracken *n* type of large fern.

bracket *n* 1 right-angled support for a shelf. 2 one of a pair of written or printed symbols used to enclose additional information, etc. 3 classified group of people, esp. an income group. *vt* 1 fix with a bracket. 2 enclose within brackets. 3 place in the same category.

brag *vi* (-gg-) boast. *n* card game similar to poker. **braggart** *n* boastful person.

braid *n* 1 plait. 2 band of material made from plaited or twisted threads. *vt* plait; interweave (strands).

Braille *n* system of writing using embossed dots enabling the blind to read by touch.

brain *n* 1 mass of nerve fibre situated inside the skull, forming the main part of the central nervous system. 2 *also* **brains** intelligence. *vt inf* kill by striking violently on the head. **brainwash** *vt* indoctrinate or condition totally. **brainwave** *n* 1 voltage and current waves produced by the brain. 2 brilliant idea or inspiration. **brainy** *adj inf* intelligent.

braise *vt,vi* cook in a small amount of liquid in an airtight container.

brake *n* device on a vehicle that stops or slows down the motion of the wheels. *vi,vt* stop or slow down by applying the brake.

bramble *n* bush with thorny stems, esp. a blackberry bush.

branch *n* 1 limb of a tree or shrub that grows from the trunk or main stem; bough. 2 subdivision; offshoot. 3 local shop, bank, etc., that is part of a larger organization. *vi* 1 produce branches. 2 *also* **branch off** subdivide, diverge; fork. **branch out** extend one's interests.

brand *n* 1 class of product, esp. one marketed under a trademark. 2 type, variety; sort. 3 identifying mark on cattle, sheep, etc. 4 *also* **branding iron** iron rod that is heated and used for marking animals for identification. 5 stigma. *vt* 1 mark with a brand. 2 denounce as; label. 3 impress permanently on the mind; scar. **brand-new** *adj* absolutely new and unused.

brandish *vt* hold or wave (a weapon) threateningly or defiantly. *n* triumphant wave; flourish.

brandy *n* spirit distilled from the fermented juice of grapes.

brash *adj* 1 coarse; loud. 2 reckless, impetuous. **brashly** *adv*. **brashness** *n*.

brass *n* 1 yellowish-gold alloy of copper and zinc. 2 family of musical instruments that includes the trumpet and trombone. 3 engraved memorial tablet made of brass. **get down to brass tacks** start to consider or discuss the most important aspects of an issue or situation. **brassy** *adj* 1 of or like brass. 2 vulgar and showy; shameless.

brassiere *n* bra.

brave *adj* courageous; not cowardly; bold. *vt* face or tackle courageously; defy. *n* warrior of an American Indian tribe. **bravely** *adv*. **bravery** *n*.

brawl *n* noisy uncontrolled fight. *vi* fight or quarrel noisily.

brawn *n* 1 well-developed muscles. 2 muscular strength. 3 dish made of chopped meat from the head of a pig or calf and compressed into a mould.

bray *n* 1 harsh cry of a donkey. 2 shout or harsh laugh. *vi,vt* 1 (of a donkey) utter a harsh cry. 2 shout or laugh harshly.

brazen *adj* 1 shamelessly defiant; bold. 2 made of or like brass; brassy. *v* **brazen out** face or carry out boldly or defiantly.

brazil *n also* **brazil nut** nut with an edible kernel and hard rough shell that grows in a cluster inside a large capsule.

breach *n* 1 infringement or violation of the terms of a contract or agreement. 2 split between factions or parties. 3 gap; hole; crack. *vt* 1 infringe; violate. 2 break open; make a hole in.

bread *n* 1 food made from flour, milk, yeast, etc., baked in the form of loaves or rolls. 2 *sl* money. **breadwinner** *n* person responsible for earning money to support a family.

breadth *n* 1 measurement or extent from one side to another; width; broadness. 2 extent. 3 open-mindedness; tolerance.

break *v* (broke; broken) *vt,vi* 1 shatter or separate into pieces; fragment; smash; burst. 2 damage or cease to function. 3 pause; adjourn; stop for a while. *vt* 1 fail to keep (a promise, agreement, etc.). **2** bankrupt; ruin financially. **3** destroy; crush. **4** fracture (a bone). **5** reveal or disclose (news, a secret, etc.). **6** succeed in giving up (a habit). **7** surpass or improve on (a previous record, achievement, etc.). **8** reduce the impact of. *vi* **1** become known; be made public. **2** change; come to an end. **3** be overcome or overwhelmed with grief, strain, etc. **4** (esp. of the male voice at puberty) undergo a change. *n* **1** fracture; split; crack. **2** pause; recess; interval. **3** disconnection; discontinuation. **4** change of routine or habit. **5** sudden escape. **6** *inf* opportunity; stroke of luck. **break away 1** escape. **2** form or join a new group. **breakaway** *n* **1** escape. **2** split. **break down 1** stop functioning because of mechanical failure. **2** fail. **3** collapse with emotion. **4** analyse. **breakdown** *n* **1** failure. **2** mental collapse; nervous breakdown. **3** analysis; detailed account. **break even** cover one's expenses with neither profit nor loss. **break in(to) 1** force entry, esp. in order to steal. **2** interrupt. **3** tame and train (a horse). **break-in** *n* forced entry. **break off 1** detach a piece (from). **2** discontinue (a relationship). **3** stop abruptly, esp. when speaking. **break out 1** escape (from prison). **2** begin suddenly or violently. **3** develop (a rash, pimples, etc.). **break through 1** penetrate. **2** achieve after a long struggle. **breakthrough** *n* important discovery or achievement. **break up 1** disintegrate. **2** split up; separate; part. **break-up** *n* **1** disintegration. **2** split; separation. **breakable** *adj*. **breakage** *n* **1** act of breaking. **2** the thing broken or its value.

breakfast *n* first meal of the day. *vi* eat breakfast.

breast *n* **1** front part of the body from the neck to the abdomen; chest. **2** mammary gland. **3** centre of affection, patriotic feelings, etc. **make a clean breast of** confess. **breaststroke** *n* stroke in swimming performed face downwards with the arms and legs making circular movements.

breath *n* **1** inhalation and exhalation of air. **2** air inhaled or exhaled. **3** slight gust of air or wind. **4** hint; suggestion; vague rumour. **out of breath** unable to breathe properly. **take one's breath away** dumbfound; astound. **under one's breath** in a

low voice or whisper. **breathless** *adj* out of breath. **breathy** *adj*. **breathtaking** *adj* amazing; thrilling.

breathe *vt,vi* **1** inhale and exhale (air). **2** whisper; murmur; blow gently. **breather** *n inf* pause for rest. **breathing space** *n* sufficient room to move or function.

breed *vt,vi* (bred) **1** bear and produce (offspring). **2** propagate; reproduce. **3** generate; give rise to. *n* **1** group within a species, having common characteristics. **2** type; variety; brand. **breeder** *n*. **breeding** *n* **1** reproduction; propagation. **2** socially acceptable upbringing or background.

breeze *n* light wind. *vi inf* move about in a carefree manner. **breezy** *adj*.

brethren *n pl* of **brother**, esp. in a religious context.

brevity *n* briefness; conciseness.

brew *vt,vi* **1** make (beer) by fermentation. **2** make (tea, coffee, etc.) by infusion. *vt* concoct. *vi* **1** undergo fermentation or infusion. **2** be in the process of formation. *n* **1** brand of beer. **2** concoction. **brewery** *n* establishment where beer is brewed.

bribe *n* payment offered in order to influence a person to act in one's favour, esp. illegally. *vt,vi* persuade with a bribe. **bribery** *n*.

brick *n* **1** block of stone or baked clay used in building. **2** small block of wood used as a toy. **3** slab. *vt also* **brick up** seal or enclose with bricks. **bricklayer** *n* person skilled in building with bricks. **bricklaying** *n*. **brickwork** *n* construction with bricks.

bride *n* woman preparing for marriage or recently married. **bridegroom** *n* husband of a bride. **bridesmaid** *n* female attendant who looks after the bride.

bridge[1] *n* **1** construction spanning a river, valley, etc. **2** top part of the nose. **3** platform from which a ship is piloted or navigated. **4** small block supporting the strings of a violin, guitar, etc. **5** something that serves to connect. *vt* **1** place a bridge over; span. **2** form a connection between.

bridge[2] *n* card game developed from whist.

bridle *n* part of a harness, including the headpiece, bit, and reins, for controlling a horse. *vt* **1** fit or control with a bridle. **2** curb; check. *vi* express contempt, anger, etc., by drawing in the chin or jerking the head. **bridlepath** n narrow track that is suitable for horses.

brief adj 1 lasting a short time. 2 concise. 3 curt; abrupt. n 1 document in which a solicitor sets out details of his client's case for a barrister. 2 set of instructions. **briefs** pl n short underpants or knickers. ~vt prepare or instruct with a brief. **briefly** adv. **briefness** n. **briefcase** n bag or case used to hold papers, documents, etc. **briefing** n meeting at which information and instructions are given, esp. for a military operation.

brigade n 1 military unit forming part of a division. 2 group of people trained to perform a special task. **brigadier** (brigə'diə) n army officer holding a rank below that of major general and above a colonel and usually in command of a brigade.

bright adj 1 giving off a strong light. 2 of a strong colour; vivid. 3 shiny; gleaming. 4 cheerful. 5 inf clever; intelligent. adv also **brightly** in a bright manner. **brightness** n. **brighten** vt,vi make or become bright (er).

brilliant adj 1 shining brightly; glittering. 2 extremely clever or talented. 3 displaying great imagination. 4 outstanding. **brilliance** n. **brilliantly** adv.

brim n 1 rim of a cup, dish, etc. 2 edge of a hat projecting from the crown. vt,vi (-mm-) fill or be full so as to overflow.

bring vt (brought) 1 carry or convey (to or towards). 2 accompany. 3 produce; yield. 4 cause. 5 force or persuade. **bring about** cause to happen. **bring back** reintroduce; restore. **bring down** 1 force down. 2 reduce. 3 humiliate or depress. **bring forward** 1 produce; present. 2 fix for an earlier time. **bring in** 1 introduce; initiate. 2 yield; earn. 3 include. **bring off** achieve by striving or by taking risks. **bring on** 1 cause to start; induce. 2 help to develop; encourage. **bring out** 1 cause to show or appear. 2 publish. **bring round** 1 make conscious again, esp. after fainting. 2 persuade; convert; convince. **bring up** 1 rear; educate from an early age. 2 vomit. 3 introduce or mention.

brink n 1 edge of a high or steep place, body of water, etc. 2 threshold; verge.

brisk adj 1 quick; lively. 2 invigorating; fresh. **briskly** adv. **briskness** n.

bristle n 1 short tough hair of an animal such as the pig. 2 hair, wire, fibre, etc., of a brush. 3 hair of a man's beard; stubble. vi 1 (of fur, hair, etc.) stand on end; be stiff or rigid. 2 display signs of annoyance, indignation, etc. **bristle with** be crowded or overrun with. **bristly** adj.

brittle adj 1 easily broken, shattered, or cracked. 2 irritable; short-tempered. **brittleness** n.

broach vt 1 introduce or suggest tentatively. 2 pierce or open in order to draw off liquid; tap.

broad adj 1 wide; not narrow. 2 extensive. 3 from one side to another; across; in width. 4 general; not specific. 5 direct; not subtle. 6 crude; coarse; vulgar. 7 displaying features of dialect or non-standard speech. 8 tolerant. **in broad daylight** openly; without attempting to conceal. **broad bean** n bean having large flat seeds, which are eaten as a vegetable. **broaden** vt,vi make or become broad(er); widen. **broad-minded** adj having tolerant or liberal views; not bigoted. **broad-mindedness** n.

broadcast v (-cast or -casted) vt,vi transmit via radio or television. vi appear on a radio or television programme. vt 1 publicize. 2 sow (seed) by hand. n radio or television transmission or programme. **broadcaster** n. **broadcasting** n.

brocade n heavy fabric woven with embossed designs.

broccoli n type of cabbage having edible green or purple flower heads.

brochure n pamphlet or booklet containing information, advertisements, etc.

broke v pt of **break**. adj penniless; bankrupt.

broken v pp of **break**. **broken-hearted** adj overwhelmed with grief, sorrow, disappointment, etc.

broker n agent for insurance, shares, securities, loans, etc.

bronchi ('brɒŋkai) pl n, s **bronchus** ('brɒŋkəs) also **bronchial tubes** two main branches of the windpipe. **bronchial** adj. **bronchitis** n inflammation of the bronchi.

bronze *n* 1 reddish-gold alloy of copper and tin, sometimes with zinc and lead added. 2 statue or ornament of bronze. *adj* 1 reddish-gold. 2 *also* **bronzed** suntanned. *vt,vi* make or become suntanned.

brooch *n* ornamental pin or clasp fastened to the front of the clothing.

brood *n* 1 group of young birds hatched at the same time. 2 *inf* children in a family; offspring. *vt,vi* 1 sit on and hatch (eggs). 2 think or worry (about) for a long time. **broody** *adj*.

brook *n* small stream.

broom *n* 1 implement for sweeping with a head of bristles or fibres and a long handle. 2 evergreen shrub with bright yellow flowers, that is able to grow on poor soil.

brother *n* 1 son of the same parents as another. 2 fellow member; comrade. 3 unordained or lay male member of a religious order. **brotherhood** *n* 1 relationship as a brother. 2 fraternity; fellowship. 3 religious community of men. **brother-in-law** *n, pl* **brothers-in-law** 1 husband of one's sister. 2 brother of one's wife or husband. 3 husband of the sister of one's wife or husband. **brotherly** *adj* affectionate or loyal as a brother

brought *v pt* and *pp* of **bring**.

brow *n* 1 eyebrow. 2 forehead. 3 crest of a hill. **browbeat** *vt* (-beat; -beaten) intimidate; oppress; bully.

brown *n* the colour of earth; very dark orange or yellow. *adj* 1 of the colour brown. 2 suntanned. *vt,vi* make or become brown. **browned off** *adj* disillusioned; bored; fed up. **brownish** *adj*.

browse *vi* 1 look through or examine a book, items for sale, etc., unhurriedly or casually. 2 feed on vegetation; graze.

bruise *n* rupture of the blood vessels causing discoloration of the skin. *vt,vi* 1 produce a bruise. 2 offend; hurt the feelings (of).

brunette *n* woman or girl with dark hair. *adj* dark; brown.

brunt *n* full impact of force, shock, etc.

brush *n* 1 implement with a head of bristles or fibres and a handle. 2 stroke made with a brush. 3 light touch. 4 short unpleasant meeting or contact. 5 fox's tail. *vt* 1 wipe, clean, apply, etc., with a brush. 2 touch lightly. **brush aside** dismiss as irrelevant; disregard. **brush up** 1 revise; refresh the memory. 2 make neat and tidy.

brusque *adj* curt; brisk; abrupt. **brusquely** *adv*. **brusqueness** *n*.

Brussels sprout *n* type of cabbage having small edible heads of tightly overlapping leaves growing on one stem.

brute *n* 1 animal, esp. when contrasted with man; beast. 2 cruel, tyrannical, or ignorant person. *adj* **brute force/strength** sheer physical force/strength; brawn. **brutal** *adj* cruel; savage; barbaric. **brutality** *n*. **brutally** *adv*.

bubble *n* 1 globule of air or gas contained within a film of liquid. 2 gurgling sound. *vt,vi* form bubbles; effervesce. *vi* gurgle.

buck *n* male of animals such as the rabbit, hare, or deer. *vi* rear in an attempt to unseat a rider. *vt* unseat; throw off. **buck up** 1 hurry. 2 cheer up.

bucket *n* container with a circular bottom and a handle. **kick the bucket** die.

buckle *n* 1 clasp with a prong used for securing a belt or strap. 2 distorted curve; bulge; twist. *vt,vi* 1 fasten with a buckle. 2 force or be forced out of shape through stress, heat, etc.; warp.

bud *n* undeveloped flower or leaf shoot. **nip in the bud** prevent the development of. ~*vi* (-dd-) produce buds. **budding** *adj* beginning to show talent; promising.

Buddhism ('budizəm) *n* Eastern religion, founded by Buddha, that teaches self-awareness through the denial of passion or desire. **Buddhist** *n,adj*.

budge *vt,vi* move; shift.

budget *n* 1 estimate of expected income and expenditure. 2 money allocated for a project. *vt,vi* 1 allow for or include in a budget. 2 spend according to a budget; economize (on).

buffalo *n* 1 African animal of the ox family having curved horns. 2 bison.

buffer *n* 1 shock absorber fitted to a train or placed at the end of a railway track. 2 person or thing that serves to reduce the threat of attack or lessen the impact of a collision.

buffet[1] ('bʌfei) *n* 1 counter or table from which refreshments are served. 2 refreshments set out for guests to help themselves.

buffet[2] ('bʌfit) *vt* 1 blow or toss about; batter. 2 fight or push through.

bug *n* **1** type of insect that feeds on plant juices or the blood of animals. **2** *inf* infection caused by certain microorganisms. **3** concealed device, such as a microphone, used to obtain secret information. **4** *sl* obsession; craze. *vt* (-gg-) **1** annoy; bother; nag. **2** conceal a microphone in.

bugle *n* brass instrument similar to the trumpet but without valves. *vi* play a bugle.

build *vt,vi* (built) **1** construct using materials such as brick, stone, or wood. **2** commission or finance a construction. *vt* **1** establish and develop (a business, etc.). **2** create or design for a particular purpose. **build up 1** work on in order to strengthen, increase, or enhance. **2** accumulate. **build-up** *n* **1** gradual increase. **2** promotion of a commodity. **builder** *n*. **building** *n* **1** construction having walls and a roof. **2** business or process of constructing houses, shops, etc. **building society** *n* company advancing loans for mortgages using funds deposited by investors. **built-in** *adj* constructed as an integral part.

bulb *n* **1** rounded organ of a plant, such as the tulip or onion, that grows underground. **2** plant growing from such an organ. **3** light bulb. **bulbous** *adj*.

bulge *n* swelling; protuberance. *vi* swell; stick out.

bulk *n* **1** large quantity or volume. **2** greater part. **3** cargo, esp. before packaging. **4** human body, esp. when large or fat. **bulky** *adj* large and cumbersome. **bulkiness** *n*.

bull *n* **1** adult male member of the ox family. **2** male of animals such as the elephant or seal. **3** person who buys stocks and sells them after the price has risen. **4** *sl also* **bullshit** nonsense; exaggerated statement. **bulldog** *n* breed of short-haired dog with a sturdy body, muscular legs, and a large head. **bulldoze** *vt* **1** demolish or clear with a bulldozer. **2** barge through; shove. **bulldozer** *n* heavy tractor used for clearing rubble, earth, etc. **bullfight** *n* public entertainment common in Spain, Portugal, and S America in which a matador fights a bull. **bullfighter** *n*. **bullring** *n* arena used for a bullfight.

bullet *n* projectile discharged from a gun. **bullet-proof** *adj* able to protect from bullets.

bulletin *n* public notice or announcement giving official news or information.

bullion *n* gold or silver, esp. before it has been minted.

bully *vt,vi* threaten or act violently towards someone weaker; intimidate. *n* person who bullies.

bum *n* *sl* buttocks.

bump *vt,vi* **1** collide (with); bang (into); knock. **2** injure or hurt by banging. *vi also* **bump along** jolt; travel jerkily. **bump into** meet unexpectedly. **bump off** *sl* murder. ~*n* **1** collision; jolt; knock. **2** swelling; lump. **3** small mound; bulge. **bumpy** *adj*. **bumper** *n* protective bar fitted to either end of a vehicle.

bun *n* **1** small sweet baked roll. **2** hair coiled into a knot at the back of the head.

bunch *n* **1** number of things growing or arranged in a cluster. **2** group of people; set. *vt,vi also* **bunch up** gather together; cluster; huddle.

bundle *n* pile of things loosely wrapped or tied together. *vt* **1** *also* **bundle up** make into a bundle. **2** push hurriedly out of sight.

bung *n* stopper for a bottle, barrel, etc. *vt* **1** *also* **bung up** stop up or seal with a bung; block. **2** *sl* throw; chuck.

bungalow *n* single-storeyed house.

bungle *vt,vi* spoil by acting clumsily or incompetently; botch.

bunk *n* **1** narrow bed, esp. on a ship. **2** *also* **bunk bed** one of a pair of beds fitted one above the other in a single framework.

bunker *n* **1** storage container for coal, oil, etc. **2** sand-filled hollow functioning as a hazard on a golf course. **3** fortified underground shelter.

buoy *n* anchored float used as a navigation guide or for mooring a vessel. *v* **buoy up 1** keep afloat. **2** sustain optimism or cheerfulness in. **buoyant** *adj* **1** able to float. **2** optimistic; light-hearted. **buoyancy** *n*. **buoyantly** *adv*.

burble *vt,vi* gurgle; babble. *n* gurgling sound.

burden *n* **1** heavy load. **2** responsibility, suffering, etc., that is hard to cope with. *vt* **1**

343

overload; weigh down with. **2** oppress; cause to suffer. **burdensome** *adj.*

bureau ('bjuərou) *n, pl* **bureaux** ('bjuərou) *or* **bureaus 1** agency or government department dealing in employment, tourist information, etc. **2** writing desk fitted with drawers, pigeonholes, etc.

bureaucracy (bjuə'rɔkrəsi) *n* **1** system of government or administration by paid officials rather than elected representatives. **2** officials working within such a system. **3** excessive use of official administrative procedures; red tape. **bureaucrat** *n.* **bureaucratic** *adj.*

burglary *n* crime of breaking into a building at night with intent to commit certain offences. **burglar** *n.* **burgle** *vt,vi* commit burglary (in or on).

burial *n* burying, esp. of a body at a funeral.

burn *v* (burnt *or* burned) *vt,vi* damage or become damaged by fire, heat, or acid. *vi* **1** be combustible or inflammable. **2** produce heat or light; blaze; glow. **3** feel painfully hot or sore; smart. **4** be consumed with desire, anger, jealousy, etc. *vt* **1** use in order to produce heat or light. **2** make (a hole, mark, etc.) by fire, heat, or acid; scorch. **burn out 1** wear out by heat or friction. **2** use up one's energy; become exhausted. ~*n* **1** injury caused by fire, heat, or acid. **2** mark or hole caused by burning. **burning** *adj* **1** urgent; vital. **2** intense; passionate.

burrow *n* underground hole or tunnel dug by an animal for shelter. *vt,vi* tunnel or dig deeply (into). *vi* delve; search.

burst *vt,vi* (burst) break or split open, esp. under pressure; explode. **burst in(to) 1** enter noisily. **2** interrupt rudely. **burst into song/tears, etc.** start to sing, cry, etc., loudly and suddenly. ~*n* **1** split; rupture. **2** sudden loud noise; explosion. **3** spurt of activity, energy, etc.; surge.

bury *vt* **1** place (a corpse) in a grave or tomb; inter. **2** place underground. **3** conceal by covering. **4** embed; stick into. **5** engross. **6** repress; forget.

bus *n, pl* **buses** *or* **busses** large motor vehicle scheduled to carry passengers along a fixed route. *vi,vt* (-ss-) travel or carry by bus.

bush *n* **1** large plant with woody stems; shrub. **2** thick mass. **the bush** area of rough uncultivated land, esp. in Australia or S Africa; scrubland. **beat about the bush** act evasively; prevaricate. **bushy** *adj* **1** thick and shaggy. **2** covered with bushes.

bushel *n* unit of capacity equal to 2219 cubic inches. **hide one's light under a bushel** be modest about one's abilities or skills.

business *n* **1** commerce; trade. **2** occupation; profession. **3** commercial company; trading organization; firm. **4** affair; matter; concern. **business-like** *adj* conforming to certain standards of business procedure; efficient. **businessman** *n, pl* **-men** man engaged in commerce or trade, esp. as an executive. **businesswoman** *f n.*

bust[1] *n* **1** bosom or breast. **2** sculpture depicting a person's head and shoulders.

bust[2] *vt,vi* (busted *or* bust) **1** break; smash. **2** ruin; make or become bankrupt. **3** *sl* raid or search, esp. in order to arrest. **bust up 1** disrupt. **2** split or part after a quarrel. **bust-up** *n* **1** brawl. **2** separation after a quarrel.

bustle *vt,vi* hurry; be or make busy. *n* busy activity; commotion.

busy *adj* **1** fully occupied; active; engaged. **2** crowded; bustling. *v* **busy oneself** take up time with; occupy oneself. **busily** *adv.* **busybody** *n* person who gossips or meddles.

but *conj* **1** however; yet; nevertheless. **2** except; apart from; other than. *prep* with the exception of. **but for** without; were it not for. ~*adv* merely, just. **all but** almost; nearly.

butane *n* flammable hydrocarbon gas used as a fuel.

butcher *n* **1** person who prepares and sells meat. **2** savage murderer. *vt* **1** slaughter and prepare (meat). **2** murder, esp. with a knife, axe, etc.; slaughter; slay. **butchery** *n.*

butler *n* male servant, usually having special responsibility for wines.

butt[1] *n* **1** blunt thick end of a rifle, tool, etc. **2** cigarette end; stub.

butt[2] *n* **1** person who bears the brunt of ridicule, scorn, etc. **2** mound situated behind the target on a shooting range. **3** target.

butt³ *vt,vi* push hard with the head or horns; ram. **butt in** interrupt; interfere. ~*n* violent push with the head or horns.

butter *n* yellowish-white solid fat produced by churning cream. *vt* spread with butter. **butter up** flatter. **buttercup** *n* wild flower with bright yellow petals. **butterscotch** *n* brittle toffee made with butter and sugar.

butterfly *n* 1 insect with large wings, which are often brightly coloured or patterned. 2 person who is unable to settle or sustain interest in anything for very long.

buttocks *pl n* fleshy lower part of the body on which a person sits; bottom.

button *n* 1 small disc sewn on to a garment and able to pass through a buttonhole or loop as a fastening, or used for decoration. 2 small knob that is pushed to operate a machine, doorbell, etc. 3 anything small and round that resembles a button. *vt also* **button up** fasten with a button. **buttonhole** *n* 1 hole edged with stitching, through which a button is passed. 2 flower or spray worn in a buttonhole. *vt* 1 stitch round a buttonhole. 2 corner in order to engage in conversation.

buttress *n* 1 structure of stone or brick built to support a wall. 2 source of strength or support. *vt* 1 strengthen with a buttress. 2 give moral support to.

buxom *adj* having a full bosom; plump.

buy *vt,vi* (bought) obtain in exchange for money; purchase. **buy up** buy all that is available of a particular commodity. ~*n* thing bought; purchase. **buyer** *n* person who buys, esp. one purchasing merchandise for resale.

buzz *n* 1 low continuous noise; hum. 2 *inf* telephone call; ring. 3 *sl* pleasant sensation caused by certain drugs, alcohol, etc. *vt,vi* 1 produce a low vibrating hum. 2 signal or call using a buzzer. 3 *inf* phone; ring. *vi* 1 move hurriedly from place to place. 2 produce an atmosphere of excitement. **buzz off** go away; leave. **buzzer** *n* electrical device producing a harsh continuous signal.

by *prep* 1 through the agency, means, or authorship of. 2 via; past. 3 beside; close to; near. 4 no later than. 5 to a greater or lesser extent than. 6 multiplied with. 7 with a second dimension of. 8 during; in the course of.

by and by eventually; after a while. **by-election** *n* election held when a particular seat becomes vacant, as after the resignation or death of a Member of Parliament. **bylaw** *n* law made by a local authority and operational only within its own area. **bypass** *n* road constructed to direct the flow of traffic away from a town centre. *vt* 1 go round in order to avoid. 2 ignore (regulations, procedures, etc.) in order to proceed without delay.

C

cab *n* 1 driver's compartment of a lorry, bus, etc. 2 taxi.

cabaret ('kæbərei) *n* entertainment provided by a nightclub, restaurant, etc.

cabbage *n* vegetable with a short stalk and a head of green or purplish tightly packed leaves.

cabin *n* 1 small functional house, hut, or shelter. 2 living quarters on a ship; berth. 3 section of an aircraft for passengers or crew. **cabin cruiser** *n* motor boat with cabin accommodation.

cabinet *n* 1 piece of furniture for storing crockery, glassware, medicine, etc.; cupboard. 2 filing cabinet. 3 outer case of a radio or television set. **the Cabinet** body of Government ministers responsible for policy-making.

cable *n* 1 strong rope of twisted wire, hemp, etc. 2 set of insulated wires used for conducting electricity. 3 overseas telegram. 4 *also* **cable stitch** knitting stitch producing a twisted pattern. *vt,vi* send an overseas telegram (to). **cable television** *n* system of transmitting television by cable to individual subscribers resulting in a greater range of programmes.

cache (kæʃ) *n* hidden supply or store.

cackle *vi* 1 squawk like a hen. 2 laugh or shriek raucously. *n* 1 squawk. 2 raucous laugh.

cactus *n, pl* **cacti** ('kæktai) *or* **cactuses** plant adapted to grow in desert regions with tough spiny stems and bright showy flowers.

cadence *n* 1 sequence of chords marking the end of a musical phrase or section. 2 modulation of the voice; intonation.

cadet *n* young trainee, esp. in the armed forces or police force.

cadge *vt,vi* acquire or ask for without intending to pay; beg. **cadger** *n* person who cadges.

café *n* small restaurant serving snacks.

cafeteria *n* self-service restaurant or canteen.

caffeine *n* mild stimulant found in some plants, esp. coffee.

cage *n* **1** enclosure or box with bars used for confining animals or birds. **2** lift in a mine shaft. *vt* put or keep in a cage.

cajole *vt,vi* wheedle; coax; persuade by flattery.

cake *n* **1** sweet food made from flour, sugar, eggs, etc., and baked. **2** flattish compact mass, as of soap. **a piece of cake** *inf* something easily achieved or obtained. ~*vt* cover with a hard dry mass.

calamity *n* disaster; misfortune. **calamitous** *adj*.

calcium *n* silvery metallic element found in limestone, marble, and other rocks and in bones and teeth.

calculate *vt,vi* work out mathematically. *vt* **1** estimate; believe; suppose. **2** design; plan; intend. **calculating** *adj* ruthless; scheming. **calculation** *n*. **calculator** *n* electronic device used for mathematical calculation.

calendar *n* **1** system for determining the length of a year, order of months, etc. **2** chart showing the divisions of a year. **3** list or diary of events and engagements.

calf[1] *n, pl* **calves 1** young of cattle. **2** young seal, whale, elephant, etc.

calf[2] *n* fleshy part of the back of the lower leg.

calibre *n* **1** diameter of a gun bore, bullet, etc. **2** worth; merit.

call *vt,vi* **1** shout out in order to summon, attract attention, etc. **2** telephone; ring. *vi* *also* **call on** visit. *vt* **1** name; christen. **2** describe as; label. **3** convene (a meeting). **call for 1** fetch; collect. **2** require; demand. **call in 1** drop by on a visit. **2** request the services of (a doctor, specialist, etc.). **call off 1** cancel or postpone. **2** order to stop attacking. **call on** appeal to; request. **call out 1** summon. **2** bring out on strike. **call to mind** recall. **call up 1** con-

script. **2** reach by telephone. ~*n* **1** characteristic cry of a bird or animal. **2** shout. **3** visit. **4** telephone conversation. **5** duty; obligation. **6** demand; need. **on call** available for duty. **caller** *n*. **callbox** *n* public telephone box. **calling** *n* vocation. **call-up** *n* conscription.

callous *adj* cruelly indifferent to suffering. **callously** *adv*. **callousness** *n*.

calm *adj* **1** not excited or anxious; serene; untroubled. **2** peaceful. **3** still; hardly moving. *n* *also* **calmness** stillness; tranquillity; peace. *vt,vi* *also* **calm down** make or become calm(er); quieten; soothe. **calmly** *adv*.

calorie *n* unit of heat energy, used esp. for measuring the energy value of foods.

came *v pt* of **come**.

camel *n* long-legged largely domesticated mammal with one or two humps on its back, commonly found in desert areas of N Africa.

camera *n* **1** optical device for producing a photographic image. **2** *also* **television camera** device for converting optical images into electrical signals. **in camera** in private; not open.

camouflage *n* **1** use of certain materials as a disguise to prevent a person, military equipment, etc., from being seen by an enemy. **2** colour or markings of an animal that make it less conspicuous in a certain environment. *vt* make less noticeable by use of camouflage.

camp[1] *n* **1** site having tents, huts, etc., for use as temporary accommodation. **2** military base housing soldiers temporarily; encampment. **3** group of people with common political views. *vi* *also* **camp out** live in a tent or other temporary living accommodation. **camper** *n*. **camping** *n*.

camp[2] *adj* of a style that exaggerates or parodies what is thought to be appropriate homosexual behaviour. *n* exaggerated or effeminate style of behaviour.

campaign *n* **1** series of planned military operations. **2** technical activities designed to promote a political cause or candidate, commercial product, etc. *vi* mount a campaign; fight. **campaigner** *n*.

campus *n* area and buildings occupied by a university or college.

can[1] *v aux* (*pt* could) **1** be able or willing to; know how to. **2** have permission or opportunity to.

can[2] *n* metal container or tin. **carry the can** accept responsibility or blame. ~*vt* (-nn-) put or store in a can.

canal *n* **1** man-made waterway or channel for navigation, irrigation, etc. **2** passage or duct in the body.

canary *n* small yellow songbird of the finch family.

cancel *vt* (-ll-) **1** prevent (a planned event) from taking place; call off. **2** stop; discontinue. **3** make invalid by crossing through or stamping with a special mark. **cancel out** offset; compensate (for). **cancellation** *n*.

cancer *n* malignant growth or tumour in the body. **Cancer** fourth sign of the zodiac represented by the crab.

candid *adj* honest; frank; open; fair. **candidly** *adv*. **candour** *n*.

candidate *n* **1** person nominated or applying for a particular office, job, or position. **2** person sitting an examination.

candle *n* cylinder of wax with a central wick, which burns slowly when lit. **burn the candle at both ends** exhaust oneself by living strenuously.

cane *n* **1** pliant hollow stem of the bamboo or various palms, often used for making furniture. **2** sugar cane. **3** thorny stem of a raspberry or blackberry bush. **4** thin rod used as a walking stick or as an implement for inflicting punishment. *vt,vi* punish by beating with a cane.

canine *adj* **1** of the dog family. **2** like a dog.

canister *n* cylindrical metal storage container; can.

cannabis *n* **1** hemp plant. **2** marijuana.

cannibal *n* **1** person who eats human flesh. **2** animal that feeds on its own kind. **cannibalism** *n*. **cannibalize** *vt* take parts from (motor vehicles, etc.) to repair others.

cannon *n, pl* **cannons** *or* **cannon** heavy mounted gun that discharges large shells. *v* **cannon into** collide with; barge into.

cannot *v aux* **1** be unable or unwilling to. **2** be forbidden or have no opportunity to.

canoe *n* small narrow portable boat propelled with a paddle. *vi* travel or transport by canoe.

canon *n* **1** ecclesiastical law. **2** list of Christian saints. **3** priest attached to a cathedral or various religious orders. **4** moral principle; standard; criterion. **5** musical form in which the same melody is introduced at overlapping intervals by two or more voices. **canonical** *adj*. **canonize** *vt* recognize officially as a saint.

canopy *n* ornamental awning suspended above a throne, bed, etc.

canteen *n* **1** restaurant for the use of employees of a company, children at school, etc. **2** box of cutlery. **3** flask carried by soldiers, campers, etc.

canter *n* gait of a horse between a trot and a gallop. *vi,vt* move or take at a canter.

canvas *n* **1** hard-wearing waterproof material of flax or hemp. **2** piece of such material used for painting on in oils.

canvass *vi,vt* seek support or opinions from (potential voters, customers, etc.). **canvasser** *n*.

canyon *n* deep narrow valley or gorge; ravine.

cap *n* **1** flat closely fitting hat, sometimes with a peak. **2** small lid or cover. **3** natural or artificial covering of a tooth. **4** *also* **dutch cap** diaphragm used as a contraceptive device. *vt* (-pp-) **1** cover the top or surface of. **2** outdo; top. **to cap it all** in addition; on top; as a finishing touch.

capable *adj* **1** having the potential or capacity for. **2** able; competent. **capability** *n*. **capably** *adv*.

capacity *n* **1** power to contain a quantity. **2** amount that a container can hold; volume. **3** maximum number that can be accommodated. **4** ability to perform or behave in a particular way. **5** power or function of an office or rank.

cape[1] *n* short cloak.

cape[2] *n* headland.

capital *n* **1** city that is the seat of government of a country. **2** wealth or assets, esp. when used for investment or profit. **3** *also* **capital letter** large or upper case form of a written or printed letter of the alphabet. *adj* **1** *inf* excellent; first-class. **2** carrying the penalty of death. **capitalism** *n* economic system whereby private owners control the means of production and distribution. **capitalist** *adj,n.* **capitalize** *vt* **1** use, provide, or convert into capital. **2** write or print in capital letters. **capitalize on** exploit; take advantage of.

caprice (kə'pri:s) *n* whim. **capricious** (kə'prifəs) *adj* subject to or indicative of whim; changeable.

Capricorn *n* tenth sign of the zodiac, represented by the goat.

capsicum *n* tropical plant bearing edible fruit (peppers).

capsize *vi,vt* overturn; upset.

capsule *n* **1** soluble shell enclosing a dose of oral medicine. **2** pressurized compartment of a space vehicle. **3** closed structure containing seeds, spores, or fruits. **capsular** *adj.*

captain *n* **1** person in charge of a vessel or aircraft. **2** naval officer ranking above a commander and below a rear admiral. **3** army officer ranking above a lieutenant and below a major. **4** leader of a sports team. *vt* act as captain of. **captaincy** *n.*

caption *n* **1** brief description accompanying an illustration. **2** heading or title; headline; subtitle. *vt* provide with a caption.

capture *vt* **1** take prisoner. **2** gain control or possession of. *n* act of capturing. **captivate** *vt* fascinate; charm; enchant. **captivation** *n.* **captive** *n* prisoner. *adj* **1** imprisoned. **2** restrained; confined. **captivity** *n.*

car *n* **1** small wheeled vehicle for personal transport. **2** vehicle containing passengers, such as a railway carriage.

carafe (kə'ræf, 'kærəf) *n* decorative bottle used for serving wine or water at the table.

caramel *n* **1** burnt sugar used for flavouring and colouring. **2** chewy kind of toffee.

carat *n* **1** measure of the purity of gold in an alloy. **2** measure of weight of precious stones, esp. diamonds.

caravan *n* **1** covered vehicle equipped for living in and capable of being drawn by a car, horse, etc. **2** company of travellers in desert regions. *vi* (-nn-) travel by caravan.

caraway *n* Eurasian plant whose aromatic fruits (caraway seeds) are used in cooking.

carbohydrate *n* organic compound, such as starch or sugar, containing carbon, hydrogen, and oxygen.

carbon *n* **1** widely distributed nonmetallic element occurring as diamond, graphite, or charcoal and forming many organic and inorganic compounds. **2** *also* **carbon paper** *n* paper coated on one side with a dark pigment, used to duplicate writing or typing. **carbon dioxide** *n* colourless incombustible gas present in the atmosphere, formed during respiration and the combustion of organic compounds.

carburettor *n* part of a petrol engine where the fuel is mixed with air.

carcass *n* dead body, esp. of an animal sold for food.

card *n* **1** piece of stiff paper used for filing, as proof of identity or membership, advertising, etc. **2** similar piece of paper, often illustrated, used for sending greetings, congratulations, etc. **3** any of a set of cardboard pieces, marked with symbols, used for playing games or telling fortunes. **a card up one's sleeve** thing or action kept in reserve to be used to gain an advantage. **on the cards** probable; likely. **put one's cards on the table** *or* **show one's cards** reveal one's intentions, plans, etc. **cardboard** *n* thin stiff board made of paper pulp.

cardigan *n* close-fitting woollen jacket.

cardinal *n* senior dignitary of the Roman Catholic Church, ranking next below the Pope. *adj* of prime importance; fundamental. **cardinal number** *n* number denoting quantity rather than order. **cardinal point** *n* one of the points of the compass, N, S, E, or W.

care *n* **1** solicitous attention. **2** caution. **3** supervision; charge; responsibility. **4** anxiety; trouble; worry. **care of** at the address of. ~*vi* feel interest or concern. **care for 1** feel affection for. **2** look after; tend. **3** wish for; want. **carefree** *adj* free from worry, anxiety, and responsibility. **careful** *adj* **1** cautious; wary. **2** meticulous; painstaking. **carefully** *adv.* **careless** *adj* **1** lacking sufficient thought or attention; negligent. **2** unconcerned; indifferent. **carelessly** *adv.* **carelessness** *n.* **caretaker** *n* person employed to look after and maintain a school, office, etc.

career n 1 pursuit of a profession or occupation. 2 course; progression. vi move rapidly, esp. in an uncontrolled way; hurtle.

caress n light gentle stroke of affection. vt stroke gently and affectionately; fondle.

cargo n goods carried in a ship or aircraft; freight; load.

caricature n satirical representation of a person that grossly exaggerates particular characteristics. vt represent as a caricature.

carnal adj sensual; not spiritual; of the flesh. **carnal knowledge** n sexual intercourse. **carnally** adv.

carnation n cultivated flower having fragrant pink, white, or red blooms.

carnival n public celebration, festivities, and revelry, esp. just before Lent.

carnivorous adj meat-eating. **carnivore** n meat-eating animal, esp. a mammal.

carol n joyous song, esp. to celebrate Christmas. vi (-ll-) sing joyfully.

carpenter n person skilled in using wood in building, making furniture, etc. vi,vt work as a carpenter. **carpentry** n.

carpet n 1 thick textile floor covering. 2 thick layer or covering. vt cover with or as if with a carpet.

carriage n 1 horse-drawn four-wheeled vehicle. 2 section of a train, often comprising several compartments. 3 movable gun-support. 4 part of a typewriter holding and moving paper. 5 deportment; bearing. **carriageway** n road, or part of a road, used by vehicles.

carrot n plant whose long orange root is eaten as a vegetable. **carroty** adj orange.

carry vt,vi take (something) from one place to another; transport; transmit; convey. vt 1 hold; bear; keep. 2 contain; include. 3 sustain; keep in operation. 4 influence. **carry oneself** conduct oneself; behave. **carry on** continue; persevere. **carrier** n 1 person or thing that carries. 2 also **carrier-bag** large paper or polythene bag with handles. 3 person or animal carrying disease.

cart n strong two-wheeled open vehicle used by farmers, tradesmen, etc. vt,vi 1 transport in a cart. 2 inf carry with difficulty.

cartilage n strong flexible tissue often developing into bone; gristle. **cartilaginous** adj.

carton n small light container, esp. of cardboard.

cartoon n 1 simple humorous or satirical drawing. 2 animated film. 3 sketch made in preparation for a painting, tapestry, etc. **cartoonist** n.

cartridge n 1 small cylindrical case containing explosives, a bullet, or shot. 2 large type of cassette for a tape recorder. 3 film cassette. 4 device fitted to the pickup arm on a gramophone that contains the stylus. 5 removable container filled with ink for a fountain pen. **cartridge paper** n strong white paper for drawing.

carve vi,vt 1 shape with a knife, chisel, etc. 2 cut (meat) into pieces or slices. **carve up** 1 inf injure by an attack with a knife. 2 sl endanger by aggressive driving. **carver** n. **carving** n 1 act of carving. 2 artefact carved from wood, stone, etc.

cascade n 1 waterfall. 2 something that falls in folds or drapes. vi fall like a cascade.

case[1] n box, container, or protective outer covering.

case[2] 1 instance; circumstance; example. 2 instance of a medical condition. 3 legal suit, or grounds for suit. 4 patient or client dealt with by a doctor, social worker, lawyer, etc. 5 grammatical relationship of a noun, pronoun, or adjective to other parts of a sentence, sometimes shown by inflectional endings. **in case** in the event that. **in any case** whatever happens.

cash n money, esp. in the form of notes and coins. vt convert into cash. **cash in on** inf profit from; exploit.

cashier[1] n person employed to receive and pay out cash in a bank, shop, etc.

cashier[2] vt discharge dishonourably from the army.

cashmere n very fine soft woven hair of the Kashmir goat.

casino n building equipped for gambling.

casket n small box or case, esp. for jewels.

casserole n 1 heavy pan or dish for long slow cooking. 2 meal cooked in a casserole. vt cook in a casserole.

cassette n sealed container holding spools of film, magnetic tape, etc., for use in a camera, tape-recorder, etc.

cassock n long black tunic worn by various members of the clergy.

cast vt (cast) 1 throw; hurl; fling. 2 discard; shed; drop. 3 project; direct. 4 make (a vote). 5 allocate (parts) for a play. 6 make (shape of metal, glass, etc.) by pouring into a mould. **cast off** discard; throw away; reject. **castoff** n discarded thing or person. **cast on/off** form the first/last row of stitches of a piece of knitting. ~n 1 all the actors in a play. 2 throw, as of dice. 3 mould. 4 casing for a broken bone. 5 slight squint.

castanets pl n pair of hollow shells of hard wood or ivory held in the hand and clicked together to accompany music and dancing.

caste n 1 one of four hereditary social divisions in Hindu society. 2 social class.

castle n 1 large fortified building functioning as a fortress or stronghold. 2 (in chess) rook. **castellated** adj having battlements, turrets, etc., as a castle.

castrate vt remove the testicles of. **castration** n.

casual adj 1 accidental; not planned; chance. 2 informal. 3 not regular; temporary. **casually** adv.

casualty n victim of a serious accident, battle, etc.

cat n 1 small domestic animal, kept esp. as a pet. 2 feline mammal, such as the lion, tiger, or leopard. **cat's eye** n glass stud set into the road surface to mark traffic lanes as a guide to motorists at night.

catalogue n comprehensive orderly list of books in a library, goods for sale, etc. vt list or insert in a catalogue.

catapult n 1 device for hurling small rocks and stones. 2 equipment for launching aircraft from ships, etc. vt throw or hurl as from a catapult.

cataract n 1 powerful waterfall. 2 heavy rainstorm or flood. 3 eye disorder in which the lens becomes opaque.

catarrh n inflammation of a mucous membrane in the nose or throat, as during a cold.

catastrophe n major disaster; calamity. **catastrophic** adj. **catastrophically** adv.

catch v (caught) vt 1 grasp (something that has been thrown or is falling). 2 capture; seize. 3 discover by surprise; detect. 4 board or take (a train, bus, etc.). 5 hear or grasp the meaning of. 6 contract (an infection or disease). 7 strike; hit. 8 portray accurately or convincingly. 9 make contact with; find. 10 deceive; swindle. vi,vt 1 ignite or become ignited by. 2 become tangled (with) or hooked up (on). **catch on** 1 learn or grasp. 2 become fashionable. **catch up** 1 reach or get level after following. 2 make up (arrears, a backlog, etc.). ~n 1 act of catching. 2 something caught. 3 device for fastening. 4 inf difficulty; snag. 5 inf highly eligible person. 6 ball game. **catchy** adj inf (esp. of a tune) easy to remember or imitate.

catechism n religious instruction, esp. in a dialogue form.

category n class; group; division. **categorical** adj absolutely; definite; explicit. **categorically** adv. **categorize** vt place in a category; classify.

cater vi provide food, entertainment, etc. **cater for** supply whatever is necessary. **caterer** n.

caterpillar n 1 larva of a moth, butterfly, etc. 2 continuous band of steel plates fitted instead of wheels to a vehicle such as a tractor or tank.

cathedral n principal church in a diocese.

catholic adj widespread; liberal; of general interest. **Catholic** adj, n Roman Catholic. **Catholicism** n.

catkin n cluster of small flowers of the willow, hazel, etc., resembling a cat's tail.

cattle pl n cows, bulls, etc., collectively.

catty adj inf spiteful.

caught v pt and pp of **catch**.

cauliflower n variety of cabbage cultivated for its large edible white flower head.

cause n 1 something that produces an effect. 2 motive; grounds; reason. 3 general aim or set of ideals for which a person or group campaigns. vt be the cause of; bring about; make happen. **causal** adj. **causation** or **causality** n.

causeway n raised road or path over treacherous ground, water, etc.

caustic adj 1 burning or corrosive. 2 cutting; sarcastic. n substance that corrodes or burns. **caustic soda** n sodium hydroxide.

caution *n* **1** prudence; care; watchfulness. **2** warning. *vt* warn; advise caution. **cautionary** *adj* advising caution; intended as a warning. **cautious** *adj* careful; prudent; wary. **cautiously** *adv.*

cavalry *n* unit of troops, originally mounted on horseback but now equipped with armoured cars, tanks, etc.

cave hollow area in a rock or under a cliff. *vt* hollow out. **cave in** collapse; give way; subside. **cavern** *n* large underground cave. **cavernous** *adj.*

caviar *n* salted roe of the sturgeon, eaten as a delicacy.

cavity *n* **1** hollow space. **2** hollow part of a tooth caused by decay.

cayenne *n* hot red pepper produced from capsicum seeds.

cease *vt,vi* stop; end; discontinue; finish. *n* **without cease** endlessly; continuously. **ceasefire** *n* truce, esp. a temporary one. **ceaseless** *adj* incessant; endless.

cedar *n* large coniferous evergreen tree with hard sweet-smelling wood.

cede *vt,vi* concede or yield territory, rights, etc.

ceiling *n* **1** upper surface of a room. **2** upper limit of prices, wages, etc.

celebrate *vt* **1** mark or honour with festivity and rejoicing. **2** officiate at a religious or public ceremony. *vi* rejoice; make merry. **celebrated** *adj* famous. **celebrity** *n* **1** well-known or famous person. **2** fame; renown; notoriety.

celery *n* vegetable grown for its long greenish-white edible stalks.

celestial *adj* heavenly; of the sky.

celibate *adj* **1** unmarried. **2** abstaining from sexual intercourse. *n* person who is celibate,-esp. one who has taken religious vows. **celibacy** *n.*

cell *n* **1** independent unit of an organism. **2** small room occupied by a monk, prisoner, etc. **3** device producing or storing electric current by chemical action. **4** small group working within a larger political or religious movement. **cellular** *adj.*

cellar *n* **1** underground room, used esp. for storage. **2** store of wine.

cello *n* musical instrument of the violin family, held between the knees when played. **cellist** *n.*

Cellophane *n Tdmk* thin transparent packaging material.

Celluloid *n Tdmk* inflammable material made from cellulose nitrate and camphor, used esp. as a coating for film.

cellulose *n* carbohydrate forming walls of plant cells.

cement *n* **1** substance made from limestone and clay mixed with water that hardens to form concrete. **2** substance used to fill cavities of the teeth. *vt* **1** join or spread with cement. **2** unite; bind together; strengthen.

cemetery *n* burial ground, esp. one not attached to a church.

censor *n* person authorized to examine and ban material in films, books, letters, etc., considered to be harmful, dangerous, or immoral. *vt* act as a censor of. **censorship** *n.* **censorious** *adj* critical; harsh.

censure *n* disapproval; blame; harsh criticism. *vt* reprimand; criticize; blame.

census *n* official population count.

cent *n* **1** US coin equivalent to one hundredth of a dollar. **2** coin of various other countries. **per cent** by the hundred; in a hundred. **hundred per cent** complete; absolute; total.

centenary *n* hundredth anniversary. *adj* relating to a period of a hundred years.

centigrade *adj* relating to a temperature scale on which the freezing point of water is 0° and its boiling point 100°.

centime *n* **1** French coin equivalent to one hundredth of a franc. **2** coin of various other countries.

centimetre *n* one hundredth of a metre.

centipede *n* small crawling animal having a body made up of several segments, each segment bearing a pair of legs.

central *adj* **1** of the centre. **2** principal; most important. **central heating** *n* system of heating a building with radiators, air vents, etc., connected to a central source. **centralize** *vt* **1** bring to a central point. **2** unite (several duties, powers, etc.) under one central authority. *vi* come to a central point. **centralization** *n.*

centre *n* **1** middle point of a circle, line, sphere, etc. **2** main point or focus of interest, attention, administration, importance, etc. *vt,vi* be concentrated (on); have a centre at or in. **centre-forward** *n* player in football, hockey, etc., positioned at the centre of the front line. **centre-half** *n, pl* **-halves** player in football, hockey, etc., positioned at the centre of the defence line.

century *n* 1 one hundred years. 2 one of the periods of a hundred years numbered before and since the birth of Christ. 3 score of a hundred runs in cricket.

ceramics *n* art of making pottery from clay, porcelain, etc. **ceramic** *adj, n.*

cereal *n* 1 crop yielding edible grain. 2 breakfast dish made from cereals.

ceremony *n* 1 formal or public act, religious rite, etc. 2 formal politeness. **stand (up)on ceremony** insist on exaggerated politeness or formality. **ceremonial** *adj* ritual; formal; pertaining to ceremony. *n* prescribed form of ceremonies; ritual. **ceremonially** *adv.* **ceremonious** *adj* elaborately correct, dignified, or precise. **ceremoniously** *adv.*

certain *adj* 1 sure; convinced; positive. 2 definite; inevitable. 3 indicating someone or something specific but unnamed. **certainly** *adv.* **certainty** *n.*

certificate *n* written declaration of a fact, such as success in an examination, ownership of shares, public status, etc. **certify** *vt* 1 declare; authorize; guarantee; endorse. 2 declare officially to be insane.

cervix *n, pl* **cervixes** *or* **cervices** ('sɜːvɪsiːz) 1 lower part of the uterus. 2 neck. **cervical** *adj.*

chafe *vt, vi* rub until sore or roughened. *n* soreness.

chaffinch *n* small European songbird of the finch family.

chain *n* 1 flexible line of connected metal links. 2 range of mountains. 3 series of connected events. *vt* fasten or restrict with or as with a chain. **chain reaction** 1 chemical or nuclear process in which the product of each step initiates the next step. 2 series of rapid interconnected events. **chain-smoke** *vi* smoke continuously, esp. by lighting one cigarette from the stub of the last. **chainsmoker** *n.* **chain-store** *n* one of a number of shops owned and managed by the same organization.

chair *n* 1 movable seat usually with four legs and a back, for one person. 2 seat of dignity or authority. 3 chairmanship. 4 profes-

sorship. *vt* preside over; act as chairman of. **chairman** *n, pl* **-men** 1 principal director of a company. 2 person presiding over a meeting, committee, etc. **chairmanship** *n.*

chalet *n* 1 wooden Swiss house with a steep overhanging roof. 2 house or bungalow built in this style, esp. for holidays.

chalk *n* 1 soft white rock consisting of calcium carbonate. 2 piece of chalk or similar material used for writing or drawing. *vt, vi* write or treat with chalk.

challenge *vt* 1 invite to a duel or other contest. 2 defy; dispute; call for an answer to. *n* 1 summons to a contest. 2 questioning of right; calling to account.

chamber *n* 1 room, esp a bedroom. 2 meeting hall. 3 enclosed cavity. **chambers** *pl* barrister's or judge's conference rooms. **chambermaid** *n* hotel maid in charge of bedrooms. **chamber music** *n* music written for a small ensemble of solo instruments.

chamberlain *n* 1 officer managing a royal household. 2 high-ranking Court official.

chameleon (kə'miːliən) *n* type of lizard capable of changing its skin colour to match its surroundings.

champagne *n* type of sparkling French wine.

champion *n* 1 winner; victor; person excelling all others. 2 upholder of a cause. *adj* excellent. *vt* defend; stand up for. **championship** *n* 1 competition or series of contests to find a champion. 2 status or conduct of a champion.

chance *n* 1 unexpected or inexplicable event. 2 risk. 3 possibility; opportunity. **by chance** accidentally; fortuitously. ~*adj* fortuitous; accidental. *vi, vt* 1 happen (to). 2 risk; dare.

chancel *n* eastern part of a church near the altar, reserved for the clergy and choir.

chancellor *n* 1 chief minister or other high official. 2 titular head of a university. **Chancellor of the Exchequer** *n* principal government finance minister.

chandelier *n* decorative branched fitting that hangs from a ceiling and supports a number of lights.

change *n* 1 substitution of one thing for another; alteration; variance. 2 money returned as balance for payment; coins of small value. *vt* 1 alter; substitute; make different. **2** give coins of smaller denomination in exchange for a larger coin or note. *vi* become different. *vt,vi* **1** put on (different clothes). **2** board (another train, bus, etc.). **changeable** *adj.*

channel *n* **1** navigable part of a harbour, river bed, etc. **2** comparatively narrow stretch of sea. **3** radio or television waveband. **4** tube; passage; groove. **5** means of communication, commerce, etc. *vt* (-ll-) **1** provide, use, or supply through a channel. **2** direct; find an outlet for.

chant *n* song, esp. intoned sacred music. *vt,vi* **1** sing, esp. in monotone. **2** recite.

chaos *n* disorder; confusion. **chaotic** *adj.*

chap[1] *vt,vi* (-pp-) (of skin) roughen and crack through excessive cold, etc.

chap[2] *n inf* man; fellow.

chapel *n* **1** small subordinate church often attached to a college, institution, etc. **2** small part of a larger church containing a separate altar. **3** association of printers or journalists.

chaplain *n* clergyman attached to a particular household, institution, unit of soldiers, etc.

chapter *n* **1** one of the principal divisions of a book. **2** governing body of a cathedral.

char[1] *vt,vi* (-rr-) scorch; singe; blacken; burn.

char[2] *n also* **charwoman** *or* **charlady** *inf* person employed to do housework. *vi* (-rr-) do rough housework.

character *n* **1** sum of particular qualities distinguishing an individual. **2** personality created by a writer. **3** distinguishing feature, mark, handwriting, etc. **4** eccentric or amusing person. **characteristic** *adj* distinctive; typical. *n* distinctive quality or trait. **characteristically** *adv.* **characterize** *vt* **1** distinguish (by); typify. **2** portray; describe. **characterization** *n.*

charcoal *n* carbon made from burnt wood, coal, etc.

charge *n* **1** price; liability to pay. **2** accusation. **3** responsibility; duty. **4** quantity, esp. of explosive, with which anything is loaded. **5** property of matter responsible for electrical phenomena and having two forms, positive and negative, which cause mutual attraction. **6** sudden attacking rush. **in charge of** with responsibility for. ~*vt,vi* **1** demand as a price. **2** rush aggressively

towards. *vt* **1** accuse. **2** burden. **3** load; fill up. **4** supply (with electricity). **charge-hand** *n* workman or assistant in charge of others; foreman.

chariot *n* two-wheeled horse-drawn vehicle formerly used for races and battle. **charioteer** *n.*

charisma *n* spiritual quality inspiring great devotion and trust. **charismatic** *adj.*

charity *n* **1** quality of love, kindness, or generosity; compassion. **2** institution or organization founded for the benefit of others. **charitable** *adj* **1** kind; lenient; generous. **2** of a recognized charity.

charm *n* **1** ability to fascinate and delight by personal qualities. **2** magic spell, act, trinket, etc., thought to bring good fortune. *vt,vi* **1** attract; delight; enthrall. **2** enchant by magic. **charming** *adj* delightful.

chart *n* graph, plan, or map. *vt* record progress by means of a chart.

charter *n* document granting a right, establishing a university, etc. *vt* **1** establish by charter. **2** let or hire, esp. a ship or aircraft. **chartered** *adj* qualified according to established rules.

chase *vt* hunt; pursue; run after; drive away. *n* pursuit; hunt.

chasm ('kæzəm) *n* deep gulf or inlet; abyss.

chassis ('ʃæsi) *n, pl* **chassis** basic frame, esp. of a motor car, on which other parts are mounted.

chaste *adj* pure or virtuous, esp. sexually. **chastity** *n.*

chastise *vt* punish, esp. by beating. **chastisement** *n.*

chat *vi* (-tt-) talk in a friendly informal way. *n* easy informal conversation. **chatty** *adj inf* talkative.

chatter *vi* **1** talk rapidly and thoughtlessly. **2** (of monkeys, birds, etc.) make an excited rapid rattling noise. *n* **1** idle talk; gossip. **2** rattling noise. **chatterbox** *n inf* talkative person.

chauffeur ('ʃoufə) *n* person employed to drive another's car; driver. *vt* act as chauffeur for.

chauvinism ('ʃouvinizəm) *n* excessive aggressive patriotism. **male chauvinism** belief of men in their superiority over women. **chauvinist** *n,adj.*

cheap *adj* **1** inexpensive; low in price. **2** inferior; vulgar; shoddy. **cheaply** *adv.* **cheapness** *n.* **cheapen** *vt,vi* decrease in price or quality.

cheat *vt* defraud; swindle; trick. *vi* attempt to succeed by dishonest means. *n* person who cheats; fraud.

check *vt* **1** restrain; hinder; halt. **2** verify; test the truth of; inspect. *n* **1** obstruction; hindrance. **2** supervision; careful watch; verification. **3** move in chess threatening the opponent's King. **4** pattern of squares. **5** *US* bill; account; cheque. **checkmate** *n* stage in chess where a threat to the King cannot be countered. *vt* defeat at checkmate. **checkpoint** *n* place where traffic is halted and inspected by police, etc. **check-up** *n* careful detailed examination, esp. for medical purposes.

cheek *n* **1** side of the face below the eye. **2** *inf* impudence; rudeness; impertinence. *vt inf* speak impertinently to. **cheeky** *adj inf* impudent; saucy. **cheekily** *adv.* **cheekiness** *n.* **cheekbone** *n* bone of the face just below the eye.

cheer *n* **1** shout of approval or joy. **2** entertainment; comfort. **3** disposition; attitude. *vt* comfort; encourage. *vi,vt* shout with joy or approval. **cheer up** become more cheerful. **cheerful** *adj* happy; jovial; lively. **cheerfully** *adv.* **cheerfulness** *n.*

cheese *n* protein-rich food of many varieties made from the curd of milk.

cheetah *n* swift-running member of the cat family, resembling a leopard.

chef *n* master cook.

chemical *adj* pertaining to chemistry. *n* substance made by or used in chemical processes. **chemist** *n* **1** one qualified to sell drugs and medicine. **2** researcher or student of chemistry. **chemistry** *n* science concerned with the properties and interactions of elements and compounds.

cheque *n* signed order, written generally on a printed form, to a bank to pay out money from a customer's account.

chequer *n* pattern of squares. **chequered** *adj* **1** variegated; diversified in colour. **2** marked by fluctuations in fortune, nature, etc.

cherish *vt* protect; preserve; hold dear; nurture.

cherry *n* small red or yellow stone fruit.

cherub *n* one of the orders of angels, generally depicted as a plump winged child.

chess *n* game of skill for two players using thirty-two pieces (chessmen) on a board with sixty-four black and white squares.

chest *n* **1** upper front part of the body. **2** large strong box. **chest of drawers** *n* piece of furniture fitted with a set of drawers, used esp. for storing clothes or linen.

chestnut *n* **1** deciduous tree (sweet-chestnut, bearing edible nut, or hor ϵ-chestnut, bearing inedible nut). **2** fruit of these trees. **3** dark reddish-brown horse. *n,adj* dark reddish-brown.

chew *vt,vi* grind between the teeth. **chew over** wonder; ruminate. $\sim n$ act of chewing. **chewing gum** *n* sweetened flavoured preparation of resin or gum for chewing.

chick *n* **1** young bird, esp. a chicken. **2** *sl* girl.

chicken *n* **1** fowl reared for its eggs and meat. **2** *inf* young person. *adj sl* cowardly. **chicken-pox** *n* mild infectious disease usually contracted by children, characterized by a blistery rash.

chicory *n* plant whose leaves are used in salads and whose root is ground to flavour coffee.

chief *adj* main; major; most important; principal. *n* **1** leader; superior head of a department, organization, etc. **2** *also* **chieftain** leader of a tribe or clan. **chiefly** *adv* mainly; principally.

chilblain *n* painful itchy red swelling on the hands and feet caused by extreme cold, bad circulation, etc.

child *n* **1** young person; infant; boy or girl. **2** son or daughter. **childbirth** *n* act of giving birth to a child. **childhood** *n* state or period of being a child. **childish** *adj* immature; foolish; naive. **childishly** *adv.* **childlike** *adj* trusting or innocent like a child.

chill *n* **1** coldness. **2** slight cold preceding fever. **3** discouraging influence. *vt,vi* make or become cold or cool. **chilly** *adj* **1** slightly cold; cool. **2** unfriendly.

chilli *n* pod of a capsicum, often dried and ground into the hot pungent spice, Cayenne pepper.

chime *n* melodious sound as of bells, esp. when ringing in sequence. *vt,vi* 1 ring musically. 2 agree; concur.

chimney *n* construction allowing smoke to escape from a fireplace, furnace, etc.

chimpanzee *n* small African ape.

chin *n* part of the face below the mouth.

china *n* crockery, esp. made of fine porcelain.

chink[1] *n* crevice; narrow opening; slit.

chink[2] *n* sharp clinking sound, as of coins or glasses struck together. *vi* clink; jingle.

chip *n* 1 small fragment or splinter of glass, wood, etc. 2 small oblong piece of deep-fried potato. 3 small crack or missing piece in china, glass, etc. 4 counter or token used in gambling games. **have a chip on one's shoulder** bear a grudge. ~*vt* (-pp-) 1 crack or break a small piece from. 2 cut (potatoes) into oblongs. 3 carve with a small tool. **chip in** contribute.

chiropody *n* treatment of minor foot disorders. **chiropodist** *n*.

chirp *vi* make the short shrill cry of a bird. *n* chirping sound. **chirpy** *adj inf* lively and cheerful.

chisel *n* steel cutting tool with wedge-shaped edge used in carpentry, masonry, etc. *vi,vt* (-ll-) cut or shape with a chisel.

chivalry *n* 1 courtesy or protectiveness, esp. as shown by men to women. 2 code of behaviour of medieval knights. **chivalrous** *adj*.

chive *n* small plant of the onion family whose leaves are used as a seasoning in cooking.

chlorine *n* greenish-yellow poisonous corrosive gaseous element, used as a disinfectant and bleach.

chlorophyll *n* green colouring matter present in plants, necessary for photosynthesis.

chocolate *n* preparation of cocoa mixed with sugar, milk, etc., eaten as a sweet, used for flavouring, etc. *adj,n* dark brown.

choice *n* 1 act of choosing. 2 variety to choose from. 3 thing chosen. *adj* of excellent quality; selected.

choir *n* 1 body of singers performing in public, esp. in a church. 2 part of a church or cathedral reserved for singers, above the nave and below the altar. **chorister** *n* member of a church choir.

choke *vt* 1 throttle or obstruct the breathing of; suffocate. 2 block; obstruct. *vi* 1 become choked. 2 become speechless through emotion. *n* 1 action or sound of choking. 2 valve controlling air supply, as in a carburettor.

cholera *n* highly infectious, often fatal disease characterized by feverish vomiting and diarrhoea.

choose *vt* select or take something in preference to something else. *vi* decide; determine.

chop[1] *vt* (-pp-) 1 cut with sharp blows. 2 cut into small pieces. *n* 1 act of chopping. 2 slice of pork or lamb containing part of a rib. **chopper** *n* axe or hatchet.

chop[2] *vi* (-pp-) make a sudden change of direction or attitude. **chop and change** change or alter repeatedly.

chopstick *n* one of a pair of small sticks used, esp. in the Far East, as an implement for eating.

choral *adj* written for or sung by a choir or chorus.

chord *n* 1 simultaneous sounding of several notes in music. 2 string of a musical instrument. 3 straight line linking two points on a curve.

chore *n* routine or repetitive task, esp. housework.

choreography *n* art of dance composition and notation. **choreographer** *n*.

chorus *n* 1 group of performers speaking, singing, or dancing together, esp. as separate from the action of a drama. 2 combined speech or song, esp. the refrain of a ballad, etc. *vt,vi* speak or sing as a group.

chose *v pt* of **choose**.

chosen *v pp* of **choose**.

Christ *n* title given to Jesus acknowledging him to be the Saviour foretold in the Old Testament.

christen *vt* give a name to, esp. at a Christian baptismal service. **christening** *n* ceremony of baptizing and naming a child in a church.

Christian *n* one professing to follow the teaching of Christ. *adj* 1 believing in Christ. 2 charitable; forgiving; unselfish. 3 of or pertaining to Christ. **Christian name** *n* personal name, esp. as given at a christening.

Christianity *n* Christian faith, teaching, spirit, or way of life.

Christmas *n* celebration of the birth of Christ. **Christmas Day** December 25th.

chromatic *adj* **1** concerned with or having colours. **2** relating to a musical scale consisting of semitones.

chrome *n* chromium.

chromium *n* silvery-white metallic element used for highly polished coatings on other metals.

chromosome *n* small rod-like body found in living cells, responsible for the transmission of genetic information.

chronic *adj* **1** (esp. of a disease) of a long-standing or constantly recurring nature. **2** *inf* dreadful; tedious; objectionable. **chronically** *adv.*

chronological *adj* in order of time; according to time of occurrence. **chronologically** *adv.* **chronology** *n.*

chrysalis *n* pupa or insect larva, esp. enclosed in a sheath during its resting stage.

chrysanthemum *n* autumn-flowering garden plant with large blooms.

chubby *adj* plump and round-faced. **chubbiness** *n.*

chuck *vt,vi inf* **1** throw; toss. **2** give up. **chuck out 1** throw away or out. **2** eject forcibly.

chuckle *n* quiet burbling laugh. *vi* laugh quietly.

chunk *n* thick piece or portion. **chunky** *adj* thick and bulky.

church *n* **1** whole body of Christians or of one of the Christian denominations. **2** building used for Christian or other religious services. **3** the clergy. **churchyard** *n* burial ground surrounding a church.

churn *n* **1** vessel used for converting milk or cream into butter. **2** large cylindrical container used for transporting milk. *vt,vi* rotate or agitate vigorously, as in a churn. **churn out** produce rapidly and in great quantity.

chute *n* **1** sloping track or passage down which water, rubbish, laundry, etc., may be shot. **2** narrow waterfall.

chutney *n* sweet spicy relish made from pickled fruit and vegetables.

cider *n* drink made from pressed fermented apples.

cigar *n* roll of tobacco leaves for smoking.

cigarette *n* shredded tobacco leaves rolled in thin paper for smoking.

cinder *n* piece of burnt or charred wood, coal, etc.

cinecamera *n* camera used for taking motion pictures.

cinema *n* **1** the film industry. **2** building in which films are shown.

cinnamon *n* sweet pungent spice made from the bark of a type of laurel.

circle *n* **1** plane figure bounded by an unbroken line, which is at every point the same distance from the centre. **2** ring. **3** group of people with a common interest. **4** gallery in a theatre. *vt,vi* move round in a circle.

circuit *n* **1** circular path; distance or way round. **2** journey taken regularly through a specific area, esp. by a judge or barrister in performance of professional duties. **3** path of an electric current. **circuitous** *adj* roundabout.

circular *adj* **1** relating to a circle. **2** round. **circulate** *vi,vt* move or pass around. **circulation** *n* **1** act of moving or passing around. **2** movement of blood through veins and arteries. **3** distribution or sale of newspapers, magazines, etc.

circumcise *vt* cut off the foreskin. **circumcision** *n.*

circumference *n* outer rim of a circle.

circumscribe *vt* **1** restrict or contain within certain limits. **2** draw a line around.

circumstance *n* incident; fact; detail. **circumstances** *n pl* **1** facts attendant on or relating to others; condition; state. **2** financial position. **circumstantial** *adj* **1** of or derived from circumstances. **2** fully detailed.

circus *n* **1** group of travelling entertainers, clowns, acrobats, performing animals, etc. **2** arena or amphitheatre. **3** place where several roads converge.

cistern *n* water tank, esp. supplying water to a lavatory.

cite *vt* **1** quote as an example or authority. **2** summon to appear in court. **citation** *n* **1** quotation. **2** summons. **3** mention, esp. for bravery, in military dispatches.

citizen *n* **1** resident of a city. **2** member of a state. **citizenship** *n.* **Citizens' Band** *n* (often **CB**) range of radio frequencies assigned for use by members of the public.

citrus *n* genus of fruit trees including orange, lemon, and lime.

city *n* large or important town, esp. containing a cathedral. **the City** financial centre of London.

civic *adj* of a city or local community. **civics** *pl n* science of government, esp. local government.

civil *adj* 1 courteous; polite. 2 of a citizen or the community. 3 not military. 4 (of legal proceedings, etc.) not criminal; disputed between ordinary citizens. **civil engineering** *n* branch of engineering concerned with designing and building roads, bridges, etc. **civil engineer** *n*. **civil service** *n* body of officials employed by the state in an administrative capacity. **civil servant** *r*. **civil war** *n* war between citizens of the same state.

civilian *n* one not in the employ of the armed forces.

civilization *n* 1 moral, social, intellectual, and artistic standards of a specific society. 2 advanced nonbarbaric condition or society. **civilize** *vt* bring out of a primitive condition; refine.

clad *adj* clothed; dressed.

claim *vt* 1 demand as a right. 2 ask or call for. *vt,vi* assert; maintain. *n* 1 demand or request by right. 2 that which is claimed or asserted. 3 right or title. **claimant** *n* person who makes a claim, esp. in law.

clam *n* edible bivalve shellfish. *v* **clam up** refuse to speak.

clamber *vi* climb, esp. with effort or difficulty. *n* awkward climb.

clammy *adj* damp and sticky.

clamour *n* raucous outcry; uproar. *vi* demand vociferously. **clamorous** *adj*. **clamorously** *adv*.

clamp *n* device used in carpentry, metalwork, surgery, etc., to hold things firmly in place. *vt* fasten or hold with a clamp. **clamp down on** *inf* suppress.

clan *n* large family or tribal group, esp. in Scotland. **clansman** *n*.

clandestine *adj* concealed; secret.

clang *n* resounding metallic sound, as of a large bell. *vt,vi* make or cause a clang. **clanger** *n* *inf* blunder.

clank *n* loud metallic sound, as of a heavy chain. *vt,vi* make or cause a clank.

clap *n* 1 sudden noise as of the palms of the hands brought sharply together. 2 sound of thunder. *vt,vi* (-pp-) 1 applaud with the hands. 2 place (down) suddenly. 3 throw (into prison, etc.). **clapper** *n* tongue suspended inside a bell. **like the clappers** very energetically or quickly.

claret *n* red wine from Bordeaux.

clarify *vt,vi* make or become clear. **clarification** *n*.

clarinet *n* musical wind instrument with a single reed. **clarinettist** *n*

clarity *n* clearness.

clash *n* 1 loud banging noise, as of colliding metal objects. 2 opposition; dispute; conflict. *vt* bang noisily together. *vi* 1 strike against. 2 come into opposition; conflict. 3 (of colours) be displeasing or disharmonious when placed together.

clasp *n* 1 hinged or interlocking fastening. 2 embrace; grasp of the hand. *vt* 1 fasten with a clasp. 2 embrace; grasp with the hand.

class *n* 1 kind; sort; category. 2 social group defined according to occupation, position, wealth, birth, social status, etc. 3 group of students or pupils undergoing the same course of instruction. 4 division denoting standard of comfort in an aeroplane, train, etc. *vt* form into or place in a class.

classic *adj* widely recognized as standard, typical, or of great merit. *n* work of art, esp. literature, noted for its lasting excellence. **classical** *adj* 1 of ancient Greece or Rome, esp. in formalized literary or architectural style. 2 (of music) belonging to great serious European tradition, esp. if composed before 1800. **classics** *pl n* language, literature, and philosophy of ancient Greece and Rome. **classicist** *n* student of classics.

classify *vt* arrange in classes or categories; place in a class. **classification** *n*.

clatter *n* loud repetitive rattling noise. *vt,vi* make or cause a clatter.

clause *n* 1 part of a sentence with a subject, predicate, and finite verb. 2 subsection in a legal contract, will, agreement, etc.

claustrophobia *n* morbid dread of enclosed or confined places. **claustrophobic** *adj*.

claw *n* hard hooked nail of an animal or bird. *vt* seize or tear with claws or nails.

clay *n* heavy sticky fine-grained soil material, plastic when moist, and used in pottery, brick-making, etc.

clean *adj* free from dirt, marks, impurity, guilt, disease, etc. *adv* completely. *vt* make clean. **clean out** clean thoroughly; empty. **clean up 1** tidy. **2** suppress crime, vice, etc. **3** gain a large profit, advantage, etc. **cleanliness** *n*.

cleanse *vt* clean (something) thoroughly; make pure. **cleanser** *n*.

clear *adj* **1** unclouded; bright; transparent. **2** obvious; distinct; straightforward. **3** net; after deductions. **4** without obstruction. *adv* completely. *vt* **1** clarify. **2** empty. **3** acquit; declare innocent. **4** pass without touching. **5** verify; justify. **6** receive (net). *vi* become clear. **clear off** *or* **out** leave hurriedly. **clear up 1** solve. **2** tidy. **3** become fine or sunny. **clearance** *n* **1** act of clearing. **2** space between moving and stationary objects. **3** certificate permitting passage through Customs, esp. of a ship. **clearheaded** *adj* lucid; intelligent; sensible. **clearing** *n* **1** act of making or becoming clear. **2** area free from trees, esp. in a forest.

clef *n* musical symbol denoting pitch of the notes written on the stave.

clench *vt* **1** grasp; grip; press (teeth, the fist, etc.) firmly together. **2** secure tightly; rivet.

clergy *n* priests and ordained ministers of a Christian church. **clergyman** *n*, *pl* **-men** priest, esp. in the Church of England.

clerical *adj* **1** of a clerk. **2** of a clergyman; religious.

clerk *n* **1** employee dealing with records, correspondence, etc., in an office. **2** person holding a particular administrative position in local government, the law, etc.

clever *adj* **1** intelligent; bright. **2** ingenious; cunning. **cleverly** *adv*. **cleverness** *n*.

cliché *n* hackneyed expression or phrase.

click *n* short sharp sound, as of a latch closing. *vi,vt* make a click.

client *n* customer; person employing another for business or professional purposes. **clientele** (kli:ɔn'tel) *n* clients.

cliff *n* steep high rock, esp. facing the sea.

climate *n* **1** general weather conditions of a region. **2** prevailing public attitude, economic situation, etc.

climax *n* **1** ultimate culmination of a series of events. **2** moment of supreme elation, terror, etc. **3** orgasm. **climactic** *adj*.

climb *vi,vt* **1** ascend or go up using hands and feet; scale. **2** rise; mount. *n* **1** distance or route to be climbed. **2** act of climbing. **climb down** admit to having been wrong; withdraw.

cling *vi* (clung) **1** adhere or stick to closely. **2** refuse to abandon a belief, idea, etc.

clinic *n* **1** hospital department or health centre for the diagnosis and treatment of specific disorders. **2** private nursing home. **clinical** *adj* **1** relating to a clinic. **2** of, used, or carried out in a hospital. **3** concerned with treatment of disease in the patient. **4** not biased or emotionally involved.

clink *n* **1** short ringing sound, as of metal, glass, etc., struck together. **2** *sl* prison. *vt,vi* make a clink.

clip¹ *n* **1** device for holding paper, etc., together. **2** hairgrip. *vt* (-pp-) fasten with a clip.

clip² *vt* (-pp-) **1** trim; cut closely; shorten. **2** smack; hit sharply. *n* **1** act of clipping. **2** piece clipped off. **3** sharp blow. **4** short extract from a film.

clitoris *n* female sexual organ similar to a rudimentary penis. **clitoral** *adj*.

cloak *n* long loose sleeveless garment fastening at the neck. *vt* disguise; mask. **cloakroom** *n* room in a public building, etc., where coats are left.

clock *n* instrument for telling or measuring time. *vt* **1** time (a runner). **2** *sl* hit; strike. **clock in** *or* **on/out** *or* **off** record the time of starting/finishing work. **clockwise** *adv* in the same direction as the hands of a clock. **clockwork** *n* mechanism of a clock or one working like that of a clock. **like clockwork** with perfect regularity and precision.

clog *n* heavy shoe with a sole and sometimes upper of wood. *vi* (-gg-) (of drains, pipes, etc.) become obstructed or blocked. *vt* block.

cloister *n* **1** covered arcade surrounding a monastery quadrangle. **2** monastery, abbey, or nunnery. **cloistered** *adj* shut away; secluded.

close *adj* (klous) **1** nearby; near. **2** mean; stingy. **3** stuffy; sultry. **4** confined; restricted. **5** thorough. **6** intimate. *n* (klous for 1,2; klouz for 3) **1** alley; dead-end street or road; enclosure. **2** cathedral precinct. **3** end. *adv* (klous) tightly; leaving no space. **close-up** *n* ('klousʌp) film-shot or photograph giving a detailed view. ~*v* (klouz) *vt* **1** shut. **2** pull together; unite. **3** finish; end; complete. *vi* come to an end; terminate. **close in** surround and move in on. **close down** terminate; cease functioning. **close up** shut completely. **closed-shop** *n* factory employing only union members. **closure** *n*.

closet *n* **1** small private room. **2** cupboard. **3.** lavatory. *adj* secret, not admitted. **closeted** *adj* shut away; kept secret.

clot *n* **1** small solidified mass of blood, mud, etc. **2** *sl* fool. *vt,vi* (-tt-) form into clots; congeal; coagulate.

cloth *n* **1** small piece of fabric used for polishing, mopping, covering, etc. **2** woven fabric from which clothing, curtains, etc., are cut and sewn.

clothe *vt* **1** provide with clothes; dress. **2** cover; disguise. **clothing** *n* clothes; garments in general. **clothes** *pl n* **1** garments; materials fashioned to be worn on the person; dress. **2** bed-coverings. **in plain clothes** (of a policeman, etc.) not wearing uniform.

cloud *n* **1** visible mass of small droplets of water floating in the sky, from which rain or snow falls. **2** mass of dust, smoke, etc., resembling a cloud. **3** anything depressing or threatening. *vt,vi* **1** fill or cover with clouds. **2** make or become murky or opaque. **3** fill or cover with gloom, doubt, etc. **cloudy** *adj* **1** covered or scattered with clouds. **2** opaque; not clear.

clove[1] *n* dried flower-bud of an aromatic tropical tree, used as a spice.

clove[2] *n* small bulb, esp. of garlic, that forms part of a larger one.

clover *n* small flowering plant with three-lobed leaves, often grown as cattle fodder.

clown *n* comic fool, esp. in a circus. *vi* play the fool.

club *n* **1** association of people with a common interest in a social, cultural, or sporting activity, etc. **2** the building, etc., used by such a group. **3** thick heavy stick. **4** stick used in golf. **clubs** *pl n* one of the four suits in cards. ~*vt* (-bb-) beat with a club. **club together** unite for a common end; contribute to a collection.

cluck *n* sound made by a hen. *vi* make such a sound.

clue *n* **1** hint or suggestion leading to the solution of a mystery. **2** information; idea. **clueless** *adj inf* stupid.

clump *n* **1** cluster of trees, bushes, etc. **2** heavy tread. *vi* **1** tread heavily. **2** group together.

clumsy *adj* **1** inclined to stumble, drop things, etc.; awkward. **2** tactless; gauche. **clumsily** *adv.* **clumsiness** *n*.

cluster *n* closely packed group, as of flowers, diamonds, stars, etc. *vi* grow or be gathered together.

clutch *vt* grasp or seize tightly. *n* **1** grasp; grip. **2** mechanical coupling device allowing gradual engagement of gears, etc. **3** number of eggs laid at one time.

clutter *n* confused jumble. *vt* crowd with a confused or untidy mass.

coach *n* **1** bus, esp. one used for long trips. **2** large horse-drawn carriage. **3** railway carriage. **4** tutor training people for exams, athletic events, etc. *vt* prepare for examination, contest, etc.; train.

coagulate *vi* solidify; clot; congeal. **coagulation** *n*.

coal *n* solid black mineral consisting of carbonized vegetation and mined for use as fuel. **coalmine** *n* workings from which coal is obtained; pit.

coalition *n* short-term alliance, esp. between political parties.

coarse *adj* **1** rough in texture; not fine. **2** vulgar; base; impolite. **coarsely** *adv.* **coarseness** *n*.

coast *n* land bordering the sea. *vi* sail or drift along. **coastal** *adj.* **coastguard** *n* person employed to watch the coast and sea for ships in danger, smuggling, etc. **coastline** *n* line of the shore, esp. as seen from the sea or air or as shown on a map.

coat *n* **1** outer garment with sleeves. **2** hair, fur, etc., covering an animal; pelt. **3** layer of paint, etc., on a surface. *vt* cover with a layer.

coax *vt* persuade, esp. by soothing or flattery; cajole.

cobble *n* rounded stone used for paving, road-making, etc. *vi,vt* mend or repair clumsily or shoddily.

cobbler *n* one who makes or mends shoes and boots.

cobra *n* poisonous hooded snake found in Asia and Africa.

cobweb *n* spider's web.

cock *n* **1** male bird, esp. of domestic fowl. **2** water-tap. **3** hammer of a gun. **4** *inf* chap; fellow. **5** *sl* penis. *vt* **1** tilt; turn to one side; set at a jaunty angle. **2** pull back the hammer of (a gun). **cocky** *adj* cheeky; self-assured; impudent. **cockiness** *n*.

cockle *n* edible bivalve mollusc with a heart-shaped shell.

Cockney *n* **1** Londoner, esp. one born within the sound of Bow Bells. **2** dialect of a Cockney.

cockpit *n* pilot's compartment in an aircraft.

cockroach *n* brown or black insect with long antennae.

cocktail *n* **1** drink made from a mixture of spirits and flavourings. **2** dish made from mixed fruit or prawns, etc.

cocoa *n* powder from the ground seeds of the cacao tree, used to make chocolate or to flavour drinks.

coconut *n* large fruit of a tropical palm-tree, with edible flesh, juice resembling milk, and a hard hairy husk.

cocoon *n* protective silky coating spun by various insect larvae before becoming pupae.

cod *n, pl* **cod** large edible sea fish.

coddle *vt* **1** boil lightly. **2** pamper; indulge; be protective towards.

code *n* **1** system of symbols for secret or esoteric communication. **2** system of regulations, laws, social customs, or moral principles. *vt* put into a code.

codeine *n* pain-killing drug obtained from opium.

coeducation *n* education of children of both sexes at the same school.

coerce (kou'ɔ:s) *vt* persuade forcefully; compel. **coercion** *n*. **coercive** *adj*.

coexist *vi* exist at the same time, esp. in harmony. **coexistence** *n*.

coffee *n* drink made from the roasted ground seeds (beans) of the coffee tree. *adj,n* light brown.

coffin *n* wooden box in which a corpse is placed for burial.

cog *n* one of the teeth on the rim of a wheel. **cogwheel** *n* wheel fitted with cogs, used in engineering, etc., for transmitting movement; gearwheel.

cognac *n* French brandy.

cohabit *vi* live together as man and wife. **cohabitation** *n*.

cohere *vi* stick together; remain consistent. **coherence** *n*. **cohesion** *n*. **coherent** *adj* clear; comprehensible; articulate; consistent.

coil *vt,vi* wind in rings; twist. *n* **1** piece of rope, string, etc., coiled into rings. **2** coil of wire in an electrical circuit.

coin *n* stamped metal disc used as official currency. *vt* **1** form or stamp coins in a mint. **2** invent (an expression or phrase). **coinage** *n*.

coincide *vi* **1** occur at the same time or place. **2** agree; concur. **coincidence** *n* **1** act or state of coinciding. **2** striking accidental concurrence of events.

colander *n* large strainer for draining vegetables.

cold *adj* **1** not hot; chilly; low in temperature. **2** unfriendly; indifferent; unemotional. *n* **1** lack of heat. **2** acute nasal inflammation. **coldly** *adv*. **coldness** *n*. **cold-blooded** *adj* **1** having a blood temperature varying with that of the surrounding water or air. **2** unemotional; callous; ruthless. **cold-bloodedly** *adv*. **cold-bloodedness** *n*. **cold war** *n* period or state of political and military hostility between nations, involving no armed conflict.

collaborate *vi* **1** co-operate; work together. **2** co-operate with an enemy. **collaboration** *n*. **collaborator** *n*.

collapse *vi* **1** break or fall down; fail totally; give up. **2** fold away. *n* **1** breakdown; physical or mental exhaustion. **2** falling down of a structure. **collapsible** *adj.*

collar *n* **1** part of a garment encircling the neck. **2** leather strap worn round the neck by a dog, horse, etc. *vt inf* seize; tackle. **collarbone** *n* prominent frontal bone linking the ribs to the shoulder blades.

colleague *n* associate, esp. someone following the same profession as oneself.

collect *vt* **1** gather together; seek out and acquire. **2** solicit (money) for a cause. **3** fetch; pick up. **collection** *n* **1** group of objects collected together. **2** act of collecting, esp. for a charity, church, etc. **collective** *adj* taken as a whole. **collectively** *adv.*

college *n* **1** place of higher or specialized education. **2** autonomous group of people. **collegiate** *adj.*

collide *vi* **1** strike violently; crash into. **2** come into conflict. **collision** *n.*

colloquial *adj* of informal everyday speech. **colloquialism** *n* informal phrase; slang; idiom.

colon *n* punctuation mark (:) used to indicate a definite pause or division in a sentence.

colonel *n* military officer of a rank between lieutenant-colonel and brigadier.

colony *n* group of settlers from another country. **colonize** *vt* take over as a colony. **colonial** *adj* from or of a colony. *n* inhabitant of a colony.

colossal *adj* extremely large; enormous; gigantic; huge.

colour *n* **1** sense impression produced by light of different wavelengths, or the property of objects or light producing this. **2** pigment; hue. **3** skin pigmentation. **4** quality of vividness or distinction. **5** false quality. **colours** *pl n* **1** military flag or standard. **2** award for membership of a team. **off colour** unwell. ~*vt* **1** impart colour to. **2** give a false or biased impression of. *vi* take on a colour. **coloration** *n.* **colour-bar** *n* discrimination against people of coloured or dark-skinned races. **colour-blind** *adj* unable to distinguish or identify specific colours. **colour-blindness** *n.* **coloured** *adj* **1** having a colour. **2** (of a person) of a non-White race. **3** deceptive; biased. **colourful** *adj* **1** full of colour. **2** picturesque; vivid.

colt *n* young male horse.

column *n* **1** tall pillar, esp. one supporting a building. **2** row or line of people, figures, etc. **3** newspaper or magazine article or report. **columnist** *n* journalist providing regular articles for a newspaper or magazine.

coma *n* condition of very deep unconsciousness. **comatose** *adj* **1** drowsy. **2** in a coma.

comb *n* **1** small toothed instrument for separating and tidying hair, wool, etc. **2** group of wax cells made by bees. **3** crest of certain birds, esp. cocks. *vt* **1** untangle and tidy hair, wool, etc. **2** search thoroughly.

combat *vt,vi* fight against; oppose. *n* fight; struggle; battle. **combatant** *n.* **combative** *adj.*

combine *vt,vi* (kəm'bain) join together; unite; amalgamate. *n* ('kɔmbain) association of several similar companies, institutions, etc. **combine harvester** *n* mechanical corn harvester. **combination** *n* mixture; amalgamation.

combustion *n* process of burning. **combustible** *adj* capable of burning; flammable.

come *vi* (came; come) **1** arrive; be delivered; reach. **2** happen; occur. **3** originate; be caused by. **4** be available; be supplied. **come across** discover or meet by chance. **come back** return. **come off 1** become separated or broken. **2** be successfully completed. **come out 1** emerge. **2** be issued. **3** erupt. **come round 1** recover consciousness. **2** be persuaded. **come to 1** recover consciousness. **2** amount to. **come up** arise; appear. **come up with** suggest; think of; produce. **comeback** *n* **1** return or success after an absence or failure. **2** retort. **comedown** *n* **1** anticlimax. **2** reduction in status, quality, etc.

comedian *n* entertainer who performs comic songs or plays, tells jokes, etc.

comedy *n* humorous, amusing, or light-hearted play.

comet *n* heavenly body having a luminous head and a long tail, which always points away from the sun.

comfort *n* **1** encouragement; relief. **2** ease; peacefulness; lack of anxiety or pain. *vt* relieve; console; cheer. **comfortable** *adj* **1** providing or enjoying comfort. **2** fairly affluent. **comfortably** *adv.*

comic *adj* **1** funny; amusing. **2** relating to comedy. *n* **1** comic person; comedian. **2** children's paper consisting mainly of strip cartoons. **comical** *adj* ridiculous; absurd; laughable. **comically** *adv.*

comma *n* punctuation mark (,) used to indicate a slight pause, to separate clauses, etc.

command *vt* order; control; have authority or influence over; dominate. *n* order; rule; authority; control. **in command** in charge. **commander** *n* **1** someone who commands; leader. **2** naval officer ranking below a captain.

commandeer *vt* take over or seize arbitrarily or by force, esp. for military purposes.

commandment *n* order; command. **Ten Commandments** *pl n* laws given by God to Moses according to the Old Testament.

commando *n, pl* **commandos** *or* **commandoes** soldier specially trained to carry out dangerous raids.

commemorate *vt* celebrate the memory of; provide a memorial to. **commemoration** *n.*

commence *vt,vi* begin; start. **commencement** *n.*

commend *vt* **1** praise; recommend. **2** entrust. **commendable** *adj.* **commendation** *n.*

comment *n* brief, critical, or explanatory remark expressing an opinion, reaction, etc. *vi* make a comment. **commentary** *n* **1** series of comments, esp. analysing a book. **2** description of and comments on a sporting event, state occasion, etc., esp. when broadcast. **commentator** *n* one who provides a commentary, esp. on radio or television.

commerce *n* business; trade. **commercial** *adj* relating to commerce or business. **commercial traveller** *n* representative employed by a firm as a salesman.

commission *n* **1** document conferring authority, position, agency, etc. **2** body of people holding an enquiry and producing a report. **3** piece of work, esp. a work of art, specifically ordered. **4** percentage payment taken by an agent, salesman, etc. *vt* **1** give authority to. **2** put in an order for. **commissioner** *n* one holding or appointed by a commission.

commit *vt* (-tt-) **1** entrust; charge with. **2** perform; do; perpetrate (a crime, etc.). **3** promise; pledge. **4** send to prison or for further trial. **commit oneself** take on an obligation or duty. **commitment** *n.*

committee *n* small group instructed by a larger organization to deal with specific matters.

commodity *n* particular type of goods, produce, or merchandise.

common *adj* **1** shared by or belonging to all or to many. **2** usual; frequent. **3** general; widespread. **4** relating to the public. **5** habitual. **6** ordinary; familiar; well-known. **7** coarse; vulgar; low. *n* piece of land belonging to the community and available for public use. **in common** in joint use; of mutual interest; shared. **commonly** *adv.* **commonness** *n.* **common law** unwritten law based on custom or tradition. **common sense** *n* practical sense; good judgment; normal mental capacity. **commonplace** *adj* ordinary; not remarkable. *n* trite remark; cliché. **commonwealth** *n* **1** people of a state or nation, esp. when viewed as a political entity. **2** federation of self-governing units or former colonies.

commotion *n* disturbance; public disorder; uproar.

communal *adj* relating to or belonging to a commune or community; public; common.

commune[1] *vi* (kə'mju:n) converse or act intimately or spiritually. *n* ('kɔmju:n) intimate conversation; communion.

commune[2] ('kɔmju:n) *n* **1** smallest administrative division of some countries, such as France or Belgium. **2** group or small community organized to promote mutual interests and goals.

communicate *vt* **1** give or transmit; impart. **2** make known. *vi* **1** exchange thoughts or information in a way that may be easily understood. **2** be connected, as by a passage. *vt,vi* administer or receive the Eucharist. **communicant** *n,adj.* **communication** *n.*

communion *n* **1** participation; act of sharing. **2** fellowship. **3** intimate exchange of thoughts and feelings. **Communion** *also* **Holy Communion** the Eucharist or its celebration.

communism *n* belief or social system based on the doctrine that all goods, property, and means of production belong to the community or state. **communist** *adj,n.*

community *n* **1** group of people living in the same area or sharing a common culture. **2** joint possession or ownership.

commute *vi* travel regularly, usually over relatively long distances, from home to work. *vt* reduce (a prison sentence, penalty, etc.). *vt,vi* transform; substitute. **commuter** *n.*

compact[1] *adj* (kəm'pækt) **1** packed neatly and closely together. **2** concentrated; dense. **3** terse; pithy. *vt* (kəm'pækt) pack closely together; condense; compress. *n* ('kɔmpækt) small hinged container, usually with a mirror, for holding face powder. **compactly** *adv.* **compactness** *n.*

compact[2] ('kɔmpækt) *n* agreement or contract between parties.

companion *n* **1** mate; comrade. **2** person who accompanies another or shares the same experience. **3** something that matches another. **companionable** *adj.* **companionship** *n* fellowship; friendship.

company *n* **1** gathering of persons, as for social purposes; group. **2** guest or guests. **3** association for business. **4** officers and crew of a ship. **5** infantry unit of two or more platoons. **6** troupe of actors, dancers, or singers. **part company** end association or friendship (with).

compare *vt* notice or identify similarities; liken. *vi* be in relation to. **comparable** *adj* capable or worthy of being compared. **comparably** *adv.* **comparative** *adj* **1** relating to or involving comparison. **2** not absolute or positive; relative. **comparatively** *adv.* **comparison** *n.*

compartment *n* **1** part or parts into which an enclosed space is partitioned or divided off; section; division. **2** section of a railway carriage.

compass *n* **1** instrument for determining bearings, usually by means of a magnetized needle that always points north. **2** limit or scope. **compasses** *pl n* small instrument with two hinged arms, used for drawing circles, arcs, etc. *vt* encircle; surround.

compassion *n* deeply felt pity or sympathy. **compassionate** *adj.*

compatible *adj* **1** able to live or exist well or harmoniously together. **2** consistent; not contradictory. **compatibility** *n.* **compatibly** *adv.*

compel *vt* (-ll-) **1** force or bring about by force. **2** subdue; overpower.

compensate *vt,vi* pay money (to) in acknowledgement of loss, damage, or injury; recompense. *vt* offset. *vi* modify or exaggerate one's behaviour to make up for a fault or shortcoming. **compensation** *n.*

compete *vi* strive against others. **competitor** *n.* **competition** *n* **1** competing; rivalry; opposition. **2** contest to show worth or ability, often with a prize for the winner. **competitive** *adj.* **competitively** *adv.*

competent *adj* **1** skilful; able; properly qualified. **2** sufficient; adequate. **competence** *or* **competency** *n.* **competently** *adv.*

compile *vt* assemble; make or put together (a book, its parts, etc.) from various materials or sources. **compilation** *n.* **compiler** *n.*

complacent *adj* self-satisfied. **complacency** *n.* **complacently** *adv.*

complain *vi* express unhappiness or lack of satisfaction; grumble; moan. **complaint** *n* **1** statement of a grievance, wrong, etc. **2** illness.

complement *n* **1** something that serves to complete or make whole or perfect. **2** full allowance, quantity, etc. **complementary** *adj.*

complete *adj* **1** whole; finished; full; perfect. **2** utter; absolute. *vt* finish; make whole, perfect, or full. **completely** *adv.* **completion** *n.*

complex *adj* **1** involved; intricate; complicated. **2** having many facets or parts. *n* **1** whole composed of many parts, often different or distinct. **2** set of mental attitudes, often subconscious, that affect personality. **complexity** *n.*

complexion *n* **1** texture, colour, and quality of the skin, esp. of the face. **2** aspect; appearance.

complicate *vt* make difficult, intricate, or involved. **complication** *n.*

compliment *n* ('kɔmplimənt) remark expressing praise, admiration, respect, etc. *vt* ('kɔmpliment) pay a compliment to; congratulate; praise. **complimentary** *adj* **1** expressing a compliment; flattering. **2** free of charge.

comply *vi* do as one is asked; consent; conform. **compliance** *n.* **compliant** *adj.*

component *n* essential or constituent part of something.

compose *vt* **1** create or write (a literary or musical work). **2** constitute; make up. **3** make of various parts or elements; fashion. **4** set type in lines. *vi* write music. **compose oneself** calm or settle oneself. **composer** *n* writer of music. **composite** *adj* made up of differen⸱ parts. **composition** *n* **1** putting together of parts or elements to form a whole. **2** parts that form the whole; make-up. **3** piece of music. **4** artistic creation. **5** short essay, esp. one written at school. **composure** *n* calmness of mind; serenity.

compost *n* decomposed matter, manure, etc., used as fertilizer.

compound[1] *adj* ('kɔmpaund) composed of separate parts or substances. *vt* **1** (kəm'paund) assemble into a whole; combine. **2** complicate; increase. *n* ('kɔmpaund) **1** something formed by putting together separate substances, ingredients, or components. **2** chemical substance composed of atoms of two or more elements held together by chemical bonds.

compound[2] ('kɔmpaund) *n* enclosure containing houses or other buildings.

comprehend *vt, vi* **1** understand; grasp. **2** include. **comprehensible** *adj.* **comprehension** *n.* **comprehensive** *adj* **1** inclusive; covering everything; broad. **2** able to understand fully. *n also* **comprehensive school** state secondary school taking in pupils from a given area irrespective of ability.

compress *vt* (kəm'pres) **1** force or squeeze together. **2** make smaller in bulk, size, etc. *n* ('kɔmpres) pad or cloth for applying pressure, moisture, etc., to a bodily part. **compression** *n.*

comprise *vt* contain; include; consist of.

compromise *n* **1** settlement of a dispute or disagreement by giving up part of a claim. **2** something between two extremes, courses of action, etc. **3** exposure to jeopardy, suspicion, loss of reputation, etc. *vi* settle a dispute through a compromise. *vt* expose to jeopardy, etc.

compulsion *n* **1** impulse or urge that cannot be resisted. **2** act of compelling. **compulsive** *adj* acting on a sudden urge or impulse. **compulsively** *adv.* **compulsiveness** *n.* **compulsory** *adj* **1** obligatory; required. **2** compelling; employing compulsion. **compulsorily** *adv.*

computer *n* electronic apparatus that performs calculations, processes data, etc., usually equipped with a memory and able to print out required information.

comrade *n* **1** close associate or companion; mate. **2** fellow member of a communist group or party. **comradeship** *n.*

concave *adj* curved inwards; being hollow and curved. *n* concave surface or part.

conceal *vt* **1** hide. **2** keep secret. **concealment** *n.*

concede *vt* admit having lost. *vt, vi* **1** acknowledge to be true. **2** yield.

conceit *n* excessive estimation of one's achievements, abilities, or worth; vanity. **conceited** *adj.*

conceive *vt, vi* **1** become pregnant with (a child). **2** form (an idea); imagine. **conceivable** *adj.*

concentrate *vt, vi* **1** direct (one's attention or energies) towards a particular objective. **2** make or become less diluted; condense. **3** place or be confined in a dense mass. *n* concentrated solution. **concentration** *n.* **concentration camp** *n* (esp. during World War II) place, such as a guarded compound, for the detention of political prisoners, racial minorities, etc.

concentric *adj* having a common centre.

concept *n* abstract notion; idea; thought. **conceptual** *adj.* **conception** *n* **1** fertilization; start of pregnancy. **2** idea; concept. **3** plan; design.

concern *vt* be of interest to; relate to; affect; worry. *n* **1** care; regard; anxiety; interest. **2** affair; matter. **3** business; firm;

company. **concerning** *prep* about; regarding; relating to.

concert *n* ('kɔnsət) **1** public musical entertainment. **2** agreement; union; harmony. *vt* (kən'sɔːt) plan together; arrange by agreement. **concerted** *adj.*

concertina *n* musical instrument with bellows and button-like keys.

concerto (kən'tʃɛətou) *n* musical piece for solo instrument and orchestra.

concession *n* **1** act of conceding or yielding. **2** that which is conceded or yielded. **3** franchise or privilege; grant. **concessionary** *adj.*

concise *adj* brief; terse; succinct. **concisely** *adv.*

conclude *vt,vi* bring or come to an end; finish. *vt* **1** settle; arrange or agree finally. **2** say or declare in ending or finishing. **conclusion** *n.* **conclusive** *adj.*

concoct *vt* **1** prepare with various ingredients; make a mixture of. **2** make up; devise; invent. **concoction** *n.*

concrete *adj* **1** real; not abstract. **2** relating to a specific object or case. *n* building material formed from sand, cement, water, etc., that hardens as it dries. *vt* cover over with concrete.

concur *vi* (-rr-) **1** agree; have the same opinion. **2** occur together; coincide. **concurrent** *adj.*

concussion *n* injury to the brain, caused by a blow, fall, etc., often causing loss of consciousness. **concuss** *vt* cause concussion in.

condemn *vt* **1** blame; find guilty. **2** pronounce judicial sentence against. **3** judge to be unfit for service or use. **condemnation** *n.*

condense *vt* **1** concentrate; make more solid, compact, or dense. **2** abridge; put into a few or fewer words. **3** change (a gas or vapour) to a liquid, esp. by cooling. *vi* become liquid or solid. **condensation** *n* anything condensed from a vapour, esp. fine droplets of water on a window, etc., condensed from the atmosphere.

condescend *vi* **1** lower oneself to the level of one's inferiors. **2** be gracious or patronizing. **condescension** *n.*

condition *n* **1** state or mode of existence. **2** state of health. **3** stipulation; restric-

tion. **conditions** *pl n* **1** circumstances. **2** terms of an agreement, contract, etc. ~*vt* **1** accustom (someone) to. **2** affect; change. **conditional** *adj* tentative; not absolute; dependent on certain conditions. **conditionally** *adv.*

condolence *n* expression of sympathetic grief.

condone *vt* overlook; forgive; pardon.

conduct *v* (kən'dʌkt) *vt,vi* **1** transmit (heat, electricity, etc.). **2** control (an orchestra) during a performance or rehearsal. *vt* **1** guide; lead. **2** direct; manage; control. *n* ('kɔndʌkt) **1** behaviour. **2** execution or handling of business. **conduction** *n* transfer of heat or electricity through a medium. **conductor** *n* **1** director of an orchestra, choir, etc. **2** leader; guide. **3** person who collects fares from passengers on public transport vehicles. **4** that which conducts electricity, heat, etc.

cone *n* **1** solid figure with a circular base and tapering to a point. **2** fruit of certain trees, such as the pine or fir. **3** anything shaped like or resembling a cone.

confectioner *n* person who makes or sells sweets, cakes, etc. **confectionery** *n* **1** sweets, chocolate, etc. **2** confectioner's trade or business.

confederate *adj* (kən'fedərit) united; allied. *n* (kən'fedərit) ally; accomplice. *vt,vi* (kən'fedəreit) unite in an alliance, conspiracy, etc. **confederation** *or* **confederacy** *n.*

confer *v* (-rr-) *vt* grant as a favour, gift, honour, etc. *vi* talk with; compare opinions.

conference *n* meeting for discussion.

confess *vt,vi* **1** admit or acknowledge (a crime, sin, etc.). **2** concede; agree. **confession** *n.* **confessor** *n* priest who gives absolution to those who confess their sins.

confetti *n* small bits of coloured paper for throwing at weddings, etc.

confide *vi* *also* **confide in** divulge information (to); disclose in secret. **confidence** *n* **1** feeling of trust, assurance, etc.; firm belief. **2** self-assurance. **confident** *adj.* **confidently** *adv.* **confidential** *adj* secret; private. **confidentially** *adv.*

confine *vt* (kən'fain) **1** imprison; shut in. **2** keep in bed or in the house. **3** limit; keep within limits. **confines** ('kɔnfainz) *pl n* limits; restrictions. **confinement** *n.*

confirm *vt* **1** verify; substantiate; make valid. **2** give a firm undertaking of. **3** administer confirmation to. **confirmation** *n* **1** verification. **2** rite by which baptized persons are admitted into full membership of the Church.

confiscate *vt* seize by authority; appropriate. **confiscation** *n*.

conflict *n* ('konflikt) **1** struggle; trial of strength. **2** opposition or clash of interests, ideas, etc. *vi* (kɔn'flikt) be inconsistent or at odds with; clash.

conform *vi* *also* **conform to** comply (with); agree to certain standards, rules, etc.; fit in (with). **conformist** *n,adj.* **conformity** *n*.

confound *vt* **1** baffle; perplex. **2** mix up; confuse. **confounded** *adj* **1** astonished; utterly confused. **2** dreadful; irritating.

confront *vt* **1** face; present. **2** bring face to face with. **confrontation** *n*.

confuse *vt* **1** throw into disorder. **2** mix mentally; obscure. **3** bewilder; muddle. **confusion** *n*.

congeal *vt,vi* **1** solidify by freezing or cooling. **2** coagulate; stiffen. **congealment** *n*.

congenial *adj* **1** pleasing; agreeable. **2** similar in disposition; compatible. **congenially** *adv.*

congenital *adj* existing at birth.

congested *adj* **1** crowded; overcrowded; blocked. **2** (of an organ or part) excessively suffused with blood. **congestion** *n*.

congratulate *vt* acknowledge the good fortunes or achievements of; praise; compliment. **congratulation** *n*.

congregate *vi* assemble; flock together; gather. **congregation** *n* **1** act of congregating. **2** assembly of people, esp. those who gather in a church to worship.

congress *n* **1** assembly; conference. **2** legislative body. **congressional** *adj.*

conical *adj* *also* **conic** relating to or having the shape of a cone.

conifer *n* tree, such as the pine or fir, having evergreen needle-shaped leaves and bearing cones. **coniferous** *adj.*

conjugal *adj* marital; relating to husband and wife.

conjugate *vt* ('kondʒugeit) inflect (a verb) in its various forms. *adj* ('kondʒugit) joined together in pairs; coupled. **conjugation** *n*.

conjunction *n* **1** union; association. **2** simultaneous occurrences; combination of events. **3** part of speech joining words, phrases, etc. **conjunctive** *adj.*

conjure *vt* *also* **conjure up** **1** call or produce as if by magic. **2** imagine; evoke; recall. *vi* practice or perform tricks of illusion or magic. **conjurer** *n*.

connect *vt,vi* link; join; fasten together. *vt* associate in the mind. **connection** *n* **1** link; joining together. **2** association; relationship. **3** public transport, esp. a train, timed to meet another train for the transfer of passengers. **connections** *pl n* influential business or social contacts.

connoisseur *n* person who is an expert, esp. in matters of taste and art.

connotation *n* suggestion or implication of a word in addition to its chief meaning. **connotative** *adj.*

conquer *vt,vi* **1** overcome (an enemy) by force; defeat. **2** surmount. *vt* gain possession of by force; take over. **conqueror** *n*. **conquest** *n*.

conscience *n* **1** mental sense of right and wrong. **2** feeling of guilt. **conscientious** *adj* **1** paying attention to conscience; scrupulous. **2** painstaking; hard-working. **conscientiously** *adv.*

conscious *adj* **1** aware of one's surroundings; awake. **2** sensitive to or recognizing some truth, fact, etc. **3** performed or registered with full awareness. **4** intended; deliberate. **consciously** *adv.* **consciousness** *n*.

conscript *vt* (kɔn'skript) enrol compulsorily into service, esp. in the armed forces; call up. *n* ('kɔnskript) person who has been conscripted. **conscription** *n*.

consecrate *vt* **1** make sacred or holy; sanctify. **2** devote; dedicate. **consecration** *n*.

consecutive *adj* in unbroken or logical order or succession. **consecutively** *adv.*

consent *vi* agree (to); give assent. *n* **1** permission. **2** agreement.

consequence *n* **1** effect or result; conclusion. **2** significance; importance. **in consequence** as a result. **consequent** *adj.*

conservative *adj* 1 opposed to change, as in social or political conditions; traditional. 2 moderate. *n* person who is conventional or opposed to change. **Conservative Party** *n* British political party which generally favours private enterprise. **conservatively** *adv.*

conservatory *n* glassed-in room for growing blooming or exotic plants, esp. one attached to an outside wall of a house.

conserve *vt* preserve; keep from decay, change, etc. *n* jam made with whole fruit. **conservation** *n* preservation, esp. of the natural environment.

consider *vt,vi* 1 think about; reflect on; contemplate; examine. 2 suppose; think to be; believe. 3 look upon with respect, sympathy, etc. **considerable** *adj* 1 somewhat large in amount, extent, or degree. 2 important; great. **considerably** *adv.* **considerate** *adj* thoughtful; kind. **consideration** *n* 1 thought; contemplation; reflection. 2 payment; financial reward. 3 thoughtfulness for others. 4 importance. **take into consideration** take into account; bear in mind. **considering** *prep* in view of.

consign *vt* 1 hand over formally; commit (to). 2 give over to another's custody; entrust. **consignment** *n.*

consist *vi* be composed or made up (of). **consistency** *n* 1 degree of solidity, density, or firmness. 2 agreement; correspondence; accordance; regularity. **consistent** *adj* harmonious; not contradictory; regular. **consistently** *adv.*

console *vt,vi* comfort in distress or grief; cheer. **consolation** *n.*

consolidate *vt,vi* 1 make or become firm or solid; strengthen. 2 combine; unite. **consolidation** *n.*

consonant *n* 1 speech sound made by constriction or stoppage of the breath stream. 2 letter or symbol representing this, such as *p*, *t*, or *s*.

conspicuous *adj* easily seen; noticeable; standing out. **conspicuously** *adv.*

conspire *vt,vi* plot (an evil or criminal act) in secret. *vi* act together; contribute in combination. **conspiracy** *n.* **conspirator** *or* **conspirer** *n.*

constable *n* police officer of the lowest rank. **constabulary** *n* local police force.

constant *adj* 1 always present, happening, or continuing. 2 unchanging; permanent. *n* quantity or value that does not vary. **constancy** *n.* **constantly** *adv.*

constellation *n* star group, esp. one with a given name.

consternation *n* dismay; anxiety.

constipation *n* difficulty or infrequency in evacuating the bowels.

constituency *n* body of electors or area served by a member of Parliament.

constituent *adj* 1 serving to make up a whole; component. 2 having power to elect. *n* 1 component or essential part. 2 elector; voter.

constitute *vt* 1 set up; establish. 2 be an element of; make up. 3 appoint; make into. **constitution** *n* 1 manner in which something is made up. 2 state of physical or mental health. 3 character; temperament; disposition. 4 principles or laws by which a state is governed. **constitutional** *adj.*

constrain *vt* 1 compel. 2 confine; restrain; restrict. **constraint** *n.*

constrict *vt* make narrower or tighter; compress. **constriction** *n.*

construct *vt* (kən'strʌkt) 1 put together; build; make. 2 devise; formulate; fabricate. *n* ('kɔnstrʌkt) something constructed; formulation. **construction** *n.* **constructive** *adj* useful; helpful.

consul *n* official state representative, residing and performing administrative duties in a foreign city. **consular** *adj.* **consulate** *n* 1 premises occupied by a consul. 2 period of office of a consul.

consult *vt* seek advice or information from; refer to. **consultant** *n* 1 person qualified to give expert professional advice. 2 medical or surgical specialist. **consultation** *n.*

consume *vt* 1 use up. 2 eat or drink up. 3 destroy as by burning or decomposition. 4 spend (time, money, etc.), esp. foolishly or wastefully. 5 engross; absorb. **consumer** *n* person who buys or uses a commodity or service. **consumption** *n.*

contact *n* 1 touching or being in touch. 2 connection; association. 3 person exposed to a contagious disease. 4 person who may be useful to one socially or for business purposes. *vt,vi* get in touch, be in contact, or communicate (with). **contact lenses** *pl n* optical lenses that fit directly on to the surface of the eye to correct visual defects.

contagious *adj* **1** (of an infectious disease) transmitted directly or indirectly from one person to another. **2** (of an infected person) able to spread disease to others. **3** tending to spread or influence; catching. **contagion** *n.*

contain *vt* **1** hold; enclose. **2** comprise; include; have room for. **contain oneself** control or restrain oneself. **container** *n* something able to hold a product, substance, etc.; receptacle.

contaminate *vt* **1** make impure by mixture or contact; pollute. **2** corrupt; spoil. **3** make dangerous or worthless by being exposed to radioactivity. **contamination** *n.*

contemplate *vt* **1** gaze upon, esp. thoughtfully. **2** meditate on. **3** intend; plan. *vi* consider carefully; meditate. **contemplation** *n.*

contemporary *adj* **1** of roughly the same date or age. **2** of the present; reflecting current styles, fashions, etc.; modern. *n* person of the same age or time as another. **contemporaneous** *adj.*

contempt *n* **1** scorn. **2** disrespect. **3** lack of regard for authority, esp. for the rules of a court or legal body. **contemptible** *adj.* **contemptuous** *adj.*

contend *vi* struggle; fight for; compete. *vt* assert; claim; maintain. **contention** *n.*

content[1] ('kontent) *n* **1** capacity. **2** proportion of a substance contained; subject matter. **contents** *pl n* **1** items placed in a container. **2** list of chapters or divisions in a book.

content[2] (kən'tent) *adj* **1** satisfied; happy. **2** willing; resigned. *vt* make content; please. *n* *also* **contentment** happiness; satisfaction.

contest *n* ('kontest) **1** competition; match. **2** conflict; struggle. *vt* (kən'test) fight for; dispute; struggle against. **contestant** *n* person who takes part in a contest; competitor.

context *n* **1** text or section preceding or following a particular passage, word, etc. **2** facts or circumstances relating to an event, situation, etc.; background. **contextual** *adj.*

continent *n* major land mass of the earth. **continental** *adj.* **Continental** *adj* relating to the mainland of Europe or to Europe-

ans. *n* inhabitant of the mainland of Europe. **continental quilt** *n* duvet.

contingency *n* chance occurrence; unforeseen event or circumstance; possibility; eventuality. **contingent** *adj* dependent upon an uncertain event or condition; possible. *n* representative group in a body of people.

continue *vt,vi* **1** go on; carry on; proceed (with). **2** remain existing; persist. **3** resume; take up again. **continual** *adj* occurring at regular intervals; constant; persistent. **continually** *adv.* **continuation** *n* **1** extended or connected part or section. **2** prolonged action. **3** resumption; renewal. **continuity** *n* **1** continuous flow; logical sequence. **2** complete film scenario, script, etc. **continuous** *adj* without interruption; unbroken. **continuously** *adv.*

contour *n* outline or shape of a body or figure. *vt* form the outline or shape of. **contour line** *n* line on a map that passes through all points that have equal elevation.

contraband *n* **1** illegal importing or exporting. **2** smuggled goods.

contraception *n* prevention of conception; birth control. **contraceptive** *adj* serving to prevent conception. *n* agent or device that prevents conception.

contract *n* ('kontrækt) agreement, esp. legally binding, between two or more persons, groups, etc. *v* (kən'trækt) *vt,vi* **1** make or become smaller or more compressed. **2** ('kontrækt) enter into or settle by agreement. **3** draw or be drawn together. *vt* **1** shorten by omitting parts, elements, etc. **2** acquire (a disease, liability, etc.). **contraction** *n.*

contradict *vt* **1** state the opposite of (a statement, etc.). **2** deny; refute. *vt,vi* be inconsistent (with). **contradiction** *n.* **contradictory** *adj.*

contralto *n* female alto voice.

contraption *n* strange or cumbersome invention, machine, etc.

contrary *adj* **1** opposite. **2** opposed in direction, tendency, or nature. **3** perverse. *n* exact opposite. *adv* in opposition.

contrast *vt,vi* (kən'tra:st) show or display dissimilarity. *n* ('kontra:st) striking difference or distinction.

contravene *vt* **1** infringe; conflict with; violate. **2** contradict; dispute. **contravention** *n.*

contribute *vt,vi* **1** pay with others to a common fund. **2** supply or give as one's share in a discussion, task, etc. **contribution** *n.* **contributor** *n.* **contributory** *adj.*

contrive *vt* **1** devise; design. **2** succeed in bringing about; manage. *vi,vt* plot; conspire. **contrivance** *n.* **contrived** *adj* unnatural; not spontaneous.

control *vt* (-ll-) **1** command; dominate. **2** check; curb; restrain. **3** verify or test by a standard comparison. *n* **1** domination; command. **2** restraint; check. **3** standard of comparison. **controls** *pl n* devices for regulating or guiding a machine, as an aircraft, car, etc.

controversy *n* debate; dispute; argument. **controversial** *adj.*

convalesce *vi* recover from illness. **convalescence** *n* period of recovery. **convalescent** *adj,n.*

convenience *n* **1** suitability; usefulness. **2** personal comfort; ease. **3** public lavatory. **convenient** *adj* **1** well adapted to one's purpose; suitable. **2** helpful; useful; handy. **conveniently** *adv.*

convent *n* **1** religious community, esp. of nuns. **2** buildings occupied by such a community.

convention *n* **1** large assembly, conference, or formal meeting. **2** traditionally observed custom or rule; norm. **conventional** *adj* conforming to accepted standards.

converge *vi* tend to meet or move towards the same point; approach. **convergence** *n.* **convergent** *adj.*

converse[1] (kən'vəːs) *vi* talk or hold a conversation (with). **conversation** *n* talk; exchange of thoughts, opinions, etc.

converse[2] ('kɔnvəːs) *adj* opposite; reverse. *n* statement with the terms of another interchanged; opposite. **conversely** *adv.*

convert *vt* (kən'vəːt) **1** modify or change into something different; adapt. **2** change in outlook, religion, opinion, etc. *n* ('kɔnvəːt) person who has been converted, esp. to a particular religion. **conversion** *n.* **convertible** *adj* capable of being converted. *n* car with a folding or removable roof.

convex *adj* curved outwards; bulging.

convey *vt* **1** carry; transport. **2** communicate. **conveyance** *n* **1** transfer of property from one person to another. **2** transportation. **conveyor belt** *n* endless flexible belt used to convey goods, esp. in a factory.

convict *vt* (kən'vikt) prove or declare guilty. *n* ('kɔnvikt) imprisoned criminal.

conviction *n* **1** firm belief; certainty. **2** verdict of guilt.

convince *vt* satisfy by argument or evidence; persuade.

convoy *n* **1** escort of naval vessels, armed forces, etc., provided for protection. **2** group of vehicles moving together.

cook *vt,vi* **1** prepare (food) by roasting, boiling, etc. **2** subject or be subjected to heat; burn. *n* person who prepares food, esp. professionally. **cooker** *n* oven; stove. **cookery** *n* art or practice of cooking.

cool *adj* **1** somewhat cold. **2** unexcited; calm. **3** lacking interest or friendliness. *vt,vi* make or become cool(er). *n* cool part, place, time, etc. **cool one's heels** be kept waiting. **coolly** *adv.* **coolness** *n.*

coop *n* pen or cage for poultry. *vt* also **coop up** confine in a small space.

cooperate *vi* work together; act jointly. **cooperation** *n.* **cooperative** *adj* helpful; willing to cooperate. *n* joint enterprise based on collective principles.

coordinate *vt* (kou'ɔːdineit) bring into order as parts of a whole; combine harmoniously. *adj* (kou'ɔːdinit) combined; harmonious. *n* (kou'ɔːdinit) combination.

cope *vi* deal with; manage satisfactorily.

copper[1] *n* **1** soft reddish lustrous metal, used in electrical wiring, plumbing, etc. **2** coin made or formerly made of copper. *adj,n* red or reddish-gold.

copper[2] *n sl* policeman.

copulate *vi* have sexual intercourse. **copulation** *n.*

copy *n* **1** reproduction or imitation; duplicate. **2** single specimen of a book. **3** matter for printing. *vt,vi* **1** make a copy (of); duplicate. **2** imitate. **copyright** *n* exclusive legal right to produce or dispose of copies of a literary or artistic work over a given period of time. *vt* secure a copyright on.

coral *n* **1** hard red or white substance secreted by sea polyps, often forming reefs or islands. **2** polyps producing this. **3** ornament, etc., fashioned from coral.

cord *n* **1** thin rope or thick string. **2** ribbed fabric, such as corduroy. *vt* furnish or fasten with cord.

cordial *adj* sincere; warm; hearty. *n* concentrated fruit juice. **cordially** *adv.*

cordon *n* **1** ornamental cord or badge. **2** line of police, troops, etc., guarding an area.

corduroy *n* thick cotton fabric with a corded or ribbed surface.

core *n* **1** central or innermost part of anything. **2** middle part of an apple or other fleshy fruit, containing the seeds. *vt* remove the core of.

cork *n* **1** porous outer bark of a certain tree (cork oak), used for making bottle stoppers, floats, etc. **2** piece of cork used as a bottle stopper. *vt* stop up with a cork. **corkscrew** *n* device for extracting corks from bottles, usually consisting of a sharp pointed metal spiral.

corn[1] *n* **1** edible grain, esp. the small hard seeds of cereal plants. **2** *US* maize. **cornflakes** *n* breakfast cereal made from flakes of roasted maize. **cornflour** *n* finely ground flour from maize, used mainly to thicken gravies, sauces, etc. **cornflower** *n* blue flower commonly found growing in cornfields.

corn[2] *n* horny growth on the toe or foot, caused by friction of shoes.

corner *n* **1** angle or area formed when two sides, surfaces, or lines meet. **2** nook; secluded place. *vt* **1** force or drive into a difficult position. **2** establish a monopoly.

cornet *n* **1** brass musical instrument with three valves, similar to but smaller and more mellow than a trumpet. **2** cone-shaped wafer for ice cream.

coronation *n* ceremony of crowning a monarch.

coroner *n* public official in charge of an inquest in cases of suspicious death.

coronet *n* small crown.

corporal[1] *adj* relating to the body; physical.

corporal[2] *n* noncommissioned officer below a sergeant in the army or airforce.

corporation *n* **1** body of persons, usually in business, legally authorized to function as an individual. **2** municipal authority or council. **corporate** *adj.*

corporeal *adj* physical; material; not spiritual.

corps (kɔ:) *n* **1** military unit comprising several divisions. **2** group of dancers, actors, etc. **3** body of officials, esp. diplomats.

corpse *n* dead human body.

corpuscle ('kɔ:pʌsəl) *n* small free-floating cell present in the blood.

correct *vt* **1** set right. **2** point out faults or errors. **3** neutralize; counteract. *adj* **1** factual; true; accurate. **2** proper; conforming to a custom or standard. **correction** *n.* **correctly** *adv.*

correlate *vt,vi* have or bring into mutual relation. *n* either of two related things that imply each other. **correlation** *n.*

correspond *vi* **1** conform; match. **2** be similar or equivalent. **3** communicate by exchanging letters. **correspondence** *n* **1** agreement; conformity. **2** communication by letters. **correspondent** *n* **1** person who communicates by letters. **2** person employed by a newspaper, etc., to cover a special area or to report from a foreign country. *adj* similar.

corridor *n* long passageway connecting rooms, railway compartments, etc.

corrode *vt* eat away; eat into the surface of. **corrosion** *n.* **corrosive** *adj,n.*

corrupt *adj* **1** dishonest; open to bribery. **2** depraved; evil. **3** rotten; putrid; tainted. *vt* **1** cause to be dishonest. **2** pervert; debase. **3** taint. **corruptible** *adj.* **corruption** *n.*

corset *n* close-fitting stiffened undergarment that supports and shapes the stomach, worn esp. by women.

cosmetic *n* preparation to beautify the complexion or the hair. *adj* relating to cosmetics.

cosmic *adj* relating to or forming part of the universe.

cosmonaut *n* Soviet astronaut.

cosmopolitan *adj* **1** relating to all parts of the world; worldwide. **2** widely travelled; urbane. *n* person who is widely travelled or sophisticated.

cosmos *n* **1** universe. **2** harmonious system; order.

cost *n* **1** price of something. **2** loss; sacrifice; penalty. **3** expenditure of time, labour, money, etc. **at all costs** *or* **at any cost** regardless of the cost. ~*vt* (cost) **1** have as the price. **2** result in a loss, sacrifice, or penalty. **3** determine or estimate the cost of. **costly** *adj*.

costume *n* style of dress, esp. one indicating a particular period, nationality, etc.

cosy *adj* snug; comfortable. *n* padded cover for keeping a teapot, boiled egg, etc., warm. **cosily** *adv*.

cot *n* **1** child's bed with high sides. **2** portable bed or hammock.

cottage *n* small house, esp. in the country.

cotton *n* **1** plant producing white downy fibres that cover its seeds. **2** thread or cloth produced from these fibres. *v* **cotton on** realize; grasp. **cotton-wool** *n* raw bleached cotton, esp. as used for surgical dressings.

couch *n* upholstered furniture that seats two or more persons. *vt* express in a particular style.

cough *vi* expel air from the lungs with effort and noise. **cough up** *sl* produce; hand over. ~*n* act or sound of coughing.

could *v pt* of **can**.

council *n* administrative or legislative body, esp. one elected to govern a town or district. **councillor** *n*.

counsel *n* **1** advice; guidance. **2** barrister. **3** consultation; debate. *vt* (-ll-) give advice to; recommend. **counselling** *n* professional guidance given by social workers, etc., to individuals seeking help with personal problems. **counsellor** *n* adviser.

count[1] *vt,vi* **1** enumerate; add; reckon up; calculate. **2** list or name numerals in sequence. *vt* take into account; consider. *vi* be of importance; matter. **count on** rely or depend on. **count out** exclude. ~*n* **1** reckoning; calculation. **2** total number. **countdown** *n* period immediately before launching a spacecraft, etc., timed by counting backwards to zero. **countless** *adj* innumerable.

count[2] *n* nobleman of certain European countries, corresponding to a British earl.

counter[1] *n* **1** table or other surface on which money is counted, business transacted, etc. **2** long narrow table at which food is served. **3** small disc used as a token.

under the counter **1** conducted in a secret or dishonest manner. **2** reserved for special persons.

counter[2] *adv* in the opposite direction. *adj,n* opposite. *vt,vi* oppose; contradict.

counterattack *n* military attack launched just after an enemy attack. *vt,vi* make such an attack (on).

counterfeit *adj* not genuine; fake; forged. *vt* imitate with intent to deceive; forge. *n* something counterfeited.

counterfoil *n* stub of a cheque, receipt, etc., kept as a record.

counterpart *n* person or thing having an identical or equivalent function.

countess *n* **1** wife or widow of a count or earl. **2** woman of a rank equivalent to a count or earl.

country *n* **1** nation; territory; state. **2** population of a nation. **3** land of birth or residence. **4** rural area as opposed to a town.

county *n* major administrative, political, or judicial division of certain countries or states.

coup (ku:) *n* successful and often unexpected attack, stroke, etc.

couple *n* **1** pair. **2** two people in a relationship. **a couple of** a small number of; a few. ~*vt* **1** link or fasten together. **2** associate mentally. *vi* **1** associate in pairs. **2** unite sexually; copulate.

coupon *n* detachable slip or ticket used when ordering goods, claiming discount, etc.

courage *n* capacity to deal with danger; bravery; boldness. **courageous** *adj*. **courageously** *adv*.

courgette *n* small vegetable marrow.

courier *n* **1** special or express messenger. **2** person employed to take care of tourists and their travel arrangements.

course *n* **1** movement in space or time. **2** direction of movement; route. **3** type of action or conduct. **4** duration. **5** area or stretch of land over which a race is run, golf is played, etc. **6** series of lessons, sessions, etc. **7** any of the sequential parts of a meal. **in the course of** during. **of course** certainly; in fact. ~*vi* move or flow quickly.

court *n* **1** *also* **courtyard** space enclosed by buildings. **2** area marked off or enclosed for playing games, such as tennis or squash. **3** household or establishment of a sovereign. **4** body with judicial powers; tribunal. **5** building or room in which a trial or tribunal is held. **6** attention; homage. *vt,vi* **1** seek the affection of (a member of the opposite sex). **2** seek the approval or support of.

courtesy *n* polite behaviour or disposition. **courteous** *adj.*

cousin *n* son or daughter of one's uncle or aunt.

cove *n* **1** small inlet; sheltered bay. **2** nook or recess.

covenant *n* **1** agreement; bargain. **2** sealed contract or one of its clauses. *vt,vi* agree to or enter into a covenant.

cover *vt* **1** place or spread over. **2** overlie. **3** shield or conceal. **4** include. **5** protect by insurance. **6** report (an event) for a newspaper, etc. *n* **1** anything that covers. **2** funds to meet possible liability or loss. **coverage** *n* extent, amount, or risk covered.

cow *n* **1** female of the ox family, esp. one kept by farmers for milk. **2** female of certain other animals, such as the elephant, whale, and seal. **cowboy** *n* herdsman in charge of cattle on the western plains of North America, esp. one on horseback.

coward *n* person given to fear. **cowardice** *n.* **cowardly** *adj.* **cower** *vi* crouch in fear or shame; tremble.

coy *adj* shy; modest; slow to respond, esp. deliberately. **coyly** *adv.* **coyness** *n.*

crab *n* **1** ten-legged shellfish. **2** flesh of the crab, used as food. **3** ill-tempered person. **4** species of small apple. *vi* (-bb-) criticize; find fault.

crack *vi,vt* **1** break into pieces; form fissures. **2** make or cause to make a sharp sound. **3** change suddenly in tone; become hoarse. *vt* **1** strike sharply. **2** *inf* open; break into. **3** *inf* find the solution to. **4** tell (a joke). *vi also* **crack up** have a physical or mental breakdown. *n* **1** sharp explosive noise. **2** split or fissure.

cradle *n* **1** infant's bed. **2** supporting frame. **3** origin or home. *vt* hold in or as if in a cradle.

craft *n* **1** skilled trade. **2** manual skill. **3** cunning. **4** boat; vessel. **craftsman** *n.* **craftsmanship** *n.* **crafty** *adj* cunning; artful. **craftily** *adv.*

cram *v* (-mm-) *vt* fill or pack tightly. *vt,vi* **1** study intensively, as just before an examination. **2** eat greedily.

cramp *n* sudden painful involuntary contraction of a muscle.

crane *n* **1** large wading bird with long legs, neck, and bill. **2** machine for moving heavy objects. *vi* stretch the neck (for a better view).

crate *n* large packing case. *vt* pack in a crate.

crater *n* **1** bowl-shaped cavity or depression, such as one made by a meteorite on the earth or moon or by an exploding bomb. **2** mouth of a volcano. **cratered** *adj.*

crave *vt,vi* have a strong desire (for); yearn (for). **craving** *n.*

crawl *vi* **1** move along on the ground, etc., on the stomach or on the hands and knees. **2** move or progress very slowly. **3** creep or go stealthily or abjectly. **4** behave abjectly. *n* **1** act of crawling. **2** *also* **front crawl** fast swimming stroke.

craze *n* **1** mania; tremendous liking. **2** temporary fashion. *vt* **1** impair mentally; drive insane. **2** make small cracks in. *vi* become insane. **crazy** *adj* **1** insane; mad. **2** eccentric; peculiar. **3** unsound; shaky. **4** *inf* wildly enthusiastic or excited (about). **crazily** *adv.* **craziness** *n.*

cream *n* **1** fatty part of milk. **2** dish or delicacy resembling or made of cream. **3** creamlike substance, esp. a cosmetic. **4** best part of anything. *n,adj* yellowish-white. *vt* **1** beat (a mixture, etc.) until light and smooth. **2** remove the cream from. **3** apply a cream to. **creamy** *adj.*

crease *n* **1** line made by folding. **2** wrinkle. *vt,vi* make or develop creases.

create *vt* **1** bring into being. **2** give rise to. **3** make; produce. **creation** *n* **1** act of creating or state of being created. **2** something created, esp. an original design, work of art, etc. **3** universe and all living creatures. **creative** *adj* having the ability to create; original; inventive. **creativity** *n.*

creature *n* **1** living being, esp. an animal. **2** contemptible or pitiful person.

crèche *n* **1** nursery for infants. **2** model of the Nativity scene.

credible *adj* believable; worthy of belief.

credit *n* **1** system of doing business without immediate receipt or payment of cash. **2** power to purchase items, services, etc., by deferred payment. **3** money at one's disposal in a bank, etc. **4** belief; trust. **5** source of honour, reputation, etc. **6** good name; reputation. **7** influence; respect; commendation. **8** acknowledgement of authorship, direction, performance, etc. *vt* **1** believe; trust; have faith in. **2** attribute; acknowledge. **3** give credit for. **credit card** *n* card that identifies and authorizes the holder to obtain goods or services on deferred payment. **creditor** *n* person, etc., to whom money is owed.

cremate *vt* dispose of (a corpse) by burning. **cremation** *n.* **crematorium** *n* place where corpses are cremated.

crescent *n* **1** waxing or waning moon. **2** narrow curved and pointed figure or symbol. **3** curved row of houses.

crest *n* **1** comb or tuft on an animal's head. **2** plume on top of a helmet. **3** top of a wave, mountain ridge, etc. *vt* reach or lie on the top of. *vi* form or rise into a crest. **crestfallen** *adj* dejected.

crevice *n* fissure; narrow split or crack.

crew *n* persons that man a boat, ship, aircraft, etc.

cricket[1] *n* chirping leaping insect.

cricket[2] *n* **1** team game played on a grass pitch with bats, ball, and wickets. **2** *inf* fair play.

crime *n* **1** serious violation of the law. **2** wicked act; sin; grave offence. **3** *inf* senseless or foolish act. **4** unlawful acts in general. **criminal** *n* person guilty or convicted of crime. *adj* **1** relating to or involving crime or its punishment; guilty of crime. **2** wicked; senseless.

cripple *n* lame or disabled person. *vt* **1** disable; maim; make a cripple of. **2** damage, esp. financially. **crippling** *adj* damaging.

crisis *n*, *pl* **crises** ('kraisi:z) **1** time of acute danger, stress, suspense, etc. **2** turning point; decisive moment.

crisp *adj* **1** brittle; dry; crackling. **2** brisk. **3** clear-cut; sharp; lively. **4** fresh. *n* fine slice of fried potato. **crisply** *adv.* **crispness** *n.*

criterion *n*, *pl* **criteria** (krai'tiəriə) standard of judgement or comparison; test.

critic *n* **1** person who passes judgment or criticizes. **2** expert in assessing the merits of works of art, literature, drama, etc. **critical** *adj* **1** given to judging, fault-finding, etc. **2** of great importance; decisive. **3** involving suspense or risk. **4** relating to critics or criticism. **critically** *adv.* **criticism** *n* **1** severe judgment; disapproval. **2** assessment; review; analysis; evaluation. **criticize** *vt,vi* **1** judge severely; censure. **2** examine critically; evaluate.

crockery *n* china or earthenware vessels.

crook *n* **1** criminal; swindler. **2** hooked staff. **3** sharp turn or bend. *vt* bend; curve; make a crook in. **crooked** *adj* **1** bent; curved. **2** set at an angle; askew. **3** *inf* dishonest.

crop *n* **1** cultivated produce. **2** harvest of this. **3** group of things occurring together. **4** pouch in a bird's gullet. **5** stock of a whip. **6** hunting or riding whip. **7** closely cut head of hair. *vt* (-pp-) **1** clip; cut short; cut off. **2** raise or harvest produce. **crop up** *inf* occur, arise, etc., unexpectedly.

cross *n* **1** upright stake with a transverse bar. **2** model, mark, or figure of a cross, esp. as a Christian emblem or symbol of Christianity. **3** sign of the Cross made with the hand. **4** intermixture of breeds, qualities, etc. **5** misfortune; trouble. **the Cross 1** cross on which Jesus died. **2** model or picture of this. ⁓ *vt* **1** place so as to intersect. **2** make the sign of the Cross on or over. **3** pass across. **4** meet and pass. **5** mark with lines across. **6** oppose; thwart. **7** modify a breed of animals or plants by intermixture. *vi* **1** intersect. **2** pass over. *adj* **1** out of

crow[1] *n* large black bird with glossy feathers.

crow[2] *vi* **1** *inf* boast. **2** utter a shrill cry.

crowd *vi* flock together. *vt* **1** cram or pack. **2** fill with people. *n* large number; throng. **crowded** *adj.*

crown *n* **1** monarch's headdress. **2** wreath for the head. **3** royal power. **4** former coin. **5** top, as of the head. **6** completion; perfection. *vt* **1** put a crown on. **2** make a king or queen. **3** honour; reward; invest with dignity, etc. **4** bring to completion or perfection.

crucial *adj* decisive; critical.

crucifix *n* cross, esp. one with a figure of Jesus crucified on it. **crucifixion** *n* crucifying, esp. of Jesus. **crucify** *vt* **1** put to death by nailing or tying to a cross. **2** treat severely; torment.

crude *adj* **1** in the natural or raw state. **2** unfinished; rough. **3** without grace; unpolished. **4** blunt; vulgar. **crudely** *adv.* **crudeness** *or* **crudity** *n.* **crude oil** *n* petroleum before it is made into petrol or other products.

cruel *adj* **1** delighting in the pain or suffering of others; heartless. **2** enjoying the infliction of pain on others. **3** distressing; painful. **cruelty** *n.*

cruise *vi* **1** sail about, esp. for pleasure. **2** fly, drive, etc., at moderate speed. *n* act of cruising. **cruiser** *n* armed high-speed naval ship of light or medium displacement.

crumb *n* small particle; fragment, esp. of bread. *vt* break into or cover with crumbs.

crumble *vt,vi* **1** break into small fragments. **2** decay; fall to pieces.

crusade *n* **1** *also* **Crusade** medieval Christian war to recover the Holy Land from the Turks. **2** campaign in favour of a cause. *vi* participate in a crusade.

crush *vt* **1** compress so as to break, bruise, or crumple. **2** break into small pieces. **3** defeat utterly. *n* **1** act of crushing. **2** crowded mass, esp. of people.

crust *n* **1** hard outer surface of bread. **2** any hard or firm outer part, deposit, or casing. **3** surface of the earth. *vt,vi* cover with

or form a crust. **crusty** *adj* **1** having or like a crust. **2** ill-tempered. **crustily** *adv.*

crutch *n* **1** support for a lame person that fits under the armpit. **2** something needed for moral or psychological support.

crux *n* **1** real issue. **2** hard problem.

crypt *n* underground chamber or vault, esp. one beneath a church, used for burials, etc. **cryptic** *adj* secret; hidden; mysterious.

crystal *n* **1** transparent piece of mineral. **2** form of certain substances having a definite internal structure and external surfaces that intersect at characteristic angles. **3** very clear glass. **4** cut-glass vessels. **5** something made of or resembling crystal. **crystalline** *adj.* **crystallize** *vt,vi* **1** form into crystals. **2** become or cause to be definite or certain.

cub *n* **1** young of certain animals, such as lions or bears. **2** inexperienced person.

cube *n* **1** regular solid figure bounded by six equal squares. **2** cube-shaped or nearly cube-shaped block. **3** product obtained by multiplying a number by itself twice. **cubic** *adj* **1** having the shape of a cube. **2** relating to volume or volume measure. **3** having three dimensions.

cubicle *n* small room or walled-off space, as for sleeping, dressing, studying, etc.

cuckoo *n* widely distributed bird named from the sound of its call.

cucumber *n* long fleshy green edible fruit, commonly used in salads.

cuddle *vt* hug; fondle. *vi* lie close. *n* hug; affectionate embrace.

cue[1] *n* **1** words or actions used as a guide or signal. **2** hint.

cue[2] *n* long tapered rod with a soft tip used to strike the ball in billiards, etc.

cuff[1] *n* end of a sleeve; wrist-band. **off the cuff** without preparation; improvised.

cuff[2] *vt* hit with the open hand. *n* such a blow.

culinary *adj* relating to or used in cooking or the kitchen.

culprit *n* guilty person; offender.

cult *n* **1** system of religious worship. **2** devotion to or pursuit of some object.

cultivate vt **1** raise (crops) on land; grow. **2** develop; improve; refine. **cultivation** n.

culture n **1** intellectual, behavioural, and artistic ideas, beliefs, etc., of a particular group, time, or place. **2** particular form or stage of civilization. **3** development and training of the mind. **4** refinement of taste, manners, etc. **5** cultivation. **cultural** adj. **cultured** adj **1** refined. **2** grown in an artificial medium.

cunning n **1** dexterity; skill. **2** skill in deceit or evasion. adj having such qualities or characteristics. **cunningly** adv.

cupboard n closed cabinet, usually with shelves.

curate n assistant to a parish priest or vicar.

curator n person in charge of a museum, a specific collection, etc.

curb n **1** check or means of restraint; control. **2** framework or border that encloses. vt restrain; control; check.

curd n substance obtained by coagulating milk, used as food or in cheese-making. **curdle** vt,vi form into curd.

cure vt **1** heal; remedy. **2** preserve (fish, skins, etc.). n **1** remedy. **2** course of medical treatment. **3** restoration to health.

curious adj **1** eager to know; inquisitive. **2** prying; tending to meddle. **3** exciting interest. **4** odd; eccentric. **curiosity** n. **curiously** adv.

curl vt,vi bend into a curved shape or spiral. n **1** spiral lock of hair. **2** spiral or curved form, state, or motion. **curly** adj.

currant n small seedless raisin.

currency n **1** time during which anything is current. **2** state of being in use. **3** money.

current adj **1** in general use or circulation. **2** going on; not yet superseded. n **1** moving body of water or air. **2** flow of something, such as a river. **3** movement of electric charge through a conductor or the rate of its flow.

curse n **1** obscene or profane utterance. **2** utterance designed to destroy or harm someone. **3** affliction; bane; scourge. vi swear. vt **1** abuse by uttering curses at. **2** call on supernatural powers to bring harm to (someone).

curt adj **1** short. **2** rudely brief. **curtly** adv. **curtness** n.

curtail vt cut short; end. **curtailment** n.

curtain n **1** cloth, etc., hung as a screen in front of a window or door. **2** screen between the audience and a stage. **3** end to an act or scene. vt provide or cover with a curtain.

curtsy n formal woman's bow made as a sign of respect, greeting, etc. vi make such a bow.

curve n **1** line with no straight parts. **2** bend in a road, etc. **3** curved form or object. vt,vi bend in a curve. **curvature** n.

cushion n **1** bag or pad filled with soft stuffing or air, used to sit on, lean against, etc. **2** something that absorbs shocks, jolts, etc. vt provide or protect with a cushion.

custody n **1** safe-keeping; guardianship. **2** imprisonment. **custodian** n person having custody of someone or something.

custom n **1** established or habitual practice, usage, etc. **2** business patronage. **3** customers of a shop, business, etc. **customs** pl n **1** duties levied on certain imports. **2** area in an airport, etc., where such duties are collected. **customary** adj usual. **customer** n **1** buyer; patron. **2** inf fellow; chap.

cutlery n **1** knives and other cutting implements. **2** eating implements.

cycle n **1** recurrent or complete series or period. **2** development following a course of stages. **3** series of poems, etc. **4** short for **bicycle**. vi **1** move in cycles. **2** ride a bicycle. **cyclic** or **cyclical** adj. **cyclist** n person who rides a bicycle.

cyclone n system of winds moving round a centre of low pressure.

cygnet n young swan.

cylinder n **1** tube-shaped figure, usually with a circular base. **2** piston chamber of an engine. **cylindrical** adj.

cymbal n saucer-shaped piece of brass used as a musical instrument of percussion.

cynic n sceptical or distrusting person. **cynical** adj. **cynicism** n.

D

dab *vt,vi* (-bb-) touch gently; apply with a light touch. *n* **1** gentle blow. **2** small lump of soft substance.

dabble *vt,vi* move about in water or other liquid. *vi* engage in some activity in a superficial manner. **dabbler** *n*.

dad *n inf* father.

daffodil *n* variety of yellow narcissus.

daft *adj* silly; feeble-minded.

dagger *n* short stabbing weapon with a double-edged blade.

daily *adj* performed, occurring, etc., every day. *adv* every day. *n* **1** daily newspaper. **2** non-resident domestic help.

dainty *adj* **1** pretty; elegant. **2** fastidious; delicate. **daintily** *adv*. **daintiness** *n*.

dairy *n* place for keeping, processing, or supplying milk and milk products. **dairy farm** *n* farm producing milk and milk products.

daisy *n* small white-petalled flower with a yellow centre.

dam[1] *n* barrier to hold back water. *vt* (-mm-) obstruct or hold back with a dam.

dam[2] *n* female parent, esp. of an animal.

damage *vt,vi* injure; harm; impair; spoil. *n* harm; injury. **damages** *pl n* financial compensation awarded by law for loss or harm.

dame *n* lady, esp. a mistress of a household or school. **Dame** title of a female member of an order of knighthood.

damn *vt* **1** curse; doom; condemn to hell. **2** censure. *interj* expression of anger or annoyance. **damnable** *adj* **1** deserving condemnation. **2** wretched. **damnation** *n* state of being damned.

damp *adj* moist; slightly wet. *n* moisture. *vt also* **dampen 1** moisten. **2** depress; discourage.

damson *n* small purple fruit of the plum family.

dance *n* **1** sequence of rhythmical steps usually performed to music. **2** social gathering for dancing. *vt,vi* **1** perform (a dance). **2** move quickly, energetically, or gracefully. **dance attendance (on)** attend constantly. **dancer** *n*.

dandelion *n* plant with bright yellow flowers and leaves with jagged edges.

dandruff *n* flakes of scurf formed on the scalp.

danger *n* exposure to risk of harm; peril; risk. **dangerous** *adj*. **dangerously** *adv*.

dangle *vt,vi* swing loosely; hang freely.

dare *vt,vi* be brave enough (to do something). *vt* challenge; defy. *n* challenge to do something. **daring** *adj* bold; adventurous. *n* boldness; audacity.

dark *adj* **1** without light. **2** deeply tinted; brown or almost black. **3** mysterious; secret; evil. *n* **1** absence of light; night. **2** ignorance; secrecy. **darkness** *n*. **darken** *vt,vi* make or become dark(er).

darling *n* person greatly loved; favourite. *adj* greatly loved or desired.

darn *vt,vi* mend (a hole in fabric) by stitching over. *n* repair so made.

dart *n* **1** small pointed missile, such as a short arrow. **2** swift sudden movement. **3** short seam or tuck in a garment. *vi,vt* move swiftly and suddenly; shoot out. **darts** *n* game in which darts are thrown at a circular board (dartboard).

dash *vi* rush hastily. *vt* **1** hurl; thrust; knock violently. **2** discourage; ruin. *n* **1** sudden rush. **2** small quantity, esp. as a flavouring in food or drink. **3** punctuation mark (-) used to indicate a pause, change of subject, etc. **4** energy; vigour. **dashing** *adj* **1** showy; stylish. **2** impetuous; spirited. **dashboard** *n* instrument panel of a motor vehicle.

data *n s or pl* facts, figures, statistics, etc., used as a basis for discussion or calculation. **data base** *n* mass of information stored in a computer from which particular items of information can be retrieved as required.

date[1] *n* **1** day on which an event occurs or a statement of this in days, months, and years. **2** *inf* appointment; rendezvous. **3** person with whom one has an appointment. *vt* **1** determine the date of. **2** *inf* make an appointment, esp. with a member of the opposite sex. **date from** originate from a certain date.

date[2] *n* sweet oblong single-stoned fruit.

daughter *n* **1** female offspring, esp. in relation to her parents. **2** any female descendant. **daughter-in-law** *n, pl* **daughters-in-law** son's wife.

dawdle *vi* move slowly; loiter; fall or lag behind. **dawdler** *n*.

dawn *n* **1** period during which the sun rises; daybreak. **2** beginning. *vi* **1** begin to grow light. **2** begin to appear or develop. **dawn upon** become evident to.

day *n* **1** period between sunrise and sunset. **2** period of 24 hours beginning at midnight. **daybreak** *n* dawn. **daydream** *n* pleasant sequence of thoughts or musing while awake. *vi* have daydreams. **daylight** *n* light from sun.

daze *vt* stupefy; bewilder; stun. *n* state of being dazed or stunned; drowsiness.

dazzle *vt* **1** blind temporarily with brilliant light. **2** surprise with brilliance, beauty, etc.

dead *adj* **1** without life; having died. **2** dull; numb; resembling death. **3** extinct; no longer active. **deaden** *vt* make insensible; numb; dull the vitality of. **deadline** *n* time by which some task must be completed. **deadlock** *n* complete standstill in which further progress is impossible. **deadly** *adj* **1** fatal; poisonous. **2** like death.

deaf *adj* **1** lacking or deficient in the sense of hearing. **2** unwilling to listen. **deafen** *vt* **1** make deaf. **2** make impervious to sound. **deafness** *n*.

deal *v* (dealt) *vt,vi* distribute, esp. playing cards to the players. *vt* inflict; deliver. *vi* do business; trade. **deal with** manage; settle. ~*n* **1** business transaction. **2** distribution of playing cards. **3** *inf* amount. **dealer** *n*.

dean *n* **1** head clergyman of a cathedral. **2** college or university official.

dear *adj* **1** much loved; precious. **2** expensive; costly. *n* someone much loved. *adv* at high cost. **dearly** *adv*. **dearness** *n*.

death *n* **1** end of life; state of being dead. **2** dying. **3** cause of death. **deathly** *adj* resembling death; lifeless; pale.

debase *vt* undervalue; lower in value; degrade.

debate *n* **1** formal public discussion. **2** argument; controversy. *vt,vi* discuss; argue (about). **debatable** *adj* open to discussion; questionable.

debit *n* **1** record in an account of money owed. **2** debt; something owed. *vt* record as money owing; charge.

debris *n* wreckage; fragments.

debt *n* **1** something owed. **2** obligation. **in debt 1** owing money. **2** having an obligation. **debtor** *n* person who is in debt to another.

decade *n* period of ten years.

decadent *adj* **1** declining or deteriorating, esp. morally. **2** corrupted. **decadence** *n*.

decant *vt* pour liquid gently from one vessel to another. **decanter** *n* glass vessel for serving wine.

decapitate *vt* ᵗ ᵣ or chop off the head of. **decapitatic..** *n*.

decay *vi* **1** decompose; rot. **2** deteriorate; decline. *n* **1** decomposition. **2** deterioration; decline.

decease *n* death. *vi* die.

deceive *vt,vi* mislead deliberately; delude; cheat. **deceit** *n*. **deceitful** *adj*. **deceitfully** *adv*.

December *n* twelfth month of the year.

decent *adj* **1** respectable; proper; modest. **2** *inf* fairly good; adequate. **decency** *n*. **decently** *adv*.

deceptive *adj* tending to deceive or give a false impression. **deception** *n*.

decibel *n* unit for measuring intensities of sounds.

decide *vt* give judgment on; settle. *vi* make up one's mind; conclude. **decided** *adj* **1** certain; definite. **2** resolute. **decidedly** *adv*.

deciduous *adj* **1** (of leaves, teeth, etc.) shed periodically. **2** (of trees) shedding leaves annually.

decimal *adj* based on the number ten; numbered or proceeding by tens. *n also* **decimal fraction** fraction having a denominator that is a power of ten, written with a dot in front of the numerator.

decipher *vt* **1** decode. **2** make out the meaning of.

decision *n* **1** judgment; settlement; conclusion. **2** firmness; determination. **decisive** *adj* **1** conclusive; deciding. **2** resolute; firm. **decisively** *adv*.

deck *n* **1** horizontal platform forming the floor of a ship, bus, etc. **2** pack of cards. *vt* adorn; decorate. **deckchair** *n* portable folding chair with a canvas back.

declare *vt,vi* **1** announce formally; proclaim; assert. **2** state that one has an income, goods, etc., on which duty or tax must be paid. **3** close an innings in cricket before all the wickets have fallen. **declaration** *n*.

declension *n* 1 change in form of a noun, pronoun, or adjective depending on its case. 2 decline; deterioration.

decline *vt,vi* 1 slope downwards. 2 deteriorate; decay. 3 refuse. *n* gradual deterioration; loss of strength, vigour, etc.

decode *vt* interpret from a code; decipher.

decompose *vt,vi* putrefy; rot; decay. **decomposition** *n*.

decorate *vt* 1 embellish; adorn. 2 restore with new paint, wallpaper, etc. 3 invest with a medal, badge, etc. **decoration** *n*. **decorative** *adj*. **decorator** *n*.

decoy *n* something used to attract others into a trap; lure.

decrease *vt,vi* diminish; make or grow less; reduce. *n* process of or amount of lessening; reduction.

decree *n* official decision, judgment, or law. *vt,vi* command; judge; order.

decrepit *adj* worn out; old and useless.

dedicate *vt* 1 devote solemnly or wholly. 2 set apart for a special purpose. 3 inscribe or address as a compliment. **dedication** *n*.

deduce *vt* draw as a conclusion from given facts; infer. **deduct** *vt* take away; subtract. **deduction** *n* 1 act of deducting. 2 amount deducted. 3 logical reasoning from given facts. 4 the conclusion reached.

deed *n* 1 something done; action; exploit. 2 legal document stating terms of a contract, rights, etc.

deep *adj* 1 extending far down, in, or across. 2 at or of a specified distance down or in. 3 profound; intense; serious. 4 absorbed; engrossed. 5 low-pitched. 6 dark-coloured. *adv also* **deeply** so as to be deep. *n* deep place, esp. in the sea. **deepness** *n*. **deepen** *vt,vi* make or become deep(er). **deep-freeze** *n* refrigerator to keep food fresh for long periods. **deeply** *adv* strongly; profoundly; extremely. **deep-seated** *adj* firmly established; not superficial.

deer *n*, *pl* **deer** ruminant, the male of which has deciduous antlers.

deface *vt* spoil the appearance or surface of; disfigure. **defacement** *n*.

defame *vt* injure the good name or reputation of, as by libel, slander, etc. **defamation** *n*. **defamatory** *adj*.

default *n* 1 absence; want. 2 failure to act or appear. *vi* fail to act or appear as required. **defaulter** *n*.

defeat *vt* conquer; vanquish; overcome; beat. *n* act of being beaten or conquered.

defect *n* ('di:fekt) failing; blemish; imperfection; fault; flaw. *vi* (di'fekt) desert one's country, duty, etc.; switch allegiance. **defection** *n*. **defector** *n*. **defective** *adj* imperfect; faulty; deficient.

defend *vt,vi* 1 protect against attack. 2 justify, as in answer to a legal charge. **defence** *n*. **defences** *pl n* 1 fortifications. 2 self-protective attitudes. **defensive** *adj* protective; resisting attack. **defensively** *adv*.

defer[1] *vt,vi* (-rr-) postpone; put off.

defer[2] *vi* (-rr-) make concessions; submit (to). **deference** *n* respectful submission to another's will. **deferential** *adj*.

defiant *adj* stubbornly or aggressively hostile; insolent. **defiance** *n*. **defiantly** *adv*.

deficient *adj* incomplete; defective; lacking. **deficiency** *n*.

deficit *n* lack or shortage, esp. of money.

define *vt* 1 mark out; show the limits of. 2 describe exactly; give the meaning of.

definite *adj* 1 certain; fixed; exact. 2 clear; distinct. **definite article** *n* the word 'the'. **definitely** *adv*.

definition *n* 1 act of defining. 2 brief description or explanation, esp. of a word or phrase. 3 quality of distinctness or clarity.

deflate *vt,vi* 1 release air from or lose air. 2 reduce economic inflation. 3 lessen the dignity or conceit of. **deflation** *n*. **deflationary** *adj*.

deflect *vt,vi* turn or move at an angle. **deflection** *n*.

deform *vt* spoil the shape of; make ugly; disfigure. **deformation** *n*. **deformity** *n*.

defraud *vt* cheat; swindle; deprive by fraud.

defrost *vt* remove ice from.

deft *adj* skilful; nimble. **deftly** *adv*. **deftness** *n*.

defunct *adj* obsolete; no longer used.

defy *vt* 1 challenge; resist stubbornly. 2 disobey.

degenerate *vi* (di'dʒenəreit) decline in standard or qualities; deteriorate. *adj* (di'dʒenərət) degraded; depraved. *n* (di'dʒenərət) degenerate person. **degeneration** *or* **degeneracy** *n.*

degrade *vt,vi* **1** reduce in grade or rank. **2** lower in character; debase; humiliate. **degradation** *n.*

degree *n* **1** grade; stage; relative position; extent. **2** academic rank awarded for proficiency or as an honour. **3** unit of measurement in temperature scales. **4** unit of angular measure; 1/360th part of a complete turn.

dehydrate *vt* remove water from. **dehydration** *n.*

deity *n* god or goddess.

dejected *adj* depressed; despondent; sad; miserable.

delay *vt* cause to be late; postpone. *vi* be late; linger. *n* act of delaying; fact or period of being delayed; postponement.

delegate *vt* ('deligeit) **1** send or elect as a representative. **2** entrust to as a deputy. *n* ('deligət) representative; deputy; agent. **delegation** *n* **1** number of delegates in a group. **2** act of delegating.

delete *vt* strike out; erase; remove. **deletion** *n.*

deliberate *vi* (di'libəreit) reflect; consider carefully. *adj* (di'libərət) **1** intentional; purposeful. **2** slow in deciding; cautious. **deliberately** *adv.* **deliberation** *n.*

delicate *adj* **1** finely made or prepared; pleasing. **2** sensitive; easily hurt or damaged. **3** refined; fastidious. **delicacy** *n* **1** sensitivity; tact. **2** refinement; gracefulness. **3** attractive and tasty food. **delicately** *adv.*

delicatessen *n* shop specializing in foreign food, cooked meats, delicacies, etc. *pl n* the foods sold.

delicious *adj* **1** pleasing, esp. to the senses of taste or smell. **2** delightful.

delight *vt* give great pleasure to. **delight in** take pleasure in. ~*n* intense pleasure or joy or a cause of this. **delightful** *adj.* **delightfully** *adv.*

delinquency *n* neglect of duty; wrongdoing; petty crime. **delinquent** *n,adj.*

deliver *vt* **1** set free; liberate. **2** hand over or distribute (mail, goods, etc.). **3** give forth; discharge. **4** pronounce; utter. **5** assist at the birth of. **deliverance** *n* liberation; rescue.

delivery *n* **1** delivering of mail, goods, a speech, etc. **2** childbirth.

delta *n* fan-shaped area of land at the mouth of a river.

delude *vt* deceive; mislead. **delusion** *n.* **delusive** *adj.*

deluge *n* violent flood. *vt* rush upon or at, as a flood; inundate.

delve *vt,vi* **1** dig. **2** *also* **delve into** research deeply (into).

demand *vt* **1** ask for; claim; request urgently. **2** require; need. *n* pressing request or requirement.

democracy *n* **1** government by the people, esp. by majority vote; equality of rights. **2** state or community so governed. **democrat** *n.* **democratic** *adj.*

demolish *vt* destroy; pull down. **demolition** *n.*

demon *n* **1** devil; evil spirit. **2** cruel or wicked person. **demonic** *adj.*

demonstrate *vt* show by reasoning or practical example; explain. *vi* manifest opposition or sympathy in public; make a protest. **demonstrable** *adj.* **demonstration** *n.* **demonstrator** *n.*

demoralize *vt* **1** lower the morale of; cause to lose courage. **2** harm morally; corrupt.

demure *adj* modest; reserved; sedate. **demurely** *adv.*

den *n* **1** wild animal's retreat or resting place. **2** hiding-place of thieves. **3** private room for work.

denial *n* **1** contradiction. **2** refutation; rejection. **3** refusal of a request.

denim *n* strong cotton fabric.

denomination *n* **1** name or designation. **2** class of units in money, weights, etc. **3** name of a group of people, esp. a religious sect.

denominator *n* lower number in a fraction; divisor. **common denominator** *n* something possessed in common by all members of a group.

denote *vt* **1** mark out; distinguish. **2** stand for; indicate. **denotation** *n.*

denounce *vt* **1** condemn strongly or publicly. **2** inform against. **3** repudiate.

dense *adj* **1** thick; closely packed. **2** opaque. **3** *inf* stupid. **density** *n* **1** thickness. **2** mass per unit volume.

dent *n* small hollow left by a blow or by pressure. *vt,vi* make a dent in or become marked by a dent.

dental *adj* of or relating to the teeth. **dentist** *n* person who treats decayed teeth, fits false teeth, etc. **dentistry** *n.* **denture** *n* set of false teeth.

deny *vt* 1 declare to be untrue; contradict. 2 reject; repudiate. 3 refuse. **deny oneself** abstain from.

deodorant *n* substance that counteracts offensive smells.

depart *vi* 1 go away; leave. 2 die. **departure** *n.*

department *n* 1 subdivision; branch; separate section of an organization. 2 field of activity; special concern.

depend *v* **depend (up)on** 1 be conditional or contingent on. 2 rely on; trust. **dependable** *adj* reliable. **dependant** *n* person relying upon another for maintenance or support. **dependent** *adj.* **dependence** *n.*

depict *vt* represent in words or pictures; portray; describe. **depiction** *n.*

deplete *vt* exhaust; empty; reduce. **depletion** *n.*

deplore *vt* 1 regret deeply; lament. 2 disapprove of. **deplorable** *adj.*

deport *vt* expel from a country; banish. **deportation** *n.*

deportment *n* manner of standing, walking, etc.; bearing.

depose *vt* remove from office, esp. from a high position. *vi* bear witness; testify. **deposition** *n.*

deposit *vt* 1 set down. 2 put aside for safekeeping or as a pledge of faith. *n* 1 money entrusted to a bank, etc., or as part-payment of a transaction. 2 layer of ore or sediment in the earth. **depository** *n* place for safekeeping, esp. a store for goods.

depot *n* 1 store or military headquarters. 2 central garage for buses.

deprave *vt* corrupt morally; pervert. **depravity** *n.*

deprecate *vt* express disapproval of.

depreciate *vt,vi* 1 lower or fall in price or value. 2 disparage. **depreciation** *n.*

depress *vt* 1 press down; lower. 2 lessen the activity of. 3 make humble or gloomy. **depression** *n* 1 lowered surface; hollow.

2 low spirits; dejection. 3 state or period of reduced economic activity; slump. 4 region of low barometric pressure in the atmosphere.

deprive *vt* prevent from possessing or using; take away from. **deprivation** *n.*

depth *n* 1 distance downwards; deepness. 2 intensity or extent, as of emotion. 3 profundity of thought or explanation. 4 lowness of pitch. 5 most extreme or intense point. **out of one's depth** unable to understand or cope with a subject, situation, etc. **the depths** *pl n* 1 deepest part. 2 condition of low spirits or dejection.

deputize *vi,vt* act or appoint as an agent or representative. **deputation** *n* body of persons sent to represent others. **deputy** *n* assistant; representative; delegate.

derail *vt* cause (a train) to leave the rails. **derailment** *n.*

derelict *adj* abandoned; in a poor condition; dilapidated. *n* something abandoned. **dereliction** *n* neglect, esp. of duty.

deride *vt* mock at; scorn. **derision** *n.* **derisive** *adj.*

derive *vt* obtain or receive from. *vi* originate (from); be descended (from). **derivation** *n.* **derivative** *n,adj.*

derogatory *adj* insulting; not complimentary; damaging.

descend *vt,vi* move, come, or bring down. *vi* 1 move or slope downwards. 2 originate (from). **descendant** *n* person descended from another; offspring. **descent** *n* 1 descending; going down. 2 downward slope or path. 3 ancestry; transmission by inheritance.

describe *vt* 1 give a detailed account of, esp. in words. 2 trace or mark out. **description** *n.* **descriptive** *adj.*

desert[1] ('dezət) *n* waterless and uninhabited region. *adj* barren; lonely.

desert[2] (di'zɔːt) *vt* abandon; leave. *vi* leave service, esp. the army, without permission. **deserter** *n.* **desertion** *n.*

desert[3] (di'zɔːt) *n* something deserved, as a reward or punishment.

deserve *vt* be entitled to by conduct or qualities; merit. *vi* be worthy.

design *vt* 1 plan; make sketches for. 2 intend. *n* 1 plan; scheme; project. 2 art of making designs or patterns. **designer** *n.*

designate vt ('dezigneit) **1** indicate; point out; name. **2** appoint to office. adj ('dezignǝt) appointed to but not yet holding office. **designation** n.

desire vt **1** wish for greatly; yearn for; want. **2** request. n **1** longing; craving; urge; appetite. **2** request. **3** thing or person desired. **desirable** adj.

desist vi refrain; cease; stop.

desk n table with a flat or sloping writing surface.

desolate adj ('desǝlǝt) **1** abandoned; lonely. **2** dreary; gloomy. vt ('desǝleit) **1** lay waste; destroy. **2** make unhappy. **desolation** n.

despair n loss of hope; hopelessness; despondency. vi lose hope.

desperate adj **1** very serious or dangerous; beyond hope. **2** reckless; violent; careless of risk. **desperation** n.

despise vt feel contempt for; scorn. **despicable** adj.

despite prep in spite of.

despondent adj dejected; lacking hope or courage. **despondency** n.

despot n tyrant; cruel ruler or master. **despotic** adj.

dessert n fruit, confectionery, etc., served as the final course of a meal. **dessertspoon** n spoon of a size between a tablespoon and a teaspoon.

destine vt **1** determine the future of; doom. **2** set apart for a special purpose; intend. **destination** n place towards which a person travels or a thing is sent; end of a journey. **destiny** n **1** fate; supernatural or divine power. **2** that which is destined to happen.

destitute adj in extreme poverty; penniless. **destitution** n.

destroy vt demolish; annihilate; ruin. **destruction** n. **destructive** adj.

detach vt separate; disconnect. **detached** adj **1** disconnected. **2** aloof; impartial. **detachment** n.

detail n small part of a whole; item; fact; piece of information. **in detail** thoroughly; fully. ~vt **1** give particulars of. **2** appoint for special duty.

detain vt **1** keep waiting; prevent from leaving; delay. **2** keep possession of; withhold. **3** hold in custody. **detainee** n. **deten-**

tion n **1** detaining or being detained. **2** holding in custody. **3** keeping in school of a pupil or pupils after normal hours as a punishment.

detect vt **1** notice; see. **2** find out; discover. **detection** n. **detective** n person, esp. a policeman, who investigates crimes.

deter vt (-rr-) discourage or dissuade from action, esp. by fear of consequences. **deterrent** n,adj.

detergent n cleansing substance. adj cleansing.

deteriorate vt,vi make or become worse; degenerate. **deterioration** n.

determine vt **1** be the cause of or deciding factor in. **2** set limits to; fix. vi resolve; decide. **determination** n resoluteness; firmness of purpose.

detest vt dislike intensely; loathe; hate. **detestable** adj.

detonate vt,vi explode. **detonation** n. **detonator** n detonating device.

detour n diversion; deviation from a usual route.

detract vt disparage. **detract from** diminish; spoil.

devalue vt reduce the value of. **devaluation** n.

devastate vt destroy wholly; demolish. **devastation** n.

develop vi evolve; grow; open out. vt **1** bring to a more advanced stage. **2** bring forth; reveal. **3** treat (photographic film) to make the image visible. **development** n.

deviate vi diverge; turn away from what is normal or expected. **deviant** adj,n. **deviation** n.

device n **1** mechanical contrivance; apparatus, appliance, or machine. **2** plot; scheme.

devil n **1** demon; wicked fiend. **2** sl lively or energetic person; rascal. **the Devil** personification of evil; Satan. **devilish** adj.

devious adj **1** roundabout; winding; erratic. **2** deceitful.

devise vt **1** invent; contrive. **2** bequeath.

devoid adj **devoid of** empty (of); lacking in.

devote vt give up wholly, esp. to some cause or person; dedicate. **devotion** n **1** great loyalty; dedication. **2** religious worship. **devotee** n.

devour *vt* **1** eat greedily; consume. **2** absorb mentally with great eagerness.

devout *adj* **1** pious. **2** earnest; solemn.

dew *n* droplets of moisture deposited on ground surfaces at night.

dexterous *adj* skilful; deft; clever. **dexterity** *n.*

diabetes (daiə'biːtis) *n* disease of the pancreas, characterized by allergy to sugar and abnormal discharge of urine. **diabetic** *n,adj.*

diagonal *adj* joining two opposite corners; slanting; oblique. *n* diagonal line. **diagonally** *adv.*

diagram *n* sketch, drawing, or plan, used esp. to illustrate or demonstrate something. **diagrammatic** *adj.*

dial *n* **1** graduated face or disc on a watch, compass, or other instrument. **2** numbered disc on a telephone. *vt* (-ll-) call using a telephone dial.

dialect *n* regional variation of a language.

dialogue *n* **1** conversation. **2** passage of written work in conversational form.

diameter *n* **1** straight line across a circle passing through the centre. **2** length of this line; thickness.

diamond *n* **1** very hard precious stone of pure carbon. **2** equilateral parallelogram. **3** playing card of the suit marked with a red diamond-shaped pip, or the symbol itself.

diaphragm *n* **1** muscular membrane between the chest and the abdomen. **2** thin vibrating disc in certain instruments. **3** contraceptive device inserted over the mouth of the cervix to act as a barrier to sperm.

diarrhoea (daiə'riə) *n* abnormal looseness of the bowels.

diary *n* daily record of events, or book in which such a record is kept.

dice *n pl or s* small cube with faces marked with between one and six spots, used in games of chance. *vt* cut into small cubes. **dice with** gamble with; deal with recklessly.

dictate *vt* (dik'teit) **1** say or read for another to write down. **2** prescribe; command. *n* ('dikteit) authoritative command. **dictation** *n* act of dictating for another to write down or the matter so dictated. **dictator** *n* absolute ruler. **dictatorial** *adj* of or resembling a dictator; autocratic. **dicta-**

torship *n* **1** office of or government by a dictator. **2** country so ruled.

dictionary *n* **1** book containing an alphabetical list of words and their meanings, pronunciation, etc. **2** reference book relating to a particular subject, with items listed in alphabetical order.

did *v pt* of **do.**

die *vi* (dying) cease to live; perish. **die down** gradually diminish or become less forceful.

diesel *n* internal-combustion engine fuelled by oil or a vehicle driven by this.

diet *n* **1** regulated allowance of food, esp. one prescribed for slimming or medical reasons. **2** the food a person normally eats. *vi* to eat a special diet.

differ *vi* be unlike; disagree. **difference** *n* degree of differing or point in which things differ; disagreement. **different** *adj.* **differently** *adv.* **differentiate** *vi* **1** constitute a difference between. **2** become unlike; diverge. *vt* distinguish between. **differentiation** *n.*

difficult *adj* not easy; hard to do or understand. **difficulty** *n.*

dig *v* (-gg-; dug) *vt,vi* cut into or remove earth, esp. with a spade; excavate. *vt* poke or prod. *n* **1** prod. **2** sarcastic remark. **3** excavation.

digest *vt* (di'dʒest) **1** dissolve (food) in the stomach for bodily absorption. **2** classify or summarize to aid mental assimilation. **3** reflect on; absorb. *n* ('daidʒest) **1** summary. **2** publication containing condensed versions of other articles, books, etc. **digestion** *n* natural assimilation of food into the bodily system.

digit *n* **1** any number from nought to nine. **2** finger or toe. **digital clock/watch** *n* clock/watch on which the time is indicated by numbers only rather than hands pointing to numbers on a dial.

dignified *adj* stately; exalted; noble.

dignity *n* **1** stateliness; gravity; distinction of mind or character. **2** high office or title.

digress *vi* stray from the main point or theme of a story, argument, etc. **digression** *n.*

dike *n,vt* dyke.

dilapidated *adj* decayed; neglected; in ruins. **dilapidation** *n.*

dilemma *n* situation in which alternative choices are equally unattractive; difficult predicament.

diligent *adj* conscientious. **diligence** *n*.

dilute *vt* reduce the strength of by adding water; water down. **dilution** *n*.

dim *adj* **1** not bright; indistinct; obscure. **2** *also* **dim-witted** *inf* stupid, not intelligent. *vt,vi* (-mm-) make or become dim(mer).

dimension *n* measurement of length, breadth, height, etc.; extent; size.

diminish *vt,vi* make or become smaller or less; lessen; reduce. **diminutive** *adj* extremely small.

dimple *n* small hollow, esp. in the surface of the skin on the face.

din *n* loud continuous noise. *vt* (-nn-) **1** subject to din. **2** repeat (facts, opinions, etc.) insistently.

dine *vi* eat dinner. *vt* entertain at dinner.

dinghy *n* small open boat.

dingy *adj* **1** shabby; dirty. **2** badly lit; gloomy. **dinginess** *n*.

dinner *n* **1** chief meal of the day. **2** formal banquet.

dinosaur *n* large extinct reptile.

diocese ('daiəsis) *n* district under a bishop's jurisdiction. **diocesan** (dai'ɔsizən) *adj*.

dip *vt* (-pp-) **1** submerge briefly in liquid; immerse. **2** lower. *vi* **1** sink briefly under the surface of a liquid. **2** slope downwards. *n* **1** act of dipping. **2** downward slope. **3** bathe.

diphthong *n* union of two vowel sounds in one syllable.

diploma *n* document conferring some privilege, title, or qualification.

diplomacy *n* **1** management of international relations. **2** tact or skill in dealing with others. **diplomat** *n* person engaged in international diplomacy. **diplomatic** *adj*.

direct *vt* **1** give orders; manage; control. **2** give directions to; point; indicate a route to. *adj* straight; straightforward; immediate. **direct object** *n* word in a sentence receiving the direct action of the main verb. **direction** *n* **1** instruction; command. **2** course to which anything moves, faces, etc. **director** *n* **1** person who directs, esp. the production of a film or play. **2** member of a board controlling a company or organi-

zation. **directory** *n* book listing names with addresses, telephone numbers, etc.

dirt *n* **1** any unclean substance; filth. **2** soil; earth. **dirty** *adj*.

disable *vt* incapacitate; cripple. **disability** *n*. **disabled** *adj*.

disadvantage *n* unfavourable circumstance or situation; handicap.

disagree *vi* **1** differ in opinion; dissent. **2** be incompatible. **disagreeable** *adj*. **disagreement** *n*.

disappear *vi* vanish; go out of sight. **disappearance** *n*.

disappoint *vt* fail to fulfil the desires or expectations of; frustrate. **disappointment** *n*.

disapprove *vt,vi* fail to approve; have an unfavourable opinion (of). **disapproval** *n*.

disarm *vt* **1** deprive of weapons; make defenceless. **2** win over; conciliate. *vi* lay down weapons; reduce national military forces. **disarmament** *n*.

disaster *n* extreme misfortune; calamity. **disastrous** *adj*.

disc *n* **1** thin flat circular plate. **2** *inf* gramophone record. **3** a disc file. **disc file** *n* set of discs coated with magnetized material on which computer data is stored in tracks. **disc jockey** *n* person who plays recorded music on the radio, at parties, etc.

discard *vt,vi* throw out; cast off; reject.

discern *vt* see clearly; detect; distinguish. **discerning** *adj* having good taste; discriminating. **discernment** *n*.

discharge *vt* (dis'tʃɑːdʒ) **1** release; send forth. **2** dismiss. **3** unload. *n* ('distʃɑːdʒ) **1** matter discharged. **2** state of being discharged.

disciple *n* follower; loyal pupil.

discipline *n* **1** obedience and orderliness; self-control. **2** training or system of rules that produces such conduct. *vt* **1** subject to strict rules of conduct; train. **2** punish.

disclose *vt* reveal; make known. **disclosure** *n*.

disconcert *vt* upset; take aback; dismay.

disconnect *vt* break connection between.

disconsolate *adj* lacking hope or comfort.

discontinue *vt,vi* cease to continue; leave off.

discord *n* lack of harmony; disagreement; strife.

discotheque *n* public place for dancing to recorded pop music.

discount *n* ('diskaunt) reduction in the price of anything. *vt* (dis'kaunt) **1** reduce the value or price of. **2** leave out of consideration; ignore.

discourage *vt* **1** lessen the courage or confidence of; dishearten. **2** oppose by expressing disapproval; deter. **discouragement** *n.*

discover *vt* **1** find out; learn about. **2** uncover; reveal. **discoverer** *n.* **discovery** *n.*

discreet *adj* careful; prudent; tactful.

discrepancy *n* difference; inconsistency; variance.

discrete *adj* separate; distinct.

discretion *n* **1** prudence; tact. **2** freedom to act or choose as one likes.

discriminate *vt,vi* **1** make or see distinctions; distinguish. **2** treat persons, groups, etc., as different from others. **discrimination** *n.*

discus *n* heavy disc thrown in athletic contests.

discuss *vt* argue or write about in detail; debate. **discussion** *n.*

disease *n* illness; condition of impaired health.

disembark *vt,vi* set or go ashore from a ship; land.

disfigure *vt* spoil the appearance of; deform. **disfigurement** *n.*

disgrace *n* shame; dishonour. *vt* bring shame or discredit on; humiliate.

disgruntled *adj* discontented; sulky.

disguise *vt* conceal the true nature or appearance of; misrepresent. *n* clothing, make-up, etc., worn to give a false appearance.

disgust *n* extreme dislike; loathing; repugnance. *vt* cause disgust in; offend greatly.

dish *n* **1** shallow vessel or basin for food. **2** particular variety or preparation of food.

dishearten *vt* discourage; make despondent.

dishevelled *adj* untidy; scruffy; bedraggled.

dishonest *adj* not honest; insincere; deceitful. **dishonesty** *n.*

dishonour *n* **1** state of shame or disgrace. **2** cause of this. *vt* **1** bring shame or discredit on; disgrace. **2** treat with disrespect. **3** fail to pay (a debt, etc.). **dishonourable** *adj.*

disillusion *vt* cause to lose illusions; disenchant. **disillusionment** *n.*

disinfect *vt* free from infection; remove infectious germs from; sterilize. **disinfection** *n.* **disinfectant** *n* substance that prevents or removes infection.

disinherit *vt* deprive of inheritance. **disinheritance** *n.*

disintegrate *vt,vi* break into fragments; crumble. **disintegration** *n.*

disinterested *adj* impartial; objective; free from selfish or private motives.

disjointed *adj* **1** disconnected. **2** incoherent.

dislike *vt* feel aversion to; disapprove of. *n* aversion; disapproval.

dislocate *vt* put out of joint; displace. **dislocation** *n.*

disloyal *adj* not loyal; unfaithful. **disloyalty** *n.*

dismal *adj* gloomy; depressing; dreary. **dismally** *adv.*

dismantle *vt* take apart, esp. carefully or piece by piece.

dismay *vt* fill with alarm or fear. *n* apprehension; anxiety.

dismiss *vt* **1** send away; discharge from a job. **2** give only brief consideration to. **dismissal** *n.*

disobey *vt* refuse or fail to obey. **disobedience** *n.* **disobedient** *adj.*

disorder *n* **1** lack of order or organization; confusion. **2** breach of the peace; riot. **3** illness; ailment. **disordered** *adj* upset; disturbed; badly arranged. **disorderly** *adj* unruly; badly organized.

disown *vt* refuse to acknowledge; repudiate.

disparage *vt* speak scornfully of; belittle. **disparagement** *n.*

dispassionate *adj* without emotion or prejudice; objective.

dispatch *vt* **1** send off. **2** finish off. *n* **1** sending off. **2** speed; promptness. **3** official message or report.

dispel *vt* (-ll-) clear away; make disappear; scatter.

dispense *vt* 1 deal out; administer. 2 make up (medicines). **dispense with** do without; get rid of. **dispensary** *n* place where medicines are made up.

disperse *vt,vi* scatter; spread widely. **dispersal** *n*.

displace *vt* 1 move out of place. 2 remove from office. 3 take the place of. **displacement** *n*.

display *vt* exhibit; show; expose to view. *n* 1 exhibition. 2 ostentatious show.

dispose *vt* 1 arrange; set in order. 2 make willing or inclined. **dispose of** get rid of; deal with. **disposal** *n*. **disposition** *n* 1 arrangement. 2 inclination; tendency. 3 temperament.

dispossess *vt* deprive of rights, possessions, etc.

disprove *vt* prove false; refute.

dispute *v* (di'spju:t) *vi,vt* argue, debate, or disagree. *vt* 1 doubt or question the truth of. 2 compete to win (something). *n* ('dispju:t) argument; quarrel.

disqualify *vt* 1 make ineligible or unsuitable. 2 ban from competing in sports, etc., for a breach of the rules. 3 deprive of legal or other rights, etc. **disqualification** *n*.

disregard *vt* 1 take no notice of; ignore. 2 treat with no respect. *n* lack of respect.

disrepute *n* ill repute. **disreputable** 1 discreditable. 2 shabby.

disrespect *vt* have or show no respect for. *n* lack of respect or courtesy. **disrespectful** *adj*.

disrupt *vt* 1 cause chaos or disorder. 2 interrupt the continuity of. **disruption** *n*. **disruptive** *adj*.

dissect *vt* 1 cut up and examine (an animal or plant). 2 analyse in detail. **dissection** *n*.

dissent *vi* 1 disagree. 2 express views opposing established or orthodox doctrines, esp. of a church. **dissension** *n*. **dissenter** *n*.

dissimilar *adj* not similar; different. **dissimilarity** *n*.

dissolve *vi,vt* 1 disperse or cause to disperse into a solution. 2 dismiss (a company, organization, etc.). *vi* vanish. **dissolution** *n*.

dissuade *vt* discourage from an intention by persuasion.

distance *n* length of a space between two points. **keep (someone) at a distance** refuse to allow someone to become friendly. **keep one's distance** behave in a reserved or formal way. **distant** *adj* 1 far away. 2 remote. 3 reserved.

distaste *n* dislike. **distasteful** *adj* unpleasant; objectionable.

distil *v* (-ll-) *vt* 1 boil (a liquid) and condense the vapour. 2 purify by this process. 3 obtain the essential part of something. *vi* undergo distillation. **distillation** *n*. **distillate** *n* product of distillation. **distillery** *n* place where alcoholic spirits are produced.

distinct *adj* 1 easily understood; clear. 2 noticeable. **distinct from** different; not the same as. **distinction** *n* 1 act of distinguishing things as different or distinct. 2 mark of difference. 3 mark of superiority or excellence. **distinctive** *adj* of distinguishing characteristic.

distinguish *vt* 1 be able to see a difference; discriminate. 2 characterize. 3 recognize; perceive. **distinguish oneself** do something with distinction.

distort *vt* 1 twist; deform. 2 give an untrue impression of. **distortion** *n*.

distract *vt* 1 divert the attention of. 2 confuse; disturb. 3 entertain or amuse. **distraction** *n*. **distractive** *adj*.

distraught *adj* 1 agitated or bewildered. 2 frantic.

distress *vt* cause acute mental or physical discomfort. *n* 1 state of acute anxiety or anguish. 2 state of danger, extreme discomfort, etc.

distribute *vt* 1 give out in shares; allot. 2 spread; scatter. 3 divide into groups or categories. **distribution** *n*.

district *n* geographical, political, or administrative region.

distrust *vt* have no trust in; suspect. *n* lack of trust.

disturb *vt* 1 interrupt; disrupt. 2 cause disorder; disarrange. 3 cause worry or anxiety. **disturbance** *n* 1 act of disturbing or being disturbed. 2 disturbing of the public peace.

ditch *n* narrow trench dug for drainage purposes. *vi* repair or dig ditches. *vt inf* throw away; abandon.

ditto *n* the same as above; used in accounts, lists, etc., to save repetition.

divan *n* 1 low backless cushioned couch set against a wall. 2 *also* **divan bed** type of bed with an enclosed base and no visible frame.

dive *vi* 1 jump into water headfirst or in a controlled fashion. 2 throw oneself forward headlong. 3 (of a submarine) submerge. *vi,vt* 1 move in a steep downward path through the air. *n* 1 act of diving. 2 *inf* shabby disreputable café, pub, etc. **diver** *n.*

diverge *vi* 1 turn off and go in different directions; move apart. 2 differ. **divergence** *n.*

diverse *adj* varied; different. **diversify** *vt,vi* make or become diverse. **diversification** *n.*

divert *vt,vi* turn (a person or thing) from a previously intended course. *vt* distract. **diversion** *n* 1 act of diverting. 2 temporary detour caused by repairs, etc., on a road. 3 distraction; amusement.

divide *vt,vi* 1 separate or split into two or more parts. 2 distribute. 3 find out how many times a number is contained in another. *vt* cause a disagreement (between).

dividend *n* 1 money paid to shareholders as interest, profit, etc. 2 number to be divided by another.

divine *adj* 1 relating to God, a god, or theology. 2 sacred; religious; heavenly. *vt,vi* guess or discover intuitively. **divinely** *adv.* **divinity** *n* 1 state or quality of being divine. 2 god; deity. 3 theology.

divisible *adj* able to be divided.

division *n* 1 act of dividing. 2 part of a unit or whole. 3 administrative or legislative body. 4 military unit larger than a regiment.

divorce *n* 1 legal termination of a marriage. 2 total or radical separation. *vt,vi* obtain a divorce (from). *vt* separate. **divorcé(e)** *n* man (woman) who is divorced.

divulge *vt* reveal; disclose; let out (a secret, etc.).

dizzy *adj* 1 experiencing a sensation of confusion, being unsteady, or whirling; giddy. 2 causing such a sensation. **dizzily** *adv.* **dizziness** *n.*

do *v* (does; did; done) *vt* 1 perform; act. 2 deal with; complete. 3 serve; provide. 4 fix; arrange. 5 have as a job or occupation. 6 *inf* swindle; defraud. *vi* 1 suffice; be accepted. 2 manage; cope. 3 make progress. *v aux* used in certain interrogative, negative, or emphatic statements. **do in** *sl* kill; murder. **do up** 1 tie; fasten. 2 make smart. **make do (with)** manage with what is available. ~*n inf* function; social event.

docile *adj* willing to be trained; tame; gentle; obedient.

dock[1] *n* area or wharf for mooring, loading, repairing ships, etc. *vt,vi* bring or come in to dock; moor. **docker** *n* person employed to load and unload cargo. **dockyard** *n* enclosure with docks for repairing, equipping, or building ships.

dock[2] *n* 1 solid part of an animal's tail. 2 stump remaining after clipping a tail. *vt* 1 cut (an animal's tail). 2 deduct from.

dock[3] *n* section in a lawcourt where the accused is seated.

doctor *n* 1 person qualified to practise medicine. 2 person holding the highest diploma or degree of a university. *vt* 1 treat medically. 2 falsify; adulterate.

doctrine *n* 1 teaching of a school, church, political group, etc. 2 dogma; belief.

document *n* ('dɔkjumənt) printed or written evidence or information. *vt* ('dɔkjument) furnish with evidence, references, etc. **documentation** *n.* **documentary** *adj* relating to a document. *n* detailed factual film.

dodge *vi,vt* move quickly, so as to avoid; evade. *n* clever plan or move.

does *v* 3rd person singular of **do** in the present tense.

dog *n* domesticated or wild four-footed animal of various breeds. *vt* (-gg-) pursue steadily; tail; hound. **dog-collar** *n inf* clergyman's collar. **dogged** ('dɔgid) *adj* persistent; stubborn; tenacious.

dogma *n* system of beliefs, such as those of a church; doctrine. **dogmatic** *adj* 1 relating to dogma. 2 asserting beliefs or opinions with persistent arrogance. **dogmatically** *adv.*

dole *n* money or food given charitably or for maintenance. **on the dole** receiving unemployment benefit. *v* **dole out** give or share out; distribute.

doll *n* 1 child's toy in the image of a person. 2 *sl* attractive girl or young woman. *v* **doll up** dress up in fine clothes.

dollar *n* unit of currency of the US and various other countries, comprising 100 cents.

dolphin *n* sea mammal resembling but larger than a porpoise.

domain *n* **1** territory ruled over, as by a sovereign. **2** field of interest, influence, etc.; province.

dome *n* large high rounded roof.

domestic *adj* **1** relating to the home or household matters. **2** not foreign. **3** (of animals) tame. **domestic science** *n* study or art of cooking, needlework, household management, etc. **domesticate** *vt* tame; train for domestic purposes. **domesticity** *n* home life; matters concerning the home or a household.

dominate *vt,vi* **1** rule; control; govern. **2** be the most important or conspicuous feature (of). **domination** *n*. **dominant** *adj* **1** prevailing; having power, authority, or priority. **2** prominent; most important. **dominance** *n*. **domineer** *vi* behave in an overbearing or arrogant manner. **dominion** *n* **1** sovereignty; governing authority; rule. **2** land controlled by a government; domain. **3** name formerly given to the self-governing countries of the Commonwealth of Nations.

domino *n, pl* **dominoes** small rectangular brick marked with various combinations of spots for use in various games.

donate *vt* give. **donation** *n* gift, esp. for charity. **donor** *n* person making a donation.

done *v pp* of **do**.

donkey *n* **1** long-eared member of the horse family, used esp. as a beast of burden; ass. **2** *sl* fool.

doodle *vi,vt* draw or scribble casually, esp. while attending to some other matter. *n* scribbled drawing or shape. **doodler** *n*.

doom *n* **1** fate; destiny. **2** unfavourable judicial sentence; condemnation. *vt* **1** sentence; condemn. **2** destine to an unhappy end or fate.

door *n* **1** hinged or sliding structure fitted across a passage or entrance. **2** *also* **doorway** entrance to a building, room, etc.

dope *n* **1** kind of varnish used for waterproofing. **2** drug, esp. a narcotic. **3** *sl* information. **4** *sl* stupid person; dunce. *vt,vi* drug or take drugs. **dopey** *adj also* **dopy** **1** drugged; drowsy. **2** stupid.

dormant *adj* inactive.

dormitory *n* large room containing a number of beds.

dormouse *n, pl* **dormice** hibernating rodent similar to but smaller than a squirrel.

dorsal *adj* relating to or on the back.

dose *n* **1** amount of a medicine, etc., to be given or taken at one time. **2** bout; spell. *vt* give medicine or doses (to). **dosage** *n* **1** giving of medicine in doses. **2** amount of medicine to be given.

dot *n* small point or spot; speck. *vt* (-tt-) **1** mark with dots; spot. **2** place a dot over a letter, after a musical note, etc.

dote *vi* be silly or mentally weak. **dote on** be excessively fond of. **dotage** *n* silliness or childishness in old age; feeble-mindedness.

double *adj* **1** two of a kind together; of two kinds. **2** twice as much. **3** having two functions, uses, etc. **4** suitable for two. **5** having extra weight, thickness, width, etc. **6** ambiguous. *adv* **1** twice. **2** in pairs. *n* **1** something or someone exactly like another. **2** quantity that is twice that of another. **3** sharp backward turn or bend. **4** evasion; trick; shift. *vt,vi* **1** make or become twice as great. **2** multiply by two. **3** fold in half. **4** turn sharply. **double up** be contorted with pain, laughter, etc. **double bass** *n* largest instrument of the violin family. **double-cross** *vt* betray. *n* betrayal. **double-dutch** *n inf* nonsense; gibberish. **doubly** *adv* to twice the extent.

doubt *vt* **1** hesitate to accept; fail to believe immediately. **2** suspect. *n* uncertainty; lack of conviction or belief. **no doubt** probably; presumably. **doubtful** *adj*. **doubtless** *adv,adj*.

dough *n* flour or meal mixed with water and kneaded before baking. **doughnut** *n* small round cake made of dough and sugar and fried in deep fat.

douse *vt,vi also* **dowse** plunge into water; immerse; drench. *vt* extinguish (a light).

dove *n* bird belonging to the pigeon family.

dowdy *adj* drab; shabby.

down¹ *adv* **1** from a higher to a lower place or position. **2** to or at the bottom; towards or on the ground. **3** below the horizon. **4** from an earlier to a later time. **5** into a worse physical or mental condition. *prep* **1**

towards, at, in, or near a lower place, rank, condition, etc. **2** in the same direction as; with. *adj* dejected; miserable; depressed.

down² *n* **1** fine soft feathers of young ducks or other birds. **2** fine hair.

downcast *adj* **1** looking or directed downwards. **2** dejected.

downfall *n* **1** ruin; destruction. **2** cause of overthrow or destruction. **3** falling, as of rain or snow.

downhearted *adj* dejected in spirits; depressed.

downhill *adv* down a hill; downwards. *adj* descending; sloping.

downpour *n* heavy fall of rain.

downright *adj* in plain terms; straightforward. *adv* absolutely; thoroughly.

downstairs *adv* **1** down the stairs. **2** towards or on a lower floor. *adj* relating to or situated on a lower floor. *n* lower floor.

downstream *adv* down or in the direction of flow of a stream. *adj* farther down or moving with the current.

downtrodden *adj* trodden or trampled down; oppressed.

downward *adj* moving or extending from a higher to a lower place. **downwards** *adv* from a higher place to a lower; in a descending course.

dowry *n* money, goods, or property that a woman brings to her husband at marriage.

dowse *vt,vi* douse.

doze *vi* sleep lightly or for a short time. *n* light or brief sleep.

dozen *n* group of twelve. **dozens** *pl n* many.

drab *adj* **1** of a dull colour. **2** monotonous; not exciting.

draft *n* **1** first or rough copy, outline, sketch, etc. **2** detachment of soldiers. **3** conscription. **4** written order for money. *vt* **1** prepare a first or rough copy of. **2** send or select (a detachment of soldiers). **3** conscript; recruit.

drag *v* (-gg-) *vt,vi* **1** pull; draw or be drawn along. **2** trail. **3** search or sweep with a net, hook, etc. *vi* move slowly; lag. **drag out** prolong, esp. unnecessarily. ~*n* **1** device used for dragging. **2** something that slows movement or progress. **3** *sl* something or someone that is tedious or a waste of time. **4** *inf* puff or inhaling of a cigarette. **in**

drag (of a man) wearing women's clothing.

dragon *n* **1** fire-breathing monster usually depicted as a winged reptile. **2** *inf* fierce or fiery person, esp. a woman; tyrant. **dragonfly** *n* long-bodied insect with large delicate wings.

drain *vt* **1** draw off (liquid) so as to empty or leave dry. **2** exhaust; consume utterly; empty. *vi* **1** flow out or away. **2** become dry or empty. *n* **1** pipe, channel, or ditch for drawing off water, sewage, etc. **2** steady depletion or expenditure. **drainage** *n* **1** act or process of draining. **2** system of pipes or channels for draining. **3** substance drained. **draining board** *n* sloping surface beside a sink on which wet dishes, etc., are placed to dry. **drainpipe** *n* pipe channelling water, sewage, etc.

drake *n* male bird of the duck family.

dram *n* **1** unit of weight, equal to one sixteenth of an ounce. **2** small amount of alcoholic drink; tot.

drama *n* **1** story performed by actors; play. **2** plays collectively. **3** compelling event or series of events. **dramatic** *adj* **1** relating to or resembling drama. **2** vivid; forceful. **dramatically** *adv.* **dramatics** *pl n* acting by an amateur company. **dramatist** *n* person who writes drama; playwright. **dramatize** *vt* **1** act out or put into the form of a drama. **2** express vividly or forcefully or in an exaggerated manner.

drank *v pt* of **drink.**

drape *vt* cover, esp. with cloth or fabric. *vt,vi* hang in folds (about). *n* arrangement of folds. **draper** *n* person who deals in cloth, linen, etc. **drapery** *n* **1** cloth or other fabrics. **2** business of a draper.

draught *n* **1** current of air, esp. in an enclosed space. **2** act of pulling or that which is pulled. **3** quantity drunk in one go. **4** drawing of beer, wine, etc., from a barrel or cask. **5** dose of medicine. **draughts** *n* game played with round flat pieces on a board marked off in squares. **draughtsman** *n, pl* **-men 1** person skilled in mechanical drawing. **2** *also* **draught** piece used in draughts.

draw *v* (drew; drawn) *vt,vi* **1** pull; haul; drag. **2** bring or come nearer; approach. **3** portray in lines; sketch. *vt* **1** pull out;

extract; withdraw; take. **2** inhale. **3** infer; deduce. **4** describe. **5** obtain by lot. **6** attract. *vi* **1** finish a game with an equal score for both sides; tie. **2** permit the circulation of air. **draw on 1** use as a resource. **2** approach. **draw up** draft (a will, contract, etc.). ~*n* **1** attraction. **2** raffle; lottery. **3** game ending in a tie. **drawback** *n* disadvantage. **drawbridge** *n* bridge that can be raised.

drawer *n* sliding compartment in a desk, chest, etc. **drawers** *pl n inf* underpants or knickers.

drawing *n* **1** art or practice of portraying in lines; sketching. **2** image or sketch so done. **drawing pin** *n* short pin with a flat head, fixed by pushing with the thumb. **drawing room** *n* room for the reception or entertaining of guests; living room.

drawl *vt,vi* speak slowly, esp. with elongated vowel sounds. *n* such speech.

dread *vt* anticipate with great fear or apprehension. *n* great apprehension or fear; terror. **dreadful** *adj* **1** causing dread. **2** *inf* unpleasant; bad. **dreadfully** *adv inf* terribly; awfully; very.

dream *n* **1** sequence of thoughts or images during sleep. **2** something hoped for. **3** vision. *vi,vt* (dreamt *or* dreamed) have dreams (of).

dreary *adj* gloomy; not exciting; dull. **dreariness** *n*.

dredge *n* device for bringing up mud and other material from the bottom of a river, etc. *vt* bring up, clean, etc., with a dredge.

dregs *pl n* sediment.

drench *vt* wet completely; soak.

dress *vt,vi* put clothes on. *vt* arrange for show; decorate; adorn. **3** prepare (meat, fish, etc.) by trimming, gutting, etc. **4** treat (a wound, etc.) by applying a dressing. *n* **1** clothing. **2** female outer garment consisting of a bodice and skirt. **3** formal evening wear. **dress circle** *n* first gallery above the floor in a theatre or cinema. **dressmaker** *n* person skilled in making dresses. **dress rehearsal** *n* final rehearsal of a stage production, in which the actors appear in full costume.

dresser[1] kitchen sideboard.

dresser[2] person assisting an actor with costume changes.

dressing *n* **1** sauce applied to various foods. **2** stuffing. **3** something applied to a wound to aid healing. **dressing-gown** *n* loosely fitting robe or gown, usually worn over night attire. **dressing-room** *n* special room, esp. in a theatre, where one dresses. **dressing-table** *n* small table, usually with a mirror, for cosmetics etc.

drew *v pt* of **draw**.

dribble *vi,vt* **1** flow or allow to flow in small drops; trickle. **2** propel (a ball) with a series of small kicks. *n* drop; trickle.

drier *n* appliance for drying clothes, hair, etc.

drift *n* **1** snow, sand, etc., piled up by the wind. **2** general meaning. **3** deviation from a plan, course, etc. **4** general movement, progress, etc. *vi* **1** be carried, as by air or water currents. **2** move without purpose or direction. **driftwood** *n* wood carried ashore by water.

drill[1] *n* **1** tool or device for boring holes. **2** routine exercises or training. *vt,vi* **1** bore (a hole) in. **2** exercise, esp. by repetition.

drill[2] *n* **1** small trench for seed. **2** machine or device for sowing seed in drills.

drink *v* (drank; drunk) *vt,vi* swallow (liquid). *vt* **1** absorb; take in. **2** consume (alcoholic drinks). *n* **1** amount of liquid suitable for consumption; beverage. **2** alcohol.

drip *vi,vt* (-pp-) fall or let fall in drops. *n* process of dripping or that which falls by dripping. **drip-dry** *adj* (of clothing, etc.) drying without creases if hung up when wet. **dripping** *n* fat that drips from a roasting joint.

drive *vt,vi* (drove; driven) **1** move by force, power, etc. **2** urge onward; compel. **3** control or steer (an animal, vehicle, etc.). **4** transport or be transported in a vehicle. **5** move or fix by striking, hitting, etc. *n* **1** act of driving. **2** trip in a vehicle. **3** road, esp. a private one leading to a house. **4** energy; force; motivation. **driver** *n*.

drivel *vi* (-ll-) **1** let secretions flow from the mouth or nose; dribble. **2** talk or act foolishly. *n* nonsense; silly talk.

drizzle *vi* rain lightly. *n* fine rain.

droll *adj* witty; satirical; wry.

dromedary *n* camel with one hump.

drone *n* **1** male bee. **2** idle person. **3** deep buzz or hum. **4** monotonous voice, tone, etc.

vi 1 buzz or hum continuously. 2 speak in a low monotonous voice.

drool *vi* 1 gloat; gush. 2 drivel; dribble.

droop *vi,vt* bend or hang down limply; sag. *vi* become disheartened; languish. *n* drooping state or condition.

drop *n* 1 small spherical amount of liquid; globule. 2 very small amount of anything. 3 steep descent; fall. 4 distance through which something falls. 5 round sweet. *v* (-pp-) *vt,vi* 1 fall or permit to fall. 2 lower; decrease; sink. *vt* 1 cease to consider or discuss. 2 mention casually. 3 allow (passengers, goods, etc.) to disembark or be unloaded. 4 omit; cease to make use of. **drop in** make a casual visit. **drop off** 1 fall asleep. 2 decline; decrease. **drop out** cease to compete, complete one's education, etc. **dropout** *n* person who rejects society's norms, fails to complete an educational course, etc.

drought *n* prolonged period during which no rain falls.

drove[1] *v pt* of **drive**.

drove[2] *n* herd or flock, esp. when on the move.

drown *vt,vi* kill or die by suffocating in water. *vt* 1 overpower; extinguish; destroy. 2 cover completely; flood. 3 shut out (sound); muffle.

drowse *vi,vt* be or make sleepy. *n* condition of being sleepy or half asleep. **drowsy** *adj* 1 sleepy or sluggish. 2 inducing sleep; soporific. **drowsily** *adv.* **drowsiness** *n.*

drudge *vi* work hard; slave. *n* person doing menial work. **drudgery** *n* hard menial work; toil.

drug *n* substance, esp. a narcotic. *vt* (-gg-) 1 mix a drug or drugs with (food, drink, etc.). 2 administer a drug (to).

drum *n* 1 percussion instrument having skin, etc., stretched tightly over a hollow chamber. 2 large cylindrical container for oil, water, etc. *vt,vi* (-mm-) 1 beat or play (a drum). 2 beat, tap, or strike continuously. *vt* instil by insistent repetition. **drummer** *n.*

drunk *adj* 1 *also* **drunken** intoxicated; inebriated. 2 emotionally overcome. *n also* **drunkard** person who is drunk, esp. habitually.

dry *adj* 1 not wet or moist. 2 having little or no rainfall; arid. 3 thirsty or causing thirst. 4 not yielding milk, water, etc. 5 not

stimulating; dull. 6 caustically clever or witty. 7 not permitting the legal sale or consumption of alcohol. *vt,vi* make or become dry(er). **dry-clean** *vt* clean with chemical solvents rather than water.

dual *adj* 1 relating to two or a pair. 2 having two parts; double. **dual carriageway** *n* major road with opposite lanes separated by a barrier, area of grass, etc. **duality** *n.* **dually** *adv.*

dubious *adj* causing doubt; suspicious; questionable.

ducal *adj* relating to a duke or duchy.

duchess *n* 1 wife or widow of a duke. 2 woman holding a rank equivalent to that of a duke. **duchy** *n* territory ruled by a duke or duchess.

duck[1] *n* wild or tame edible bird with webbed feet. **duckling** *n* young duck.

duck[2] *vi* 1 bend down or lower suddenly; bob. 2 plunge temporarily under water. 3 avoid; dodge.

duct *n* channel or tube for conveying liquid, secretions, etc. **ductile** *adj* 1 (of gold, copper, etc.) capable of being drawn out into wire or hammered very thin. 2 flexible; pliant.

due *adj* 1 payable at once. 2 fitting; usual; proper; adequate. 3 expected to arrive or be ready. **due to** attributed or ascribed to. ~*n* fair share. **dues** *pl n* fee; charges.

duel *n* 1 fight with pistols, swords, etc., between two persons. 2 contest between two parties. *vi* (-ll-) fight a duel.

duet *n* composition for two musicians or performers.

dug *v pt* and *pp* of **dig**.

duke *n* 1 nobleman ranking next below a prince. 2 ruler of a small state (duchy).

dulcimer *n* percussion instrument having a set of strings, which are struck with hammers.

dull *adj* 1 lacking intelligence; stupid. 2 having no feelings; insensible. 3 not clear or sharp. 4 tedious. 5 moving slowly; sluggish. 6 overcast. 7 blunt. *vt,vi* make or become dull. **dullness** *n.* **dully** *adv.*

duly *adv* as expected; properly; in a fitting manner.

dumb *adj* 1 incapable of uttering speech sounds. 2 temporarily unable to speak. 3 silent. 4 *sl* stupid. **dumbfound** *vt* amaze into silence; astound. **dumbly** *adv.* **dumbness** *n.*

dummy *n* **1** model of a human being used esp. for displaying clothes. **2** imitation; copy. **3** *inf* inactive or silent person. **4** rubber teat sucked by a baby.

dump *vt* **1** throw down in a pile or heap. **2** unload; dispose of. *n* **1** place where rubbish is dumped; tip. **2** *inf* messy, dirty, or ugly place, room, etc. **down in the dumps** depressed; dejected; miserable. **dumpling** *n* ball of dough cooked in a stew, etc. **dumpy** *adj* short and fat; plump.

dunce *n* person who is slow to learn or mentally dull.

dune *n* ridge or hill of sand.

dung *n* excrement; manure.

dungeon *n* underground cell or prison, esp. in a castle.

duplicate *adj* ('dju:plikət) **1** resembling or exactly like another. **2** occurring in pairs; double. *n* ('dju:plikət) exact copy. *vt* ('dju:plikeit) reproduce exactly; copy. **duplication** *n.* **duplicator** *n* machine for producing stencilled copies.

durable *adj* resisting decay or wear; lasting. **durability** *n.*

duration *n* period of time that something lasts.

during *prep* **1** throughout the period, existence, or activity of. **2** in the course of.

dusk *n* period of the evening before darkness falls; twilight. **dusky** *adj* **1** darkskinned. **2** dim; shadowy.

dust *n* dry fine particles of earth, mineral deposits, etc. *vt,vi* wipe the dust (from). *vt* sprinkle; powder. **dusty** *adj.* **dustbin** *n* container for refuse, ashes, etc. **duster** *n* cloth used to wipe dust from furniture, etc. **dustman** *n, pl* **-men** person employed to remove refuse, empty dustbins, etc.

duty *n* **1** obligation, esp. of a moral or legal nature. **2** allocated work or task. **3** tax on imported or exported goods; tariff. **on/ off duty** at work/not at work, esp. as a nurse, doctor, soldier, etc. **duty-free** *adj* requiring no duty to be paid. **dutiful** *adj* respectful; obedient. **dutifully** *adv.*

duvet ('du:vei) *n* quilt for a bed, padded with feathers, down, etc.; continental quilt.

dwarf *n, pl* **dwarfs** or **dwarves** **1** person of exceptionally small stature or size. **2** plant or animal of a smaller type than average. **3** supernatural being in the form of a small ugly man. *vt* **1** restrict the growth of. **2** cause to appear relatively small, insignificant, etc., by comparison.

dwell *vi* (dwelt *or* dwelled) reside as a permanent occupant; live (in). **dwell (up)on** emphasize; concentrate on. **dwelling** *n* place where someone lives; abode; house.

dwindle *vi* grow gradually less in size, number, etc.; decrease.

dye *n* substance used for colouring fabric, the hair, etc. *v* (dyeing; dyed) *vt* colour (fabric, hair, etc.) with a dye. *vi* become coloured with a dye.

dying *v pres p* of **die**. **dying to/for** having a strong desire to/for.

dyke *n also* **dike** **1** embankment for holding back sea or river water. **2** ditch; trench. *vt* hold back or drain with a dyke.

dynamic *adj* **1** relating to force or energy; not static. **2** forceful; ambitious. **dynamically** *adv.* **dynamics** *n* branch of science concerned with forces and their effects on motion.

dynamite *n* high explosive of nitroglycerine and other substances.

dynamo device that converts mechanical energy into electrical energy.

dynasty *n* **1** unbroken line of hereditary rulers of the same family. **2** period of their rule.

dysentery *n* disease of the intestines.

dyslexia *n* condition leading to impaired reading ability. **dyslexic** *adj,n.*

E

each *adj,pron,adv* every separate one considered individually.

eager *adj* **1** strongly desirous. **2** keen; willing. **eagerly** *adv.* **eagerness** *n.*

eagle *n* large bird of prey having very keen eyesight.

ear[1] *n* **1** one of two organs of hearing, situated on either side of the head. **2** sense of hearing or appreciation of sound, esp. music. **3** attention. **be all ears** be listening attentively. **eardrum** *n* membrane in the inner part of the ear that vibrates when struck by sound waves. **earmark** *vt* designate for a special purpose. **earphone** *n* small loudspeaker placed in or over the ear for listening to a radio or telephone communication. **earring** n jewellery worn on or hanging from the ear lobe.

ear[2] n spike of a cereal plant containing the seed.

earl n British nobleman ranking next above a viscount.

early adj,adv **1** before the expected or appointed time. **2** at or near the beginning of a period or season. **earliness** n.

earn vt,vi gain (money, etc.) by working. vt deserve. **earnings** pl n wages or salary.

earnest adj **1** sincere; serious. **2** zealous; determined. **earnestly** adv.

earth n **1** third planet from the sun, lying between Venus and Mars and orbited by the moon, on which life has developed; world. **2** surface of this planet. **3** soil; ground. **4** home of a fox, etc. **5** connection of an electrical apparatus to the ground, assumed to be at zero voltage. **down-to-earth** sensible; realistic. **earthenware** n domestic pottery of coarse baked clay. **earthly** adj **1** of the earth or world. **2** likely; conceivable. **earthquake** n violent natural movement of the earth's crust; tremor. **earthworm** n worm that lives in and eats soil. **earthy** adj coarse; basic; crude.

earwig n small insect having pincers on the tail.

ease n **1** freedom from work, pain, or exertion; comfort; relaxation. **2** lack of difficulty (in doing something). vt,vi make or become less painful, difficult, etc.

easel n frame for supporting a blackboard or artist's canvas.

east n **1** one of the four cardinal points of the compass situated to the front of a person facing the sunrise. **2** part of a country, area, etc., lying towards the east. adj also **eastern** of, in, or facing the east. adv,adj also **easterly 1** towards the east. **2** (of winds) from the east. **easterner** n. **eastward** adj facing or moving towards the east. **eastwards** adv in the direction of the east.

Easter n annual Christian festival in the spring, celebrating Christ's resurrection.

easy adj **1** requiring little effort; not difficult. **2** relaxed; comfortable. **3** tolerant; casual. **easily** adv. **easiness** n. **easygoing** adj tolerant; relaxed.

eat v (ate; eaten) vt,vi consume (food) through the mouth; have (a meal). vt **1** corrode; wear away. **2** use up in great quantities.

eavesdrop vi (-pp-) listen secretly to a private conversation. **eavesdropper** n.

ebb n **1** tidal falling back of the sea away from land. **2** decline; decay. vi **1** flow back from the land. **2** decline; diminish; wane.

ebony n hard almost black wood, obtained from a tropical or subtropical tree.

ebullient adj fervent; enthusiastic; full of life. **ebullience** n.

eccentric adj **1** not having the same centre; having a noncentral axis. **2** unconventional; odd. n eccentric person. **eccentricity** n.

ecclesiastic adj also **ecclesiastical** of or relating to the Church or clergymen. n clergyman.

echo n, pl **echoes 1** sound like or repeating a first sound, caused by reflection of sound waves by a solid object. **2** anything that repeats or mimics. vt,vi reverberate; repeat; imitate.

éclair n cake of light pastry filled with cream.

eclipse n phenomenon in which light from one heavenly body is blocked by another, esp. a **solar eclipse,** where the moon moves between the earth and the sun. vt **1** cause an eclipse of. **2** throw into obscurity; surpass.

ecology n **1** relationship between natural things and their surroundings, and the effect of technology on this. **2** study of this. **ecological** adj. **ecologist** n.

economic adj **1** of or relating to economics. **2** worth doing; profitable. **3** economical. **economical** adj **1** frugal; thrifty. **2** not wasteful; giving value for money. **economically** adv. **economics** n study of the causes of and relationships between production, exchange, distribution, and consumption. **economize** vt,vi reduce expenditure or consumption to save money. **economy** n **1** arrangement or condition of trade, production, and commerce of an area. **2** thrift; frugality.

ecstasy n **1** intense joy; bliss. **2** state of extreme religious fervour. **ecstatic** adj.

edge *n* **1** outer side or margin. **2** cutting side of a blade. **3** keenness; sharpness. **4** slight advantage. **on edge** tense. *~vt* **1** sharpen. **2** be or provide the border of. *vi,vt* move gradually; inch. **edgy** *adj* tense.

edible *adj* that may be eaten; not poisonous; not disgusting to the palate.

edit *vt* **1** prepare (a manuscript) for publication. **2** prepare the final form of (a film).

edition *n* set of books, newspapers, etc., printed at the same time. **editor** *n* **1** person who edits. **2** person who directs content and coverage of a newspaper, etc. **editorial** *adj* of or relating to the task of an editor. *n* newspaper article containing the opinions of its editor. **editorialize** *vi* introduce personal opinions or bias into reporting events etc.

educate *vt* **1** give teaching to; instruct. **2** bring up; raise. **3** refine; improve. **education** *n* **1** process of gaining knowledge; training; schooling. **2** state of being educated. **3** upbringing. **educational** *adj*.

eel *n* snakelike fish.

eerie *adj* frighteningly strange; weird; ghostly. **eerily** *adv.* **eeriness** *n.*

effect *n* **1** change produced by an action; result. **2** impression on the mind, eyes, etc. **in effect** actually; virtually. **take effect** start; become operative. *~vt* bring about; cause. **effective** *adj* **1** producing a result, esp. a considerable one. **2** causing a pleasant or striking effect or impression. **3** taking effect. **effectively** *adv.*

effeminate *adj* (of a man) like a woman; not masculine or virile.

effervesce *vi* (of a liquid) give off bubbles of gas; fizz. **effervescent** *adj* **1** bubbling; fizzy. **2** merry; lively. **effervescence** *n.*

efficient *adj* producing the desired effect without waste; competent; effective. **efficiency** *n.* **efficiently** *adv.*

effigy *n* model or solid representation of a person.

effort *n* **1** exertion of energy. **2** attempt; try. **effortless** *adj* needing or using little effort; easy. **effortlessly** *adv.*

egg[1] *n* **1** oval object consisting of the embryo of birds, reptiles, etc., within a protective shell. **2** egg of certain birds, esp. hens, eaten as food.

egg[2] *v* **egg on** encourage or incite; urge.

ego *n* **1** the self; part of the mind that is conscious of itself. **2** self-centredness; conceit. **egocentric** *adj* self-centred; conceited. **egoism** *n* characteristic of thinking only of oneself; self-centredness. **egoist** *n.* **egoistic** *adj.* **egotism** *n* characteristic of talking only or too much about oneself; arrogance; conceit. **egotist** *n.* **egotistic** *or* **egotistical** *adj.* **ego-trip** *n sl* action or experience that increases one's own high opinion of oneself.

eiderdown *n* **1** fine down from the eider duck. **2** bed cover or quilt filled with down, feathers.

eight *n* **1** number equal to one plus seven. **2** group of eight things or people. **3** *also* **eight o'clock** eight hours after noon or midnight. *adj* amounting to eight. **eighth** *adj* **1** coming between seventh and ninth in sequence. *n* **1** eighth person, object, etc. **2** one of eight equal parts; one divided by eight. *adv* after the seventh.

eighteen *n* **1** number that is eight more than ten. **2** eighteen things or people. *adj* amounting to eighteen. **eighteenth** *adj,adv,n.*

eighty *n* **1** number equal to eight times ten. **2** eighty things or people. *adj* amounting to eighty. **eightieth** *adj,adv,n.*

either *adj,pron* one or each of two. *conj* used to introduce a choice between alternatives. *adv* (after negatives) as well; furthermore; anyway.

ejaculate *vt,vi* **1** say (something) suddenly; exclaim. **2** discharge; eject. **ejaculation** *n.*

eject *vt* throw out; expel; send forth; discharge. **ejection** *n.*

eke *v* **eke out** cause to last; supplement; draw out.

elaborate *adj* (i'læbərət) complicated; intricate; detailed. *vt,vi* (i'læbəreit) make more detailed; give further explanation of. **elaborately** *adv.* **elaboration** *n.*

elapse *vi* (of time) pass; go by.

elastic *adj* easily stretched; flexible; able to return to its original shape after being distorted, etc. *n* material made elastic by interwoven strips of rubber, used in clothes. **elasticity** *n.*

elated *adj* very happy and excited; overjoyed; high-spirited. **elatedly** *adv.* **elation** *n.*

elbow *n* **1** joint between the forearm and upper arm. **2** part of a coat, etc., covering this. **elbow grease** *n inf* hard work. ~*vt* push (one's way) through, towards, etc.

elder[1] *adj* older of two, esp. two brothers or sisters; senior. *n* **1** older person. **2** official in some churches. **elderly** *adj* old; aged.

elder[2] *n* bush or small tree with whitish flowers and purple or black berries.

eldest *adj* oldest of three or more people.

elect *vt* appoint or choose by voting. *vi* choose; decide. **elector** *n.* **election** *n* process of choosing and voting for candidates for office, esp. for Parliament.

electric *adj* **1** *also* **electrical** of, relating to, or worked by electricity. **2** charged with emotion; tense. **electrically** *adv.*

electrician *n* person whose job is to install or mend electrical equipment.

electricity *n* **1** phenomenon caused by motion of electrons or by excess of electric charge. **2** electric current; electric charge.

electrify *vt* **1** supply with or adapt to work by electric power. **2** startle; shock; thrill. **electrification** *n.*

electrocute *vt* kill by passing an electric charge through the body. **electrocution** *n.*

electrode *n* metal plate or wire by which an electric current enters or leaves a device.

electron *n* elementary particle with negative electric charge that moves round the nucleus of an atom.

electronic *adj* relating to or operated by the conduction of electrons through a vacuum, gas, or semiconductor. **electronics** *n* **1** *s* study and technology of electronic equipment. **2** *pl* circuits in electronic equipment.

elegant *adj* tasteful; refined; graceful. **elegance** *n.* **elegantly** *adv.*

element *n* **1** constituent part. **2** chemical substance that cannot be broken down into simpler substances by chemical reactions. **3** small amount; suggestion. **elements** *pl n* **1** weather; rain, wind, etc. **2** basic ideas. **elemental** *adj.*

elementary *adj* **1** easy; simple; basic. **2** relating to the earliest stages of teaching or development.

elephant *n* largest land mammal, found in India and Africa, having a trunk and two tusks of ivory. **elephantine** *adj* enormous.

elevate *vt* **1** make higher in physical position; raise; lift up. **2** promote in rank. **3** make more refined or cultured. **elevation** *n* **1** act of elevating or state of being elevated. **2** altitude; height. **elevator** *n US* **lift** (def. 2).

eleven *n* **1** number that is one greater than ten. **2** eleven things or people. *adj* amounting to eleven. **eleventh** *adj,adv,n.*

elf *n, pl* **elves** small magical being in human form; fairy. **elfin** *adj.*

eligible *adj* having the necessary qualities or qualifications to be chosen; suitable.

eliminate *vt* get rid of; remove. **elimination** *n.*

elite *n* select group of people.

ellipse *n* geometric figure having an oval shape. **elliptical** *adj also* **elliptic** oval-shaped.

elm *n* tall deciduous tree.

elope *vi* run away with one's lover to get married secretly. **elopement** *n.*

eloquent *adj* speaking persuasively or expressively. **eloquence** *n.* **eloquently** *adv.*

else *adv* **1** other; different. **2** more. **or else** otherwise; if not. **elsewhere** *adv* to, in, or at another place.

elucidate *vt* explain the meaning of; clarify. **elucidation** *n.*

elude *vt* **1** escape from; avoid capture. **2** escape (a person's mind or memory). **elusive** *adj* **1** hard to find, catch, or see. **2** evasive.

emaciated *adj* very thin, esp. through starvation or illness. **emaciation** *n.*

emanate *vi* come from; originate from. **emanation** *n.*

emancipate *vt* free from slavery or legal or social restraint, esp. by giving the right to vote. **emancipation** *n.*

embalm *vt* preserve (a corpse) by removing internal organs and applying chemicals, etc.

embankment *n* artificial mound or ridge piled up to carry a railway, etc., or hold back water, as along a river.

embargo *n, pl* **embargoes** order prohibiting ships from entering or leaving port; veto; prohibition (esp. on trade).

embark *vi,vt* go or put on board a ship, aircraft, etc. **embark on** begin; start. **embarkation** *n.*

embarrass *vt* 1 cause awkwardness or shyness in; disconcert. 2 hinder; hamper. **embarrassment** *n.*

embassy *n* 1 ambassador's official residence. 2 staff of an ambassador. 3 mission or message of an ambassador.

embellish *vt* 1 make more beautiful; decorate; adorn. 2 add greater detail or description to. **embellishment** *n.*

ember *n* piece of wood or coal in a dying fire; glowing cinder.

embezzle *vt* misuse or misappropriate (money in one's care); defraud. **embezzlement** *n.* **embezzler** *n.*

embitter *vt* cause to feel bitterness or rancour.

emblem *n* sign or symbol representing an idea, principle, etc. **emblematic** *adj.*

embody *vt* 1 represent in physical form. 2 include; comprise. **embodiment** *n* person or thing representing a quality, etc.; personification.

emboss *vt* impress (a raised design, lettering, etc.) on (a surface).

embrace *n* clasp; hug. *vt,vi* hug, as to show affection or welcome. *vt* 1 take up (a religion, etc.); adopt. 2 include; cover.

embroider *vt,vi* sew (a pattern) on to (fabric) using coloured silks and fancy stitches. *vt* add untrue details to. **embroidery** *n.*

embryo *n* 1 unborn young of animals during early stages of development. 2 early stage of development. **embryonic** *adj.*

emerald *n* bright green precious stone. *n,adj* bright green.

emerge *vi* 1 come into view, as from concealment; appear. 2 become revealed or known. **emergence** *n.* **emergent** *adj* beginning to develop.

emergency *n* unforeseen and dangerous situation requiring immediate action; crisis.

emigrate *vi* leave a country to live permanently in another. **emigrant** *n,adj.* **emigration** *n.*

eminent *adj* 1 famous and respected; distinguished; high; exalted. 2 outstanding or obvious. **eminence** *or* **eminency** *n.* **eminently** *adv.*

emit *vt* (-tt-) give forth; make (sounds, etc.). **emission** *n.*

emotion *n* feeling, esp. strong feeling; anger, hate, love, etc. **emotional** *adj* given to strong or changeable emotion. **emotionally** *adv.* **emotive** *adj* arousing emotion; provocative.

empathy *n* ability to imagine and share the feelings of another person.

emperor *n* ruler of an empire.

emphasis *n* 1 calling of special attention to an important fact, etc.; stress. 2 accent on a particular or important word, phrase in music, etc. **emphasize** *vt* represent as important; give emphasis to; lay stress on. **emphatic** *adj* 1 stressed; accented. 2 sure; decided. **emphatically** *adv.*

empire *n* group of territories or countries ruled by one person or government.

empirical *adj* based on experience or experiment; not theoretical. **empirically** *adv.*

employ *vt* 1 hire (a person) to work for money; provide work for. 2 make use of. 3 occupy; use. **employment** *n.* **employee** *n* person hired to work for money. **employer** *n* person, firm, etc., employing people.

empower *vt* invest with the power (to); authorize.

empress *n* 1 female ruler of an empire. 2 wife or widow of an emperor.

empty *adj* 1 containing nothing; unoccupied. 2 lacking significance or feeling; meaningless; dull. 3 lacking force or substantiation. *vt,vi* discharge; vacate; leave empty; evacuate. **emptiness** *n.* **empty-handed** *adj* 1 carrying nothing. 2 having won or gained nothing. **empty-headed** *adj* not thinking deeply about important matters; silly.

emu *n* large flightless Australian bird.

emulate *vt* imitate (a person or thing admired or envied); try to equal. **emulation** *n.*

emulsion *n* 1 mixture in which one liquid is suspended in the form of tiny droplets in another. 2 household paint consisting of an emulsion of oil paint in water. 3 light-sensi-

tive coating on photographic film or plates.
emulsify *vt,vi* make into or become an emulsion.

enable *vt* make able (to); make possible for (a person) to do something.

enact *vt* **1** make into a law or statute. **2** represent on or as if on a stage; perform. **enactment** *n.*

enamel *n* **1** opaque glossy substance applied by fusion to metal for protection or decoration. **2** glossy paint. **3** protective outer layer of the teeth. *vt* (-ll-) coat or decorate with enamel.

enchant *vt* **1** cast a magic spell on; charm. **2** be delightful or fascinating to; bewitch. **enchantment** *n.*

encircle *vt* **1** make a circle round; surround. **2** pass round (the waist, etc.).

enclose *vt* **1** place within a surround, wall, etc.; shut in. **2** put in an envelope for posting, esp. as an additional item. **enclosure** *n* **1** act of enclosing or something enclosed. **2** fencing off of land, esp. common land. **3** area of a sports ground, etc., reserved for spectators, officials, or others.

encore *interj* call from an audience to a performer to repeat a piece of music, etc., or perform an additional item. *n* song or item so performed.

encounter *vt* **1** meet unexpectedly; come across. **2** be faced or confronted with. *n* meeting or confrontation.

encourage *vt* cause to feel more hopeful or confident. **encouragement** *n.*

encroach *vi* overstep the proper limits; intrude on (another's property, area of responsibility, etc.).

encumber *vt* **1** weigh down; be a burden to. **2** hamper; impede. **encumbrance** *n.*

encyclopedia *n* reference book or books giving information on a wide range of topics or on one particular subject. **encyclopedic** *adj.*

end *n* **1** final or last part; furthest point. **2** conclusion or completion. **3** aim; object. **4** death. **at a loose end** having nothing to do. **in the end** finally; at last. ~*vi,vt* come or bring to an end; finish; conclude. **endless** *adj* without end; never ceasing. **endlessly** *adv.*

endanger *vt* bring into danger; put at risk.

endeavour *vt,vi* try hard (to do something); attempt. *n* act of trying; attempt.

endemic *adj* always present in a particular country or area.

endorse *vt* **1** sign the back of (a cheque, etc.). **2** enter a motoring offence in (a driving licence). **3** support; uphold. **endorsement** *n.*

endow *vt* **1** give money or property to (a college, etc.). **2** bestow (beauty, kindness, etc.) upon; bless with. **endowment** *n.*

endure *vi* last; continue in existence. *vt* tolerate; bear. **endurance** *n.* **endurable** *adj* bearable. **enduring** *adj* longlasting.

enemy *n* **1** person hostile to or hated by one; foe; opponent; antagonist. **2** nation with which one is at war.

energy *n* **1** capacity to do work. **2** physical strength; vitality; force. **energetic** *adj.* **energetically** *adv.*

enfold *vt* fold in; hold tightly; embrace.

enforce *vt* **1** force (a law) to be carried out or obeyed. **2** force; compel. **enforcement** *n.*

engage *vt* **1** hire; employ. **2** promise; pledge, esp. to marry someone. **3** occupy. **4** begin fighting against; attack. *vt,vi* (of gears, etc.) lock in position; mesh. **engagement** *n* **1** state of being engaged; act of engaging. **2** appointment to meet; date. **3** military encounter; battle.

engine *n* **1** machine able to convert energy into mechanical work. **2** railway locomotive. **3** any mechanical apparatus or device. **engineer** *n* **1** person skilled in a branch of engineering. **2** someone in charge of engines, esp. on a ship. **3** planner or organizer. *vt* **1** plan, supervise, or construct as an engineer. **2** plan or arrange skilfully; contrive. **engineering** *n* **1** practical application of scientific knowledge in the design, construction, or management of machinery, roads, bridges, buildings, etc. **2** planning or contrivance.

engrave *vt* **1** cut (letters, designs, etc.) into a hard surface. **2** print from an engraved and inked surface. **3** make a deep impression on. **engraver** *n.* **engraving** *n* **1** print made from an engraved surface. **2** engraved surface. **3** art of engraving.

engross *vt* occupy the attention of; absorb.

engulf *vt* swallow up. **engulfment** *n.*

enhance *vt* raise in importance or prominence; heighten; intensify. **enhancement** *n.*

enigma *n* 1 puzzle; riddle. 2 baffling or perplexing person, situation, etc. **enigmatic** *or* **enigmatical** *adj.* **enigmatically** *adv.*

enjoy *vt* 1 take pleasure in. 2 have the use or benefit of; possess. **enjoy oneself** feel pleasure, amusement, satisfaction, etc. **enjoyable** *adj.* **enjoyment** *n.*

enlarge *vt,vi* make or become larger; increase in size, scope, extent, etc. **enlarge on** *or* **upon** treat more fully. **enlargement** *n.*

enlighten *vt* impart knowledge or information to, esp. to free from ignorance, superstition, etc. **enlightenment** *n.*

enlist *vt,vi* 1 enrol in some branch of the armed forces. 2 secure or join in support of a person, cause, etc. **enlistment** *n.*

enmity *n* hatred between enemies; hostility; animosity.

enormous *adj* very great; huge; gigantic. **enormity** *n.* **enormously** *adv.*

enough *adj* adequate for the purpose; sufficient. *n* adequate amount; sufficiency. *adv* 1 sufficiently; adequately; tolerably. 2 fully.

enquire *vt,vi* 1 ask questions or seek information (about). 2 inquire. **enquiry** *n* 1 act of enquiring. 2 question. 3 inquiry.

enrage *vt* fill with rage; anger.

enrich *vt* 1 make wealthy or wealthier. 2 make more splendid in appearance; adorn. 3 increase the value or quality of.

enrol *v* (-ll-) *vt* place (a name) or write the name of (a person) on a list, register, etc. *vt,vi* make or become a member; enlist. **enrolment** *n.*

ensemble (ɑ:n'sɑ:mbəl) *n* 1 collection of parts. 2 group of performers. 3 outfit; set of matching clothes and accessories.

ensign *n* 1 flag of a nation, regiment, etc. 2 badge or emblem of office.

enslave *vt* make a slave of. **enslavement** *n.*

ensue *vi* come about or follow, esp. as a consequence.

ensure *vt* 1 make sure or certain. 2 make safe; secure.

entail *vi* have as a consequence; inevitably involve. **entailment** *n.*

entangle *vt* 1 catch or snare in a mesh, net, etc. 2 make tangled. 3 involve in difficulties, complications, etc. **entanglement** *n.*

enter *vt,vi* 1 come or go in(to). 2 penetrate; pierce. 3 be or cause to be admitted (to). *vt* 1 put into; insert. 2 become a member of. 3 write down in a record, list, etc. 4 begin upon. **enter into** take part in; become a party to. **enter upon** 1 begin; set out on. 2 come into enjoyment or possession of.

enterprise *n* 1 undertaking or project, esp. an important one. 2 boldness, daring, or adventurousness; initiative. 3 commercial undertaking; business.

entertain *vt,vi* 1 divert, amuse, or interest. 2 give hospitality (to); receive (guests). *vt* consider; cherish. **entertainment** *n.*

enthral *vt* (-ll-) captivate; enchant. **enthralment** *n.*

enthusiasm *n* intense interest, admiration, approval, etc.; zeal; fervour. **enthusiast** *n.* **enthusiastic** *adj.* **enthusiastically** *adv.* **enthuse** *vi* display enthusiasm.

entice *vt* lure or attract by exciting hope of reward, gratification, etc.; tempt. **enticement** *n.* **enticingly** *adv.*

entire *adj* 1 whole; complete; undivided; unbroken; intact. **entirely** *adv.* **entirety** *n.*

entitle *vt* 1 give a particular title or name to. 2 give a right, claim, or legal title to. **entitlement** *n.*

entity *n* 1 something that has real existence; thing; object. 2 being; existence.

entrails *pl n* 1 internal organs of an animal, esp. the intestines. 2 internal parts of anything.

entrance[1] ('entrəns) *n* 1 act of entering. 2 place of entry, such as a doorway, passage, etc. 3 admission. 4 act or instance of an actor coming on stage.

entrance[2] (en'trɑ:ns) *vt* delight; charm; captivate; enthral.

entreat *vt,vi* beseech; implore; beg. **entreaty** *n.*

entrench *vt* 1 fortify or defend by digging trenches. 2 establish firmly and securely. **entrenchment** *n.*

entrepreneur (a:ntrəprə'nə:) *n* someone who sets up and organizes business enterprises.

entrust *vt* give into the care of; trust with; invest or charge with a duty, etc.

entry *n* 1 act or instance of entering. 2 place for entering, esp. a passageway or hall; entrance. 3 access or admission. 4 entering of an item in a record, ledger, etc., or the item entered. 5 contestant in a race, competition, etc.

entwine *vt,vi* twist or tangle together; interweave (with).

enumerate *vt* 1 mention or specify one by one, as in a list; itemize. 2 count. **enumeration** *n.*

enunciate *vt,vi* say or pronounce (a word or words). *vt* state, declare, or proclaim, esp. clearly and carefully. **enunciation** *n.*

envelop (en'veləp) *vt* 1 wrap or cover up. 2 surround, enclose, or engulf. 3 obscure; conceal. **envelopment** *n.*

envelope ('envəloup) *n* 1 covering or container for a letter. 2 any enclosing structure, etc.

environment *n* all the external influences, surroundings, conditions, etc., immediately affecting a person or other organism. **environmental** *adj.*

envisage *vt* contemplate as actual or real; visualize.

envoy *n* 1 diplomatic representative ranking just below an ambassador. 2 any messenger or agent.

envy *n* 1 feeling of discontent caused by the possessions, status, etc., of someone else. 2 desire to have or enjoy an advantage, possession, etc., of another. 3 object of such feelings. *vt* view with envy. **enviable** *adj.* **envious** *adj.* **enviously** *n.*

enzyme *n* any of numerous organic substances that are produced in living cells and act as catalysts for biochemical changes.

epaulet *n also* **epaulette** decorative shoulder piece, esp. as worn on military uniforms.

ephemeral *adj* lasting only for a short time; transitory; fleeting.

epic *n* 1 long narrative poem in formalized style relating the exploits of a hero or heroes. 2 film, novel, etc., resembling this in style or content.

epidemic *adj* spreading rapidly among people in a certain area. *n* widespread occurrence of a disease, etc.

epilepsy *n* disorder of the nervous system characterized by convulsions and, usually, loss of consciousness. **epileptic** *adj,n.*

epilogue *n* 1 speech made to an audience at the end of a play by one of the actors. 2 concluding part of a novel, television or radio broadcast, etc.

episcopal *adj* 1 of or relating to a bishop. 2 governed by bishops.

episode *n* 1 incident or occurrence in the course of a series of events. 2 digression in a narrative, piece of music, etc. 3 instalment of a book, play, etc., serialized on television or radio. **episodic** *adj.*

epitaph *n* 1 inscription on a tomb or other monument. 2 anything serving as a memorial.

epitome (i'pitəmi) *n* 1 summary; abstract. 2 representative or typical characteristic. **epitomize** *vt* 1 summarize; abstract. 2 typify.

epoch *n* 1 period of time, esp. one considered as distinctive; era. 2 beginning of an important era in the history of anything.

equable *adj* 1 uniform or steady in effect, operation, motion, etc.; unvarying. 2 tranquil; even; serene.

equal *adj* 1 as great as another in extent, size, degree, etc.; equivalent. 2 having the same rank, value, quality, etc., as another. 3 evenly proportioned. 4 uniform; equable. 5 adequate in quantity, powers, ability, etc. 6 smooth; even; level. *n* someone or something equal to another. *vt* (-ll-) be equal to or the same as. **equality** *n.* **equalize** *vt* make equal. *vi* reach a score equal to an opponent's.

equate *vt* 1 treat or regard as equal or equivalent. 2 put in the form of an equation. **equation** *n* 1 mathematical expression of the equality of two quantities. 2 representation in symbols of a chemical reaction.

equator *n* circle round the earth dividing the Northern hemisphere from the Southern hemisphere. **equatorial** *adj.*

equestrian *adj* 1 of or relating to horses, horsemen, or the skill of riding. 2 on horseback. *n* rider on horseback, esp. an entertainer or competitor.

equilateral *adj* having all sides equal.

equilibrium *n* 1 state of poise or balance prevailing when equal and opposing forces, influences, etc., counter each other in effect. 2 mental composure or stability.

equinox *n* either of the two dates in the year, at the beginning of spring and auntumn, when day and night are of equal length.

equip *vt* (-pp-) provide with necessary equipment, skills, etc. **equipment** *n* 1 equipping or being equipped. 2 collection of tools, implements, resources, etc., necessary for a task or undertaking.

equity *n* 1 fairness; impartiality. 2 system of law co-existing with and supplementing Common Law. 3 total ordinary shares of a limited company. **equitable** *adj.*

equivalent *adj* 1 equal in value, significance, force, etc. 2 corresponding in meaning, function, etc. *n* something equivalent. **equivalence** *n.*

equivocal *adj* 1 uncertain; ambivalent. 2 ambiguous; debatable.

era *n* 1 period of time with its own distinctive flavour, trends, characteristics, etc.; age; epoch. 2 system of dating from a particular event, etc., in the past.

eradicate *vt* wipe out; destroy; obliterate. **eradication** *n.*

erase *vt* 1 rub or scratch out (something written). 2 remove all trace of; wipe out. **eraser** *n.*

erect *adj* 1 upright; vertical. 2 raised or directed upwards. 3 stiff or firm. *vt* 1 build, construct, or elevate. 2 set up; establish. **erection** *n.*

ermine *n* 1 stoat with a brown summer coat and white winter fur. 2 white fur of the animal used to trim judges' robes, etc. 3 rank or functions of a judge.

erode *vt* wear or eat away by gradual action. **erosion** *n.*

erotic *adj* of, relating to, or exciting sexual desire. **eroticism** *n.*

err *vi* 1 be mistaken; make an error. 2 deviate from a moral code; sin.

errand *n* short task entrusted to someone, esp. a short journey to deliver or fetch something.

erratic *adj* 1 irregular; random. 2 irresponsible; unpredictable.

error *n* 1 something incorrect; mistake. 2 sin.

erudite *adj* learned; having great knowledge or wisdom. **erudition** *n.*

erupt *vi* 1 (of a volcano) emit lava, etc. 2 burst out; emit suddenly. **eruption** *n.*

escalate *vt,vi* increase by stages or in intensity. **escalator** *n* moving staircase consisting of steps in an endless belt.

escape *vt,vi* 1 free oneself from; get away (from). 2 avoid (harm, punishment, etc.). *vi* become free; leak out. *vt* be forgotten by; elude. *n* 1 act of escaping or means by which this occurs. 2 sport, pastime, or other release from pressure or reality. **escapism** *n* avoidance of unpleasant reality by fantasy, etc. **escapist** *adj,n.*

escort *n* ('eskɔ:t) 1 person or group acting as guard or protection for others on a journey. 2 man accompanying a woman to a social function. *vt* (e'skɔ:t) accompany as an escort.

esoteric *adj* 1 restricted to a specialized group. 2 difficult to understand; obscure in meaning.

especial *adj* 1 outstanding; notable; special. 2 particular. **especially** *adv.*

espionage *n* spying; obtaining secret information.

esplanade *n* wide level road or walk, esp. one constructed along the shore.

essay *n* 1 ('esei) short prose composition. 2 (e'sei) attempt; try; test. *vt,vi* (e'sei) attempt; try; test.

essence *n* 1 characteristic fundamental feature or nature of something. 2 oil or other constituent of a plant, extracted as a perfume, flavouring, etc. **essential** *adj* 1 highly important; indispensable; necessary. 2 constituting the essence; fundamental. 3 absolute; perfect. *n* something that is essential.

establish *vt* 1 make secure or permanent. 2 found; bring about. 3 set up in a position, business, etc. 4 cause to be accepted. **establishment** *n* 1 act or an instance of establishing something. 2 permanent large business or government organization. 3 institution. 4 small business premises, club, hotel, etc. 5 large private household. **the Establishment** *n* group of people and institutions thought of as holding the power in a country.

estate *n* **1** country property with extensive land. **2** new building development for housing or light industry. **3** person's collective assets and liabilities. **4** position in society; social standing. **estate agent** *n* person whose business is the management, lease, and sale of houses and land. **estate car** *n* car with a long body and rear doors, designed to carry goods as well as passengers.

esteem *vt* **1** think highly of; respect. **2** consider; regard. *n* judgment or opinion, esp. a favourable one.

estimable *adj* **1** deserving respect; worthy. **2** able to be estimated; calculable.

estimate *vt* ('estimeit) **1** calculate roughly; gauge. **2** judge. *n* ('estimət) **1** approximation. **2** judgment. **estimation** *n* **1** act or result of estimating. **2** regard; esteem.

estuary *n* tidal mouth of a river.

etch *vt* **1** produce (a design, picture, etc.) on a metal plate by cutting into a wax coating and removing exposed metal with acid. **2** eat away by chemical action. **etching** *n* etched plate or a print made from this.

eternity *n* **1** endless time. **2** time after death. **eternal** *adj* **1** lasting for ever; timeless; without end. **2** continual; incessant. **eternally** *adv.*

ether ('i:θə) **1** volatile highly flammable liquid formerly used as an anaesthetic. **2** hypothetical weightless substance once thought to permeate all space. **ethereal** (i'θiəriəl) *adj* **1** light and airy. **2** spiritual; heavenly.

ethics *n* **1** *s* branch of philosophy concerned with moral conduct, right and wrong, etc. **2** *pl* moral principles; rules or standards of conduct. **ethical** *adj.* **ethically** *adv.*

ethnic *adj* **1** relating to a group of people of a particular culture, religion, language, etc. **2** relating to the racial classification of man.

etiquette *n* customs and rules determining good behaviour; manners.

etymology *n* study of the derivation of words and changes in their meaning and form. **etymological** *adj.* **etymologist** *n.*

eucalyptus *n* tree native to Australasia yielding an aromatic oil, which is used medicinally.

Eucharist *n* **1** Christian sacrament of communion, commemorating the Last Supper. **2** consecrated bread or wine offered at communion.

eunuch *n* male who has been castrated.

euphemism *n* **1** socially acceptable word or phrase used in place of one considered offensive or impolite. **2** practice of using euphemisms. **euphemistic** *adj.*

euphoria *n* feeling of bliss or elation. **euphoric** *adj.*

euthanasia *n* act of killing a person, esp. one experiencing intense pain or suffering; mercy killing.

evacuate *vi,vt* leave or remove from (an unsafe place). *vt* empty; discharge; vacate. **evacuation** *n.*

evade *vt* avoid; escape; elude.

evaluate *vt* **1** determine the quantity or worth of. **2** judge critically; appraise. **evaluation** *n.*

evangelist *n* preacher, esp. one not attached to a particular church. **Evangelist** any one of the four writers of the Gospels. **evangelical** *adj* **1** relating to the Gospels. **2** relating to certain Protestant groups that stress the importance of personal religious experiences and missionary work.

evaporate *vt,vi* **1** change from a solid or liquid state to a vapour. **2** lose or cause to lose some liquid, leaving a concentrated residue. **3** disappear; vanish. **evaporation** *n.*

eve *n* **1** evening or day before a holiday, festival, etc. **2** period immediately preceding an event.

even *adj* **1** level; flat; plane. **2** uniform; regular. **3** calm; placid. **4** equally balanced; fair. **5** (of numbers) divisible by two. **6** exact. *adv* **1** still; yet. **2** used to emphasize comparative forms. **3** used when the content of a phrase or sentence is unexpected. **4** used to modify a statement or add precision to it. *vt,vi* make or become even; balance. **evenly** *adv.* **even-tempered** *adj* calm; not easily upset or angered.

evening *n* **1** latter part of the day or early night. **2** concluding or final period.

event *n* **1** anything that takes place; occurrence. **2** outcome; result. **3** sports contest.

eventual *adj* final; ultimate; last. **eventually** *adv*.

ever *adv* 1 at any time.» 2 by any possibility. 3 always. **evergreen** *adj* (of trees, shrubs, etc.) having foliage that remains green throughout the year. *n* evergreen tree or shrub. **everlasting** *adj* 1 endless; unending. 2 perpetual; of long duration. **evermore** *adv* always; forever; constantly.

every *adj* 1 each. 2 all possible. **every other** every second or alternate. **everybody** *pron* each person; everyone. **everyday** *adj* 1 daily. 2 commonplace; ordinary. 3 suitable for normal days; not special. **everyone** *pron* each person; everybody. **everything** *pron* 1 each thing, aspect, factor, etc. 2 a great deal; something very important. **everywhere** *adv* towards or in all places, parts, etc.

evict *vt* eject or expel (a person) from a house, building, etc. **eviction** *n*.

evidence *n* proof; ground for belief. **evident** *adj* apparent; obvious; plain. **evidently** *adv*.

evil *adj* 1 wicked; sinful. 2 harmful; malicious. 3 offensive; vile. *n* wickedness; sin; depravity.

evoke *vt* 1 summon; call forth. 2 excite; provoke. **evocation** *n*.

evolution *n* 1 natural process of very gradual continuous change in all plants and animals. 2 development; unfolding. **evolutionary** *adj*.

evolve *vt,vi* develop; unroll. *vi* undergo evolution.

ewe *n* female sheep.

exacerbate *vt* 1 aggravate; heighten. 2 exasperate; irritate; provoke. **exacerbation** *n*.

exact *adj* 1 completely correct. 2 precise. 3 very same; particular. 4 rigorous; strict. *vt* 1 extort. 2 demand; require authoritatively. **exactly** *adv*.

exaggerate *vt,vi* represent (something) as being greater or more than it really is. *vt* make more noticeable. **exaggeration** *n*.

exalt *vt* 1 raise; elevate. 2 praise. **exaltation** *n*.

examine *vt* 1 inspect; observe. 2 investigate; study. 3 test (a person's skill, knowledge, etc.). **examiner** *n*. **examination** *n* 1 act of being examined. 2 questions or tasks

intended to test skill or knowledge. 3 medical inspection of the body.

example *n* 1 specimen; sample. 2 someone or something worthy of emulation. 3 precedent.

exasperate *vt* irritate; provoke; incense. **exasperation** *n*.

excavate *vt,i*. 1 dig out. 2 hollow out. 3 expose (buried objects) by digging. **excavation** *n*. **excavator** *n* machine for digging and moving soil, gravel, etc.

exceed *vt,vi* be greater than (another). *vt* overstep the limit of. **exceedingly** *adv* very; greatly.

excel *v* (-ll-) *vt,vi* surpass; be superior to. *vi* do extremely well (in).

excellency *n* term of address used for ambassadors, governors, high-ranking government officials, etc.

excellent *adj* of the best quality; thoroughly good and praiseworthy. **excellence** *n*.

except *prep* with the exception of; save. *vt* exclude; omit. **exception** *n* 1 act of being excepted. 2 instance to be excepted; unusual situation, person, thing, etc. **exceptional** *adj* 1 relating to an exception; irregular. 2 having higher than average intelligence, skill, talent, etc. **exceptionally** *adv*.

excerpt *n* selected passage from a book; extract.

excess *n* (ek'ses) 1 surplus. 2 amount, degree, etc., by which something is exceeded by another. *adj* ('ekses) over and above what is normal, necessary, or required. **excessive** *adj*. **excessively** *adv*.

exchange *vt* 1 barter; trade for something. 2 interchange; trade (information). 3 replace; substitute. *n* 1 act of exchanging. 2 anything that substitutes for or replaces something offered. 3 argument. 4 central office or station. 5 place where brokers, dealers, etc., buy and sell securities and certain commodities.

exchequer *n* 1 department of the treasury dealing with accounting. 2 treasury or government department of a country, state, etc., controlling financial matters.

excise *n* ('eksaiz) 1 tax levied on certain commodities or for certain licences. 2 branch of the civil service responsible for collecting such taxes. *vt* (ek'saiz) impose excise on; tax; levy.

excite *vt* 1 arouse; awaken; provoke. 2 stir up; instigate. 3 disturb; agitate. **excitable** *adj*. **excitement** *n*.

exclaim *vt* cry out; shout. **exclamation** *n* 1 act of exclaiming; outcry. 2 interjection; emphatic word, phrase, or sentence. **exclamation mark** *n* punctuation mark (!) used after an exclamation.

exclude *vt* 1 keep out; bar. 2 deny inclusion or consideration of. **exclusion** *n*. **exclusive** *adj* 1 barring or excluding everything else. 2 sole; not shared; individual. 3 fashionable; select. **exclusively** *adv*.

excommunicate *vt* bar (someone) from church membership or receiving certain sacraments. **excommunication** *n*.

excrete *vt* (of an animal) discharge (waste, such as urine, sweat, etc.) from the body. **excrement** *n* waste matter, esp. solid, discharged from the body. **excreta** *pl n* waste matter discharged from the body.

excruciating · *adj* agonizing; tortuous; intensely painful.

excursion *n* 1 short journey, pleasure trip, or outing. 2 group or party taking an excursion.

excuse *vt* (ik'skju:z) 1 pardon; forgive. 2 justify or make allowances for. 3 exempt or release (from). *n* (ik'skju:s) 1 justification; reason. 2 explanation offered to explain bad behaviour, rudeness, etc. 3 pretext; pretence. **excusable** *adj*.

execute *vt* 1 kill, esp. following a legal decision; put to death. 2 perform; achieve; carry out. 3 administer; enforce. **execution** *n*. **executive** *adj* relating to administration, the execution of a duty, etc. *n* person or group running or administrating a company, project, etc. **executor** (ig'zekjutə) *n* person who carries out a duty, esp. someone responsible for dealing with the provisions of a will.

exempt *vt* release or excuse from a duty, obligation, etc. *adj* released from a duty, obligation, etc. **exemption** *n*.

exercise *n* 1 physical exertion, esp. for the purpose of training or to maintain health. 2 task undertaken to improve one's skill or competence. 3 operation or use of one's power, right, etc. *vt,vi* give exercise to or

take exercise. *vt* 1 use; employ. 2 put into action; carry out. 3 exert; wield.

exert *vt* use the power of (strength, influence, etc.); exercise. **exert oneself** make an effort; strive. **exertion** *n*.

exhale *vi,vt* breathe out; force (air) out of the lungs. **exhalation** *n*.

exhaust *vt* 1 drain; empty; consume completely. 2 use, discuss, etc., to the full. *n* 1 gases that are expelled from an engine as waste. 2 expulsion of such gases. **exhaustion** *n*. **exhaustive** *adj*. **exhaustively** *adv*.

exhibit *vt* 1 present for viewing or inspection. 2 indicate; disclose; demonstrate. *n* something presented for public viewing. **exhibitor** *n*. **exhibition** *n* 1 act of exhibiting. 2 public show or display. **exhibitionism** *n* practice of or tendency towards showing off or drawing undue attention to oneself in public. **exhibitionist** *adj,n*.

exhilarate *vt* enliven; animate; stimulate. **exhilaration** *n*.

exhume *vt* dig up (a corpse) after burial.

exile *n* 1 banishment; ostracism. 2 banished person; outcast. *vt* banish; expel (from a country).

exist *vi* 1 be; have reality. 2 endure; continue. 3 be present in a particular place or situation. **existence** *n* life; state of being. **existent** *adj*.

exit *n* 1 way out. 2 departure; withdrawal. *vi* go out or away; depart.

exonerate *vt* 1 absolve; acquit. 2 release; exempt. **exoneration** *n*.

exorbitant *adj* excessive; extravagant; enormous. **exorbitantly** *adv*.

exorcize *vt* deliver from evil spirits, demons, etc. **exorcism** *n*. **exorcist** *n*.

exotic *adj* unusual; foreign; not native.

expand *vt,vi* 1 make or become greater in size, range, scope, etc. 2 swell; fill out; extend. 3 develop (a theme, story, etc.). **expansion** *n*. **expansive** *adj*. **expanse** *n* continuous surface that extends or spreads; stretch.

expatriate *vt* (eks'peitrieit) 1 banish; exile. 2 move (oneself) away from one's own country. *adj* (eks'peitriit) expatriated. *n* (eks'peitriit) expatriated person. **expatriation** *n*.

expect *vt* **1** consider as probable. **2** await; look forward to. **3** rely on; require; want. *vt,vi* be pregnant (with). *vi* suppose; anticipate. **expectant** *adj*. **expectation** *n* **1** act of expecting. **2** goal; aim; hope. **3** something expected or anticipated.

expedient *adj* **1** proper; suitable. **2** advantageous; profitable. **expediency** *n*.

expedition *n* **1** organized journey for exploration, hunting, etc. **2** group or party on such a journey.

expel *vt* (-ll-) eject; drive out; ban.

expend *vt* use up; spend; consume. **expenditure** *n* money spent; outgoings.

expense *n* **1** cost; charge; outlay. **2** something costing a great deal. **expensive** *adj* costly; high-priced; dear.

experience *n* **1** direct personal observation, knowledge, practice, etc. **2** specific situation that one has undergone. **3** process of gaining knowledge, esp. when not through study. **4** acquired knowledge. *vt* **1** undergo; encounter. **2** feel; be moved by. **experienced** *adj* fully trained or qualified; expert.

experiment *n* **1** trial, test, or examination to discover something by observation. **2** original or new attempt. *vi* perform an experiment. **experimental** *adj*. **experimentation** *n*. **experimenter** *n*.

expert *n* person having great knowledge, experience, skill, etc., in a particular subject. *adj* **1** relating to an expert. **2** knowledgeable; specialist; skilled. **expertise** *n* specialist skill or knowledge.

expiate *vt* atone for; redeem. **expiation** *n*.

expire *vi* **1** end; terminate; conclude. **2** exhale. **3** die. **expiry** *n* termination; lapsing; end.

explain *vt,vi* **1** make clear or understandable. **2** interpret; expound. **3** account for; justify. **explanation** *n*. **explanatory** *adj*. **explicable** *adj*.

expletive *n* exclamation; swearword or curse.

explicit *adj* **1** clear; precise; definite. **2** open; unreserved. **explicitly** *adv*.

explode *vt,vi* **1** burst; blow up. **2** destroy or be destroyed by bursting. *vi* suddenly or violently display anger, rage, etc. **explosion** *n* **1** act of exploding. **2** any rapid or very large increase, as in population.

explosive *adj* **1** characterized by or capable of explosion. **2** potentially violent, turbulent, or dangerous. *n* substance or device capable of exploding. **explosively** *adv*.

exploit *n* ('eksplɔit) heroic act, deed, or feat. *vt* (ik'splɔit) **1** take unjust advantage of. **2** utilize fully. **exploitation** *n*. **exploitative** *adj*.

explore *vt* investigate thoroughly and methodically. *vt,vi* go to or into (distant lands, areas, etc.) to investigate. **exploration** *n*. **explorer** *n*.

exponent *n* person or thing that functions as an example, representation, or symbol.

export *vt,vi* (ik'spɔːt) sell or send (goods) out of a country for foreign sale. *n* ('ekspɔːt) commodity sold or sent to a foreign country. **exporter** *n*.

expose *vt* **1** uncover; disclose; lay open. **2** subject; make liable. **3** make familiar with. **4** subject (camera films, etc.) to light. **exposure** *n* **1** act of exposing. **2** direction in which the main wall of a house or building faces. **3** frame of photographic film that has been exposed to light.

expound *vt* explain in detail.

express *vt* **1** utter; verbalize; speak. **2** represent or symbolize as in a painting, piece of music, etc. *adj* **1** clear; plain; definite. **2** special; particular. *n* train, bus, etc., stopping only at major stations. **expression** *n* **1** verbal communication. **2** manifestation; representation. **3** saying; phrase; term. **4** look on the face that expresses a particular emotion. **expressionless** *adj*. **expressive** *adj*. conveying emotion. **expressly** *adv* particularly; especially; explicitly.

exquisite *adj* delicate; refined; excellent; rare. **exquisitely** *adv*.

extend *vt,vi* **1** stretch; reach out; spread. **2** prolong or last (for). *vt* **1** offer; give. **2** expand; broaden. **extension** *n* **1** act of extending. **2** additional room(s) built on to a house, etc. **3** additional telephone apparatus connected to a central switchboard or having the same number as another. **4** delay or additional period. **extensive** *adj* **1** wide; large. **2** comprehensive; far-reaching. **extensively** *adv*. **extent** *n* degree to which something extends; range; scope.

exterior n outside; outward appearance. adj outer; outside; external.

exterminate vt annihilate; destroy or kill. **extermination** n.

external adj 1 situated at or coming from the outside; outer. 2 foreign; alien. 3 (of medicines, etc.) not to be taken internally. **externally** adv.

extinct adj 1 (of plants, animals, etc.) no longer existing. 2 obsolete; out-of-date. 3 (of volcanoes) inactive; incapable of further eruption. **extinction** n.

extinguish vt 1 put out or suppress (fire, lights, etc.). 2 destroy completely. **extinguisher** n.

extort vt obtain by force or threats. **extortion** n.

extra adj additional; supplementary. n 1 something additional. 2 special edition of a newspaper. 3 actor taking part in crowd scenes, etc.

extract vt (ik'strækt) 1 draw or pull out; remove. 2 derive or develop (an idea, theory, etc.). 3 select (from a written work). n ('ekstrækt) 1 quotation; excerpt. 2 essence; vital principle or substance. **extraction** n.

extramural adj related to but not under direct control of an academic institution.

extraneous (ik'streiniəs) adj not strictly necessary or central; external; extra.

extraordinary adj remarkable; unusual; amazing. **extraordinarily** adv.

extravagant adj 1 wasteful. 2 free or generous. 3 excessive; inordinate; exorbitant. 3 ornate; fussy. **extravagance** n. **extravagantly** adv.

extreme adj 1 greatest; highest; most intense. 2 immoderate; unreasonable. 3 drastic; radical. 4 most distant or remote; utmost. n 1 highest or greatest degree. 2 upper or lower limit of a scale, range, etc. **extremely** adv. **extremity** n 1 utmost or farthest point or degree. 2 end part of a limb; hand or finger or foot or toe.

extricate vt disengage; clear; set free (from). **extrication** n.

extrovert n gregarious outgoing person. adj also **extroverted** gregarious; outgoing; not shy.

exuberant adj 1 joyful; vigorous; lively. 2 lavish; prolific; abundant. **exuberance** n. **exuberantly** adv.

exude vt,vi emit; ooze; gush.

eye n 1 organ of sight. 2 also **eyesight** sight; vision. 3 gaze; look; glance. 4 ability to inspect, judge, or observe. 5 aperture in a camera, etc., through which light can pass. 6 small hole in a needle, etc. 7 calm centre of a hurricane, tornado, etc. 8 bud on a potato, etc. vt inspect carefully; scrutinize. **eyeball** n round ball-shaped part of the eye. **eyebrow** n 1 fringe of hair growing on the ridge above the eye. 2 ridge above the eye; brow. **eye-catching** adj stunning; attracting attention. **eyelash** n short hair growing out of the edge of the eyelid. **eyelid** n fold of skin that can be closed over the eyeball. **eye-opener** n revelation; startling occurrence. **eye shadow** n cosmetic applied to colour the eyelids and draw attention to the eyes. **eyesore** n extremely ugly or offending building, object, etc. **eyestrain** n fatigue and tiredness of the eye. **eye-witness** n someone who has been present at and has observed a particular event.

F

fable n 1 tale with a moral, whose characters are often animals. 2 fictional story or account.

fabric n 1 woven or knitted cloth. 2 structure or basis, as of society, personality, etc. **fabricate** vt 1 manufacture or construct, esp. by putting together components. 2 invent; give a false account of. **fabrication** n.

fabulous adj 1 wonderful; marvellous. 2 almost impossible; unbelievable. 3 mythical. **fabulously** adv.

facade (fə'sɑːd) n 1 front of a building, esp. when considered for its artistic merit. 2 image that a person presents, esp. when misleading.

face n 1 front part of the head, including the mouth, nose, eyes, etc. 2 particular expression of the face. 3 outward attitude or pose, as of self-confidence. 4 any outward appearance. 5 most prominent or front part, as of a cliff, building, etc. 6 dial of a clock or watch. 7 flat surface of something, such as a coin, crystal, etc. **save/lose face** maintain/lose one's dignity or prestige. ~vt,vi position or be positioned to point in a particular direction. *vt* 1 come into contact with; meet. 2 confront; challenge. 3 apply to or cover (a surface). **face up to** accept and deal with realistically. **faceless** *adj* anonymous. **facelift** *n* 1 surgical operation to tighten the skin on the face and improve the appearance. 2 any improvement in appearance, as by decoration; renovation. **facepack** *n* cream or paste applied to the face to improve the skin. **face value** *n* 1 stated monetary value. 2 apparent value or meaning of something. **facial** *adj* relating to the face. *n* cosmetic treatment for the face.

facet *n* 1 flat surface of a polished gem. 2 aspect of a situation, subject, or personality.

facetious (fə'si:ʃəs) *adj* meant or attempting to be amusing, sometimes inappropriately. **facetiously** *adv*.

facile *adj* 1 easy; simple. 2 glib; superficial; too easy.

facility *n* 1 ease or skill. 2 equipment or means enabling execution of an action. **facilitate** *vt* make easier or simpler.

facsimile (fæk'simili) *n* copy; reproduction.

fact *n* something that actually happened, existed, or exists; provable statement. **in fact** *or* **as a matter of fact** really; truly. **factual** *adj* true or truthful; actual.

faction[1] *n* dissenting group within a larger group.

faction[2] *n* piece of writing, play, etc., that is a blend of fact and fiction.

factor *n* 1 something that contributes towards a result. 2 number that can be divided into another number evenly.

factory *n* building equipped with manufacturing machinery.

faculty *n* 1 ability or power, as the senses, etc. 2 department of a university or its staff.

fade *vt,vi* make or become pale, less clear, etc. **fade out** disappear gradually.

fag *n* 1 difficult chore. 2 *sl* cigarette. *vt,vi* (-gg-) *also* **fag out** make or become tired through arduous work; exhaust.

Fahrenheit *adj* relating to a temperature scale on which the freezing point of water is 32° and its boiling point 212°.

fail *vi,vt* have no success (at). *vi* 1 become inoperative; break down. 2 be inadequate or insufficient. 3 omit; forget. *vt* 1 judge to have failed. 2 disappoint; let down. *n* instance of failing. **without fail** certainly;

definitely. **failing** *n* inadequacy; fault. **failure** *n* person or thing that fails.

faint *adj* 1 lacking in clarity, contrast, etc. 2 without conviction; weak; feeble. 3 feeling as though one is going to lose consciousness. 4 cowardly; timid. *vi* lose consciousness for a short time. *n* short period of loss of consciousness. **faint-hearted** *adj* cowardly; timid.

fair[1] *adj* 1 impartial; just; without bias. 2 conforming to regulations. 3 (of a person) having light colouring. 4 beautiful or unblemished. 5 acceptable; good. 6 sunny; cloudless. **fair and square** legitimate; correct. **fairness** *n*. **fairly** *adv* 1 moderately; rather. 2 justly; deservingly. **fair-minded** *adj* just.

fair[2] *n* 1 event, usually out of doors, with various entertainments and sideshows. 2 cattle market. 3 gathering of people dealing in similar products for trade purposes. **fairground** *n* place where a fair is held.

fairy *n* imaginary being having small human form and supernatural or magical powers. **fairytale** *n* a story containing imaginary or supernatural characters, usually intended for children.

faith *n* 1 belief; trust. 2 any religion. **faithful** *adj* 1 loyal; true. 2 remaining close to the original. **faithfully** *adv*. **faith-healing** *n* healing by means of supernatural or religious powers.

fake *vt,vi* forge; pretend. *n* counterfeit; forgery. *adj* not real; counterfeit.

falcon *n* bird of prey, which is sometimes trained for sport.

fall *vi* (fell; fallen) 1 descend quickly; drop. 2 collapse from an upright position. 3 decrease; decline. 4 diminish in tone. 5 extend towards a lower level; hang down. 6 be defeated or overthrown; submit. 7 pass into sleep or a similar condition. 8 occur at a specified time. 9 be transferred. 10 be classified into. **fall back on** have recourse to for support. **fall for** *inf* 1 be deceived by. 2 develop a deep affection for. **fall in with** 1 become acquainted with. 2 agree to. **fall on one's feet** emerge successfully from a precarious situation. **fall out** quarrel; disagree. ~*n* 1 act or instance of falling or dropping. 2 lowering; decline. 3 distance over or through which something falls. 4 capture or decline of a city, civilization, etc. **falls** *pl n* waterfall; cataract. **fallout** *n* descent of particles of radioactive substances, which contaminate the air after a nuclear explosion.

fallacy *n* incorrect opinion or belief; deceptive notion. **fallacious** *adj.*

fallible *adj* 1 liable to make mistakes or be deceived. 2 likely to contain errors.

fallow *adj* (of land) left uncultivated for one or more seasons.

false *adj* 1 untrue; incorrect. 2 unfaithful; given to deceit. 3 synthetic; not genuine; artificial. **falsehood** *n* lie or fallacy. **false pretences** *pl n* forgeries and misrepresentations for illegally obtaining money, property, etc. **falsify** *vt* 1 make false or incorrect, esp. to mislead. 2 prove incorrect; disprove.

falsetto *n* male voice pitched within a range that is higher than normal. *adj,adv* using such a voice.

falter *vi* hesitate; waver; stumble. *vt* say with hesitation; stammer.

fame *n* state of being well known; reputation. **famed** *adj* acknowledged; recognized.

familiar *adj* 1 well-known or easily recognizable. 2 often used or frequented; customary. **familiar with** well acquainted with. **familiarize** *vt* make knowledgeable about a subject, place, etc.

family *n* 1 group consisting of parents and their children. 2 group of related people. 3 any interrelated group of things.

famine *n* widespread shortage of food, esp. because of drought or crop failure.

famished *adj* extremely hungry; starved.

famous *adj* 1 well-known; celebrated. 2 *inf* fantastic; splendid.

fan[1] *n* 1 device for causing a flow of air for cooling, such as a folding wedge-shaped device held in the hand. 2 anything shaped like a fan. *vt,vi* (-nn-) 1 cool by means of a fan. 2 *also* **fan out** spread or move in the shape of a fan; separate.

fan[2] *n* enthusiastic admirer of a pop star, actor, etc.

fanatic *n* 1 person with extreme and irrational dedication to a cause. 2 *inf* person dedicated to a particular pastime. **fanatical** *adj.*

fancy *adj* 1 elaborate, decorated, or ornamental. 2 high in quality. 3 coming from the imagination. *n* 1 whim; pleasure. 2 poetic imagery. *vt* 1 imagine; picture in the mind. 2 like; be attracted by. **fancy dress** *n* costume worn for a masquerade. **fanciful** *adj* 1 not factual; imaginary. 2 produced creatively or imaginatively.

fanfare *n* short musical piece played on trumpets.

fang *n* long pointed tooth, as of a snake or dog.

fantasy *n* 1 unrestrained imagination. 2 something imagined, esp. when bizarre. 3 imagined sequence that fulfils some unsatisfied need; daydream. 4 hallucination. 5 notion that is not based on fact. **fantastic** *adj* 1 strange or eccentric in design, appearance, etc. 2 exaggerated or incredible. 3 *inf* very large or great. 4 *inf* fabulous; splendid.

far *adv* 1 at, to, or from a long way or great distance. 2 at or to a distant time. 3 very much. **as far as** to the point that. **by far** by a great deal. **far and near** *or* **far and wide** everywhere; over a great distance or area. **far gone** 1 in an advanced condition. 2 mad; crazy. 3 *inf* drunk. **far out** *sl* strange; unconventional. **in so far as** to the extent that. ~*adj* 1 long way away. 2 extending or protruding a great distance. 3 remote; isolated. **far-away** *adj* 1 distant; removed. 2 preoccupied; daydreaming. **far-fetched** *adj* improbable; exaggerated. **far-off** *adj* distant; remote. **far-reaching** *adj* having extensive effects or importance.

farce *n* 1 form of drama in which characters, plot, etc., are presented as highly comical or ridiculous. 2 absurdly silly event or situation. **farcical** *adj.*

fare *n* 1 amount of money paid for a journey, etc. 2 menu; type of food.

farewell *interj,n* goodbye.

farinaceous *adj* made of or containing flour or grain.

farm *n* tract of land, with buildings, used for the rearing of livestock or cultivation of crops. *vi,vt* rear livestock or cultivate (land) for a living. **farm out** distribute. **farmer** *n.* **farmyard** *n* enclosed area adjacent to farm buildings.

farther *adv* 1 to or at a distant place or time; further. 2 in addition (to). **farthest** *adv* to or at the most distant place or time; furthest. *adj* most remote in place or time.

fascinate *vt* make curious or interested; captivate. **fascination** *n*.

fascism *n* ideology or government that is authoritarian and undemocratic. **fascist** *adj,n*.

fashion *n* 1 style of dress, makeup, etc. 2 custom; behaviour. 3 kind; type. *vt* make or form. **fashionable** *adj* relating to a current trend, style, or fashion.

fast[1] *adj* 1 moving or able to move rapidly; quick. 2 lasting only a short period. 3 (of a timepiece) indicating a more advanced time than is accurate. 4 promiscuous. 5 retaining colour; not prone to fading. *adv* 1 quickly; rapidly; swiftly. 2 securely; tightly. 3 soundly.

fast[2] *vi* abstain from food, esp. for religious reasons or as a protest. *n also* **fasting** abstinence from food.

fasten *vt,vi* attach; secure; tie.

fastidious *adj* difficult to please; fussy.

fat *n* 1 greasy semi-solid chemical substance. 2 animal tissue containing such substances. *adj* 1 overweight; obese. 2 containing fat. 3 thick. 4 rewarding or promising. **fatten** *vt,vi* make or become fat(ter). **fatty** *adj*.

fatal *adj* 1 leading to death. 2 disastrous; tragic. **fatality** *n* 1 accident that has resulted in death. 2 person so killed. 3 condition causing death.

fate *n* 1 force or power that determines events. 2 fortune; destiny. **fated** *adj* determined by fate. **fateful** *adj* awful; dreadful.

father *n* 1 male parent. 2 person who has founded a field of study, movement, etc. *vt* be the father (of). **father-in-law** *n*, *pl* **fathers-in-law** father of one's husband or wife. **fatherland** *n* person's native country or that of his ancestors.

fathom *n* unit used to measure depth of water, equal to 6 feet. *vt* 1 measure the depth of (water). 2 probe into (a problem, situation, etc.) and discover its meaning.

fatigue *n* 1 tiredness; weariness. 2 strain, esp. in fibres, metals, etc. *vt* make tired or weak.

fatuous *adj* silly; foolish.

fault *n* 1 flaw; defect. 2 mistake. 3 misdemeanour; wrong. 4 accountability for a mistake or error. **at fault** to blame. **find fault** criticize; find a mistake in. **to a fault** excessively. ~*vt* find a mistake in. **faulty** *adj*.

fauna *n*, *pl* **faunas** *or* **faunae** ('fɔːniː) all animal life of a particular time or region.

favour *n* 1 kind gesture of good will. 2 good will. 3 partiality. 4 token or gift. **in favour of** 1 commending. 2 to the advantage of. *vt* 1 prefer. 2 advocate or endorse. **favourable** *adj* advantageous; encouraging. **favourably** *adv*. **favourite** *adj* given preference to over others; best liked. *n* someone or something regarded preferentially.

fawn[1] *n* young deer. *adj,n* greyish or yellowish brown.

fawn[2] *vi* seek attention or favour servilely.

fear *n* 1 feeling of alarm or terror. 2 something causing this. 3 reverence. 4 anxiety; apprehension. **for fear of** so as to avoid. ~*vt,vi* feel fear (of). **fearless** *adj*. **fearful** *adj* 1 afraid. 2 *inf* very great.

feasible *adj* 1 able to be done. 2 suitable or likely. **feasibility** *n*.

feast *n* 1 lavish meal; banquet. 2 periodic religious celebration. 3 something lavishly pleasing. *vi* 1 eat at a feast. 2 take extreme pleasure in. *vt* 1 provide with a feast. 2 please; delight.

feat *n* deed or action, esp. when noteworthy.

feather *n* one of the external structures that form a bird's outer covering. *vt* cover or fill with feathers. **feathery** *adj*.

featherweight *n* 1 boxer of a weight under 126 lbs. 2 something extremely lightweight or of little consequence.

feature *n* 1 part of the face, such as mouth, eyes, etc. 2 characteristic or quality. 3 full-length cinema film. 4 particular article in a periodical. *vi* be a distinctive characteristic of. *vt* offer as or make a feature; give main importance to.

February *n* second month of the year.

feckless *adj* weak; ineffectual.

federal *adj* 1 relating to a league of nations or states. 2 relating to a system of government in which states retain a degree of autonomy under a central government. **federally** *adv*. **federate** *vi,vt* join in a federation or league. **federation** *n*.

fee *n* amount of money due for a service, right of entrance, etc.

feeble *adj* 1 weak or exhausted, either physically or mentally. 2 deficient in strength or force. **feeble-minded** *adj* lacking in intelligence.

feed *v* (fed) *vt* 1 offer food or other essential materials to. 2 offer as food. *vi* eat. *n* 1 food, esp. as for infants, livestock, etc. 2 amount of food or material allowed. **fed up** disgruntled with a particular situation.

feel *v* (felt) *vt* 1 sense or examine by touching. 2 experience (an emotional or physical sensation). 3 have an emotional or physical reaction to. *vi* produce a sensation as specified. **feel for** sympathize with. **feel like** want. **feel up to** be well enough to. ~*n* 1 instance of feeling. 2 nature of something as perceived by touch or by intuition. **feeler** *n* organ in some animals especially adapted for touch. **feeling** 1 ability to experience a sensation or a sensation itself. 2 mood; attitude; emotion. 3 impression; premonition. *adj* 1 sensitive; sympathetic. 2 showing emotion.

feet *n pl* of **foot.**

feign *vt* pretend; invent; imitate.

feint *n* deceptive movement, action, etc. *vi* make such a movement.

feline *adj* 1 of the cat family. 2 like a cat. *n* animal in the cat family.

fell[1] *v pt* of **fall.**

fell[2] *vt* bring down or cause to fall.

fellow *n* 1 man; boy. 2 companion; colleague. 3 member of the same class, kind, etc. 4 member of a learned society. **fellowship** *n* 1 sharing of interests, activities, etc. 2 group sharing such things; brotherhood. 3 position of being a fellow, esp. in a learned society, university, etc. 4 religious communion.

felon *n* criminal. **felony** *n.*

felt[1] *v pt* and *pp* of **feel.**

felt[2] *n* fabric whose fibres have not been woven but joined together by pressure.

female *n* person or animal of the sex that conceives and gives birth. *adj* designating a female. **feminine** *adj* 1 considered suitable to or representative of women or girls. 2 of a grammatical gender normally denoting females. **feminism** *n* 1 ideology or movement that advocates the equality of women. **feminist** *n,adj.*

fence *n* 1 structure enclosing an area or forming a barrier. 2 *inf* distributor of illegally obtained goods. **on the fence** indecisive; neutral. ~*vt* build a fence around or on. *vi* 1 participate in the sport of fencing. 2 evade questions or arguments. **fencing** *n* sport or activity of fighting with swords.

fend *v* **fend off** ward off (something). **fend for** provide for; support.

ferment *vt,vi* (fə'ment) undergo or cause fermentation. *n* ('fə:ment) 1 agent, such as yeast, that causes fermentation. 2 tumult; commotion. **fermentation** *n* chemical reaction in which sugar is changed into alcohol by action of microorganisms.

fern *n* plant with green feathery leaves that forms spores.

ferocious *adj* fierce; savage.

ferret *n* weasel-like animal used for hunting rabbits and rats. *vt* 1 drive out from cover. 2 *also* **ferret out** find; search out; seek.

ferry *n* boat or service used for transportation across a body of water. *vt,vi* transport or travel over water.

fertile *adj* 1 able to produce young. 2 capable of sustaining vegetation. **fertility** *n.* **fertilize** *vt* 1 cause the union of (a female reproductive cell) with sperm or a male reproductive cell. 2 make fertile. **fertilizer** *n* substance added to soil to increase crop yield.

fervour *n* ardour; zeal; passion. **fervent** *adj.*

fester *vi* 1 form pus. 2 become gradually resentful, bitter, etc.

festival *n* 1 celebration or feast. 2 series of cultural performances. **festivity** *n* 1 gaiety; merry-making. 2 feast or celebration.

festoon *n* 1 decorative chain of flowers, foliage, etc.; garland. 2 something that resembles a festoon. *vt,vi* decorate with or form festoons.

fetch *vt* 1 go and get; bring. 2 cost or sell for. **fetching** *adj* becoming or charming.

fete (feit) *n* 1 festival or celebration, esp. in aid of charity. 2 holiday. *vt* 1 entertain. 2 celebrate with a fete.

fetid *adj* smelling stale or rotten.

fetish *n* 1 object believed to have magic powers in certain cultures. 2 object or activity to which one is blindly devoted.

fetlock *n* part of a horse's leg above the hoof.

fetter *n* chain fastened to the ankle; shackle. *vt* restrain with fetters; shackle.

feud *n* long bitter hostility between two families, factions, etc. *vi* participate in a feud.

feudal *adj* of a social system based on land ownership and on ties between lords and vassals. **feudalism** *n.*

fever *n* 1 abnormally high body temperature. 2 disease characterized by fever. 3 extreme excitement. **feverish** *adj.*

few *adj* not many; small number of. *n* small number. **quite a few** large number.

fiancé *n* engaged man. **fiancée** *f n.*

fiasco *n* disaster; absolute failure.

fib *inf n* harmless lie. *vi* (-bb-) tell fibs. **fibber** *n.*

fibre *n* 1 yarn or cloth or the filaments from which they are made. 2 thread; filament. 3 structure or substance. 4 character; nature. **fibreglass** *n* 1 fabric made from pressed or woven glass fibres. 2 material made by binding glass fibres with synthetic resin.

fickle *adj* not faithful; changeable.

fiction *n* 1 literary works not based on fact. 2 falsehood; lie. 3 act of lying. **fictional** *adj.* **fictitious** *adj* not genuine; false.

fiddle *n* 1 *inf* violin. 2 *inf* illegal or fraudulent dealing or arrangement. *vi* 1 play on a fiddle. 2 fidget or tamper with. *vt* do something deceptively or illegally.

fidelity *n* 1 faithfulness or devotion to duty, a cause, person, etc.; loyalty. 2 truthfulness. 3 faithfulness of reproduction in sound recording.

fidget *vi* 1 be restless or uneasy. 2 play with or handle something in a restless manner. **fidgety** *adj.*

field *n* 1 open plot of land, esp. one for pasture or crops. 2 tract of land on which sports are played; pitch. 3 battleground. 4 area rich in minerals, etc. 5 area of knowledge, study, etc. 6 area away from normal working quarters where new data or material can be collected. 7 the side that is not batting in a game of cricket. *vt* stop or recover (the ball) in cricket. **fieldwork** *n* work done away from normal working

quarters for purposes of research, investigation, etc.

fiend *n* 1 evil spirit. 2 wicked or cruel person. 3 *inf* fanatic; addict. **fiendish** *adj* cruel; wicked.

fierce *adj* savage; wild; ferocious.

fiery *adj* 1 of or like fire. 2 emotional; passionate. 3 causing a feeling of burning.

fifteen *n* 1 number that is five more than ten. 2 fifteen things or people. *adj* amounting to fifteen. **fifteenth** *adj,adv,n.*

fifth *adj* coming between fourth and sixth in a sequence. *n* 1 one of five equal parts; one divided by five. 2 fifth person, object, etc. *adv* after the fourth.

fifty *n* 1 number equal to five times ten. 2 fifty things or people. *adj* amounting to fifty. **fiftieth** *adj,adv,n.*

fig *n* plant bearing sweet fleshy fruit, which is sometimes dried.

fight *n* 1 battle; combat. 2 quarrel; conflict. 3 boxing contest. *vt,vi* (fought) 1 struggle against (a person) in physical combat. 2 contend with (a person, situation, etc.). 3 support or campaign (for). 4 box. **fighter** *n.*

figment *n* invention; fiction.

figurative *adj* not literal; metaphorical.

figure *n* 1 symbol for a number. 2 amount; number. 3 shape; form. 4 person. 5 pattern; design. *vt,vi* 1 calculate. 2 mark with a pattern, diagram, etc. *vi* be important; feature. **figure out** *inf* solve; think out. **figurehead** *n* person who is an apparent leader, but with no real power.

filament *n* 1 thin wire inside a light bulb. 2 single strand of fibre.

file¹ *n* 1 holder for the orderly storage of documents. 2 correspondence or information on a particular subject, person, etc. 3 row or line. **on file** in a file; recorded. ~*vt* 1 keep or put in a file. 2 institute (a legal suit). *vi* proceed in a row. **filing cabinet** *n* cabinet designed for orderly storage of documents.

file² *n* 1 hand tool with a blade that has small cutting teeth. 2 nailfile.

filial *adj* of or suitable to a son or daughter.

fill *vt* 1 make full to capacity. 2 extend; permeate. 3 insert material into (an opening). 4 fulfil (a requirement). 5 cover, as with writing, etc. 6 do or perform the duties of (a job). 7 hire or elect for. **fill in** 1 supply information on a form. **2** be a substitute for. **3** insert. **4** fill up (a hole, gap, etc.). **fill out** become or make fuller. **n one's fill** enough; one's limit.

fillet *n* piece of boneless meat or boned fish. *vt* remove the bones from (meat or fish).

filly *n* female horse or pony of under four years.

film *n* **1** cellulose that has been specially treated for making photographs, negatives, etc. **2** sequence of pictures projected onto a screen in a cinema or transmitted on television, etc. **3** thin layer or coating. *vt* take moving pictures with a cinecamera. *vt,vi* cover or be covered with a film.

filter *n* **1** substance or device through which fluid is passed to remove particles, impurities, etc. **2** device which allows only certain signals, kinds of light, etc., to pass through. *vt,vi* pass through a filter. *vi* become known or occur slowly.

filth *n* **1** dirt, squalor, or pollution. **2** obscenity. **filthy** *adj*.

fin *n* wing-like organ of a fish, used for locomotion.

final *adj* **1** last; ultimate. **2** decisive; conclusive. **finally** *adv*. **finalize** *vt* conclude or arrange.

finance (fi'næns, 'fainæns) *n* study or system of public revenue and expenditure. *vt* provide funds for. **finances** *pl n* monetary affairs, resources, etc. **financial** *adj*. **financially** *adv*. **financier** *n* person engaged in finance, esp. on a large scale.

finch *n* small bird that feeds mainly on seeds.

find *vt* (found) **1** discover or come upon. **2** become aware of. **3** regard or consider as being. **4** determine; arrive at (a conclusion). **5** provide. *n* lucky discovery, bargain, etc.

fine[1] *adj* **1** superior in quality, skill, or ability. **2** pleasurable. **3** minute, powdered, or thin. **4** (of weather) clear and dry. **5** in good health or condition. **6** subtle or acute. **7** refined; well-mannered. *adv inf* very well; in good health. **finely** *adv*. **fine arts** *pl n* painting, sculpture, architecture, etc.

fine[2] *n* amount of money paid as a penalty for a crime, offence, etc. *vt* impose a fine on.

finery *n* showy or elaborate dress, jewellery, etc.

finesse (fi'nes) *n* delicate or subtle skill.

finger *n* any of the five appendages attached to the hand. *vt* handle; touch with the fingers. **fingermark** *n* smudge made by a finger. **fingerprint** *n* impression of the pattern on the underside of the end joint of a finger.

finish *vt,vi* end; complete; conclude; terminate. *vt* **1** use up; consume. **2** perfect. **3** put a finish on. *n* **1** final stage; completion; conclusion; end. **2** surface or texture of a material or a preparation used to produce this. **3** refinement; elegance.

finite *adj* bounded or limited.

fiord *n also* **fjord** narrow inlet of the sea between high cliffs.

fir *n* coniferous tree with needle-like leaves.

fire *n* **1** state of burning or combustion. **2** mass of burning material. **3** any device for heating a room. **4** something that resembles a fire. **5** discharge of a firearm. **6** passion or enthusiasm. **7** liveliness or brilliance. *vt,vi* (of a firearm or explosive) discharge or be discharged. *vt* **1** *inf* terminate (someone's) employment. **2** expose to heat, as clay in a kiln. **3** provide the fuel for. **firearm** *n* weapon from which a bullet, etc., is propelled by means of an explosion. **fire brigade** *n* group of persons trained in firefighting. **fire drill** *n* practice of emergency measures to be taken in case of fire. **fire engine** *n* motor vehicle equipped with fire-fighting apparatus. **fire-escape** *n* staircase or other means of escape in the event of a fire. **fireman** *n, pl* **-men** man specially trained in fire-fighting. **fireplace** *n* recess in a wall for a fire. **fire station** *n* building where fire engines are housed and where firemen are stationed. **firework** *n* device made from combustible material that is lit for entertainment. **firing squad** *n* group of men who carry out a death sentence by shooting.

firm[1] *adj* **1** hard; solid. **2** stationary; secured. **3** settled; established. **4** steadfast; resolute. **firmly** *adv*. **firmness** *n*.

firm[2] *n* business concern; company.

first *adj* coming before all others. *adv* **1** before any other. **2** for the first time. *n* **1** beginning. **2** highest honours degree. **first**

aid *n* emergency medical aid administered before professional help is available. **first-class** *adj* best or most expensive; belonging to the highest grade. *adv* by first-class means. **first-hand** *adj,adv* from the original source. **first person** *n* form of a pronoun or verb when the speaker is the subject. **first-rate** *adj* of the best kind or class.

fiscal *adj* relating to state finances.

fish *n, pl* **fish** *or* **fishes** 1 any of a large group of aquatic animals, usually having gills and fins. 2 flesh of this animal used for food. *vi* 1 catch or attempt to catch fish. 2 *also* **fish out** obtain from an inaccessible place. 3 draw out, as by hinting or questioning. *vt* fish in (a particular body of water). **fisherman** *n, pl* **-men** man who catches fish for a living. **fishmonger** *n* person who sells fish.

fission *n* 1 breaking into parts or bits. 2 *also* **nuclear fission** splitting of the nucleus of atoms, used in atom bombs and as a source of energy.

fist *n* closed or clenched hand.

fit[1] *vt,vi* (-tt-) 1 make or be suitable or well adapted for. 2 be proper or correct for. 3 adjust to make (something) appropriate. 4 qualify or make competent. 5 alter (clothing) for a particular person. *adj* 1 suitable or well adapted. 2 competent. 3 healthy; well. 4 worthy. 5 ready or inclined to. *n* 1 way in which something fits. 2 something that fits. 3 process of fitting. **fitting** *adj* appropriate; suitable.

fit[2] *n* 1 attack; seizure; convulsion. 2 period or spell of emotion, activity, etc. **fitful** *adj* coming on in or characterized by sudden irregular spells.

five *n* 1 number equal to one plus four. 2 group of five persons, things, etc. 3 *also* **five o'clock** five hours after noon or midnight. *adj* amounting to five.

fix *vt,vi* fasten; secure; attach. *vt* 1 settle; determine. 2 assign; allot. 3 repair; mend; correct. *n* 1 *inf* predicament; dilemma. 2 *sl* injection of a narcotic. **fixation** *n* compulsive preoccupation with or concentration on (a particular object, idea, etc.). **fixture** *n* 1 household appliance that is firmly or permanently attached. 2 person regarded as being permanently installed in a particular place,

position, etc. 3 scheduled football match, sports meeting, etc.

fizz *vi* bubble; effervesce. *n* 1 hiss. 2 effervescence. 3 drink containing soda water or sparkling wine.

fizzle *vi* 1 hiss; make bubbling sounds. 2 *inf also* **fizzle out** die out after an energetic start.

fjord *n* fiord.

flabbergasted *adj* amazed; astonished.

flabby *adj* 1 without firmness; soft. 2 having limp flesh. 3 listless. **flabbiness** *n*.

flag[1] *n* piece of cloth decorated with an emblem or symbol. *vt* (-gg-) 1 decorate with flags. 2 signal with flags.

flag[2] *vi* (-gg-) become limp or weak; tire.

flagon *n* vessel for holding liquids.

flagrant *adj* blatant; glaring.

flair *n* 1 ability or aptitude. 2 style; elegance.

flak *n* 1 antiaircraft fire. 2 *sl* adverse criticism.

flake *n* thin layer or piece. *vt,vi* 1 peel off in flakes or chips. 2 cover with flakes. **flaky** *adj*.

flamboyant *adj* showy; ostentatious; extravagant. **flamboyance** *n*.

flame *n* 1 blaze or fire. 2 ardour; passion. *vt,vi* burn. *vi* flash; be inflamed.

flamingo *n, pl* **flamingos** *or* **flamingoes** large wading bird with bright pinkish red plumage and long legs.

flammable *adj* capable of burning; inflammable.

flan *n* open tart, either savoury or sweet.

flank *n* 1 part of the body of man or animals between the ribs and hip. 2 cut of beef from this area. 3 either side of a body of armed troops, ships, etc. *vt,vi* 1 place or be next to. 2 go round the flank of (an enemy).

flannel *n* 1 light fabric with a short nap. 2 piece of cloth used for washing the body. 3 *inf* evasive speech, explanation, etc. *vt* (-ll-) clean or polish with a flannel.

flap *v* (-pp-) *vt,vi* swing or flutter. *vi* panic; become agitated or upset. *n* 1 action or sound made by flapping. 2 flat sheet attached at one end, used to cover an opening, etc. 3 *inf* panic.

flare *vt,vi* 1 burn with an unsteady or sudden flame. 2 spread outwards in a wedge shape. *vi* develop quickly; break out. **flare**

up suffer a sudden outburst of anger, violence, etc. ~*n* **1** sudden burst of flame, sometimes used as a signal. **2** spreading or tapering section. **3** sudden burst of emotion, etc.

flash *n* **1** flame; flare. **2** outburst. **3** instant; moment. **4** display. *adj also* **flashy** **1** ostentatious or gaudy. **2** counterfeit; false. *vi* **1** move quickly; race. **2** occur suddenly. **3** send out a sudden intermittent bright light. *vt* **1** send a signal or message by means of a flash. **2** *inf* display ostentatiously. **flashback** *n* abrupt change of scene to one earlier in time in a play, film, etc. **flashbulb** *n* bulb producing a bright flash used to take photographs. **flashlight** *n* **1** source of intermittent or flashing light. **2** electric torch.

flask *n* bottle or similar container for liquids.

flat[1] *adj* **1** horizontal; level; even or smooth. **2** low; prostrate. **3** collapsed or deflated. **4** unqualified; outright. **5** dull; lifeless. **6** insipid; stale. **7** pointless. **8** having a pitch below the true pitch; half a semitone below a specified note. *adv* **1** horizontally. **2** absolutely; definitely. *n* **1** flat surface, piece of land, etc. **2** deflated tyre. **3** flat musical note. **flatfish** *n, pl* -**fish** fish that swims horizontally and has both eyes on the uppermost side of the body, such as plaice, sole, etc. **flat-footed** *adj* having feet with flattened arches. **flatten** *vt,vi* make or become flat.

flat[2] *n* room or set of rooms in a building, used as a self-contained dwelling.

flatter *vt,vi* **1** praise insincerely or immoderately. **2** show to advantage. **3** please by paying compliments or attention to. **flattery** *n*.

flaunt *vt,vi* **1** show off. **2** wave or flutter.

flautist *n* person who plays the flute.

flavour *n* **1** taste. **2** seasoning or extract. **3** essence; characteristic quality. **4** smell; aroma. *vt* give a flavour to. **flavouring** *n* seasoning.

flaw *n* defect; imperfection; blemish. **flawless** *adj*.

flax *n* plant producing fibres used in the manufacture of linen, paper, etc.

flea *n* small blood-sucking insect, a parasite on mammals and birds, noted for its ability to leap.

fleck *n* speck; spot.

flee *vt,vi* (fled) run away (from).

fleece *n* **1** woollen coat of a sheep, etc. **2** something resembling this. *vt* **1** shear (a sheep). **2** swindle.

fleet[1] *n* **1** large number of warships functioning as a unit. **2** nation's navy. **3** group of aeroplanes, motor vehicles, ships, etc., operated by the same company.

fleet[2] *adj* moving quickly; fast. **fleeting** *adj* passing quickly; transitory.

flesh *n* **1** soft body tissue of animals or man. **2** skin; body surface. **3** thick pulpy part of a fruit or vegetable. **4** man's physical nature, as opposed to his spiritual side. **5** one's family. **fleshy** *adj*.

flew *v pt* of **fly**[1].

flex *vt,vi* bend. *n* insulated cable for connecting an appliance with a source of electricity. **flexible** *adj* **1** pliable; supple. **2** adaptable or yielding. **flexibility** *n*.

flick *n* sudden light stroke. *vt* strike, move, or remove with a sudden jerky movement. **the flicks** *pl n inf* cinema.

flicker *vi,n* **1** flash; glimmer. **2** flutter; flap.

flight[1] *n* **1** act, ability, or manner of flying. **2** route taken by an airborne animal or object. **3** trip or journey of or on an aircraft or spacecraft. **4** soaring mental digression. **5** fin fitted to a dart, arrow, etc., to stabilize its flight. **6** set of steps or stairs. **flighty** *adj* irresponsible; frivolous or erratic.

flight[2] *n* act of fleeing, as from danger.

flimsy *adj* **1** weak or insubstantial. **2** (of paper, fabrics, etc.) thin.

flinch *vi* **1** withdraw suddenly, as if from pain or shock; wince. **2** avoid; shirk.

fling *v* (flung) *vt* **1** toss or hurl; throw forcefully. **2** cast aside; abandon. *vi* move quickly and violently. *n* **1** instance of flinging. **2** period of unrestrained or irresponsible behaviour. **3** any of several lively Scottish dances.

flint *n* **1** hard dark grey stone. **2** small piece of this stone used for striking fires.

flip *v* (-pp-) *vt* toss lightly or carelessly. *vt,vi* move with a jerky motion; flick. *n* **1** tap; flick. **2** alcoholic drink containing egg.

flipper *n* **1** broad flat limb of certain

aquatic animals, used for swimming. 2 paddle-like device worn on the feet for use in swimming.

flippant *adj* impertinent or impudent. **flippancy** *n.*

flirt *vi* 1 behave as if one is amorously attracted to another person. 2 trifle or toy (with an idea, situation, etc.). **flirtation** *n.* **flirtatious** *adj.*

flit *vi* (-tt-) 1 dart; skim along; flutter. 2 pass or pass away quickly. *n* rapid movement; flutter.

float *vt,vi* 1 suspend or be suspended on the surface of a liquid. 2 move lightly through the air or through a liquid. 3 come or bring to mind vaguely. *vt* 1 circulate (a rumour, idea, etc.). 2 offer (stocks, bonds, etc.) for sale on the market. *n* 1 something that floats. 2 small floating object attached to a fishing line. 3 light electrically powered vehicle, as for delivering milk, etc.

flock[1] *n* 1 group of sheep, goats, birds, etc., that keep or are kept together. 2 crowd of people. *vi* 1 gather or cluster together. 2 go or attend in large numbers.

flock[2] *n* 1 tuft of wool, cotton, etc. 2 wool remnants used for mattress stuffing, etc.

flog *vt* (-gg-) 1 beat or whip. 2 *sl* sell.

flood *n* 1 overflowing of water on usually dry ground. 2 great outpouring or gush. 3 rising tide. *vt,vi* 1 cover or be covered in quantities of water. 2 overflow or cause to overflow. 3 overwhelm or be overwhelmed with a great quantity of something. 4 cover or fill completely; saturate. *vi* flow copiously; gush. **floodlight** *n* artificial light that illuminates an area evenly. *vt* illuminate with or as if with a floodlight.

floor *n* 1 lowest horizontal surface of a room, compartment, etc. 2 storey. 3 bottom of a river, ocean, cave, etc. 4 area used for a particular purpose. *vt,vi* cover with or make a floor. *vt* 1 knock over or down. 2 defeat or confound. **floorboard** *n* board in a wooden floor.

flop *v* (-pp-) *vi,vt* 1 fall or drop quickly or clumsily. 2 flap; flutter clumsily. *vi inf* fail. *n* failure.

flora *n, pl* **floras** *or* **florae** ('flɔːriː) 1 plant life of a particular area or time period. 2 catalogue of such plant life. **floral** *adj* of flowers. **florist** *n* person who sells flowers or plants.

flounce[1] *vi* move or go with angry or jerky movements. *n* instance of flouncing.

flounce[2] *n* ruffle used to ornament a garment, etc.

flounder[1] *vi* stumble or plod; move or act with difficulty.

flounder[2] *n* common marine flatfish.

flour *n* powdered wheat or other grain, used in baking and cooking. *vt* 1 make into flour or a fine powder. 2 sprinkle or cover with flour.

flourish *vi* 1 thrive; prosper. 2 make a display; show off. *vt* wave in the air. *n* 1 ostentation; show. 2 embellishment. 3 showy musical passage.

flout *vt,vi* mock; show contempt (for).

flow *vi* 1 (of liquids) move in a stream; circulate. 2 move or proceed as if in a stream. 3 hang loosely. 4 abound. *n* 1 act or rate of flowing. 2 current; stream. 3 continuity. 4 amount that flows. 5 outpouring; flood; overflowing.

flower *n* 1 blossom or a plant that bears a blossom. 2 finest period, part, example, etc. 3 ornament or embellishment. *vi* 1 bear flowers; blossom. 2 mature; develop fully. *vt* cover or adorn with flowers. **flowery** *adj* 1 covered with flowers. 2 ornate; highly embellished.

flown *v pp* of **fly**[1].

fluctuate *vi* waver; change; vary. **fluctuation** *n.*

flue *n* pipe or passage conducting hot gases, air, etc., from a fireplace or boiler.

fluent *adj* 1 speaking or writing a foreign language well. 2 spoken or written well and with ease. 3 flowing, smooth, or graceful. **fluency** *n.* **fluently** *adv.*

fluff *n* light downy particles or material. *vi,vi* make or become fluffy or like fluff. **fluffy** *adj.*

fluid *n* 1 liquid substance. 2 (in physics) liquid or a gas. *adj* 1 capable of flowing. 2 changing; not stable.

flung *v pt* and *pp* of **fling**.

fluorescent *adj* giving off light by the influence of radiation, electrons, etc.; luminous. **fluorescence** *n.*

fluoride *n* **1** chemical compound of fluorine. **2** sodium fluoride added to the water supply to reduce tooth decay.

fluorine *n* yellow poisonous corrosive gaseous element.

flush[1] *vt,vi* **1** blush or make blush; glow. **2** flow or cause to flow with water, etc. *vt* excite; exhilarate. *n* **1** blush; rosy colour; ruddiness. **2** emotion; exhilaration. **3** hot feeling; fever.

flush[2] *adj,adv* level; even. *adj* **1** *inf* affluent. **2** *inf* plentiful; easily obtainable. **3** vigorous. **4** full; almost overflowing.

fluster *vt,vi* make or become nervous or confused. *n* state of nervousness or confusion.

flute *n* **1** musical wind instrument made of wood or metal. **2** narrow rounded channel or groove, as in pillars, etc. *vt* cut flutes in.

flutter *vt,vi* **1** wave or flap. **2** make or be nervous; fluster. *vi* **1** fall or move with irregular motion. **2** move uneasily or aimlessly. *n* **1** flap; wave. **2** state of nervousness. **3** excitement; sensation. **4** distortion of higher frequencies in record-players, radios, etc. **5** *inf* gamble; wager.

flux *n* **1** flow. **2** continuous change.

fly[1] *v* (flew; flown) *vi* **1** move through the air; take wing; soar. **2** move quickly or rapidly. **3** vanish; disappear. *vt,vi* **1** travel in or operate (an aircraft). **2** float; glide; flutter. **3** transport or be transported by aircraft. *n* strip of fabric concealing the zip on trousers. **flyover** *n* road intersection having a bridge that passes over another road.

fly[2] *n* any of certain two-winged insects, such as the housefly.

foal *n* horse, ass, etc., less than one year old. *vt,vi* (of horses, etc.) give birth (to).

foam *n* **1** mass of tiny bubbles, as soap suds. **2** sweat of a horse. **3** frothy saliva. **4** lightweight porous substance made from rubber, plastic, etc. *vi,vt* produce foam; froth; lather.

focus *n, pl* **focuses** *or* **foci** ('fousai) **1** point to which light converges or from which it appears to diverge by the action of a lens or curved mirror. **2** central point, as of attraction or interest. *vt,vi* **1** bring or come to a focus. **2** concentrate (on). **focal** *adj*.

fodder *n* feed for livestock.

foe *n* enemy; opponent.

foetus *n* young of an animal or person while still developing in the womb.

fog *n* **1** cloudlike mass of water vapour near the ground. **2** bewilderment; confusion. *vt,vi* (-gg-) **1** surround or be surrounded with fog. **2** blur; confuse; obscure. **foggy** *adj*. **foghorn** *n* loud horn used to signal warning to ships, etc., in foggy weather.

foible *n* slight weakness or fault; failing.

foil[1] *vt* frustrate; thwart.

foil[2] *n* thin flexible metal sheet.

foil[3] *n* light flexible sword used in fencing.

foist *vt* impose or force (unwanted or inferior goods, etc.).

fold[1] *vt,vi* bend or double (paper, etc.) over itself. *vt* **1** position (the arms) with one round the other. **2** wrap up. **3** wind; bend; enclose. *vi* *inf* fail; flop. *n* **1** section or mark made by folding. **2** act of folding.

fold[2] *n* enclosure for livestock, esp. sheep.

foliage *n* leaves of a plant.

folk *n* **1** people in general. **2** family; relatives. **folkdance** *n* traditional dance having common or popular origins. **folklore** *n* traditional legends, proverbs, etc., of a people. **folksong** *n* **1** song whose words and music have been passed down through the common people. **2** composition imitating such a song. **folktale** *n* traditional legend or tale.

follicle *n* small cavity or gland, such as that from which a hair grows.

follow *vt,vi* **1** go or come after. **2** result from; ensue. **3** comprehend or understand. **4** watch closely; monitor. *vt* **1** accompany. **2** keep to (a path, road, etc.); trace. **3** comply with; observe; conform to. **4** be interested in. **follower** *n*.

folly *n* **1** foolishness. **2** elaborate nonfunctional building erected to satisfy a whim, fancy, etc.

fond *adj* **1** affectionate; loving. **2** doting; indulgent. **be fond of** have a liking for; be pleased by. **fondness** *n*.

fondant *n* creamy sugary paste, used for sweets, icing, etc.

fondle *vt* touch or handle tenderly or with affection.

font *n* receptacle for baptismal water in a church.

food *n* 1 substance, esp. when solid, eaten for nourishment. 2 something that provides nourishment or stimulation.

fool *n* 1 senseless, silly, or stupid person. 2 jester; buffoon. *vt* deceive; trick; take in. *vi* act like a fool; joke or tease. **fool (around) with** behave stupidly or irresponsibly with. **foolish** *adj* 1 silly; senseless. 2 unwise; thoughtless. **foolishly** *adv.*

foot *n*, *pl* **feet** 1 part of the end of the leg below the ankle. 2 similar part in animals. 3 unit of length equal to 12 inches (30.48 centimetres). 4 anything resembling a foot in form or purpose. 5 bottom or base. 6 way of walking. **on foot** walking or running. **football** *n* any of various team games in which a ball is kicked towards a goal. **footballer** *n*. **footbridge** *n* bridge for pedestrians. **foothold** *n* 1 place capable of providing support for a foot. 2 secure situation or position. **footing** *n* 1 foothold. 2 foundation or base. 3 status or level. **footlights** *pl n* row of lights along the front of the stage floor in a theatre. **footnote** *n* note printed on the bottom of a page giving additional information to the main text. **footprint** *n* mark made by a foot. **footwear** *n* articles worn on the feet, as shoes, boots, etc.

for *prep* 1 with the intention of. 2 intended to belong to. 3 towards. 4 over or across. 5 in support of. 6 to obtain. 7 suited to. 8 over a particular period or length of time. 9 instead of. 10 because of. 11 with regard to a norm. 12 as. 13 at a particular time. 14 to join in. 15 in spite of. *conj* because.

forage *n* 1 fodder. 2 search for food. *vt,vi* search for food, etc.

forbear *vt,vi* (-bore; -borne) abstain or refrain (from).

forbid *vt* (-dd-; -bad *or* -bade; -bidden) 1 prohibit. 2 hinder.

force *n* 1 strength; intensity; energy. 2 power or might. 3 power to affect; influence. 4 organized military group. 5 group of people organized for a particular purpose. 6 violence; coercion. 7 effectiveness; potency. 8 influence producing motion or strain in an object or material. *vt* 1 compel or oblige. 2 obtain through effort or by overpower-

ing. 3 propel or drive. 4 break down or open; overpower. 5 impose; urge upon. 6 strain; labour. **forceful** *adj*. **forcefully** *adv*. **forcible** *adj* having or done through force. **forcibly** *adv*.

forceps *pl n* surgical pincers.

ford *n* area of a river, etc., shallow enough to be crossed on foot, horseback, etc. *vt* cross (a river, etc.) in this manner.

fore *adj* at or towards the front. *n* front section or area. *adv* at or towards the bow of a ship or boat.

forearm[1] ('fɔ:rɑ:m) *n* part of the arm between the elbow and wrist.

forearm[2] (fɔ:r'ɑ:m) *vt* arm beforehand.

forebear *n* ancestor.

forecast *vt,vi* predict; foretell. *vt* herald; anticipate. *n* prediction; estimate.

forecourt *n* court in front of a building, petrol station, etc.

forefather *n* ancestor; forebear.

forefinger *n* finger next to the thumb; index finger.

forefront *n* most outstanding or advanced position.

foreground *n* nearest part of a scene or view.

forehand *adj* 1 made or relating to the right side of a right-handed person or the left side of a left-handed person. 2 foremost; most important. *n* forehand stroke in tennis, squash, etc.

forehead *n* part of the face between the hairline and eyebrows.

foreign *adj* 1 in, from, dealing with, or relating to another country, people, or culture. 2 not familiar; alien. 3 not coming from or belonging to the place where found. 4 not pertinent or applicable; inappropriate. **foreigner** *n*.

foreleg *n* one of the front legs of a four-legged animal.

forelock *n* lock of hair growing above the forehead.

foreman *n*, *pl* **-men** person who supervises workers.

foremost *adj,adv* first in order, prominence, etc.

forensic *adj* relating to courts of law.

forerunner *n* 1 predecessor; forebear. 2 herald.

foresee *vt* (-saw; -seen) see or realize beforehand; anticipate.

foresight *n* 1 prudence, forethought, or precaution. 2 forecast.

forest *n* 1 large tree-covered tract of land. 2 anything resembling this in appearance, density, etc.

forestall *vt* 1 thwart or foil beforehand. 2 anticipate; consider in advance.

foretaste *n,vt* sample or taste in advance.

foretell *vt* (-told) predict; prophesy.

forethought *n* foresight; anticipation.

forfeit *n* 1 fine or penalty. 2 something lost in order to pay a fine or penalty. *vt* surrender or lose (something) as a forfeit. **forfeiture** *n*.

forge[1] *n* 1 place or furnace where metal is heated and worked. 2 device for hammering heated metal into shape. *vt* 1 hammer (heated metal) into a form. 2 make or produce. 3 invent or make up (a story, etc.). 4 duplicate or copy (a signature, money, etc.) **forgery** *n* act or result of illegally duplicating (a signature, money, etc.).

forge[2] *vi* move ahead or make progress, esp. slowly and with difficulty.

forget *v* (-got; -gotten) *vt,vi* fail to remember or recall. *vt* 1 neglect or ignore. 2 leave behind unintentionally. **forget oneself** 1 behave improperly. 2 forget one's position or station.

forgive *vt,vi* (-gave; -given) 1 pardon; excuse; acquit. 2 cease to blame or harbour ill will (for). **forgiveness** *n*.

forgo *vt* (-went; -gone) do without; deny oneself.

fork *n* 1 pronged instrument for holding and lifting, esp. one used at table or for gardening. 2 branching or dividing of a road, river, etc. 3 tuning fork. *vi,vt* divide as or with a fork.

forlorn *adj* 1 abandoned; deserted; forsaken. 2 desolate; miserable.

form *n* 1 shape; structure. 2 variety; type. 3 nature. 4 printed document with blank spaces to be filled in. 5 long backless bench. 6 class in a school. 7 conventional social behaviour. 8 formula; conventional procedure. 9 fitness or level of performance, as in a sport. *vt,vi* 1 make into or assume a particular shape, arrangement, or condition. 2 develop. 3 constitute; make up. **formation** *n*.

formal *adj* 1 relating or adhering to set conventions, rituals, behaviour, etc. 2 precise or symmetrical in form. **formally** *adv*.

formality *n* 1 something done solely for the sake of custom or appearance. 2 state of being formal. 3 rigorous observation of ceremony, protocol, etc.

formation *n* 1 forming. 2 arrangement, as of a group of soldiers, aircraft, etc.

formative *adj* 1 relating to growth or development. 2 giving form.

former *adj* previous. *n* first of two things mentioned. **formerly** *adv*.

formidable *adj* 1 fearful; threatening; menacing. 2 difficult to resolve, conquer, etc. 3 awe-inspiring.

formula *n, pl* **formulas** *or* **formulae** ('fɔːmjuliː) 1 standard procedure or method for doing or expressing something. 2 mathematical relationship expressed, esp. in the form of an equation. 3 representation of the chemical structure of something. **formulaic** *adj*. **formulate** *vt* express in exact form or formula. **formulation** *n*.

forsake *vt* (-sook; -saken) 1 leave; desert; abandon. 2 renounce; forgo.

fort *n also* **fortress** fortified building or enclosure. **hold the fort** maintain or control during the absence of those usually in charge.

forte (fɔːt, 'fɔːtei) *n* person's strong point or particular ability.

forth *adv* 1 forwards; onwards. 2 out or away from. **forthcoming** *adj* 1 happening soon; imminent. 2 willing to talk; open; forward.

fortify *vt* strengthen or enrich. **fortification** *n*.

fortnight *n* two weeks; fourteen days. **fortnightly** *adv* every two weeks.

fortress *n* fort.

fortune *n* 1 amount of great wealth; bounty. 2 fate; destiny. 3 good luck. **fortunate** *adj* lucky; happy; favourable. **fortunately** *adv*. **fortune-teller** *n* person who predicts future events.

forty *n* 1 number equal to four times ten. 2 forty things or people. *adj* amounting to forty. **fortieth** *adj,adv,n*.

forum *n, pl* **forums** *or* **fora** ('fɔːrə) 1 meeting for discussion. 2 court or tribunal.

forward *adv* **1** onward; ahead; in advance. **2** out or forth. *adj* **1** well-advanced; ahead. **2** ready; prompt; eager. **3** bold; impertinent. **4** radical; progressive. **5** early; premature. *n* an attacking player in certain team games. *vt* send (a letter) on to a new address. **forwards** *adv* **1** towards the front; ahead. **2** into the future.

forwent *v pt* of **forgo.**

fossil *n* **1** remains or impression of a plant or animal of an earlier geological age. **2** *inf* old-fashioned person or thing. **fossilize** *vt,vi* make into or become a fossil.

foster *vt* **1** promote; encourage; further. **2** bring up; rear; nourish. **3** cherish; care for. **fosterparent** *n* person who takes care of another's child.

fought *v pt* and *pp* of **fight.**

foul *adj* **1** offensive; disgusting; repulsive. **2** filthy; squalid; polluted. **3** stormy; tempestuous. **4** wicked; shameful; infamous. **5** obscene; smutty; profane. **6** unfair; dishonourable; underhanded. *n* breaking of the rules (of a sport, game, etc.). *vt* **1** soil; defile; stain. **2** commit a foul on. *vt,vi* entangle or clog. *adv* unfairly. **foul play** *n* unfair or underhanded goings-on or behaviour.

found¹ *v pt* and *pp* of **find.**

found² *vt* set up; establish; organize. *vt,vi* base (on). **founder** *n.* **foundation** *n* **1** base or basis. **2** supporting base of a building, structure, etc. **3** organization or institution supported by an endowment. **4** cosmetic used to cover the skin.

founder *vt,vi* sink; fill with water. *vi* **1** break down or collapse. **2** stumble or fail.

foundry *n* place where metal is cast.

fountain *n* **1** jet or gush of water. **2** decorative structure producing jets of water. **fountain pen** *n* pen with a built-in ink reservoir or cartridge.

four *n* **1** number equal to one plus three. **2** group of four persons, things, etc. **3** *also* **four o'clock** four hours after noon or midnight. *adj* amounting to four. **fourth** *adj* coming between third and fifth in sequence. *adv* after the third. **four-poster** *n* bed having a post at each corner and sometimes a canopy. **foursome** *n* group of four.

fourteen *n* **1** number that is four more than ten. **2** fourteen people or things. *adj*

amounting to fourteen. **fourteenth** *adj,adv,n.*

fowl *n* **1** hen or cock; chicken. **2** any bird that is hunted as game or used or bred for food. **3** flesh of these birds.

fox *n* **1** undomesticated doglike mammal having pointed ears and muzzle and a bushy tail. **2** fur of this animal. **3** sly or crafty person. *vt inf* trick or perplex. **foxhound** *n* hound trained and kept for foxhunting. **foxhunting** *n* sport in which people on horseback pursue a fox that is being chased by a pack of hounds.

foxglove *n* wild flower having trumpet-like purple or white flowers.

foyer ('fɔijei) *n* lobby or entrance hall.

fraction *n* **1** small part of something. **2** quantity that is not a whole number, often expressed as one number divided by another. **fractional** *adj* being a part, esp. a small part.

fracture *n* act of breaking or something broken, esp. a bone. *vt,vi* break.

fragile *adj* easily broken, marred, or damaged; frail. **fragility** *n.*

fragment *n* ('frægmənt) **1** broken-off part; chip. **2** incomplete portion or part. *vt,vi* (fræg'ment) break into fragments or bits. **fragmentation** *n.*

fragrant *adj* perfumed; sweet-smelling; aromatic. **fragrance** *n.*

frail *adj* **1** weak; delicate; feeble. **2** fragile; breakable; brittle. **frailty** *n.*

frame *n* **1** supporting structure of anything. **2** form; basis. **3** surrounding structure, such as a border around a picture or mirror. **4** small glass structure for growing plants. **5** single picture in a film or television transmission. *vt* **1** surround with a frame. **2** support with a frame. **3** form the basic outlines of (a plan, theory, etc.). **4** *sl* incriminate (someone) by falsifying evidence. **framework** *n* **1** basis or outline. **2** structure that supports or sustains.

franc *n* monetary unit of France, Belgium, Switzerland, and several other countries.

franchise *n* **1** rights of citizenship, esp. the right to vote. **2** privilege granted by the government. **3** permission to market a product in a specified area.

frank *adj* **1** straightforward; honest; candid. **2** blunt; unrestrained; outright. **3** undisguised; avowed. *vt* mark (mail) so as to authorize for free delivery.

frankfurter *n* thin smoked sausage made of beef or pork that is served hot, usually in a roll.

frantic *adj* agitated; frenzied; raving. **frantically** *adv*.

fraternal *adj* 1 of or relating to a brother. 2 brotherly; showing affection or support. **fraternally** *adv*. **fraternity** *n* 1 group of people with common interests or goals. 2 brotherhood; brotherly consideration and affection. **fraternize** *vi* associate or be friendly (with). **fraternization** *n*.

fraud *n* 1 deceit; trickery; deception. 2 something false or forged; counterfeit. 3 person who practises fraud. **fraudulent** *adj*.

fraught *adj* abounding in; full of.

fray[1] *n* noisy argument or brawl.

fray[2] *vt,vi* 1 unravel or wear away. 2 strain; vex; annoy. 3 rub or rub against.

freak *n* 1 deformed person, animal, or plant. 2 abnormal or odd thing, event, etc. 3 *sl* person deeply interested in something.

freckle *n* small brownish spot on the skin. *vt,vi* cover or be covered with freckles.

free *adj* 1 at liberty; independent; unfettered. 2 not restricted or regulated. 3 clear, immune, or exempt. 4 easy; firm or unimpeded. 5 loose; unattached. 6 available; unoccupied. 7 costing nothing; without charge. 8 frank or open. 9 liberal; generous. *vt* (freed) 1 liberate; set free; release. 2 exempt. 3 rid; clear. *adv* 1 *also* **freely** in a free manner. 2 without cost. **freedom** *n* 1 state or quality of being free; liberty. 2 immunity or privilege. 3 ease; facility. 4 frankness. 5 familiarity; lack of formality. **freehand** *adj* done by hand without the use of other aids. **freehold** *n* absolute ownership of land, property, etc. **freeholder** *n*. **freelance** *n* *also* **freelancer** self-employed writer, artist, etc. *adj* relating to a freelance. *adv* in the manner of a freelance. **free will** *n* doctrine that people have free choice and that their actions are not predetermined.

freeze *v* (froze; frozen) *vt,vi* 1 change into a solid by a drop in temperature. 2 cover, be, or become covered or blocked with ice. 3 attach (to). 4 be or cause to be motionless

through terror, fear, surprise, etc. 5 be or make very cold. *vt* 1 preserve (food) by subjecting to extreme cold. 2 stabilize and prevent increases in (prices, incomes, etc.). *n* fixing of levels of prices, incomes, etc. **freezer** *n* refrigerator in which food can be deep-frozen; deep freeze. **freezing point** *n* temperature at which a liquid freezes.

freight *n* 1 cargo; shipment; load. 2 transportation of goods.

French bean *n* thin green seed pod used as a vegetable.

French dressing *n* salad dressing made from oil and vinegar and usually seasoned.

French horn *n* coiled brass instrument with a mellow tone.

French window *n* door made of glass and wood that opens outwards.

frenzy *n* wild excitement or enthusiasm; rage. *vt* make very excited; enrage. **frenzied** *adj*.

frequent *adj* ('fri:kwənt) 1 occurring often and at short intervals. 2 habitual; usual. *vt* (fri'kwent) visit regularly or repeatedly. **frequently** *adv*. **frequency** 1 state of being frequent. 2 rate of occurrence. 3 rate of repetition of a periodic process per unit time.

fresco *n*, *pl* **frescoes** *or* **frescos** technique or example of wall-painting in which pigments are applied to the plaster before it has dried.

fresh *adj* 1 new; recent. 2 additional; more. 3 (of food) not preserved in any way. 4 (of water) not salt. *adv* in a fresh manner. **freshly** *adv*. **freshness** *n*. **freshen** *vt,vi* make or become fresh. **freshwater** *adj* relating or indigenous to fresh water.

fret[1] *vt,vi* (-tt-) 1 worry; irritate; vex. 2 wear away; erode. *n* 1 annoyance; irritation; vexation. 2 erosion; eating away. **fretful** *adj*.

fret[2] *n* ornamental geometric pattern. *vt* (-tt-) adorn with such a pattern. **fretsaw** *n* fine narrow saw with a curved frame used for cutting designs. **fretwork** *n* interlacing geometric designs cut in thin wood.

friar *n* male member of a religious order supported by alms.

friction *n* 1 resistance met when two surfaces are rubbed together. 2 discord; conflict.

Friday n sixth day of the week.

fridge n inf refrigerator.

friend n 1 companion; intimate. 2 acquaintance; colleague. 3 ally. **friendly** adj 1 relating or fitting to a friend. 2 amicable or helpful. **friendliness** n. **friendship** n 1 being friends or a friend. 2 goodwill; benevolence.

frieze n ornamental band or border on a column, wall, etc.

fright n scare; alarm; dismay. **look a fright** look terrible or grotesque. **frighten** vt 1 scare; terrify. 2 cause to worry or feel apprehensive about something. **frightful** adj dreadful; terrible. **frightfully** adv 1 dreadfully; terribly. 2 inf very.

frigid adj cold in manner, feeling, temperature, etc. **frigidity** n.

frill n 1 decorative ruffle. 2 trimming; ornamentation. vt decorate with frills.

fringe n 1 border or edging having hanging thread, tassels, flaps, etc. 2 section of hair cut short to hang over the forehead. 3 outer region; margin. vt provide with a fringe. adj additional; supplementary.

frisk vi,vt move about playfully. vt inf search or rob (a person) by examination of clothing. **frisky** adj.

fritter[1] vt waste (money, time, etc.).

fritter[2] n type of pancake dipped in batter and deep-fried.

frivolity n gaiety; revelry; merriment. **frivolous** adj 1 unimportant; trifling; petty. 2 idle; silly; foolish.

frizz vt,vi make or become tightly curled or kinky. **frizzy** adj.

frizzle[1] vt,vi frizz. n tight wiry curl.

frizzle[2] vi emit a hiss or sizzling noise. vt cook (meat, etc.) until crisp and dry.

fro adv from or back. **to and fro** back and forth.

frock n 1 dress. 2 monk's cloak. vt install (a cleric) in office.

frog n smooth-skinned web-footed amphibian. **have a frog in one's throat** speak hoarsely. **frogman** n, pl -men underwater diver.

frolic n gaiety or merry occasion. vi (-ck-) act in a lively playful manner. **frolicsome** adj.

from prep 1 indicating the original place or circumstance. 2 starting at. 3 indicating a distance between (two places). 3 indicating removal or restraint.

front n 1 forward position or side that is usually closest to a viewer or user. 2 beginning or opening part or section. 3 leading position. 4 separating area between two different masses of air. 5 inf cover; outward appearance. 6 alliance; coalition. vt,vi face (on). **frontal** adj. **frontally** adv.

frontier n 1 unexplored or unsettled area. 2 boundary.

frost n 1 (formation of) ice particles that are white in appearance. 2 below-freezing temperature. 3 inf coldness of attitude, manner, etc. vt,vi coat or be coated with frost or something similar. **frostbite** n injury to the body caused by exposure to extreme cold. **frostbitten** adj. **frosty** adj.

froth n,vi,vt foam.

frown vi,n scowl. **frown on** disapprove of.

froze v pt of **freeze**. **frozen** v pp of **freeze**.

frugal adj economical; thrifty. **frugality** n. **frugally** adv.

fruit n 1 produce of a plant, usually eaten raw or cooked as a sweet. 2 result; product. vi bear fruit. **fruit machine** n gambling machine with pictures of fruits as variables. **fruitful** adj prolific; fertile; productive. **fruitfully** adv. **fruitfulness** n. **fruitless** adj 1 yielding nothing; useless. 2 barren; sterile. **fruitlessly** adv. **fruition** (fru:'iʃən) n 1 fulfilment or maturity. 2 bearing of fruit.

frustrate vt baffle; disconcert; foil. **frustration** n.

fry vt,vi cook in oil or fat.

fuchsia ('fju:ʃə) n ornamental plant or shrub yielding hanging red, purple, or white flowers.

fudge n thick sweet made of butter, sugar, cream, and flavouring.

fuel n substance that can be used to supply energy. vt,vi (-ll-) provide with or receive fuel.

fugitive n person who flees or hides.

fulcrum n, pl **fulcrums** or **fulcra** ('fulkrə) 1 pivot. 2 support; prop.

fulfil vt (-ll-) 1 carry out; complete. 2 perform; do; obey. 3 satisfy; gratify. 4 complete; terminate. **fulfilment** n.

full *adj* 1 filled to capacity. 2 having eaten as much as one can. 3 entire; complete. 4 enjoying all rights and privileges. 5 ample or plump. **full of** preoccupied with. ~*adv also* **fully** entirely; exactly. *n* **in full** in entirety. **to the full** to capacity. **full-length** *adj* 1 relating to the complete length; unabridged. 2 (of dresses and skirts) reaching the floor. **full stop** *n* punctuation mark (.) used to mark the end of a sentence. **full-time** *adj,adv* relating to or lasting normal working hours.

fumble *vi* 1 handle something clumsily. 2 grope; find one's way clumsily. *vi,vt* utter (something) in an awkward manner. **fumbler** *n.*

fume *vi* storm; rage. *vt,vi* smoke; give off (smoke). *n* smoke; vapour.

fun *n* enjoyment; pleasure; amusement. **make fun of** ridicule; tease. **funfair** *n* fair; amusement park.

function *n* 1 purpose; special or natural activity. 2 formal gathering. 3 variable factor. *vi* perform (as). **functional** *adj* 1 relating to a function. 2 useful rather than decorative or ornamental. **functionally** *adv.*

fund *n* store or reserve, esp. of money, resources, etc. *vt* supply with a fund or funds.

fundamental *adj* 1 basic; underlying; principal. 2 original; first. *n* principle; rule. **fundamentally** *adv.*

funeral *n* burial ceremony.

fungus *n, pl* **fungi** ('fʌndʒai) plant lacking chlorophyll, such as a mould, mushroom, etc.

funnel *n* 1 hollow tapering apparatus for transferring a substance to a more narrow-necked container. 2 something shaped like a funnel. *vt,vi* (-ll-) 1 pour through a funnel. 2 direct or channel. 3 fix attention or focus (on).

funny *adj* amusing; comical; humorous. **funnily** *adv.*

fur *n* 1 dense coat of an animal. 2 *inf* sediment caused by hard water. *v* (-rr-) *vt* decorate with fur. *vi,vt inf* cover or be covered with sediment.

furious *adj* raging; angry; violent. **furiously** *adv.*

furnace *n* apparatus equipped to produce steam, etc., by burning fuel.

furnish *vt* 1 provide furniture, carpets, etc., for. 2 equip or supply (with).

furniture *n* movable items such as tables, chairs, or beds, found in a house, office, etc.

furrow *n* 1 trench. 2 groove or line, esp. in the forehead. *vt,vi* make or become wrinkled or lined.

further *adv* 1 *also* **furthermore** moreover. 2 to a greater degree or distance. *adj* more. *vt* assist; help along. **furthest** *adv* to the most extreme degree or place. *adj* most.

furtive *adj* secret; sly. **furtively** *adv.*

fury *n* 1 passion; anger; frenzy. 2 violence; turbulence.

fuse[1] *vi,vt* 1 melt. 2 combine; blend. *n* safety device in plugs, electric wiring, etc. **fusion** *n* act of fusing; coming together.

fuse[2] *n* combustible wire or device leading to and capable of setting off an explosive. *vt* provide with a fuse.

fuselage *n* body of an aeroplane.

fuss *n* activity; ado; bustle. *vi* worry; be unduly preoccupied with. **fussy** *adj* 1 fussing; worrying. 2 preoccupied with petty details. 3 particular.

futile *adj* 1 ineffective; useless; unsuccessful. 2 trivial; frivolous. **futility** *n.*

future *n* 1 time that is yet to come. 2 prospects. *adj* yet to come.

fuzz *n* 1 fluffy or curly hairy mass. 2 blur. *vt,vi* make or become like fuzz. **fuzzy** *adj.*

G

gabble *vi,vt* speak rapidly and inarticulately. *n* rapid inarticulate speech.

gable *n* triangular part of a wall immediately below that part of a pitched roof that juts out.

gadget *n* ingenious, novel, or useful tool, device, or appliance. **gadgetry** *n* gadgets collectively.

gag[1] *n* something placed in or over the mouth in order to silence or control. *vt* (-gg-) place a gag on.

gag[2] *n inf* comedian's joke.

gaiety *n* jollity; light-heartedness; merriment.

gaily *adv* in a gay manner; light-heartedly.

gain *vt* 1 obtain; acquire; win; earn. 2 reach; attain. *vi* 1 increase; gather speed. 2

profit. *n* **1** advantage; win; profit. **2** increase; advancement. **gainful** *adj* profitable.

gait *n* manner of walking.

gala *n* special performance or display; festival.

galaxy *n* **1** large grouping of stars, such as the Milky Way. **2** impressive group of famous people. **galactic** *adj*.

gale *n* strong wind.

gallant *adj* ('gælənt) **1** dashing and brave; courageous. **2** ('gælənt, gə'lænt) chivalrous. *n* ('gælənt) **1** brave knight or nobleman. **2** attentive suitor. **gallantly** *adv*. **gallantry** *n*.

galleon *n* large sailing ship originally used by Spain.

gallery *n* **1** building or room(s) exhibiting works of art. **2** block of seats above the circle in a theatre. **3** upper floor or section opening out on to the interior of a hall, church, etc.

galley *n* **1** ship's kitchen. **2** warship propelled by oars. **3** long tray for holding metal type.

gallon *n* measure of liquid equal to approx. 4.5 litres (8 pints).

gallop *n* **1** the fastest gait of a horse or similar animal. **2** rapid movement or course. *vi,vt* ride at a gallop. *vi* race; move rapidly.

gallows *s n* wooden structure used for execution by hanging.

galore *adv* in abundance.

galvanism *n* process of producing electricity by chemical action. **galvanize** *vt* **1** coat with a metal by galvanism. **2** stimulate into action. **galvanic** *adj*.

gamble *vi,vt* **1** place a bet (on); stake. **2** risk; hazard; speculate. *vi* play at games of chance, esp. in order to win money. *n* risk; something of uncertain outcome; chance. **gambler** *n*.

game *n* **1** something played for amusement or sport. **2** match; contest. **3** certain wild animals that are hunted for sport or food. *vi* take part in games of chance such as roulette. *adj* willing; plucky. **gamekeeper** *n* person employed to take care of animals, fish, etc., on an estate, to prevent poaching, etc.

gammon *n* lower end of a side of bacon.

gander *n* male goose.

gang *n* **1** group of people, esp. one engaged in unlawful activity. **2** band of workers. *v* **gang up (on)** band together in order to attack. **gangster** *n* armed criminal, usually operating in a gang.

gangrene *n* death and putrefaction of part of a living organism caused by lack of blood supply.

gangway *n* **1** aisle or passageway separating blocks of seats. **2** movable bridge placed between a ship and the quay.

gaol *n,vt* jail. **gaoler** *n*.

gap *n* **1** opening; hole or space between two things. **2** interval; pause.

gape *vi* **1** stare in a stupid way, with astonishment, etc. **2** be wide open. *n* **1** open-mouthed stare. **2** split; hole; breach.

garage *n* **1** small building or shelter for a vehicle, esp. a car. **2** commercial premises selling petrol, repairing motor vehicles, etc.; service station.

garble *vt* give a muddled or misleading account of.

garden *n* **1** plot of land adjoining a house, where flowers, vegetables, etc., are cultivated. **2** small park. *vi* engage on work in a garden. **gardener** *n*. **gardening** *n*.

gargle *vi* rinse out the mouth and throat with liquid, which is kept moving by the action of air drawn up from the lungs. *n* mouthwash; rinse.

gargoyle *n* carved stone face, usually of a grotesque form and often functioning as a waterspout.

garish ('gɛərɪʃ) *adj* gaudy; vulgar in taste, colour, etc.

garland *n* flowers, leaves, etc., woven into a ring and worn for decoration round the neck or on the head. *vt* decorate with a garland.

garlic *n* plant with a pungent bulbous root, which is used as a seasoning.

garment *n* item of clothing.

garnish *vt* add extra decoration, seasoning, etc., to (food). *n* trimmings or seasoning used to decorate or enhance the flavour of food.

garrison *n* military establishment where troops are stationed. *vt* station (troops, etc.) in a garrison.

garter *n* elasticated band worn round the leg to hold up a stocking or sock.

gas *n* **1** substance, such as nitrogen, oxygen, or carbon dioxide, that has no fixed volume or shape. 2 fuel in the form of gas. *vt* (-ss-) poison or asphyxiate with gas. **gaseous** ('gæsiəs, 'geifəs) *adj*.

gash *n* deep cut, wound, or tear. *vt* cut deeply; slash.

gasket *n* asbestos sheet used as a seal in an engine cylinder.

gasp *vi* 1 struggle to breathe; pant. 2 catch one's breath in surprise, shock, etc. 3 *inf* crave; long (for). *n* 1 sudden sharp intake of air. 2 strangled cry of surprise, etc.

gastric *adj* relating to the stomach.

gastronomic *adj* relating to the art of good eating. **gastronomy** *n*.

gate *n* wooden or metal structure forming a barrier across an opening in a fence, wall, etc. **gatecrash** *vt,vi* force one's way into (a party, meeting, etc.) as an uninvited guest. **gatecrasher** *n*.

gâteau *n, pl* **gâteaus** *or* **gâteaux** ('gætou) rich cake decorated with cream, fruit, nuts, etc.

gather *vi,vt* 1 collect together in a crowd or group; assemble; congregate. 2 increase in speed, intensity, etc. 3 draw thread through material to form pleats or folds. *vt* 1 amass; accumulate; collect. 2 pick or pluck (flowers, berries, etc.). 3 assume; understand; believe. **gathering** *n* assembly of people; congregation.

gauche (gouf) *adj* awkward; clumsy; ill at ease. **gaucheness** *n*.

gaudy *adj* brightly coloured; showy; garish. **gaudiness** *n*.

gauge (geidʒ) *n* 1 instrument for measuring speed, temperature, pressure, etc. 2 standard or criterion. 3 thickness of metal. 4 width of a railway track. *vt* 1 measure or estimate the measurement of. 2 assess; judge.

gaunt *adj* thin and bony; haggard; angular.

gauze *n* thin loosely woven fabric used for surgical dressings, curtains, etc.

gave *v pt* of **give**.

gay *adj* 1 cheerful; bright; light-hearted; merry. 2 vivid; of a bright colour. *adj,n sl* homosexual.

gaze *vi* stare fixedly or for a considerable time. *n* fixed or long look or stare.

gazelle *n* small antelope of Africa and Asia.

gear *n* 1 mechanism consisting of a set of toothed wheels, such as that on a motor vehicle used for transmitting motion from the engine to the road wheels. 2 the engaging of a particular gear. 3 *inf* equipment or apparatus required for a particular activity. *vt* set up or arrange one thing to fit in with another.

geese *n pl* of **goose**.

gelatine *n also* **gelatin** yellowish protein obtained by boiling animal bones and skin, used in the manufacture of glue, jellies, etc. **gelatinous** *adj*.

gelignite *n* type of dynamite.

gem *n also* **gemstone** jewel created from a polished stone.

Gemini *n* third sign of the zodiac, represented by the Twins.

gender *n* 1 category, such as masculine, feminine, or neuter, into which nouns may be placed in some languages. 2 sexual identity.

gene *n* part of a chromosome carrying hereditary information.

genealogy *n* 1 descent through a line of ancestors; lineage. 2 family tree. **genealogical** *adj*.

general *adj* 1 not specific or particular; broad. 2 common; widespread; usual. 3 vague; indefinite. *n* military officer of a rank below that of field marshal. **general election** *n* nationwide election held to elect parliamentary representatives. **generalize** *vi,vt* come to a general conclusion from particular statements or facts. **generalization** *n*. **generally** *adv* 1 usually. 2 widely; commonly. **general practitioner** *n* doctor dealing with a wide range of cases rather than specializing in any particular area of medicine.

generate *vt* 1 create. 2 produce (electricity). **generation** *n* 1 production; creation. 2 whole range of people within the same general age group. 3 particular genealogical stage. 4 span of about 30 years. **generator** *n* machine producing electrical energy.

generic *adj* 1 relating to a genus. 2 representing a whole group or class.

generous *adj* 1 unselfish; not mean; kind. 2 tolerant; liberal. 3 ample; lavish. **generosity** *n*. **generously** *adv*.

genetic *adj* relating to genes or genetics. **genetics** *n* study of heredity.

genial *adj* amiable; friendly; warm. **geniality** *n.*

genitals *pl n* male or female sexual organs. **genital** *adj.*

genius *n* 1 person of exceptionally high intelligence or talent. 2 remarkable talent or ability.

genteel *adj* displaying extremely refined manners or taste.

gentile *n* non-Jewish person, esp. a Christian. *adj* non-Jewish.

gentle *adj* 1 not rough or violent. 2 mild. 3 docile; tame. 4 gradual. **gentleness** *n.* **gently** *adv.* **gentleman** *n, pl* **-men** 1 man who is cultured and well-mannered. 2 aristocrat or nobleman.

genuine *adj* 1 real; authentic; not false or artificial. 2 sincere. **genuinely** *adv.*

genus ('dʒenəs, 'dʒiːnəs) *n, pl* **genera** ('dʒenərə) biological subdivision containing one or more species.

geography *n* 1 study of the features of the earth's surface. 2 physical features of a region. **geographer** *n.* **geographical** *adj.*

geology *n* study of the composition and evolution of the earth. **geological** *adj.* **geologist** *n.*

geometry *n* branch of mathematics concerned with the properties of figures in space. **geometric** *or* **geometrical** *adj.*

geranium *n* garden or house plant having pink, scarlet, or white flowers and roundish leaves.

germ *n* any microbe that causes disease.

German measles *n* contagious disease characterized by a rash and swelling of the glands.

germinate *vi,vt* 1 develop through warmth and moisture from a seed into a plant. 2 create; spring up. **germination** *n.*

gesticulate *vi* make wild or broad gestures. **gesticulation** *n.*

gesture *n* 1 movement of the arms or head. 2 act of friendship, sympathy, etc. *vi,vt* express by means of gestures.

get *v* (-tt-; got) *vt* 1 obtain; acquire; gain possession of. 2 fetch. 3 cause to happen or be done. 4 *inf* grasp; understand. 5 make; force; persuade. *vi* 1 become; grow. 2 start. 3 go; proceed. **get about** *or* **around** 1 be active. 2 move about; circulate. **get across** communicate so as to be understood. **get ahead** progress; continue. **get along** 1 manage; cope. 2 succeed. **get at** 1 reach. 2 intend; imply. **get away** escape. **get away with** remain undetected or unpunished. **get by** just about manage to cope adequately. **get down** 1 descend. 2 depress; make unhappy. **get down to** begin to concentrate on. **get off** 1 dismount or disembark. 2 be permitted to leave. 3 escape punishment. **get on** 1 board (a bus, train, etc.). 2 mount (a horse, etc.). 3 make successful progress. 4 have a friendly relationship (with). **get over** recover from; come to terms with. **get round** 1 cajole; persuade; bribe. 2 solve or resolve (a difficulty, problem, etc.) by using a different technique or approach. **get round to** find time for. **get through (to)** 1 contact by telephone. 2 make (someone) understand or listen. **get up** 1 stand up. 2 get out of bed. 3 organize; arrange. **get up to** engage in, esp. when not being watched or controlled. **getaway** *n* escape.

geyser *n* 1 natural hot spring. 2 gas-fuelled water heater.

ghastly *adj* dreadful; shocking; gruesome; horrific.

gherkin *n* small cucumber used for pickling.

ghetto *n, pl* **ghettos** *or* **ghettoes** 1 poor district or quarter in a city; slum area. 2 (formerly) poor Jewish quarter in a city.

ghost *n* supernatural being believed to be a dead person's soul, which returns to haunt the living; spirit. *vt,vi* write (a book) for another person, who is then acknowledged as the author.

giant *n* 1 abnormally tall person. 2 prominent or powerful person. 3 one of a race of huge mythological people with superhuman powers. *adj* huge; enormous.

gibberish *n* nonsense; gabbling speech.

gibbon *n* small long-armed ape.

giddy *adj* 1 dizzy. 2 frivolous. **giddiness** *n.*

gift *n* 1 present; donation. 2 talent. **gifted** *adj* talented.

gigantic *adj* very large; huge.

giggle *vi* laugh in a silly or uncontrolled manner. *n* silly laugh; chuckle.

gild *vt* (gilded *or* gilt) coat with gold, gold paint, etc.

gill[1] (gil) *n* respiratory organ of aquatic animals.

gill[2] (dʒil) *n* liquid measure equal to one quarter of a pint.

gimmick *n* device or method used to gain publicity, promote sales, etc.

gin *n* alcoholic drink made by distilling barley or rye and flavoured with juniper berries.

ginger *n* plant whose pungent root is used as a flavouring for drinks, confectionery, etc. *n,adj* reddish-orange; auburn. *v* **ginger up** *inf* enliven; give energy to.

gingerly *adv* cautiously; warily; uncertainly.

gingham *n* cotton fabric patterned with coloured checks or stripes.

Gipsy *n* Gypsy.

giraffe *n* African mammal with a mottled hide and very long neck.

girder *n* iron or steel beam; joist.

girdle *n* 1 cord or thin belt worn round the waist. 2 light corset. 3 band or circle. *vt* 1 fasten with a girdle. 2 encircle.

girl *n* 1 female child; young woman. **girlish** *adj.* **girlhood** *n.* **Girl Guide** *n* female member of an organization with aims similar to those of the Scouts.

giro *n* banking system whereby transfers between accounts may be made by special cheques.

girth *n* 1 leather strap secured under a horse's belly to hold a saddle in position. 2 measurement of circumference. *vt* secure with a girth.

give *v* (gave; given) *vt* 1 present as a gift; donate. 2 place into the hands of; offer; hand. 3 provide; supply. 4 be the cause of. 5 transmit or transfer. 6 yield; produce. 7 *also* **give out** emit or radiate. 8 grant; award; confer. 9 pay; make to buy for. 10 set aside; allow; spare. 11 act as the host for (a party, meal, etc.). 12 administer (drugs, a punishment, etc.). 13 communicate; make known; tell. 14 inflict; cause to suffer. 15 utter. *vi* 1 donate. 2 be flexible or elastic. 3 *also* **give way** collapse or break under strain or pressure. **give away** 1 dispose of; offer for no payment. 2 reveal; disclose. **give in** submit; surrender. **give up** abandon; cease to

do, study, care for, etc. ~*n* elasticity; flexibility.

glacier *n* mass of ice extending over a large area. **glacial** *adj.*

glad *adj* happy; pleased. **gladly** *adv.* **gladness** *n.* **gladden** *vt,vi* make or become glad; cheer.

gladiolus *n, pl* **gladioli** (glædi'oulai) *or* **gladioluses** plant with long narrow leaves and one stem bearing a brightly coloured flower.

glamour *n* attraction or attractiveness; allure; glittering charm. **glamorous** *adj.* **glamorize** *vt* make attractive or glamorous; exaggerate the charms of; idealize.

glance *vi* 1 take a brief look. 2 flash; shine. **glance off** bounce off sharply. ~*n* 1 brief look; glimpse. 2 quick movement of the eyes. 3 flash; spark.

gland *n* one of various organs in the body that secrete different substances. **glandular** *adj.*

glare *vi* 1 shine fiercely or dazzlingly. 2 stare angrily; glower; scowl. *n* 1 harsh blinding light; dazzle. 2 angry look.

glass *n* 1 hard brittle transparent material used in windows, vessels, etc. 2 drinking vessel made of glass. 3 mirror. 4 telescope. *vt* glaze. **glasses** *pl n* 1 spectacles. 2 binoculars. **glasshouse** *n* greenhouse or conservatory. **glassy** *adj* of or like glass.

glaze *vt,vi* 1 fit with glass. 2 apply or have a thin glassy coating. *n* shiny coating, esp. on ceramics.

gleam *n* beam of light; glow. *vi* shine; beam; glow.

glean *vt,vi* 1 gather (remnants of corn) after reaping. 2 collect painstakingly.

glee *n* mirth; cheerfulness; joy. **gleeful** *adj.* **gleefully** *adv.*

glen *n* (in Scotland) narrow valley.

glib *adj* smooth but insincere in manner. **glibly** *adv.* **glibness** *n.*

glide *vi,vt* move smoothly and noiselessly. *n* smooth flowing movement. **glider** *n* aircraft without an engine that moves according to air currents.

glimmer *vi* shine dimly or faintly. *n* 1 faint light. 2 slight hint or suggestion of hope, intelligence, etc.

glimpse *n* fleeting look; glance; brief view. *vt* see very briefly; get a partial view of.

glint *n* flash; sparkle; gleam. *vi* sparkle; glitter.

glisten *vi* sparkle; shine brightly.

glitter *vi* shine brilliantly; flash; twinkle. *n* sparkle; twinkle.

gloat *vi* take malicious pleasure in one's own greed, another's misfortune, etc.

globe *n* 1 the earth. 2 model of the earth. 3 spherical object; ball. **global** *adj*. **globule** *n* small drop, particle, or bubble.

gloom *n* 1 dim light; semi-darkness; shadow. 2 pessimism; cynicism; despondency; depression. **gloomy** *adj*. **gloomily** *adv*.

glory *n* 1 state of being highly honoured, revered, etc.; exaltation. 2 magnificence; splendour. 3 fame; renown. **glorify** *vt* exalt; treat with great reverence; worship or admire. **glorification** *n*. **glorious** *adj* 1 overwhelmingly beautiful; magnificent. 2 stunning. 3 highly distinguished; great. **gloriously** *adv*.

gloss *n* 1 bright or reflective surface or appearance; sheen; lustre. 2 *also* **gloss paint** type of paint giving a smooth shiny finish. *vt* polish; shine. **gloss over** try to hide; cover up mistakes, etc. **glossy** *adj* shiny.

glossary *n* explanatory list of specialist or technical terms or words.

glove *n* covering for the hand with individual sections for each finger and the thumb. *vt* cover with a glove.

glow *vi* 1 burn with a steady light; shine warmly or brightly. 2 radiate excitement, pride, enthusiasm, etc. *n* steady bright light; blaze. **glow-worm** *n* small beetle, the female of which possesses organs that give off a luminous greenish light.

glower ('glauə) *vi* scowl; frown; stare angrily. *n* angry stare; scowl.

glucose *n* type of sugar obtained from grapes and other fruits.

glue *n* substance used as an adhesive, made from gelatine, resin, etc. *vt* 1 stick with glue. 2 attach firmly.

glum *adj* disconsolate; unhappy; gloomy; sullen. **glumly** *adv*. **glumness** *n*.

glut *n* surfeit; excess. *vt* (-tt-) supply with an excess amount; provide with too much. *vi* gorge; overeat. **glutton** *n* 1 excessively

greedy person; one who habitually overeats. 2 fanatic. **gluttony** *n*.

gnarled *adj* twisted and knotty; misshapen; lumpy.

gnash *vt* grind or clench (the teeth); grate. *n* grinding action or sound.

gnat *n* small mosquito.

gnaw *vt,vi* 1 bite continuously (on); chew. 2 corrode; wear away. 3 torment persistently. *n* act of gnawing.

gnome *n* mythological being living underground and having a dwarflike appearance.

go *v* (went; gone) *vi* 1 move; proceed. 2 function; work; operate. 3 depart; leave. 4 make a trip or take a walk with a particular purpose. 5 vanish; disappear. 6 extend as far as; reach. 7 become. 8 be put; belong. 9 be ordered; have as a sequence. 10 be used for. 11 fail; break down; collapse. 12 attend; be a member of. 13 be decided (by). 14 be able to fit. 15 be applicable or relevant. 16 be awarded. 17 be allowed to escape. *vt* 1 take or follow (a route, path, etc.). 2 travel (a specified distance). **go against** defy; infringe. **go down** 1 descend. 2 be reduced. 3 deflate. 4 be received or appreciated by an audience. **go for** 1 aim at. 2 attack suddenly. **go in for** take up as a hobby, career, etc. **go off** 1 explode. 2 cease to be interested in. 3 happen. 4 (of food) turn bad. **go on** 1 proceed; continue. 2 criticize or nag incessantly. 3 appear (on stage, TV, etc.). 4 take place; occur. **go out** 1 be extinguished. 2 cease to be fashionable. 3 attend a social function. **go over** 1 repeat; re-examine. 2 cross. 3 be communicated. **go slow** work slowly to enforce one's demands for more pay, etc. **go through** 1 suffer; have to bear; experience. 2 make a search of. 3 inspect. **go under** succumb; sink. ~*n* 1 turn. 2 *inf* energy; drive. **go-between** *n* person acting as a messenger between parties; intermediary.

goad *n* 1 sharp pointed stick used for driving cattle. 2 provocation; stimulus. *vt* 1 drive or prod with a goad. 2 urge; incite; provoke.

goal *n* 1 area between two posts through which a ball must pass in games such as football or hockey in order to score. 2 winning post on a race track. 3 point scored by getting a ball through the goal. 4 aim;

object; target. **goalkeeper** *n* player who guards the goal area.

goat *n* brownish-grey mammal often domesticated for its milk or wool. **get one's goat** irritate; annoy.

gobble[1] *vt,vi* eat quickly or greedily; gulp; bolt.

gobble[2] *vi* (of a turkey cock) make a harsh gurgling sound. *n* harsh gurgling sound.

goblet *n* drinking vessel with a long stem.

goblin *n* mythological being that is malevolent or mischievous; demon.

god *n* 1 supernatural being having power over mankind who is worshipped and revered; deity. 2 any object of worship or idolatry. **God** *n* spiritual being who is the creator and ruler of mankind. *interj* exclamation of disgust, horror, surprise, etc. **the gods** highest gallery in a theatre. **godchild** *n, pl* **-children** child for whom a godparent acts. **goddaughter** *n* female godchild. **godfather** *n* male godparent. **godfearing** *adj* intensely religious; pious. **godless** *adj* 1 having no religious beliefs. 2 wicked; evil. **godmother** *n* female godparent. **godparent** *n* person who acts as a sponsor for a child at baptism. **godsend** *n* timely and fortunate event or gift. **godson** *n* male godchild.

goddess *n* 1 female god. 2 beautiful woman.

goggle *vi* 1 stare stupidly; gape. 2 roll the eyes. **goggles** *pl n* protective covering worn over the eyes.

going *n* 1 departure; leaving. 2 manner of travelling. *adj* thriving. **going to** intending to.

gold *n* 1 valuable yellow metal used for coins, jewellery, etc. 2 coins of this metal. 3 wealth; money; riches. *adj,n* bright yellowish-orange. **golden** *adj* 1 made of gold. 2 of the colour of gold. 3 valuable; precious. **golden handshake** *n* sum of money given to an employee on leaving a company. **golden syrup** *n* kind of treacle of a pale golden colour. **goldfinch** *n* European finch with gold and black plumage. **goldfish** *n* reddish-gold freshwater fish. **goldmine** *n* 1 place where gold ore is mined. 2 source of great wealth. **goldsmith** *n* craftsman who works with gold.

golf *n* sport played on a grass course with the aim of driving a small ball into a succession of holes with a long club. **golfer** *n*.

gondola *n* long narrow open boat traditionally used on the canals in Venice. **gondolier** *n* person who makes a living by transporting passengers in a gondola.

gone *v pp* of **go**.

gong *n* percussion instrument consisting of a large metal disc, struck with a hammer.

gonorrhoea (gɔnə'riə) *n* type of venereal disease.

good *adj* 1 of a high quality; not bad. 2 obedient; not naughty. 3 pleasing; attractive. 4 virtuous. 5 efficient; suitable. 6 kind; benevolent. 7 beneficial. 8 correct; accurate. 9 able; competent. 10 fitting; apt. 11 considerable. 12 safe; not harmful. 13 full; complete. *n* 1 use; point. 2 benefit; advantage. 3 virtue. **for good** for ever; definitely and finally. **Good Friday** *n* Friday before Easter when Christ's Crucifixion is commemorated. **good-humoured** *adj* affable; in a good mood. **good-looking** *adj* handsome; attractive. **good-natured** *adj* kind; genial; easygoing. **goods** *pl n* 1 merchandise; products. 2 items; articles. 3 possessions; property. **good will** *n* 1 generosity; kindness. 2 assets, such as clientele, reputation, etc., taken into consideration when a business is bought or sold.

goose *n, pl* **geese** 1 web-footed bird that is similar to but larger than a duck. 2 foolish or timid person.

gooseberry *n* small edible green berry that grows on a bush with thorny stems.

gore[1] *n* blood that flows from a wound.

gore[2] *vt* stab and wound by ramming with horns or tusks.

gorge *n* 1 steep-sided river valley; ravine. 2 lavish feast. *vi,vt* stuff (oneself) with food; overeat; glut.

gorgeous *adj* very beautiful; magnificent; wonderful.

gorilla *n* large African ape.

gorse *n* prickly evergreen shrub with bright yellow flowers.

gory *adj* 1 covered with blood. 2 bloodthirsty; involving bloodshed. 3 horrifying.

gosh *interj* exclamation of surprise.

gosling *n* young goose.

gospel *n* something taken as the truth; doctrine. **Gospel** *n* one of the first four books of the New Testament, namely Matthew, Mark, Luke, and John.

gossip *vi* talk, esp. in a way that spreads scandal, rumours, etc. *n* **1** act of gossiping. **2** casual or malicious talk; news; scandal. **3** person who gossips.

got *v pt* and *pp* of **get. have got** possess; hold; own. **have got to** must.

gouge *vt* **1** carve a deep hole in with a sharp instrument. **2** tear or scoop out.

goulash *n* stew seasoned with paprika that is a traditional Hungarian dish.

gourd *n* large fruit of various plants, having a tough outer skin and a large number of seeds.

gourmand *n* glutton.

gourmet *n* connoisseur of good food and wine.

govern *vt,vi* **1** rule; reign (over); control. **2** participate in a government. *vt* **1** check; restrain. **2** determine; influence completely. **governess** *n* woman employed as a tutor in a private household. **government** *n* **1** control; rule. **2** body of representatives who govern a country, state, etc. **governor** *n* **1** ruler, esp. of a colony, province, etc. **2** person in charge of a prison. **3** chief controller of a state in the US. **4** *inf* boss. **governorship** *n.*

gown *n* **1** woman's dress, esp. for evening wear. **2** loose light garment, often signifying academic or official status; robe.

grab *vt,vi* (-bb-) **1** take hold of hastily, clumsily, or greedily; seize; snatch. **2** take possession of by force; confiscate. *n* **1** act of grabbing. **2** mechanical device for gripping large objects.

grace *n* **1** elegance, beauty, or charm of movement, style, etc. **2** good will; magnanimity; mercy. **3** short prayer of thanks offered before or after a meal. *vt* serve to add elegance or beauty to; adorn. **graceful** *adj.* **gracefully** *adv.* **gracious** *adj* **1** elegant; dignified. **2** benevolent; courteous; kind. *interj also* **good gracious!** expression of surprise or alarm.

grade *n* **1** position on a scale or in a category. **2** mark or score awarded in an examination, test, etc. *vt* **1** place in a category according to size, quality, etc. **2** award a mark or score to. **gradation** *n* **1** step or stage within a system or on a scale. **2** gradual progression or transition.

gradient *n* slope of a road, railway, etc., measured by the increase in height per distance travelled.

gradual *adj* **1** slowly changing. **2** not steep. **gradually** *adv.*

graduate *vi* ('grædju:eit) **1** receive a degree or diploma from a university, college, etc. **2** change gradually; move along a scale. **3** progress. *n* ('grædju:it) person holding a degree, diploma, etc. **graduation** *n.*

graffiti *pl n* scribbled messages or drawings on walls, public buildings, etc.

graft *n* **1** small plant shoot that is united with another plant in order to produce a new plant. **2** transplanted bone or skin tissue. *vt,vi* **1** propagate by means of a graft. **2** transplant or be transplanted.

grain *n* **1** fruit or seed of a cereal plant. **2** cereal crops. **3** small particle or granule of sand, sugar, etc. **4** pattern, texture, or arrangement of layers of a piece of timber, rock, etc. **5** minute quantity or proportion.

gram *n also* **gramme** metric unit of weight equivalent to approx. 0.035 ozs.

grammar *n* **1** system of rules governing the correct use of a language. **2** branch of linguistics concerned mainly with syntax and word formation. **grammar school** *n* (in Britain) state secondary school that selects pupils at the age of eleven by means of examination. **grammatical** *adj* relating or conforming to the rules of grammar. **grammatically** *adv.*

gramophone *n* machine for playing records, having a turntable, amplifier, and pick-up arm fitted with a stylus; record player.

granary *n* storage place for grain.

grand *adj* **1** impressively large; magnificent; tremendous. **2** haughty; elegant. **3** marvellous; great. **4** admirable; worthy. **5** final and complete. *n also* **grand piano** large piano whose strings are arranged horizontally rather than vertically. **grandeur** *n.* **grandly** *adv.* **grandchild** *n* grandson or granddaughter. **granddaughter** *n* daughter of one's son or daughter. **grandfather** *n* father of one's father or mother. **grandmother** *n* mother of one's father or mother. **grandparent** *n* grandfather or grandmother. **grandson** *n* son of one's son or daughter. **grandstand** *n* covered block of seats for spectators at a race meeting, football match, etc.

granite *n* hard greyish-white crystalline rock.

granny *n inf* grandmother.

grant *vt* 1 give as a favour. 2 admit; concede. 3 give (a sum of money). *n* sum of money given for research, education, etc.

granule *n* small grain. **granular** *adj*.

grape *n* small sweet green or purple fruit that is eaten raw, dried, or pressed to make wine. **grapevine** *n* 1 vine producing grapes. 2 informal or underground information network.

grapefruit *n* large round citrus fruit with a yellow peel.

graph *n* chart or diagram for depicting the relationship between variables, particular sets, quantities, etc. **graphic** *adj* 1 clearly or imaginatively expressed. 2 relating to writing or drawing. 3 in graph form.

graphite *n* soft black carbon, used in pencils, electrodes, etc.

grapple *vi* struggle physically; wrestle; tussle. **grapple with** attempt to deal with (a problem, difficult situation, etc.). ~*n* 1 iron hook. 2 grip in wrestling; hold.

grasp *vt,vi* 1 take hold (of) firmly in the hands; grip; clasp. *vt* understand; comprehend. *n* 1 firm grip. 2 knowledge; understanding. 3 power to dominate.

grass *n* 1 plant with green spiky blades. 2 lawn, field, or pasture of such plants. 3 *sl* marijuana. *vt,vi* sow with grass. *vi sl* act as an informer, esp. to the police. **grassy** *adj*. **grasshopper** *n* greenish-brown insect renowned for its characteristic chirping sound produced by friction of the hind legs against the wings. **grass roots** *pl n* 1 section of the population regarded as representing true political or public opinions at a local level. 2 underlying or essential principles.

grate[1] *vt* cut or shred (cheese, vegetables, etc.) by rubbing against a rough surface. *vt,vi* 1 produce a harsh squeak by scraping. 2 annoy; jar. *n* harsh squeak.

grate[2] *n* iron structure or rack placed in a fireplace to hold fuel and allowing air to circulate underneath.

grateful *adj* thankful; appreciative of kindness, a gift, opportunity, etc. **gratefully** *adv*.

gratify *vt* 1 seek or obtain satisfaction of (one's desires); indulge. 2 please; make happy. **gratification** *n*.

grating *n* cover or guard made of a network of metal bars; grille.

gratitude *n* feeling or expression of appreciation; thankfulness.

gratuity *n* gift of money; tip. **gratuitous** *adj* 1 free of charge. 2 not asked for or solicited; unjustified.

grave[1] *n* trench or hole dug in the ground for a coffin. **have one foot in the grave** be feeble or near to death.

grave[2] *adj* 1 serious; solemn. 2 dangerous; bad. **gravely** *adv*.

gravel *n* coarse mixture of fragments of rock.

gravity *n* 1 force of attraction between objects with mass, exerted by the earth, moon, etc., to pull objects towards their centre. 2 seriousness; solemn importance. **gravitate** *vi* 1 be drawn by the force of gravity. 2 be attracted to a certain place. **gravitation** *n*.

gravy *n* stock or juice produced by cooking meat, often thickened for a sauce.

graze[1] *vi,vt* feed or allow to feed on grass or other vegetation in a pasture.

graze[2] *vt,vi* touch lightly; scrape. *vt* produce a scratch or cut on the skin by scraping. *n* abrasion; scratch.

grease *n* 1 melted animal fat. 2 lubricant; oil. *vt* 1 cover or smear with grease. 2 lubricate. **greasy** *adj*. **greasepaint** *n* waxy substance used by actors as make-up for the stage.

great *adj* 1 large; big; huge; vast; tremendous. 2 excellent. 3 famous. 4 important; significant. 5 impressive; grand. **greatly** *adv*. **greatness** *n*.

greed *n* 1 desire to overeat; gluttony. 2 desire to take more than one's fair share of wealth, power, etc. **greedy** *adj*. **greedily** *adv*.

green *n* 1 colour of grass; spectral colour. 2 grass pitch or field. *adj* 1 of the colour green. **2** inexperienced; naive. **3** jealous; envious. **4** unripe. **greenery** *n* green vegetation; foliage. **greenfly** *n* green aphid. **greengage** *n* fruit of the plum family with a yellowish-green skin. **greengrocer** *n* person who sells fruit and vegetables. **greengrocery** *n*. **greenhouse** *n* shed with walls and roof mainly of glass, used for housing and cultivating plants. **greens** *pl n* leaves of green vegetables, such as cabbage.

greet *vt* **1** welcome. **2** send good wishes to. **3** be present at the arrival of; meet. **greeting** *n* statement or act of welcome, good wishes.

gregarious *adj* enjoying other people's company; sociable.

grenade *n* small explosive shell thrown by hand or fired from a gun.

grey *n* colour between black and white, having no hue. *adj* **1** of a grey colour. **2** having grey hair. **3** dull; gloomy. **greyish** *adj*.

grey area *n* **1** area, etc., between two extremes having characteristics of both of these. **2** area, situation, etc., lacking clearly defined characteristics. **greyhound** *n* breed of smooth-haired dog with a slender body and pointed muzzle, often used for racing.

grid *n* **1** network of squares printed or placed over a map or drawing. **2** network of electricity cables, water pipes, etc.

grief *n* sorrow; distress; remorse. **grief-stricken** *adj* suffering intense grief; heart-broken. **grievance** *n* complaint; feeling of being hurt or offended. **grieve** *vi,vt* feel or cause grief, etc.

grill *n* rack or section of an oven on or under which food is cooked. *vt,vi* cook on or under a grill. *vt inf* interrogate; cross-question.

grille *n* framework of metal bars forming an ornamental screen or grating.

grim *adj* **1** bleak; unpleasant; formidable. **2** stern; unbending; severe. **grimly** *adv*.

grimace *n* facial expression of disgust, hatred, etc. *vi* screw up the face in a grimace.

grime *n* **1** soot. **2** dirt. **grimy** *adj*.

grin *n* broad happy smile. *vi,vt* (-nn-) smile with the lips widely parted.

grind *vt,vi* (ground) **1** crush or pound into powder or small particles. **2** sharpen (a blade) or smooth by friction. **3** oppress;

enslave. **4** grate or gnash (the teeth). *n* hard toil; repetitive routine. **grinder** *n* appliance for grinding coffee beans, etc.

grip *n* **1** firm hold or clasp; grasp. **2** strength of the fingers. **3** handle of a racquet or bat. **4** understanding; comprehension. **5** holdall; bag. **get** *or* **come to grips with** learn to control; master; tackle. ~*vt,vi* (-pp-) **1** hold firmly; clasp. **2** mesmerize; enthrall.

gripe *vi* moan; nag; complain. *vi,vt* feel or cause sudden pain.

gristle *n* cartilage, esp. when present in meat.

grit *n* **1** small pieces of gravel, sand, etc. **2** *inf* courage; stamina. *v* **grit one's teeth** (-tt-) **1** clench the teeth. **2** bear suffering bravely and without complaint.

groan *n* **1** low cry of pain, distress, disappointment, etc. **2** harsh noise made by the wind. **3** complaint; grumble. *vi,vt* **1** utter or sound like a groan. **2** complain; moan.

grocer *n* shopkeeper selling food, household articles, etc. **grocery** *n* trade or business of a grocer. **groceries** *pl n* items purchased from a grocer.

groin *n* part of the body where the legs join the abdomen.

groom *n* **1** person employed to look after horses. **2** bridegroom. *vt* **1** rub down (a horse). **2** keep (hair, clothes, etc.) clean and neat. **3** train or instruct for a particular role.

groove *n* **1** narrow channel cut into the surface of something; rut; furrow. **2** monotonous routine. *vt* cut a groove (into).

grope *vi* **1** search by touch; handle uncertainly; fumble. **2** seek (a solution) with difficulty. *n* fumbling touch.

gross *adj* **1** offensively fat. **2** vulgar; crude. **3** excessive; extreme. **4** before deductions. *n* **1** *pl* **gross** quantity of 144 (12 dozen). **2** majority; bulk. *vt* earn before deductions. **grossly** *adv*.

grotesque *adj* extremely ugly; bizarre.

grotto *n* small cave; cavern.

ground[1] *n* **1** surface of the earth; land; soil. **2** enclosure or pitch. **3** area of knowledge; field. **down to the ground** perfectly; entirely. ~*vt* **1** prevent the take-off of (an aircraft). **2** give basic but thorough instructions to. **grounds** *pl n* **1** justification; valid reasons. **2** land attached to a large house, castle, etc. **3** coffee dregs. **groundsheet** *n* waterproof sheet used when camping in a tent. **groundsman** *n, pl* -**men** caretaker or gardener employed on an estate, park, sports ground, etc. **groundwork** *n* basic preparation for a job or project.

ground² *v pt* and *pp* of **grind.**

group *n* number of people or things placed or classed together; set. *vt,vi* form into a group or set; assemble.

grouse¹ *n* game bird with reddish-brown or black plumage.

grouse² *vi* grumble; nag; complain. *n* complaint; grievance.

grove *n* area of trees; plantation.

grovel *vi* (-ll-) **1** humiliate oneself; behave in a servile manner. **2** crawl in an undignified manner.

grow *v* (grew; grown) *vi* **1** become larger, taller, etc.; mature. **2** increase in size or number. **3** develop; arise; become. *vt* produce; bring forth; yield. **grow up** become adult. **grown-up** *n* adult person. *adj* mature; adult. **growth** *n* **1** process of growing. **2** amount by which something grows. **3** increase; development. **4** cancer or tumour.

growl *vt,vi* **1** (esp. of an animal such as a dog) utter a low warning or hostile sound. **2** say in a low angry voice. *vi* rumble; grumble. *n* low hostile sound.

grub *n* **1** larva of certain insects, esp. a beetle. **2** *sl* food. *vt,vi* (-bb-) dig or root (in).

grubby *adj* dirty; grimy; soiled. **grubbiness** *n*.

grudge *n* grievance; feeling of resentment. *vt* resent; feel grieved about; begrudge. **grudgingly** *adv*.

gruelling *adj* extremely strenuous; exhausting; taxing; rigorous.

gruesome *adj* ghastly; horrible; spine-chilling.

gruff *adj* rough in manner or voice; rough. **gruffly** *adv*.

grumble *vt,vi* express dissatisfaction; groan; complain. *vi* rumble. *n* **1** expression of discontent; groan. **2** rumble.

grumpy *adj* inclined to grumble; cross; bad-tempered. **grumpiness** *n*.

grunt *vi,vt* **1** (esp. of a pig) snort. **2** say in a low incoherent manner. *n* **1** snort. **2** low incoherent noise.

guarantee *n* **1** statement that goods supplied conform to a certain standard or that they will be repaired or replaced. **2** formal undertaking to honour another's debts. **3** assurance that something is right or will happen. *vt* give a guarantee of; assure; undertake. **guarantor** *n* person giving a guarantee.

guard *vt,vi* **1** keep watch (over) in order to defend, protect, or prevent entry or escape. **2** shield; protect. *vt* restrain; control. **guard against** take precautions to avoid. ~*n* **1** person who guards, esp. a warder. **2** military or police escort. **3** sentry; keeper. **4** person officially in charge of a train. **5** safety device fitted to a machine, fire, etc. **6** safeguard; precaution. **on/off one's guard** alert or watchful/unwary. **guarded** *adj* cautious. **guardian** *n* **1** person having custody of another, esp. a minor. **2** defender; protector; keeper.

guerrilla *n also* **guerilla** member of a group of fighters waging war against regular military forces, using tactics of ambush, sabotage, etc.

guess *vt,vi* **1** attempt to judge or find an answer or solution (to) without having sufficient information; estimate. **2** give the right answer (to); discover correctly. *n* attempt at solving; estimate. **guesswork** *n* **1** process of guessing. **2** conclusion reached by guessing.

guest *n* **1** person invited as a visitor. **2** person whom one entertains or treats to a meal. **3** person staying at a hotel. **guesthouse** *n* small private hotel or boarding house.

guide *vt* **1** lead; show the way to; conduct. **2** influence; direct. **3** steer; control the movement of. *n* **1** person who guides, esp. one who conducts tourists or sightseers round places of interest. **2** *also* **guidebook** book giving information on places of interest. **3** book containing practical information on a subject; manual. **4** *also* **guideline** suggested principle or standard. **5** Girl Guide. **guidance** *n*.

guild *n* **1** society of craftsmen or merchants of the Middle Ages. **2** association; society.

guile *n* cunning; slyness; deceit. **guileless** *adj*.

guillotine *n* **1** execution device used to behead people. **2** machine fitted with a sharp blade for cutting and trimming paper, metal, etc. *vt* use a guillotine on.

guilt *n* **1** fact of having committed a criminal or other offence. **2** deep feeling of shame or remorse at having been responsible for a crime, error, omission, etc. **guiltless** *adj*. **guilty** *adj*. **guiltily** *adv*.

guinea *n* former British gold coin worth 21 shillings (£1.05).

guinea pig *n* **1** small tailless rodent often kept as a pet or used for experiments. **2** person used as the subject of experiment.

guitar *n* long-necked musical instrument, usually with six strings, which are plucked. **guitarist** *n*.

gulf *n* **1** large bay or inlet of the sea. **2** chasm or abyss. **3** great discrepancy; irreconcilable difference. *vt* engulf.

gull *n* seabird with white or grey plumage and webbed feet.

gullet *n* **1** oesophagus. **2** throat.

gullible *adj* easily cheated or taken in. **gullibility** *n*.

gulp *vt,vi* **1** swallow (food) quickly and noisily; bolt. **2** inhale noisily; choke; gasp. *n* act of gulping.

gum¹ *n* **1** sticky substance produced by various plants and used as an adhesive. **2** chewing gum. *v* (-mm-) *vt* stick with gum. *vt,vi also* **gum up** smear or become smeared with gum; clog.

gum² *n* pink fleshy tissue in which the teeth are rooted.

gun *n* any type of weapon capable of discharging bullets or shells from a barrel. **jump the gun** begin too soon or without adequate preparation. **stick to one's guns** keep to one's opinions or principles; persevere. ~*vt* (-nn-) *also* **gun down** shoot at with a gun. **gun for** pursue with determination. **gunman** *n, pl* **-men** person who uses a gun to commit a crime. **gunpowder** *n* explosive mixture of sulphur, charcoal, and saltpetre. **gunrunning** *n* smuggling of firearms. **gunrunner** *n*.

gurgle *vi* **1** (esp. of flowing water) make a bubbling or rushing sound. **2** produce a throaty chuckle; bubble. *n* gurgling sound.

guru *n* Hindu or Sikh religious teacher.

gush *vt,vi* **1** pour out with great force; flow; stream. **2** utter with exaggerated enthusiasm or sentiment. *n* sudden stream or flow.

gust *n* blast of wind, smoke, etc.

gut *n* **1** alimentary canal or any part of it. **2** strong type of thread made from an animal's intestines. *vt* (-tt-) **1** remove the entrails of (fish). **2** reduce to a shell; destroy. **guts** *pl n* **1** intestines or bowels. **2** courage; tenacity; determination. **3** essential part; core.

gutter *n* drainage channel at the side of a road or attached to the eaves of a roof.

guy¹ *n* **1** *inf* man. **2** effigy of Guy Fawkes that is burnt on Nov. 5th.

guy² *n* rope or chain used to keep a tent, mast, etc., in position.

guzzle *vt,vi* eat or drink greedily or noisily.

gymkhana (dʒim'kɑːnə) *n* horseriding event in which competitors are judged for their skill or speed in various contests.

gymnasium *n, pl* **gymnasiums** *or* **gymnasia** (dʒim'neiziə) building or hall equipped with gymnastic apparatus and also used for various indoor sports. **gymnastics** *n* method of physical training that includes exercises in balance, vaulting, etc. **gymnast** *n*. **gymnastic** *adj*.

gynaecology *n* branch of medicine concerned with diseases peculiar to women. **gynaecological** *adj*. **gynaecologist** *n*.

gypsum *n* white mineral consisting of calcium sulphate, used to make plaster of Paris.

Gypsy *n also* **Gipsy** member of a nomadic race living in many parts of Europe and N America.

gyrate (dʒai'reit) *vi* rotate. **gyration** *n*.

H

haberdasher *n* shop or shopkeeper selling pins, thread, lace, etc. **haberdashery** *n*.

habit *n* **1** custom; usual practice or way of behaving. **2** type of garment worn by monks, nuns, etc. **habit-forming** *adj* causing addiction. **habitual** *adj* **1** usual; customary. **2** having a specified habit or addiction. **habitually** *adv*.

habitable *adj* fit to be lived in.

hack[1] *vi,vt* cut, chop, or strike roughly or clumsily. *vi inf* cough dryly and spasmodically. *n* rough cut or blow. **hacksaw** *n* saw for cutting metal, consisting of a narrow blade in a U-shaped frame.

hack[2] *n* **1** horse that can be hired. **2** old overworked horse. **3** writer or journalist who produces poor work fast and for little money. **hackneyed** *adj* unoriginal; said too often; trite.

had *v pt* and *pp* of **have.**

haddock *n, pl* **haddock** common N Atlantic food fish, related to the cod.

haemorrhage *n* profuse bleeding. *vi* to bleed profusely.

hag *n* ugly old woman; witch.

haggard *adj* looking ill, tired, or pale; gaunt.

haggis *n* Scottish dish of sheep's offal and oatmeal boiled in a sheep's stomach.

haggle *vi* dispute noisily (over) a price, etc.; wrangle.

hail[1] *n* **1** *also* **hailstones** pellets of frozen rain. **2** shower of hail. **3** profusion or shower of insults, abuse, or bullets. *vi* fall as hail.

hail[2] *vt* **1** greet or salute. **2** call out to; attract the attention of. **hail from** be a native of. *n* shout; greeting.

hair *n* **1** threadlike growth on or from the skin of mammals. **2** mass of hairs, esp. that on the human head. **hair's breadth** very short distance or margin. **keep your hair on!** keep calm! **let one's hair down** act informally and without reserve. **not turn a hair** show no fear or surprise. **split hairs** make petty unimportant distinctions. **hairy** *adj.* **hairdo** *n* arrangement of a woman's hair, esp. by a hairdresser. **hairdresser** *n* **1** person who cuts and arranges hair. **2** shop employing such persons. **hairdressing** *n.* **hairgrip** *n also* **hairpin** clip for securing women's hair. **hairpiece** *n* false hair worn to hide baldness, etc. **hair-raising** *adj* frightening; terrifying.

half *n, pl* **halves** **1** amount obtained by dividing a whole into two equal or nearly equal parts. **2** either of the parts. **3** half a pint, esp. of beer. **better half** one's wife or husband. **go halves** share equally. ~*adv* **1** to the extent of a half. **2** partially; nearly. *adj* amounting to a half in number. *pron* amount of half in number. **half-and-half** *adj* neither one thing nor the other. **half-back** *n* player or position in rugby, soccer, etc., behind the forwards. **half-baked** *adj* foolish; not properly thought out. **half-breed** *n* **1** person having parents of different races; half-caste. **2** domestic animal having parents of different breeds. *adj* relating to a half-breed. **half-brother** *n* brother related through only one parent. **half-caste** *n,adj* half-breed. **half-hearted** *adj* not enthusiastic. **half-heartedly** *adv.* **half-sister** *n* sister related through only one parent. **half-term** *n* point or holiday in the middle of a scholastic term. **half-time** *n* point or interval in the middle of a football match, etc. **halfway** *adv,adj* equally far from two points. **halfwit** *n* **1** idiot; cretin. **2** stupid or foolish person. **halfwitted** *adj.*

halibut *n, pl* **halibut** large N Atlantic flat fish, important as a food fish.

hall *n* **1** large room for dining, lectures, etc. **2** public building for dances, meetings, etc. **3** *also* **hallway** passage or room leading from an entrance to other rooms. **4** large country house. **5** students' residence, hostel, or college.

hallelujah *interj,n,* *also* **alleluia** cry of praise to God.

hallmark *n* **1** stamp of an official body on a silver or gold article, indicating its purity. **2** typical characteristic proving authenticity; distinguishing feature.

hallowed *adj* **1** holy; consecrated. **2** revered; respected.

Hallowe'en *n* Oct 31st, eve of All Saints Day, when witches are supposed to ride at night and graves give up their dead.

hallucination *n* **1** alleged but imaginary perception of an object, sound, etc., because of illness or through taking certain drugs. **2** act of such perception. **hallucinate** *vi* experience hallucinations.

halo *n* **1** circle of light around the head of Christ, an angel, saint, etc., as shown in paintings. **2** circle of light around the sun or moon, caused by refraction by ice particles.

halt *vi,vt* stop. *n* **1** act of stopping; stop. **2** place, as on a train or bus route, at which it stops briefly.

halter *n* **1** rope by which horses, etc., can be led or tethered. **2** *also* **halterneck** neckline of a woman's dress that leaves the back bare.

halve *vt* **1** divide in half; share equally. **2** cut by half.

ham *n* **1** salted, sometimes smoked meat from the thigh of a pig. **2** back of the thigh; thigh and buttocks. **3** actor who overacts. **4** amateur radio operator. **ham-fisted** *adj* clumsy.

hamburger *n* fried cake of seasoned minced beef often served in a bread roll.

hammer *n* **1** tool with a head fitted at right angles to a handle for driving in nails, beating metal, etc. **2** any device for striking, knocking, etc. **3** heavy metal sphere with a flexible wire handle, thrown by athletes. **go at it hammer and tongs** argue or fight fiercely. ~*vt,vi* strike or pound with a hammer. *vt* **1** strike violently. **2** defeat conclusively. **3** criticize severely. **hammer away at** work hard to do or produce. **hammer in(to)** teach by repetition. **hammer out** settle or work out after much discussion or dispute.

hammock *n* bed of canvas, rope, etc., suspended between two supports.

hamper[1] *vt* prevent from moving or working easily; hinder; impede.

hamper[2] *n* basket or case in which food and other things can be packed.

hamster *n* tailless ratlike animal with pouched cheeks, kept as a pet.

hand *n* **1** part of the arm below the wrist. **2** help; assistance; role. **3** manual worker; labourer. **4** indicator, esp. on a clock. **5** single game at cards or the cards so dealt. **6** position or direction. **change hands** pass to another owner. **a free hand** complete freedom. **from hand to mouth** precariously; in poverty. **hand and foot** completely. **hand in glove** in close cooperation. **in good hands** well cared for. **in/out of hand** under/beyond control. **on/at/to hand** near; close by. **on the other hand** in contrast. **take in hand** discipline; control. **wash one's hands of** disclaim responsibility. **win hands down** win easily. ~*vt* **1** pass to; give. **2** *also* **hand on, hand down** pass on; transmit. **handbag** *n* small bag for carrying personal items, etc.

handbook *n* book of useful hints or information; manual; guide. **handbrake** *n* manual brake on cars, etc. **handful** *n* **1** small amount or number. **2** person that is difficult to control. **handmade** *adj* made by a person rather than a machine. **hand-pick** *vt* select very carefully. **handstand** *n* vertical upside-down position maintained by balancing on one's hands. **handwriting** *n* **1** writing done by hand. **2** individual's style of handwriting. **handwritten** *adj*.

handicap *n* **1** something that hinders; disadvantage; defect; drawback. **2** mental or physical defect or disability. **3** disadvantage given to certain sports competitors to equalize everybody's chances. *vt* (-pp-) be a disadvantage to. **handicapped** *adj*.

handicraft *n* skilled manual work, often artistic.

handiwork *n* **1** skilled or artistic manual work. **2** result of someone's actions or plans.

handkerchief *n* piece of absorbent material on which to blow or wipe one's nose.

handle *n* part of a tool, machine, case, etc., by which to hold, carry, or control it. **fly off the handle** lose one's temper. ~*vt* **1** hold or feel with one's hands. **2** control or use (a machine, etc.). **3** deal with; cope with; manage. **handlebars** *pl n* metal crosspiece by which a bicycle, etc., is steered.

handsome *adj* **1** good-looking. **2** generous or ample. **handsomely** *adv*.

handy *adj* **1** useful; easy or convenient to use. **2** capable of doing manual jobs well. **3** easily accessible. **handyman** *n*, *pl* **-men** person adept at odd jobs.

hang *vi,vt* (hung *or for def.* 2 hanged *or* hung). **1** suspend or be suspended from above. **2** execute or be executed by strangling with a noose. *vt* **1** suspend by a hook; attach, fix or stick in position. **2** keep (meat, esp. game) suspended until ready for eating. **hang around** *or* **about** linger; loiter; wait without purpose. **hang back** hesitate. **hang on** wait; persevere; cling to. **hang out 1** live; frequent. **2** display; hang outside. **hang up** replace (telephone receiver). *n* **get the hang of** understand or begin to be able to do. **hanger** *n* coathanger. **hangover** *n* after-effects of excessive drinking, esp. a headache.

hanker *vi* desire persistently; yearn (for). **hankering** *n* lingering desire or wish.

haphazard *adj* happening or arranged without planning, by chance, or at random. *adv also* **haphazardly** by chance; at random.

happen *vi* occur; take place, esp. by chance. **happen to (one)** befall; affect. **happen to** chance to (be, do, know, etc.). **happening** *n* occurrence; event.

happy *adj* 1 feeling, indicating, or causing contentment, pleasure, or joy. 2 fortunate. 3 willing (to). 4 suitable; apt. 5 mildly drunk. **happily** *adv.* **happiness** *n.* **happy hour** *n* time usually in early evening when drinks are sold at reduced prices in bars, etc.

harass *vt* annoy, pester, or pursue (someone) continually. **harassed** *adj* nervous; irritated; bothered. **harassment** *n.*

harbour *n* 1 sheltered coastal area providing safe anchorage for ships, etc. 2 place for shelter or safety. *vt* 1 give refuge to (a hunted criminal, etc.); shelter. 2 cherish or maintain secretly. *vi* take shelter (in).

hard *adj* 1 not easily cut, dented, etc.; rigid. 2 difficult to do or understand. 3 violent or strenuous; arduous. 4 unfair; harsh or strict; severe; distressing. 5 unfeeling or insensitive. 6 (of water) impairing the lathering of soap. **hard and fast** strict; rigid. **hard cash** paper money and coins rather than cheques, etc. **hard to come by** difficult to obtain. **hard drugs** addictive drugs. **hard of hearing** deaf or slightly deaf. **hard up** having little money. ~*adv* 1 with force; violently. 2 with effort or vigour. 3 closely; with careful scrutiny. **hard at it** working strenuously. **hard put to** finding difficulty in. **harden** *vt,vi* 1 make or become hard(er). 2 make or become insensitive or accustomed to pain or suffering.

hardback *n* book with stiff cardboard covers.

hardboard *n* sheeting formed from compressed sawdust and woodchips, used as a building material, etc.

hard-boiled *adj* 1 (of eggs) boiled until the whole inside is solid. 2 cynical; callous.

hard-headed *adj* practical or shrewd, esp. in business. **hard-headedness** *n.*

hard-hearted *adj* not feeling or showing sympathy for the sufferings of others; cruel.

hard-heartedly *adv.* **hard-heartedness** *n.*

hardly *adv* scarcely; not quite; barely.

hardship *n* lack of material comforts; deprivation; suffering.

hardware *n* 1 household utensils, tools, etc.; ironmongery. 2 computer equipment.

hardy *adj* 1 able to tolerate difficult physical conditions; tough; robust. 2 (of plants) able to survive outdoors all year round.

hare *n* animal resembling a rabbit but having longer legs and ears. *vi* rush (about, after, etc.), esp. in a confused manner. **harebrained** *adj* stupid; rash; foolish.

hark *vi* listen (to). **hark back** revert (to a previous question or topic).

harm *n* damage or injury. *vt* cause damage or injury to. **harmful** *adj.*

harmonic *adj* relating to or characterized by harmony. *n* component of a musical note whose frequency is a multiple of the note's pitch. **harmonically** *adv* with or in harmony. **harmonics** *n* study of musical sounds.

harmonica *n* small musical instrument played by blowing into a small case in which metal reeds are set; mouth-organ.

harmony *n* 1 pleasant relationship of musical sounds. 2 friendly agreement in personal relationships. 3 pleasant arrangement, as of colours. **harmonious** *adj.* **harmoniously** *adv.* **harmonize** *vt,vi* come or bring into harmony; reconcile. *vi* sing or play in harmony (with). **harmonization** *n.*

harness *n* 1 complete set of straps and other parts fitted to a working horse. 2 fitment for a baby, etc., used for controlling, guiding, etc. *vt* 1 put a harness on (a horse). 2 gain control over (a form of energy, etc.).

harp *n* triangular musical instrument played by plucking or drawing the fingers over strings. *v* **harp on** talk repeatedly about.

harpoon *n* spear with a line attached that is fired or thrown when hunting whales, etc. *vt,vi* catch (whales, etc.) using a harpoon.

harpsichord *n* pianolike musical instrument.

harsh *adj* 1 not soft; coarse; rough. 2 severe; cruel; unkind. 3 jarring on the senses; strident; too bright or loud. **harshly** *adv.* **harshness** *n.*

harvest *n* **1** act of cutting and gathering ripe crops. **2** the crop itself. **3** result; product. *vt,vi* **1** gather in ripe crops. **2** get the benefit from.

has *v* 3rd person singular of **have** in the present tense.

hashish *n also* **hash** intoxicating drug prepared from dried leaves, flower tops, etc., of Indian hemp.

hasten *vi,vt* hurry or cause to hurry; rush. **haste** *n* **1** speed; hurry; urgency. **2** rashness. **hastily** *adv.* **hasty** *adj.*

hat *n* shaped covering for the head. **keep (something) under one's hat** keep secret. **old hat** old-fashioned; no longer novel.

hatch[1] *vi,vt* to emerge or cause to emerge from an egg. *vt also* **hatch up** think up (a plot, surprise, or idea).

hatch[2] *n* **1** small door covering an opening in a wall, esp. between two rooms. **2** cover for an opening on the deck of a boat or ship providing access below decks.

hatchet *n* small axe. **bury the hatchet** make peace after a quarrel.

hate *vt,vi* dislike fiercely; abhor. *n* **1** *also* **hatred** feeling of strong dislike or abhorrence. **2** person or thing so disliked. **hateful** *adj* loathsome.

haughty *adj* proud and arrogant; condescending; supercilious. **haughtily** *adv.* **haughtiness** *n.*

haul *vt,vi* pull or drag along with great effort; transport. *n* **1** something hauled. **2** act of hauling or the effort involved. **3** distance hauled or travelled. **4** result or amount obtained from an enterprise.

haunch *n* part of the body from the hip to the thigh.

haunt *vt,vi* visit as or be visited by a ghost. *vt* **1** go to habitually; frequent. **2** be continually in the thoughts of; obsess. **3** pester. **4** pervade. *n* place one frequents.

have *v* (*3rd person s pres* has; *pp and pt* had) *vt* **1** be characterized by. **2** own, possess. **3** hold; keep. **4** experience or undergo. **5** bear (children or young). **6** eat or drink (something). **7** take or receive. **8** must; be forced (to). **9** cause to happen or be done. **10** tolerate; put up with; allow. **11** cheat

or deceive. *v aux* (used to form the perfect and pluperfect tenses). **have had it** be near death, no longer usable, tolerable, etc. **have on 1** wear. **2** fool; hoax.

haven *n* **1** place of shelter; refuge. **2** harbour.

haversack *n* canvas bag carried on the back or over the shoulder while hiking, etc.

havoc *n* disorder or confusion.

hawk *n* type of small long-tailed bird of prey.

hawthorn *n* thorny tree or bush with white, pink, or red flowers.

hay *n* dried grass used as fodder. **hayfever** *n* allergic reaction to inhaled pollen or dust, causing sneezing, runny eyes, etc. **haystack** *n* pile of hay in a field. **haywire** *adj.* **go haywire** go badly wrong; become disorganized.

hazard *n* **1** danger; peril; risk. **2** something causing danger or risk; obstacle. *vt* **1** risk; gamble. **2** venture (an opinion, etc.). **hazardous** *adj.*

haze *n* **1** light mist that impairs visibility. **2** vague or confused state of mind. **hazy** *adj* **1** slightly misty. **2** dimly or imperfectly remembered or remembering. **hazily** *adv.* **haziness** *n.*

hazel *n* small tree producing edible nuts. *adj,n* light to medium brown.

he *pron* male person or animal.

head *n* **1** part of the body above the neck. **2** intelligence; mental power. **3** chief person; commander; ruler. **4** highest or foremost point or part; top. **5** *pl* **head** person or animal considered as a unit in a group. **6** short for **headmaster** or **headmistress**. **bite someone's head off** rebuke sharply. **come to a head** reach a critical point. **give someone his head** allow greater freedom. **go to one's head** make proud, rash, etc. **head over heels (in love)** madly in love. **keep/lose one's head** keep calm/become flustered. **not make head nor tail of** completely fail to understand. **off one's head** crazy. **over someone's head** to someone of greater authority. ~*vt,vi* be, form, or put at the head of. *vt* hit (a football) with one's head. **head for** be directed towards (a place, trouble, etc.). **heady** *adj* intoxicating; affecting the mind or senses.

headache *n* **1** pain in the head. **2** troublesome person or thing.

headgear *n* any covering for the head.

heading *n* title at the beginning of an article, chapter of a book, etc.

headland *n* area of land jutting out to sea; cape.

headlight *n* *also* **headlamp** powerful light on the front of a car, etc.

headline *n* words in large or heavy type at the top of a newspaper article.

headlong *adv* *also* **headfirst** **1** with the head foremost. **2** rashly; impetuously.

headmaster *n* chief male teacher in a school. **headmistress** *f n*.

headphones *pl n* pair of receivers fitted over the ears for communications purposes.

headquarters *pl n* chief office of a military force or other organization.

headstrong *adj* **1** obstinate; wilful. **2** rash; impetuous.

headway *n* **1** movement forward by a vessel. **2** progress, as in a struggle or problem.

heal *vt* cure; restore to health. *vi* (of a wound) close up.

health *n* **1** person's general bodily condition. **2** condition of being well; freedom from illness. **3** general condition of a business, country, etc. **healthy** *adj* **1** in good health. **2** conducive to good health. **3** promising or encouraging. **healthily** *adv*.

heap *n* **1** jumbled mass; pile; mound. **2** *also* **heaps** great deal. **3** something no longer useful. *vt* place (things) in a heap.

hear (heard) *vt,vi* **1** perceive (sound) with the ears. **2** become informed (about news). *vt* listen to. **hear from** receive news, etc., from. **hear of 1** obtain news or information about. **2** allow the possibility of. **hear out** allow (a person) to finish what he is saying. **hear, hear!** exclamation of agreement, approval, etc. **hearing** *n* **1** sense by which one hears; ability to hear. **2** range in which a person may be heard. **3** chance or opportunity to be heard.

hearse *n* car or carriage for carrying a corpse to burial or cremation.

heart *n* **1** muscular internal organ that pumps blood round the body. **2** symbolic seat of love, sympathy, or courage; these feelings themselves. **3** soul; inner thoughts. **4** centre; core. **5** heart-shaped symbol. **6** playing card marked with one or more red hearts. **hearts** *pl or s n* suit of cards each marked thus. **after someone's own heart** exactly of the type someone likes or approves of. **break someone's heart** upset or disappoint someone, esp. in love. **by heart** from memory. **heart of hearts** inmost feelings. **heart to heart** (discussion that is) intimate. **set one's heart on** want very much. **take to heart** be greatly influenced by. **wear one's heart on one's sleeve** make one's feelings, esp. of love, very obvious. **with all one's heart 1** with deep love. **2** willingly.

heart attack *n* sudden very painful, often fatal, malfunction of the heart.

heartbeat *n* single pulsation of the heart.

heartbroken *adj* very unhappy, disappointed, etc.

hearth *n* **1** place where a domestic fire is lit. **2** the whole fireplace. **3** the home.

heartless *adj* cruel; unfeeling; unsympathetic. **heartlessly** *adv*.

hearty *adj* **1** jovial; cheerful. **2** cordial; sincere. **3** in good health; vigorous. *n* fellow; comrade. **heartily** *adv*.

heat *n* **1** form of energy resulting from the motion of atoms and molecules in an object, etc. **2** degree of hotness, esp. when great. **3** hot weather. **4** strong or deep feeling; anger; enthusiasm. **5** pressure; intensity. **6** period of sexual excitement in female animals. **7** preliminary race or contest. *vt,vi* make or become hot. *vi* become agitated or nervous. **heated** *adj*. **heater** *n* domestic appliance for heating rooms, water, etc. **heatwave** *n* period of very hot weather.

heath *n* **1** area of open uncultivated ground. **2** heather.

heathen *adj* **1** not believing in the same god or religion as oneself; pagan. **2** uncivilized; barbaric. *n* person who is heathen.

heather *n* *also* **heath** small evergreen plant having small purplish or white bell-shaped flowers. **heathery** *adj*.

heave *vt,vi* pull or drag (something heavy); haul. *vt* **1** throw with great effort. **2** give out (a sigh, etc.). *vi* **1** move up and down rhythmically. **2** retch. *n* act of heaving.

heaven *n* **1** abode of God, the angels, and the good after death. **2** great happiness; intense pleasure. **3** place or state that induces this. **4** *also* **heavens** sky. **move heaven and earth** do everything possible to effect. **heavenly** *adj.*

heavy *adj* **1** of great or considerable weight. **2** difficult to move or lift because of weight. **3** serious; weighty; considerable. **4** difficult to bear, fulfil, digest, read, etc. **5** violent; of great force. *n* **1** role of a villain in a play or film. **2** actor playing this. **heavily** *adv.* **heaviness** *n.* **heavyweight** *n* boxer who weighs 175 pounds or more.

Hebrew *n* **1** language of the ancient Jews and modern Israel. **2** Jew; Israelite.

heckle *vt,vi* try to disconcert a public speaker by continual taunts. **heckler** *n.*

hectic *adj* **1** very busy or active. **2** hurried and confused; agitated. **hectically** *adv.*

hedge *n* **1** closely planted row of bushes and small trees forming a fence, etc. **2** barrier. *vt* **1** provide or surround with a hedge. **2** give an answer that does not reveal one's true thoughts. **hedge one's bets** make a safe bet, investment, etc., to protect oneself. **hedgehog** *n* small animal with long prickles on its back.

heed *vt,vi* take careful notice of. *n* **1** attention; notice. **2** caution; care. **take heed!** be careful!

heel[1] *n* **1** back part of a the foot. **2** part of a sock, stocking, etc., that covers the heel. **3** part of a shoe or boot beneath the heel. **4** despicable man. **Achilles' heel** person's only weak point. **down at heel** shabbily dressed. **cool one's heels** be kept waiting. **take to one's heels** run away. **to heel** under control. *~vt* repair the heel of (a shoe).

heel[2] *vi also* **heel over 1** tilt to one side; list. **2** fall to the ground.

hefty *adj* **1** strong and muscular. **2** forceful.

height *n* **1** distance from bottom to top. **2** altitude. **3** most successful point; culmination. **4** most extreme or exaggerated form. **heights** high place or point. **heighten** *vt,vi* **1** make or become higher. **2** accentuate; be increased.

heir *n* **1** male person who inherits the wealth, rank, etc., of another when the latter dies. **2** successor, as to a tradition. **heiress** *f n.* **heirloom** *n* object passed down to succeeding generations in a family.

held *v pt* and *pp* of **hold.**

helicopter *n* aircraft powered by large overhead horizontally rotating blades.

helium *n* light inert rare gaseous element.

hell *n* **1** abode of Satan; place of eternal damnation for the wicked after death. **2** extreme suffering; torture; difficulty. **3** place or situation causing this. **a hell of a** very much of a. **for the hell of it** for fun. **give someone hell 1** cause much trouble to. **2** scold severely. **like hell 1** very much, fast, etc. **2** certainly not.

hello *interj* exclamation of greeting, surprise, etc.

helm *n* **1** steering device on a boat; tiller or steering-wheel. **2** position of control or authority. **helmsman** *n.*

helmet *n* **1** soldier's protective metal headgear worn during battle. **2** protective headgear worn by miners, firemen, motorcyclists, etc.

help *vt,vi* **1** give assistance (to); aid. **2** cause improvement in. *vt* **1** be of use in (doing). **2** avoid (doing); prevent oneself from. **3** serve with food or drink. **it can't be helped** it cannot be avoided or rectified. **help oneself (to) 1** take without permission, payment, etc. **2** serve oneself. **help out** give assistance to, esp. in time of need. *~n* **1** assistance; aid; cooperation. **2** domestic servant. **helper** *n.* **helpful** *adj.* **helpfully** *adv.* **helpless** *adj* **1** weak; dependent. **2** powerless.

hem *n* edge of a piece of cloth or clothing turned over and sewn. *vt* (-mm-) sew a hem on. **hem in** surround; encircle.

hemisphere *n* **1** half a sphere. **2** half of the earth. **hemispherical** *adj.*

hemp *n* **1** tough-fibred Asian plant from which the drug cannabis is obtained. **2** cannabis. **3** rope or coarse cloth made from the fibres.

hen *n* **1** female bird, esp. a chicken. **2** old woman. **hen party** *n* gathering for women only.

hence *adv* **1** and so; therefore; for this reason. **2** from this time forward. **3** from this place.

henna *n* reddish dye for hair, etc., obtained from an Asiatic shrub.

her *adj* belonging to a female person. *pron* that particular woman or girl. **herself** *r pron* **1** her own self. **2** her normal self.

herald *n* **1** official who makes public or ceremonial announcements. **2** person or thing that indicates the approach of something. *vt* usher in; proclaim.

heraldry *n* practice and rules governing official coats of arms, etc. **heraldic** *adv.*

herb *n* plant, such as parsley, that can be used as a flavouring in cooking, as a medicine, etc. **herbal** *adj.* **herbaceous** *adj* relating to plants with fleshy stems that die down after flowering. **herbivore** *n* animal feeding on plants. **herbivorous** *adj.*

herd *n* **1** large group of wild or domestic animals that live and feed together. **2** mass of people; rabble. *vt, vi* **1** gather or be gathered into a herd. **2** drive or be driven (forward or back). **herdsman** *n* man who tends a herd.

here *adv* **1** in or to this place. **2** at this point in time or space. **here and there 1** in or to several places. **2** scattered around. **be neither here nor there** be irrelevant or unimportant. ~*n* this place.

heredity *n* **1** biological process by which characteristics, etc., are transmitted from parents to children in the genes. **2** characteristics so transmitted. **hereditary** *adj.*

heresy *n* belief or doctrine, esp. religious, that is contrary to established order. **heretic** *n* person originating or believing a heresy. **heretical** *adj.* **heretically** *adv.*

heritage *n* **1** culture or tradition passed on to successive generations. **2** something inherited at birth, esp. property or family characteristics.

hermit *n* **1** person living completely alone to pray or undergo mystic experiences. **2** person who lives a solitary life; recluse. **hermitage** *n* dwelling of a hermit.

hero *n, pl* **heroes 1** man admired for his courage, nobleness, or fortitude. **2** central male character in a book, play, or film. **3** person who suffers much without complaint. **heroic** *adj.* **heroically** *adv.* **heroine** *f n.* **heroism** *n.*

heroin *n* addictive narcotic drug obtained from morphine.

heron *n* long-legged wading bird.

herring *n, pl* **herring** *or* **herrings** marine food fish. **red herring** misleading fact or argument.

hers *pron* belonging to her. **herself** *r pron* her own self; her normal self.

hesitate *vi* pause through doubt; waver; falter; be unwilling (to). **hesitancy** *n.* **hesitant** *adj.* **hesitation** *n.*

heterosexual *n* person sexually attracted to members of the opposite sex. **heterosexuality** *n.*

hexagon *n* six-sided geometric figure. **hexagonal** *adj.*

hibernate *vi* (of animals) spend the winter in a sleeplike state. **hibernation** *n.*

hiccup *n also* **hiccough** one of a series of sudden involuntary coughlike noises. *vi* (-pp-) *also* **hiccough** experience such a spasm; make such a noise.

hide[1] *vt* (hid; hidden) **1** keep from sight; conceal. **2** keep secret. *vi* conceal oneself. *n* place where someone is concealed, esp. for observing birds.

hide[2] *n* skin of some large animals, usually hairless, esp. when tanned. **tan someone's hide** beat or flog someone.

hideous *adj* **1** extremely ugly. **2** morally repulsive. **3** of an extreme nature. **hideously** *adv.*

hiding[1] *n* act or place of concealment.

hiding[2] *n* **1** beating or thrashing. **2** conclusive defeat in a contest.

hierarchy *n* strictly graded structure, as of society or some other system. **hierarchical** *adj.*

high *adj* **1** having or being at a considerable or specified height. **2** being at a peak; considerable; relatively great in value or amount. **3** important; exalted. **4** main; chief. **5** noble; lofty; admirable. **6** slightly intoxicated by liquor or drugs. **high and dry** stranded; abandoned. **high and low** in every place possible. **high time** the correct or appropriate time. ~*adv* **1** at or to a high point or place. **2** for considerable gambling stakes. *n* **1** high point; peak. **2** high place. **highly** *adv* greatly; considerably.

highbrow *adj* relating to very intellectual tastes in music, literature, art, etc. *n* person having such tastes.

high-fidelity *adj* reproducing sounds electronically without distortion.

high jump *n* athletic event in which competitors leap over a high, continuously elevated bar. **be for the high jump** be in trouble.

highland *n also* **highlands** hilly or mountainous region, esp. in Scotland.

highlight *n* 1 small concentration of light on something shiny. 2 best or most impressive or enjoyable part. *vt* 1 put highlights in. 2 put emphasis on; accentuate.

highness *n* 1 condition of being high. 2 honorary address to a royal person.

high-tech *adj also* **hi-tech** of a style of furnishing, etc., involving or imitating (sophisticated) industrial equipment.

highway *n* public road, esp. a main road.

hijack *vt* 1 board and capture (an aeroplane, etc.) and threaten to destroy it or kill its passengers unless one's demands are met. 2 steal (a lorry, etc.) with its load. *n* instance of hijacking. **hijacker** *n*.

hike *n* long walk or walking holiday in the country; ramble. *vi* go for a hike. **hiker** *n*.

hilarious *adj* very funny; causing much amusement. **hilariously** *adv*. **hilarity** *n*.

hill *n* 1 elevated area of ground; small mountain. 2 slope, as in a road. **hilly** *adj*.

him *pron* that particular man or boy. **himself** *r pron* 1 his own self. 2 his normal self.

hind *adj* in or at the back or rear; posterior. **hindsight** *n* ability to guess or act correctly when looking back on an event.

hinder *vt* cause obstruction or delay to; impede. **hindrance** *n* 1 obstruction; delay. 2 person or thing causing this.

hinge *n* 1 joint by which a door, lid, etc., is attached to a frame, container, etc., so that it can open and close. 2 central fact or argument on which all else depends. *vi* **hinge on** depend on.

hint *n* suggestion; piece of helpful advice. *vt,vi* make suggestions (about).

hip *n* side of body from upper thigh to waist.

hippopotamus *n, pl* **hippopotamuses** *or* **hippopotami** (hipə'pɔtəmai) very large thick-skinned African mammal living around rivers.

hire *vt* obtain the temporary use or services of, for payment. *n* 1 act of hiring. 2 charge of hiring.

his *pron* belonging to him.

hiss *vi* 1 produce a whistling sound like a prolonged *s*. *vt,vi* display scorn or disapproval (for) by making such a noise. *n* such a noise.

history *n* 1 development and past events of a country, etc. 2 study concerned with this. 3 book, play, or other chronological account about past events. **make history** do something important or influential. **historian** *n* scholar or student of history. **historic** *adj* 1 important or memorable in history. 2 *also* **historical** relating to history.

hit *vt,vi* (-tt-; hit) 1 give a blow to; knock; strike. 2 reach (a target, etc.). *vt* 1 come upon by chance; find. 2 wound; injure. **hit it off with** get on well (with somebody). **hit on** *or* **upon** guess or find (an answer, etc.) by chance. **hit out (at** *or* **against)** speak angrily or critically (about). ~*n* 1 blow or knock. 2 act of reaching a target. 3 great success.

hitch *vt* pull up roughly. *vt,vi* 1 fasten or become fastened (on to); become entangled or caught. 2 procure (a lift) from a driver. *n* 1 abrupt pull. 2 unexpected difficulty or obstacle causing a delay. 3 type of knot. **hitched** *adj* married. **hitch-hike** *vi* 1 procure free travel in a motor vehicle. 2 travel around by such means. **hitch-hiker** *n*.

hive *n* 1 structure in which bees are kept. 2 bees kept in a hive. 3 very busy or industrious place. *vt* gather (bees) into a hive.

hoard *n* 1 accumulated store, often hidden or secret. 2 hidden or buried treasure. 3 *also* **hoards** great quantity (of). *vt,vi* amass (a hoard). **hoarder** *n*.

hoarding *n* 1 temporary wooden fence on which advertising posters are often stuck. 2 structure intended for posters, etc.

hoarse *adj* 1 coarse and husky; raucous. 2 having a harsh voice, esp. from shouting or due to a cold. **hoarsely** *adv*.

hoax *n* mischievous deception; practical joke. *vt,vi* play a hoax on.

hobble *vi* walk lamely or clumsily; limp. *vt* tie together two legs of a horse, etc., to prevent it from straying. *n* clumsy or lame walk.

hobby *n* favourite leisure occupation; pastime.

hockey *n* 1 team game in which a ball is hit with curved wooden sticks into opposing goals. 2 ice hockey.

hoe *n* long-handled horticultural tool with transversely set blade, used to weed, break up ground, etc. *vt,vi* weed, break up, etc., with a hoe.

hoist *vt* raise or lift, esp. using a mechanical device. *n* 1 act of hoisting. 2 device for doing this.

hold[1] (held) *vt* 1 grasp, grip, or support. 2 reserve or keep; maintain; control. 3 have; occupy; use. 4 contain. 5 cause to take place; conduct. 6 think that; consider. *vi* 1 withstand. 2 remain in a certain attitude or condition; remain valid. 3 maintain beliefs, etc. 4 refrain; forbear. **hold back** restrain; hesitate. **hold down** keep a job, esp. when difficult. **hold forth** talk at length or pompously. **hold good** remain valid. **hold off** 1 keep or stay at a distance. 2 stay aloof. **hold on** 1 cling to. 2 wait. **hold one's own** maintain one's position, as in an argument. **hold one's tongue** say nothing. **hold out** 1 resist successfully; remain firm. 2 last; be sufficient. **hold up** 1 cause delay in. 2 rob while threatening with a gun. **holdup** *n* 1 delay. 2 armed robbery. **hold water** remain true or logical under analysis. **hold with** agree with out of principle. ~*n* 1 act or method of holding. 2 something to grasp. 3 control or influence. **get hold of** 1 grasp. 2 get in contact with. **holdall** *n* large bag or case.

hold[2] *n* cargo storage area below the deck of a vessel.

hole *n* 1 empty or hollow space in something; cavity; gap; opening; rupture or tear. 2 animal's burrow. 3 squalid or dingy room or house. 4 dull place. 5 predicament; difficulty. **make a hole in** use up a large part. **pick holes in** find faults with. ~*vt,vi* produce a hole in.

holiday *n* 1 time or period of rest from work, esp. when spent away from home. 2 day of rest or recreation, esp. a public one. 3 day for celebrating a religious event; festival. *vi* spend a holiday.

hollow *adj* 1 having an empty interior or a cavity inside. 2 having a depression in it; sunken. 3 insincere; flattering. 4 without substance; unreal. 5 dull or muffled. 6 hungry. *n* 1 hollow part of something. 2 sunken place; depression; cavity. 3 shallow valley. *vt also* **hollow out** scoop out a hollow in. *adv* in a hollow way. **beat hollow** defeat completely. **hollowness** *n.*

holly *n* evergreen tree or shrub having shiny prickly leaves and red berries.

hollyhock *n* tall garden plant having large showy open flowers.

holster *n* leather case for a pistol.

holy *adj* 1 of God or a religion; sacred. 2 worshipped as sacred; sanctified. 3 saintly; pious. **holiness** *n* condition of being holy. **Holiness** title or term of address of the Pope.

homage *n* 1 loyalty; allegiance; reverence. 2 act of respect or reverence rendered to someone.

home *n* 1 place where a person lives; family residence. 2 place where something originated or is situated. 3 native country or town. 4 institution for the old or infirm. **at home** feeling comfortable. **at home with** familiar with. ~*adv* 1 at or towards home. 2 to a required point, target, etc. **come/bring home to** realize/cause to realize fully. **homely** *adj* plain; simple; unpretentious. **homeliness** *n.* **homesick** *adj* feeling great longing or nostalgia for one's home or native country. **homework** *n* pupil's work that is to be done outside school hours.

homosexual *n* person sexually attracted to members of his or her own sex. *adj* relating to such people. **homosexuality** *n.*

honest *adj* 1 not lying, deceiving, or cheating. 2 not given to stealing or other criminal activities. 3 sincere; open; frank. 4 trustworthy or conscientious. **honestly** *adv.* **honesty** *n.*

honey *n* 1 sweet liquid made from nectar by bees. 2 something sweet, soothing, flattering, etc. **honeycomb** *n* 1 waxy structure of hexagonal cells in which bees store their honey and eggs. 2 intricate system of passages and tunnels. **honeymoon** *n* holiday of a newly married couple. *vi* spend one's honeymoon (in). **honeysuckle** *n* sweet-smelling climbing shrub.

honorary *adj* **1** given or conferred as an honour. **2** acting or done without pay.

honour *n* **1** good reputation; public esteem; integrity; respect. **2** person or thing bringing honour. **3** mark of respect, etc. **4** act of courtesy. **5** title or address, esp. of a judge. **do the honours** act as host. ~*vt* **1** treat with honour; show respect or courtesy for. **2** confer an honour on. **3** keep a promise or bargain. **4** accept as valid. **honourable** *adj.* **honourably** *adv.*

hood *n* **1** loose covering for the head and neck. **2** collapsible or removable cover for a car or pram. **3** hood-shaped structure. **hooded** *adj* (of the eyes) half closed.

hoof *n* horny part of the foot of horses, cows, etc.

hook *n* **1** small implement curved or bent at one end, by which something is hung, pulled, fastened, etc. **2** something shaped like a hook. **3** swerving blow or stroke. **off the hook** out of trouble or difficulty. ~*vt* **1** connect, hang, fasten, catch, etc., with a hook. **2** put in the shape of a hook; crook. **hooked on** addicted to.

hooligan *n* wild, violent, or destructive person; vandal. **hooliganism** *n.*

hoop *n* circular band or ring, used as a binding, toy, etc. *vt* bind with a hoop.

hoot *vi* **1** make or give out a hollow noise like the cry of an owl. **2** laugh noisily. **3** express derision with a hoot. *n* **1** such a noise. **2** cause of great amusement. **hooter** *n* **1** mechanical device giving out a hoot as a time signal. **2** *inf* nose.

hop[1] *vi* (-pp-) **1** jump on one leg. **2** move by hopping or jumping. **hop it!** go away! ~*n* **1** act of hopping. **2** short distance or journey. **3** small dance. **on the hop** unprepared.

hop[2] *n* climbing plant whose flowers are used in flavouring beer.

hope *n* **1** desire; expectation. **2** person or thing expected to bring desired success, etc. *vt,vi* wish (for); expect or trust (that). **hopeful** *adj.* **hopefully** *adv.*

horde *n* large number or group; throng; gang. *vi* gather together in a horde.

horizon *n* **1** line where the sea or land appears to meet the sky. **2** limit of a person's hopes, intellect, or ambition. **horizontal** *adj* parallel to the horizon; lying flat; level. **horizontally** *adv.*

hormone *n* biochemical substance produced in certain glands and secreted into the blood to trigger or stimulate certain processes. **hormonal** *adj.*

horn *n* **1** hard pointed growth projecting from the head of certain animals. **2** drinking vessel made from a hollowed horn. **3** curved projection. **4** metal musical wind instrument. **5** siren or hooter on a car, etc. **draw in one's horns** reduce one's expenditure. ~*vt* injure with a horn.

hornet *n* large wasp.

horoscope *n* astrological prediction.

horrible *adj* **1** causing horror or great fear. **2** horrid. **horribly** *adv.*

horrid *adj* **1** unpleasant; nasty; cruel. **2** shocking; repulsive. **horridly** *adv.*

horrify *vt* cause to feel horror; shock. **horrific** *adj.*

horror *n* **1** great fear; disgust. **2** thing causing such feeling. **3** ugly thing. **4** annoying or disagreeable person. **horror-struck** *adj* overwhelmed with horror.

hors d'oeuvres *n* (ɔ:'də:v) course before the main course of a meal, esp. a light savoury or appetizing fruit dish.

horse *n* **1** large hoofed domestic animal that may be ridden or used as a draught animal. **2** wooden frame for drying or airing clothes. **3** large wooden box over which gymnasts vault. **dark horse** person with hidden or unknown merit. **flog a dead horse** work at or revive a lost or hopeless cause. *vi* **horse about** act noisily or foolishly. **horsy** *adj* **1** relating to a horse. **2** interested in horses and riding. **horsebox** *n* large trailer or van for transporting horses. **horse chestnut** *n* large tree with clusters of white or red flowers and shiny brown nuts enclosed in a prickly case. **horsepower** *n* unit of power, as of a car engine. **horseradish** *n* plant whose pungent root is made into a thick sauce.

horticulture *n* growing of flowers, fruit, and vegetables; gardening. **horticultural** *adj.* **horticulturist** *n.*

hose *n* long narrow flexible pipe for transporting liquids, directing water, etc. *vt* direct water at.

hospitable *adj* offering a friendly welcome to guests; sociable. **hospitably** *adv.* **hospitality** *n.*

hospital *n* institution where the sick or injured are cared for or treated by doctors, nurses, etc.

host[1] *n* **1** person who receives and entertains guests. **2** person who runs an inn, hotel, etc. **3** animal or plant on which parasites live.

host[2] *n also* **hosts** large number of people, such as an army.

hostage *n* person seized and kept under threat until his captors' demands are fulfilled.

hostel *n* residential house or hall for students, hikers, or workers.

hostess *n* **1** female host. **2** female attendant on an aeroplane, etc.

hostile *adj* showing enmity or opposition; aggressive; unfriendly. **hostility** *n.*

hot *adj* **1** having a high temperature; very warm. **2** highly spiced; pungent. **3** violent; passionate. **4** recently occurring, produced, etc.; following closely. **hot air** meaningless or boastful talk. **hot stuff** person or thing exciting or excellent. **hot water** trouble. ~*adv* in a hot manner; hotly. **blow hot and cold** repeatedly enthuse then hesitate. *vt,vi* (-tt-) **hot up** make or become more exciting, powerful, etc. **hotly** *adv* with ardour or deep feeling. **hot-blooded** *adj* passionate. **hot dog** *n* hot sausage in a bread roll or sandwich. **hothouse** *n* artificially heated greenhouse. **hot-tempered** *adj* losing one's temper easily.

hotel *n* building offering accommodation and service to travellers, etc.

hound *n* **1** dog that hunts by following the scent of its quarry. **2** despised person. *vt* pursue or persecute ruthlessly.

hour *n* **1** unit or period of time; sixty minutes. **2** correct or appointed time. **3** destined time, as of a person's death. **hours** *pl n* **1** normal time of operation, as of a shop. **2** long time. **the eleventh hour** the last possible moment. **hourly** *adj* **1** occurring or done every hour. **2** measured by the hour.

house *n* (haus) **1** building designed for living in; residence; home. **2** building used for a special purpose. **3** household. **4** important or noble family. **5** part of a school. **6** business firm. **7** legislative assembly. **8** theatre audience. **bring the house down** cause great merriment or applause. **get on like a house on fire** get on very well. **on the house** free. **safe as houses** very safe. ~*vt* (hauz) **1** contain; enclose. **2** put in a house; provide shelter for.

housebound *adj* unable to leave the house.

household *n* those living together in a house. **household word** *or* **name** very well-known name, as of a product.

housekeeper *n* **1** woman hired to cook and look after someone else's house. **2** woman servant in charge of other servants in a large household. **housekeeping** *n* **1** domestic management. **2** money allowed or required for this.

houseman *n, pl* **-men** junior resident doctor in a hospital.

House of Commons *n* lower house of the British legislative assembly consisting of representatives elected by the people; parliament.

House of Lords *n* upper house of the British legislative assembly consisting of non-elected hereditary peers and life peers and acting also as the supreme court of judicial appeal.

housewife *n, pl* **-wives** married woman who stays at home to run the house instead of working.

housing *n* **1** houses collectively. **2** provision of houses by the government, etc.

hover *vi* **1** remain suspended in air, almost motionless. **2** remain close, as to help or protect. **hovercraft** *n* passenger craft that moves above a water or land surface on a cushion of air.

how *adv* **1** in what way or manner; by what method or means. **2** in what condition. **3** to what extent or degree. **4** why; for what reason. **5** to what a great degree or amount. **however** *conj* nevertheless; in spite of this. *adv* in any way; by whatever means.

howl *vi* **1** make a prolonged mournful cry. **2** cry loudly. **3** laugh uncontrollably. *n* **1** loud or mournful cry. **2** loud laugh. **howler** *n* ridiculous or amusing mistake.

hub *n* **1** centre of a wheel from which the spokes radiate. **2** central point, as of activity.

huddle *vi,vt* crowd or be crowded together, as for warmth or protection. *n* confused heap. **in/into a huddle** in/into a private discussion.

hue *n* **1** attribute of colour that enables different colours, red, yellow, blue, etc., to be distinguished. **2** colour; shade. **hue and cry** public outcry.

huff *n* angry, offended, or sulky fit of temper. **huffish** *or* **huffy** *adj.*

hug *v* (-gg-) *vt,vi* clasp affectionately; cuddle. *vt* keep close to. *n* affectionate clasp; cuddle.

huge *adj* extremely large; vast; immense. **hugely** *adv* very much.

hulk *n* **1** old, useless, abandoned, or partially dismantled ship. **2** large clumsy person. **hulking** *adj* large and clumsy.

hull *n* basic frame of a ship, without masts, etc.

hum *v* (-mm-) *vi* **1** make a continuous musical sound like singing but with the mouth shut. **2** make a prolonged low buzzing noise. **3** be alive with activity, rumour, etc. *vt* sing (a tune, etc.) by humming. *n* **1** sound like a prolonged 'm'. **2** low buzz or drone. **3** sound of great activity.

human *adj* **1** relating to man or mankind. **2** having or appealing to human kindness, weakness, etc. *n also* **human being** person; man or woman. **humane** *adj* sympathetic; merciful; kind; compassionate. **humanely** *adv.* **humanity** *n* **1** mankind. **2** compassion for others.

humble *adj* **1** not proud or conceited; modest. **2** unimportant or lowly; subjected; submissive. *vt* **1** cause to feel humble; shame. **2** make humble or lowly. **eat humble pie** apologize in a humble way. **humbly** *adv.*

humdrum *adj* commonplace; dull; monotonous.

humid *adj* damp; moist. **humidity** *n.*

humiliate *vt* cause to feel humble, foolish, or ashamed. **humiliation** *n.*

humility *n* condition of being humble; meekness; modesty.

humour *n* **1** ability to see or appreciate what is funny. **2** humorous or amusing quality. **3** temper; mood. *vt* indulge someone's whims or ideas. **humorous** *adj* causing laughter; funny; amusing; droll; witty. **humorously** *adv.*

hump *n* **1** natural lump on the backs of camels. **2** rounded deformity on the back of humans. **3** any curved protuberance, such as a small hill. *vt* lift clumsily. *vt,vi* arch.

hunch *n* suspicion; intuitive guess. *vt* **1** draw (one's shoulders) up, as when sitting. **2** thrust out or arch (one's back). **hunchback** *n* **1** lumplike deformity on the back. **2** person with such a deformity.

hundred *n* **1** number equal to ten times ten. **2** hundred things or people. **hundreds** very many. *adj* consisting of or amounting to a hundred or about a hundred. **hundredth** *adj,adv,n.* **hundredweight** *n* measure of weight equal to 112 pounds; one twentieth of a ton.

hung *v pt* and *pp* of **hang.**

hunger *n* **1** sensation that one needs or desires to eat. **2** lack of food; famine. **3** deep desire or need; craving. *vi* **1** feel hungry. **2** lack food. **hunger for** *or* **after** desire or crave. **hunger-strike** *n* refusal to eat, as when in prison, as a protest. **hungry** *adj.*

hunt *vt,vi* **1** chase or pursue wild animals to kill them for food or sport. **2** search (for); seek. *vt* chase or pursue a criminal, etc. **hunt down** capture after pursuing ruthlessly. ~*n* **1** practice or instance of hunting animals. **2** group of people and working animals so involved. **3** search; pursuit. **hunter** *n.*

hurdle *n* **1** light frame used as a temporary fence. **2** framelike barrier over which an athlete (**hurdler**), show jumper, etc., must leap. **3** problem to be overcome; obstacle. *vi,vt* jump over (hurdles) in a race.

hurl *vt* **1** throw with great effort or force. **2** shout; yell.

hurrah *interj,n also* **hurray** exclamation of pleasure or applause.

hurricane *n* **1** very strong wind. **2** violent storm; tropical cyclone.

hurry *vi,vt* **1** move or cause to move more quickly or with haste. **2** do quickly. *n* **1** haste; bustle. **2** need for haste; urgency.

hurt *vt,vi* (hurt) **1** cause physical pain or injury (to). **2** offend; distress. **3** affect adversely; damage. *n* **1** pain; injury; wound. **2** harm; damage. *adj* **1** injured. **2** offended.

hurtle *vi* rush violently; move very fast.

husband *n* man to whom a woman is married.

hush *vt,vi* **1** make or become quiet or silent. **2** make or become soothed. **hush up** keep secret; suppress. ~*n* quiet; silence. *interj* be quiet!

husk *n* dry outer covering of some seeds. *vt* remove the husk from.

husky *adj* hoarse or whispery. **huskily** *adv*.

hustle *vt,vi* hurry along or be hurried along roughly. *vi* act quickly and efficiently. *n* rush of activity; bustle; jostling.

hut *n* small wooden building, esp. a temporary or ramshackle one.

hutch *n* small wooden cage for pet rabbits, etc.

hyacinth *n* plant that grows from a bulb and produces a spike of white, pink, or blue fragrant flowers in spring.

hybrid *n* **1** plant or animal that is a cross between two different species or varieties. **2** blend of two dissimilar things.

hydraulic *adj* **1** worked by the flow or pressure of fluids, esp. water. **2** relating to fluids and their use in engineering. **hydraulics** *n* study of fluid flow.

hydrocarbon *n* organic compound containing only carbon and hydrogen.

hydro-electric *adj* relating to the generation of electricity by the force of falling water. **hydro-electricity** *n*.

hydrogen *n* inflammable gas that is the lightest element and occurs in water and most organic compounds.

hyena *n* doglike carnivorous animal.

hygiene *n* **1** cleanliness; healthy practices. **2** science of preserving health. **hygienic** *adj*.

hymn *n* religious song; song of praise to God.

hyphen *n* mark (-) in writing or printing used to compound two words or syllables or when a word is split at the end of a line. **hyphenate** *vt* insert a hyphen in. **hyphenation** *n*.

hypnosis *n* **1** induced relaxed state of semiconsciousness during which a person will obey suggestions or commands made to him. **2** hypnotism. **hypnotic** *adj* **1** having the power to hold the attention; fascinating.

2 of or like hypnosis; lulling or trancelike. **hypnotism** *n* induction of hypnosis. **hypnotist** *n*. **hypnotize** *vt* **1** induce hypnosis in. **2** fascinate; dominate the will or mind of.

hypochondria *n* obsessive concern with one's own health. **hypochondriac** *adj,n*.

hypocrisy *n* **1** feigning of beliefs or feelings one does not have; insincerity. **2** false virtue. **hypocrite** *n*. **hypocritical** *adj*. **hypocritically** *adv*.

hypodermic *n* **1** syringe or needle used to administer injections below the skin. **2** such an injection. *adj* relating to the tissue area below the skin.

hypothesis *n* idea or suggestion put forward for discussion or verification; proposition. **hypothetic** *or* **hypothetical** *adj* not based on facts. **hypothetically** *adv*.

hysterectomy *n* surgical removal of the womb or part of the womb or uterus.

hysteria *n* **1** neurotic uncontrollable outbursts of panic or other emotions. **2** any uncontrollable emotion. **hysterical** *adj* **1** relating to hysteria. **2** extremely funny. **hysterically** *adv*.

I

I *pron* used as the subject to refer to oneself.

ice *n* **1** water frozen until solid. **2** ice-cream. *vt* **1** produce ice in; freeze. **2** put icing on (a cake). **3** chill (a drink) with ice. **iceberg** *n* large floating mass of ice in the sea. **ice-cream** *n* dessert made of flavoured frozen cream, custard, etc. **ice lolly** *n* confectionery consisting of flavoured ice on a short stick. **ice hockey** *n* team game similar to hockey, played on ice. **ice rink** *n* an area of ice for skating, esp. one kept frozen artificially. **ice-skate** *vi* skate on ice. *n* **1** shoe fitted with a narrow metal runner for skating on ice. **2** such a runner.

icicle *n* thin tapering piece of hanging ice.

icing *n* mixture of fine sugar (icing sugar) and water, egg whites, etc., spread over cakes as a decoration.

icon *n* sacred image of Christ, saints, angels, etc.

icy *adj* **1** so cold as to cause ice. **2** relating to ice. **3** (of roads) slippery. **4** unfriendly; aloof; distant. **icily** *adv.* **iciness** *n.*

idea *n* **1** mental concept; anything thought of in the mind. **2** opinion; belief. **3** plan or suggestion. **4** impression of what something is like.

ideal *adj* **1** of the best that could be imagined; perfect. **2** conforming to a notion of excellence or purity. *n* **1** standard of excellence or complete perfection. **2** principle or aim that is pure or noble. **3** concept of perfection in a person, object, etc. **ideally** *adv.* **idealistic** *adj* **1** having or cherishing ideals or high-minded principles. **2** relating to such principles. **idealist** *n,adj.* **idealism** *n.* **idealize** *vt* **1** consider that (a person or thing) conforms to an ideal or standard of excellence. **2** present or write about (a person or thing) as if ideal. **idealization** *n.*

identical *adj* exactly the same. **identically** *adv.* **identify** *vt* recognize or prove the identity of. **identify with** associate oneself or give support to (a group, person, etc.). **identity** *n* **1** fact of being who one is or what something is. **2** exact sameness.

ideology *n* body of related ideas or doctrines of a religious, political, or economic system. **ideological** *adj.* **ideologically** *adv.*

idiom *n* **1** phrase or expression meaning something other or more than its literal meaning. **2** language restricted to a particular type of speaker, period, group, etc. **idiomatic** *adj.* **idiomatically** *adv.*

idiosyncrasy *n* individual and unusual tendency or characteristic. **idiosyncratic** *adj.*

idiot *n* **1** foolish or stupid person. **2** mentally subnormal person. **idiotic** *adj* foolish; silly. **idiotically** *adv.*

idle *adj* **1** not doing anything; inactive. **2** (of a machine) not in use. **3** lazy. **4** vain or ineffectual; useless. **5** frivolous. *vi,vt* waste (time) doing nothing. *vi* (of an engine) turn over gently while not providing drive. **idleness** *n.* **idly** *adv.*

idol *n* **1** image, esp. a sculpture, of a god or something that is worshipped as a god. **2** god of another religion from one's own. **3** very popular or admired person or thing, esp. a pop star or film star. **idolatry** *n* **1** worship of idols. **2** excessive admiration. **idola-**ter *n.* **idolatrous** *adj.* **idolize** *vt* treat or worship as an idol.

idyllic *adj* charmingly simple, peaceful, or poetic. **idyllically** *adv.*

if *conj* **1** in case that; supposing that. **2** whether. **3** even though; allowing that.

igloo *n* Eskimo's dome-shaped hut made of blocks of hard snow.

ignite *vt,vi* **1** set or be set on fire; kindle. **2** cause or reach a temperature at which combustion takes place. **3** arouse the passion of or be so aroused. **ignition** *n* **1** act or fact of igniting. **2** starting system in an internal-combustion engine.

ignorant *adj* **1** lacking knowledge. **2** lacking education or upbringing. **ignorance** *n.*

ignore *vt* **1** fail to notice or take into account; disregard. **2** refuse to acknowledge or greet.

ill *adj* **1** in bad health; sick. **2** bad; wicked. **3** hostile; malicious. **4** rude. **5** unfavourable; indicating misfortune. **ill at ease** embarrassed; uneasy. ~*adv* badly. *n* misfortune; harm. **ill-bred** *adj* lacking good manners or refinement; badly brought up. **illness** *n* **1** state of being ill; sickness; ill health. **2** specific complaint or disease. **ill-treat** *vt* treat cruelly or carelessly; abuse. **ill-treatment** *n.* **ill will** *n* feeling of dislike, jealousy, or hatred; malice.

illegal *adj* not in accordance with the law; unlawful. **illegally** *adv.*

illegible *adj* not able to be read; badly written; partially obliterated.

illegitimate *adj* **1** born of parents who are not married to each other. **2** contrary to the law; unlawful. **illegitimacy** *n.*

illicit *adj* not permitted or authorized; unlawful. **illicitly** *adv.*

illiterate *adj* **1** unable to read or write. **2** ignorant, uneducated, or uncultured. **illiteracy** *n.*

illogical *adj* **1** contrary to logic; irrational. **2** not thinking logically. **illogically** *adv.*

illuminate *vt* **1** light up; provide light for. **2** clarify. **3** decorate with bright gay lights or floodlighting. **4** decorate (a manuscript) by adding painted ornamentation. **illumination** *n.*

illusion *n* **1** something that is falsely or mistakenly thought to exist or be so. **2** deception; delusion; hallucination. **3** conjuring trick. **illusionist** *n* conjurer. **illusory** *adj* based on illusion; not real; deceptive.

illustrate *vt* **1** provide pictures for (a book, talk, etc.). **2** provide examples for; clarify. **illustration** *n.*

Illustrious *adj* eminent.

image *n* **1** representation or likeness of a person or thing. **2** exact likeness. **3** view of an object as seen in a mirror, lens, etc. **4** mental concept; idea. **5** figure of speech, esp. a metaphor or simile in poetry, etc. **6** way the personality or character of a person, company, etc., is presented to others, esp. the general public. **7** symbol; emblem. **imagery** *n* **1** metaphorical language. **2** repetition or use of certain symbols, as in a cultural tradition.

imagine *vt,vi* **1** form a mental image or idea (of). **2** suppose; believe. **imaginary** *adj* created by the imagination; not real. **Imagination** *n* **1** power or ability to create mental concepts or images. **2** act of imagining. **3** baseless or fanciful belief or idea. **imaginative** *adj* **1** having considerable powers of creative imagination. **2** relating to or characterized by imagination. **imaginatively** *adv.*

imbecile *n* idiot.

imitate *vt* **1** copy the behaviour, appearance, etc., of; take as a model. **2** impersonate or mimic. **3** be or look like. **imitation** *n* **1** act of imitating. **2** impersonation or copy. *adj* made of a synthetic material.

immaculate *adj* **1** completely free from dirtiness or untidiness. **2** free from sin; pure. **immaculately** *adv.*

immature *adj* **1** not yet fully grown or developed. **2** lacking adult judgment or stability. **immaturity** *n.*

immediate *adj* **1** without delay; instant. **2** very close or near. **3** without another intervening; next. **immediacy** *n.* **immediately** *adv.*

immense *adj* **1** very large; vast; huge. **2** very great in number, quantity, etc. **immensely** *adv* **1** to an immense degree. **2** very greatly; very much. **immensity** *n.*

immerse *vt* **1** put into water or other liquid; plunge or steep. **2** absorb or engross. **3** involve (someone) in an affair; entangle. **4** baptize (a person) by plunging him in a river, special bath, etc. **immersion** *n.*

immigrate *vi* come to a country other than one's own in order to take up permanent residence. **immigration** *n.* **immigrant** *n* person who immigrates.

imminent *adj* likely to happen very soon. **imminence** *n.* **imminently** *adv.*

immobile *adj* **1** not moving; still or fixed. **2** not capable of moving or being moved. **immobility** *n.* **immobilize** *vt* make incapable of moving. **immobilization** *n.*

immoral *adj* not in accordance with morals; against moral laws. **immorality** *n.*

immortal *adj* **1** never dying or ceasing. **2** never forgotten. **immortality** *n.*

immovable *adj* unable to be moved or altered; rigid. **immovably** *adv.*

immune *adj* **1** protected from a disease, etc., esp. because of previous exposure or inoculation. **2** not affected or moved emotionally (by). **3** free or safe (from). **immunity** *n.* **immunize** *vt* render immune to a disease. **immunization** *n.* **immunology** *n* science dealing with immunity to disease.

imp *n* **1** mischievous small fairy; sprite; goblin. **2** naughty, impudent, or mischievous child. **impish** *adj.*

impact *n* ('impækt) **1** act of one object colliding with another. **2** force with which an object collides with something. **3** effect or impression. *vt* (im'pækt) press forcefully into something or together.

impair *vt* reduce the effectiveness, value, or strength of. **impairment** *n.*

impart *vt* give (information, news, enthusiasm, etc.) to.

impartial *adj* not favouring either side; fair; disinterested; not biased. **impartiality** *n.* **impartially** *adv.*

impatient *adj* **1** not willing to wait or delay. **2** irritated; vexed. **3** intolerant (of). **impatience** *n.* **impatiently** *adv.*

impeach *vt* **1** charge with (a crime, esp. of treason). **2** cast doubt on; call in question. **3** accuse or try to discredit. **impeachment** *n.*

impeccable *adj* without fault; perfect. **impeccably** *adv.*

impediment *n* **1** something that prevents something happening or working properly; obstacle. **2** speech defect, such as a stammer or lisp.

imperative *adj* **1** urgent or necessary; essential. **2** commanding; authoritative. **3**

designating that form of a verb used in commands. *n* **1** command. **2** form of a verb used in commands.

imperfect *adj* not perfect; defective, faulty, or incomplete. **imperfection** *n* defect or flaw.

imperial *adj* **1** relating to an emperor or empire. **2** commanding in manner; majestic. **imperialism** *n* form of government in which one state establishes and extends its rule over foreign lands and people. **imperialist** *n,adj.*

impermeable *adj* impervious.

impersonal *adj* **1** not personal; formal; unfriendly. **2** (of verbs) limited in use to the third person singular form with *it* as the subject. **3** (of pronouns) not specifying; indefinite. **impersonally** *adv.*

impersonate *vt* pretend to be (another person). **impersonation** *n.*

impertinent *adj* rude; cheeky; impudent. **impertinence** *n.* **impertinently** *adv.*

impervious *adj* **1** not absorbing liquid; watertight. **2** not affected by criticism, etc.; insensitive.

impetuous *adj* done or acting without due consideration; rash. **impetuosity** *n.* **impetuously** *adv.*

impetus *n* **1** driving force or momentum. **2** incentive.

impinge *vi* come into contact or collision (with). **impinge (up)on 1** have an effect or bearing on. **2** encroach or infringe on. **impingement** *n.*

implement ('impləmənt) *n* tool; instrument. *vt* ('impləment) put (a law, etc.) into force. **implementation** *n.*

implicit *adj* **1** implied though not expressly stated. **2** unquestioning; unqualified; absolute. **implicitly** *adv.*

implore *vt* beg or plead.

imply *vt* **1** state or show in an indirect way. **2** insinuate; suggest; hint at. **3** indicate as a logical consequence. **implication** *n.*

import *vt* (im'pɔːt) **1** bring (goods) into a country from another for resale, etc. **2** mean; signify. *n* ('impɔːt) **1** imported commodity. **2** act or practice of importing. **3** importance. **4** meaning; consequence. **importer** *n.*

important *adj* **1** of significance or consequence; notable. **2** wielding power or influ-

ence. **3** pompous; self-satisfied. **importance** *n.* **importantly** *adv.*

impose *vt* **1** force to comply with. **2** force to pay (a tax). **3** take advantage of. **4** foist (one's company) on. **imposition** *n.* **imposing** *adj* of grand or impressive appearance or nature.

impossible *adj* **1** not possible; unable to be done. **2** difficult to deal with; annoying. **impossibility** *n.* **impossibly** *adv.*

impostor *n* person who pretends to be someone else in order to cheat or defraud.

impotent *adj* **1** not able to act; powerless or helpless. **2** (of men) not able to have an erection of the penis. **impotence** *or* **impotency** *n.* **impotently** *adv.*

impound *vt* **1** take legal possession of; confiscate. **2** confine; enclose.

impress *vt* **1** have a great effect or influence on the mind or feelings of. **2** cause to remember. **3** press a mark into; stamp. **impressive** *adj* producing a great or lasting effect; remarkable. **impressively** *adv.*

impression *n* **1** effect on the mind or feelings. **2** idea or memory, esp. when vague or general. **3** mark or stamp left when something is pressed on something. **4** imitation or impersonation. **5** printing of a book, esp. a subsequent one with no amendments. **impressionable** *adj* easily impressed. **impressionism** *n* late 19th-century movement in the arts, using effects of light, sound, form, etc., to give a general impression of the subject.

imprint *vt* (im'print) **1** stamp or print on to. **2** make a lasting impression on. *n* ('imprint) **1** mark or print on something. **2** publisher's or printer's mark, as on the title page of a book.

improbable *adj* unlikely; not very probable. **improbability** *n.*

impromptu *adj,adv* made or done without preparation, rehearsal, or consideration. *n* short piece of music.

improper *adj* **1** not proper; not conforming to rules of etiquette, morality, etc. **2** unsuitable; inappropriate. **improperly** *adv.*

improve *vi,vt* become or make better or more valuable. **improvement** *n.*

improvise *vt,vi* **1** make or do (something) without preparation or proper materials. **2**

play (music) without rehearsal or with the addition of one's own embellishments. **Improvisation** n.

impudent adj rude; cheeky; insolent; impertinent. **Impudence** n. **impudently** adv.

impulse n 1 sudden desire for something; whim. 2 thing that drives or forces something to happen. 3 electrical signal in certain machines. **Impulsive** adj done or acting on impulse. **Impulsively** adv.

impure adj 1 not pure; mixed with other substances. 2 not chaste; indecent. **Impurely** adv. **Impurity** n.

In prep 1 on the inside of; within. 2 at or to (a place). 3 during. 4 according to. 5 involved with. 6 through the medium of; using. 7 made of. 8 wearing. adv 1 inside; on the interior. 2 at home. 3 so as to have power. 4 so as to be fashionable. 5 accepted as a friend. **In for** going to receive or experience. **In on** knowing about. n **ins and outs** complicated details.

Inability n lack of ability, power, or means.

inaccurate adj not accurate; wrong; incorrect. **Inaccuracy** n. **inaccurately** adv.

inadequate adj 1 not adequate; insufficient. 2 not able to cope or deal with a task, etc. **Inadequacy** n. **Inadequately** adv.

inadvertent adj 1 done, said, etc., by accident. 2 not paying attention; careless; heedless. **Inadvertently** adv.

inane adj 1 having no sense; silly. 2 having no content; empty; void. **Inanely** adv. **Inaneness** or **Inanity** n.

inarticulate adj 1 not able to voice one's thoughts or feelings fluently. 2 not clearly said or expressed. **Inarticulately** adv.

inasmuch adv **Inasmuch as** since; because.

inaugurate vt 1 declare open or in use with ceremony. 2 install in office ceremonially. **Inaugural** adj. **Inauguration** n.

incapable adj 1 not able (to). 2 not capable; lacking the necessary powers. **Incapacity** n. **Incapacitate** vt render incapable or unfit; disable.

incendiary adj 1 relating to fires, esp. intentional fires. 2 stirring up strong feelings, esp. of revolt against authority. n 1 person who illegally sets fire to buildings, etc. 2 person who stirs up revolt, violence, etc. 3 type of bomb causing fires.

incense[1] n ('insens) substance that gives off sweet or aromatic smells when burnt.

incense[2] vt (in'sens) enrage.

incessant adj never-ending; constant; ceaseless. **Incessantly** adv.

incest n illicit sexual intercourse between closely related members of the same family. **Incestuous** adj.

Inch n unit of length equal to one twelfth of a foot or 2.54 centimetres. vi move forward very slowly.

incident n event or occurrence. **Incidence** n degree or scope of occurrence of something. **Incidental** adj 1 happening at the same time as or as a natural part of. 2 not specially planned; chance; casual. 3 less important or significant. **Incidentally** adv 1 in an incidental manner. 2 by the way.

incisor n tooth adapted for cutting.

incite vt stir up in; inflame; urge on. **Incitement** n.

incline v (in'klain) vt,vi 1 slope or slant. 2 tend or cause to tend towards. vt 1 bend or bow (the head, etc.). 2 influence (someone) towards; dispose. n ('inklain, in'klain) slope; gradient. **Inclination** n.

include vt 1 contain as a part or member; comprise. 2 regard as a part of a category, class, etc. **Inclusion** n. **Inclusive** adj.

incognito adj,adv in disguise; under an assumed identity.

incoherent adj not easy to understand because of being rambling, inconsistent, or illogical. **Incoherently** adv.

income n money gained, esp. regularly, from work done, investments, etc.

incompatible adj 1 not able to agree or remain on friendly terms together. 2 not capable of or suitable for existing, working, etc. (with or together). **Incompatibility** n.

incompetent adj 1 lacking the necessary skill or knowledge. 2 not capable or able; inefficient. n person who is incapable or inefficient. **Incompetence** or **Incompetency** n. **Incompetently** adv.

incongruous adj out of place; irrelevant; not suitable. **Incongruously** adv.

inconsistent adj 1 not consistent. 2 changing one's opinions often. 3 not agreeing or compatible. **Inconsistency** n. **Inconsistently** adv.

Inconvenient adj not convenient; causing trouble or difficulty. **Inconvenience** n. **Inconveniently** adv.

Incorporate vt,vi unite, blend, or mix into another body or thing. **Incorporation** n.

Increase vt,vi (in'kri:s) make or become more, larger, or greater; multiply; enlarge. n ('inkri:s) 1 act or fact of increasing. 2 amount increased by. **Increasingly** adv more and more.

Incredible adj 1 not able to be believed; unlikely or amazing. 2 very surprising; extraordinary. **Incredibly** adv.

Incubate vt (of birds, reptiles, etc.) sit on eggs to hatch them. vi 1 (of eggs) hatch. 2 undergo incubation. **Incubation** n 1 hatching of eggs. 2 stage of a disease between infection and the appearance of symptoms. **Incubator** n 1 heated apparatus in which delicate or premature new-born babies are protected. 2 similar device for hatching eggs, growing bacteria, etc.

Incur vt (-rr-) bring upon oneself; become liable or responsible for.

Indecent adj 1 shameful; immodest. 2 improper or unseemly. **Indecency** n. **Indecently** adv.

Indeed adv 1 certainly. 2 in fact. interj really!

Indefinite adj 1 not clearly or exactly stated, limited, or defined. 2 not precise or fixed; vague; unsure. 3 (of pronouns) impersonal. **Indefinite article** n 'a' or 'an'. **Indefinitely** adv 1 in an indefinite manner. 2 for an unknown, esp. a long, period of time.

Indent vt 1 put or cut notches or regular recesses in. 2 set lines (such as the first line of a paragraph) in printed or written matter further from the margin than the rest. **Indentation** n 1 act of indenting. 2 notched portion as formed. 3 series of such notches or recesses.

Independent adj 1 not under the control or authority of someone or something else; free; self-governing. 2 not relying or dependent on other people or things; self-sufficient. 3 without any connection (with) or reference (to). **Independence** n. **Independently** adv.

Index n, pl **index** or **indices** ('indisi:z) 1 alphabetical list of names, subjects, etc., at the end of a book, indicating where or on what page they are mentioned. 2 pointer on a dial, etc. 3 indication; sign. vt provide an index for (a book). **index finger** n finger next to the thumb.

Indicate vt 1 show, as by sign or gesture; point out. 2 imply; mean. **Indication** n. **Indicative** adj suggestive (of); meaning or implying (that). adj,n (of or designating) grammatical mood of verbs expressing simple statements, not wishes, etc. **Indicator** n 1 person or thing that indicates, esp. a directional signal on a car. 2 chemical substance that changes colour when certain reactions take place.

Indifferent adj 1 not caring (about); not interested (in). 2 mediocre. **Indifference** n. **Indifferently** adv.

Indigenous adj originally belonging (to); native.

Indigestion n 1 inability to digest food or difficulty in digesting. 2 pain in the stomach caused by this. **Indigestible** adj not easy to digest.

Indignant adj righteously angry, as at something one considers justifies anger. **Indignantly** adv. **Indignation** n.

Indirect adj not direct, straightforward, or explicit. **Indirectly** adv.

Individual adj of, for, or characteristic of one particular person or thing. n 1 single person, as distinguished from a group. 2 any person. **Individuality** n. **Individually** adv.

Indoctrinate vt teach (someone) rigidly so that he does not question or think for himself. **Indoctrination** n.

Indolent adj lazy; idle. **Indolence** n. **Indolently** adv.

Indoor adj done or suitable for inside a house or other building. **Indoors** adv in, into, or inside a house or other building.

Induce vt 1 have the effect of; cause; produce. 2 persuade or influence. **Inducement** n.

Indulge vi,vt yield to or satisfy (a desire, whim, etc.). vt pamper; spoil. **Indulgence** n. **Indulgent** adj.

Industry n 1 system of manufacturing goods using mechanization. 2 particular branch of this; trade. 3 hard work or diligent application. **Industrial** *adj* relating to industry. **Industrially** *adv.* **industrialism** *n.* **Industrialist** *n.* **Industrialize** *vt* bring industry, factories, etc., to. **Industrialization** *n.*

inebriate *vt* intoxicate.

inept *adj* **1** not suitable or appropriate. **2** stupid; slow, as to learn. **ineptly** *adv.* **ineptness** *n.* **Ineptitude** *n* **1** ineptness. **2** inept remark, etc.

Inequality *n* state or instance of a person or thing being unequal, esp. in having fewer rights or advantages.

Inert *adj* **1** not showing movement, activity, or change; sluggish. **2** not chemically active. **Inertly** *adv.* **inertia** *n* lack of activity or movement.

inevitable *adj* unavoidable; certain to happen. **inevitability** *n.* **inevitably** *adv.*

inextricable *adj* unable to be separated, parted, or solved. **inextricably** *adv.*

infallible *adj* **1** never failing; always successful, correct, or effective. **2** certain; inevitable. **infallibility** *n.* **infallibly** *adv.*

infamous ('infəməs) *adj* **1** notorious; disreputable. **2** shocking; scandalous. **infamy** *n.*

infant *n* **1** small child. **2** person under eighteen and therefore not legally independent or responsible; minor. **infancy** *n* **1** period of being an infant. **2** early stages of development. **infantile** *adj* childishly immature.

infantry *n* foot soldiers.

infatuated *adj* wildly or foolishly in love or obsessed, esp. temporarily. **infatuation** *n.*

infect *vt* **1** transmit a disease or germs to. **2** communicate a feeling to. **3** pollute; contaminate. **infectious** *adj.* **infection** *n* **1** act of infecting or state of being infected. **2** disease or organism causing disease.

infer *vt* (-rr-) deduce; conclude. **inference** *n.*

inferior *adj* lower in position, rank, value, or quality. *n* person lower in rank or authority; subordinate. **inferiority** *n.*

infernal *adj* **1** of, like, or found in hell or the underworld. **2** wicked; diabolical. **3** annoying; confounded. **infernally** *adv.*

infest *vt* (of vermin, pests, etc.) swarm over or into; overrun. **infestation** *n.*

infidelity *n* **1** unfaithful or disloyal act or behaviour. **2** adultery.

infiltrate *vt* enter (a country, political group, etc.) gradually and stealthily as to subvert it. **infiltration** *n.* **infiltrator** *n.*

infinite *adj* without end or limit; boundless or countless. **infinity** *n.* **infinitely** *adv* **1** without limit or end. **2** extremely; very.

infinitive *n* grammatical form of verbs, usually preceded by *to,* and not indicating tense, person, or subject.

infirm *adj* **1** in poor health; ill or weak. **2** not resolute; uncertain. **infirmity** *n.*

inflame *vt* **1** cause a part of the body, etc., to become red and swollen, as when hit or infected. **2** anger or excite. **3** make more intense or worse. **inflammable** *adj* **1** likely to ignite; easy to burn. **2** excitable. **inflammation** *n* **1** act of inflaming or state of being inflamed. **2** swelling or redness.

inflate *vt,vi* **1** fill with gas; blow or swell up. **2** raise (prices) or increase in price. **inflation** *n* persistent fall in the value of money leading to continuously rising prices. **inflationary** *adj.*

inflection *n* **1** modulation of tone and stress in speech. **2** alteration in the form of a word to denote a grammatical change, as in the tense, number, case, etc.

inflict *vt* make (a person) suffer, undergo, or endure (something unpleasant); impose. **infliction** *n.*

influence *vt* have an impression on; affect; persuade, often indirectly. *n* **1** power to influence others. **2** person or thing that influences. **influential** *adj.*

influenza *n* *also inf* **flu** contagious viral disease characterized by fever, breathing difficulties, and muscular aches and pains.

influx *n* sudden abundant flow or large increase.

inform *vt* **1** tell; instruct; impart knowledge (to). **2** give character to; inspire. **inform on** reveal a person's activities, esp. secret or discreditable ones, to a higher authority. **informer** *n* person who informs on others. **information** *n* knowledge acquired from another source; news; relevant facts. **informative** *adj.*

informal *adj* casual; easy-going; not formal. **informality** *n.* **informally** *adv.*

infringe *vi* go beyond the limits or boundaries of. *vt* break or disobey (a law or rule). **infringement** *n*.

infuriate *vt* annoy or irritate intensely.

infuse *vt* impart; inspire. *vt,vi* soak or steep in a liquid, esp. to extract flavour. **infusion** *n*.

ingenious *adj* inventive; cleverly contrived; resourceful; cunning. **ingenuity** *n*.

ingenuous *adj* innocent or naive; not sophisticated.

ingredient *n* constituent; something that forms part of a mixture.

inhabit *vt* live or reside in. **inhabitable** *adj*. **inhabitant** *n* person living in a place; occupier.

inhale *vt,vi* draw into the lungs; breathe in.

inherent *adj* existing as an essential part (of). **inherently** *adv*.

inherit *vt,vi* have as a legacy; become heir (to). *vt* possess (a family trait); derive from one's family. **inheritance** *n*.

inhibit *vt* prevent; restrain; hold back. **inhibition** *n*.

inhuman *adj* cruel; barbarous; unfeeling. **inhumanity** *n*.

initial *adj* existing at the beginning or outset; early; first. *n* first letter of a name. *vt* (-ll-) sign one's initials on.

initiate *vt* (i'niʃieit) 1 begin; originate. 2 introduce; admit. *n* (i'niʃiit) initiated person. **initiation** *n*.

initiative *n* 1 capacity to be enterprising and efficient. 2 first step; introductory move.

inject *vt* 1 drive (liquid) into living tissue using a syringe. 2 introduce vigorously. **injection** *n*.

injure *vt* hurt; harm; damage. **injury** *n* 1 damage. 2 wound. 3 something causing damage or offence.

injustice *n* 1 lack of fairness; practice of being biased or unjust. 2 wrong; unjust act.

ink *n* coloured liquid used in writing, printing, etc.

inkling *n* hint; vague idea; notion.

inland *adj* 1 situated in the interior of a country or region; away from the coast. 2 operating inside a country; domestic. *adv* towards an inland area. *n* interior of a country or region. **Inland Revenue** *n* 1 money obtained by taxes and duties levied within a country and on residents living abroad. 2 government body that collects and administers this money.

inmate *n* 1 person confined to an institution. 2 occupant.

inn *n* public house, esp. one that serves meals and offers lodgings.

innate *adj* inherent in one's nature. **innately** *adv*.

inner *adj* 1 situated or occurring further in, inside, or within. 2 not superficial; hidden.

innings *n pl or s* turn of a batsman or team of batsmen in cricket.

innocent *adj* 1 ignorant of evil; uncorrupted; naive; unsophisticated. 2 not guilty. 3 not harmful. *n* innocent person. **innocence** *n*. **innocently** *adv*.

innocuous *adj* totally harmless.

innovation *n* a newly introduced device, procedure, method, or change. **innovate** *vt,vi* make an innovation.

innuendo *n, pl* **innuendoes** malicious or obscene implication or reference.

innumerable *adj* too many to be calculated; countless.

inoculate *vt,vi* introduce a vaccine into the body to immunize against a specific disease. **inoculation** *n*.

input *n* amount, material, or data put into or supplied to a machine, factory, project, etc.

inquest *n* 1 judicial inquiry, esp. one into an unnatural death. 2 any official investigation.

inquire *vi* investigate; request information. *vt,vi* enquire. **inquiry** *n* 1 investigation; official examination of the facts. 2 enquiry.

inquisition *n* lengthy, thorough, and painful investigation or interrogation. **The Inquisition** tribunal set up by the Roman Catholic Church to abolish heresy. **inquisitor** *n*.

inquisitive *adj* 1 fond of inquiring into other people's affairs; curious. 2 eager to learn. **inquisitively** *adv*. **inquisitiveness** *n*.

insane *adj* 1 mentally ill or out of control; mad; crazy. 2 dangerously foolish. **insanely** *adv*. **insanity** *n*.

insatiable *adj* unable to be satisfied; voracious; greedy.

Inscribe *vt* write, engrave, or mark (names, words, etc.). **Inscription** *n.*

Insect *n* **1** invertebrate animal or class of animals with six legs, a segmented body, and wings, such as beetles, butterflies, flies, and ants. **2** *inf* any similar animal, such as a spider. **Insecticide** *n* substance used to kill insects.

Insecure *adj* **1** not balanced; wobbly; unsafe. **2** lacking confidence or stability. **Insecurely** *adv.* **Insecurity** *n.*

Inseminate *vt* implant semen into (a female). **Insemination** *n.*

Insensible *adj* **1** insensitive; indifferent. **2** unconscious; unable to experience sensations.

Insensitive *adj* **1** thick-skinned; not sensitive. **2** heartless; cruel; ruthless.

Insert *vt* put or place in, among, or between; introduce into. **insertion** *n.*

Inside *n* **1** inner area, surface, or side; interior. **2** *inf* stomach. *adj* relating to the inside. *adv* **1** on or in the inside; indoors. **2** *inf* in prison. *prep* also **inside of** within; on the inside of.

Insidious *adj* **1** secretly spreading; tending to corrupt or destroy. **2** intended to trap; treacherous. **insidiously** *adv.* **Insidiousness** *n.*

Insight *n* **1** perception; discernment; sympathetic understanding. **2** sudden revealing glimpse.

Insinuate *vt* **1** imply or hint (something unpleasant). **2** introduce covertly or gradually. **Insinuation** *n.*

insist *vt,vi* **1** declare or assert emphatically or repeatedly. **2** demand strongly; persist in urging. **insistence** *n.* **Insistent** *adj* persistent; demanding attention.

Insolent *adj* insulting; impertinent; rude. **Insolence** *n.* **Insolently** *adv.*

Insoluble *adj* **1** not soluble. **2** unable to be solved.

Insolvent *adj* unable to meet debts; bankrupt. *n* insolvent person. **Insolvency** *n.*

Insomnia *n* inability to get to sleep. **Insomniac** *n* person suffering from insomnia.

Inspect *vt* examine; scrutinize; look into; investigate. **Inspection** *n.* **Inspector** *n* **1** person, esp. an official, who inspects. **2** police officer inferior in rank to a superintendent and superior to a sergeant.

Inspire *vt* **1** stimulate; fill with creative or intellectual urges or impulses. **2** arouse; excite. **3** communicate or produce by superhuman influence. **Inspiration** *n* **1** artistic genius or impulse. **2** sudden bright idea.

Instability *n* lack of stability, esp. in mood or character.

Install *vt* **1** fix (apparatus) in position ready for use. **2** place in office. **3** settle; set (oneself) down. **installation** *n.*

Instalment *n* one portion of something that appears, is sent, or paid in parts at regular intervals or over a period of time.

Instance *n* example; illustration of a general statement or truth. **for instance** for example. **in the first instance** to begin with; firstly.

Instant *adj* **1** occurring immediately or at once; immediate; urgent. **2** requiring little or no preparation. *n* **1** precise moment. **2** brief time. **instantaneous** *adj* occurring or done immediately or with little delay. **Instantaneously** *adv.* **Instantly** *adv* immediately; at once.

Instead *adv* as an alternative. **Instead of** in place of; rather than.

Instep *n* **1** top part of the foot between the toes and ankle. **2** part of a shoe, etc., that covers the instep.

Instigate *vt* stir up; urge; incite; bring about. **Instigation** *n.* **Instigator** *n.*

Instil *vt* (-ll-) gradually introduce (ideas, values, etc.) into the mind. **Instillation** *n.*

Instinct *n* **1** innate impulse or feeling. **2** mode of behaviour that is innate and not learned or acquired through experience. **Instinctive** *adj.* **Instinctively** *adv.*

Institute *vt* establish; start up. *n* society or establishment, esp. for promoting the arts or sciences or for education. **Institution** *n* **1** act of instituting. **2** established law, procedure, custom, or practice. **3** establishment set up for educational, medical, social, or corrective purposes. **Institutional** *adj.*

Instruct *vt* teach; direct; order. **Instruction** *n* **1** act of instructing. **2** information. **Instructions** *pl n* directions as to use, etc.; orders. **Instructive** *adj* informative.

Instrument *n* **1** implement; tool; mechanical device. **2** object played to produce music.

3 person exploited by another as a means to an end. **instrumental** *adj.* **Instrumentalist** *n* person who plays a musical instrument. **Instrumentation** *n* arrangement of music for instruments; orchestration.

Insubordinate *adj* disobedient; rebelling against authority. *n* insubordinate person. **Insubordination** *n.*

Insular *adj* **1** inward-looking; narrow-minded; remote; aloof. **2** relating to an island. **Insularity** *n.*

Insulate *vt* **1** protect against heat or sound loss or the passage of electric current by means of nonconducting material. **2** isolate or separate by means of a barrier. **Insulation** *n.*

Insulin *n* hormone secreted by the pancreas to control blood sugar levels.

Insult *vt* (in'sʌlt) speak or act in order to hurt a person's pride or dignity; abuse. *n* ('insʌlt) insulting remark or action.

Insure *vt* **1** safeguard against loss, damage, illness, etc., by paying insurance. **2** ensure. **insurance** *n* **1** act, system, or business of insuring. **2** state of being insured. **3** money paid to provide financial compensation in the event of illness, injury, loss of or damage to property, etc. **4** financial protection so obtained.

intact *adj* **1** whole; complete. **2** unharmed; untouched.

Intake *n* amount or number taken in, admitted, or consumed.

Integer ('intidʒə) *n* whole number.

Integral *adj* **1** being an essential part (of). **2** complete; entire.

Integrate *vt* combine or mix parts to make a whole; coordinate; unify. **integration** *n.*

Integrity *n* **1** uprightness; honesty; soundness of character. **2** unity; wholeness.

Intellect *n* **1** ability to absorb knowledge and think rationally; intelligence. **2** person of great intelligence; brilliant mind. **Intellectual** *adj* **1** relating to the intellect. **2** having or revealing great powers of mind. *n* person of high intellect and cultural tastes, esp. one interested in ideas.

Intelligence *n* **1** ability to learn, to reason, and to use the mental faculties. **2** information, esp. secret information about an enemy. **Intelligent** *adj* possessing or showing intelligence; clever. **Intelligently** *adv.*

Intelligible *adj* comprehensible; capable of being easily understood.

Intend *vt* have as a purpose; mean.

Intense *adj* **1** extreme. **2** strenuous; strong. **3** violent; deeply felt; passionate. **4** unable to relax; tense. **intensely** *adv.* **intensify** *vt,vi* make or become stronger, greater, brighter, or more extreme. **Intensification** *n.* **intensity** *n* **1** quality or state of being intense. **2** strength; power; concentration. **Intensive** *adj* **1** thorough and organized; exhaustive; concentrated. **2** requiring and using large amounts of labour or capital. **Intensively** *adv.*

Intent *adj* **1** determined; resolved; having in mind. **2** concentrating (on). *n* purpose; motive. **to all intents and purposes** as good as; more or less; pretty well. **Intention** *n* aim; purpose; plan of action; design; motive. **Intentional** *adj* meant; on purpose. **Intentionally** *adv.*

Inter (in'tə:) *vt* (-rr-) bury.

Interact *vi* have an effect upon other things; influence. **Interaction** *n.*

Intercept *vt* stop or seize during transit; interrupt the progress of. **Interception** *n.*

Interchange *vt,vi* **1** exchange; switch. **2** substitute; alternate. *n* **1** exchange; alternation. **2** motorway junction of interconnecting roads and bridges. **Interchangeable** *adj.*

Intercourse *n* **1** dealings; interchange of ideas, benefits, etc. **2** *also* **sexual intercourse** copulation.

Interest *n* **1** curiosity; concern; involvement. **2** cause of such a feeling. **3** pursuit; pastime; hobby. **4** personal advantage. **5** right, share, or claim, as in a business. **6** charge or payment for a financial loan. *vt* arouse the curiosity of; take an interest in. **Interested** *adj* **1** having or showing interest. **2** personally involved.

Interfere *vi* meddle; concern oneself with others' affairs. **Interfere with** have a bad effect on; impede; hinder; molest. **Interference** *n* **1** act of interfering. **2** interruption of broadcast signals by atmospheric conditions, etc.

Interim *n* time between; time that has elapsed; meantime. *adj* temporary.

interior *n* **1** inside, esp. of a house or room. **2** inland regions of a country. *adj* of, on, or in the interior.

interjection *n* exclamation; sudden interrupting remark. **interject** *vt* interpose; interrupt with.

interlock *vi,vt* lock together; join firmly or inextricably.

interlude *n* **1** intermission; interval. **2** intervening period or episode of contrasting activity.

intermediary *n* go-between; mediator. *adj* **1** acting as an intermediary. **2** intermediate.

intermediate *adj* coming or existing between; in between.

intermission *n* **1** short interval; pause between the parts of a performance, film show, etc. **2** respite; rest.

intermittent *adj* occurring at intervals; sporadic; periodic. **intermittently** *adv.*

intern *vt* confine to a particular area, camp, or prison, esp. during wartime. **internee** *n.*

internal *adj* **1** concerning the interior workings or inside of something. **2** domestic; within a country. **3** essential; intrinsic. **internally** *adv.*

international *adj* of, between, or shared by a number of countries. *n* **1** member of a national team. **2** international match or contest.

interpose *vt,vi* **1** put in or between; interrupt (with). **2** intervene; mediate.

interpret *vt,vi* **1** translate. **2** reveal the meaning or significance of. **3** take to mean; understand. **interpretation** *n.* **interpreter** *n* person who makes an immediate verbal translation of speech.

interrogate *vt* ask (a prisoner or suspect) a series of questions; cross-examine; cross-question. **interrogation** *n.* **interrogator** *n.*

interrogative *adj* **1** questioning; in the form of a query. **2** describing a word, such as *who* or *which*, used in or forming a question. *n* interrogative word.

interrupt *vt,vi* **1** stop the flow, passage, or progress (of). **2** break in (on); disturb. *vt* obstruct. **interruption** *n.*

intersect *vt,vi* divide by crossing; cut across; cross. **intersection** *n* **1** act of intersecting. **2** place or point where two things cross.

interval *n* **1** period of time between two events, acts, or parts; intermission. **2** intervening space.

intervene *vi* **1** occur or come between. **2** interfere or step in in order to prevent, hinder, or protest. **intervention** *n.*

interview *n* **1** formal meeting or discussion. **2** conversation between a journalist and a newsworthy person. **3** article resulting from this. *vt* have an interview with. **interviewer** *n.*

intestines *pl n* portion of the digestive tract between the stomach and anus. **intestinal** *adj.*

intimate[1] ('intimit) *adj* **1** close; dear; being a good friend. **2** deep; profound; private. **3** sexual; having sexual relations. *n* close friend. **intimacy** *n.*

intimate[2] ('intimeit) *vi* hint; imply.

intimidate *vt* **1** frighten; make nervous or timid; bully. **2** discourage by threats. **intimidation** *n.*

into *prep* **1** in; to the inside of. **2** to; from one point or condition to another.

intolerable *adj* **1** unbearable; unendurable. **2** extremely annoying. **intolerably** *adv.*

intolerant *adj* not tolerant; narrow-minded; bigoted. **intolerance** *n.*

intonation *n* **1** variation of pitch in the speaking voice. **2** correct pitching of musical notes.

intoxicate *vt* **1** make drunk; inebriate. **2** excite; inflame; exhilarate. **intoxication** *n.*

intransitive *adj* describing a verb that does not take or need a direct object.

intricate *adj* complex; complicated; difficult to work out or solve. **intricacy** *n.* **intricately** *adv.*

intrigue *n* ('intri:g) **1** plot; conspiracy; secret plan. **2** illicit love affair. *v* (in'tri:g) *vt* fascinate; stimulate the curiosity or wonder of. *vi* plot; conspire.

intrinsic *adj* real; fundamental; essential. **intrinsically** *adv.*

introduce *vt* **1** bring in; put forward. **2** bring into use; first establish. **3** present and identify (a stranger) to another or others; make acquainted. **4** insert. **introduction** *n* **1** act of introducing. **2** something introduced. **3** preface; foreword; opening. **4** preliminary guide; basic handbook. **introductory** *adj.*

introspective *adj* mentally inward-looking; aware of and critical of one's mental processes.

introvert *n* withdrawn or introspective person.

intrude *vt,vi* force (one's presence, etc.) uninvited. **intruder** *n.* **intrusion** *n.* **intrusive** *adj.*

intuition *n* **1** ability to perceive and understand things instinctively. **2** knowledge acquired through this ability; hunch. **intuitive** *adj* using or revealing powers of intuition rather than logic or rationality. **intuitively** *adv.*

inundate *vt* flood; overwhelm; swamp. **inundation** *n.*

invade *vt,vi* attack or forcibly enter (another's country or territory). *vt* violate; intrude or encroach on. **invader** *n.* **invasion** *n.*

invalid[1] ('invəliːd) *n* sick, disabled, or permanently bedridden person. *vt also* **invalid out** send home or retire (military personnel) because of ill health or injury.

invalid[2] (in'vælid) *adj* not valid; not legally justifiable or effective. **invalidate** *vt* render invalid. **invalidation** *n.*

invaluable *adj* of great worth or usefulness; priceless.

invariable *adj* constant; unvarying; not changing; usual. **invariably** *adv* always; constantly.

invent *vt* **1** think up (something untrue or imaginary). **2** design or devise (something new or original). **inventor** *n.* **invention** *n* **1** act of inventing. **2** thing invented. **3** ability to invent; ingenuity. **inventive** *adj* good at thinking up or creating new ideas or things; ingenious.

invert *vt* turn upside down; put back to front; reverse. **inverse** *adj* inverted; back to front; contrary. **inversion** *n.*

invertebrate *adj* having no backbone. *n* invertebrate animal.

invest *vt,vi* put in (money, capital, time, effort, etc.) in order to make a profit. *vt* **1** endow; provide. **2** confer a rank or office upon with ceremony. **investor** *n.* **investiture** *n* ceremonial conferring of office. **investment** *n* **1** act of investing. **2** thing invested.

investigate *vt* make enquiries about; look into; examine; inquire into. **investigation** *n.* **investigator** *n.*

invincible *adj* unconquerable.

invisible *adj* **1** incapable of being seen. **2** hard to see; not conspicuous. **invisibility** *n.*

invite *vt* **1** request (a person) to be present or take part. **2** ask for (comments, questions, etc.). **3** court; provoke. **invitation** *n* **1** act of inviting. **2** spoken or written request for a person's presence.

invoice *n* bill listing goods sold or services rendered with prices charged. *vt* present with or make an invoice of.

invoke *vt* summon the powers of; appeal or call for. **invocation** *n.*

involve *vt* **1** include. **2** embroil; entangle. **3** engross. **4** entail; mean. **involvement** *n.*

inward *adj* **1** inner. **2** existing in the mind or emotions; situated within. **inwardly** *adv* inside; deep down. **inwards** *adv* towards the inside or middle.

iodine *n* chemical element found in seawater and seaweed and used in photography and the manufacture of antiseptics and dyes.

ion *n* positively or negatively charged atom or group of atoms. **ionize** *vt,vi* convert into ions.

iridescent *adj* shimmering with rainbow colours. **iridescence** *n.*

iris *n* **1** circular coloured area around the pupil of the eye. **2** garden plant with narrow leaves and purple or yellow flowers.

iron *n* **1** malleable magnetic metallic element that is easily corroded and widely used in alloyed form, esp. steel. **2** heated appliance for removing creases from clothes, etc. **3** iron or steel tool, usually heated. **4** great hardness, strength, or resolution. **5** golf club with a metal head. *vt,vi* remove creases from (clothes, etc.) with a hot iron. **iron out** settle; put right. **Iron Curtain** *n* the ideological, cultural, and social barrier that exists between the Soviet dominated countries of Eastern Europe and most of Western Europe. **ironmonger** *n* person selling hardware, tools, etc. **ironmongery** *n* **1** hardware, tools, etc. **2** shop or business of an ironmonger.

irony *n* **1** subtle use of words to imply a meaning opposite to the literal one. **2** incongruous usually unfortunate situation or sequence of events. **Ironic** or **ironical** adj. **ironically** adv.

irrational adj not rational or consistent; illogical. **irrationality** n. **irrationally** adv.

irreconcilable adj not capable of being reconciled or made compatible. **irreconcilably** adv.

irregular adj 1 not occurring regularly. 2 not symmetrical; uneven; not uniform. 3 contravening customs, rules, or laws. 4 not following the usual grammatical pattern. **irregularity** n. **irregularly** adv.

irrelevant adj not relevant or applicable. **irrelevance** n.

irresistible adj 1 impossible to resist. 2 extremely delightful or charming; fascinating. **irresistibly** adv.

irrespective adv **irrespective of** not taking into consideration; regardless of.

irresponsible adj not behaving in a responsible manner; unreliable. **irresponsibly** adv.

irrevocable (i'revəkəbəl) adj unable to be reversed; unalterable. **irrevocably** adv.

irrigate vt keep (land) constantly supplied with water using ditches, pipes, etc. **irrigation** n.

irritate vt 1 annoy; exasperate. 2 sore; itch; chafe. **irritation** n. **irritable** adj easily annoyed.

is v 3rd person singular form of **be** in the present tense.

Islam n 1 Muslim faith based on a belief in one God, Allah, and on the teachings of his prophet, Mohammed, set down in the Koran. 2 Muslim culture; Muslim world. **Islamic** adj.

island n 1 area of land surrounded by water. 2 anything resembling an island in being isolated from its surroundings. **islander** n. **isle** n small island.

isolate vt 1 set apart or keep separate. 2 put in quarantine. **isolation** n.

issue vi 1 emerge; come, go, or pour out. 2 result; be derived. vt 1 give out; offer; distribute. 2 publish. n 1 something issued at one time, such as stamps or copies of a magazine or journal. 2 outflow; discharge. 3 disputed point; question; topic. 4 result. 5 offspring. **at issue** in dispute; under discussion. **take issue** disagree; dispute.

it pron 1 that or this thing, animal, group, etc., when not specified or identified precisely or when previously mentioned. 2 used as the subject with impersonal verbs such as 'rain', 'snow', etc. 3 used as the subject or object when referring to a following clause or phrase.

italic adj in or denoting a style of type with letters sloping to the right. n also **italics** italic type, sometimes used to isolate or emphasize a word or phrase.

itch n 1 irritating sensation of the skin causing a desire to scratch. 2 constant craving; restless desire. vi have or feel an itch. **itchy** adj.

item n 1 one unit or object from a list or collection. 2 piece of news or information. **itemize** vt list.

itinerary n 1 detailed plan of a journey; route. 2 account of a journey. **itinerant** adj travelling from place to place. n itinerant worker.

its adj belonging to it. **itself** r pron of its own self.

ivory n hard smooth cream-coloured highly prized material forming the tusks of the elephant, walrus, etc.

ivy n trailing evergreen plant with shiny leaves.

J

jab vt,vi (-bb-) poke; thrust; stab. n 1 sharp thrust or poke. 2 inf injection.

jack n 1 tool used for raising heavy objects, esp. a vehicle. 2 lowest court card in a pack; knave. vt,vi also **jack up** raise by using a jack. **jackpot** n accumulated sum of money given as a prize.

jackal n wild animal of the dog family.

jackdaw n large black bird of the crow family.

jacket n 1 short coat. 2 also **dust jacket** detachable paper cover of a book. 3 skin of a baked potato.

Jacuzzi n Tdmk bath or small pool containing a mechanism that agitates the water.

jade n semiprecious hard stone of a green or whitish colour, valued as a gemstone.

jaded adj worn out or stale; weary.

jagged ('dʒægid) adj having rough sharp edges.

jaguar *n* wild animal of the cat family.

jail *or* **gaol** *n* prison. *vt* imprison. **jailer** *n.*

jam[1] *v* (-mm-) *vt* **1** crush or squeeze into a confined space; cram; clog. **2** *also* **jam on** apply (brakes) suddenly and forcefully. *vt, vi* stick or become stuck; wedge. *n* congestion or blockage, esp. of a number of vehicles on the road.

jam[2] *n* preserve made by boiling fruit and sugar together. **jam tomorrow** a promise that things will be better in the future although gloomy at present.

jangle *vi, vt* produce a harsh or discordant metallic ringing sound. *n* harsh metallic ringing sound.

janitor *n* caretaker; porter; warden.

January *n* first month of the year.

jar[1] *n* glass or earthenware vessel used for preserves, pickles, etc.

jar[2] *vi, vt* (-rr-) **1** vibrate with an unpleasant grating sound. **2** grate (on the nerves). *n* jolt; grating vibration.

jargon *n* **1** idiomatic or specialized language developed by a particular group, trade, or profession. **2** any talk or writing difficult to understand.

jasmine *n* shrub of the olive family having sweet-scented yellow, red, or white flowers.

jaundice *n* disease caused by excessive bile pigment in the blood, characterized by a yellowing of the skin. **jaundiced** *adj* affected or distorted by prejudice, jealousy, etc.

jaunt *n* **1** short trip or excursion. **2** spree; carefree adventure.

jaunty *adj* sprightly; brisk; lively. **jauntily** *adv.*

javelin *n* long slender spear thrown as a field event in athletics.

jaw *n* bony structure forming the bottom of the face or head in which the teeth are set. **jaws** *pl n* gripping part of a machine, tool, etc. ~*vi inf* gossip; chatter. **jawbone** *n* either of the two bones of the jaw.

jazz *n* popular music of Negro origin, often improvised and making use of syncopation.

jealous *adj* experiencing strong feelings of resentment or envy, esp. towards a rival in love. **jealously** *adv.* **jealousy** *n.*

jeans *pl n* trousers of a strong cotton or denim.

jeep *n* open-sided motor truck used esp. by military personnel.

jeer *vi* shout insults; scorn; scoff; mock. *n* mocking remark or shout; taunt.

jelly *n* **1** type of confectionery made from gelatin, sugar, and fruit flavouring. **2** gelatinous substance produced when meat is boiled. **jellyfish** *n* small marine creature with tentacles and a soft gelatinous body.

jeopardize *vt* place at risk; endanger. **jeopardy** *n.*

jerk *vt* pull or push sharply; tug. *vi* move quickly and suddenly; jolt. *n* **1** sharp tug. **2** spasm. **jerky** *adj.* **jerkily** *adv.* **jerkiness** *n.*

jersey *n* **1** woollen jumper. **2** type of knitted fabric. **Jersey** breed of dairy cattle.

jest *n* witty or amusing joke or trick. *vi* joke light-heartedly. **jester** *n* **1** clown or fool formerly employed at the court of a king or nobleman. **2** joker in a pack of cards.

Jesuit ('dʒezjuit) *n* member of a religious order (Society of Jesus) founded by Ignatius Loyola.

Jesus *n* *also* **Jesus Christ** founder of Christianity.

jet[1] *n* **1** fast stream of water, gas, etc., forced by pressure through a nozzle. **2** aircraft propelled by means of a gas turbine.

jet[2] *n* type of hard black coal used for jewellery. **jet black** *adj, n* deep glossy black.

jetty *n* small pier.

Jew *n* person belonging to or following the religion of the race which is descended from the ancient Israelites. **Jewish** *adj.*

jewel *n* precious stone worn or used for adornment; gem. **jewellery** items such as necklaces, rings, or brooches; jewels. **jeweller** *n.*

jig[1] *n* **1** lively folk-dance. **2** music for such a dance, usually in triple time. *vi, vt* (-gg-) **1** dance or play (a jig). **2** bounce or jog up and down.

jig[2] *n* cutting tool or a guide for such a tool. **jigsaw** *n* *also* **jigsaw puzzle** puzzle consisting of a number of specially shaped pieces of cardboard or wood, which interlock to make up a complete picture.

jiggle *vt, vi* jerk or shake up and down; rattle.

jilt *vt* forsake (a lover, etc.).

jingle *vt,vi* produce a light ringing sound; tinkle. *n* **1** light metallic sound. **2** catchy tune or song.

job *n* **1** employment; occupation; work. **2** specific task; assignment. **a good job** a fortunate thing or occurrence.

jockey *n* professional rider of racehorses. *vt,vi also* **jockey for** jostle; manoeuvre.

jocular *adj* given to joking; jolly. **jocularity** *n*.

jodhpurs ('dʒɔdpɔz) *pl n* type of close-fitting trousers worn when riding a horse.

jog *v* (-gg-) *vi* **1** knock or push lightly; nudge; jerk. **2** move slowly but steadily; trot or plod. *vt* stimulate (the memory). *n* nudge; light blow. **jogging** *n* running at a slow steady pace for exercise.

joggle *vt,vi* jolt; jerk; jiggle; shake; jog. *n* slight shake or jolt.

join *vt,vi* **1** bring or come together; fasten; connect. **2** become a member (of). **3** *also* **join up** enlist (in). *vt also* **join in** accompany; take part in with. *n* seam. **joinery** *n* craft of making wooden doors, window frames, etc. **joiner** *n*.

joint *n* **1** connection of two parts or components. **2** junction at which two bones connect. **3** large piece of meat including a bone. **4** *inf* marijuana cigarette. **5** *inf* bar or club. **6** *inf* place. *adj* shared; combined. *vt* cut up (meat) into joints. **jointly** *adv*.

joist *n* steel or timber beam or girder.

joke *n* something done or said to cause amusement or laughter; jest. *vi* speak or act amusingly or wittily. **joker** *n* **1** person who jokes. **2** one of two extra cards in a pack with a picture of a clown or jester.

jolly *adj* cheerful; funny; jovial. *adv* very. **jollity** *n*.

jolt *vt,vi* shake or bump sharply; lurch; jerk. *n* **1** sudden sharp jerk. **2** shock.

jostle *vi,vt* push or move so as to gain more room or a better position. *n* rough push.

journal *n* **1** periodical; newspaper or magazine. **2** diary or logbook recording daily events. **journalism** *n* art or practice of writing for the press. **journalist** *n*.

journey *n* process of travelling or distance travelled; trip; voyage; excursion. *vi* travel; take a trip.

jovial *adj* hearty; jolly; good-humoured.

joy *n* delight; pleasure; gladness. **joyful** *or* **joyous** *adj*. **joyfully** *adv*.

jubilant *adj* joyful; rejoicing; triumphant. **jubilance** *or* **jubilation** *n*.

jubilee *n* celebration of a particularly significant anniversary.

Judaism *n* Jewish religion or tradition.

judge *n* **1** person presiding over a trial in a court of law. **2** person who chooses the winner(s) of a competition; adjudicator. **3** critic; assessor. *vt,vi* act as a judge (for). **judgment** *or* **judgement** *n*. **judicial** *adj* relating to a judge, court of law, or justice. **judiciary** *adj* relating to judgment. *n* **1** method or administration of justice. **2** judges collectively. **judicious** *adj* wise; well-judged; sensible. **judiciously** *adv*.

judo *n* Japanese sport embracing certain principles of self-defence by unarmed combat.

jug *n* vessel with a handle and spout or lip, used for holding or serving liquids.

juggernaut *n* large articulated lorry.

juggle *vi,vt* **1** perform tricks (with) by tossing and catching (various objects). **2** manipulate or rearrange, esp. in order to deceive. **juggler** *n*.

juice *n* liquid from fruit, vegetables, etc. **juicy** *adj* **1** containing plenty of juice. **2** suggesting scandal. **juiciness** *n*.

jukebox *n* coin-operated record-player found mainly on commercial premises.

July *n* seventh month of the year.

jumble *vt,vi* mix up; place or be out of sequence. *n* muddled heap or mixture. **jumble sale** *n* sale of second-hand articles, which have been donated, esp. in aid of charity.

jump *vi* **1** leap into the air, spring. **2** move involuntarily, esp. in reaction to a noise, shock, etc. **3** jerk. **4** increase, rise, or switch suddenly. *vt* leap over or across; clear. **jump at** take advantage of or seize (an opportunity) eagerly. ~*n* **1** leap; spring. **2** obstacle to be cleared by jumping. **3** spasm; jerk. **4** sudden increase, rise, or switch. **jumpy** *adj* nervous; tense.

jumper *n* garment fitting the upper part of the body, often made of wool; sweater.

junction *n* **1** joining place or point of intersection. **2** place where railway lines converge or intersect. **3** point of contact between different electrical circuits.

juncture *n* **1** critical point in time. **2** junction; connection.

June *n* sixth month of the year.

jungle *n* **1** area of land in tropical regions, having thick dense vegetation and undergrowth. **2** situation or environment characterized by ruthless competition, lack of law and order, etc.

junior *adj* of a lower rank or status; not senior. *n* person who is younger or of a lower rank or status; subordinate. **junior school** *n* school for children after primary but before secondary levels.

juniper *n* conifer producing pungent purple cones, which are used in medicines, distilling, etc.

junk[1] *n* discarded articles regarded as worthless; rubbish; trash. **junkie** *n* *also* **junky** *sl* drug addict.

junk[2] *n* flat-bottomed square-sailed ship of Chinese origin.

junta *n* **1** self-appointed group that seizes political power. **2** administrative council in some parts of Latin America.

Jupiter *n* largest of the planets, orbiting between Mars and Saturn.

jurisdiction *n* legal power, authority, or administration.

jury *n* **1** body of persons required to hear evidence and deliver a verdict at a trial. **2** panel of judges. **juror** *n* member of a jury.

just *adj* **1** fair in the administration of justice; impartial; unbiased. **2** deserved; proper. *adv* **1** a moment earlier; recently. **2** exactly; precisely. **3** barely; hardly. **4** at the same time (as). **5** merely; only. **justly** *adv*.

justice *n* moral or legal correctness; fairness; lawfulness. **do justice to** treat according to merit.

justify *vt* give sufficient or valid reasons for; uphold; defend. **justifiable** *adj*. **justification** *n*.

jut *vi* (-tt-) *also* **jut out** stick out; extend beyond a particular point; protrude.

jute *n* strong natural fibre used for ropes or sacking.

juvenile *adj* **1** immature; young; childish. **2** intended for young people. *n* young person; child or adolescent. **juvenile delinquency** *n* criminal behaviour by young offenders. **juvenile delinquent** *n*.

juxtapose *vt* place immediately next to. **juxtaposition** *n*.

K

kaftan *n* *also* **caftan** traditional loose full-length tunic of the Near East.

Kaiser *n* (formerly) German emperor.

kaleidoscope (kǝ'laidǝskoup) *n* sealed tube containing at one end pieces of coloured glass whose reflections produce patterns when the tube is turned or shaken.

kangaroo *n* Australian marsupial with powerful hind limbs and a broad tail.

karate (kǝ'rɑːti) *n* Oriental system of self-defence by unarmed combat employing smashes, chops, or kicks with the hands, elbows, head, or feet.

kebab *n* Middle Eastern dish of small cubes of meat and vegetables cooked on a skewer over a charcoal grill.

keel *n* timber or plate running along the length of the bottom of a ship's hull. **on an even keel** maintaining a steady course; stable. *v* **keel over** capsize; overturn.

keen *adj* **1** enthusiastically willing or interested. **2** anxious; eager. **3** perceptive; observant; shrewd. **4** having a sharp cutting edge. **5** bitingly cold. **6** intense; strong. **keen on** very interested in. **keenly** *adv*. **keenness** *n*.

keep *v* (kept) *vt* **1** hold in one's possession; retain. **2** detain. **3** maintain in a particular state or condition. **4** own and look after or care for. **5** abide by; observe; comply with. **6** store; have in stock. **7** restrain; deter; prevent. **8** provide for; earn money for. **9** make a record in. *vi* **1** remain; stay. **2** carry on; continue to. **3** stay fresh. **keep on 1** continue to employ. **2** nag; persist. **3** proceed. **keep to** proceed as planned; stick or adhere to. **keep up (with)** maintain the same rate of progress (as). ~*n* **1** cost of maintaining. **2** fortified central tower of a castle. **keeper** *n* **1** person in charge of animals in a zoo. **2** museum or gallery attendant. **3** warder; jailer. **keeping** *n* **in keeping with** in accordance with; conforming or appropriate to. **keepsake** *n* memento; token gift or souvenir.

keg *n* small barrel.

kennel *n* **1** small shed for housing a dog. **2** *also* **kennels** establishment breeding and caring for dogs.

kerb *n* edge of a pavement.

kernel *n* edible central part of a nut or fruit stone.

kestrel *n* small falcon.

kettle *n* metal vessel with a lid, spout, and handle, used for boiling water. **kettledrum** *n* large percussion instrument having a hollow body with a skin stretched tightly over the top.

key *n* **1** metal instrument cut and shaped to fit a particular lock. **2** lever on a typewriter. **3** lever on a piano and certain woodwind instruments. **4** set of notes in a musical scale. **5** crucial piece of information, component, etc. **6** guide to coded information or symbols used. *adj* most important or vital. **keyed up** tense with anticipation. **keyboard** *n* set of levers or keys on a piano, typewriter, etc.

khaki ('ka:ki) *adj,n* yellowish-brown, often used as the colour for military uniforms.

kibbutz (ki'buts) *n, pl* **kibbutzim** (kibut-'si:m) collective farm in Israel.

kick *vt,vi* strike or aim (at) with the foot. *vi* raise or shake the feet or legs. **kick up** create (a fuss, trouble, etc.). ~*n* **1** blow or jerky movement of the foot. **2** *inf* thrill. **kick-off** *n* start of play in football.

kid[1] *n* **1** young goat. **2** *inf* child; young person. **3** soft goatskin.

kid[2] *vt,vi* (-dd-) *inf* deceive by teasing; hoax.

kidnap *vt* (-pp-) seize and carry off (a person), esp. in order to obtain ransom. **kidnapper** *n*.

kidney *n* one of a pair of bodily organs that filters the blood and removes waste products, which are discharged to the bladder as urine. **kidney bean** *n* reddish-brown kidney-shaped bean.

kill *vt,vi* **1** cause the death (of). **2** destroy completely. **3** *inf* cause pain, suffering, etc., to; exhaust. **kill time** find something to do whilst waiting. ~*n* act of killing, esp. a hunted animal or prey. **killer** *n*.

kiln *n* large oven used for baking clay, bricks, etc.

kilogram *n* also **kilogramme** *or* **kilo** one thousand grams (approx. 2.2 lbs.).

kilometre ('kiləmi:tə, ki'ləmitə) *n* one thousand metres (approx. 0.6 miles).

kilowatt *n* one thousand watts.

kilt *n* pleated tartan skirt, traditionally worn by Highland Scotsmen.

kimono *n* full-length wide-sleeved dress with a wide sash, traditionally worn by Japanese women.

kin *n* also **kindred** one's relatives.

kind[1] *adj* **1** *also* **kind-hearted** friendly; generous; helpful; considerate. **2** mild; not harmful. **kindness** *n*. **kindly** *adj* sympathetic; warm-hearted. *adv* **1** in a kind manner; sympathetically. **2** please.

kind[2] *n* sort; type; class.

kindergarten *n* nursery group or school for children under primary school age.

kindle *vt* **1** set light to. **2** arouse or excite (interest, passion, etc.). *vi* catch fire.

kindred *adj* **1** of one's kin. **2** compatible; in sympathy. *n* kin.

kinetic *adj* relating to motion.

king *n* **1** male monarch or sovereign. **2** most influential or prominent person or thing. **3** highest court card ranking above a queen and often below an ace. **4** key chess piece, able to move one square at a time in any direction. **kingdom** *n* **1** nation ruled by a king or queen; realm. **2** one of three major divisions into which animals, plants, or minerals may be classified. **kingfisher** *n* fish-eating river bird having bright blue and orange plumage. **king-size** *adj also* **king-sized** of a larger than average size.

kink *n* **1** twist, loop, or curl in a piece of rope, string, hair, etc. **2** *inf* perversion. *vi,vt* form into kinks; bend; curl. **kinky** *adj sl* sexually deviant; perverted.

kiosk *n* **1** public telephone booth. **2** small open-fronted shop selling newspapers, cigarettes, etc.

kipper *n* herring or similar fish that has been salted and smoked.

kiss *vt,vi* caress or touch with lips as a token of love, affection, reverence, etc. *n* act of kissing.

kit *n* **1** items of clothing and equipment issued to a member of the armed forces. **2** equipment or tools used by a workman, sportsman, etc. **3** collection of parts sold for assembly by the purchaser. *vt* (-tt-) *also* **kit out** supply or issue with a kit.

kitchen *n* room equipped for cooking. **kitchen garden** *n* garden where vegetables, herbs, etc., are grown.

kite *n* **1** light framework of wood, paper, etc., that can be flown in the air at the end of a long string. **2** type of hawk.

kitten *n* young cat.

kitty *n* pooled sum of money; fund.

kiwi *n* large bird native to New Zealand that is unable to fly.

kleptomania *n* compulsion to steal. **kleptomaniac** *n,adj*.

knack *n* skilful or intuitive ability; aptitude; flair.

knave *n* **1** jack in a pack of cards. **2** rogue; scoundrel.

knead *vt* shape and mould (dough, clay, etc.) with the hands.

knee *n* joint connecting the upper and lower leg. **kneecap** *n* flat bone at the front of the knee. **kneedeep/kneehigh** *adj* so deep/high as to reach the knees.

kneel *vi* (knelt *or* kneeled) rest or bend with the knees on the ground.

knickers *pl n* woman's undergarment covering the lower half of the body.

knife *n, pl* **knives** cutting implement consisting of a sharpened blade set into a handle. *vt* stab or wound with a knife. **on a knife-edge** in a state of extreme tension or anxious anticipation.

knight *n* **1** medieval nobleman of high military rank. **2** person honoured by the sovereign with a non-hereditary rank below that of the nobility. **3** chess piece usually in the shape of a horse's head. **knighthood** *n* rank of a knight.

knit *vi,vt* (-tt-; knitted *or* knit) **1** make (a garment, fabric, etc.) by winding and looping wool or yarn round two or more long needles in a particular way. **2** join together; mesh; interlock. **knitwear** *n* knitted garments.

knob *n* **1** rounded handle on a door, drawer, etc. **2** round switch on a radio, TV set, etc. **3** lump; swelling. **knobbly** *adj also* **knobby** lumpy; bumpy; having knobs.

knock *n* **1** blow; bang; tap. **2** tapping noise. *vt,vi* **1** tap; bang; hit; strike. **2** produce a tapping sound; rattle. **3** *inf* criticize; find

fault (with). **knock about** *or* **around 1** travel around. **2** be in a group (with). **3** beat; batter. **knock down 1** hit and push over. **2** sell in an auction. **3** reduce in price. **knock off** *sl* **1** finish work. **2** pilfer; steal. **3** complete hurriedly. **4** deduct. **knock out 1** cause to lose consciousness. **2** exhaust; tire. **knockout** *n* **1** blow that renders (someone) unconscious. **2** contest in which competitors are eliminated by heats. **3** person of stunningly attractive appearance. **4** overwhelming experience. **knock up 1** assemble quickly. **2** rouse; waken. **knocker** *n* hinged metal bar attached to a door and used for knocking.

knot *n* **1** tight loop tied in a piece of rope, string, ribbon, etc. **2** small bunch of people. **3** irregular lump in a piece of wood. **4** unit used to measure the speed of a ship or aircraft equal to one nautical mile per hour. *vt,vi* (-tt-) form into a knot; tangle; tie.

know *v* (knew; known) *vt,vi* **1** be aware or certain of (a fact). **2** understand; have experience (of). *vt* **1** be acquainted or familiar with. **2** have a grasp of or skill in. **3** be able to distinguish. **know how** be able (to); have the skill (to). **knowhow** *n inf* skill; ability. **knowing** *adj* **1** shrewd; aware. **2** intentional; deliberate. **knowingly** *adv.* **knowledge** *n* **1** information or facts. **2** experience; awareness; consciousness. **3** familiarity; understanding. **4** learning; wisdom. **knowledgeable** *adj* well-informed. **knowledgeably** *adv.*

knuckle *n* joint of the finger. *v* **knuckle down** get on with a task. **knuckle under** submit to authority or pressure.

kosher *adj* conforming to the requirements for the preparation of food under Jewish law.

kung fu *n* Chinese system of self-defence combining the principles of both karate and judo.

L

label *n* **1** slip of paper, card, etc., affixed to luggage, a parcel, etc., for identification; tag. **2** name or description. *vt* (-ll-) **1** affix a label to. **2** describe as; name.

laboratory n room or building equipped for scientific experiments, manufacture of drugs, etc.

laborious adj 1 requiring great effort or hard work. 2 painstaking; hardworking. **laboriously** adv.

labour n 1 work; toil; task. 2 period of childbirth. 3 body of people available for employment; workers. vi 1 work hard; toil. 2 move with difficulty; struggle. vt go into excessive detail about. **labourer** n unskilled manual worker. **Labour Party** n British political party representing the interests of the working class and trade unions.

laburnum n small tree bearing clusters of drooping yellow flowers.

labrador n breed of dog with a golden or black coat.

labyrinth n 1 complex network of paths, tunnels, caves, etc. 2 complicated system, situation, etc.

lace n 1 delicate fabric woven from cotton, silk, etc. 2 cord for fastening a shoe or boot. vt 1 also **lace up** tie (footwear) with a lace. 2 add a dash of alcohol to. **lacy** adj.

lack n deficiency; absence; shortage. vt,vi be without or short (of).

lacquer n 1 resinous substance for varnishing wood. 2 hairspray. vt,vi coat or spray with lacquer.

lad n inf boy or young man.

ladder n 1 framework for climbing consisting of two uprights fitted with horizontal bars or rungs. 2 flaw in knitting where vertical threads have unravelled. 3 means of moving within a social structure. vt produce a ladder in (stockings, tights, etc.).

laden adj 1 loaded; weighed down. 2 overburdened.

ladle n spoon with a long handle and deep bowl for serving soups, stews, etc. vt also **ladle out** serve by using a ladle.

lady n woman, esp. one who is wealthy or noted for her good manners. **Lady** title, rank, or form of address of certain female members of the nobility. **ladylike** adj refined and well-mannered as befits a lady. **Your/Her Ladyship** n form of address used to/of certain women with the rank of Lady.

ladybird n small beetle having a red back with black spots.

lag[1] vi (-gg-) fall behind. n interval; lapse.

lag[2] vt (-gg-) protect (pipes, etc.) with insulating material.

lager n type of beer stored in a cool place and served chilled.

laid v pt and pp of **lay**[1].

lain v pp of **lie**[2].

laity n persons who are not members of the clergy; laymen.

lake n inland expanse of water.

lamb n young sheep or its meat.

lame adj 1 unable to walk properly; crippled or limping. 2 feeble; unconvincing. vt make lame; cripple. **lame duck** n liability, worthless cause, etc.

lament (lə'ment) vi,vt express great sorrow or grief (for); mourn. n song or poem expressing grief or mourning. **lamentable** ('læməntəbəl) adj deplorable.

lamp n device producing light by electricity, oil, etc., usually having a shade for protection.

lance n 1 long spear. 2 also **lancet** sharp surgical knife. vt pierce with a lance. **lance corporal** n noncommissioned officer of the lowest rank in the British Army.

land n 1 solid mass forming the earth's surface. 2 country; nation. 3 soil; ground. 4 domain; sphere. vi 1 arrive on the shore or ground after a journey by ship or aircraft; disembark. 2 come to the ground after falling or jumping. vt 1 bring (a ship) to shore or (an aircraft) to the ground. 2 catch (a fish). 3 obtain (a job, contract, etc.). vt,vi place or be in a difficult situation. **landing** n 1 flat area at the top of a flight of stairs. 2 act of bringing a ship or aircraft to land. **landlady** n 1 woman who rents out rooms to tenants or guests. 2 female owner or manager of a public house. **landlord** n 1 person who owns and rents out property, land, rooms, etc. 2 male owner or manager of a public house. **landmark** n 1 prominent feature of the landscape. 2 significant historical event or achievement. **landscape** n 1 scenery of an area. 2 painting, drawing, etc., depicting this. vt,vi design and lay out (a park, garden, etc.).

lane n 1 narrow road, esp. in the country. 2 marked division of a motorway, racing track, etc. **3** prescribed route for shipping or aircraft.

language n **1** structured system of speech sounds used by a community. **2** written form of such a system. **3** any system of communication. **4** style of expression of speech or writing.

languid adj lacking energy; weakened; listless; inert. **languish** vi become languid; lose strength through neglect, deprivation, etc. **languor** n.

lanky adj tall and thin.

lantern n lamp with a light enclosed in a glass case.

lap[1] n **1** part formed by the area from the waist to the thighs when a person is sitting down. **2** comfortable or safe place.

lap[2] vt,vi (-pp-) **1** drink by licking up with the tongue. **2** wash gently against with a soft slapping sound. **lap up** take in (information) greedily. ~n gentle slapping movement or sound.

lap[3] n one circuit of a racing track. vt (-pp-) **1** wrap round; overlap; envelop. **2** overtake so as to be one or more laps ahead.

lapel n front part of a garment that folds back to join the collar.

lapse n **1** error; deviation; aberration; fault. **2** decline to a lower standard. **3** interval or passing of time. vi **1** decline; fall into disuse. **2** cease to subscribe to or be a member of a club, organization, religion, etc. **3** elapse; pass slowly. vt cancel the subscription of.

larceny n theft.

larch n type of deciduous conifer.

lard n pig fat melted down for use in cooking. vt **1** smear with lard. **2** embellish (a speech, story, etc.).

larder n room used for storing food; pantry.

large adj of considerable size, weight, extent, etc.; great; big. **at large 1** free; unchecked. **2** on the whole; generally. **largely** adv mostly; to a great extent.

lark[1] n small songbird; skylark.

lark[2] n piece of fun or mischief; prank; spree. v **lark about** act mischievously.

larva n, pl **larvae** ('lɑːviː) immature form of an insect such as the butterfly or an animal such as the frog. **larval** adj.

larynx n organ containing the vocal cords, situated at the base of the tongue. **laryngitis** n inflammation of the larynx resulting in temporary loss of voice.

lascivious (ləˈsɪvɪəs) adj lewd; lustful; lecherous.

laser n electronic device for producing a narrow parallel very intense beam of light of a single wavelength.

lash[1] n **1** whip, esp. the flexible part or thong. **2** stroke of a whip. **3** cutting remark. **4** beating or impact of waves, rain, etc. **5** eyelash. vt **1** whip; thrash. **2** scold; criticize sharply. **3** strike forcefully and repeatedly. **4** move like a whip. **lash out 1** attack wildly. **2** spend extravagantly.

lash[2] vt bind with ropes.

lass n inf girl or young woman.

lasso n, pl **lassoes** or **lassos** long rope with a noose for catching horses, etc. vt catch with a lasso.

last[1] adj **1** coming at the end; final. **2** most recent; latest. **3** one remaining. **4** ultimate; most conclusive. adv **1** at the end; after the rest. **2** most recently. n person or thing at the end. **at last** finally; eventually. **lastly** adv as a conclusion.

last[2] vi **1** exist or continue for a specified time. **2** endure; remain useful or in good condition; keep. **lasting** adj permanent; continuing.

latch n bar or lever for securing a door or gate. vt fasten with a latch. **latch on (to)** inf **1** attach oneself to. **2** grasp; come to understand.

late adj **1** not punctual. **2** happening or continuing after the normal or expected time. **3** occurring towards the end of a period, stage, etc. **4** former; recent. **5** deceased. adv **1** after the expected time. **2** at an advanced stage. **lately** adv also **of late** recently.

latent adj present but not yet developed or apparent; potential. **latency** n.

lateral adj directed to or coming from the side.

lathe n machine for holding and shaping or cutting wood, metal, etc.

lather n **1** foam produced by soap or detergent; suds. **2** frothy sweat, esp. of a horse. vi,vt produce lather; foam; froth.

latitude *n* angular distance north or south of the equator.

latrine *n* lavatory, esp. a temporary one for use at a camp site, barracks, etc.

latter *adj* 1 relating to the second of two things. 2 occurring in the second half. **latterly** *adv* lately.

lattice *n* network of strips of wood, metal, etc., arranged to form a pattern of squares, diamonds, etc.

laudable *adj* praiseworthy; commendable.

laugh *vi,vt* utter a sound of amusement, scorn, etc. **laugh at** make fun of; mock. *n* 1 single sound uttered in amusement, scorn, etc. 2 *inf* something that is fun to do or watch. **laughable** *adj* ridiculous. **laughter** *n* act or sound of laughing.

launch[1] *vt* 1 send (a ship) into the water for the first time. 2 send (a rocket) into space. 3 propel; hurl. 4 start off on a new course or enterprise. **launch into** start without hesitation or introduction.

launch[2] *n* small open motorboat.

launder *vt,vi* wash and press or iron (clothes, sheets, etc.). **Launderette** *n Tdmk* public laundry equipped with coin-operated machines. **laundry** *n* 1 place where clothes, sheets, etc., are laundered. 2 items to be laundered.

laurel *n* evergreen tree with smooth broad aromatic leaves; bay. **laurels** *pl n* honours; credit for achievement. **rest on one's laurels** cease to strive after having attained victory or success.

lava *n* molten rock from an erupting volcano.

lavatory *n* water-closet or the room where it is situated; toilet.

lavender *n* bush bearing fragrant mauve flowers. *n,adj* mauve.

lavish *adj* done on a generous scale; abundant; lush. *vt* bestow; spend generously. **lavishly** *adv.*

law *n* 1 binding regulation laid down by a government, council, or sovereign. 2 scientific rule or principle. 3 code of behaviour. **the law** 1 legal profession. 2 body of legal regulations. 3 *inf* police. **lay down the law** behave domineeringly, dogmatically, or tyrannically. **law-abiding** *adj* obedient according to the law. **lawful** *adj* permitted by law; legal; legitimate. **lawsuit** *n* instance of bringing a case before a court of law; action. **lawyer** *n* practising member of the legal profession.

lawn *n* area of grass laid out in a garden or park. **lawn-mower** *n* machine for cutting grass.

lax *adj* 1 not strict. 2 loose; slack. 3 having open or loose bowels. **laxative** *n* medicine taken to relieve constipation.

lay[1] *v* (laid) *vt* 1 place gently on the ground or a surface; rest; deposit. 2 set (a table) for a meal. 3 fit (a carpet). 4 place a bet on; stake. 5 *tab* copulate with. *vt,vi* produce (eggs). **lay down** surrender; sacrifice; relinquish. **lay off** 1 dismiss (workers) temporarily. 2 *sl* stop; desist. **lay on** provide; organize. **lay out** 1 spread out; arrange for display. 2 prepare (a body) for burial. 3 spend. **lay up** incapacitate. **layabout** *n* lazy person. **layby** *n* parking space at the side of a road. **layout** *n* arrangement of material for a book, newspaper, etc.

lay[2] *v pt* of **lie**[2].

lay[3] *adj* relating to people, duties, etc., concerned with the laity. **layman** *n, pl* **-men** 1 person who is not a member of the clergy. 2 person who has an amateur rather than a professional knowledge of something.

layer *n* 1 coating spread over a surface. 2 stratum; band. 3 strip placed over or resting on another. 4 shoot of a plant pegged underground so that it will produce its own roots. *vi,vt* form or place in layers. *vt* propagate by means of a layer.

lazy *adj* not inclined to work; idle; inactive. **lazily** *adv.* **laziness** *n.* **laze** *vi,vt* be lazy; spend (time) idly.

lead[1] (led) *n* 1 tough malleable bluish-grey metal, used for pipes, as a roofing material, etc. 2 graphite used for pencils. **leaden** *adj* 1 made of lead. 2 heavy or sluggish.

lead[2] (li:d) *v* (led) *vi,vt* 1 show the way (to); guide; conduct. 2 act as the leader or head (of); control. 3 be in or take first place; be ahead (of). *vi* 1 be a means of reaching. 2 follow a particular direction. *vt* live; follow (a particular way of life). **lead astray** persuade to do wrong; corrupt. **lead on** entice; provoke. **lead up to** move towards; prepare for; approach. ~*n* 1 clue; hint; guideline. 2 position in front or ahead of others. 3 main role in a play, film, etc. **4** flex, cord, or cable for an electrical appliance. **5** leash. **leader** *n* **1** person in charge; head of a political party, movement, etc. **2** person in a winning position. **3** principal violinist in an orchestra. **4** editorial in a newspaper. **leadership** *n*. **leading** *adj* main; principal; chief.

leaf *n, pl* **leaves 1** flat photosynthetic organ of a plant. **2** page of a book. **turn over a new leaf** make a fresh start by reforming one's behaviour. ~*vi* produce leaves. **leaf through** glance through (a book, papers, etc.) by turning the pages quickly. **leaflet** *n* **1** advertisement or notice printed on a single sheet of paper. **2** small undeveloped leaf.

league *n* **1** political alliance; coalition. **2** association of sports teams. **in league (with)** conspiring (with); allied (to). ~*vt,vi* bring or come together in a league.

leak *n* **1** crack or hole through which liquid, gas, etc., escapes. **2** disclosure of confidential information. *vi,vt* **1** escape or allow to escape through a leak. **2** divulge; disclose. **leaky** *adj*. **leakage** *n* process of leaking or the amount leaked.

lean[1] *vt,vi* (leaned *or* leant) place or be in a sloping position; tilt; incline. **lean on 1** rest against; use for support. **2** rely or depend on. **3** *sl* threaten; intimidate. **lean towards** favour; have a bias towards. **leaning** *n* tendency; bias; inclination.

lean[2] *adj* **1** (of meat) having very little fat. **2** thin; skinny. **3** not productive; barren; of a poor quality or standard. **leanness** *n*.

leap *vi,vt* (leapt *or* leaped) **1** jump or spring high into the air; bound. **2** increase sharply. *n* **1** high or sudden jump. **2** abrupt change of position. **leap at** take advantage of eagerly. **leapfrog** *n* game in which one person bends over for another to leap or vault over him. *vi* (-gg-) **1** play leapfrog. **2** move erratically. **leap year** *n* year having one day (i.e. Feb. 29th) more than the usual 365.

learn *vi,vt* (learned *or* learnt) **1** acquire knowledge (of) or skill by studying or being taught. **2** experience. **3** obtain information (of); hear (about). **learned** ('lɔ:nid) *adj* scholarly; wise; having great learning. **learning** *n* academic knowledge or study; scholarship.

lease *n* contract drawn up between a landlord and tenant. *vt* grant or take possession of by lease. **leasehold** *adj* held by lease. *n* tenure by lease. **leaseholder** *n*.

leash *n* strap for attaching to a dog's collar as a means of control; lead. *vt* attach a leash to.

least *adj* smallest in amount or importance. *n* smallest amount. **at least 1** as a minimum. **2** even if nothing else. **not in the least** not at all; not in the slightest; not to any extent. ~*adv* of the lowest amount.

leather *n* strong material made from the cured hide of certain animals. **leathery** *adj* of or resembling leather.

leave[1] *v* (left) *vt,vi* **1** go away or depart (from). **2** cease to attend. **3** cease to be a member (of) or participant (in). *vt* **1** forget to take; lose. **2** deposit; place. **3** result in. **4** cause a visible sign (of). **5** bequeath. **6** cause to remain. **7** fail to complete; postpone. **8** keep open, free, or vacant. **9** abandon; forsake. **leave out** omit; fail to consider.

leave[2] *n* **1** permission. **2** time off from duty or work. **take one's leave (of)** depart (from); say goodbye (to).

leaves *n pl* of **leaf**.

lecherous *adj* lewd; lascivious; lustful. **lecher** *n*. **lechery** *n*.

lectern *n* stand for the Bible in a church.

lecture *n* **1** formal talk given to instruct an audience, esp. as part of a university course. **2** rebuke; reproof; scolding; reprimand. *vt,vi* deliver a lecture (to). **lecturer** *n*. **lectureship** *n*.

ledge *n* narrow horizontal shelf projecting from a wall, window, cliff, etc.

ledger *n* book in which credits and debits of an account are recorded.

leech *n* **1** blood-sucking wormlike animal living usually in water. **2** person who lives off another's efforts.

leek *n* vegetable related to the onion, having a long edible greenish-white bulb.

leer *vi* stare lustfully, mockingly, or slyly. *n* lascivious, mocking, or sly look. **leery** *adj*.

left[1] *v pt* and *pp* of **leave**[1].

left[2] *adj* of or on the side of a person or thing that is turned towards the west when facing north. *adv* towards the left side. *n* direction, location, or part that is on the left side. **the Left** party or political group following radical or socialist policies. **left-hand** *adj* on the side towards the left. **left-handed** *adj* using the left hand for writing, etc. **left w'ng** *n* the Left. *adj* **left-wing** relating to the left wing.

leg *n* **1** limb used for walking, standing, running, etc. **2** upright support of a chair, table, etc. **3** part of a garment covering the leg. **4** particular stage of a journey, race, or competition. **not have a leg to stand on** be unable to defend oneself; have no justifiable case. **on its/one's last legs** about to disintegrate or collapse; worn out. **pull someone's leg** hoax; tease; deceive jokingly. *v* **leg it** (-gg-) walk; go on foot.

legacy *n* gift of property left by will; bequest.

legal *adj* **1** relating to law. **2** authorized or required by law; legitimate; lawful. **legality** *n*. **legally** *adv*. **legalize** *vt* make legal; sanction by law. **legalization** *n*.

legend *n* traditional story popularly believed to concern actual people or events. **legendary** *adj* known from legend; renowned.

legible *adj* written so as to be clear to read; easily deciphered.

legion *n* **1** military unit of Ancient Rome comprising several thousand soldiers. **2** vast number; multitude.

legislate *vi,vt* formulate officially and pass laws (about). **legislation** *n*. **legislative** *adj*. **legislator** *n*. **legislature** *n* body of statesmen who pass laws; parliament.

legitimate *adj* **1** permitted by law; legal. **2** conforming to rules; allowable; permissible. **3** logical; justifiable. **4** born of parents who are legally married. **legitimacy** *n*. **legitimately** *adv*.

leisure *n* period outside working hours; free time. **at leisure** when free; at a convenient time. **leisurely** *adj* without haste; unhurried. *adv* at an easy or unhurried rate or pace.

lemon *n* sharp-tasting citrus fruit with a bright yellow skin. *n,adj* bright light yellow.

lend *vt* (lent) **1** give with the expectation of repayment or return; loan. **2** add to the quality or character of; impart. **lend a hand** help; cooperate; assist. **lender** *n*.

length *n* **1** measurement of something from one end to another. **2** time taken from beginning to end; duration. **3** piece of cloth, rope, wire, etc. **at arm's length** at a distance; apart. **at length 1** in great detail; for a long time. **2** eventually. **lengthen** *vt,vi* make or become longer. **lengthways** *adj,adv also* **lengthwise** measured from one end to another. **lengthy** *adj* long and detailed.

lenient *adj* not strict; inclined not to punish severely. **leniency** *n*. **leniently** *adv*.

lens *n* piece of transparent material with curved surfaces for converging or diverging a beam of light.

Lent *n* period of forty days before Easter, traditionally observed by Christians as a time for fasting and penitence.

lentil *n* plant producing brownish-orange seeds, which are eaten as a vegetable, used to thicken soups, etc.

Leo *n* fifth sign of the zodiac, represented by the Lion.

leopard *n* large animal of the cat family having a yellowish coat with black markings.

leprosy *n* infectious disease characterized by skin inflammation and disfigurement. **leper** *n* person suffering from leprosy.

lesbian *n* woman who has a sexual relationship with someone of her own sex; female homosexual. **lesbianism** *n*.

less *adj,adv* not as much; to a smaller extent; not as often. *prep* minus. *pron* a smaller amount. **lessen** *vt,vi* make or become less; reduce; decrease. **lesser** *adj* smaller; less important.

lesson *n* **1** period of time spent learning or teaching. **2** something that is learned or taught. **3** short reading from the Bible given during a service.

lest *conj* in case; for fear that; so as to avoid.

let *vt* (-tt-; let) **1** allow; permit. **2** rent or hire (accommodation, etc.). **let alone 1** leave alone. **2** not to mention; apart from. **let down 1** lower; take down. **2** deflate. **3** disappoint; fail to keep a promise. **let (someone) know** inform; tell. **let off 1** excuse; pardon; refrain from punishing. **2** cause to explode. **3** release; allow to escape. **let on** divulge; tell; reveal. **let out 1** allow to leave. **2** divulge; leak. **3** alter (a garment) so as to be larger. **4** utter; emit. **let up**

cease; become less persistent. **let-down** *n* disappointment; anticlimax.

lethal *adj* likely to cause death; highly dangerous.

lethargy ('leθədʒi) *n* extreme lack of energy or vitality; inertia; sleepiness; idleness; sluggishness. **lethargic** (le'θɑːdʒik) *adj*.

letter *n* 1 written message or account that is sent to someone. 2 written or printed alphabetical symbol or character. **letter of the law** the law when interpreted literally. **lettering** *n* art or practice of inscribing letters.

lettuce *n* vegetable with broad green leaves used in salads.

leukaemia *n* disease in which an excessive number of white corpuscles in the blood is produced.

level *adj* 1 having an even surface or plane; horizontal. 2 not tilted or sloping. 3 equal; even. 4 *also* **level-headed** calm and sensible; not inclined to panic. *n* 1 measured height or altitude. 2 flat even surface or area. 3 standard or status; grade. 4 instrument or device for measuring or checking that something is horizontal or level. 5 layer; stratum. **on the level** *inf* honest; straightforward. ~*vt* (-ll-) 1 make level or horizontal; line up. 2 equalize; bring to the same standard or status; even up. 3 raze; demolish. 4 take aim with; point. 5 direct (a remark, gaze, etc.). **levelly** *adv.* **levelness** *n.* **level crossing** *n* intersection of a road and railway track.

lever *n* 1 bar or rod used to move a heavy object, set machinery in motion, etc. 2 means of persuasion or coercion. *vt,vi* use a lever (on); prise. **leverage** *n* 1 force or action of a lever. 2 means of exerting power or influence.

levy *n* tax; duty; toll. *vt,vi* impose a levy (on).

lewd *adj* 1 lecherous; lustful. 2 vulgar; crude; obscene; indecent.

liable *adj* 1 obliged by law; subject (to). 2 likely; apt; inclined. **liability** *n* 1 legal obligation. 2 likelihood; probability. 3 tendency; inclination. 4 responsibility; burden; disadvantage; drawback.

liaison *n* 1 close working relationship; association; cooperation. 2 illicit sexual rela-

tionship. **liaise** *vi* work together; cooperate.

liar *n* person who tells lies.

libel *n* 1 written defamatory statement. 2 crime of publishing such a statement. *vt* (-ll-) publish libel about. **libellous** *adj.*

liberal *adj* 1 tolerant, esp. on political or religious matters. 2 progressive; enlightened. 3 generous; free. **Liberal** *n* member or supporter of the Liberal Party. **Liberal Party** *n* British political party advocating individual freedom and occupying a position to the right of the Labour Party but to the left of the Conservative Party.

liberate *vt* set free; release; emancipate. **liberation** *n.*

liberty *n* freedom from restraint, restriction, or control. **take liberties (with)** take unfair advantage (of).

Libra *n* seventh sign of the zodiac, represented by the Scales.

library *n* 1 room or building housing a collection of books. 2 collection of films, documents, etc. **librarian** *n* person working in a library. **librarianship** *n.*

libretto *n* text of an opera, operetta, etc.

lice *n pl* of **louse**.

licence *n* 1 official document or certificate of authorization. 2 permission granted by an authority. 3 misuse of freedom; lack of self-control. 4 allowable deviation from a particular convention, esp. in art or literature.

license *vt* grant or authorize a licence (for). **licensee** *n* person holding a licence, esp. to sell alcoholic drinks.

lichen ('laikən, 'litʃən) *n* moss-like plant that grows on tree-trunks, rocks, etc.

lick *vt,vi* 1 touch or stroke with the tongue. 2 *inf* beat or defeat soundly. 3 *inf* thrash; flog. **lick into shape** improve or groom by special training or instruction. ~*n* 1 stroke of the tongue. 2 *inf* pace; rate; speed.

lid *n* 1 cover for a container. 2 eyelid.

lie[1] *n* untrue statement, esp. one deliberately intended to deceive. *vi* (lying) tell a lie or lies.

lie[2] *vi* (lying; lay; lain) 1 be stretched out or placed in a horizontal position; rest. 2 be situated. 3 be buried. 4 be the responsibility (of). **lie in** remain in bed for longer than usual. **lie low** remain in hiding.

lieu (lu:) *n* **in lieu of** instead of; in place of.

lieutenant (lef'tenənt) *n* **1** military officer of a rank below that of captain. **2** naval officer of a rank below that of lieutenant commander. **lieutenant colonel** *n* military officer of a rank below that of colonel. **lieutenant commander** *n* naval officer of a rank below that of commander.

life *n, pl* **lives 1** condition of existing or being alive; being. **2** *also* **lifetime** period of existence; length of time lived. **3** all living things. **4** biographical account. **5** liveliness; vivacity; vitality. **6** way of living; mode of existence. **7** maximum prison sentence that can be awarded. **come to life 1** recover consciousness; be revived. **2** become lively or animated. **lifeboat** *n* boat used for searching for those in distress at sea or one carried by a ship in case of emergency. **lifeguard** *n* person who patrols the shore, attends a swimming pool, etc., for the safety of swimmers. **lifelike** *adj* resembling something real. **lifeless** *adj* **1** dead. **2** motionless; seemingly dead. **3** dull; uninspired. **lifeline** *n* **1** rope used in life-saving. **2** something that ensures survival. **lifelong** *adj* lasting throughout one's life; permanent. **life-saving** *n* practice or method of rescuing someone in distress, esp. at sea. *adj* able to save life.

lift *vt* **1** take or carry upwards; pull up; haul; raise. **2** turn or direct upwards. **3** put into a happy or cheerful mood; gladden. **4** exalt; elevate. **5** revoke or cancel (a ban, restriction, etc.). **6** *inf* steal; shoplift. **7** *inf* copy or borrow (an idea, piece of text, etc.). **8** dig up (plants). *vi* **1** move upwards; rise. **2** (of fog, mist, etc.) clear; disperse. *n* **1** act of lifting or raising. **2** boxlike compartment driven hydraulically, mechanically, or by electricity that moves vertically between floors of a building. **3** free ride in someone else's vehicle. **4** something that gives one energy or makes one cheerful or happy. **lift-off** *n* launching of a rocket; blast-off.

light¹ *n* **1** brightness emitted by the sun, a lamp, etc. **2** daylight. **3** source of illumination. **4** match, etc., that produces a flame. **5** aspect; context; view. **6** enlightenment; knowledge. **7** small window pane. **bring/ come to light** make/become known or apparent. **in the light of** taking into account; with the knowledge of. **set light to** ignite or kindle. **shed** *or* **throw light on** clarify; explain. ~*adj* **1** not dark; illuminated. **2** of a pale or pastel shade or colour. **3** fair-haired. *vt, vi* (lit *or* lighted) **1** set light to; ignite. **2** provide with light or illumination. **light up 1** illuminate; make bright. **2** apply a match to. **3** cause to sparkle or shine; brighten. **light bulb** *n* glass bulb containing a metal filament, which lights up when an electrical current is passed through it. **lighten** *vt, vi* brighten; make or become light(er). **lighter** *n* device producing a flame for lighting cigarettes, etc. **lighthouse** *n* tower situated on or near the coast that sends out a powerful light as a guide or warning to shipping.

light² *adj* **1** not heavy; weighing little. **2** not forceful; gentle; not hard. **3** of a small amount; slight. **4** not overpowering; subtle. **5** buoyant. **6** *also* **light-headed** giddy; faint; dizzy. **7** *also* **light-hearted** cheerful; not serious; happy. **8** not severe or strict; lenient. **9** airy; spongy; porous. **10** not classical or highbrow. **11** nimble; graceful or quick. **12** not arduous; simple or easy. **make light of** treat as unimportant; make no fuss about. ~*adv* without being weighed down; comfortably. *vi* (lighted *or* lit) settle or perch; alight. **light (up)on** come across by chance; discover. **lightly** *adv.* **lightness** *n.* **lighten** *vt, vi* **1** make or become less heavy. **2** make or become more cheerful, optimistic, etc.; lift. **lightweight** *adj* **1** light in weight. **2** not intellectually demanding; superficial. *n* boxer whose weight is between 126 lbs and 135 lbs.

lightning *n* electricity discharged in the atmosphere producing a flash of light and usually accompanied by thunder. **like lightning** with tremendous speed.

like¹ *prep* **1** very similar to; in the manner of; the same as. **2** for example; such as. **3** as though; as if. **feel like 1** desire; want; be tempted or inclined to. **2** have the sensation of; resemble; feel similar to. **like-minded** *adj* having the same or similar views or opinions. **liken** *vt* compare; draw an analogy or find a resemblance (between). **likeness** *n* **1** resemblance; similarity. **2** representation in a painting, photograph, etc.

likewise *adv* **1** similarly; in the same way. **2** moreover; furthermore; also.

like² *vt* be fond of; find pleasing, attractive, agreeable, etc. *vi,vt* wish; prefer; choose.

likely *adj* probable; to be expected; liable. *adv* probably; possibly. **likelihood** *n*.

lilac *n* hardy shrub having fragrant purple, mauve, or white flowers.

lilt *n* **1** rhythmic or melodious quality in speech or music. **2** tune or song with such a quality. *vi,vt* sing, speak, or sound with a lilt.

lily *n* bulb producing large white, purple, yellow, or orange flowers. **lily-of-the-valley** *n* small plant having fragrant white bell-shaped flowers and broad leaves.

limb *n* **1** part of the body attached to the trunk, such as an arm or leg. **2** branch; bough. **(out) on a limb** isolated and vulnerable.

limbo *n* **1** supposed state of those who have died without being baptized. **2** state of being unwanted, cast aside, or without a proper place.

lime¹ *n* **1** *also* **quicklime** calcium oxide; white substance made from limestone. **2** *also* **slaked lime** calcium hydroxide; white substance produced by adding water to quicklime. *vt* treat with lime. **limelight** *n* **in the limelight** attracting a great deal of public notice or acclaim. **limestone** *n* whitish rock composed of calcium carbonate.

lime² *n* green-skinned citrus fruit similar to a lemon.

limerick *n* humorous five-lined poem.

limit *n* **1** extent to which something is possible or permissible. **2** most acceptable amount; minimum or maximum. **3** boundary. *vt* place a restriction on. **limitation** *n* restriction; limiting circumstance.

limp¹ *vi* walk in an abnormal way because of injury or disablement; be lame. *n* act of limping.

limp² *adj* **1** sagging; not rigid; floppy. **2** feeble; weak.

limpet *n* marine mollusc having a conical shell that clings to rocks, etc.

line¹ *n* **1** mark drawn in pencil, paint, etc., across a surface. **2** groove; crease; furrow. **3** row; column. **4** outline; edge. **5** boundary; limit. **6** cable, rope, cord, or string used for a particular purpose. **7** means of transport; route. **8** railway track. **9** policy; method or system. **10** direction taken by a missile. **11** field of research; area of interest. **12** single horizontal row of written or printed words. *vt* **1** draw lines on. **2** produce grooves or furrows in. **3** form a row along; border. **line up 1** set in a straight or orderly row or line. **2** provide; organize.

line² *vt* provide with an inside covering or layer of material.

lineage *n* line of descent from a common ancestor.

linear ('liniə) *adj* **1** relating to a line. **2** made up of lines. **3** of one dimension only.

linen *n* **1** strong fabric of woven flax. **2** sheets, tablecloths, etc., made esp. of linen.

liner *n* ship designed to carry a large number of passengers.

linger *vi* **1** be reluctant to hurry away; stay behind; loiter. **2** remain or persist, esp. as a memory.

lingerie ('lɑːnʒəri) *n* women's underwear and nightwear.

linguist *n* **1** person who is able to speak one or more foreign languages skilfully. **2** student of linguistics. **linguistic** *adj* relating to language, linguistics, or speech. **linguistics** *n* study of the structure or history of language.

lining *n* material used to line a coat, curtain, etc.

link *n* **1** single loop forming part of a chain. **2** connecting part or piece in a mechanism. **3** connection or relationship between people, different places, times, etc. *vt,vi* form a link (between); connect; relate.

linoleum *n* *also* **lino** material having a canvas backing coated with linseed oil, cork, etc., used as a floor covering.

linseed *n* seed of flax from which oil is extracted.

lion *n* **1** large mammal of the cat family, the male of which has a shaggy mane. **2** powerful or strong person. **lioness** *f n*.

lip *n* **1** one of two fleshy parts surrounding the opening of the mouth. **2** that part of the rim of a jug, etc., that channels liquid being poured out. **3** *sl* impudent remark. **lip-read** *vi,vt* (-read) interpret (speech) by following a person's lip movements. **lipstick** *n* cosmetic used to add colour to the lips.

liqueur *n* sweet alcoholic drink generally taken after a meal.

liquid *n* substance that can flow but cannot easily be compressed. *adj* 1 relating to a liquid; capable of flowing. 2 harmonious; flowing. 3 (of assets) readily convertible into cash. **liquidate** *vt* 1 settle (debts). 2 dissolve (a company) by realizing assets in order to pay off creditors, shareholders, etc. 3 dispose of (an enemy, spy, etc.) by violent means. **liquidize** *vt,vi* *also* **liquefy** make or become liquid.

liquor *n* any alcoholic drink, esp. a spirit.

liquorice *n* black substance extracted from the root of a shrub for use in medicines, confectionery, etc.

lira ('liərə) *n, pl* **lire** ('liəri) *or* **liras** standard monetary unit of Italy.

lisp *n* manner of pronunciation in which *s* and *z* sound like *th*. *vt,vi* pronounce or speak with a lisp.

list¹ *n* record or statement placing a number of items one after the other. *vt* place on a list; make a list of.

list² *vi* (of a ship) lean to one side. *n* leaning to one side.

listen *vi* 1 pay attention or concentrate in order to hear. 2 take notice; heed. **listener** *n.*

listless *adj* not energetic; lethargic; weary.

lit *v* a *pt* and *pp* of **light¹** and **light²**.

literal *adj* 1 not metaphorical. 2 interpreted or translated word for word. **literally** *adv.*

literary *adj* concerning literature, authorship, or scholarship.

literate *adj* able to read and write. **literacy** *n.*

literature *n* body of written material, such as novels, poetry, or drama.

lithe *adj* supple; moving easily or gracefully.

litmus *n* type of vegetable dye that turns red in acids and blue in alkalis.

litre *n* unit of volume equal to one thousand cubic centimetres.

litter *n* 1 rubbish or refuse that is dropped or left lying about, esp. in a public place. 2 set of offspring produced by a sow, bitch, etc., at one birth. *vt* 1 cover or make untidy with litter. 2 scatter or be scattered untidily on.

little *adj* 1 small; tiny; not big or tall. 2 not important; trivial. 3 brief; not lasting long. *pron* not much. *adv* not often; hardly at all. **a little** *pron* a small number or quantity. *adv* to a small extent. **little by little** gradually.

live¹ (liv) *vi* 1 exist; be alive; have life. 2 have one's home (in); reside; stay. 3 continue; flourish. 4 make a living. *vt* 1 spend (one's life). 2 have as a fundamental part of one's life. **live up to** match (required standards or expectations).

live² (laiv) *adj* 1 alive; not dead; living. 2 stimulating; interesting. 3 (of a shell, cartridge, etc.) not yet exploded. 4 broadcast directly without being previously recorded. 5 carrying electric current. **livestock** *n s or pl* animals kept or reared on a farm, such as cattle, pigs, or poultry.

livelihood *n* means of earning a living.

lively *adj* 1 active; having energy; vigorous. 2 busy; fully occupied. 3 alert; quick. 4 bright; cheerful. **liveliness** *n.*

liver *n* reddish-brown organ situated below the diaphragm in the body that secretes bile, neutralizes toxic substances, etc.

livid *adj* 1 extremely angry; furious. 2 discoloured, as when bruised.

living *adj* still alive; not yet dead or extinct. *n* 1 livelihood. 2 way of life. **living room** *n* room in a house used for recreation, receiving guests, etc.

lizard *n* reptile having four limbs, a long tail, and a scaly body.

llama *n* mammal related to but smaller than a camel, valued for its fleece.

load *n* 1 something carried or transported. 2 cargo. 3 burden; weight of responsibility, etc. 4 *inf* large amount; lot; heap. *vt,vi* 1 place a load on or in (a lorry, ship, etc.). 2 burden. 3 put ammunition in (a gun).

loaf¹ *n, pl* **loaves** baked bread in a particular shape.

loaf² *vi* pass time idly; lounge; loiter.

loan *n* something lent, such as a sum of money or a book from a library. **on loan** borrowed. ~*vt,vi* lend.

loathe *vt* hate; detest; abhor. **loathsome** *adj* detestable; abhorrent.

lob *vt,vi* (-bb-) hit or bowl (a ball) so as to form a high arc. *n* ball hit or bowled in such a way.

lobby *n* 1 entrance hall, waiting room, or corridor. 2 group seeking to persuade officials, members of parliament, etc., to support or oppose a particular policy or piece of legislation. *vt,vi* seek to influence as a lobby.

lobe *n* 1 lower fleshy part of the ear. 2 subdivision of certain organs such as the lung or brain.

lobster *n* large edible crustacean with long claws or pincers.

local *adj* 1 belonging to or concerning a particular district or locality. 2 affecting a particular part of the body. *n* 1 person belonging to the locality. 2 *inf* public house nearest to one's home or place of work. **locality** *n* neighbourhood; vicinity; district. **localize** *vt* 1 limit to a particular part of the body. 2 make local.

locate *vt* 1 look for and find the position of. 2 situate; place; position. **location** *n* 1 place; site; position. 2 act of locating or finding. 3 place other than a studio, where a film is shot.

loch *n* (in Scotland) lake or narrow sea inlet.

lock¹ *n* 1 device for securely fastening a door, drawer, box, etc., operated usually by means of a key. 2 section of a canal or river enclosed within a barrier or gate, which can be opened or shut to control the water level. 3 wrestling hold in which a limb or the head is unable to move. *vt,vi* 1 fasten or become secure with a lock. 2 jam; fix so as to be unable to move. 3 interlock.

lock² *n* length or curl of hair from or on the head.

locker *n* cupboard provided esp. in a public building, used for storing personal property, clothes, etc.

locket *n* small case containing a portrait, memento, etc., attached to a chain and worn as a necklace.

locomotion *n* power of motion. **locomotive** *n* engine driven by steam, electricity, or diesel power, used to draw a train along a railway track.

locust *n* insect of the grasshopper family that travels in swarms stripping vegetation over a wide area.

lodge *vt,vi* 1 provide or be provided with accommodation, esp. in a private household. 2 embed or become embedded (in); wedge. *vt* 1 make (a formal complaint). 2 deposit for safekeeping. *n* 1 small house located near or at the gate of a park, estate, etc. 2 cabin or house used by hunters, skiers, etc. **lodger** *n* person lodging in a private household. **lodgings** *pl n* accommodation, such as rented rooms in a private household.

loft *n* 1 room or space immediately below the roof of a house. 2 upper floor of a barn, stable, etc., where hay is stored. 3 building constructed as a shelter for racing pigeons. **lofty** *adj* 1 high and imposing. 2 idealistic; noble. 3 haughty; arrogant.

log *n* 1 section of a felled branch or tree trunk. 2 regular or daily record kept during a voyage, flight, etc. *vt* (-gg-) 1 fell or saw (logs). 2 record as a log. **logbook** *n* book in which records or logs are kept.

logarithm *n* power to which a base number, usually 10, is raised to give a specified number, tabulated as an aid to calculation. **logarithmic** *adj*.

logic *n* 1 branch of philosophy concerned with determining the validity of particular statements according to certain principles of reasoning. 2 consistency of method or practice; validity of reasoning. **logical** *adj*. **logically** *adv*.

loins *pl n* lower part of the back and sides of the body.

loiter *vi* lurk; linger; move about aimlessly. **loiterer** *n*.

loll *vi* laze; lounge. *vt,vi* droop; sag; hang loosely.

lollipop *n* 1 boiled sweet on a small stick. 2 ice lolly.

lonely *adj* 1 without friends; isolated; alone. 2 remote; desolate. **loneliness** *n*. **lone** *adj* solitary; single.

long¹ *adj* 1 of considerable extent from one end to another; not short. 2 lasting for a considerable time. 3 of a particular length or duration. 4 having a large number of entries, parts, etc. **in the long run** over a long period. *adv* for a particular time. **as long as** on condition that; provided that. *n* **before long** after a short time; soon. **for long** for a long time. **no/any longer** no/any more. **long-sighted** *adj* 1 able to see clearly at a distance. 2 having imagination or foresight. **long-standing** *adj* having been in effect over a long period. **long-**

winded *adj* using an excessive number of words; tediously long.

long² *v* **long for** crave; yearn for; desire. **longing** *n.*

longevity *n* relatively long life span or state of living to a great age.

longitude *n* angular distance east or west of a standard meridian (through Greenwich).

loo *n inf* lavatory or toilet.

look *vi* **1** *also* **look at** direct the eyes (towards) in order to see. **2** *also* **look at** begin to examine; attend (to). **3** seem; appear; be likely to be. **4** face; overlook. **5** *also* **look for** search (for); seek. **6** *also* **look through** read; glance at; scan. *vt* **1** direct one's gaze at; stare or glance at. **2** have the appearance of being; correspond to. **look after** take care of; tend; be in charge of. **look down on** regard as inferior or worthy of contempt. **look forward (to)** anticipate with pleasure. **look out** be cautious; heed. **look up** begin to improve. **look up to** admire; respect. ~*n* **1** act of looking. **2** appearance; impression. **lookout** *n* **1** person placed on guard, to watch out for danger, etc. **2** *inf* matter for personal concern; affair. **looks** *pl n* physical appearance.

loom¹ *n* machine for weaving by hand or mechanically.

loom² *vi* **1** approach or appear menacingly. **2** give an impression of greatness; dominate.

loop *n* shape of a circle, oval, spiral, etc., formed by string, wire, etc.; coil. *vt,vi* form a loop.

loophole *n* flaw or ambiguity in a law, contract, etc., that enables one to evade obligations, penalties, etc.

loose *adj* **1** not tight; slack. **2** not fastened or fitted securely. **3** not put in a bundle or tied together. **4** free; not confined. **5** not compact. **6** approximate; rough. **7** promiscuous. **8** not careful; sloppy. **9** not controlled. **at a loose end** having nothing in particular to do; not occupied. ~*adv also* **loosely** in a loose manner. *vt* **1** liberate; set free; allow to escape. **2** loosen; slacken. **loosen** *vt,vi* make or become loose(r); slacken; unfasten.

loot *n* money, property, etc., stolen or seized, esp. during a battle or riot. *vt,vi* steal; plunder. **looter** *n.*

lop *vt* (-pp-) chop or sever (branches, a limb, etc.) swiftly and in one movement.

lopsided *adj* tilted to one side; uneven or crooked; not symmetrical.

lord *n* nobleman. **Lord 1** title, rank, or form of address of certain male members of the nobility. **2** title of certain high officials in the Church or of the law. **the Lord 1** God. **2** Jesus Christ. **the Lords** House of Lords. *v* **lord (it) over** be master of; dominate. **lordship** *n* rank of a lord. **Your/His Lordship** form of address used to/of certain men with the rank of Lord and also bishops and judges of the high court.

lorry *n* motor vehicle for carrying heavy loads, transporting goods, etc.; truck.

lose *v* (lost) *vt* **1** drop or leave (something) and be unable to find it again. **2** decrease in power, speed, etc. **3** be deprived of as through death, accident, etc. **4** be unable to maintain (a particular state, belief, etc.). **5** fail to take advantage of or use. *vt,vi* **1** fail to win; suffer defeat (in). **2** (of a watch, clock, etc.) be slow (by). **loser** *n.* **loss** *n* act of losing or that which is lost. **at a loss** helpless; incapable.

lot *pron* **a lot** a large number or quantity; much or many; a great deal. *n* **1** group; collection; bunch. **2** assigned task. **3** article or set of items in an auction. **draw lots** select at random by using tickets, slips, etc. *adv* **a lot 1** to a great extent. **2** often; regularly.

lotion *n* liquid preparation used as a skin cleanser, antiseptic, etc.

lottery *n* **1** system of raising money by selling tickets, one or more of which are drawn at random to entitle the holder to a prize. **2** situation governed by luck or chance.

lotus *n* **1** mythical fruit that induces laziness or forgetfulness. **2** variety of tropical water lily.

loud *adj* **1** of a relatively high volume of sound; not quiet. **2** of a vulgar style; garish. *adv also* **loudly** in a loud manner. **out loud** aloud. **loudness** *n.* **loud-mouthed** *adj* rude; abusive; brash. **loudspeaker** *n* device for converting electrical signals into sound that can be heard over a wide area.

lounge n 1 sitting room. 2 room or area at an airport, hotel, etc., where one may sit or wait. 3 also **lounge bar** saloon bar. vi laze; move or sit idly.

louse n, pl **lice** wingless bloodsucking insect that is a parasite of mammals. **lousy** adj 1 infested with lice. 2 inf very bad; awful.

lout n uncouth person.

love n 1 feeling of deep passion, desire, affection, or fondness. 2 score of nil in tennis, squash, etc. **make love (to)** have sexual intercourse (with). ~vt,vi feel love (for). **lover** n. **lovesick** adj pining; suffering through love.

lovely adj 1 giving pleasure; nice; highly enjoyable. 2 beautiful; attractive. **loveliness** n.

low[1] adj 1 not tall or high; relatively close to the ground. 2 close to the bottom of a particular scale, grade, etc.; poor. 3 inferior; below average. 4 mean; despicable. 5 depressed or ill. 6 almost empty; having only a small amount left. 7 deep and quiet. adv towards or into a low position, state, or condition. **lie low** remain hidden, esp. to avoid capture. **lowness** n. **lowbrow** adj relating to a style or taste, esp. in the arts, that is not very sophisticated or intellectual; not highbrow. **lower** vt,vi 1 decrease; reduce. 2 move downwards. **lower case** n printed letters of the alphabet that are not capitals. **lowland** n region or area that is relatively flat. **lowlander** n.

low[2] vt,vi,n (of cattle) moo.

loyal adj faithful; maintaining allegiance; patriotic. **loyally** adv. **loyalty** n.

lozenge n 1 small tablet eaten as a sweet for medicinal purposes. 2 diamond-shaped equilateral figure.

LSD n **lysergic acid diethylamide**: synthetic hallucinatory drug.

lubricate vt apply oil or grease to. **lubrication** n. **lubricant** n lubricating substance; oil. adj serving to lubricate.

lucid adj 1 expressed in a way that is easily understood; clear. 2 shining; bright. **lucidity** n.

luck n 1 state of affairs, event, etc., apparently occurring at random; chance; fortune. 2 good fortune. **lucky** adj having or bringing good luck; fortunate. **luckily** adv fortunately.

lucrative adj profitable.

ludicrous adj absurd; ridiculous.

lug vt (-gg-) pull or carry with effort; drag.

luggage n suitcases, bags, etc., carried on a journey; baggage.

lukewarm adj 1 tepid; moderately warm. 2 not enthusiastic.

lull vt soothe; make calm or drowsy. n brief respite or period of tranquillity. **lullaby** n soothing song intended to lull a child to sleep.

lumbago n backache.

lumber[1] n 1 (esp. in North America) timber or logs. 2 large unwanted furniture or other household articles. vt 1 store or fill with household lumber. 2 inf burden with an unpleasant duty, boring person, etc. **lumberjack** n (esp. in North America) person who fells trees and cuts timber.

lumber[2] vi move clumsily and heavily.

luminous adj reflecting light.

lump n 1 solid mass, usually irregular in shape. 2 swelling; bump. vt also **lump together** place in or consider to be one group or mass. **lumpy** adj having many lumps; bumpy.

lunar adj relating to the moon.

lunatic n insane person. **lunacy** n madness; insanity.

lunch n also **luncheon** midday meal. vi eat lunch.

lung n one of a pair of respiratory organs situated in the thorax that oxygenates the blood.

lunge n 1 thrust of a sword in fencing. 2 sudden forward movement. vi make or move with a lunge.

lupin n plant with a tall stem bearing bright flowers of various colours.

lurch[1] vi stagger; sway; jerk or jog violently. n sudden violent jerk or stagger.

lurch[2] n **leave in the lurch** abandon at a critical time; forsake.

lure vt entice in order to trap; tempt.

lurid adj 1 sensational; shocking; scandalous. 2 having strange bright colours.

lurk vi loiter; lie in wait; remain hidden.

luscious adj 1 gorgeous; delightful. 2 having a rich flavour; succulent.

lush *adj* **1** characterized by rich dense growth; luxuriant; abundant. **2** luxurious.

lust *n* **1** strong sexual desire. **2** craving; passion; greed. **lustful** *adj* consumed with lust. **lusty** *adj* robust; hearty; vigorous.

lustre *n* brightness or gloss of a surface; sheen; shine; radiance. **lustrous** *adj*.

lute *n* pear-shaped stringed instrument of the 14th–17th centuries, related to the guitar. **lutenist** *n*.

luxury *n* **1** condition of having all that one needs to gratify one's desires. **2** item not regarded as a necessity. **luxuriant** *adj* abundant; lush. **luxurious** *adj* providing luxury. **luxuriously** *adv*.

lynch *vt* (of a mob) hunt down and kill without legal trial.

lynx *n* long-eared wild cat inhabiting forest regions in parts of Europe, North America, and Africa.

lyre *n* stringed instrument of ancient Greece, resembling a small harp.

lyric *adj* relating to a style of poetry expressing personal feelings, originally recited to a lyre accompaniment. **lyrical** *adj* **1** expressive of the emotions of love, sorrow, etc. **2** enthusiastically eloquent. **lyrics** *pl n* words of a song.

M

mac *n* short for **mackintosh**.

macabre (mə'ka:brə) *adj* suggesting or associated with death; frightening.

macaroni *n* type of pasta shaped into thin tubes.

mace[1] *n* **1** hammer-like medieval weapon with a spiked metal head. **2** ceremonial staff that is a symbol of office.

mace[2] *n* spice produced from nutmeg.

machine *n* **1** apparatus that performs useful work using applied forces. **2** mechanism, such as a car or aeroplane. **3** highly organized controlling body. *vt,vi* use a machine to shape, cut, or work on something. **machine gun** *n* automatically loaded and repeatedly firing gun. **machine-gun** *vt* (-nn-) shoot at with a machine gun. **machinery** *n* **1** machines or machine parts. **2** system or way of organization. **machinist** *n* person who makes or works on machines.

mackerel *n, pl* **mackerel** *or* **mackerels** marine food fish with a silvery belly and green stripes on its back.

mackintosh *n* light coat worn esp. as protection from rain; raincoat.

mad *adj* **1** mentally disturbed; insane. **2** eccentric; crazy. **3** *inf* extremely pleased, angry, enthusiastic, noisy, etc. **drive** *or* **make someone mad** annoy. **go mad** become very excited, angry, pleased, etc. **madly** *adv*. **madness** *n*. **madden** *vt,vi* anger; excite; irritate.

madam *n* polite form of address to a woman.

made *v pt* and *pp* of **make**.

Madonna *n* Virgin Mary, esp. when painted or a statue.

madrigal *n* **1** love poem or song. **2** part song performed usually by six or seven voices without musical accompaniment.

magazine *n* **1** paper-covered periodical containing contributions from various writers and usually illustrated. **2** place where arms, explosives, etc., are stored. **3** replaceable metal containers for cartridges inserted into some automatic guns or rifles.

maggot larva of a housefly, etc., often breeding in decaying matter.

magic *n* **1** art of producing certain effects with the help of supernatural forces; witchcraft. **2** art of producing seemingly inexplicable results by means of tricks. **3** mysterious power or agency. *adj* **1** relating to magic. **2** *also* **magical** as if by magic; miraculous; enchanting. **magician** *n* person who is skilled in tricks or in spells.

magistrate *n* person who officiates in a lower court of law; justice of the peace. **magisterial** *adj* **1** relating to a magistrate. **2** dictatorial; authoritative.

magnanimous *adj* generous; noble; not petty. **magnanimity** *n*. **magnanimously** *adv*.

magnate *n* wealthy highly influential person, esp. in industry.

magnet *n* piece of iron or steel that can attract iron or steel objects and point north when suspended. **magnetic** *adj* **1** relating to a magnet or magnetism. **2** attractive; alluring. **magnetism** *n* **1** science or attractive properties of magnets. **2** charm; attractiveness. **magnetize** *vt* **1** make magnetic. **2** attract.

magnificent *adj* remarkable; splendid. **magnificence** *n.* **magnificently** *adv.*

magnify *vt* **1** make apparently larger, esp. by means of a lens or microscope. **2** exaggerate. **magnification** *n.*

magnitude *n* **1** size; extent. **2** importance; significance.

magnolia *n* shrub or tree with large, usually sweet-smelling creamy-pink flowers.

magpie *n* bird with a long tail, black-and-white plumage, and a chattering call.

mahogany *n* tropical American tree, the hard reddish-brown wood of which is used for furniture.

maid *n* **1** girl. **2** female servant. **old maid** old unmarried woman; spinster. **maiden** *n* young single woman. **maiden aunt** *n* unmarried aunt. **maiden name** *n* family name before a woman marries. **maiden speech** *n* first speech.

mail *n* **1** letters, parcels, etc., sent or received by post. **2** postal service. **mailing list** *n* list of names and addresses of persons to whom specific information is regularly sent. **mail order** *n* order and delivery of goods by post.

maim *vt* disable; cripple.

main *adj* chief; principal; most important. *n also* **mains** principal pipe or cable for gas, water, or electricity supply. **mainly** *adv.* **mainframe** *adj* of a large powerful type of computer as opposed to a smaller model. **mainland** *n* land mass, such as a country or continent, excluding its islands. **mainspring** *n* **1** chief spring of a clockwork mechanism. **2** driving force. **mainstream** *n* leading trend.

maintain *vt* **1** keep going; keep in fair condition; support. **2** assert. **maintainance** *n* **1** act or way of keeping or supporting a person or thing. **2** financial support, as after a divorce.

maize *n* tall annual grass grown for its yellow grain, used as food and fodder, and for its oil.

majesty *n* grandness; splendour; stateliness. **Majesty** term of address for a queen or king or the spouse or widow of a sovereign. **majestic** *adj* stately; dignified.

major *adj* **1** of greater importance, extent, size, etc. **2** of or relating to a musical scale in which the third and fourth and the seventh and eighth notes are a semitone apart. *n* military officer ranking below a lieutenant colonel and above a captain. **major general** *n* military officer ranking above a brigadier.

majority *n* **1** greater number, part, etc.; more than half. **2** number by which a winning vote in an election, etc., exceeds the runner-up. **3** state or time of reaching full legal age.

make *v* (made) *vt* **1** create; produce; construct; form; prepare; establish. **2** cause to be, become, or seem. **3** cause; force. **4** amount to; constitute. **5** earn; acquire. **6** develop into. **7** do; perform. **8** appoint. *vt,vi* cause to become or become (happy, sad, merry, etc.). *n* brand; style; way things are made. **on the make** *inf* seeking an easy profit or conquest. **make do (with)** be content with; improvise with. **make for** go towards. **make good 1** repair. **2** be successful in. **make it** achieve or reach a goal. **make off (with)** go or run off (with). **make out 1** understand. **2** see; discern. **3** write out or fill in (a cheque, etc.). **4** attempt to establish; represent as. **make up 1** complete; form. **2** invent; compose; fabricate. **3** reconcile or become reconciled. **4** apply cosmetics to the face, esp. for theatrical effect. **make-up** *n* **1** cosmetics. **2** person's constitution or personality. **make up for** compensate or atone for. **make up one's mind** decide; resolve.

make-believe *n* pretence; fantasy.

makeshift *adj* provisional; acting as a substitute. *n* makeshift object, method, etc.

maladjusted *adj* not adjusted or adapted properly to personal environment. **maladjustment** *n.*

malaria *n* infectious tropical disease transferred by mosquitoes and characterized by chills and high fever.

male *adj* **1** of or related to the sex that produces young by fertilizing the female; masculine. **2** composed of or for men or boys. *n* male person or animal.

malevolent *adj* harmful; evil; spiteful; malicious. **malevolence** *n.* **malevolently** *adv.*

malfunction *vi* fail to function properly. *n* failure to function properly.

malice *n* intention to inflict harm on another; spite. **malicious** *adj*. **maliciously** *adv*.

malignant *adj* **1** inclined to cause suffering; showing ill will. **2** (of disease) likely to cause death if not treated successfully. **malign** *vt* insult; slander. *adj* evil. **malignancy** *n*.

malleable *adj* (esp. of metal) easily shaped or treated.

mallet *n* hammer-shaped tool, usually with a wooden head.

malnutrition *n* defective or inadequate nutrition.

malt *n* grain, often barley, soaked then dried for use in brewing beers or distilling spirits.

maltreat *vt* treat in an abusive or cruel manner. **maltreatment** *n*.

mammal *n* any of the class of warm-blooded animals whose offspring are fed by mother's milk. **mammalian** *adj*. **mammography** *n* examination of the breast by X-rays usually to check for cancer.

mammoth *n* huge extinct elephant. *adj* huge.

man *n, pl* **men 1** human male adult. **2** individual; person. **3** mankind. **4** husband or lover. **5** workman; male employee. **6** piece in draughts, chess, etc. **man in the street** *n* person considered as representative of an average member of society. **to a man 1** unanimously. **2** completely; utterly. ~*vt* (-nn-) supply with people for a specific purpose. **manly** *adj* denoting conduct and qualities expected of a man. **manliness** *n*.

manage *vt,vi* control; be in charge (of); handle. *vt* succeed in; be successful in. *vi* cope. **manageable** *adj*. **management** *n* **1** managing techniques. **2** body of persons in charge of a business. **3** administration. **manager** *n* person managing or controlling a business, etc. **manageress** *f n*. **managerial** *adj*.

mandarin *n* **1** high-ranking official in imperial China. **2** high-ranking or pompous official. **3** small orange-like fruit. **Mandarin** *n* official Chinese dialect.

mandate *n* **1** authorization; official command. **2** sanction or support given to a gov-

ernment by the electorate. **mandatary** ('mændətəri) *n* person, body, or state holding a mandate. **mandatory** ('mændətəri) *adj* **1** having the nature or command of a mandate. **2** compulsory.

mandolin *n* musical instrument of the lute family with eight strings tuned and plucked in pairs.

mane *n* long growth of hair on the back of the neck of a horse, lion, etc.

mange *n* contagious skin disease of domestic animals, esp. dogs. **mangy** *adj* **1** having mange. **2** scruffy.

mangle[1] *vt* **1** disfigure as by severe cuts, etc; mutilate. **2** spoil by errors.

mangle[2] *n* machine with two rollers used for removing water from and smoothing clothes, etc. *vt* put through a mangle.

mango *n, pl* **mangos** *or* **mangoes** pear-shaped tropical fruit with sweet yellowish flesh, borne on an evergreen tree.

manhandle *vt* **1** treat roughly; use physical violence on. **2** use physical rather than mechanical force.

manhole *n* hole, covered by a lid, that serves as an access to a sewer, pipe, etc.

mania *n* **1** excessive excitement. **2** obsession or excessive liking for something. **3** condition characterized by abnormal excitement and often manifestations of violence. **maniac** *n* **1** person showing excessive enthusiasm for something; fanatic. **2** mad person; lunatic. **manic** *adj* relating to mania.

manicure *n* care or treatment of hands and fingernails. *vt* treat (fingernails) by cutting, varnishing, etc.

manifest *adj* quite apparent and obvious; visible. *vt* reveal clearly. **manifest itself** show itself; appear. **manifestation** *n*. **manifestly** *adv*.

manifesto *n* written declaration by a sovereign or body of people proclaiming certain principles or rights.

manifold *adj* of many parts, aspects, or uses; varied. **manifoldly** *adv*.

manipulate *vt* **1** operate skilfully; use; handle. **2** exercise shrewd control over; influence cleverly. **3** exercise treatment on. **manipulation** *n*. **manipulator** *n*.

mankind *n* human race.

man-made *adj* artificially produced.

manner *n* **1** way something happens or is done. **2** style. **3** particular way a person behaves towards others. **4** kind; sort. **manners** *pl n* social conduct. **mannerism** *n* gesture, speech habit, etc., particular to an individual.

manoeuvre (mə'nu:və) *n* planned, calculated, or strategic movement, as in a war; clever plan. *vt,vi* **1** make or perform manoeuvres. **2** move or cause to move into a desired direction or position.

manor *n* **1** feudal territorial unit occupied and worked by serfs paying rent in crops and service to their lord. **2** *also* **manor house** residence of the lord with its grounds. **3** mansion on an estate.

manpower *n* number of people needed or supplied for something.

mansion *n* large stately residence; manor house.

manslaughter *n* unlawful but unintentional killing of a person.

mantelpiece *n* structure above and around a fireplace, often incorporating a shelf.

mantle *n* **1** loose sleeveless cloak. **2** something covering or concealing. **3** net-like luminous cover over a gas lamp. *vt* cover with or in a mantle.

manual *adj* of the hands; done or operated by hand; not mechanical. *n* book containing fundamentals of a subject; textbook; handbook. **manually** *adv*.

manufacture *n* **1** commercial production or processing of goods, usually on a large scale. **2** manufactured product. *vt,vi* make (goods); produce; process. *vt* fabricate; concoct. **manufacturer** *n*.

manure *n* animal excrement used for fertilizing soil. *vt* apply manure to (soil).

manuscript *n* author's original piece of writing or document before its printing.

many *adj* much more than few; numerous. *n,pron* large number of people or things.

map *n* two-dimensional representation of a geographical area. *vt* (-pp-) produce a map of.

maple *n* deciduous tree or shrub with hard close-grained wood, used for furniture, etc.

mar *vt* (-rr-) spoil; ruin.

marathon *n* **1** long-distance race run over a distance of 42 km. **2** any long and trying task or contest.

marble *n* **1** hard, usually veined, limestone rock, used in a polished form, esp. in architecture. **2** small glass ball. **marbles** *n* game played with such balls.

march *vi* **1** walk with regular steps in an orderly military fashion. **2** proceed steadily. *vt* force to go or march. *n* **1** act or instance of marching. **2** distance or route marched. **3** piece of music composed for marching.

March *n* third month of the year.

marchioness *n* (ma:ʃə'nes) wife or widow of a marquess.

mare *n* female horse.

margarine *n* food product, similar to butter, usually made from vegetable fats.

margin *n* **1** border. **2** empty space on the sides of a text. **3** vertical line bordering this. **4** limit of something. **5** tolerable excess. **marginal** *adj* **1** relating to a margin. **2** close to a limit. **3** insignificant. **marginally** *adv*.

marguerite *n* garden plant resembling a large daisy.

marigold *n* plant having orange or yellow flowers.

marijuana (mæri'wa:nə) *n* dried hemp leaves or flowers smoked for euphoric effect.

marinade *n* **1** seasoned mixture of vinegar or wine with oil in which meat, vegetables, etc., are steeped before cooking. **2** food thus steeped. **marinate** *vt,vi also* **marinade** soak (meat, fish, etc.) in marinade.

marine *adj* **1** of or relating to the sea and sea life. **2** of navigation and shipping or the navy. *n* **1** soldier trained to serve both on land and the sea. **2** sea vessels collectively.

marital *adj* relating to marriage.

maritime *adj* **1** relating to the sea, shipping, or navigation. **2** of a place or area by the sea.

marjoram *n* plant with sweet-scented leaves, which are used in cooking.

mark[1] *n* **1** visible trace on a surface, such as a stain, dot, scratch, etc. **2** sign or symbol indicating or distinguishing something. **3** figure or letter evaluating a piece of work, examination, etc. **4** distinguishing quality. **5** target. *vt* **1** put a mark on. **2** distinguish, characterize, indicate, or show, as by a mark. **3** select; designate. *vt,vi* **1** stain; scratch. **2** evaluate and correct (an examination paper, essay, etc.). **marked** *adj* **1** noticeable; evident. **2** watched with suspicion; singled out. **markedly** *adv.* **marksman** *n, pl* **-men** a person who shoots a gun skilfully and accurately.

mark[2] *n* German monetary unit.

market *n* **1** place, usually with outdoor stands, where food, clothes, etc., are sold. **2** area of trade in certain goods. **3** demand for goods. *vt,vi* offer for sale. **market garden** *n* establishment where fruit and vegetables are grown for sale. **market research** *n* research into consumers' needs and preferences.

marmalade *n* jelly-like preserve usually made from oranges.

maroon[1] *n,adj* brownish-red.

maroon[2] *vt* abandon or isolate on an island, etc., without resources.

marquee *n* large tent used for exhibitions, etc.

marquess *n also* **marquis** ('mɑːkwis) nobleman ranking below a duke and above an earl or count. **marquise** (mɑːˈkiːz) *n* wife of a marquess.

marriage *n* **1** relationship or legal bond between a man and woman, making them husband and wife. **2** harmonious union of two things.

marrow *n* **1** soft nutritious tissue inside bones that is vital for production of certain blood cells. **2** *also* **vegetable marrow** plant with a long, rounded, and usually green striped fruit, eaten as a cooked vegetable. **marrowbone** *n* bone containing marrow used in cooking, esp. for making stock.

marry *vi* become husband and wife. *vt* **1** make (a person) one's spouse; join or take in marriage. **2** unite.

Mars *n* fourth planet from the sun, lying between earth and Jupiter. **Martian** *adj.*

Marseillaise (mɑːsɔˈleiz) *n* French national anthem.

marsh *n* low, poorly drained, and usually very wet ground. **marshy** *adj.*

marshal *n* **1** highest military rank in certain countries. **2** official in charge of ceremonies, parades, etc. *vt* (-ll-) **1** arrange in proper order. **2** assemble. **3** conduct.

marshmallow *n* sweet with a soft spongy texture.

marsupial *n* any of the group of mammals, including the kangaroo, whose young are carried in and complete their development in a pouch.

martial *adj* relating to war.

martin *n* kind of swallow.

martini *n* drink made of gin and vermouth.

martyr *n* person who endures suffering out of religious or some other conviction. *vt* kill, torture, or persecute as a martyr. **martyrdom** *n.*

marvel *n* something wonderful. *vi,vt* (-ll-) feel wonder or surprise (at). **marvellous** *adj* wonderful; excellent. **marvellously** *adv.*

Marxism *n* political theory describing the historical change of capitalism into a classless society as the outcome of the struggle of the working classes against their exploitation. **Marxist** *n,adj.*

marzipan *n* sweet paste of ground almonds and sugar, moulded into small fruits or used in cakes, etc.

mascara *n* cosmetic for painting eyelashes.

mascot *n* object believed to bring luck.

masculine *adj* **1** relating to or characteristic of a man. **2** of a grammatical gender normally denoting males. **masculinity** *n.*

mash *n* **1** mixture of warm water and crushed grain, etc., used as fodder, in brewing, etc. **2** mashed potatoes. *vt* crush into a soft pasty mass.

mask *n* **1** facial covering, worn, esp. as a disguise. **2** pretence; disguise. *vt* **1** put a mask on. **2** disguise; hide.

masochism *n* condition in which a person suffers voluntarily in order to experience pleasure, esp. sexual. **masochist** *n.* **masochistic** *adj.*

mason *n* person who works with building stone. **masonry** *n* profession or work of a mason.

masquerade *n* **1** ball, etc., where people wear masks, costumes, and other disguises. **2** pretence; false show. *vi* wear a disguise.

mass[1] *n* **1** bulk of matter that is not particularly shaped. **2** large number or quantity of something. **3** measure of the amount of matter in a body. *vt,vi* form or gather into a large crowd. **mass media** *pl n* newspapers, television, radio, etc., informing and influencing the public. **mass-produce** *vt* manufacture on a very large scale. **mass production** *n*.

mass² *n* **1** *also* **Mass** celebration of the Eucharist, esp. in the Roman Catholic Church. **2** music composed for this occasion.

massacre *n* ruthless killing, esp. of innocent people; slaughter. *vt* kill indiscriminately.

massage *n* treatment of muscles in order to relax them by rubbing and kneading. *vt* give a massage to. **masseur** *n* person who practises massage. **masseuse** *f n*.

massive *adj* **1** large and solid. **2** considerable.

mast *n* **1** vertical pole for supporting a vessel's sails and rigging. **2** any high upright pole.

mastectomy *n* surgical removal of a breast.

master *n* **1** person who controls others. **2** expert in a special field. **3** employer of servants. **4** male teacher. **5** form or mould for making duplicates; original. *vt* **1** become highly skilled in. **2** gain control over; overcome. **masterful** *adj* **1** highly capable; skilful. **2** showing authority; dominant. **mastermind** *n* person who creates or plans a major project or activity. *vt* plan with great skill. **masterpiece** *n* great work of art; example of excellence or skill.

masturbate *vi,vt* excite oneself or another to orgasm by manipulation or rubbing of the genitals. **masturbation** *n*.

mat¹ *n* **1** piece of fabric, used to cover floors, stand or sit on, wipe shoes on, etc. **2** piece of material placed under vases, plates, etc. **3** tangled mass. *vi* (-tt-) become tangled.

mat² *adj* matt.

matador *n* man who kills the bull in bullfights.

match¹ *n* slender strip of wood with a coated head that bursts into flame when rubbed.

match² *n* **1** person or thing that resembles or corresponds to another. **2** contest; team game. **3** marriage or person eligible for marriage. *vt* **1** equal or be equal to. **2** be the match of. **3** make to fit or correspond; adapt.

vi correspond in shape, size, colour, etc.; harmonize. **matchless** *adj* incomparable; having no equal.

mate *n* **1** one of a couple or pair, esp. a pair of breeding animals. **2** husband or wife. **3** friend; one's equal; fellow worker. **4** officer of a merchant ship ranking below a captain. *vt,vi* **1** join or pair. **2** (of animals) unite in order to produce young.

material *n* **1** stuff or substance of which anything is made. **2** raw data; facts. **3** cloth; fabric. **materials** *pl n* elements or tools required to make or perform something. ~*adj* **1** composed of matter; not spiritual; relating to physical well-being or wealth. **2** essential; important. **materialist** *n* person who values possessions and physical wellbeing more than ideas or spiritual beliefs. **materialism** *n*. **materialistic** *adj*. **materialize** *vi,vt* appear or cause to appear out of nothing. *vi* assume solid, material, or bodily form; become fact.

maternal *adj* **1** relating to a mother or mothers; motherly. **2** related through a mother. **maternalistic** *adj*.

maternity *n* state of being a mother. *adj* relating to mothers or the period of their pregnancy.

mathematics *n* science concerned with the logical study of space, numbers, relationships, etc., using various forms of analysis and special symbols. **mathematical** *adj*. **mathematician** *n*.

matinée *n* afternoon or first evening performance at a theatre, cinema, etc.

matrimony *n* state of being married. **matrimonial** *adj*.

matrix *n, pl* **matrices** ('meitrisi:z) **1** mould for casting or shaping objects. **2** anything that encloses or gives form to something.

matron *n* **1** married woman, esp. one of at least middle age. **2** woman in charge of nurses or domestic arrangements in a school, hospital, or other institution. **matronly** *adj* of or like a matron; dignified.

matt *adj also* **matte, mat** dull; without lustre; not shiny.

matter *n* **1** stuff or substance of which the physical universe is composed. **2** any physical or bodily substance. **3** topic or issue; thing; concern. **4** difficulty or trouble. **5**

content of a book, etc. *vi* be of significance or importance.

mattress *n* flat case filled with soft or firm supporting material, used as a bed or placed on a bed frame.

mature *adj* **1** fully developed; ripe. **2** complete in growth; grown-up. **3** characteristic of an adult; mentally developed; sensible. **4** perfected; complete. *vi,vt* become or make mature. **maturity** *n*.

maudlin *adj* over-sentimental; tearfully drunk.

maul *vt* treat roughly; attack savagely; injure badly.

mausoleum *n* **1** stately building used as a tomb or housing tombs. **2** large depressing building.

mauve *n,adj* pale bluish purple.

maxim *n* condensed general truth or principle of conduct.

maximum *adj* greatest; highest. *n, pl* **maximums** *or* **maxima** ('mæksimə) greatest or highest amount, extent, degree, etc. **maximize** *vt* **1** increase to a maximum. **2** make the most of.

may *v aux* (*pt* might) **1** be able or permitted to. **2** be likely or probable that. **maybe** *adv* perhaps; possibly.

May *n* fifth month of the year. **May Day** *n* first day of May, celebrated with various festivities, parades, etc. **maypole** *n* decorated pole around which persons dance on May Day.

mayonnaise *n* thick dressing for salads, etc., consisting usually of egg yolk, oil, and vinegar.

mayor *n* official head of a town corporation. **mayoress** *f n*.

maze *n* **1** intricate network of interconnecting paths, passages, etc. **2** confused state.

me *pron* form of **I** when used as the object.

meadow *n* grassland, often used for grazing or growing hay.

meagre *adj* lacking quality or quantity; insufficient; scanty; thin.

meal[1] *n* **1** food, esp. when eaten at regular times during the day. **2** occasion or time of eating.

meal[2] *n* coarsely ground grain, used esp. as fodder.

mean[1] *vt,vi* (meant) **1** signify; intend; intend to express; denote. **2** be resolved to; be serious about.

mean[2] *adj* **1** stingy; petty; not generous. **2** low in quality, character, rank, or performance. **3** not important; having little consequence. **4** offensive; nasty. **meanly** *adv*. **meanness** *n*.

mean[3] *adj* **1** halfway between two extremes, values, numbers, etc.; intermediate. **2** average. *n* anything intermediate or between two extremes, values, etc.; average.

meander (mi'ændə) *vi* wander; move about aimlessly; follow a winding course. *n* winding course of a river or stream.

meaning *n* **1** significance; import. **2** sense of a word, phrase, etc.; definition. **meaningful** *adj*. **meaningless** *adj*.

means *pl n* **1** method for achieving a purpose or function. **2** financial or material resources. **by all means** certainly; without fail or hesitation. **by no means** most definitely not; on no account; not at all.

meantime *n* intervening time. *adv also* **meanwhile** during or in an intervening time; at the same time.

measles *n* **1** infectious viral disease producing a red rash, common in childhood. **2** German measles.

measure *n* **1** size, quantity, extent, etc., of something, determined by comparing it with a standard. **2** unit of size, quantity, etc. **3** criterion. **4** vessel or instrument for determining size, quantity, etc. **5** certain amount, extent, or degree. **6** regular beat or movement in music, poetry, etc.; rhythm. **for good measure** as something extra; as an addition. **take measures** do things to achieve some goal or purpose. ~*vt* determine the size or quantity of; judge; estimate. *vi* have a specified measure. **made to measure** (of clothes) fitted to the individual. **measure up** live up to expectations; be adequate for. **measurement** *n*.

meat *n* **1** flesh of animals used as food, often excepting fish and poultry. **2** edible part of anything. **3** main principle of something; essence.

mechanical *adj* **1** relating to machinery. **2** operated or produced by machines; automatic. **3** not requiring thought; spontaneous. **mechanic** *n* person skilled in repairing, building, or using machinery. **mechanics 1** *s n* study of the action of forces on physical bodies and the motions they produce. **2** *pl n* technical aspects or workings of something.

mechanism *n* **1** machine or its structure or parts. **2** means by which a machine works. **3** way in which anything works or operates.

mechanize *vt* **1** make mechanical. **2** substitute mechanical power as a source of production or energy. **3** operate by machines or machinery. **mechanization** *n.*

medal *n* flat piece of metal, usually round, with a design or inscription to commemorate an event or given as an award. **medallion** *n* **1** large medal. **2** circular decorative design or panel.

meddle *vi* **1** *also* **meddle in** concern oneself with things that are not one's business. **2** *also* **meddle with** interfere; tamper.

media *pl n* newspapers, radio, and television; collective means of communication.

medial *adj also* **median** relating to or situated in the middle. **median** *n* middle point, part, value, etc.; dividing line or plane.

mediate *vt* **1** settle; reconcile. **2** serve as the medium for communicating, conveying, etc. *vt,vi* intervene to bring about a reconciliation or compromise. **mediation** *n.*

medicine *n* **1** practice and profession of preserving or restoring health. **2** drugs or other agents used to treat bodily diseases or disorders. **medicinal** *adj.* **medical** *adj* **1** relating to medicine. **2** relating to treatment that does not require surgery. *n* physical examination by a doctor. **medication** *n* **1** use of medicine or medical agents. **2** drug or other medical agent.

medieval *adj* **1** relating to the Middle Ages. **2** *inf* primitive; crude.

mediocre *adj* between good and bad; of only average quality or excellence; ordinary. **mediocrity** *n.*

meditate *vi* engage in deep mental reflection; contemplate. *vt* think about doing; plan. **meditation** *n.* **meditative** *adj.*

medium *n* **1** means; agency. **2** middle degree or quality; mean. **3** substance through or in which something is transmitted, conveyed, or effected. **4** material used by an artist. **5** environment. **6** person claim-

ing to be able to communicate with spirits. **7** *pl* **media** means of mass communication, such as the press, radio, or television. *adj* average; intermediate.

meek *adj* humble; submissive; lacking in spirit; mild. **meekly** *adv.*

meet *v* (met) *vt* **1** encounter; come across. **2** be present at the arrival point of. **3** satisfy; handle; cope with. *vi* come together; come into contact; join. *vt,vi* **1** be introduced (to). **2** gather for a meeting, etc. (with). **3** fight; confront. *n* assembly of people and animals prior to a hunt. **meeting** *n* **1** coming together; encounter. **2** gathering; assembly of persons, esp. for a common cause. **3** joining of things.

megaphone *n* instrument shaped like a funnel, used to amplify the voice or direct sound.

melancholy *n* depression; sadness; tendency to be morose. *adj* depressing; sad; gloomy. **melancholic** *adj.*

mellow *adj* **1** not harsh; rich and full. **2** genial; warm. **3** rendered receptive and friendly, as through advancing years, alcoholic drink, etc. *vt,vi* make or become mellow.

melodrama *n* **1** play or drama displaying violent or exaggerated emotions. **2** overemotional language or behaviour. **melodramatic** *adj.*

melody *n* **1** agreeable or pleasing music or tune. **2** recognizable sequence of musical notes. **melodic** *adj* relating to melody. **melodious** *adj* pleasing to listen to; tuneful.

melon *n* plant of the gourd family, the edible fruit of which has a hard rind and juicy flesh.

melt *vi,vt* **1** liquefy by heat; thaw; pass or convert from solid to liquid. **2** soften; dissolve. **3** disappear; disperse. **4** blend; merge. *n* act of melting or state of being melted. **melting point** *n* temperature at which a solid becomes liquefied.

member *n* **1** person who belongs to a group, society, or organization. **2** distinct part of a whole. **3** limb or other bodily organ. **membership** *n* **1** state of being part of a group or society. **2** total number of persons who are part of a group, etc.

membrane *n* thin pliable sheet of tissue that lines, connects, or covers an organ or part.

memento *n, pl* **mementoes** *or* **mementos** reminder; souvenir; keepsake.

memoir *n* record of facts or events written from experience or gathered through research. **memoirs** *pl n* biography or autobiography; published reminiscences.

memorable *adj* easily or worthy to be remembered.

memorandum *n, pl* **memorandums** *or* **memoranda** (memə'rændə); *also* **memo** 1 note to aid the memory. 2 short informal communication to colleagues, business firms, clients, etc.

memorial *n* object or custom in memory of a person, event, etc.; monument. *adj* preserving the memory of a person or event; commemorative.

memory *n* 1 faculty of recalling to mind or recollecting. 2 something remembered. 3 capacity to remember. 4 commemoration. 5 part of a. computer where information is stored. **memorize** *vt* commit to memory.

men *n pl* of **man**.

menace *n* something that threatens or constitutes a threat. *vt* threaten; intimidate.

menagerie *n* exhibition of caged animals.

mend *vt* 1 repair; make whole; put right. 2 make better; improve; correct. *vi* improve in health. *n* improvement; repair. **on the mend** recovering; improving in health.

menial *adj* lowly; servile. *n* servile person; domestic servant.

menopause *n* time of life during which women cease to menstruate, usually between the ages of 45 and 50.

menstrual *adj* relating to the monthly discharge from the womb of blood and cellular material in women. **menstruate** *vi* produce menstrual discharge. **menstruation** *n*.

mental *adj* 1 relating to the mind or intellect; done or existing in the mind. 2 *sl* insane; mad; crazy. **mental hospital** *n* institution for treating persons with disorders of the mind. **mentality** *n* mental or intellectual capacity; mind.

menthol *n* substance obtained from peppermint oil, used esp. as a flavouring.

mention *vt* speak of; refer to. *n* remark about or reference to a person or thing.

menu *n* 1 list of dishes available to be served, with their prices. 2 dishes served.

mercantile *adj* 1 relating to merchants or commerce; commercial. 2 engaged in commerce or trade.

mercenary *adj* working simply for reward or gain. *n* professional soldier serving a foreign country.

merchandise *n* 1 goods or commodities bought and sold in commerce or trade. 2 stock of a store. *vt,vi* buy and sell; promote the sale (of).

merchant *n* wholesale trader, esp. with foreign countries. **merchant bank** *n* bank chiefly involved in foreign commerce. **merchant navy** *n* 1 ships of a nation engaged in commerce. 2 officers and crews of merchant ships.

mercury *n* heavy silvery toxic metallic element, normally liquid, used in thermometers, barometers, etc. **Mercury** nearest planet to the sun. **mercurial** *adj* lively; changeable.

mercy *n* 1 compassion; kindness; pity. 2 forgiveness of an injustice, transgression, or injury by someone with the power to inflict punishment. 3 act of compassion, kindness, etc. **at the mercy of** completely in the power of; defenceless. **merciful** *adj* compassionate. **mercifully** *adv.* **merciless** without mercy; cruel. **mercilessly** *adv.*

mere *adj* nothing more than; only. **merely** *adv.*

merge *vt,vi* 1 blend; mingle. 2 combine; unite. **merger** *n* commercial combination of two or more companies.

meridian *n* 1 position of the sun at noon. 2 highest point or period of development of something. 3 imaginary circle encompassing the earth and passing through both poles. *adj* 1 relating to a meridian. 2 relating to or at noon.

meringue (mə'ræŋ) *n* 1 mixture of sugar and beaten egg whites, slightly browned, used as an icing, etc. 2 small cream-filled cake of meringue.

merit *n* 1 worth; excellence. 2 commendable quality. *vt* be worthy of. **meritorious** *adj.*

mermaid *n* mythical sea creature with the head, arms, and torso of a woman and the tail of a fish.

merry *adj* **1** joyous; cheerful; festive; happy; gay. **2** slightly drunk. **merry-go-round** *n* fairground amusement consisting of a rotating platform fitted with models of animals, cars, etc., on which one may ride; roundabout. **merrily** *adv.* **merriment** *or* **merriness** *n.*

mesh *n* net; network. *vt* catch in a mesh. *vi* **1** (of gearwheels) engage. **2** merge; blend; harmonize.

mesmerize *vt* **1** hypnotize. **2** fascinate greatly.

mess *n* **1** untidy state or condition. **2** state of confusion or disorder. **3** difficult or embarrassing situation. **4** place where military personnel, etc., take their meals. **5** meals taken by military personnel, etc. **6** *inf* person who is untidy, sloppy, or dirty. *vt also* **mess up** make dirty or untidy. **mess around** *or* **about** busy oneself in an ineffective or aimless manner.

message *n* **1** spoken or written communication. **2** moral conveyed in a literary or artistic work. **messenger** *n* person who conveys a message, does errands, etc.

metabolism *n* sum of the chemical changes in an animal or plant that result in growth, production of energy, etc. **metabolic** *adj.*

metal *n* **1** chemical element, such as iron, tin, or silver, that is usually lustrous, easily worked, and often a good conductor of heat and electricity. **2** alloy. **metallic** *adj.* **metallurgy** *n* study and technology of metals. **metallurgical** *adj.* **metallurgist** *n.*

metamorphosis *n* **1** complete change in form. **2** marked change in character, etc. **3** relatively rapid transformation of certain larvae into adults, as tadpole to frog. **metamorphic** *adj.*

metaphor *n* figure of speech in which a word is applied to something for which it does not literally stand. **metaphorical** *adj.*

meteor *n* small body from space that burns up in the earth's atmosphere producing a bright streak. **meteoric** *adj* **1** relating to meteors. **2** rapid; transient. **meteorite** *n* larger body able to reach earth.

meteorology *n* study of the earth's atmosphere, climate, and weather. **meteorological** *adj.* **meteorologist** *n.*

meter *n* measuring or recording instrument or device. *vt* measure with a meter.

methane *n* inflammable gas occurring in natural gas and used as a fuel and in chemical manufacture.

method *n* **1** way of doing something. **2** systematic or orderly procedure. **methodical** *adj* systematic; orderly.

Methodist *n* adherent of the Christian beliefs and tenets (Methodism) of a Protestant nonconformist denomination founded by John Wesley. *adj* relating to Methodists.

meticulous *adj* extremely careful about detail.

metre *n* **1** unit of length equal to 1.09 yards. **2** rhythmic arrangement of syllables in verse. **metric** *adj.* **metric system** *n* system of scientific units based on the metre, the kilogram or gram, and the second. **metrication** *n* conversion to the metric system.

metropolitan *adj* **1** relating to or characteristic of the capital or any large city. **2** relating to the characteristics or attitudes of a city dweller; sophisticated. **metropolis** *n* chief or major city; capital.

miaow *n* sound a cat makes. *vi* make such a sound.

mice *n pl* of **mouse.**

microbe *n* microorganism, esp. one causing disease; germ.

microcomputer *n* a type of small computer usually functioning as a single unit and often used for domestic purposes.

microorganism *n* microscopic animal or plant, such as a bacterium or virus.

microphone *n* instrument for converting sound waves into electrical currents or voltages that can then be amplified.

microscope *n* instrument for magnifying very small objects, usually consisting of at least two lenses mounted in a tube. **microscopic** *adj* visible only under a microscope; tiny.

microwave *n* wave in the radiation spectrum between normal radio waves and infrared. **microwave oven** *n* oven in which food is cooked by heat produced by microwaves.

midday *n* noon.

middle *adj* **1** equidistant from two extremes; intermediate; mean. **2** central. *n* **1** something intermediate or equidistant from two extremes. **2** central area of the body; waist. **middle-aged** *adj* relating to the age between youth and old age; aged about 40 to 65. **Middle Ages** *n* historical period now usually regarded as being from about the fifth to the late fifteenth century. **middle class** *n* generally well-educated class of people in commerce, the professions, etc., who often hold conformist views.

midget *n* very small person or thing.

midnight *n* 12 o'clock at night.

midst *n* middle; central part, stage, or point. **in the midst of** surrounded by; among.

midwife *n, pl* **-wives** woman who assists others in childbirth. **midwifery** *n.*

might[1] *v pt* of **may**. *v aux* used to express likelihood or possibility.

might[2] *n* strength; power. **mighty** *adj.*

migraine *n* severe headache.

migrate *vi* **1** leave one country, region, etc., to settle or work in another. **2** (of certain birds, animals, etc.) move seasonally from one region to another. **migrant** *n.* **migration** *n.* **migratory** *adj.*

mike *n sl* microphone.

mild *adj* **1** moderate; gentle; not harsh or drastic. **2** not having a sharp taste. **mildly** *adv.*

mildew *n* destructive fungus or fungal disease that attacks plants or objects exposed to damp.

mile *n* **1** unit of length equal to 1760 yards or 1.61 kilometres. **2** *also* **miles** great distance. **mileage** *n* **1** total number of miles travelled. **2** distance in miles between two points. **3** travel expenses based on a given sum per mile. **mileometer** *n* device for measuring and recording the number of miles travelled. **milestone** *n* **1** roadside stone showing number of miles to the next large city or town. **2** important event or turning point in history, a person's life, etc.

militant *adj* **1** aggressive; forceful. **2** engaged in warfare. *n* aggressive person. **militancy** *n.*

military *adj* relating to the armed forces, soldiers, or warfare. *n* soldiers collectively; armed forces.

milk *n* **1** whitish liquid produced in the mammary glands of female mammals, used to feed their young. **2** cow's or goat's milk, used as food. **3** whitish juice of various plants or fruits. **cry over spilt milk** regret or complain about something that cannot be undone or remedied. ~*vt* **1** extract milk from the udder of. **2** draw off from. **milkman** *n, pl* **-men** person who sells or delivers milk. **Milky Way** *n* faint band of light in the night sky that consists of millions of stars and is part of our galaxy.

mill *n* **1** machinery for grinding grain into flour. **2** machinery for manufacturing paper, textiles, steel, etc. **3** building containing such machinery. **4** small machine for grinding pepper corns, coffee beans, etc. *vt* grind, work, or shape in or as if in a mill. **millstone** *n* **1** either of two large round slabs of stone between which grain, etc., is ground. **2** heavy emotional burden.

millennium *n, pl* **millenniums** *or* **millennia** (mi'leniə) thousand years.

millet *n* cereal grass cultivated for its small seeds or grain.

milligram *n* one thousandth of a gram.

millimetre *n* one thousandth of a metre.

million *n* **1** number or numeral, 1 000 000, equal to 1000 multiplied by 1000. **2** *also* **millions** extremely large number or amount. **3** million units of money, etc. *adj* amounting to a million. **millionth** *adj,n.* **millionaire** *n* **1** person worth a million pounds, dollars, etc. **2** very rich person.

mime *n* **1** art or practice of wordless acting. **2** person who performs wordless acting. *vt,vi* act or express in mime.

mimic *n* person or animal that imitates or copies others. *vt* (-ck-) imitate in action, speech, etc.; copy; caricature. **mimicry** *n.*

minaret *n* slender tower of a mosque, from which the faithful are called to prayer.

mince *vt* **1** cut or chop into small pieces. **2** utter with affected carefulness. *vi* speak or act in an affected way. *n* minced meat.

mind *n* **1** thinking faculties or consciousness. **2** intellect. **3** memory. **4** person of great intelligence. **5** sanity; reason. **6** way of thinking; opinion; temper. **7** attention. **bear in mind** continue to remember. **be of one mind** be in total agreement with. **be of two minds** be undecided. **make up one's mind** decide. **out of one's mind** mad; highly agitated; confused. **take (someone's) mind off** help (someone) stop worrying about something; distract. ~*vt,vi* **1** object (to); be upset or concerned (about). **2** pay attention (to). **3** be careful (about). *vt* attend to; look after. **mind out** be careful; watch.

mine[1] *pron* that belonging to me.

mine[2] *n* **1** deep hole or shaft in the ground for extracting coal, metals, etc. **2** associated buildings, etc. **3** underground or surface deposit of minerals. **4** rich source of something. **5** explosive device, detonated on impact. *vt,vi* **1** dig or extract (minerals) from a mine. **2** make a mine in or under.

mineral *n* **1** inorganic substance that occurs in the earth and has a definite chemical composition. **2** nonliving matter. **mineralogy** *n* study of minerals. **mineral water** *n* **1** water containing dissolved minerals or gases. **2** fizzy nonalcoholic drink.

minestrone (mini'strouni) *n* Italian soup containing vegetables, etc.

mingle *vt,vi* **1** blend; mix; combine. **2** mix in company.

miniature *n* **1** very small painting, esp. a portrait. **2** model, copy, etc., greatly reduced in size. *adj* small-scale; reduced; tiny.

minim *n* musical note half the length of a semibreve.

minimum *n* least possible or lowest quantity, number, degree, etc. **minimal** *adj*. **minimize** *vt* **1** reduce to or estimate at a minimum. **2** belittle; underestimate.

mining *n* act, process, or industry of extracting minerals, coal, etc., from mines.

minister *n* **1** person authorized to conduct religious services; clergyman. **2** person in charge of a government department. **3** diplomatic representative. *vi* give aid or service (to). **ministerial** *adj*.

ministry *n* **1** functions or profession of a clergyman or clergyman. **2** profession or department of a government minister. **3** building in which government offices are located. **4** act of giving service.

mink *n* **1** animal of the weasel family with highly valued brownish fur. **2** garment made of mink fur.

minor *adj* **1** lesser in size, extent, significance, etc. **2** of or relating to a musical scale in which the second and third and the fifth

and sixth notes are a semitone apart. *n* **1** person under full legal age. **2** person or thing of inferior importance, rank, etc. **minority** *n* **1** smaller number, part, etc.; less than half. **2** group whose race, religion, etc., is different from most others in the same country or community. **3** state or period of being under full legal age.

minstrel *n* medieval musician or singer.

mint[1] *n* **1** aromatic herb. **2** sweet with a peppermint or similar flavouring.

mint[2] *n* **1** place where money is officially minted. **2** large amount, esp. of money. *vt,vi* make (coins and paper money) under government authority. **mint condition** perfect condition.

minuet *n* **1** slow stately dance in triple time. **2** music in the rhythm of this dance.

minus *prep* **1** less by the deduction of; decreased by. **2** without; lacking. *adj* **1** indicating deduction or subtraction. **2** negative. **3** lacking. *n also* **minus sign** symbol denoting subtraction.

minute[1] ('minit) *n* **1** one sixtieth of an hour; 60 seconds. **2** short time. **3** one sixtieth of a degree of angular measure. **4** memorandum. **up to the minute** current; very latest; modern. **minutes** *pl n* summary of a meeting.

minute[2] (mai'nju:t) *adj* **1** very small. **2** insignificant; trivial. **3** precise; detailed. **minutely** *adv*.

miracle *n* **1** supernatural event. **2** something wonderful; marvel. **miraculous** *adj*.

mirage *n* **1** optical illusion caused by intense heat, etc. **2** something unreal or illusory.

mirror *n* **1** polished surface that reflects images of objects, esp. glass backed with metal. **2** any reflecting surface, as of water. **3** something that gives a true representation or portrayal. *vt* reflect or represent faithfully.

mirth *n* merriment; festive or joyous gaiety.

misbehave *vi* behave badly. **misbehaviour** *n*.

miscarriage *n* **1** expulsion of a foetus from the womb before it is capable of living independently. **2** failure to carry out or attain a desired result. **miscarry** *vi* **1** undergo a miscarriage. **2** fail; go wrong.

miscellaneous *adj* **1** varied; mixed; assorted. **2** having various qualities or aspects; many-sided. **miscellany** *n* miscellaneous collection.

mischance *n* bad luck; misfortune; unlucky accident.

mischief *n* **1** teasing or annoying conduct. **2** source of annoyance or harm. **mischievous** *adj.* **mischievously** *adv.*

misconceive *vt,vi* misunderstand; interpret incorrectly. **misconception** *n.*

misconduct *n* improper conduct.

misdeed *n* evil or criminal deed.

miser *n* person who hoards money. **miserly** *adj.*

miserable *adj* **1** extremely unhappy or uncomfortable. **2** causing misery. **3** characterized by wretched poverty and neglect. **4** pitiable. **miserably** *adv.* **misery** *n* condition or cause of great suffering or distress.

misfire *vi* **1** fail to fire correctly or on time. **2** fail to be successful or have a desired effect. *n* failure to fire.

misfit *n* **1** person who does not fit in socially with others. **2** something that does not fit properly.

misfortune *n* bad luck; calamity.

misgiving *n* feeling of fear, doubt, or mistrust.

misguided *adj* mistaken; misled.

mishap *n* unlucky or unfortunate accident.

mislay *vt* (-laid) put something in a place later forgotten.

mislead *vt* (-led) lead astray; deceive, esp. by giving incorrect or inadequate information or advice.

misplace *vt* **1** lose; put in the wrong place. **2** place or bestow unwisely or improperly.

misprint *n* mistake in printing.

miss¹ *vt* **1** fail to hit, find, reach, notice, catch, etc. **2** *also* **miss out** omit; pass over. **3** notice or regret the absence of. **4** fail. **5** escape; avoid. *vi* **1** (of an engine) fail to fire. **2** fail to hit or attain something. **miss the boat** fail to take advantage of an opportunity. ~*n* failure.

miss² *n* girl; young woman. **Miss** form of address for an unmarried young woman or girl.

missile *n* object or weapon that can be thrown or fired, esp. a rocket-propelled weapon.

mission *n* **1** group of persons sent to a foreign country as envoys or missionaries. **2** official business or task of an envoy or missionary. **3** aim or calling in life. **4** military operation against an enemy. **5** any duty, esp. one that has been assigned. **missionary** *n* person sent to convert natives or primitive peoples to his religion, educate them, etc.

mist *n* **1** water vapour in fine drops; thin fog. **2** something that blurs or dims. *vt,vi* be, become, or make dim or blurred. **misty** *adj.*

mistake *n* error in thought or action. *vt* (-took; -taken) **1** form a wrong opinion about; misunderstand. **2** take (a person or thing) for another; confuse.

Mister *n* form of address for an adult male: normally written *Mr.*

mistletoe *n* evergreen plant with white berries that grows as a partial parasite on other trees.

mistress *n* **1** woman teacher. **2** woman who employs others. **3** woman with whom a man has a continuing sexual relationship outside marriage.

mistrust *n* lack of trust. *vt* regard with lack of trust; distrust.

misunderstand *vt,vi* (misunderstood) fail to understand correctly or properly. **misunderstanding** *n* **1** failure to understand. **2** slight quarrel.

misuse *n* (mis'ju:s) wrong or improper use. *vt* (mis'ju:z) **1** use wrongly. **2** treat badly.

mitre *n* **1** bishop's tall pointed hat. **2** corner joint formed by two pieces of wood, etc., that meet at equal angles. *vt* join so as to form a mitre joint.

mitten *n* glove with one compartment for the four fingers and a separate one for the thumb.

mix *vt,vi* combine; blend. *vi* associate with others freely or easily. *vt* form by blending. **mix up 1** confuse. **2** blend. **mixture** *n* **1** product of mixing. **2** combination of two or more ingredients, elements, types, qualities, etc. **mix-up** *n* confusion; muddle.

moan *n* low sound, usually indicating pain or suffering. *vi,vt* **1** utter or say with a moan. **2** grumble; complain.

moat *n* deep wide ditch, originally filled with water, round a castle or town.

mob *n* disorderly crowd of people. *vt* (-bb-) crowd round; attack in a crowd.

mobile *adj* 1 capable of movement. 2 easily moved. 3 expressive. *n* ornament consisting of a delicate hanging construction of balanced parts, which move with the air current. **mobility** *n*. **mobilize** *vt* 1 prepare (armed forces) for active service. 2 organize for a task. 3 put into motion or use. *vi* be ready or assembled for battle.

mock *vt,vi* make fun of by imitating; scoff or jeer (at). **mockery** *n* 1 ridicule. 2 derisive action or imitation.

mode *n* manner; style; method; fashion.

model *n* 1 representation of an object made to scale. 2 pattern to be followed; design; style. 3 person or object worthy of imitation. 4 person who poses for an artist, etc. 5 person who wears and displays clothing for potential customers. *v* (-ll-) *vt,vi* 1 make a model (of). 2 form or work (clay, etc.). 3 wear and display (clothing) for potential customers. *vi* pose for an artist, etc.

moderate *adj* ('mɔdərit) 1 not going to extremes. 2 of medium quantity, quality, or extent; not excessive. *n* ('mɔdərit) person of moderate views. *vt,vi* ('mɔdəreit) make or become less violent or excessive. **moderately** *adv*.

modern *adj* relating to or characteristic of present and recent time. **modernize** *vt* make modern; bring up to date. **modernization** *n*.

modest *adj* 1 unassuming; shy; not vain. 2 free from pretension; not showy. 3 moderate. **modestly** *adv*. **modesty** *n*.

modify *vt* 1 make small changes in. 2 tone down. 3 qualify. 4 make less severe. **modification** *n*.

modulate *vt* 1 vary the tone, pitch, or volume of. 2 regulate; adjust; soften. *vi* change from one musical key to another. **modulation** *n*.

module *n* 1 separable compartment of a space vehicle. 2 standard or unit of measurement. 3 removable framework or assembly.

mohair *n* yarn or fabric made from the soft silky hair of the Angora goat or made to resemble it.

moist *adj* damp; slightly wet. **moistly** *adv*. **moisten** *vt,vi* make or become moist. **moisture** *n* 1 water or other liquid diffused as a vapour or condensed on a surface. 2 dampness. **moisturize** *vt* give or restore moisture to.

mole[1] *n* small dark birthmark on the skin.

mole[2] *n* small nocturnal burrowing animal with a smooth silky pelt.

molecule *n* simplest unit of a chemical compound, consisting of two or more atoms. **molecular** *adj*.

molest *vt* 1 disturb or annoy by interfering with. 2 interfere with improperly, esp. sexually.

mollusc *n* soft-bodied invertebrate, such as the snail, oyster, or octopus, usually with a hard shell.

molten *adj* liquefied by intense heat.

moment *n* 1 very short space of time. 2 appropriate time. **at the moment** now. **in a moment** 1 soon; shortly. 2 quickly; instantly. **momentary** *adj* lasting a moment. **momentarily** *adv*. **momentous** *adj* important.

momentum *n* 1 mass multiplied by velocity of a moving body. 2 impetus; driving strength.

monarch *n* sovereign head of a country; king or queen. **monarchic** *or* **monarchical** *adj*. **monarchy** *n* 1 form of government in which authority is vested, constitutionally or traditionally, in the monarch. 2 country of a monarch.

monastery *n* house occupied by a community of monks. **monastic** *adj* relating to monks or their way of life.

Monday *n* second day of the week.

money *n* 1 official medium of exchange of a country, consisting of coins and paper currency of various denominations. 2 amount or sum of money; income. 3 funds; assets. **monetary** *adj* relating to money.

mongrel *n* dog of mixed breeds.

monitor *n* 1 pupil appointed to special duties in a school. 2 person who warns or advises. 3 control or checking device on a machine or system. 4 person who officially listens to and records foreign broadcasts. *vt* listen to in order to record or check.

monk *n* member of a male community, having taken final religious vows.

monkey *n* **1** long-tailed primate usually living in forests. **2** mischievous child. *vi also* **monkey around** *or* **about** play or fool (with).

monochrome *n* something of one colour or in black and white.

monogamy *n* custom or state of being married to only one person at a time. **monogamous** *adj*.

monologue *n* **1** prolonged talk by a single speaker. **2** dramatic work or part to be performed by one speaker.

monopoly *n* exclusive control or possession of a trade, privilege, etc. **monopolize** *vt* obtain or exercise sole control or possession of.

monosyllable *n* word of one syllable. **monosyllabic** *adj*.

monotone *n* sound, note, or voice of an unvaried pitch. **monotonous** *adj* lacking variation; dull; tedious. **monotonously** *adv*. **monotony** *n*.

monsoon *n* **1** seasonal wind of S Asia and the Indian Ocean, blowing from the southwest in summer. **2** rainy season that accompanies the wind from this direction.

monster *n* **1** legendary animal of a combination of forms. **2** grossly deformed animal or plant. **3** evil person. **4** something huge. **monstrous** *adj* **1** very great; huge. **2** ugly; hideous. **3** outrageous; revolting.

month *n* any of the 12 periods into which a year is divided. **monthly** *adj* **1** occurring, done, etc., once a month. **2** lasting a month. *adv* once a month.

monument *n* **1** something, esp. a statue, that commemorates. **2** statue, structure, etc., of historical importance. **3** written record. **monumental** *adj* **1** colossal; massive; stupendous. **2** relating to or serving as a monument.

moo *n* sound a cow makes. *vi* make a sound like a cow.

mood[1] *n* **1** state of mind and feelings. **2** depressed or sulky state of mind. **moody** *adj* changeable in mood.

mood[2] *n* form of a verb that indicates a particular function, such as the imperative, subjunctive, conditional, etc.

moon *n* **1** cratered and mountainous body that revolves around the earth in about 27.3 days, changing in apparent shape. **2** apparent shape of the moon; phase. *vi also* **moon around** *or* **about** go about idly, dreamily, listlessly, etc. **moonlight** *n* light from the sun reflected from the moon to the earth.

moor[1] *n also* **moorland** tract of open waste land, often hilly and covered with heather. **moorhen** *n* black red-billed water bird living on rivers, etc.

moor[2] *vt,vi* secure or fasten (a ship, etc.) with cables or ropes or be secured so. **mooring** *n* place for securing a vessel. **moorings** *pl n* ropes, etc., used in securing a vessel.

mop *n* sponge or bundle of yarn, cloth, etc., fastened to the end of a handle for cleaning floors, etc. *vt* (-pp-) *also* **mop up** clean or wipe with a mop.

mope *vi* be depressed. **mope about** *or* **around** act aimlessly. **mopes** *pl n* dejected state.

moped *n* motorized bicycle.

moral *adj* **1** relating to or concerned with right and wrong conduct; ethical. **2** of good conduct; virtuous; honest. *n* practical lesson, esp. one taught by a fable or other story. **morally** *adv*. **morale** (məˈrɑːl) *n* discipline and spirit of a group of persons. **morality** *n* **1** virtuous conduct. **2** moral principles. **moralize** *vt* interpret or explain in a moral sense; derive a moral from. *vi* make moral reflections; talk about morality. **morals** *pl n* personal conduct or principles.

morbid *adj* **1** gloomy; unpleasant. **2** unhealthy. **morbidly** *adv*.

more *adj* **1** greater in quantity, number, or degree. **2** additional; extra. *n* additional quantity, number, or degree. *adv* to a greater extent; in addition. **more or less** approximately; roughly. **moreover** *adv* besides; further.

morgue *n* room or building where dead bodies are taken to await identification before burial.

morning *n* early part of the day, usually up to noon or lunchtime.

moron *n* 1 mentally deficient person. 2 foolish person. **moronic** *adj.*

morose *adj* sullen; gloomy; unsociable.

morphine *n* drug to relieve severe pain.

Morse Code *n* signalling system in which numbers and letters are represented by combinations of dots and dashes.

mortal *adj* subject to or causing death. *n* human being. **mortality** *n* 1 condition of being subject to death. 2 large loss of life. 3 frequency of death; death rate.

mortar *n* 1 mixture of lime, sand, and water for holding bricks and stones together. 2 vessel in which substances are pounded or ground. 3 short cannon for throwing shells at high angles. *vt* fix or plaster with mortar.

mortgage *n* conveyance of property pledged as security for a debt until the loan is repaid. *vt* pledge (property) by mortgage.

mortify *vt* 1 humiliate. 2 subdue by self-denial. **mortification** *n.*

mortuary *n* place where dead bodies are temporarily kept before burial.

mosaic *n* picture or pattern made of small pieces of coloured stone, glass, etc.

Moslem *n,adj* Muslim.

mosque *n* Muslim place of worship.

mosquito *n, pl* **mosquitoes** *or* **mosquitos** blood-sucking insect that can transmit a disease such as malaria.

moss *n* small plant that grows in dense clumps on moist surfaces. **mossy** *adj.*

most *adj* greatest in size, number, or degree; nearly all. *n* greatest amount or degree. **at (the) most** not over; at maximum. **make the most of** use to the greatest advantage. ~*adv* in the greatest degree. **mostly** *adv* mainly; almost entirely; usually.

motel *n* roadside hotel, often consisting of private cabins with parking space in front.

moth *n* usually nocturnal insect similar to the butterfly. **motheaten** *adj* decrepit; damaged; filled with holes.

mother *n* 1 female parent. 2 head of a religious community of women. *vt* care for or protect as a mother. **motherhood** *n* state or qualities of being a mother. **mother-in-law** *n, pl* **mothers-in-law** mother of one's husband or wife. **mother superior** *n* head of a religious community of women.

motion *n* 1 movement. 2 manner or power of movement. 3 formal proposal at a meeting. **in motion** in operation; functioning. ~*vi* make a gesture, as with the hand. *vt* direct or guide by a gesture. **motionless** *adj* not moving; still.

motive *n* 1 reason; cause; intention; incentive. 2 chief idea in a work of art. *adj* causing motion or action. **motivate** *vt* provide with a motive. **motivation** *n.*

motor *n* 1 engine. 2 machine that transforms electrical into mechanical energy to produce motion. *vi* travel by car. **motorboat** boat powered by a motor. **motor car** *n* car. **motorcycle** *n also* **motorbike** two-wheeled road vehicle, heavier and more powerful than a moped. **motorist** *n* person who drives a (motor) car. **motorway** *n* main road with separate carriageways of several lanes and limited access.

motto *n, pl* **mottoes** *or* **mottos** 1 saying adopted as a rule of conduct. 2 short phrase or sentence inscribed on a coat of arms, etc.

mould[1] *n* 1 hollow form or container in which molten metal, plastic, etc., is cast or shaped. 2 anything cast or shaped in a mould. 3 character; type. *vt* form; shape; model.

mould[2] *n* fungal growth caused by dampness; mildew. **mouldy** *adj.*

moult *vi,vt* shed (feathers, skin, fur, etc.). *n* act or process of moulting.

mound *n* 1 pile, as of earth or stones; heap. 2 small hill. *vt* form into a mound.

mount[1] *vt,vi* 1 go up; ascend; climb. 2 get up on (a horse, platform, etc.). *vt* 1 set at a height or elevation. 2 provide with or place on a horse. 3 fix in a setting, backing, or support. *vi* rise; increase. *n* 1 act of mounting. 2 something mounted. 3 setting, backing, or support on which something is mounted.

mount[2] *n* mountain; hill.

mountain *n* 1 natural and usually very high and steep elevation of the earth's surface. 2 large pile or heap. **mountainous** *adj.* **mountaineer** *n* person who climbs mountains. *vi* climb mountains.

mourn *vi* feel sorrow. *vt* grieve for.

mouse *n, pl* **mice** small long-tailed rodent. **mousy** *adj* 1 like or suggestive of a mouse. 2 (of hair) fair but not blond(e).

mousse *n* dish made with whipped cream, beaten eggs, etc.

moustache *n* hair growing on the upper lip.

mouth *n* (mauθ) **1** cavity between the lips and the throat, containing the teeth, tongue, etc., in which food is chewed and speech sounds are formed. **2** opening into anything hollow. **3** entrance to something. **4** part of a river where its waters empty into a sea, lake, etc. *v* (mau) *vt* form (words) with the lips without speaking. *vi* declaim. **mouthpiece** *n* **1** end of something intended to be put between or near the lips. **2** person who speaks for others. **mouth-watering** *adj* appetizing.

move *vt,vi* **1** change the place or position (of). **2** stir. *vt* **1** propose. **2** affect with emotion. *vi* **1** change one's place of residence. **2** make progress; advance. *n* act of moving; movement. **get a move on** *inf* hurry up. **movable** *adj* capable of being moved; not fixed. **movement** *n* **1** process or act of moving. **2** moving parts of a mechanism, as of a watch. **3** main division of a musical work, esp. of a symphony. **4** group engaged in or activities directed towards some goal or end. **5** trend.

mow *vt,vi* (mowed; mown *or* mowed) cut or cut down (grass, grain, etc.). **mower** *n*.

Mr abbreviation for **Mister**.

Mrs abbreviation for **mistress**; used as a form of address for a married woman.

much *adj* in great quantity or degree. *n* **1** large amount. **2** notable or important matter or thing. *adv* in or to a great degree. **as much** exactly that. **make much of 1** make sense of. **2** give importance to. **not much of** not really. **not think much of** have a poor opinion of.

muck *n* **1** manure. **2** filth; dirt. *vt* make dirty. **muck about** *sl* mess or fool about. **muck in** *sl* join in to achieve something. **muck out** clean out; remove muck from. **muck up** *sl* ruin; spoil. **mucky** *adj*.

mud *n* wet soft earth. **mudguard** *n* guard over a wheel to protect against mud. **mudslinging** *n* reckless accusations or abuse. **muddy** *adj* **1** covered with or abounding in mud. **2** mudlike in colour or texture. **3** vague; obscure; not clear. *vt,vi* make or become muddy.

muddle *vt* **1** confuse; bewilder. **2** mismanage; mix up in a confused way. **muddle through** succeed in spite of inadequate planning, etc. ~*n* muddled state or condition; mess.

muffle *vt* **1** wrap or cover up with something warm. **2** wrap up to deaden sound. **3** deaden (sound). **4** conceal. *n* something that muffles.

mug *n* **1** large drinking cup with a handle. **2** *sl* face or mouth. **3** fool; gullible person. *vt,vi* (-gg-) *sl* attack and rob. **mug up** obtain (information) or study during a short intensive period. **mugger** *n sl* person who assaults and robs someone.

mulberry *n* tree that bears dark red edible berries.

mule[1] *n* sterile offspring of a mare and a donkey. **mulish** *adj* stubborn.

mule[2] *n* slipper with an exposed heel.

multiple *adj* have many parts, elements, etc. *n* quantity that contains another quantity an exact number of times.

multiply *vt,vi* **1** find the mathematical product of two or more numbers or quantities. **2** increase or cause to increase in number or amount. **multiplication** *n*.

multitude *n* **1** great number of persons; crowd; throng. **2** the common people.

mum *n inf* mother.

mumble *vt,vi* speak or utter indistinctly. *n* indistinct talk or sound.

mummy[1] *n* dead body preserved by embalming or other techniques. **mummify** *vt* preserve as a mummy.

mummy[2] *n inf* mother.

mumps *n* contagious viral disease, esp. of children, marked by a swelling of the glands in the neck.

munch *vt,vi* chew vigorously and often noisily.

mundane *adj* ordinary; everyday; common.

municipal *adj* relating to the local government of a city or town. **municipality** *n* city or town with local self-government.

mural *n* painting executed on a wall.

murder *n* **1** unlawful and deliberate killing of a human being. **2** *inf* difficult or unpleasant task. *vt* **1** kill. **2** *inf* ruin; destroy. *vi* commit murder. **murderer** *n*. **murderess** *f n*.

murmur n 1 low and continuous sound. 2 grumble; complaint. vt utter in a low voice. vi 1 make a murmur. 2 complain.

muscle n 1 specialized body tissue that produces movement by contracting. 2 strength; brawn. **muscular** adj.

muse vi ponder; meditate; be lost in thought.

museum n building housing objects or illustrations of art, science, history, etc., for observation and study.

mushroom n fungus, esp. an edible variety, having a cap on the end of a stem. vi 1 increase, grow, or expand rapidly. 2 gather mushrooms.

music n 1 organization of vocal or instrumental sounds into a pleasing or stirring rhythm or harmony. 2 sequence of pleasing sounds. 3 art of producing music. 4 record of notes for reproducing music. **musical** adj 1 relating to music. 2 liking or skilled in music. n light stage or film entertainment with songs and dancing. **musician** n composer or performer of music.

Muslim n also **Moslem** adherent of Islam. adj also **Moslem** relating to the religion or culture of Islam.

muslin n fine cotton fabric.

mussel n mollusc with a dark elongated hinged shell.

must v aux be obliged to; be certain to; be resolved to. n something imperative.

mustard n strong-flavoured yellowish or brownish paste or powder prepared from the seeds of the mustard plant, used as a condiment and seasoning.

mute adj 1 silent; soundless. 2 dumb; not capable of speech. n person unable to speak. vt deaden the sound of; soften.

mutilate vt injure, disfigure, or make imperfect, as by damaging parts, removing a limb, etc. **mutilation** n.

mutiny n revolt or rebellion against authority, esp. by soldiers or sailors. vi engage in mutiny. **mutinous** adj.

mutter vt,vi utter indistinctly or in a low tone; mumble. n muttered sound; complaint.

mutton n flesh of mature sheep, used as food.

mutual adj done, felt, possessed, etc., by each of two with respect to the other; common to both or all. **mutually** adv.

muzzle n 1 open end of the barrel of a firearm. 2 projecting nose and mouth of an animal. 3 device placed over the mouth of an animal to prevent it from biting. vt 1 put a muzzle on. 2 prevent from speaking.

my pron belonging to or associated with me. **myself** pron reflexive or emphatic form of me or I.

myrrh (mə:) n aromatic gum exuded from certain shrubs, used as perfume, incense, etc.

mystery n secret, puzzling, or obscure thing. **mysterious** adj. **mysteriously** adv.

mystic n person who claims spiritual knowledge or insight, as by following mysticism. **mystical** adj also **mystic** 1 of hidden, spiritual, or occult nature or significance. 2 mysterious. 3 relating to mysticism. **mysticism** n belief in direct communion with God and awareness of divine truth by means of contemplation and love alone.

mystify vt 1 bewilder; confuse; perplex. 2 make obscure or mysterious. **mystification** n.

mystique n atmosphere of mystery associated with or investing certain activities, doctrines, arts, etc.

myth n 1 ancient story or legend, usually with supernatural characters or events. 2 imaginary or fictitious event, person, or thing. **mythical** adj. **mythology** n 1 collection of myths. 2 study of myths. **mythological** adj.

N

nag vt,vi (-gg-) annoy, pester, or be troubled with constant complaints, reminders, worries, or pain.

nail n 1 narrow flat-headed piece of metal hammered in as a means of joining or for use as a peg. 2 hard horny covering on the tip of a finger or toe. **as hard as nails** cold; ruthless; tough. **hit the nail on the head** describe exactly; pinpoint (a problem, situation, etc.). ~vt 1 join or fasten with a nail. 2 inf get hold of (a person); catch. **nail down** make (a person) declare his aims or opinions. **nailfile** *n* small metal file for shaping fingernails.

naive *adj* 1 unsophisticated; ingenuous. 2 credulous; gullible. **naively** *adv.* **naiveté** *or* **naivety** *n.*

naked *adj* without clothes or protection; bare. **nakedly** *adv.* **nakedness** *n.*

name *n* 1 word or words by which a person or thing is known or identified. 2 reputation. 3 *inf* celebrity. *vt* 1 give a name to; identify. 2 declare (a price, terms, etc.). **namely** *adv* that is to say. **namesake** *n* person or thing having the same name as another.

nanny *n* 1 woman employed to look after children, esp. in a private household. 2 *inf* grandmother.

nap[1] *n* short period of sleep, esp. during the day. *vi* (-pp-) sleep for a short period.

nap[2] *n* surface fibres on cloth.

napalm *n* jellied mixture of petrol and acids used in bombs, etc.

nape *n* back of the neck.

napkin *n* square of cloth or paper used for protecting clothes and wiping the mouth and fingers during meals.

nappy *n* square of cloth or disposable pad worn by a baby to absorb excreta.

narcissus *n, pl* **narcissi** (nɑːˈsisai) bulb producing yellow or white flowers.

narcotic *n* addictive drug, such as morphine, that induces sleep and dulls the senses. *adj* inducing sleep or insensibility.

narrate *vt* relate or tell (a story). **narration** *n.* **narrator** *n.* **narrative** *n* story; account. *adj* consisting of or relating to a narrative.

narrow *adj* 1 measuring little across. 2 strict; accurate. 3 bigoted; not liberal. 4 limited; restricted. *vt,vi* make or become narrow or narrower. **narrowly** *adv.* **narrowness** *n.* **narrow-minded** *adj* having rigid and narrow views.

nasal *adj* 1 relating to the nose. 2 (of sounds) formed by breathing through the nose.

nasturtium *n* garden plant having orange, yellow, or red flowers and roundish leaves.

nasty *adj* 1 unpleasant. 2 spiteful. 3 offensive; disgusting. **nastily** *adv.* **nastiness** *n.*

nation *n* 1 country; land. 2 large group of people having a common cultural background, history, and language. **nationwide** *adj,adv* throughout the country.

national *adj* 1 relating to a country as a whole. 2 typical of a particular country. 3 controlled by the government. **nationally** *adv.* **national anthem** *n* country's official song. **national insurance** *n* state scheme to provide financial aid during unemployment, sickness, widowhood, etc. **national service** *n* compulsory military training. **nationalism** *n* patriotism; belief in national unity. **nationalist** *n,adj.* **nationality** *n* citizenship of a particular country. **nationalize** *vt* transfer (an industry or property) to public ownership and control. **nationalization** *n.*

native *adj* 1 relating to the place of birth or origin. 2 innate. 3 indigenous. 4 relating to the indigenous population. *n* 1 person born or living in or animal found in a certain country or area. 2 person belonging to a race of original inhabitants of a country. **nativity** *n* 1 birth. 2 *also* **nativity play** play or artistic representation of the birth of Christ.

natural *adj* 1 produced by, present in, or relating to the physical world; not artificial. 2 innate. 3 normal; to be expected; automatic. 4 unaffected. 5 not domesticated or civilized. *n* 1 *inf* person naturally equipped for a particular skill or job. 2 musical note or key that is neither sharp nor flat. **naturally** *adv.* **natural gas** *n* gas formed like oil in natural deposits and burned for cooking, heating, etc. **natural history** *n* study of animals and plants. **natural science** *n* science, such as chemistry or zoology, that is concerned with laws and processes of the external physical world. **naturalize** *vt,vi* 1 confer or adopt citizenship of a country. 2 introduce or adapt to another country or area. **naturalization** *n.*

nature *n* 1 external physical world and its laws, plants, and animals. 2 character or temperament; characteristics. 3 kind or sort.

naughty *adj* 1 mischievous. 2 indecent; suggestive. **naughtily** *adv.* **naughtiness** *n.*

nausea *n* 1 feeling of sickness; desire to vomit. 2 absolute disgust. **nauseous** *adj.* **nauseate** *vt* 1 induce a feeling of sickness. 2 disgust; repel.

nautical *adj* relating to ships, seamen, or navigation.

naval *adj* relating to the equipment, personnel, or activities of a navy.

nave *n* central seating area of a church up to the chancel.

navel *n* small pit in the abdomen left by the severed umbilical cord.

navigate *vt,vi* direct or plan the course or route of (a ship, car, etc.). *vt* **1** follow the course of (a river). **2** sail across. **navigator** *n*. **navigable** *adj* **1** (of water) deep enough to admit ships. **2** able to be navigated. **navigation** *n* **1** theory and practice of navigating. **2** shipping.

navy *n* **1** fleet of warships with sea aircraft. **2** personnel of the fleet. **navy blue** *n,adj* dark blue.

near *prep* at or within a short time or distance. *adj* **1** close in position or time. **2** intimate; dear. **3** only just avoided; narrow. *adv* close (to). **nearness** *n*. **nearby** *adv,adj* close by; not far away. **nearly** *adv* almost. **nearside** *n* the side of a car, traffic lane, etc., nearest to the kerb. **near-sighted** *adj* short-sighted.

neat *adj* **1** tidy; carefully arranged. **2** skilful; deft. **3** well-planned; clever. **4** precise. **5** undiluted. **neatly** *adv*. **neatness** *n*. **neaten** *vt* make neat; tidy up.

necessary *adj* **1** essential; needed. **2** logical. **necessarily** *adv*. **necessity** *n* **1** essential requirement. **2** pressing need. **3** logical consequence.

neck *n* **1** part of the body connecting the head and shoulders. **2** *also* **neckline** part of a garment round the neck and shoulders. **3** long narrowed portion of land, slender part of a bottle, etc. **neck and neck** abreast in a race or contest. **stick one's neck out** act defiantly and risk censure. ~*vi inf* kiss and cuddle lengthily (with). **necklace** *n* neck ornament.

nectar *n* **1** sweet liquid that bees obtain from certain flowers for making honey. **2** very sweet, soothing drink.

née (nei) *adj* having a maiden name of; born.

need *vt* require; lack. *vi* be obliged to; be necessary to. *v aux* **need I, you, he?, etc.** must I, you, he?, etc. **I, you, he, etc., need not** I, you, he, etc., do/does not have to. ~*n* **1** circumstances in which something is needed. **2** misfortune; poverty. **3** requirement. **needy** *adj* poor.

needle *n* **1** sharp pointed sliver of steel with a hole at one end to take thread for sewing. **2** plastic or metal rod for knitting. **3** gramophone stylus. **4** indicator arrow on a compass, dial, etc. **5** pointed part of a hypodermic syringe. **6** sharply pointed leaf of a conifer. **needlework** *n* hand-sewing.

negate *vt* **1** deny. **2** cancel out; make void. **negation** *n*.

negative *adj* **1** indicating *no*; not affirmative. **2** not productive or positive. **3** indicating opposition or disapproval. **4** denoting numbers less than zero. **5** with light and dark areas reversed. **6** designating the electrical charge carried by an electron. *n* **1** word(s) indicating a denial or refusal. **2** negative number. **3** negative photographic plate.

neglect *vt* **1** fail to care for. **2** omit; overlook. *n* act or result of neglecting. **negligent** *adj* careless; not paying proper attention. **negligence** *n*. **negligently** *adv*. **negligible** *adj* so minor as to be not worth considering. **negligibly** *adv*.

négligé ('negliʒei) *n* woman's dressing gown, usually of a light or flimsy material.

negotiate *vi* reach an agreement through discussion. *vt* **1** settle through discussion. **2** successfully come through or deal with (an obstacle). **3** obtain cash settlement for. **negotiation** *n*. **negotiator** *n*.

Negro *n, pl* **Negroes** black-skinned person of African descent.

neigh *vi* (of a horse) produce a braying sound. *n* cry of a horse; bray.

neighbour *n* **1** person living nextdoor or nearby. **2** thing situated near or adjacent to another. *v* **neighbour on** border on; adjoin. **neighbourhood** *n* (people living in) the vicinity; surrounding area.

neither *adj,pron* not either (one). *conj* nor yet.

neon *n* gaseous element used in strip lighting and advertising display.

nephew *n* son of one's brother or sister, or of one's husband's or wife's brother or sister.

nepotism *n* favouritism shown to relatives in unfairly procuring positions or promotion for them. **nepotist** *n*.

Neptune *n* outer giant planet lying beyond Uranus.

nerve *n* **1** bundle of fibres that connects the central nervous system with all parts of the body transmitting sensory and motor impulses. **2** courage; confidence. **3** *sl* impudence; cheek. **nerves** *pl n* anxiety; hysteria; irritability. **get on one's nerves** irritate. **nervy** *adj* anxious; tense. **nerve-racking** *adj* causing emotional strain; worrying.

nervous *adj* **1** tense; excitable. **2** timid; anxious. **3** vigorous; spirited. **4** relating to the nerves. **nervous breakdown** *n* severe mental and emotional collapse. **nervous system** *n* body mechanism coordinating internal functions and external impulses.

nest *n* **1** shelter made of twigs, grass, etc., where birds, reptiles, mice, etc., lay eggs or give birth. **2** protective or comfortable place in which young animals are reared. *vi* **1** make a nest. **2** look for nests. **nest egg** *n* savings.

nestle *vi* cuddle; settle comfortably.

net[1] *n* **1** *also* **netting** open mesh of knotted string, wire, etc., used for catching fish, birds, etc., or to protect against birds, insects, etc. **2** mesh barrier dividing playing areas in tennis and other games or to enclose a goal area. *vt, vi* (-tt-) **1** catch or cover with nets. **2** snare. **3** construct a net. **netball** *n* sport in which goals are scored by throwing a ball into a net. **network** *n* **1** complex connected pattern or system of wires, roads, etc. **2** series of linked radio or television stations.

net[2] *adj* remaining after deductions. *vt* (-tt-) earn as net profit or income.

nettle *n* plant with toothed leaves and stinging hairs. *vt* irritate.

neurosis *n* nervous disorder involving irrational anxiety, obsessions, or other abnormal behaviour. **neurotic** *adj* **1** relating to a neurosis or to the nerves. **2** prone to anxiety or hysteria. *n* neurotic person.

neuter *adj* **1** of neither masculine nor feminine gender. **2** sexually underdeveloped. **3** deprived of sexual organs. *n* neuter word, animal, plant, etc. *vt* make neuter.

neutral *adj* **1** impartial; not taking sides. **2** belonging to neither side. **3** having no definite characteristics. **4** neuter. **5** neither alkali nor acid. **6** neither positive nor negative. **7** (of gears) not engaged. *n* **1** person, country, etc., who favours no side or who does not take part in an argument, war, etc. **2** (of gears) state of being not engaged. **neutrality** *n*. **neutralize** *vt* **1** make neutral. **2** render powerless; deaden.

neutron *n* minute uncharged particle occurring in the nuclei of all atoms except hydrogen.

never *adv* **1** at no time. **2** not at all. **never mind!** don't worry! **well I never!** how surprising!

nevertheless *adv* even so; in spite of that.

new *adj* **1** of recent origin or existence; not old; freshly produced. **2** recently acquired or discovered. **3** modern; novel; different. **4** another. **new at** *or* **to** unaccustomed to; unfamiliar with. ~*adv also* **newly** freshly; recently. **newcomer** *n* recently arrived person; beginner. **New Year** *n* **1** coming year. **2** first or first few days of January.

news *s n* **1** current information about recent events. **2** broadcast information about local, national, and international events. **newsagent** *n* shopkeeper who sells newspapers, journals, etc. **newspaper** *n* daily or weekly publication containing news, features, specialist information, and advertisements. **newsreel** *n* filmed report of current events.

newt *n* small lizard-like amphibian.

next *adj* **1** following; subsequent. **2** adjacent; neighbouring. **3** closest. *adv* after this or that.

nib *n* pointed writing end of a pen.

nibble *n* **1** small bite. **2** morsel. *vt, vi* take a nibble (at); eat in nibbles.

nice *adj* **1** pleasant; attractive. **2** good; virtuous. **3** refined. **4** precise; subtle; delicate. **nicely** *adv*.

niche *n* **1** alcove or recess, often used for shrines or statues. **2** suitable or comfortable place or position.

nick *n* tiny notch. **the nick** *sl* jail. **in the nick of time** just in time. ~*vt* **1** make a nick in. **2** *sl* steal; pinch.

nickel *n* **1** hard silvery metal used for plating and coin-making. **2** *US* five-cent coin.

nickname *n* name by which a person is known affectionately or mockingly. *vt* give a nickname to.

nicotine *n* narcotic found in tobacco.

niece *n* daughter of one's brother or sister, or of one's husband's or wife's brother or sister.

night *n* period of time between evening and morning; darkness. **nightclub** *n* place of entertainment open at night providing food and drink. **nightdress** *n also* **nightgown** woman's sleeping garment. **nightly** *adv* 1 during the night. 2 every night. **nightmare** *n* 1 terrifying dream. 2 frightening experience; trauma. **night-time** *n* period of darkness between sunset and sunrise. **night watchman** *n* person employed to guard premises at night.

nightingale *n* red-brown European songbird noted for its nocturnal trilling song.

nil *n* nothing.

nimble *adj* agile; deft; quick. **nimbly** *adv*.

nine *n* 1 number equal to one plus eight. 2 group of nine persons, things, etc. 3 *also* **nine o'clock** nine hours after noon or midnight. *adj* amounting to nine. **nine days wonder** something that causes short-lived excitement or admiration. **ninth** *adj* coming between eighth and tenth in sequence. *n* 1 ninth person, object, etc. 2 one of nine equal portions; one divided by nine. *adv* after the eighth.

nineteen *n* 1 number that is nine more than ten. 2 nineteen things or people. **talk nineteen to the dozen** talk fast and unceasingly. ~*adj* amounting to nineteen. **nineteenth** *n,adj,adv*.

ninety *n* 1 number equal to nine times ten. 2 ninety things or people. *adj* amounting to ninety. **ninetieth** *adj,adv,n*.

nip *vt,vi* (-pp-) 1 catch, pinch, or bite sharply. 2 check the growth (of). *vi inf* go quickly; pop. *n* 1 small bite or pinch. 2 touch of frost. **nippy** *adj* cold; sharp; frosty.

nipple *n* 1 suckling teat of a breast or bottle. 2 device similar in shape or function to a nipple.

nit *n* 1 egg of a head louse or other parasite. 2 *sl* fool. **nit-picking** *n sl* petty criticism of small unimportant details.

nitrogen *n* colourless gas forming 78 per cent of the air and used esp. in the manufacture of fertilizers.

nitroglycerine *n* unstable chemical used in dynamite and other explosives.

no *adv* 1 not any; not one. 2 not in any way; not at all. 3 not. 4 expressing denial, refusal, etc. *n* statement of denial, refusal, etc.; negative.

noble *adj* 1 courageous; worthy; high-minded. 2 aristocratic. 3 stately; splendid. *n also* **nobleman** member of the nobility; aristocrat; peer. **nobility** *n* 1 hereditary class of the highest status; aristocracy. 2 moral courage, worthiness, or endurance.

nobody *pron* 1 no-one. 2 person of no importance or of low birth.

nocturnal *adj* of, occurring in, or active during the night. **nocturnally** *adv*.

nod *vt,vi* (-dd-) bend (the head) forward to indicate (agreement or approval). *vi* doze. *n* nodding motion.

noise *n* sound. **noisy** *adj* loud. **noisily** *adv*. **noisiness** *n*.

nomad *n* 1 member of a tribe constantly on the move in search of new pasture. 2 habitual wanderer; roamer. **nomadic** *adj*.

nominal *adj* 1 not actual; existing in name only. 2 very small; token. **nominally** *adv*.

nominate *vt* 1 propose as a candidate. 2 appoint. **nomination** *n*. **nominee** *n* person who is nominated.

non- *prefix* indicating negation, absence, etc.

nonchalant *adj* coolly casual; offhand. **nonchalance** *n*. **nonchalantly** *adv*.

nondescript *adj* having no distinguishing characteristics; dull.

none *pron* 1 not any (of them or it). 2 no part or section. 3 no such person. *adv* not at all; in no way.

nonentity *n* 1 insignificant person or thing. 2 non-existent thing.

nonsense *n* 1 meaningless or foolish words or ideas. 2 trifle. **nonsensical** *adj*.

noodle *n* thin strip of pasta.

nook *n* secret or sheltered corner or hiding place.

noon *n* midday; 12 o'clock in the daytime.

no-one *pron* no person at all; nobody.

noose *n* loop of rope with a slipknot to tighten it, used esp. for execution by hanging.

nor *conj* also not; not either.

norm *n* 1 usual or recognized standard or pattern. 2 expected or potential output.

normal *adj* **1** usual; ordinary; average. **2** not physically or mentally handicapped. **normality** *n.* **normally** *adv.*

north *n* **1** one of the four cardinal points of the compass situated to the left of a person facing the sunrise. **2** part of a country, area, etc., lying towards the north. *adj also* **northern** of, in, or facing the north. *adv,adj also* **northerly 1** towards the north. **2** (of winds) from the north. **northerner** *n.* **northeast** *n* point situated midway between the north and east. *adj also* **northeastern** of, in, or facing the northeast. *adv,adj also* **northeasterly 1** towards the northeast. **2** (of winds) from the northeast. **northward** *adj* facing or moving towards the north. **northwards** *adv* in the direction of the north. **northwest** *n* point situated midway between north and west. *adj also* **northwestern** of, in, or facing the northwest. *adv,adj also* **northwesterly 1** towards the northwest. **2** (of winds) from the northwest.

nose *n* **1** central projection in the face used for breathing and smelling. **2** ability to smell out or discover. **be led by the nose** follow blindly. **keep one's nose to the grindstone** work persistently. **pay through the nose** pay too much. **poke one's nose into** interfere in. **turn one's nose up (at)** reject contemptuously. **under one's (very) nose** in one's presence; in full view. *~vt,vi* smell or sniff (at).

nostalgia *n* **1** sentimental longing for things past. **2** homesickness. **nostalgic** *adj.*

nostril *n* one of the two openings of the nose.

nosy *adj* unpleasantly inquisitive. **nosiness** *n.*

not *adv* expressing negation, denial, refusal, etc.

notable *adj* important; remarkable; conspicuous. *n* important person. **notably** *adv.*

notation *n* **1** act or process of organizing a scheme of signs that represent scientific, musical, or other concepts. **2** such a scheme or method.

notch *n* V-shaped cut in a piece of wood, etc. *vt* cut a notch in, esp. as a way of keeping count. **notch up** score.

note *n* **1** short written record, summary, or comment. **2** short letter. **3** piece of paper money. **4** written promise to pay. **5** (symbol indicating) a musical sound of a certain pitch. **6** distinction; fame; importance. **7** notice; attention. **8** certain quality. *vt* **1** make a note of. **2** take note of; observe. **noteworthy** *adj* **1** deserving attention; worth noting. **2** remarkable.

nothing *n* **1** not anything; no thing. **2** no part. **3** something of no importance or value. **4** something requiring no effort. **5** zero; nought. **for nothing 1** free of charge. **2** with no purpose. **think nothing of** do without hesitation. *~adv* not in any way.

notice *vt,vi* **1** observe; take note of. **2** comment on, esp. favourably. *n* **1** attention; observation. **2** piece of displayed written information. **3** public announcement. **4** warning. **5** official announcement or notification of the termination of employment. **6** critical review. **at short notice** with little warning or preparation time. **noticeable** *adj.*

notify *vt* let (a person) know; inform officially. **notification** *n.*

notion *n* impression; view; idea; concept. **notional** *adj* **1** expressing a concept; not based on fact. **2** nominal.

notorious *adj* infamous; having a bad reputation. **notoriety** *n.* **notoriously** *adv.*

notwithstanding *adv* nevertheless. *prep,conj* in spite of.

nougat *n* chewy white sweet containing nuts.

nought *n* zero; nothing. **noughts and crosses** *n* game played on a criss-cross grid in which the object is to get three noughts or crosses in a row.

noun *n* word used to denote a thing, person, concept, act, etc.

nourish *vt* **1** give food to. **2** encourage or harbour (feeling). **nourishment** *n* food.

novel[1] *adj* new and different. **novelty** *n* **1** quality of being novel. **2** cheap often gaudy small article for sale.

novel[2] *n* sustained work of prose fiction longer than a short story. **novelist** *n.*

November *n* eleventh month of the year.

novice *n* **1** beginner; learner. **2** nun or monk who has not yet taken final vows.

now *adv* **1** at present. **2** immediately; this minute. **3** recently. **4** presently. **5** at this point; currently. **6** consequently. **now and then** every so often; occasionally. ~*conj* *also* **now that** since; as a consequence of. **nowadays** *adv* these days; in modern times.

nowhere *adv* not in any place; not anywhere. **get nowhere** be unsuccessful.

noxious *adj* poisonous.

nozzle *n* tube or spout through which liquid or gas is let out.

nuance *n* subtle variation in meaning, shade, etc.

nuclear *adj* **1** of, forming, or relating to a nucleus or central core. **2** relating to the structure or splitting of atoms. **nuclear fission/fusion** *n* splitting of a heavy atom/fusion of light atoms attended by enormous release of energy. **nuclear physics** *n* science relating to the behaviour of atoms. **nuclear reactor** *n* device for generating power from nuclear fission. **nuclear weapon** *n* bomb or missile using energy from nuclear fission or fusion.

nucleus *n*, *pl* **nuclei** ('nju:kliai) *or* **nucleuses 1** central or most active part of a movement, organization, etc. **2** positively charged central mass of an atom consisting of protons and neutrons.

nude *adj* naked. *n* naked figure, esp. one depicted in a painting, sculpture, etc. **in the nude** naked. **nudity** *n*.

nudge *n* deliberate slight push with the elbow; prod. *vt* give a nudge (to).

nugget *n* **1** small hard irregularly shaped lump, esp. of gold. **2** small valuable piece.

nuisance *n* thing or person causing annoyance, trouble, or offence.

null *adj* **1** without value or feeling. **2** having no legal force. **null and void** legally invalid. **nullity** *n*. **nullify** *vt* make null. **nullification** *n*.

numb *adj* without feeling, sensation, or emotion. *vt* make numb or insensitive. **numbness** *n*.

number *n* **1** mathematical concept of quantity, each unit of which has a unique value, enabling them to be used in counting. **2** numeral. **3** sum; quantity; aggregate. **4** one of a series; issue. **5** short musical piece. **6** exclusive article. **a number of** several.

number one oneself. **without** *or* **beyond number** too many to be counted. ~*vt* **1** assign a number to. **2** add up to. **3** enumerate; list. **numberless** *adj* countless; innumerable.

numeral *n* symbol or group of symbols, such as 6 or VI, denoting a number.

numerate *adj* ('nju:mərət) able to understand and use mathematical concepts. *vt* ('nju:məreit) number; count. **numeracy** *n*.

numerical *adj* relating to or consisting of numbers. **numerically** *adv*.

numerous *adj* great in number; abundant.

nun *n* woman who has taken final vows in a religious order. **nunnery** *n* community of nuns; convent.

nurse *n* **1** person trained and employed to care for the sick under the direction of doctors. **2** woman employed to look after very small children. *vt,vi* **1** act as a nurse (to). **2** suckle. *vt* cherish; foster; nurture; encourage. **nursing home** *n* small privately run hospital for convalescent, aged, or chronically ill patients.

nursery *n* **1** playroom. **2** place for growing or stocking plants. **nursery rhyme** *n* traditional children's song or verse. **nursery school** *n* school for children under five, kindergarten.

nurture *vt* foster; rear; feed. *n* upbringing; education.

nut *n* **1** hard shelled fruit with a single sometimes edible kernel. **2** small regularly shaped metal block with a central threaded hole used for securing bolts. **3** *sl* fanatic; enthusiast. **4** *sl* insane or peculiar person. **nuts** *sl adj* crazy. **nutcracker** *n* *also* **nutcrackers** device having pincers for cracking nutshells. **nutmeg** *n* seed of an East Indian tree, ground as a spice. **nutshell** *n* woody covering of a nut kernel. **in a nutshell** precisely; concisely expressed. **nuts and bolts** the basic facts; the essential points.

nutrient *n* nourishing substance taken in, esp. by a plant.

nutrition *n* **1** digestion and assimilation of food. **2** feeding; nourishment. **nutritious** *adj* nourishing; health-giving.

nuzzle *vt,vi* rub or push (against) with the nose.

nylon *n* synthetic plastic fibre or material made from it. **nylons** *pl n* woman's stockings.

nymph *n* 1 minor Greek or Roman goddess inhabiting and guarding trees, rivers, etc. 2 beautiful young girl.

O

oak *n* deciduous acorn-bearing tree with hard wood and jagged leaves.

oar *n* wooden pole with one end flattened into a blade, used to propel a boat through water. **put one's oar in** interfere. **oarsman** *n pl* **-men** one who rows with an oar.

oasis *n*, *pl* **oases** (ou'eisi:z) fertile area in a desert.

oath *n* 1 solemn binding declaration of the truth of one's statement. 2 casual use of a solemn word or name in anger or irritation; swearword. **on** *or* **under oath** sworn to tell the truth.

oats *pl n* grains of a hardy cereal plant, widely used as human and animal food. **sow one's wild oats** indulge in pleasures, esp. irresponsible sexual relationships, while young. **oatmeal** *n* coarse flour made from oats used for porridge, biscuits, etc.

obese *adj* extremely fat; gross. **obesity** *n*.

obey *vt,vi* do what is commanded by a person, law, instinct, etc. **obedient** *adj* ready and willing to obey; dutiful. **obedience** *n*. **obediently** *adv*.

obituary *n* notice of death, esp. in a newspaper, often including a short biography.

object *n* ('ɔbdʒekt) 1 thing discernible by the senses. 2 aim, goal, or intention. *vt,vi* (əb'dʒekt) oppose, disapprove, or protest against. **objection** *n* 1 act of or reason for objecting. 2 feeling or statement of dislike or disapproval. **objective** *adj* 1 separate; detached. 2 impartial; viewed fairly and dispassionately. *n* point or situation to be aimed at; goal. **objectively** *adv*. **objectivity** *n*.

oblige *vt* 1 allow no choice; insist or force. 2 do a favour for. 3 make indebted to. **obligation** *n* duty enforceable by law, morality, a contract, promise, etc. **obligatory** (ə'bligətəri) *adj* necessary and binding.

oblique 1 slanting away from the horizontal or vertical. 2 indirect; devious; not straightforward. **obliquely** *adv*.

obliterate *vt* leave no trace of; destroy; blot out. **obliteration** *n*.

oblivion *n* state of forgetfulness or lack of awareness. **oblivious** *adj* 1 absent-minded; unaware. 2 unaffected by; impervious to. **obliviously** *adv*.

oblong *n* figure, esp. a rectangle, longer than it is broad. *adj* shaped like an oblong.

obnoxious *adj* 1 repulsive; causing disgust. 2 extremely rude or insulting.

oboe *n* woodwind instrument having a mouthpiece fitted with a double reed. **oboist** *n*.

obscene *adj* offending against decency or morality; vulgar; lewd. **obscenely** *adv*. **obscenity** *n*.

obscure *adj* 1 vague; enigmatic; not easily understood. 2 dim; gloomy; indistinct. 3 not famous or well-known. **obscurely** *adv*. **obscurity** *n*.

observe *vt,vi* 1 see, notice, or watch. 2 keep to the rules of a custom, law, religion, etc. 3 remark or comment. **observer** *n*. **observance** *n* adherence to the rules of law, religion, custom, etc. **observant** *adj* attentive; taking notice. **observation** *n* 1 careful watching; recognizing and noting. 2 comment or remark. **observatory** *n* building used for astronomical observation.

obsess *vt* be an obsession of; preoccupy. **obsessive** *adj*. **obsession** *n* fixed idea or addiction that fascinates and preoccupies the mind to an exaggerated or dangerous extent.

obsolete *adj* out-of-date; antiquated; disused. **obsolescent** *adj* becoming obsolete. **obsolescence** *n*.

obstacle *n* any snag or obstruction hindering progress or action.

obstinate *adj* stubborn; hard to persuade; unyielding. **obstinacy** *n*. **obstinately** *adv*.

obstruct *vt,vi* 1 block off; prevent access or progress. 2 impede or delay any action. **obstruction** *n*.

obtain *vt,vi* gain possession (of); get; secure or acquire. **obtainable** *adj*.

obtrusive *adj* interfering; impertinent. **obtrusion** *n*.

obtuse *adj* dull; blunt; not sharp or acute. obtuse angle *n* angle greater than 90° but less than 180°.
obvious *adj* evident; clear; apparent. obviously *adv.*
occasion *n* 1 particular time of an event, ceremony, etc. 2 suitable opportunity or chance. 3 reason; need. rise to the occasion display the necessary or suitable qualities. ~*vt* give rise to; bring about or cause. occasional *adj* infrequent; sporadic. occasionally *adv.*
Occident *n* the West, esp. W. Europe and America. Occidental *adj,n.*
occult *adj* supernatural; magical; mysterious. the occult *n* supernatural or magical knowledge or experience.
occupy *vt* 1 take or hold possession of (a country, building, etc.). 2 employ. occupant *n* one who possesses or lives in a particular place. occupancy *n.* occupation *n* 1 employment; pastime; job. 2 state or act of occupying or being occupied.
occur *vi* (-rr-) 1 happen; take place. 2 exist; be found at. 3 come into the mind. occurrence *n.*
ocean *n* one of the five vast areas of sea surrounding the continents of the globe. oceanic *adj.*
octagon *n* geometric figure, design, building, etc., having eight sides. octagonal *adj.*
octane *n* inflammable hydrocarbon present in petrol. high-octane *adj* denoting a superior grade of petrol.
octave *n* 1 range of eight notes in a musical scale. 2 set of eight.
October *n* tenth month of the year.
octopus · *n, pl* octopuses *or* octopi ('ɔktəpai) eight-armed mollusc.
odd *adj* 1 strange; bizarre; peculiar. 2 uneven; irregular. 3 (of a number) not divisible by two. odd man out one remaining when others have formed a pair, class, group, etc. oddly *adv.* oddity *n* 1 strangeness; peculiarity. 2 remarkable or unlikely event, person, object, etc. oddment *n* scrap; remnant; leftover. odds *pl n* 1 chances; possibilities. 2 ratio between two stakes in a wager. at odds in disagreement. odds and ends small miscellaneous scraps.
ode *n* poem addressed to a particular person or object.

odious *adj* hateful; loathsome. odium *n.*
odour *n* smell; fragrance.
oesophagus (i:'sɔfəgəs) *n, pl* oesophagi (i:'sɔfəgai) tube running from the pharynx to the stomach; gullet.
oestrogen *n* female sex hormone.
oestrus *n* period of sexual receptiveness in most female mammals.
of *prep* 1 belonging to. 2 originating from. 3 created or produced by. 4 from the period relating to. 5 made with. 6 containing; holding. 7 towards or away from a specified place. 8 that is the same as. 9 for. 10 separated from.
off *prep* 1 so as to be away or distant from. 2 not present at or attending to. 3 removed or deducted from. 4 no longer interested in. 5 by the means of. *adv* 1 distant; away. 2 so as to be removed or rid of. 3 so as to stop or disengage. *adj* 1 cancelled or postponed. 2 not attached. 3 not working or turned on. on the off chance with the possibility or hope.
offal *n* edible internal organs or parts of an animal.
offend *vt* cause displeasure or pain to. *vi* sin; do wrong. offence *n* 1 crime or infringement of the law. 2 any cause of anger, grievance, or pain. to take/give offence to be/cause hurt. offensive *adj* aggressive; repellent; obnoxious. *n* attack.
offer *vt* give; present or hold out for acceptance. *vi* volunteer; be available or on hand. *n* 1 act of offering. 2 something offered.
offhand *adj* 1 impromptu; unprepared. 2 casual; impolite.
office *n* 1 position of authority, esp. public or governmental. 2 place of business. 3 government department. 4 rite or religious service. officer 1 person holding a responsible position in a government, club, organization, etc. 2 holder of a commission in the armed forces. 3 policeman. official *n* one who holds an office. *adj* 1 authorized or vouched for. 2 relating to an office. officially *adv.* officious *adj* bossy; interfering.
offing *n* in the offing in view; near; likely to happen.
off-licence *n* shop licensed to sell alcoholic drink for consumption off the premises.

off-peak *adj,adv* at a less popular or less busy time.

off-putting *adj* discouraging; repelling.

offset *vt* (-tt-; -set) compensate for; balance out.

offshore *adj,adv* from or far from the shore or land.

offside *adj* in a part of a football field, etc., between the ball and the opponents' goal, where it is not allowable to kick the ball. *n* the right-hand side of a vehicle, horse, etc.

offspring 1 child or children. 2 any issue or result.

offstage *adj,adv* not visible to the audience.

often *adv* frequently; repeatedly.

ogre *n* 1 monstrous man-eating giant of fairy tales and folklore. 2 cruel person; tyrant.

oil *n* viscous liquid obtained from many mineral and vegetable sources, lighter than and insoluble in water. **burn the midnight oil** work or study until late at night. ~*vt* apply oil to. **oily** *adj*. **oil painting** *n* 1 picture painted in oil-based paints (oils). 2 art or practice of painting such pictures. **oilskin** *n* cloth or clothing treated with oil to make it waterproof.

ointment *n* soothing or medicated cream applied to the skin.

old *adj* 1 aged; having existed for many years. 2 out-of-date; obsolete; belonging to an earlier age; stale. **old age** *n* last years of life. **old-fashioned** *adj* out-of-date; obsolete; quaint. **old hand** *n* experienced person.

olive *n* small oily Mediterranean fruit eaten either unripe (green olive) or ripe (black olive). *n,adj also* **olive green** brownish green.

omelette *n* eggs beaten together, fried, and flavoured with herbs, vegetables, cheese, etc.

omen *n* sign supposedly prophesying a future event.

ominous *adj* threatening; suggesting trouble.

omit *vt* (-tt-) leave out; fail to do. **omission** *n*.

omnibus *n* bus. *adj* containing several assorted ingredients, items, etc.

omnipotent *adj* all-powerful. **omnipotence** *n*.

on *prep* 1 placed or being in contact with the top or surface of. 2 supported by or attached to. 3 during a particular day. 4 close to or by the side of; along. 5 being broadcast by or performed at. 6 at the time or occasion of. 7 with the support of. 8 concerning; about. 9 by means of. *adv* 1 so as to work or function. 2 so as to be covered with. 3 ahead. **on and off** sporadically. **on and on** repeatedly; continuously. ~*adj* 1 taking place; planned. 2 attached. 3 working; functioning; performing.

once *adv* 1 on a single occasion. 2 in the past. **at once** 1 immediately. 2 simultaneously. **once and for all** finally.

oncology *n* branch of medicine dealing with the study of cancer. **oncologist** *n*.

one *adj* 1 single; individual. 2 only. 3 being a united entity. *n* 1 the smallest whole number represented by the symbol 1 or I. 2 particular or specified single person, thing, example, etc. 3 *also* **one o'clock** the first hour after noon or midnight. *pron* 1 a person; any person; each person. 2 *formal* I or me. **one another** each other; one to or with the other. **oneself** *r pron* 1 a or any person's own self. 2 yourself. **be/feel oneself** be/feel normal, natural, etc. **one-sided** *adj* unfairly biased. **one-way** *adj* 1 allowing traffic in one direction only. 2 not reciprocal.

onion *n* vegetable whose rounded pungent bulb is used in cooking.

onlooker *n* spectator; observer.

only *adj* being a single one or one of few; sole. *adv* 1 exclusively; solely. 2 merely; just. *conj* but; however.

onset *n* beginning; start; attack.

onslaught *n* violent assault.

onus *n* responsibility; duty; burden.

onward *adj* moving forwards. **onwards** *adv* forwards; towards the front.

onyx ('oniks) *n* quartz having bands or layers of different colours.

ooze *vi,vt* seep; leak; flow gradually.

opal *n* quartz-like mineral characterized by iridescent colours, often used as a gemstone.

opaque *adj* obscure; transmitting no light. **opacity** *n*.

open *adj* 1 not closed or sealed. 2 allowing access. 3 ready or available for business or trade. 4 free from obstruction. 5 vacant; unoccupied; free. 6 not yet settled or decided. 7 candid; honest; not prejudiced. 8 vulnerable; liable. *vt,vi* 1 make or become open. 2 undo; unfold. 3 start; give an introduction (to). *vt* 1 disclose; reveal. 2 declare officially to be open to the public. *n also* **the open air** outdoors; outside. **in the open** so as to be known or made public. **openly** *adv.* **openness** *n.* **open-ended** *adj* limitless. **opener** *n* gadget for opening tins, bottles, etc. **open-handed** *adj* generous. **open-hearted** *adj* frank; sincere. **opening** *n* 1 gap; space. 2 start; beginning. 3 opportunity; chance. **open-minded** *adj* not biased or prejudiced; liberal. **open-mouthed** *adj* astonished; aghast. **open-plan** *adj* having few or no internal walls to separate rooms.

opera *n* musical drama, largely or wholly sung. **operatic** *adj.*

operate *vi,vt* 1 work or function. 2 perform surgery (on). **operative** *adj.* **operator** *n.* **operation** *n* 1 working; action; function; effect. 2 instance of surgery. **operational** *adj.*

operetta *n* short, light, or comic opera.

ophthalmology *n* branch of medicine dealing with eye disorders. **ophthalmologist** *n.*

opinion *n* judgment; view; belief. **opinionated** *adj* dogmatic; stubborn. **opinion poll** *n* organized questioning to determine public opinion on a particular issue.

opium *n* narcotic, sedative, or stimulant drug prepared from juice of certain poppies. **opiate** *n* drug containing opium. *adj* made from opium; inducing sleep.

opponent *n* antagonist; one who opposes. *adj* opposing; adverse.

opportunity *n* favourable chance or occasion. **opportune** *adj* lucky; well-timed.

oppose *vt* set against; resist; obstruct or contest. **opposite** *adj* 1 facing; in front of. 2 opposed or contrary (to). *n* opposite person or thing; antithesis. *adv,prep* in an opposite position, direction, etc. **opposite number** *n* person holding a similar or equivalent position in another country, company, etc. **opposition** *n* 1 resistance; hostility. 2 state or position of being opposite. 3 most

distant positioning of two stars or planets. **the Opposition** major political party not in office.

oppress *vt* 1 weigh down or overwhelm. 2 persecute severely. **oppression** *n.* **oppressive** *adj* 1 harsh; cruel. 2 (of weather) sultry.

opt *vt* choose; settle for; decide between. **option** *n* 1 choice; alternative. 2 right, freedom, or opportunity to purchase. **optional** *adj* not obligatory.

optical *adj* relating to the eyes; visual. **optician** *n* person who makes or sells glasses, lenses, etc.

optimism *n* feeling or belief that the best will happen; hopefulness. **optimist** *n.* **optimistic** *adj.*

opulent *adj* rich; lavish; sumptuous. **opulence** *n.*

or *conj* 1 with the alternative of. 2 and also; as well as.

oral *adj* 1 spoken. 2 relating to the mouth.

orange *n* round juicy citrus fruit with reddish-yellow peel. *n,adj* reddish-yellow. **orangeade** *n* orange-flavoured fizzy drink.

oration *n* eloquent public speech or address. **orator** *n.* **oratory** *n.*

orbit *n* 1 path followed around a planet or star by a satellite. 2 sphere of influence. 3 eye socket. **orbital** *adj.*

orchard *n* enclosed area of fruit trees.

orchestra *n* 1 company of instrumental musicians. 2 *also* **orchestra pit** semicircle between the stage and seats in a theatre. **orchestra stalls** *pl n* front seats in a theatre. **orchestral** *adj.* **orchestrate** *vt* arrange (music) for an orchestra. **orchestration** *n.*

orchid *n* one of a family of perennial plants with complicated specialized, often exotic, flowers.

ordain *vt* 1 decree; order. 2 appoint as a priest or minister. **ordination** *n.*

ordeal *n* severe trial of stamina or endurance.

order *n* 1 arrangement; sequence. 2 command; rule. 3 tidiness. 4 class or group. 5 religious body. **in order** 1 in a proper state or condition. 2 correct or appropriate. **in order to** so as to; with the intention or purpose of. ~*vt* 1 command; instruct. 2

arrange; organize. **3** send for. **orderly** *adj* methodical; tidy; well-controlled. *n* **1** soldier serving an officer. **2** attendant in a hospital.

ordinal number *n* number, such as first, second, etc., that denotes order, quantity, or rank in a group.

ordinary *adj* usual; common; familiar; plain. *n* **out of the ordinary** unusual; exceptional. **ordinarily** *adv*.

ore *n* mineral from which metal may be obtained.

organ *n* **1** differentiated part of an animal or plant performing a particular function. **2** large musical wind instrument with a keyboard and pipes, often used in churches. **3** means or method of communication. **organist** *n*.

organic *adj* **1** relating to or derived from plants or animals. **2** inherent; structural. **3** (of food) grown without application of any non-organic fertilizer, pesticide, etc. **4** relating to chemical compounds of carbon. **organically** *adv*.

organism *n* any animal, plant, bacterium, or virus.

organize *vt* arrange, group, classify, or prepare. *vi* form a political group, union, etc. **organization** *n* **1** organized group, system, company, etc. **2** act of organizing.

orgasm *n* culmination of a sexual act, characterized by ejaculation in the male and vaginal contractions in the female.

orgy *n* drunken riotous revelry. **orgiastic** *adj*.

Orient *n* the East or the countries of Asia. **Oriental** *adj,n*.

orientate *vt* find the bearings of in relation to surroundings, conditions, etc. **orientation** *n*.

origin *n* source; beginning; starting point. **original** *adj* **1** existing since the beginning. **2** new; not copied; novel; creative. *n* the source from which copies, translations, etc., are made. **originate** *vt,vi* start or initiate; have as a source. **origination** *n*.

Orlon *n Tdmk* lightweight synthetic fibre used for clothing, etc.

ornament *n* ('ɔːnəmənt) **1** decoration; adornment. **2** item or article used for show. *vt* ('ɔːnəment) embellish; decorate. **orna-**

mentation *n*. **ornamental** *adj* decorative.

ornate *adj* elaborately or flamboyantly decorative.

ornithology *n* study of birds. **ornithologist** *n*.

orphan *n* child whose parents have died. *adj* bereaved of parents. *vt* leave bereaved of parents. **orphanage** *n* institution for bringing up orphans.

orthodox *adj* having sound, correct, or established views, esp. in religion. **orthodoxy** *n*.

orthopaedic *adj* intended to cure deformity.

oscillate *vi* **1** move from side to side as a pendulum. **2** waver; fluctuate. **oscillation** *n*.

ostensible *adj* apparent; seeming. **ostensibly** *adv*.

ostentatious *adj* showy; flamboyant; vulgar. **ostentation** *n*.

osteopath *n* one who manipulates the bones and muscles in order to cure diseases. **osteopathy** *n*.

ostracize *vt* isolate, shun, or bar from society. **ostracism** *n*.

ostrich *n* large fast-running long-necked bird that is native to Africa.

other *adj* alternative; remaining; different; additional. **on the other hand** alternatively. **the other day** recently. ~*pron* second or additional person or thing. *adv* **other than 1** in addition to; apart from. **2** in a different way from. **others** *pl pron* remaining, different, or additional ones. **otherwise** *conj* or else. *adv* in a different way; in other respects. *adj* different.

otter *n* fish-catching aquatic mammal having a smooth coat and webbed feet.

ought *v aux* **1** have an obligation or duty. **2** need; will be wise or advised. **3** will be likely or liable. **4** will be pleased.

ounce *n* unit of weight equal to one sixteenth of a pound (approx. 28 grams).

our *adj* belonging to us. **ours** *pron* something or someone belonging to us. **ourselves** *r pron* **1** our own selves. **2** our normal selves.

oust *vt* eject or dispossess; usurp or replace.

out *adv* **1** away; towards the outside. **2** not present. **3** no longer in power. **4** on strike. **5** not accurate. **6** available to the public. **7** not alight or switched on. **8** no longer in fashion. **9** so as to eliminate or omit. **10** so as to project or protrude. **11** so as to appear. **12** acting with the intention of. **13** into a state of unconsciousness. *prep* away through. **out-of-date** *adj,adv* old-fashioned; obsolete.

outboard motor *n* engine that can be attached to the exterior of a small boat.

outbreak *n* eruption, epidemic, or sudden appearance.

outburst *n* sudden or violent expression of feelings.

outcast *n* one rejected by society; exile.

outcome *n* result; consequence.

outcry *n* eruption of public protest.

outdo *vt* (-does; -did; -done) excel or surpass.

outdoor *adj* used or existing outdoors. **outdoors** *adv* in the open air; outside any building.

outer *adj* external; further out. **outermost** *adj* furthest out or away. **outer space** *n* vast untravelled area beyond the known planets.

outfit *n* **1** complete equipment, such as a suit of clothes, for a specific purpose. **2** *inf* gang; group of people. **outfitter** *n* shop or dealer selling men's clothes.

outgoing *adj* **1** resigning; retiring; departing. **2** extrovert; gregarious. *n* expenditure.

outgrow *vt* (-grew; -grown) **1** grow larger or taller than. **2** grow too large for. **outgrowth** *n* something growing from a main stem, part, etc.

outhouse *n* shed; small building separate from larger one.

outing *n* excursion; pleasure trip.

outlandish *adj* extraordinary; eccentric; bizarre.

outlaw *n* fugitive from justice; bandit. *vt* ban; prohibit.

outlay *n* expenditure. *vt* (-laid) spend; expend.

outlet *n* **1** means of escape, expression, etc. **2** market or shop handling a particular commodity.

outline *n* **1** rough sketch or draft. **2** silhouette. *vt* **1** produce an outline of. **2** give a preliminary account of.

outlive *vt* live longer than; survive.

outlook *n* **1** mental attitude; point of view. **2** prospect; forecast.

outlying *adj* remote; on the outside; far away.

outnumber *vt* surpass in number; be more than.

outpatient *n* non-resident patient who visits hospital for treatment.

outpost *n* position or station far away from headquarters.

output *n* quantity or amount produced by a factory, industry, person, etc.

outrage *n* **1** atrocity; intolerable act. **2** indignation or anger over such an act. *vt* shock; scandalize. **outrageous** *adj* **1** monstrous; appalling; horrifying. **2** absurdly ridiculous. **outrageously** *adv*.

outright *adj* **1** direct; thorough. **2** blatant; total. *adv* at once; completely.

outshine *vt* (-shone) be more successful than; surpass; overshadow.

outside *n* outer surface or side. *adj* exterior; on the outside. *adv* out of doors; inside. *prep* beyond. **outsider** *n* **1** one not belonging to a particular group, society, party, etc. **2** competitor in a race, etc., considered to have very little chance of winning.

outsize *adj* larger than average.

outskirts *pl n* outer surrounding area or district; suburbs.

outspoken *adj* exceedingly frank and candid; forthright.

outstanding *adj* **1** prominent; conspicuous; exceptional. **2** not yet paid.

outstrip *vt* (-pp-) **1** do better than; surpass. **2** run faster than.

outward *adj* **1** towards the outside. **2** superficial; apparent; external. *adj,adv* away from home. **outwardly** *adv* ostensibly; apparently; on the surface. **outwards** *adv* out; away from the centre.

outweigh *vt* be more important, valuable, or heavy than.

outwit *vt* (-tt-) defeat by superior cunning or ingenuity.

oval *adj* egg-shaped. *n* something that is oval.

ovary *n* **1** one of the two female reproductive organs producing eggs. **2** part of a flower containing ovules.

ovation *n* enthusiastic applause.

oven *n* compartment enclosed by metal, brick, etc., and heated for baking, roasting, etc.; kiln; furnace.

over *prep* **1** above; higher than. **2** on the top or surface of; so as to cover. **3** across; on the other side of. **4** during. **5** in excess of; more than. **6** throughout. **7** about; concerning. **8** recovered from; finished with. **9** better than. **10** superior in rank to. **11** by means of. **12** whilst occupied with. *adv* **1** across. **2** throughout; during. **3** from start to finish. **4** so as to fall or bend. **5** so as to remain. **6** so as to be finished. **over and over (again)** repeatedly. ~*n* series of six balls bowled in cricket.

overall *adj,adv* including or considering everything. *n* light coat or apron worn to protect clothes from dirt. **overalls** *pl n* hard-wearing trousers with a high front and straps over the shoulders.

overbearing *adj* domineering; bossy.

overboard *adv* over the side of a boat or ship. **go overboard** enthuse.

overcast *adj* cloudy; gloomy.

overcharge *vt,vi* charge too much money.

overcoat *n* heavy coat.

overcome *vt* (-came; -come) **1** conquer; vanquish; get the better of. **2** overwhelm; affect totally.

overdo *vt* (-does; -did; -done) **1** do something to excess; exaggerate. **2** cook for too long.

overdose *n* too large a dose.

overdraw *vt,vi* (-drew; -drawn) draw from a bank more money than exists to one's credit. **overdraft** *n* amount by which debit exceeds credit in a bank account.

overdue *adj* late; past the time when due.

overeat *vi* (-ate; -eaten) eat excessively; gorge.

overestimate *vt* value too highly.

overfill *vt* flood; fill too full.

overflow *vt* (-flowed; -flown) flow over the edge of; reach beyond the limits of; be excessively full of. *n* **1** flood or profusion. **2** outlet for excess water.

overgrown *adj* covered with vegetation, weeds, etc.

overhang *vt,vi* (-hung) jut over. *n* jutting ledge.

overhaul *vt* **1** check thoroughly for faults. **2** repair; renovate; restore. *n* check-up; service.

overhead *adv,adj* above the head; in the sky. **overheads** *pl n* regular unavoidable expenses of administration.

overhear *vt* (-heard) eavesdrop; hear words intended for others by accident or design.

overjoyed *adj* ecstatic; thrilled; delighted.

overland *adj,adv* mainly or entirely by land.

overlap *vt,vi* (-pp-) **1** extend partly beyond the edge of. **2** coincide partly. *n* overlapping part or area.

overlay *vt* (-laid) **1** cover the surface of. **2** cover; disguise with. *n* something laid over as a cover, decoration, etc.

overleaf *adv* on the other side of the page.

overload *vt* load, fill, or weigh down excessively.

overlook *vt* **1** view from a higher place. **2** disregard or take no notice of; choose to ignore.

overnight *adv,adj* **1** during the night. **2** all night. **3** lasting for one night.

overpower *vt* **1** conquer by superior strength, weight, etc. **2** subdue; overwhelm; overcome.

overrate *vt* overestimate.

overreach *vt* **1** reach or extend too far for comfort. **2** outwit.

overrule *vt* rule against or annul by virtue of greater authority.

overrun *vt* (-nn-; -ran; -run) **1** swarm over and take possession of; infest. **2** extend beyond.

overseas *adv,adj* abroad; across the sea.

overshadow *vt* **1** cast a shadow over. **2** outshine.

overshoot *vt* (-shot) shoot or go over or beyond.

oversight *n* **1** omission; mistake; failure to take into account. **2** supervision.

oversleep *vi* (-slept) sleep longer than intended.

overspill *n* surplus, esp. of the population of a town.

overstep *vt* (-pp-) exceed; go beyond (a limit, constraint, etc.).

overt *adj* openly done; public; not concealed. **overtly** *adv*.

overtake *vt* (-took; -taken) **1** catch up with and pass. **2** come up on suddenly.

overthrow *vt* (-threw; -thrown) **1** defeat utterly. **2** overturn; demolish. *n* defeat; ruin.

overtime *n* time worked beyond usual working hours or payment for this.

overtone *n* implication; suggestion.

overture *n* **1** instrumental prelude to an opera, ballet, etc. **2** opening negotiations or approach.

overturn *vt* upset, overthrow, or abolish.

overweight *adj* heavier than permissible or normal. *n* excess weight.

overwhelm *vt* **1** conquer by superior might. **2** overpower emotionally. **overwhelmingly** *adv*.

overwork *vt,vi* work or cause to work too hard. *n* excess work.

overwrought *adj* over-excited; in a state of nervous agitation.

ovulate *vi* produce and discharge an egg from an ovary. **ovulation** *n*.

ovule *n* part of a plant that contains the egg cell, which develops into a seed after fertilization.

owe *vt* be indebted for; be under an obligation. **owing to** because of.

owl *n* nocturnal bird of prey with a large head and eyes, small hooked beak, and a hooting cry.

own *adj* relating to oneself, itself, etc. **get one's own back** take revenge. **hold one's own** succeed in keeping one's position; acquit oneself well. **on one's own** by oneself; independently. ~*vt* possess; have. **own up** confess. **owner** *n*. **ownership** *n*.

ox *n pl* **oxen** castrated male of domestic cattle. **oxtail** *n* tail of an ox used esp. in soups and stews.

oxygen *n* colourless tasteless gaseous element present in air, water, and most minerals. **oxygenate** *vt,vi also* **oxygenize** fill with oxygen.

oyster *n* edible marine bivalve mollusc.

P

pace *n* **1** single step or its approximate length. **2** speed, esp. of walking or running.

put through one's paces test (someone) for speed, talent, etc. ~*vi* walk with a regular step. *vt* measure out (distance) by pacing.

pacifism *n* opposition to or nonparticipation in warfare or violence. **pacifist** *n,adj*. **pacify** *vt* calm; soothe; placate; appease.

pack *n* **1** bundle; load; heap. **2** container; small package, as of cigarettes. **3** set of playing cards. **4** group of wolves, hounds, etc. **5** gang of people. **6** forwards in a Rugby team. **pack of lies** false story. ~*vt,vi* arrange (clothes, etc.) in a case, etc. *vt* **1** form into a bundle; roll up; put away. **2** crowd into; press together; cram. **3** make compact. **pack off** send away. **send packing** send away abruptly; dismiss. **packhorse** *n* horse used to carry supplies, goods, etc.

package *n* **1** parcel; object or objects in a container, wrapping, etc. **2** group of separate items, services, ideas, etc., offered for sale or acceptance as a single unit. *vt* make a package of or for; wrap. **packaging** *n* materials or containers and wrappings used to package goods.

packet *n* **1** small package. **2** *sl* large sum of money.

pact *n* agreement; treaty; contract.

pad[1] *n* **1** piece of material used to fill out, cushion, or protect. **2** fleshy cushion on the underside of an animal's paw or foot. **3** covering or guard to protect part of the body. **4** sheets of writing paper fastened together. **5** *sl* flat or residence, esp. a small one. *vt* (-dd-) **1** stuff, fill, or protect with soft cushionlike material. **2** expand or extend with irrelevant or unnecessary information. **padding** *n*.

pad[2] *vt,vi* (-dd-) traverse on foot; trudge. *n* soft dull sound.

paddle[1] *n* **1** short oar flattened at one or both ends used without rowlocks in small boats, canoes, etc. **2** structure or implement shaped like a paddle. **3** spell of paddling. *vt,vi* move on water using a paddle.

paddle[2] *vi* dabble one's feet or hands in shallow water. *n* act or instance of paddling.

paddock *n* **1** small field used for grazing horses. **2** enclosure where racehorses assemble before a race.

paddyfield *n also* **paddy** field used for growing rice.

padlock *n* detachable lock having a hinged loop released by a key. *vt* secure with a padlock.

paediatrics *n* branch of medicine dealing with children and childhood diseases. **paediatric** *adj.* **paediatrician** *n.*

pagan *adj* heathen; relating to a religion other than Christianity, Judaism, or Islam. *n* pagan person.

page[1] *n* one side of a leaf of a book, newspaper, etc.

page[2] *n* 1 attendant in a hotel, etc. 2 junior servant of a king or nobleman. 3 boy attendant at a wedding. *vt* summon by calling out a name over a public address system.

pageant *n* lavish public spectacle, procession, or play, esp. of historical significance. **pageantry** *n.*

pagoda *n* Oriental temple with a tower of concave sloping roofs.

paid *v pt* and *pp* of **pay**.

pain *n* 1 physical or mental distress or discomfort. 2 *sl also* **pain in the neck** irritating or annoying person or thing. *vt* hurt; cause to feel physical or mental distress. **painful** *adj.* **painfully** *adv.*

painstaking *adj* careful; meticulous. **painstakingly** *adv.*

paint *n* colouring or covering matter on or for a surface. *vt* 1 apply paint or liquid to. 2 represent or depict in words. *vt, vi* portray or design using paint. **painter** *n.* **painting** *n* 1 picture; artist's representation in paint. 2 art or procedure of applying paint to a canvas.

pair *n* 1 two matched objects designed to be used or worn together. 2 two persons, animals, things, etc., normally found together. 3 single object consisting of two similar interdependent parts. *vt, vi* arrange in twos; make a pair.

pal *n inf* friend; mate; chum. *v* (-ll-) **pal up** *inf* become friends.

palace *n* present or former residence of a royal family, bishop, or archbishop. **palatial** *adj.*

palate *n* 1 roof of the mouth. 2 sensitive or refined sense of taste, esp. for wine. **palatable** *adj* 1 agreeable to the taste. 2 acceptable to the mind.

pale *adj* 1 light in shade; lacking in colour. 2 faint; dim. *vi* lose importance or significance (before). **paleness** *n.*

palette *n* 1 flat board used by artists for mixing colours. 2 range of colours used by a particular artist or school of painters.

pallid *adj* pale; sickly looking. **pallor** *n.*

palm[1] *n* cushioned underside of the hand between the fingers and wrist. *v* **palm off (on)** pass to or impose by trickery; get rid of.

palm[2] *n* tropical and subtropical tree with a straight branchless trunk and a crest of large fan-shaped leaves at the top. **Palm Sunday** *n* Church festival on the Sunday before Easter commemorating Christ's triumphal entry into Jerusalem.

palmistry *n* practice or skill of foretelling the future by inspecting lines on the palm of the hand. **palmist** *n.*

pamper *vt* spoil; over-indulge.

pamphlet *n* leaflet or short publication containing information of current interest.

pan *n* 1 metal or earthenware vessel in which food is cooked or served. 2 container resembling such a vessel. *vt, vi* (-nn-) wash (sand, gravel, etc.) in a pan to separate out any gold, silver, etc. **pancake** *n* thin round cake of batter that is fried on both sides.

pancreas *n* gland situated near the stomach that secretes insulin.

panda *n* large black and white bearlike mammal that is native to China.

pander *v* **pander to** minister to or gratify vices, weakness, etc.

pane *n* sheet of glass cut to fit a window or door.

panel *n* 1 section of a wall, door, etc., when framed, raised, or sunk. 2 vertical strip of material in a dress, skirt, etc. 3 small group of persons meeting for a specific purpose. *vt* (-ll-) cover with or provide panels for.

pang *n* sharp stabbing pain.

panic *n* fear or terror, often resulting in rash ill-considered behaviour. *vi, vt* (-ck-) feel or cause to feel panic. **panic-stricken** *adj.*

panorama *n* uninterrupted view of a landscape spread over a wide area. **panoramic** *adj.*

pansy *n* 1 garden plant with white, yellow, purple, or red flowers. 2 *sl* homosexual.

pant *vi, vt* gasp for breath. *vi* long or yearn (for). *n* gasping noise.

panther *n* leopard, esp. a black leopard.

pantihose *n* tights.

pantomime *n* traditional English Christmas entertainment for children.

pantry *n* room adjoining a kitchen with shelves for storing provisions, etc.

pants *pl n* undergarment covering area of the body from the waist to the thighs.

papal *adj* relating to the Pope.

paper *n* **1** material produced by processing wood, rags, etc., used for books, packaging, etc. **2** examination; essay; report. **3** newspaper. *vt* cover with paper or wallpaper. **paperback** *n* book in a cheap edition with a paper cover. **paperclip** *n* piece of twisted wire used to fasten single sheets of paper together. **paperwork** *n* routine clerical work.

papier-mâché *n* pulped paper used in making models, masks, etc.

papist *n* *abusive* follower of the Pope and the Roman Catholic faith.

paprika *n* powdered sweet red pepper.

par *n* **1** equality; equal or even footing; average or usual value or level. **2** (in golf) standard score. **at par** (of shares, etc.) at face value. **on a par with** equal or equivalent to.

parable *n* story designed to illustrate a moral or philosophical point; allegory.

parachute *n* device that assumes an umbrella shape to slow down the descent of a person jumping from an aircraft, etc. *vi,vt* descend or land by parachute.

parade *n* **1** procession; march. **2** show; ostentatious display. **3** promenade. *vi* walk or march (through) in or as in a procession. *vt* flaunt; exhibit openly.

paradise *n* heaven; state of bliss.

paradox *n* **1** statement that appears self-contradictory or absurd. **2** person or thing having self-contradictory qualities. **paradoxical** *adj.* **paradoxically** *adv.*

paraffin *n* light oil distilled from petroleum, used for domestic heating and as aircraft fuel.

paragraph *n* subdivision of the printed page containing several sense-connected sentences and indicated by indentation of the first word.

parallel *adj* **1** remaining equidistant to infinity. **2** similar; analogous. *n* **1** comparable situation. **2** circle marking a degree of latitude. *vt* (-ll-) compare with; correspond to.

paralyse *vt* **1** immobilize or cripple through damage to or destruction of a nerve function. **2** transfix; make immobile. **paralysis** *n, pl* **paralyses** (pə'rælisiːz) pathological condition of crippling due to loss of muscle control. **paralytic** *adj,n.*

paramount *adj* chief; supreme; most important.

paranoia *n* mental disorder characterized by delusions of grandeur, persecution, etc. **paranoid** *adj,n.*

parapet *n* low protective wall built along the edge of a balcony, bridge, etc.

paraphernalia *n* **1** equipment; assorted personal possessions. **2** complicated procedure; rigmarole.

paraphrase *vt* express the sense of a passage by using other words. *n* passage thus reworded.

parasite *n* **1** animal or plant depending on another for sustenance. **2** person who lives off others. **parasitic** *adj.*

paratrooper *n* member of an army unit trained in parachute jumping.

parcel *n* wrapped object, esp. in paper. *vt* (-ll-) **1** make a parcel of. **2** divide (up); apportion.

parch *vt,vi* dry up. *vt* make thirsty.

parchment *n* **1** skin of a sheep or goat processed for use as paper. **2** old document.

pardon *vt* **1** forgive; excuse. **2** waive legal consequences of an offence for (a prisoner). *n* **1** forgiveness. **2** waiver of a penalty.

pare *vt* peel; skin; trim. **pare down** make smaller or more compact.

parent *n* **1** mother or father. **2** animal or plant that has produced one of its kind. **parental** *adj.* **parenthood** *n* state of being a parent.

parenthesis *n, pl* **parentheses** (pə'renθisiːz) either of a pair of characters used to separate or enclose matter in a written or printed text.

parish *n* ecclesiastical subdivision of a county with its own church and clergyman.

park *n* large enclosed area of land laid out for ornamental or recreational purposes. *vt,vi* position or leave (a car, etc.) in a place temporarily. *vt inf* put or leave.

parliament *n* democratic assembly of elected representatives constitutionally empowered to govern by legislation following free discussion. **parliamentary** *adj.*

parlour *n* sitting room or lounge.

parochial *adj* 1 relating to a parish. 2 provincial; limited; narrow.

parody *n* 1 imitation of a work or of an author or musician's style with comic or satirical intent. 2 poor imitation; travesty. *vt* imitate; mock.

parole *n* 1 early or temporary release from prison on condition of good behaviour. 2 period of such release. *vt* grant parole to.

parrot *n* brightly coloured tropical bird capable of imitating human speech.

parsley *n* mildly aromatic herb with curly green leaves.

parsnip *n* white tapering root vegetable.

parson *n* clergyman; minister. **parsonage** *n* residence of a clergyman.

part *n* 1 portion; piece; segment; component. 2 role; responsibility; duty. 3 actor's role. 4 melodic line in choral or orchestral music. 5 *also* **parts** region; area. **take part in** become involved in; join in. ~*vt,vi* 1 divide; separate; come, break, or take apart. 2 leave or stop seeing one another; keep apart. **part with** give up; relinquish. ~*adv* partially; in part. **partly** *adv.* **parting** *n* 1 leave-taking; separation. 2 division; splitting up. 3 line between two sections of hair that have been combed in opposite directions. **part-time** *adj,adv* for or during less than normal working time.

partake *vi* (-took; -taken) 1 participate. 2 have or receive a share or portion.

partial *adj* 1 incomplete; relating to a part. 2 biased; unfair. 3 having a liking for; fond of. **partially** *adv.*

participate *vi* take part (in); share (in). **participant** *n.* **participation** *n.*

participle *n* adjective derived from various verb forms, e.g. *laughing, loving, given,* or *written.*

particle *n* 1 tiniest visible portion; speck. 2 microscopic body of matter.

particular *adj* 1 relating to a single person, object, etc. 2 extraordinary; notable. 3 careful; fastidious; exact. **particulars** *pl n* details; features. **particularly** *adv.*

partisan *n* 1 supporter of a party, cause, etc. 2 guerrilla fighter in enemy-occupied territory.

partition *n* 1 division; separation into parts. 2 structure erected to separate rooms, areas, etc. *vt* divide into parts; separate.

partner *n* 1 associate; colleague; member of a partnership. 2 one of a pair in dancing, cards, etc. *vt* join with someone, esp. in a game or dance. **partnership** *n* legal relationship between two or more persons operating a joint business venture.

partridge *n* small European game bird.

party *n* 1 group united by a common belief or purpose, esp. political. 2 social gathering. 3 person or persons involved in a legal action.

pass *vt,vi* 1 go by or through; move ahead or on; proceed. 2 move or cause to move. 3 exchange or be exchanged. 4 undergo (an exam, trial, etc.) with favourable results. 5 elapse or allow to elapse. *vt* 1 hand over; transfer; throw. 2 surpass; exceed. 3 pronounce; utter. 4 adopt; approve (legislation, etc.). *vi* happen; occur; come to an end. **pass out** faint. ~*n* 1 favourable examination result, without honours. 2 ticket, authorization, etc., to enter or leave at will, without charge, etc. 3 critical position. 4 narrow passage between mountains. 5 amorous advance. **passable** *adj* 1 able to be crossed, passed, etc. 2 mediocre; fairly good.

password *n* prearranged word used as a code for entry, etc.

passage *n* 1 corridor; channel; route. 2 state of transit; voyage; journey. 3 section of a book, etc. **passenger** *n* 1 person travelling in but not controlling a motor vehicle, boat, etc. 2 *sl* person in a team, etc., who does not do his share of the work.

passion *n* 1 intense or ardent emotion. 2 strong liking or enthusiasm. 3 object of such liking. **passionate** *adj.* **passionately** *adv.*

passive *adj* 1 inactive; inert; not participating. 2 submissive; yielding. 3 denoting a sentence or construction in which the logical subject of a verb is the recipient of the action. **passively** *adv.*

Passover *n* Jewish festival commemorating the deliverance of the Hebrews from Egypt.

passport *n* official document issued by a country that identifies the bearer, permits his travel abroad, and requests safe passage while there.

past *adj* **1** relating to an earlier time; gone by; just over; finished. **2** previous; former. **3** relating to a verb tense used to express an action or condition occurring in the past. *n* **1** period prior to the present; past time. **2** person's past life, career, activities, etc. *prep* beyond. *adv* by; ago. **past participle** *n* verb form functioning as an adjective or used with an auxiliary verb to denote past or completed action, e.g. grown, written, or spoken.

pasta *n* food, such as spaghetti, macaroni, etc., made from a flour and water dough and boiled.

paste *n* **1** pliable, malleable, or sticky mess. **2** preparation of meat, fish, etc., mashed to a spreadable consistency. **3** glue; adhesive. *vt* stick; fix or cover with paste.

pastel *n* **1** crayon made from colour pigments and gum. **2** drawing made with these crayons. *adj* pale; light.

pasteurize *vt* partially sterilize (milk, beer, etc.) by heating in order to kill bacteria, limit fermentation, etc. **pasteurization** *n*.

pastime *n* recreation; amusement; hobby.

pastoral *adj* **1** of the country; rural. **2** (of land) used for grazing. **3** peaceful; idyllic. **4** relating to a clergyman or his duties.

pastry *n* **1** flour paste used for pies, tarts, etc. **2** baked foods.

pasture *n* **1** grass, etc., suitable for grazing cattle. **2** meadow; field. *vt* put to pasture.

pasty[1] ('peisti) *adj* **1** relating to paste. **2** (of a person's appearance) pale; unhealthy; white-skinned.

pasty[2] ('pæsti) *n* small pie filled with meat, vegetables, etc.

pat[1] *vt* (-tt-) **1** tap; touch lightly. **2** stroke softly; caress. **3** flatten by beating gently. *n* light blow; slap; tap.

pat[2] *adj* **1** apt; perfect. **2** presumptuous; glib. *adv* **1** exactly; perfectly. **2** aptly.

patch *n* **1** piece of material used to repair something. **2** irregular or small area, piece, plot of land, etc. **3** protective covering for an eye, etc. *vt* repair; mend. **patchwork** *n* **1** patches of material stitched together to form a pattern. **2** something made of different parts, pieces, etc.

pâté *n* paste or spread made from liver, meat, fish, etc.

patent ('pætnt) *n* **1** government permit granting sole rights for an invention, process, etc., for a set period of time. **2** something under such a permit. *adj* ('peitnt) obvious; evident. **patent leather** *n* leather treated to produce a hard lacquered appearance. ∼*vt* obtain a patent for.

paternal *adj* **1** fatherly; characteristic of a father. **2** pertaining to a father or a father's side of a family. **paternally** *adv*. **paternity** *n* **1** fatherhood. **2** descent from a father.

path *n* **1** *also* **pathway** track worn by pedestrians, animals, etc. **2** walk in a park, garden, etc. **3** means; procedure; course of action.

pathetic *adj* **1** pitiful; evoking sadness. **2** *inf* poor; of low quality. **pathetically** *adv*.

pathology *n* study of diseases. **pathological** *adj*. **pathologist** *n*.

patience *n* ability to persevere or endure without complaint.

patient *n* person under the care of a doctor, dentist, etc. *adj* marked by or exhibiting patience. **patiently** *adv*.

patio *n* paved area adjoining a house.

patriarch *n* **1** male head of a family, tribe, etc. **2** elder; senior member of a community. **3** any of several Old Testament personages regarded as a father of the human race. **4** bishop of the Eastern Orthodox Church. **patriarchal** *adj*.

patriot *n* person who loves his country intensely. **patriotic** *adj*. **patriotism** *n*.

patrol *n* **1** regular inspection of an area or building to ensure security, orderliness, etc. **2** person or persons carrying out this inspection. **3** military detachment with the duty of reconnaissance. *vt,vi* (-ll-) take part in a patrol (of).

patron *n* **1** regular customer of a shop, etc. **2** one who offers financial support to a cultural or educational enterprise. **patronage** *n* **1** support given by a patron. **2** trade given a business by its customers. **3** power to bestow political favours, make appointments, etc. **patronize** *vt* **1** visit regularly; support. **2** behave condescendingly (towards someone). **3** be a benefactor of; sponsor.

patter[1] *n* **1** glib inconsequential speech. **2** rapidly delivered lines of a salesman, comedian, etc. **3** *inf* jargon; expressions used by a clique. *vi,vt* talk glibly, rapidly, etc.

patter[2] *vi* **1** make a sound like tapping. **2** walk with a patter. *n* light tapping sound.

pattern *n* **1** design; arrangement. **2** example; model; plan. **3** usual way of doing something. *vt* model after a pattern; imitate.

pause *n* temporary stop or break. *vi* **1** stop temporarily. **2** hesitate; linger.

pave *vt* **1** cover (a road, etc.) with a hard surface. **2** prepare; facilitate. **pavement** *n* paved path for pedestrians alongside a road.

pavilion *n* **1** building on a sportsground housing changing rooms, etc. **2** large tent erected temporarily at fairs, weddings, etc. **3** summerhouse; light ornamental building or structure.

paw *n* foot of certain mammals, esp. cats and dogs. *vi,vt* touch or strike with a paw or leg. *vt inf* caress clumsily; grope.

pawn[1] *vt* leave (an article) as security in exchange for a loan until repayment is made. **pawnbroker** *n* person who lends money on security of personal possessions.

pawn[2] *n* **1** chessman of least value whose second and subsequent moves are limited to one square in a forward direction. **2** manipulated person.

pay *v* (paid) *vt,vi* **1** give (money, etc.) to for, or in return for; recompense. **2** discharge (a debt, etc.). **3** *also* **pay off** be profitable or worthwhile; benefit. *vt* **1** bestow; give. **2** make (a visit, etc.). **pay back 1** repay (a loan, etc.). **2** retaliate against. **pay for** suffer or be punished because of. **pay off 1** pay wages of and discharge. **2** pay in total. ~*n* **1** money paid for work; salary; wages. **2** paid employment. **payment** *n* **1** act of paying. **2** sum of money paid. **3** due reward. **payoff** *n* **1** *inf* outcome; climax of events. **2** full payment. **payroll** *n* **1** list of employees to be paid and their salaries or wages. **2** total of or amount equal to a company's salary or wage expenditure.

pea *n* annual climbing plant whose round green seeds are eaten as a vegetable.

peace *n* **1** state of amity; absence of war. **2** tranquillity; period of rest or quiet. **peaceful** *adj*. **peacefully** *adv*.

peach *n* tree yielding a round juicy yellowish fruit with down-covered skin. *n,adj* bright pinkish-yellow.

peacock *n* brightly coloured male of a large pheasant with a crested head and a tail which can fan out to display bright blue and green markings. **peahen** *f n*.

peak *n* **1** any pointed edge or projection. **2** top of a mountain; summit. **3** projecting brim of a cap. **4** sharp increase or the highest point or value reached. *vi* reach the highest point or value. **peaked** *adj*.

peal *n* loud resounding sound, such as bells ringing, laughter, or thunder. *vt,vi* sound with a peal; ring out.

peanut *n* edible seed rich in food value and yielding oil.

pear *n* tree yielding a sweet juicy fruit whose shape is rounded and tapers towards the stalk.

pearl *n* **1** smooth lustrous creamy precious gem formed on the inside of a clam or oyster shell or synthesized. **2** highly valued person or thing. **pearly** *adj*.

peasant *n* **1** agricultural labourer; countryman; rustic. **2** *inf* uncultured and unsophisticated person. **peasantry** *n*.

peat *n* solid partially carbonized and decomposed vegetable matter used as a garden fertilizer and a fuel. **peaty** *adj*.

pebble *n* small rounded stone. *vt,vi* pave or cover with pebbles. **pebbly** *adj*.

peck *vt* **1** strike with the beak or something sharp. **2** *inf* kiss quickly on the cheek. *n* **1** quick strike or blow. **2** *inf* quick kiss on the cheek.

peckish *adj inf* hungry.

peculiar *adj* strange; odd; unusual. **peculiar to** special or specific to. **peculiarity** *n*. **peculiarly** *adv*.

pedal *n* foot lever of a machine, bicycle, piano, etc. *vt,vi* (-ll-) **1** operate by using pedals. **2** ride a bicycle.

peddle *vt,vi* sell from door to door; hawk. **pedlar** *n*.

pedestal *n* **1** plinth or base supporting an upright object. **2** position of superiority or eminence.

pedestrian *n* person who goes about on foot. *adj* plodding; dull; unimaginative.

pedigree *n* **1** record of an animal's ancestors, kept esp. for animals of good breeding.

2 animal of pedigree stock. 3 ancestral line. **pedigreed** adj.

peel n rind; outer layer of fruit, vegetables, etc. vt,vi strip or whittle (off) an outer skin or surface.

peep vi 1 look quickly or furtively. 2 appear briefly or partially. n quick look or glance.

peer[1] n 1 member of the nobility. 2 person equal in rank or social standing. **peerage** n 1 nobility as a group. 2 position, rank, or title of a peer.

peer[2] vi 1 look closely or intently (at). 2 appear partially; peep.

peevish adj irritable; bad-tempered. **peevishly** adv. **peevishness** n.

peg n 1 small piece of wood or metal used for hanging or fastening things. 2 pin or stake pushed into the ground, a scoreboard, or other surface. 3 pin on a guitar, violin, etc., used for tuning the strings. 4 hinged or grooved pin for hanging clothes on a line. **take down a peg** teach a lesson; humble. **off the peg** (of clothes) ready-made. ~vt (-gg-) 1 pierce with or insert a peg. 2 secure with a peg.

pejorative adj deprecatory; uncomplimentary.

pelican n water bird with white plumage and a large beak with a pouch used for catching fish.

pellet n 1 small ball of something solid. 2 piece of shot.

pelmet n wood or fabric used to conceal a curtain rail.

pelt[1] n skin or hide of a fur-bearing animal.

pelt[2] vt assail with a shower of missiles, blows, abuse, etc. n blow; knock; stroke.

pelvis n cavity or structure found in the lower part of the trunk in most vertebrates. **pelvic** adj.

pen[1] n instrument with a pointed nib used for writing with ink. **penfriend** n person, often living in a different country, with whom one corresponds. **penknife** n small folding knife usually carried in the pocket.

pen[2] n small enclosure for farm animals. vt (-nn-) enclose in a pen; confine.

penal adj relating to punishment, esp. for breaking a law. **penal code** n body of criminal law. **penalize** vt 1 punish; subject to

penalty. 2 handicap; disadvantage. 3 award a point or points to an opposing team. **penalization** n. **penalty** n 1 punishment; price exacted as a punishment. 2 loss; suffering. 3 free kick at goal afforded to one football team because of a breach of rules by the other. **penance** n 1 self-imposed punishment. 2 regret; sorrow.

pence n pl of **penny** (def. 3).

penchant ('pɑːnʃɑːn) n liking; strong inclination.

pencil n writing instrument consisting of a thin rod of graphite encased in wood. vt (-ll-) write or draw with a pencil.

pendant n 1 hanging ornament, esp. on a necklace. 2 hanging lamp or chandelier.

pending adj about to be decided, confirmed, completed, etc. prep while waiting for.

pendulum n suspended weight that swings back and forth under the influence of gravity.

penetrate vt,vi 1 pass into or through. 2 enter or permeate. vt 1 see through. 2 unravel; understand. vi be understood. **penetrable** adj. **penetration** n.

penguin n large flightless black and white aquatic bird of Antarctica.

penicillin n antibiotic drug produced from a mould and capable of preventing the growth of certain bacteria.

peninsula n strip of land jutting into the sea. **peninsular** adj.

penis n male organ of copulation.

penitent adj repentent; remorseful. n penitent person. **penitence** n. **penitently** adv.

penniless adj having no money; very poor; destitute.

penny n 1 also **new penny** bronze coin worth one-hundredth of a pound sterling. 2 former bronze coin worth one-twelfth of a shilling. 3 pl **pence** unit of currency of such a value. **not worth a penny** worthless. **spend a penny** inf urinate.

pension n periodical payment by state or employer to the retired, disabled, widowed, etc. vt grant a pension to. **pensioner** n person receiving a pension.

pensive adj engaged in serious or sad thought. **pensively** adv.

pentagon n five-sided figure. **pentagonal** adj.

penthouse *n* subsidiary structure attached to the main part of a building, often a small house or flat on the roof.

penury *n* poverty; destitution.

people *pl n* **1** human beings in general. **2** racial group. **3** one's family. *vt* populate; fill as with people.

pepper *n* **1** pungent condiment made from the dried berries of a pepper plant. **2** red or green slightly pungent fruit of other types of pepper plant. *vt* flavour with pepper. **peppercorn** *n* dried berry of the pepper plant. **peppermill** *n* instrument for grinding peppercorns. **peppermint** *n* **1** aromatic and pungent herb of the mint family. **2** lozenge flavoured with oil from this mint.

per *prep* **1** for each. **2** by means of.

perambulator *n formal* pram.

perceive *vt* **1** see; discern. **2** be or become aware of. **3** understand. **perceivable** *adj*.

per cent *adv* in each hundred.

percentage *n* **1** number forming a proportion in each hundred. **2** interest paid per hundred.

perception *n* **1** process or power of becoming aware of something. **2** insight; discernment. **perceptible** *adj* noticeable; discernible. **perceptive** *adj* **1** able or quick to notice. **2** intelligent. **perceptively** *adv*.

perch[1] *n, pl* **perch** edible spiny-finned freshwater fish.

perch[2] *n* **1** pole, bar, or branch for birds to roost or sit on. **2** secure seat in a high position. *vi,vt* sit or place on a perch.

percolate *vt,vi* filter or trickle (through). *vi* gradually become known. **percolator** *n* apparatus for percolating water through coffee grounds.

percussion *n* **1** impact; collision. **2** production of noise by striking or tapping. **3** musical instruments, such as the drum, that are struck to produce a note.

perennial *adj* **1** continuing through the year or from year to year. **2** (of plants) living more than two years. **3** perpetual. **perennially** *adv*.

perfect *adj* ('pə:fikt) faultless; complete; functioning correctly; exact. *vt* (pə'fekt) make perfect or complete; finish. **perfection** *n*. **perfectly** *adv*.

perforate *vt,vi* make a hole or holes through, often in a line for easy separation. **perforation** *n*.

perform *vt,vi* **1** do; carry out; complete. **2** act. **performer** *n*. **performance** *n* **1** act of performing; carrying out of something. **2** piece of work; exhibition or entertainment. **3** manner or achievement in working.

perfume *n* **1** sweet-smelling substance applied to the body. **2** pleasant odour; fragrance. *vt* impart fragrance to.

perhaps *adv* maybe; possibly.

peril *n* danger; risk. **perilous** *adj*. **perilously** *adv*.

perimeter *n* circumference; boundary; length of outline of a plane figure.

period *n* **1** stretch of time; phase; era. **2** interval between recurrent phases. **3** full stop. **4** *inf* menstruation. **periodic** *adj*. **periodical** *adj* periodic; issued or occurring at roughly regular intervals. *n* magazine published at stated intervals of more than one day. **periodically** *adv*.

peripheral *adj* **1** of or on the circumference, boundary, or outskirts. **2** of less than central importance. **periphery** *n*.

periscope *n* tube with mirrors for viewing objects above eye level.

perish *vt* destroy; ruin; cause to decay. *vi* **1** die; decay; be ruined or destroyed. **2** distress with hunger and cold. **perishable** *adj*.

perjure *vt* **perjure oneself** lie deliberately under oath. **perjurer** *n*. **perjury** *n*.

perk *v* **perk up** **1** look up jauntily. **2** make (oneself) smarter. **3** recover spirits or energy. *n inf* legitimate extra gain attached to a job, not included in wages.

permanent *adj* lasting or intended to last indefinitely. *n also inf* **perm** artificially induced and long-lasting waving of the hair. **permanently** *adv*.

permeate *vt,vi* spread through, pervade, or be pervaded. **permeation** *n*.

permission *n* act of permitting; allowing; consent. **permissible** *adj*. **permissive** *adj* granting permission or liberty; lenient; tolerant. **permissively** *adv*. **permissiveness** *n*.

permit *vt,vi* (pə'mit) (-tt-) grant leave; allow; concede; make possible. *n* ('pə:mit) written permission; warrant; licence.

permutation *n* **1** changing of the order of a set of objects. **2** each arrangement of these objects.

peroxide *n* **1** oxide containing more oxygen than normal oxide. **2** *inf* hydrogen peroxide, an antiseptic and bleach.

perpendicular *adj* upright; vertical; at right angles (to). *n* vertical position; perpendicular line. **perpendicularly** *adv.*

perpetual *adj* **1** never ceasing; not temporary. **2** continuously blooming through the growing season. **3** applicable or valid for ever or for an indefinite time. **perpetually** *adv.* **perpetuate** *vt* **1** make perpetual. **2** prolong indefinitely. **3** preserve from extinction or oblivion. **perpetuity** *n* quality or condition of lasting indefinitely.

perplex *vt* confuse; present difficulties or intricacies to bewilder; tease with suspense or doubt. **perplexity** *n.*

persecute *vt* **1** harass; treat cruelly; persistently attack. **persecution** *n.*

persevere *vi* continue in spite of obstacles; keep on striving. **perseverance** *n.*

persist *vi* **1** continue firmly or obstinately, esp. against opposition. **2** continue to exist; remain. **persistence** *n.* **persistent** *adj.* **persistently** *adv.*

person *n* **1** human being. **2** body of a person. **in person** physically present or active. **personal** *adj* **1** one's own; individual; of private concern. **2** relating to bodily appearance. **3** offensive to an individual; insulting. **personally** *adv.* **personality** *n* **1** state of having an identity. **2** celebrity. **3** total intellectual, emotional, or physical qualities of an individual, esp. as presented to others. **personify** *vt* **1** regard as a person. **2** embody; symbolize in human form. **personification** *n.*

personnel *n* persons engaged together in some work; work force.

perspective *n* **1** method of portraying relative size and distance of objects on a plane surface. **2** relative importance and true relationship of facts, ideas, etc.

perspex *n* tough transparent unsplinterable plastic material.

perspire *vi,vt* exude moisture through skin pores; sweat. **perspiration** *n.*

persuade *vt* induce by argument; cause to believe; convince. **persuasion** *n.* **persuasive** *adj.* **persuasively** *adv.*

pert *adj* **1** forward; saucy; cheeky. **2** open; brisk; flourishing. **pertly** *adv.*

pertain *vi* **1** belong as part of; be connected with. **2** have reference or relevance to. **3** be suitable for or appropriate to. **pertinent** *adj.* **pertinently** *adv.*

perturb *vt* disturb greatly; cause alarm or anxiety to. **perturbation** *n.*

pervade *vt* penetrate; diffuse through the whole of; permeate. **pervasion** *n.* **pervasive** *adj.*

perverse *adj* obstinately turning aside from right or truth; unreasonably contradictory. **perversely** *adv.* **perversion** *n.* **pervert** *vt,vi* (pə'vɔ:t) turn from proper use or sense; corrupt or be corrupted. *n* ('pə:vɔ:t) one who is thought to deviate in sexual desires or practice. **perversion** *n.*

peseta *n* monetary unit of Spain.

peso *n* monetary unit of Argentina, Mexico, the Philippines, and various other countries.

pessimism *n* tendency to look on the worst side of things; despondency. **pessimist** *n.* **pessimistic** *adj.*

pest *n* **1** troublesome or destructive person, etc. **2** insect, fungus, etc., destructive of cultivated plants. **pesticide** *n* chemical for destroying pests.

pester *vt* cause slight but repeated annoyance to.

pet[1] *n* **1** tame animal kept as a companion, etc. **2** favourite; dearly-loved and pampered person, esp. a child; darling. *v* (-tt-) *vt* treat as a pet; pamper; fondle. *vi* indulge in amorous caressing.

pet[2] *n* childish fit of aggrieved sulkiness; huff. *vi* (-tt-) be peevish; sulk.

petal *n* leaflike part, sometimes brightly coloured, of a flower.

peter *v* **peter out** gradually diminish to nothing; fade away.

petition *n* **1** humble or solemn entreaty. **2** formal request to an authority often signed by a number of persons. *vt,vi* make or receive a humble or formal request.

petrify *vt,vi* **1** turn into or become like stone; fossilize. **2** fix in amazement or horror.

petrol *n* inflammable liquid from refined petroleum, used esp. as fuel in motor-vehicle engines.

petroleum *n* dark thick oily mixture of hydrocarbons, other organic compounds, etc., found in rock deposits.

petticoat *n* woman's underskirt.

petty *adj* **1** unimportant; trivial; insignificant. **2** contemptible, spiteful, or mean over small matters. **petty cash** *n* cash fund in an office for small items of receipt or expenditure. **petty officer** *n* noncommissioned naval officer. **pettiness** *n.*

petulant *adj* peevishly impatient, irritated, or capricious. **petulance** *n.* **petulantly** *adv.*

pew *n* enclosed compartment or fixed bench with a back and sides, as in a church.

pewter *n* **1** alloy of tin and lead and sometimes other metals. **2** vessel, plate, or utensil made of pewter.

pfennig *n, pl* **pfennigs** *or* **pfennige** ('pfenigə) West German copper coin equal to one hundredth of a mark.

phallus *n* **1** male sexual organ; penis. **2** representation of the penis. **phallic** *adj.*

phantom *n* **1** supernatural apparition; ghost; immaterial form. **2** visual illusion.

pharmacy *n* **1** art or practice of preparing and dispensing medicines. **2** chemist's dispensary. **pharmacist** *n.* **pharmaceutical** *adj* relating to medical drugs.

pharynx *n* cavity behind nose and mouth forming the upper part of the gullet and the opening into the larynx.

phase *n* **1** transitory stage in a cycle. **2** appearance of a moon or planet at a particular stage of its orbit. **3** aspect or appearance of anything at any stage. *vt* separate into stages of activity or development. **phase out** bring to terminal stage; extinguish gradually; discontinue.

pheasant *n* **1** long-tailed game bird, brightly coloured in the male. **2** flesh of this bird as food.

phenomenon *n, pl* **phenomena** (fə-'nominə) **1** anything perceived by the senses; observed event. **2** anything striking or exceptional. **phenomenal** *adj* of or like a phenomenon; extraordinary; exceptional; remarkable. **phenomenally** *adv.*

philanthropy *n* benevolence; active generosity in social action; love of mankind. **philanthropic** *adj.* **philanthropist** *n.*

philately *n* study and collection of postage and revenue stamps. **philatelist** *n.*

philosophy *n* **1** study of the ultimate nature of existence. **2** any specified system of thought in this. **3** general mental and moral outlook on life; reasoning. **philosopher** *n.* **philosophical** *adj* **1** relating to philosophy or philosophers. **2** calmly reasonable; wise. **3** stoical; bearing misfortune well.

phlegm (flem) *n* **1** thick slimy fluid secreted in the throat and chest and discharged by coughing. **2** apathy; sluggish indifference. **phlegmatic** (fleg'mætik) *adj* **1** not easily excited or perturbed; placid. **2** sluggish; apathetic; stolid. **phlegmatically** *adv.*

phobia *n* fear, often irrational; dread; dislike.

phoenix *n* bird fabled to burn itself to death every 500 years and be reincarnated from its own ashes.

phone *n, vt, vi* short for **telephone.**

phonetic *adj* relating to the sounds of spoken language. **phonetically** *adv.* **phonetics** *n* study of speech sounds.

phoney *adj* counterfeit; unreal; insincere.

phosphate *n* chemical salt containing phosphorus, used in fertilizers.

phosphorescent *adj* emitting a faint light, similar to fluorescence, esp. after bombardment by radiation. **phosphorescence** *n.*

phosphorus *n* nonmetallic chemical element having an unreactive red form and a toxic inflammable phosphorescent white form, used in matches.

photo *n* short for **photograph.**

photocopy *vt* reproduce an exact copy of by a photographic process. *n* copy produced in this way.

photogenic *adj* suitable for and making a pleasing photograph.

photograph *n* image of something produced by the action of light on chemically sensitized surfaces. *vt* make a photographic image of. **photographer** *n.* **photography** *n* art or process of producing photographs. **photographical** *adj.*

phrase n 1 group of words forming a subdivision of a sentence. 2 idiomatic expression. vt choose fitting words to express. **phrasebook** n collection of idioms and commonly used phrases of a language.

physical adj 1 pertaining to the natural world of matter and energy or its study. 2 relating to the body. **physically** adv. **physical education** n promotion of bodily fitness by exercising the body.

physician n doctor; person legally qualified to treat disease by medicines but not surgery.

physics n study of the properties of matter and energy. **physicist** n.

physiology n study of physical processes in living beings. **physiological** adj. **physiologist** n.

physiotherapy n treatment of disease, weakness, or disability by exercise, massage, heat, etc. **physiotherapist** n.

physique n bodily appearance and constitution.

pi n ratio of the circumference of a circle to its diameter, equal to about 3.142.

piano n keyboard instrument with strings struck by hammers. **pianist** n.

piccolo n small high-pitched woodwind instrument of the flute family.

pick[1] vt, vi 1 choose; select carefully. 2 gather (fruit, etc.). vt 1 poke at with the fingers. 2 provoke. 3 steal from (a pocket, etc.). **pick and choose** select with excessive care. **pick at** nibble at food, esp. due to loss of appetite. **pick on** select, esp. to blame be unpleasant to. **pick out** 1 select. 2 recognize; distinguish; make obvious. **pick up** 1 lift or gather in the hands. 2 improve. 3 take on (passengers, etc.). 4 learn gradually and casually. 5 inf meet casually and get acquainted. 6 inf arrest. ~n 1 choice; selection. 2 best choice. **pickpocket** n one who steals from others' pockets. **pick-up** n 1 device for converting vibrations, as of a record-player stylus, into electric current. 2 recovery. 3 act of picking up or one picked up.

pick[2] n 1 also **pickaxe** tool having a long cross-bar with sharp or pointed ends, used for breaking up stone, etc. 2 any sharp or pointed instrument for picking.

picket n 1 striker or group of strikers outside their workplace to dissuade other workers from working. 2 vigil in a public place by a person or group expressing political or social protest. vt, vi surround with or act as a picket.

pickle n 1 brine or vinegar solution in which food is preserved. 2 vegetable so preserved. 3 inf plight. vt preserve in pickle. **pickled** adj sl drunk.

picnic vi (picnicking; picnicked) take a casual meal outdoors for pleasure. n 1 meal so eaten. 2 outing for such a purpose.

pictorial adj 1 having or expressed by pictures. 2 relating to painting or drawing. n magazine comprising mainly pictures. **pictorially** adv.

picture n 1 two-dimensional arrangement of lines and colours intended to have aesthetic value. 2 embodiment; representation; mental image. 3 impressive sight. 4 film shown at a cinema. 5 vivid verbal description. **in the picture** well-informed; in possession of the facts. **the pictures** pl n cinema. ~vt depict or represent in a picture, the mind, or in words.

picturesque adj suitable for a picture; graphic; quaint.

pidgin n trade language or jargon having elements from two or more languages.

pie n dish of meat, fish, vegetables, or fruit baked with a pastry covering. **easy as pie** very easy.

piece n 1 part or item of a whole; bit; portion. 2 example; specimen. 3 musical, artistic, or literary composition. 4 small object, as used in board games. **go to pieces** 1 lose one's self-control. 2 disintegrate. **piecemeal** adv bit by bit; in pieces. **piecework** n work paid according to the amount done rather than the time taken. v **piece together** assemble; fit together; mend.

pier n 1 jetty; landing stage; breakwater. 2 column supporting an arch or bridge. 3 load-bearing brickwork between windows or doors.

pierce vt 1 penetrate; make a hole in; enter or force a way into. 2 be seen, heard, or felt through. 3 afflict; touch or move deeply.

piety n willing and devout observance of religious duties; devotion to God.

pig *n* **1** domesticated mammal with thick bristly skin and a long snout, bred for its meat. **2** coarse, dirty, or greedy person. **pig in a poke** something bought without examination. **pig-headed** *adj* stupidly stubborn; obstinate. **pigheadedly** *adv.* **pig-iron** *n* iron in rough bars as first extracted from its ore. **piglet** *n* young pig. **pigsty** *n* **1** pen in which pigs are kept. **2** very untidy or dirty house or room. **pigtail** *n* hair twisted into a bunch to form a plait or hang loose.

pigeon *n* widely distributed bird of the dove family. **pigeonhole** *n* **1** small compartment for storing or classifying papers. **2** compartment of the mind. **3** entrance to a dovecote or pigeon's nest. *vt* **1** put in a pigeonhole. **2** put aside; defer considering. **3** classify methodically.

piggyback *n* ride astride someone's back or shoulders. *adv* on someone's back or shoulders.

pigment *n* paint; any colouring matter; substance giving colour to living tissue. **pigmentation** *n* coloration by pigments.

pike *n, pl* **pike** large voracious freshwater fish with a pointed snout.

pilchard *n* small food fish, similar to the herring.

pile[1] *n* **1** heap of objects. **2** *inf* large sum or amount of money, work, etc. *vt,vi also* **pile up.** heap up; collect into a mound. *vi* move quickly and haphazardly as in a group. **pile-up** *n inf* accumulation of things, esp. of cars as a result of a multiple crash, traffic jam, etc.

pile[2] *n* post driven into the ground to support a structure. **piledriver** *n* **1** machine for driving piles into the ground. **2** (in games) powerful stroke; kick.

pile[3] *n* **1** fine soft hair; down. **2** raised yarn on cloth such as velvet or towelling.

pilfer *vt,vi* steal petty articles in small quantities.

pilgrim *n* **1** person journeying to a shrine for religious reasons. **2** wanderer. **pilgrimage** *n* journey to a sacred or revered place. **Pilgrim Fathers** *pl n* original settlers of New England.

pill *n* oral medicine formed into or contained in a small ball, capsule, etc. **bitter pill** something disagreeable that has to be accepted. **the pill** contraceptive pill.

pillar *n* **1** column supporting a structure or standing alone as a monument. **2** person who is a prominent supporter. **pillar-box** *n* short hollow red pillar in which letters are posted; letter box.

pillion *n* seat for a second person on a horse or motorcycle behind the rider or driver. *adv* on a pillion.

pillow *n* soft cushion to support a sleeper's head; padded support. *vt* rest one's head; serve as a pillow for. **pillowcase** *n* washable cover for a pillow.

pilot *n* **1** person qualified to conduct ships in harbours, channels, etc. **2** person qualified to operate flying controls of an aircraft. **3** person steering a ship. *vt* steer; navigate; guide. **pilot scheme** preliminary, experimental, or trial approach or procedure.

pimento *n* red pepper used for stuffing olives, in salads, and as a vegetable.

pimple *n* small swelling on the skin. **pimply** *adj.*

pin *n* **1** short stiff pointed piece of wire with a rounded or flat head. **2** anything resembling a pin in form or function. **3** brooch; badge. *vt* (-nn-) **1** fasten, attach, or secure by a pin. **2** hold or fix in position; immobilize. **pin down 1** force to keep a promise, agreement, etc. **2** define exactly. **pin on** attribute to; blame. **pinpoint** *n* **1** point of a pin. **2** anything very tiny or minute. *vt* locate; define very exactly. **pinstripes** *n* repeated narrow stripes in a material pattern, etc. **pin-up** *n* **1** picture of a nude or seminude girl pinned up on wall. **2** one whose picture is thus displayed.

pinafore *n* apron. **pinafore dress** *n* sleeveless dress worn over a jumper, etc.

pincers *pl n* **1** gripping tool with jaws and handles on a pivot. **2** pair of grasping claw-like parts, as in a crab. **pincer movement** *n* attack by two converging forces.

pinch *vt,vi* **1** squeeze sharply between finger and thumb or be squeezed between two hard objects. **2** inconvenience or be inconvenienced by a lack (of something). *vt* **1** *sl* steal. **2** *sl* arrest. *n* **1** squeeze. **2** emergency. **3** small amount. **at a pinch** if absolutely necessary.

pine[1] *n* coniferous tree with evergreen needle-shaped leaves.

pine[2] *vi* 1 become feeble from mental or physical suffering. 2 languish with longing; yearn (for).

pineapple *n* tropical plant yielding a large edible fruit having yellow flesh and a tuft of leaves on top.

Ping-Pong *n Tdmk* table-tennis.

pinion *n* small wheel with teeth engaging with a larger wheel or rack, one imparting motion to the other.

pink *adj,n* pale red; light rose. *n* garden plant resembling the carnation.

pinnacle *n* 1 small ornamental turret or spire. 2 slender mountain peak. 3 highest point or degree. *vt* 1 set on a pinnacle. 2 adorn with pinnacles.

pint *n* 1 measure of liquid capacity equal to an eighth of a gallon (0.57 litre). 2 *inf* this amount of beer.

pioneer *n* one of the first to attempt, explore, research, or colonize; one who takes the lead. *vt,vi* be or act as a pioneer.

pious *adj* devout; faithful in religious duties. **piously** *adv.*

pip[1] *n* small seed of fleshy fruits.

pip[2] *n* shrill note repeated as a signal in broadcasting or telephoning.

pip[3] *n* spot on a playing card, domino, or die.

pipe *n* 1 tube for conveying water, etc. 2 vessel for smoking loose tobacco. 3 simple wind instrument. 4 note of a bird; shrill voice. **pipes** *pl n* bagpipes. ~*vt* 1 convey by pipe. 2 provide pipes or piping for. 3 play on a pipe. **pipe down** make less noise. **pipe up** begin to speak unexpectedly. **pipe-dream** *n* wishful daydream; futile hope or plan. **pipeline** *n* 1 long line of pipes conveying water or oil. 2 direct communication line. **in the pipeline** on the way.

piquant *adj* 1 pleasantly pungent; tasty. 2 rousing keen interest. **piquancy** *n.*

pique *n* ill-feeling; resentment; anger. *vt* 1 annoy; offend. 2 arouse (interest, etc.).

pirate *n* 1 one who attempts robbery or unlawful capture of ships at sea. 2 privately owned radio transmitter or operator without a licence. 3 one who infringes copyright or trading rights. *vt* infringe copyright or trading laws. **piracy** *n.*

pirouette *n* act of spinning on tiptoe, esp. in dancing. *vi* spin thus.

Pisces *n* twelfth sign of the zodiac, represented by the Fishes.

pistol *n* small hand gun.

piston *n* short cylinder moving to and fro in a cylindrical tube as part of an engine or pump.

pit *n* 1 hole; sunken area; depression. 2 mine shaft. 3 sunken area for an orchestra in front of a stage. 4 area near a race track in which cars are serviced or refuelled. **pit of the stomach** hollow below the breastbone. ~*vt,vi* (-tt-) make a hole in or become marked with hollows. **pit against** set to fight against; match against. **pitfall** *n* hidden danger or unexpected difficulty.

pitch[1] *vt,vi* 1 throw; fling. 2 set up (camp); erect (a tent). *vt* 1 set the slope or level of. 2 give a particular slant or character to. 3 sing or play (a note, etc.) accurately. *vi* toss up and down, as by waves. *n* 1 slope; gradient. 2 playing field. 3 frequency of a musical note. 4 *inf* persuasive sales talk. **pitchfork** *n* long-handled two-pronged fork for pitching hay. *vt* 1 lift and throw with a pitchfork. 2 assign work or responsibility to hastily or roughly.

pitch[2] *n* black viscous tarry liquid that sets hard on cooling and is used for roads, paths, etc. *vt* apply pitch to.

piteous *adj* arousing pity; pathetic.

pith *n* 1 core of spongy tissue in plant stems, feathers, etc. 2 white fibre inside the rind of oranges, lemons, etc. 3 essence; concentrated meaning; importance. 4 physical strength; mastery. **pithy** *adj.*

pitta bread *n* type of slightly leavened bread in the form of flat cakes.

pittance *n* meagre allowance or portion.

pituitary gland *n* small gland in the brain that controls or influences hormone action.

pity *n* 1 compassion for suffering and the misfortunes of others; mercy. 2 cause of disappointment or regret. *vt* feel pity for. **pitiful** *adj* 1 arousing pity; pathetic; miserable. 2 contemptible. **pitifully** *adv.* **pitiless** *adj* merciless; cruel.

pivot *n* 1 pin or fixed point on which something turns. 2 person or thing on which all depends. *vt,vi* mount or turn on a pivot. *vi* depend on.

pizza *n* Italian dish consisting of a bread-like base with a topping of tomato sauce, cheese, and garnishes.

placard *n* public notice; written or printed display. *vt* **1** publicize by a placard. **2** fix a placard to.

placate *vt* appease hostility or resentment of.

place *n* **1** geographical point; location; area. **2** position; state; rank. **3** space; room; seat. **4** house; residence. **5** duty; right. **6** job; appointment. **7** relative position in a race. **go places** *inf* become successful. **out of place** unsuitable; inappropriate. **in place of** instead of. **take place** occur; happen. ~*vt* **1** put or set in a particular or suitable position or order. **2** identify by some past link. **3** make; put. **4** appoint. **place with** put under the care of.

placenta *n* mass of tissue within the womb by which a connection is made between the foetus and the mother and which is discharged after birth. **placental** *adj.*

placid *adj* calm; unruffled. **placidly** *adv.*

plagiarize *vt,vi* steal from writings or ideas of another and use as one's own. **plagiarism** *n.* **plagiarist** *n.*

plague *n* **1** deadly highly infectious epidemic disease. **2** calamity; curse. **3** troublesome or annoying person or thing. *vt* be a persistent trouble to; pester.

plaice *n* edible flatfish having a brown body marked with orange spots.

plaid *n* cloth with a tartan pattern.

plain *n* **1** tract of level land; open country. **2** simple knitting stitch. *adj* **1** level; flat; even. **2** clear; obvious. **3** simple; not ornate, decorated, or embellished. **4** neither beautiful nor ugly. **5** outspoken; straightforward. *adv also* **plainly** distinctly; bluntly; frankly. **plain-clothes** *adj* (of police, etc.) wearing ordinary clothes as opposed to a uniform. **plain sailing** *n* smooth and unhindered progress.

plaintive *adj* mournful; lamenting; complaining. **plaintively** *adv.*

plait *n* braid in which three or more strands or bunches of hair, etc., are passed over one another in turn. *vt* braid; intertwine.

plan *n* **1** scheme; project; method. **2** map of an area. **3** diagram of a structure. *vt,vi* (-nn-) **1** make a plan of or for; devise methods of doing. **2** regulate by a central authority.

plane[1] *n* **1** level or even surface. **2** level of existence or standard of performance, etc. **3** short for **aeroplane**. *adj* level; flat. *vi* skim over a water surface.

plane[2] *n* tool for levelling or smoothing surfaces, cutting grooves, etc. *vt* **1** use a plane on. **2** shave off by means of a plane.

planet *n* nonluminous celestial body that orbits around a star, esp. the nine bodies, including earth, that orbit around the sun. **planetary** *adj.*

plank *n* long broad length of cut timber. *vt* cover or supply with planks.

plankton *n* small animals and plants that inhabit the surface of a body of water and on which many larger animals feed.

plant *n* **1** living organism that synthesizes its own food from inorganic substances and lacks sense organs and powers of locomotion. **2** any herbaceous plant, as distinct from a tree or shrub. **3** factory; manufacturing works. **4** *inf* person or thing introduced into a group, place, etc., to throw guilt on innocent people. *vt* **1** put in the ground to grow. **2** establish; fix. **plantation** *n* large estate, esp. in tropical countries, where crops are grown. **planter** *n* **1** owner or supervisor of a plantation. **2** decorative holder for a house plant.

plaque 1 ornamental plate or disc intended to be mounted or hung for display. **2** hard white deposit that forms around the teeth.

plasma *n* clear yellowish fluid part of blood or lymph in which cells are suspended.

plaster *n* **1** mixture of sand, lime, and water that is applied to walls and ceilings to make them smooth. **2** self-adhesive bandage for minor wounds. *vt* cover or coat with or as if with plaster. **plaster of Paris** *n* hard refined plaster suitable for use in sculptures, casts, etc.

plastic *n* widely used synthetic material that can be moulded into a desired shape when soft. *adj* **1** made of plastic. **2** pliable; elastic. **3** easily influenced. **plastic money** *n* credit cards, etc. **plastic surgery** *n* surgery concerned with the repair, sometimes cosmetic, of external tissue.

Plasticine *n* *Tdmk* soft modelling material.

plate *n* **1** shallow dish or receptacle. **2** thin coating of metal, esp. gold or silver. **3** item or items coated with gold or silver. **4** illustration or print in a book. **5** thin sheet, esp. of glass. *vt* coat with a thin layer of metal. **platelayer** *n* person who lays and maintains railway tracks.

plateau *n* **1** large level area of high land. **2** long stable period during development.

platform *n* **1** raised area, as for a speaker at a meeting. **2** waiting area at a railway station, etc. **3** statement of policy of a political party.

platinum *n* pliable silvery precious metal that is very durable and much used, esp. in jewellery.

platonic *adj* without physical desires.

platter *n* large dish or plate, used esp. for serving food.

plausible *adj* reasonable, likely, or believable. **plausibility** *n*. **plausibly** *adv*.

play *vt,vi* **1** occupy or amuse oneself (in a game, sport, etc.). **2** fill a particular role in a team game. **3** act as; imitate. **4** operate a musical instrument, radio, record player, etc., or be operated. *vt* **1** compete with. **2** act the part of. **3** give a dramatic performance of. *n* **1** drama; dramatic production. **2** games, diversions, etc. **3** manner or way of playing. **4** fun; light-heartedness. **5** liberty of action; scope. **playable** *adj*. **player** *n*. **playboy** *n* man who devotes himself to the pursuit of irresponsible pleasures. **playground** *n* outdoor area for children to play in. **playgroup** *n* nursery group for very young children. **playhouse** *n* **1** theatre for live drama. **2** toy house for children. **playing card** *n* one of a pack of fifty-two cards having a set value in one of the four suits into which the cards are divided. **playing field** *n* field used for playing team games. **playmate** *n* companion in play, esp. for children. **playschool** *n* playgroup. **playwright** *n* writer of plays; dramatist.

plea *n* **1** sincere claim or appeal. **2** something pleaded on behalf of a defendant in a legal trial.

plead *vt,vi* **1** appeal (to); beseech; implore. **2** offer an argument (for). *vt* **1** give as an excuse or justification. **2** declare oneself as being (guilty or not guilty) in a court of law.

pleasant *adj* pleasing; agreeable; enjoyable. **pleasantly** *adv*. **please** *vt,vi* gratify or delight (someone). *adv* used in making polite requests, asking favours, etc. **pleasure** *n* **1** delight; happiness; enjoyment. **2** something giving these things.

pleat *n* permanent fold or repeated crease in a fabric, esp. in skirts or dresses. *vt* make pleats in.

plectrum *n,pl* **plectrums** *or* **plectra** ('plektrə) implement or pick for plucking a musical string.

pledge *n* **1** solemn oath or promise. **2** guarantee; security. **3** token; symbol. *vt,vi* **1** promise solemnly. **2** give as a pledge. *vt* bind or secure by a pledge.

plenty *n* **1** enough; adequate supply. **2** abundance; profusion; large number. *adj* enough; very many. **plentiful** *adj*.

pliable *adj* **1** flexible; easily bent. **2** compliant; yielding; manageable.

plight *n* dilemma; difficult situation.

plimsoll *n* rubber-soled canvas shoe worn for sport.

plod *v* (-dd-) *vt,vi* walk along in a slow dogged manner. *vi* work slowly and steadily. *n* act or sound of plodding.

plonk *n* *inf* cheap wine.

plop *n* sound made by dropping an object into water. *v* (-pp-) *vt,vi* drop or make fall with a plop. *vi* make a plop.

plot[1] *n* **1** secret plan; outline; scheme. **2** story of a play, novel, etc. *v* (-tt-) *vt,vi* plan or conspire secretly. *vt* chart (a course) or make a map of.

plot[2] *n* small patch of ground.

plough *n* device for turning over soil when planting crops. *vt,vi* till or make a furrow with a plough.

pluck *vt* **1** pick off (feathers, flowers, etc.) from. **2** draw sound from (the strings) of (a musical instrument) by pulling them. **3** pull; tug. *n* courage. **plucky** *adj* brave; courageous.

plug *n* **1** piece of material used to fill a hole or stop up a gap. **2** device that connects an electrical appliance to an electricity supply. **3** *inf* unscheduled advertisement for or mention of a product. *vt* (-gg-) **1** attach to an electricity supply by means of a plug. **2** stop up or fill. **3** *inf* mention favourably or advertise.

plum *n* small tree bearing purple or green fruit with an oval stone. *adj inf* comfortable; pleasant.

plumage *n* feathers on a bird.

plumb *n* lump of heavy material, esp. when attached to a length of string (**plumbline**) and used to ensure that a wall, etc., is vertical. *vt* measure the depth of (the sea, etc.) with or as if with a plumb.

plumber *n* person who installs and repairs water pipes, baths, sinks, etc. **plumbing** *n* **1** profession of a plumber. **2** pipes and other appliances connected with the supply of water to a building.

plume *n* feather, esp. a long ornamental one.

plump[1] *adj* fleshy; chubby; fat. *vt,vi* make or become plump.

plump[2] *vi* fall or drop heavily or noisily. **plump for** choose; select.

plunder *vt,vi* steal (from) by force; rob. *n* **1** anything stolen or taken by force; loot. **2** act of plundering.

plunge *vt,vi* **1** thrust or be thrust, esp. into a liquid. **2** bring or be brought suddenly (into a certain condition). **3** rush madly in a certain direction. **4** throw oneself enthusiastically (into). *n* **1** act of plunging. **2** leap; mad dash.

plural *adj* consisting of or relating to more than one. *n* **1** linguistic number category in which plural nouns are placed. **2** plural form of a noun.

plus *prep* added to; with. *adv* or more. *n also* **plus sign** sign indicating addition.

plush *adj also* **plushy** very comfortable and expensive; luxurious.

Pluto *n* ninth and furthest known planet from the sun.

ply[1] *vt* **1** travel regularly around (an area) selling (goods, etc.). **2** supply continuously. **3** work at; engage in.

ply[2] *n* layer of material, esp. wood, or a strand of yarn. **plywood** *n* material consisting of layers or strips of wood glued together.

pneumatic *adj* relating to or operated by air, esp. compressed air.

pneumonia *n* disease marked by inflammation of the lungs, usually caused by bacteria or a virus.

poach[1] *vi,vt* **1** catch or take (game, fish, etc.) illegally. **2** trespass; encroach. **3** steal; pinch. **poacher** *n.*

poach[2] *vt* cook in gently boiling liquid.

pocket *n* **1** small pouch or bag, esp. one sewn into a garment. **2** cavity; hollow. **3** isolated area of group of people. **out of pocket** having made a financial loss. ~*vt* steal; appropriate. **pocket money** *n* small weekly sum of money given by parents to a child.

pod *n* fruit of the pea, bean, and related plants.

poem *n* composition usually written in regular rhythmic lines and often employing rhyme, metaphor, etc., to stimulate the imagination. **poetic** *adj.* **poet** *n* writer of poems. **poetess** *n f.* **poetry** *n* **1** verse. **2** art or work of a poet. **3** poetic qualities.

point *n* **1** sharp tapering end. **2** any projection, esp. a tapering one, such as a piece of land jutting out into the sea. **3** mark or dot made by something with a sharp point. **4** punctuation mark or accent used in writing, esp. a full stop. **5** something that has a position but no spatial extent. **6** definite place on a scale; specific moment. **7** stage in a course of action, procedure, etc., esp. an important or decisive stage. **8** element or part of something, esp. the most essential part, as of a topic, joke, etc. **9** reason; aim; meaning; significance. **10** unit of counting used in scoring games; mark. **on the point of** about to commit the act of. **make a point of** insist on as being important. **point of view** outlook; personal position or attitude. **stretch a point** be prepared to make an exception to one's usual practice. **to/off the point** relevant/irrelevant. **point-blank** at a range so close that one cannot miss; directly. ~*vt,vi* direct or aim (one's finger, etc.) at. *vt also* **point out 1** indicate the position of. **2** turn someone's attention to. *vi* indicate or face in the direction of. **pointed** *adj* **1** having a point. **2** referring obviously to someone or something; emphatic; incisive. **pointer** *n* **1** something used for pointing. **2** indicator on a dial. **3** hint; suggestion. **4** breed of hunting dog. **pointless** *adj* lacking relevance, meaning, significance, etc.

poise *n* **1** calmness of manner; composure. **2** balance; stability. *vt,vi* **1** balance or be balanced. **2** hold a position, esp. in mid-air; hover.

poison *n* substance that causes illness or death because of its chemical properties. *vt* **1** kill or injure by administering poison. **2** put poison into (food, water, etc.). **poisonous** *adj.*

poke *vt,vi* **1** probe; prod; pierce. **2** push or thrust. *n* prod; push; thrust.

poker[1] *n* metal rod used for stirring the embers of a fire.

poker[2] *n* gambling card game.

pole[1] *n* long usually slender cylindrical rod used for support, measurement, propulsion, etc. **pole-vault** *n* athletic event in which a competitor propels himself over a high bar by means of a pole. *vt,vi* perform the pole-vault over a barrier.

pole[2] *n* **1** either of the two extreme ends of the axis of a planet or other globe. **2** two ends of a magnet, terminals of an electric battery, etc. **Pole Star** star almost directly over the earth's North Pole. **polar** *adj.* **polarize** *vt,vi* form into two or more distinct opposing groups.

polemic *n* controversial dispute or argument or an article, essay, etc., containing this. *adj also* **polemical** of or concerning a polemic.

police *n* **1** authority in a country responsible for keeping order, preventing crime, and enforcing laws. **2** *pl* members of this authority. *vt* control or keep law and order in. **policeman** *n,* *pl* **-men** police officer. **police station** *n* headquarters of a local branch of the police.

policy[1] *n* **1** course or line of action, esp. one adapted by a government in running state affairs. **2** wise or sensible way of doing things.

policy[2] *n* document stating the details of a contract between an individual and an insurance company.

polio *n also* **poliomyelitis** acute infectious disease, usually of children, that can paralyse various muscle groups.

polish *vt,vi* put a shine on something. *vt* improve (one's language, manners, etc.). *n* **1** substance applied to something to make it smooth or shiny. **2** shine or smoothness resulting from polishing. **3** act of polishing. **4** elegance or superior quality, as of a person's behaviour.

polite *adj* **1** demonstrating good manners and good behaviour; courteous. **2** refined and elegant. **politely** *adv.* **politeness** *n.*

politic *adj* **1** wise. **2** clever; cunning.

political *adj* **1** of or connected with politics or a party in politics. **2** of or relating to a state government or its administration. **politically** *adv.* **politician** *n* person concerned with politics, esp. one who holds a public office in a government. **politics** *n* **1** s science or profession concerned with government. **2** *pl* political affairs, principles, or ideas.

polka *n* **1** lively Bohemian dance. **2** music composed for this dance. *vi* dance a polka.

poll *n* **1** mass vote, as at an election. **2** number of votes cast. **3** list of people drawn up for voting or taxation purposes. **4** *also* **opinion poll** process in which a selection of people are interviewed as a means of assessing public opinion. *vt* **1** receive votes in an election. **2** interview to test public opinion.

pollen *n* dustlike material produced by flowering plants that serves as a fertilizing agent. **pollinate** *vt* transfer pollen to (a plant) for purposes of fertilization. **pollination** *n.*

pollute *vt* **1** make foul or poisonous; contaminate. **2** corrupt the morals of. **pollutant** *n* something that pollutes. **pollution** *n.*

polygamy *n* practice of marrying or the situation of being married to more than one woman at a time. **polygamist** *n.* **polygamous** *adj.*

polygon *n* geometric figure having three or more sides.

polymer *n* substance containing long chains of atoms joined together, as in cellulose, plastics, synthetic fibres, etc.

polyp *n* **1** type of individual of such organisms as corals or sea anemones, having tentacles and a mouth. **2** *also* **polyps** small pathological growth, as in the nose.

polytechnic *n* type of college of higher education originally set up to teach scientific subjects but now also teaching social sciences.

polythene *n* widely used type of plastic. *adj* made of polythene.

pomegranate *n* large round usually red fruit with a tough rind and inner parts divided into chambers containing edible seeds.

pommel *n* **1** raised front end of a saddle. **2** knob on the top of a sword.

pomp *n* **1** stately splendour. **2** ostentatious or empty show; vain display. **pompous** *adj* **1** overdignified; self-important. **2** ostentatious or inflated. **pompously** *adv.*

pond *n* small lake; pool.

ponder *vt,vi* reflect or think deeply; meditate.

pony *n* small horse.

poodle *n* breed of dog having thick curly hair.

pool[1] *n* **1** small body of water; pond; puddle. **2** any small amount of liquid. **3** still deep part in a river.

pool[2] *n* **1** group or association of mutually cooperative members. **2** combination of things, esp. a set of services or financial facilities shared by a number of people or groups. **3** all the stakes in a game. *vt,vi* combine to form a pool. **the pools** *n* system of betting on the results of football matches.

poor *adj* **1** having or characterized by little wealth or resources. **2** deficient in something necessary or desirable; inferior; unsatisfactory; scanty. *n* **the poor** poor people in general. **poorly** *adv* badly. *adj inf* ill.

pop[1] *v* (-pp-) *vt,vi* **1** make or cause to make a short sharp sound. **2** burst open or cause to burst open with a pop. *vi* come or go quickly. *n* **1** popping sound. **2** nonalcoholic fizzy drink. **pop off 1** depart. **2** die suddenly. **pop the question** propose marriage. ~*adv,interj* with or expressing a popping sound. **popcorn** *n* type of maize that bursts and puffs up when roasted.

pop[2] *n* type of music usually having a distinctive and persistent rhythmic beat and making extensive use of electronically aided instruments.

Pope *n* head of the Roman Catholic Church.

poplar *n* tall tree of the willow family having a spirelike appearance.

poppy *n* plant bearing red, orange, or white flowers.

popular *adj* **1** liked or enjoyed by a large number of people. **2** of or connected with the people. **3** normal among or suitable for the people. **popularity** *n.* **popularly** *adv.* **populate** *vt* **1** live in; inhabit. **2** introduce a population into; people. **population** *n* people considered collectively, esp. all the people living in a town, city, country, etc.

porcelain *n* type of delicate pottery; china.

porch *n* **1** exterior roofed entrance to a house. **2** veranda.

porcupine *n* animal of the rodent family whose body is covered with stiff sharp spines or quills.

pore[1] *v* **pore over** think or ponder deeply about; study.

pore[2] *n* tiny opening, esp. in the skin or a leaf, to allow the passage of perspiration or other moisture.

pork *n* flesh or meat obtained from pigs. **porker** *n* pig being fattened for slaughter.

pornography *n* literature or art dealing with obscene subjects and intended to arouse sexual desires. **pornographic** *adj.*

porous *adj* full of little holes like a sponge, which allow the passage of water or air.

porpoise *n* aquatic mammal with a blunt snout, related to the whale.

porridge *n* breakfast dish consisting of oatmeal, water, and often milk.

port[1] *n* a place, city, etc., where ships may load or unload cargoes.

port[2] *n* left side of a ship or aeroplane for someone facing towards the front.

port[3] *n* sweet fortified usually dark red wine.

portable *adj* able to be carried easily by hand. *n* portable object.

porter[1] *n* person employed to carry people's luggage, as at a railway station or hotel.

porter[2] *n* dark bitter ale.

portfolio *n* **1** large flat case for carrying documents, drawings, etc. **2** collection of documents concerned with a government department. **3** office of a government minister. **4** list of securities held by a person, bank, etc.

porthole *n* opening in a ship's side fitted with glass to let in air and light.

portion *n* 1 piece; share. 2 amount of food served to one person. *vt* 1 give as a share. 2 divide or share.

portrait *n* 1 picture of a person, usually a painting. 2 lively written description of a person. **portraiture** *n* 1 art of producing portraits. 2 portraits collectively.

portray *vt* 1 play the part of (someone), as in a play. 2 describe a person or his character. **portrayal** *n*.

pose *n* 1 way of standing or behaving deliberately adopted to give an effect. 2 pretence. *vi* 1 act (as something one is not). 2 stand or sit in a certain way to be photographed or painted. *vt* ask (a question); present (a problem).

posh *adj inf* 1 smart; showing style. 2 upper-class; snobbish.

position *n* 1 place. 2 situation or condition. 3 opinion; attitude. 4 way of standing, sitting, etc. 5 job; employment; office; rank. *vt* 1 put into place. 2 find the place of. **positional** *adj*.

positive *adj* 1 definite. 2 certain; sure. 3 real, true, or actual. 4 useful or helpful. 5 hopeful; optimistic. 6 denoting numbers greater than zero. 7 designating or having the electric charge of a proton. 8 (of a photograph) corresponding in colour or tone to the scene photographed. *n* positive photograph, electric terminal, etc. **positively** *adv*. **positive discrimination** *n* provision of special opportunities for an acknowledged disadvantaged group.

possess *vt* have or control; own. **possessed** *adj* mad or frenzied, esp. when under the control of an evil spirit. **possession** *n* 1 something one owns. 2 act of possessing or state of being possessed. 3 condition of occupying property. 4 overseas colony. **possessive** *adj* 1 concerning possession. 2 selfishly dominating or controlling a person. 3 denoting the case or form of a word used to indicate possession.

possible *adj* 1 able to exist, occur, be done, etc. 2 that may perhaps happen. 3 potential. *n* person or thing that is possible. **possibly** *adv*. **possibility** *n* something that is possible. **possibilities** *pl n* likely prospects.

post¹ *n* 1 stout wooden pole driven into the ground, esp. to support a roof, gate, or door. 2 place where a race starts or ends. *vt* 1 put up (a notice) on a wall, etc. 2 announce to the public by putting up a notice or sign.

post² *n* 1 job or duty. 2 place where a soldier carries out his duties. 3 fort or military camp. 4 remote settlement. *vt* 1 assign a task or duty to. 2 send to (a military camp). 3 appoint to.

post³ *n* 1 national system or organization for carrying letters, parcels, etc. 2 letters and parcels handled for delivery; mail. 3 act or time of collecting or delivering mail. *vt* send through the post. **keep posted** keep informed. **postage** *n* money paid for the use of the post. **postal** *adj*. **postal order** *n* money order that can be bought or cashed only at a post office. **postbox** *n* box in which letters are placed for collection. **postcard** *n* card, sometimes having a picture on one side, used to send short messages. **postman** *n, pl* **-men** official who delivers letters.

poster *n* placard, esp. used as an advertising announcement.

posterior *adj* placed or following behind something else. *n* buttocks.

posterity *n* future generations.

postgraduate *adj* relating to studies carried out by a student who has already gained his first degree. *n* postgraduate student.

posthumous *adj* 1 happening or produced after a person's death. 2 published after an author's death. **posthumously** *adv*.

postmortem *n* 1 medical examination of a corpse to find out the cause of death. 2 analysis of reasons for failure of a plan, etc., of something after it is over. *adj,adv* after death.

postpone *vt* delay; put off; defer. **postponement** *n*.

postscript *n* additional note added at the end of a letter or document, after the signature.

postulate *n* ('pɔstjulit) 1 idea or principle temporarily adopted as the basis of an argument, etc.; assumption. 2 unproved or self-evident scientific statement. *vt* ('pɔstjuleit) 1 claim; demand. 2 adopt as a postulate.

posture *n* 1 way of standing or walking. 2 situation or condition. *vi* act in an unnatural way to achieve an effect.

posy *n* small bunch of flowers.

pot¹ *n* 1 round vessel or container. 2 vessel used for cooking food or from which tea or coffee is served. 3 jar. **go to pot** fall into a state of ruin. **pot shot** easy shot with a gun, etc. ~*v* (-tt-) *vt,vi* 1 place plants, etc., in a pot. 2 put food in jars to preserve it. *vt* strike (a billiard ball) into a pocket.

pot² *n* marijuana.

potassium *n* soft silvery-white metallic element whose compounds are much used in drugs and fertilizers.

potato *n, pl* **potatoes** tuber of certain plants used as a vegetable.

potent *adj* 1 powerful; strong; influential. 2 (of men) able to perform sexually. **potency** *n*.

potential *adj* 1 capable of existing, becoming effective, etc. 2 not yet using one's power. *n* capacity or ability not yet realized or used. **potentiality** *n*. **potentially** *adv*.

pothole *n* 1 small pit in a road. 2 deep hole in rock, often large enough to be explored. **potholer** *n*.

potion *n* drink of a medicinal, magical, or poisonous nature.

potter¹ *n* person who makes pottery.

potter² *vi* move or act aimlessly.

pottery *n* 1 earthenware vessels. 2 material from which such vessels are made. 3 factory where pots are made.

pouch *n* 1 small bag, esp. one for carrying money, food, tobacco, etc. 2 baglike or pocket-like part of the body on certain animals, esp. the one in which kangaroos, wallabies, etc., carry their young.

poultice *n* soft moistened mass applied to the body for medicinal purposes. *vt* place a poultice on.

poultry *n* domesticated fowls. **poulterer** *n* person who sells poultry and game.

pounce *vi* leap suddenly (upon); swoop. *n* sudden leap or swoop.

pound¹ *vt,vi* beat with a succession of heavy blows. *vt* reduce to dust; crush. *vi* thump; throb. *n* thump.

pound² *n* 1 unit of weight, divided into sixteen ounces, equivalent to 0.45 kilograms. 2 basic unit of British currency or the system of currency used in Great Britain (**pound sterling**) and several other countries.

pound³ *n* enclosure, esp. one for sheltering, confining, or catching animals.

pour *vt,vi* 1 flow or cause to flow out. 2 emit or cause to emit continually and quickly. 3 rain heavily.

pout *vi* push out the lips as when angry, sullen, etc. *vt* say in a sulky manner. *n* 1 act or gesture of pouting. 2 sulk.

poverty *n* state or condition of being poor; lack of wealth. **poverty-stricken** *adj* without means; destitute.

powder *n* 1 solid substance in the form of tiny loose particles, usually produced by grinding or crushing. 2 type of powder used as a cosmetic, medicine, etc. *vt,vi* make into or become a powder; crush or be crushed. *vt* apply powder to. **powdery** *adj*.

power *n* 1 ability or means to do something. 2 capacity of mind or body. 3 strength, energy, or force. 4 control; influence; authority. 5 country or state having international influence. 6 divine or supernatural being. 7 rate at which work is done or energy is transferred. *vt* 1 provide energy, force, etc., for. 2 provide with an engine or motor. **powerful** *adj*. **powerfully** *adv*. **powerless** *adj*.

practicable *adj* able to be done or used.

practical *adj* 1 concerned with practice or action. 2 capable of or suitable for use. 3 concerned with the ordinary activities in the world. 4 inclined towards actual or useful work; not philosophical or interested in theory. 5 aware of possibilities; experienced. **practically** *adv* 1 almost; nearly. 2 in a practical manner.

practice *n* 1 custom; habit. 2 exercises done to gain skill in something. 3 action that corresponds to a theory. 4 work or clients of a lawyer, doctor, etc. **practise** *vt,vi* 1 do as a habit or do repeatedly to gain skill. 2 train (at). 3 take an action that corresponds to a theory. 4 work as a lawyer, doctor, etc. **practitioner** *n* person who works at a profession, esp. a doctor.

pragmatic *adj* 1 making judgments based on causes and results. 2 acting in a practical manner. **pragmatically** *adv*.

prairie *n* large usually fertile area of grassland without trees.

praise *vt* 1 show approval or admiration for. 2 give glory to (God, etc.). *n* 1 admiration or approval. 2 glory or homage expressed to God. **praiseworthy** *adj.*

pram *n* wheeled carriage for a baby.

prance *vi* 1 jump or move by jumping from the hind legs, as a horse does. 2 walk about pompously; swagger. *n* jump; spring; swagger.

prank *n* childish trick.

prattle *n* meaningless chatter. *vi* chatter meaninglessly.

prawn *n* edible marine animal resembling but larger than a shrimp.

pray *vt,vi* make an earnest request for, esp. to God or a god; make a prayer. **prayer** *n* 1 earnest request made to God or a god. 2 special set of words used in praying. 3 strong wish or desire.

preach *vt,vi* 1 speak publicly on a religious theme or in support of a religion. 2 give strong moral encouragement (to); advocate. 3 give unwelcome moral advice (to). **preacher** *n.*

precarious *adj* insecure; unsafe; uncertain. **precariously** *adv.* **precariousness** *n.*

precaution *n* action taken to stop something unpleasant or dangerous from happening. **precautionary** *adj.*

precede *vt* 1 go in front of. 2 be earlier than. 3 be more important or of higher rank than. **precedence** *n* 1 act of preceding. 2 relative importance or rank. 3 right resulting from rank, birth, or important office. **precedent** *n* earlier case or decision that is taken as guidance in dealing with subsequent situations.

precept *n* rule or guide for behaviour; maxim.

precinct *n* enclosed area, esp. the grounds of a cathedral, school, etc.

precious *adj* 1 valuable; of great price. 2 well loved. 3 affected; excessively refined. *adv* very. **preciously** *adv.*

precipice *n* high, vertical, and steep cliff.

precipitate (pri'sipiteit) *vt* 1 cause to happen before required or expected; hasten. 2 throw down; hurl. 3 cause dissolved matter to separate from solution in solid form. *n*

(pri'sipitit) solid precipitated matter. **precipitation** *n.*

précis *n* shortened form of a longer statement, document, etc. *vt* make a summary of.

precise *adj* 1 accurate; exact. 2 clear; definite. **precisely** *adv.* **precision** *n.*

precocious *adj* advanced in development.

preconceive *vt* form an opinion beforehand. **preconception** *n.*

predator *n* 1 animal that lives by hunting and killing other animals for food. 2 plunderer; thief. **predatory** *adj.*

predecessor *n* person who precedes someone else in a particular office, job, or duty.

predestine *vt* decide the fate of beforehand. **predestination** *n.*

predicament *n* awkward or dangerous situation.

predicate *n* ('predikit) 1 part of a sentence that contains what is said about the subject. 2 statement relating to something. *vt* ('predikeit) declare as a characteristic. **predication** *n.* **predicative** *adj.*

predict *vt* describe future events before they happen; foretell; prophesy. **predictable** *adj.* **prediction** *n.*

predominate *vi* 1 be the most numerous. 2 have the most power or strength. **predominance** *n.* **predominant** *adj.*

pre-eminent *adj* better than anyone or anything else; excellent; very distinguished. **pre-eminence** *n.* **pre-eminently** *adv.*

preen *vt,vi* 1 (of a bird) clean and straighten the feathers with the beak. 2 prepare or dress oneself tidily. 3 show self-satisfaction.

prefabricate *vt* manufacture parts or sections of (a building, etc.) ready for assembling and erection.

preface *n* 1 written introduction in a book; foreword. 2 similar introduction to a speech or play. *vt* introduce with a preface. **prefatory** *adj.*

prefect *n* senior pupil with some authority over other pupils at a school.

prefer *vt* (-rr-) 1 like better. 2 give special attention to. 3 present or make (a statement, charge, etc.). 4 promote. **preferable** *adj.* **preference** *n* 1 preferring or being preferred. 2 something preferred. 3 advantage or right granted to particular people, countries, etc. **preferential** *adj.*

prefix *n* affix added to the beginning of a word to alter or otherwise affect its meaning. *vt* attach at the beginning of something.

pregnant *adj* 1 (of a woman or female animal) being with child or young. 2 full of; abounding in. 3 very significant. **pregnancy** *n*.

prehistoric *adj* of or occurring in the period before history was written down.

prejudice *n* 1 judgment or opinion reached prematurely or on insufficient evidence. 2 unfavourable opinion or bias. *vt* 1 cause to be prejudiced; bias. 2 injure; harm. **prejudicial** *adj*.

preliminary *adj* occurring beforehand; introductory. *n* first action or occurrence; introductory or preparatory step, event, etc.

prelude *n* 1 short piece of music, esp. introducing an opera, suite, or fugue. 2 any introduction. *vt* form a prelude or introduction to.

premarital *adj* before marriage.

premature *adj* before the right time; too early.

premeditate *vt* think of or decide upon beforehand; plan. **premeditation** *n*.

premier *adj* of the highest importance; first; leading. *n* prime minister.

premiere *n* first showing or performance of a film, play, etc.

premise *n* 1 *also* **premiss** assumption. 2 introduction to a document, such as a lease. **premises** *pl n* house or other building, including the grounds. ~*vt* state as a premise.

premium *n* 1 prize; bonus. 2 additional payment to a standard rate, wage, etc. 3 amount paid periodically to renew an insurance policy. **at a premium** very valuable. **premium bond** government bond that pays no interest but offers the chance of monthly cash prizes.

preoccupied *adj* 1 concentrating on one thought above others; engrossed; absorbed. **preoccupation** *n*.

prepare *vt,vi* 1 make or become ready or suitable for something. 2 make; manufacture; construct. 3 equip. **preparatory** *adj*. **preparation** *n* 1 preparing or being prepared. 2 something prepared, esp. a medicine or cosmetic. 3 *also inf* **prep** school work done by a pupil at home; homework.

preposition *n* word placed before a noun or pronoun indicating relationship in time, space, etc. **prepositional** *adj*.

preposterous *adj* ridiculous; stupid; absurd. **preposterously** *adv*.

prerogative *n* privilege; right.

Presbyterian *adj* relating to a Protestant Church governed by elders (presbyters), traditionally following the teachings of Calvin. *n* member of such a Church.

prescribe *vt,vi* 1 order or require (medicine, treatment, etc.). 2 make certain rules about. **prescription** *n* 1 written instructions issued by a doctor indicating required medicine, treatment, etc. 2 act of prescribing.

presence *n* 1 state or condition of being present. 2 closeness; nearness. 3 demeanour; bearing. 4 dignity; importance. **presence of mind** ability to act quickly and intelligently when faced by difficulty or danger.

present[1] ('prezənt) *adj* 1 being here within sight or hearing. 2 being at a particular place at a certain time. 3 existing now; indicating this time now. *n* 1 time being lived through now. 2 tense in a language indicating this. **presently** *adv* soon; before long. **present participle** *n* verb form functioning as an adjective or used with an auxiliary verb to denote continuous action, e.g. *changing, living,* or *speaking.*

present[2] *n* ('prezənt) gift. *vt* (prə'zent) 1 give, esp. formally; bestow. 2 introduce, esp. in a formal way. 3 organize (a performance, etc.). 4 show to the public. 5 offer or put forward for consideration, etc. 6 raise (a weapon) in salute. **presentation** *n*. **presentable** *adj* fit to be introduced, displayed, etc.

preserve *vt* 1 keep safe or undamaged. 2 save from decay, change, etc. *n* 1 preserved food, such as jam. 2 area of country protected or kept private, as for hunting. 3 right; privilege. **preservation** *n*. **preservative** *n,adj*.

president *n* 1 person having highest authority in a republic. 2 someone presiding over an assembly, society, company, etc. **presidency** *n*. **preside** *vi* 1 sit in authority over a meeting, debate, etc. 2 exercise control or authority.

press[1] *vt,vi* 1 apply weight, force, or pressure to, so as to squeeze, crush, flatten, etc. 2 obtain liquid, juice, oil, etc., by pressure. 3 hold close; grasp. 4 attack hard, as in battle. 5 insist on; compel; urge; entreat. 6 oppress; harass. 7 *iron.* **press on** continue with an activity. ~*n* 1 machine for printing. 2 newspapers and magazines collectively. 3 machine for exerting pressure, as in extracting liquids. 4 large crowd of people. **press stud** *n* fastener for clothes having two parts pressed together.

press[2] *vt* force into service, esp. military service. **pressgang** *n* men formerly employed to force people into the army or navy. ~*vt* force (someone) into doing something.

pressure *n* 1 act of pressing. 2 force exerted by pressing; force per unit area acting on a surface. 3 compulsion; constraint. 4 cause of distress; burden. **pressure group** *n* group of people seeking to influence public opinion, government, etc. **pressure cooker** *n* special pot in which food is cooked at a high temperature under pressure. **pressurize** *vt* 1 maintain normal air pressure in (an aircraft cabin, etc.). 2 urge or compel, esp. to a course of action.

prestige *n* 1 high reputation gained through success, rank, etc.; status. 2 power to influence and impress. **prestigious** *adj*.

presume *vt,vi* 1 assume; suppose. 2 dare or venture, esp. with excessive boldness. **presumption** *n.* **presumable** *adj.* **presumably** *adv.*

pretend *vt,vi* 1 feign or affect (to do or be something). 2 lay claim to, esp. dubiously. 3 state or profess falsely. 4 venture; attempt. 5 fancy or imagine oneself as being. **pretender** *n* 1 claimant to a throne, inheritance, etc. 2 someone who pretends. **pretence** *n.*

pretentious *adj* 1 claiming or attempting things beyond one's ability. 2 affecting dignity, importance, etc. 3 ostentatious; showy. **pretentiousness** *n.* **pretentiously** *adv.* **pretension** *n* 1 laying claim to something. 2 dubious or unsupportable claim, esp. made indirectly, to some merit, importance, etc. 3 pretentiousness.

pretext *n* pretended reason or motive that conceals the real one; excuse.

pretty *adj* 1 attractive, charming, or appealing in a delicate way. 2 neat; dainty. 3 *inf* fine; good. 4 *inf* considerable. **a pretty penny** great deal of money. ~*adv* fairly; quite. **prettily** *adv.* **prettiness** *n.*

prevail *vi* 1 be or prove dominant, effective, superior, etc.; be victorious. 2 be used or exist widely; predominate. **prevail on** persuade.

prevalent *adj* used or occurring widely; common. **prevalence** *n.*

prevaricate *vi* make misleading statements; answer evasively. **prevarication** *n.*

prevent *vt* make impossible; hinder; stop. **prevention** *n.* **preventive** *adj.*

preview *n* advance showing of a play, film, exhibition, etc., before presentation to the public. *vt* see in advance.

previous *adj* 1 before something else in time or position; prior. 2 *inf* too early; premature. **previously** *adv.*

prey *n* 1 animal hunted for food. 2 habit of hunting for prey. 3 victim, as of an enemy, illness, etc. *v* **prey on** 1 hunt for food. 2 make profits out of; exploit. 3 have a destructive or depressing influence (on); weigh heavily (on).

price *n* 1 amount of money, goods, etc., for which something is bought or sold. 2 cost at which something is acquired. 3 value, worth. *vt* 1 set a price on. 2 estimate or find out the price of. **priceless** *adj* 1 valuable beyond price; invaluable. 2 *inf* very funny or absurd. **pricey** *adj inf* expensive.

prick *vt* pierce; puncture; make holes in with a sharp point. *vi,vt* feel or cause to feel sharp mental or physical pain; sting. **prick up one's ears** listen attentively. ~*n* 1 pricking or being pricked. 2 small injury or puncture caused by a sharp point. 3 sharp painful sensation. 4 *sl* penis. **prickle** *n* 1 small sharp thorn or spine. 2 tingling or prickling sensation. *vt,vi* tingle. **prickly** *adj*.

pride *n* 1 self-respect based on a true sense of personal worth. 2 arrogance about or exaggerated belief in one's own merits, achievements, etc. 3 satisfaction. 4 source of pride, esp. something splendid. 5 group of lions. **take pride in** be proud about.

priest *n* minister who officiates at religious ceremonies and rituals. **priestess** *f n.* **priesthood** *n.*

prim *adj* excessively formal or proper in attitude or behaviour.

primary *adj* **1** first or most important. **2** simple; elementary; basic; fundamental. **primarily** *adv.* **primary colours** *pl n* three colours, for example red, green, and blue, that can be combined to give any other colour. **primary school** *n* school for children below the age of eleven (or sometimes nine).

primate *n* **1** high-ranking clergyman, such as an archbishop. **2** member of the order of mammals that includes man, apes, and monkeys.

prime *adj* **1** first or most important; primary. **2** excellent; very good. **3** necessary; essential. *n* period when something is at its best or strongest, usually the earliest period. *vt,vi* **1** put explosive into. **2** fill with food. **3** supply with information. **prime minister** *n* chief minister; leader of the government. **prime number** *n* number, such as seven, able to be divided only by itself and one. **primer** *n* **1** book for beginners. **2** cap or tube containing explosive used to set off a charge. **3** first coat of paint.

primitive *adj* **1** at the beginning of development. **2** barbarous; savage. **3** not sophisticated; rough; simple. *n* primitive person or thing.

primrose *n* wild plant bearing pale yellow flowers. *n,adj* pale yellow.

prince *n* **1** son or close male relative of a king or queen. **2** nobleman. **3** ruler of a minor state. **princely** *adj.* **princess** *n* **1** daughter or close female relative of a king or queen. **2** wife of a prince.

principal *adj* **1** chief; main. **2** of the highest rank. *n* **1** person who plays a leading part in an activity. **2** head of a university, college, or school. **3** capital sum that is borrowed or lent at interest. **principally** *adv.*

principality *n* rule of a prince or the country or state over which he rules.

principle *n* **1** basic rule, esp. one that governs one's life. **2** fundamental truth or doctrine. **3** important element of something. **4** moral behaviour.

print *vt,vi* **1** produce (letters, text, pictures, etc.) by pressing inked types, plates, etc., directly onto paper. **2** publish (a book, magazine, etc.) in this way. **3** write in separated letters or block capitals. **4** produce a picture from a negative. **5** leave (a mark, etc.) by or as if by pressing or stamping. *n* **1** printed text. **2** picture produced from an engraved or etched plate or a photographic negative. **3** cloth with a pattern printed on it. **4** mark made by or as if by pressure. **out of print** (of a book, etc.) sold out; not available. **printable** *adj* fit to appear in print. **printer** *n.*

prior[1] *n* head of a monastery.

prior[2] *adj* **1** coming before; earlier. **2** of greater importance. **prior to** before; previous to. **priority** *n* **1** greater importance; superiority. **2** state of being earlier. **3** condition of being or right to be dealt with earlier.

priory *n* religious house presided over by a prior, often attached to an abbey.

prise *vt* lift or open by means of a lever, etc.

prism *n* **1** solid figure usually having rectangular sides and triangular ends of equal size. **2** triangular prism of transparent material, used esp. for splitting light into its component colours. **prismatic** *adj.*

prison *n* **1** building used for the confinement of convicted criminals. **2** any place of confinement. **prisoner** *n* criminal or other captive kept in prison.

private *adj* **1** not public or official; secret; confidential. **2** connected with an individual; personal. **3** out of the way; isolated. *n* soldier of the lowest army or marine rank. **privacy** *n.* **privately** *adv.* **privatize** *vt* remove from public or state ownership. **privatization** *n.*

privet *n* evergreen shrub commonly used for hedges.

privilege *n* **1** right granted to a person or group. **2** advantage connected with such a right. *vt* grant a privilege to; give a special advantage.

prize[1] *n* **1** reward won in a competition. **2** something valuable captured in war, etc.

prize[2] *vt* hold in high estimation; place a high value on.

probable *adj* likely to occur or be true. **probability** *n* likelihood, esp. when mathematically calculated. **probably** *adv.*

probation *n* **1** period during which a person is tested for his ability or suitability. **2** system by which a convicted offender is set free on condition that he reports regularly to an official and behaves well. **probationary** *adj.*

probe *vt,vi* seek for information; investigate; examine. *n* 1 investigation. 2 surgical instrument used to probe wounds, etc. 3 spacecraft capable of exploration.

problem *n* 1 difficult issue or situation. 2 matter deserving profound consideration. 3 question requiring a solution by calculation. **problematic** *adj*.

procedure *n* 1 method of doing something; technique. 2 established manner of behaviour in a given situation. 3 rules governing the conduct of business, as in parliament. **procedural** *adj*.

proceed *vi* 1 go forward; advance. 2 start or continue a course of action. **proceed from** be the result of. **proceed against** bring a legal action against. **proceeds** *pl n* profit from a sale, etc.

process *n* 1 series of connected actions; course of action. 2 method by which legal action is conducted. 3 method of making or manufacturing something. 4 bone, organ, or part that sticks out or projects. *vt* 1 preserve (food), as by drying, freezing, etc. 2 use special methods to manufacture or do something.

procession *n* 1 large number of people moving along in an ordered manner. 2 long series of things or events.

proclaim *vt* announce or make known officially or openly. **proclamation** *n*.

procreate *vt,vi* give birth to or produce (offspring). **procreation** *n*. **procreator** *n*.

procure *vt* 1 get; obtain. 2 bring about; cause. **procurement** *n*.

prod *vt* (-dd-) 1 poke; nudge. 2 urge; encourage; rouse; stir. *n* 1 poke; nudge. 2 reminder.

prodigy *n* 1 wonder; marvel; miraculous event or thing. 2 person, esp. a child, having exceptional ability or talent. **prodigious** *adj* 1 enormous. 2 extraordinary; wonderful.

produce *v* (prə'dju:s) *vt,vi* bring forth; bear; yield. *vt* 1 cause; bring into existence. 2 manufacture or make. 3 organize or finance (a play, film, etc.). 4 bring out; show. *n* ('prɔdju:s) anything that is produced, brought forth, or made, esp. fruit or crops. **producer** *n*. **production** *n*. **product** *n* 1 something produced. 2 result of multiplying two or more numbers. **productive** *adj* able

to produce, esp. effectively or efficiently. **productivity** *n*.

profane *adj* 1 showing contempt or disrespect for sacred or holy things. 2 vulgar or coarse, esp. in language. *vt* 1 defile or otherwise spoil (something holy, sacred, or pure). 2 treat with callous disrespect. **profanely** *adv*. **profanity** *n*.

profess *vt* 1 declare or claim in public. 2 pretend; declare falsely.

profession *n* 1 job or career for which special training and mental skills are required. 2 body of people in a particular profession. 3 public declaration or claim. **professional** *adj* 1 connected with a profession or those who practise it. 2 earning one's living by playing a sport. *n* professional person.

professor *n* 1 head of a teaching department in a university or similar institution. 2 someone who professes a religious belief.

proficient *adj* skilled; capable; expert; experienced. **proficiency** *n*.

profile *n* 1 view or drawing of a face seen from the side. 2 outline or sectional drawing. 3 journalistic character outline of someone; brief biography. *vt* give, present, or draw an outline of.

profit *n* 1 advantage; benefit. 2 money left over after the necessary expenses of a transaction have been paid. *vt,vi* 1 gain advantage (from). 2 be of advantage. 3 obtain profits. **profitable** *adj*.

profound *adj* 1 extremely deep. 2 felt deeply; strong; intense. 3 requiring considerable concentration; obscure; difficult. **profoundly** *adv*. **profundity** *n*.

profuse *adj* 1 unrestrained; lavish; generous. 2 very plentiful; abundant to the point of excess. **profusely** *adv*. **profusion** *n*.

programme *n* 1 list of items or events in a theatrical performance, concert, etc., or at a meeting. 2 performance consisting of several items or parts. 3 radio or television broadcast. **program** *n* list of operations and data used in or prepared for a computer. *vt,vi* (-mm-) prepare data for a computer. **programmer** *n*.

progress *n* ('prougres) 1 forward motion. 2 advance; development; increase or growth. *vi* (prə'gres) 1 move forward; advance. 2 improve; get better. **progres-**

sion *n.* **progressive** *adj* **1** characterized by progress. **2** supporting political or social reforms; enlightened. **3** increasing regularly; accumulative. *n* person supporting social and political reform. **progressively** *adv.*

prohibit *vt* forbid or prevent, esp. by law; stop; ban; restrict. **prohibition** *n.* **prohibitive** *adj.*

project *n* ('prɔdʒekt) scheme being planned or already being worked on. *v* (prɔ'dʒekt) *vt,vi* stick out; protrude; jut out. *vt* **1** throw; thrust; drive forward. **2** cast (the mind) forward to think about the distant future; plan ahead. **3** shine light or an image on something, as with a film projector. **projection** *n.* **projectile** *n* object propelled through the air; missile. **projectionist** *n* person who works a projector at a cinema. **projector** *n* machine for projecting films or picture slides on a screen.

proletariat *n* social class that owns no property and earns its living by the sale of its labour; working class.

proliferate *vt,vi* bring or come forth in increasing abundance; produce or reproduce more and more. **proliferation** *n.* **prolific** *adj* **1** plentiful; abundant. **2** producing much. **3** having numerous offspring.

prologue *n* **1** section of a book, play, poem, etc., that comes before the main part; introduction. **2** any preliminary to something more important.

prolong *vt* make longer in time or space.

promenade *n* **1** place along which one may walk, esp. near the sea. **2** short walk; stroll. *vi* walk along freely; stroll.

prominent *adj* **1** famous; well-known. **2** obvious; clear. **3** projecting; sticking out. **prominence** *n.* **prominently** *adv.*

promiscuous *adj* **1** indiscriminate, esp. in sexual relations. **2** confused; lacking order; casual. **promiscuity** *n.* **promiscuously** *adv.*

promise *n* **1** declaration; vow. **2** assurance given to do or not to do something. **3** grounds or hope for future excellence, achievement, etc. *vt,vi* make a promise (of).

promote *vt* **1** advance to a higher or more important rank, position, etc. **2** encourage the development, progress, or growth of. **3** work to make successful, acceptable, or popular. **promotion** *n.*

prompt *adj* **1** quick to act, respond, or do. **2** punctual. **3** acted on or accomplished without delay. *vt* **1** instigate; incite. **2** inspire. *vi,vt* provide or help by providing cues or suggestions. *n* act of prompting or something that prompts. **promptly** *adv.*

prone *adj* lying with the face or front of the body downwards; stretched out. **prone to** liable, inclined, or disposed (to).

prong *n* pointed end, as of a fork; spike; narrow projection.

pronoun *n* word, such as you, my, who, or someone, used as a substitute for a noun.

pronounce *vt,vi* make a speech sound, esp. in a specific manner; utter; articulate. *vt* state formally; declare officially. *vi* voice an opinion (on). **pronounced** *adj* obvious; marked. **pronouncement** *n* declaration. **pronunciation** *n* act or manner of making speech sounds, esp. with regard to correctness.

proof *n* **1** irrefutable evidence, reasoning, or facts. **2** anything that serves to establish validity or truth. **3** trial; demonstration; test. **4** alcoholic strength proved or maintained by certain standards. *adj* of standard or proved strength or quality. **proof against** unable to be penetrated; invulnerable. **proofread** *vt,vi* (-read) read and correct (trial printed matter).

prop[1] *n* **1** rigid support, such as a beam or pole. **2** person or thing giving support. *vt* (-pp-) **1** *also* **prop up** prevent from caving in or falling; support. **2** place or rest against something.

prop[2] *n* object placed on stage or used by actors.

propaganda *n* false, biased, or self-serving information, usually designed to harm or discredit another person, group, etc.

propagate *vt* **1** cause to increase or multiply. **2** reproduce or transmit in reproduction. **3** spread. *vi* **1** breed; multiply. **2** move (through); be transmitted. **propagation** *n.*

propel *vt* (-ll-) cause to move forwards; drive. **propeller** *n* powered device, usually consisting of blades mounted on a revolving shaft, for propelling aircraft, ships, etc.

proper *adj* **1** suitable; appropriate; right; apt. **2** having good manners; correct. **3**

within the technical or strict meaning of a term, etc. **properly** *adv.* **proper noun** *n* also **proper name** noun that refers to a specific person, place, or thing.

property *n* **1** possession(s). **2** piece of land; estate. **3** ownership. **4** quality or characteristic associated with something.

prophecy ('prɔfisi) *n* **1** prediction. **2** divine revelation. **3** prophetic declaration. **prophesy** ('prɔfisai) *vt* **1** predict; proclaim; foretell. **2** reveal by divine inspiration. *vi* declare what is to come. **prophet** *n* **1** person who speaks by divine inspiration. **2** person who predicts future events, etc. **3** inspired leader, etc. **prophetic** *adj.*

proportion *n* **1** relative size or magnitude; ratio; comparative relation. **2** symmetry; harmony. **3** part of a whole; share; portion. **proportions** *pl n* size. ~*vt* adjust or arrange proportions of. **proportional** *adj.*

propose *vt* **1** submit for consideration; suggest. **2** recommend for membership, office, etc. **3** intend; plan to do. *vi* make a proposal of marriage. **proposal** *n* **1** act of proposing. **2** plan; scheme. **3** offer of marriage.

proposition *n* **1** suggested plan; scheme. **2** statement; assertion. **3** point or subject offered for discussion. *vt* suggest a plan, scheme, etc., to.

proprietor *n* person who owns a business.

propriety *n* **1** suitability; correctness; aptness. **2** good conduct.

propulsion *n* **1** act of propelling or state of being propelled. **2** impulse; force.

prose *n* speech, writing, or printed matter, esp. as distinguished from poetry.

prosecute *vt* bring legal action against. *vi* seek legal redress. **prosecutor** *n.* **prosecution** *n* **1** act of prosecuting or state of being prosecuted. **2** lawyers acting for the Crown in a criminal lawsuit.

prospect *n* **1** expectation; probability; future outlook. **2** scenic view; outlook. **prospects** *pl n* chances of success, good fortune, etc. ~*vt,vi* search, esp. for oil or valuable minerals; explore. **prospective** *adj* anticipated; expected; likely.

prospectus *n* statement or pamphlet giving details of a coming event or of school or academic courses or describing an organization, etc.

prosperous *adj* **1** successful; flourishing. **2** having plenty of money; well-off. **3** favourable; promising. **prosperity** *n* wealth; success. **prosper** *vi* be successful; thrive.

prostitute *n* woman who charges money for sexual intercourse. *vt* **1** offer (oneself) for sexual intercourse for money. **2** sell for immediate gain; put to a base or unworthy use. **prostitution** *n.*

prostrate *adj* ('prɔstreit) **1** lying with the face downwards. **2** helpless; defenceless; exhausted. *vt* (prɔ'streit) **1** throw (oneself) down in an act of submission, humility, etc. **2** force or throw to the ground. **3** render helpless; overcome.

protagonist *n* leading character, actor, participant, spokesman, etc.

protect *vt* guard; defend; shield from harm, etc. **protection** *n.* **protective** *adj.*

protégé *n* person under the protection or guidance of another.

protein *n* type of complex organic compound, found esp. in meat, eggs, and milk, essential for metabolism.

protest *n* ('proutest) **1** serious or formal objection, disapproval, or dissent. **2** act of objecting or declaring formally. *vt,vi* (prou'test) **1** object; complain. **2** affirm seriously or solemnly.

Protestant *n* member or adherent of any of various Christian Churches outside the Roman Catholic Church.

protocol *n* etiquette, esp. in formal or diplomatic situations.

proton *n* stable positively charged particle that occurs in the nucleus of an atom.

prototype *n* first model, design, or pattern; original.

protrude *vt,vi* project or thrust out. **protuberance** *n.*

proud *adj* **1** feeling intensely pleased with an achievement, etc. **2** showing or having self-esteem, often excessive. **3** very creditable. **proudly** *adv.* **proudness** *n.*

prove *vt* **1** demonstrate to be true or genuine. **2** test; verify; demonstrate by using, etc. **3** show to be as expected or specified. *vi* turn out (to be).

proverb *n* short common saying, expressing a general truth. **proverbial** *adj.*

provide *vt* **1** equip; supply; furnish. **2** yield. *vi* supply money or means of support (for). **providing** *conj also* **provided** on condition (that).

province *n* 1 administrative division of a country. 2 area of learning, interest, or activity. **provinces** *pl n* parts of a country distinct from the leading financial, cultural, or government centres. **provincial** *adj* 1 relating to a province; not national. 2 lacking sophistication; rustic. *n* unsophisticated person.

provision *n* 1 supplying of something needed. 2 arrangement in advance. 3 stipulation. 4 something provided. **provisions** *pl n* food and other necessities. **provisional** *adj* temporary; serving only a limited function, need, etc.

proviso *n* condition; stipulation.

provoke *vt* 1 make angry; irritate; enrage. 2 arouse; move to action. 3 cause to happen; induce. **provocation** *n*. **provocative** *adj*.

prow *n* front part of a ship or boat; bow.

prowess *n* 1 bravery; courage. 2 accomplishment, esp. showing unusual ability.

prowl *vt,vi* move about stealthily, esp. in search of something. *n* act of prowling.

proximity *n* nearness; near neighbourhood.

prude *n* person who is excessively prim or modest. **prudish** *adj*.

prudent *adj* 1 wisely cautious or careful. 2 showing caution, good judgment, etc. **prudence** *n*.

prune[1] *n* dried plum, dark brown in colour.

prune[2] *vt* 1 trim; cut off, esp. from trees and shrubs. 2 remove (excesses, etc.).

pry *vi* look inquisitively; enquire closely or furtively; examine with intrusive curiosity.

psalm *n* religious song or hymn.

pseudonym *n* false name used by a writer, etc., to conceal his identity.

psychedelic *adj* relating to or producing a joyful state of expanded consciousness.

psychiatry *n* branch of medicine concerned with treating mental illness. **psychiatric** *adj*. **psychiatrist** *n*.

psychic *adj* 1 relating to the mind or mental activities. 2 relating to unusual mental powers, such as telepathy. 3 involving a nonphysical force or influence.

psychoanalysis *n* technique or system of bringing subconscious conflicts into aware-

ness. **psychoanalyst** *n*. **psychoanalyse** *vt* treat by psychoanalysis.

psychology *n* scientific study of mental attitudes and human or animal behaviour. **psychologist** *n*. **psychological** *adj* 1 relating to psychology. 2 arising in the mind; irrational.

psychopath *n* person suffering from severe mental and emotional instability. **psychopathic** *adj*.

psychosis *n* serious mental illness. **psychotic** *adj*.

psychosomatic *adj* relating to a physical disorder that is caused or aggravated by the emotional state.

pub *n inf also* **public house** building licenced for the sale and consumption of alcoholic drinks. **publican** *n* person responsible for running a pub.

puberty *n* age at which a person becomes sexually mature.

public *adj* 1 relating or belonging to the people of a community, country, etc. 2 general; available to all; not private. *n* 1 people in general. 2 followers; admirers. **public relations** *n* business or activity of promoting goodwill for an organization, individual, etc. **public school** *n* private independent fee-paying school.

publication *n* act or product of publishing.

publicity *n* 1 state or condition of being generally known. 2 business, activity, or methods of informing the public about a person, product, campaign, etc.

publicize *vt* make public; bring to general notice.

publish *vt,vi* produce and issue (books, etc.) for sale. *vt* make known to the public. **publisher** *n*.

pucker *vt,vi* gather into wrinkles or folds. *n* uneven fold; wrinkle.

pudding *n* 1 cooked dish of various ingredients, such as suet or sponge with fruit or meat. 2 course following the main meal; sweet; dessert.

puddle *n* small pool of water or other liquid.

puff *n* 1 brief burst of air, smoke, vapour, etc.; gust of wind. 2 draw at a cigarette, cigar, or pipe. *vi,vt* 1 send out puffs of air, smoke, etc. 2 *also* **puff up** *or* **out** swell;

inflate. **3** smoke. *vi* breathe in short gasps; pant.

pull *vt,vi* tug (at) forcefully; haul; jerk. *vt* **1** move forward by means of or using force; draw. **2** tear or rip (apart, out, etc.). **3** remove from the natural or normal position by pulling. **pull apart** criticize severely. **pull faces** grimace. **pull a fast one** trick; deceive. **pull in 1** draw into a station, kerb, etc., and stop. **2** attract. **pull off** succeed in accomplishing something. **pull oneself together** regain self-control. **pull one's weight** make a significant contribution towards a common task. **pull out** withdraw; abandon; leave. **pull someone's leg** tease. **pull strings** use personal influence. **pull through** recover. **pull up 1** stop. **2** draw level in a race. ~*n* act or force of pulling. **pullover** *n* sweater; jumper.

pulley *n* wheel for raising weights by pulling downwards on a cord, etc., passing over its grooved rim.

pulp *n* **1** mass of soft moist matter. **2** moist mixture of wood particles, rags, etc., from which paper is made. *vt,vi* reduce or be reduced to pulp.

pulpit *n* raised stand or platform from which a clergyman preaches.

pulsate *vi* beat or throb, esp. rhythmically; quiver; vibrate. **pulsation** *n.* **pulse** *n* **1** periodic throbbing of the arteries, caused by successive contraction and relaxation of the heart. **2** transient change in voltage, current, etc.

pulverize *vt,vi* grind or pound to a fine powder or be so reduced. *vt* demolish.

pump *n* machine for forcing liquids or gases to a different level, container, etc., for reducing fluid pressure, etc. *vt,vi* raise, clear, inflate, etc., with a pump. *vt* **1** move up and down repeatedly. **2** elicit by repeated questioning. **3** question for information.

pumpkin *n* large orange-coloured edible gourd.

pun *n* play on words, esp. those with similar sounds. *vi* (-nn-) make puns.

punch[1] *n* **1** sharp forceful blow, esp. with the fist. **2** forcefulness; drive. **3** tool for stamping, piercing, etc. *vt* **1** hit sharply, esp. with the fist. **2** prod; poke. **3** stamp, pierce, etc., with a punch.

punch[2] *n* drink usually made in quantity by mixing wine or spirits with fruit, spices, etc.

punctual *adj* on time; prompt. **punctuality** *n.*

punctuate *vt* **1** mark (sentences, etc.) with full stops, commas, brackets, etc. **2** give emphasis to; stress. **3** interrupt at intervals. *vi* use punctuation. **punctuation** *n* **1** various marks inserted in sentences, etc., to clarify meaning. **2** act of punctuating.

puncture *n* **1** tiny hole made by pricking or piercing. **2** loss of pressure in a tyre resulting from this. *vt* **1** prick; pierce. **2** deflate by a puncture.

pungent *adj* **1** smelling or tasting sharp or acrid. **2** caustic; biting. **pungency** *n.* **pungently** *adv.*

punish *vt* **1** inflict a penalty on; make to suffer for some offence, fault, etc.; discipline. **2** hurt; injure. **punishment** *n.*

punt[1] *n* boat with a flat bottom, moved by aid of a pole. *vt,vi* propel (a boat) by using a pole.

punt[2] *vi,n* gamble; bet.

pup *n* young dog, seal, or similar animal.

pupa *n, pl* **pupae** ('pju:pi:) inactive stage of development of an insect, between larva and adult forms. **pupal** *adj.*

pupil[1] *n* student; schoolchild.

pupil[2] *n* variable aperture in the iris of the eye through which light enters.

puppet *n* **1** figure with movable limbs controlled by strings or wires; marionette. **2** person, group, etc., under the control of another.

puppy *n* **1** young dog. **2** conceited young man.

purchase *vt* buy; obtain by payment. *n* **1** something bought. **2** act of buying. **3** leverage. **4** hold; grip. **purchase tax** *n* tax levied on purchased goods, being added to the selling price.

pure *adj* **1** not contaminated; free from mixture with anything else. **2** simple; not complicated. **3** innocent; chaste. **4** mere. **purely** *adv* entirely; solely. **purity** *n.*

purgatory *n* **1** place where souls of the dead go for punishment of earthly sins before entering heaven. **2** state or condition of temporary pain, suffering, etc.

purge *vt* 1 cleanse; remove by cleaning. 2 rid of waste, unwanted elements, etc.; clear; eliminate; remove. *vi* become cleansed, purified, etc. *n* 1 act of purging. 2 something that purges. 3 *also* **purgative** drug or agent aiding defecation.

purify *vt,vi* make or become pure. *vt* free from undesirable elements, etc. **purification** *n.*

Puritan *n* member of an extreme reform group of 16th- and 17th-century Protestants. **puritan** person who is excessively strict, esp. in matters of religion or morals. **puritanical** *adj.*

purl *n* knitting stitch that is an inverted plain stitch. *vt,vi* knit in purl.

purple *n,adj* reddish-blue or bluish-red. **purplish** *adj.*

purpose *n* 1 end or aim towards which any view, action, etc., is directed; intention. 2 reason. **on purpose** intentionally.

purr *n* low murmuring sound, as made by a contented cat. *vi* utter such a sound.

purse *n* small pouch or bag for holding coins, etc.

pursue *vt* 1 trail; follow closely; chase. 2 attend. 3 seek to gain or accomplish. 4 continue (with or on). **pursuit** *n* 1 act of pursuing. 2 hobby; pastime.

pus *n* yellowish-white matter discharged from an infected wound.

push *vt,vi* 1 press (against) forcefully; impel by pressure. 2 urge; promote. *vt* thrust (away, through, forward, etc.) with or by force. **pushed (for)** *inf* short of. ~*n* 1 act of pushing. 2 *inf* drive; self-assertion. 3 *inf* special effort. 4 *inf* dismissal. **pushchair** *n* small chair on wheels for carrying infants.

pussy *n inf* cat.

put *vt* (-tt-; put) 1 place, deposit, lay, set, or cause to be in any position, situation, or place. 2 render; transform. 3 express; propose. **put across** *or* **over** communicate. **put (it) at** estimate (it) as. **put away** 1 store. 2 save. 3 imprison; lock up. **put down** 1 record; write. 2 quell. 3 kill (an animal). **put forward** suggest; propose. **put off** 1 delay; defer. 2 discourage. 3 switch off. **put on** 1 dress in. 2 assume; adopt. 3 wager; bet. 4 switch on. **put out** 1 annoy; disturb. 2 extinguish; switch off. **put up** 1 build. 2 accommodate. 3 provide; give. **put up with** tolerate. **stay put** remain; not move.

putrid *adj* 1 rotten; decaying. 2 having a foul smell. 3 *inf* awful; of poor quality. **putrefy** *vi,vt* rot; decompose. **putrefaction** *n.*

putt *vt,vi* hit a golfball so that it rolls towards the hole. *n* putted stroke. **putting** *n* game like golf involving putted strokes only.

putty *n* pliable material that sets rigid, used for holding panes of glass in frames, etc. *vt* repair, fill, etc., with putty.

puzzle *vt,vi* confuse or perplex or be confused or perplexed. **puzzle over** strain to discover a solution; expend effort to find a meaning. ~*n* 1 something that poses a problem to be worked out. 2 something that perplexes. 3 jigsaw.

PVC *n* polyvinyl chloride: man-made plastic material, either flexible or rigid, with a wide variety of uses.

Pygmy *n* member of a central African hunting people of small stature. **pygmy** very small person.

pyjamas *pl n* loose trousers and jacket for sleeping in.

pylon *n* tall structure, used esp. to convey high-voltage electric cables over open country.

pyramid *n* 1 solid figure consisting usually of a square base and triangular sloping faces that meet at the top. 2 enormous pyramid-shaped stone monument, esp. of ancient Egypt.

Pyrex *n Tdmk* heat-resistant glass or glassware.

python *n* large snake that kills its prey by squeezing.

Q

quack[1] *n* harsh cry of a duck. *vi* make such a sound.

quack[2] *n* medical practitioner who is unqualified or unreliable.

quadrangle *n* 1 quadrilateral. 2 *also inf* **quad** quadrilateral courtyard, esp. within a school. **quadrangular** *adj.*

quadrant *n* quarter section of a circle.

quadrilateral *n* figure with four sides and four angles. *adj* having four sides and four angles.

quadruped *n* animal with four legs. *adj* having four legs.

quadruple *vt,vi* increase fourfold. *adj* **1** four times as much. **2** having four members, parts, etc.

quadruplet *n* **1** *also inf* **quad** one of four children born at the same time to the same mother. **2** group having four members or parts.

quail[1] *n* small game bird.

quail[2] *vi* shrink with dread or fear; tremble.

quaint *adj* pleasingly odd or old-fashioned. **quaintly** *adv.*

quake *vi* tremble or shake. *n inf* short for **earthquake.**

Quaker *n* member of a pacifist Christian sect advocating simplicity of worship, dress, etc.

qualify *vt,vi* make or become suitable, appropriate, or acceptable (for). *vi* reach a required standard or level. *vt* **1** restrict or modify (a statement, proposal, etc.). **2** temper or moderate. **qualification** *n.*

quality *n* **1** distinguishing attribute or characteristic. **2** degree of fineness or excellence. **3** excellence. **4** accomplishment. **qualitative** *adj.*

qualm *n* pang of conscience; misgiving.

quandary *n* dilemma; perplexed turmoil.

quantify *vt* assess or ascertain the amount of. **quantification** *n.*

quantity *n* **1** amount. **2** large amount.

quarantine *n* careful isolation imposed on people, animals, etc., to prevent the spread of an infectious disease. *vt* put into quarantine; isolate.

quarrel *n* **1** disagreement or dispute. **2** cause for complaint. *vi* (-ll-) argue or disagree; squabble; dispute.

quarry[1] *n* shallow mine or pit from which stone, slate, etc., is excavated. *vt* mine (stone, etc.) from a quarry.

quarry[2] *n* animal, person, or other object of pursuit; game; prey.

quart *n* liquid or dry measure equal to two pints (approx. 1.1 litres) and one quarter of a bushel respectively.

quarter *n* **1** one of four equal parts or portions; one divided by four. **2** *US* twenty-five cents or a coin having this value. *vt* **1** cut or divide into quarters. **2** place or provide someone, esp. soldiers, with lodgings. **quarterly** *adj,adv.* **quarterdeck** *n* rear section of the upper deck of a ship, often reserved for officers. **quartermaster** *n* **1** petty officer on a ship responsible for steering, signals, etc. **2** officer, esp. in the army, responsible for the provision of food, clothing, lodging, etc. **quarters** *pl n* living accommodation.

quartet *n* group of four persons or things, esp. four singers or musicians.

quartz *n* common colourless crystalline mineral.

quash *vt* **1** subdue; suppress. **2** annul or invalidate (a decision, law, etc.).

quaver *n* musical note lasting one eighth the time of a semibreve. *vi* quiver; quake; tremble.

quay *n* man-made landing place to which ships may come to load or unload; wharf.

queasy *adj* **1** feeling or causing nausea; sickly. **2** ill at ease. **queasily** *adv.* **queasiness** *n.*

queen *n* **1** female monarch or wife of a king. **2** woman, thing, etc., regarded as very fine or outstanding. **3** fertile female in a colony of wasps, bees, ants, etc. **4** court card whose value is higher than the jack and lower than the king. **5** most powerful chess piece able to move any distance in a straight or diagonal line. **6** *sl* homosexual male. **queenly** *adj.*

queer *adj* **1** odd; peculiar; strange. **2** *sl* homosexual. *n sl* homosexual. *vt sl* ruin or spoil. **queerly** *adv.*

quell *vt* suppress; subdue; calm.

quench *vt* **1** satisfy (a thirst, etc.). **2** extinguish or smother something such as a fire.

query *n* **1** question. **2** point of doubt. **3** question mark. *vt,vi* raise (a question); ask for (an answer or clarification).

quest *n* search or hunt, esp. one carried on fervently. *vi* engage in a quest; search.

question *n* **1** request for information, a decision, clarification, etc. **2** point of doubt; uncertainty. **3** problem or matter for discussion; issue. *vt,vi* ask questions (of). *vt* cast doubt upon; challenge. **beyond question** indisputable. **call into question** cast doubt upon. **out of the question** impossible. **question mark** n mark (?) used at the end of a sentence, phrase, or word to indicate a question. **questionnaire** n written list of questions used to gather information, obtain opinions, etc.

queue n line of people or things waiting their turn to do or obtain something. vi form or wait in a queue.

quibble n trivial or petty objection, criticism, evasion, etc. vi argue about trivial points; evade by petty criticism or objection.

quick adj fast or sudden; swift. adv rapidly; swiftly. n sensitive flesh at the edge of a fingernail or toenail. **the quick and the dead** the living and the dead. **cut to the quick** hurt or offend deeply. **quicken** vt,vi 1 hasten; accelerate. 2 stimulate; revive. **quicksand** n soft wet sand into which objects are liable to sink. **quicksilver** n mercury. **like quicksilver** moving very swiftly. **quickstep** n 1 quick marching step. 2 fast ballroom-dancing step. **quick-tempered** adj having a hasty or hot temper; easily angered. **quick-witted** adj thinking swiftly; alert.

quid n, pl **quid** sl pound (money).

quiet adj 1 free from harsh noise or disturbance. 2 tranquil; calm. 3 subdued; restrained. n calmness; stillness; tranquillity. **quietly** adv. **quieten** vt,vi also **quiet** make or become quiet; subdue; ease.

quill n 1 large feather from the wing or tail of a bird. 2 such a feather made into a pen for writing. 3 one of the spines of a hedgehog, porcupine, etc.

quilt n bed covering made of two layers of material filled with some soft fabric and sewn together. vt,vi make a quilt (of).

quinine n alkaline substance originally obtained from the bark of a tree and used medicinally, esp. in treating malaria.

quintet n group of five persons or things, esp. five singers or musicians.

quirk n 1 unusual or odd trait or characteristic. 2 sudden twist or turn.

quit vt,vi (-tt-; quitted or quit) 1 stop; cease. 2 give up; relinquish; resign. 3 discharge (a debt, etc.). 4 depart (from); leave.

quite adv 1 wholly or entirely. 2 inf fairly; moderately. 3 positively. interj expression of agreement or concurrence.

quiver[1] vi shake; tremble; quake. n act of quivering; tremble.

quiver[2] n case or sheath for holding arrows.

quiz n series of questions, often taking the form of a competition between two or more people. vt (-zz-) question closely.

quizzical adj 1 comical or odd. 2 questioning; perplexed. 3 teasing. **quizzically** adv.

quoit n ring of rubber, metal, etc., used in a game by being thrown at an upright peg in an attempt to encircle it.

quota n prescribed share or amount of something that is allotted to or expected from a person, group, etc.; allotment.

quote vt 1 repeat (a passage, sentence, etc.) from a written or spoken source. 2 cite as an example. 3 state the price or cost of. vi use a quotation or quotations. n quotation. **quotation** n 1 also **quote** something quoted. 2 act of quoting. **quotation marks** pl n punctuation marks ' and ' or " and " used to enclose and indicate a quotation.

R

rabbi n 1 Jewish priest. 2 scholar and teacher of the Jewish law.

rabbit n small burrowing animal of the hare family with long ears, a short tufty tail, and soft fur. vi hunt rabbits.

rabble n noisy crowd or throng; mob.

rabid adj 1 fervent; wildly enthusiastic. 2 raging; violent. 3 relating to or having rabies.

rabies n fatal viral disease that is transmitted by the bite of an infected animal, esp. a dog.

race[1] n 1 contest of speed between people or animals in running, swimming, driving, etc. 2 any contest in which people compete to be the first to do or achieve something. vi 1 take part in a race. 2 hurry; go quickly. vt 1 run a race or compete with. 2 cause (a horse, car, etc.) to take part in a race. **racecourse** n track on which races, esp. horseraces, are held. **racehorse** n horse trained and used for racing.

race[2] n 1 group of people connected by common ancestry or blood. 2 subdivision of mankind to which people belong by virtue of their hereditary physical characteristics. **3** any group of people, plants, or animals regarded as a distinct class. **race relations** *pl n* relationships between people of different races, esp. within a single society. **racial** *adj* of or relating to race or races. **racially** *adv.*

rack *n* **1** framework, holder, or container; storage or display unit. **2** former instrument of torture on which people were tied and stretched. *vt* **1** torture on the rack. **2** torment. **3** arrange on or in a rack. **rack one's brains** strive to remember or understand something.

racket[1] *n* **1** noisy disturbance; uproar. **2** *sl* any illegal or dishonest scheme, activity, business, etc.

racket[2] *n* bat used in tennis, squash, etc., consisting of a rounded frame across which strings are stretched. **rackets** *n* kind of tennis played in a walled court.

radar *n* system for determining the presence and position of an object, such as a ship, by transmitting a beam of radio waves and measuring the direction and time taken for the echo to return from the object.

radial *adj* **1** branching out from a central point; radiating. **2** of or relating to a radius.

radiant *adj* **1** glowing with heat or brightness; shining. **2** glowing with happiness, joy, hope, etc. **3** emitted in rays.

radiate *v* ('reidieit) *vt,vi* **1** emit radiation. *vt* transmit or give out a particular emotion or feeling. *vi* spread or branch out from a central point. *adj* ('reidiit) having rays or radiating from a centre. **radiation** *n* **1** emission of energy in the form of light, heat, sound, electrons, etc. **2** energy so emitted and propagated. **3** radiate arrangement. **radiator** *n* **1** heating device through which hot air, water, steam, etc., passes. **2** device by which a car engine is kept cool.

radical *adj* **1** basic; fundamental. **2** essential; complete. **3** favouring fundamental political, social, or other reforms. **4** of or arising from a root. *n* person favouring radical reforms.

radio *n* **1** transmission of information by waves transmitted through the atmosphere. **2** device for receiving radio broadcasts; wireless. **3** broadcasts so received. *vt,vi* transmit a message, etc., by radio.

radioactivity *n* spontaneous disintegration of unstable atomic nuclei with the emission of radiation. **radioactive** *adj* undergoing or relating to radioactivity.

radish *n* small crisp white or red root of a plant of the mustard family, usually eaten raw.

radium *n* radioactive metallic element.

radius *n, pl* **radii** ('reidiai) *or* **radiuses** **1** line from the centre of a circle or sphere to its perimeter or surface. **2** length of such a line. **3** any radiating or raylike part. **4** circular area defined by the length of its radius. **5** range or extent of experience, influence, activity, etc.

raffia *n* fibre obtained from the leafstalks of a Madagascan palm, used for weaving baskets, matting, etc.

raffle *n* scheme for raising money in which tickets give the purchaser the chance of winning a prize, the winning tickets being randomly selected. *vt* offer as a prize in a raffle.

raft *n* buoyant material, such as logs, fastened together into a platform to transport goods or people by water.

rafter *n* sloping timber or beam on which a roof is supported.

rag[1] *n* **1** scrap of cloth; torn, dirty, or worthless fragment. **2** *sl* newspaper or magazine, esp. one of poor quality. **rags** *pl n* old or tattered clothing. **ragged** *adj* **1** rough, tattered, or torn. **2** uneven; jagged. **3** irregular or imperfect.

rag[2] *vt* (-gg-) **1** tease or play jokes on. **2** scold. *n* **1** joke or escapade. **2** organized series of games, events, etc., by students to publicize the collection of money for charity.

rage *n* **1** extreme anger; fury. **2** violence or intensity of fire, wind, disease, etc. **3** intensity of emotion, appetite, or enthusiasm. **4** anything arousing widespread enthusiasm. *vi* **1** display violent anger. **2** move, continue, prevail, etc., with great intensity or violence.

raid *n* surprise attack, esp. one undertaken to capture goods, personnel, etc. *vt,vi* make a surprise attack (on).

rail *n* **1** horizontal bar of wood or metal acting as a barrier, support, etc. **2** fence. **3** one of a pair of parallel metal bars laid as a track for trains, etc. **4** railway transportation. *vt* enclose with a rail; fence. **railing** *n* fence or framework of rails. **railway** *n* **1** permanent track of rails on which trains may transport passengers, goods, etc. **2** complete network of such tracks together with stations, land, etc.

rain *n* **1** drops of water falling from clouds, condensed from atmospheric water vapour. **2** an instance of this; shower. **3** rapid heavy fall or occurrence of anything. *vt,vi* fall or cause to fall as or like rain. *vt* give (praise, gifts, etc.) in large quantities. **rain cats and dogs** rain very heavily. **rainbow** *n* banded arc of spectral colours visible in the sky during or just after a shower of rain. **rainfall** *n* **1** fall of rain; shower. **2** amount of water falling as rain, snow, etc., in a given area within a given period of time.

raise *vt* **1** elevate; lift up. **2** build; erect. **3** bring up for consideration. **4** initiate or inspire; provoke. **5** bring up (children, etc.); rear. **6** collect or gather. **7** increase in degree, size, intensity, etc. **8** evoke; suggest. **9** promote in rank, dignity, etc. **10** summon up. **11** bring back to life. **12** remove or lift (a ban, siege, etc.).

raisin *n* sweet dried grape.

rajah *n* king, prince, or chief, esp. in India.

rake *n* tool with a long handle and teeth or prongs at one end used for gathering leaves, etc. *vt* **1** gather, collect, or smooth with a rake. **2** gather in or collect up. **3** search through carefully. *vi* use a rake. **rake up** bring up or reveal (something, esp. from the past).

rally *vt,vi* **1** reassemble. **2** bring or come together for some common purpose. *vi* **1** gather to support or assist a person, cause, etc. **2** regain strength or vigour; recover. *n* **1** recovery. **2** gathering of people supporting a cause, taking part in a sporting event, etc.

ram *n* **1** male sheep. **2** device used to batter, crush, or drive against something. *vt* (-mm-) **1** strike or crash against with great force. **2** force, cram, or press.

ramble *vi* **1** wander about; stroll. **2** grow in or follow a meandering course. **3** talk or write aimlessly or incoherently. *n* walk taken for pleasure. **rambler** *n.*

ramp *n* sloping surface joining two levels.

rampage *vi* rush about wildly or destructively. *n* wild, violent, or destructive beha-viour. **on the rampage** very angry; engaged in destructive behaviour.

rampant *adj* **1** rife; unchecked. **2** violent in opinion, action, etc.

rampart *n* **1** mound of earth, usually surmounted by a parapet, fortifying a castle, fort, etc. **2** any defence or protection.

ramshackle *adj* loosely constructed or held together; shaky; derelict.

ran *v pt* of **run**.

ranch *n* large farm, esp. in America, for rearing cattle, horses, or sheep. **rancher** *n.*

rancid *adj* having an unpleasant stale smell or taste; rank.

rancour *n* angry resentment; bitterness.

random *adj* happening, done, etc., without aim or purpose; chance; haphazard. *n* **at random** without choice, purpose, method, etc. **randomly** *adv.*

rang *v pt* of **ring**.

range *n* **1** limits within which variation is possible. **2** extent or scope. **3** possible distance of movement, flight, etc. **4** place with targets for shooting practice. **5** chain of mountains. **6** row or line. **7** class, set, or series. **8** large cooking stove. *vt* **1** arrange in order, esp. in rows or lines. **2** dispose or place in a particular group, class, etc. **3** travel through or over; roam. *vi* **1** vary within specified limits. **2** extend or run, esp. in a given direction. **3** roam or wander (over). **4** occur within a certain area or time. **5** have a particular range.

rank[1] *n* **1** position or standing in a scale or graded body. **2** row or line, esp. of soldiers. *vt* **1** arrange in a row or rank. **2** assign to a certain position, station, class, etc. *vi* hold a certain position. **rank and file** *n* body of soldiers in an army or people in any other organization, as opposed to the officers or leaders. **ranks** *pl n* soldiers as opposed to officers.

rank[2] *adj* **1** growing vigorously or producing luxuriant vigorous growth. **2** having a strong unpleasant smell or taste. **3** utter; complete. **rankly** *adv.* **rankness** *n.*

rankle *vi* annoy; hurt one's pride.

ransack *vt* **1** search thoroughly or energetically. **2** plunder.

ransom *n* **1** redeeming of a kidnapped person, captured goods, etc., for a price. **2** price paid or demanded. *vt* release from captivity, detention, etc., by paying the price demanded.

rant *vi* shout angrily; rage.

rap *vt,vi* (-pp-) **1** knock, strike, or tap, esp. quickly. **2** *also* **rap out** say sharply. *n* **1** quick light blow; tap. **2** sound of this. **3** *sl* blame or punishment, esp. a prison sentence.

rape *n* **1** crime of having sexual intercourse with a woman without her consent. **2** act of taking by force. *vt,vi* commit rape (on). **rapist** *n*.

rapid *adj* quick; fast; swift. **rapids** *pl n* part of a river where the water flows very swiftly. **rapidity** *n*. **rapidly** *adv*.

rapier *n* sword with a slender pointed blade used for thrusting.

rapt *adj* **1** enthralled; enchanted. **2** totally absorbed or engrossed.

rapture *n* ecstatic delight; joy; pleasure. **rapturous** *adj*.

rare[1] **1** seldom occurring, found, experienced, etc. **2** remarkable or unusual, esp. in excellence. **3** of low density. **rarely** *adv*. **rarity** *n*.

rare[2] *adj* not completely cooked; underdone.

rascal *n* **1** scoundrel; rogue. **2** mischievous child or animal. **rascally** *adj,adv*.

rash[1] *adj* hasty in speech or action; reckless.

rash[2] *n* skin eruption, as of spots.

rasher *n* thin slice of bacon.

rasp *vt,vi* grate; sound harsh. *n* harsh grating sound.

raspberry *n* shrub of the rose family producing small juicy red edible fruit.

rat *n* **1** long-tailed rodent resembling but larger than the mouse. **2** *sl* despicable person. **smell a rat** be suspicious about. ~*v* (-tt-) **rat on** *sl* desert or betray (friends, a cause, etc.).

rate *n* **1** quantity, amount, degree, etc., relative to a unit of something else. **2** price. **3** speed of movement, action, etc. **4** tax paid by householders, companies, etc., to cover the supply of local services and amenities. *vt* **1** appraise the value or worth of. **2** esteem; consider. **3** deserve. **4** determine (prices, etc.) at a certain rate. *vi* **1** be classed or ranked. **2** have status, value, position, etc.

rather *adv* **1** more readily; preferably. **2** somewhat; quite. **3** with more reason, justice, etc. **4** more accurately or properly. **5** on the contrary.

ratio *n* fixed numerical relation between two similar magnitudes; proportion.

ration *n* fixed allowance; share. *vt* **1** apportion; share out. **2** restrict to or provide with rations.

rational *adj* **1** of, relating to, or based on reason. **2** able to reason. **3** reasonable; sensible. **rationality** *n*. **rationally** *adv*. **rationalize** *vt* **1** make rational; justify unconscious behaviour. **2** make (an industry, process, etc.) more efficient; streamline. *vi* think in a rational manner; reason.

rattle *vi,vt* make or cause to make a series of short sharp sounds; vibrate noisily. *vi also* **rattle on** chatter. *vt* **1** say or do rapidly. **2** *sl* confuse or disturb (someone). *n* **1** rapid succession of short sharp sounds. **2** device producing a rattling sound, such as a baby's toy.

raucous *adj* rough or harsh sounding. **raucously** *adv*.

ravage *n* **1** violent destructive action. **2** devastation; damage. *vt* damage or devastate. *vi* cause great damage.

rave *vi,vt* talk or utter wildly or incoherently. *vi also* **rave about** talk or write very enthusiastically (about). *n* **1** act of raving. **2** extravagant praise.

raven *n* large bird of the crow family with shiny black plumage and a harsh cry. *adj,n* shiny black.

ravenous *adj* **1** extremely hungry. **2** greedy for praise, recognition, etc. **ravenously** *adv*.

ravine steep valley; gorge; canyon.

ravioli *n* small pieces of pasta enclosing chopped meat, etc., usually served in a tomato sauce.

ravish *vt* **1** seize and carry away forcibly. **2** rape. **3** enrapture.

raw *adj* **1** not cooked. **2** in a natural state; unprocessed. **3** inexperienced. **4** painfully open or exposed, as a wound. **5** crude; vulgar. **6** harsh; unfair; unpleasant. **rawness** *n*.

ray *n* **1** narrow beam of light, etc. **2** tiny amount of hope, comfort, etc.; spark. **3** line or structure radiating from a centre. *vi,vt* radiate.

rayon *n* man-made textile or fibre made from cellulose.

raze *vt* demolish or destroy (buildings, etc.) completely.

razor *n* instrument fitted with cutting edges, used esp. for shaving hair.

reach *vt* 1 get to; arrive at; attain; come to. 2 establish contact with. 3 amount to; total. *vt,vi* extend as far as. **reach for** stretch up or out for in order to grasp and bring closer. ~*n* 1 act of reaching. 2 range; extent covered.

react *vi* 1 reciprocate. 2 respond to a stimulus. 3 act in opposition or in reverse. 4 interact. **reaction** *n* 1 reciprocal action, movement, or tendency. 2 response to a stimulus. 3 response to an event, idea, etc. 4 tendency or movement in politics towards extreme conservatism. 5 interaction between chemicals. **reactionary** *adj* relating to reaction, esp. in politics. *n* reactionary person.

read *v* (read) *vt,vi* 1 apprehend the meaning of (letters, words, etc.). 2 *also* **read out** utter (printed or written matter) aloud. 3 be occupied in reading. 4 study (a subject). 5 learn of by reading. *vt* 1 interpret. 2 register; indicate. 3 predict; foretell. *vi* have a certain wording. **read between the lines** deduce an implied meaning not openly stated. ~*n* act of reading. **reader** *n*.

readjust *vt* adjust again or afresh; rearrange; readapt.

ready *adj* 1 fully prepared. 2 willing. 3 prompt; quick. 4 inclined; apt. 5 likely or liable (to). 6 immediately available. **get ready** 1 prepare. 2 dress oneself. *n* **at the ready** in position. **readily** *adv* willingly; without delay.

real *adj* 1 true; genuine; authentic. 2 actual; not imaginary or fictitious. **really** *adv* 1 in fact; actually. 2 truly; genuinely. **reality** *n*. **realism** *n* interest in or concern for the real or actual. **realist** *n*. **realistic** *adj*. **realistically** *adv*.

realize *vt,vi* comprehend; appreciate; be aware. *vt* 1 bring to fruition. 2 convert into cash. *vi* be sold for; bring as proceeds; gain. **realization** *n*.

realm *n* 1 kingdom; domain. 2 region or sphere in which something rules or predominates.

reap *vt,vi* cut or harvest (grain). *vt* obtain as a result or recompense.

rear[1] *n* 1 back part of anything. 2 position behind or in the rear. 3 buttocks. *adj* of, at, or in the rear. **rear admiral** *n* naval officer ranking immediately below a vice-admiral. **rearguard** *n* military detachment that brings up and protects the rear, esp. in retreat.

rear[2] *vt* 1 care for and bring to maturity. 2 lift up; erect. *vi* rise up on the hind legs. **rear up** rise up in anger, resentment, etc.

reason *n* 1 ground, cause, or motive. 2 justification; explanation. 3 mental ability of logical argument. 4 good sense. 5 sanity. *vi,vt* 1 think or argue logically (about). 2 conclude or infer (that). 3 urge or persuade by reasoning. **reasonable** *adj* 1 amenable to reason. 2 based on reason; sensible or sound. 3 able to reason. 4 not excessive; moderate. **reasonably** *adv*.

reassure *vt* allay (fears, doubts, etc.); restore confidence or tranquillity to. **reassurance** *n*.

rebate *n* return of part of an amount paid for goods, a service, etc.

rebel *n* ('rebəl) person who defies authority or control. *vi* (ri'bel) (-ll-) resist; oppose. **rebel against** show or feel strong aversion (for). **rebellion** *n*. **rebellious** *adj*.

rebound *vt,vi* (ri'baund) spring back or cause to spring back. *n* ('ri:baund) act of rebounding; recoil.

rebuff *vt* treat scornfully; turn away; snub. *n* rejection; abrupt dismissal.

rebuke *vt,n* reprimand.

recalcitrant *adj* unwilling to submit; wayward; wilful; stubborn. **recalcitrance** *n*.

recall *vt* 1 remember. 2 call back. 3 revoke or withdraw. *n* 1 act or instance of recalling. 2 memory.

recede *vi* 1 move back; retreat. 2 become more distant. 3 slope backwards. 4 withdraw from a bargain, promise, etc. 5 decline in value, etc.

receipt *n* 1 written acknowledgement of payment or delivery. 2 act of receiving; fact of being received. *vt* mark (a bill) as paid. *vt,vi* write or give a receipt for. **receipts** *pl n* amount received.

receive *vt* **1** take into one's possession; gain; get. **2** encounter, experience, or undergo. **3** bear; sustain. **4** gain knowledge of; learn. **5** welcome; admit. *vi* **1** receive something. **2** buy and sell stolen goods. **receiver** *n* **1** someone or something that receives. **2** device for converting electrical signals into their desired form.

recent *adj* occurring, appearing, done, etc., just before the present time; fresh; not remote. **recently** *adv.*

receptacle *n* **1** container. **2** portion of a plant stem bearing a flower or flower head.

reception *n* **1** act of receiving or being received. **2** manner of being received. **3** formal social gathering. **4** area in an office, hotel, etc., where visitors are received. **5** quality attained in receiving radio signals, etc. **receptionist** *n* person employed to receive visitors, answer the telephone, etc. **receptive** *adj* able, quick, or willing to receive suggestions, requests, etc.

recess (ri'ses, 'ri:ses) **1** part or area that is set back; alcove. **2** *also* **recesses** secluded inner place or area. **3** *US* temporary break; holiday. *vt* **1** place in a recess. **2** make a recess in or of.

recession *n* **1** withdrawal. **2** receding part. **3** decline or falling off in business activity.

recipe *n* formula or method, esp. for preparing a dish in cookery.

recipient *n* person who receives.

reciprocal *adj* **1** given, felt, etc., on both sides; mutual. **2** given, done, etc., in return. *n* reciprocal relationship; equivalent; counterpart. **reciprocate** *vt,vi* **1** do, feel, etc., (something similar) in return. **2** give and receive; interchange.

recite *vt,vi* repeat aloud, as from memory. *vt* read or narrate before an audience. **recital** *n* **1** musical performance, poetry reading, etc. **2** detailed account; statement; description.

reckless *adj* careless of consequences; heedless; rash. **recklessly** *adv.*

reckon *vt,vi* add (up); calculate. *vt* consider; regard as; think. **reckon with 1** settle accounts with. **2** take into consideration.

reclaim *vt* **1** render useable for cultivation, habitation, etc. **2** recover from waste products. **3** bring back from error, sin, etc. **reclamation** *n.*

recline *vi,vt* lean back or cause to lean back. **reclinable** *adj.*

recluse *n* hermit.

recognize *vt* **1** identify; know again. **2** perceive; realize. **3** acknowledge or accept the existence, truth, etc., of. **4** show appreciation of by a reward, etc. **recognition** *n.* **recognizable** *adj.*

recoil *vi* **1** draw or shrink back, as in fear, horror, etc. **2** spring back when released, as a firearm. **3** rebound or react upon. *n* act or instance of recoiling.

recollect *vt,vi* recall; remember. **recollection** *n.*

recommend *vt* **1** speak or write of favourably; commend. **2** urge as advisable; advise. **3** entrust to. **4** make acceptable or likeable. **recommendable** *adj.* **recommendation** *n.*

recompense *vt* **1** compensate, repay, or reward. **2** compensate for (a loss, etc.). *n* compensation; repayment; remuneration.

reconcile *vt* **1** make no longer opposed or hostile. **2** settle. **3** make consistent or compatible. **reconciliation** *n.*

reconstruct *vt* **1** rebuild. **2** recreate from surviving information. **reconstruction** *n.*

record *v* (ri'kɔːd) *vt* **1** set down for future reference, esp. in writing. **2** produce in a lasting form, as on magnetic tape. **3** register; indicate. *vi* record music, etc. *n* ('rekɔːd) **1** written account. **2** something preserving evidence of the past. **3** aggregate of past achievements, actions, etc.; career. **4** attainment, occurrence, etc., that surpasses all others. **5** flat disc with a spiral groove played on a gramophone to reproduce music, etc. **6** list of a person's crimes. **on record** stated or known publicly. **recorder** *n* wind instrument similar to the flute.

recount *vt* **1** relate or tell in detail. **2** enumerate.

recover *vt* **1** regain; retrieve; reclaim. **2** secure compensation for; make up for. *vi* **1** regain health, composure, balance, etc. **2** get back to a former or normal position, state, etc. **recovery** *n.*

recreation *n* **1** refreshment and relaxation afforded by exercise, a pastime, etc. **2**

hobby, exercise, or other diversion providing this. **recreational** *adj.*

recriminate *vi* accuse one's accuser. **recrimination** *n.*

recruit *n* recently enlisted member, esp. of the armed forces. *vt,vi* enlist (new personnel, etc.). **recruitment** *n.*

rectangle *n* four-sided figure with four right angles. **rectangular** *adj.*

rectify *vt* set or put right; remedy; correct. **rectification** *n.*

rector *n* clergyman of a parish formerly returning tithes. **rectory** *n* residence of a rector.

rectum *n* lower end of the intestine.

recuperate *vi* recover from illness or fatigue. *vt* recover (financial losses). **recuperation** *n.*

recur *vi* (-rr-) 1 occur again; be repeated. 2 return to the mind, in conversation, etc. **recurrence** *n.*

red *n* 1 colour of the spectrum that is the colour of fresh blood, ripe tomatoes, etc. 2 *also* **Red** someone who is radical in politics, esp. a communist. **in the red** in debt. **see red** become very angry. ~*adj* of the colour red. **reddish** *adj.* **redness** *n.* **redcurrant** *n* shrub bearing small red edible berries. **redden** *vt,vi* make or become red. *vi* blush. **red-handed** *adj,adv* in the act of performing a deed, committing a crime, etc. **red tape** *n* complicated official or administrative procedure.

redeem *vt* 1 buy or get back; recover; pay off. 2 convert (bonds, etc.) into cash. 3 fulfil (a pledge, etc.). 4 make amends for. 5 deliver from sin. **redemption** *n.*

redress *vt* set right; remedy; repair; adjust. *n* compensation; reparation.

reduce *vt,vi* make or become smaller or less; diminish; decrease. *vt* 1 bring or force into a certain state, form, etc. 2 lower; weaken; subdue. **reduction** *n.*

redundant *adj* 1 excessive; superfluous; unnecessary. 2 deprived of a job through being superfluous, etc. **redundancy** *n.*

reed *n* 1 hollow straight stem of any of various tall grasses. 2 vibrating piece of cane or metal in some wind instruments. 3 wind instrument that sounds by means of a reed.

reef *n* narrow ridge of sand, rocks, etc., at or just under the surface of water.

reek *vi* smell strongly or unpleasantly; stink. *vt* emit (smoke, etc.). *n* strong unpleasant smell.

reel[1] *n* cylinder, frame, or spool on which thread, wire, film, etc., may be wound. *vt* wind on a reel. **reel off** say, write, or produce easily and quickly.

reel[2] *vi* sway; rock; stagger; whirl. *n* act of reeling; stagger.

refectory *n* large communal dining hall.

refer *v* (-rr-) *vt,vi* direct attention, etc., (to). *vt* submit; assign. **refer to 1** be concerned with; relate to. 2 resort to for help, information, etc. 3 mention or allude (to). **referee** *n* 1 person to whom something is referred for decision. 2 umpire in certain games. 3 person who supplies a written reference. *vi* act as a referee. **reference** *n* 1 act of referring. 2 mention or allusion. 3 direction of attention to a person or thing. 4 written statement as to character, abilities, etc. 5 relation; regard. **referendum** *n, pl* **referendums** *or* **referenda** (refə'rendə) referring of legislative measures to the direct vote of the electorate for approval or rejection.

refine *vt,vi* 1 make or become fine; purify; separate out. 2 make or become more polished, elegant, etc. **refined** *adj.* **refinement** *n.* **refinery** *n* establishment for refining oil, sugar, etc.

reflation *n* government action taken to stimulate the economy. **reflationary** *adj.*

reflect *vt,vi* 1 cast or throw back light, heat, etc. 2 produce an image (of). *vt* 1 mirror; express; reproduce. 2 rebound; bring as a consequence. *vi also* **reflect on 1** think about; contemplate. 2 cast credit, dishonour, etc., on. **reflection** *n.* **reflector** *n* surface or device that reflects light, heat, sound, etc.

reflex *n* involuntary reaction; automatic response. **reflexive verb** *n* verb having an identical subject and direct object.

reform *vt* improve by removing abuses, inequalities, etc.; change for the better. *vi,vt* abandon or cause to abandon (evil habits, crime, etc.). *n* act or instance of reforming; improvement. **reformation** *n.*

refract *vt,vi* appear to bend or be bent by the action of light or other waves. **refraction** *n.*

refrain¹ *vi* keep oneself from; forbear.

refrain² *n* recurring phrase or verse.

refresh *vt,vi* revive; restore; renew. *vt* stimulate or revive (the memory). **refreshment** *n* food or drink. **refreshments** *pl n* light meal.

refrigerator *n* cabinet in which food, drink, etc., may be kept at a low temperature. **refrigerate** *vt,vi* freeze, chill, or keep cool in a refrigerator. **refrigeration** *n.*

refuge *n* 1 shelter or protection from danger, trouble, etc. 2 place or person affording this. **refugee** *n* person who flees from warfare, persecution, etc., esp. to a foreign country.

refund *vt* (ri'fʌnd) pay back; reimburse. *n* ('ri:fʌnd) repayment; sum repaid.

refuse¹ (ri'fju:z) *vt* decline to do, accept, give, grant, etc. *vi* withhold or decline acceptance, consent, compliance, etc.

refuse² ('refju:s) *n* rubbish; waste.

refute *vt* prove to be false or in error.

regain *vt* 1 win or get back; recover. 2 reach or attain again.

regal *adj* 1 of, like, or befitting a king; royal. 2 stately; dignified; elegant.

regard *vt* 1 consider; look upon; take into account; heed. 2 have or display respect for; esteem. 3 relate to; concern. *vt,vi* look steadily (at). *n* 1 attention; heed. 2 respect; esteem. 3 reference; connection. **regards** *pl n* greetings. **regardless** *adj* heedless or careless (of). *adv* without regard for expense, difficulties, etc.

regatta *n* event in which yachts and other boats are raced.

regent *n* person ruling in a kingdom during the minority, illness, incapacity, etc., of the sovereign. **regency** *n,adj.*

regime *n* 1 system or method of government. 2 prevailing system or authority.

regiment *n* ('redʒimənt) 1 military unit of ground forces commanded by a colonel. 2 large quantity. *vt* ('redʒiment) organize strictly, esp. into disciplined groups. **regimentation** *n.*

region *n* 1 part; area; district. 2 range; scope. 3 sphere of activity. **regional** *adj.*

register *n* 1 official record or list of names, items, etc. 2 book in which this is kept. 3 range of a voice or an instrument. *vt,vi* 1 enter in a register. 2 record. 3 show by facial expression, reaction, etc. **registration** *n.* **registrar** *n* official keeper of a register or record.

regress *vi* 1 move or go backwards. 2 revert to a former, esp. worse, state. **regression** *n.* **regressive** *adj.*

regret *vt* (-tt-) 1 feel sorrow or remorse for. 2 remember with sadness or remorse. 3 mourn. *n* 1 remorse. 2 sorrow or grief, esp. for a loss. **regretful** *adj.* **regrettable** *adj.*

regular *adj* 1 usual; normal. 2 conforming to a rule, principle, etc. 3 symmetrical. 4 recurring at fixed times or distances; unvarying; periodic. 5 habitual. *n* 1 soldier in a permanent army. 2 habitual customer or visitor of a place. **regularity** *n.* **regularly** *adv.*

regulate *vt* 1 control by rule, principle, etc. 2 adjust to function accurately, conform to some standard, etc.; put in order. **regulatory** *adj.* **regulation** *n* 1 rule; law; requirement. 2 control; adjustment.

rehabilitate *vt* 1 restore to normal by treatment or training. 2 restore to a former position or standing. **rehabilitation** *n.*

rehearse *vt,vi* practise in private before giving a public performance. **rehearsal** *n.*

reign *n* 1 period of rule, esp. of a sovereign. 2 dominance or rule. *vi* 1 rule as a sovereign. 2 prevail; predominate.

reimburse *vt* repay or refund, esp. for expense incurred, time lost, etc. **reimbursement** *n.*

rein *n* 1 long narrow strap fastened to a bit for controlling a horse. 2 restraint; curb. **give free rein to** allow complete freedom or licence. ~*vt* 1 put a rein on. 2 check; guide.

reincarnation *n* 1 belief that the soul returns after death in a new bodily form. 2 rebirth of the soul in a new body. 3 new bodily form taken.

reindeer *n, pl* **reindeer** large deer having branched antlers, found in arctic regions.

reinforce *vt* strengthen; give support to; stress. **reinforcement** *n.*

reinstate *vt* restore to a former state or position.

reject *vt* (ri'dʒekt) refuse to take, keep, accept, grant, etc. *n* ('ri:dʒekt) something rejected as imperfect, useless, etc. **rejection** *n.*

rejoice *vt,vi* make or become joyful; gladden.

rejuvenate *vt,vi* make or become young again; restore or be restored in vigour, freshness, etc. **rejuvenation** *n.*

relapse *vi* 1 fall or slip back to a former state or condition. 2 become ill again after apparent recovery. *n* act of relapsing.

relate *vt* 1 tell of; recount. 2 establish or perceive connection or relationship. *vi* refer to; have relation to. **relation** *n* 1 connection; association. 2 kinship. 3 relative. 4 reference; respect. 5 narration. **relations** *pl n* connections, feelings, etc., between people, countries, etc. **relationship** *n* connection; relation; mutual response.

relative *adj* 1 considered or existing in relation to something else; comparative. 2 related to; connected with. 3 relevant. 4 proportionate. *n* someone connected to another by birth or marriage. **relatively** *adv.* **relative pronoun** *n* word, such as *who* or *which*, that introduces a subordinate clause and refers back to a previous word or words.

relax *vt,vi* 1 make or become less rigid, tense, or firm. 2 make or become less strict, severe, or intense. 3 rest from or cease (work, effort, worry, etc.). **relaxation** *n.*

relay *n* 1 fresh supply or group of horses, men, etc., relieving others. 2 *also* **relay race** race between teams, each member covering part of the distance before being relieved by another. 3 broadcast; transmission. *vt* broadcast; transmit.

release *vt* 1 free; let go; give up; surrender. 2 permit to be issued, published, etc. 3 discharge. *n* 1 act of releasing; discharge. 2 something released for public sale, exhibition, publication, etc.

relent *vi* become less severe, firm, or harsh; soften; abate. **relentless** *adj* ruthless.

relevant *adj* to the point; pertinent. **relevance** *or* **relevancy** *n.*

reliable *adj* dependable; trustworthy. **reliability** *n.* **reliant** *adj* dependent. **reliance** *n.*

relic *n* 1 something associated with or surviving from the past. 2 object treasured in remembrance. 3 something associated with a saint, martyr, etc., revered as holy.

relief *n* 1 easing or alleviation of pain, distress, etc. 2 feeling resulting from this. 3 anything that eases. 4 aid; assistance. 5 pleasing change. 6 release from a post or duty. 7 person taking over. 8 raising of a siege. 9 elevation of figures, forms, etc., from a flat surface or the appearance of this. 10 distinct contrast. **relieve** *vt* 1 ease; lessen; alleviate. 2 help; aid. 3 free from anxiety, etc. 4 break the monotony of. 5 bring into relief; provide contrast. 6 release from duty; take over the duties of. 7 deprive.

religion *n* 1 belief in and worship of a god or gods. 2 a particular system of belief and worship. 3 associated ritual, conduct, doctrines, etc. 4 anything revered or zealously pursued. **religious** *adj* 1 relating to religion. 2 pious. 3 conscientious. **religiously** *adv.*

relinquish *vt* 1 give up; abandon. 2 let go; release. 3 surrender.

relish *vt* take delight in; enjoy; look forward to. *n* 1 enjoyment; keen anticipation. 2 appetizing taste or flavour. 3 sauce; spicy food.

relive *vt* experience again through the imagination or memory.

relocate *vt,vi* move (a firm, workers, etc.) to a different area or site. **relocation** *n.*

reluctant *adj* unwilling; marked by unwillingness. **reluctance** *n.* **reluctantly** *adv.*

rely *v* **rely on** trust in; depend on; have confidence in.

remain *vi* 1 stay behind in a place. 2 be left over or behind. 3 continue to be. **remains** *pl n* 1 remnants; relics; surviving fragments. 2 dead body; corpse. **remainder** *n* 1 something remaining or left over. 2 quantity remaining after subtraction or division.

remand *vt* send (a prisoner or accused person) back to prison pending further inquiries or proceedings. *n* act of remanding or state of being remanded. **remand home** *n* home for juvenile offenders.

remark *n* comment; observation. *vt,vi* say; comment (about). *vt* notice; perceive. **remarkable** *adj* worthy of notice; striking; unusual. **remarkably** *adv.*

remedy *n* 1 medicinal cure or treatment. 2 cure or correction for a wrong, evil, etc. 3 legal redress. *vt* 1 cure or heal. 2 put right; correct; redress. **remedial** *adj.*

remember *vt* retain in or recall to the memory. *vi* hold in one's memory. **remembrance** *n* memory; keepsake.

remind *vt* cause to remember or think of again. **reminder** *n* thing that reminds.

reminiscence *n* thing remembered or act of evoking old memories. **reminiscent** *adj.*

remiss *adj* negligent; at fault.

remission *n* 1 forgiveness; pardon. 2 reduction of a prison sentence.

remit *v* (-tt-) *vt* 1 send, esp. money. 2 pardon; refrain from inflicting (a sentence, etc.). *vt,vi* slacken. **remittance** *n* money sent; payment.

remnant *n* fragment; remainder; relic.

remorse *n* feeling of deep regret, guilt, etc. **remorseful** *adj.* **remorseless** *adj* 1 relentless. 2 not penitent.

remote *adj* 1 far away; removed; isolated. 2 slight; unlikely. **remotely** *adv.*

remove *vt* 1 take away or off; withdraw. 2 dismiss from a post or appointment. **removal** *n.*

remunerate *vt* grant as earnings, reward, etc.; pay or repay. **remuneration** *n.* **remunerative** *adj.*

renaissance *n* revival, esp. of learning. **the Renaissance** *n* period of radical artistic, scientific, and social development in Europe from the 14th to 16th centuries.

renal *adj* relating to the kidney.

render *vt* 1 give back; return. 2 serve; present for approval, action, etc.; supply with. 3 give a version or interpretation of; represent. 4 melt down. **rendition** *n.*

rendezvous *n* meeting place or time of meeting. *vi* meet by appointment.

renew *vt,vi* make or become new again; revive. *vt* 1 restore; replace; repair; renovate. 2 grant for a further period. 3 begin again. **renewal** *n.*

renounce *vt* 1 give up; abandon, esp. formally. 2 disown; break ties with. **renunciation** *n.*

renovate *vt* make fit or habitable again; restore. **renovation** *n.*

renown *n* fame; great distinction; notoriety.

rent *n* regular payment for the use of land, a house, buildings, etc. *vt* grant or use in exchange for rent; hire. **rental** *n* amount charged or paid in rent.

rep *n* short for (sales) **representative** or **repertory** (company).

repair *vt* 1 mend; restore; renew. 2 make up for; make good; remedy. *n* 1 mend. 2 act or process of repairing. **reparation** *n* compensation; amends; remedy.

repartee *n* witty reply or retort.

repatriate *vt* send (someone) back to his own country. **repatriation** *n.*

repay *vt,vi* (-paid) 1 pay back; refund. 2 return (a kindness, compliment, etc.).

repeal *vt* annul; revoke; cancel. *n* annulment; cancellation.

repeat *vt* say or do again; reproduce; echo. *n* second performance; something repeated. **repeatedly** *adv.*

repel *vt* (-ll-) 1 drive or force back or away; resist. 2 disgust. **repellent** *adj* 1 revolting; disgusting. 2 unpleasant. *n* substance used to keep flies, pests, etc., away.

repent *vi,vt* feel penitent (about); regret (one's sins). **repentance** *n.* **repentant** *adj.*

repercussion *n* 1 indirect or unintended consequence or result. 2 recoil.

repertoire *n* stock of plays, songs, etc., that a theatrical company, singer, etc., can offer.

repertory *n* 1 theatrical company performing a selection of plays, operas, etc., over a relatively short period. 2 repertoire; stock.

repetition *n* 1 act of repeating or being repeated. 2 something said or done again. **repetitious** *adj* repeated in a boring manner. **repetitive** *adj* 1 having a constant rhythm or beat. 2 characterized by repetition.

replace *vt* 1 put back. 2 find or be a substitute for. **replacement** *n.*

replenish *vt* fill up or supply again.

replica *n* copy or reproduction, esp. of a work of art.

reply *vi,vt* answer; respond. *n* answer; response.

report *vt,vi* 1 relate. 2 make, give, or bring back an account (of). 3 take down or write for publication. *vt* name as an offender; inform against. *vi* present (oneself); register (with). *n* 1 rumour. 2 account of something. 3 bang; sharp noise. **reporter** *n* person who reports, esp. for a newspaper.

repose *vi,vt* take rest or give rest to; recline; relax. *n* 1 rest; sleep; relaxed state. 2 tranquillity; composure.

represent *vt* 1 depict; stand for; symbolize. 2 act as a deputy or agent for. 3 portray; describe. **representation** *n*. **representative** *adj* serving to represent; typical. *n* 1 person or thing that represents or typifies. 2 *also* **sales representative** person selling a company's products. 3 agent; delegate.

repress *vt* keep down or under. **repressive** *adj*. **repression** *n* 1 restraint. 2 exclusion of thoughts and tendencies from consciousness.

reprieve *vt* 1 suspend execution of. 2 relieve temporarily from harm, punishment, etc. *n* 1 respite from punishment. 2 temporary relief.

reprimand *n* sharp rebuke; severe scolding. *vt* give a reprimand to.

reprint *vt* print again; print a new copy of. *n* reproduction or copy of something previously printed.

reprisal *n* retaliation; vengeful action.

reproach *vt* scold; rebuke. *n* scolding; rebuke. **reproachful** *adj*.

reproduce *vt* 1 produce again. 2 make a copy of; duplicate; imitate. *vt,vi* produce (offspring). **reproduction** *n*. **reproductive** *adj*.

reptile *n* cold-blooded egg-laying vertebrate, such as a snake, lizard, or turtle. **reptilian** *adj*.

republic *n* form of state in which supreme power rests in the people and their elected representatives. **republican** *adj,n*.

repudiate *vt* 1 reject. 2 disown; cast off. **repudiation** *n*.

repugnant *adj* distasteful; offensive. **repugnance** *n*.

repulsion *n* distaste; aversion. **repulsive** *adj*.

reputation *n* 1 what is generally thought about a person or thing. 2 good repute. **reputable** *adj* of good repute; respectable. **repute** *n* reputation, esp. a favourable one. **reputed** *adj* considered; reckoned.

request *n* act of asking for something or a thing asked for; demand. *vt* ask for (something) or ask (someone) to do something, esp. a favour.

requiem *n* 1 mass for the dead. 2 music composed for this.

require *vt* 1 need. 2 demand; order. **requirement** *n*.

rescue *vt* save or deliver from danger, etc. *n* delivery or release from harm or danger.

research *n* investigation, esp. into a scientific field in order to discover facts. *vt,vi* investigate. **researcher** *n*.

resemble *vt* look like or be similar to. **resemblance** *n*.

resent *vt* feel indignant at; dislike; be bitter about. **resentful** *adj*. **resentment** *n*.

reserve *vt* 1 hold back; set apart; keep for future use. 2 book (tickets, seats, etc.) in advance. *n* 1 something reserved. 2 part of an army, etc., kept back for use in emergency. 3 self-restraint; lack of familiarity. **in reserve** kept back for future use. **reservation** *n* 1 act of reserving; something reserved. 2 advance booking. 3 qualification; limitation. **reserved** *adj* 1 set aside for future use; held back. 2 booked in advance. 3 quiet; self-restrained; reticent.

reservoir *n* 1 place functioning as a store. 2 place for holding a large quantity of water.

reside *vi* dwell; have as one's home; live. **reside in** live in; be present or inherent. **residence** *n* state of residing or the place where a person resides. **resident** *adj* residing. *n* person staying in a place permanently or for a long time. **residential** *adj* relating to housing, residences, etc.; not commercial.

residue *n* what is left over; remainder. **residual** *adj*.

resign *vt* give up; surrender; relinquish. *vi* give up an office, commission, employment, etc. **resign oneself (to)** accept as unavoidable. **resignation** *n*.

resilient *adj* 1 elastic; rebounding. 2 capable of recovering quickly from a shock, injury, etc. **resilience** *n*.

resin *n* 1 sticky substance manufactured or obtained from various plants or trees. 2 synthetic substance used in making plastics, varnish, etc.

resist *vt,vi* 1 withstand; oppose. 2 overcome (a temptation). **resistance** *n*. **resistant** *adj*.

resit *vt* (-tt-; -sat) take (an examination) again after failing it.

resolute *adj* firm; determined. **resolutely** *adv.*

resolution *n* 1 firmness; determination; resolve. 2 act or state of resolving or being resolved. 3 decision of a court. 4 vote of an assembly, etc. 5 explanation; solution.

resolve *vt* 1 make clear. 2 determine; decide. 3 form by a vote or resolution. 4 find a solution to (a problem, etc.). 5 agree to (an action, course, etc.) formally. *vt,vi* separate into component parts; analyse. *n* 1 something resolved. 2 determination; strong intention.

resonance *n* increase or prolonging of vibrations, as of sound. **resonant** *adj.* **resonate** *vi,vt* undergo or cause resonance.

resort *vi* also **resort to** go for help to; turn to. *n* holiday or recreation place.

resound *vi* echo; ring; continue sounding.

resource *n* skill in devising means. **resources** *pl n* 1 means of supplying a want. 2 supplies, etc., that can be drawn on. **resourceful** *adj.*

respect *n* 1 reference; relation. 2 deference; esteem. 3 point or aspect. *vt* treat with esteem; admire. **respectable** *adj.* **respectability** *n.* **respectful** *adj.* **respective** *adj* relating to two or more persons or things regarded individually. **respectively** *adv* individually in the order mentioned.

respite ('respit) *n* 1 delay. 2 period of rest or relief. 3 suspension of execution; reprieve.

respond *vi* 1 answer; reply. 2 react. **response** *n.*

responsible *adj* 1 liable to answer for something. 2 of good credit or position. **responsibility** *n.*

responsive *adj* 1 answering; making reply. 2 acting in response.

rest[1] *n* 1 quiet repose; sleep. 2 refreshing break from activity. 3 freedom or relief. 4 calm; tranquillity. 5 stopping or absence of motion. 6 prop or support; something that steadies. 7 pause in music, rhythm, etc. *vi,vt* 1 take rest or give rest to. 2 support or steady or be supported or steadied. **restful** *adj.* **restless** *adj* 1 unable to remain at rest. 2 uneasy; unquiet. 3 never still or motionless. 4 without rest. 5 characterized by constant activity.

rest[2] *n* 1 remainder; that which is left. 2 others; everyone else. *vi* remain; continue to be.

restaurant *n* place where meals are bought and eaten.

restore *vt* 1 build up again; repair; renew. 2 establish again. 3 give back. **restoration** *n.* **restorative** *adj,n.*

restrain *vt* check; hold back; repress. **restraint** *n.*

restrict *vt,vi* place limits (on); confine; restrain. **restriction** *n.* **restrictive** *adj.*

result *n* 1 thing caused or produced; effect; outcome; consequence. 2 solution; answer. 3 final score. *vi* be the result **result in** end in.

resume (ri'zju:m) *vt,vi* start to take up again after an interval or pause. *vt* occupy (a seat) again. **resumption** *n.*

résumé ('rezju:mei) *n* summary, esp. of one's career or background.

resurrect *vt* 1 bring to life again. 2 use again; express new interest in. **resurrection** *n.*

retail *n* sale of goods in small quantities to the public, usually through a shop; not wholesale. *adv* sold in such a way. *vt,vi* sell or be sold by retail. **retailer** *n.*

retain *vt* 1 keep back; continue to hold. 2 hold in the mind or memory. 3 continue to employ; keep for future use. **retention** *n.* **retentive** *adj.*

retaliate *vi* fight back; answer an attack. **retaliation** *n.*

retard *vt* hold back or slow down the development of; delay. **retardation** *n.*

retch *vi* attempt or begin to vomit.

reticent *adj* reserved; modest; shy; not forthcoming. **reticence** *n.*

retina *n, pl* **retinas** *or* **retinae** ('retini:) membrane of the eyeball that is sensitive to light and transmits images to the brain.

retire *vi* 1 leave one's employment at the end of one's working life. 2 go to bed. 3 leave or withdraw. *vt* cease to employ after a certain age. **retirement** *n.*

retort[1] *vi,vt* reply rudely or abruptly; answer back. *n* rude or angry reply.

retort[2] *n* round glass vessel with a long neck attached at an angle, used esp. in a laboratory for distilling or heating certain substances.

retrace *vt* **1** follow (a route) again in exactly the same way. **2** go over again; recount or recall.

retract *vt,vi* **1** draw or pull inwards. **2** withdraw (an earlier statement, promise, etc.); go back on. **retractable** *or* **retractible** *adj.* **retraction** *n.*

retreat *vi* **1** move back, esp. from an advancing army. **2** seek shelter or refuge. *n* **1** act of retreating. **2** safe place; refuge; haven; sanctuary.

retribution *n* punishment; revenge.

retrieve *vt* **1** fetch; find again; recover; regain. **2** rescue from difficulty or harm. **retrieval** *n.*

retrograde *adj also* **retrogressive 1** moving or pointing backwards; reverse. **2** tending to retrogress or decline into a worse condition. **retrogress** *vi* **1** move backwards; recede. **2** revert; decline; deteriorate. **retrogression** *n.*

retrospect *n* **in retrospect** looking back in time; with hindsight. **retrospective** *adj.*

return *vi* **1** come or go back to a former place, situation, etc. **2** reappear. **3** reply; answer back. *vt* **1** give, send, or take back. **2** respond to; react to; acknowledge. **3** yield as a rate of interest. **4** elect by voting. *n* **1** act of coming or going back. **2** yield on investment; revenue. **3** reappearance. **4** form to be filled in for tax purposes. **returnable** *adj.*

reveal *vt* **1** display; show. **2** divulge; disclose; betray. **revelation** *n* dramatic or sudden disclosure of the truth, esp. as revealed by God to mankind.

revel *v* (-ll-) **revel in** derive enormous satisfaction or pleasure from; bask in. **revels** *pl n also* **revelry** merrymaking; festivities.

revenge *n* act of retaliation to offset a previous crime or wrong; vengeance. *vt* avenge; retaliate for.

revenue *n* income, esp. from taxation or goods sold.

reverberate *vi* vibrate noisily; resound; echo. **reverberation** *n.*

reverence *n* feeling or act of deep respect, esp. towards something sacred. **Reverence** title used when addressing a priest or high-ranking clergyman. **reverent** *adj.* **revere** *vt* treat with reverence; idolize or worship.

reverse *vt* **1** change the direction or order of; turn back. **2** revoke; alter (a former decision, attitude, etc.). *vi* drive or move backwards. *n* **1** opposite side of a coin, sheet of paper, etc. **2** gear engaged on a vehicle for moving backwards. **3** opposite of what has been stated. *adj* opposite. **reversal** *n* **1** turning round; reversing. **2** revoking of a law, etc.; cancellation.

revert *vt* return to a former state or condition. **reversion** *n.*

review *vt* **1** look back over; examine, check, or consider again. **2** give a critical report of (a book, play, etc.). *n* **1** critical report. **2** general analysis or report; survey. **reviewer** *n.*

revise *vt* **1** alter (one's attitudes, opinions, etc.). **2** rewrite. *vi,vt* study in preparation for an examination. **revision** *n.*

revive *vt,vi* **1** bring or return to consciousness. **2** introduce again; restore. **revival** *n.*

revoke *vt* cancel, esp. a law or rule; repeal.

revolt *vi* rebel; protest or act against authority. *vt* disgust; repel. *n* rebellion; uprising; mutiny. **revolting** *adj* disgusting; repulsive.

revolution *n* **1** large-scale rebellion resulting in the overthrowing of those in power and radical social and political change. **2** dramatic change. **3** movement around a point or axis; orbit or rotation. **revolutionary** *n* person in favour of or working for political revolution. *adj* **1** relating to political revolution. **2** radical; changing dramatically. **3** revolving or rotating. **revolutionize** *vt* cause a radical change in; alter dramatically.

revolve *vt,vi* move around a point or axis; orbit or rotate. **revolve around** be centred on or totally engaged with. **revolver** *n* small firearm capable of discharging several shots before reloading.

revue *n* light entertainment with music, satirical or comic sketches, etc.

revulsion *n* **1** repugnance; feeling of extreme distaste or hatred. **2** violent withdrawal or recoil.

reward *n* **1** something, such as a sum of money or prize, awarded in acknowledgment of a particular deed, act of service, etc. **2** profit; gain; benefit. *vt* repay; give a reward to. **rewarding** *adj* satisfying.

rhetoric n 1 art of public speaking; oratory. 2 eloquence. **rhetorical** adj 1 relating to rhetoric. 2 concerned more with style or effect of language than with meaning or content. **rhetorical question** n question to which no answer is required, used esp. as a literary device for its dramatic effect.

rheumatism n inflammation of the muscles, joints, etc. **rheumatic** adj.

rhinoceros n large mammal inhabiting tropical or subtropical regions, having one or two horns and a tough hide.

rhododendron n evergreen shrub having showy red, pink, or white flowers.

rhubarb n plant with large flat leaves and edible pink stalks.

rhyme n 1 identical or similar form of sounds occurring esp. at the end of two or more words, e.g. try and buy or relieve and believe. 2 verse using rhymes. vi,vt occur or make use of as a rhyme.

rhythm n 1 alternation of strong and weak stress or beats in music, speech, etc. 2 recurring pattern or form of movement, flow, etc. **rhythmic** or **rhythmical** adj.

rib n 1 one of the curved bones forming the wall of the chest. 2 anything resembling such a bone. 3 ridged stitch in knitting. vt (-bb-) 1 knit using alternate plain and purl stitches. 2 inf tease; make fun of in a gentle way.

ribbon n 1 strip of satin, cotton, etc., used for decoration, trimming, etc. 2 long narrow strip of land, water, etc. 3 narrow band impregnated with ink for use on a typewriter or similar machine.

rice n type of grass whose grains are used as a staple food.

rich adj 1 having a large amount of money; wealthy. 2 having an abundant supply. 3 sumptuous; luxurious. 4 having a high proportion of cream or fat. 5 having a full flavour or consistency. 6 of a deep or vivid colour. **richly** adv. **richness** n. **riches** pl n wealth; valuable possessions.

rickety adj liable to collapse or break.

rickshaw n two-wheeled passenger vehicle drawn by hand, traditionally used in parts of Asia.

rid vt (-dd-; rid or ridded) free; clear away completely. **get rid of** dispose of entirely; do away with; banish or abolish. **good riddance (to)** n welcome relief (from).

riddle[1] n complicated puzzle or problem in the form of a verse or question, employing puns, hidden meaning, etc.

riddle[2] vt make a series of holes in.

ride v (rode; ridden) vi 1 be carried on the back of a horse, donkey, etc. 2 travel in a vehicle. 3 inf continue without interference. vt 1 travel by sitting on an animal's back. 2 drive or propel (a vehicle). n journey on horseback, in a vehicle, etc. **take for a ride** swindle; defraud. **rider** n 1 person who rides. 2 additional remark, observation, etc.

ridge n 1 long elevated stretch of land; range. 2 furrow; raised or projecting section. 3 area of high atmospheric pressure between two depressions.

ridicule n mockery; scorn. vt treat as absurd; mock; deride. **ridiculous** adj stupid; extremely silly; absurd; ludicrous. **ridiculously** adv.

rife adj prevalent; rampant; widely distributed.

rifle[1] n firearm that is effective over a relatively long range, having spiral grooves cut inside a long barrel.

rifle[2] vt ransack; loot; plunder.

rift n 1 crack or opening caused by a geological fault. 2 split or disagreement.

rig vt (-gg-) 1 equip (a vessel) with sails, masts, etc. 2 fix (prices, an election, etc.) by fraudulent means. **rig up** construct or set up, esp. in a makeshift fashion. ~n 1 arrangement of sails, masts, etc. 2 equipment or installation used in drilling for oil or gas. **rigging** n ropes, chains, etc., supporting sails or masts on a ship.

right adj 1 correct; accurate. 2 true; of an expected standard. 3 suitable; appropriate. 4 normal. 5 on the side of the body opposite the heart. 6 conservative or reactionary. adv 1 accurately; correctly; properly. 2 directly; all the way. 3 completely; totally. 4 towards the right side. 5 immediately. n 1 legal or moral entitlement; due. 2 direction, location, or part that is on the right side. 3 conservative or reactionary group. vt correct; restore. vt,vi make or become upright again. **rightly** adv. **rightful** adj proper; entitled; justified. **right angle** n angle of 90°. **right-hand** adj on the side towards the right. **right-handed** *adj* using the right hand for writing, etc. **right wing** *n* political group representing conservative attitudes. *adj* **right-wing.**

righteous ('raitʃəs) *adj* virtuous; pious; upright. **righteousness** *n.*

rigid *adj* 1 straight and stiff; not flexible. 2 strict; not allowing variation. **rigidity** *n.* **rigidly** *adv.*

rigour *n* harshness; severity; hardship. **rigorous** *adj.* **rigorously** *adv.*

rim *n* outer or top edge of a container, wheel, etc.

rind *n* 1 tough outer skin of certain fruits; peel. 2 hard layer or coating of a piece of bacon or cheese.

ring[1] *n* 1 circle. 2 band worn on the finger. 3 circular course, track, route, etc. 4 group of people in a circle. 5 circular arena, esp. for a circus performance. 6 raised platform for a boxing match. *vt,vi* 1 encircle; surround. 2 fit rings on (birds, etc.) for identification. **ringleader** *n* main organizer, esp. of crime, etc. **ringlet** *n* long curl of hair. **ringpull** *n* piece of metal with ring attached pulled to open a can of beer, etc. **ringside** *n* seats nearest the ring at a boxing match.

ring[2] *v* (rang; rung) *vt,vi* 1 produce a clear metallic sound. 2 sound (a bell). 3 *also* **ring up** telephone; call. *vi* 1 resound. 2 experience a vibrating hum in the ears. **ring true/false** sound right/wrong. ~*n* 1 sound produced by a bell, telephone, etc. 2 echo. 3 telephone call. 4 quality; characteristic; hint.

rink *n* building or arena used for ice-skating.

rinse *vt* wash through in water, esp. in order to remove soap. *n* 1 application of clean water. 2 temporary dye for the hair; tint.

riot *n* 1 public disturbance causing a breakdown of law and order; uprising. 2 showy display; blaze. 3 *inf* hilarious occasion or person. *vi* participate in a riot. **rioter** *n.* **riotous** *adj* uproarious; disorderly.

rip *vt,vi* (-pp-) tear clumsily or violently. *n* torn part; split. **rip off** *sl* 1 cheat; overcharge. 2 steal. **rip-off** *n sl* 1 swindle. 2 exploitation for profit.

ripe *adj* 1 ready to be eaten or harvested. 2 fully matured. 3 having reached the appropriate stage of development. **ripen** *vi,vt* become or make ripe.

ripple *n* 1 slight movement of liquid; small wave. 2 continuous gentle sound. *vi* 1 form small waves; undulate. 2 gently rise and fall.

rise *vi* (rose; risen) 1 move upwards; ascend. 2 stand up; arise. 3 get out of bed. 4 progress to a higher rank or status. 5 become more cheerful, animated, etc. 6 increase in price or value. 7 rebel; revolt. 8 be able to tackle or cope. *n* 1 pay increase. 2 upward movement or progression; ascent. 3 slope; incline. **give rise to** cause; produce.

risk *n* possibility of harm, loss, etc.; gamble; chance. *vt* take a chance on; gamble; hazard. **risky** *adj.*

rissole *n* ball of minced meat fried with a coating of egg and breadcrumbs.

rite *n* formal ceremony having deep religious or cultural significance. **ritual** *adj* relating to rites. *n* 1 formalized procedure for performing certain rites or ceremonies. 2 rigid routine.

rival *n* person, organization, etc., in competition with others. *vt* (-ll-) 1 compete with. 2 be equal to. **rivalry** *n.*

river *n* 1 body of fresh water flowing usually into the sea or a lake. 2 flow; stream.

rivet *n* short bolt or nail. *vt* fasten with rivets. **riveted** *adj* unable to move or avert one's gaze; fixed.

road *n* 1 *also* **roadway** stretch of prepared land for vehicles. 2 street. 3 way.

roam *vi,vt* wander freely (over); travel widely. *n* leisurely walk; ramble. **roamer** *n.*

roar *vi* (esp. of lions) utter a loud noise. *vi,vt* 1 bellow; produce a loud angry or wild sound. 2 burn fiercely. *n* 1 loud cry of a lion, bull, etc. 2 angry or wild noise of a crowd, the wind, etc. **roaring trade** brisk profitable trade.

roast *vt,vi* 1 cook in an oven. 2 brown; scorch. *n* joint of meat for roasting.

rob *vt* (-bb-) 1 steal from. 2 deprive of. **robbery** *n* stealing by force or by threat of violence. **robber** *n.*

robe *n* long loose gown, often signifying office held. *vt,vi* dress, esp. officially.

robin *n* small brown songbird, the male of which has a red breast.

robot *n* man-like machine capable of performing certain human tasks and functions.
robust *adj* strong; healthy; vigorous. **robustly** *adv.*
rock[1] *n* 1 large solid mass of minerals. 2 cliff; boulder; large stone. 3 hard stick of sugar. **on the rocks** 1 in serious financial trouble. 2 served with ice-cubes. **rock-bottom** *n* lowest possible level. **rockery** *n* also **rock garden** area in which small plants grow between specially placed rocks. **rocky** *adj* having or strewn with rocks.
rock[2] *vt,vi* sway; move gently from side to side; shake. **rocker** *n* curved wooden or metal support for a rocking-chair, cradle, etc. **off one's rocker** mentally unbalanced. **rocky** *adj* shaky; unsteady.
rocket *n* cylindrical object propelled at speed into the sky to launch spaceships, direct bombs, or act as a warning or decorative firework. *vi* move like a rocket.
rod *n* 1 long straight stick of wood, bar of metal, etc. 2 also **fishing rod** rod used to suspend a line over water.
rode *v pt* of **ride.**
rodent *n* mammal, such as a rat, vole, or squirrel, with four strong incisors for gnawing and no canine teeth.
roe *n* 1 also **hard roe** 1 mass of eggs in a female fish. 2 also **soft roe** sperm of a male fish.
rogue *n* villain; rascal; scoundrel; criminal. **roguery** *n.* **roguish** *adj.*
role *n* 1 actor's part. 2 function; task.
roll *vt,vi* 1 move along by rotating; turn over. 2 move on wheels. 3 billow; undulate. 4 rotate; move up and down. 5 sway or move from side to side. 6 form into a ball or cylinder; coil. 7 produce a loud noise; roar. *vi* pass; move onwards. *vt* use a roller on. **roll in** *or* **up** arrive; turn up. ~*n* 1 act of rolling. 2 something rolled into a cylinder or ball. 3 small round or oblong of baked dough. 4 undulation. 5 roar. 6 rapid drumbeat. **rollcall** *n* calling of names to check attendance. **rolling pin** *n* cylindrical kitchen utensil for rolling pastry, dough, etc.
roller *n* 1 cylindrical part of a machine for pressing, rolling, winding, etc. 2 small cylindrical hair-curler. 3 long swelling wave. **roller-skate** *n* skate with wheels. *vi* move on roller-skates.
Roman Catholic *n* member of that part of the Christian Church owing allegiance to the Pope. *adj* relating to the Roman Catholic Church. **Roman Catholicism** *n.*
romance *n* 1 love affair; idealized love. 2 inclination for adventure, excitement, etc. 3 atmosphere of mystery, nostalgia, etc. 4 love story, esp. remote and idealized. 5 heroic medieval legend, verse, etc. 6 flight of imagination or fancy. *vi* tell extravagant or untrue stories. **romantic** *adj* 1 concerned with or given to romance. 2 fantastic; extravagant; imaginative. *n* person with romantic views. **romanticize** *vt,vi* attach romantic qualities to an otherwise unromantic object, story, etc.
romp *vi* frolic and play together, esp. boisterously. **romp home** win easily. ~*n* boisterous game. **rompers** *pl n* one-piece garment for a young child.
roof *n* 1 upper covering of a building, vehicle, etc. 2 top limit; highest point. **hit the roof** become furious. **raise the roof** 1 complain noisily. 2 cause confusion. ~*vt* cover with a roof.
rook[1] 1 black raucous gregarious type of crow. 2 *sl* swindler; cheat. *vt sl* swindle; cheat; overcharge. **rookery** *n* tree-top colony of rooks.
rook[2] *n* also **castle** chess piece that can move forwards, backwards, or sideways over any number of empty squares.
room *n* 1 unoccupied space. 2 partitioned part of a building with a specific purpose. 3 opportunity; scope. **make room** clear a space; bring about an opportunity. **roomy** *adj* spacious.
roost *n* bird's perch or sleeping place. **rule the roost** be in charge; dominate. ~*vi* settle for sleep.
root[1] *n* 1 part of a plant anchoring it to the ground and through which it absorbs water and nutrients. 2 essential element; basic part or cause; origin. 3 one of a specified number of equal factors of a number or quantity. *vi* 1 form roots; become established. 2 have a basis or origin (in). **root out** 1 dig out. 2 remove; destroy.

root² *v* **root about** *or* **around** search (for).
rope *n* thick twisted cord. **give enough rope** allow enough freedom. **know the ropes** be familiar with the method, rules, etc. ~*vt* catch or tie with rope. **rope in** persuade to take part; enlist. **rope off** partition or enclose with a rope. **ropy** *adj sl* meagre; of poor quality.

rosary *n* **1** series of Roman Catholic prayers, counted on a string of beads. **2** beads so used.

rose¹ *n* **1** prickly shrub or climbing plant having red, yellow, pink, or white flowers, often fragrant. **2** rose-shaped ornament, window, etc. *n,adj* deep pink. **bed of roses** luxurious state. **through rose-coloured spectacles** *or* **glasses** with unjustified optimism. **rosette** *n* **1** cluster of ribbons in the shape of a rose, often worn or presented as a trophy. **2** carving in the shape of a rose. **rosy** *adj* **1** rose-coloured. **2** promising; hopeful.

rose² *v pt* of **rise.**

rot *vi,vt* (-tt-) decay or cause to decay; deteriorate; putrefy. *n* **1** decay; corruption. **2** disease causing localized decay in plants, animals, timber, etc. *n,interj inf* nonsense! rubbish!

rota *n* list of duties, names, etc., which may be performed or used in rotation.

rotate *vt,vi* **1** move or cause to move on an axis; spin. **2** recur or cause to recur in regular succession. **rotation** *n.* **rotary** *adj* **1** turning like a wheel; moving round an axis. **2** acting by rotation. **rotor** *n* rotating part of a machine.

rotten *adj* **1** unsound; decayed; putrefied. **2** corrupt; contemptible. **3** *inf* unfortunate; annoying; badly done.

rouge *n* pink cosmetic powder for the cheeks.

rough *adj* **1** not smooth; coarse; uneven. **2** turbulent; violent. **3** unkind; rude. **4** harsh; grating. **5** unfinished; casual. **rough and ready** primitive but effective. **rough and tumble** *or* **rough house** disorderly brawling behaviour. **rough diamond** person who is worthy but lacking refinement. **rough on 1** unfortunate for. **2** severe towards. ~*n* **1** rough ground. **2** preliminary sketch, stage, etc. *v* **rough it** live primitively. **rough up 1** *sl* attack; beat up. **2** produce a preliminary sketch, etc. **roughen** *vt,vi* make or become rough. **roughly** *adv* **1** in a rough way. **2** approximately. **roughness** *n.*

roulette *n* gambling game in which bets are laid on which numbered socket a ball will find when dropped onto a rotating wheel.

round *adj* **1** circular; ring-shaped; spherical; curved. **2** complete; whole. *n* **1** habitual journey; single circuit, turn, session, etc. **2** meeting; session. **3** outburst; volley. **4** distribution of drinks to members of a group. **5** song in which voices sing in turn. *adv,prep* **1** continuously. **2** around; about; from place to place. **3** in a reverse or sideways direction. **4** with a circular movement. **5** so as to arrive. **6** so as to be conscious again. **round the bend** crazy. **get round** persuade; overcome. ~*vt,vi* make or become round, curved, etc. *vt* go or move around. **round off** bring to completion. **round on** attack, esp. verbally. **round up** gather or collect together. **roundup** *n* gathering; collection.

roundabout *n* **1** merry-go-round at a fairground. **2** road junction where traffic circulates in only one direction. *adj* indirect; circuitous.

rouse *vt,vi* **1** waken from sleep; stir. **2** incite to fury, passion, etc.; provoke. **rousing** *adj* exciting; thrilling; vigorous.

route *n* course or way to be followed to a destination. *vt* direct along or plan (a particular route).

routine *n* regular unvarying repeated course of action.

rove *vt,vi* stray; wander; ramble.

row¹ (rou) *n* line of several persons, objects, etc.

row² (rou) *vt,vi* propel by oars. *vt* carry or transport in a boat propelled by oars. *vi* take part in races in such a boat. *n* act or instance of rowing.

row³ (rau) *n* **1** noisy brawl; squabble. **2** disturbance; noise; din. *vi* quarrel noisily.

rowdy *adj* noisily boisterous and exuberant. **rowdiness** *n.*

royal *adj* **1** of or relating to a king or queen; regal; majestic. **2** splendid; lavish; magnificent. **royally** *adv.* **royalty** *n* **1** the rank of a king or queen. **2** member(s) of a reigning family. **3** share of profits made on the sale of books, records, etc., paid to the author, composer, etc.

rub *vt,vi* (-bb-) **1** move a hand, cloth, etc., briskly or forcefully over the surface (of); polish; smooth. **2** irritate; grate. **rub (it) in** emphasize. **rub off on** affect through association. **rub out** obliterate; erase. **rub up** polish; improve. **rub up the wrong way** annoy. ~*n* act of rubbing; massage.

rubber *n* **1** elastic material made from the milky juice of certain tropical trees or synthesized. **2** piece of rubber used to erase pencil marks, etc.

rubbish *n* **1** waste materials; litter. **2** nonsense.

rubble *n* loose fragments of stone, rock, etc., esp. from demolished buildings.

ruby *n* deep red precious stone. *n,adj* deep red.

rucksack *n* large bag carried on the back by walkers, etc.

rudder *n* vertical pivoted piece of wood, metal, etc., at the stern of a boat or aircraft, used to steer it.

rude *adj* **1** impolite; impertinent. **2** primitive; unsophisticated. **3** vulgar; coarse. **rudely** *adv.* **rudeness** *n.*

rudiments *pl n* **1** basic elements; first principles of a subject. **2** undeveloped form. **rudimentary** *adj* undeveloped; primitive; elementary.

rueful *adj* regretful; repentant. **ruefully** *adv.*

ruff *n* **1** starched lacy collar or frill. **2** prominent growth of feathers or hair around the neck of a bird or animal.

ruffian *n* rogue; villain; bully.

ruffle *vt,vi* **1** disturb; wrinkle; rumple. **2** annoy or become annoyed. **3** erect (feathers) in anger or display. *n* frill at the neck or wrist.

rug *n* **1** small thick carpet. **2** thick woollen blanket.

rugby *n* also **rugby football** or **rugger** form of football in which players may use their hands to carry the ball or to tackle opponents.

rugged *adj* **1** uneven; rough; craggy. **2** strong; unbending; harsh. **ruggedly** *adv.* **ruggedness** *n.*

ruin *n* **1** collapse; devastation; total destruction. **2** complete loss of social, financial, or moral reputation. *vt* bring to ruin; spoil; destroy. **ruins** *pl n* remains of a partly destroyed or derelict building, etc. **in ruins** destroyed; decayed. **ruinous** *adj.*

rule *n* **1** regulation; law; maxim; code of discipline; procedure. **2** period of control, authority, etc. **as a rule** generally. **work to rule** decrease efficiency or output by observing rules precisely. ~*vt,vi* **1** govern; dominate. **2** decree (that); decide officially (that). *vt* draw a straight line. **rule out** exclude. **ruler 1** person who rules. **2** instrument for measuring, drawing straight lines, etc.

rum *n* alcoholic drink distilled from sugar cane.

rumble *vi* make a low rolling noise, as of distant thunder. *vt sl* see through; guess correctly. **rumble along** or **past** move or pass making a rumble. ~*n* low rolling noise.

ruminant *n* any of various cud-chewing, hoofed animals, such as the cow, sheep, or deer. **ruminate** *vi* **1** chew the cud. **2** meditate; ponder; consider carefully.

rummage *vt,vi* ransack; search (through).

rumour *n* hearsay; gossip; unverified talk.

rump *n* rear part of a person or animal; buttocks.

rumple *vt,vi* crease; crumple; ruffle.

run *v* (-nn-; ran; run) *vi* **1** proceed on foot at a fast pace. **2** gallop or canter. **3** make a quick journey. **4** function; operate. **5** be valid; endure or last. **6** go; proceed. **7** be inherited from. **8** fall in a stream; flow. **9** spread; become diffused. *vt* **1** do whilst running. **2** roll; push; drive. **3** cover quickly. **4** operate; manage; control. **5** be affected by. **6** cause to flow. **run across** or **into** meet unexpectedly. **run away** escape; abscond. **run down 1** slow down. **2** find or capture. **3** criticize; speak badly of. **run for** seek election for. **run out** become exhausted; have no more. **run to** be adequate for. ~*n* **1** act or pace of running; race. **2** continuous series. **3** sort; type. **4** unlimited freedom or access. **5** strong demand. **6** score of one in cricket. **in the long run** eventually; after a long while. **on the run** escaping from the police, etc.

rung[1] *n* bar forming a spoke of a wheel, step of a ladder, crosspiece on a chair, etc.

rung[2] *v pp* of **ring**.

runner *n* 1 person that runs; athlete. 2 lateral shoot of a plant. 3 narrow strip of wood, metal, or cloth on which something is supported or runs. **runner bean** *n* climbing bean plant with scarlet flowers and long edible green pods. **runner-up** *n* competitor finishing just after the winner.

running *adj* 1 continuous; without interruption. 2 taken at a run. 3 moving easily; flowing. *n* 1 condition of the ground on a race course. 2 management; operation. **in/out of the running** with a/no chance of winning.

runny *adj* discharging liquid; streaming.

runway *n* 1 long wide track used by aircraft for landing or taking off. 2 ramp. 3 channel; groove.

rupture *n* act of bursting; state of being burst or broken; breach; split. *vt,vi* break; burst.

rural *adj* 1 of the countryside. 2 rustic.

rush[1] *vi,vt* hurry or cause to hurry; hasten; proceed recklessly. *vi* come, flow, etc., quickly. *vt* make a sudden attack on. *n* sudden speedy advance. **rush hour** *n* time of day when traffic is heaviest.

rush[2] *n* plant growing in wet places, the stems of which can be used for chair seats, baskets, etc.

rust *n* powdery brownish coating formed on iron and steel by the action of air and moisture. *vi,vt* become or make rusty; corrode. **rusty** *adj* 1 covered in rust; corroded. 2 inefficient through disuse; spoilt by neglect. **rustiness** *n.*

rustic *adj* unsophisticated; rural; simple. *n* 1 country dweller. 2 unsophisticated person.

rustle *vi,vt* make or cause to make a soft sound, as of dry leaves, silk, etc. *vt* steal (cattle, etc.). **rustle up** improvise; procure hastily. ~*n* rustling sound.

rut *n* 1 sunken furrow in a path or track; groove. 2 dreary or boring way of life.

ruthless *adj* without mercy or pity; cruel; heartless. **ruthlessly** *adv.* **ruthlessness** *n.*

rye *n* cereal grain used as animal fodder and for making flour and whisky.

S

Sabbath *n* day set aside for rest and worship, Saturday for Jews and Sunday for Christians.

sabotage *n* deliberate destruction for political, military, or private ends. *vt* destroy or disrupt by sabotage. **saboteur** *n.*

saccharin *n* intensely sweet powder used as a non-fattening sugar substitute. *adj* cloyingly sweet.

sachet *n* small sealed bag containing perfume, shampoo, etc.

sack *n* 1 large coarse bag made of flax, hemp, etc., used for coal, flour, corn, etc. 2 *inf* dismissal from employment. *vt inf* dismiss from employment.

sacrament *n* religious ceremony (Baptism, Matrimony, Holy Orders, etc.) regarded as conferring an outward sign of inward divine grace. **sacramental** *adj.*

sacred *adj* holy; dedicated to God; inviolate. **sacredly** *adv.* **sacredness** *n.*

sacrifice *vt* 1 give up (something) so that greater good or a different end may result. 2 offer to or kill in honour of a deity. *n* 1 offering of something to a god. 2 giving or offering up (anything), esp. with a worthy motive. **sacrificial** *adj.*

sacrilege *n* desecration of a sacred place, person, or thing. **sacrilegious** *adj.*

sad *adj* 1 sorrowful; dejected; downcast. 2 unfortunate. **sadly** *adv.* **sadness** *n.* **sadden** *vt,vi* make or grow sad.

saddle *n* rider's seat fitted to a horse, bicycle, etc. *vt* 1 put a saddle on. 2 load or burden (with).

sadism *n* perversion in which pleasure, esp. sexual pleasure, is derived from inflicting pain. **sadist** *n.* **sadistic** *adj.*

safari *n* expedition, esp. for hunting big game.

safe *adj* 1 secure; free from danger. 2 dependable; reliable. **safe and sound** unharmed. ~*n* strong box for keeping valuables secure against theft. **safely** *adv.* **safeguard** *n* proviso; precaution. *vt* protect; guard. **safekeeping** *n* custody.

safety *n* security; freedom from danger or risk. **safety belt** *n* strong strap to secure a passenger in the seat of an aircraft, car, etc.

safety pin *n* bent pin with the point protected by a guard. **safety valve** *n* **1** machine valve that opens when pressure becomes too great for safety. **2** harmless outlet for anger, passion, etc.

sag *vi* (-gg-) **1** droop; bend; sink. **2** give way under weight or pressure.

saga *n* **1** heroic prose tale in old Norse literature. **2** long chronicle, esp. of generations of one family.

sage[1] *n* very wise man. *adj* of great wisdom, discretion, prudence, etc. **sagacity** *n.* **sagely** *adv.*

sage[2] *n* grey-green aromatic herb widely used in cookery.

Sagittarius *n* ninth sign of the zodiac, represented by the Archer.

said *v pp* and *pt* of **say.**

sail *n* **1** large sheet of canvas, etc., spread to catch the wind and propel a boat. **2** arm of a windmill. **3** trip in a sailing vessel. *vt,vi* **1** move by sail power; travel by sea. **2** glide or pass smoothly and easily. **set sail** start on a voyage. **sail close to the wind** narrowly avoid danger, ruin, etc. **sailor** *n* member of ship's crew. **good/bad sailor** one not/very liable to seasickness.

saint *n* holy person canonized or famous for extreme virtue. **saintly** *adj.*

sake *n* purpose; benefit; behalf. **for the sake of** for the advantage or purpose of; in order to help, protect, etc.

salad *n* cold meal of vegetables seasoned and served raw. **fruit salad** mixture of raw fruits. **salad dressing** *n* mixture of oil, vinegar, seasoning, herbs, etc., used to flavour salad.

salamander *n* lizard-like creature of the newt family.

salary *n* fixed payment given periodically for non-manual work. **salaried** *adj* earning a salary.

sale *n* **1** exchange of goods for money. **2** fast disposal of unwanted stock at reduced prices or by auction. **saleable** *adj* easy to sell. **salesman** *n, pl* **-men** person employed to sell. **saleswoman** *f n.* **salesmanship** *n* skill in persuading customers to buy.

saline *adj* of or containing salt. **salinity** *n.*

saliva *n* spittle; colourless odourless juice secreted into the mouth, esp. for moistening food. **salivate** *vi* produce saliva, esp. in excess. **salivation** *n.*

sallow *adj* **1** with skin of a pale yellow colour. **2** unhealthy looking.

salmon *n, pl* **salmon** *or* **salmons** large fish, popular as a food, that goes up rivers to spawn. **salmon pink** *n,adj* orange-pink colour of salmon flesh.

salon *n* **1** large elegant reception room. **2** regular gathering of distinguished guests. **3** exhibition of paintings. **4** premises or shop where dressmakers, hairdressers, etc., receive clients.

saloon *n* **1** large public room in a hotel, ship, train, etc. **2** *also* **saloon bar** more comfortably furnished bar room in a public house. **3** car with an enclosed body.

salt *n* **1** white crystalline compound, sodium chloride, used as food seasoning, preservative, etc. **2** any crystalline compound formed from an acid and base. *vt* season or treat with salt. **salt-cellar** *n* small container for holding salt. **saltpetre** *n* nitrogen compound used in explosives, fertilizers, etc.

salute *n* gesture of greeting, recognition, or respect. *vt,vi* make a salute (to).

salvage *n* act of or reward for saving a ship, property, etc., from destruction or waste. *vt* save from loss or destruction.

salvation *n* act of saving from loss, destruction, or sin.

salve *vt* anoint, heal, or soothe. *n* ointment; balm; whatever soothes or heals.

same *adj* **1** identical. **2** indicating no change. *adv* **the same** in an identical manner; with no change. **all the same** even so; in spite of that; nevertheless. ~*pron* that same or identical thing or person.

sample *n* specimen; example; small quantity showing properties of something. *vt* test or try a sample.

sanatorium *n, pl* **sanatoria** (sænə'tɔːriə) *or* **sanatoriums 1** hospital, esp. for convalescent, tubercular, mentally unbalanced, or chronically ill patients. **2** place where sickness is treated in a school, college, etc.

sanctify *vt* make holy or sacred; revere.

sanction *vt* allow; authorize; confirm. *n* **1** penalty or reward intended to enforce a law. **2** confirmation; authorization; permission.

sanctity *n* holiness; sacredness.

sanctuary *n* 1 recognized place or right of refuge. 2 part of a church beyond the altar rails. 3 protected reserve for birds, animals, etc.

sand *n* mass of tiny fragments of crushed rocks covering deserts, seashores, etc. *vt* rub with sandpaper. **sandpaper** *n* heavy paper coated with sand or other abrasive and used for smoothing, polishing, etc. **sandy** *adj* 1 covered in sand. 2 of the colour of sand.

sandal *n* open shoe secured by straps.

sandwich *n* two slices of bread enclosing jam, meat, etc. *vt* squeeze (one thing) between two others.

sane *adj* of sound mind; sensible; rational. **sanely** *adv*. **sanity** *n*.

sang *v pt* of **sing**.

sanitary *adj* concerning or conducive to health, esp. in regard to cleanliness and hygiene. **sanitary towel** *n* absorbent pad for use during menstruation. **sanitation** *n* sanitary methods and equipment, esp. concerning sewage disposal, drainage, clean water, etc.

sank *v pt* of **sink**.

sap *n* vital juice, esp. of plants. *vt* (-pp-) drain the sap or energy from. **sapling** *n* young tree.

sapphire *n* gemstone, usually brilliant blue, akin to the ruby. *adj* brilliant blue.

sarcasm *n* mocking, sneering, or ironic language. **sarcastic** *adj*. **sarcastically** *adv*.

sardine *n* young pilchard often packed tightly with others and tinned in oil.

sari *n* Indian or Pakistani woman's garment, worn over a blouse, consisting of a long bolt of cloth that is wrapped around the waist and over the shoulder.

sash[1] *n* band of material worn around the waist or over the shoulder.

sash[2] *n* sliding frame holding panes of glass in a window.

sat *v pt* and *pp* of **sit**.

Satan *n* the Devil. **satanic** *adj*.

satchel *n* small bag with shoulder straps, esp. for holding school books.

satellite *n* 1 heavenly body or spacecraft revolving round a planet or star. 2 disciple; hanger-on; underling.

satin *n* glossy closely woven silk fabric. *adj* of or like satin.

satire *n* 1 use of irony, ridicule, or sarcasm to mock or denounce. 2 literary work exhibiting this. **satirical** *adj*.

satisfy *vt,vi* fulfil the needs or wishes of. *vt* be sufficient for; give enough to; appease. **satisfaction** *n*. **satisfactory** *adj*.

saturate *vt* imbue or soak completely; cause to be thoroughly absorbed in. **saturation** *n*.

Saturday *n* seventh day of the week.

Saturn *n* outer giant planet lying between Jupiter and Uranus and having a system of rings around its equator.

sauce *n* 1 liquid poured over food to add piquancy or relish. 2 *inf* cheeky impudence. **saucy** *adj* 1 cheeky; impertinent; bold. 2 smart; pert. **saucily** *adv*. **sauciness** *n*.

saucepan *n* long-handled cooking pan.

saucer *n* 1 shallow indented dish placed under a cup. 2 anything of similar shape.

sauna *n also* **sauna bath** 1 steam bath. 2 room used for this.

saunter *vi* wander idly; stroll; amble. *n* gentle stroll; ramble.

sausage *n* short tube, esp. of animal gut, stuffed with minced seasoned meat.

savage *adj* ferocious; violent; uncivilized. *n* 1 primitive person. 2 one with savage characteristics; brute. *vt* attack and wound.

save[1] *vt* rescue or protect from evil, danger, loss, damage, etc. *vt,vi* 1 store up; set aside for future use. 2 be economical or thrifty. **savings** *pl n* sum of money set aside for future use.

save[2] *prep* except; not including.

saviour *n* one who saves another person, etc., from serious trouble; redeemer. **Saviour** *n* Christ.

savoury *adj* not sweet but with a pleasant appetizing taste. *n* savoury course of a meal.

saw[1] *n* tool with a long toothed metal blade used for cutting wood, etc. *vt,vi* use a saw (on). **sawdust** *n* tiny fragments of wood produced by sawing and used in packaging, etc.

saw[2] *v pt* of **see**.

saxophone *n* brass wind instrument with a single reed and about twenty keys. **saxophonist** *n*.

say *vt,vi* (said) **1** state, utter, or speak in words. **2** declare; tell; repeat. **3** assume; take as an example. *n* **1** chance or turn to speak. **2** authority. **saying** *n* maxim; proverb; something commonly said.

scab *n* **1** crust formed over a healing wound. **2** *sl* blackleg.

scaffold *n* **1** temporary raised platform, esp. for supporting workmen. **2** platform on which criminals are executed. **scaffolding** *n* scaffold or system of scaffolds.

scald *vt* **1** burn with hot liquid. **2** clean or cook with boiling water. **3** bring (milk, etc.) almost to boiling point. *n* burn caused by hot liquid.

scale¹ *n* **1** graded table used as a scheme for classification or measurement. **2** series of musical notes ascending at fixed intervals. **3** range; compass; scope. *vt* clamber up; climb. **scale down** make smaller proportionately.

scale² *n* **1** one of the small thin plates protecting fish, reptiles, etc. **2** thin film or layer. *vt,vi* peel off (scales). **scaly** *adj* dry; flaky; hard.

scale³ *n* **1** dish forming one side of a balance. **2** *also* **scales** weighing machine.

scalp *n* skin covering the head. *vt* tear off scalp and hair from.

scalpel *n* small surgical knife.

scampi *pl or s n* large prawns.

scan *v* (-nn-) *vt* **1** scrutinize carefully. **2** glance briefly over. **3** cast a beam over. **4** classify (verse) by metre. *vi* follow metrical pattern. *n* act of scanning.

scandal *n* **1** act or behaviour outraging public opinion. **2** malicious gossip; slander. **scandalize** *vt* shock by scandal. **scandalous** *adj*. **scandalously** *adv*.

scant *adj* scarcely enough; not plentiful. **scanty** *adj* meagre; inadequate.

scapegoat *n* one forced to bear the blame for others' faults.

scar *n* mark left by a wound. *vt* (-rr-) mark with a scar.

scarce *adj* in short supply; rare. **make oneself scarce** *inf* go away. **scarcely** *adv* **1** hardly; barely; only just. **2** not quite. **scarcity** *n*.

scare *vt* startle; frighten away; alarm. *n* sudden or unreasonable panic. **scary** *adj inf* frightening. **scarecrow** *n* device, often resembling a man, to frighten birds away from crops.

scarf *n, pl* **scarves** piece of material worn over the head or around the neck.

scarlet *adj* brilliant red.

scathing *adj* scornful; showing contempt.

scatter *vt* strew; sprinkle; throw loosely about. *vi* disperse; separate. **scatterbrained** *adj* easily distracted; unable to concentrate.

scavenge *vt,vi* search through litter and rubbish and take (anything of value). **scavenger** *n*.

scenario *n* outline of the plot of a film or play.

scene *n* **1** setting for an action, play, film, etc. **2** short division of an act in a play or film. **3** description of an incident. **4** noisy public outburst. **behind the scenes** not for public view or knowledge. **scenery** *n* **1** theatrical backdrops, properties, etc. **2** natural features of landscape. **scenic** *adj* **1** concerning natural scenery. **2** dramatic; theatrical.

scent *n* **1** individual smell, aroma, or fragrance. **2** mixture of fragrant essences; perfume. **3** sense of smell. *vt* **1** perceive odour of. **2** sense; suspect. **3** impart scent to.

sceptic *n* one unwilling to believe and inclined to question or doubt. **sceptical** *adj*. **scepticism** *n*.

sceptre *n* staff carried as a symbol of regal or imperial power.

schedule *n* **1** timetable; order of events. **2** inventory or list. *vt* make a schedule of; plan; arrange. **on schedule** as arranged; on time.

scheme *n* **1** planned systematic arrangement. **2** cunning plot. *vt,vi* plan; contrive; plot.

schizophrenia *n* psychosis marked by delusions and inability to distinguish fantasy from reality and often leading to a double personality. **schizophrenic** *adj,n*.

scholar *n* **1** learned person. **2** student or holder of a scholarship. **scholarly** *adj* studious; learned; intellectually thorough. **scholarship** *n* **1** grant awarded to a promising student. **2** erudition; learning.

school¹ *n* **1** place of education, esp. for children. **2** group of students of a particular branch of learning. **3** followers or imitators of a particular theory, artist, etc. *vt* **1** instruct. **2** control. **scholastic** *adj* of schools, learning, etc.

school² *n* large body of fish, whales, etc.

schooner *n* **1** swift two-masted sailing ship. **2** large beer or sherry glass.

science *n* knowledge or branch of knowledge obtained by experiment, observation, and critical testing. **science fiction** *n* fiction based on imagined sensational changes or developments of environment, space travel, etc. **scientific** *adj* **1** to do with science. **2** systematic, careful, and exact. **scientist** *n.*

scissors *pl n* cutting tool with two pivoted blades.

scoff¹ *vi* mock or jeer; show scorn and derision. *n* expression of contempt.

scoff² *vt sl* eat greedily, ravenously, or quickly. *n sl* food.

scold *vt* find fault with; reprimand.

scone *n* small round plain cake eaten with butter and jam.

scoop *n* **1** small short-handled shovel. **2** journalist's exclusive story. *vt* hollow out or lift as with a scoop.

scooter *n* **1** child's two-wheeled vehicle with handles and a platform, propelled by pushing against the ground with one foot. **2** small low-powered motorcycle.

scope *n* range; extent; field of action.

scorch *vt,vi* **1** burn slightly, so as to discolour but not destroy. **2** dry up with heat; parch.

score *n* **1** tally or record of relative charges, achievements, or points gained. **2** incised line. **3** written musical composition. **4** set of twenty. *vt* **1** gain and record points. **2** furrow or mark with lines. **3** orchestrate. *vi inf* achieve a success. **know the score** know the hard facts. **scoreboard** *n* board on which a score is recorded.

scorn *vt* **1** despise; hold in contempt. **2** refuse contemptuously; disdain to. *n* derision; contempt; mockery. **scornful** *adj.* **scornfully** *adv.*

Scorpio *n* eighth sign of the zodiac, represented by a scorpion.

scorpion *n* member of the spider family with pincers and a joined head and thorax.

scoundrel *n* rascal; villain; rogue.

scour¹ *vt* clean or polish thoroughly by rubbing. *n* act of scouring. **scourer** *n.*

scour² *vt* search thoroughly through.

scout *n* one sent out or ahead to bring back information. *vi* act as scout. **Scout** *also* **Boy Scout** boy belonging to an organization founded to encourage high principles, self-reliance, etc.

scowl *vi* frown angrily or sullenly. *n* bad-tempered sullen frown.

scramble *vi* make one's way fast and awkwardly, esp. as to race others to a goal. *vt* **1** mix or muddle. **2** alter the frequencies of (a radio message, etc.) so as to render it unintelligible. *n* **1** undignified rush. **2** motor-cycle race over rough ground. **scrambled eggs** eggs beaten and cooked.

scrap *n* **1** morsel; fragment. **2** rubbish; left-overs. **3** *inf* fight; quarrel. *vt* (-pp-) discard; throw away. **scrapbook** *n* blank book into which newspaper cuttings, photographs, etc., are pasted. **scrap iron** *n* fragments of metal useful only for remelting.

scrape *vt* smooth or damage by rubbing with a sharp edge. **scrape through** succeed by a narrow margin. **scrape up** *or* **together** gather with difficulty, diligence, or thrift. ~*n* **1** scratch. **2** *inf* awkward predicament.

scratch *vt,vi* **1** mark or cut with something sharp or be susceptible to such marking. **2** rub the nails over (the skin) to relieve itching. *vt* cancel; erase. *n* mark or sound made by scratching. **from scratch** from the very beginning. **up to scratch** *inf* acceptable; up to standard. **scratchy** *adj* **1** marked with scratches. **2** ragged; irregular. **3** irritable.

scrawl *vt,vi* scribble; write fast and unintelligibly. *n* illegible writing.

scream *vt,vi* shriek or cry out in a high loud voice. *n* **1** piercing cry. **2** *inf* hilarious joke. **screamingly** *adv* hilariously.

screech *vi* cry out in a harsh shrill voice. *n* sound made by screeching.

screen *n* movable board or partition acting as a room divider, surface to project films, protection from heat or observation, etc. *vt* **1** hide or shelter. **2** display on a cinema or television screen. **3** subject to tests to

determine weakness, disease, qualities, etc.
screenplay *n* script for a film.

screw *n* spiral grooved metal shaft used as a fastening device. **have a screw loose** be mentally deficient. **put the screws on** extort by blackmail. ~*vt* fasten; tighten; compress with a screw. *vt,vi tab* have sexual intercourse (with). **screw up 1** tighten firmly with a screw. **2** twist; distort; crumple. **3** summon up. **screwdriver** *n* tool with metal wedge-shaped blade, which slots into the groove on the head of a screw to turn it. **screwy** *adj sl* crazy.

scribble *vt,vi* write carelessly, fast, or meaninglessly. *n* careless or meaningless writing. **scribbler** *n.*

script *n* **1** text of a film, play, speech, etc. **2** handwriting or print resembling it. **scriptwriter** *n* one who writes scripts, dialogues, television series, etc.

scripture *n* the Bible. **scriptural** *adj.*

scroll *n* **1** roll of parchment or paper. **2** ornamental design resembling a scroll.

scrounge *vt,vi inf* cadge; sponge; wheedle or scrape together. **scrounger** *n.*

scrub[1] *vt,vi* (-bb-) clean by rubbing hard with a brush and water. *n* act of scrubbing.

scrub[2] *n* landscape of low stunted trees, bushes, and shrubs.

scruffy *adj* untidy; unkempt; messy. **scruffily** *adv.* **scruffiness** *n.*

scruple *n* moral doubt or hesitation. *vi* hesitate because of scruple.

scrupulous *adj* conscientious; attentive to details. **scrupulously** *adv.*

scrutinize *vt* examine closely, critically, or in great detail. **scrutiny** *n.*

scuffle *n.* close confused struggle or fight. *vi* fight in a disorderly manner.

scullery *n* small room for rough kitchen work, dish washing, etc.

sculpture *n* **1** art of making figures, statues, etc., by carving or moulding. **2** work or works made in this way. **sculpt** *vt,vi* make a sculpture (of). **sculptor** *n.*

scum *n* **1** foam on the surface of a liquid. **2** worthless or disgusting residue.

scurf *n* crust of small flakes of dead skin, esp. on the scalp; dandruff.

scythe *n* implement with a large curved blade for cutting grass. *vt* cut with a scythe.

sea *n* **1** continuous expanse of salt water that covers most of the earth's surface. **2** large body of salt water partially bounded by land. **3** large lake. **4** condition, turbulence, waves, etc., of an ocean or sea. **5** something suggestive of the sea in being vast or overwhelming. **at sea 1** on the ocean. **2** confused. **go to sea 1** become a sailor. **2** start an ocean voyage. **put to sea** leave port.

sea anemone *n* common marine animal whose arrangement of tentacles resembles a flower.

seacoast strip of land bordering on an ocean or sea.

seafront *n* area of a seaside resort directly facing the sea and having a promenade, hotels, etc.

seagull *n* gull frequenting the sea or coast.

seahorse *n* **1** marine fish that swims in an upright position and has a head shaped like that of a horse. **2** walrus.

sea-kale vegetable having broad green leaves.

seal[1] *n* **1** impression on wax or metal serving as an authorization, guarantee, etc. **2** anything used to close tightly to prevent leaking or opening. *vt* mark, attest, or close firmly with a seal. **set the seal on** formally conclude.

seal[2] *n* carnivorous marine mammal with flippers, a short tail, and a long body covered in dense fur. **sealskin** *n* close short furry hide of the seal, sometimes used for clothing.

sea-level *n* level of the sea midway between high and low tide.

sea-lion *n* large seal having visible external ears.

seam *n* join formed by sewing together or attaching two pieces of material. **seamy** *adj* squalid.

seaman *n, pl* -men sailor, esp. below the rank of officer. **seamanship** *n* skill or techniques of ship management, operation, and navigation.

seaplane *n* aeroplane equipped to land on or take off from the water.

search *vt,vi* examine, probe, or investigate closely hoping to find something. *n* investigation; exploration; enquiry. **search me!** *sl* I have no idea! **searchlight** *n* lamp emitting a strong beam of artificial light used to scan an area, the sky, etc.

seashore *n* seacoast.

seasick *adj* nauseated by the movement of a vessel at sea. **seasickness** *n*.

seaside *n* seacoast. *adj* relating to or located at the seacoast.

season *n* **1** one of the four climatic divisions of the year. **2** appropriate time; short spell. **in season 1** (of game, fish, foxes, etc.) allowed to be legally hunted or caught. **2** ripe; ready for use. ~*vt* **1** flavour with salt, pepper, etc. **2** accustom; mature. **seasonable** *adj* appropriate to the moment or occasion; timely. **seasonal** *adj* occurring at or changing with the season. **seasoned** *adj* **1** experienced. **2** flavoured; tempered. **seasoning** *n* **1** food flavouring, such as salt, pepper, or herbs. **2** processing of timber. **season ticket** *n* ticket valid for repeated use over a set period.

seat *n* **1** chair or part of a chair; place to sit. **2** position in Parliament, a council, etc., to which one is elected or appointed. **3** basis; central location or site. **4** manner of sitting (on a horse, etc.). **5** buttocks; bottom. *vt* place on a seat; accommodate in a chair or chairs. **seat-belt** *n* safety belt.

seaweed *n* plant or alga growing in the ocean.

seaworthy *adj* (of a vessel) fit for sailing. **seaworthiness** *n*.

secluded *adj* hidden or shut off from observation or company. **seclusion** *n* privacy; solitude.

second[1] *adj* **1** coming between the first and the third. **2** another; additional; extra. **3** alternate; alternative. *adv* in second place. *n* person or thing in second place. *vt* support (another's proposal or nomination). **secondly** *adv*. **second best** *adj* inferior to the best. **second-class** *adj* of second or inferior class, quality, etc. **second-hand** *adj* not new; having belonged to another. **second nature** *n* habit or tendency that has become automatic or instinctive. **second-rate** *adj* of inferior quality or value; shoddy.

second[2] *n* **1** period of time equal to one sixtieth of a minute. **2** moment; instant. **3** unit by which time is measured.

secondary *adj* subordinate; of less importance; coming second. **secondary school** *n* school teaching children over the age of eleven.

secret *adj* concealed; hidden; private; not made known. *n* whatever is made or kept secret. **secrecy** *n*. **secretly** *adv*. **secret agent** *n* spy.

secretary *n* **1** one employed to help with correspondence, keep records, etc. **2** principal assistant to a minister, ambassador, etc. **secretarial** *adj*.

secrete *vt* (of a gland, cell, etc.) produce and release (substances such as saliva, etc.). **secretion** *n*.

secretive *adj* reticent; given to undue secrecy; uncommunicative.

sect *n* group of people following a particular leader or holding specific views. **sectarian** *n,adj*.

section *n* division or portion; part. *vt* cut or separate into parts.

sector *n* **1** part of a circle bounded by two radii and an arc. **2** area; part; scope of activity.

secular *adj* temporal; lay; not spiritual or monastic. *n* priest bound by no monastic rule.

secure *adj* **1** safe; free from danger. **2** reliable; certain. **3** not movable. *vt* **1** make safe, certain, or sure. **2** obtain. **securely** *adv*. **security** *n* **1** safety; freedom from anxiety, danger, or want. **2** pledge, document, or certificate of ownership; bond or share. **3** precautions against espionage, theft, etc.

sedate *adj* **1** calm; placid; tranquil. **2** staid; dignified. **sedately** *adv*. **sedateness** *n*. **sedation** *n* act of calming or state of calmness induced by sedatives. **sedative** *adj* calming; soporific. *n* sedative drug.

sediment *n* dregs or residue at the bottom of a liquid. **sedimentary** *adj*.

seduce *vt* **1** entice, lure, or tempt, esp. into evil. **2** persuade to have sexual intercourse. **seducer** *n*. **seduction** *n*. **seductive** *adj*.

see[1] *v* (saw; seen) *vi* **1** have the power of sight. **2** find out; investigate. **3** attend (to). *vt* **1** look at; perceive; be aware of; observe. **2** experience. **3** visit. **4** realize; consider. **5** discover. **6** consult. **7** make sure; check; take care. *vt,vi* understand; comprehend. **see through** 1 fail to be deceived by. 2 finish; remain with until completion.

see[2] *n* office or diocese of a bishop.

seed *n* 1 tiny cell containing an embryonic plant. 2 germ; first principle. *vt* 1 sow. 2 remove the seed from. **run to seed** deteriorate; decay. **seedling** *n* young plant grown from seed.

seedy *adj* shabby.

seek *vt,vi* (sought) look for; try to find; search (for).

seem *vi* appear to be; give the impression of being. **seeming** *adj* apparent. **seemingly** *adv.* **seemly** *adj* appropriate; decent.

seep *vi* ooze; percolate; leak through. **seepage** *n.*

seesaw *n* plank so balanced that children seated on either end can ride up or down alternately. *vi* move or vacillate like a seesaw.

seethe *vi* surge or be agitated (with extreme fury, excitement, etc.).

segment *n* 1 part of a circle bounded by a chord and arc. 2 section; portion. *vt,vi* divide into segments. **segmentary** *adj.* **segmentation** *n.*

segregate *vt* separate from others; isolate; group apart, esp. racially. **segregation** *n.*

seize *vt* take possession of, esp. suddenly or by force. **seize up** become jammed or stuck. **seizure** *n* 1 act of seizing. 2 sudden attack of illness; fit.

seldom *adv* rarely; only occasionally.

select *vt* choose; pick out for preference. *adj* choice; exclusive. **selection** *n* 1 act or result of choice; discrimination. 2 item or items selected. 3 scope or range of selected items. **selective** *adj* 1 able to select or discriminate. 2 tending to select very carefully. **selectively** *adv.*

self *n, pl* **selves** 1 person or thing regarded as individual. 2 personality or ego.

self-assured *adj* confident; not shy. **self-assurance** *n.*

self-aware *adj* able to view oneself objectively. **self-awareness** *n.*

self-centred *adj* preoccupied with oneself; selfish. **self-centredness** *n.*

self-confident *adj* having confidence in oneself. **self-confidence** *n.*

self-conscious *adj* shy; embarrassed. **self-consciously** *adv.* **self-consciousness** *n.*

self-contained *adj* 1 reserved; absorbed in oneself. 2 (of accommodation) complete; not approached through another's property.

self-defence *n* protection of oneself or one's rights, property, etc.

self-discipline *n* control of one's own behaviour, emotions, etc. **self-disciplined** *adj.*

self-employed *adj* working for oneself; freelance.

self-expression *n* voicing or demonstrating one's own personality or beliefs.

self-interest *n* desire for benefit or advantage to oneself.

selfish *adj* motivated by self-interest; showing little regard for others. **selfishly** *adv.* **selfishness** *n.*

self-pity *n* pity for oneself; feeling of being sorry for oneself. **self-pitying** *adj.*

self-portrait *n* picture painted by an artist of himself.

self-respect *n* pride; dignity; integrity.

self-righteous *adj* excessively confident in one's own merits, judgment, etc.; hypocritical. **self-righteously** *adv.* **self-righteousness** *n.*

self-sacrifice *n* subordination of one's own desires or rights to another's.

selfsame *adj* (the) very same; exactly the same.

self-satisfied *adj* smug; conceited.

self-service *adj* (of a restaurant, shop, etc.) where the customer serves himself.

self-sufficient *adj* 1 needing nothing from outside oneself. 2 economically independent. **self-sufficiency** *n.*

self-will *n* obstinacy. **self-willed** *adj.*

sell *vt* (sold) 1 exchange for money. 2 betray for an ignoble motive. 3 extol; praise the virtues of. **sell off** sell cheaply to clear stock. **sell out** 1 sell whole stock in trade. 2 betray for profit. **sell up** 1 sell a debtor's goods in settlement. 2 sell a business.

Sellotape *n Tdmk* transparent adhesive cellulose tape. *vt* attach, stick down, etc., with adhesive tape.

selves *n pl* of **self.**

semaphore *n* means of signalling by flags. *vt,vi* signal using flags.

semen *n* fluid and cells produced by the male reproductive organs.

semibreve *n* musical note equal to two minims or four crotchets.

semicircle *n* half a circle. **semicircular** *adj.*

semicolon *n* punctuation mark (;) showing a sentence division that is stronger than a comma but less marked than a colon.

semiconductor *n* substance whose electrical conductivity increases with added impurities, used in transistors and other electronic components.

semidetached *adj* (of a house) joined to another on one side.

semifinal *n* last round of a tournament before the final. **semifinalist** *n.*

seminar *n* class of advanced students working on a specific subject.

semiprecious *adj* (of stones) valuable, but not rare or valuable enough to be classed as precious.

semiquaver *n* musical note half the length of a quaver.

semitone *n* musical interval between a note and its sharp or flat.

semolina *n* particles of fine hard wheat used for making milk puddings, pasta, etc.

senate *n* *also* **Senate 1** legislative or governing body of ancient Rome, modern British universities, etc. **2** upper house of government of the US, Australia, Canada, etc. **senator** *n.*

send *vt* (sent) **1** cause (mail, goods, a message, etc.) to be transmitted or taken. **2** direct; convey. **3** drive or force into a particular condition or state. **send for** ask to come; demand the services of.

senile *adj* weak or deteriorating through old age. **senility** *n.*

senior *adj* older, higher, or more experienced or advanced. *n* one who is senior. **seniority** *n.*

sensation *n* **1** feeling; perception through the senses. **2** public or melodramatic excitement. **sensational** *adj* exciting; thrilling; startling. **sensationally** *adv.*

sense *n* **1** faculty of sight, hearing, smell, touch, or taste. **2** sensation; feeling. **3** awareness; perception. **4** intelligence; common sense. **5** meaning or definition, esp. of a word or phrase. **make sense** be logical, reasonable, or coherent. ~*vt* **1** feel; be aware of. **2** comprehend, esp. intuitively.

senseless *adj* **1** meaningless; motiveless; foolish. **2** unconscious.

sensible *adj* **1** wise; reasonable; practical. **2** aware. **3** appreciable by the senses. **sensibly** *adv.* **sensibility** *n* delicacy or capacity of emotional, mental, or moral responses.

sensitive *adj* **1** easily affected by another's emotions, actions, plight, etc. **2** easily irritated by certain stimuli. **sensitively** *adv.* **sensitivity** *or* **sensitiveness** *n.*

sensual *adj* **1** relating to the senses. **2** seeking pleasure or gratification of the senses. **3** voluptuous; licentious. **sensuality** *n.* **sensually** *adv.*

sensuous *adj* relating or pleasing to the senses. **sensuously** *adv.* **sensuousness** *n.*

sent *v pt* and *pp* of **send.**

sentence *n* **1** number of words forming a grammatical unit, usually containing a subject, predicate, and finite verb. **2** punishment allotted to an offender in court. *vt* pronounce judgment on (a person) in a court of law.

sentiment *n* thought or opinion at least partly dictated by emotion. **sentimental** *adj* **1** over-emotional; mawkish. **2** having romantic or tender feelings. **sentimentality** *n.*

sentry *n* soldier, etc., posted to stand guard.

separate *v* ('sepəreit) *vt* set or keep apart; divide. *vi* go, move, or live apart. *adj* ('seprit) distinct; divided; individual. **separable** *adj.* **separately** *adv.* **separation** *n.*

September *n* ninth month of the year.

septic *adj* putrefying because of the presence of bacteria.

sequel *n* result; consequence; whatever succeeds, follows, or happens next.

sequence *n* **1** order of succession; series. **2** scene from a film. **sequential** *adj.* **sequentially** *adv.*

sequin *n* tiny sparkling piece of foil used to decorate clothing.

serenade *n* piece of music traditionally played at night by a lover under his lady's window. *vt* entertain with a serenade.

serene *adj* tranquil; calm; placid. **serenely** *adv*. **serenity** *n*.

serf *n* medieval farm labourer or peasant bound to the land. **serfdom** *n*.

sergeant *n* 1 noncommissioned officer ranking above a corporal. 2 police officer ranking between constable and inspector. **sergeant-major** *n* highest grade of noncommissioned officer.

serial *adj* forming a series; in instalments. *n* story told in instalments. **serialize** *vt* divide (a story, film, etc.) into instalments or episodes.

series *n*, *pl* **series** sequence; succession of things, episodes, etc., with similar characters, subjects, or purposes.

serious *adj* solemn; grave; earnest; not comic or frivolous. **seriously** *adv*. **seriousness** *n*.

sermon *n* speech, esp. one delivered from a pulpit, with a strong scriptural or moral lesson.

serpent *n* snake. **serpentine** *adj* 1 relating to serpents. 2 twisting; convoluted.

servant *n* person employed to serve another.

serve *vt,vi* 1 work for; wait upon. 2 be of use to; help. 3 act or offer as a host. 4 deliver (the ball) in certain games. 5 spend (a specified period of time, enlistment, etc.). *vt* 1 obey or honour. 2 deliver (a summons, etc.) to. **serve someone right** be an appropriate punishment. ~*n* act or turn of delivering the ball in certain games.

service *n* 1 work, position, or duty of a servant. 2 religious rite or ceremony. 3 supply, maintenance, or repair. 4 set of dishes, etc. 5 act of serving or turn to serve the ball in tennis, etc. 6 supply or system of a public utility. 7 branch of government or public employment. 8 help; assistance. **(the) services** *pl n* Army, Navy, and Air Force. ~*vt* do maintenance work on. **serviceable** *adj* useful; durable but not decorative. **service station** *n* roadside garage providing petrol and repair services.

serviette *n* table napkin.

servile *adj* 1 of servants or slaves. 2 menial; cringing. **servility** *n*.

session *n* period during which a court, Parliament, etc., sits, universities function, or meetings or interviews take place.

set *v* (-tt-; set) *vt* 1 place; position; put. 2 cause or prompt. 3 fix; regulate; mend. 4 make firm or hard. 5 put (hair) in rollers, etc., to produce waves or curls. 6 bring into contact with fire; ignite; light. 7 establish as a standard, record, etc. 8 require the completion of (an examination, task, etc.). *vi* 1 become firm or hard; solidify. 2 (of the sun) fall below the horizon. 3 (of bones, etc.) mend. **set about** begin to deal with. **set in** become established. **set off** *or* **out** begin a journey; leave. **set up** start (a business, scheme, etc.); establish; found. ~*adj* 1 fixed; settled; determined; not alterable. 2 ready; prepared. *n* 1 group of people; class. 2 number of things that match or are designed to be used together. 3 scenery used for a play. 4 studio or area used when making a film, TV broadcast, etc. **setback** *n* relapse; check; halt. **setting** *n* frame, background, scenery, environment, etc., in which anything is set.

settee *n* long upholstered seat with a back and arms; couch; sofa.

settle *vt* 1 place at rest or in comfort, peace, order, etc. 2 decide finally. 3 give money to; resolve (debts). *vi* 1 subside; come to rest; sink. 2 take up residence. 3 reach a decision. **settle down** take up a settled normal established way of life. **settle for** agree to accept. **settle in** adapt to a new environment, circumstances, etc. **settle up** balance accounts; pay. **settlement** *n* 1 act or state of settling, paying, etc. 2 group of social workers in an underprivileged community. 3 newly established colony. 4 sinking or subsidence.

seven *n* 1 number equal to one plus six. 2 group of seven persons, things, etc. 3 *also* **seven o'clock** seven hours after noon or midnight. *adj* amounting to seven. **seventh** *adj* coming between sixth and eighth in sequence. *n* 1 seventh person, object, etc. 2 one of seven equal parts; one divided by seven.

seventeen *n* 1 number that is seven more than ten. 2 seventeen things or people. *adj* amounting to seventeen. **seventeenth** *adj,adv,n*.

seventy *n* 1 number equal to seven times ten. 2 seventy things or people. *adj* amounting to seventy. **seventieth** *adj,adv,n*.

sever *vt,vi* separate; cut; end. **severance** *n.*

several *adj* **1** more than one; a few. **2** separate; distinct; various.

severe *adj* **1** harsh; strict; violent. **2** grave; serious. **3** unadorned; plain; austere. **severely** *adv.* **severity** *n.*

sew *vt,vi* (sewed; sewn *or* sewed) work on, fasten, join, embroider, etc., with a needle and thread; stitch.

sewage *n* used water supply containing domestic refuse and waste matter. **sewer** *n* underground pipe or drain for carrying sewage. **sewerage** *n* provision or system of sewers.

sex *n* **1** characteristics distinguishing male from female. **2** males or females. **3** sexual desires, instincts, or intercourse.

sextet *n* **1** group of or work composed for six musicians. **2** group of six.

sexual *adj* relating to sex or sex organs. **sexuality** *n* awareness of one's own sexual characteristics.

sexy *adj* sexually attractive or stimulating. **sexily** *adv.* **sexiness** *n.*

shabby *adj* **1** worn; dilapidated; ragged. **2** despicable; dishonourable. **shabbily** *adv.* **shabbiness** *n.*

shack *n* rough hut.

shade *n* **1** comparative darkness caused by shelter from light or sun. **2** screen against light. **3** gradation of colour. **4** small amount; tiny degree. *vt* shield from light; darken. **shady** *adj* **1** out of bright sunlight. **2** *inf* dishonest; of dubious reputation.

shadow *n* **1** dark outline of an object placed in front of light or sun. **2** mere insubstantial copy. **3** constant companion. *vt* **1** shade from light. **2** follow closely and secretly. **shadowy** *adj.* **shadow cabinet** *n* group of leading Opposition politicians determining policy should their party return to power.

shaft *n* **1** long straight narrow rod, handle, beam of light, column, etc. **2** vertical passage into a mine.

shaggy *adj* unkempt; tangled. **shaggily** *adv.*

shake *v* (shook; shaken) *vt* agitate; move with small fast gestures. *vi* tremble; be agitated. **shake off** get rid of. **shaky** *adj* unreliable; precarious; wobbling.

shall *v aux* used to express future probability or intention.

shallot *n* small onion similar to but milder than garlic.

shallow *adj* **1** not deep. **2** not profound; superficial. **shallowness** *n.*

shame *n* **1** feeling of humiliation caused by guilt, failure, disgrace, etc. **2** sense of modesty, pride, or dignity. **3** disappointing or unlucky event. *vt* bring shame upon. **put to shame** cause to feel inferior. **shameful** *adj.* **shamefully** *adv.* **shamefaced** *adj* embarrassed; humiliated; ashamed.

shampoo *n* preparation for washing hair, carpets, upholstery, etc. *vt* rub clean with shampoo.

shamrock *n* type of small three-leaved plant, used as the Irish emblem.

shandy *n* drink made by mixing beer with lemonade or ginger beer.

shanty[1] small roughly built cabin or shack.

shanty[2] *n* rousing sailors' song.

shape *n* **1** external appearance of an object or figure; outline; form. **2** condition; situation; state. **take shape** begin to develop or take on a definite form. ~*vt* **1** make a particular shape of. **2** develop; fit. **shapeless** *adj* not having the proper or appropriate shape. **shapely** *adj* well shaped.

share *n* **1** part; portion or division given to or contributed by an individual. **2** fixed equal part of a company's capital. *vt* divide into shares. **share out** distribute; allot. **shareholder** *n* one holding a share, esp. in a company.

shark *n* large long-bodied voracious and often dangerous marine fish.

sharp *adj* **1** having a fine edge or point; cutting; piercing. **2** acid; shrill; painful; intense. **3** clear-cut. **4** quick; lively. **5** artful; dishonest. **6** (in music) above true pitch; a semitone higher than the note. *adv* **1** punctually. **2** too high in pitch. **look sharp** hurry. **sharp-sighted** *adj* **1** having excellent eyesight. **2** shrewd; sharp-witted. **sharpen** *vt,vi* become or make sharp.

shatter *vt,vi* **1** smash or break into fragments. **2** wreck; exhaust; destroy.

shave *vt,vi* scrape off a superficial layer, esp. of facial hair. *n* act of shaving. **close shave** narrow escape; near miss.

shawl *n* folded square of material worn loosely around the shoulders or wrapped around a baby.

she *pron* female person; the 3rd person singular as the subject.

sheaf *n, pl* **sheaves 1** large bundle of cereal crops tied together after reaping. **2** bundle of papers.

shear *vt* (sheared; shorn *or* sheared) clip or cut off hair or wool, esp. from sheep. **shears** *pl n* cutting implement resembling large scissors.

sheath *n* tightly fitting case or covering for a blade, insects' wings, etc. **sheathe** *vt* enclose in a sheath.

shed[1] *vt* (-dd-; shed) cast off; let fall; pour out. **shed light on** reveal; illuminate.

shed[2] *n* small simple building; hut.

sheen *n* glow; radiance; lustre.

sheep *n, pl* **sheep** wild or domesticated ruminant mammal reared for meat and wool. **black sheep** rogue. **sheepish** *adj* embarrassed through being wrong, etc. **sheepishly** *adv.* **sheepdog** *n* dog trained to herd sheep. **sheepskin** *n* skin of a sheep used for rugs, coats, etc.

sheer[1] *adj* **1** perpendicular; very steep. **2** unqualified; complete; utter. *adv* **1** vertically. **2** outright.

sheer[2] *vi* swerve; deviate. **sheer off 1** move away. **2** snap off with a clean break.

sheet[1] **1** large thin rectangle of cotton, linen, nylon, etc., for a bed. **2** thin rectangular piece of paper, metal, etc.

sheet[2] *n* rope attached to a sail of a boat.

sheikh *n* head of an Arab family or tribe. **sheikhdom** *n* area ruled by a sheikh.

shelf *n, pl* **shelves** horizontal board set into a wall, bookcase, cupboard, etc. **on the shelf** (usually of a woman) not married and unlikely to be so.

shell *n* **1** hard outer case enclosing an egg, nut, shellfish, tortoise, etc. **2** framework; outline. **3** explosive device fired from heavy guns. *vt* **1** remove shell from. **2** bombard. **shell out** *inf* pay. **shellfish** *n* aquatic mollusc or crustacean with a shell.

shelter *n* place or thing providing safety from weather, attack, danger, etc. *vt* shield; protect. *vi* take cover.

shelve *vt* **1** provide with or put on a shelf. **2** postpone indefinitely.

shepherd *n* one who guards and herds sheep. *vt* guide and herd like a shepherd. **shepherdess** *ʃ n.*

sherbet *n* fizzy drink or powder for making it.

sheriff *n* chief Crown officer of a county, responsible for keeping the peace, administering courts, etc.

sherry *n* fortified wine, esp. from Spain.

shield *n* **1** broad piece of armour carried to protect the body. **2** anything serving as shelter, protection, or defence. *vt* protect; screen.

shift *vt,vi* move; change position (of). *vi* manage; make do. *n* **1** movement; change of position. **2** period of work on a rota or relay system. **3** undergarment.

shilling *n* former British coin or unit of currency worth five new pence.

shimmer *vi* glisten; gleam with faint diffuse light. *n* faint light.

shin *n* **1** front of the human leg below the knee. **2** beef from the lower part of the leg. *vi* climb up (a tree, rope, etc.) quickly, using only the arms and legs.

shine *vi* (shone) **1** give off or reflect light; beam; glow. **2** excel; be conspicuous or animated. *vt* (shined) polish (shoes, etc.). *n* sheen; lustre. **shiny** *adj.*

ship *n* large floating sea-going vessel. *vt* (-pp-) carry or send by ship. **shipment** *n* **1** cargo; goods shipped together. **2** shipping goods. **shipping** *n* **1** business of transporting goods by sea. **2** number of ships, esp. of a country or port. **shipshape** *adj* well-ordered; clean; neat. **shipwreck** *n* destruction or loss of a ship at sea. *vt,vi* cause or suffer shipwreck; ruin. **shipyard** *n* dock or yard where ships are built and repaired.

shirk *vt,vi* evade (duties or obligations). **shirker** *n.*

shirt *n* loose garment covering the top half of the body, esp. with sleeves, collar, and cuffs. **shirty** *adj sl* bad-tempered; irritable.

shiver *vi* tremble or quiver with cold, excitement, or fear. *n* tremble; shivering motion.

shock[1] *n* **1** alarming startling experience. **2** violent collision or impact. **3** bodily condition of near or complete collapse because of rapid falling of blood pressure. **4** *also* **electric shock** condition resulting from bodily contact with a strong electric current. *vt* shake or alarm by violent impact, frightening experience, improper outrageous behaviour, etc. **shock absorber** *n* device for diminishing vibration in vehicles.

shock[2] *n* thick shaggy mass, esp. of hair.

shoddy *adj* of inferior quality; cheap and nasty. *n* cloth made from scraps of other materials. **shoddily** *adv.* **shoddiness** *n.*

shoe *n* 1 outer covering for the foot. 2 anything resembling a shoe. *vt* (shod) provide shoes for.

shone *v pt* and *pp* of **shine**.

shook *v pt* and *pp* of **shake**.

shoot *v* (shot) *vt,vi* 1 fire (a gun). 2 propel (a bullet, arrow, etc.). 3 send out suddenly; project. 4 sprout; put out buds. 5 photograph or film. *vt* injure or kill with a gun. *vi* hunt game for sport with a gun. *n* 1 young branch or sprout. 2 hunting or shooting party. 3 inclined plank or trough down which water, rubbish, coal, etc., may be thrown; chute. **good/bad shot** good/bad marksman.

shop *n* 1 place where goods are sold. 2 place where industrial work is carried out. **on the shop floor** amongst the workers in a factory, workshop. etc. **talk shop** discuss one's own occupation or job. ~*vi* (-pp-) visit shops to buy goods. **shop around** compare values at different shops. **shopkeeper** *n* owner or manager of a shop. **shoplifter** *n* one who steals goods from a shop. **shoplifting** *n.* **shop steward** *n* trade union's elected departmental delegate.

shore[1] *n* land bordering a river, lake, or sea.

shore[2] *vt* support or prop up (a building, ship, etc.). *n* prop.

shorn *v pp* of **shear**.

short *adj* 1 of relatively little length; not long or tall. 2 lasting for a little while; brief. 3 brusque; abrupt; curt. 4 not plentiful; sparse; inadequate; insufficient. 5 abbreviated; cut. *adv* abruptly. *n* **in short** as a summary; briefly. **shorts** *pl n* short trousers, worn esp. when participating in certain sports. **shortness** *n.* **shortage** *n* lack; deficiency. **shortbread** *n* crisp biscuit made from butter, flour, and sugar. **shortcoming** *n* failure; deficiency. **shorten** *vt,vi* decrease;

reduce. **shorthand** *n* system of symbols used for writing at speed. **shorthanded** *adj* short of staff; undermanned. **shortlived** *adj* transitory; brief. **shortly** *adv* 1 soon; in a short time. 2 briefly; abruptly. **shortsighted** *adj* 1 unable to see clearly at a distance. 2 without imagination or foresight. **short-sightedly** *adv.* **short-sightedness** *n.* **short-tempered** *adj* liable to lose one's temper easily; irritable. **short-term** *n* immediate future.

shot *n* 1 act of shooting or the missile shot. 2 photograph. 3 attempt; try. 4 hypodermic injection. **be/get shot of** be/get rid of. **like a shot** with great speed. **shot in the arm** encouragement. **shot in the dark** mere guess. ~*adj* of changing colour. *v pt* and *pp* of **shoot**. **shotgun** *n* smooth bore gun firing small shot.

should *v aux* 1 used to express obligation, duty, or likelihood. 2 used to form the conditional tense. 3 used in indirect speech.

shoulder *n* 1 part of the body where the arm is attached. 2 corresponding part in animals and birds. 3 prominent part of a hillside, bottle, vase, etc. 4 roadside verge. **give the cold shoulder to** snub. **rub shoulders with** mix with; get to know. ~*vt* 1 push, lift, or jostle with the shoulder. 2 accept (responsibility). **shoulder-blade** *n* broad flat bone of the upper back.

shout *n* loud cry or call. *vt,vi* utter (with) a shout.

shove *vt,vi* push; thrust; jostle. *n* hard push. **shove off** 1 push a boat away from the shore. 2 *sl* leave.

shovel *n* broad often short-handled spade for lifting coal, earth, etc. *vt* (-ll-) move with or as if with a shovel.

show *v* (showed; shown) *vt* 1 display; allow to be seen. 2 conduct; guide. 3 reveal; indicate. 4 demonstrate; instruct. 5 prove; give evidence of. *vi* 1 be able to be seen; be revealed or displayed. 2 be evident; prove. **show off** behave in a pretentious way. ~*n* 1 exhibition or display. 2 entertainment with dancers, singers, etc. **show business** *n* profession of theatrical entertainers, variety artists, etc. **showcase** *n* glass-fronted display cabinet. **showdown** *n* open conflict or challenge. **show-jumping** *n* horse-jumping displayed in competition.

showmanship *n* skill in displaying goods, theatrical productions, etc., to the best advantage. **showroom** *n* room in which goods may be viewed.

shower *n* **1** short fall of rain, bullets, blows, etc. **2** large supply; abundant flow. **3** bathroom fitting from which water is sprayed from above. *vt* fall or pour out, as in a shower. **showery** *adj.* **showerproof** *adj* impervious to showers.

shrank *v pt* of **shrink**.

shred *n* strip; fragment. *vt* (-dd-; shredded *or* shred) cut or tear into shreds.

shrew *n* **1** small mammal resembling a mouse and also having an elongated snout. **2** bad-tempered woman.

shrewd *adj* **1** discerning; astute; wise. **2** cunning; sly. **shrewdly** *adv.* **shrewdness** *n.*

shriek *n* high piercing cry or scream. *vt,vi* utter (with a shriek).

shrill *adj* high-pitched, piercing, and insistent. *vt,vi* utter in a shrill manner. **shrillness** *n.* **shrilly** *adv.*

shrimp *n* **1** tiny edible crustacean smaller than and similar to a prawn. **2** *inf* small person.

shrine *n* **1** place hallowed by associations with a saint. **2** casket containing holy relics.

shrink *vi* (shrank; shrunk *or* shrunken) become smaller; contract, esp. when wet. **shrink (back) from** recoil or flinch from; shun.

shrivel *vi* (-ll-) *also* **shrivel up** become shrunken, withered, and wrinkled.

shroud *n* **1** sheet wrapped around a dead body. **2** anything that veils or wraps round. **3** set of ropes forming part of a ship's rigging. *vt* cloak or cover (in secrecy, antiquity, etc.).

Shrove Tuesday *n* day of confession and subsequent merrymaking before Lent.

shrub *n* low bush with no central trunk. **shrubbery** *n* area or group of shrubs.

shrug *vt,vi* (-gg-) raise the shoulders to express indifference, doubt, or dislike. *n* act of shrugging. **shrug off** shake off with indifference.

shrunk *v a pp* of **shrink**.

shrunken *v a pp* of **shrink**.

shudder *vi* shiver, esp. with horror, fear, etc. *vi* **1** tremble as with horror. **2** vibrate.

shuffle *vt,vi* **1** move slowly without lifting the feet from the ground. **2** mix randomly, esp. playing cards. *n* act of shuffling.

shun *vt* (-nn-) avoid; stay away from.

shunt *vt,vi* **1** divert (a train) to another track. **2** bypass; sidetrack. *vi inf* move; go away. *n* **1** act of shunting. **2** electrical conductor diverting current.

shut *v* (-tt-; shut) *vt* **1** move (a door, the eyes, mouth, etc.) so as to be no longer open; close. **2** fasten; secure; lock or bolt. **3** cease to operate, trade, etc. *vi* become closed. **shut up 1** become silent. **2** lock up or in. **shutter** *n* **1** wooden or metal window covering. **2** device controlling light admitted to a camera lens.

shuttlecock *n* small piece of cork, plastic, etc., stuck with feathers and struck by a racket in badminton, etc.

shy *adj* bashful; timid; lacking self-confidence. *vi* move (away from); recoil (from). **shyly** *adv.* **shyness** *n.*

sick *adj* **1** unwell; ill. **2** inclined to vomit. **3** gruesome; macabre. **sick of** tired of; bored with. **sicken** *vi,vt* become or make sick, weary, or disgusted. **sickening** *adj* nauseating; annoying. **sickly** *adj* **1** prone to ill-health; feeble. **2** so sweet as to be nauseating. **sickness** *n* **1** illness; disease. **2** vomiting; nausea.

side *n* **1** one of the surfaces of an object. **2** that part of something other than the top and bottom or back and front. **3** surface of a piece of paper, cloth, etc. **4** left or right part of the body, face, etc. **5** area to the left or right of the centre of something. **6** one of the teams or groups in a match, competition, debate, etc. **7** facet; aspect; part. **side by side** together; in juxtaposition. **take sides** favour one side more than the other in a dispute. *v* **side with** take sides with one rather than the other. **sideboard** *n* piece of dining-room furniture holding or displaying plates, cutlery, etc. **sideboards** *pl n* side whiskers on the face. **side effect** *n* secondary unplanned and often undesirable effect of an action, drug, etc. **sideline** *n* subsidiary or additional occupation. **sideshow** *n* minor show or fairground entertainment. **sidestep** *vt* (-pp-) neatly evade; avoid or step aside from. **sidetrack** *vt* lead away from a subject; divert. **side-**

ways *adv,adj* on or towards one side.
siding *n* short stretch of railway track used for shunting.
sidle *vi* **1** move sideways; edge along. **2** fawn; cringe.
siege *n* attempt to conquer a fortified place by surrounding and preventing access to it.
sieve *n* utensil with a perforated container for straining liquids, separating coarse from fine grains, or pulping solids. *vt* put through a sieve; sift.
sift *vt* **1** pass through or separate with a sieve. **2** examine minutely.
sigh *n* long deep breath expressing weariness, sadness, relief, etc. *vt,vi* utter (with) a sigh.
sight *n* **1** ability or power to see; vision. **2** something seen or viewed. **3** something that is messy, ugly, or untidy; mess. **4** appearance. **5** *inf* a lot; much more. **at first sight** on the first occasion of seeing. *~vt* see; observe; spot. **sightless** *adj* blind. **sight-read** *vt,vi* (-read) read, play, or sing music at first sight. **sightseeing** *n* visiting tourist attractions, beauty spots, etc. **sightseer** *n*.
sign *n* **1** symbol. **2** gesture; gesticulation. **3** hint; implication; clue; trace. **4** recognizable symptom. **5** advertisement or notice. *vt,vi* **1** write one's name or signature (on). **2** signal; communicate with signs. **sign on** *or* **up** enrol; enlist.
signal *n* visible or audible sign, esp. prearranged or well-known. *vt,vi* (-ll-) make signals (to).
signature *n* **1** signed name, esp. for use as authentication. **2** act of signing. **3** mark showing key and time at the beginning of a musical score. **signature tune** *n* tune used to announce and identify a particular performer or programme on stage, radio, television, etc.
significant *adj* meaningful; noteworthy; important. **significance** *n*. **significantly** *adv*. **signify** *vt* mean; indicate; be a sign of. *vi* matter; be important.
silence *n* absence of sound, speech, or communication. *vt* make silent; suppress. **silencer** *n* device rendering car exhaust, a gun, etc., more quiet. **silent** *adj* without a sound; noiseless; quiet. **silently** *adv*.

silhouette *n* outline figure, esp. in black on a white background. *vt* show in silhouette.
silk *n* fine soft fibre spun by silkworms and woven into fabric. **silkworm** *n* caterpillar of the mulberry-eating moth, which spins silk. **silky** *adj* soft, fine, and gleaming like silk. **silkiness** *n*.
sill *n* ledge or slab below a window or door.
silly *adj* foolish; fatuous; imprudent; unwise. **silliness** *n*.
silo *n* granary.
silt *n* sediment left by water in a river, harbour, etc. *vt,vi* fill (up) with silt.
silver *n* **1** white shining malleable valuable metallic element, widely used in coinage, jewellery, tableware, electrical contacts, alloys, etc. **2** *also* **silverware** cutlery, dishes, etc., made from silver or an alloy of silver. *adj* **1** made of silver. **2** of the colour of silver. **silver wedding** *n* twenty-fifth wedding anniversary. **silvery** *adj* **1** looking like silver. **2** having a clear soft sound.
similar *adj* like; resembling; exactly the same. **similarity** *n*. **similarly** *adv*.
simile *n* figure of speech in which two apparently unlike things are compared.
simmer *vi,vi* **1** cook slowly at boiling point. **2** have emotions (esp. anger) barely in check. **simmer down** calm down. *~n* state of simmering.
simple *adj* **1** easy; plain; ordinary. **2** not complex. **3** mere. **simple-minded** *adj* ingenuous; foolish. **simple-mindedly** *adv*. **simple-mindedness** *n*. **simplicity** *n* condition of being simple. **simplify** *vt* make less complicated; clarify. **simplification 3** absolutely.
simulate *vt* feign or reproduce (a situation, condition, etc.). **simulation** *n*.
simultaneous *adj* occurring at the same time. **simultaneously** *adv*.
sin *n* moral or religious offence. *vi* (-nn-) commit a sin. **sinful** *adj*.
since *adv* from that time until now; subsequently; ago. *prep* after; from the time of. *conj* **1** from the time that. **2** because; seeing that.
sincere *adj* honest; straightforward; genuine. **sincerely** *adv*. **sincerity** *n*.
sinew *n* tendon joining a muscle to a bone. **sinewy** *adj* wiry; muscular.

sing *vi,vt* (sang; sung) **1** utter (words or a tune) melodiously; produce musical notes. **2** celebrate in poetry. **singer** *n.*

singe *vt,vi* scorch or burn (the surface, edge, or end of). *n* slight burn.

single *adj* **1** individual; only one. **2** separate; solitary. **3** unmarried. **4** unique. *n* **1** short gramophone record played at 45 revolutions per minute. **2** one-way train or bus ticket. **3** single thing, event, etc. **singles** *pl n* tennis match, etc., between two players. *v* **single out** select from many for a specific purpose. **singly** *adv.* **single-handed** *adj* alone; unaided. **single-minded** *adj* intent; with one driving force or set aim. **single-mindedly** *adv.* **single-mindedness** *n.*

singular *adj* **1** indicating a single person, place, or thing. **2** odd; extraordinary; unusual. **singularity** *n.* **singularly** *adv.*

sinister *adj* malignant; suggestive of evil.

sink *v* (sank; sunk) *vt,vi* **1** submerge. **2** drop; lower. **3** lower or become lower in cost, value, etc. *vi* **1** pass (into) a state, condition, etc. **2** become weaker, unwell, etc. *vt* drive (a stake, post, etc.) into the ground. *n* fitted basin for washing, etc. **sink or swim** fail or succeed.

sinner *n* one who commits sin.

sinus *n* bodily cavity or passage, esp. communicating with the nose. **sinusitis** *n* inflammation of the sinus.

sip *vt,vi* (-pp-) drink in small mouthfuls. *n* small mouthful of liquid.

siphon *n* **1** bent pipe or tube for drawing off liquids. **2** bottle for dispensing soda water, etc., by means of a siphon. *vt,vi* draw (off) using a siphon.

sir *n* title used in a formal letter or to address a knight, baronet, or a man superior in age, rank, dignity, etc.

siren *n* apparatus producing a loud wailing noise or signal.

sirloin *n* upper part of a loin of beef.

sister *n* **1** daughter of the same parents as another. **2** nun. **3** nurse in charge of a hospital ward. **sisterhood** *n* community of nuns or other women. **sister-in-law** *n, pl* **sisters-in-law** brother's wife or husband's or wife's sister. **sisterly** *adj.*

sit *v* (-tt-; sat) *vi* **1** be in the position of having one's buttocks resting on the ground,

a chair, etc. **2** be placed; rest. **3** be a member (of a committee, etc.). *vt* **1** seat; place in a sitting position. **2** allocate a place at table to. *vt,vi* take (an examination). **sit-in** *n* mass occupation of premises as a form of protest.

site *n* place, setting, or ground on which a building, town, etc., stands. *vt* locate.

sitting *n* **1** session; business meeting. **2** time spent posing for a portrait, etc. **sitting room** *n* room used for sitting comfortably; living room.

situated *adj* **1** located; sited. **2** placed with respect to money, housing, or other considerations. **situation** *n* **1** position; condition. **2** job.

six *n* **1** number equal to one plus five. **2** group of six persons, things, etc. **3** *also* **six o'clock** six hours after noon or midnight. **at sixes and sevens** confused; in a muddle. ~*adj* amounting to six. **sixth** *adj* coming between fifth and seventh in sequence. *n* **1** sixth person, object, etc. **2** one of six equal parts; one divided by six. *adv* after the fifth.

sixteen *n* **1** number that is six more than ten. **2** sixteen things or people. *adj* amounting to sixteen. **sixteenth** *adj,adv,n.*

sixty *n* **1** number equal to six times ten. **2** sixty things or people. *adj* amounting to sixty. **sixtieth** *adj,adv,n.*

size *n* **1** extent; dimensions; importance. **2** measurement categorizing individual proportions. *vt* categorize by size. **size up** judge roughly; weigh up. **sizable** *adj* of considerable size or importance.

sizzle *vi* **1** hiss and splutter as during frying. **2** *inf* be very hot. *n* sizzling noise.

skate[1] *n* boot fitted with a blade or wheels allowing the wearer to glide smoothly over ice or other hard surfaces. *vi* move on or as if on skates. **skate on thin ice** deal with or be in a precarious situation. **skater** *n.*

skate[2] *n* large flatfish with an elongated snout.

skeleton *n* **1** framework of bones within a human or animal body. **2** outline, sketch, nucleus, or framework of anything. **skeleton in the cupboard** secret domestic disgrace.

sketch *n* **1** rough or unfinished drawing, draft, or outline. **2** very short usually amusing play. *vt,vi* draw or outline roughly.

sketchy *adj* incomplete; rough; inadequate. **sketchily** *adv*.

ski *n* 1 one of two long narrow pointed pieces of wood, metal, etc., attached to boots allowing wearer to slide quickly over snow. 2 short for **water-ski**. *vi* (skiing; skied *or* ski'd) travel on skis. **skier** *n*. **ski-lift** *n* seats slung on a cable transporting skiers up slopes.

skid *n* 1 wooden or metal support on which a ship, aeroplane, car, etc., may be rested, moved, or slid. 2 act of skidding. *vi* (-dd-) (of a vehicle, etc.) slide sideways, esp. out of control. **skid row** haunt or condition of vagrants, drunkards, etc.

skill *n* accomplishment; craft; expert knowledge. **skilled** *adj*. **skilful** *adj*. **skilfully** *adv*.

skim *vt* (-mm-) 1 remove scum, cream, etc., from the surface of a liquid. 2 pass over lightly, scarcely touching. **skim over** *or* **through** read cursorily; glance at. **skimmed milk** milk without cream.

skin *n* 1 tissue forming the outer covering of the body. 2 outer covering of a fruit. 3 leather pelt obtained from an animal. 4 layer; thin coating. *vt* (-nn-) remove the skin of or from. **skinny** *adj* unpleasantly thin. **skin-tight** *adj* extremely close-fitting.

skip *vt,vi* (-pp-) 1 jump or hop lightly, esp. from one foot to the other or over a twirling rope. 2 omit; leave out. *n* skipping movement.

skipper *n* captain of a ship, aircraft, etc.

skirmish *n* small unplanned fight or clash, as between hostile armies, etc. *vi* engage in a skirmish.

skirt *n* 1 woman's garment extending downwards from the waist or this part of a dress. 2 edge; extremity; border. *vt* pass around or along the edge of.

skittle *n* bottle-shaped target used in ninepin or tenpin bowling.

skull *n* bony framework of the head enclosing the brain.

skunk *n* small carnivorous black North American mammal with bushy tail, white-striped back, and a gland that sprays a powerful offensive scent.

sky *n* upper atmosphere; heavens; apparent canopy of air seen from the earth. **sky-high** *adj,adv* extremely high. **skylark** *n* lark that

sings while hovering in the air. *vi inf* indulge in practical jokes, frolics, etc. **skyscraper** *n* very tall building of many storeys.

slab *n* thick flat piece of stone, metal, cake, chocolate, etc.

slack *adj* 1 loose; not taut or stretched; limp. 2 lazy; remiss. *n* slack part of a rope. **slacks** *pl n* trousers for casual or informal wear. **slacken** *vi,vt* 1 make or become slack(er). 2 relax; abate; delay.

slam *vt,vi* (-mm-) shut or put down violently and noisily. *n* noise of something slammed.

slander *n* false, defamatory, or injurious report. *vt* injure by spreading false malicious gossip. **slanderer** *n*. **slanderous** *adj*.

slang *n* colloquial language not regarded as good, educated, or acceptable. *vt* berate abusively. **slanging match** bitter exchange of verbal insults.

slant *vt,vi* 1 slope; turn obliquely. 2 write or present (material) in a biased or prejudiced manner. *n* 1 slope. 2 angle of approach; attitude.

slap *n* blow with hand or anything flat. **slap in the face** insult; rebuff. ~*vt* (-pp-) smack; strike with a slap. **slapdash** *adj* careless; haphazard. **slapstick** *n* rough boisterous comedy.

slash *vt,vi* 1 cut with long violent random strokes. 2 economize or reduce drastically. *n* long cut or slit.

slat *n* narrow strip of wood, metal, etc.

slate *n* 1 dull grey fine-grained rock that can be split into smooth even pieces. 2 thin piece of this used as a writing tablet, roofing tile, etc.

slaughter *n* killing, esp. of many people or animals at once; massacre. *vt* 1 kill or slay ruthlessly, esp. in large numbers. 2 kill (an animal) for market. **slaughterhouse** *n* place where animals are killed for market; abattoir.

slave *n* 1 person legally owned by another. 2 person forced to work against his will. 3 person under the control or influence of someone or something. *vi* work like a slave. **slavery** *n* 1 state or condition of being a slave. 2 extremely hard unrewarding work.

sledge n vehicle on runners for transporting goods or people over snow; sleigh.

sledgehammer n large heavy hammer.

sleek adj 1 smooth and glossy. 2 suave; elegant. vt make smooth and glossy. **sleekly** adv. **sleekness** n.

sleep n resting state during which the body is relaxed and consciousness is suspended. vi (slept) take rest in sleep. **sleep on it** postpone a decision overnight. **sleepless** adj. **sleepily** adv. **sleepiness** n. **sleepy** adj. **sleeper** n 1 one who sleeps. 2 horizontal beam supporting the rails of a railway track. 3 sleeping car or compartment on a train. **sleepwalk** vi walk while asleep. **sleepwalker** n.

sleet n rain falling as half-melted hail or snow. vi fall as sleet.

sleeve n 1 part of a garment covering the arm. 2 tube covering a rod, pipe, etc. 3 cover for gramophone record. **up one's sleeve** held secretly in reserve.

sleigh n sledge, esp. one pulled by horses.

slender adj 1 slim; thin. 2 meagre; insufficient.

slice n 1 thin flat piece cut from something. 2 utensil for lifting and serving fish, etc. vt 1 cut into slices. 2 cut a slice from. 3 hit (a golfball, tennis ball, etc.) so that it curves in flight.

slick adj 1 sleek; smooth. 2 deft; cunning. **slickness** n.

slide v (slid) vt,vi 1 move or glide smoothly over a surface. 2 move or be moved unobtrusively. vi 1 pass gradually. 2 slip or fall. **let slide** allow to take a natural course. ~n 1 transparent photograph. 2 smooth inclined surface for children, goods, etc., to slide down. 3 clasp for the hair. **slide-rule** n mechanical device used for calculating.

slight adj 1 frail; slim; flimsy. 2 insignificant; unimportant. n snub; hurtful act. vt disregard; treat as if of no importance. **slightly** adv a little; somewhat.

slim adj 1 slender; thin. 2 small; slight; meagre. vi (-mm-) try to lose weight by means of diet, exercise, etc. **slimmer** n. **slimness** n.

slime n thin oozing mud or anything resembling it. **slimy** adj 1 resembling or covered with slime. 2 vile; repulsive.

sling n 1 piece of material for supporting an injured arm, hand, etc. 2 band or pocket attached to strings for throwing stones, hoisting or supporting weighty objects, etc. vt (slung) 1 throw casually. 2 support with or hang from a sling.

slink vi (slunk) move stealthily and quietly; sneak. **slinky** adj 1 close-fitting. 2 sinuous and graceful.

slip^1 v (-pp-) vi 1 slide; glide. 2 become unfastened or less secure. 3 lose one's balance, grip, etc. 4 become less efficient, careful, etc. 5 move quietly or without being noticed. 6 forget; make a mistake. vt 1 pull or push easily or hastily. 2 drop; let fall. **slip up** make a mistake. ~n 1 sliding; act of slipping. 2 mistake; small error. 3 petticoat. **slipway** n sloping area from which a vessel is launched.

slip^2 n narrow strip of wood, paper, etc.

slipper n loose comfortable indoor shoe.

slippery adj 1 so smooth, greasy, etc., as to make slipping likely. 2 elusive; unstable. **slipperiness** n.

slit n 1 long cut. 2 narrow opening. vt (-tt-) 1 make a long cut in. 2 cut into long strips.

slither vi slide unsteadily.

slog vi,vt (-gg-) 1 hit violently. 2 work hard and determinedly. n 1 long spell of hard work. 2 heavy blow.

slogan n catchy word or phrase used in advertising, etc.

slop n 1 liquid waste. 2 semiliquid unappetizing food. vt,vi (-pp-) spill carelessly and messily. **sloppy** adj 1 messy; careless; untidy. 2 muddy, slushy, or watery. 3 sentimental; maudlin. **sloppily** adv. **sloppiness** n.

slope n 1 inclined surface. 2 deviation from the horizontal; slant. vi have or take a sloping position or direction.

sloshed adj inf drunk.

slot n groove, channel, or slit into which a bolt, coin, etc., may fit or be inserted. vt (-tt-) 1 make fit into. 2 provide with or pass through a slot. **slot together** fit neatly together.

slovenly adj 1 careless; slipshod. 2 lazy and dirty. **slovenliness** n.

slow adj 1 taking a long time. 2 not quick; gradual. 3 behind correct time. 4 dull-witted or unresponsive. *vt* delay; retard. **slow down** *or* **up** lessen; slacken in speed. **slowly** *adv.* **slowness** *n.*

slug small shell-less mollusc, destructive to garden plants.

sluggish *adj* lazy; slow-moving. **sluggishly** *adv.* **sluggishness** *n.*

sluice *n* sliding gate or valve controlling a flow of water in a channel, drain, etc. *vt,vi* flush or wash down with running water.

slum *n* squalid overcrowded housing.

slump *n* 1 sudden fall or decline. 2 economic depression. *vi* 1 collapse in a heap. 2 suddenly lose value.

slung *v pt* and *pp* of **sling.**

slunk *v pt* and *pp* of **slink.**

slur *vt,vi* (-rr-) 1 sound (words) indistinctly. 2 pass over lightly. 3 disparage. *n* 1 smudge; blur. 2 indistinct noise. 3 slight, insult, or blame.

slush *n* 1 watery mud or snow. 2 excessive sentimentality. **slushy** *adj.*

sly *adj* 1 cunning. 2 devious; deceitful. **slyly** *adv.* **slyness** *n.*

smack[1] *vt* strike sharply with the palm of the hand. **smack the lips** make a smacking sound with the lips. ∼*n* act or sound of smacking. *adv inf* immediately; directly.

smack[2] *n* slight trace or flavour. *vi* suggest; have the flavour (of).

small *adj* not large; of little size, strength, importance, quantity, etc. **feel small** feel humiliated. **small talk** polite trivial conversation. ∼*n* narrow part (of the back, etc.). **smallness** *n.* **smallholding** *n* small farm or rented plot of agricultural land. **small-minded** *adj* petty; narrow-minded. **smallpox** *n* serious contagious disease causing eruptions and subsequent scars on the skin.

smart *adj* 1 fashionable; elegant. 2 clever; ingenious; witty. *vi* feel sharp pain or resentment. **smartly** *adv.* **smartness** *n.* **smarten** *vt* make cleaner, tidier, more fashionable, etc.

smash *vt,vi* 1 shatter; break into fragments. 2 hit or throw violently. *n* 1 sound or act of smashing. 2 violent collision, esp. of motor vehicles. **smashing** *adj inf* wonderful; excellent.

smear *n* 1 dirty greasy mark. 2 slur on one's reputation. 3 specimen taken for pathological testing. *vt* 1 spread or cover with something thick or greasy. 2 discredit publicly. 3 blur by smearing.

smell *n* 1 odour; stink; fragrance. 2 ability to distinguish smells. 3 suggestion; hint. *vt* detect or distinguish by the sense of smell. *vi* give off a smell. **smell out** discover by investigation. **smell a rat** become suspicious. **smelly** *adj* having a strong or unpleasant smell.

smile *vi* turn up the corners of the lips to express pleasure, approval, amusement, etc. *n* act of smiling; happy expression. **smilingly** *adv.*

smirk *vi* give an unpleasant, knowing, silly, or self-satisfied smile. *n* act of smirking; smirking expression.

smock *n* full long loose shirt.

smog *n* combination of smoke and fog. **smoggy** *adj.*

smoke *n* 1 visible cloud of fine particles given off during burning. 2 cigarette, cigar, etc. *vi* give off smoke. *vi,vt* inhale fumes of burning tobacco in a cigarette, pipe, etc. *vt* cure (meat, fish, etc.) by treatment with smoke. **smoker** *n* 1 person who smokes tobacco. 2 train compartment where smoking is allowed. **smoky** *adj.*

smooth *adj* 1 having an even surface. 2 level; even. 3 unruffled; calm. 4 easy; comfortable. *vt,vi also* **smoothen** make or become smooth. *vt* 1 soothe; comfort. 2 facilitate; make easy or easier. **smoothly** *adv.* **smoothness** *n.*

smother *vt* 1 suffocate; prevent access of air with a thick covering, heavy smoke, etc. 2 suppress or conceal.

smoulder *vi* 1 burn slowly without a flame. 2 exist in a suppressed or undetected condition.

smudge *n* smear; dirty mark. *vt* mark or be marked with a smudge; smear.

smug *adj* self-satisfied; complacent. **smugly** *adv.* **smugness** *n.*

smuggle *vt,vi* import or export (goods) illegally. *vt* bring or take in secretly or illegally. **smuggler** *n.*

smut *n* 1 particle of soot or dust. 2 small dark mark. 3 bawdiness; obscenity. **smutty** *adj.*

snack *n* light quick meal.

snag *n* small problem, hitch, drawback, etc. *vt* (-gg-) **1** hinder; prevent. **2** catch or tear on a small sharp protuberance.

snail *n* small slow-moving hard-shelled mollusc.

snake *n* **1** long scaly legless reptile with a forked tongue and neither eyelids nor ears. **2** treacherous deceitful person.

snap *vt,vi* (-pp-) **1** bite suddenly. **2** speak sharply or irritably. **3** shut or break suddenly. **snap up** seize hastily. ∼*n* **1** act or sound of snapping. **2** simple card game. **3** *inf* snapshot. **snapshot** *n* informal photograph.

snarl *vi* growl, speak, or show the teeth threateningly or angrily. *n* act, sound, or expression of snarling.

snatch *vt,vi* seize or grab suddenly, violently, or when an opportunity arises. *n* **1** act of snatching. **2** fragment or bit.

sneak *vi* move or creep in a furtive cowardly or underhand way. *vt* take secretly; steal. *n* one who sneaks.

sneer *n* cynical contemptuous expression or remark. *v* **sneer at** scorn; mock.

sneeze *vi* eject sudden convulsive involuntary breath through the nose. **not to be sneezed at** not to be treated as insignificant. ∼*n* act or sound of sneezing.

sniff *vi* inhale sharply and noisily through the nose. *vt* smell. **sniff at** show scorn. ∼*n* act or sound of sniffing.

snip *vt,vi* (-pp-) clip or cut off with or as with scissors. *n* **1** act of snipping. **2** small piece snipped off.

snipe *vi* shoot at an enemy or enemies from a concealed position. *n* long-billed wading bird. **sniper** *n.*

snivel *vi* (-ll-) **1** have a runny nose. **2** whine or whimper tearfully. *n* act or sound of snivelling. **sniveller** *n.*

snob *n* one who admires and imitates those he considers his superior in class, wealth, or rank and who despises his inferiors. **snobbish** *adj.* **snobbery** *n.*

snooker *n* game resembling billiards using fifteen red balls and six of other colours.

snoop *vi* pry; investigate secretly. **snooper** *n.*

snooty *adj* supercilious; haughty; disdainful. **snootily** *adv.* **snootiness** *n.*

snooze *n* short sleep; cat nap. *vi* doze; take a snooze.

snore *vi* breathe noisily while asleep. *n* act or sound of snoring.

snort *vi* exhale noisily and sharply through the nose, often in anger. *n* act or sound of snorting.

snout *n* **1** animal's projecting nose. **2** part of machinery, etc., resembling a snout.

snow *n* atmospheric vapour frozen and falling as flakes of white crystals. *vi* shower or fall as snow. **snowed under** overwhelmed with work, problems, etc. **snowed up** confined in a house, car, etc., by fallen snow. **snowy** *adj.*

snowdrop *n* tiny white-flowered bulbous plant of early spring.

snub *vt* (-bb-) humiliate or slight pointedly or sarcastically. *n* snubbing act or rebuff. **snub-nosed** *adj* having a short turned-up nose.

snuff[1] powder (esp. tobacco) inhaled through the nose.

snuff[2] *vt* extinguish (a candle).

snug *adj* cosy, comfortable, and warm. **snugly** *adv.*

snuggle *vt,vi* cuddle closely together or into blankets, etc., for warmth and comfort.

so *adv* **1** to such an extent; very. **2** in such a manner. **3** consequently; then. **4** also; as well. **and so on** and continuing; et cetera. ∼*pron* **1** something similar. **2** as anticipated. *adj* correct; right; true. **so-and-so** *n* **1** particular but unnamed person. **2** awkward or difficult person; nuisance.

soak *vt,vi* steep or be steeped in liquid. *vt* drench; permeate. **soak up** draw into itself; absorb. ∼*n* **1** act of soaking. **2** heavy downpour.

soap *n* substance used for cleansing, forming a lather with water. **soap opera** *n* serialized drama, esp. broadcast on daytime television. ∼*vt* **1** rub with soap. **2** *inf* flatter. **soapy** *adj.*

soar *vi* rise upwards; fly or glide at great height. *n* act of soaring.

sob *v* (-bb-) *vi* catch one's breath noisily in involuntary spasms as a result of emotion; weep; cry. *vt* utter while sobbing. *n* act of sobbing.

sober *adj* **1** not drunk. **2** temperate in the use of intoxicants. **3** moderate; well-bal-

anced. **4** serious; sedate. *vt,vi* make or
become sober. **soberly** *adv.* **sobriety** *or*
soberness *n.*

sociable *adj* **1** friendly. **2** fond of or conducive to social interaction. **sociability** *n.*
sociably *adv.*

social *adj* **1** of or concerning interaction or
relations between persons. **2** forming a society, group, or community. **3** gregarious;
convivial. **4** pertaining to fashionable circles. *n* gathering for companionship.
socially *adv.* **social class** *n* members
of a community sharing a similar position in
economic and social structure. **social
security** *n* scheme(s) providing for the
welfare of the public. **social work** *n* social
service to improve the welfare of the public.
social worker *n.*

socialism *n* political and economic theory
of society which tends towards centralized
planning and ownership of the means of
production, distribution, and exchange and
operation of the free market. **socialist**
adj,n.

society *n* **1** group sharing territory, language, customs, laws, and political and economic organization. **2** fellowship; companionship. **3** any group of people organized for
a purpose. **4** rich, aristocratic, and exclusive
social group.

sociology *n* study of human societies,
their structure, organization, and customs.
sociological *adj.* **sociologist** *n.*

sock[1] *n* short stocking. **pull one's socks
up** make greater efforts.

sock[2] *vt,n sl* punch; hit.

socket *n* **1** device which receives an electric plug. **2** natural or artificial indentation
functioning as a receptacle.

soda *n* term applied to compounds of
sodium. **soda-water** *n* aerated solution of
sodium bicarbonate.

sodium *n* soft silvery reactive metallic element.

sofa *n* upholstered couch with a back and
arms.

soft *adj* **1** yielding; malleable; smooth. **2**
gentle. **3** lenient. **4** tender; sympathetic. **5**
(of sound) low in volume. **6** (of colour) not
very bright. **7** *inf* feeble-minded; foolish.
softly *adv.* **softness** *n.* **soften** *vt,vi*
make or become soft(er). **soft-hearted** *adj*

easily moved to tenderness, pity, etc. **soft-
heartedly** *adv.* **soft-heartedness** *n.*

software *n* written or printed data used
in the operation of computers; program.

soggy *adj* soaked; marshy; sodden. **soggily**
adv. **sogginess** *n.*

soil[1] *n* top layer of the earth, composed of
organic and inorganic substances; ground.

soil[2] *vt,vi* make or become dirty, or polluted.

solar *adj* **1** of or from the sun. **2** measured
by the movement of the earth relative to the
sun. **3** radiating like the sun's rays. **solar
energy** *n* energy obtained from the rays
of the sun, used for home heating. **1 solar
system** *n* our sun with the planets,
asteroids, comets, etc., that revolve round it.
solar plexus *n* network of nerves radiating from behind the stomach.

sold *v pt* and *pp* of **sell.**

solder *n* alloy with a low melting temperature used for joining metals. *vt* join, mend,
or patch with solder.

soldier *n* noncommissioned member of an
armed force. *v* **soldier on** keep fighting or
struggling towards something. **soldierly**
adj.

sole[1] *n* flat underside of a foot, shoe, etc.
vt put a sole on.

sole[2] *n* edible flatfish.

sole[3] *adj* only; single; solitary. **solely** *adv.*

solemn *adj* **1** grave; serious. **2** marked by
formal or religious ceremony; arousing awe
and reverence. **3** impressive; dignified; pompous. **solemnity** *n.* **solemnly** *adv.*

solicit *vt,vi* **1** ask (for) persistently. **2** make
unlawful sexual offers or requests (to).

solicitor *n* lawyer who prepares deeds,
manages cases, and who acts in lower courts
only but prepares cases for barristers.

solicitous *adj* considerate; concerned;
eager; anxious. **solicitude** *n.*

solid *adj* **1** firm; compact. **2** having three
dimensions; not hollow. **3** heavy; strongly
built. **4** reliable; steady. **5** unanimous. *n*
solid substance; substance that is neither liquid nor gaseous. **solidity** *n.* **solidly** *adv.*
solidarity *n* unanimous whole-hearted
coherence in action or attitude. **solidify**
vt,vi make or become solid.

solitary *adj* **1** existing, living, or going
without others. **2** happening, done, or made

alone. **3** secluded. **4** lonely; single; sole. **solitary confinement** n isolation of a prisoner from all others. **solitude** n absence of company.

solo n **1** musical composition for a single voice or instrument. **2** card game in which players act individually and not in partnership. **3** flight during which the pilot is unaccompanied. adv alone; by oneself. **soloist** n.

solstice n time of year when the sun reaches its farthest points north and south of the equator, producing the shortest or longest day.

soluble adj **1** capable of being dissolved. **2** capable of being solved. **solubility** n.

solution n **1** method or process of solving a problem. **2** explanation or answer. **3** liquid containing a dissolved solid.

solve vt find the correct solution to; settle; clear up; explain.

solvent adj **1** able to pay debts. **2** able to dissolve another substance. n liquid capable of dissolving another substance. **solvency** n ability to pay off debts. **solvent abuse** n practice of inhaling fumes from glue, petrol, etc., leading to intoxication and hallucination.

sombre adj dark; dismal; gloomy. **sombrely** adv. **sombreness** n.

sombrero n wide-brimmed hat with a tall crown, traditionally worn in Spain and Latin America.

some adj **1** certain (people or things). **2** a few; a number; an amount or quantity. **3** particular proportion. pron a number of people or things. adv about; approximately. **somebody** pron **1** particular but unnamed person. **2** important or famous person. **somehow** adv **1** in some way or other. **2** for some reason. **someone** pron somebody. **something** pron particular but unnamed thing, action, characteristic, etc. **something like** approximately; about; almost. adv to a certain extent. **sometime** adv on some occasion; at some time. **sometimes** adv occasionally; from time to time. **somewhat** adv to a certain extent; rather. **somewhere** adv **1** in or to some particular but unspecified place. **2** placed approximately.

somersault n **1** leap or roll in which one turns heels over head. **2** complete reversal of opinion or attitude. vi make a somersault.

son n **1** male offspring, esp. in relation to his parents. **2** any male descendant. **son-in-law** n, pl **sons-in-law** daughter's husband.

sonata n musical composition of three or four movements and featuring a solo instrument.

song n **1** musical piece that is sung. **2** songs in general. **3** characteristic call of certain birds. **song and dance** inf fuss.

sonic adj **1** relating to sound. **2** having a speed approximately equal to the speed of sound.

sonnet n poem of fourteen lines with a set rhyming pattern.

soon adv in a short time; without delay; quickly. **as soon as** at the moment that.

soot n black powdery substance given off by burning coal, wood, etc. **sooty** adj.

soothe vt calm; comfort; allay.

sophisticated adj **1** refined or cultured in taste and manner; urbane. **2** attractive to refined tastes. **3** over-refined; unnatural. **4** (of machines, etc.) complex. **sophistication** n.

soprano n **1** highest range of an adult female voice. **2** singer capable of this range of notes. **3** part written for this voice.

sordid adj **1** filthy; squalid. **2** degrading; base. **3** greedy or selfish. **sordidly** adv. **sordidness** n.

sore adj **1** painful; tender; inflamed. **2** grieved, vexed, or bitter. n injured or diseased spot; wound. **soreness** n. **sorely** adv severely; distressingly; greatly.

sorrow n mental pain caused by loss or misfortune. **sorrowful** adj. **sorrowfully** adv.

sorry adj **1** feeling pity, regret, sadness, sympathy, etc. **2** pitiful; miserable. **3** poor; shabby. interj expression of apology.

sort n **1** class; kind; type. **2** character; nature. **sort of** inf in some way; rather. **out of sorts** not in good health or spirits. ~vt,vi **1** classify. **2** group (with). **sort out 1** separate out. **2** solve (a problem); resolve (a situation). **3** inf punish; reprimand.

soufflé *n* light fluffy dish made with eggs.

sought *v pt* and *pp* of **seek.**

soul *n* **1** immortal spiritual part of man. **2** innermost depth, being, or nature; core. **3** nobler feelings and capacities of the human being; conscience. **4** person. **5** music derived from Black American gospel singing. **soul-destroying** *adj* eroding identity; sapping effort or vigour; making inhuman. **soulful** *adj* having, expressing, or affecting deep or lofty feelings. **soulfully** *adv.* **soulless** *adj* inhuman; mechanical; lacking emotion or identity.

sound[1] *n* **1** noise perceptible to the ear. **2** mere noise without meaning. *vt,vi* **1** cause or emit a sound. **2** signal by a sound. *vi* seem; give an impression of being. **soundless** *adj.* **soundlessly** *adv.*

sound[2] *adj* **1** in good condition; healthy; whole and complete. **2** reasoned; prudent; reliable. **3** (of sleep) deep; unbroken. **soundly** *adv.* **soundness** *n.*

soup *n* liquid food made by boiling meat or vegetables in water. **in the soup** *sl* in trouble or difficulties.

sour *adj* **1** sharp or acid to the taste; not sweet. **2** turned or rancid. **3** embittered; morose. **sour grapes** pretending to dislike what one cannot have. **sourly** *adv.* **sourness** *n.*

source *n* **1** spring; origin; starting point or cause. **2** document or work providing authority, validity, or inspiration.

south *n* **1** one of the four cardinal points of the compass situated to the right of a person facing the sunrise. **2** part of a country, area, etc., lying towards the south. *adj also* **southern** of, in, or facing the south. *adv,adj also* **southerly 1** towards the south. **2** (of winds) from the south. **southerner** *n.* **southeast** *n* point situated midway between the south and east. *adj also* **southeastern** of, in, or facing the southeast. *adv,adj also* **southeasterly 1** towards the southeast. **2** (of winds) from the southeast. **southward** *adj* facing or moving towards the south. **southwards** *adv* in the direction of the south. **southwest** *n* point situated midway between south and west. *adj also* **southwestern** of, in, or facing the southwest. *adv,adj also* **southwesterly 1** towards the southwest. **2** (of winds) from the southwest.

souvenir *n* memento or keepsake by which memory of some person, place, or event is cherished.

sovereign *n* **1** monarch; supreme ruler. **2** former English gold coin worth a pound. *adj* **1** supreme; utmost. **2** excellent. **sovereignty** *n.*

sow[1] (sou) *v* (sowed; sown *or* sowed) *vt,vi* scatter or put (seeds, plants, etc.) in the ground. *vt* disseminate; suggest. **sower** *n.*

sow[2] (sau) *n* adult female pig.

soya bean *n* seed of an east Asian plant, rich in oil and protein.

spa *n* resort having mineral water springs in its locality.

space *n* **1** three-dimensional expanse. **2** period of time or the distance between events, places, etc. **3** blank or unused area. **4** universe; area beyond the earth's atmosphere. *vt* arrange at or divide into intervals. **spacecraft** *n* vehicle launched into space for research purposes, exploration, etc. **spacious** *adj* having ample room; extensive; wide. **spaciously** *adv.*

spade[1] *n* digging tool with a broad flat blade.

spade[2] *n* playing card of the suit marked with a black heart-shaped pip and a stem or the symbol itself.

spaghetti *n* pasta in the form of long thin cords.

span *n* **1** extent of something stretched out; stretch of space or time. **2** distance between two points, as between pillars, supports of arches, bridges, etc. *vt* **1** extend; stretch across. **2** measure with an extended hand.

spaniel *n* breed of medium-sized dog with long drooping ears and a silky coat.

spank *vt* strike with the open hand, a slipper, etc., esp. on the buttocks; slap. *n* blow or series of blows with the flat of the hand, etc.; smack.

spanner *n* tool for manipulating nuts and bolts. **spanner in the works** deliberate hindrance; sabotage.

spare *vt* **1** be merciful to; refrain or release from punishment, suffering, etc. **2** give away freely; be able to do without. *adj* **1** left over; not used or needed; extra. **2** freely available; kept in reserve. **3** lean; thin. **4** scanty; meagre. *n* spare part. **sparing** *adj* thrifty; economical.

spark *n* **1** glowing particle thrown out by a burning substance. **2** brief flash of light, as that accompanying an electric discharge. **3** vitality; life. *vi* emit sparks. *vt* **1** produce (sparks). **2** kindle; excite.

sparkle *vi* **1** glitter; twinkle; emit sparks or flashes. **2** be gay, clever, or witty. *n* **1** act of glittering; brilliance. **2** gaiety; wit; lively intelligence. **3** appearance of effervescence, as in champagne.

sparrow *n* any of various small brown birds.

sparse *adj* thinly distributed; scanty. **sparsely** *adv.* **sparseness** *or* **sparsity** *n.*

spasm *n* **1** involuntary muscular contraction. **2** strong but short-lived movement, action, or emotion. **spasmodic** *adj* **1** intermittent; not continuous. **2** relating to spasms. **spasmodically** *adv.*

spastic *adj* suffering from spasms and lack of muscular control due to damage to the brain. *n* person who suffers so.

spat *v pt* and *pp* of **spit.**

spatial *adj* of, in, or concerning space or the placement of objects in space. **spatially** *adv.*

spatula *n* broad blunt-bladed knife or flattened spoon.

spawn *n* eggs of fish, frogs, molluscs, etc., laid in water. *vt,vi* deposit (eggs).

speak *v* (spoke; spoken) *vi* **1** utter words; talk. **2** give a speech, lecture, sermon, etc. *vt* declare; pronounce. **nothing to speak of** nothing worth mentioning. **so to speak** as one might put it. **speak for** speak on behalf of. **speak for oneself** express personal views. **speak up** speak so as to be sure to be heard. **speak up for** speak in favour of; defend. **speaker** *n.*

spear *n* **1** long weapon consisting of a shaft with a sharp pointed head. **2** anything so shaped. *vt,vi* kill or pierce with a spear.

spearmint *n* aromatic garden mint or the flavour of this.

special *adj* **1** distinctive; peculiar; for a particular purpose. **2** detailed; exceptional. *n* special thing or person. **specially** *adv.* **specialist** *n* person having comprehen-

sive knowledge of a subject, etc.; authority. **speciality** *n* particular characteristic, product, etc., for which a person, shop, etc., is renowned. **specialize** *vi* limit oneself to one particular area for intensive study. **specialization** *n.*

species *n, pl* **species** group of animals or plants of the same genus, capable of interbreeding.

specific *adj* **1** of or particular to one definite kind or type. **2** explicit; precise; exact. **specifically** *adv.* **specify** *vt* **1** make explicit; mention particularly. **2** set down as a requisite. **specification** *n.*

specimen *n* individual, object, or portion regarded as typical or a sample for purposes of study or collection.

speck *n* small spot; minute particle. *vt* mark with specks.

spectacle *n* **1** exhibition; show; pageant. **2** unusual or ridiculous sight. **spectacles** *pl n* glasses worn to correct vision, etc. **spectacular** *adj* impressive; outstanding; amazing. *n* flamboyant show. **spectacularly** *adv.*

spectator *n* person watching a show, contest, etc.; onlooker.

spectrum *n* **1** range of colours in order of wavelength produced when sunlight is split into colours on passing through a prism. **2** wide range; graduated series. **spectral** *adj.*

speculate *vi* **1** theorize; reflect; make conjectures. **2** take risks, esp. in buying and selling, in the hope of quick gain. **speculation** *n.* **speculative** *adj.* **speculator** *n.*

speech *n* **1** that which is spoken; language. **2** act or faculty of speaking; manner of speaking. **3** oration; talk addressed to an audience. **speechless** *adj* **1** temporarily deprived of speech. **2** unable to speak.

speed *n* rate of movement; quickness; velocity. *v* (sped *or* speeded) *vi,vt* move rapidly or quickly. *vi* drive a vehicle at high speed or in excess of the speed limit. *vt* **1** further; hasten. **2** send forth with good wishes. **speedy** *adj.* **speedily** *adv.*

spell[1] *v* (spelt *or* spelled) *vt,vi* say or write in order the letters that constitute (a word). *vt* **1** (of letters) form; make up. **2** amount to. **spell out** explain in very simple and exact terms.

spell[2] *n* **1** magical formula or incantation. **2** enchantment; irresistible attraction. **spellbound** *adj* under a spell or influence; fascinated.

spell[3] *n* short period of time; bout.

spend *vt* (spent) **1** give; pay out. **2** expend; use; exhaust. **3** pass (time). **spendthrift** *n* person who wastes money.

sperm *n* **1** semen. **2** male reproductive cell.

sphere *n* **1** ball; globe. **2** scope; range. **3** field of activity or influence; world. **spherical** *adj*.

spice *n* **1** strong aromatic and pungent seasoning of vegetable origin. **2** that which adds excitement or interest. *vt* season with spice. **spicy** *adj*. **spicily** *adv*. **spiciness** *n*.

spider *n* eight-legged insect-like animal that spins webs to catch prey. **spidery** *adj* **1** spider-like. **2** having thin angular lines.

spike *n* sharp pointed rod, esp. of metal. *vt* fix or pierce with a spike. **spiky** *adj*.

spill *vt,vi* (spilt *or* spilled) **1** allow (liquid) to fall, esp. by accident. **2** overflow or cause to overflow. **spill the beans** reveal a secret. ~*n* **1** fall from a vehicle, horse, etc. **2** spilling.

spin *vt,vi* (spun) **1** rotate rapidly. **2** draw out and twist (wool, etc.) into thread. **3** (of spiders, etc.) form webs or cocoons. *n* **1** act or speed of rotating. **2** *inf* pleasure drive in a vehicle, etc.

spine *n* **1** backbone surrounding and protecting nerve tissue. **2** long thin ridge. **3** spiked extremity on a plant, fish, etc. **4** bound edge of a book. **spinal** *adj*. **spiny** *adj*. **spine-chilling** *adj* terrifying. **spineless** *adj* **1** having no spine. **2** weak; irresolute.

spinster *n* unmarried woman.

spiral *n* **1** curve that winds around and away from a fixed point or axis. **2** upward or downward trend in prices, wages, etc. *adj* resembling a spiral; twisting. *v* (-ll-) *vt,vi* take or make into a spiral course or shape. *vi* increase or decrease with ever-growing speed.

spire *n* **1** tall slender tower tapering to a point. **2** long slender flower or stalk; shoot.

spirit *n* **1** moving force; inner life; soul. **2** underlying meaning; true significance. **3** vitality; courage. **4** mood. **5** any distilled alcoholic beverage. **6** active essence of a drug, compound, etc. **spirited** *adj* lively; animated. **spirited away** *adj* mysteriously or secretly carried off.

spiritual *adj* **1** of or like a spirit or soul. **2** religious; sacred. **3** ideal; unworldly; not materialistic. *n* American Negro religious song originating in the time of slavery. **spiritually** *adv*.

spit[1] *n* saliva. *v* (-tt-; spat *or* spit) *vt,vi* eject (something) from the mouth. *vi* drizzle lightly and irregularly.

spit[2] *n* spike for roasting meat.

spite *n* malevolence; vindictiveness; desire to injure. **in spite of** notwithstanding; in defiance of. ~*vt* injure or grieve maliciously. **spiteful** *adj*. **spitefully** *adv*.

splash *vt,vi* **1** scatter or cause (a liquid) to scatter; spatter. **2** fall or cause to fall on in drops or waves. *n* **1** act or sound of splashing. **2** liquid splashed. **3** mark so made. **make a splash** cause a sensation.

splendid *adj* **1** magnificent; brilliant. **2** *inf* excellent; very good. **splendidly** *adv*. **splendour** *n* glory; brilliance; magnificence.

splint *n* rigid piece of wood tied to a limb to keep a broken bone in place. *vt* support with splints.

splinter *n* sliver of wood, glass, metal, etc. *vt,vi* break up into splinters. **splinter group** *n* members who break away from a main group.

split *vt,vi* (-tt-; split) **1** break or divide into separate pieces, groups, etc. **2** break off from a whole. **3** tear; rend. **4** separate because of disharmony, disagreement, etc. **5** share or divide among persons. **6** *sl* go away; leave. *n* **1** act or process of splitting. **2** result of splitting; division; gap.

splutter *vi* **1** gasp and spit jerkily. **2** speak incoherently as in rage. **3** eject drops of liquid. *n* act or noise of spluttering.

spoil *v* (spoilt *or* spoiled) *vt* **1** damage, destroy, or impair the beauty, usefulness, or value of. **2** cause (a child, etc.) to become selfish by excessive indulgence. *vi* deteriorate. **spoils** *pl n* plunder; booty. **spoilsport** *n* person who spoils the enjoyment of others.

spoke[1] *v pt* of **speak.**

spoke[2] *n* **1** bar radiating from the hub towards the rim of a wheel. **2** rung of a ladder.

spoken *v pp* of **speak.**

spokesman *n, pl* **-men** person authorized to speak on behalf of others.

sponge *n* **1** pad of any porous elastic substance. **2** marine animal with fibrous skeleton. **3** act of applying or removing liquid with a sponge. **4** light baked or steamed pudding. *vt,vi* **1** apply a sponge to absorb; wipe off. **2** *inf* live or obtain by presuming on the generosity of others. **spongy** *adj.*

sponsor *vt* **1** vouch for good character of; act as surety. **2** act as godparent. **3** finance; fund. *n* person who sponsors. **sponsorship** *n.*

spontaneous *adj* **1** impulsive; uninhibited; unconstrained. **2** produced of itself without external cause. **spontaneity** *n.* **spontaneously** *adv.*

spool *n* small cylinder, bobbin, or reel for winding yarn, photographic film, etc., on.

spoon *n* utensil consisting of a small bowl on a handle. *vt,vi* transfer with or as if with a spoon.

sporadic *adj* occasional; occurring irregularly. **sporadically** *adv.*

sport *n* **1** activity or game indulged in for pleasure. **2** amusement; fun; joke. **3** *inf* good-humoured person. *vt* wear conspicuously. **sporty** *adv.* **sportive** *adj* merry; playful. **sports car** *n* low-bodied usually two-seater car with high acceleration. **sportsman** *n* **1** person fond of sport. **2** one who bears defeat, inconvenience, etc., cheerfully. **sportsmanship** *n.*

spot *n* **1** small mark or patch. **2** small area or quantity. **3** skin blemish. **in a spot** in difficulties. **soft spot** liking; fondness. ~*vt* (-tt-) **1** mark with spots. **2** notice; observe; discover. **spotless** *adj* **1** without blemish. **2** very clean. **spotlight** *n* strong beam of light focused on one spot. **spotty** *adj* having spots, esp. on the face.

spouse *n* wife or husband of someone.

spout *n* **1** narrow projecting tube through which contents of a vessel are poured. **2** jet of liquid. *vt,vi* pour out conspicuously.

sprain *vt* twist or wrench muscles or ligaments (of a foot, hand, etc.) without disloca-

tion of a joint. *n* **1** act of spraining muscles. **2** swelling and pain caused by this.

sprang *v pt* of **spring.**

sprawl *vi* **1** lie or sit with stretched-out limbs. **2** be spread untidily over a wide area. *n* **1** act or position of sprawling. **2** untidy spread, esp. of buildings.

spray[1] *n* **1** fine drops of liquid blown through the air. **2** apparatus for doing this. *vt,vi* squirt, disperse, or become spray.

spray[2] small shoot or branch of a plant; sprig.

spread *vt,vi* (spread) **1** extend or cause to extend or cover widely; stretch or be stretched. **2** circulate. *n* **1** extent. **2** act or degree of spreading or the area covered. **3** feast. **4** substance for spreading on bread, etc.

spree *n* lively outing; session of reckless activity or amusement.

sprig *n* small shoot; twig.

sprightly *adj* vivacious; brisk; lively. **sprightliness** *n.*

spring *v* (sprang; sprung) *vi* **1** leap; jump. **2** bounce; rebound; recoil. **3** move suddenly or violently. **4** have as a cause; originate; start. **5** produce shoots, leaves, etc.; sprout. *vt* **1** leap over; jump. **2** produce suddenly. *n* **1** leap; jump; bounce. **2** season following winter and preceding summer. **3** coil of wire, metal, etc., that cushions impact, causes movement of parts in a mechanism, etc. **4** natural flow of water forced by pressure from underground. **spring-clean** *n* thorough house-cleaning associated with springtime. *vt* clean in this way. **springy** *adj* **1** elastic; resilient; well-sprung. **2** able to leap or recoil.

springbok *n* African antelope.

sprinkle *vt,vi* scatter in small drops. *n* small quantity dispersed in drops; light shower.

sprint *vi* race or run very fast for a short distance. *n* short race at full speed.

sprout *vt* develop (shoots or buds). *vi* begin to grow; send forth. *n* **1** young bud or shoot. **2** short for Brussels sprout.

sprung *v pp* of **spring.**

spun *v pt* and *pp* of **spin.**

spur *n* **1** spiked or pointed device on the heel of a rider's boot for urging a horse on. **2** incitement; stimulus. **3** projecting small branch or hill range. **on the spur of the moment** on impulse. ~*vt,vi* (-rr-) goad; hasten.

spurt *vt,vi* 1 make a sudden intense effort. 2 send out a sudden jet or stream; spout. *n* 1 brief spell of intense activity. 2 sudden jet of liquid.

spy *n* secret agent watching others and collecting information. *vi* 1 watch. 2 ascertain; detect.

squabble *vi* dispute in a noisy way. *n* petty quarrel; wrangle. **squabbler** *n.*

squad *n* 1 small group of soldiers. 2 group or working party acting together.

squadron *n* 1 group of military aircraft. 2 group of warships forming part of a fleet.

squalid *adj* sordid; dirty; uncared for. **squalidly** *adv.* **squalor** *n* state of being squalid; repulsive dirtiness.

squander *vt* spend carelessly and wastefully.

square *n* 1 right-angled figure having four equal sides. 2 total obtained by multiplying a number by itself. 3 area of land, courtyard, etc., usually bounded on four sides by buildings. *adj* 1 of the shape of a square. 2 broad and straight. 3 relating to a measurement of area. 4 equal or fair. *adv* so as to be square. *vt* 1 form into a square. 2 multiply (a number) by itself. 3 make equal or fair. **square with** be equal or in agreement with; match up to. **squarely** *adv.* **squareness** *n.*

squash *vt,vi* crush or become crushed into or as if into a pulp. *n* 1 drink made from diluted fruit juice. 2 ball game played with racquets. 3 crushed mass or tight-packed crowd.

squat *vi* (-tt-) 1 sit down with knees bent up and heels against buttocks; crouch. 2 occupy a building or land without the consent of the legal owner. *adj* short and thick. **squatter** *n.*

squawk *vi* utter a loud raucous cry. *n* loud harsh cry.

squeak *vi* emit shrill note or cry. *n* shrill weak cry or grating noise. **squeaky** *adj.* **squeakiness** *n.*

squeal *vi* utter a long shrill cry of pain, terror, or excitement. *n* long shrill cry.

squeamish *adj* easily distressed, shocked, or disgusted; too sensitive.

squeeze *vt,vi* 1 subject or be subjected to pressure; press or be pressed out. 2 pack tightly; cram. 3 extort by threats. *n* 1 act of squeezing; state of being tightly pressed or packed. 2 government restrictions placed on commercial or financial activities.

squid *n* edible marine mollusc having a slender body and triangular tail fins.

squiggle *n,vi* twist; wriggle.

squint *vi* 1 be unable to focus both eyes in the same direction. 2 look obliquely; glance. *n* 1 defect in the alignment of the eyes. 2 sidelong or stealthy glance.

squire *n* country landowner, esp. of an old established family. *vt* attend or escort (a lady).

squirm *vi* 1 twist and turn; wriggle. 2 feel embarrassed or humiliated. *n* wriggling movement.

squirrel *n* 1 small nimble bushy-tailed rodent. 2 *inf* person who hoards.

squirt *vt,vi* eject or be ejected in a stream. *n* jet; stream.

stab *v* (-bb-) *vt* 1 wound or pierce with a pointed weapon. 2 give a sharp throbbing pain. *vt,vi* jab or strike (at). *n* act of stabbing; blow or wound.

stable[1] *adj* 1 firmly established or steady; unchanging. 2 not easily upset or overturned; constant. **stably** *adv.* **stability** *n* quality or state of being stable; steadiness. **stabilize** *vt,vi* make or become stable or permanent. **stabilizer** *n.*

stable[2] *n* 1 building where horses, etc., are kept. 2 group of horses, etc., kept by a particular owner or trainer. *vt,vi* provide with or keep in a stable.

stack *n* orderly pile or heap. *vt* 1 place in a stack; heap. 2 load; fill. **stack the cards** dishonestly or unfairly arrange (something) against the interests of others.

stadium *n, pl* **stadiums** *or* **stadia** ('steidiə) sports arena.

staff *n, pl* **staffs** *or* (for 3-6) **staves** 1 people employed by a company, individual, authority, etc. 2 officers appointed to assist a commanding officer. 3 rod; stick. 4 flag pole. 5 something capable of sustaining or supporting. 6 series of horizontal lines used in musical notation. *vt* provide with a staff.

stag *n* adult male deer. **stag party** *n* social gathering of men only.

stage *n* **1** elevated or allocated arena on which a performance takes place. **2** theatrical profession. **3** stopping place on a journey. **4** level or period of development. *vt* **1** put (a play, etc.) on the stage before an audience. **2** do for effect; contrive dramatically. **3** arrange and carry out. **stage manager** *n* person who organizes rehearsals, scenery, staging, etc., of a play.

stagger *vi,vt* move or walk unsteadily; totter. *vt* **1** startle; shock. **2** arrange at intervals. *n* unsteady movement; tottering gait. **staggeringly** *adv.*

stagnant *adj* **1** still; not flowing. **2** foul; putrid from standing still. **3** inert; languid. **stagnantly** *adv.* **stagnate** *vi* **1** cease to flow; putrefy. **2** fail to develop; become sluggish. **stagnation** *n.*

stain *n* **1** discoloration; spot; blemish. **2** dye or tint. *vi,vt* soil or discolour. *vt* **1** taint. **2** colour or dye. **stainless** *adj.* **stained glass** *n* glass coloured by metallic pigments fused into its surface.

stair *n* one in a series of steps. **stairs** *pl n* series of steps from one level to another. **staircase** *n* flight of stairs usually having a banister and containing structure.

stake[1] *n* **1** pointed stick or post for fixing into the ground. **2** post to which persons were tied and burnt to death. *vi* **1** tie or join with or to a stake. **2** mark a boundary with stakes. *vt* **1** register (a claim) to a plot of land, rights, etc. **2** support by tying to a stake.

stake[2] *n* **1** money risked in gambling. **2** amount that may be won. **at stake** in danger of being lost; at risk, at issue. ~*vt* bet; wager; risk.

stale *adj* **1** (of food, etc.) not fresh; altered by age. **2** out of condition or practice. **staleness** *n.*

stalemate *n* **1** one type of draw in a game of chess. **2** deadlock. *vt* cause to suffer a stalemate.

stalk[1] *n* **1** stem of a plant. **2** slender support; shaft.

stalk[2] *vt,vi* **1** walk stealthily (after); go after (prey). **2** walk stiffly or haughtily.

stall *n* **1** place for a single animal in a stable. **2** bench, table, booth, or barrow for displaying goods for sale. **3** theatre seat on the ground floor. **4** church seat, esp. for the choir. **5** covering for a finger or toe. *vt,vi* **1** stop (a car, motor, etc.) or make stop because of incorrect adjustment or handling. **2** put off; evade; delay.

stallion *n* male horse, esp. one kept for breeding.

stamina *n* power of endurance; strength.

stammer *n* speech defect in which particular sounds are uttered falteringly and sometimes repeated involuntarily. *vi,vt* speak or say with a stammer; utter brokenly.

stamp *vt,vi* crush or tread (on) heavily with the feet. *vt* **1** make a mark, symbol, or design on. **2** affix a postage stamp to. **3** make a deep impression; scar. **stamp out** suppress or abolish completely. ~*n* **1** heavy tread or pressure with the feet. **2** *also* **postage stamp** small piece of paper printed with a design, for affixing to mail as proof of postage paid. **3** seal, symbol, or mark. **4** device for producing a particular symbol or mark. **5** characteristic quality.

stampede *n* **1** sudden rush of frightened animals. **2** any impulsive action by a mass of people. *vi,vt* flee or cause to flee in panic. *vt* press a person into rash action.

stand *v* (stood) *vi* **1** be erect with the feet supporting the weight of the body. **2** move into such a position; rise; get up. **3** be positioned or located. **4** have a particular point of view. **5** remain; stay; adhere (to). **6** be a candidate; be nominated. *vt* **1** place; position; rest. **2** take the strain of; bear. **3** tolerate; put up with. **4** treat; pay for. **5** be subjected to (a trial). **stand by 1** be ready to act if needed. **2** remain loyal to. **stand down** give up a post, claim, etc. **stand for** represent; tolerate. **stand out** be conspicuous or prominent. **stand up for** defend; protect; fight for. ~*n* **1** platform. **2** article or piece of furniture for supporting something. **3** stall at a market, exhibition, etc. **4** position or point of view to be defended. **stand-by** *n* person or thing that may be relied upon in an emergency. **standing** *n* **1** rank; status; reputation. **2** duration; length of experience, etc. *adj* **1** erect. **2** permanent or continuing. **3** stagnant. **standstill** *n* complete cessation of movement or progress.

standard *n* **1** guideline; example. **2** principle; integrity. **3** flag; banner; emblem. **4** commodity on which a monetary system is based. **5** fruit or rose tree having a straight stem and no lower branches. *adj* serving as or conforming to a standard; average; accepted. **standardize** *vt* cause to conform to a standard; remove variations from. **standardization** *n.*

stank *v pt* of **stink.**

stanza *n* group of lines of verse forming a division of a poem.

staple[1] *n* bent length of wire for fastening. *vt* fasten with a staple or staples. **stapler** *n.*

staple[2] *n* **1** basic essential food. **2** grade of fibre in wool, flax, etc. *adj* basic; indispensable; standard.

star *n* **1** incandescent body in outer space seen in the night sky as a twinkling light. **2** figure with five or six pointed rays. **3** highly popular public entertainer. **4** asterisk. **5** planet influencing one's luck according to astrology; fate. *vt* (-rr-) **1** mark or cover with stars. **2** play the leading part or present as the leading performer. **3** mark with an asterisk. **starfish** *n* star-shaped invertebrate fish. **starry** *adj.*

starboard *n,adj* right-hand side of a vessel when one is facing forward.

starch *n* **1** carbohydrate present in many plants and vegetables. **2** this substance used as a stiffener after laundering fabrics. *vt* stiffen with starch. **starchy** *adj.* **starchily** *adv.* **starchiness** *n.*

stare *vi* look with fixed eyes. *n* act of staring.

stark *adj* **1** bleak; harsh; grim. **2** unelaborated; blunt. *adv* completely. **starkly** *adv.* **starkness** *n.*

starling *n* small gregarious bird with blackish feathers.

start *vt* **1** begin; set up. **2** set in motion. *vi* jump involuntarily as because of fright. *n* **1** beginning. **2** jerk; jump. **starter** *n.*

startle *vt* give a shock to; alarm; take aback. *vi* feel slight shock or alarm; be taken aback. **startlingly** *adv.*

starve *vi,vt* **1** die or make die from lack of food. **2** suffer or make suffer from hunger. *vi* be very hungry. **starvation** *n.*

state *n* **1** condition; situation; circumstances. **2** form; structure. **3** political community under a government. **4** status; rank. **5** splendour; dignified style. **6** *inf* distressed or anxious condition. *vt* declare; specify; utter. **stately** *adj* imposing; magnificent; dignified. **stateliness** *n.* **statement** *n* **1** act of stating. **2** something stated. **3** formal account. **4** financial account in detail.

statesman *n* wise revered politician. **statesmanlike** *adj.* **statesmanship** *n* skill and abilities involved in being a statesman.

static *adj* **1** at rest; unmoving. **2** not causing movement. **3** relating to interference in reception of radio signals. *n* disturbance in radio or television reception caused by electrical disturbances.

station *n* **1** fixed stopping place for a bus, train, etc. **2** position; status. **3** office or headquarters of the police, etc. *vt* assign a place or post to. **station-master** *n* official in charge of a railway station.

stationary *adj* fixed; still; permanently located.

stationer *n* person who sells writing materials, etc. **stationery** *n* writing materials, esp. note-paper and envelopes.

statistics *pl n* numerical data used to make analyses. *s n* study of the analysis of numerical data. **statistical** *adj* relating to numerical data. **statistically** *adv.* **statistician** *n* expert in statistics.

statue *n* sculpture or representation of a person, group, or an animal.

stature *n* **1** height of a person or animal standing upright. **2** moral or intellectual greatness.

status *n* **1** official or social position. **2** prestige; high rank. **status quo** the existing situation. **status symbol** object desired or owned for prestige purposes.

statute *n* **1** act, law, or decree made by Parliament or some other legislative body. **2** rule laid down by an institution or authority. **statutory** *adj* prescribed; authorized by statute.

stave *n* **1** strip of wood, esp. on the side of a barrel. **2** series of five lines on which music is written. **staves** *pl* of **staff** (defs 3–6).

stay[1] *vi* remain or be (for a time). *vt* check; delay. **stay the course** be able to finish in spite of difficulties. ~*n* **1** period of time spent; visit. **2** postponement.

stay² *n* support; prop; rope or cable supporting a ship's mast, etc. **stays** *pl n* corsets.

steadfast *adj* **1** unwavering. **2** resolute; loyal. **steadfastly** *adv*. **steadfastness** *n*.

steady *adj* **1** firmly balanced or supported. **2** regular; controlled; fixed. **3** constant. **4** reliable; sober. *vt,vi* make or become steady. **steadily** *adv*. **steadiness** *n*.

steak *n* thick slice of meat or fish.

steal *v* (stole; stolen) *vt* **1** unlawfully take away (another person's property). **2** obtain secretly; snatch. *vi* **1** thieve. **2** move quietly and unobtrusively; creep. **stealth** *n* furtive behaviour; secrecy; evasion. **stealthy** *adj*. **stealthily** *adv*.

steam *n* **1** vapour produced by boiling water. **2** mist left by water vapour. **get up steam** become excited or emotional. **let off steam** release pent-up emotion or energy harmlessly. ～*vi* **1** emit steam. **2** move by steam power. *vt* cook, iron, etc., using steam. **steamy** *adj*.

steel *n* **1** widely used strong hard alloy of iron and carbon. **2** quality of toughness. **3** steel weapon, esp. a sword. *vt* toughen; strengthen. **steel oneself** prepare oneself (to do something difficult or unpleasant). **steely** *adj* **1** of or like steel. **2** unwavering.

steep¹ *adj* **1** rising or sloping sharply; precipitous. **2** exorbitant; outrageous. **steeply** *adv*. **steepness** *n*. **steepen** *vi* become steep(er).

steep² *vt* soak thoroughly; immerse.

steeple *n* spire. **steeplechase** *n* horse race in which ditches, fences, etc., must be jumped.

steer *vt* guide; direct the course of (a vehicle, etc.). *vi* manoeuvre; guide. **steer clear of** keep away from.

stem¹ *n* **1** stalk of a plant. **2** anything resembling a stalk, such as the shaft of a pipe or wine glass. **3** unchanging part of a word to which inflexions are added. *v* (-mm-) **stem from** arise out of.

stem² (-mm-) *vt* stop the flow of; plug.

stencil *n* sheet of card, paper, or metal in which patterns or lettering have been cut in order to transfer the design to a further sheet or sheets. *vt* (-ll-) use or apply with a stencil.

Sten gun *n* lightweight machine gun.

step *n* **1** movement made by lifting the foot; pace. **2** manner of walking, dancing, etc. **3** single section of a flight of stairs. **4** single grade or stage on a scale. **5** short distance. **step by step** gradually. **take steps (to)** begin to control; initiate action (on). ～*vi* (-pp-) move by steps; walk. **step on 1** trample on; walk on or rest the foot on. **2** *inf* accelerate; go fast. **step up** increase; intensify activity. **step-ladder** *n* folding ladder with wide flat rungs.

stepbrother *n* son of one's stepmother or stepfather by another marriage.

stepdaughter *n* daughter of one's spouse by another marriage.

stepfather *n* man married by one's mother after the death or divorce of one's father.

stepmother *n* woman married by one's father after the death or divorce of one's mother.

stepsister *n* daughter of one's stepmother or stepfather by another marriage.

stepson *n* son of one's spouse by another marriage.

stereo *adj* short for **stereophonic**. *n* apparatus for reproducing stereophonic sound. **stereophonic** *adj* (of music, etc.) recorded through separate microphones and relayed through separate loudspeakers to give an impression of natural distribution of sound.

stereotype *n* **1** conventionalized idea, conception, or person that lacks variation or individuality. **2** solid metal printing plate cast from a mould made from movable type.

sterile *adj* **1** free from live bacteria. **2** unable to produce offspring, seeds, or crops; barren; unproductive. **sterility** *n*. **sterilize** *vt* **1** destroy bacteria in. **2** render incapable of producing offspring, seeds, or crops. **sterilization** *n*.

sterling *adj* **1** relating to British money. **2** (of silver) conforming to a special standard. **3** valuable; reliable; excellent. *n* British money.

stern¹ *adj* strict; severe; grim. **sternly** *adv*. **sternness** *n*.

stern² *n* **1** back section of a ship or aircraft. **2** rear; rump.

stethoscope *n* medical instrument for listening to the sounds of the body.

stew *vt* cook by long slow boiling or simmering. *n* dish, usually of meat, cooked by stewing.

steward *n* 1 person organizing the catering, seating, and sleeping arrangements, esp. on a ship; passenger attendant. 2 estate or household manager; organizer or helper at a public function, etc. **stewardess** *n* female attendant on a ship or airliner.

stick¹ *v* (stuck) *vt* 1 join or attach by using glue, paste, nails, pins, etc. 2 pierce; prod; thrust. 3 put or place carelessly or absent-mindedly. *vi* 1 become fixed, attached, or jammed; wedge. 2 remain close to. **stick out** 1 protrude; jut. 2 be conspicuous. **stick to** concentrate on for a length of time; adhere to. **stick up for** defend or support (a person, one's rights, etc.). **sticky** *adj* 1 tending to stick. 2 covered with glue, paste, etc. 3 *inf* awkward; tricky.

stick² *n* 1 wooden rod; thin detached branch; staff or cane. 2 rod used in certain sports. 3 anything resembling a stick in shape.

stiff *adj* 1 difficult to move, bend, or twist; rigid; not flexible. 2 (of persons) not moving easily; formal; not at ease socially. 3 strong. 4 (of prices) high. **stiff upper lip** stoicism. ~*n sl* corpse. **stiffly** *adv*. **stiffness** *n*. **stiffen** *vt,vi* make or become stiff. **stiffening** *n* substance used to stiffen something.

stifle *vt* 1 suffocate; choke. 2 suppress; put down. *vi* 1 die from suffocation; choke. 2 have a suffocating impression.

stigma *n* 1 mark or sign of disgrace; social blot. 2 that part of a flower that receives pollen. **stigmata** *pl n* marks of Christ's crucifixion. **stigmatize** *vt* denounce; brand.

stile *n* permanent set of steps or railings for climbing over a hedge, fence, etc.

still¹ *adv* 1 even now; yet. 2 even more. *conj* in spite of that. *adj* 1 quiet; hushed; calm; not agitated. 2 not fizzy. *vt* calm; subdue. *n* single photograph taken from a film. **stillborn** *adj* 1 born dead. 2 (of ideas, etc.) conceived but not put into practice. **still life** *n* painting or photograph of inanimate things.

still² *n* apparatus for distilling liquids by vaporizing and condensing.

stilt *n* 1 one of a pair of poles with platforms for the feet for walking above the ground. 2 supporting pole or pillar for a house, pier, etc.

stilted *adj* stiff; artificial; pompous.

stimulate *vt* 1 persuade; encourage; arouse. 2 inspire; excite mental activity in. 3 increase. **stimulation** *n*. **stimulant** *n* 1 anything, esp. a drink or drug, that produces extra mental or physical activity. 2 stimulus; spur. **stimulus** *n*, *pl* **stimuli** ('stimjulai) something that encourages, persuades, spurs on, or excites a response.

sting *vt,vi* (stung) 1 hurt by piercing the skin and secreting poison. 2 feel or cause to feel a piercing pain. 3 hurt (a person's feelings). 4 *sl* extort money (from), esp. by overcharging. *n* 1 act of or pain from stinging. 2 part of an insect, fish, or plant that causes a sting.

stink *vi* (stank *or* stunk; stunk) 1 smell disgusting or offensive. 2 *inf* (of a situation) be offensive or unpleasant. *n* disgusting smell. **stinker** *n* offensive person or thing.

stint *n* fixed amount; quota (of work). *vt* give small amounts to reluctantly; be ungenerous towards.

stipulate *vt,vi* insist (on) as a condition of agreement; require. **stipulation** *n*.

stir *v* (-rr-) *vt* 1 move or agitate (a mixture) with a spoon, etc. 2 move (slightly). 3 rouse; incite. *vi* move; become active. *n* 1 stirring movement. 2 disturbance; sensation. **stir-fry** *vt* fry (food, esp. vegetables) rapidly while stirring in pan.

stirrup *n* hooped metal footrest hanging either side of a horse's saddle.

stitch *n* 1 one unit in a row of sewing or knitting. 2 particular kind of stitch. 3 loop of thread used in surgery to close a wound, etc. 4 *inf* piercing pain in one's side. *vt,vi* sew using stitches.

stoat *n* small fur-covered mammal similar to but larger than a weasel.

stock *n* 1 store or supply of goods. 2 persons, animals, etc., having a common ancestor. 3 livestock. 4 unspecified number of shares. 5 liquid derived by cooking meat, bones, etc., in water. 6 flower having purple or white scented flowers. *vt* keep in supply; store. **stockbreeding** *n* breeding and rearing of livestock. **stockbroker** *n* person who

deals professionally in stocks and shares.
stock exchange *n* place or association for the buying and selling of stocks and shares. **stockpile** *n* store set aside for future use. *vt,vi* build a stockpile (of). **stocktaking** *n* making of an inventory of goods or assets in a shop or business.

stocking *n* tight-fitting nylon, woollen, or cotton covering for the leg and foot.

stodge *n inf* heavy not easily digestible food. **stodgy** *adj* thick and heavy; unpalatable.

stoical *adj* bearing suffering without showing pain or emotion; being resigned to one's lot. **stoically** *adv.* **stoicism** *n.*

stoke *vt,vi* tend and pile fuel into (a fire or furnace).

stole[1] *v pt* of **steal.**

stole[2] *n* woven or knitted shawl, scarf, or fur collar worn round the shoulders.

stolen *v pp* of **steal.**

stomach *n* **1** principal digestive organ lying between the gullet and the intestines. **2** appetite. *vt* **1** digest. **2** bear; tolerate.

stone *n* **1** hard compact rock material, used in building, etc. **2** lump of rock. **3** jewel. **4** hard-shelled part of certain fruit. **5** anything resembling a stone or made of stone. **6** unit of weight equal to 14 pounds (6.3 kilograms). *adj* made of stone. *vt* **1** throw stones at. **2** remove stones from. **stony** *adj* **1** made of, covered with, or like stone(s). **2** hostile; cold. **stony broke** completely penniless.

stood *v pt* and *pp* of **stand.**

stool *n* **1** backless seat for one person; footstool. **2** solid excreta.

stoop *vt,vi* bend (one's head and body) forward and down. *vi* lower oneself morally; demean oneself. *n* **1** act of stooping. **2** habitually bent posture.

stop *v* (-pp-) *vt,vi* cease; bring or come to an end; halt. *vt* **1** discontinue; cut off; prevent. **2** prevent the passage of air, liquid, etc., through; block; plug. **stop off** call (at); visit. ~*n* **1** halt; end; finish. **2** place at which a bus, train, etc., stops to let passengers enter or leave. **3** full stop. **stopgap** *n* temporary measure or substitute in an emergency, etc. **stoppage** *n* **1** act of stopping; state of being stopped. **2** obstruction. **3** cessation of work. **stopper** *n* **1** person or thing

that stops. **2** plug for a bottle or vessel. *vt* close with a stopper. **stopwatch** *n* watch that can be stopped and restarted for timing races, etc.

store *n* **1** stock set aside for future use; reserve supply; accumulation. **2** shop with several departments. **3** place where stock is kept. **in store 1** expected to happen. **2** set aside. **set store by** value greatly. ~*vt* make a store of. **store up** reserve for a future occasion; stock up. **storage** *n* keeping of stocks of goods for future use.

storey *n* floor or level of a building.

stork *n* large long-legged long-billed wading bird.

storm *n* **1** weather condition including a strong wind and often rain and thunder. **2** sudden outburst of noise, feelings, etc. **storm in a teacup** a lot of fuss over something unimportant. **take by storm 1** capture (a fortress) by a sudden massed attack. **2** bowl over; captivate. ~*vt* attack and capture suddenly. *vi* rage. **stormy** *adj* violent; tempestuous; relating to or portending a storm.

story *n* **1** tale; short narrative. **2** plot of a novel, etc. **3** *inf* lie; fib.

stout *adj* **1** fat; portly. **2** strong; sturdy. **3** brave. *n* strong dark ale. **stoutly** *adv.* **stoutness** *n.*

stove *n* device for cooking or heating, using gas, electricity, paraffin, etc.

stow *vt* put away; store. **stowaway** *n* person who hides on a ship or aircraft in order to avoid paying the fare.

straddle *vt,vi* stand or sit with one leg on either side (of); stand or sit astride.

straggle *vi* **1** sprawl; be scattered. **2** fall behind the main group; continue in small irregular groups.

straight *adj* **1** not crooked or curved. **2** direct. **3** rigid or erect. **4** honest; correct. *adv* **1** directly; in a straight line. **2** honestly. **straight away** immediately. **straighten** *vt,vi* make or become straight. **straighten out 1** make straight. **2** sort out or deal with (a problem). **straightforward** *adj* **1** uncomplicated; not difficult. **2** honest; open.

strain[1] *vt,vi* harm by stretching, exerting force, etc.; stress. *vt* **1** filter (a liquid). **2** make tense; demand excessive effort of. *n* tension; stress; act or instance of straining; demand.

strain² *n* 1 breed. 2 hereditary trait or tendency.

strand¹ *n* single thread from a wire, rope, etc.

strand² *vt,vi* run aground; beach. **stranded** *adj* abandoned; cut off; left helpless. ~*n* beach; shore.

strange *adj* 1 odd; peculiar. 2 unfamiliar; unusual; extraordinary. 3 foreign. **strangely** *adv.* **strangeness** *n.* **stranger** *n* person foreign to or not familiar with a particular place, area, or society.

strangle *vt* kill by throttling. **strangler** *n.* **stranglehold** *n* 1 choking grip. 2 force that suppresses freedom of movement or growth.

strap *n* thin strip, esp. of leather and with a buckle, for holding objects together. *vt* (-pp-) 1 bind with a strap. 2 beat with a strap.

strategy *n* overall plan of attack or campaign, esp. military; set of tactics. **strategic** *adj* relating to or important to an overall strategy.

stratum *n, pl* **strata** ('strɑːtə) *or* **stratums** 1 layer of rock. 2 level of society.

straw *n* 1 single dried stem of grain. 2 such stems used as a material for baskets, mats, etc., for packing, or as bedding for cattle, etc. 3 narrow tube of paper or plastic used for drinking. **the last straw** a final blow that makes a situation no longer tolerable.

strawberry *n* creeping plant bearing soft reddish edible fruit.

stray *vi* wander; digress; err; go astray. *n* homeless animal or child. *adj* strayed; lost; scattered.

streak *n* 1 narrow irregular stripe (of colour, etc.). 2 flash (of lightning). 3 slight surprising tendency or trace. *vt* mark with streaks. *vi* 1 dash. 2 *inf* run naked in public in order to amuse or shock. **streaky** *adj.* **streakiness** *n.*

stream *n* 1 flow (of water, blood, etc.); current. 2 brook. 3 educational division according to ability. *vi* 1 flow in a steady stream; pour out. 2 (of hair, a flag, etc.) wave in the air. *vt* divide (children) into educational groups according to ability. **stream-**

line *vt* 1 design (cars, aircraft, etc.) in a smooth narrow shape to give minimum air resistance. 2 remove inefficient areas from an operation or process.

street *n* road with houses along one or both sides. **streets ahead** wholly superior. **up one's street** in one's line or area of interest.

strength *n* 1 quality of being strong; power; force. 2 support; aid. 3 effectiveness. 4 potency; degree of concentration. **on the strength of** based on; relying on. **strengthen** *vt,vi* make or become strong (er).

strenuous *adj* vigorous; diligent; energetic. **strenuously** *adv.* **strenuousness** *n.*

stress *n* 1 anxiety or distress caused by pressure or tension. 2 importance; weight; emphasis. 3 emphasis put on a word or syllable. 4 deforming force applied to an object. *vt* emphasize; put the stress on.

stretch *vt* pull or push out; extend; pull taut. *vi* 1 extend. 2 be elastic. 3 flex one's muscles. *n* 1 act of stretching. 2 expanse. 3 continuous period of time. 4 *sl* term of imprisonment. **stretcher** *n* framework covered in canvas, etc., and used for transporting the sick or injured.

strict *adj* 1 accurate; precisely defined. 2 stern; severe; requiring complete obedience. **strictly** *adv.* **strictness** *n.*

stride *n* long step. **take in one's stride** cope with easily and without worrying. ~*vt,vi* (strode; stridden) walk (over) in strides.

strident *adj* harsh; grating.

strike *v* (struck) *vt* 1 hit; touch violently; collide with; beat. 2 light (a match). 3 occur to; remind; seem to. 4 reach suddenly or unexpectedly. *vt,vi* chime. *vi* 1 attack. 2 collide. 3 take part in a strike. **strike out** 1 delete; cross out. 2 embark on a new venture. **strike up** begin; set up; establish. ~*n* 1 stoppage of work by employees in support of a claim, etc. 2 discovery of oil, etc.

string *n* 1 twine or cord used for tying, binding, etc. 2 string-like object, such as a tendon or fibre. 3 taut cord of wire, catgut, etc., fitted to a musical instrument and producing a note when caused to vibrate. 4 linked series; chain; line. **strings** *pl n* stringed instruments of an orchestra. **no**

strings attached with no restricting factors or conditions. **pull strings** use influence in order to better oneself. ~*vt* (strung) fit strings to; thread. **string along** keep happy with false promises. **string out 1** spread out over a long area. **2** make (something) last a long time.

stringent *adj* strict; harsh; rigorous. **stringency** *n*. **stringently** *adv*.

strip[1] *v* (-pp-) *vt* **1** remove (the covering, outer layer, or clothes) from; lay bare. **2** take (an engine, etc.) apart. *vi* remove one's clothes. **striptease** *n* cabaret act in which the performer seductively removes clothing piece by piece.

strip[2] *n* narrow band; long piece. **strip cartoon** cartoon made up of a sequence of drawings.

stripe *n* **1** band of contrasting colour or texture. **2** band worn to show military rank. **striped** *adj* marked with stripes.

strive *vi* (strove; striven) try hard; endeavour; labour (to do something).

strode *v pt* of **stride**.

stroke[1] *n* **1** hit; blow. **2** single controlled movement in sports such as tennis, golf, etc. **3** style of swimming. **4** individual mark made by a brush or pen. **5** one of a series of movements. **6** apoplexy; damage to the brain's blood supply causing paralysis. **7** oarsman facing the cox. **8** chime of a clock.

stroke[2] *vt* caress with the hand; smooth. *n* act of stroking.

stroll *vi* walk for pleasure; saunter. *n* leisurely walk.

strong *adj* **1** physically powerful; forceful; difficult to break down, overcome, capture, or injure. **2** sound; healthy; vigorous. **3** positive; persuasive; drastic; effective; convincing. **4** concentrated; intense. *adv* **going strong** doing well; flourishing. **strongly** *adv*. **stronghold** *n* **1** fortress; garrison. **2** area where something prevails or has gained control. **strong-minded** having a powerful will; able to resist temptation.

struck *v pt* and *pp* of **strike**.

structure *n* **1** way in which things are put together; internal organization; make-up. **2** something constructed, esp. a building. *vt* give structure or form to; organize. **structural** *adj*. **structurally** *adv*.

struggle *vi* **1** fight hand to hand; wrestle; grapple. **2** labour; make great efforts; endeavour. *n* fight; strenuous effort.

strum *vt,vi* (-mm-) play (a stringed instrument) idly; sound a few chords (on).

strung *v pt* and *pp* of **string**. *adj* **highly strung** very nervous or tense.

strut[1] *vi* (-tt-) walk proudly to show off; swagger. *n* pompous gait.

strut[2] *n* supporting bar of wood, iron, etc.; slat; rung.

stub *n* piece left after something has been used or worn down, esp. a cigarette end or counterfoil of a ticket or cheque. *vt* (-bb-) accidentally strike (one's foot or toe) against. **stub out** crush and extinguish (a cigarette).

stubborn *adj* obstinate; difficult to persuade or influence; strong-willed. **stubbornly** *adv*. **stubbornness** *n*.

stuck *v pt* and *pp* of **stick**[1].

stud[1] *n* **1** ornamental heavy-headed nail or peg; flat knob. **2** button-like device for fastening collars or fronts to shirts. **3** threaded pin or bolt. *vt* (-dd-) **1** put studs into. **2** dot or cover (with jewels, stars, etc.).

stud[2] *n* **1** establishment for breeding pedigree animals, esp. horses. **2** horse or group of horses kept for breeding.

student *n* person who studies, esp. one following a course at a college or institute of further education.

studio *n* **1** artist's or craftsman's workroom. **2** place where broadcasts, recordings, or films are made. **studio couch** sofa that doubles as a bed.

studious *adj* **1** hard-working; fond of studying. **2** deliberate.

study *vt* **1** examine closely; peer at. **2** give special attention to; learn about; devote oneself to (a particular subject). *vi* follow a course of instruction; devote oneself to learning from books. *n* **1** act or process of studying; learning. **2** book, etc., produced by study. **3** room intended for study, reading, etc. **studied** *adj* deliberate; intentional; carefully considered; elaborately executed.

stuff *n* any type of material or substance. *vt* **1** cram full; overfill. **2** fill with stuffing. *vi* overeat. **stuffing** *n* **1** material with which objects are stuffed. **2** seasoned filling for meat, poultry, vegetables, etc.

stuffy adj **1** close; poorly-ventilated; oppressive. **2** inf prim and proper; easily shocked. **stuffily** adv. **stuffiness** n.

stumble vi trip and lose one's balance. **stumble on** or **across** discover by chance; come across. ~n act of stumbling. **stumbling block** obstacle; something that causes hesitation or doubt.

stump n **1** portion remaining after the main part of a limb or tree has been removed. **2** one of the three posts of a cricket wicket. vt inf puzzle; outwit. vi walk slowly and heavily. **stump up** inf produce or come up with (money).

stun vt (-nn-) **1** knock senseless; make unconscious. **2** amaze or shock. **stunning** adj inf extremely attractive.

stung v pt and pp of **sting**.

stunk v pt and pp of **stink**.

stunt[1] vt impede the growth or development of.

stunt[2] n dangerous, sensational, or acrobatic feat; anything done to attract attention or publicity. **stunt man** n person employed to perform dangerous feats in films or for entertainment.

stupid adj foolish; silly; not clever; dim-witted. **stupidity** n. **stupidly** adv.

sturdy adj strong; stout; solid. **sturdily** adv. **sturdiness** n.

sturgeon n large edible fish whose roe is eaten as caviar.

stutter n speech impediment causing hesitation or constant repetition of a word or syllable; stammer. vt,vi speak or say with a stutter.

sty[1] n pen for pigs.

sty[2] n small inflamed swelling on an eyelid.

style n **1** characteristic manner or fashion, esp. of practising a particular art, craft, or sport. **2** fashion; mode. **3** elegance; luxury; grandeur. **4** form; kind; sort. **5** title; mode of address. vt fashion or shape (hair, clothes, etc.). **stylist** n. **stylistic** adj relating to artistic style. **stylish** adj fashionable; smart.

stylus n **1** sapphire or diamond point used as a gramophone needle. **2** pointed writing or engraving instrument.

subconscious n area of one's mind, memory, and personality of which one is not aware. adj unconscious; stemming from the subconscious. **subconsciously** adv.

subcontract n (sʌb'kɔntrækt) agreement assigning part of the work specified in a contract to another party. vt,vi ('sʌbkɔntrækt) make a subcontract (regarding). **subcontractor** n person accepting a subcontract.

subcutaneous adj situated or introduced beneath the skin.

subdue vt suppress; put down; quieten.

subject n ('sʌbdʒikt) **1** something dealt with; object of study, analysis, discussion, examination, etc.; topic. **2** citizen under the authority of a state or ruler. **3** grammatical term for word(s) about which something is predicated or for the noun or pronoun acting as the doer of the verb in a sentence. **4** central musical theme of a composition. **subject to** adj **1** liable or prone to. **2** owing allegiance to. **3** conditional; dependent. adv conditionally. ~vt (səb'dʒɛkt) **1** force to experience or undergo. **2** bring under the control (of). **subjection** n. **subjective** adj **1** influenced by or arising from personal feelings rather than external evidence. **2** (in grammar) of the subject. **subjectively** adv.

sublime adj **1** of great moral or spiritual worth; majestic; awe-inspiring; supreme. **2** utter; extreme. n anything majestic or inspiring awe. vt,vi change directly from a solid to a gas. **sublimely** adv.

submachine gun n lightweight automatic gun.

submarine n vessel that can operate underwater. adj relating to or intended for use below water level.

submerge vt place under water; flood; cover with liquid. vi dip or go under water. **submergence** or **submersion** n.

submit vt,vi (-tt-) **1** surrender; yield. **2** put forward for consideration; suggest. **submit to** give in to; allow oneself to be under the control of. **submission** n **1** act of submitting. **2** suggestion. **submissive** adj timid and yielding.

subnormal adj mentally handicapped; below average intelligence.

subordinate adj (sə'bɔːdinit) **1** junior; inferior in rank, position, or importance. **2** (in grammar) subsidiary; dependent on a main clause. n (sə'bɔːdinit) person in an inferior position or rank. vt (sə'bɔːdineit) **1**

reduce to a lower rank or position; assign to a lesser place. **2** subdue. **subordination** n.

subscribe vt,vi pledge a regular sum of money (to). vi **subscribe to 1** agree to buy (a magazine, etc.) regularly. **2** approve of; agree with. **subscriber** n. **subscription** n **1** act of subscribing. **2** amount subscribed. **3** regular monetary contribution.

subsequent adj later; following or coming afterwards. **subsequently** adv.

subservient adj **1** showing exaggerated feelings of humility; obsequious. **2** serving an end; useful as a means. **subservience** n.

subside vi **1** sink in; collapse. **2** die down; decrease. **subsidence** n.

subsidiary adj supporting; supplementary; secondary. n thing that is subsidiary, esp. a company that is part of a group.

subsidy n state grant for an industry, cultural organization, etc.; official financial assistance. **subsidize** vt support with a subsidy; assist financially.

substance n **1** stuff; matter; material. **2** chief part; importance; essence; gist. **3** worth; value; foundation. **substantial** adj **1** ample; large; considerable. **2** solid; well-established; wealthy. **substantially** adv. **substantiate** vt provide proof of (a claim, charge, etc.); establish; show to be true.

substitute vt put (one person or thing) in place of another. vi serve as. n person or thing substituted. **substitution** n.

subtitle n **1** title, often explanatory, subsidiary to the main one. **2** caption translating dialogue in a foreign film. vt provide a subtitle for.

subtle adj **1** delicate; slight; not gross; hard to detect or perceive. **2** ingenious; perceptive; complex. **subtlety** n. **subtly** adv.

subtract vt take (an amount) away from; deduct. **subtraction** n.

suburb n residential area on the outskirts of a town or city. **suburban** adj **1** conventional; narrow-minded. **2** relating to a suburb.

subway n **1** underground passage enabling pedestrians to cross a busy road. **2** US underground railway.

succeed vi achieve one's purpose; be able; manage. vt come after; follow and take the place or position of.

success n **1** achievement of one's purpose. **2** achievement of fame and wealth. **3** triumph; anything that succeeds. **successful** adj. **successfully** adv.

succession n **1** series of things coming one after another. **2** act or process of succeeding to a title or position. **successive** adj happening one after another or in sequence. **successively** adv. **successor** n person taking over the position or rank of another.

succulent adj **1** juicy. **2** fleshy-leaved, as a cactus. **succulence** n. **succulently** adv.

succumb vi **1** yield or give in, esp. to powerful persuasion. **2** die.

such adj **1** of a particular kind. **2** so much or so many. pron **1** those who or that which. **2** the same. **as such 1** by or in itself. **2** in that role or capacity. **such as** for example; like. ~adv this or that amount of.

suchlike pron things of a similar sort. adj similar; of that sort.

suck vt,vi draw (liquid) into the mouth by action of the lips and tongue. vi **1** draw milk (from a mother's breast, an udder, etc.). **2** absorb; draw up (liquid). **3** hold in the mouth and lick. **4** make sucking actions. n act of sucking. **sucker** n **1** person that sucks. **2** sl person easily deceived. **3** device or organ, usually disc-shaped, that sticks to surfaces by suction. **4** shoot growing from the root of a plant.

suckle vt,vi give or suck milk from the breast.

suction n **1** action or process of sucking. **2** force causing a flow of liquid or gas or the adhesion of two surfaces.

sudden adj unexpected; happening quickly or without warning. n **all of a sudden** unexpectedly. **suddenly** adv. **suddenness** n.

suds pl n froth on the surface of soapy water; lather.

sue vt,vi take legal action (against). **sue for** beg; petition (for).

suede n soft leather with a velvety surface.

suet n hard fat found round the kidneys of sheep and cattle.

suffer vt,vi **1** endure; undergo mental or physical pain. **2** bear; tolerate. **suffer from** be ill, usually periodically, with. **suffering** n mental or physical pain; anguish.

sufficient *adj* enough; adequate for the purpose. **sufficiency** *n.* **sufficiently** *adv.*

suffix *n* letter(s) or syllable(s) put at the end of a word to change its part of speech, meaning, or grammatical inflexion.

suffocate *vt* kill by preventing or restricting breathing; smother. *vi* suffer restriction of one's breathing; die through lack of air; stifle. **suffocation** *n.*

sugar *n* sweet crystalline white or brown carbohydrate obtained from plants such as sugar cane or sugar beet. *vt* sweeten or coat with sugar. **sugary** *adj.* **sugar beet** *n* plant from the roots of which sugar is obtained. **sugar cane** *n* tall tropical grass from the canes of which sugar is obtained.

suggest *vt,vi* 1 propose; submit for consideration. 2 imply; intimate. 3 evoke; bring to mind; make (a person) think of. **suggestible** *adj* easily persuaded by suggestion. **suggestion** *n* 1 proposal; act of suggesting. 2 hint; trace. 3 implication. 4 production of an idea through association. **suggestive** *adj* 1 provoking thoughts (of). 2 having sexual overtones or implications.

suicide *n* 1 act of intentionally killing oneself. 2 person who has committed suicide. 3 action likely to ruin oneself or one's interests. **suicidal** *adj.*

suit *vt* 1 be convenient for; be acceptable to; satisfy. 2 (of clothes, colours, etc.) look attractive on or with. 3 be or make appropriate. 4 equip; adapt. *n* 1 matching jacket and trousers or skirt. 2 matching set or series, esp. of playing cards. 3 court case involving a claim. 4 wooing. **follow suit** copy; follow the example. **suitable** *adj* appropriate; proper; fitting. **suitably** *adv.* **suitability** *n.* **suitor** *n* 1 one who courts a woman. 2 petitioner. **suitcase** *n* portable case for luggage.

suite *n* 1 set of rooms. 2 set of furniture designed for one room. 3 group of attendants; retinue. 4 musical work of several connected movements, esp. based on dance forms.

sulk *vi* show offence or resentment by refusing to speak or cooperate. *n* act of sulking. **sulky** *adj* glumly withdrawn; sullen. **sulkily** *adv.* **sulkiness** *n.*

sullen *adj* silently unfriendly or uncooperative; morose and resentful; gloomy. **sullenly** *adv.* **sullenness** *n.*

sulphur *n* yellow nonmetallic element, used in making sulphuric acid. **sulphurous** *adj.*

sultan *n* the head of the Turkish empire.

sultana *n* 1 sweet seedless raisin. 2 wife, mother, or daughter of a sultan.

sultry *adj* 1 hot and humid. 2 sexually exciting; voluptuous.

sum *n* 1 result obtained from addition; total or whole. 2 amount of money. 3 simple arithmetical problem. *vt* (-mm-) find the sum of. **sum up** make a summary; review; appraise; judge. **summary** *n* review of the main points; précis. *adj* hasty and unceremonious. **summarily** *adv.* **summarize** *vt* make a summary of.

summer *n* season of the year between spring and autumn. **summery** *adj* characteristic or suggestive of summer.

summit *n* 1 highest point; peak. 2 zenith; highest point, esp. of a career. **summit conference** *n* high level discussion(s) between governments.

summon *vt* demand the presence of; call forth; call upon. **summons** *n* order to appear, esp. in court. ~*vt* issue a summons to.

sumptuous *adj* lavish; luxurious. **sumptuously** *adv.*

sun *n* star about which the earth rotates and from which it receives heat and light. *v* (-nn-) **sun oneself** expose one's body to the sun's warmth. **sunflower** *n* tall plant with large yellow flowers. **sunglasses** *pl n* spectacles with tinted lenses for protection from the sun's rays. **sunny** *adj* 1 exposed to the sun; full of or characterized by sunshine. 2 cheerful. **sunrise** *n* 1 daily appearance of the sun above the eastern horizon. 2 time when this occurs. **sunset** *n* 1 daily disappearance of the sun below the western horizon. 2 time when this occurs. **sunshine** *n also* **sunlight** light and warmth received from the sun.

Sunday *n* first day of the week; day of Christian worship.

sundry *adj* various; miscellaneous. **sundries** *pl n* miscellaneous articles; extras.

sung *v pp* of **sing.**

sunk *v pt* and *pp* of **sink. sunken** *adj* 1 situated below the surface; lying underwater; hollowed into the ground or floor. 2 fallen in.

super *adj inf* splendid; wonderful; first-rate.

superannuation *n* retirement pension. **superannuated** *adj* obsolete; out of date; antiquated.

superb *adj* excellent; splendid. **superbly** *adv.*

superficial *adj* shallow; perfunctory; of or on the surface; not probing or thorough. **superficiality** *n.* **superficially** *adv.*

superfluous (su:ˈpɔːfluəs) *adj* more than is wanted; unnecessary; left over. **superfluity** *n.* **superfluously** *adv.*

superhuman *adj* greater or more intense than seems humanly possible.

superimpose *vt* place (something) on top of something else.

superintendent *n* 1 official in charge of an institution, department, building, etc. 2 high-ranking police officer. **superintend** *vt* supervise; direct.

superior *adj* 1 greater; higher; better. 2 excellent; of high quality; high-ranking. 3 disdainful; conceited; indifferent. *n* person above one in rank or status. **superiority** *n.*

supermarket *n* large self-service food store.

supernatural *adj* 1 existing outside or beyond the laws of nature; magical; ghostly. 2 unnatural. *n* **the supernatural** supernatural creatures and happenings.

supersonic *adj* travelling faster than sound.

superstition *n* irrational or uninformed belief or fear, esp. in or of the supernatural or magic. **superstitious** *adj.* **superstitiously** *adv.*

supervise *vt,vi* 1 direct (work and workers); control. 2 act as a tutor (to). **supervision** *n.* **supervisor** *n.*

supper *n* light evening meal.

supple *adj* easily bent or manipulated; physically agile; flexible. **suppleness** *n.*

supplement *n* ('sʌplimənt) 1 something added to complete or extend something else. 2 additional section of a book, news-paper, etc. *vt* ('sʌpliment) add to; make supplements to. **supplementary** *adj.*

supply *vt* 1 provide; keep provided with. 2 fulfil; satisfy. *n* 1 stock; amount stored; something supplied. 2 availability or production of goods, esp. in relation to demand. **supplies** *pl n* stored goods; provisions.

support *vt* 1 hold up; bear the weight of. 2 back; stand up for; favour the cause of; assist. 3 maintain financially; provide for. 4 tolerate. *n* 1 act of supporting. 2 person or thing that supports. **supporting** *adj* secondary; not principal.

suppose *vt,vi* imagine; be inclined to think; assume. **supposition** *n.* **supposed** *adj* presumed. **supposed to** expected or obliged to. **supposedly** *adv* said or thought to be.

suppress *vt* 1 put down; crush. 2 keep concealed; withhold; stifle. **suppression** *n.* **suppressive** *adj.*

supreme *adj* most powerful; absolute; highest; greatest. **supremely** *adv.* **supremacy** *n* state of being supreme; dominance.

surcharge *n* extra amount added to the main bill, total, or cost. *vt* 1 impose a surcharge. 2 overload.

sure *adj* 1 convinced; having no doubt; confident. 2 certain; inevitable. 3 reliable; proven. **make sure (of)** 1 satisfy oneself (about); check. 2 make certain. ~*interj inf* certainly! of course! **surely** *adv* 1 in a sure way. 2 certainly; without doubt. **surety** *n* 1 pledge; guarantee; guarantor. 2 certainty.

surf *n* foam made by waves breaking along the shoreline; breakers. *vi* engage in surfing. **surfing** *n* sport of riding large waves while balancing on a board.

surface *n* 1 topmost or outer covering, layer, or edge. 2 outward appearance. *vt* provide with a surface; improve the surface (of). *vi* rise to the surface; emerge.

surfeit *n* excessive or superfluous amount; overabundance; excess, esp. of food consumed.

surge *vi* drive or press forward in a rush or flood. *n* surging action; gush; swell; onrush.

surgeon *n* 1 doctor who performs medical operations. 2 military or police doctor. **surgery** *n* 1 medical treatment involving operations. **2** doctor's consulting-room; hours for visiting a doctor. **surgical** *adj* used in or relating to surgery.

surly *adj* bad-tempered and unhelpful; sullen.

surmount *vt* overcome (an obstacle or problem); climb over. *vt,vi* be above; place on top of. **surmountable** *adj.*

surname *n* hereditary family name.

surpass *vt* excel; outdo; exceed; transcend. **surpassing** *adj* extraordinary.

surplus *n* **1** excess amount. **2** portion that remains after needs have been supplied, expenses subtracted, etc. *adj* extra; left over.

surprise *vt* **1** astonish; amaze. **2** take unawares. *n* **1** something unexpected. **2** amazement; astonishment. **surprised** *adj* revealing or expressing surprise. **surprising** *adj* causing surprise. **surprisingly** *adv.*

surrender *vt,vi* yield; give in; give up; abandon. *n* act of surrendering.

surreptitious *adj* done clandestinely; furtive; deliberately concealed. **surreptitiously** *adv.* **surreptitiousness** *n.*

surrogate *n* a person who acts in place of another or fills the role of another. **surrogate mother** *n* a woman who bears a child to give to another woman, often for money.

surround *vt* encircle; extend right round; crowd around. **surrounding** *adj* situated around or nearby. **surroundings** *pl n* environment; objects or area immediately surrounding one.

survey *vt* (sə'vei) **1** scan; look over carefully. **2** measure and record the area, elevations, and other geographical features of a piece of land. **3** make a detailed inspection of the condition of a building, etc. *n* ('sə:vei) **1** act or process of surveying. **2** review; analysis. **3** surveyor's report. **surveying** *n* study or practice of surveying land. **surveyor** *n* person employed to survey areas of land or buildings.

survive *vt,vi* continue to exist (following); come through; outlive. **survival** *n.* **survivor** *n.*

susceptible *adj* **1** prone (to); easily affected or influenced (by). **2** easily stricken by emotion; sensitive. **susceptibility** *n* **1** quality of being susceptible to. **2** weakness (for).

suspect *vt,vi* (sə'spekt) **1** believe to be true without proof; have a feeling (about); suppose. **2** be doubtful about. **3** think (a person) guilty of. *n* ('sʌspekt) person thought to have committed a crime, etc. *adj* ('sʌspekt) dubious; arousing suspicion.

suspend *vt* **1** hang (one object from another); hang from above. **2** postpone; defer; delay; keep unresolved. **3** remove temporarily from office, etc.; withdraw (someone's privileges). **suspension** *n* **1** act of suspending; condition of being suspended. **2** postponement; temporary dismissal. **3** mixture consisting of one substance dispersed in small particles in another. **suspension bridge** *n* bridge suspended from steel cables hung between two towers.

suspense *n* feeling of tension.

suspicion *n* **1** act of suspecting; doubt or mistrust. **2** hint; trace; vague idea. **suspicious** *adj* **1** dubious; likely to cause suspicion. **2** mistrustful; doubtful; likely to suspect. **suspiciously** *adv.*

suss *vt sl also* **suss out** **1** find out; discover. **2** investigate.

sustain *vt* **1** keep alive; maintain. **2** support; hold up. **3** endure; suffer; bear. **4** give strength to. **sustenance** *n* nourishment; food.

swab *n* **1** piece of cotton wool, etc., used in medicine to absorb liquid, blood, etc., or to take specimens. **2** mop; cloth used for washing floors, etc. *vt* (-bb-) mop up; wash.

swagger *vi* strut about; show off; behave conceitedly. *n* swaggering walk or manner.

swallow[1] *vt,vi* **1** take into the stomach through the throat; gulp. **2** *inf* believe or accept (something unlikely). **swallow up** consume; engulf. ~*n* act of swallowing.

swallow[2] *n* migratory bird with a forked tail.

swam *v pt* of **swim.**

swamp *n* permanently waterlogged ground, often overgrown. *vt* **1** drench with water; fill with water and sink. **2** overwhelm; flood.

swan *n* large long-necked water-bird. **swansong** final appearance; last work.

swank *vi* boast; show off. *n* **1** person who swanks. **2** act of swanking. **swanky** *adj.*

swap *vt,vi* (-pp-) *also* **swop** *inf* exchange (one thing for another). *n* 1 act of exchanging. 2 thing exchanged.

swarm *n* 1 dense mass of insects, esp. bees. 2 large crowd or throng. *vi* 1 flock or surge; be crowded (with). 2 (of bees) leave the hive in a swarm with a new queen.

swat *vt* (-tt-) strike or slap (an insect, etc.) with the hand, a newspaper, etc. *n* sharp slap.

sway *vt,vi* 1 swing, move, or bend to and fro; lean to one side. 2 persuade; influence. *n* 1 act of swaying. 2 rule; power. **hold sway** rule (over); be in control; dominate.

swear *vi* (swore; sworn) 1 use obscene or insulting language; utter curses or oaths. 2 declare or promise solemnly; make a binding legal promise or oath. **swear by** 1 take an oath on (a sacred object, etc.). 2 rely on absolutely. **swearword** *n* socially unacceptable word; profane or obscene word.

sweat *n* 1 moisture secreted from the pores of the skin; perspiration. 2 *inf* hard work; trouble. *vi* 1 exude sweat; perspire. 2 *inf* work hard; labour.

sweater *n* woollen garment covering chest, back, and arms; jersey; jumper; pullover.

swede *n* pale orange root vegetable related to the turnip.

sweep *vi,vt* (swept) 1 clean or clear with a broom, brush, etc. 2 proceed or move rapidly (through). 3 extend; curve. *n* 1 sweeping movement. 2 person who cleans chimneys. **sweeper** *n*.

sweet *adj* 1 tasting sugary; not sour. 2 kind; likeable; charming; cute. *n* 1 any type of small confection made principally from sugar. 2 pudding; dessert. **sweetly** *adv*. **sweetness** *n*. **sweeten** *vt* 1 make sweet (er). 2 make more acceptable. **sweetheart** *n* person who loves and is loved in return; darling. **sweet pea** *n* climbing garden plant with sweet-smelling flowers.

swell *vt,vi* (swelled; swollen) expand; bulge out; increase in size, volume, etc. *n* 1 act of swelling. 2 waves; action of waves when not breaking. 3 gradual increase in sound. **swelling** *n* 1 act of swelling. 2 something swollen, esp. a bruised or infected area of the body. **swollen-headed** *adj* conceited.

swerve *vi* make a sudden or abrupt sideways turn. *n* act of swerving.

swift *adj* speedy; rapid; prompt. *n* small widely distributed bird capable of fast sustained flight. **swiftly** *adv*.

swig *inf* *vt,vi* (-gg-) swallow; take gulps (from). *n* draught; gulp.

swill *vt,vi* 1 drink large quantities (of). 2 wash or slop down. *n* liquid food for animals, esp. pigs.

swim *v* (swam; swum) *vi* 1 move in or under water by movement of the body, limbs, tail, or fins, etc. 2 float; drift; appear to swim. 3 feel dizzy; swirl. *vt* cross by swimming. *n* act or period of swimming.

swindle *vt,vi* obtain by fraud; cheat; exploit unfairly. *n* instance of swindling. **swindler** *n*.

swine *n*, *pl* **swine** 1 pig. 2 brutish or beastly person.

swing *vt,vi* (swung) 1 move; sway; rock back and forth. 2 whirl about. 3 veer; turn. **swing round** turn suddenly in a sweeping movement. ~*n* 1 swinging movement or action. 2 seat suspended on ropes, etc., on which a person can swing himself.

swipe *n* lunging blow. *vt,vi* 1 make a swipe (at). 2 *inf* seize; steal.

swirl *vi* move round in a slow whirl, eddy, or series of curves. *n* 1 swirling action. 2 eddy; whirl.

swish *n* whistling sound as of a thin rod swung through the air; rustle; hiss. *vi,vt* make a swishing sound (with).

switch *vt,vi* exchange; transfer; shift; make a change. **switch on/off** turn on/off (an electric appliance, etc.). ~*n* 1 act of switching. 2 device for turning an electrical appliance, etc., on or off. 3 thin flexible cane or whip. **switchboard** *n* device fitted with many switches, esp. one used for relaying telephone calls.

swivel *vt,vi* (-ll-) turn (round) on a pivot. *n* device for joining two objects to allow one to move independently of the other.

swollen *v* *pp* of **swell**.

swoop *vt,vi* plunge or sweep down (on), as of a bird of prey, esp. to attack or carry off. *n* act of swooping.

swop *vt,vi,n* swap.

sword *n* weapon with a long pointed blade set in a handle. **swordfish** *n* edible marine fish with a long pointed jaw resembling a sword. **swordsman** *n* person skilled in the use of a sword.

swore *v pt* of **swear**.

sworn *v pp* of **swear**.

swot *vt,vi* (-tt-) *inf* study hard, esp. for an examination. *n* person who swots.

swum *v pp* of **swim**.

swung *v pt* and *pp* of **swing**.

sycamore *n* any of various kinds of deciduous tree having large indented leaves.

syllable *n* word or part of a word uttered as a single unit of sound.

syllabus *n, pl* **syllabuses** *or* **syllabi** ('siləbai) outline of work to be studied; summary of a course.

symbol *n* sign or object that represents something else, esp. something abstract. **symbolic** *adj.* **symbolically** *adv.* **symbolism** *n* the use of symbols to express abstract concepts, esp. in the arts. **symbolize** *vt* represent; stand for; act as a symbol of.

symmetry *n* harmonious balance between parts; regularity or correspondence of a pattern within a whole. **symmetrical** *adj.*

sympathy *n* quality of feeling for people's suffering or understanding their attitude; compassion; understanding. **sympathetic** *adj* 1 having sympathy. 2 understanding; congenial. **sympathetically** *adv.* **sympathize** *vi* share a person's feelings, esp. during suffering; have understanding; show sympathy. **sympathizer** *n* one who approves of or sanctions a cause, political party, etc., without being a member or an active supporter.

symphony *n* major orchestral composition in three or more movements.

symptom *n* 1 physical or mental change indicative of or due to a malfunction. 2 any sign indicative of a change, disorder, or condition. **symptomatic** *adj.*

synagogue *n* place of worship and instruction for members of the Jewish religion.

synchronize *vt,vi* work, operate, or occur at the same time or in harmony. **synchronization** *n.* **synchronous** *adj.*

syndicate *n* 1 association of people carrying out a business or joining in an enterprise. 2 agency that sells articles, etc., to several newspapers for simultaneous publication. *vt* publish through a syndicate.

syndrome *n* combination of symptoms or signs indicating a certain condition or disorder.

synopsis *n, pl* **synopses** (si'nɔpsi:z) brief summary, précis, or outline, esp. of the plot of a novel, play, etc.

synthesis *n, pl* **syntheses** ('sinθəsi:z) combination or fusing of parts into a whole; whole thus formed. **synthetic** *adj* 1 artificial; false; man-made. 2 produced by or relating to a synthesis.

syphilis *n* serious contagious type of venereal disease. **syphilitic** *adj.*

syringe *n* device for sucking in liquid and/or forcing it out in a spray or jet, esp. one used for injecting fluid into the body. *vt* clean out or spray using a syringe.

syrup *n* thick solution of sugar and water or juice; treacle. **syrupy** *adj.*

system *n* 1 group of coordinating parts forming a whole. 2 carefully organized set of related ideas or procedures. **systematic** *adj* methodical; regular; following a system.

T

tab *n* small flap or strip of cloth, paper, etc. **keep tabs on** keep a check or watch on.

tabby *adj* (of cats) brown or grey with dark stripes or blotches. *n* tabby cat.

table *n* 1 piece of furniture with a flat top and legs or supports, usually high enough to sit at. 2 organized list, chart, index, etc. **turn the tables on** place in an inferior or losing position. ~*vt* put forward for future discussion. **tablespoon** *n* large spoon used for serving food. **table tennis** *n* game played with round bats and a small light ball on a table fitted with a low net.

tablet *n* 1 pill. 2 inscribed stone slab or plaque. 3 cake (of soap).

taboo *n also* **tabu** act, object, or word that is forbidden in a particular society or religion. *adj* forbidden.

tack *n* 1 large-headed short nail for fastening things. 2 direction taken by a sailing ship according to the angle of the wind. 3 method of approach; course of action. *vt* 1 fasten with tacks. 2 sew together with loose temporary stitching; gather together loosely. *vi* steer a course along a different tack.

tackle *n* 1 gear or equipment, esp. for fishing. 2 set of ropes used in a pulley system. 3 (in rugby football) act of seizing a player's legs so that he will give up the ball. 4 attempt to get the ball from another player in football. *vt* 1 attempt or attack (something difficult). 2 approach or deal with (a difficult or unwilling person, situation, etc.). 3 perform a tackle on in football.

tact *n* sensitivity to other people's feelings or to situations that require delicate and discreet handling. **tactful** *adj.* **tactfully** *adv.*

tactic *n* manoeuvre; act directed towards a goal. **tactics** *pl n* strategy; plan of action. **tactical** *adj.* **tactically** *adv.*

tadpole *n* completely aquatic stage in a frog's or toad's life during which the legs develop and the tail and gills disappear.

taffeta *n* strong stiff satin-like cloth.

tag *n* small label or indentity disc. *vt* (-gg-) label; identify. **tag along** accompany; go along.

tail *n* 1 end part of an animal's body that is an elongation of the backbone. 2 back or end part, section, or projection. **turn tail** flee; run away. ~*vt,vi* 1 follow and observe (a person's actions), esp. without being noticed. 2 take the tail from. **tail off** gradually diminish or deteriorate. **tailback** *n* line of vehicles stretching back from something blocking or slowing down traffic flow. **tails** *s n* side of a coin not bearing the sovereign's head.

tailor *n* 1 person employed to make garments which require careful fitting, esp. those for men. 2 person selling men's clothes. *vt,vi* 1 make and fit (suits, etc.). 2 adapt; alter to suit individual needs.

taint *n* trace of some defect, infection, corrupting influence, etc. *vt* infect; stain; spoil.

take *vt* (took; taken) 1 receive or accept (something offered). 2 bring into one's possession; help oneself to; remove. 3 accompany to a particular destination. 4 capture; seize. 5 grasp; grip; hold. 6 eat, drink, or swallow (medicine, tablets, etc.). 7 steal. 8 select; use. 9 transmit; transport; convey. 10 keep a record of. 11 last; be the time required for. 12 require; be necessary for.

13 have accommodation for. 14 regard; consider. 15 subtract; deduct. 16 study. **take in** deceive; swindle. **take off** 1 remove. 2 become airborne. 3 impersonate; mimic. **take on** accept as a duty or commitment. **take out** 1 extract; delete. 2 escort. 3 acquire (a licence, insurance, etc.). **take over** assume control. **take to** find pleasure in; develop a liking or skill for. **take up** pursue; adopt; become involved in. **take-off** *n* 1 act of jumping or lifting off the ground. 2 satirical imitation. **take-over** *n* act of taking over and assuming control, esp. of a business, government, etc. **takings** *pl n* money obtained in the course of business during a particular period.

talcum powder *n* very fine scented body powder.

tale *n* story; narrative; legend. **tell tales** 1 report another's misdoings. 2 tell lies.

talent *n* ability; skill; special gift or aptitude.

talk *vi,vt* 1 communicate by means of speech. 2 discuss; express by speaking. 3 chatter; gossip. *n* 1 manner of speaking. 2 speech or brief lecture. 3 gossip. **talkative** *adj* tending to talk a lot; chatty.

tall *adj* large in height; not small. **tall order** difficult commission. **tall story** *or* **tale** *n* unlikely or exaggerated account or story.

tally *vi* correspond; agree. *vt* add up; reckon. *n* 1 reckoning; score; bill. 2 notched stick for recording numbers.

talon *n* claw, esp. of a bird of prey.

tambourine *n* small shallow drum with metal discs, which clink when shaken.

tame *adj* 1 (of animals) not wild; not aggressive towards or frightened of humans. 2 unexciting; unadventurous. *vt* make tame.

tamper *vi* interfere; meddle.

tan *n,adj* light brown. *n* skin browned by the sun. *vt,vi* (-nn-) 1 make or go brown. 2 turn (hides) into leather.

tang *n* sharp taste.

tangent *n* straight line that touches but does not intersect a curve. **go off at a tangent** digress; change the subject or line of thought. **tangential** *adj* 1 relating to tangents. 2 connected but irrelevant.

tangerine *n* type of small sweet orange.

tangible *adj* 1 able to be touched. 2 visible; factual; real.

tangle *n* muddle; confused web of knots; intricate mass. *vt,vi* make into a tangle; muddle.

tango *n* Latin-American ballroom dance.

tank *n* 1 large container for keeping or storing liquids. 2 large armour-plated military vehicle.

tankard *n* large mug with a handle, used esp. for beer.

tanker *n* ship or lorry built for carrying liquids in bulk.

tantalize *vt* tease by offering or presenting something desirable that cannot be attained.

tantrum *n* hysterical fit of bad temper.

tap[1] *vt,vi* (-pp-) strike a quick gentle blow (on). *n* tapping action or sound. **tap dancing** *n* style of dancing involving complicated heel and toe tapping steps.

tap[2] *n* device with a screw and washer for controlling the flow of liquid from a pipe or container. **on tap** constantly available. ~*vt* (-pp-) 1 sap; drain off; extract. 2 fit a bugging device to (a telephone, etc.) so as to intercept or overhear calls.

tape *n* 1 strip of flexible resistant material for binding, mending, etc. 2 length of tape stretched across the finishing line of a race track or cut symbolically to open a fête, etc. 3 strip of plastic magnetized recording tape. *vt* 1 bind or stick together with tape. 2 record on tape. **tape-measure** *n* length of tape marked off with measurements; flexible rule. **tape-recorder** *n* device for recording sound on magnetic tape.

taper *vt,vi* make or become gradually thinner at one end; tail off. *n* very thin candle.

tapestry *n* heavy fabric having a picture or design woven by hand in coloured threads.

tar *n* thick black sticky coal-based substance used in road building, wood preserving, etc. *vt,vi* (-rr-) cover with tar.

target *n* 1 object or person to be aimed at or attacked. 2 goal or objective.

tariff *n* 1 tax or list of taxes levied on imported goods. 2 fixed schedule of charges or prices.

tarnish *vt,vi* spoil the shine or lustre (of). *n* loss of shine or lustre.

tart[1] *adj* 1 sharp to the taste; acid. 2 sarcastic.

tart[2] *n* 1 small pie or flan with a sweet filling. 2 *sl* prostitute.

tartan *n* woollen plaid fabric in different patterns and colours corresponding to those of various Highland Scottish clans.

task *n* particular job or piece of work; chore. **take to task** reprove; censure.

tassel *n* ornamental knot with a bunch of loose threads.

taste *vt,vi* 1 sense the flavour (of) with one's tongue. 2 try; have a short experience of. 3 have the flavour (of). *n* 1 flavour. 2 sense by which one perceives flavour. 3 ability to make aesthetic judgment; discernment. 4 fineness or elegance of style, manners, etc. 5 particular preference. 6 small amount; trace; hint. **tasteful** *adj* elegant; fitting. **tasteless** *adj* 1 not strongly flavoured; insipid. 2 not tasteful; tactless. **tasty** *adj* good to eat.

tattoo[1] *vt* permanently mark (the skin) by putting indelible stains into pricked designs. *n* design made by tattooing.

tattoo[2] *n* 1 military entertainment involving marching and music, usually at night. 2 signal sounded on a drum or bugle recalling soldiers to their quarters for the night. 3 continuous drumming.

taught *v pt* and *pp* of **teach.**

taunt *vt* jeer at; provoke; tease. *n* jeer; insulting remark.

Taurus *n* second sign of the zodiac, represented by the Bull.

taut *adj* tightly stretched; having no slack; tense. **tautness** *n.*

tavern *n* public house; inn.

tax *n* 1 money demanded by law to be paid according to income, assets, goods purchased or imported, etc. 2 difficult or onerous obligation, demand, etc.; burden. *vt* 1 impose a tax on. 2 put a burden on; strain. **taxation** *n* system of imposing taxes or the amount of tax payable.

taxi *n* car with a driver for public hire. *vi* (of aircraft) move along the ground on landing or before take-off. *vt* cause (an aircraft) to taxi.

tea *n* 1 evergreen shrub grown in East Asia for its pungent leaves. 2 drink made from infusing dried tea leaves in boiling water. **3** meal between lunch and supper at which tea is drunk. **tea-cloth** *n also* **tea-towel** cloth for drying dishes.

teach *vt,vi* (taught) instruct; give lessons (in); show (a person) how to do something. **teacher** *n.* **teaching** *n* **1** ability to teach; knowledge or practice of teaching. **2** set of doctrines.

teak *n* large tree found in SE Asia with hard orange-brown wood, used for furniture, etc.

team *n* **1** group of people working together, esp. in order to compete against others. **2** group of horses, dogs, etc., pulling together. *v* **team up with** join with in order to pool resources and work in harmony.

tear¹ (tiə) *n also* **teardrop** drop of salty liquid that falls from the eye. **tearful** *adj* **1** liable to cry. **2** sad. **tear-gas** *n* type of gas that makes the eyes water, used to disperse rioting crowds, etc.

tear² (tɛə) *v* (tore; torn) *vt,vi* divide; split; rip. *vi* hurry; rush. **tear down** pull down; destroy. **tear off 1** pull or pluck off, esp. violently. **2** *inf* do in a great hurry. **tear up 1** divide into small pieces, strips, etc. **2** pull up; destroy. ~*n* torn hole; slit.

tease *vt,vi* **1** torment by joking; mock; make fun of. **2** draw out; comb out; disentangle. *n* person given to teasing others.

teat *n* **1** nipple. **2** feeding nipple on a baby's bottle.

technical *adj* **1** relating to a technique, method, or skill. **2** relating to specialized industrial or mechanical skills and crafts or to technology. **technically** *adv.*

technician *n* person skilled in the technical processes of a craft, science, or industry.

technique *n* **1** method of performing some skill; system of practical procedures. **2** skill.

technology *n* **1** application of scientific ideas to industry or commerce. **2** methods and equipment so used. **technological** *adj.* **technologist** *n.*

tedious *adj* **1** boring; monotonous. **2** tiresome. **tediously** *adv.* **tedium** *n.*

tee *n* **1** small peg that supports a golf ball for the first stroke at each hole. **2** elevated area from which this stroke is played. *v* **tee off 1** drive the ball from the tee. **2** start.

teenager *n* person aged between 13 and 19.

teeth *n pl* of **tooth. get one's teeth into** begin to cope with or tackle seriously. **teethe** *vi* (esp. of babies) produce teeth.

teetotal *adj* refusing to drink or serve alcoholic drinks. **teetotaller** *n* teetotal person.

telegram *n* message transmitted by telegraph.

telegraph *n* method of or apparatus for transmitting messages using radio signals or electric impulses sent along wires. *vt,vi* send a telegram to. **telegraphy** *n.*

telemessage *n* message sent by telex or telephone.

telepathy *n* human communication through inexplicable channels. **telepathic** *adj.*

telephone *n* system or apparatus for verbal communication over a distance, usually using electric impulses sent back and forth along a wire. *vt,vi* call or talk to by telephone; phone. **telephonist** *n* operator of a telephone switchboard.

telescope *n* **1** optical instrument using lenses or mirrors to magnify distant objects. **2** instrument, esp. one using radio or light waves, to study astronomical bodies. *vt,vi* make or become shorter, compressed, or crushed. **telescopic** *adj.*

teletext *n* written data, such as business news, transmitted by companies for viewing on a television screen.

television *n* **1** process of or apparatus for using high-frequency radio waves to transmit and receive visual images with accompanying sound. **2** radio broadcasts received on a television. **televise** *vt,vi* record or broadcast by means of television.

telex *n* telegraph service or apparatus for transmitting printed messages.

tell *v* (told) *vt,vi* inform; let know. *vt* **1** relate; recount; express in words; describe. **2** order; instruct. **3** disclose; reveal; confess. *vi* reveal secrets; inform against someone. **can tell** be able to discover, understand, distinguish, etc. **tell off** scold. **telltale** *adj* betraying; serving to reveal something hidden. *n* person given to informing on others.

temper *n* **1** state of mind; mood. **2** angry fit; rage; tendency to become angry. *vt* **1** modify; moderate; alleviate. **2** strengthen (metal) by sudden changes of temperature.

temperament *n* nature; disposition; person's style of thinking and behaviour. **tem-**

peramental *adj* **1** given to violent changes of mood; excitable. **2** unreliable.

temperate *adj* **1** mild in temperature. **2** moderate; restrained; even-tempered.

temperature *n* **1** measured or approximate degree of hotness of something. **2** fever.

tempestuous *adj* stormy; violent.

temple[1] *n* **1** place of worship dedicated to a particular deity. **2** sacred place.

temple[2] *n* flat area on either side of the forehead.

tempo *n* speed at which a conductor or performer chooses to play a piece of music.

temporal *adj* existing in or limited by time; not spiritual; earthly. **temporally** *adv.*

temporary *adj* intended to be used for a short time; not permanent; passing. **temp** *n* *inf* person not employed on a permanent basis. **temporarily** *adv.*

tempt *vt* persuade or induce (a person) to try or do something undesirable; attract; seduce; influence. **temptation** *n.*

ten *n* **1** number equal to one plus nine. **2** group of ten persons, things, etc. **3** *also* **ten o'clock** ten hours after noon or midnight. *adj* amounting to ten.

tenacious *adj* holding or sticking firmly; stubbornly persisting. **tenaciously** *adv.* **tenacity** *n.*

tenant *n* person who occupies a house, flat, farm, etc., for payment of rent. **tenancy** *n* state of being a tenant or the period during which this occurs.

tend[1] *vt* look after; care for.

tend[2] *vi* be inclined or likely (to); have the effect of. **tendency** *n.*

tender[1] *adj* **1** soft; delicate; not hardy. **2** gentle; loving; compassionate. **3** painful when touched; sensitive. **4** easily chewed. **5** youthfully innocent; vulnerable. **tenderly** *adv.* **tenderness** *n.* **tender-hearted** *adj* easily moved to pity. **tenderize** *vt,vi* make (food) soft and easy to chew.

tender[2] *vt,vi* offer for acceptance or settlement. *n* offer of goods or services at a fixed rate.

tendon *n* band or sheet of fibrous tissue by which muscle is attached to bone.

tendril *n* threadlike shoot of a plant enabling it to cling to a support while climbing.

tenement *n* **1** rented room or flat in a block, esp. one in a poor quarter of a city. **2** property held by a tenant.

tennis *n* game for two or four players played by hitting a ball over a net with rackets.

tenor *n* **1** general meaning; tone; direction. **2** instrument or male voice with a range between that of baritone and alto.

tense[1] *adj* **1** anxious; in suspense; overwrought. **2** taut; strained; stretched. *vt* make tense. **tensely** *adv.* **tenseness** *n.* **tensile** *adj* able to be stretched. **tension** *n* **1** stretching or state of being stretched or strained. **2** excitement; suspense. **3** anxiety or unease caused by suppressed emotion.

tense[2] *n* form of a verb indicating the time of action.

tent *n* canvas portable shelter for camping, etc.

tentacle *n* slender flexible organ of various invertebrates, used for feeding, grasping, etc.

tentative *adj* **1** hesitating; cautious. **2** provisional.

tenth *adj* coming between ninth and eleventh. *n* **1** tenth person, object, etc. **2** one of ten equal parts; one divided by ten. *adv* after the ninth.

tenuous *adj* **1** thin; slender; flimsy. **2** subtle; weak.

tenure *n* holding of land or office.

tepid *adj* **1** slightly warm; lukewarm. **2** unenthusiastic.

term *n* **1** period of time for which something occurs or is in force, as a period of teaching in a college, school, etc. **2** word used in specialized field. **3** end of pregnancy. **terms** *pl n* **1** conditions of an agreement, bargain, etc. **2** relationships between people. **come to terms** form an agreement; reconcile. **in terms of** as expressed by. ~*vt* define (something) as; call.

terminology *n* set of terms specific to any particular field of study. **terminological** *adj.*

terminate *vt,vi* bring or come to an end. **termination** *n.* **terminal** *adj* of, at, or marking an end or limit; final. *n* **1** end of a transport route. **2** either end of an open electrical circuit. **terminally** *adv.*

terminus *n, pl* **termini** ('tɔːminai) *or* **terminuses** 1 boundary points; final point reached. 2 end of a railway, airline, or bus route.

terrace *n* 1 raised bank or walk in a garden. 2 flat area cut into a slope, often for crop cultivation. 3 balcony; flat rooftop. 4 row of similar adjoined houses.

terrestrial *adj* 1 of or on earth; earthly. 2 living or growing on land rather than in the sea or air.

terrible *adj* 1 causing terror; appalling; very bad. 2 *inf* excessive; outstanding. **terribly** *adv*.

terrier *n* small dog of various breeds originally used in hunting out animals underground.

terrific *adj* 1 frighteningly large; instilling terror. 2 *inf* amazingly good; enjoyable. **terrifically** *adv*.

terrify *vt* cause terror in; frighten.

territory *n* area regarded as owned by the state or a social group or individual or animal. **territorial** *adj*. **territorially** *adv*.

terror *n* 1 extreme fear. 2 anything causing fear or dread. 3 *inf* nuisance; troublesome person. **terrorist** *n* person employing organized violence and intimidation to obtain political objectives. **terrorism** *n*. **terrorize** *vt* manipulate by inspiring terror.

terse *adj* concise; curt.

Terylene *n Tdmk* type of synthetic fibre used as textile yarn.

test *n* any critical trial or examination to determine the merit or nature of something. *vt* conduct a test on; examine. **test case** *n* legal case that establishes a precedent. **test match** *n* international cricket match. **test-tube** *n* glass tube used in conducting chemical experiments.

testament *n* 1 one of the two major divisions of the Bible (the Old Testament and the New Testament). 2 act of testifying, as to religious faith. 3 (in law) will.

testicle *n* one of two glands in males producing sperm and male sex hormones.

testify *vi,vt* bear witness; affirm; give evidence.

testimony *n* evidence; proof; declaration. **testimonial** *n* 1 written testimony of character. 2 gift presented as a tribute or token of respect.

tether *n* rope or chain by which an animal is secured. **at the end of one's tether** at the end of one's patience or ability to withstand. ~*vt* fasten with a tether; tie.

text *n* 1 main section of written or printed words of a book as distinguished from illustrations, the index, etc. 2 passage from the Bible. **textual** *adj*. **textbook** *n* book used as a standard source for a particular course of study.

textile *n* woven fabric or cloth.

texture *n* 1 surface, arrangement of strands, etc., of a material, esp. as perceived by the sense of touch. 2 quality, esp. of music.

than *conj* 1 expressing the second stage of a comparison. 2 expressing an alternative after *rather, sooner,* etc.

thank *vt* 1 express gratitude to. 2 blame. **thankful** *adj*. **thankless** *adj*. **thanks** *pl n, interj* expression of gratitude, relief, etc.

that *adj* relating to the person or thing specified, esp. one further away than or different from another. *pron* 1 the particular person or thing so specified. 2 who(m) or which. *adv* so; to such an extent. *conj* introducing a noun clause. **that's that** there is ‧ more to be said or done.

thatch *n* arrangement of straw, reeds, etc., used as a roof covering. *vt,vi* cover with a thatch.

thaw *vt,vi* 1 melt after being frozen. 2 make or become less hostile, frigid, etc. *n* period or process during which snow or ice melts.

the *def art* preceding a noun. *adv* used for emphasis or to express a comparative amount or extent.

theatre *n* 1 building in which plays, operas, etc., are performed. 2 lecture hall. 3 *also* **operating theatre** room equipped for carrying out surgery. 4 drama. 5 business of working in or for a theatre. **theatrical** *adj*.

theft *n* crime of stealing another's property.

their *adj* belonging to them. **theirs** *pron* those things belonging to them.

them *pron* those people or things. **themselves** *r pron* 1 their own selves. 2 their normal selves.

theme *n* 1 main idea or concept with which a work of art, discussion, etc., is concerned; topic. 2 recurring melody.

then *adv* **1** at the particular time referred to. **2** immediately afterwards; next. **3** in that case. *adj* functioning at that time. *n* that time.

theology *n* study of religion and the nature of God. **theological** *adj.* **theologian** *n.*

theorem *n* statement that is to be proved by logical reasoning.

theory *n* **1** system or formula as an explanation of a particular phenomenon. **2** body of abstract ideas or principles, esp. as distinguished from practice. **theoretical** *adj.* **theoretically** *adv.* **theorize** *vi* speculate; formulate a theory.

therapy *n* course of treatment designed to cure various disorders of the body or mind. **therapeutic** *adj.* **therapist** *n.*

there *adv* **1** in, to, at, or towards that place. **2** at that point. *pron* used with forms of *be, can,* etc., to introduce a sentence or clause. *n* that position. *interj* expression of consolation, victory, pride, etc. **thereabouts** *adv also* **thereabout** in that approximate place or position. **thereafter** *adv* after that time; from then on. **thereby** *adv* thus; by those means. **therefore** *adv* so; consequently; for that reason. **thereupon** *adv* at which point; after which.

thermal *adj* of or relating to heat. *n* rising current of warm air.

thermodynamics *n* study of the relationships between work, heat, and other forms of energy.

thermometer *n* any instrument used to measure temperature.

thermonuclear *adj* involving fusion of two atomic nuclei, with consequent production of large amounts of heat. **thermonuclear bomb** *n* hydrogen bomb.

Thermos flask *n also* **Thermos** *Tdmk* container with double walls enclosing a vacuum to prevent heat transfer, used for keeping food or drink hot or cold.

thermostat *n* automatic device to maintain a room, enclosure, etc., at a constant temperature. **thermostatic** *adj.* **thermostatically** *adv.*

these *adj* form of **this** used with a plural noun.

thesis *n, pl* **theses** ('θi:si:z) **1** original work submitted by a candidate for an academic degree. **2** hypothesis; proposition.

they *pron* **1** two or more persons or things when used as the subject in a sentence or clause. **2** people in general.

thick *adj* **1** relatively deep, wide, or fat; not thin. **2** measured by width or diameter. **3** densely layered, arranged, etc. **4** not watery or runny. **5** *inf* stupid. **6** having a broad accent. **a bit thick** unfair; unreasonable. **through thick and thin** throughout both good and bad periods. *adv also* **thickly** so as to be thick. **thickness** *n.* **thicken** *vt,vi* make or become thick(er). **thick-skinned** *adj* **1** insensitive, esp. to criticism. **2** having a thick hide or outer layer.

thief *n, pl* **thieves** person committing theft. **thieve** *vt,vi* commit theft; steal.

thigh *n* that part of the leg above the knee.

thimble *n* small cap worn over the fingertip whilst sewing.

thin *adj* **1** relatively narrow; not thick. **2** slim; slender; not fat. **3** not densely layered, arranged, etc.; sparse. **4** watery or runny. **5** lacking depth of quality; not rich. *adv also* **thinly** so as to be thin. *vt,vi* (-nn-) **1** make or become thin(ner). **2** dilute. **thinness** *n.* **thin-skinned** *adj* sensitive, esp. to criticism.

thing *n* **1** inanimate object; entity. **2** course or action; act; deed. **3** person or animal, esp. when referred to with affection, sympathy, etc. **have a thing about** be preoccupied with. **the thing** fashionable trend. **things** *pl n* **1** possessions. **2** points; matters; ideas. **3** conditions or circumstances.

think *v* (thought) *vi* use one's mind or power of reason. *vt,vi* **1** believe; consider. **2** be aware (of); regard. **think about 1** reflect or ponder on. **2** *also* **think of** have an opinion of. **think of 1** bring to mind; imagine or remember. **2** plan; anticipate; consider. ~*n inf* concentrated effort to examine or analyse an idea, suggestion, etc.

third *adj* coming between second and fourth in sequence. *n* **1** third person, object, etc. **2** one of three equal parts; one divided by three. **3** gear above second on a motor vehicle. *adv* **1** after the second. **2** *also* **thirdly** as a third point. **third party** *n* person only marginally involved in a case or affair. **third person** n category of pronouns or verbs other than the person speaking or addressed. **third rate** adj also **third-class** of a very poor standard; mediocre.

thirst n 1 desire for water or other liquids. 2 craving; yearning. vi have a thirst (for). **thirsty** adj.

thirteen n 1 number that is three more than ten. 2 thirteen things or people. adj amounting to thirteen. **thirteenth** adj,adv,n.

thirty n 1 number equal to three times ten. 2 thirty things or people. adj amounting to thirty. **thirtieth** adj,adv,n.

this adj relating to the person or thing specified, esp. one closer than or different from another. pron the particular person or thing so specified. adv to a specified extent.

thistle n plant with a purple flower and prickly leaves.

thong n thin strip of leather used in a whip, as a fastening, etc.

thorax n, pl **thoraxes** or **thoraces** ('θɔːrəsiːz) 1 part of the body containing the heart, lungs, etc.; chest. 2 part of an insect bearing the wings and legs.

thorn n 1 sharp woody point occurring on a stem or leaf. 2 bush, esp. the hawthorn, having thorns. **thorny** adj 1 having thorns. 2 difficult to solve.

thorough adj 1 completed carefully and painstakingly; meticulous. 2 utter; absolute. **thoroughly** adv. **thoroughness** n. **thoroughbred** n animal of a pure breed; pedigree. adj relating to such an animal. **thoroughfare** n 1 road or street. 2 access; passage.

those adj form of **that** used with a plural noun.

though conj in spite of the fact that; although. **as though** as if. ~adv nevertheless; on the other hand.

thought v pt of **think**. n 1 idea, notion, concept, etc., produced by thinking. 2 act or process of thinking. 3 attention; consideration. 4 body of ideas relating to a particular period, movement, etc. **thoughtful** adj 1 considerate. 2 engaged in thought. **thoughtfully** adv. **thoughtfulness** n. **thoughtless** adj tactless; careless; inconsiderate. **thoughtlessly** adv. **thoughtlessness** n.

thousand n 1 number equal to ten times one hundred. 2 thousand people or things. **thousands** pl n huge number. adj amounting to a thousand. **thousandth** adj,adv,n.

thrash vt 1 flog; whip; beat. 2 defeat overwhelmingly. vi make a violent movement with the arms or legs, esp. in water. **thrash out** settle by debate or intense discussion. ~n beating; violent blow.

thread n 1 strand of cotton, yarn, wool, etc. 2 spiral groove of a screw, bolt, etc. 3 central idea running through a story, argument, etc. vt 1 pass (a thread) through (a needle). 2 make (a way) through (obstacles, etc.). **threadbare** adj 1 worn; having no pile or nap. 2 shabby; poor.

threat n 1 statement or indication of future harm, injury, etc. 2 person or thing likely to cause harm, injury, etc.; danger. **threaten** vt,vi make threats (to); be a threat (to); menace.

three n 1 number equal to one plus two. 2 group of three persons, things, etc. 3 also **three o'clock** three hours after noon or midnight. adj amounting to three. **three-dimensional** adj also **3-D** having three dimensions; solid or apparently so . **threesome** n group of three; trio.

thresh vt,vi beat or shake (corn) so as to separate the grain from the husks. **thresher** n person or machine that threshes.

threshold n 1 slab or board placed at a doorway or entrance. 2 starting point or verge. 3 point at which a stimulus produces an observable effect.

threw v pt of **throw**.

thrift n economic or careful use of resources. **thrifty** adj.

thrill n 1 tingle of excitement; flush of enthusiasm; intense emotion or sensation. 2 event causing this. vt,vi cause or experience a thrill. **thriller** n book, film, etc., arousing strong excitement and suspense.

thrive vi 1 grow healthily and well. 2 prosper.

throat n 1 front of the neck. 2 passage connecting the mouth and stomach. 3 narrow part, passage, or opening. **cut one's throat** pursue a disastrous course. **jump down someone's throat** attack verbally with sudden vehemence. **ram down some-**

one's throat assert or force upon without allowing response. **throaty** *adj* hoarse, as if with a sore throat.

throb *vi* (-bb-) beat strongly and rhythmically. *n* strong pulsating beat.

throne *n* **1** monarch's, pope's, or bishop's seat. **2** sovereign power.

throng *n* crowd; mass of people. *vi,vt* form or fill with a throng.

throttle *n* valve that regulates an engine's fuel supply. *vt* **1** choke; strangle. **2** regulate or restrict (power supply).

through *prep* **1** along the length of; from one end to the other of. **2** in one side and out of the other side of. **3** during; from the beginning to the end of. **4** via. **5** with the influence of; by the means or agency of. **6** because of. *adv* **1** from one side or end to another. **2** from start to finish. **3** throughout; completely. **4** no longer functioning or successful. **throughout** *prep* right through; during the whole of. *adv* in every part.

throw *v* (threw; thrown) *vt,vi* **1** send (a missile) through the air. **2** toss; fling. *vt* **1** baffle; perplex; confuse; take aback. **2** place in a particular situation. **throw away** discard as useless; reject; get rid of. **throw out 1** eject; remove by force. **2** expel; dismiss. **throw up 1** vomit. **2** produce unexpectedly. **3** leave or reject (a job). ~*n* **1** act of throwing. **2** toss; pitch.

thrush *n* songbird with brown plumage and speckled underparts.

thrust *vt,vi* **1** push with force. **2** stab; pierce. **3** force (a situation) upon (someone). *n* **1** violent lunge or push. **2** force of the propulsion of an engine. **3** *inf* ruthless drive to succeed.

thud *n* dull heavy sound of impact. *vi* (-dd-) make such a sound.

thumb *n* **1** short thick digit of the human hand. **2** corresponding digit in other mammals. **rule of thumb** practical method based on experience. **under the thumb of** under (someone's) control. ~*vt* **1** mark or touch with the thumb. **2** use the thumb as a signal, esp. as a hitch-hiker.

thump *n* **1** dull heavy blow. **2** sound made by such a blow. *vt,vi* strike; pound; beat.

thunder *n* loud rumbling noise caused by movement of air after lightning. *vi,vt* **1** make a sound like thunder; roar. **2** speak loudly and angrily. **thunderous** *adj*. **thunderstorm** *n* thunder and lightning accompanied by heavy rain.

Thursday *n* fifth day of the week.

thus *adv* **1** in the meantime. **2** to this extent or degree. **3** therefore.

thwart *vt* prevent; frustrate.

thyme (taim) *n* fragrant herb with a minty odour.

thyroid *n* *also* **thyroid gland** gland whose hormones regulate metabolism and growth.

tiara *n* jewelled head ornament worn by women.

tick[1] *n* **1** light tapping or clicking noise of a watch, clock, etc. **2** mark or symbol used to indicate approval or acknowledgment of having been noted. *vi* make a ticking sound. *vt* mark with a tick. **tick off** rebuke; scold. **tick over** (of an engine) idle.

tick[2] *n* any of a number of parasites of warm-blooded animals.

ticket *n* **1** card or slip indicating right to entry, service, etc. **2** price label. **3** slip issued for any of certain motoring offences.

tickle *vt* **1** touch lightly so as to cause laughter, pleasure, etc. **2** amuse; please. *vi* tingle; be the location of an itching sensation. *n* itching sensation. **ticklish** *adj* **1** susceptible or sensitive to tickling. **2** precarious; difficult to handle.

tide *n* **1** twice daily movement of the sea caused by the gravitational pull of the moon. **2** turning point in time. *v* **tide over** enable to cope until help or relief comes. **tidal** *adj*.

tidy *adj* neat; orderly. *vt,vi* make tidy. **tidily** *adv*. **tidiness** *n*.

tie *v* (tying) *vt* **1** fasten with a knot, bow, etc. **2** bind or secure with string, rope, etc. **3** restrict the freedom or mobility of. *vi* **1** fasten. **2** obtain an equal score or number of marks as someone else; draw. *n* **1** fastening such as string or rope. **2** obligation; restriction of freedom, etc.; commitment. **3** draw; equal score. **4** shaped piece of material worn with a shirt, fastened in a large knot at the throat.

tier *n* **1** row (of seats, etc.) above and slightly behind another or others. **2** level; layer.

tiger *n* Asiatic feline mammal with a yellow and black striped coat.

tight *adj* 1 taut; not loose. 2 fitting snugly; constricting. 3 compact. 4 strict; hard. 5 *inf also* **tight-fisted** stingy; mean; miserly. 6 *inf* drunk. **tightly** *adv.* **tightness** *n.* **tighten** *vt,vi* make or become tight(er). **tightrope** *n* taut rope or wire on which an acrobat performs. **tights** *pl n* close fitting sheer garment covering the lower part of the body, legs, and feet.

tile *n* thin flat slab used for covering roofs, floors, etc. *vt* cover with tiles.

till¹ *prep* until.

till² *n* box or receptacle into which money is put behind the sales counter in a shop, etc.

till³ *vt* cultivate or work (land). **tillable** *adj.*

tiller *n* lever attached to a rudder.

tilt *vi,vt* incline; slant; lean. *n* slope; inclination.

timber *n* wood cut into planks for use in building. *vt* provide with timber.

time *n* 1 system that relates successive events, occurrences, or changes in terms of the past, present, or future. 2 measurement by means of a clock. 3 period; age. 4 period for which something lasts; duration. 5 tempo. 6 instance; moment. 7 experience of an event, emotion, etc. 8 leisure; freedom from other tasks or duties. 9 period allotted or taken to complete something. 10 occasion. **from time to time** occasionally. **in time** not late or overdue. **on time** at precisely the time fixed; punctual. ~*vt* 1 keep a record of (the amount of time needed or taken). 2 fix the time of. **time bomb** *n* bomb detonated by a timing device. **time-keeper** *n* person or mechanism that records time. **timely** *adj* happening at a fortunate or suitable time. **times** *prep* multiplied by. *pl n* period; era. **time-sharing** *n* scheme by which someone buys the right to use a holiday house, etc., for the same period each year. **timetable** *n* schedule of times of events, arrivals, etc.

timid *adj* easily frightened; shy. **timidity** *n.* **timidly** *adv.*

timpani *pl n* kettledrums.

tin *n* 1 soft silvery metal. 2 container for food, etc., made of iron and plated with tin. *vt* (-nn-) 1 cover with tin. 2 preserve (food) in airtight containers.

tinge *vt* colour faintly. *n* 1 faint colour or tint. 2 small trace; hint.

tingle *vi* experience a prickling or mildly vibrating sensation. *n* prickling feeling.

tinker *n* itinerant craftsman who mends or sells pots and pans. *vi* 1 work as a tinker. 2 work in a haphazard fashion. 3 meddle; interfere.

tinkle *n* light metallic bell-like sound. *vi,vt* make or produce such a sound.

tinsel *n* ornamental string of glittering metal threads used as a festive decoration.

tint *n* 1 shade of a colour produced by mixture with white. 2 dye; pigment. *vt* give a tint to; colour; dye.

tiny *adj* very small; minute.

tip¹ *n* end; extremity, esp. of anything tapering to a point. **tiptoe** *vi* walk very quietly. *n* **on tiptoe** standing or walking on the balls of the feet; straining to reach up.

tip² *v* (-pp-) *vt,vi* lean or tilt to one side. *vt* 1 pour out or dump by tipping the container. 2 touch or raise (one's hat). **tip over** topple; overturn. ~*n* place where rubbish is dumped.

tip³ *n* 1 extra payment in appreciation of services rendered. 2 useful hint or advice. *vt,vi* (-pp-) give a tip (to). **tip off** give a tip-off to. **tip-off** *n* advance warning or confirmation of advantage to the recipient.

tipsy *adj* inebriated; tight; slightly drunk.

tired *adj* 1 weary; suffering from fatigue; sleepy. 2 bored; fed up; no longer interested. **tire** *vt,vi* make or become tired. **tireless** *adj* unwearying. **tiresome** *adj* wearying; trying; irritating.

tissue *n* 1 finely woven thin paper. 2 substance consisting of cells forming the structure of plants and animals.

tithe *n* (formerly) tenth part of agricultural produce, levied as a tax.

title *n* 1 name by which a person or thing may be distinguished. 2 heading by which a novel, play, etc., is known. 3 position or mode of address, esp. of a member of the nobility. 4 legal right to possess something.

to *prep* 1 in the direction of. 2 as far as. 3 into the state of. 4 giving the result of. 5 near or in contact with. 6 in comparison with. 7 with the extent of. 8 conforming with. 9 for use with or on. 10 in the opinion of. 11 until. 12 into the possession of. 13

used before the infinitive form of a verb. *adv*
1 fixed; closed. **2** into consciousness. **to
and fro** alternately backwards and forwards. **to-do** *n* fuss; bother; commotion.

toad *n* **1** small tailless greenish-brown
amphibian with a dry warty skin. **2** unpleasant person. **toadstool** *n* umbrella-shaped
fungus living on dead organic matter.

toast[1] *n* slice of bread browned by heat on
each side. *vt,vi* crisp; brown under heat.

toast[2] *vt* drink to the health of (a person,
etc.). *n* drink in honour of a person, country, etc., or words proposing such a drink.

tobacco *n* **1** tall annual plant with large
broad leaves. **2** cured leaves of this plant
used in cigarettes, cigars, etc. **tobacconist**
n person or shop selling tobacco.

toboggan *n* small sledge used on snow
slopes for winter sport. *vi* ride on a toboggan.

today *n* this present day. *adv* **1** now; on
this very day. **2** nowadays; at the present
time.

toddle *vi* walk with an unsteady uneven
gait, as a child learning to walk. **toddle
along** *inf* go at an easy unhurried pace.
toddler *n* child between the ages of one
and three approximately, who is beginning
to walk.

toe *n* **1** digit of the foot. **2** part of a shoe,
stocking, etc., covering this. *v* **toe the line**
obey; do as one is told. **toenail** *n* nail covering the toe.

toffee *n* sweet made of boiled sugar. **tof-
fee-apple** *n* apple coated in toffee. **tof-
fee-nosed** *adj sl* snobbish; conceited.

together *adv* **1** in close proximity. **2** in the
company of one or more other persons. **3**
simultaneously; at the same time.

toil *vi* **1** work hard and long. **2** proceed
slowly and with difficulty. *n* labour; hard
work.

toilet *n* **1** process of washing, combing
one's hair, etc. **2** lavatory; W.C. **toilet
water** *n* dilute solution of perfume.

token *n* **1** something used to represent or
serve as a substitute. **2** symbol; gesture. **3**
small gift; memento. **4** metal or plastic
voucher used in place of money. *adj* **1** serving as a token. **2** in name only; having little
practical effect.

told *v pp* and *pt* of **tell.**

tolerate *vt* allow; permit; endure. **tolerable** *adj* bearable. **tolerably** *adv* moderately; to a certain extent. **tolerance** *n* **1** *also*
toleration forbearance; fair-mindedness;
freedom from bigotry. **2** degree to which
something can withstand specified conditions, etc.

toll[1] *n* **1** payment exacted for use of a
bridge, road, etc., in certain circumstances.
2 price paid; number or amount sacri-
ficed.

toll[2] *vt,vi* ring or cause to ring with slow
heavy strokes.

tomato *n, pl* **tomatoes** juicy red fruit usually served as a vegetable with seasoning.

tomb *n* place where the dead are buried or
laid out in a hollow chamber.

tomorrow *n* **1** the day after today. **2** the
future. *adv* on the day after today.

ton *n* measure of weight equivalent to 2240
pounds (approx. 1016 kilograms).

tone *n* **1** quality of a musical note. **2** pure
musical note. **3** manner of speaking, writing,
etc., indicating attitude or emotion. **4** general physical or moral condition. **5** shade of
colour; tint. *v* **tone down** reduce; soften;
calm. **tonal** *adj.* **tonality** *n* system of musical keys, esp. in traditional Western music.

tongs *pl n* instrument consisting of two
hinged arms for grasping objects.

tongue *n* **1** flexible organ in the mouth
used in eating and in forming speech. **2** language; method or tone of speaking. **3** anything shaped like a tongue. **tongue in
cheek** insincerely or ironically. **tongue-
tied** *adj* **1** suffering from a speech defect.
2 speechless; inarticulate. **tongue-twister**
n phrase or sentence that is difficult to pronounce because of unusual sound combinations.

tonic *n* **1** medicine used to stimulate and
invigorate. **2** anything with this effect. **3**
key on which a musical work is primarily
based.

tonight *n* the night of the present day. *adv*
on this night or evening.

tonsils *pl n* pair of oval-shaped organs situated on each side of the back of the throat.
tonsillitis *n* enlargement or inflammation
of the tonsils due to infection.

too *adv* **1** also; in addition; as well. **2** to an excessive extent.

took *v pt* of **take**.

tool *n* **1** instrument used in making or doing something; implement. **2** person used to serve another's purpose. **3** useful device; means. *vt,vi* use a tool (on).

tooth *n, pl* **teeth 1** hard projection in the jaws of humans and most vertebrates, used for biting, chewing, etc. **2** any similar projection, as on a comb. **toothbrush** *n* brush used for cleaning the teeth.

top[1] *n* **1** highest point; peak. **2** upper part. **3** highest position. **4** cap or cover of a bottle, jar, box, etc. **blow one's top** lose one's temper. ~*adj* best; highest. *vt* (-pp-) **1** take the top off. **2** cover or form the top of. **3** surpass. **top up** add extra liquid to so as to fill. **top hat** *n* tall cylindrical hat worn by men on formal occasions. **top-heavy** *adj* **1** disproportionately heavier or thicker above than below and thus unstable. **2** with too much emphasis on certain parts. **topmost** *adj* highest. **topsoil** *n* uppermost and most fertile layer of the earth's crust.

top[2] *n* small shaped object made to balance by spinning on a point, used esp. as a toy.

topic *n* subject; theme. **topical** *adj* of current interest.

topography *n* detailed geographical description or representation of the features of an area.

topple *vi,vt* fall or cause to fall over; overturn. *vt* overthrow; depose.

topsy-turvy *adj,adv* **1** upside down. **2** confused; muddled.

torch *n* **1** burning material held on a stick. **2** device carried by hand for giving light, usually operated by a battery.

tore *v pt* of **tear**[2].

torment *n* ('tɔːment) severe mental or physical distress; anguish. *vt* (tɔːˈment) **1** torture; distress. **2** pester; harass.

torn *v pp* of **tear**[2].

tornado *n, pl* **tornadoes** *or* **tornados** violent storm of short duration with a characteristic rotating movement and funnel-shaped cloud.

torpedo *n, pl* **torpedoes** self-propelled missile carried by a submarine for use against ships. *vt* hit with or as if with a torpedo.

torrent *n* **1** rapidly flowing stream of large quantities of water. **2** any copious rapid flow, as of words, abuse, etc. **torrential** *adj*.

torso *n* trunk of the human body.

tortoise *n* slow-moving reptile with a bony shell and scaly head and legs.

tortuous *adj* **1** twisting; winding; snakelike. **2** devious; unnecessarily complicated.

torture *n* **1** severe pain inflicted as a punishment or method of persuasion. **2** any extreme physical or mental distress. *vt* **1** inflict torture on. **2** cause extreme agony, pain, or distress in. **torturous** *adj*.

Tory *n* supporter of the Conservative party. *adj* belonging or relating to this party.

toss *vt* **1** throw into the air. **2** move (the head, hair, etc.) upwards with a jerk. *vt,vi* **1** move about or up and down quickly and in an irregular manner; pitch; jerk. **2** move restlessly, as in sleep. **3** *also* **toss up** spin (a coin) in the air to decide something. **toss off** finish quickly. ~*n* act of tossing or being tossed.

tot[1] *n* **1** small child. **2** small measure of alcoholic liquor.

tot[2] *v* **tot up** (-tt-) add up; count.

total *n* **1** complete whole as compared with a part. **2** final figure obtained by addition. *adj* **1** complete; final. **2** absolute; unrestrained. *vt,vi* (-ll-) add up (to).

totalitarian *adj* (of a government) characterized by absolute authority; allowing no opposition. **totalitarianism** *n.*

totem *n* object, esp. an animal, regarded as having special significance for a clan, tribe, etc. **totem-pole** *n* carved post used as a totem by North American Indians.

totter *vi* **1** walk unsteadily. **2** be in a precarious state.

touch *vt,vi* **1** bring or come into contact with. **2** bring the hand into contact with; feel. **3** *also* **touch (up)on** allude to; mention in passing. *vt* **1** affect; influence. **2** deal with; be associated with. **3** *sl* borrow money from. *n* **1** sense by which objects in contact with the body are felt. **2** act of touching, esp. a light brush or blow. **3** small amount of something. **4** knack; ability. **5** *sl* act of borrowing money or the person borrowed from. **In touch 1** aware. **2** having correspondence or contact (with). **touched** *adj* **1** emotionally moved. **2** slightly mad. **touch-**

Ing *adj* producing pity or sympathy; moving. **touchy** *adj* easily offended.

tough *adj* **1** strong; hard-wearing. **2** hardy; robust; capable of suffering hardship. **3** (of food) difficult to chew. **4** stubborn; uncompromising. **5** difficult. **6** vicious; rough. *n* ruffian; lout. **toughness** *n.* **toughen** *vt* make tough(er); strengthen.

toupee *n* small patch of false hair worn to cover a bald spot.

tour *n* journey through several places, usually for sightseeing. *vt,vi* make a tour (through). **tourism** *n* business catering for the needs of tourists. **tourist** *n* person, esp. a holidaymaker, visiting a city, foreign country, etc.

tournament *n* **1** medieval contest between armed horsemen. **2** organized competition involving several matches, as in tennis, chess, etc.

tow *vt* pull along behind, as with a rope. *n* act of towing.

towards *prep also* **toward 1** in the direction of. **2** close to; in the vicinity of. **3** as a contribution to.

towel *n* cloth or paper for drying things. **throw in the towel** surrender; concede. ~*vt,vi* (-ll-) dry with a towel. **towelling** *n* type of absorbent cloth used for towels.

tower *n* tall cylindrical or square-shaped construction, forming part of a church, castle, etc. **tower of strength** strong reliable person. **in an ivory tower** insulated from reality. ~*vi* rise up to great heights. **tower above** *or* **over 1** be much higher than. **2** be greatly superior to.

town *n* **1** group of houses, shops, etc., larger than a village and smaller than a city. **2** inhabitants of a town. **go to town** act in a wholehearted or unrestrained manner. **town clerk** *n* official in charge of civic records. **town hall** *n* public building used as the administrative centre of a town.

toxic *adj* poisonous.

toy *n* **1** plaything of a child. **2** trifle; something treated lightly. *adj* **1** relating to or like a toy. **2** (esp. of a dog) bred specially to be smaller in size than average. *v* **toy with 1** play or trifle with. **2** consider; ponder about.

trace *vt* **1** follow (a track, path, etc.). **2** discover or find by careful searching. **3** copy by overlaying a transparent sheet and mark-

ing the lines. **4** draw; sketch. *n* **1** trail; track. **2** sign showing former presence of something. **3** small amount; vestige.

track *n* **1** mark or marks left by the passage of something; trail. **2** path. **3** path designed for guiding something, as in a railway. **4** course on which races are held. **5** series of metal plates fitted instead of wheels to vehicles such as tractors, tanks, etc. *vt,vi* follow the track of. **track down** find by searching. **tracksuit** *n* loose-fitting garment fastened at the neck, wrists, and ankles, worn by athletes in training.

tract[1] *n* **1** large area of water or land; expanse. **2** bodily structure or system serving a specialized function. **3** bundle of nerve fibres.

tract[2] *n* treatise or pamphlet.

tractor *n* vehicle with large wheels or tracks, for use esp. on farms.

trade *n* **1** business; commerce. **2** interchange of goods and money on an agreed basis. **3** skilled manual craft. *vt,vi* exchange for money or other goods; barter. *vi* engage in a business. **trade in** give in part exchange for something. **trade on** exploit. **trader** *n.* **trademark** *n* **1** mark or name registered by a manufacturer for a product. **2** characteristic trait. **tradesman** *n, pl* **-men 1** person engaged in trade, esp. a small shopkeeper. **2** skilled worker. **trade union** *n* association of people engaged in the same trade pledged to protect standards of wages, working conditions, etc.

tradition *n* beliefs and practices passed down from earlier generations. **traditional** *adj.* **traditionally** *adv.*

traffic *n* **1** motor vehicles using a road. **2** movement of ships, aircraft, etc. **3** trade; commerce. *vi* (-ck-) trade (in), esp. illicitly.

tragedy *n* **1** prose or drama with an inevitable unhappy ending. **2** sad event; great misfortune. **tragic** *adj* **1** in the style of a tragedy. **2** sad; moving; calamitous. **tragically** *adv.*

trail *n* track left behind by a person, animal, or thing. *vt* **1** drag or pull behind. **2** track; pursue. **3** hang loosely. *vi* **1** walk wearily with lagging steps. **2** hang or grow downwards. **trailer** *n* **1** vehicle attached to and pulled by another. **2** series of short extracts used to advertise a film.

train *n* **1** number of railway carriages or wagons coupled together and drawn by an engine. **2** succession of things, persons, or events. **3** part of a gown or robe trailing behind. *vt* **1** impart skill or knowledge to. **2** teach (an animal) to obey commands or perform tricks. **3** encourage (plants) to grow as required. **4** point (a gun, camera, etc.) at. *vi* **1** receive instruction. **2** exercise regularly to increase fitness. **trainee** *n.* **trainer** *n.*

traipse *vi* trudge; follow a long or circuitous route; wander about aimlessly; trek. *n* long tiring walk or journey.

traitor *n* person who betrays a trust, esp. one who commits treason. **traitorous** *adj.*

tram *n* passenger car running on a metal track on a road. **tramlines** *pl n* **1** tracks on which trams run. **2** parallel lines on a tennis court marking the boundaries of the singles court.

tramp *vi* walk with heavy tread. *vi,vt* walk (a certain distance), as for recreation. *n* **1** itinerant vagrant living by casual work or begging. **2** sound of someone tramping. **3** walk, esp. a long recreational walk.

trample *vt,vi* tread under foot; crush with the feet.

trampoline *n* gymnasium apparatus consisting of a sheet attached to a framework by springs, used for jumping, performing somersaults, etc. *vi* exercise on a trampoline.

trance *n* dreamlike semi-conscious state produced by hypnotism, drugs, etc.

tranquil *adj* calm; peaceful; unruffled. **tranquillity** *n.* **tranquillize** *vt* make tranquil; calm down. **tranquillizer** *n* drug used to reduce anxiety.

transact *vt,vi* perform; carry out (something, esp. a business deal). **transaction** *n.*

transatlantic *adj* **1** across or beyond the Atlantic Ocean. **2** relating to North America.

transcend *vt,vi* excel; surpass; exceed. **transcendent** *adj.* **transcendental** *adj* of or connected with the philosophy of seeking after truth by exploring the inner self. **transcendentalism** *n.*

transcribe *vt* copy out in writing. **transcription** *n.*

transfer *vt,vi* (træns'fɔ:) (-rr-) **1** move from one place to another. **2** change from one position, job, responsibility, etc., to another.

3 make over (power, responsibility, etc.) to another. *n* ('trænsfɔ:) **1** act of transferring. **2** prepared design or picture on paper that can be transferred to another surface.

transform *vt,vi* change in character, nature, shape, etc. **transformation** *n.*

transfusion *n* transfer of blood from one person to another or injection of other fluids to make up loss of blood. **transfuse** *vt* give a transfusion of.

transient *adj* transitory.

transistor *n* small electronic component made of certain solid materials. **transistorized** *adj* (of a piece of electronic equipment) using transistors rather than valves.

transit *n* **1** act of crossing or being conveyed from one place to another. **2** act of moving across. **transition** *n* **1** change from one place or set of circumstances or conditions to another. **2** process of continuous change or development. **transitory** *adj* changing; of limited duration.

transitive *adj* designating a verb that takes a direct object.

translate *vt,vi* **1** express in another language. **2** interpret; explain the meaning of. **translation** *n.* **translator** *n.*

translucent *adj* allowing light to pass through but not allowing a clear image of an object to be seen.

transmit *vt* (-tt-) **1** send across; pass on; communicate. **2** act as a condition or medium for. **transmission** *n.* **transmitter** *n* device used to broadcast radio or television signals.

transparent *adj* **1** transmitting rays of light; clear. **2** easily seen or detected. **transparently** *adv.* **transparency** *n* **1** quality of being transparent. **2** transparent photographic print projected or viewed by transmitted light.

transplant *vt* (træns'plɑ:nt) **1** dig up and plant elsewhere. **2** transfer (living tissue or an organ) from one person to another. *n* ('trænsplɑ:nt) act of transplanting or something transplanted.

transport *n* ('trænspɔ:t) **1** means of conveying a person or thing from one place to another. **2** vehicle used for this purpose. *vt* (træn'spɔ:t) **1** carry; move from one place to another. **2** carry away, as with emotion.

transpose *vt* **1** cause to exchange positions. **2** rewrite (music) in a different key. **transposition** *n.*

trap *n* **1** device for catching an animal. **2** trick to place someone in an unfavourable position. **3** hazard; pitfall. **4** device to prevent passage of gas, impurities, etc. **5** light open horse-drawn carriage. **6** stall from which greyhounds are released for a race. **7** *also* **trap door** door in a floor or ceiling. *vt* (-pp-) catch or remove by means of a trap. **trapper** *n* person who traps animals for fur.

trapeze *n* apparatus used by gymnasts or acrobats, consisting of two suspended ropes carrying a horizontal crossbar.

trash *n* **1** rubbish; refuse. **2** anything considered worthless or shoddy.

trauma *n* violent emotional shock or experience. **traumatic** *adj.*

travel *v* (-ll-) *vi* **1** go on a journey; make a trip. **2** go abroad frequently or regularly. **3** move; proceed. **4** move from place to place selling goods. *vt* cover (a specified distance). **traveller** *n* **1** person who travels. **2** person employed to travel in goods; travelling salesman. **travels** *pl n* trips or journeys, esp. abroad.

traverse *vt,vi* cross from one side or corner to another. *n* act of crossing over or through.

trawl *n* large net pulled behind a boat to catch fish. *vi,vt* catch (fish) with a trawl. **trawler** *n* fishing boat equipped with a trawl.

tray *n* flat piece of wood, metal, etc., often with a raised edge, for carrying objects.

treacherous *adj* **1** deceitful; betraying a trust. **2** dangerous; hazardous. **treachery** *n.*

treacle *n* thick sticky syrup obtained by refining sugar.

tread *v* (trod; trod *or* trodden) *vi,vt* put the foot down on (something) or apply pressure to (something) with the foot. *vi* walk. *vt* **1** walk on (a path, road, etc.). **2** mark a floor with (mud, dirt, etc.) carried on the feet. **tread on 1** oppress. **2** crush; stamp out. ~*n* **1** act or manner of treading. **2** part of a tyre that makes contact with the ground, usually having a patterned surface to improve the grip. **3** horizontal part of a step.

treason *n* disloyalty to a sovereign or the state.

treasure *n* object or collection of objects of value. *vt* value or regard greatly; cherish. **treasurer** *n* person in charge of funds of a society, group, etc. **treasury** *n* storehouse for treasure. **the Treasury** government department responsible for finance.

treat *vt* **1** deal with; handle. **2** prescribe medicine or medical care for. **3** act towards or regard. **4** buy something for. **5** act upon; apply a process to. *n* **1** entertainment or a gift paid for by someone else. **2** something producing joy or pleasure. **treatment** *n* **1** act or manner of treating a person or thing. **2** course of medical care.

treaty *n* formal agreement between nations.

treble *vt,vi* multiply or be multiplied by three. *n* soprano or a voice or instrument in this range. *adj* threefold; multiplied by three.

tree *n* perennial plant with a thick trunk of wood topped by branches and leaves.

trek *vi* (-kk-) make a long slow journey, esp. through difficult country. *n* journey of this kind.

trellis *n* framework of criss-crossed bars used as a plant support, decorative screen, etc.

tremble *vi* **1** shake or quiver, as from cold, fear, etc. **2** be afraid. **3** vibrate. *n* act or an instance of trembling.

tremendous *adj* **1** overpowering; astonishing. **2** *inf* great; considerable. **tremendously** *adv.*

tremor *n* trembling; shaking; quivering.

trench *n* **1** narrow ditch dug in the ground. **2** ditch with soil parapets, used by soldiers during battle. *vi,vt* dig a trench (in).

trend *n* **1** movement or tendency in a particular direction. **2** *inf* fashion. **trendy** *adj* *inf* up-to-date; fashionable.

trespass *vi* **1** intrude upon private property without permission. **2** encroach upon. *n* act of trespassing. **trespasser** *n.*

trestle *n* structure consisting of a beam with hinged legs, used to support a plank, table top, etc.

trial *n* **1** test; experiment. **2** trying experience; hardship. **3** formal inquiry in court.

triangle *n* **1** plane figure bounded by three straight lines. **2** steel musical instrument of this shape sounded by striking with a small rod. **triangular** *adj.*

tribe *n* **1** group of people, usually primitive, with a common ancestry, culture, etc. **2** group of related animals or plants. **tribal** *adj.*

tribunal *n* **1** court of justice. **2** board or group appointed to settle any matter in dispute.

tributary *n* small river flowing into a larger one.

tribute *n* **1** payment in money or kind made by one ruler or country to another as an act or submission. **2** mark or expression of respect.

trick *n* **1** action or device intended to deceive. **2** skill; knack. **3** prank; joke. **4** cards played in one round. *vt,vi* deceive; delude; cheat. **trickery** *n.* **tricky** *adj* **1** crafty; deceitful. **2** difficult; complicated.

tricycle *n* vehicle with three wheels propelled with pedals.

trifle *n* **1** small object. **2** matter of little value or importance. **3** cold dessert sweet consisting of layers of cream, custard, fruit, and sponge. *v* **trifle with** act insincerely towards.

trigger *n* **1** device releasing the spring mechanism of a gun. **2** any device that sets off or initiates something. *vt also* **trigger off** set off; cause; initiate.

trill *n* high-pitched vibrating sound. *vi,vt* utter or sing with a trill.

trim *vt* (-mm-) **1** make neat or tidy, as by clipping. **2** cut away (superfluous material) from. *adj* **1** neat; tidy. **2** smart; in good condition. *n* **1** correct condition; good order. **2** act of trimming, esp. the hair. **trimmings** *pl n* additional decoration or garnish.

trio *n* group of three, esp. three singers or musicians.

trip *n* **1** journey; excursion. **2** stumble or fall. **3** mistake; slip. **4** sudden starting of a mechanism. *v* (-pp-) *vi,vt* **1** stumble or cause to stumble. **2** make or cause to make a mistake. **3** release (a mechanism) or (of a mechanism) be released. *vi* dance; skip.

tripe *n* **1** white lining of the stomach of a ruminant, used for food. **2** *sl* rubbish; worthless material.

triple *adj* **1** three times as great; threefold. **2** of three parts or kinds. *n* anything that

is a group of three. *vt,vi* multiply or be multiplied by three. **triplet** *n* **1** one of three children born at the same birth. **2** any one of a group of three.

tripod *n* stand with three legs, for supporting a camera, etc.

trite *adj* commonplace; hackneyed.

triumph *n* **1** victory. **2** notable achievement; great success. *vi* **1** gain a victory; win. **2** achieve great success. **3** rejoice in something; exult. **triumphant** *adj* **1** victorious. **2** exultant.

trivial *adj* insignificant; of no account. **triviality** *n.*

trod *v pt* and a *pp* of **tread. trodden** *v* a *pp* of **tread.**

trolley *n* **1** small hand-drawn wheeled vehicle for carrying goods, dishes, etc. **2** wheel on the end of a pole running on an overhead cable, used to draw electric current to drive a bus (trolleybus) or tram.

trombone *n* long brass instrument, usually having a moving slide to control the notes. **trombonist** *n.*

troop *n* **1** body of soldiers. **2** group of people or animals. *vi* march or proceed in a group. **troops** *pl n* soldiers.

trophy *n* memento of a victory; prize; award.

tropic *n* one of two lines of latitude, either 23°28' north (tropic of Cancer) or 23°28' south (tropic of Capricorn) of the equator. **tropical** *adj* relating to the tropics. **tropics** *pl n* region between these lines of latitude.

trot *n* **1** pace between walking and running. **2** pace of horses with diagonal pairs of legs moving together. *vi* (-tt-) move with a trot. **trot out** produce; introduce. **trotter** *n* **1** horse bred for trotting. **2** foot of a pig or certain other animals.

trouble *n* **1** disturbance; uneasiness. **2** affliction; distress. **3** person or thing causing trouble or worry. **4** care; pains; effort. *vt* afflict; annoy; inconvenience. *vi* take pains; bother; make an effort.

trough (trɔf) *n* **1** long narrow vessel holding food or drink for animals. **2** area of low barometric pressure.

troupe *n* group of performers.

trousers *pl n* garment designed to cover the legs and lower part of the body.

trout *n, pl* **trout** *or* **trouts** brownish speckled edible fish of the salmon family.

trowel *n* **1** flat-bladed tool with a pointed tip, used to spread mortar. **2** hand tool used by gardeners. *vt* (-ll-) use a trowel on.

truant *n* child absenting himself from school without permission. **truancy** *n.*

truce *n* temporary cessation of hostilities by mutual agreement.

truck *n* strong vehicle for carrying heavy loads.

trudge *vi* walk wearily. *n* long or tiring walk.

true *adj* **1** relating to truth; in accordance with facts; not false. **2** legitimate; rightful. **3** real; genuine. **4** exact; precise; correct. **5** faithful; reliable. **truly** *adv* **1** sincerely; honestly; truthfully. **2** really; absolutely.

trump *n* card of a suit ranking above the others for the duration of a game or round. *vt,vi* defeat by playing a trump.

trumpet *n* long funnel-shaped brass wind instrument, usually having three valves. *vi* make a loud noise similar to that of a trumpet. **trumpeter** *n.*

truncheon *n* short wooden club used esp. by policemen.

trundle *vt,vi* roll along or propel on or as if on wheels or castors.

trunk *n* **1** large strong box with a hinged lid for storing or transporting goods. **2** main stem of a tree. **3** human body, excluding the head and limbs; torso. **4** main telephone line. **5** long flexible snout of an elephant. **trunk call** *n* long distance call on a main telephone line.

trust *n* **1** belief in someone's honesty or something's reliability. **2** responsibility. **3** good faith. **4** association of companies combining for trade. **hold in trust** take legal charge for benefit of another. ~*vt,vi* place or have trust (in). **trustee** *n* person holding property or money in trust for another. **trustworthy** *adj* deserving of trust; reliable; dependable.

truth *n* fact, statement, or concept that is known to be true or can be verified. **truthful** *adj* given to speaking the truth. **truthfully** *adv.*

try *vt,vi* **1** attempt or make an effort to do (something). **2** test, as by experiment. *vt* **1** irritate; strain. **2** subject to a trial. **try on** put

(a garment) on to test the fit. ~*n* **1** attempt; effort. **2** score of four points in rugby made by grounding the ball behind the opponent's line.

tsar *n also* **czar** Russian emperor.

T-shirt *n* short-sleeved shirt without buttons or collar.

tub *n* **1** small barrel. **2** bath, esp. one filled by hand. **tubby** *adj* shaped like a tub; chubby; rotund.

tuba *n* large low-pitched brass instrument.

tube *n* **1** long hollow cylinder. **2** narrow flexible container for toothpaste, etc. **the Tube** London's underground railway. **tubular** *adj.*

tuber *n* thick underground stem of certain plants on which buds are formed at or below ground level.

tuberculosis *n* disease produced by bacteria attacking body tissues, esp. the respiratory tract.

tuck *vt,vi* **1** fold under. **2** push or fit into a small space. **3** draw (the legs or arms) in close to the body. **4** make folds in (a material). **tuck in** eat heartily. ~*n* **1** small fold sewn into a garment. **2** position in which the knees are drawn up close to the chest.

Tuesday *n* third day of the week.

tuft *n* bunch of strands, hairs, etc.

tug *vt,vi* (-gg-) pull sharply or with force. *n* **1** act of tugging. **2** small boat used to tow larger boats. **tug-of-war** *n, pl* **tugs-of-war** sporting contest between two teams, each holding one end of a rope and trying to pull the other over a line between them.

tuition *n* instruction; teaching.

tulip *n* bulb producing a brightly coloured bell-shaped flower on a single upright stem.

tumble *vi,vt* **1** fall or cause to fall; topple. **2** move in an ungainly manner. **3** roll or toss about. **4** decrease or lose value sharply. *n* fall. **tumbler** *n* **1** acrobat who performs somersaults, etc. **2** stemless drinking glass.

tummy *n inf* stomach.

tumour *n* local swelling from a benign or malignant growth.

tumult ('tju:mʌlt) *n* noisy or violent disturbance, as of a crowd; uproar. **tumultuous** *adj.*

tuna *n also* **tunny** large ocean fish of the mackerel family with pinkish edible flesh.

tune n 1 sequence of musical notes forming a melody. 2 piece of music, song, etc. **out of/in tune** having the incorrect/correct pitch. **out of/in tune with** unsympathetic/sympathetic to. ~vt 1 adjust (a musical instrument) so as to obtain the correct pitch. 2 adjust (a radio, etc.) so as to obtain the correct setting. 3 adjust (a car engine) to improve performance. **tune in** adjust a radio to receive a particular programme. **tune up** (of an orchestra) check instruments to ensure that they are in tune before performing. **tuneful** adj melodious. **tunefully** adv. **tuning fork** n device with two prongs, which produce a sound of a set pitch when vibrated.

tunic n loose-fitting kneelength garment.

tunnel n underground passage. vi,vt (-ll-) make a tunnel (through).

turban n 1 headdress consisting of a long scarf wound around a cap, traditionally worn by men in parts of N Africa, India, etc. 2 woman's hat resembling this.

turbine n engine in which a wheel is turned by the direct force of steam, water, etc.

turbulent adj 1 restless; disturbed; tumultuous. 2 (of liquids) not flowing smoothly; agitated. **turbulence** n.

tureen (tju'ri:n) n large dish from which soup is served.

turf n, pl **turves** or **turfs** 1 ground covered with short close-growing springy grass. 2 single piece of grass and soil cut from the ground. **the turf** horseracing. ~vt cover with turf. **turf accountant** n bookmaker; person who takes legal bets on horseraces.

turkey n large domesticated bird used for food.

turmoil n state of confusion or anarchy; turbulence.

turn vt,vi 1 rotate; move around; spin. 2 face or cause to face a different direction. 3 go around (a corner). 4 move in a different direction. 5 change (into a specified state or condition); transform. vt 1 move (a page) over so as to display the other side. 2 dig or plough (the soil). 3 shape on a lathe. 4 reach (a specified age). vi 1 become sour, rancid, etc. 2 change colour. **turn away** send away; refuse. **turn down** 1 refuse. 2 reduce the volume or intensity of. 3 fold down. **turn in**

1 hand in; deliver. 2 go to bed. 3 finish; give up. **turn off** 1 branch off; deviate. 2 cause to stop operating. 3 sl repel; disgust. **turn on** 1 cause to operate. 2 produce automatically. 3 sl arouse; attract. 4 attack without warning. 5 sl initiate, esp. into the use of drugs. **turn out** 1 stop (a light, gas burner, etc.) operating. 2 produce; make. 3 expel. 4 become; develop into. 5 assemble; gather. 6 dress; array. 7 clear out the contents of. **turn over** 1 move so as to reverse top and bottom; shift position. 2 start (an engine). 3 deliver; hand over. 4 (of an engine) function correctly. 5 handle (a specified amount of stock or money) in a business. **turn tail** run away; flee. **turn to** have recourse to; seek help from. **turn up** 1 appear; attend. 2 be found or discovered as if by chance. 3 increase the volume or intensity of. 4 point upwards. ~n 1 act or instance of turning. 2 one of a number of successive periods during which different people have the right or responsibility of doing something. 3 short spell of work, etc. 4 distinctive style. 5 something done to affect someone. 6 need; requirement. 7 inf shock; surprise. 8 short walk. **at every turn** on all occasions; in all directions. **to a turn** perfectly. **turn-off** n road branching off from a main road. **turn-out** n 1 group of people appearing at a gathering. 2 output. 3 style in which someone is dressed or something is equipped. 4 act of clearing out the contents of something. **turnover** n 1 small pastry containing fruit or jam. 2 amount handled, produced, used, etc., during a specified period. **turntable** n 1 revolving circular table of a record player. 2 revolving platform for turning a locomotive. **turnup** n 1 cloth folded up at the bottom of a trouser leg. 2 chance occurrence.

turnip n vegetable having a rounded purplish edible root.

turpentine n also inf **turps** oily resin of several types of conifers, used in mixing paints.

turquoise n opaque greenish-blue stone. adj,n blue-green.

turret n 1 small round or square tower attached to a larger building. 2 revolving structure for a gun on a ship, tank, etc.

turtle *n* large marine reptile similar to a tortoise.

turves *n* a *pl* of **turf.**

tusk *n* long pointed tooth of an elephant, walrus, etc., protruding from the closed mouth.

tussle *vi,n* struggle; scuffle; fight.

tutor *n* **1** private teacher. **2** university teacher in charge of the studies of individual students or small groups. **tutorial** *n* teaching session run by a university tutor.

twang *n* resonant sound of the type produced by plucking a string. *vi,vt* produce a twang.

tweed *n* rough woollen fabric made from interwoven colours, used esp. for clothing.

tweezers *pl n* small metal tongs, used to lift small objects or pull out splinters, hairs, etc.

twelve *n* **1** number equal to one plus eleven. **2** group of twelve people, things, etc. **3** *also* **twelve o'clock** noon or midnight. *adj* amounting to twelve. **twelfth** *adj* coming between eleventh and thirteenth in sequence. *adv* after the eleventh. *n* **1** twelfth person, thing, etc. **2** one of twelve equal parts; one divided by twelve.

twenty *n* **1** number equal to twice ten. **2** twenty things or people. *adj* amounting to twenty. **twentieth** *adj,adv,n*

twice *adv* **1** two times. **2** multiplied by two. **3** on two occasions. **4** doubly; two times as much or many.

twiddle *vt,vi* twirl; turn to and fro; fidget (with).

twig *n* small shoot of a branch of a tree or bush. *vt* (-gg-) *inf* catch the significance of.

twilight *n* evening light as the sun is setting; dusk.

twin *n* **1** one of two children born at one birth. **2** one of any identical or closely related pair. *adj* relating to a twin or pair. *vt* (-nn-) bring together as a couple or pair; match exactly.

twine *n* string made up of twisted strands. *vt,vi* wind; coil; entwine.

twinge *n* **1** sudden shooting pain. **2** sudden pang as of conscience, regret, etc.

twinkle *vi* **1** sparkle; glitter; flash intermittently. **2** move lightly and rapidly. *n* single flash; gleam.

twirl *vt,vi* revolve or cause to revolve; turn in rapid circles. *n* single rapid turn or flourish.

twist *vt,vi* **1** alter in shape by a rotating or screwing motion; wrench; contort. **2** wind or twine. *vt* **1** alter or misinterpret the meaning of. **2** *inf* deceive; cheat. *vi* **1** rotate or turn sharply. **2** writhe. *n* **1** twisting movement; turn; rotation. **2** anything twisted, as in a spiral. **3** unexpected turn of events.

twitch *vt,vi* **1** make spasmodic or convulsive muscle movements. **2** pull; jerk; pluck. *n* act of twitching; jerk.

twitter *vi,vt* chirp; produce a continuous chattering sound. *vi* tremble.

two *n* **1** number equal to one plus one. **2** group of two persons, things, etc. **3** *also* **two o'clock** two hours after noon or midnight. *adj* amounting to two. **two-faced** *adj* hypocritical; deceitful. **twosome** *n* **1** pair; couple, esp. when exclusive of others. **2** game with two players. **two-way** *adj* **1** operating in two directions. **2** reciprocal; of mutual benefit.

tycoon *n* wealthy powerful businessman.

type *n* **1** kind; sort. **2** class; category. **3** block of material carrying relief characters for printing. **4** printed characters considered collectively. *vt,vi* use a typewriter (for). *vt* assign to a type; classify. **typecast** *vt* (-cast) cast (an actor) in a part similar to parts he has played before. **typewriter** *n* machine for printing characters on paper, operated by pressing keys, which strike an ink-impregnated ribbon. **typical** *adj* **1** characteristic; normal or average. **2** showing the essential properties of a category. **typically** *adv.* **typify** *vt* represent; be typical of. **typist** *n* person who uses a typewriter, esp. a person employed to type.

typhoid *n* *also* **typhoid fever** infectious intestinal disease caused by bacilli growing in contaminated food or water.

typhoon *n* violent cyclonic storm occurring in the W Pacific Ocean.

tyrant *n* harsh ruler or master; despot. **tyranny** *n*. **tyrannical** *adj*. **tyrannize** *vt* treat tyrannically; terrorize.

tyre *n* solid or air-filled rubber tube held round the circumference of a vehicle wheel.

U

ubiquitous *adj* present everywhere. **ubiquity** *n*.

udder *n* external organ of cows, goats, etc., through which milk is secreted.

ugly *adj* 1 unpleasant to look at; repulsive; offensive. 2 threatening; angry. **ugliness** *n*.

ukulele *n* four-stringed instrument resembling but smaller than a guitar.

ulcer *n* open sore on the skin or an internal membrane, which is slow to heal.

ulterior *adj* 1 further away in time or space; distant. 2 not disclosed; deep-seated.

ultimate *adj* 1 last; final. 2 most desirable or significant. *n* 1 basis; final stage. 2 best; greatest; most desirable. **ultimately** *adv* eventually; in the end. **ultimatum** *n* final proposal of terms whose rejection will cancel further negotiations; deadline.

ultraviolet *n* invisible radiation having wavelengths between that of violet light and x-rays.

umbrella *n* portable collapsible object used as protection against rain or sun.

umpire *n* impartial person who enforces rules and settles disputes in cricket, tennis, etc. *vt,vi* act as umpire (for).

umpteen *adj inf* large number of; countless.

unaccompanied *adj* 1 alone. 2 singing or playing without instrumental accompaniment.

unanimous *adj* having the support and agreement of all concerned. **unanimity** *n*. **unanimously** *adv*.

unarmed *adj* without weapons.

unavoidable *adj* inevitable.

unaware *adj* ignorant; not aware. **unawares** *adv* by surprise; without warning or previous knowledge.

unbalanced *adj* not sane; mentally disturbed.

unbearable *adj* intolerable; beyond endurance. **unbearably** *adv*.

unbend *vt,vi* (-bent) 1 straighten. 2 *inf* relax or become relaxed, friendly, etc. **unbending** *adj* 1 stiff; rigid. 2 stubborn; formal.

unbutton *vt,vi* 1 undo the buttons (of). 2 *inf* unbend.

uncalled-for *adj* unwarranted; out of place; gratuitously rude.

uncanny *adj* weird; strange; irrational.

uncertain *adv* doubtful; undecided; variable; unpredictable. **uncertainty** *n*.

uncle *n* brother of one's father or mother; aunt's husband.

uncomfortable *adj* 1 not comfortable. 2 uneasy; awkward; embarrassing.

unconscious *adj* 1 unaware; unintentional. 2 having lost consciousness; insensible; in a faint, coma, etc. *n* part of the mind concerned with instincts, impulses, repressed feelings, etc., not normally accessible to the conscious mind. **unconsciously** *adv*.

unconventional *adj* not conforming; bizarre; eccentric.

uncouth *adj* ill-mannered; awkward; boorish.

uncut *adj* 1 entire; not abridged. 2 natural; unpolished and without facets.

undecided *adj* uncertain; hesitant; in two minds.

undeniable *adj* definite; obviously true. **undeniably** *adv*.

under *prep* 1 below the surface of; beneath; in a lower position than. 2 covered or concealed by. 3 lower in rank than; inferior to. 4 less in price or value than. 5 with the classification of. 6 in; according to. 7 influenced by; subject to. *adv* 1 in or to a lower or inferior place or position. 2 younger than. 3 less than. *adj* lower; low; inferior.

underclothes *pl n* underwear.

undercoat *n* coat of paint below the top or final coat. *vt* apply an undercoat to.

undercover *adj* secret; disguised.

undercut (-tt-; -cut) *vt,vi* sell at lower prices than competitors.

underdeveloped *adj* 1 not fully developed; developing; of unrealized potential. 2 primitive; backward.

underdone *adj* lightly cooked; rare.

underestimate *vt* (ʌndərˈestimeit) estimate at too low a value; underrate. *n* (ʌndərˈestimət) estimate that is too low.

underfoot *adv* 1 under the feet; on the ground. 2 in a subservient position.

undergo *vt* (-goes; -went; -gone) experience; submit oneself to; endure; suffer.

undergraduate *n* student who has not yet taken a degree.

underground *adj,adv* **1** below ground level. **2** secret; hidden. *n* **1** secret political resistance movement. **2** underground railway.

undergrowth *n* shrubs and plants growing under trees in a wood, etc.

underhand *adj* sly; dishonest; furtive. *adv* secretly; fraudulently.

underline *vt* **1** draw a line under. **2** stress; emphasize.

undermine *vt* **1** tunnel beneath; wear away. **2** destroy or weaken by subtle or insidious methods.

underneath *adv,prep* below; beneath; lower than. *n* lower part.

underpants *pl n* man's undergarment covering the waist to the thighs.

underpass *n* road or path crossing underneath another road, a railway, etc.; subway.

underrate *vt* underestimate; rate too low.

understand *v* (-stood) *vt,vi* know or grasp the meaning (of); comprehend; realize. *vt* **1** infer; believe. **2** sympathize with; tolerate. **understanding** *n* **1** sympathy. **2** comprehension; intelligence. **3** agreement; pact. *adj* sympathetic; wise.

understatement *n* expression with less force or completeness than merited or expected. **understate** *vt* express by understatement; minimize.

understudy *n* actor or actress prepared to take another's part when necessary. *vt* be ready to act as understudy to; learn a part as understudy.

undertake *vt* (-took; -taken) commit oneself (to); attempt to; accept; promise. **undertaker** *n* person who arranges funerals. **undertaking** *n* **1** task; venture. **2** promise.

undertone *n* **1** low, suppressed, or hidden tone of voice or feeling. **2** pale or subdued colour.

undervalue *vt* place too low a value on.

underwear *n* clothing worn under outer clothing, next to the skin; underclothes.

underweight *adj* of less than average or required weight.

underwent *v pt* of **undergo**.

underworld *n* **1** place of departed spirits. **2** section of society controlled by criminals, gangsters, etc.

underwrite *vt* (-wrote; written) accept liability; insure; guarantee. **underwriter** *n*.

undesirable *adj* not desirable; unpleasant; offensive.

undo *v* (-does; -did; -done) *vt,vi* open; loosen; unfasten. *vt* **1** cancel; reverse. **2** ruin the reputation of.

undoubted *adj* certain; sure. **undoubtedly** *adv.*

undress *vt,vi* remove the clothes (of). *n* state of being naked or partly clothed.

undue *adj* excessive; unnecessary. **unduly** *adv.*

undulate *vi* move in a wavelike or rolling manner. **undulation** *n*

unearth *vt* dig up; uncover; reveal; bring to light. **unearthly** *adj* **1** ethereal; supernatural; uncanny. **2** ridiculous; unreasonable.

uneasy *adj* anxious; apprehensive; uncomfortable; awkward. **uneasily** *adv.*

unemployed *adj* **1** out of work. **2** not in use. *n* those without jobs. **unemployment** *n.* **unemployment benefit** *n* regular payments made to the unemployed; dole.

unequal *adj* not equal, similar, or uniform; not evenly balanced. **unequal to** lacking necessary strength, ability, etc., to. **unequalled** *adj* supreme; without rivals. **unequally** *adv.*

uneven *adj* **1** not level or straight; rough. **2** not uniform or well balanced; patchy. **3** odd; not divisible by two. **unevenly** *adv.*

unfailing *adj* dependable; continuous; certain.

unfair *adj* not fair; unjust; dishonest. **unfairly** *adv.* **unfairness** *n.*

unfaithful *adj* **1** not faithful; disloyal. **2** adulterous. **3** inaccurate; unreliable.

unfamiliar *adj* strange; not known or experienced. **unfamiliar with** having little knowledge of.

unfit *adj* **1** not fit; unhealthy. **2** unsuitable; incapable; not worthy.

unfold *vt,vi* **1** spread or open out. **2** reveal or be revealed; relate; develop.

unfortunate *adj* unlucky; unsuccessful; undesirable; regrettable. **unfortunately** *adv.*

ungainly *adj* awkward; gauche; clumsy.

unhappy *adj* 1 not happy; sad; miserable. 2 unfortunate; unlucky. 3 tactless. **unhappily** *adv.* **unhappiness** *n.*

unhealthy *adj* 1 not healthy; sick; diseased; abnormal. 2 threatening physical, mental, or moral damage; harmful.

unicorn *n* fabulous animal resembling a white horse with a single horn on its forehead.

uniform *adj* exactly similar in appearance, quality, degree, etc.; unvarying; regular. *n* distinctive outfit worn by all members of a school, nursing staff, police force, etc. **uniformity** *n.* **uniformly** *adv.*

unify *vt,vi* unite. **unification** *n.*

unilateral *adj* one-sided; of, affecting, or carried out by one side only.

uninterested *adj* not interested; bored. **uninteresting** *adj* arousing no interest; dull.

union *n* 1 act or condition of becoming united or joined together. 2 association or confederation of people, companies, countries, etc., formed for the common good. 3 trade union. **Union Jack** *n* national flag of Great Britain, combining the crosses of the patron saints Andrew, Patrick, and George.

unique *adj* 1 single; sole. 2 unequalled; remarkable. **uniquely** *adv.* **uniqueness** *n.*

unison *n* **in unison** 1 sounding or speaking the same notes or words simultaneously. 2 in agreement.

unit *n* 1 single item; undivided entity. 2 standard amount such as the metre or second, by which a physical quantity, such as length or time, may be measured. 3 small part of a larger scheme, organization, etc. 4 apparatus; mechanical assembly; functional system. **unit pricing** *n* method of pricing foodstuffs, etc. by showing the cost per specified unit, e.g. kilogram, as well as total cost of item.

unite *vt,vi* 1 join together; combine; cooperate. 2 unify; come or bring to agreement. **unity** *n* 1 state of being united; amalgamation; continuity; harmonious agreement. 2 number one.

universe *n* 1 whole system of matter, energy, and space, including the earth, planets, stars, and galaxies. 2 field of human experience. **universal** *adj* 1 relating to all mankind, to nature, or to every member of a specific group. 2 widespread; general; applicable to most situations, conditions, etc.

university *n* institution of higher education empowered to confer degrees and having research facilities.

unkempt *adj* not cared for; neglected; untidy; messy.

unkind *adj* not kind; inconsiderate; hurtful. **unkindly** *adv.* **unkindness** *n.*

unknown *adj* not known, recognized, or identified. *n* unknown thing, state, etc.

unlawful *adj* against the law; illegal.

unless *conj* except on condition or under the circumstances that.

unlike *adj* not like; dissimilar; different. *prep* not like; not typical of.

unlikely *adj* not likely; improbable.

unload *vi,vt* remove a load (from). *vt* sell in bulk.

unlucky *adj* not successful; unfortunate; bringing misfortune or failure.

unnatural *adj* 1 not natural; artificial; unusual; abnormal; forced. 2 wicked; vile.

unnecessary *adj* not necessary; superfluous.

unofficial *adj* not official or confirmed; informal. **unofficially** *adv.*

unorthodox *adj* not orthodox; unconventional.

unpack *vt,vi* remove (items) from a case, box, package, etc.

unpleasant *adj* not pleasant; nasty; impolite; disagreeable. **unpleasantly** *adv.* **unpleasantness** *n.*

unravel *v* (-ll-) *vt* 1 disentangle; undo a piece of knitting. 2 sort out; straighten. *vi* become unravelled.

unreasonable *adj* not guided by reason; not justified; excessive; illogical.

unrest *n* state of discontent; disturbance; anxiety.

unruly *adj* difficult to control; not disciplined; wild; disorderly.

unscrew *vt* 1 unfasten or loosen by turning a screw. 2 loosen or detach by rotating. *vi* become unscrewed.

unsettle *vt* disturb; make uncertain or insecure; upset.

unsightly *adj* unpleasant to look at; ugly.

unsound *adj* not stable or reliable.

unstable *adj* **1** not firm or reliable, esp. mentally or emotionally. **2** decomposing spontaneously; radioactive. **3** readily decomposing into other chemicals.

unsteady *adj* not steady or firm; rocky; precarious. **unsteadily** *adv.*

untidy *adj* not tidy; disordered; slovenly. *vt* make untidy; mess up. **untidily** *adv.* **untidiness** *n.*

untie *vt* (-tying) unfasten; undo (a knot).

until *prep* during the time preceding; up to the time of. *conj* up to the time or stage that. **not...until** only...when.

untrue *adj* **1** not true; incorrect; false. **2** unfaithful. **3** diverging from a standard, rule, etc. **untruth** *n* lie; falsehood. **untruthful** *adj* **1** given to lying. **2** untrue.

unusual *adj* not usual or common; strange; remarkable. **unusually** *adv.*

unwarranted *adj* uncalled for; unnecessary.

unwell *adj* sick; ill.

unwieldy *adj* difficult to handle or use; awkward; clumsy; cumbersome.

unwind *vt,vi* (-wound) **1** unroll; uncoil; slacken; untangle. **2** relax; calm down.

unworldly *adj* unearthly; spiritual. **2** not sophisticated; not materialist.

unworthy *adj* not worthy or deserving; lacking merit. **unworthily** *adv.*

unwrap *vt* (-pp-) remove the wrapping from.

up *adv* **1** in or to a higher position; further away from the ground. **2** in or to a higher status or rank. **3** into a hotter condition. **4** into a more intense emotional state. **5** no longer in bed. **6** so as to be equal to. **be up to 1** be the responsibility of. **2** be secretly engaged in. **up against** involved in a struggle with; face to face with. **up to date 1** modern; fashionable; current. **2** complete up to the present time; not in arrears. ~*prep* **1** to a higher position on. **2** further along. **3** to a place level with. *adj* moving or directed towards the top or north. *n* **ups and downs** fluctuations; alternate good and bad periods. ~*v* (-pp-) *vi* rise; get or stand up. *vt* make larger; increase or raise.

upbringing *n* education and rearing of children.

upheaval *n* great disturbance; commotion; eruption.

uphill *adj* **1** going or sloping upwards. **2** very difficult and exhausting. *adv* upwards; towards higher ground.

uphold *vt* (-held) maintain or defend against opposition; sustain.

upholstery *n* **1** coverings, padding, springs, etc., of chairs, sofas, etc. **2** business, trade, or skill of upholstering. **upholster** *vt,vi* provide or work with upholstery. **upholsterer** *n.*

upkeep *n* **1** maintenance; keeping in good condition. **2** cost of maintenance.

uplift *vt* **1** elevate; raise. **2** raise spiritually, morally, etc.; exalt. *n* **1** raising; elevation. **2** improvement; encouragement; enlightenment. **3** moment of joy.

upon *prep* on; on top of.

upper *adj* **1** higher in position, rank, status, etc. **2** further upstream or inland. **upper hand** position of control. ~*n* upper part of a shoe, boot, etc., above the sole. **on one's uppers** reduced to desperate poverty. **uppermost** *adj* highest in position, power, etc. *adv* in the highest position, rank, etc.

upright *adj* **1** vertical; erect. **2** honest; worthy; righteous. *adv* vertically. *n* **1** vertical post, beam, etc. **2** *also* **upright piano** piano with vertical strings.

uproar *n* **1** loud clamorous noise. **2** angry protest. **uproarious** *adj* **1** hilarious. **2** accompanied by uproar; tumultuous. **uproariously** *adv.*

uprising *n* revolt; rebellion.

uproot *vt* **1** dig up by the roots. **2** displace or remove from native surroundings. **3** destroy.

upset (-tt-; -set) *vt,vi* **1** overturn; knock or be knocked over; spill. **2** distress; disturb; confuse. **3** make or become ill. *n* **1** act of upsetting. **2** quarrel; disturbance. *adj* **1** annoyed; unhappy; disturbed. **2** overturned. **3** ill; sick.

upshot *n* consequence; outcome.

upside down *adj* **1** turned over completely; inverted. **2** confused; chaotic. *adv* in an upside down position or fashion.

upstairs *adv* up the stairs; to, in, or on a higher level. *n* upper part or floor.

upstream *adv,adj* against the current of a river; nearer or towards the source.

upward *adj* facing or moving towards a higher place, level, etc. **upwards** *adv* 1 to or towards a higher place, level, etc. 2 onwards; further along a scale. **upwards of** more than.

uranium *n* radioactive metallic element, used in nuclear reactors.

Uranus *n* outer giant planet lying between Saturn and Neptune.

urban *adj* relating to a town or city.

urbane *adj* sophisticated; suave; refined.

urge *vt* 1 entreat; plead with; press; strongly advise. 2 drive or force forward. *n* impulse; strong tendency; yearning. **urgent** *adj* pressing; demanding immediate action or attention. **urgency** *n*. **urgently** *adv*.

urine *n* fluid containing waste products excreted by the kidneys that is stored in the bladder before being discharged from the body. **urinate** *vi* discharge urine. **urination** *n*.

urn *n* 1 large metal container for heating and dispensing tea, etc. 2 vase or vessel, esp. for holding the ashes of a dead person.

us *pron* form of **we** when used as the object.

use *vt* (ju:z) 1 employ; put to some purpose. 2 handle; treat. 3 exploit. 4 expend; consume. *v aux* **used** to expressing past habits or regular occurrences. **use up** finish; exhaust. **used to** *adj* accustomed to; in the habit of. ~*n* (ju:s) 1 act of using; state of being used; usage. 2 right of using. 3 need; purpose; point of using. 4 custom; familiar practice. **usage** *n* manner of use; employment; treatment. **useful** *adj* of use; convenient; serviceable; helpful. **usefully** *adv*. **usefulness** *n*. **useless** *adj* of no use or help; incompetent; hopeless.

usher *n* 1 person employed to show people to their seats. 2 minor official at a law court, parliament, etc. *vt* 1 act as usher to; escort; lead in or to. 2 precede; herald. **usherette** *n* female usher in a cinema, theatre, etc.

usual *adj* habitual; customary; ordinary. **usually** *adv*.

usurp *vt* oust or take forcibly; seize without legal authority. **usurper** *n*.

utensil *n* tool or implement, esp. used in cookery.

uterus *n* womb; organ in female mammals where an embryo develops.

utility *n* 1 usefulness. 2 something useful or practical. 3 *also* **public utility** public service, such as the railway or electricity supply. **utilize** *vt* make practical or worthwhile use of.

utmost *adj also* **uttermost** furthest; outermost; maximum; most extreme. *n* greatest possible amount, degree, extent, etc.; best.

utter[1] *vt,vi* give audible voice to; say or speak.

utter[2] *adj* extreme; complete; total; absolute. **utterly** *adv*.

U-turn *n* 1 turn in the shape of the letter U made by a vehicle reversing its direction of travel. 2 reversal of policy or direction.

V

vacant *adj* 1 empty; unoccupied; not in use. 2 blank; stupid. **vacantly** *adv*. **vacancy** *n* 1 position, job, etc., that is not yet filled. 2 stupidity; blankness. **vacate** *vt* make empty; leave. **vacation** *n* holiday period for universities, law courts, etc.

vaccinate *vt* produce immunity against a specific disease by inoculating with vaccine. **vaccination** *n*. **vaccine** *n* dead microorganisms used in vaccination to produce immunity by stimulating antibody production.

vacillate *vi* 1 oscillate; fluctuate. 2 waver; hesitate; prevaricate. **vacillation** *n*.

vacuum *n* 1 space devoid of air or containing air or other gas at very low pressure. 2 feeling of emptiness. **vacuum cleaner** *n* equipment for removing dust, etc., by suction. **vacuum flask** *n* container in which the contents are kept at constant temperature by means of the insulating effect of the vacuum between its two walls.

vagina (və'dʒainə) *n* passage from an exterior orifice to the uterus in female mammals. **vaginal** *adj*.

vagrant *n* person with no fixed abode or job; tramp. *adj* wandering; unsettled; erratic. **vagrancy** *n*.

vague *adj* lacking precision or clarity; uncertain; indefinite. **vaguely** *adv.* **vagueness** *n.*

vain *adj* **1** conceited; excessively proud of one's appearance, possessions, etc. **2** useless; futile; worthless; empty. **in vain** to no purpose. **vainly** *adv*

valiant *adj* brave; strong; heroic. **valiantly** *adv.*

valid *adj* based on truth; logically sound; having legal force. **validity** *n.* **validate** *vt* confirm; make valid. **validation** *n.*

valley *n* **1** trough between hills, often containing a river. **2** land area drained by a river.

value *n* **1** worth; market price; fair equivalent. **2** quality that makes something estimable, desirable, or useful. **3** degree of this quality. *vt* **1** assess the value of; assign a value to. **2** esteem; prize. **valuable** *adj* **1** of great worth; costing much money. **2** very useful; having admirable qualities, etc. *n* article of high value.

valve *n* **1** device or structure that seals, opens, or regulates fluid flow, usually in one direction. **2** electronic device in which current flows in one direction only, used esp. to amplify signals. **3** device on some brass instruments by which the tube length and hence pitch may be varied.

vampire *n* creature of folklore that rises by night from the grave to suck the blood of humans.

van *n* **1** covered motor vehicle for transporting or delivering goods. **2** railway wagon for luggage, goods, etc.

vandal *n* person who deliberately destroys or spoils something of value. **vandalism** *n.* **vandalize** *vt* destroy by vandalism.

vanilla *n* flavouring obtained from the bean of a tropical climbing orchid.

vanish *vi* disappear; become invisible; cease to exist.

vanity *n* **1** exaggerated opinion of oneself; conceit; excessive pride. **2** worthlessness; futility.

vapour *n* **1** moisture in the air, seen as mist, smoke, clouds, etc. **2** substance in a gaseous state, esp. when its temperature is below its boiling point. **vaporize** *vt, vi* turn into or become a vapour.

variable *adj* liable to change; not constant; inconsistent; unreliable. *n* something that can change value, etc.

variant *adj* showing discrepancy or difference; varying. *n* *also* **variance** different form of the same thing; variation; deviation.

variation *n* **1** change; modification. **2** departure from a standard type or norm.

variety *n* **1** state or quality of having many forms or versions; diversity; versatility. **2** different form or version of something. **3** assorted collection. **4** theatrical presentation of assorted turns.

various *adj* several; of different kinds; displaying variety. **variously** *adv.*

varnish *n* **1** oil-based solution that dries to provide a hard glossy skin. **2** glossy surface so produced. **3** superficial attractiveness. *vt* **1** coat with varnish. **2** conceal under superficial gloss.

vary *vt* make different; alter; diversify; modify. *vi* become different or altered; disagree; deviate.

vase *n* ornamental container, often used for holding flowers.

vasectomy *n* sterilization of men by surgical cutting of the spermatic duct.

vast *adj* boundless; immense; exceedingly great. **vastly** *adv.* **vastness** *n.*

vat *n* large vessel or cask for holding liquids.

VAT *n* *also* **value-added-tax** tax on the rise in value of a product caused by manufacturing and marketing processes.

Vatican *n* **1** palace and principal residence and administrative centre of the Pope, in Rome. **2** Papal authority.

vault[1] *vi, vt* spring; leap over, esp. with the aid of the hands or a pole. *n* act of vaulting.

vault[2] *n* **1** underground room, often a burial chamber. **2** arched roof or ceiling. **3** strongroom in which valuables may be safely stored. **vaulted** *adj* arched. ~*vt, vi* cover with, construct, or curve like a vault.

veal *n* calf's flesh, prepared as food.

veer *vi, vt* change direction or course; swing.

vegetable *n* **1** plant having various parts that may be used for food. **2** *inf* person entirely dependent on others due to loss of mental faculties, etc.

vegetarian n person who eats no meat but only vegetable foods and sometimes fish, eggs, and dairy produce. **vegetarianism** n.

vegetation n plants in a mass; plant life.

vegetate vi lead a boring, empty, inactive life.

vehement adj marked by strong feelings; forceful; passionate; emphatic. **vehemence** n. **vehemently** adv.

vehicle n 1 means of transport or communication; conveyance. 2 medium for conveying or expressing ideas, etc. **vehicular** adj.

veil n 1 covering for a woman's head or face. 2 something flat that covers or conceals. vt cover with a veil; conceal; disguise.

vein n 1 vessel conducting oxygen-depleted blood to the heart. 2 fluid-conducting vessel in plant leaves. 3 fine tube in the framework of an insect's wing. 4 streak in marble, wood, etc. 5 trait in a person's character.

velocity n speed; rate of change of position.

velvet n 1 silk, cotton, or nylon fabric with soft thick pile on one surface. 2 soft smooth surface or covering.

vendetta n private feud; rivalry.

veneer n 1 thin layer of wood, plastic, etc., bonded to a surface. 2 superficial covering. vt cover with veneer.

venerate vt worship; have great respect or reverence for. **veneration** n.

venereal disease n disease transmitted by sexual intercourse.

vengeance n infliction of injury in return for injury suffered; revenge. **with a vengeance** thoroughly. **vengeful** adj vindictive; desiring revenge.

venison n deer's flesh prepared as food.

venom n 1 poison, esp. that of a snake. 2 spite. **venomous** adj.

vent n narrow opening or outlet; ventilating duct. **give vent to** allow free expression of. ~vt give expression to.

ventilate vt 1 allow free passage of air into; drive stale or foul air out. 2 expose to public examination and discussion. **ventilation** n.

venture n hazardous or speculative course of action; attempt. vt 1 risk. 2 dare to put forward. vi also **venture out** brave the dangers of something.

Venus n conspicuous bright planet, lying between Mercury and the earth.

veranda n also **verandah** covered terrace along the outside of a house.

verb n word expressing action, occurrence, or existence. **verbal** adj. **verbally** adv. **verbatim** adj word for word. **verbiage** n excess of words. **verbose** adj using an excessive number of words. **verbosity** n.

verdict n conclusion of a jury; decision.

verge n 1 limit; boundary; edge; margin. 2 grass border. v **verge on** approach; border on.

verger n person acting as an official attendant and usher in a church. ·

verify vt ascertain or confirm the truth of. **verifiable** adj. **verification** n.

vermin pl n 1 animals, esp. rodents, that are destructive or dangerous to man. 2 obnoxious people; scum.

vermouth n white wine flavoured with aromatic herbs.

vernacular n 1 spoken language or dialect of a people. 2 jargon or idiom.

versatile adj capable of many activities or uses; adapting readily. **versatility** n.

verse n 1 subsection of a poem; stanza. 2 metrical composition of a line of poetry. 3 poetry as opposed to prose. 4 unit into which chapters of the Bible are divided. **versed** adj acquainted with; skilled in.

version n one of a number of possible accounts, renderings, or interpretations.

vertebrate n animal having a backbone. adj having a backbone.

vertex n, pl **vertexes** or **vertices** ('vɔːtisiːz) apex; topmost point; meeting point of two intersecting lines.

vertical adj 1 upright; at right angles to the horizon. 2 extending at right angles from a surface; directly above or overhead. n vertical line or position. **vertically** adv.

verve n vigour; zest.

very adv used to add emphasis to an adjective. adj used with a noun to give emphasis to a quality inherent in the meaning of the noun.

vessel n 1 container or receptacle, esp. for a liquid. 2 ship or boat, usually large. 3 tube for conducting fluid in animals or plants.

vest n undergarment covering the upper half of the body. vt invest, confer on, or endow with (rights, property, etc.). **vest in place** in the control of.

vestige *n* faint trace or hint of proof, evidence.

vestment *n* ceremonial garment as worn by clergy.

vestry *n* room in or attached to a church where vestments and church documents are kept.

vet *n* short for **veterinary surgeon.** *vt* (-tt-) examine; check.

veteran *n* **1** person with great or long experience in something. **2** old and experienced soldier. **veteran car** *n* old car constructed before 1905 or sometimes before 1919.

veterinary surgeon *n also* **vet** person having specialized medical training in the treatment of sick or injured animals.

veto *vt* forbid absolutely; withhold assent; reject. *n, pl* **vetoes 1** right to veto, esp. the passing of a law. **2** act of vetoing.

vex *vt* distress; tease; annoy. **vexation** *n*.

via *prep* through; by way of.

viable *adj* **1** capable of sustaining existence. **2** capable of being effected, validated, etc.; feasible; workable. **viability** *n*.

viaduct *n* structure bridging a valley, etc., bearing a road or railway.

vibes *pl n sl* feelings, sensations, reactions, etc., to a particular situation.

vibrate *vt,vi* **1** move rapidly to and fro; oscillate; quiver. **2** resound; resonate. **vibration** *n*.

vicar *n* clergyman of a parish having the same spiritual status as a rector. **vicarage** *n* residence of a vicar.

vicarious *adj* deriving pain, pleasure, etc., from another's experiences. **vicariously** *adv*.

vice[1] *n* evil practice or trait; wickedness; immorality; bad habit.

vice[2] *n* adjustable tool for gripping an object that is being worked on.

vice-chancellor *n* active head of a university.

vice-president *n* president's immediate deputy.

vice versa *adv* conversely.

vicinity *n* surrounding or adjacent area; neighbourhood; proximity.

vicious *adj* wicked; cruel; violent; harsh; spiteful. **viciously** *adv*. **viciousness** *n*.

victim *n* object of attack; person suffering from an accident or from ill treatment by others. **victimize** *vt* make a victim of. **victimization** *n*.

victory *n* defeat of an enemy; success in a contest or struggle. **victor** *n* person gaining victory; winner. **victorious** *adj*.

video *n* **1** a video-tape. **2** a video-recorder. **video game** *n* electronically operated game played on a screen. **video-recorder** *n* device for recording and playing back television programmes, etc. on video-tape. **video-tape** *n* magnetic tape on which television programmes, films, etc., may be recorded for subsequent transmission.

view *n* **1** act of seeing or observing; examination; inspection. **2** prospect of the surrounding countryside, etc. **3** range or field of vision. **4** mental attitude; opinion. **5** survey. **6** intention. **in view of** considering. ~*vt,vi* watch, esp. a film or television; inspect; judge. **viewer** *n*. **view-finder** *n* device in a camera through which the area to be photographed can be established.

vigil *n* act of or time spent keeping watch, esp. at night. **vigilance** *n* alertness. **vigilant** *adj*.

vigour *n* energy; power; strength; forcefulness; good health. **vigorous** *adj*. **vigorously** *adv*.

vile *adj* **1** disgusting; despicable. **2** abominable; shameful; sinful. **3** unpleasant; objectionable. **vilify** *vt* speak ill of; abuse. **vilification** *n*.

villa *n* luxurious house, esp. one by the sea or in the country.

village *n* **1** group of rural dwellings with a smaller population than that of a town. **2** inhabitants of a village. **villager** *n*.

villain *n* **1** wicked person; scoundrel; evildoer. **2** character whose evil is central to the plot in a story, play, etc. **villainous** *adj*.

vindictive *adj* spiteful. **vindictively** *adv*.

vine *n* woody climbing plant, esp. one bearing grapes. **vineyard** *n* plantation of grapevines.

vinegar *n* sour-tasting acidic liquid used for pickling, as a seasoning, etc.

vintage *n* **1** age as an indication of quality. **2** time of origin. **3** harvesting or harvest of grapes and the making of wine. **4** wine obtained from grapes grown in a specified year, esp. one of good quality. *adj* **1** old and of good quality. **2** dated. **vintage car** *n* old car, esp. one built between 1919 and 1930.

vinyl *adj* containing an organic group of atoms that form the basis of many plastic and resins.

viola *n* four-stringed instrument resembling but slightly larger than a violin.

violate *vt* **1** do violence to; abuse; defile; treat disrespectfully. **2** rape or assault. **3** disregard or break (a rule, promise, etc.). **violation** *n.*

violence *n* **1** assault; use of excessive unrestrained force. **2** great force; intensity; fervour. **violent** *adj* **1** impetuously forceful; overwhelmingly vehement. **2** using or needing great physical strength. **violently** *adv.*

violet *n* **1** small purple spring flower. **2** spectral colour of a bluish-purple hue. *adj* of a violet colour.

violin *n* musical instrument having a hollow wooden waisted body and four strings, played with a bow. **violinist** *n.*

viper *n* small venomous snake; adder.

virgin *n* person, esp. a woman, who has never had sexual intercourse. *adj* **1** *also* **virginal** pure; chaste. **2** in the original condition; untouched; not yet used, cultivated, etc. **virginity** *n.*

Virgo *n* sixth sign of the zodiac, represented by the Virgin.

virile *adj* sexually potent; displaying traditional masculine characteristics. **virility** *n.*

virtual *adj* existing in effect or essence, but not in fact. **virtually** *adv* in effect; practically.

virtue *n* **1** goodness; moral excellence. **2** chastity; sexual purity. **by virtue of** by reason of; on the grounds of. **virtuous** *adj.*

virus *n* microorganism causing various infectious diseases. **viral** *adj.*

visa *n* stamp or endorsement on a passport permitting the bearer to enter a particular country.

viscount ('vaikaunt) *n* nobleman ranking between a baron and an earl in the British peerage. **viscountess** *n* wife or widow of a viscount.

viscous *adj* thick; sticky; slow to flow. **viscosity** *n.*

visible *adj* **1** capable of being seen. **2** apparent; obvious. **visibility** *n* **1** state of being visible. **2** clearness of the atmosphere; range of vision.

vision *n* **1** act or power of seeing; sight; range of sight. **2** beautiful person or object. **3** mystical experience or prophetic dream. **4** imagination; foresight.

visit *vt,vi* go or come to see for pleasure, business, etc.; call (on). *n* act of visiting; call. **visitor** *n.*

visual *adj* of or by sight; capable of being seen; visible. **visually** *adv.* **visualize** *vt* form a clear mental image of.

vital *adj* **1** necessary to or sustaining life; living. **2** lively. **3** very important; essential. **vitality** *n* strength; vigour; energy. **vitally** *adv* critically.

vitamin *n* substance found in food and essential in small quantities to health.

vivacious *adj* lively; sprightly; full of vitality. **vivaciously** *adv.* **vivacity** *n.*

vivid *adj* **1** very bright; intense. **2** graphic; distinct; clear. **3** vigorous; lively. **vividly** *adv.*

vivisection *n* practice of performing surgical operations on living animals, esp. for medical research.

vixen *n* female fox.

vocabulary *n* **1** total number of words used or understood by a person, group, etc., or contained in a language. **2** listing of words or phrases given with meanings, translations, etc.

vocal *adj* **1** relating to or produced by the voice. **2** readily disposed to express opinions; outspoken. **vocalist** *n* singer. **vocal cords** *pl n* vibrating membranes in the larynx that are responsible for vocal production.

vocation *n* **1** course of action or occupation to which a person feels called by God, duty, or conscience. **2** profession or occupation, esp. when viewed as a career. **vocational** *adj.*

vodka *n* traditional Russian alcoholic drink distilled from rye or potatoes.

voice *n* **1** sound produced by the vocal cords. **2** tone, quality, etc., of a voice; person's characteristic speech sounds. **3** musical sound of a singing voice. **4** faculty of speech or singing. **5** expression of opinion. *vt* express.

void *adj* **1** empty; vacant. **2** not binding; null; invalid. *vt* make empty, invalid, or ineffective. *n* **1** empty space. **2** painful awareness of a lack of something or someone.

volatile *adj* **1** changeable; lively but unstable. **2** readily forming a vapour.

volcano *n, pl* **volcanoes** *or* **volcanos** outlet in the earth's crust for erupting subterranean matter (lava, rocks, dust, and gases), which forms into a conical mountain. **volcanic** *adj*.

vole *n* small rodent resembling a rat.

volition *n* power or exercise of the will.

volley *n* **1** series of things discharged simultaneously or rapidly. **2** return of a ball in cricket, tennis, etc., before it bounces. *vt,vi* **1** return (a ball) before it bounces. **2** discharge in a volley.

volt *n* unit for measuring voltage. **voltage** *n* force producing an electric current in a circuit.

volume *n* **1** measure of the space occupied by or enclosed inside something; quantity; amount. **2** intensity of sound. **3** book; one of a series of books forming one work. **voluminous** *adj* **1** sufficient to fill many volumes. **2** ample; large.

voluntary *adj* **1** done willingly or by one's own choice or desire; not compulsory. **2** given or offered for no payment; supported by donations. **voluntarily** *adv*. **volunteer** *vi,vt* freely offer (oneself, one's help, etc.) for something; enlist for service without compulsion. *n* person who makes a voluntary offer or enlists voluntarily.

voluptuous *adj* full of or suggesting sensual pleasure; alluring; provocative. **voluptuously** *adv*.

vomit *vi,vt* eject the contents of the stomach through the mouth. *n* **1** matter ejected. **2** act of vomiting.

voodoo *n* religious cult, esp. of Negroes in Haiti, involving belief in spirits, who possess the worshippers, and other rituals.

vote *n* **1** indication of preference or opinion; formal decision. **2** right to express such. **3** act of voting. *vt* **1** determine, decide on, or elect by a vote or general opinion. **2**

inf suggest. *vi* express one's preference, etc., by a vote. **voter** *n*.

vouch *vi* *also* **vouch for** guarantee; confirm; bear witness to. **voucher** *n* **1** written evidence supporting a claim. **2** ticket acting as a substitute for cash.

vow *n* solemn promise; pledge. **take vows** enter and commit oneself to a religious order. ~*vt,vi* make a vow (that); solemnly promise (to).

vowel *n* speech sound represented by the letters a, e, i, o, u, or a combination of these.

voyage *n* journey of some distance, esp. by water. *vi* make a voyage.

vulgar *adj* **1** lacking in taste; crude; coarse; unrefined. **2** of the common people. **vulgarity** *n*.

vulnerable *adj* open to attack or injury; easily hurt. **vulnerability** *n*.

vulture *n* **1** large predatory bird, feeding mainly on dead flesh. **2** person who preys on others.

vulva *n, pl* **vulvae** ('vʌlvai) *or* **vulvas** external female genitals.

W

wad *n* **1** mass of soft material. **2** bundle; roll. *vt,vi* (-dd-) pack, pad, or stuff with a wad. **wadding** *n* material for padding, packing, etc.

waddle *vi* take short steps, swaying from side to side. *n* swaying walk.

wade *vi* **1** step forward through water, mud, etc. **2** progress with difficulty; labour. *vt* cross by wading.

wafer *n* **1** thin light crisp biscuit. **2** thin disc of bread or biscuit used in the Eucharist.

waft *vi,vt* convey or cause to move smoothly through the air, over water, etc. *n* **1** whiff or scent carried through the air. **2** rush of air.

wag *vt,vi* (-gg-) move or cause to move from side to side or up and down. *n* act of wagging.

wage *n* rate of pay for a job, manual work, etc. *vt* engage in; carry on. **wager** *n,vt,vi* bet; stake. **wages** *pl n* payment for a job; earnings.

waggle *vt,vi,n* wag.

wagon *n* four-wheeled vehicle, such as a cart or open lorry.

wail *vi* lament; moan; express grief in long plaintive cries. *n* cry of grief.

waist *n* 1 narrowest part of the human body between the ribs and hips. 2 *also* **waistband** part of a garment covering the waist. 3 narrow middle part of an object, such as a violin. **waistcoat** *n* sleeveless close-fitting garment covering the chest and back. **waistline** *n* 1 junction of the skirt and bodice of a garment. 2 level of or length around a waist.

wait *vt,vi* defer action; remain in the same place (until, for, etc.); delay or be delayed. *vi* act as a waiter or waitress. *n* act or period of waiting. **lie in wait** prepare an ambush. **waiter** *n* male person employed to serve meals and wait at table in restaurants, etc. **waitress** *f n*.

waive *vt* refrain from insisting on, claiming, or enforcing; defer.

wake[1] *vi,vt* (woke; woken) *also* **wake up** disturb or be disturbed from sleep or inactivity; arouse; excite. *n* vigil beside a corpse before the funeral. **waken** *vt,vi* rouse or be roused; wake.

wake[2] *n* 1 disturbed water waves produced by a moving boat, etc. 2 disturbed track left by a hurricane, etc.

walk *vi* 1 move, pass through, or travel to on foot at a moderate pace. 2 stroll; ramble; hike. *vt* 1 pass through, pace, or traverse on foot. 2 cause to walk; accompany. **walk out** *v* 1 go on strike. 2 leave or abandon as a protest. **walkout** *n* industrial strike. **walk out on** *inf* abandon; desert. **walk over** *v* 1 beat or win easily. 2 *inf* take advantage of. **walkover** *n* easy victory; unopposed win. ~*n* 1 act or manner of walking. 2 leisurely excursion. 3 path; route.

wall *n* 1 upright construction of brick, stone, etc., forming part of a room or building, marking a boundary, etc. 2 containing surface or membrane. 3 barrier. *vt* surround, divide, fortify with, or confine within a wall. **wallflower** *n* 1 cultivated plant with fragrant yellow, brown, or red flowers. 2 *inf* spectator at an essentially participatory event. **wallpaper** *n* paper, usually decorated, for pasting to a wall or ceiling. *vt,vi* cover with wallpaper.

wallet *n* folding case for bank notes, etc.

wallop *inf* *vt,vi* beat soundly; thrash. *n* heavy blow.

wallow *vi* 1 indulge or delight (in). 2 roll about in mud, etc. *n* act of wallowing.

walnut *n* tree yielding highly esteemed hardwood for furniture, etc., and a nut with a wrinkled shell and edible kernel.

walrus *n* amphibious mammal related to the seal, having two long tusks.

waltz *n* 1 dance in three-four time performed in pairs. 2 music for this dance or having this rhythm. *vi* dance the waltz.

wand *n* slender and supple stick used as symbol of power or authority.

wander *vi* 1 roam without purpose or plan; stroll; meander. 2 deviate from the line of argument. 3 become delirious; talk incoherently. *n* ramble. **wanderer** *n*. **wanderlust** *n* urge to travel.

wane *vi* diminish in observed size, esp. after a peak; decrease; decline. *n* act of waning.

wangle *inf* *vt,vi* manipulate to suit oneself; use craft or irregular means to achieve ends. *n* act or instance of wangling.

want *vt* feel a need for; long for. *vt,vi* need; desire. **want for lack**. ~*n* 1 something wanted. 2 lack; shortage. **in want** destitute; requiring help.

war *n* 1 armed conflict between nations, groups of people, etc. 2 bitter conflict; hostility. *vi* (-rr-) make war; fight. **warfare** *n* act or process of waging war. **warlike** *adj* 1 hostile; belligerent. 2 military.

warble *vi,vt* sing with trills. *vi* produce a quavering note. *n* sound of such singing.

ward *n* 1 hospital room with beds for patients. 2 area of a city, borough, etc., for administrative purposes. 3 minor entrusted to the care of a guardian or a court of law. **ward off** protect against. **warden** *n* 1 guardian; guard; custodian. 2 superintendent or head of certain colleges and schools. **warder** *n* person in charge of prisoners in a gaol. **wardress** *f n*.

wardrobe *n* 1 cupboard in which clothes are kept. 2 range and extent of clothing or costumes of an individual or theatrical group.

warehouse *n* building used for storage of goods before their sale, distribution, etc. **wares** *pl n* goods for sale.

warm *adj* **1** having or maintaining a pleasant temperature; moderately hot. **2** affectionate; kind. **3** enthusiastic; passionate; lively. **4** red, yellow, or orange coloured. **5** near to discovery, guessing, etc. *vt,vi* **1** *also* **warm up** raise or be raised to medium temperature. **2** make or become livelier or happier. **warm to** become enthusiastic about or friendly towards. ~*n* process of warming. **warm up 1** make receptive to a performance on television, etc. **2** exercise before a sporting contest. **3** run until operating conditions are achieved. *n* **warm-up** process of warming up. **warmly** *adv.* **warmth** *n.* **warm-blooded** *adj* able to maintain a constant body temperature. **warm-hearted** *adj* generous; sympathetic; kindly.

warn *vt,vi* **1** give an indication of approaching danger, adverse results, etc.; threaten. **2** advise against or in advance. **warning** *n* indication of a likely course of events or state of affairs; caution.

warp *vt,vi* **1** twist or cause to twist out of shape; distort. **2** make or become full of misconceptions; pervert. *n* **1** threads running along the length of woven material. **2** distortion of wood, etc., caused by heat, damp, etc.

warrant *n* **1** authorization, esp. for police to make an arrest, search property, etc. **2** guarantee. *vt* authorize; guarantee. *vt,vi* declare; affirm. **warrant officer** *n* officer in the armed services holding a rank, authorized by warrant, between commissioned and noncommissioned officers.

warren *n* **1** interconnecting underground tunnels inhabited by rabbits. **2** overcrowded living quarters.

warrior *n* man who is skilled in or experienced in warfare or fighting.

wart *n* horny protuberance on the skin. **warty** *adj.*

wary *adj* cautious; careful of deception or danger. **warily** *adv.* **wariness** *n.*

was *v* 1st and 3rd person form of **be** in the past tense.

wash *vt,vi* make or become clean using water and usually soap. *vt* **1** remove with soap and water. **2** flow over. **3** cover with a thin layer of paint, etc. *vi inf* bear examination. **wash away** move or remove by the force of water. ~*n* **1** act of washing. **2** collection of articles for washing. **3** flow or wake of water. **4** medical lotion. **washing** *n* clothes, etc., washed or to be washed. **washout** *n inf* total failure.

washer *n* flat ring under a bolt head or nut to distribute pressure or provide a seal.

wasp *n* winged stinging insect, usually with black and yellow stripes on its body.

waste *vt* use carelessly; squander. **waste away** deteriorate in health; dwindle. ~*n* **1** misuse; neglect; act of wasting. **2** something squandered, neglected, discarded, worthless, superfluous, etc. **3** rubbish. **wasteful** *adj* causing or tending to waste.

watch *vt,vi* **1** look (at) or observe carefully or closely. **2** wait attentively (for); keep a look-out (for). **3** guard. *vi* keep guard or vigil. *n* **1** small mechanism, worn esp. on the wrist, registering the passage of time. **2** act or instance of watching; period of vigil. **3** person or persons performing this duty. **watchdog** *n* dog kept for guarding property. **watchful** *adj* vigilant; awake.

water *n* colourless liquid that consists of hydrogen and oxygen and forms ice below its freezing point and steam above its boiling point. **2** impure water, as found in rivers, oceans, etc. **3** large expanse of water. **4** solution of something in water. *vt* **1** supply or add water to; make wet. **2** irrigate. **3** dilute. *vi* **1** (of the mouth) secrete saliva at the sight of food. **2** (of the eyes) secrete tears.

watercolour *n* **1** painting in water-soluble pigments. **2** those pigments.

watercress *n* freshwater plant with edible leaves.

waterfall *n* precipitous descent of water in a river course.

watering-can *n* vessel with a handle, spout, and nozzle for watering plants, etc.

water lily *n* aquatic plant whose large leaves and showy flowers float on the surface of water.

waterlogged *adj* saturated with water.

watermelon *n* melon plant bearing large edible fruit with reddish watery flesh.

waterproof *adj* not allowing water through. *n* waterproof garment; raincoat. *vt* make waterproof.

water-ski *vi* travel over the surface of water on skis holding a rope pulled by a speedboat. *n* ski used for this purpose. **water-skier** *n*.

watertight *adj* **1** impervious to water. **2** irrefutable; allowing no points of dispute.

waterworks *n* **1** establishment for supplying water to a community. **2** *sl* shedding of tears. **3** *sl* urinary system.

watery *adj* **1** of, like, or containing water. **2** weak; pale; insipid.

watt *n* unit of electrical, mechanical, and thermal power.

wave *n* **1** undulation on the surface of a liquid, esp. the sea. **2** any undulation, as in the hair. **3** oscillating disturbances by which radio energy, sound energy, light energy, etc., is carried through air or some other medium. **4** surge of events, emotions, people, etc. **5** to-and-fro movement of the hand expressing greeting, etc. *vt,vi* move or cause to move to and fro. *vi* greet or signal by a wave. *vt* **1** direct by a wave. **2** set waves in (hair). **waveband** *n* range of wavelengths used in radio transmission. **wavelength** *n* distance between two successive peaks of an energy wave. **wavy** *adj* undulating; full of waves; swaying to and fro.

waver *vi* **1** be unsteady. **2** oscillate; vary. **3** hesitate; falter.

wax[1] *n* solid or viscous insoluble natural substance that softens at low temperatures. *vt* smear or rub with wax. **waxy** *adj*.

wax[2] *vi* become larger or apparently larger; increase.

way *n* **1** route; direction; path. **2** progress; distance; journey. **3** manner; style; method; characteristic behaviour, etc. **4** condition; state. **by the way** incidentally. **give way (to) 1** yield. **2** stop for. **in a way** in certain respects. **in the way** impeding progress. **out of the way 1** so as not to obstruct. **2** unusual. **3** not easily accessible. **under way** in progress; in motion. **wayside** *n* edge of a road or route.

waylay *vt* **1** intercept so as to attack; ambush. **2** detain in order to speak with.

wayward *adj* wilful; capricious; selfish.

we *pron* used as the subject to refer to oneself and another person or all other people including oneself.

weak *adj* **1** not strong; frail. **2** very diluted; insipid. **3** below expected standard. **4** lacking moral, mental, or political strength. **weakly** *adv*. **weakness** *n*. **weaken** *vt, vi* make or become weaker; reduce or be diminished in stature, strength, or resolve. **weak-kneed** *adj* lacking resolution or firmness; timid. **weakling** *n* person or animal that gives way easily or lacks strength. **weak-minded** *adj* **1** mentally deficient. **2** lacking resolution; easily persuaded. **weak-willed** *adj* easily deterred, dissuaded, or distracted.

wealth *n* **1** aggregate of valuable property; affluence; riches. **2** abundance. **wealthy** *adj*.

weapon *n* object, device, or other means used for attack or defence or to injure another.

wear *v* (wore; worn) *vt* **1** be dressed in; have on. **2** carry; bear; display; present. *vt,vi* **1** produce or be produced by constant rubbing, long use, etc.; impair or deteriorate. **2** reduce or be reduced to a certain condition. *n* **1** act of wearing. **2** clothing. **3** damage; wastage caused by use. **4** lasting quality. **wearable** *adj*.

weary *adj* **1** tired; reduced in strength or patience. **2** tedious; causing or caused by fatigue. *vt,vi* make or become tired or impatient. **wearily** *adv*. **weariness** *n*.

weasel *n* **1** small nimble carnivorous animal with a long slender brownish body. **2** treacherous, furtive, or sharp-featured person.

weather *n* local current atmospheric conditions of temperature, humidity, cloudiness, rainfall, wind, etc. *vt* come safely through. *vt,vi* expose or be exposed to the air or the weather.

weave *v* (wove *or* weaved; woven *or* weaved) *vt,vi* **1** interlace by passing threads alternately below and above other threads. **2** make fabric in this way. **3** create or move by winding in and out. *vt* **1** construct; fabricate. **2** introduce; combine. *n* texture or pattern of a woven fabric. **weaver** *n*.

web *n* **1** something woven. **2** fine filmy net spun by a spider to trap its prey. **3** membrane between the digits of a bat, duck, etc. **webbed** adj.

wedding n marriage ceremony.

wedge n 1 piece of solid material tapering towards one end. 2 anything of this shape. vt 1 fix firmly by positioning a wedge. 2 split; force apart. vt,vi squeeze or be squeezed into a space.

Wednesday n fourth day of the week.

weed n 1 wild prolific plant, esp. one growing where it is not wanted by man. 2 inf person of puny stature. 3 sl tobacco; cigarette. vt,vi remove weeds from (ground).

week n 1 period of seven days, usually from Sunday to Saturday. 2 working days of the week. **weekday** n any day of the week except Sunday and usually Saturday. **weekend** n period from Friday night to Sunday night.

weep v (wept) vi,vt 1 shed tears of sorrow, joy, etc; grieve (for). 2 exude moisture. n act of grieving or crying.

weft n threads running across the width of woven material.

weigh vt 1 ascertain the weight of. 2 compare against; counterbalance. 3 have a weight of. 4 estimate weight by holding or balancing in the hands. 5 consider carefully. 6 draw in an anchor. vi 1 have weight; be heavy. 2 be considered important or to have value. **weigh down** press down; oppress. **weigh out** measure by weight. ~n process of weighing. **weighbridge** n machine for weighing vehicles and their loads.

weight n 1 heaviness. 2 standardized piece of metal used for weighing. 3 force by which a mass is attracted by gravity to the earth. 4 anything heavy or oppressive. 5 power; impressiveness; significance. vt load with a weight. **weighty** adj. **weight-lifting** n sport consisting of competitive attempts at lifting increasingly heavier weights.

weird adj odd; uncanny; unreal. **weirdly** adv.

welcome n cordial greeting or reception. adj agreeable; giving pleasure; gladly received; willingly permitted. **make welcome** treat hospitably. ~vt greet cordially; be glad of.

weld vt join (metals, plastics, etc.) by applying heat or pressure; unite. vt,vi bring or be brought together. n welded joint or union.

welfare n 1 well-being; state or condition of life; freedom from want, sickness, or ignorance. 2 work or plans to improve people's welfare.

well[1] n 1 underground source of water; spring. 2 deep sunken shaft through which oil, water, gas, etc., may be extracted. vi pour forth; flow; gush.

well[2] adv 1 satisfactorily; correctly; thoroughly. 2 intimately. 3 clearly; easily. 4 with reason or consideration. 5 fully; abundantly. 6 generously; kindly; with care. **as well** also; too; in addition. adj 1 healthy. 2 right; favourable; satisfactory. interj expression of surprise, etc. **well-being** n state of good health, happiness, etc.; good. **well-bred** adj of good stock; properly reared; having good manners, etc. **well-built** adj of generous proportions and stature. **well-known** adj celebrated; famous; notorious. **well-off** adj rich; fortunate. **well-spoken** adj 1 speaking with a sociably acceptable accent. 2 spoken fittingly or appropriately. **well-worn** adj 1 thoroughly used. 2 trite; hackneyed.

wellington n also **wellington boot** knee-length footwear, esp. of rubber.

went v pt of **go**.

wept v pt and pp of **weep**.

were v 1 2nd person singular and 1st, 2nd, and 3rd person plural form of **be** in the past tense. 2 form of **be** in the subjunctive.

west n 1 one of the four cardinal points of the compass situated to the rear of a person facing the sunrise. 2 part of a country, area, etc., lying towards the west. adj also **western** of, in, or facing the west. adv,adj also **westerly** 1 towards the west. 2 (of winds) from the west. **western** n story, film, etc., taking place in the American West during pioneering times. **westerner** n. **westward** adj facing or moving towards the west. **westwards** adv in the direction of the west.

wet adj 1 covered or saturated with liquid; not yet dry. 2 rainy. 3 inf sentimental; feeble; lacking spirit; naive. vt (-tt-) make wet. n rain; moisture; dampness. **wetness** n.

whack vt strike; hit. n 1 sharp blow or the sound of this. 2 inf share. **whacked** adj inf exhausted. **whacking** n beating. adj inf very large.

whale n very large marine mammal that breathes through a blowhole on its head. vi hunt whales.

wharf n, pl **wharves** or **wharfs** landing-stage for mooring, loading, and unloading boats. vt,vi 1 berth. 2 unload (cargo).

what adj,pron used as an interrogative to request further information. adj that which. interj exclamation of surprise, dismay, etc. **whatever** pron 1 anything or all that. 2 what. adj,pron whichever; no matter which. adj at all.

wheat n cereal grass or its grain used for flour to make bread, etc.

wheedle vt,vi persuade by devious means; cajole.

wheel n 1 circular frame attached by radial supports to a central axis around which it rotates, used to aid movement, transportation, etc. 2 thing of similar shape or function. vt,vi 1 move on wheels; push along. 2 change direction; pivot. **wheelbarrow** n barrow supported on one wheel in front and two legs behind, which may be lifted by two handles. **wheelchair** n chair on two wheels, used by invalids, etc.

wheeze vi breathe with difficulty, making a rattling or hissing sound. n 1 sound of difficult breathing. 2 inf ruse; clever scheme; dodge.

whelk n edible marine mollusc with a snail-like shell.

when adv 1 at what time. 2 in or during which period. conj at the time that. pron from or until what time. **whenever** conj,adv at any or whatever time that. adv when.

where adv 1 in, at, or to what or which place or position. 2 from which place. conj to or in the place or situation that. **whereabouts** adv in what place; near where. n place where something or someone is located or hidden. **whereas** conj but; though; while. **whereby** adv by which means. **whereupon** conj,adv at which point. **wherever** conj,adv in or to any or whatever place that. adv where.

whether conj used to introduce an indirect question, esp. implying an alternative or choice and sometimes substitutable by 'if'.

which adj,pron used as an interrogative to request further information, esp. so as to distinguish between things. pron used to introduce a relative clause when referring to inanimate objects. **whichever** adj,pron 1 any one(s) that. 2 no matter which.

whiff n 1 puff; gust. 2 slight smell. vt,vi 1 puff. 2 smell.

while conj also **whilst** as long as; during the time that; at the same time as; although. n space of time. v **while away** spend or pass idly.

whim n caprice; fancy. **whimsical** adj capricious; fanciful.

whimper n feeble cry; whine. vi utter a whimper; plaintively moan or whine.

whine n 1 wailing high-pitched cry or note. 2 undignified complaint. vi,vt make or utter in a whine.

whip v (-pp-) vt 1 beat with a lash to punish or cause (a horse, etc.) to move forward. 2 whisk into froth. vi move or act quickly. **whip out** produce suddenly. ~n 1 lash on a handle for whipping. 2 stroke of a lash. 3 person responsible for a political party's discipline. 4 call on members to vote according to party policy. 5 confection of whipped ingredients. **whip-round** n informal collection of money for a present, etc.

whippet n thin long-legged dog similar to a greyhound.

whir vi (-rr-) move rapidly with a buzzing sound.

whirl vi,vt 1 move or cause to move in a circle; spin very fast. 2 move away quickly. vi swing round quickly. n 1 rapid circular movement; rush; agitation. 2 state of bewilderment. **whirlpool** n circular current of water. **whirlwind** n moving spiral of air into which surrounding air can be drawn.

whisk vt 1 move or remove swiftly and lightly; brush, swing, or toss briskly. 2 beat lightly introducing air so as to make froth. vi move or pass quickly. n 1 rapid sweeping motion. 2 light stiff brush. 3 instrument for beating.

whisker n 1 firm sensitive hair at the side of an animal's mouth. 2 hairs on a person's upper lip or side of the face.

whisky n alcoholic drink, distilled esp. from malted barley.

whisper *vi,vt* **1** speak in very low tones; murmur. **2** converse in secret. *vi* spread rumours. *n* **1** soft speech; murmur; rustle. **2** hint; rumour.

whist *n* card game played in pairs.

whistle *vi* make a shrill sound by forcing breath through almost sealed lips or teeth, or air through a crack, etc. *vt* use this method for rendering a tune. *n* **1** sound of whistling. **2** device making a similar sound.

white *n* **1** colour of fresh snow, having no hue. **2** something coloured or characteristically white. *adj* **1** of the colour white or nearly white; pale; colourless. **2** pure; unblemished. **White** *n* person with a pale skin colour, esp. a European. *adj* having skin colour of Europeans. **whiten** *vt* make white. *vi* grow pale. **whitewash** *n* substance for whitening walls, etc. *vt* **1** cover with whitewash. **2** *inf* gloss over; conceal (errors, faults, etc.).

whiting *n* marine food fish.

Whitsun *n* **1** *also* **Whit Sunday** seventh Sunday after Easter when the Christian Church celebrates Pentecost, the inspiration of the disciples by the Holy Spirit. **2** week following Whit Sunday.

whiz *vi,vt* (-zz-) **1** move quickly, making a buzzing whirring sound. **2** *inf* move or go rapidly. *n* buzzing sound.

who *pron* **1** what or which person. **2** used to introduce a relative clause when referring to a person or people. **whoever** *pron* **1** anyone at all that. **2** no matter who. **3** who.

whole *adj* complete; total; undamaged; healthy *adv* in a complete or unbroken piece. *n* entire or undivided thing; total of all parts. **wholefood** *n* food produced without artificial fertilizers, etc., and with the minimum of processing. **wholehearted** *adj* sincerely and enthusiastically felt, done, etc. **wholeheartedly** *adv.* **wholesale** *n* sale of goods in bulk rather than retail selling. *adj* **1** relating to sales in bulk. **2** large-scale; indiscriminate. *adv* on a wholesale basis. **wholesome** *adj* **1** containing good value. **2** healthy in body, mind, morals, etc. **3** conducive to such. **wholly** *adv* completely; altogether.

whom *pron* form of **who** as the object.

whooping cough *n* infectious disease characterized by bouts of coughing, respiratory difficulties, etc.

whore (hɔ:) *n* female prostitute.

whose *pron* belonging to whom; of whom or which.

why *adv,conj* for what reason; from what cause.

wick *n* stringlike cord that burns in a candle.

wicked *adj* **1** sinful; evil; extremely bad. **2** mischievous; roguish. **wickedly** *adv.* **wickedness** *n.*

wickerwork *n* craft of making furniture, etc., from twisted twigs or branches, or the objects so made.

wicket *n* **1** three pointed stumps with two bails resting on top, at which the bowler aims in a game of cricket. **2** strip of turf between two wickets. **3** batsman or batsman's turn. **4** small gate or door. **wicketkeeper** *n.*

wide *adj* **1** broad; of considerable dimension from side to side. **2** roomy; extensive; including much. *adv* **1** to the full extent. **2** widely. **widely** *adv* over a large area or extent; considerably; spreading far from. **widen** *vt,vi* make or grow wide(r). **widespread** *adj* found over a considerable area; distributed far.

widow *n* woman whose husband has died and who has not remarried. **widower** *m n.*

width *n* **1** distance or measurement between sides. **2** state of being wide.

wield *vt* hold and use; possess; exercise.

wife *n, pl* **wives** female partner in a marriage; married woman. **wifely** *adj.*

wig *n* hairpiece for the whole head made of artificial or real hair.

wiggle *vt,vi* move or cause to move to and fro jerkily. *n* wiggling movement.

wigwam *n* light conical dwelling used by North American Indians.

wild *adj* **1** uncivilized; undomesticated or uncultivated. **2** uncontrolled; boisterous; extremely excited or angry. **3** untidy; dishevelled. **4** lacking judgment; random; erratic; fantastic. **wildly** *adv.* **wildness** *n.* **wildlife** *n* animals, birds, plants, etc., that are undomesticated and live in their natural habitat.

wilderness *n* large desolate area; uncultivated and uninhabited region.

wilful *adj* headstrong; obstinately self-willed. **wilfully** *adv.*

will[1] *v aux* **1** used to form the future tense. **2** used to emphasize an intention. **3** used to express willingness or ability. **4** used to express probability or likelihood.

will[2] *n* **1** faculty by which decisions are made. **2** conscious choice; intention; inclination; moral strength. **3** intended distribution of one's property at death. **4** legal document expressing this. *vt,vi* **1** bequeath in a will. **2** compel by using the will; desire. **willpower** *n* strength of mind; firmness; control.

willing *adj* without reluctance; in agreement; eager; cooperative. **willingly** *adv.* **willingness** *n.*

willow *n* tree with slender pliant branches and long slender leaves, often found near rivers. **willowy** *adj* flexible; graceful; slender.

wilt *vt,vi* droop, as through lack of moisture, energy, etc.; fade.

win *v* (-nn-; won) *vi* reach a goal, esp. before anyone else; come first. *vt* secure or gain by effort or contest; obtain by gambling. **win over** persuade. ~*n* act of winning; victory; success. **winner** *n.*

wince *vi* draw back; flinch. *n* involuntary movement resulting from pain, etc.

winch *n* hauling or hoisting machine consisting of a drum on a rotating axle.

wind[1] (wind) *n* **1** current of air usually moving with speed. **2** gas produced in the alimentary canal. **3** empty meaningless words. **4** wind instruments in an orchestra. **5** *inf* hint; suggestion. **get/put the wind up** become frightened or alarmed/frighten or alarm. **in the wind** about to happen. ~*vt* cause to be short of breath. **windbag** *n* **1** *sl* person who talks a lot but says little of interest. **2** bag in bagpipes from which air can be squeezed to maintain a continuous sound. **windfall** *n* **1** fruit blown off a tree. **2** unexpected good fortune, often a receipt of money. **wind instrument** *n* musical instrument played by blowing or using an air current. **windmill** *n* mill with rotating sails driven by wind power. **windpipe** *n* passage between the mouth and lungs through which breath is inhaled or exhaled. **wind-**

screen *n* protective plate of glass in front of a vehicle. **windswept** *adj* exposed to or disordered by wind. **windy** *adj* like, characterized by, or exposed to wind.

wind[2] (waind) *v* (wound) *vt* **1** turn; twist; **2** *also* **wind up** tighten the spring of (a watch, etc.) by turning something. **3** make into a ball; coil. *vi* change direction constantly; meander.

windlass *n* machine with a revolving cylinder for hauling or hoisting. *vt* hoist by means of a windlass.

window *n* **1** opening in a wall, etc., to let in air and light. **2** frame of a window or the glass in it. **window-dressing** *n* **1** displaying of goods in a shop window. **2** art of doing this. **3** skill in emphasizing the best features of something. **window-shop** *vi* (-pp-) scrutinize goods in shop windows without buying.

wine *n* alcoholic drink made from fermented grape juice or sometimes from other fruits.

wing *n* **1** limb or organ by which a bird, insect, etc., flies. **2** similarly shaped structure on an aeroplane. **3** any side structure, as of a building or stage. **4** player on the extreme right or left of the forward line in football, etc. **wing-commander** *n* airforce officer similar in rank to lieutenant colonel or naval commander. **wingspan** *n* length from tip to tip of wings.

wink *vi,vt* **1** rapidly shut and open (one or both eyes), often to convey complicity, etc. *n* act or instance of winking.

winkle *n* edible shellfish. *v* **winkle out** extract with difficulty.

winter *n* coldest season of the year. *adj* of, like, happening, used, or sown in winter. *vi* spend the winter (in). *vt* feed and shelter (animals) through winter. **wintry** *adj.*

wipe *vt* clean or dry by drawing a cloth over or rubbing lightly. **wipe out** obliterate. ~*n* act of wiping; clean; rub.

wire *n* **1** flexible strand or rod of metal or a group of strands plaited or twisted together. **2** insulated wire for carrying an electric current. **3** *inf* telegram. *vt* join, fasten, support, protect, equip, etc., with wire. *vi* telegraph. **wireless** *n* radio. **wiry** *adj* sinewy; tough.

wise *adj* **1** having knowledge, perception, or judgment; clever. **2** sensible; discreet. **3** *sl* knowing the whole situation; warned about. **wisdom** *n.* **wisely** *adv.*

wish *vt* **1** desire; long for. **2** request; want. *vt,vi* express or have a desire for. *n* **1** desire. **2** thing desired. **wishful** *adj* desirous; hoping.

wisp *n* **1** thin strand or streak of something. **2** small bundle of straw, hay, etc.

wisteria *n* climbing plant with blue flowers hanging in clusters.

wistful *adj* yearning, with little hope of satisfaction; thoughtful. **wistfully** *adv.*

wit *n* **1** ability to think quickly and pertinently and say clever amusing things. **2** person with this ability. **3** *also* **wits** intelligence; resourcefulness.

witch *n* **1** woman believed to have supernatural powers through contact with evil spirits. **2** ugly malevolent woman. **witchcraft** *n* craft or practice of supernatural powers for evil purposes.

with *prep* **1** in the company of. **2** by means of; using. **3** bearing; possessing. **4** displaying; showing. **5** in relation to. **6** among; in the midst of. **7** at the same time as.

withdraw *v* (-drew; -drawn) *vi* draw back or away; retire. *vt* take out; take back; retract; remove. **withdrawal** *n.* **withdrawn** *adj* unsociable; very reserved.

wither *vi,vt* shrivel; dry (up); fade; decay. **withering** *adj* crushingly sarcastic.

withhold *vt* (-held) keep from; hold back; restrain; refuse to grant.

within *adv* inside; internally; indoors. *prep* **1** not out of or beyond. **2** in; inside; to the inner part.

without *adv* outside. *prep* **1** outside. **2** not having; free from; in the absence of. **3** beyond the limits of. *conj* unless; but.

withstand *vt* (-stood) maintain; endure; oppose successfully.

witness *n* **1** person who is present and perceives a fact or event. **2** person who gives evidence, esp. in court. **3** person who attests another's signature. *vt,vi* give testimony; observe personally; act as witness. **witness box** *n* place in a lawcourt where witnesses give evidence.

witty *adj* capable of verbal wit; amusing. **wittily** *adv.*

wives *n pl* of **wife.**

wizard *n* **1** man having supernatural powers; magician. **2** expert. **wizardry** *n.*

wobble *vi* **1** move unsteadily; rock; shake; tremble. **2** be uncertain; vacillate. *n* unsteady motion. **wobbly** *adj.*

wok *n* frying pan with round bottom used in Chinese cookery.

woke *v pt* of **wake. woken** *v pp* of **wake.**

wolf *n, pl* **wolves 1** gregarious carnivorous predatory animal of the dog family. **2** person who is greedy and cunning. **cry wolf** raise a false alarm. ~*vt also* **wolf down** eat rapidly and ravenously.

woman *n, pl* **women 1** adult female human being. **2** women collectively. **womanhood** *n.* **womanly** *adj.*

womb *n* uterus.

won *v pt* and *pp* of **win.**

wonder *n* **1** emotion of delighted surprise and admiration. **2** object or person that excites this. **no wonder** not surprising(ly). **work wonders** achieve great results. ~*vt,vi* **1** be curious or seek to find out (about). **2** doubt. **3** marvel (at). **wonderful** *adj* **1** amazing. **2** *inf* very good; marvellous. **wonderfully** *adv.*

wonky *adj sl* unsound; shaky; not right or well.

wood *n* **1** collection of growing trees and other plants over an extensive area. **2** hard fibrous material in the trunks and branches of trees, used as a building material, in furniture, etc. **woody** *adj.* **wooden** *adj* **1** made of wood. **2** stiff; clumsy. **3** showing no emotion. **4** stupid; insensible. **woodpecker** *n* bird with a chisel-like bill, which it uses for drilling the bark of trees for insects. **woodwind** *n* section of an orchestra containing wind instruments with the exception of brass instruments. **woodwork** *n* anything made of wood; carpentry. **woodworm** *n* **1** larva of certain beetles laid in, boring through, and eating wood. **2** resulting damage in wooden furniture, etc.

wool *n* **1** hair-covering of sheep and other animals. **2** yarn spun from this. **3** garment, etc., made from the yarn. **woollen** *adj* made from wool. *n also* **woollens** woollen cloth or garments. **woolly** *adj* **1** made of or like wool. **2** lacking clearness or precision. *n* jersey.

word *n* 1 unit of spoken language or a written symbol of this, expressive of some object, idea, or relation. 2 brief conversation; remark. 3 news; message. 4 decree; promise; recommendation. **have words** argue. **in a word** in short. ~*vt* express in words; phrase. **wordy** *adj* using too many words. **word-perfect** *adj* memorized accurately. **word processor** *n* electronic device, esp. a microcomputer with a screen, that performs such routine tasks as typing, editing, storage of information, etc.

wore *v pt* of **wear.**

work *n* 1 effort exerted in purposeful activity; expenditure of energy. 2 task; occupation for gain; employment. 3 product of one's efforts; creation. 4 place of employment or where activity takes place. *vt* 1 bring into action; effect. 2 handle; shape. *vi* 1 labour; expend energy; be occupied; be employed (at or in). 2 behave in a desired way when started; operate; function. **worked up** *adj* angry; excited. **work out** solve; develop. **working class** *n* workers, usually implying those in manual work. **workman** *n, pl* -**men** labourer; skilled manual worker. **workmanlike** *adj* efficient; of a high standard. **workmanship** *n* level of competence or skill in a product. **workshop** *n* place where goods are made, manual work is carried on, etc.

world *n* 1 universe; all that exists. 2 earth and its inhabitants; part of the earth. 3 mankind; public; society. 4 present state of existence; public life; sphere of interest or activity; environment. 5 materialistic standards or system; secular life. 6 large amount or quantity. **worldly** *adj* 1 familiar with public life and the ways of society. 2 adhering to materialistic standards; not idealistic or religious. **worldliness** *n*. **worldwide** *adj* applying to the whole planet.

worm *n* 1 long slender usually limbless invertebrate animal, esp. an earthworm. 2 internal parasite. *vt* wriggle; squirm; make (one's way) slowly or secretly; extract insidiously.

worn *v pp* of **wear.** *adj* 1 well used; long used; exhausted. 2 worried; haggard.

worry *vi* be anxious; fret. *vt* make anxious; disturb; pester; harass; be a trouble to. *n* 1 act of worrying. 2 cause of this.

worse *adj* less good; poorer in health; more inferior or severe in condition or circumstances. *adv* in a worse way; with more severity. **worsen** *vt,vi* make or become worse.

worship *v* (-pp-) *vt* 1 accord religious honour and supreme esteem to. 2 adore; idolize. *vi* attend religious worship. *n* 1 act of worshipping; religious service. 2 adoration.

worst *adj* of the extreme degree of badness. *adv* in the worst way. *n* worst part, state, etc.; least good part. *vt* get an advantage over.

worth *adj* 1 having a value of. 2 deserving; justifying. *n* intrinsic value; value in money; merit. **worthwhile** *adj* warranting the time, effort, etc; sufficiently important. **worthy** *adj* of sufficient merit; deserving; commendable. **worthily** *adv*.

would *v aux* form of **will**[1] in the past tense, conditional, or subjunctive.

wound[1] *vt,vi* (wu:nd) hurt; injure. *n* injury.

wound[2] *v* (waund) *pt* and *pp* of **wind**[2].

wove a *pt* of **weave. woven** a *pp* of **weave.**

wrangle *vi* argue; dispute doggedly. *n* angry dispute.

wrap *vt* (-pp-) cover; fold round or together; wind; envelop in. *vi* 1 enfold. 2 package. *n* 1 covering, such as a shawl or rug. 2 single turn or fold.

wreath *n* 1 arrangement, often circular, of intertwined leaves and flowers, often in memory of a deceased person; garland. 2 wisp or curl of smoke or vapour. **wreathe** *vt,vi* twist; entwine; interweave.

wreck *vt* ruin; damage or destroy; sabotage. *n* 1 ship that has foundered or sunk. 2 broken or damaged remains after a disaster; destruction. 3 person enfeebled mentally or physically. **wreckage** *n* 1 act of wrecking. 2 remains of a wrecked thing or person.

wren *n* small brown songbird with short erect tail.

wrench *vt* pull sharply and with a twist; force by violence; sprain; distort. *vi* undergo violent pulling, tugging, or twisting. *n* 1 act of wrenching; twist; sprain. 2 difficult parting; pain at parting. 3 adjustable spanner.

wrestle *vi,vt* struggle to overcome. *vi* contend in an organized fight by holding and throwing, without punching. *n* bout of wrestling; struggle. **wrestler** *n*. **wrestling** *n*.

wretch *n* 1 miserable unfortunate person. 2 worthless despicable person. **wretched** *adj* 1 miserable; dismal. 2 of poor quality; contemptible.

wriggle *vi,vt* squirm or make short twisting movements. **wriggle into/out of** *inf* insinuate oneself deviously into or extricate oneself out of. *n* act, motion, or shape of wriggling movement.

wring *v* (wrung) *vt,vi* twist and squeeze out moisture (from). *vt* 1 twist. 2 clasp in anguish. 3 grip in a friendly manner. 4 extract. *n* act of wringing.

wrinkle *n* small ridge or furrow on a surface; crease. *vt,vi* crease.

wrist *n* 1 joint between the hand and lower arm. 2 part of a garment covering this. **wristwatch** *n* watch worn at the wrist.

writ *n* legal or formal document summoning or requiring a person to take some course of action.

write *v* (wrote; written) *vt,vi* 1 mark letters, words, numbers, etc., usually on paper, to communicate ideas, thoughts, etc. 2 correspond (with) by letter. 3 be an author (of). *vt* state in a letter, book, etc. **write down** *or* **out** put in writing. **write off** consider a loss or failure. **write-off** *n* complete loss or failure; wreck. **write up** describe or bring up to date in writing. **write-up** *n* written account in a newspaper, etc., of a book, film, etc.; review. **writing** *n* 1 written work, book, etc. 2 act of writing. 3 style of handwriting.

writhe *vi* 1 twist or roll about as if suffering pain; squirm. 2 suffer mentally.

wrong *adj* 1 not correct, accurate, or true; mistaken. 2 wicked; unjust. 3 not suitable; not wanted. *n* injustice; wrong action. **in the wrong** mistaken. *adv also* **wrongly** in a wrong way. **get wrong** 1 misunderstand. 2 produce an incorrect answer. ~*vt* do injustice or harm to; think ill of unjustifiably. **wrongdoing** *n* improper, illegal, or immoral action. **wrongdoer** *n*.

wrought iron *adj* malleable pure iron, often drawn out into decorative shapes.

wry *adj* 1 twisted; contorted. 2 ironical; dryly humorous. **wryly** *adv*.

X

xenophobia *n* irrational fear or hatred of foreigners or things foreign or strange.

xerography *n* copying process in which images are produced using electrically charged surfaces.

Xerox *n Tdmk* process or machine employing xerography.

Xmas *n* Christmas.

X-ray *n* 1 wave of radiation of considerable energy that can penetrate matter, used esp. in medical diagnosis and treatment. 2 image, esp. of bone structure, produced on film sensitive to X-rays. *vt,vi* irradiate with X-rays.

xylophone *n* musical instrument consisting of a graduated series of wooden bars struck by wooden hammers.

Y

yacht *n* light sailing vessel for racing, cruising, etc. *vi* sail in a yacht. **yachtsman** *n, pl* **-men** person who keeps or sails a yacht.

yank *vt,vi* pull sharply; jerk. *n* sharp tug.

yap *n* short sharp high-pitched bark; yelp. *vi* (-pp-) 1 bark in yaps. 2 *inf* chatter stupidly or at length.

yard¹ *n* 1 unit of length, equivalent to 0.91 metres (three feet). 2 piece of material of this length. **yardstick** *n* 1 graduated stick, one yard long, used for measuring. 2 any standard used for comparison.

yard² *n* enclosed area, usually adjoining a building and having a hard surface.

yarn *n* 1 continuous thread made from twisted fibres of wool, cotton, synthetic materials, etc. 2 story spun out to some length. *vi* tell stories.

yawn *vi* 1 breathe in through a wide open mouth, usually as a result of tiredness or boredom. 2 be open wide. *n* act of yawning.

year *n* 1 *also* **calendar year** period of time of 365 days (or 366 in a leap year) from Jan 1 to Dec 31. 2 period of twelve months. 3 period of time (365.256 days) taken by the earth to complete one orbit of the sun. **yearly** *adj,adv*.

yearn *vi* 1 have a great longing; crave. 2 feel pity or tenderness. **yearning** *n*.

yeast *n* fungus or a preparation of this fungus, used in brewing and for raising bread.

yell *vi,vt* scream; shout loudly. *n* scream of anger, pain, or excitement; loud cry.

yellow *n* spectral colour, as that of gold or a daffodil. *adj* **1** of the colour yellow. **2** *inf* cowardly.

yelp *n* short sharp cry of pain, surprise, or excitement, esp. by a dog. *vi* utter a yelp.

yes *adv,interj* expression of affirmation, consent, etc. *n* affirmative reply.

yesterday *n* day before today. *adv* **1** on or during yesterday. **2** not long ago.

yet *adv* **1** up to that or this time. **2** now; at this moment. **3** still; even. *conj* but; nevertheless; however.

yew *n* coniferous tree with dark needle-shaped leaves and red cones.

yield *vt* **1** produce; supply. **2** give up under pressure; concede. *vi* submit; give way under pressure; comply. *n* amount yielded; product.

yodel *vi,vt* (-ll-) alternate in singing between a normal and falsetto voice. **yodeller** *n.*

yoga *n* type of oriental meditation. **yogi** *n* person who practises yoga.

yoghurt *n* also **yogurt, yoghourt** thickly clotted milk curdled by bacteria.

yoke *n* **1** wooden neckpiece holding together two draught oxen. **2** something resembling this. **3** fitted part of a garment, esp. for the chest and shoulders. **4** oppressive force; slavery. **5** bond of union. *vt* put a yoke on; join together.

yolk *n* yellow centre of an egg.

yonder *adv* over there. *adj* distant but in sight.

you *pron* **1** used to refer to one or more persons addressed directly, excluding the speaker. **2** people in general; one.

young *adj* having lived a relatively short time; undeveloped; immature; not old. *pl n* young people; offspring. **youngster** *n* young person.

your *adj* belonging to you. **yours** *pron* something or someone that belongs to or is associated with you. **yourself** *r pron, pl* **-selves** **1** of your own self. **2** your normal self.

youth *n* **1** age between childhood and adulthood; early life. **2** quality or condition of being young, inexperienced, etc. **3** young man. **4** young people collectively. **youthful** *adj* fresh; vigorous; optimistic; buoyant.

Z

zeal *n* enthusiasm; fervour; passionate ardour.

zebra *n* black-and-white striped animal of the horse family, originating in Africa. **zebra crossing** *n* black-and-white striped path used by pedestrians to cross a road.

zero *n* nought; nothing; nil; figure 0; point separating positive and negative values or quantities, as on a temperature scale.

zest *n* **1** gusto; keen interest; obvious enjoyment. **2** anything that gives added zest.

zigzag *n* **1** line that forms a series of sharp alternately right and left turns. **2** something having this form. *vt,vi* (-gg-) move or cause to move along such a line.

zilch *n* nothing; zero.

zinc *n* hard bluish-white metal, used ɔ. in alloys and in galvanizing iron.

zip *n* **1** interlocking fastener for openings in clothes. **2** whizzing sound. **3** energy; vigour. *v* (-pp-) *vt also* **zip up.** fasten with a zip. *vi* **1** hurry or rush (through, etc.). **2** move with a whizzing sound.

zither *n* musical instrument consisting of numerous strings stretched over a wooden frame.

zodiac *n* belt or zone of the heavens divided into twelve parts, each accorded a sign, in which the paths of the sun, moon, and planets appear to lie.

zone *n* area; region; belt; characteristic or distinctive section, as of the earth. *vt* divide into or mark with zones.

zoo *n* enclosure where wild animals are kept for display to the public, for c eeding, etc.

zoology *n* scientific study of animals and animal life. **zoological** *adj.* **zoologist** *n.*

zoom *vi,vt* produce a loud buzzing noise. *vi* move or rise rapidly.

Index